COLD WAR CULTURE

OTHER BOOKS BY THE AUTHOR

The Cold War Reference Guide

COLD WAR AMERICA

COLD WAR CULTURE

Media and the Arts, 1945–1990

Richard A. Schwartz, Ph.D.
Florida International University

Facts On File, Inc.

To Ana-Maria

For all the voodoo that you do.

Cold War America
Cold War Culture: Media and the Arts, 1945–1990

Copyright © 1998 by Richard A. Schwartz

Facts On File, Inc.
11 Penn Plaza
New York NY 10001

Library of Congress Cataloging-in-Publication Data

Schwartz, Richard Alan, 1951–
    Cold War culture / Richard A. Schwartz.
      p.   cm.
    Includes bibliographical references and index.
    ISBN 0-8160-3104-5 (acid-free paper)
    1. United States—Civilization—1945– —Encyclopedias. 2. Popular culture—United States—History—20th century—Encyclopedias. 3. United States—Intellectual life—20th century—Encyclopedias. 4. Cold War—Social aspects—United States—Encyclopedias. I. Title.
E169.12.S39 1997   96-29642
973.92′03—dc21

You can find Facts On File on the World Wide Web at http://www.factsonfile.com

Cover design by Whizbang! Studios

Printed in the United States of America

VB VCS 10 9 8 7 6 5 4 3 2 1

This book is printed on acid-free paper.

CONTENTS

ACKNOWLEDGMENTS

I wish to thank everyone who helped me complete *Cold War Culture*. In particular, Asher Milbauer, my colleague at Florida International University, gave me valuable advice when I was planning the initial project. Donald Watson, the chairman of the English Department, was also supportive, as was the university, which granted me a sabbatical leave to write the book. My editor at Facts On File, Drew Silver, helped me conceive the encyclopedia and assisted me along the way.

Line editor Rachel Kranz and copy editor Paul Scaramazza corrected my mistakes and drew on their own wealth of knowledge to enhance the book significantly. Nat Andriani of World Wide Photos assisted me in selecting the illustrations, and John Barth, Robert Coover and William F. Buckley Jr. graciously provided me with photos as well. Most importantly, my parents, my sister and my wife Ana-Maria provided unbounded encouragement and love.

INTRODUCTION

On November 17, 1990, President George Bush declared, "The Cold War is over." The Cold War was a fluid, multinational conflict between Western capitalist democracies and the communist regimes of Eastern Europe and Asia, led by the Soviet Union. It lasted some 44 years and dominated the lives of Americans in both explicit and implicit ways. Though it remained mostly "cold"—that is, America and the Soviet Union never went to war—the Cold War also subsumed the Korean and Vietnam Wars as well as the invasion of Grenada, U.S. interventions in the Dominican Republic and Lebanon, and various covert or clandestine military actions on both sides. The ever-present threat of imminent nuclear annihilation was an outstanding Cold War characteristic that set this period apart from any other in history. In addition to shaping U.S. foreign policy and much of its domestic policy during the second half of the 20th century, the Cold War helped define American national values and identity. These, in turn, influenced virtually every public and private aspect of American life, from aviation, shipping and space exploration, the development of an interstate highway system, public school education, to the development of nuclear power to advertising, arts and letters (both "high-brow" and "popular") and other forms of expression intended for mass audiences.

Cold War Culture describes the various people, works of art and literature, movements and influences in American culture that significantly reflected or responded to the Cold War. The book shows how American culture was informed by Cold War sensibilities, values and events, via an encyclopedia format that presents the many outlets through which the American body politic manifested its Cold War attitudes, beliefs and concerns. Examining the fine arts and literature, popular culture and consumer culture from 1945 to 1990, individual entries range from such real and fictional personalities as Arthur Miller, James Bond, Rocky and Bullwinkle, Allen Ginsberg and Lenny Bruce to Paul Robeson, Mikhail

Baryshnikov and Nadia Comaneci; from movies, theater, art, novels, folk music, rock and roll and televised Billy Graham crusades to happenings and the counterculture.

The book discusses Cold War culture in the following broad categories: art, cartoons, consumer goods, dance, film, games and toys, language, literature, magazines, music, journalists, sports, television and theater. Nuclear apocalypse and the Red scare comprise the other two broad subject listings. A general article is included for each major category. Individual entries within each category are cross-referenced and indicated by small capital letters. Thus, for example, the long entry on FILM refers to SPY FILMS, which in turn discusses JAMES BOND. And the JAMES BOND entry refers back to SPY FILMS, which, in turn, alludes to FILM.

The subjects covered in this book constitute the fabric of Americans' daily lives: Citizens interact intellectually, emotionally and experientially through these domains to create society. These cultural arenas helped express and shape national values during the Cold War and render American beliefs and attitudes into actual words, images, sounds, deeds and products. In general, the narrative arts—novels, non-fiction, television, theater and film—allowed for more direct expression of Cold War issues, attitudes and events than other forms of popular culture. Storytelling is fundamentally about people and the circumstances of their lives; consequently, narratives more readily gravitate to politics and ideology than most other forms of cultural expression. Other aspects of popular culture do not so readily allow for explicit expression of political attitudes and responses to political events, though they are nonetheless affected by current attitudes and events. For example, the commonplace observation that hemlines rise during prosperity and fall during times of economic depression indicates a connection between fashion and the economy. Yet this connection alone tells nothing about the specific relation between fashion and the economic climate; without further analysis, the fashion trend is not very precise as an expression of a particular era. Therefore, this book contains a proportionately greater number of entries on the narrative arts than on other aspects of American culture.

Following this introduction is the main body of the text: A-to-Z entries describing relevant works, personalities, move-ments and influences that constituted Cold War culture from 1945 to 1990. The titles listed for additional reading are fully cited in the bibliography at the end of the book.

Aczel, Tamas A Hungarian EXILED WRITER (to the United States). Aczel immigrated to London in 1956 after the Soviets squelched the Hungarian Revolution and initiated the political crackdown that followed. He came to the United States in the early 1960s, when he was appointed professor of English at the University of Massachusetts at Amherst. He had joined the Communist Party in Hungary shortly after World War II and in 1952 won the Stalin Prize for literature for his first novel, *In the Shadow of Liberty*, which had been published in 1948. However, Hungarian officials severely criticized that work as well as his second novel, *Storm and Sunshine* (1950), because these books allegedly failed to exemplify "socialist realism" and did not overcome Aczel's bourgeois upbringing. In the United States, Aczel's poetry broke with the traditions of literary realism and became more abstract and metaphysical. In 1959, he coauthored *Revolt of the Mind* with Tibor Meray. The book provides an account of pre-revolutionary intellectual activity in Hungary and the attraction communism held for the intelligentsia there. Some consider this a classic work of intellectual history. His American novels, written in English, employ an experimental and exuberant style despite their chilling subject matter. These works include *The Ice Age* (1965), which depicts Hungary during Stalin's reign of terror, and *Illuminations* (1981), which comically depicts life behind the Iron Curtain and his life in London. *The Hunt* (1989) is a contemporary fable about the show trials in Communist Hungary. After the fall of communism Aczel returned to Hungary, where he was treated as a national hero. Famous for coining the term "the aristocracy of the proletariat," Aczel died in 1994.

For further reading see Tucker's *Literary Exile in the Twentieth Century*.

"Adlai Stevenson Reports" A biweekly TELEVISION NEWS show that ran on ABC from 1961 to 1963. Stevenson, then the Kennedy administration's ambassador to the United Nations, focused on the current activities of the UN through interviews with prominent public figures. Among the individuals and issues featured were U Thant, the Burmese ambassador who became UN secretary general after the death of Dag Hammarskjöld; Edward R. MURROW, the former journalist who headed the U.S. Information Agency; the crisis in the Congo; potential peaceful uses for outer space; arms control and nuclear testing; the Cuban Missile Crisis; and the shifting alliances and changing nature of the Cold War.

"Adventures of Superman, The" A TELEVISION SCIENCE FICTION SHOW starring George Reeves that ran in syndication from 1951 to 1957. The show was repeated in syndication thereafter. It was revived in cartoon form from 1966 to 1970. Reeves also starred in a 1951 film, *Superman and the Mole Men*. In addition, Christopher Reeve (no relation) starred in four Superman films between 1978 and 1987. In the last of these movies, Superman rids the world of atomic weapons, only to see them return through the efforts of international arms dealers.

Adlai Stevenson. Courtesy Library of Congress.

Based on the comic book character from DC Comics' *Action Comics* periodical, originating in the 1930s, Superman was an invincible superhero who came to Earth after his parents launched him into outer space in a rocket ship to spare him from the impending destruction of their planet, Krypton. Superman was able to fly (originally, merely to "leap tall buildings in a single bound"), was "faster than a speeding bullet, more powerful than a locomotive" and was impervious to attacks from fists, guns, bombs or any substance other than Kryptonite (fragmented debris from his destroyed planet). He also possessed super-hearing and "X-ray vision" that allowed him to see at great distances and through walls or any other unleaded structures.

Disguised as Clark Kent, "mild-mannered" newspaper reporter for the *Daily Planet,* Superman was dedicated to preserving "Truth, Justice, and the American Way." Superman first appeared in a comic book in 1938, at a time of great international tension and expectation of war. He flourished throughout World War II and after in a newspaper comic strip, a radio show, feature-length cartoons, a novel and two movie serials. His continued attraction for Cold War audiences lay at least partially in his identification with the innocent and his continued defense of American values at a time when the "American way of life" was again threatened, this time by communism. The superhero provided a certain level of wish fulfillment for audiences that were anxious about threats to their personal and national security, including the possibility of nuclear annihilation. Much as the super-creature RODAN evolved as a savior of Japan from its nuclear-armed enemies, Superman embodied an American desire for a protector against aggressors who would destroy what the United States was considered to stand for.

For additional reading see the Stern's *Encyclopedia of Pop Culture* and McNeil's *Total Television.*

Advise and Consent   A 1959 POLITICAL NOVEL by Allen DRURY and a 1962 POLITICAL FILM starring Henry Fonda, Walter Pidgeon, Charles Laughton and Gene Tierney, directed by Otto Preminger. The novel spent 102 weeks on the *New York Times* best-seller list and won the 1959 Pulitzer Prize. *Advise and Consent* is the first in Drury's series of six political novels dealing with the struggle between liberals and conservatives to lead the country through the Cold War.

The story centers on the political battle surrounding the nomination of a liberal candidate for secretary of state, Robert Leffingwell, who is based loosely on Alger Hiss. It describes the various political machinations involved in the Senate confirmation hearings, including political blackmail over alleged homosexuality and allegations of Leffingwell's past affiliations with a communist cell when he was teaching at the University of Chicago. Drury's values are strongly conservative, and the book introduces his vilification of the liberal press, a persistent theme throughout the series. Several of the characters, including Leffingwell, Vice President Harley Hudson and Senators Orrin Knox, Seabright Cooley, Robert Munson and Fred Van Ackerman are also prominent in these subsequent novels: A SHADE OF DIFFERENCE (1962), CAPABLE OF HONOR (1967), PRESERVE AND PROTECT (1968), COME NINEVEH, COME TYRE (1973) and THE PROMISE OF JOY (1975). The choice of Fonda to play Leffingwell in the movie mirrored Fonda's own identification with liberal causes.

For additional reading see Kemme's *Political Fiction, The Spirit of the Age, and Allen Drury.*

Air America   A 1990 MILITARY FILM starring Mel Gibson, Robert Downey Jr. and Nancy Travis, directed by Roger Spottiswoode. This late Cold War film provides an unsympathetic view of the CIA as it chronicles the exploits of two agency pilots working from an illegal base in Southeast Asia during the Vietnam War. Years of revelations about the activities of the CIA, including the then still-unfolding Iran-contra scandal, in which CIA director William Casey was alleged to have played a major role, may have contributed to the decision to make a film that depicts the CIA operatives as opportunistic and reckless.

Air Power   A TELEVISION DOCUMENTARY series that ran on CBS from 1956 to 1958. Narrated by Walter CRONKITE and produced with the cooperation of the U.S. Air Force, *Air Power* was the first documentary series to explore the ramifications of nuclear warfare. The series traced the history of the airplane and described its impact on 20th-century history. Representations of the airplane as a necessary weapon in wartime, with supporting footage provided by the air force, suggested to American audiences the importance of maintaining a fleet of technologically advanced aircraft throughout the Cold War conflict. The show's initial segment described the defensive action that the air force would take in the event of an air attack, a much-feared possibility in 1956. That episode concluded with an atomic explosion—minus the beginning frames of the blast: Officials feared that enemy scientists could identify the bomb's content and performance by viewing the first few seconds of the explosion.

Airwolf   A TELEVISION SPY SHOW that ran on CBS from 1984 to 1986. The show reappeared in syndication on cable television in 1987 with a different cast but similar premise. The eponymous Airwolf was a high-tech helicopter of the future possessing enormous firepower, tremendous range and greater speed than a jet. Stolen by its creator, who tried to sell it to Libya, Airwolf was stolen back again at the behest of a U.S. government agency known as the "Firm" (and later as the "Company") by loner Stringfellow Hawke. Hawke, however, refused to surrender the helicopter to the Firm until the government found his brother, who was missing in action in Vietnam. In the interim the strong, silent Hawke, who spent his off-hours playing a cello in a mountain cabin filled with Impressionist paintings, conducted missions for the Firm. Produced during the Reagan administration's military buildup in the 1980's, *Airwolf* appealed to the interest attracted by the real-world Apache attack helicopter, which was developed during this period. Clandestine military missions were another trademark of the Reagan years, and concern for missing soldiers from the Vietnam War remained an emotional and politically sensitive issue even beyond the end of the Cold War. The 1987 change of name from the Firm to the Company, when the series appeared on cable, made even more thinly veiled the show's allusion to the CIA, which was informally known as the Company.

Aksyonov, Vassily Pavlovich   A Soviet EXILED WRITER (to the United States). Aksyonov's parents were arrested in the 1937 Stalinist purges; his mother, Eugenia Ginsburg, later achieved worldwide recognition for her two-volume account of her 18-year prison term, *Journey into the Whirlwind* (1967) and *Within the Whirlwind* (1979, in English, 1981). After graduating from the Leningrad Medical Institute in 1956, Aksyonov practiced medicine in the Soviet Union until 1960, when he became a full-time writer. Written during the Khrushchev years of de-Stalinization, his first two novels, *Colleagues* (1960; published in English, 1962) and *A Starry Ticket* (1961; published in English, 1962), portrayed young intellectuals discarding the restrictions of Stalinist regulations. Characterized by energetic wordplay, literary experimentation and the influence of Mikhail Bakhtin's literary theories, particularly the notion of carnival, Aksyonov's early work revels in its rejection of Soviet social realism. In 1966, two years after the fall of Khrushchev, Aksyonov was stripped of his Soviet citizenship. In 1976, he published *Non-Stop Round the Clock*, a satiric account of his experience as a visiting professor at the University of California at Los Angeles. The book describes the fast-paced American lifestyle in circus-like terms. *Crimea Island* (1980) also satirizes the amoral nature of American life by describing a mythical island close to the U.S.S.R. that becomes an independent capitalist democracy.

However, when he turned his satiric vision to the Soviet Union during the final years of détente, Aksyonov fell into political disfavor. He participated in the 1979 publication of *Metropol*, a collection of banned Soviet writings, and in 1980 he published *The Burn*, a mock portrait of contemporary life in the Soviet Union. Aksyonov immigrated to the United States in the summer of 1980, after he was expelled from the Writers Union and removed from the editorial board of the periodical, *Yunost*. His U.S. writings continued to satirize the Soviet Union in such works as *Say Cheese!* (1989) and *In Search of Melancholy* (1987), which he described as the "story of my emigration, alienation, and acceptance of a new home." In 1990 Mikhail Gorbachev ordered that Aksyonov's full Soviet citizenship be restored, but the writer continues to reside in the United States.

For additional reading see Tucker's *Literary Exile in the Twentieth Century*.

Alamo, The   A 1960 MILITARY FILM starring John WAYNE, Richard Widmark and Laurence Harvey. Wayne also produced and directed the movie. The action centers on the heroics of Davy Crockett (Wayne), Jim Bowie (Widmark), Col. William Travis and the other outnumbered Americans during their brave but ultimately futile attempt to defend the Texas mission from Mexican armies in 1836. The film depicts Americans as tough, dedicated and unyielding in their commitment to the cause of freedom, just as Wayne appeared to be in his real-life attacks on communists and communism and those he believed associated with them. Released during the second Berlin crisis, when Cold War tensions were especially high and the possibility of a nuclear war with the U.S.S.R. seemed quite real, *The Alamo* celebrates Americans who stand up for their beliefs, even in the face of overwhelming adversity. (The film did not delve into the reasons for the American presence in Texas, which had to do with extending slavery.) As in Berlin, the American Alamo fighters are surrounded and vastly outnumbered by the enemy, but they remain firm in their commitment to their cause.

Alas, Babylon   A popular 1959 APOCALYPTIC NOVEL by Pat Frank. The book went through 31 printings and sold over two million copies through 1975 and remained in print throughout the Cold War. The book tells the story of a small Florida town that survives a major nuclear war. In the foreword Frank, a military writer who had assignments at the Strategic Air Command (SAC) and the Missile Test Center at Cape Canaveral, states that "the H-bomb is beyond the imagination of all but a few Americans, while the British, Germans, and Japanese can comprehend it, if vaguely. And only the Japanese have personal understanding of atomic heat and radiation." He claims he wrote the book after answering a business acquaintance who wanted to know what would happen "if the Russkies hit us when we weren't looking—you know, like Pearl Harbor?" When Frank conservatively estimated that some 50 or 60 million Americans would die but the United States would probably win the war, the businessman replied, "What [an economic] depression that would make!" Frank claims, "I doubt if he realized the exact nature and extent of the depression—which is why I am writing this book."

Alas, Babylon thus plays out a post-apocalypse scenario in the central Florida town of Fort Repose. The book begins with a tense international situation resulting from the Soviet launch of *Sputnik 23*, a threatening spy satellite. At the same time, the superpowers clash in the Middle East. The protagonist, Randy Bragg, receives a coded message, "Alas, Babylon," from his brother at SAC Headquarters, indicating that a Soviet nuclear strike is imminent. The gossipy, small-town telegraph operator mentions the message to her librarian friend who recognizes it as a biblical quote referring to destruction. The women pass the word and Fort Repose prepares for an attack. Since Fort Repose is far enough from the local military base to avoid actual destruction, the survivors' main challenge is to deal with the threat of radiation and the transition to a post-nuclear society. The town is cut off from its outside sources of food, fuel and other staples. Provisions become increasingly hard to come by and money rapidly loses value. High-priced luxury items like Cadillacs and fancy homes become virtually worthless in comparison to more practical necessities: bicycle tires, evaporated milk and safety pins. In what may be a swipe at the business acquaintance who inspired the book, a bank president commits suicide because he cannot accept a world without money.

Nonetheless, private property is still respected, and the novel's moral universe punishes the wicked when recipients of looted jewelry suffer burns on the wrists and neck from radioactive contamination. The dedicated local doctor helps most of the townspeople pull through, and the survivors begin to rebuild society and reassert basic American values. They form vigilante groups for their mutual protection, rediscover the Yankee wisdom of Ben Franklin and return to church; their "faith had not died under the bombs and the missiles." Moreover in the post-nuclear society women must assume more crucial roles. A female Cabinet member becomes acting president and the gossipy telegraph operator and the heroic librarian, who at the beginning of the book was resisting right-wing efforts to remove objectionable books from the shelves, are now "practically our whole education system, and they keep all the records." They have never "worked so hard or accomplished so much in their whole lives."

Earlier in the novel Bragg asks his brother how the country had allowed itself to become vulnerable to an attack.

> It wasn't lack of money . . . It was state of mind. Chevrolet mentalities shying away from a space-ship world. Nations are like people. When they grow old and rich and fat they get conservative. They exhaust their energy trying to keep things the way they are—and that's against nature. Oh, the services were to blame too. Maybe even SAC. We designed the most beautiful bombers in the world, and built them by the thousands . . . We couldn't bear the thought that jet bombers themselves might be out of style . . . It's a state of mind that money alone won't cure.

The solution lies in empowering "bold men, audacious men, tenacious men. Impatient, odd-ball men like Rickover pounding desks for his atomic sub. Ruthless men who will fire the deadheads and ass-kissers . . . Young men because we've got to be a young country again. If we get that kind of men we may hack it—if the other side gives us time." Finally, America wins the war—"not that it matters"—and young, audacious men like Randy Bragg bring hope for a post-nuclear future in which America will return to the traditional small-town values and attitudes that, in the universe of *Alas, Babylon,* made it a great power in the first place. (See also NUCLEAR APOCALYPSE.)

For additional reading see Dowling's *Fictions of Nuclear Disaster* and Anisfield's *The Nightmare Considered.*

Aleshkovsky, Yuz   A Soviet EXILED WRITER (to the United States). Born in 1929, Aleshkovsky had been sent to a Soviet prison camp in his youth because of his "anti-social" views.

His early poems and fictional portraits draw on those experiences and on his acquaintance with criminals and their wardens. During the 1970s he appeared as an underground writer in the U.S.S.R. He reprinted much of his work in the United States after emigrating in 1979, at the end of United State-Soviet détente. He has published children's books as well as adult novels.

An extremely harsh critic of the Soviet system, Aleshkovsky declared at a Writers in Exile conference in 1982 that, "Having escaped from Dracula, from the Soviet regime, I suddenly began to encounter its closest blood relatives in the amazingly beautiful expanses of the New and Old worlds. Trembling with horror and loathing, I see *Sovieticus draculat* in the talentless specimens of mass culture that truly ravage the human spirit, in the obtuseness and blindness of independent politicians surrendering one after another the bastions of freedom to world totalitarianism . . . I think that one of the greatest ironies in history is that the peoples of the Soviet Empire, having long ago overcome the seduction of evil at the cost of unimaginable sacrifices, watch in horror as the West, as the entire free world, heads in the direction from which they have come, at least morally— toward the epicenter of seductive evil, where the free creative spirit of man resides behind heavy bars."

The Hand, or the Confession of an Executioner (1980; published in English, 1990) describes the brutality of the Stalinist regime and the efforts of a victim to achieve revenge against his tormentors by becoming a KGB agent.

For additional reading see Tucker's *Literary Exile in the Twentieth Century.*

"All in the Family"   A TELEVISION SITUATION COMEDY that ran on CBS from 1971 to 1991. Produced by Norman Lear, "All in the Family" was one of the most successful and significant shows in television history. Not only did it endure for a remarkable 20 years and spin off two other successful comedies, "Maude" and "The Jeffersons," and the less successful "Gloria," it brought political content and conflicts over political and social values to American situation comedies, which hitherto had been exclusively the domain of the noncontroversial. In addition to addressing racial and ethnic prejudices and labor-management confrontations, the show also humorously pitted Cold War liberal and conservative values against one another as Archie (Carroll O'Connor), a blue-collar conservative, exchanged barbs with the liberals in his family: his daughter Gloria (Sally Struthers), son-in-law Mike (Rob Reiner) and, in the early episodes, his wife's cousin Maude (Bea Arthur). Mediating between them was Archie's kindly wife, Edith (Jean Stapleton). Over the years, alterations in the cast and setting changed some of the particulars, and the show changed its name to "Archie Bunker's Place" in 1979. But it retained its premise of generating humor from the differences in backgrounds, attitudes and values among the characters. Begun during the Vietnam War, the show represented generational differences as Gloria and Mike maintained an antiwar perspective, while Archie held fast to the traditional Cold War ideology that accepted the necessity of fighting the communist menace throughout the world. In this respect "All in the Family" provided one of the few non-news television presentations of the political and social diversity that characterized the United States during the final 20 years of the Cold War.

"All the King's Horses" A 1953 story by Kurt VONNEGUT Jr. First published in *Collier's* magazine in the same year the Korean War concluded, it appears in Vonnegut's collection of short stories, *Welcome to the Monkey House* (1968). "All the King's Horses" centers on Colonel Bryan Kelley, a U.S. military attaché who is shot down over Asia with his wife, two sons and 12 soldiers by a sadistic communist guerrilla, Pi Ying. Though advised by Major Barzov, a Soviet military officer whom he wants to impress, Pi is autonomous and, because he is not really aligned to any nation-state, he is essentially immune to outside political pressures. "He's an outlaw. He hasn't a thing to lose by getting the United States sore at him." To satisfy his vanity in his intellectual superiority, Pi forces Kelley to participate in a game of chess, played on a life-sized board, in which the American prisoners are Kelley's chess pieces. Major Barzov and Pi's mistress, "a delicate young Oriental woman," look on dispassionately as captured pieces are summarily executed. Eventually an opportunity emerges for Kelley to sacrifice one of his sons in order to gain a quick victory. Though he agonizes over the decision, he orders his son onto a vulnerable square and then pretends to be horrified when Pi captures him. Pi taunts Kelley, but Pi's mistress kills Pi and herself rather than allow the boy to be slain. Barzov then resumes the game in Pi's place. He decides not to kill the captured pieces but sadistically declines to announce his decision. He offers to let Kelley take back his move and save his son, but the attaché declines. The Soviet then captures the boy and falls into the American's trap. Eventually all of the American survivors are freed.

The story expresses Vonnegut's view of the difficulties in conducting foreign policy in "feudal, barbaric" Asia. It also presents a contrast in U.S. and Soviet stereotypes commonly found in American Cold War culture: the communist is a cold, dispassionate professional who cares solely about his specific mission, while the American is a deeply feeling family man who loves his wife and children but can switch off his emotions and retain his professional cool when crises require it. He can therefore master his inner anguish and do what he must—deliberately sacrifice his son in order to save everyone else. Ironically, the American must become like the Soviet in order for the American community to survive; the difference is that for the American, the suppression of his fatherly love is unnatural and requires a supreme act of will, while the communist seems to come by it naturally. The story's pro-U.S. sentiment also appears when Barzov fails to recognize the trap Kelley has set and loses the game. Thus, his community's survival at stake, the American outwits the Soviet.

In 1991 "All the King's Horses" was one of several selections from *Welcome to the Monkey House* made into a short made-for-television film. Introduced by Vonnegut himself and directed by Allan King, it starred Len Cariou, Don S. Davis, Linda Darlow and Miguel Fernandes. In this version, set in Latin America instead of Asia, an American ambassador, his family and military guard are flying to the capital city of an unnamed country. The accompanying major points out that they had to sneak in the preceding ambassador in the middle of the night, while the new ambassador will be greeted by a brass band. He adds, "I used to worry about what I'd say when my grandchildren asked, 'What did you do in the Cold War, Grandpa?' Now I can just tell them I won. I stared down my enemy until he blinked." The ambassador replies that such U.S. consumer goods as VCRs, shiny cars and refrigerators helped make the enemy blink. Soon after this conversation, revolutionaries fighting the U.S.-backed government shoot down the plane and capture the American contingent. The guerrillas are running desperately short of supplies since they no longer receive aid from Cuba, because Cuba in turn no longer receives massive assistance from the U.S.S.R.

Vaccarro, the idealistic rebel leader, debates political philosophies with the pro-capitalist ambassador. The ambassador points to the failure of the communist experiment in Eastern Europe, and Vacarro scolds him for his delight that the end of the Cold War seems to prove that greed and self-interest motivate humanity more strongly than altruism and the common interest. Vaccarro, a chess master whose beloved son had been killed by U.S.-supplied weapons, then demands that the ambassador play the chess match. He forces the ambassador into sacrificing his son in order to save the others, then has the boy and the other captured "pieces" carried behind a wall, from which sounds of a firing squad are heard. But unlike in the original story, where vanity and sadism motivate Pi, a noble idealism prompts Vaccarro, who wants to teach the ambassador a lesson in how even the most committed materialist will sacrifice what he loves most for the good of the larger community. He tells the ambassador that he may be a fanatic but he is not a monster, and he then releases the boy and the other captives; their executions had been simulated in order to trick the ambassador. The film concludes with a TELEVISION NEWS account of how government troops raided the rebel headquarters and killed the leader, whom the U.S. major denounces as a "madman, a crazed, sadistic lunatic." The audience and ambassador, however, have a deeper understanding of Vaccarro, and the major's declaration comes across as government distortion. Thus the values in this post–Cold War film question U.S. Cold War ideology, while the original story from the beginning of the Cold War affirmed it. (See also MILITARY NOVELS.)

All the President's Men A 1974 NONFICTION book by Carl Bernstein and Bob Woodward and a 1976 POLITICAL FILM starring Dustin Hoffman, Robert Redford and Jason Robards Jr. and directed by Alan Pakula. Appearing shortly after President Nixon's resignation, the book narrates the story of the investigative efforts of Woodward and Bernstein, the *Washington Post* reporters who broke the story of the Watergate coverup. The Watergate scandal brought down the president and revealed a complex web of illegal acts, dirty money, abuse of power and political intrigue that had important ramifications for the Cold War and subsequent U.S. policies and actions. These included illegal covert actions by U.S. intelligence agencies and instances in which the CIA illegally spied on U.S. citizens. As a result of these revelations, covert activities by the intelligence agencies were curtailed during the 1970s.

Allende, Isabel   A Chilean NOVELIST and the niece of Chile's assassinated president, Salvador Allende. Born in Lima, Peru, in 1942, the daughter of Chilean diplomat Tomas Allende, Allende was brought to Chile when she was three years old, after her parents divorced. She grew up there with her maternal grandparents, who inspired her first novel, *The House of the Spirits* (1982; published in English, 1985). Allende's grandfather was highly autocratic; her grandmother, after whom Isabel was named, was a spiritualist who practiced seances in their home. When her mother married another diplomat, Allende first traveled with her but later attended private schools. While in school she began corresponding daily with her mother, a habit that influenced her later writing. Upon graduating she became a journalist, wrote several unsuccessful plays and married Michael Frias, an engineer whom she subsequently divorced.

Allende greatly admired her uncle, Salvador, who was the first freely elected, openly avowed Marxist head of state in the Western Hemisphere. Elected president in 1970, he attempted to turn Chile into a socialist state by nationalizing numerous industries and promoting extensive land reform. However, as a minority president in a coalition government, he faced powerful opposition to much of his program. Following a period of crippling strikes and public violence, fomented at least in part by covert activities of the CIA, a military coup directed by army commander General Augusto Pinochet, with American support, overthrew Allende and constitutional democracy. Pinochet established a pro-American military dictatorship that quickly became notorious for its brutality and widespread human rights violations. The U.S.-supported coup was certainly a Cold War event, as it eliminated from the Western Hemisphere a leftist government unsympathetic to American political and economic power.

Isabel Allende exiled herself shortly afterward to Venezuela, where she wrote *The House of the Spirits* upon learning of her grandfather's death. Influenced by the magical realism of Gabriel GARCIA MARQUEZ's *One Hundred Years of Solitude* (1970), which blends fantasy and realism, Allende's novel describes four generations of a Latin American family. The chronicle includes the overthrow of Salvador Allende. Allende has since published other, less well-received novels, including *Of Love and Shadow* (1987) and *Eva Luna* (1988). She is now married to William Gordon, a San Francisco lawyer, with whom she lives in Marin County, California.

For further reading, see Tucker's *Literary Exile in the Twentieth Century.*

Alsop, Joseph   A JOURNALIST. Born in 1910 to a wealthy New York family, Alsop attended the exclusive Groton School and graduated from Harvard University in 1932. He then joined the *New York Herald-Tribune* and within five years was writing his own Washington-based syndicated column. During World War II, Alsop worked as a publicist for General Claire Chennault in China, and he emerged from the war a strong supporter of Chinese Nationalist Chiang Kai-shek and an ardent opponent of Mao Zedong's communist revolution. Following the war he and his brother Stewart ALSOP collaborated on a syndicated column, and they continued their anti-communist stand in the formative

years of the Cold War. In 1947 Alsop predicted the communist takeover in Czechoslovakia, and in 1948 he warned that an American troop withdrawal from Korea would make that country vulnerable to "the expanding Soviet Empire." He therefore called for increased defense spending in 1950 and supported the U.S. policy of "containment." He criticized U.S. foreign policy under President Eisenhower as too weak, and his New Year's message for 1954 was "All is Lost." That year he unsuccessfully advocated U.S. intervention in Vietnam on behalf of the French and against the communist insurgents, and he was later a strong advocate of the Vietnam War. Though a Cold War "superhawk," Alsop opposed the RED SCARE, and he and his brother denounced Senator Joseph McCarthy and regularly defended his victims. They maintained that the chief communist danger came from China and the Soviet Union and not from within the United States. In 1953 they coauthored *We Accuse!*, a denunciation of the Atomic Energy Commission's refusal to reinstate the security clearance of J. Robert Oppenheimer, who had headed the commission from 1946 to 1952 and had previously directed the wartime Manhattan Project, which developed the atomic bomb. However, by the 1960s, Alsop came to believe that domestic communists had infiltrated the civil rights movement and were fomenting the racial strife that was erupting throughout the nation.

In 1958 Stewart left the column to become an editor for the *Saturday Evening Post*. Joseph continued their hard-line anti-Soviet position, arguing in the late 1950s that the United States lagged behind the Soviets militarily and suffered from a "missile gap." Senator John F. Kennedy adopted the missile gap (which turned out not to exist) as one of his issues in the 1960 presidential campaign, and Alsop became an influential adviser to the new president. He recommended that Kennedy select Lyndon Johnson as his running mate and, after the election, successfully promoted Republican C. Douglas Dillon as secretary of the treasury, although his efforts to have David Bruce named secretary of state failed. Following Kennedy's assassination in 1963, Alsop was the first to advocate that a blue-ribbon panel investigate the circumstances surrounding the president's murder. Though less friendly toward President Johnson, whom Alsop criticized for not being "forthright, either with the country, or with his associates, or even, one suspects, with his nearest or dearest," he staunchly supported Johnson's prosecution of the Vietnam War and criticized journalists David HALBERSTAM, Malcolm Browne and Neil Sheehan, whose reporting from Vietnam contradicted official representations; he accused them of painting a "dark, indignant picture" of the situation in Southeast Asia. He compared them to the journalists in the 1940s who had called Mao an "agrarian reformer." Alsop's antipathy for the Chinese communists was long-lived. In 1962 he criticized a suggestion by Supreme Court associate justice William O. Douglas that the United States send aid to China in order to avert a widespread famine, saying "Sentimentalists are beginning to talk of feeding starving China, which would simply mean getting Mao Tse-tung off his self-created hook." In 1973 Alsop retired to devote himself to studies of Greek antiquities. He died in 1989.

Alsop, Stewart A JOURNALIST. Born in 1914 to a wealthy New York family, Alsop attended the exclusive Groton School and graduated from Yale University in 1936. During World War II he served with the Office of Strategic Services (OSS), the agency that later became the CIA. He parachuted into occupied France soon after the D-Day invasion and later described his experiences in *Sub Rosa: the OSS and American Espionage.* In 1945 he joined the syndicated column written by his older brother, Joseph ALSOP. They took a strong anti-communist hard line, and in 1949 Soviet foreign minister Andrei I. Vishinsky denounced them for advocating new American air bases in the Middle East, India and North Africa. Though they opposed what they believed to be a genuine threat from international Soviet and Chinese expansionism, the brothers also spoke out against the abuses of Senator Joseph McCarthy, and they frequently defended victims of the domestic RED SCARE in their column. In 1953 they coauthored *We Accuse!,* a denunciation of the Atomic Energy Commission's refusal to reinstate the security clearance of J. Robert Oppenheimer, former head of the commission and director of the wartime Manhattan Project that developed the atomic bomb.

Alsop left the column in 1958 to become a contributing editor of the *Saturday Evening Post.* He held that position until 1968, when he became a political columnist for *Newsweek.* In 1962 he and Charles Bartlett claimed that UN ambassador Adlai Stevenson had strongly disagreed with President Kennedy's decision to blockade Cuba during the Cuban Missile Crisis. Stevenson and other members of the administration vehemently denied the charge, though Alsop and Bartlett stood by their claim. Like his brother, Alsop was a strong supporter of the Vietnam War, and his book *The Center* (1968) attacks academics and liberal intellectuals who criticized the administration's war policy. In *Stay of Execution* (1973) Alsop described his long struggle with the terminal cancer from which he died in 1974.

Always Coming Home A 1985 APOCALYPTIC NOVEL by URSULA LE GUIN. Written toward the end of the most bellicose era in the Cold War since the 1962 Cuban Missile Crisis, *Always Coming Home* features two alternative human societies following a nuclear disaster of an undisclosed nature. Reflecting many of the feminist sentiments of the era, the story centers on a tribe known as the Kesh. Unlike their aggressive, patriarchal neighbors they have recognized the dangers of technological violence and sexual inequality and have created instead a society predicated on female principles of kinship, nurturing behavior and respect for nature. Like such other contemporary apocalyptic novels as WARDAY (1984), THE WILD SHORE (1984), FISKADORO (1985) and THE POSTMAN (1986), *Always Coming Home* offers the hope that the nuclear holocaust will engender a leap in human consciousness, and it suggests that the enlightened consciousness involves a more complete acceptance and integration of feminine principles into the collective consciousness. Michael Dorris and Louise Erdrich conclude in *The Nightmare Considered,* "*Always Coming Home* . . . finds the seeds of a superior, less dangerous revitalization in the treasury of culture's traditional values. Its perspective is as nostalgic as a memory of childhood—filled with straightforward sim-

plicity and clarity of choice . . . even *with* 'big brains,' there is no chance that this branch of humankind will elect to reinvent weapons capable of its own destruction."

For additional reading, see Anisfield's *The Nightmare Considered.*

Amalrik, Andrei Alekseyvich A Soviet EXILED WRITER (to the United States), playwright, historian and human rights advocate. As a result of his controversial dissertation and his early efforts to publish his work abroad in the early 1960s, Amalrik was forced to forfeit his degree from Moscow University. In lieu of the academic career he had aspired to, he found employment performing menial jobs in order to sustain himself. During this period he surreptitiously wrote a series of experimental, absurdist plays akin to those of Eugene Ionesco and Samuel BECKETT, though Amalrik was unfamiliar with their Western literary tradition, the THEATER of the Absurd. He later published these works in a collection entitled, *Nose! Nose? No-se! and Other Plays* (1973). Because of his history of dissidence, the KGB kept him under constant surveillance and arrested him in 1965 after a search of his apartment revealed copies of his plays illustrated by the avant-garde artist Anatoly Zverev. Amalrik was charged first with disseminating pornographic and anti-Soviet material and then with "parasitism." He was sentenced to two-and-a-half years of forced labor in Siberia, where he began to write of his arrest, trial and internment. After 16 months he was released, and he returned to Moscow to live with his wife, the painter Gyusel Makudinova. In 1970 his autobiographical account, *Involuntary Journey to Siberia,* and an historical essay, *Will the Soviet Union Survive Until 1984,* were published abroad. As a result, Amalrik was arrested, tried and sentenced to prison. Released in 1976 after international protest on his behalf, Amalrik was allowed to leave the U.S.S.R. with his wife. The two immigrated first to the Netherlands, then to the United States and finally to France. In 1980, Amalrik completed a history of his last 10 years in the Soviet Union, shortly before his death in an automobile accident in Spain, where he was traveling to take part in an international conference organized by dissident groups. That work, *Notes of a Revolutionary,* appeared posthumously in 1982. (See also THEATER.)

For additional reading, see Tucker's *Literary Exile in the Twentieth Century.*

Amazing Grace and Chuck A 1987 FILM DRAMA starring Gregory Peck, Jamie Lee Curtis and Alex English, directed by Mike Newell. The story centers on a young boy who gives up Little League baseball to launch a one-person protest against nuclear weapons. Soon professional athletes join him, and he gains the attention and respect of world leaders.

"American Parade, The" A TELEVISION magazine show that ran on CBS for six months in 1984. It was retitled "Crossroads" midway through its brief life span. Anchored by correspondents Charles Kuralt and Bill Moyers, the show also included reports by Morton Dean, Bill Kurtis, Diane Sawyer, Maria Shriver and Andrew Lack, with Art Buchwald presenting satirical commentary. The Reagan-era program was dedicated to exploring the "vitality of the American spirit." Patriotic in nature, it featured uplifting pieces on both well-known American figures and obscure individuals. As a product of the Cold War and of the Reagan era, the show supported President Reagan's campaign to restore America's confidence in itself and to overcome the negativity and doubt spawned by the Vietnam War and such subsequent demoralizing events as Iran's hostage-taking.

"America's Town Meeting" A radio and TELEVISION TALK show that ran on ABC in 1948 and 1949 and during the winter and spring of 1952. It originated as a radio broadcast that ran from 1935 to 1956. The television show was moderated by George V. Denny Jr. and later by John Daly. It featured debates between prominent writers, politicians and public personalities over such questions as "Are We Too Hysterical About Communism?" and "Has the Korean War Been a Failure?" The show originated from New York's Town Hall auditorium, where a live and very vocal audience also participated. Stephen J. Whitfield suggests in *The Culture of the Cold War* that network officials terminated the show in 1952 in order to eliminate a possible forum for communists or others on the political left wing.

Amerika A TELEVISION DOCU-DRAMA that aired February 15 to 22, 1987. The 14½-hour program purported to depict what the United States would be like under Soviet occupation. The show began with the premise that an apathetic America had succumbed without a fight to Soviet aggression. The U.S.S.R. had essentially employed the United Nations as its puppet organization in order to achieve its conquest. Once the occupation was complete, the American government and social institutions radically changed. Communist Party officials were in charge of every level of bureaucracy, the Bill of Rights was suppressed and basic freedoms of speech, press and assembly were eradicated. Consumer goods were scarce and difficult to acquire. Set in the Midwest, America's so-called "heartland," the show was filmed to emphasize the purportedly drab nature of life under communist rule: Colors were muted; clothing was plain and inexpressive; and common household appliances were unavailable. The filmmakers evoked images from the Great Depression, as farm families huddled around old-fashioned coffee percolators, their Mr. Coffee machines presumably having been confiscated and shipped to Russia. The show's overriding tone was a pervasive gray. The heavy-handed message was that being a patriotic American meant actively opposing communism and being willing to take a military stand against it.

Amerika stirred considerable controversy in the press. Liberals called it "a hate film that evokes fear and hostility toward the Soviets," and they charged that ABC was pandering to "right-wing interests who loudly objected to the anti-nuclear message of ABC's THE DAY AFTER." (*The Day After* [1983] had graphically shown the devastation that a nuclear attack would wreak upon a Midwest city.) Conservatives, on the other hand, argued that the portrayal of Soviet occupation was too mild.

Both *Amerika* and *The Day After* were products of the Reagan era when, after a decade of détente, the Cold War heated up again. President Reagan's military buildup, his support of the right-wing Nicaraguan Contras and the military government of El Salvador, his invasion of the Caribbean island of Grenada, and his strident anti-Soviet rhetoric depicting the U.S.S.R. as "an evil empire" created a climate in which the possibility of a military confrontation with the U.S.S.R. seemed more likely than at any time since the 1962 Cuban Missile Crisis. The renewed Cold War tensions were depicted in a new round of films and television specials, one of which, the 1984 film RED DAWN, also depicts a defeated United States under Soviet occupation.

Anastasia A 1956 FILM DRAMA starring Ingrid Bergman, Helen Hayes and Yul Brynner, directed by Anatole Litvak. The movie tells the story of an amnesiac girl living in Germany who may be the surviving daughter of Czar Nicholas II, who was forced to abdicate in 1917 during the Russian Revolution and later executed along with his family. By generating sympathy for a victim of the revolution that brought the communists to power, the film reinforced anti-Soviet sentiment at a time when Cold War tensions were strong. (See also ANASTASIA: THE MYSTERY OF ANNA.) Bergman received an Academy Award for her portrayal of Anastasia.

Anastasia: The Mystery of Anna A 1986 FILM DRAMA starring Amy Irving, Olivia de Havilland, Claire Bloom, Rex Harrison and Omar Sharif and directed by Marvin Chomsky. Made 30 years after Ingrid Bergman's award-winning performance as Anastasia, this film about the purported surviving daughter of Czar Nicholas II also appeared during a tense period of the Cold War. Like the earlier film, it reinforced anti-Soviet sentiment by depicting the slaughter involved in the revolution that brought the communists to power in Russia.

Both films were based on a real person, Anna Anderson, who maintained that she was the princess Anastasia. A posthumous comparison in the 1990s of genetic material from Anderson and from undisputed Romanovs proved that she could not have been Anastasia, who was in fact killed along with her family in 1918. (See also ANASTASIA.)

And Now the War Is Over . . . The American Military in the 1970s A 1973 NBC TELEVISION DOCUMENTARY produced by Fred FREED. It premiered as a two-part "NBC White Paper." Narrated by Floyd Kalber, the film asks what will happen to the nuclear arsenals once the Cold War ends. It points out three paradoxes of the Cold War nuclear stalemate: that citizens have become accustomed to it; that each side can ensure the other's complete destruction even after suffering a successful first strike; and that despite the growth in nuclear arsenals, U.S. citizens have become less secure with each passing year. Kalber goes on to describe the logic behind the then-new philosophy of Mutually Assured Destruction (MAD), that the nuclear stockpile's primary purpose is not to fight a war but to prevent a nuclear attack. MAD, an outgrowth of Nixon and Kissinger's policy of détente with the Soviet Union in the early 1970s, replaced the doctrine of massive retaliation articulated by the Eisenhower administration in the 1950s.

"And Now the War Is Over" was criticized for being unfocused and oversimplified and for failing to answer, or even state clearly, the important questions it raises. (See also APOCALYPTIC FILMS.)

For additional reading, see Shaheen's *Nuclear War Films.*

Apocalypse Now A 1979 VIETNAM WAR FILM starring Marlon Brando, Martin Sheen, Robert Duvall and Dennis Hopper, directed by Francis Ford Coppola. *Apocalypse Now* is based on Joseph Conrad's 1902 short novel *Heart of Darkness,* about a steamboat pilot who has been hired to sail up the Congo River to bring back a company business agent who has assumed god-like powers over the natives and exceeded the company's control. As Marlowe, the pilot, goes farther upriver, he finds that the "light of reason," which illuminates and orders experience in the Western world, has gradually become replaced by a darker, more primitive, more visceral force. And he recognizes that Kurtz, the business agent, has been won over by that force. Though in Western eyes Kurtz has ceased to be civilized, when he expresses his newly acquired point of view he is often eloquent. Moreover, Conrad suggests, the brutal Kurtz represents the horrors of which the European colonialists were capable when released from the fragile hold of civilization.

Apocalypse Now restages the story during the Vietnam War. It shows the inadequacy of the classic liberal view of progress that informed many of the decisions to prosecute the war and suggests that apparently rational efforts become twisted and doomed when they fail to acknowledge the presence and power of deeper, more primal human forces. The plot centers on Captain Willard (Sheen), an army assassin traveling up the Mekong River into Cambodia, where he plans to kill Kurtz (Brando), an out-of-control Green Beret colonel who has established himself as a god among a tribe of Montagnard warriors. Things become increasingly surreal as Willard moves upstream in a small navy gunboat. In one village he witnesses a squadron of helicopters attack a Viet Cong–held village while blasting Wagner's "Ride of the Valkyries" over loudspeakers. Once the village has been secured, the commander of the helicopter squad (Duvall) takes time off from the war to organize a surfing party, even while sporadic fighting continues. Echoing the My Lai massacre and recalling the famous remark by an American officer that "we had to destroy the village in order to save it," which for many people summed up the absurdity of the war, Americans are shown killing the South Vietnamese civilians they have ostensibly come to protect. When Willard finally reaches the last American outpost on the river, it is in utter confusion. Just so the generals can claim that it is open, soldiers battle every day to restore a bridge that the Viet Cong destroy every night. When Willard asks a soldier who is in command, the man answers, "I don't know—I thought you were." Shot with eerie lighting, the scene appears almost hallucinogenic, as if imagined on the LSD one of the American sailors has taken. Once Willard passes beyond the final outpost, the world of logic, order, cause-and-effect and military procedure gives way entirely to the primitive and irrational forces that Kurtz seems to have harnessed.

Made at the end of détente, six years after the Vietnam War concluded, *Apocalypse Now* sought to express the confu-

sion and insanity that characterized the war for so many of those who experienced it, and to show the cynical, confused and conflicting motives of the powerful men who directed it. Like many other major works of contemporary literature and film, *Apocalypse Now* addresses the problem of how to act morally and properly in a realm of moral uncertainty, where our knowledge of crucial facts and situations is guaranteed to be incomplete and inaccurate. It also underscores the contrast between the Americans, who put their faith in advanced technology but had no strong motivation for their participation in the war, and the Viet Cong, who employed low-level technology but were fiercely dedicated to their cause.

apocalyptic films With the exception of APOCALYPTIC NOVELS, FILM dealt more directly than any other art form with the Cold War possibility of NUCLEAR APOCALYPSE. Generally, apocalyptic films either presented scenarios culminating with nuclear war or depicted the possible aftermath of a nuclear confrontation. In the former category are such MILITARY FILMS as FAIL-SAFE (1964) and THE BEDFORD INCIDENT (1965), the BLACK HUMOR film satire DR. STRANGELOVE (1964) and the Bush-era BY DAWN'S EARLY LIGHT (1990). All three of the earlier films come from the middle 1960s, within two or three years of the Cuban Missile Crisis, when nuclear war loomed as a distinct possibility. Each deals with an unintentional U.S. strike against Soviet targets, and each raises the possibility of the superpowers being drawn almost accidentally into a nuclear confrontation that the top leaders do not seek. *Dr. Strangelove* shows inept U.S. and Soviet military and political leaders trying unsuccessfully to stop an attack launched by an insane air force general, suggesting that there is a strong affinity among sexual power, political power and the bomb—that the military and political leaders of both countries have a "strange love" for the awesome possibility of annihilation. The disaster in *The Bedford Incident* also stems from independent actions taken by a field-level military commander, a navy captain who becomes emotionally caught up in his quest to chase a Soviet submarine from NATO-protected waters and who drives his men past the breaking point. In *Fail-Safe* the nuclear attack stems purely from a mechanical failure. Events get out of control once the American bombers proceed past their fail-safe points beyond which they cannot turn back, and the joint efforts of top U.S. and Soviet leaders are unable to avert the nuclear destruction of a Soviet city.

Some earlier films also imagine nuclear scenarios but do not address the dynamics that instigate the war, probably because the U.S.-Soviet antagonisms in the 1950s were so strong and the possibility of war was so ever-present that the particular events that might spark an attack attracted less attention than the possible outcome. INVASION U.S.A. (1952) depicts a hypnotist in a New York bar who helps patrons imagine what might happen to them in an atomic war. As they feel the stress of the imagined combat the patrons become militaristic; in the final moments the protagonists rush to convert tractor plants into tank factories. ON THE BEACH (1959) centers on the lives of Americans and Australians who are awaiting the arrival of a lethal radioactive cloud that has already wiped out the entire Northern

Hemisphere and is now progressing southward. Made during one of the most intense periods of the Cold War, *On the Beach* concludes with a shot of a religious banner proclaiming "There's still time." Though the message proves brutally ironic for the characters in the film, it serves as a warning for viewers.

According to directors Ingmar Bergman and Akira Kurosawa, the seemingly imminent possibility of nuclear apocalypse inspired their films THE SEVENTH SEAL (1956) and THE SEVEN SAMURAI (1954). Set in Sweden during an outbreak of the plague in the Middle Ages, Bergman's *The Seventh Seal* explores several different philosophical approaches to life in an environment in which death always hovers nearby. His later film *Shame* (1968) also develops apocalyptic themes as it depicts the deleterious effects on the personalities and marriage of a man and woman who become enmeshed in the horrors of warfare. *Shame* concludes with the pair fleeing through a vast sea saturated with human corpses. Set in 17th-century Japan, Kurosawa's *The Seven Samurai* features a new, technologically advanced weapon, the gun, which serves as a metaphor for nuclear weaponry. The swordwielding samurai are vulnerable only to this new weapon. The film also reveals the different motivations of the defenders (the samurai) and the defended (the townspeople) and thus implicitly raises some important questions about the relationship between standing Cold War armies and the citizens they serve.

The films that depict human survival after a nuclear war also fall into two categories. Some, like the 1959 film drama THE WORLD, THE FLESH AND THE DEVIL and the 1962 survivalist film, PANIC IN YEAR ZERO (based on Dean Owen's 1962 novel THE END OF THE WORLD), try to imagine a realistic account of survivors in a lawless, postnuclear society without normal food supplies, medical treatment, transportation or other forms of social support. *The World, The Flesh and the Devil*, addressing more than one social anxiety of the time, considers the possibility that the small number of survivors may be racially mixed and that human repopulation will require interracial coupling. That theme is also suggested but less fully developed in Hollywood's first postapocalyptic film, FIVE. Made in 1951, *Five* centers on the five survivors of an atomic war, a diverse group comprised of an idealistic college graduate, a hysterical, pregnant young woman, a bank worker, an elderly cashier and a fascist sportsmanexplorer—all white except for the bank worker. THE LAST WOMAN ON EARTH (1960) also deals with postnuclear sexual dynamics in its presentation of a love triangle among the only three survivors of a nuclear war—two men and a woman. The 1963 film LORD OF THE FLIES, based on the 1954 novel by William Golding, shows a community of British schoolboys degenerating into primitive behavior when they are abandoned on an ocean island after they flee England to avoid nuclear war. DAMNATION ALLEY (book, 1969; film, 1977) is about survivors attempting to reach a colony populated by other survivors. Similarly, GLEN AND RANDA (1971) follows a young couple as they wander through the United States seeking remnants of civilization. OMEGA MAN (1971) concerns the survivor of germ warfare, a topical issue in the early 1970s when the movie appeared.

The Australian film MAD MAX (1979) and its sequels *The Road Warrior* (1982) and *Mad Max: Beyond Thunderdome*

(1985), depict life in a violent postnuclear society that has reverted to tribalism. Based on a science fiction story by Harlan Ellison, A BOY AND HIS DOG (1975) became an underground hit. The black humor story is set in a postnuclear wasteland and focuses on a survivor and his dog. It culminates in an act of cannibalism. DEF-CON 4 (1985) imagines the fates of astronauts who return to Earth after a nuclear war and must try to survive in a lawless, chaotic America. RADIOACTIVE DREAMS (1986) is a Reagan-era teen comedy about the efforts of two boys raised on detective fiction to survive in a postnuclear-war environment. THE DAY AFTER (1983) attempts to depict the horror, chaos and confusion in a midwestern city following a nuclear attack. It was made for television during the most intense year of the Cold War since the Cuban Missile Crisis, when the Reagan administration was speaking publicly of "winnable" nuclear war; in opposition, the movie presents a strong antinuclear message. British director Peter Watkins had earlier made THE WAR GAME (1966) for the BBC as a pseudo-documentary based on a similar premise—a nuclear strike against a British town. At the time, the BBC declined to air it because it was fatalistic, bitter, hopeless and cruel—"too horrifying" and unsuitable for family viewing. AMERIKA, which aired on U.S. television in 1987, presented a conservative response to the antinuclear *Day After*. That movie shows life in a Sovietoccupied America after the United States has capitulated to the U.S.S.R. rather than fight a nuclear war. RED DAWN (1984) also depicts portions of the United States under communist occupation after the Soviets and their Latin American allies launch a surprise nuclear attack.

In addition to these more or less realistic attempts to imagine postnuclear scenarios, several SCIENCE FICTION FILMS raised the possibility of human survivors having to confront monsters and mutants formed by radiation. These films include THE DAY THE WORLD ENDED (1955) and the Japanese films GODZILLA (1955) and RODAN (1957). PLANET OF THE APES (1968) imagines a postnuclear world in which apes have become the dominant species and enslave humans. CAFE FLESH (1960s) is a pornographic film centering around mutants from nuclear fallout who can enjoy sex only vicariously because physical touching nauseates them.

Films in which nuclear apocalypse is narrowly avoided include THE DAY THE EARTH CAUGHT FIRE (1961), a science fiction movie in which nuclear testing threatens to throw the Earth out of its orbit; CRACK IN THE WORLD (1965), in which a scientist nearly destroys the Earth by launching a missile into its core; and the JAMES BOND films DR. NO (1962), GOLDFINGER (1964) and THUNDERBALL (1965), in which various evildoers gain control of nuclear weapons. Another SPY FILM, THE KREMLIN LETTER (1970), presents the possibility of a joint U.S.-Soviet nuclear attack against China. The 1966 novel on which the film was based appeared two years after China exploded its first atomic bomb and at the beginning of Mao Zedong's Cultural Revolution, when both superpowers had strained relations with the increasingly hostile Asian nation. The film appeared at the beginning of the U.S.-Soviet détente, during the final stages of the Cultural Revolution but before the thawing of relations between the United States and China. THE DAY THE FISH CAME OUT is a 1967 Greek-British satire directed by Michael Cacoyannis. The story spoofs attempts by the military to retrieve nuclear material dropped near a Greek island. In the Reagan-era WARGAMES (1983) a teenage computer hacker accidentally taps into the U.S. nuclear defense system and mistakenly believes he has discovered a sophisticated computer game. He then unknowingly issues a number of commands to the military, setting a doomsday scenario in motion. Also from the Reagan administration, THE FOURTH PROTOCOL (1987) presents a competition between two master spies who narrowly forestall a nuclear disaster.

Several FILM DOCUMENTARIES address the beginnings of atomic warfare. ATOMIC POWER (1946), THE DAY THE SUN BLOWED UP (1976) and FAT MAN AND LITTLE BOY (1989) depict the World War II–era Manhattan Project, which produced the atomic bomb, as does the 1947 film drama THE BEGINNING OR THE END (1947). THE DECISION TO DROP THE BOMB (1965), HIROSHIMA, A DOCUMENT OF THE ATOMIC BOMBING (1970), HIRO-SHIMA-NAGASAKI—AUGUST, 1945 (1968) and HIROSHIMA-NAGA-SAKI (1970) document the atomic bombings of Japan at the conclusion of World War II. In TO DIE, TO LIVE (1976) Robert Vas, a Hungarian concentration camp survivor, intercuts between black-and-white shots of Hiroshima immediately after the bombing in 1945 and color footage of Hiroshima in 1975. The film is based on DEATH IN LIFE, Dr. Robert Jay Lifton's 1962 study of the survivors' psychological responses to the bombing. A THOUSAND CRANES: CHILDREN OF HIROSHIMA appeared in 1962, the year of the Cuban Missile Crisis. Its stated purpose was "To inform American children what it is like to be a child in Hiroshima . . . to make a plea for peace." Alain Resnais's French-made film drama HIROSHIMA, MON AMOUR (1959) centers on a Japanese architect and a French actress who have a short love affair in Hiroshima after the war. The film intercuts documentary footage of the destruction caused by the atomic bomb with tender shots of the protagonists' lovemaking, both with each other and with lost lovers from the war.

PATTERN FOR SURVIVAL is a 1950 documentary intended to prepare the United States for a possible atomic attack by "an aggressor nation." The made-for-television documentaries COUNTDOWN TO ZERO (1966) and FOOTNOTES ON THE ATOMIC AGE (1969) describe the arms race in the middle and late 1960s. *Footnotes* points out some of the less well-known dangers of nuclear testing and nuclear policy and highlights several nuclear accidents that had gone largely unreported, such as the fire that contaminated a plutonium plant in Rocky Flats, Colorado, one of the most serious accidents in the nuclear weapons program during the Cold War. The film also addresses the financial interests at stake within the nuclear armaments industry and plays off scenes from *Dr. Strangelove* against interviews with former defense secretary Robert McNamara and the "father of the hydrogen bomb," Edward Teller. The BBC-produced RUMOURS OF WAR (1972) offers a cynical and bleak assessment of the superpowers' nuclear buildup in the early 1970s. It follows one of the officers assigned to a Minuteman missile silo in Albuquerque, New Mexico, and documents the procedures for ensuring that no missile will be launched by mistake or without proper authorization. ONLY THE STRONG was produced in 1972 by the conservative Institute for American Strategy, which opposed the arms limitation treaties that President Nixon had just submitted to Congress. It represents Soviet military strength as superior to that of the United States

and claims that peace can be ensured only by a strong, well-armed U.S. military. None of the major television networks would air the film, which was attacked by other political organizations and in newspaper editorials as biased propaganda. Nonetheless, church groups, veterans' organizations, service clubs and schools screened it extensively, using the 16mm prints that were made available for a nominal fee. In addition, over 400 local and independent television stations broadcast the program as a public service.

ARMS AND SECURITY: HOW MUCH IS ENOUGH? (1972) appeared on television the same year, three days after the Senate overwhelmingly approved the anti-ballistic missile (ABM) treaty, which forbade the U.S. and U.S.S.R. from building extensive missile defense capabilities. The film traces the nuclear arms race back to its post-World War II beginnings and covers the various arms limitation agreements that the superpowers had signed so far. AND NOW THE WAR IS OVER (1973) is a made-for-television documentary that also examines nuclear issues. The film asks what will happen to the nuclear arsenals once the Cold War ends and points out three paradoxes contained within the Cold War nuclear stalemate: that U.S. citizens have become accustomed to it; that each side can ensure the other's complete destruction even in the event of a successful first strike; and that despite the growth in nuclear arsenals U.S. citizens have become less secure with each passing year. THE ATOMIC CAFE (1982), in an apparent effort to undermine current Reagan administration claims about survivable nuclear war, edits clippings from 1950s government documentary films that present unrealistically optimistic assessments and ludicrously useless and erroneous advice for surviving a nuclear attack. In MISSILE (1988), Frederick Wiseman documents the training program for the air force officers in charge of the nuclear-armed Minuteman missile silos in the late 1980s.

The 1962 Cuban Missile Crisis became the subject of a limited number of documentaries and film dramas, though surprisingly, the most dangerous and dramatic moment in the Cold War has inspired relatively few literary or cinematic treatments. Fred FREED documented the event on NBC two years after it occurred in THE MISSILE CRISIS (1964), which aired on television; 10 years later, THE MISSILES OF OCTOBER (1974) reenacted the event in a made-for-television movie. LADYBUG, LADYBUG, a 1963 drama inspired by the missile crisis, explores the emotional turmoil suffered by a group of schoolchildren who are sent home from school in anticipation of a nuclear attack that ultimately does not come. And Alfred HITCHCOCK also treats the missile crisis in his 1969 spy film TOPAZ, which he adapted from the 1967 SPY NOVEL by Leon URIS.

For additional reading see Broderick's *Nuclear Movies*; Shaheen's *Nuclear War Films*.

apocalyptic novels   A subgenre of Cold War LITERATURE and a significant part of a body of Cold War culture dealing with the implications of a NUCLEAR APOCALYPSE. Because it is inherently hypothetical, often futuristic, and concerned with the products of science and technology, the subgenre frequently overlaps with SCIENCE FICTION NOVELS AND STORIES. Apocalyptic fiction breaks down into two broad categories. The first deals mostly with the buildup to a nuclear attack, the nuclear disaster itself and its immediate aftermath. The second addresses the new attitudes, beliefs, values, motivations, social organizations and forms of livelihood that might emerge in postapocalyptic societies. Several books in the second category also address the changes to language and storytelling that a nuclear holocaust might bring about, and some call for new mythologies to redirect the human conscious and subconscious in less violent and more nurturing ways. In feminist literature this redirection usually requires the replacement of patriarchal values, if not the patriarchy itself, with a world view and social organization that are more fully informed by a feminine perspective.

In HIROSHIMA, a work of NONFICTION first published in the *New Yorker* in 1946, John Hersey describes the actual experiences of six survivors of history's first atomic bombing. Other survivors' experiences appear in THE CRAZY IRIS AND OTHER STORIES OF THE ATOMIC BOMB (1984), a collection of eight Japanese short stories edited by Kenzaburo Oe and published in the United States. Although the prospect of worldwide nuclear apocalypse did not widely capture the literary imagination until after the U.S. developed the vastly more potent hydrogen bomb in 1952, the literary community quickly recognized that the emerging nuclear age would affect literature. In his 1950 Nobel Prize acceptance speech William FAULKNER declared, "Our tragedy today is a general and universal fear so long sustained by now that we can even bear it. There are no longer problems of the spirit. There is only the question: When will I be blown up? Because of this, the young man or woman writing today has forgotten the problems of the human heart in conflict with itself which alone can make good writing because only that is worth writing about, worth the agony and the sweat."

The fear of being blown up intensified after the Soviets exploded their first hydrogen bomb in 1953 and again in 1957 when they launched *Sputnik I,* the first human-made space satellite, and demonstrated their capacity to attack the U.S. mainland with intercontinental ballistic missiles (ICBMs). From then on, postnuclear literature acquired a more apocalyptic tone.

The preponderance of apocalyptic fiction appeared during or shortly after the most hostile and bellicose periods of the Cold War. The first of these occurred between 1958 and 1962 when the second Berlin Crisis and the Cuban Missile Crisis threatened to trigger global nuclear war and the Soviet Union was mistakenly thought to enjoy missile superiority over the United States. During this period many Americans believed that nuclear war was close to inevitable and possibly imminent.

The next most belligerent period lasted from 1980 to 1985, after the Soviet invasion of Afghanistan destroyed détente and before Mikhail Gorbachev became the Soviet leader. During this time President Ronald Reagan called the Soviet Union an "evil empire" and accused it of abandoning its commitment to the balance of power implicit in the stalemate concept known as Mutually Assured Destruction (MAD), and accused it as well of preparing to prevail in a protracted nuclear war. Reagan launched a massive defense buildup and advocated that the United States pursue its own policy of winnable nuclear war. The year 1983 was especially intense. In early spring Reagan proposed developing the Strategic Defense Initiative (SDI—more popularly known as STAR WARS), a laser-armed satellite shield that Reagan hailed for its defensive capabilities but that the Soviets feared for its potential offensive abilities. That summer the Soviets shot down a Korean civilian airliner that had strayed over their airspace, and the West decried their "barbarism." On September 8 Soviet foreign minister Andrei Gromyko cautioned, "The world situation is now slipping toward a very dangerous precipice. Problem number one for the world is to avoid nuclear war." The following month a terrorist car bomb in Beirut killed 241 American marines who had been sent there as peacekeepers in the Lebanese civil war. Two days later, Reagan ordered a full-scale U.S. invasion of the Marxist-led Caribbean island of Grenada. Less than a week after that, scientists from the United States, the Soviet Union and other nations met in Washington at the World After Nuclear War Conference, where they warned that a "nuclear winter" might follow a large-scale nuclear war. In November the first nuclear-armed intermediate-range American cruise missiles arrived in England, sparking massive protests, especially by women. That month U.S.-Soviet arms limitation negotiations also broke down, and the Soviet Union announced its intention to increase its nuclear forces. Less well known to the public, in October the Soviets feared that a planned NATO military exercise in command and control, Able Archer 83, might be the prelude to an actual NATO attack against the Warsaw Pact countries. During the exercise the Soviet KGB mistakenly notified its intelligence stations that American military bases had been put on alert.

Tensions remained high between the superpowers until 1985 when Gorbachev took office. He soon introduced economic and political reforms that were welcomed in the West, and he and Reagan conducted several summit conferences that promoted more peaceful relations to restrict, and in some cases reverse, the nuclear buildup. Thus, unlike the final Brezhnev years, the last five years of the Cold War were less dominated by fears of a devastating nuclear war, though these were never absent. Consequently, less apocalyptic fiction appears after about 1987.

Among pre-hydrogen bomb literary works was THE MANIAC'S DREAM (1946). Its author, F. H. Rose, claimed it was "the first novel about the atomic bomb." It alludes to Joseph Conrad's 1902 novel, *Heart of Darkness,* as a detached narrator observes Thara, a mad scientist at work deep in a tropical jungle. The Faustian scientist who suffers from hubris heretically likens himself to God: "Mankind harnessing to his own uses the power of Atomic Energy, will prove once and for all, that there is no other God but Man, and that he himself is God." The author's postscript makes explicit his admonition about science gone amok. Rose condemns "the ruthlessness with which Science goes forward in its search for truth, brushing aside every obstacle, and caring for nothing but to search and find . . . Does not his [Thara's] attitude toward God and Man typify the attitude, and foretell the doom, of all men and nations who exalt Man and despise God?" *The Maniac's Dream* thus introduces the debate over science that informs much apocalyptic literature. Poul Anderson's science fiction story "Tomorrow's Children," written two years after the Hiroshima attack, also describes the effects of a worldwide atomic war, and his

1952 novel *Vault of the Ages* likewise deals with nuclear issues. George ORWELL's futuristic, totalitarian society in NINETEEN EIGHTY-FOUR (1949) emerges in the aftermath of atomic wars although its inspiration is largely the totalitarian Soviet bureaucracies of the 1930s.

Judith Merril was the first woman to publish a popular novel dealing with the prospect of surviving an atomic attack. SHADOW ON THE HEARTH (1950) centers on Gladys, a suburban housewife whose life is entirely absorbed by the day-to-day demands of suburban living. She pays little attention to politics or the news and is woefully uninformed about radiation and survival techniques. Her home is far enough away from ground zero not to be harmed when a nuclear attack destroys New York, and her initial response is largely denial. However, she and her teenage daughter Virginia acquire the necessary survival skills as they await the return of her husband who, we learn, is safe in another part of town. One of the book's themes is that women, too, must become knowledgeable about nuclear war in the Cold War era. Unlike apocalyptic novels from the era of the hydrogen bomb, *Shadow on the Hearth* pictures a postnuclear society that recovers relatively quickly from the attack, which, though devastating, directly affects only a comparatively small area. Society remains intact after the bombing, the danger from radioactive fallout is minimal and the authorities remain largely in control. Even though lawlessness increases, neighbors also work together to help each other. The story reaches a comparatively happy ending as a much more savvy, independent and capable Gladys reunites with her husband and begins a new life.

Most apocalyptic literature from the era of the hydrogen bomb presents a far more gruesome prospect for both short-term and long-term survival, though some stories depict the bomb as a kind of moral cleansing agent that will wipe the slate clean and give humanity a new start. Most stories concentrate more on the long-term impact on society than on the specific horrors of the attack, something to which Herman Kahn alludes in his 1960 study, ON THERMONUCLEAR WAR: THINKING ABOUT THE UNTHINKABLE, in which he remarks that "it is characteristic of our time that many intelligent and sincere people are willing to agree that it is immoral to think and even more immoral to write in detail about having to fight a thermonuclear war." There are some notable exceptions, however. Philip Wylie's TOMORROW! (1954), a novel whose rhetorical purpose is to promote construction of fallout shelters and a comprehensive civil defense system, details the destruction of a small midwestern town in which most people had been living orderly, routine lives.

> In a part of a second, he was gas, incandescent, hotter than the interior of any furnace. In the same part of a second the proud skyline of River City and Green Prairie smoked briefly, steamed a little, and no shadows were thrown anywhere in the glare. The facades—stone, concrete, brick-glazed, crinkled and began to slip as they melted. But the heat penetrated, too. The steel frames commenced to sag and buckle; metal, turned molten, ceased to sustain the floors.

The narrator points out that the buildings would have collapsed but gravity was not quick enough, so the build-ings vaporized before they could fall. "On the sidewalks, for a part of a second, on sidewalks boiling like forgotten tea, were dark stains that had been people, tens of thousands of people . . . The heart of the cities was gone. A third of their people were dead or dying or grievously hurt." Survivors are reduced to looting and plundering and quickly fall into a mob psychology.

In the 1940s Wylie had popularized MOMISM, a belief that overbearing, emasculating mothers were responsible for many of the nation's ills, including its presumed failure to "stand up" to communism. In *Tomorrow!* the nuclear bomb serves as the moral agent that punishes such failings. Three domineering mothers oppose the civil defense program, largely because they resent the inconvenience it causes to their shopping routines and social engagements. When the nuclear attack comes, none takes shelter, and each is duly punished and humbled. Wylie's support for nuclear armament becomes evident as a secret cobalt bomb saves the United States from almost certain conquest by the underhanded Soviets, who had introduced germ warfare. The decision to use the bomb had been complicated by scientific predictions that it might destroy the entire world, but Wylie's novel supports the president's decision to employ it, and the bomb destroys only the Soviet Union. *Tomorrow!* concludes optimistically as the survivors, free of their domineering wives and mothers, work to build a better world under the supervision of those "able to dream and put the dreams on paper." Thus the bomb becomes "no catastrophe at all, but pure benefit. 'End of an era,' they would say. 'Good thing too,' they'd add."

Pat Frank's best-selling ALAS, BABYLON (1959) similarly depicts the before, during and after phases of a nuclear attack on a small community and suggests hope for a postnuclear future in which America will return to the traditional small-town values and attitudes that, in the view of *Alas, Babylon,* made it a great power in the first place. Nevil Shute's earlier best-seller, ON THE BEACH (1957), is not so hopeful. It begins after a nuclear war has destroyed all life in the Northern Hemisphere and follows a group of characters in Australia awaiting the inevitable arrival of a lethal cloud of radiation that will kill them as well. In INTENSIVE CARE (1970) New Zealand writer Janet Frame likewise resists suggestions by Aldous Huxley and others that the Southern Hemisphere may be immune from nuclear disaster. So too does David Graham's DOWN TO A SUNLESS SEA (1979), which follows the fates of airplane passengers who were airborne when the nuclear attacks began and thus were saved from immediate destruction. The passengers take refuge in Antarctica, but the radioactivity ultimately destroys them as well. Mordecai Roshwald's LEVEL 7 (1959) follows the postnuclear fate of military personnel deep in an underground command bunker that controls the U.S.'s ICBMs. Also published in 1959, Helen Clarkson's THE LAST DAY, like *Shadow on the Hearth*, presents an account of the nuclear apocalypse from the perspective of a housewife. However, like *On the Beach,* its perspective is bleak.

RED ALERT (1958) imagines a deranged military officer who orders a nuclear strike; it became the basis for a FILM SATIRE, the highly acclaimed 1964 classic of BLACK HUMOR, DR. STRANGELOVE. In Eugene BURDICK and Harvey Wheeler's 1962 MILITARY NOVEL, FAIL-SAFE, Moscow and New York suffer nuclear annihilation after a mechanical error launches an American strike against the Soviet Union. Influenced by the 1960s psychedelic drug culture, BAREFOOT IN THE HEAD (1969) imagines a global war fought with mind-altering drugs that takes place totally within the protagonist's imagination. Doris Lessing's five-volume *Children of Violence* follows the life of a white South African woman from the 1920s through the postwar era. The final volume, *The Four-Gated City* (1969), concludes with a 60-page appendix that chronicles a nuclear war that destroys the British Empire. Robert Merle's MALEVIL (1973) follows the fates of a group of friends who survive the nuclear attack by hiding in wine vats in an old family castle.

Yorick Blumenfeld's JENNY: MY DIARY (1981) chronicles the experiences of a mother who takes refuge in a communal shelter with her two children before a nuclear attack. The sexually promiscuous postnuclear society that develops underground initially repels her: ". . . as if this shelter were some kind of suburban swapclub." Eventually she becomes more tolerant, and her antipathy for "life forces" disintegrates when she finds a Jewish lover with whom she can discuss the Holocaust. The ending suggests that a successful new society can be rebuilt from the ashes. Carolyn See's GOLDEN DAYS (1987) also posits a happy future as it depicts a group of Reagan-era Californians whose pop psychology and Eastern mysticism enable them to face the postapocalyptic world with a positive attitude. The reviewer for the *New York Times Book Review* declared, "In its weird way, this may be the most life-affirming novel I've ever read." The title comes from Book III of Milton's *Paradise Lost,* in which Jesus saves humanity by offering himself as a sacrifice. Another book featuring Californian survivors of nuclear war is Robert Silverberg's *Tom o' Bedlam* (1986), in which the survivors dream of exotic alien worlds. Their dreams give rise to a cult whose leader may or may not be describing hallucinations. Bernard Malamud's GOD'S GRACE (1982) also draws on the Bible as it presents the story of a postnuclear Noah, a paleontologist who tries to breed an improved species of human-chimpanzee in the aftermath of a nuclear war.

Dean Ing's 1983 survivalist novel PULLING THROUGH reflects the attitudes and values of contemporary "survivalists," who were then arming and training themselves to survive in a lawless, hostile postnuclear-war environment. Its hero, a pragmatic, cheetah-owning bounty hunter named Harve Rackham, relies on his resourcefulness, intelligence and ability to discard liberal "nonsense" and assess situations clearly and astutely. Ing's other work on similar themes includes *Systemic Shock* (1981), *Single Combat* (1983) and *Wild Country* (1985). In this respect Ing's work mirrors Dean Owen's earlier survivalist novel, THE END OF THE WORLD (1962), which was the basis for the FILM DRAMA, PANIC IN YEAR ZERO. Robert Heinlein's FARNHAM'S FREEHOLD (1965) also presents a survivalist scenario, as does Ryder Stacy's DOOMSDAY WARRIOR (1984) and its 1984 sequel, *Doomsday Warrior No. 2: Red America.*

Most of the rest of apocalyptic literature focuses on postapocalyptic society rather than on the actual nuclear attack that created it. Bernard Wolfe's LIMBO '90 (1953) presents an early example of several common themes and issues. It projects the emergence of a highly religious/superstitious postapocalyptic culture that rejects science; it suggests that the impulse toward violence and self-destruction is an innate feature of the human psyche; and it employs linguistic experimentation and exploration to create an appropriate medium for rendering the postapocalyptic experience. The story focuses on an American surgeon who was on an island, lobotomizing natives when the war broke out in 1990. He returns home to a land of mutilated people who deify him in a religion of prostheses that promotes the voluntary amputation of their limbs. He rejects their attempt to excise the human proclivity for destruction by eliminating body parts.

> There's only one thing . . . that has any chance of saving man before he's annihilated through his own masochism, it's to get behind his shows of violence and pound it home to him that 99 per cent of them are phony, masochistic in inception and masochistic in aim, born of death and striving for death. That'll work, and only that, all the rest is suicide disguised as science and humanitarianism.

Wolfe thus suggests that the nuclear threat stems from deep, unconscious forces pulling humanity toward self-destruction. In this respect he anticipates William Golding's LORD OF THE FLIES (1954) and Arthur Kopit's play END OF THE WORLD (1984). L. Sprague de Camp's short story JUDGMENT DAY (1955) also rests on the premise that humans are inevitably drawn to their own destruction. Like James Joyce's earlier *Finnegans Wake,* Orwell's more contemporary *Nineteen Eighty-Four* and such later apocalyptic novels as Russell Hoban's RIDDLEY WALKER (1981), Anthony Burgess's THE END OF THE WORLD NEWS (1982), Whitley Strieber and James Kunetka's WARDAY (1984), Tim O'Brien's THE NUCLEAR AGE (1985), David Brin's THE POSTMAN (1985), Denis Johnson's FISKADORO (1985) and James Morrow's *This Is the Way the World Ends* (1986), *Limbo '90* treats the power of language to shape reality and is deeply concerned with the power of the unconscious mind. Because words can mediate between the conscious and unconscious, language itself emerges as an important element of the book. The wordplay lightens the tone of an otherwise demoralizing subject and thus endows the novel with elements of black humor. The new religion is predicated on puns: "arms means armaments, legs mean marching order" and even the title is a sick pun on body parts.

Other works focus more on storytelling and mythmaking than on language per se as they consider which accounts from the preapocalyptic past are worth preserving for postapocalyptic society. Some, like Edgar Pangborn's DAVY (1964), take a humanist approach and hope to retain the best of the earlier civilization, including the writings of Pangborn's contemporary, John BARTH. Stephen Minot's CHILL OF DUST (1964) also encourages saving elements from the past, as leaders representing the humanistic, religious and scientific traditions collectively furnish the reemerging society with what it will require to survive and flourish. By contrast, the need for new myths appears in Ursula LE GUIN's ALWAYS COMING HOME (1985), *Riddley Walker, Warday, The Wild Shore, Fiskadoro* and *The Postman.*

In 1955, three years after the United States developed the hydrogen bomb, Walter Miller published A CANTICLE

FOR LEIBOWITZ in *Fantasy and Science Fiction* magazine. The novella became the first part of his three-part 1959 novel of the same title. (The other two parts also appeared as separate stories, in 1956 and 1957.) This novel became a prototype of postapocalyptic fiction predicated on a cyclic view of history. In such literature society devolves into either lawless anarchy, as in *The End of the World;* medieval feudalism, as in Leigh Brackett's THE LONG TOMORROW (1955), C. S. Casewit's THE PEACEMAKERS (1960), *Doomsday Warrior, Davy, Riddley Walker, The Postman* and *Warday;* or fascistic dictatorship as in *Nineteen Eighty-Four,* N. B. Williams's ATOM CURTAIN (1956), Alfred Coppel's DARK DECEMBER (1958), L.P. Hartley's FACIAL JUSTICE (1960), Norman Spinrad's THE IRON DREAM (1972) and Suzy McKee Charnas's WALK TO THE END OF THE WORLD (1979). In *Always Coming Home* and *Fiskadoro*, postapocalyptic society returns to tribalism, as do the upper-class British schoolboys who are deserted on an ocean island in *Lord of the Flies.* Many of these stories depict a brutal, capricious, superstitious, male-dominated world, but some, like *A Canticle for Leibowitz,* suggest that eventually human society will resume its evolution and undergo a new Enlightenment in which it will again embrace science but learn to harness it with better success: Thus *Canticle* concludes with a futuristic colony of priests taking off for the stars in a spaceship. Other postapocalyptic books that project an eventual positive role for science in postnuclear society include *Chill of Dust, The Long Tomorrow,* Poul Anderson's ORION SHALL RISE (1983) and *Riddley Walker.* Robert Sheckley treats technology in an absurdist manner in JOURNEY BEYOND TOMORROW (1964), and in MILLENNIUM (1983), John Varley imagines time travel as a way to save the species. *The Iron Dream* posits a parallel universe in which Adolf Hitler is a science fiction writer imagining a male-dominated, postapocalyptic Nazi motorbike gang that celebrates science and power. The gang escapes the effects of the nuclear war it has waged by cloning themselves and colonizing space. Hitler, the writer, describes the settlers who, like the priests in *Canticle,* are leaving Earth aboard a spaceship: "The seed of the Swastika rose on a pillar of fire to fecundate the stars."

By contrast, many books with feminist sympathies depict the dangers of technological violence and sexual inequality and promote a society predicated on the presumably female principles of kinship, nurturing behavior and respect for nature. These include *The Long Tomorrow, Always Coming Home, The Wild Shore* and *Walk to the End of the World,* which appears to have been inspired by the machinations of the real Hitler. In that novel, women in the postnuclear society are made into slaves who work underground and are processed and delivered as food when they die. "Some man must have designed the process; it was too beautiful, too efficient to be a product of the fems' [women's] own thinking." Likewise, in *Nineteen Eighty-Four,* science and technology serve as tools of oppression and repression and help those in power construct an easily manipulated citizenry that neither wants nor is capable of enlightenment. Two novels by Native Americans, Leslie M. Silko's CEREMONY (1977) and Martin Cruz Smith's STALLION GATE (1986), also decry the impact of Western science as they describe the effect of the Manhattan Project upon the New Mexico tribes during the development and testing of the atomic bomb.

Perhaps more than any other mainstream popular American author, Kurt VONNEGUT Jr. addresses the theme of human-made apocalypse. In Vonnegut's novels the disaster or potential disaster typically stems from science and technology gone amok. *Player Piano* (1952), for instance, features a supercomputer capable of waging totally efficient war. The story climaxes with the destruction of all forms of technology, but even this solution seems inadequate, as people begin eagerly to reconstruct the very technology that has nearly destroyed them. In CAT'S CRADLE (1963), which appeared the year after the Cuban Missile Crisis, Felix Hoenikker, the father of the atom bomb, has invented *ice-nine.* A unique isotope of water, ice-nine reconfigures the molecules in ordinary water so that they turn into ice at temperatures below 114 degrees Fahrenheit, instead of 32 degrees. Dropped into the ocean, a single crystal of ice-nine can solidify the entire sea, and touched to someone's lips it freezes the blood, killing the person. When he dies, Hoenikker leaves a piece of ice-nine to his three maladjusted children who divide it among themselves and then proceed to trade the crystal for personal gratification. Ultimately ice-nine falls into irresponsible hands, freezes over the sea and brings about an apocalypse. Thus Vonnegut warns that science will inevitably be abused because it is human nature to treat it carelessly and apply it for selfish reasons. Moreover the flukes of nature ensure that people's best efforts to control the dangerous products of science will inevitably fail. Nonetheless, the novel's black-humor playfulness and pleasure in creative imagination render this bleak theme palatable, even fun.

Vonnegut's *Deadeye Dick* (1982) addresses the question of moral responsibility by comparing the fate of a boy who has accidentally killed a woman to that of the U.S. government, which may have deliberately destroyed an American city to test the neutron bomb, a weapon whose development in the real world President Carter had canceled but whose resumption of development the Reagan administration was then considering. "My own guess is that the American Government . . . set one off in a small city which nobody cared about, where people weren't doing all that much with their lives anyway, where businesses were going under or moving away. The Government couldn't test a bomb on a foreign city, after all, without running the risk of starting World War Three." In the end the government suffers no repercussions for its action, while the boy is stigmatized for life and his family is ruined. *Galapagos* (1986) also features nuclear destruction. The book begins with an apocalyptic nuclear war and then moves forward a million years to the renewed evolution of the species. However, the law of natural selection this time reduces human brain size since the earlier, excessively large brains were most responsible for the nuclear holocaust. The old-time big brains "would tell their owners, in effect, 'Here is a crazy thing we could actually do, probably, but we would never do it, of course. It's just fun to think about.' And then, as though in trances, the people would really do it—have slaves fight each other to the death in the Colosseum . . . or build factories whose only purpose was to kill people in industrial quantities, or to blow up whole cities, and on and on." As Tom Hearron points out in *The Nightmare Considered* (1991), Vonnegut shows that "the essential paradox of our time [is] that people are equipped with such large brains that they have become extremely stupid when it comes to foreseeing the consequences of their action." Elsewhere Vonnegut, writing about the comedy team Bob and Ray, seems to be commenting on his own work: "Man is not evil, they seem to say. He is simply too hilariously stupid to survive." However, the hilarity has redemptive value in its own right, and like John Barth, Thomas PYNCHON, Robert COOVER and other black humorists, Vonnegut derives a life-affirming spirit of play and energy from the bleak world he perceives.

For additional reading see Dowling's *Fictions of Nuclear Disaster,* Anisfield's *The Nightmare Considered* and Scheick's "Continuative and Ethical Predictions: The Post-Nuclear Holocaust Novel of the 1980s."

Arabesque A 1966 SPY FILM starring Gregory Peck, Sophia Loren and Alan Badel and directed by Stanley Donen. It is based on Gorden Cotler's novel *The Cipher.* The story concerns an Oxford professor who deciphers a hieroglyphic that proves to contain valuable information sought by international spies, oil sheiks and Middle Eastern political figures.

Are You Now Or Have You Ever Been A 1972 play by Eric Bentley. This play is a dramatic representation of the investigation of communist influences in the entertainment industry by the HOUSE COMMITTEE ON UN-AMERICAN ACTIVITIES (HUAC). The dialogue is comprised entirely of the actual words of the participants, taken from transcripts of the committee hearings, though the committee members and investigators have been identified only by number (Committee Member 1, Investigator 2 and so on). The testimonies of 18 witnesses, given between 1947 and 1956, are merged into a single session for purposes of dramatic unity. Bentley cites the theatrical nature of the hearings to justify his treatment of them as drama. He points out that the 1947 hearings were punctuated by applause, boos, cheers, hisses and laughter and that Chairman Parnell Thomas (R., New Jersey) presided with rhetorical flourish. He further claims that, "Though I did abridge and tidy up the record, I did not write in additional dialogue. Transpositions—of words within a sentence or of sentences within a sequence—I tried to hold down to a minimum lest there be any distortion of the sense." The 18 testimonies presented are by HOLLYWOOD TEN members Edward DMYTRYK and Ring LARDNER Jr.; Sam G. Wood, the founder of the MOTION PICTURE ALLIANCE FOR THE PRESERVATION OF AMERICAN IDEALS, who testified as a "friendly witness"; and actors and writers Larry PARKS, Sterling Hayden, Jose Ferrer, Abe Burrows, Tony Kraber, Jerome Robbins, Elliott Sullivan, Martin Berkeley, Lillian Hellman (whose SCOUNDREL TIME [1976] presents her autobiographical account of her testimony), Marc Lawrence, Lionel Stander, Zero MOSTEL, Arthur MILLER and Paul ROBESON. (See also THEATER; RED SCARE; BLACKLISTING.)

Armageddon: A Novel of Berlin A 1964 POLITICAL NOVEL by Leon URIS. The story depicts the political and social developments in Berlin from the end of World War II to the end of the Berlin airlift in 1949. The brutal treatment of German women by the Soviet occupiers is highlighted in a story that centers on an American military administrator who, despite his antipathy for Germans, falls in love with a German girl. The book was praised for its journalistic detail but criticized for its flat characters and other literary failings. (See also LITERATURE ABOUT COLD WAR EVENTS.)

"Armed Forces Hour, The" A musical variety TELEVISION show that ran on NBC in 1949–50 and on the DuMont network in 1951. Produced by the Defense Department, this show was a promotional program for the U.S. Armed Forces. Acts by professional entertainers and such military performers as the Singing Sergeants and the U.S. Navy Dance Band were intermingled with films about the army, navy and air force.

Arms and Security: How Much Is Enough? A 1972 FILM DOCUMENTARY written and produced by James Benjamin and directed by Howard Enders. Narrated by Frank Reynolds, the critically acclaimed film premiered as an ABC Special Report three days after the Senate overwhelmingly approved the antiballistic missile (ABM) treaty, which forbade the United States and U.S.S.R. from constructing extensive defensive missile capabilities. The film traces the nuclear arms race back to its post-World War II beginnings. It discusses failed proposals by Bernard Baruch and Andrei Gromyko to control atomic energy in 1946 and moves through the arms race of the 1950s, the 1963 Nuclear Test Ban Treaty that outlawed above-ground testing, the UN Sea Bed Treaty, the ABM Treaty and an interim strategic weapons agreement that established a five-year freeze on deployment of intercontinental ballistic missiles (ICBMs). The film also shows underground silos housing Minuteman ICBMs and features two air force officers simulating launch procedures. Also featured are the "father" of the hydrogen bomb, physicist Edward Teller, Defense Secretary Melvin Laird and Dr. Jerome Frank, a professor of psychiatry at Johns Hopkins University. (See also APOCALYPTIC FILMS.)

For additional reading, see Shaheen's *Nuclear War Films.*

Army-McCarthy hearings Televised 1954 Senate hearings investigating allegations that Senator Joseph McCarthy (R. Wisconsin) had tried to blackmail the army into commissioning as an officer McCarthy's recently drafted aide, G. David Schine. According to the allegations, McCarthy had threatened to "wreck the Army" by holding hearings to investigate McCarthy's own claims that Secretary of the Army Robert T. Stevens had attempted to conceal communist subversive activity at the U.S. Army's Signal Corps Center at Fort Monmouth, New Jersey. The hearings were notable because, for the first time since his rise to power in 1950, McCarthy was effectively challenged and placed on the defensive. Though the Republican-dominated subcommittee ultimately exonerated McCarthy of the charges, McCarthy's outrageous performance at the investigation led directly to the diminution of his power and his formal censure by the Senate. The hearings were also significant because they were among the earliest instances of congressional deliberations receiving live television coverage (the 1950 investigation of organized crime by Senator Estes Kefauver's special committee was the first). As such, the Army-McCarthy hearings were a major political event and have become an indelible part of American public memory.

The television coverage allowed some 20 million Americans to witness McCarthy's bullying style, his threats, his incessant use of points of order and points of personal privilege to interrupt and discombobulate his opponents, and his incoherent rambling. The carefully controlled, soft-spoken manner of army counsel Joseph Welch, a patrician Republican lawyer from a conservative establishment Boston law firm, further highlighted McCarthy's cynical, unrestrained outbursts and ungrounded accusations. The impact of viewing these performances on television, as opposed to reading accounts of them in newspapers and magazines, was tremendous.

The hearings climaxed when Welch challenged McCarthy's aide, Roy Cohn, to provide the FBI with the names of the communists and possible spies whom Cohn and McCarthy had alleged were at Fort Monmouth. As Welch prodded Cohn to give the names "before the sun goes down," McCarthy interrupted with a wholly unrelated accusation: "I think we should tell Mr. Welch that he has in his law firm a young man named Fisher who has been for a number of years a member of an organization named as the legal bulwark of the Communist Party [Fisher had once belonged to the National Lawyers Guild; Welch had so informed McCarthy and the committee, and McCarthy had agreed not to mention it] . . . Mr. Welch, I just felt that I had a duty to respond to your urgent request that before sundown, when we know of anyone serving the Communist cause, we let the agency know . . . I have been rather bored with your phony requests to Mr. Cohn here that he personally get every Communist out of government before sundown."

Welch's famous reply is part of America's political folklore. "Until this moment, Senator, I think I never really gauged your cruelty or your recklessness. Fred Fisher is starting what looks to be a brilliant career with us. Little did I dream you could be so reckless and so cruel as to do an injury to that lad. I fear he shall always bear a scar needlessly inflicted by you . . . Let us not assassinate this lad further, Senator. You have done enough. Have you no sense of decency, sir, at long last? Have you no sense of decency?"

art In several respects art in the Cold War was a site of ideological contention, where differences between, and assumptions about, communism and capitalism were enacted.

Communist leaders behind the Iron Curtain showed great respect for the political power of art and therefore worked hard to control it. The communist parties officially subordinated aesthetics to thematic content and discouraged experimentation, especially with abstraction, Expressionism and other forms of modern art then popular in the West. In 1946 Andrei Zhdanov, Stalin's heir apparent, insisted that all Soviet arts adhere strictly to the Communist Party line. Zhdanov rejected modernism and abstraction as "decadent"; moreover, he insisted that artists who focused on negative or personal aspects of life were expressing "relics of the capitalist mentality." Such artists were subject to arrest, imprisonment, exile and/or "professional suicide." In this period of Soviet history, intellectuals and Jews were often considered especially suspect, intellectuals for their presumed inability to participate in the creation of a true

Henry Moore, Nuclear Energy. Photo by Linda and Bernard Bergmann.

workers' state, Jews for their alleged "cosmopolitan" allegiance to movements or ideas that came from outside the Soviet Union.

Under these conditions Soviet art, which had once been at the forefront of the modern art movement, now took on a uniformly representational style, and socialist realism dominated art within communist-ruled Eastern Europe. Since communist ideology pointed to an ever-improving existence under Soviet rule, *socialist* "realism" was interpreted as portraits of happy and prosperous workers taking satisfaction from life-affirming labor. Thus socialist realism had a propagandistic function. It sought to unify Soviet citizens in their approval of the workers' state and to define their vision of what that state should look like. In this respect, the function of art in communist societies echoed that of art from earlier noncapitalistic European cultures. Like Greek art, which depicted the culture's central myths; Roman art, which celebrated the empire; and medieval art, which communicated the vision of the Catholic Church, communist art served to express to a mass audience a communal vision, communal values and communal aspirations. As in the earlier cultures, the dominant social authority, in this case the Communist Party, determined the specific nature of the communal vision. Thus communist art was inherently political and stylistically conservative, since it served to affirm rather than to challenge the ruling authority.

Though restraints on Soviet artistic expression loosened after Stalin's death in 1953, renewed East-West confrontations quickly led to their return, and socialist realism remained the dominant communist artistic style throughout the Cold War. Between 1946 and 1953 Zhdanov's harsh policies succeeded in squelching most forms of unorthodox and unsanctioned art. With the ascension of Khrushchev in 1953, the penalties for artistic heterodoxy became less severe, and underground artists began experimenting with modernist forms. As early as the middle 1960s, artists also began staging occasional underground exhibits that lasted anywhere from 15 minutes to a few days. Unlike such literary counterparts as Aleksandr SOLZHENITSYN and Irina RATUSHINSKAYA, Soviet underground artists rarely expressed political themes in their work. Nonetheless, unsanctioned art could still provoke the wrath of the communist regime, which, for example, broke up a 1974 outdoor exhibit with bulldozers and arrested several artists. However, after Mikhail Gorbachev introduced his policy of *glasnost* (openness) in 1985, artistic censorship was abolished and Soviet artists were allowed to expand their range of subjects and themes, as well as forms and techniques. Soviet work also became available in the West, so that by the late 1980s New York galleries were routinely selling works by Soviet artists.

By contrast, citizens of the capitalist democracies typically regarded art as a form of individual rather than communal expression, and their governments tolerated a much more divergent range of styles, subjects and themes. Indeed, the extensive experimentation in form, content and artistic intention characteristic of post-Renaissance Western art resulted partly from the rise of capitalism in the 17th century. By freeing artists from the aristocratic patronage system and enabling them to sell their work to a wider and more diverse audience—a growing class of large and small owners—capitalism both encouraged greater aesthetic variety and gave artists more latitude for personal expression. At the same time, however, most artists in capitalist societies were politically and economically marginalized because they were no longer attached to the social power structure. Consequently, their political views carried no greater authority than those of anyone else, and rather less authority than, say, those of a newspaper editor or political pundit. Thus artists' antiestablishment views could be tolerated in capitalist societies because they were largely irrelevant. Despite limited efforts during the Cold War to draw attention to social and political concerns through HAPPENINGS, performance art and other innovative forms, American artists generally remained apolitical in their work and they exerted minimal influence on the political scene. Abe Ajay reflected the general artistic sentiment in 1971 when he stated, "An artist's work should be clean as a hound's tooth of politics and social protest imagery. It is always bad art, sad and dreary and witless . . . Good art is never social work. There is no message in the medium." (This attitude is in marked contrast to a 1930s and 1940s American tradition of left- and labor-oriented art, as well as liberal art that was politically engaged.)

This is not to say that there was no Western counterpart to socialist realism. Mass-market advertising came close to serving some of the same communal functions. Advertising was a form of expression that developed within capitalism mainly during the 20th century. It flourished during the Cold War and, like socialist realism, served the dominant power structure. Through this medium, corporations helped create a common set of national aspirations, beliefs and values that mirrored their own worldview and served their economic, political and social interests. Like socialist realism but unlike modern and postmodern art, which addressed an elite audience, advertising appealed to a mass working-class and middle-class audience. Advertising art did not express the personality, viewpoint or beliefs of the individual artist; rather, it reflected the viewpoint of the corporation, a communal entity. Moreover, advertising in this period typically shunned abstraction and expressionism in favor of traditional realism—"realism" here suggesting happy citizens thriving in a capitalist society. As with communist art, early Cold War commercial art showed contented people enjoying the fruits of their society's dominant political power and social authority—in this case the corporation.

Toward the end of the Cold War, advertising became more abstract and expressionistic—but always with the same goals of selling a product and promoting consumerism. This modernist trend in advertising had its roots in the 1950s and early 1960s, when Robert Rauschenberg, Andy Warhol, Roy Lichtenstein, Claes Oldenburg, Richard Hamilton and other practitioners of pop art somewhat ironically transformed advertising and the mass-produced products of consumer capitalism into objets d'art, works that sometimes included subtle political overtones. Lichtenstein's *Blam!* (1962), for example, highlights military violence via a cartoon drawing of a fighter plane. In the 1960s, Oldenburg presented deformed images of the American flag, echoing earlier pieces by Jasper Johns and Wally Hedrick; painting of an American flag with "Peace" written across it.

Generally, though, pop art and abstract expressionism highlighted aspects of capitalist society that set it apart from communist society. For instance, Warhol celebrated Hollywood glitz and glamor in his paintings of Marilyn MONROE, and his Campbell soup cans foregrounded the products of American industry and the packaging of consumer goods. Thus Warhol, Johns and other pop artists drew attention to America's abundance and its unbounded pursuit of sensual pleasure, entertainment and consumption. By contrast, the Soviets deemed abundant consumer goods and material glamor "decadent," not least because shoppers behind the Iron Curtain had a far more limited selection of products to choose from. Such abstract expressionists as Jackson Pollock, Arshile Gorky and Willem de Kooning in their often baffling attempts both to explore personal concerns and extend what they understood to be the course of art history, moved into territory that was off-limit to communist artists. In this way they exemplified, even from the margins of society, the emphasis on personal development that characterizes capitalist society. As Christine Lindey points out in *Art in the Cold War*, "While Jackson Pollock sought personal expression through his painting, [Soviet artist] V.A. Serov painted history paintings which sought to educate and elevate the masses. Pollock would have derided Serov's varnished canvases as nothing but retrogressive, illustrational propaganda; Serov would have dismissed Pollock's paintings as meaningless, elitist and self-indulgent daubs."

In general, modern and postmodern art have been considered apolitical. "Realistic" fine artists were often viewed as liberal or left-wing because of their concern for the poor, the disenfranchised and social injustices. Though tolerated and even encouraged in the Depression-era Federal Art Project, social realists came under a double-sided attack during the Cold War. The elitist New York art establishment, which had embraced modernist formalism at the expense of social content, criticized the realists' thematic narrative as inherently propagandistic, rather than esthetically essential. On the other hand, critics from the political right regarded many realists' social criticisms and concern for the working class as pro-communist. (They also rejected abstract art as an attack on "culture.") Thus realistic fine art did not thrive during the 1950s RED SCARE, though some practitioners persevered. Ralph Fasanella, Ben Shahn and William Gropper and the artists from the Kitchen Sink School maintained that modernism's obsessive concern for form and its corresponding apparent disregard for content reduced art to meaninglessness. These artists were championed by Marxist critic John Berger who believed "the Realist must look at the modern world, which has so unnerved the Formalists, and come to terms with it."

On the other hand mass-produced reproductions of popular art works typically provided reassuring, realistic representations of comfortable and pleasing scenes. Sold in department stores, drugstores and five-and-tens and hung in the homes of middle- and lower-middle-class citizens, prints of works by such popular artists as Norman Rockwell, Andrew Wyeth, Huldah and the Russian emigré Vladimir Tretchikoff, by masters from the 17th, 18th and 19th centuries, and by engravers like Currier and Ives, reinforced traditional middle-class values. The best-selling prints were rarely experimental, nor did they criticize capitalist society. Instead they portrayed patriotic scenes from American history, religious figures, episodes from the Bible and comforting images from middle-class life: dancers, sailboats, animals, nature scenes, picturesque street scenes, dolls and nonthreatening but interesting-looking people. Reproductions of such 19th-century paintings as Emanuel Leutze's *Washington Crossing the Delaware* and James Whistler's *Arrangement in Grey and Black* (known as *Whistler's Mother*) looked to art of the past to express middle-American sensibilities with comforting images of strength, stability, security and love. Moreover, these works celebrated family, country and often Christianity, areas where Americans believed they differed from atheistic communists. Thus prints and similar forms of popular art were essentially conservative in their complacent and approving representations of middle-class life. Like socialist realism, they reaffirmed the way of life in their society.

By contrast, in 1959 the so-called March Gallery Group, also known as the Doom artists, presented exhibits in New York exploring the theme of nuclear destruction. Prominent among these artists were Boris Lurie, Sam Goodman and Stanley Fisher, and their work, intended to shock audiences, featured destroyed artifacts from American society: bloody and dismembered dolls, sensational photographs from the *National Enquirer* and erotic pictures from men's magazines.

Goodman's *The Cross* (1969), for example, groups a model of a bomb with a rocking horse, a model fighter plane, a horn, a telephone receiver and a drawing of a mushroom cloud with the words "Stop Testing" written on the page.

Among the few other notable pieces of Western art that directly address the Cold War are Pablo Picasso's *Massacre in Korea* (1951) and James Rosenquist's *F-111* (1965), an exhibit of a larger-than-life-sized bomber, orange canned spaghetti that suggested entrails, a mushroom cloud beneath an umbrella and various artifacts from consumer culture. Rosenquist, who wanted to suggest the connection between militarism and consumerism, later explained, "A man has a contract from the company making the bomber . . . and he plans his third automobile and fifth child because he . . . has work for the next couple of years." Henry Moore's bronze sculpture *Nuclear Energy* (1965) commemorates the first sustained atomic chain reaction at the University of Chicago's Stagg Field, now the site of the Regenstein Library. Located in front of the library, the piece merges the image of the atomic bomb's characteristic mushroom cloud with references to a human skull. Moore, a supporter of the Campaign for Nuclear Disarmament in Britain, had originally entitled the sculpture *Atom Piece* but changed the name because he feared some people might confuse "piece" for "peace." Jean Tinguely's sculpture *Homage to New York* (1960) self-destructed in the garden of the Museum of Modern Art as a sort of political statement about the possibilities of human self-destruction in the nuclear age. It appeared during the Second Berlin Crisis, one of the most intense moments of the Cold War, when nuclear war appeared possible, even probable.

Between 1988 and 1990 the Rosenberg Era Art Project exhibited *Unknown Secrets: Art and the Rosenberg Era.* Project director Rob A. Okun published the contents under the title *The Rosenbergs: Collected Visions of Artists and Writers* (1988); Margaret RANDALL wrote the introduction. The exhibit included, among others; Picasso's untitled sketch of the alleged atomic bomb spies, Julius and Ethel Rosenberg (1952); Paul Marcus's *The Greatest Show on Earth* (1987), depicting the trial as a circus overseen by Eisenhower, Nixon and other powerful government figures; Arnold Mesches's *The Kiss* (1954) showing Julius and Ethel kissing; Alice Neel's *Eisenhower, McCarthy and Dulles* (1953), in which the three leaders appear as winged devils hovering over the world; David Wojnarowicz's surreal rendering of the Rosenbergs' electrocution, *The Anatomy and Architecture of June 19, 1953* (1987); Peter Saul's brightly colored *Ethel Rosenberg in Electric Chair* (1987); Deborah Small's *Witch Hunt* (1987) and Robert Arneson's *2 Fried Commie Jew Spies* (1987), a bronze sculpture that fuses the Rosenbergs' faces. Attached to Julius's ear is a small American flag with "I like Ike" printed on it.

The Vietnam War occasioned much antiwar art in the West, as many prominent U.S. and European artists opposed the U.S. military involvement in Southeast Asia. In 1966 the approximately one hundred artists of the Los Angeles Artists Protest Committee collected $10,000 to fund the Tower for Peace, which sculptor Mark di Suvero constructed on land rented with money advanced by Robert Rauschenberg and William Copley. Alongside the abstract steel edifice were billboards exhorting "STOP THE WAR IN VIETNAM." Attached below the slogan were pictures by some 400 artists from throughout the country, most notably including Roy Lichtenstein, Frank Stella, Sam Francis, Louise Nevelson, Larry Rivers and Mark Rothko. In 1967 New York artists organized an Angry Arts Week, which included work by some 600 artists and featured FILM, DANCE, MUSIC, THEATER and poetry as well. The week of protest drew some 50,000 viewers and spawned similar activities in Chicago, Philadelphia, Washington, D. C. and London. The Art Workers Coalition (AWC), founded in New York in 1969, took a strong antiwar stand and tried to pressure the Museum of Modern Art into exhibiting antiwar works. The museum had earlier exhibited *Paris, May 1968, Posters of Student Revolt* (1968), but the trustees overruled an agreement by the staff and the AWC to coproduce a poster condemning the My Lai massacre. Subsequently, the AWC produced the poster independently. In 1990 the Indochina Arts Project sponsored a retrospective exhibit of Vietnam War art featuring works by Americans and Vietnamese. It opened in the Arvada Center for the Arts and Humanities in Arvada, Colorado, had its national opening at the Boston University Art Gallery and traveled through the United States and Vietnam. The exhibit is chronicled and art works are reproduced in *As Seen By Both Sides: American and Vietnamese Artists Look at the War,* edited by artist and project director C. David Thomas. The American artists featured are war veterans Thomas, Michael Aschenbrenner, John Plunkett, David Schirm, David Smith, Richard J. Olsen, William Short and Rick Droz, as well as Leon Golub, Cliff Joseph, James Cannata, May Stevens, Arnold Trachtman, Cynthia Norton, Rudolf Baranik, Kate Collie, Wendy V. Watriss and Nancy Spero.

For additional reading, see Lindey's *Art in the Cold War;* Thomas's *As Seen By Both Sides;* Seitz's *Art in the Age of Aquarius;* Sandler's *American Art of the 1960s;* and Okun's *The Rosenbergs: Collected Visions of Artists and Writers.*

Ashby, Hal   A FILM DIRECTOR. Ashby made several FILM COMEDIES and FILM SATIRES relating to the Cold War. These include THE RUSSIANS ARE COMING! THE RUSSIANS ARE COMING! (1966), about the reception given the crew of a Soviet submarine that runs aground off Nantucket Island; HAROLD AND MAUDE (1971), an antiwar BLACK HUMOR comedy about the 1960s COUNTERCULTURE; and BEING THERE (1979), about a mentally retarded man with a short attention span who is obsessed by gardening and television and who becomes an influential political adviser to the president. *Being There* is based on the book by Jerzy KOSINSKI, who also wrote the movie's screenplay. In addition Ashby directed *Bound for Glory* (1976), a biography of left-wing FOLK SINGER Woody Guthrie, and COMING HOME (1977), a powerful antiwar film featuring an affair between a sensitive antiwar Vietnam veteran and a middle-class housewife (played by JANE FONDA), whose husband, an officer, remains strongly prowar.

Ashes and Diamonds   A 1958 Polish-made film starring Zbigniew Cybulski, Eva Krzyzewski and Adam Pawlikowski and directed by Andrzej Wajda. It was released in the United States in 1961, the year that the second Berlin crisis culminated in the erection of the Berlin Wall and the standoff between U.S. and Soviet tanks at Checkpoint Charlie. The appearance in the United States of an Eastern European film was unusual during this heating up of the Cold War. Made when Poland was permitting new freedoms to its film directors and other artists, *Ashes and Diamonds* completed Wajda's war trilogy, which also included *A Generation* (1954) and *Kanal* (1957). Set immediately after the conclusion of World War II, the film studies the remaining conflicts among the various political factions then ready to compete for control of Poland's postwar destiny. *Ashes and Diamonds* has been critically acclaimed, especially for its visual effects. (See also FOREIGN FILMS.)

"Asia Perspective"   A series of four TELEVISION NEWS shows shown on CBS in September 1966. Reported by several CBS correspondents, the documentaries covered China's Cultural Revolution, focusing on its ideological turmoil and social upheaval; the elections in South Vietnam; and a two-part history of the social, economic and political changes in mainland China since the fall of Manchuria in 1931. The interest in China and Vietnam reflected both the escalating American military involvement in Vietnam (400,000 troops by the end of the year, double the number of 1965) and the increasingly bellicose rhetoric from China that accompanied the Chinese acquisition of nuclear weaponry in 1964.

"Assignment Vienna"   A TELEVISION SPY SHOW that ran on ABC in 1972–73. The show starred Robert Conrad as Jake Webster, an American expatriate with a shady past who operated Jake's Bar and Grill in Vienna. However, the restaurant was actually a cover for Jake's secret work for the U.S. government. Each week Jake foiled enemy spies and international criminals while maintaining an uneasy relationship with his government contact, Major Caldwell (Charles Cioffi), who kept him out of jail. With a main character derived from Humphrey Bogart's Rick in the 1942 film *Casablanca,* the Vietnam-era show tried to reconcile the protagonist's independence and resistance to social institutions with his fundamental patriotism.

"At the Bomb Testing Site"   A 1960 poem by William Stafford. Stafford, who had been a conscientious objector during World War II, depicts the nuclear age from the viewpoint of a reptile: "At noon in the desert a panting lizard/ waited for history, its elbows tense,/ watching . . . as if something might happen./ It was looking for something farther off/ than people could see . . . Ready for a change, the elbows waited./ The hands gripped hard on the desert." The poem first appeared in Stafford's collection, *Stories that Could Be True* (1960), and was anthologized throughout the Cold War in textbooks used in university literature classes.

"A-Team, The"   A TELEVISION SPY SHOW that ran on NBC from 1983 to 1987, starring George Peppard and Mr. T. The show presented the adventures of a group of Vietnam veterans united under the command of Col. John "Hannibal" Smith (Peppard). Having robbed the Bank of Hanoi shortly after the final American pullout from Vietnam, the team members had been caught and imprisoned by the U.S. government. They escaped and thereafter were pursued by both the government and various criminals. Weekly they traveled throughout the country and to exotic foreign locations, eluding their pursuers while serving the cause of justice. The action-packed show required ex-soldiers to employ their combat skills and mastery of high-technology warfare to defeat their enemies and evade their would-be captors. The cigar-smoking Col. Smith was a master of disguises. Sgt. Bosco "B.A." Baracus (Mr. T) provided muscle and mechanical expertise. Their pilot, Howling Mad Murdock, was borderline insane but could fly virtually any aircraft, and Lt. Templeton "Faceman" Peck was a smooth-talking pretty boy who could hustle whatever supplies or equipment they required. In 1986, after the team was finally captured by the mysterious Gen. Stockwell, they were coerced into working for the U.S. government. As a Cold War phenomenon, "The A-Team" celebrated such legendary American traits as courage, resourcefulness, mastery of gadgetry and technology, and indomitable spirit. The A-Team never gave up in the face of adversity—although the earlier episodes of the show presented the team with considerable irony and a kind of self-mocking humor. The insane pilot, for example, was a virtual caricature of a movie "tough guy," as Mr. T was a self-parody of (black) machismo.

atom bomb   Slang for a potent mixture of heroin and marijuana. (See also LANGUAGE.)

Atom Curtain   A 1956 APOCALYPTIC NOVEL by N. B. Williams. Following the nuclear World War III, the world is literally divided by a curtain of radiation, the metaphoric extension of Winston Churchill's 1946 image of an IRON CURTAIN extending across Europe. O'Hara, the novel's protagonist, flies through the atomic curtain and discovers that, as in H. G. Wells's *Time Machine*, American society is comprised of aboveground and belowground populations. Those aboveground are subject to deadly radiation, while the subterranean group lives in fallout shelters and is led by a dictator. Eventually O'Hara seizes control of the latter group and devises a plan to have the "Twelve Old Men of Geneva" oversee an armistice.

For additional reading, see Dowling's *Fictions of Nuclear Disaster*.

atomic bombs   Cinnamon-flavored hard candies, sometimes called "atomic fire ball" or "jawbreakers." First marketed in 1954, the name alludes to the burning sensation in the mouth from the cinnamon. (See also CONSUMER GOODS.)

Atomic Cafe, The   A 1982 FILM DOCUMENTARY directed by Kevin Rafferty, Pierce Rafferty and Jayne Loader. This feature-length documentary appeared in the aftermath of détente, during one of the most bellicose periods of the Cold War since the Cuban Missile Crisis of 1962, a period when top members of the Reagan administration were speaking publicly of winnable nuclear war. *The Atomic Cafe* looks back at the early era of nuclear terror in the United States, the middle 1950s. It shows civil defense information and training films from that time, as well as a simulation of a family comfortably weathering a nuclear attack in the security of their fallout shelter. *The Atomic Cafe* also documents more lighthearted—or light-minded—treatments of the nuclear threat in popular culture, such as the

song "Atomic Love" by Little Caesar and drive-in restaurants with atomic themes and decorations. Though everything in the film is archival, and it is indeed a documentary, *The Atomic Cafe* presents an absurdist, BLACK HUMOR view of the optimistic way the U.S. government represented civil defense and the dangers of nuclear warfare in the 1950s. The film builds to a powerful concluding sequence that intercuts upbeat official 1950s representations of nuclear warfare with film footage showing the awesome devastation of actual nuclear tests. Presumably the intended effect of the film was to create public cynicism about then-current claims that WITH ENOUGH SHOVELS most Americans could survive a nuclear attack. (See also APOCALYPTIC FILMS.)

Atomic City, The   A 1952 FILM DRAMA starring Gene Barry, Lydia Clarke and Milburn Stone and directed by Jerry Hopper. The story is about the extortion of atomic secrets via the kidnapping of a top physicist's son. *The Atomic City* appeared the same year that the United States and Great Britain exploded their first hydrogen bombs and a year before the Soviets exploded theirs. It was also a year after Julius and Ethel Rosenberg were convicted of giving atomic secrets to the Soviets.

Atomic Kid, The   A 1954 FILM COMEDY starring Mickey Rooney, Robert Strauss and Elaine Davis and directed by Leslie Martinson. The story concerns a man who survives an atomic explosion but becomes radioactive. His radioactivity produces comic results.

Atomic Man, The   A 1956 FILM DRAMA starring Gene Nelson and Faith Domergue and directed by Ken Hughes. The story involves a reporter and his girlfriend who uncover a mystery surrounding a suspicious scientist.

Atomic Power   A 1946 FILM DOCUMENTARY. Presented as an episode of *The March of Time* (a newsreel), the film chronicles the development of atomic weaponry, featuring several of the men who helped develop nuclear bombs.

Attack of the Crab Monsters, The   A 1956 SCIENCE FICTION FILM starring Richard Garland, Pamela Duncan and Russell Johnson and directed by Roger Corman. Twenty-five-foot crabs, the product of genetic mutations caused by nuclear testing, cause giant landslides on a Pacific island. During the 1980s this became a cult film, perhaps in response to fears generated by politicians' talk of a winnable nuclear war and widespread concern over a nuclear winter.

Attack of the Killer Tomatoes   A 1978 SCIENCE FICTION FILM starring David Miller, George Wilson and Sharon Taylor and directed by John de Bello. A straight-faced takeoff of the atomic mutant films of the 1950s, this parodic tale of giant carnivorous tomatoes became a détente-era cult film.

"Avengers, The"   A TELEVISION SPY SHOW that ran on ABC from 1966 to 1969. It first appeared on British television five years earlier. Honor Blackman played the lead in the first season. Essentially a television takeoff on the highly popular James BOND movies of the 1960s, "The Avengers" presented the adventures of Jonathan Steed (Patrick

Macnee), a cosmopolitan and very proper British secret agent, and his sexy but highly competent partner, Mrs. Peel (Diana Rigg). In the show's last year Mrs. Peel was "reunited" with her long-lost husband and excised from the show, while the younger and more docile Tara King (Linda Thorson) became Steed's partner. Like the Bond films, "The Avengers" featured diabolic geniuses bent on world domination and/or destruction, clever dialogue, unflappable protagonists, fantastic schemes and ingenious technology. Shown in America during the period between the resolution of the Cuban Missile Crisis and the beginning of détente, the popular show depicted a world continuously threatened by evil but brilliant villains who were, nonetheless, never a match for Steed and Mrs. Peel, who barely even rumpled their clothes as they managed to keep the world safe for democracy.

Baby Doll A 1956 FILM COMEDY starring Karl Malden and Carroll Baker, directed by Elia KAZAN and based on the Tennessee Williams play *27 Wagons Full of Cotton* (1946). Though not political or directly related to Cold War events, *Baby Doll* represented for some right-wing critics the decline in American morals that allegedly made the United States vulnerable to communist domination. By more recent standards, the film is not sexually explicit, but in 1956 *Time* magazine called it "possibly the dirtiest American picture ever legally exhibited." The anti-communist cardinal Francis Spellman of New York condemned the film from the pulpit, though he had not personally viewed it, and he ordered priests to stand in theater lobbies and write down the names of parishioners who attended it under "pain of sin." Although Spellman did not explicitly link the film to communism, this type of religious objection to "dirty films" was typical of the 1950s.

For additional reading, see Whitfield's *The Culture of the Cold War.*

Baez, Joan A FOLK SINGER. Baez was born in 1941 on Staten Island, in New York City. Her father was a Mexican-born physicist while her mother was Scotch-Irish. The dark-skinned Baez experienced racial discrimination at an early age: "As far as they [the townspeople] knew we were niggers." She began singing folk songs, blues and spirituals in coffeehouses in Cambridge, Massachusetts, and played a major role in establishing the popularity of folk music in the early 1960s. Her first major national appearance came

at the 1959 Newport Folk Festival when Bob Gibson invited her to sing with him. Their duet "Jordan River" was one of the highlights of the festival. Prompted by her own experiences of discrimination, Baez soon became a highly visible figure in the social protest movements of the 1960s; she was a vocal proponent of civil rights and an early opponent of the Vietnam War. The right-wing cartoonist Al Capp satirized her in his popular, nationally syndicated comic strip CARTOON *Li'l Abner,* calling her Joanie Phonie. In 1964 Baez helped organize the Free Speech Movement at the University of California at Berkeley in response to a ban on students' political activities there, and in 1965 she founded the Institute for the Study of Nonviolence, in Carmel, California. She performed widely at rallies and concerts that protested the war and applied such civil rights songs as "We Shall Overcome" to the antiwar effort. During the early 1960s Baez appeared at concerts with her then boyfriend Bob DYLAN, but the couple, who were known as the King and Queen of Folk Rock, broke up in 1965 as Dylan withdrew from politics and otherwise became more self-absorbed.

Baez remained active in the peace movement and related political causes throughout the Cold War and in the early 1980s participated in concerts organized to protest the renewed buildup of nuclear weapons by the first Reagan administration. She also wrote a song inspired by the way Nicaraguan minister of the interior Tomas Borge, who had been imprisoned and tortured under the regime of the dictator Anastasio Somoza, confronted one of his torturers after the Sandinista revolution. Borge reportedly declared,

Joan Baez, 1966. Courtesy American International Pictures.

"My revenge is to have you shake my hand." Baez performed the song in Spanish in Nicaragua in the early 1980s. In 1968 she published an autobiography, *Daybreak.*

For additional reading, see Szatmary's *Rockin' in Time* and Ward et al.'s *Rock of Ages: The Rolling Stone History of Rock & Roll.*

Baldwin, James A NOVELIST and essayist, born in New York in 1924. One of the most respected black American writers of the Cold War era, Baldwin lived in Paris from 1948 to 1957, when he returned to the United States. The assassination of civil rights leader Martin Luther King in 1968 provoked Baldwin to return a few years later to France, where he lived until his death in 1987. Baldwin's books rarely deal with the Cold War directly, but his public remarks on American racism place the civil rights/black liberation struggles within a Cold War context. In 1963 he defended William Worthy, a black JOURNALIST who had traveled to Cuba and the People's Republic of China without a passport and in violation of a State Department ban. That year Baldwin further attacked the travel ban on Cuba declaring that, for a black person, vacationing in Cuba was better than in Miami Beach, notwithstanding Cuba's supposedly repressive political system. Likewise, in a speech about oppression of black people in the United States, Baldwin claimed, "I have never been afraid of Russia, China, or Cuba, but I am terrified of this country." Much of Baldwin's writing calls for harmony, acceptance and understanding among the races; *The Fire Next Time* (1963), for instance, describes his rejection of the black separatist movement. But later in the 1960s Baldwin adopted a more militant posture. He also opposed the Vietnam War.

Baldwin regarded FBI director J. Edgar Hoover as a major impediment to civil rights; Hoover, in turn, regarded the civil rights movement as a communist-inspired attempt to spread chaos in the United States and undermine U.S. standing among the emerging African countries in order to drive them into the Soviet camp. Baldwin's open homosexuality may also have contributed to the suspicion by some, mostly on the right, that Baldwin was an anti-American, communist sympathizer, since in the popular culture and in public statements by several prominent public officials homosexuals were often linked with communism. (See MOM-ISM.) Baldwin's FBI file reflects the bureau's concern in 1964 that he was planning to write for the *New Yorker* magazine a book on the role of the FBI in the South. The entry in the file comments, "*The New Yorker* has over the years been irresponsible and unreliable with respect to references concerning the Director and the FBI. [The FBI office in] New York has previously been instructed to follow the publication of this book and to remain alert to any possibility of securing galley proofs for the Bureau." However, the book never appeared.

For additional reading, see O'Reilly's *Black Americans: The FBI Files.*

Ball, Lucille A popular television comedienne and star of the top-rated 1950s TELEVISION SITUATION COMEDY, "I Love Lucy." Predicated on the marriage of the American Lucy to Cuban-born band leader Ricky Ricardo (played by Ball's real-life husband, Desi Arnaz), "I Love Lucy" ran on CBS from 1951 to 1961. The domestic comedy possessed virtually no overt political content. However, in 1953 newspaper columnist Walter WINCHELL revealed that "America's top comedienne has been confronted with her membership in the Communist Party." Subsequent headlines proclaimed, "Lucille Ball Named Red." In fact, in 1952 Ball had told the HOUSE COMMITTEE ON UN-AMERICAN ACTIVITIES (HUAC) that she had registered as a Communist in 1936 "to please my grandfather." HUAC cleared her of all charges of communist activity, and because the show's ratings were so strong, its sponsor, Philip Morris, continued to support "I Love Lucy" even after Winchell's revelation. After the column came out, Arnaz went before a live audience gathered at the Desilu Playhouse in California to watch the filming of the show. Arnaz declared, "Lucille Ball is no Communist. Lucy has never been a Communist, not now and never will be. I was kicked out of Cuba because of Communism. We both despise the Communists for everything they stand for. Lucille is 100 percent American. She's as American as Barney Baruch and Ike Eisenhower. Please, ladies and gentlemen, don't believe every piece of bunk you read in today's papers." The audience gave a standing ovation to Arnaz, who then called out his wife, introducing her as "my favorite redhead . . . in fact, that's the only thing red about her, and even *that's* not legitimate." Thus ended Ball's brush with the RED SCARE; she was not subject to BLACKLISTING. Arnaz's claim to having been kicked out of Cuba by communists is dubious, since his 1933 departure to Miami preceded Castro's communist revolution by some 26 years. The birth of their son in January 1953 was a significant enough media event to distract attention from the presidential inauguration of Lucy's fan, Dwight D. Eisenhower.

Bananas A 1971 FILM COMEDY starring Woody Allen, Louise Lasser, Carlos Montalban and Howard Cosell. Allen wrote and directed the film. The story centers on Fielding Mellish (Allen), a bumbling loser who tests experimental products for a living. (Allen pays tribute to Charles CHAPLIN's *Modern Times* [1936] when Mellish is attacked by one of the gadgets he is testing.) Mellish falls in love with Nancy, a girl collecting petitions to support a revolutionary movement in the mythical republic of San Marcos. The movement has sprung up to oppose a cruel dictator who gunned down the freely elected president during a televised assassination covered by sports commentator Howard Cosell. When his intended lover spurns him, Mellish travels to San Marcos, where he narrowly escapes a cynical plot by the reigning dictator and joins the rebels in the mountains. However, after the revolution's success, its leader immediately becomes power-crazed, demanding among other

things that everyone change underwear several times a day—and wear it on the outside so authorities can check. Against his will, Mellish agrees to help the revolutionary movement by overthrowing the crazed leader and becoming the new head of state himself. Eventually he returns to the United States, where he stands trial for subversion and faces hostile testimony from FBI agents and Miss America. Finally, he is reunited with Nancy, and Howard Cosell calls the play-by-play on their wedding night.

Bananas is not so much satiric as absurdist. The characters are too inane to be taken seriously, though the transformation of the revolutionary leader certainly points to Allen's jaundiced view of Fidel Castro, and agents of the U.S. government typically seem disorganized, vindictive and eager to see subversion in the most ridiculous places. Nonetheless, Allen's main concern is to turn the Cold War scenario into a slapstick, absurdist playground, not to make moral judgments or overtly political statements. For instance, the cruel dictator becomes upset because he doesn't like the dessert Mellish brings when invited to the presidential palace for dinner. During the revolution U.S. troops discover that their government is not taking any chances this time; it is sending soldiers to fight on both sides. The dictator's henchman accidentally calls on the UJA for support, instead of the CIA. Consequently, during the street fighting on the night of the revolution, the soldiers are interrupted by Hasidic men dressed in traditional garb and holding out collection cans for the United Jewish Appeal. In general, *Bananas* shares the absurdist sensibility behind such contemporary works as M*A*S*H and CATCH-22, but it does not share their dark criticism of the American military's cruelty and waste. Rather, Allen's view in this film is a kind of lighthearted "a plague on both your houses" equally skeptical of U.S. patriotism and foreign revolution.

Baranczak, Stanislaw A Polish EXILED WRITER (to the United States). A professor at Adam Mickiewicz University, Baranczak fell afoul of the Polish authorities in the middle 1970s because of his involvement with the emerging human rights movement and because he had edited several underground publications, including the uncensored literary quarterly *Zapis*. Fired from his teaching post in 1977, Baranczak was offered a temporary position at Harvard University; however, Polish authorities denied him an exit visa eight times, despite Harvard's attempts to intervene through diplomatic channels. In August 1980 the Poznan chapter of the Solidarity trade union specifically included Baranczak's reinstatement at Mickiewicz University as one of its political demands, but to no avail. Finally, in 1981, Baranczak, his wife and his two children were given passports to go to America, where he began teaching at Harvard. At that time, optimistic about the prospects for political reform, he expected to return to Poland in three to five years. However, in December 1981, General Jaruzelski, who was backed by the Soviets, assumed control of the Polish government, imposed martial law, banned Solidarity and imprisoned many of Baranczak's friends. Baranczak thus came to view his exile to the United States as more or less permanent. While working full-time at Harvard he toured campuses throughout the United States to give talks on Solidarity and Polish culture, as well as writing articles on Poland for U.S.

and Western European journals. Informed in 1983 by the Polish consulate in New York that his passport had expired, Baranczak ignored his government's directive to return to Poland with his family. Instead, he applied for permanent U.S. residency. In addition to a large number of publications in Polish, he has written several articles and three books in English, *A Fugitive from Utopia: The Poetry of Zbigniew Herbert* (1988), *Selected Poems: The Weight of the Body* (1989) and *Breathing Under Water and Other East European Essays* (1990).

For additional reading, see Tucker's *Literary Exile in the Twentieth Century.*

Barefoot in the Head

A 1969 APOCALYPTIC NOVEL by Brian Aldiss. Influenced by the COUNTERCULTURE that sprung up partly in response to the Vietnam War, the BLACK HUMOR novel imagines a global war fought with psychedelic drugs. "When the Acid Head War broke out . . . Britain had been the first nation to suffer the PCA bomb—the Psycho Chemical Aerosols that propagated psychotomimetic states." Thus Aldiss relates to the Cold War the contemporary interest in LSD, which the counterculture used to "expand consciousness" and which the CIA also experimented with for political reasons. The Acid War proves to take place only in the mind of the protagonist, whose epitaph reads "The bombs were only / In his head." The title alludes to a popular play of the time, *Barefoot in the Park.*

For additional reading, see Dowling's *Fictions of Nuclear Disaster.*

"Barney Miller"

A TELEVISION SITUATION COMEDY that ran on ABC from 1975 to 1982. Starring Hal Linden as police captain Barney Miller, the show centered on the eccentric police officers and criminals that came into New York's 12th Precinct station house. Though "Barney Miller" did not address the Cold War directly, occasionally individual episodes dealt with Cold War problems. On one episode Detective Wojohowicz (Max Gail) created confusion among Carter administration bureaucrats when he attempted on his own initiative to grant a defector political asylum; on another a retiring CIA agent confronted his counterpart, a retiring KGB agent. Another time a college student built an atomic bomb as a project for his physics class. The student warned of the potential spread of atomic technology among civilians, pointing out that he was only a B student and that the officers should imagine what the A students could do.

Barth, John

American NOVELIST. Most of Barth's books address the Cold War either directly or indirectly. He treats it most forthrightly in GILES GOAT-BOY (1966), an intricately developed BLACK HUMOR allegory of the Cold War employing the metaphor of the universe as university. The double allegory reenacts the journey of the mythic hero in a Cold War scenario: The "university" teeters on the brink of annihilation as the East and West campuses threaten to destroy each other. Among the Cold War figures represented are Presidents Eisenhower and Kennedy and physicists Albert Einstein and J. Robert Oppenheimer. Barth's first novel, a work of black humor entitled *The Floating Opera* (1956), likewise reflects a vision of the Cold War in which extremely rational, intelligent, but emotionally disconnected men make insane apocalyptic decisions. In this comically mean-

John Barth, 1994. Courtesy Teturo Maruyama.

dering novel that revels in digressions, a brilliant but depressed and emotionally detached lawyer concludes that life has no intrinsic meaning and that, logically, there is no reason to live. So he sets about to blow up himself along with his entire community. Thus Barth suggests that when people in power have sharp intellects but no capacity for sympathetic emotion, they may destroy the world. *The Sot-Weed Factor* (1967) and *Letters* (1979) present highly imaginative revisionist histories of early America. Written in a Cold War environment where fabricated and/or disputed accounts of history played integral roles in superpower policy and propaganda, these novels parody the very act of reconstructing and recounting history. Barth suggests that history—and the present—must always remain murky and amorphous, incompletely knowable and highly dependent on the circumstances of its narration. Yet despite the epistemological uncertainty that renders life a bewildering maze, Barth insists on the need for individuals to seize responsibility for their lives and act decisively and to enact their good intentions.

Barth's early fiction, especially *The Floating Opera, The End of the Road* (1958), *The Sot-Weed Factor, Lost in the Funhouse,* (1968) and *Chimera* (1972), is populated with characters suffering from despair; emotional disconnection;

physical and spiritual impotence; inability to choose or act; and a felt absence of meaning in their lives. Their feelings of emptiness and despair reflect one common response to the 1950s and 1960s Cold War atmosphere of imminent nuclear destruction and of a seemingly endless political stalemate resulting from policies of massive retaliation and what later came to be called mutually assured destruction. Though some critics have labeled Barth a nihilist, his humor and vitality allow him to celebrate life even as he regards it from what he calls "the tragic view." As a Cold War–era writer, his artistic goal is to "make us merry with the pain of insight, wise and smiling in the terror of our life."

For additional reading, see *Dictionary of Literary Biography* (vol. 2, *American Novelists Since World War II*).

Baryshnikov, Mikhail   A DANCE performer and Soviet defector. Baryshnikov was born in 1948 to Russian parents in Riga, Latvia, a region annexed by the Soviet Union following World War II. In 1963 he entered the Vaganova Ballet, the training company for the Kirov Ballet of Leningrad (St. Petersburg) and was placed in the class of Alexander Pushkin, the famous teacher who had also taught Rudolf NUREYEV. At age 18 Baryshnikov joined the Kirov as a soloist and won the gold medal at the international competition in Varna, Bulgaria, in 1966. Over the next several years, Baryshnikov garnered many more honors. He debuted in the West in 1970, performing in London and Amsterdam and later in Japan, Australia and Spain, and he became the most highly acclaimed dancer of his generation.

Mikhail Baryshnikov with Natalia Makarova, 1974. Photo by Dina Makarova; courtesy AP/Wide World.

He was often paired with Irina Kolpakova, the Kirov's female star whom many considered the greatest living classical ballerina.

Despite his success, acclaim and special treatment by the Soviet government, Baryshnikov felt restricted by the Kirov's limited repertoire and the Soviet Union's refusal to permit the performance of contemporary ballets from the West. This led to his decision to defect on June 30, 1974, while touring Canada. His defection was arranged by Christina Berlin, the daughter of a former Hearst Corporation executive he had met while touring in London in 1970. A week later he told the press, "I realized finally that if I didn't take advantage of all the opportunities that came my way and that I felt capable of, I would remain unsatisfied for the rest of my life . . . All that I am is bound up in ballet, nothing else really exists form me than this art." He insisted that the reasons for his defection were artistic and not political, and he hoped his action would not harm Soviet-Canadian relationships. "No other country in the world will be my home but Russia. You can be a citizen anywhere, but my soul will always be a Russian one".

Baryshnikov's first post-defection performance was with the National Ballet of Canada in the television film version of *Les Sylphides*. He debuted in New York on July 27, 1974, and danced before a sold-out audience at Lincoln Center with Natalia MAKAROVA, another defector and a former partner at the Kirov. The performance was an enormous success. Baryshnikov first danced with the American Ballet Theater (ABT) in Washington, D.C., in October and was one of its top attractions during the company's 35th anniversary season in New York. He quickly expanded his repertoire to include choreography by George Balanchine, Jerome Robbins, Kenneth MacMillan, Martha Graham and later Twyla Tharp. Baryshnikov served as the ABT's artistic director from 1980 to 1990 and starred in three movies, *The Turning Point* (1977), WHITE NIGHTS (1985) and *Company Business* (1991). *White Nights,* which costars tap dancer Gregory Hines and Isabella Rossellini, is about a ballet star who has defected from the Soviet Union but is returned in a plane crash. The film plays out what must have been one of Baryshnikov's worst nightmares, but it makes his case for the importance of artistic freedom and creative expression, even for those who otherwise enjoy a privileged existence within a totalitarian state. In *Company Business* Baryshnikov plays a spy who reluctantly returns to the U.S.S.R.

Baseball and the Cold War   A 1977 NONFICTION book by Howard Senzel. Published early in the Carter administration, when détente was still strong and prospects for renewed ties between the United States and Cuba were encouraging, the book discusses the historic role of baseball in U.S.-Cuban relations and in the lives of Cold War-era Americans. Senzel, an American Jew born near the beginning of the Cold War, describes the importance of baseball to him when he was a child growing up in Rochester, New York; his disaffiliation from the sport as he became politically active in the COUNTERCULTURE during the Vietnam War era; and his renewed interest in the game following the 1975 World Series between the Boston Red Sox and Cincinnati Reds. He remembers watching the minor-league Havana Sugar Kings play in the United States prior to

Castro's 1959 revolution and recalls that the last game between a U.S. and a Cuban team ended in a draw shortly thereafter when Frank Verdi, the Rochester Red Wings' third baseman, was shot in the head in Havana. Senzel then suggests that concluding that game would be the ideal symbolic action for introducing a new era of détente between the two nations: "The time has come to finish that last . . . game. What a theater for baseball. What a shtick for détente." Later he adds, "For America, détente with Cuba should be a time of confession and catharsis, a time when America comes to understand the self-destructive delusions of the imperial mentality. But instead of self-understanding, America is anxious merely to resume trade and forget the whole thing."

Baseball and the Cold War thus occasions Senzel's reflections about his personal past and the U.S. role in the Cold War. He overlays his autobiography with the development of the Cold War in general and U.S.-Cuban antagonisms in particular. Baseball is the thread that holds them together. For instance, in his review of history, Senzel presents three newspaper articles from May 3, 1954. The first describes how "red-led masses of Vietminh unleased a new assault" against French forces at Dienbienphu in Vietnam; the second reports on a civil defense exercise in which Rochester high school students served as stretcher bearers; and the third describes a game between the Sugar Kings and Red Wings. Senzel traces the Cold War through other aspects of his life. He recounts watching the ARMY-MCCARTHY HEARINGS on television as a young boy incapable of understanding their significance but aware of his mother's concern that some of those involved were Jewish. His childhood participation in the Cold War–era middle-class migration from the inner cities to the suburbs meant that he was no longer able to go to the ballpark every day. At the book's end, Senzel describes his disappointment when Henry Kissinger squelched a popular 1975 proposal to finish the Sugar Kings-Red Wings game because President Ford feared losing the Cuban vote in the Florida presidential primaries and because Castro had supported an anti-Zionist UN resolution and advocated Puerto Rican independence.

Basic Training (1) A 1970 FILM DOCUMENTARY produced, edited and directed by Frederick Wiseman. Filmed at the U.S. Army Training Center at Fort Knox, Kentucky, the piece documents the army's basic training program during the Vietnam War. The film first appeared as a public television broadcast in 1971.

For additional reading, see Benson and Anderson's *Reality Fictions: The Films of Frederick Wiseman*.

Basic Training (2) A 1986 FILM COMEDY starring Ann Dusenberry, Rhoda Shear and Angela Ames, directed by Andrew Sugarman. The film adds a feminist dimension to the Cold War as a clever secretary of defense appoints to the Pentagon a woman who outsmarts the top brass of both the Soviet Union and the United States.

"Battle Report" A TELEVISION NEWS show that ran on NBC in 1950 and 1951. The show documented the U.S. involvement in the Korean War, featuring filmed interviews and reports from the battlefronts as well as reports from the home front. President Truman's assistant, Dr. John Steelman, provided a regular weekly commentary, and other high-ranking government officials made frequent appearances.

"Battlestar Galactica" A TELEVISION SCIENCE FICTION SHOW that ran on ABC from 1978 to 1980. Based so closely on the movie STAR WARS (1977) that the producers of the film sued ABC for plagiarism, "Battlestar Galactica" played out a high-tech struggle between good and evil set in outer space. Starring Lorne Greene as Commander Adama, the show was premised on a sneak attack against the human species by the cynical Cylons, who were committed to wiping out the humans' sole remaining starship, the *Battlestar Galactica*. Made during the collapse of the U.S.-Soviet détente at the end of the 1970s, the show revived the image of a sinister empire dedicated to destroying well-intentioned protagonists who survived because they possessed such presumed American qualities as innocence, courage, cleverness, mechanical know-how and regard for truth and fair play.

Beast, The A 1988 MILITARY FILM starring George Dzundza, Jason Patric and Steven Bauer and directed by Kevin Reynolds. The film, which establishes significant parallels between the U.S. war in Vietnam and the Soviet war in Afghanistan, centers on a Soviet tank crew that becomes increasingly confused about its mission and the purpose of the war. One crew member becomes sympathetic to the rebel cause and eventually decides to fight against his own tank, named "the Beast" by Afghan rebels. The film creates sympathy for the Russian soldier who rejects his country's effort to prop up the pro-Soviet regime it had installed in Afghanistan.

The Beast presents a rare film treatment of a major Cold War event, the 1979 Soviet invasion of Afghanistan. A pivotal moment in the Cold War, the Afghanistan war ended U.S.-Soviet détente and the decade-long attempt of the superpowers to reach greater harmony and deeper levels of cooperation. Its more immediate effects were a U.S. grain embargo and a U.S. boycott of the 1980 Moscow OLYMPIC GAMES. The 10-year war proved to offer many parallels to the U.S. experience in Vietnam. Unpopular at home, both wars went on seemingly endlessly, incurred a substantial number of casualties, substantially crippled or destroyed the countries in whose interests they were ostensibly fought, drained precious resources, diverted funds from domestic programs and ultimately failed to achieve their missions, which were in both cases vague, confused and conflicting. *The Beast* emphasizes those parallels.

Beat movement A literary and political movement that began in the late 1940s. It gave rise to the much-publicized "beatniks" who populated coffeehouses in the 1950s, reciting unconventional poetry and making various kinds of antiestablishment statements. Jack Kerouac and Allen GINSBERG were among the movement's founders. Other prominent figures included Gregory CORSO, who joined them in 1951, Lawrence FERLINGHETTI and Kenneth Rexroth. Both a social and literary phenomenon, the Beats rebelled against the constraints of the tightly structured poetry and fiction then celebrated by academic critics and against the social and political restrictions of middle-class American society. As the modernist writers of the earlier part of the century attempted to impose order on chaos, insisted on intricate formal structure and often celebrated social order and political conservatism (Ezra Pound's sestinas and his support of fascism represented the extreme of the modernist literary and political call for order), the Beats celebrated the liberal outpouring of emotion unfettered by excessive structure and generally endorsed leftist political positions. In Freudian terms, modernist literature aligned itself with the forces of the superego, which assert self-restraint, in order to build a cohesive society, while Beat literature identified with the libido in its celebration of emotions, sexuality and the individual's desires. Similarly, literary modernists tended to be highly self-conscious, often ironic writers who carefully crafted each line, while the Beats sought to unleash the anarchic forces of the unconscious. Thus, in contrast to the studied craft of modernists like James Joyce, Virginia Woolf and William FAULKNER, Kerouac wrote *On the Road* (1957) in three weeks, typing on a continuous roll of teletype paper. In many ways Beat literature harkens back to the Dada of the early 20th century, though it was more concerned with attacking the culture of emotionally detached rationality, what Gregory Corso called "calculative thinking," than with assaulting meaning per se.

Like the Dadaists, the Beats favored poetry readings to supplement the written publication of their work, and they sought to liberate literature from the universities and the precincts of high culture in order to make it accessible to ordinary citizens. The Beats' performance poetry led to the HAPPENINGS of the late 1960s, in which poets and artists made political statements through theatrical gestures.

Ironically, despite their rejection of academe, some of the major Beat writers had considerable formal education. For instance, Ferlinghetti holds a doctorate from the Sorbonne and Ginsberg and Kerouac attended Columbia University. Moreover, although the Beats may have fancied themselves populists of sorts, they were never widely embraced by middle- or working-class Americans, who were most likely to have heard of them through magazine articles emphasizing their social nonconformity as a kind of entertainment, rather than through reading their work. Ordinary readers of popular journalism were likely to perceive the Beats as bizarre, obscene, immoral and/or unpatriotic. Their use of marijuana, peyote, LSD and other "mind-expanding" drugs; their promotion of homosexuality and sexual freedom; their championing of criminals, misfits, individuals institutionalized for insanity and other social outcasts; and their rejection of the work ethic also offended the sensibilities of many "middle Americans."

The political agenda of the Beats was to reaffirm the basic values of humanism—sanctity of human life, free expression of the individual and respect for nature—in the face of an evolving Cold War American society that seemed to organize itself increasingly around militarism and depersonalizing technology and bureaucracy, and that demanded social and political conformity. It was not uncommon for the Beats to label America's growing Cold War militarism and its foreign military and covert operations as fascist. The movement opposed the RED SCARE, which was at its height during the early 1950s and which sought to suppress the left in all its forms—political, social, cultural. Ferlinghetti's City Lights Bookstore, an early gathering place for leftists and intellectuals that opened in San Francisco in 1953, became one of the few places during the Red Scare where antiestablishment publications could be purchased. The store also served as an unofficial headquarters for the Beat movement in the West, just as Ferlinghetti's press, City Lights Books, published many important works of Beat literature, most notably Ginsberg's *Howl and Other Poems* (1956), whose publication led Ferlinghetti to be arrested on obscenity charges in 1957. (The court eventually ruled that the work was not obscene.)

The United States developed its first hydrogen bomb in 1952, and nuclear weapons became a frequent target of the Beat poets. Ginsberg minces no words in expressing his attitudes about the bomb in "America" (1956): "Go fuck yourself with your atom bomb." Ferlinghetti's *A Coney Island of the Mind* (1958), published at the outset of the second Berlin crisis when the prospect of nuclear war seemed not only possible but almost inevitable, depicts the probable nuclear destruction of people, nature and machines: "Oh it was a spring/ of fur leaves and cobalt flowers/ when cadillacs fell through the trees like rain/ drowning the meadows with madness/ while out of every imitation cloud/ dropped myriad wingless crowds/ of nutless nagasaki survivors." Corso's poem "Bomb" (1960), which also appeared during the Berlin crisis, likewise describes the immense damage to nature that nuclear war would create: "Turtles exploding over Istanbul/ The jaguar's flying foot/ soon to sink in arctic snow/ Penguins plunged against the sphinx/ The top of the Empire State/ arrowed in a broccoli field in Sicily."

During the 1960s the Beat movement evolved into or was absorbed by the COUNTERCULTURE, a cultural and political movement that emerged from the protest to the Vietnam War. Ginsberg, Ferlinghetti and other Beat writers were early, vocal critics of that war: Ferlinghetti's *Where Is Vietnam?* (1965) lambastes President Johnson as "Colonel Cornpone" who callously orders the suffering and death of people on the other side of the earth; his *Tyrannus Nix* (1969) accuses President Nixon of promoting the "nazification" of America. In 1965, the year Johnson first ordered combat troops into Vietnam, Ginsberg toured several communist countries, and as a result of being censored in Czechoslovakia, he rejected Marxism-Leninism. On his return, he became involved with the nascent Vietnam War protest movement and helped originate the concept of "flower power" as a means of achieving peace. He participated in a 1967 "life festival," which offered chanting, rock music and poetry readings as alternatives to war, and he was arrested with Dr. Benjamin Spock for blocking access to a military induction center. He continued his social criticism in *Planet News* (1968), a collection of poetry written from 1961 to 1967, and in *The Fall of America* (1972), which won the National Book Award.

Though the Beats had ceased to exist as an identifiable movement by the late 1960s, the major Beat poets continued to take strong political positions against the Cold War. Ginsberg's 1982 collection *Plutonium Ode* appeared during the massive arms buildup in the first Reagan administration, when Cold War tensions rapidly escalated after the failed détente of the 1970s. Politically Ginsberg declares a pox on both Cold War houses. In "Capitol Air" he declares:

No hope Communism no hope Capitalism Yeah
Everybody's lying on both sides Nyeah nyeah nyeah
The bloody iron curtain of American Military Power
Is a mirror image of Russia's red Babel-Tower.

At the same time Ginsberg continued his interest in Eastern philosophy as an attempt to achieve spiritual wholeness, which he believes is the ultimate solution to human violence and aggression. He first became attuned to this philosophy after talking with philosopher Martin Buber and Hindu holy men during his travels in the early 1960s. Buber counseled him to concentrate on personal relationships, and the holy men advised him to concentrate on matters of the heart instead of the mind and to seek contentment within his own body. In Japan in 1963 the meaning of their advice became suddenly clear to him. He describes his spiritual transformation in his poem "The Change."

In 1984, while President Reagan was sponsoring the revolt by the Contras against the leftist Sandinista government in Nicaragua and warning that communist forces were only a day's drive from Texas, Ferlinghetti traveled to that country at the invitation of the Nicaraguan government. Subsequently, he published SEVEN DAYS IN NICARAGUA LIBRE (1984), an account of his journey with photographs by Chris Felver. In contrast to the picture of oppression painted by the Reagan administration Ferlinghetti represents Nicaragua under the Sandinistas as a country dedicated to sincerely motivated social reform and equal rights for women. Furthermore, Ferlinghetti's Nicaragua values poetry and elevates poets to high positions in the government.

Though never widely embraced by middle America, the Beats provided some of the most forceful and expressive literary responses to the Cold War.

For additional reading, see Foster's *Understanding The Beats.*

Beckett, Samuel An Irish-born playwright and novelist who expatriated to France. The GROVE PRESS introduced American audiences to Beckett's work in the 1950s. He died in 1989 during the final stage of the Cold War. Beckett was one of the dominating figures in Western THEATER from the Cold War era. He also wrote fiction, poetry, criticism, a film scenario, and plays for radio and television, and he won the Nobel Prize for literature in 1969. Though he rarely addressed politics directly in his work, Beckett's recurrent themes of confusion, insanity, imminent death and silence in an absurd and empty universe expressed commonly felt Cold War sensibilities.

Born outside of Dublin on Good Friday, 1906, Beckett graduated from Trinity College in 1928, after which he moved to Paris, where he taught school and joined James Joyce's literary circle. He lived in Ireland, England and France between 1932 and 1937 before settling again in Paris. Active in the French Resistance during World War II, he narrowly escaped arrest by the German Gestapo after his group was betrayed by an informer. In 1945 Beckett volunteered to work for an Irish Red Cross hospital in Normandy. Before the end of World War II he wrote most of his work

in English; afterward he wrote almost exclusively in French and then translated his work into English. He claimed to prefer French because he believed it was easier "to write without style in French."

Beckett's most famous work, *Waiting for Godot* (1952; first published in English by Grove Press in 1954), portrays humanity's desire for a confident, commanding, authoritarian, god-like figure who is never forthcoming. A major contribution to the Theater of the Absurd, the darkly humorous play depicts an indifferent universe in which human life lacks intrinsic meaning. The characters' unsettling plight of endless waiting for a resolution of their situation may be said to parallel the condition of the world caught in an unresolvable stalemate between nuclear-armed superpowers, although the play itself contains no specific allusions to politics or history. His later absurd play *Endgame* (1957) uses a CHESS metaphor to allude to eventual NUCLEAR APOCALYPSE.

One response to such an absurd world is to turn increasingly inward, which Beckett did in his writing. During the early 1950s he wrote a trilogy of novels in which he presents the human consciousness questing for its essential self. Rejecting the external world, he demonstrates how the inner self structures all human experience. The trilogy is comprised of *Molloy* (1951; published in English in 1955), *Malone Dies* (1951; in English, 1956) and *The Unnameable* (1953; in English, 1958). Like many other literary works of the Cold War period, such as George ORWELL's NINETEEN EIGHTY-FOUR, (1949) Joseph Heller's CATCH-22, (1961) Arthur Kopit's END OF THE WORLD (1984) and LE CARRE's THE SPY WHO CAME IN FROM THE COLD (1963), Beckett's writings question the very definitions of sanity and insanity and challenge the authorities who define those terms. Throughout his career, Beckett shows the world of human affairs to exist on confusing and uncertain terrain, with death always hovering nearby. Though the human desire for redemption is always strong, God remains unavailable, perhaps absent altogether.

Though Beckett rarely addressed politics directly, he remained concerned with social injustice and political repression—and *Rough for Radio II* (1976) and *What Where* (1984) do have some political elements. In 1984 he dedicated *Catastrophe* to Vaclav Havel, the dissident Czech writer who became the president of Czechoslovakia after the fall of communism.

For additional reading, see Tucker's *Literary Exile in the Twentieth Century.*

Bedford Incident, The A 1963 MILITARY NOVEL by Mark Rascovich and a 1965 MILITARY FILM starring Richard Widmark and Sidney Poitier, directed by James B. Harris. Widmark plays Finlander, the captain of a U.S. Navy destroyer chasing a Soviet submarine in the North Atlantic. Sidney Poitier appears as a journalist writing a story about the captain, who is known for his tough ways and solid military record. Finlander disdains the liberal pacifism of Poitier's magazine, proclaiming the absolute necessity of taking a consistent hard line against the Soviets. Finlander's destroyer relentlessly pursues the submarine, trying to catch it within the territorial limits of a NATO country. However, after the submarine escapes into international waters, the American ship triggers a possible nuclear war between the United States and U.S.S.R. when a sailor on the battle-ready vessel incorrectly hears a command not to fire as a command to fire.

The film was made a little more than two years after the Cuban Missile Crisis and only a few months after the 1964 presidential election. Widmark based Captain Finlander's character on the Republican nominee, Barry Goldwater, who had stated in his acceptance speech that "extremism in the defense of liberty" was "no vice." Goldwater embodied extreme patriotism, suggesting his willingness to risk nuclear war for his country. Running for election to a full term, President Lyndon Johnson exploited the perception of Goldwater as a warmonger; so the issue was firmly in the public mind when *The Bedford Incident* appeared. In many ways Finlander functions like the tragic hero of classical Greek drama. He is an essentially good leader whose personal downfall and that of his community are precipitated by a tragic flaw in his personality—in this case, Finlander's inability to subordinate his primal, emotional need to hunt down his enemy to the more abstract needs of international diplomacy. Moreover, in his pride, he refuses to heed the advice of his officers, who suggest he is subjecting his crew to a dangerous level of stress. Finlander disdains civilian authority, and his prejudice against people with high levels of education and intellectual or humane dispositions blinds him to the value of their observations.

Made during the height of the Civil Rights movement, the film is also notable for presenting Poitier in his first role that does not specifically call for a black character, thereby highlighting the fact that African Americans can be articulate, insightful professionals. (See also APOCALYPTIC FILMS.)

Beginning or the End, The A 1947 FILM DRAMA starring Brian Donlevy, Robert Walker and Tom Drake and directed by Norman Taurog. The first Hollywood film about nuclear warfare, *The Beginning or the End* presents the story of the Manhattan Project, which developed the atomic bomb during World War II. Much of the film centers on major figures involved in the process that led to the development and use of the bomb: J. Robert Oppenheimer, Albert Einstein, President Roosevelt and Colonel Paul Tibbetts (Taylor) who piloted the *Enola Gay,* the plane that dropped the bomb. Another plot line centers on Matt (Drake), a young scientist who questions the morality of the bomb, as do other scientists. But he and they ultimately subordinate their misgivings to the claims of their military superiors that the bomb is necessary for the war effort and the cause of freedom: "Get it done before the Germans and Japs, then worry about the bomb." Matt eventually dies after accidentally receiving a lethal dose of radiation (as did an actual scientist on the project), but his final words reiterate his support of the project and his hope that atomic energy will ultimately be used for peaceful purposes. Elsewhere, the film shows even greater dangers associated with the project: When a colonel asks Matt what will happen if the safety rods on the atomic pile were to fail, Matt replies that "We might lose something." When the colonel asks what they might lose, Matt answers, "Chicago."

The pseudo-documentary is not always historically accurate. It presents Matt, not Leo Szilard, as the man who convinces Einstein to write the famous letter to President Roosevelt urging development of the bomb. It also inaccu-

rately shows the *Enola Gay* encountering anti-aircraft fire on its bombing mission. *The Beginning or the End* was not well-received critically. The reviewer for *Time* wrote, "The picture will do no great harm unless it discourages the making of better pictures on the same subject." (See also APOCALYPTIC FILMS.)

For additional reading, see Shaheen's *Nuclear War Films.*

"Behind Closed Doors" A TELEVISION SPY SHOW that ran on NBC in 1958 and 1959. Based on the files of Rear Admiral Ellis M. Zacharias, USN (retired), the show dramatized American counterespionage activities in the Cold War. Bruce Gordon played Commander Matson, who hosted the show and appeared in some of the episodes. Admiral Zacharias served as technical consultant for the series.

"Behind the News" A TELEVISION NEWS show that ran on CBS from January to September, 1959. Produced by William Weston and hosted on Sunday afternoons by Howard K. Smith, it provided background reports on Cold War issues and events: the visit to the United State of Soviet deputy premier Anastas Mikoyan, the rise of Charles de Gaulle, the growing Berlin crisis, the Tibetan revolt against communist China, the dangers of radioactive fallout, the difficulties of space exploration, Cuba's drift toward communism, Nikita Khrushchev's visit to the United States, his meeting with President Eisenhower and the Cold War itself.

Being, The A 1983 SCIENCE FICTION FILM starring Martin Landau, José Ferrer, Dorothy Malone and Ruth Buzzi and directed by Jackie Kong. This Reagan-era attempt to rejuvenate the 1950s nuclear-born monster movies centers on a creature that terrorizes a middle American town. In this case, however, the mutant results not from atomic testing but from nuclear waste, a more recently recognized danger of the Cold War arms program and of the growing use of nuclear energy. Like the APOCALYPTIC FILMS of the 1950s, this 1983 depiction of massive destruction and possible annihilation caused by misapplied nuclear energy appeared at a time of heightened Cold War tensions: Top government officials were speaking of winnable nuclear war, and President Reagan was denouncing the U.S.S.R. as an "evil empire."

Being There A 1970 Literary SATIRE by Jerzy KOSINSKI and a 1979 FILM COMEDY starring Peter SELLERS, Melvyn Douglas and Shirley MacLaine and directed by Hal ASHBY. The novel and film treatments of the story are remarkably close, though the film feels more lighthearted. The action centers on a mentally deficient man named Chance who knows about the world only from his work as a gardener and from television, which he watches with a short attention span. Through a chain of accidents and misunderstandings Chance becomes attached to a wealthy and politically powerful family and gains enormous political influence. The media and members of the ruling political inner circle come to regard him as a man of great wisdom, able to communicate effectively to the nation through his simple-minded platitudes—unbeknownst to them, references to gardening and to television. Kosinski won an Academy Award for the 1979 film treatment. The release of the movie coincided with the campaign for the presidency of Ronald Reagan, whom many viewers compared to Chance, although this may not have been the film's intention.

Bell, The   A 1950 FILM DOCUMENTARY produced by the Crusade for Freedom, which was chaired by General Lucius D. Clay, USA (retired), the former American high commissioner in occupied Germany. Using the Liberty Bell as its starting point, the short educational film was used to encourage moviegoers to purchase savings bonds. Made in cooperation with the Defense Department, the film includes footage from the 1949 Berlin Airlift and depicts the evils of communism and the dangers of Soviet aggression. The film was released in coordination with a nationwide radio address by then-General Eisenhower in support of the Crusade for Freedom, a project of the National Committee for a Free Europe, Inc. Other leading members of the committee included Major General C. L. Adcock, USA (retired), executive vice-chairman, DeWitt C, Poole, and the future head of the CIA, Allen Dulles.

For additional reading, see Suid's *Film and Propaganda in America* (vol. 4).

"Bell & Howell Close-Up!"   A TELEVISION NEWS show that ran from 1960 to 1963 on ABC. Produced primarily by ABC News, but sometimes by independent production teams, "Close-Up" provided background reports on Cold War issues: the conflicting goals and interests between advocates of communism and democracy in Haiti, the rising influence of communism in Latin America, the growing communist influence in Africa, the conversion of Cuba to communism, the war in Algieria, East and West Berlin, Eastern Europe, Italy, Cambodia, the Middle East, Chinese refugees, Soviet university students, the Chinese border war with India, the rocket-powered X-15 airplane and the personal problems facing U.S. ambassadors overseas. The independently produced feature about communism in Latin America, "Yanki No!", prompted the resignation of John Daly, the network's vice president for news and public affairs, who objected to the show's use of independent producers.

For additional reading, see Einstein's *Special Edition: A Guide to Network Television Documentary Series and Special News Reports, 1955–1979.*

Ben-Hur   A 1959 EPIC FILM starring Charlton HESTON, Jack Hawkins, Stephen Boyd and Haya Harareet and directed by William Wyler, based on the 1880 best-selling novel by Lew Wallace. Depicting the conflict between Romans and Jews at the time of Jesus, *Ben-Hur* received popular attention for its epic scope and climactic 20-minute chariot race. Like such other film epics as QUO VADIS (1951), THE TEN COMMANDMENTS (1956), SPARTACUS (1960) and *Samson and Delilah* (1949), *Ben-Hur* established parallels between ancient despotism and contemporary communist tyranny. And as in those epics, the protagonists in *Ben-Hur* asserted their Judeo-Christian religious values in their struggle against oppression. Moreover, the epic-sized cast, the vast sets and expensive props and the film's enormous scope reflected the seemingly endless resources of capitalist America.

Berrigan, Daniel   A POET, priest and political activist. Born in 1921 to a devout Catholic family, Berrigan joined the Society of Jesus in 1939. "I was acquainted with no Jesuits, so it was a matter of an act of faith on both sides. Not a bad arrangement." He was ordained as a priest in 1952. After fulfilling several teaching assignments during the 1950s and early 1960s, he traveled to Eastern Europe in 1964 and Latin America in 1965 on church business. In 1965 he founded Clergy and Laymen Concerned About Vietnam, and in February 1968 traveled to Hanoi to receive three captured American pilots. In May 1968 Berrigan, his brother Philip Berrigan, also a Catholic priest, and seven others protested the war by pouring napalm on Selective Service records in Catonsville, Maryland. After the Catonsville 9 were convicted, Berrigan went underground but was arrested four months later by the FBI. He served a 19-month term in federal prison. His experiences became the basis for his play, *The Trial of the Catonsville Nine* (1970). Berrigan continued to oppose U.S. involvement in Vietnam. After the war, he worked with Thich Nhat Hahn, a Buddhist monk, to facilitate a reconciliation between the people of Vietnam and the United States. Throughout the Cold War, he continued to protest nuclear warfare and participate in several demonstrations.

Though much of Berrigan's poetry centers on religious themes, his war-era poetry expresses his protest against the U.S. involvement in Vietnam. His first book to address political issues was *No One Walks Waters* (1966), which includes such poems as "Holy Week, 1965 (The Vietnam Raids Go On)" and "A Pittsburgh Beggar Reminds Me of the Dead of Hiroshima." In 1968 Berrigan published *Night Flight to Hanoi*, which includes "Children in the Shelter," a description of his experience with three children in a Hanoi bomb shelter: "I bore, reborn / a Hiroshima child from Hell." Several poems from *Night Flight* were republished in *False Gods, Real Men* (1969), which also describes the burning of the draft records at Catonsville. Berrigan won the 1971 Milker Book Award for three volumes of poetry, *Trial Poems, No Bars to Manhood* and *The Trial of the Catonsville Nine*, all of which were published in 1970. *The Dark Night of Resistance* (1971), in which Berrigan patterns himself after St. John of the Cross, won the Thomas More Association Medal. Berrigan also received several National Book Award nominations. (See also VIETNAM WAR LITERATURE.)

For additional reading, see *Dictionary of Literary Biography* (vol. 5, *American Poets Since World War II*).

Bessie, Alvah   A SCREENWRITER and NOVELIST and member of the HOLLYWOOD TEN. Born in New York City in 1904, Bessie graduated from Columbia College in 1924. Afterward he moved to Paris, where he worked on the newspaper *Paris Times*. He returned to the United States in 1929 and worked during the Depression with his wife at the home of a wealthy family in Vermont. During this period he became attracted to Marxism, whose anti-fascism and philosophy of equality appealed to him. In 1935 Bessie received a Guggenheim Fellowship, which allowed him to complete his first novel, *Dwell in the Wilderness*, the story of an American family from 1876 to 1925. That year he also joined the staff of the *Brooklyn Daily Eagle* as an assistant editor. Motivated by his support of the communist-backed Republican forces during the Spanish Civil War, Bessie worked for the Spanish Information Bureau in 1937 and fought against the Nazi-supported forces of General Franco in 1938 as a member of the Abraham Lincoln Brigade, a unit of international volunteers. He described his wartime experiences in his memoir *Men in Battle* (1939) and later edited *The Heart of Spain* (1952), a collection of memoirs published by the veterans of the Abraham Lincoln Brigade. In 1943 Bessie received a contract from Warner Brothers, for whom he wrote four screenplays: *Northern Pursuit* (1943), *The Very Thought of You* (1944), *Hotel Berlin* (1945) and *Objective, Burma!* (1945), a World War II film that earned an Academy Award nomination. After leaving Warner Brothers he wrote the screenplay for *Smart Woman* (1948).

In 1946 Bessie, along with John Howard LAWSON, Howard FAST and other communists viciously attacked future Hollywood Ten member Albert MALTZ for an article in *New Masses* calling for greater artistic and aesthetic freedom for communist writers. Maltz later recanted, but the savagery of the attack provoked other members to leave the party. In 1947 Bessie, who was an active member of the Communist Party, was called to testify at the HOUSE COMMITTEE ON UN-AMERICA ACTIVITIES (HUAC) hearings on alleged communist influences in Hollywood films. Like the other members of the Hollywood Ten, Bessie refused to testify, citing his First Amendment right of free speech. As a result he was eventually sentenced to a one-year prison term, which he served in 1950. Bessie wrote two accounts of his experiences with HUAC, a largely autobiographical POLITICAL NOVEL entitled *The Un-Americans* (1957) and the NONFICTION book *Inquisition in Eden* (1965).

Subjected to BLACKLISTING after his appearance before HUAC, Bessie wrote the story for the screenplay of *Passage West* (1951) under a false name. Subsequently, he turned away from film and worked first for a union newspaper and later for a theater company in San Francisco. His novel *The Symbol* (1967), based on the life of Marilyn MONROE, became the basis of a heavily edited made-for-television movie, *The Sex Symbol* (1974). In 1968 Bessie worked on the script for and appeared in the Spanish-made film *Spain Again,* which deals with the experiences of a doctor who returns to Spain 30 years after fighting against Franco during the revolution. Though entered as Spain's Academy Award nominee for best foreign film, it was not screened in the United States. Bessie later worked with fellow Hollywood Ten writer Dalton TRUMBO on the film *Executive Action* (1973), which suggests that right-wing corporate and military figures were responsible for the assassination of President Kennedy.

For additional reading, see *Dictionary of Literary Biography* (vol. 26, *Screenwriters*) and Navasky's *Naming Names.*

Best and the Brightest, The

A bestselling 1972 NONFICTION book about the early years of the Vietnam War, by David HALBERSTAM. Earlier Halberstam had won a Pulitzer Prize for his coverage in the *New York Times* of the American involvement in Vietnam; written a previous nonfiction book on Vietnam, *The Making of a Quagmire* (1965); and published a novel, ONE VERY HOT DAY (1967). *The Best and the Brightest* appeared during the "Vietnamization" of the war then being carried out by the Nixon administration. Halberstam was

motivated by the disparity between the well-publicized optimism of U.S. officials about the progress of the war and his own firsthand perception that it would remain a stalemate because, despite their military superiority, the United States and the South Vietnamese were overwhelmed by the total political superiority of the enemy. To make his case, Halberstam provides a detailed account of the war during the Kennedy and Johnson years and describes the individuals responsible for planning and prosecuting it. The title is an indictment of the traditional liberal assumption, dating from the 18th-century Enlightenment, which maintained that virtually any problem could be resolved by the appropriate application of knowledge, reason and scientific methodology. Halberstam goes to great lengths to show that Kennedy and Johnson indeed employed "the best and the brightest," many from the faculties of Harvard and other leading universities, to formulate Vietnam policies that were nonetheless confused, misguided and ineffective. Halberstam suggests that hubris and self-deception were at the root of the policies' failure.

Among those profiled by Halberstam were national security adviser McGeorge Bundy, General Maxwell Taylor, CIA director John McCone, press secretary Pierre Salinger, Walt Rostow of the State Department and, perhaps most impressive of all, Defense Secretary Robert McNamara (who in 1995 published *In Retrospect: The Tragedy and Lessons of Vietnam,* in which he admits believing that the war was a mistake and that U.S. policies had been confused almost from the beginning). Halberstam describes McNamara as a highly practical man who, as president of Ford Motor Company, believed customers should be and were utilitarian and that car purchasing was a rational and not impulsive decision. McNamara thus opposed developing a convertible version of the Ford Falcon since "the idea that a customer would pay $200 more for a dangerous car that would deteriorate more rapidly offended him." McNamara brought his belief that people are fundamentally motivated by reason rather than emotion to his new job as secretary of defense, along with his keen intellect and his predilection for statistics and quantifiable information. This predilection manifested itself in Vietnam as enemy body counts, quantifiable data that ignored the commitment and morale of civilians and combatants and that became the basis for erroneous administration declarations that the United States and South Vietnam were winning the war.

Much to the surprise of the author, who had assumed there was little public interest in the origins of the war, the book sold some 180,000 copies in hardback and 1.5 million in paperback and was well received critically, especially among opponents to the war, which was ongoing when *The Best and the Brightest* appeared.

Biberman, Herbert

A FILM DIRECTOR and member of the HOLLYWOOD TEN. Biberman, a member of the Communist Party, had directed only three films before being called to testify before the 1947 HOUSE COMMITTEE ON UN-AMERICAN ACTIVITIES (HUAC) hearings on alleged communist influences in Hollywood films. Like the other nine "unfriendly" witnesses who comprised the Hollywood Ten, Biberman refused to testify, citing his First Amendment right of free speech. As a result, he was eventually sentenced to a six-month prison term, after which he was blacklisted and unable to direct in Hollywood again (see BLACKLISTING). Biberman's wife, Academy Award–winning Actress Gale Sondergaard, was also a communist who was likewise blacklisted. When called to testify before HUAC in the early 1950s she invoked her Fifth Amendment rights.

In 1954 Biberman directed the internationally acclaimed, independently produced SALT OF THE EARTH. Made in association with the International Union of Mine, Mill and Smelter Workers, the simulated FILM DOCUMENTARY sympathetically portrayed a 1951–52 strike by Mexican-American zinc workers. Biberman, producer Paul Jarrico, actor Will Geer and screenwriter Michael Wilson (another member of the Ten) were all on blacklists. Rosaura Revueltas, the female lead, was deported by the Immigration and Naturalization Services (INS) for a minor passport violation before the shooting was finished. She was subsequently blacklisted in both the United States and Mexico and never made another film.

Salt of the Earth was attacked as the work of communists even before it was completed. Congressman Donald Jackson, a member of HUAC, argued that the film was "a new weapon for Russia" that might somehow instigate copper miners to strike and thereby block the production of weapons for the Korean War. When the film debuted it was screened in only 10 American cities, but it became popular among some liberal and left-wing viewers when it was re-released in 1965. It was acclaimed once again by feminists in the 1970s (the film celebrates the role of the mineworkers' wives, who, when the mineworkers were prevented by an injunction from picketing, conducted the strike in their husbands' place).

Jarrico and Biberman had wanted to create an independent film company to employ blacklisted artists and draw "from the living experiences of people long ignored in Hollywood—the working men and women of America." However, *Salt of the Earth* was their only production.

"Biff Baker, U.S.A."   A TELEVISION SPY SHOW that ran on CBS in 1952–53. The show featured Alan Hale Jr. as Biff Baker, an American businessman who traveled throughout the world with his wife Louise (Randy Stuart) to purchase goods for his import business. Though he did not seek it out, intrigue followed Baker throughout the world as he became enmeshed in various espionage activities that developed around him.

Big Jim McClain   A 1952 FILM DRAMA starring John WAYNE, Nancy Olson and James Arness and directed by Edward Ludwig. Wayne appears as Jim McClain, a congressional committee investigator assigned to foil a communist plot in Hawaii. William Wheeler, the chief investigator for the HOUSE COMMITTEE ON UN-AMERICAN ACTIVITIES (HUAC), consulted on this film, which glorifies the work of HUAC and attacks what Senator Joseph McCarthy (R., Wisconsin) called "Fifth Amendment Communists" who invoked their constitutional protection against self-incrimination to avoid participating in committee interrogations. The film begins by praising the work of HUAC and condemning those who criticized the committee members. Equating domestic

communists with "agents of the Kremlin," the opening narrative declares that "anyone who continued to be a Communist after 1945 is guilty of high treason."

The plot centers around Jim McClain's efforts to uncover a secret, underground communist cell in Hawaii that is committed to domestic sabotage. It deals with communist infiltration of labor unions, though most union leaders are shown to be patriotic Americans. (The 1947 Taft-Hartley Act had denied the facilities of the National Labor Relations Board to unions that failed to file affidavits that their officers were non-communists, and most unions subsequently eliminated communists from their leadership). The movie characterizes communist leaders as cold-hearted and emotionally neutral. They take their orders from Moscow and plan to eliminate domestic American communists after they take over the country. On the other hand, several of the more positive characters are former communist dupes who have seen through the duplicity of the Communist Party and cooperated fully with HUAC and the FBI. Throughout the movie, local and federal government agents are shown to be responsible figures, and figures of authority appear in a favorable light. The film also gives passing tribute to religion, and it frequently alludes to the then-current Korean War and celebrates the efforts of patriotic Americans during World War II. McClain, for example, is an ex-marine who served in World War II; his partner, played by Arness, was wounded in Korea fighting communists. Interestingly, McClain, who apparently hails from east Texas, exercises considerable professional restraint throughout the movie, even when he confronts a communist doctor who has inadvertently killed the Arness character while administering a truth serum. But McClain loses his cool and strikes another communist who accuses everyone from east Texas of being "niggers and white trash." Though the incident highlights McClain's pride in being neither of those, it also belies the communist claim to being on the side of poor and black Americans, since the statement was clearly intended as an insult. Elsewhere, the film makes the passing suggestion that communism and homosexuality are linked. (See MOM-ISM.) On the other hand, the film's final sequence celebrates American marines of every ethnicity, including African Americans and Asian Americans.

The object of McClain's investigation was apparently to expose the cell leaders as communists, and he is stymied when they invoke their Fifth Amendment protections against self-incrimination. The film thus equates being a communist with being a criminal and suggests that the cell leaders have managed to escape justice by avoiding having to acknowledge their communist affiliation. In fact, however, it was legal to be a communist, even though the Communist Party was outlawed. Therefore, even had HUAC demonstrated that they were communists, no criminal charges could have been filed against them. On the other hand, by invoking the Fifth Amendment they would have been publicly perceived to be communists and subject to the social ostracism and job discrimination experienced by others who invoked the Fifth. And the FBI and police agencies would have known to keep them under surveillance. Nonetheless, a frustrated McClain feels defeated by their ability to escape being officially labeled communists. He praises the Constitution, but resents when the Bill of

Rights is used to protect those who wish to undermine the Constitution.

Bikini A skimpy two-piece women's bathing suit named after Bikini Atoll in the Pacific Ocean. Part of the Marshall Island chain, Bikini Atoll was the site of 23 U.S. atomic and hydrogen bomb tests between 1946 and 1958. A 1954 Bikini test created an international incident when radioactive fall-out fell on a Japanese fishing boat, causing radiation sickness among members of the crew. Prior to a highly publicized Bikini bomb test on June 30, 1946, someone attached a photograph of movie "bombshell" Rita Hayworth to the bomb, thereby explicitly establishing an association of nuclear explosions with sexuality. (See also DR. STRANGELOVE.) Four days afterward the bathing suit's designer, Louis Réard, selected the name "bikini" to suggest the scanty bathing suit's "explosive" potential.

For additional reading, see Elaine Tyler May, "Explosive Issues: Sex, Women and the Bomb," in May's *Recasting America.*

"Biography" A TELEVISION DOCUMENTARY that ran in syndication from 1962 to 1964. It was revived in 1979 and again in 1987. The original show was hosted by Mike Wallace, who also served as the script consultant. David Janssen hosted the 1979 revival, and Peter Graves was host in 1987. Relying on film clips, photographs and recordings, the show presented biographies of famous men and women from the 20th century. The biographical subjects included political figures, generals, sports figures, scientists, explorers, actors and other prominent personalities, including such Cold War subjects as presidents Truman, Eisenhower and Kennedy, Senator Joseph McCarthy, General Douglas MacArthur, Josef Stalin, Mao Zedong, Fidel Castro, Konrad Adenauer, Madame Chiang Kai-shek, Charles de Gaulle and Dag Hammarskjöld. The show frequently took a patriotic slant, praising great Americans and condemning the treachery of America's enemies.

"Bionic Woman, The" A TELEVISION SPY SHOW that ran on ABC in 1976–77 and NBC in 1977–78. A spin-off of THE SIX MILLION DOLLAR MAN, (ABC, 1973–78) "The Bionic Woman" starred Lindsay Wagner as Jaime Sommers, the former fiancée of "The Six Million Dollar Man's" protagonist, Steve Austin. Almost killed in a skiing accident, Sommers was bionically reconstructed with superhuman legs and a superhuman ear and right arm. These gave her great speed, acute powers of hearing and enormous strength. Sommers became an agent for the U.S. government's Office of Scientific Information, for whom she fought international spies and criminals. Like "The Six Million Dollar Man," this Cold War–era show depicted the fruits of American science being applied to the protection of the United States and the virtues of the American way. The series was based on Martin Caidin's novel, *Cyborg.*

"Bishop Sheen Program, The" See LIFE IS WORTH LIVING.

black humor A dark humor that generates laughter from dangers that in the real world would be disturbing rather than funny. During the Cold War, black humor appeared in many media, including FILM, TELEVISION, THEATER, CARTOONS, LITERATURE, MUSIC, SATIRE, stand-up comedy and even fashion. Sometimes called "gallows humor" because of its propensity for laughing about death and horror, black humor provided an outlet for Cold War anxieties. The ability to laugh at something implies the recognition of an incongruous situation, and Cold War black humor typically served as a coping mechanism for those who perceived that the world's destiny—conventionally represented as being in the hands of rational people—was actually being determined by sex-crazed megalomaniacs, out-of-control machines and unwieldy bureaucracies capable of creating a nuclear apocalypse at any time. Black humor was not invented during the Cold War; it flourished in Europe during the plague years of the late Middle Ages and early Renaissance. But such humor experienced a revival during the Cold War, especially in the period before détente, between the 1950s and early 1970s.

DR. STRANGELOVE (1964), a FILM SATIRE, may represent the epitome of Cold War black humor: An insane U.S. Air Force general orders a nuclear strike against the Soviet Union, and bumbling, sex-crazed American and Soviet leaders are unable to prevent a Russian "doomsday" machine from going off in retaliation. In the same dark and gruesome vein, Robert Altman's M*A*S*H (1970) generates humor even as the camera shows spurting blood and battlefield carnage. Like *Dr. Strangelove*, M*A*S*H depicts a world run by insane, sexually crazed, sexually frustrated and/or sexually perverted men (and to a lesser extent women), but the horror behind its humor is more immediate and more frightening. *Dr. Strangelove* appeared in a relatively benign period in the Cold War—after U.S.–Soviet tensions had subsided from the 1962 Cuban Missile Crisis and before the major U.S. escalation in Vietnam. On the other hand, M*A*S*H, though set during the Korean War, was made during the height of the Vietnam War, when the TELEVISION NEWS shows and TELEVISION DOCUMENTARIES were regularly sending home pictures of dead and wounded Americans. Its antiwar message thus had a more direct target, and its grotesque images had more immediate correlatives in the real world.

Another powerful black humor film from 1970 was CATCH-22, based on Joseph Heller's 1961 MILITARY NOVEL. Like M*A*S*H and the earlier FOREIGN FILM, KING OF HEARTS, (1967) *Catch-22* uses a setting from an earlier conflict (World War II) to depict warfare as an insane enterprise run by power-hungry men with twisted values. Hal ASHBY'S HAROLD AND MAUDE (1971) is another black humor film of the era that celebrates COUNTERCULTURE values and attacks the war.

The Vietnam War spawned black humor in other media too, as war protesters perceived the absurdity of destroying villages in order to "save" them and the obscenity of having American soldiers kill and be killed in order to prop up cruel and corrupt South Vietnamese regimes that lacked support from the South Vietnamese people and denied them human rights. Among the most forceful black humor lyrics to come from the war were those sung by Country Joe Mcdonald in his "I-Feel-Like-I'm-Going-To-Die Rag." Over an upbeat melody, Country Joe employs the language of 1950s television commercials to urge "Mothers and fathers throughout the land/ Send your son off to Vietnam . . . Be the first one on your block/ To have your boy come home in a box."

Among the best examples of Cold War black humor in literature are *Catch-22*, Robert COOVER's THE PUBLIC BURNING (1976), which treats the execution of convicted atomic spies Julius and Ethel Rosenberg, and Coover's short story, THE CAT IN THE HAT FOR PRESIDENT (1968) which addresses American presidential politics. John BARTH, Terry SOUTHERN, Kurt VONNEGUT Jr. and Bruce Jay Friedman also employ black humor in Cold War-related settings. Barth's GILES GOAT-BOY (1966) evokes U.S.-Soviet brinkmanship in an allegorical setting: The world is a large university controlled by a supercomputer; the East and West campuses are locked in a dangerous cold war; and the new messiah is a Grand Tutor whose destiny is to Pass All/Fail All. The punning wordplay in Bernard Wolfe's APOCALYPTIC NOVEL, LIMBO '90, (1953) and the treatment of nuclear war as a bad acid trip in Brian Aldiss's BAREFOOT IN THE HEAD (1969) also draw on the tradition of black humor. Thomas PYNCHON and John Hawkes likewise create nightmare worlds drawn with an uneasy humor, though these portrayals usually relate to the Cold War only indirectly.

The role of black humor in the novel and TELEVISION SITUATION COMEDY "M*A*S*H" (novel 1968, TV 1972–83 on CBS) was greatly diminished by comparison to the film. In general, black humor appeared infrequently on network television, which of all the media was the least daring and most concerned with remaining inoffensive. However, the droll satire of "THAT WAS THE WEEK THAT WAS" (NBC, 1964–65), a short-lived television show featuring political satire, often had a black humor edge, as did some skits from the variety shows THE SMOTHERS BROTHERS COMEDY HOUR (CBS, 1967–68) and SATURDAY NIGHT LIVE (NBC, 1975–present). CHINA BEACH (ABC 1988), a TELEVISION MILITARY DRAMA from the late 1980s, included elements of black humor in its otherwise somber portrayal of the Vietnam War, especially through the comments of Private Sam Beckett who ran the morgue and Red Cross worker Holly the Donut Dolly.

Arthur Kopit's 1984 play, END OF THE WORLD, uses black humor to examine the then-current policies of Mutually Assured Destruction (MAD) as well as Reagan administration attempts to break the nuclear balance by regaining nuclear superiority. The play convincingly concludes that within the framework of MAD the very existence of nuclear weapons implies their eventual use in a nuclear war, whereas any attempt to escape from the framework of MAD will also result in nuclear war. Moreover, humans are drawn to the awesome power of the bomb and are thrilled as well as horrified by the prospect of their own destruction. Thus Kopit's play communicates both intellectually and emotionally the horrifying reality of the nuclear situation and at the same time leaves the audience with something more uplifting than the despair that the situation would seem to warrant. He employs black humor to accomplish his goal, substituting life-affirming laughter for life-denying despair.

Such magazines as *The National Lampoon, Mad, The Realist, Screw* and, less consistently, PLAYBOY, *Penthouse, Hustler* and other men's magazines also featured black humor, especially in cartoons. Garry Trudeau's nationally syndicated comic strip *Doonesbury* also occasionally served as a vehicle for black humor. Englishman Raymond Briggs's 1982 WHEN THE WIND BLOWS is a black humor cartoon book about a middle-class British couple that is helpless to prevent a NUCLEAR APOCALYPSE brought about by "The Powers That Be." As he suns himself in radioactive air, the husband declares with preposterous cheerfulness, "We'll just have to acclimatise ourselves to the Post-Nuclear Area. It could be OK—wiping the slate clean . . . starting afresh—a New Fire of London! The New Elizabethan Age will dawn." The couple dies absurdly quoting passages from the Bible and "The Charge of the Light Brigade."

Other Cold War examples of black humor include Tom LEHRER's songs about nuclear destruction, WE WILL ALL GO TOGETHER WHEN WE GO (1959), "The Wild West Is Where I Want to Be" (1953) and "Who's Next" (1965), and Lenny BRUCE's stand-up comedy routines in which, for example, the comedian asks whether a true patriot would reveal state secrets if subjected to a hot-lead enema. Black humor even appeared in fashion during the 1970s and 1980s as T-shirts appeared with Pop art drawings. One shows a sobbing woman saying, "Nuclear War?! There Goes My Career!" Other black humor T-shirts proclaimed "One Nuclear Bomb Ruins Your Whole Day," "Cobaltone . . . For the Tan of Your Life" and the exit line from the Looney Tunes cartoons, "That's All, Folks!" superimposed over a mushroom cloud.

One of the most positive characteristics of black humor is its capacity to generate a redeeming spark of creativity and lightness of spirit from even the bleakest circumstances. In this way, black humor produces a spiritual energy without which, in the words of *Catch-22*, "man is garbage."

For additional reading, see Blair and Hill's *America's Humor*.

Blacker, Irwin An author of VIETNAM WAR LITERATURE. A prolific novelist, Blacker's Vietnam stories typically center on secret assignments behind enemy lines. His novel *Search and Destroy* (1966), for instance, describes the activities of a five-man commando team that parachutes into North Vietnam. Their mission is to prevent an anticipated invasion of South Vietnam by destroying key North Vietnamese strategic targets. Other books he has written or edited include *Behind the Lines: Twenty-Eight Stories of Irregular Warfare* (1956) and *Irregulars, Partisans, Guerrillas* (1954).

blacklisting During the RED SCARE, the entertainment industry practiced widespread blacklisting—that is, an industry-wide policy of refusing to hire alleged communists, former communists and communist sympathizers, though formal blacklists were not admitted to exist. SCREENWRITERS and FILM ACTORS AND ACTRESSES were especially affected, but so too were FILM DIRECTORS and writers, performers, commentators and announcers in FILM, TELEVISION and radio. Because live THEATER was not as vulnerable to boycotts and picketing as were movies and television shows, blacklisting rarely occurred in that medium, not least because the Actors' Equity Association (stage actors' union) and the Theater League of New York formulated an anti-blacklisting agreement and scrupulously abided by it.

For legal reasons and fear of reprisals from unions, entertainment industry officials publicly denied the existence of a formal blacklist. In fact, they relied on lists compiled by such private citizens' groups as the American Legion, which published *Firing Line* and whose Syracuse Post #41 published the newsletter *Spotlight;* the Wage Earners Committee; Aware Inc.; and American Business Consultants, a firm formed by three former FBI agents who published the magazine COUNTERATTACK and the 1950 booklet RED CHANNELS. Private individuals who influenced industry blacklisting decisions included Rabbi Benjamin Schultz, who directed the American Jewish League Against Communism; Laurence A. Johnson, a Syracuse businessman; and Vincent Hartnett, who wrote the introduction to *Red Channels,* assembled and distributed *File 13* (a more comprehensive sequel to *Red Channels*) and formed Aware, Inc., which published a series of bulletins distributed to industry executives.

These private individuals and groups, in turn, relied on various public documents that listed individuals and identified alleged communist and communist-front organizations. The common practice was to list the names of supposed communists or communist sympathizers and indicate the groups to which they allegedly belonged, usually with a citation documenting the allegation. For example, *Red Channels* lists actor Lee J. COBB to be "reported as" a sponsor of the American Peace Mobilization Committee and the League of American Writers, among other suspect organizations. As evidence of his participation in the first organization, the entry cites the HOUSE COMMITTEE ON UN-AMERICAN ACTIVITIES' (HUAC) suppressed Appendix IX, (see below); it cites an article from the American Communist Party newspaper, *The Daily Worker,* to document the second affiliation. Likewise, *Red Channels* cites government documents to verify that the American Peace Mobilization Committee was a "Communist front" and mentions eight government sources to support claims that the League of American Writers was either a communist or communist-front organization.

The most frequently cited government sources used for documenting communist affiliation were Attorney General Tom Clark's letters to the Loyalty Review Board, released in 1947 and 1948, which identified "subversive" and "Communist-front" organizations; reports from the 1938 Massachusetts House Committee on Un-American Activities; the 1947 and 1948 reports from the California state Senate Committee on Un-American Activities chaired by Senator Jack Tenney; and, of course, HUAC, a congressional committee that conducted hearings on the Hollywood film industry in 1947 and 1951–52 and additional hearings on the entertainment industry throughout the 1950s.

HUAC's Appendix IX was another significant government source for documentary "evidence" of communist affiliation. J. B. Matthews and Benjamin Mandel prepared it in 1944 for the Costello subcommittee of HUAC. Appendix IX was a seven-volume compilation of some 2,000 pages listing the names of thousands of people who participated in alleged communist-front organizations between 1930 and 1944. The first six volumes identify and document some 245 organizations; the last volume contains 22,000 names of individuals. According to Mandel, the inclusion of a name in Appendix IX did not necessarily indicate that the person was "subversive"; however, the document itself contains no disclaimer to that effect or any other explanation of its

purpose or proper use. When the full committee learned of the report, it ordered that Appendix IX be restricted and that all existing copies be destroyed. Consequently, during the Red Scare there were no copies in the Library of Congress or such public repositories as the New York Public Library. However, prior to the committee's order, several of the 7,000 printed copies had been distributed to private individuals or organizations, including the editors of *Red Channels* and such government agencies as the FBI, the State Department and Army and Navy Intelligence. Thus, in most instances, people cited for their inclusion in Appendix IX did not have access to it, even to verify that they were, in fact, listed in the document, let alone to review the source behind the accusation.

Blacklists were developed from several sources and were continually revised throughout the Red Scare. As a consequence of the 1947 HUAC hearings, each of the HOLLYWOOD TEN was denied employment throughout the industry, as were several of the other nine "unfriendly" witnesses whom the committee never called. The 19 included actor Larry PARKS, writer Robert Adrian Scott and director Edward DMYTRYK. Others to be blacklisted as an outgrowth of the 1947 hearings included some of the signers of a Committee for the First Amendment advertisement in behalf of the Hollywood Ten, 208 actors who had bought an ad supporting the unfriendly witnesses and attacking HUAC, and signers of an amicus curiae brief submitted to the Supreme Court requesting that it review the case of the Hollywood Ten. Among those to lose their livelihoods for supporting the Ten were Anne Revere, an Academy Award winner and two-time nominee, and Gale Sondergaard, also an Academy Award winner and wife of Herbert BIBERMAN, one of the Hollywood Ten.

The year 1951 brought a new round of Hollywood hearings and the emergence of a new blacklist, compiled by the American Legion. J. B. Matthews, compiler of Appendix IX, wrote "Did the Movies Really Clean House?" for *American Legion Magazine,* naming 66 movie personalities whom Matthews alleged to have communist sympathies. (Seventeen were listed solely because they had signed the amicus curiae brief, and several others appeared solely because they had signed the advertisement criticizing HUAC.) One result of the article was a meeting between the American Legion and the studio heads, who feared widespread boycotts and demonstrations against movies featuring alleged communists listed by the Legion. The studios relied on bank financing of films, and banks were reluctant to finance films that were certain to be boycotted. Consequently, the studio heads were under pressure to refuse employment to anyone of whom the Legion did not approve. With the understanding that access to the list would be limited to top studio executives and to the named individuals themselves, the Legion presented the studios with the names of some 300 people, with the proviso that the studios would "check for any factual errors and make such reports to us as [they] deem[ed] proper." According to the Legion, the list was almost immediately abused. It quickly became a de facto blacklist. Those listed were given an opportunity to write a letter explaining the charges against them. If they refused to write such a letter, they were fired. The letters from those who cooperated were submitted to the American Legion, which passed judgment on their acceptability. Difficult cases were sent to George SOKOLSKY, a Hearst newspaper JOURNAL-IST based in New York who possessed sterling anti-communist credentials and an apparently sincere desire to assist those who truly repented their earlier political "errors." Sokolsky either rendered a decision or consulted Roy BREWER, president of the AFL's International Alliance of Theater and Stage Employees, and/or actor Ward BOND in Hollywood. Brewer was the first and Bond the second president of the anti-communist MOTION PICTURE ALLIANCE FOR THE PRESERVATION OF AMERICAN IDEALS. Of those who wrote letters, only 30 failed to produce satisfactory explanations. However, individuals who were not currently under contract were never asked to write a letter and were thus not informed of their presence on the American Legion's list or given an opportunity to "clear" themselves.

Other de facto blacklists include HUAC's 1952 and 1953 annual reports, which released 212 names of individuals in the movie industry named by "friendly" witnesses as having been communists. Evidence indicates that in having witnesses name their associates in communist-supported activities, HUAC was intentionally trying to create a blacklist by introducing the names into the public record. (See *Report on Blacklisting,* vol. one on testimony of Larry Parks.) Whether or not this was the case, the HUAC listings in fact functioned as a blacklist, as all 212 people named there lost their livelihoods in Hollywood by having their contracts either canceled, bought up or not renewed. Once without a contract, they were unable to get new work in the Hollywood studios under their own names for several years. (Writers sometimes submitted work under pseudonyms or through "fronts." See THE FRONT.)

Red Channels was the predominant list used by the television and radio industry. Published as a special report by *Counterattack* magazine in 1950, the booklet listed 151 men and women who the editors claimed were currently or had once been linked with communist causes. The editors cited the links in each instance, documenting them with citations from the attorney general's list, HUAC, the California Un-American Activities Committee, American Legion reports and other official and private sources. Because *Red Channels* began with a disclaimer stating that the listed activities or associations *may* have been free of subversive intentions, and it purported only to report factual information from the public domain, the publication avoided legal liability for damages suffered by those listed. As Merle Miller documents in *The Judges and the Judged, Red Channels* consistently failed to include anti-Communist activities in which the people it had listed also participated, and it made little effort to authenticate the accuracy of its sources. Among other sources, *Red Channels* relied freely on HUAC's restricted and often unreliable Appendix IX. Once listed in *Red Channels,* an individual became "controversial" and therefore undesirable for employment.

Even after blacklisted individuals were cleared, industry officials were often leary of hiring them because their reputations remained tainted or because their careers had lost momentum while they were removed from the public eye and they no longer held popular appeal. Ireene WICKER, who was inaccurately included in *Red Channels,* is a prime example. Though she proved that the charges against her were inaccurate, television executives deemed her too controversial and refused to offer her work again for several years, by which time her popularity had faded. Prominent names listed in *Red Channels* include Larry Adler, Leonard Bernstein, Aaron Copland, Howard Duff, José Ferrer, John GARFIELD, Will Geer, Morton Gould, Dashiell Hammett, Lillian Hellman, Judy Holliday, Lena HORNE, Langston Hughes, Burl Ives, Gypsy Rose Lee, Philip LOEB, Burgess Meredith, Arthur MILLER, Henry Morgan, Zero MOSTEL, Jean MUIR, Dorothy Parker, Edward G. Robinson, Anne Revere, Hazel SCOTT, Pete SEEGER, Artie Shaw, William Shirer, Howard K. Smith, William SWEETS, Louis Untermeyer and Orson Welles. Singer and actor Paul ROBESON was another highly successful performer whose ability to practice his craft and earn a living was greatly restricted by blacklisting.

One technique that anti-communist groups used effectively to ensure that the radio and television industries complied with the blacklists was to threaten boycotts of the sponsoring companies' products if a show featured someone who appeared on one of the lists. Rabbi Schultz used this technique with considerable success. Laurence Johnson, who owned a chain of supermarkets, employed a similar effective strategy: He would send letters informing a sponsor of a performer's alleged communist affiliations and then propose placing a questionnaire next to the company's products in his stores. The questionnaire would ask whether consumers wanted any part of their purchase price to be used to hire "Communist Front talent." The consumer would then mark "Yes" or "No." Fearful of this kind of adverse publicity, the sponsors would then pressure the broadcast company to fire the performer.

People whose names appeared on a blacklist could become eligible for jobs again if they "cleared" themselves. To be cleared, a person usually had either to provide indisputable evidence that the basis for the blacklisting was incorrect (as in a case of mistaken identity, in which two people shared the same name) or repudiate the earlier "subversive" activities, publicly repenting "mistakes" and making a show of support for anti-communist efforts. Those who were called to testify before HUAC were also expected to "name names"—to identify others in the industry who had belonged to communist-front organizations or participated in communist-supported activities. Often the clearance process involved the intervention of well-known anti-communist intermediaries, such as Hartnett, Sokolsky, Brewer, Bond, Jack Wren ("security officer" at the BBD&O advertising agency) or Daniel T. O'Shea and Alfred Berry (security officers at CBS). These men claimed they were performing a beneficial service, without remuneration, and typically made themselves easily available to listed individuals. Such "clearance men" were known for their strong anti-communist sympathies. Their certification could make listed individuals eligible for reemployment, as the clearance men met with listed people to work out a mutually acceptable ritual of atonement. Among those rehabilitated in this way was Edward Dmytryk, who, after reversing his 1947 "unfriendly" position, atoned by naming names to HUAC in 1951. Moreover, Dmytryk convinced Brewer that "the people who had broken with the Party had to be helped, both because it was the right thing to do and because it hurt the Communist Party." Brewer concurred and signaled Dmytryk's rehabilitation by arranging for a favorable article about him to appear in *The Saturday Evening Post.* The director returned to work shortly thereafter. Brewer likewise arranged for John Garfield to publish an article entitled "I Was a Sucker for a Left Hook," as part of a rehabilitation process that was cut short by the actor's death. (Garfield's friends maintained that his fatal heart attack resulted from the stress caused by his blacklisting and his efforts to clear himself.) Brewer also arranged for the clearances of Gene Kelly, Jose Ferrer and John Huston.

Brewer, Sokolsky and most of the other prominent clearance men pointed out that they themselves had never blacklisted anyone and insisted that their activity was a humanitarian service that gave employment to people who otherwise would not be permitted to work. On the other hand, anyone who failed to receive their approval was doomed to unemployment. For instance, Brewer turned down one writer cited by the American Legion. Although the writer had written the requisite letter answering the charges against him, described his anti-communist activities and publicly stated anti-communist sentiments, Brewer claimed that his letter was not sufficiently penitent or humble. Even after the writer filed a 64-page document with the FBI listing his political advocacies and activities, Brewer failed to clear him, and he remained out of the film industry from 1951 to 1955.

The clearing process sometimes required listed individuals to hire the organization that blacklisted them to perform an "investigation" in order to certify that they were indeed "clean." Thus, between selling the lists to government agencies and businesses and performing "security investigations" and "clearing" operations, some people were able to earn a living from blacklisting, though the most prominent clearance men—Brewer, Sokolsky, Bond et al.—performed their work for free. On the other hand, Ken Bierly, a former editor of *Counterattack,* became a public relations consultant who cleared people. He thus earned money by causing people to be blacklisted and then again by clearing them. Among his clients was Judy Holliday, who was listed in *Counterattack's* publication, *Red Channels.*

Many blacklisted individuals were willing to testify about their own activities but would not testify about others because they did not want their friends or former associates to be blacklisted in turn. Such individuals were not usually considered acceptable for clearance from the blacklists because they were not properly atoning for their mistakes and were inhibiting the anti-communist efforts of the committees. In 1947 the Hollywood Ten were cited for contempt of Congress when they refused to answer HUAC's questions about their political beliefs, citing their First Amendment constitutional protections. However, the Supreme Court denied their claim to First Amendment protection and upheld their convictions, and the Ten had to serve terms in federal prison. In order to avoid that fate, some witnesses testifying at the 1951–52 HUAC hearings chose to refuse to answer by "taking the Fifth Amendment." However, after the Supreme Court ruled that individuals could not invoke the Fifth Amendment if they had already testified about themselves, witnesses were compelled to choose between incurring potential criminal penalties for remaining silent or implicating other people. Thus a witness's price for using a committee

hearing as a forum for defending his or her views was either to inform on friends and colleagues or face a jail sentence. Otherwise witnesses had to invoke the Fifth Amendment from the outset and thereby lose the opportunity to make their case for themselves. "Fifth Amendment Communists," as Senator Joseph McCarthy labeled them, were routinely denied employment within the entertainment industry. Among those who refused to name names were playwright and screenwriter Lillian Hellman, writer-producer Carl FOREMAN, director Robert ROSSEN, actor Jose Ferrer and playwright Arthur Miller who, because he did not invoke a constitutional right, was cited for contempt of Congress, fined $500. and given a 30-day suspended jail sentence.

The television blacklist came to an end when the blacklisters began to be held financially liable for the consequences of their listings. In 1955 the Texas broadcast humorist John Henry Faulk sued Johnson and Hartnett for libel after Aware, Inc., in a case of mistaken identity, inaccurately publicized his alleged communist associations. After a seven-year trial, a jury awarded Faulk $3.5 million. Though the award was later greatly reduced, the precedent did much to end the television and radio blacklist. Faul described his ordeal in *Fear on Trial* (1964).

The film blacklist ended in 1960 when director Otto Preminger publicly announced that Dalton TRUMBO, of the Hollywood Ten, had written the screenplay for EXODUS. The same year Trumbo received credit for his work on another major film, Stanley KUBRICK'S SPARTACUS (1960), which president-elect John F. Kennedy crossed American Legion picket lines to view. In 1970 Trumbo, who had vehemently attacked blacklisting in his 1949 pamphlet, "Time of the Toad," received the Screen Writers Guild's highest honor, the Laurel Award. In his acceptance speech he addressed those who were too young to remember the Red Scare: "To them I would say only this: that the blacklist was a time of evil, and that no one on either side who survived it came through untouched by evil . . . There was bad faith and good, honesty and dishonesty, courage and cowardice, selflessness and opportunism, wisdom and stupidity, good and bad on both sides; and almost every individual involved . . . combined some or all of these antithetical qualities in his own person, in his own acts . . . in the final tally we were *all* victims because . . . each of us felt compelled to say things we did not want to say . . . none of us—right, left, or center—emerged from that long nightmare without sin."

For additional reading, see Cogley's *Report on Blacklisting,* Vaughn's *Only Victims,* Miller's *The Judges and the Judged,* and Whitfield's *The Culture of the Cold War.*

Blob, The   A 1958 SCIENCE FICTION FILM starring Steve McQueen and Aneta Corseaut and directed by Irvin Yeaworth. Chuck Russell's 1988 remake, starring Kevin Dillon, Shawnee Smith and Donovan Leitch, employs special effects that are far more sophisticated and successful than those of the original in creating a Jell-O-like creature that slogs its way through city streets engorging all who fall into its path. The 1950s version, however, makes literal the common RED SCARE metaphor of "creeping communism," a concept that had lost its force by 1988. Like INVASION OF THE BODY SNATCHERS (1956), *The Blob* centers on the protagonist's struggle to persuade his fellow citizens that a dangerous and imminent threat exists. The film thus reflects the right-wing fear that its warnings about the communist menace are not being heeded. (See also FILMS ASSOCIATED WITH THE RED SCARE.)

For additional reading, see Biskind's *Seeing Is Believing.*

Bly, Robert   A POET. Born in Madison, Minnesota, in 1926, Bly graduated magna cum laude from Harvard University in 1950. In 1956 he received a master's degree from the University of Iowa and a Fulbright grant to travel to Norway and translate Norwegian poems into English. He subsequently founded *The Fifties* magazine to provide an outlet for poetry in translation; the publication later evolved into *The Sixties* and *The Seventies.* Bly rebelled against the formal poetry that dominated the American literary scene in the 1950s as too removed from life, too intellectual and insufficiently passionate. Though much of his work seeks to bring out "more of the joy of the unconscious," Bly was also politically aware, and during the Vietnam War much of his poetry concerned antiwar themes. In 1966 he coedited with David Ray a volume entitled *A Poetry Reading Against the Vietnam War.* His second book of poetry, *The Light Around the Body* (1967), received the 1968 National Book Award for poetry. It mixes introspective poems revealing and celebrating the unconscious with attacks on the war and on other aspects of American Cold War politics. These latter include "Listening to President Kennedy Lie about the Cuban Invasion," "Johnson's Cabinet Watched by Ants," "Those Being Eaten by America," "The Great Society," "Asian Peace Offers Rejected without Publication," "Hatred of Men with Black Hair" and "Driving through Minnesota during the Hanoi Bombings."

According to C. Michael Smith, "The images of destruction apparent in Bly's antiwar poems portray a society too oriented toward the outward world, too ignorant of the other side of life. His purpose in this volume is to show both languages, to show that the problems of one world [the external world of political events] come from an inability to deal with the other [the realm of the unconscious]." Bly's subsequent poetry continued to move "from political and social issues back to the landscapes of the mind and of nature." "The Teeth Mother Naked at Last" connects American prosperity to the horrors of the war: "It's because taxpayers move to the suburbs/ that we transfer populations./ The Marines use cigarette lighters/ to light the thatched-roofed huts/ because so many Americans own their/ own homes." Following the war, Bly's poetry became less overtly political, though he retains the belief that nurturing unconscious forces and achieving inner harmony can bring about a more peaceful and harmonious world. In the 1980s he became known as a New Age guru when he put his beliefs into practice in televised seminars offered specifically to men. (See also VIETNAM WAR LITERATURE.)

For additional reading, see *Dictionary of Literary Biography* (vol. 5, *American Poets Since World War II*).

Bond, James   The protagonist of a series of SPY NOVELS and SPY FILMS. The suave, virile and deadly British secret agent had a "license to kill." He first appeared in Ian

Sean Connery as James Bond in Goldfinger, *1964. Courtesy AP/Wide World.*

Fleming's 1953 novel *Casino Royale;* subsequently the James Bond stories became the most successful series of spy novels and films in history. Fleming published 12 Bond novels between 1953 and 1965. After his death, John Gardner and other writers created additional Bond stories. During the Cold War era, over 15 Bond movies were produced in Great Britain. Sean Connery, the first film Bond, appeared in six Bond movies between 1962 and 1971, most notably DR. NO (book 1958, film 1962), FROM RUSSIA WITH LOVE (book 1957, film 1963), GOLDFINGER (book 1960, film 1926) and THUNDERBALL (book 1961, film 1965). Perhaps the best of the Bond films, *Goldfinger* introduced the general public to lasers. In 1983 Connery returned to play Bond in *Never Say Never Again.* Roger Moore appeared as Bond seven times, notably in THE SPY WHO LOVED ME (book 1962, film 1977), MOONRAKER (book 1955, film 1979) *Octopussy* (film 1983) and *Live and Let Die* (book 1959, film 1989). George Lazenby starred in *On Her Majesty's Secret Service* (book 1964, film 1969), and Timothy Dalton was Agent 007 in THE LIVING DAYLIGHTS (film 1987) and *License to Kill* (film 1989). The film version of *Casino Royale* (1967) parodied the Bond character, starring David Niven as the retired Sir James Bond and Woody Allen as his nephew. In the post–Cold War era, the series remains successful as drug barons, organized criminals and disaffected military officers from the former Soviet Union serve as enemies.

The spy genre flourished during the Cold War, possibly because so much of the Cold War was fought through covert actions and secret maneuvering rather than direct military confrontation. The action-packed Bond stories purported to depict the sexy and exciting extra-legal life of a Cold War secret agent. Unlike spy stories by such authors as John LE CARRE and Graham GREENE, which portray the complex mix of right and wrong on both sides, the Bond stories clearly distinguish between good and evil, and no doubt ever exists that Bond is working not only to save the West but also to preserve all that is valuable in the entire world. Although he often lacks compassion and his methods are sometimes brutal, Bond is never sadistic and everything he does is ultimately "for God and country," even if he enjoys himself immensely along the way.

The qualities that make Bond a successful secret agent, hence a successful world savior, are his physical prowess, sexual attractiveness and performance, elegant dress, polished manners, sophistication and high levels of skill, intelligence, resourcefulness and good luck. Moreover, he drives high-performance cars and has access to other state-of-the-art technology. As a superior man, Bond is clearly someone who rose from the masses, not with them; he showcases the virtues of consumer capitalism over communism. While Bond never loses touch with his animal nature, which makes him strong and virile, he balances it with the refinement and high fashion that are the pride of Western achievement, along with its superior technology. In this regard the Bond stories create images of success and masculine desirability similar to those cultivated by PLAYBOY magazine, which also first appeared during the early 1950s. Bond's sexual prowess plays a large role in his success over rival agents, and the plots often turn on his ability to seduce and control women, many of whom come to disastrous ends in the course of his adventures. His emotional detachment usually enables him to recover quickly from their loss, though in the novels that detachment is treated more ambivalently than in the films. On the other hand, Bond's willingness to seek out and submit to pleasure demonstrates that a person can successfully be responsible and self-indulgent at the same time, so long as he never loses sight of his primary mission. Moreover, for Bond, seeking out pleasure becomes a virtue that enables him to complete his task by frequently placing him in the right place at the right time and by winning him useful female friends. Bond's acceptance of the pleasure principle thus endorses the consumerism of the Cold War era, even as it reverses the Puritan ethic of denial and refutes communist self-denial.

The novels also suggest that female sexuality is a potent but potentially dangerous force that must be safely harnessed. Though some women in the Bond stories are weak and compliant, others are strong and influential. Therefore Bond's ability to control women is another important weapon in his personal arsenal for fighting the Cold War. When Bond seduces and wins over the villain's girlfriend, the audience understands that Bond has become the dominant male. Moreover, the woman's defection usually plays a crucial role in determining the outcome. Thus Bond's virility is one of his chief virtues, and his ability to control women through his sexuality plays an important role in his success and therefore in the survival of the Western world.

As the Cold War progressed, Bond's antagonists changed accordingly. In the earliest novels the Soviets are typically the enemy. However, after the 1962 Cuban Missile Crisis, U.S.-Soviet relations became less bellicose, and China be-

came more hostile. Thus in *Goldfinger* the antagonist is a criminal who has been given an atomic bomb by the Chinese; his right-hand man is a North Korean. (The Chinese exploded their first atomic device in 1964.) During the détente of the 1970s the enemy was often an agent of S.P.E.C.T.R.E., a highly organized, highly disciplined international criminal organization. In *Octopussy*, whose appearance coincided with the Soviet war in Afghanistan, the villain is an evil Afghan prince attempting to plunder treasures that once belonged to the czar. *The Living Daylights* also takes place partly in Afghanistan, and Afghan rebels help Bond fight against the Soviets. The film's ambivalent attitude toward the U.S.S.R. reflects the more conciliatory Western feelings about the Soviet Union under Gorbachev, who had been in power and introducing his reforms for two years when *The Living Daylights* appeared. Here the villain is a rogue Soviet military officer, and Bond works in limited cooperation with a ranking Soviet official to foil him. Thus the U.S.S.R. itself is not vilified for its sinister intentions, as it was earlier in the Cold War, except for its involvement in Afghanistan. Instead, the top-level Soviet officials appear responsible and even somewhat compassionate, and the danger comes from their inability to control a wayward subordinate. On the other hand, *Dr. No* and *Thunderball* deal with the problems that might arise when nuclear weapons or other advanced military technology fall into the hands of villains who operate as individuals or members of criminal organizations instead of agents of a nation-state. In *License to Kill* (1989), Bond addresses a new world enemy, an international consortium of drug lords.

For additional reading see Cawelti and Rosenberg's *The Spy Story*.

Bond, Ward A FILM ACTOR. Bond was active in anti-communist activities in Hollywood during the RED SCARE. He was an early member of the right-wing MOTION PICTURE ALLIANCE FOR THE PRESERVATION OF AMERICAN IDEALS and became its president after Roy BREWER's departure in 1955. Both Brewer and Bond were influential in helping to "clear" individuals who had been blacklisted (see BLACKLISTING) but who were willing to demonstrate their anti-communist sympathies through various public acts of contrition that usually involved identifying any members of the Communist Party known to them. Bond was a popular character actor who appeared in numerous films. He also starred as the wagonmaster on the television show "Wagon Train" (NBC / ABC, 1957–65).

Book of Daniel, The A 1971 POLITICAL NOVEL by E. L. Doctorow. The book presents a fictitious account of the case of Julius and Ethel Rosenberg, who were executed as spies in 1953. The novel is set in 1967 as Daniel Lewin, a 27-year-old graduate student at Columbia, tries to come to terms with the lives and fate of his parents, the Isaacsons, who, like the historical Rosenbergs, were Jewish communists from New York executed for passing atomic bomb secrets to the Russians. Daniel's younger sister is mentally ill, and his narrative represents his effort to discover the truth about his parents and his relationship to them, and to help his sister regain her sanity. Daniel tries to comprehend who his parents were, what they believed, what they actually did and why, the role their trial played in 1950s American culture and its current significance for himself and his country. Stanley Kauffmann, in *The New Republic,* called the book "the political novel of our age, the best American work of its kind . . . since Lionel Trilling's THE MIDDLE OF THE JOURNEY," and in *Newsweek* Peter S. Prescott describes the novel as "a purgative book, angry and more deeply felt than all but a few contemporary American novels, a novel about defeat, impotent rage, the passing of the burden of suffering through generations and 'the progress of madness inherited through the heart.' " The characters' Jewishness plays an important role as Daniel inherits the burden of suffering passed on by the Isaacsons. Their name, of course, means "the sons of Isaac"; Isaac was the son of Abraham chosen by God for sacrifice. Sidney Lumet's 1983 film adaptation, *Daniel,* appeared during an especially tense period in the Cold War. It concludes with actual footage from antinuclear demonstrations of June 12, 1982.

See also RED SCARE.

Book of Lights, The   A 1981 MILITARY NOVEL by Chaim Potok set in the early 1950s, shortly after the conclusion of the Korean War. The story centers on Gershon Loran, a quiet Jewish seminary student who is drawn to study the mystical writings of the Kabbalah, and his moody roommate Arthur Leiden, the unforgiving son of a brilliant physicist who helped make the atomic bomb. Leiden's mother, an art historian, indirectly used her influence to spare the beautiful city of Kyoto from atomic annihilation. In the novel's first section, Loran becomes increasingly attuned to and accepting of the Kabbalah, and Leiden's inability to come to terms with his father's responsibility for the bomb becomes evident. In the second section, all of the seminarians are coerced into joining the military services as chaplains, and Loran is assigned to a front-line medical unit in South Korea. The responsibilities he assumes in this hostile environment mature him, give him new self-confidence and allow him to integrate his understanding of the Kabbalah more richly into his life. By the time he reunites with Leiden, who is also assigned to Korea, Loran has accrued the wisdom to accompany his former roommate to Hiroshima and Kyoto, where Leiden begins to come to terms with his parents' legacies. By experiencing the Cold War and its historical antecedents in such a raw and forceful fashion, both men come to know themselves better.

Born on the Fourth of July   A 1989 VIETNAM WAR FILM starring Tom Cruise, Bryan Larkin and Raymond J. Barry and directed by Oliver STONE, a Vietnam veteran who received an Academy Award for this movie. Based on the memoirs of activist Ron Kovic, the story follows a patriotic, religious, macho all-American athlete who enlists in the Marines to fight in Vietnam because he wants to contribute to what he sees as a noble cause. The experience of the war disorients him, especially after he accidentally kills one of his own men in combat. He is later wounded in the back and paralyzed from the waist down. Back home Kovic feels alienated and misunderstood. He begins to drink heavily and remove himself from society until he recognizes that the war is wrong. Becoming an antiwar activist redeems Kovic, allowing him to recognize and express his deepest

feelings and renewing the sense of purpose and mission he had possessed when he enlisted. Moreover, his macho attitude changes as his outlook on the war does.

For additional reading see Kagan's *The Cinema of Oliver Stone.*

Boy and His Dog, A   A 1975 SCIENCE FICTION FILM starring Don Johnson, Susan Benton and Jason Robards Jr. and directed by L. Q. Jones. Based on a science fiction story by Harlan Ellison, *A Boy and His Dog* became an underground cult hit. The story, which concludes with a sick joke involving cannibalism, concerns the adventures of a survivor and his dog in a postnuclear-war wasteland. The film manages to walk a thin line between serious drama and self-parody until the end, when it gives in to BLACK HUMOR and self-parody. (See also APOCALYPTIC FILMS.)

Brecht, Bertolt   A German playwright who immigrated to the United States during World War II and later returned to East Germany after being compelled to testify before the HOUSE COMMITTEE ON UN-AMERICAN ACTIVITIES (HUAC). The GROVE PRESS published his plays in the United States in the 1950s. Born in Augsburg, Germany, in 1898, Brecht became affiliated with the famed Deutsches Theater in Berlin during the 1920s and early 1930s. He achieved both popular and critical success for his experimental THEATER, through which he sought to express his Marxism and bring about social change. *The Threepenny Opera* (1928), on which he collaborated with the composer Kurt Weill, was his most enduring work of this period. However, Brecht's Marxist ideology put him in disfavor with the rising Nazi power structure, severely limiting his opportunities to have his plays produced. He and his family fled to Sweden after the burning of the Reichstag in 1933, and he eventually immigrated to the United States in 1941, settling in Santa Monica, California, where he resided through 1947. During this period he completed *The Visions of Simone Machard* (1941–43), *Mother Courage* (1941), *The Good Woman of Setzuan* (1943) and *The Caucasian Chalk Circle* (1944–45). He also wrote the script for Fritz Lang's anti-Nazi film, *Hangmen Also Die* (1942).

American audiences were not highly receptive to Brecht's theatrical experimentation or to his didactic, Marxist message. *The Caucasian Chalk Circle,* for example, eschews a traditional dramatic story line and features instead a dispute between Soviet land owners dispossessed by war and the new settlers who have replaced them. Each side argues why it should control the land, and, to resolve the dispute, a visiting Communist Party official tells a story that, acted out, becomes the bulk of the play. After the play-within-the-play the former owners acknowledge that the property should belong to whoever puts it to the most productive use, and the two sides are happily reconciled. Thus individual property rights are subjugated to common cause.

In 1947, while Brecht was preparing a revised production of his dramatic portrayal of the iconoclastic scientist, *Galileo* (1938–39), HUAC subpoenaed him to testify as part of its highly politicized and sensational investigation of communist influence in the motion picture industry. He was the eleventh of 19 so-called "unfriendly witnesses" identified by the committee. *Galileo* addresses the failure of individuals to confront an unjust, repressive and unimaginative authority. However, both the avowedly Marxist Brecht and his hero, Galileo, fail to take a strong public stand against their inquisitors. Brecht answered their query about whether he had ever been a member of the Communist Party, "No, no, no, no, no, never." In *Galileo* he presents a disillusioned follower who reproaches the scientist after Galileo has capitulated to the Church: "Pity the land that has no heroes." "Pity the land that *needs* a hero," the astronomer replies. The other 10 witnesses called by the committee were the writers and directors who became knows as the HOLLYWOOD TEN. They served prison sentences and had their careers curtailed because of their refusal to comply with the committee's interrogation.

Although HUAC cleared him of any criminal charges, Brecht left the United States immediately after testifying and soon after settled in East Germany, whose government provided him with his own theater and a generous subsidy to continue his work. Ironically, this Marxist playwright was responsible for the longest-running musical up to that time in American history. *The Threepenny Opera* enjoyed over 2,000 off-Broadway performances in New York from 1954 to 1961, during the height of the Cold War. Its hit song, "Mack the Knife," sung by Bobby Darin, sold over 10 million copies in 1959, surpassed only by "White Christmas." Brecht was the subject of a 1988 film, *My Name Is Bertolt Brecht—Exile in the U.S.A.,* in which Hollywood Ten member Ring LARDNER Jr. appeared. (See also EXILED WRITERS [from the United States].)

For additional reading, see Tucker's *Literary Exile in the Twentieth Century;* Cook's *Brecht in Exile;* Navasky's *Naming Names.* For a partial transcript of Brecht's testimony before HUAC, see Bentley's THIRTY YEARS OF TREASON.

Brewer, Roy The president of the AFL's International Alliance of Theatrical Stage Employees (IATSE) and president of the MOTION PICTURE ALLIANCE FOR THE PRESERVATION OF AMERICAN IDEALS (MPA) during much of the RED SCARE. Brewer came to Hollywood in 1945 as an IATSE troubleshooter. An interunion jurisdictional dispute between IATSE and the Conference of Studio Unions (CSU) culminated in a series of strikes from which IATSE, under Brewer's leadership, emerged victorious. Brewer quickly aligned himself with the anti-communist forces in Hollywood, including the MPA. He testified as a "friendly" witness before the HOUSE COMMITTEE ON UN-AMERICAN ACTIVITIES (HUAC) in 1947, when the committee was investigating allegations of communist influence in the content of Hollywood films. Brewer stated, "We hope . . . that with the help of the committee, the Communist menace in the motion picture industry may be successfully destroyed."

After HOLLYWOOD TEN member Edward DMYTRYK reversed his 1947 position and cooperated with HUAC in 1951 by identifying alleged communists, Brewer met with him and Dmytryk convinced Brewer that "the people who had broken with the Party had to be helped, both because it was the right thing to do and because it hurt the Communist Party." According to *The Report on Blacklisting,* Brewer then began using his influence to "clear" penitent ex-communists and ex-communist sympathizers whose careers had been ruined by BLACKLISTING. Brewer would meet with blacklisted individuals and, if convinced they were sincere,

would arrange for them to make some public display of their anti-communist sentiments. After Brewer had cleared someone, he or she was once more eligible for employment. Among those Brewer is said to have helped clear were Gene Kelly, John GARFIELD, José Ferrer and John Huston. Brewer himself denied playing such a role. Testifying before HUAC in 1956 he stated, "I did not want, I did not seek . . . any power over anyone . . . any influence that I had came from the fact that I was willing to work at the job of countermanding the influence of what I consider to be a very evil force [communism]."

For additional reading, see Cogley's *Report on Blacklisting* (vol. 1); Vaughn's *Only Victims.*

Bridge at Andau, The A 1957 NONFICTION book by James MICHENER. The book presents a series of stories about ordinary people who were involved in the failed 1956 Hungarian Revolution and describes how some 20,000 people fled from Hungary into Austria across a frail wooden bridge in the weeks immediately following the revolt. Michener, who interviewed many of the refugees and visited the sites himself, helped some of the refugees escape into Austria, even carrying one on his back.

The book, which was generally well received, begins with a powerful indictment of communism: "At dawn, on November 4, 1956, Russian communism showed its true character to the world. With a ferocity and barbarism unmatched in recent history, it moved its brutal tanks against a defenseless population seeking escape from the terrors of communism, and destroyed it."

Bridge Over the River Kwai, The A 1952 MILITARY NOVEL by Pierre Boulle. An English translation was published in the United States in 1954. It was made into a 1957 MILITARY FILM entitled *The Bridge on the River Kwai,* starring William Holden, Alec Guinness, Jack Hawkins and Sessue Hayakawa and directed by David Lean. Boulle received credit for the screenplay, which was actually written by two blacklisted SCREENWRITERS, Michael Wilson, who had been the scenarist for SALT OF THE EARTH, and Carl FOREMAN, then in exile in England. (See also BLACKLISTING.) Boulle, who could not write in English at the time, received an Academy Award, which, as Foreman later said, "He had the good taste not to return in person to accept." The film won six additional Academy Awards, including best film, best actor and best director.

Set in Burma in a Japanese prison camp for British soldiers during World War II, *The Bridge on the River Kwai* shows the ranking British officer, Colonel Nicholson (Guinness), strictly adhering to military discipline and protocol as he and his men construct a railway bridge that is crucial for Japanese supply and troop movements. The film explores the conflict between the duty to undermine the enemy and the innate need to take pride in one's work, doing a job as well as it can be done. The latter is a military value that Nicholson rigidly imposes in order to maintain order and sanity among his troops. Through this conflict, the story implicitly criticizes the high cost of maintaining strict military values during World War II. Such criticisms were rare in the 1950s, when World War II was still revered as a "good war" and when military values were popularly seen to be a bulwark against communist tyranny and domination.

Bridges at Toko-Ri, The A 1953 MILITARY NOVEL by James MICHENER and a 1954 KOREAN WAR FILM starring William Holden, Fredric March, Grace Kelly and Mickey Rooney and directed by Mark Robson. Michener wrote the novel at the suggestion of the editors of *Life* magazine. The story focuses on Lieutenant Harry Brubaker, a World War II veteran and Navy Reserve pilot who is called up to serve in the Korean War. Though he feels he has already done more than his share in the service of his country, and though he deeply resents this second intrusion into his family life, Brubaker nonetheless subordinates himself to military authority, follows orders and does his share to fight the war. The extremely popular film won an Academy Award for the special effects used in the aerial combat sequences. The novel was published during the year the Korean War ended, and the film appeared a year after. Their impact on audiences was timely, as were the themes they raised about various Cold War issues. For instance, in having the World War II veteran serve in Korea, the story links the two wars. Initially Brubaker resents being called up to fight a war in such a remote and seemingly irrelevant region. But eventually he comes to accept the necessity of his task, the importance of which Admiral Tarrant (March) makes clear in the film: "Son, whatever progress this world has made has been because of the efforts of the few . . . If we did [pull out of Korea], they'd take Japan, Indo-China, the Philippines . . ." *The Bridges at Toko-Ri* thus suggests that the American mission in the Cold War is as important as its mission in World War II. At the same time, the story presents the ambivalent feelings experienced by war veterans who were once again called upon to fight for their country.

President Ronald REAGAN quoted from the film at the fortieth anniversary of the D-Day invasion, asking "Where do we find such men?" He used these words as his own, however, without attribution.

Bright Shining Lie, A a 1988 NONFICTION book by Neil Sheehan. *A Bright Shining Lie* presents the biography of Lt. Col. John Paul Vann, an American officer who first went to Vietnam in 1962 as a military adviser to the South Vietnamese Army. Originally convinced of the appropriateness of the U.S. mission, Vann became disillusioned and spoke out against the ineffective U.S. strategy and the brutality it entailed. Since his senior officers ignored his protests, he resigned from active duty in 1963 so that he could state his positions publicly in newspaper and magazine articles and in television interviews and speeches. He returned to Vietnam as a civilian provincial "pacification" representative for the Agency for International Development (AID) in March 1965, a month before the introduction of the first U.S. combat troops, and by the end of 1966 he was promoted to chief of the civilian pacification program for 11 provinces surrounding Saigon. During that time, he charged that U.S. bombing and shelling of the countryside was both cruel and counterproductive, as was its policy of driving peasants into urban slums and refugee camps in an unsuccessful effort to deprive the Viet Cong of its population base.

Despite his criticisms of the military establishment, Vann's leadership capabilities and dedication to the war resulted in his continued promotions, and by 1971 he became senior adviser in the central highlands and central coast. Though remaining a civilian working for AID, he assumed authority over all U.S. military forces in the area, as well as the civilians and military personnel in the pacification program. Because of his unusually close relationship with the South Vietnamese general who was his counterpart, Vann also in effect shared the command of the 158,000 South Vietnamese troops in the region. According to Sheehan, Vann was the most important American in South Vietnam after the ambassador and commanding general in Saigon, and his control as a civilian over U.S. military troops was unprecedented. He wielded power equivalent to that of a major general. "His accumulated expertise and aptitude for this war made him the one irreplaceable American in Vietnam."

Though he found fault with much of the way the war was handled Vann never concluded that the war itself was wrong. "He saw the United States as a stern yet benevolent authority . . . to him all Communists were enemies of America and thus enemies of order and progress." In 1972 Vann led a successful defensive action against a major North Vietnamese offensive that threatened to win the war; he was killed shortly afterward in a helicopter crash. The book jacket describes Vann as "the closest the United States came in Vietnam to a Lawrence of Arabia," and *A Bright Shining Lie* presents a detailed account of his career. Vann's papers were Sheehan's primary source. The title comes from a comment Vann made to a U.S. Army historian, "We had also, to all the visitors who came over there, been one of the bright shining lies."

Brodsky, Joseph A Soviet EXILED WRITER (to the United States) who won the 1987 Nobel Prize for literature for his poetry. Born in Leningrad in 1940, Brodsky first received international recognition in 1964 when Soviet authorities put him on trial for "social parasitism." Despite the support of such prominent cultural figures as composer Dmitri Shostakovich, Brodsky was sentenced to five years at hard labor in a remote village in the northern Soviet Union. His sentence was reduced to a year and a half, after which he returned to Leningrad, where he made a sparse living as a translator. Though he had difficulty publishing in the U.S.S.R., his poetry was well received in the United States, where it first appeared in a 1968 anthology, *Poets on Street Corners*. After he was anthologized in the U.S. volume, *The Living Mirror: Five Young Poets from Leningrad* (1972), Soviet officials expelled him from the country. His collection, published in English in 1973, *Selected Poems,* earned the praise of W. H. Auden, among other prominent literary figures.

After his exile, Brodsky held faculty positions at the University of Michigan and Cambridge University and traveled widely in Europe and the United States before settling in New York in 1977. His verse collection *A Part of Speech* (1980) was translated into English by such leading poets as Derek Walcott and Richard Wilbur. Brodsky's themes ranged from the metaphysical to the political. A 1980 poem expresses his reaction to the Soviet invasion of Afghanistan; other poems deal with individual human suffering. Brodsky received several honors, including an honorary doctorate from Yale University (1978), membership in the American Academy and Institute of Arts and Letters (1979), a MacArthur Foundation "genius" fellowship (1981) as well as the Nobel Prize. Written in English in tribute to Auden, George ORWELL and others to whom he felt indebted, Brodsky's collection of autobiographical and literary essays, *Less Than One*, received the National Book Critics Circle award for criticism for 1976. Also written in English is *Democracy*, a play that was produced in London in 1990. Brodsky died in New York in 1996.

For additional reading, see Tucker's *Literary Exile in the Twentieth Century.*

Bruce, Lenny   A stand-up comedian and social and political satirist. Born in 1925 as Leonard Albert Schneider, the son of immigrant Jewish parents, Bruce ran away from home in 1941 at age 16 and joined the navy the next year. He served as a shell-passer during World War II and participated in four major invasions. After the war

Lenny Bruce, 1963. Courtesy AP/Wide World.

concluded he walked on deck dressed as a woman in order to be caught and dismissed from the service. He denied being a homosexual but maintained that he enjoyed wearing women's clothing. His undesirable discharge was later upgraded to honorable after a Red Cross lawyer noted that his service record had been good and no charges had been filed against him.

Subsequently Bruce began his career as a comedian, first serving as a master of ceremonies for variety acts and as a contestant in rigged amateur shows. These experiences helped him shape his material, which was indebted to contemporary Jewish stand-up comedians who played with the nuances of language and interacted directly with their audiences. Bruce recognized the political and social power of language, and many of his routines, particularly those that were labeled obscene, demonstrate how language shapes our view of the world and of what we consider moral and true. In this respect he anticipated such political figures of the late 1960s and early 1970s as Abbie Hoffman and Jerry Rubin who recognized the importance of manipulating symbols to expose and undermine the establishment's control of political terminology and signification.

Though most of his SATIRE and stand-up comedy were directed at the social hypocrisy inherent in middle-class attitudes toward race, religion and sexuality, Bruce also touched on more obvious Cold War issues. For instance, in his routine, "Would You Sell Out Your Country?" he claims that no one has the right to denounce the patriotism of anyone else unless the accuser is willing to submit himself to a hot-lead enema. Elsewhere Bruce ridicules Presidents Truman and Kennedy for using the same kind of "obscene" language in the White House that he was prosecuted for using onstage. He claims that Truman is going to be arrested for saying, "Drew Pearson is a sonofabitch" and notes that "That word is pretty popular in the White House, sonofabitch. Why do they say that? That some secret ritual they go through? 'Nyanyanyanyablahblah *sonofabitch.*' " After pointing out that capitalism doesn't always rely on the competition it claims to pride itself on, as with the then-monopolistic telephone system, for example, Bruce goes on to lambaste the communist system. "Communism is like one big phone company—you're screwed . . . All those other things [i.e., that communism is "godless"] don't count." Bruce also mockingly complains that Castro has ruined Cuba for vacationers. "Tell you what a bad guy Castro is. Since Castro came, you can get no narcotics, no abortions, and there's no prostitutes there . . . He's really an asshole, this guy."

In addition to ridiculing the Cold War presidents, whose sexuality—or lack thereof—he highlights as a major component of their political appeal, Bruce also satirizes antibomb protesters. He imagines a scenario in which President Johnson confronts the leader of a student protest:

STUDENT: Mr. Johnson, I represent 17,000 students. We're here to stamp out the bomb. We wanna get some pictures of it too.
LBJ: Son, ah dunno what ta hell ya think's goin on here. Ya see, this place is a *shithouse*—they steal linen, silverware here. Ah cain't find a damn thing. Whaddayou wanna, bomb? That's bullshit . . . never was

no bomb. Two Jew writers from Hollywood made up a story about a bomb and that was it . . .

STUDENT: I'm not gonna tell those kids that—that there's no bomb. They marched from Maryland! . . . Come on, you got a piece of a bomb, something that looks like a bomb.

LBJ: Son, ah ain't got a damn thing, I ain't got a popped piston . . . Now if I *had* a bomb, I'd give it to ya.

STUDENT: Well, give us a button, then.

LBJ: What button izzat?

STUDENT: The madmen are always gonna push a button.

LBJ: Okay, son. Turn around. Here it is.

STUDENT: That's the button? "USN." Your pants are falling down! That's a button on your fly!

LBJ: That's right. I kept it there all during the war. My wife was frigid and she would never touch it.

STUDENT: *That's* the bomb button, eh?

In addition to ridiculing Johnson's Southern heritage, Bruce here and elsewhere joins Stanley KUBRICK who, in his FILM SATIRE DR. STRANGELOVE (1964), suggests that sexual politics and the need to assert male sexual domination underlie Cold War politics, including nuclear politics.

Bruce was arrested frequently on charges of obscenity and narcotics use. His successful defenses in court, in which he likened himself to Aristophanes, Rabelais and Jonathan Swift, helped broaden the definition of acceptable speech and thus opened doors for later comedians and protesters. He died in 1966 of what the Los Angeles police immediately declared was a drug overdose, though the medical report stated that the cause of death was unknown, and the medical analysis was inconclusive. His books include *How to Talk Dirty and Influence People* (1963, revised 1964), *Stamp Out Help* (1964) and two posthumous volumes, *The Essential Lenny Bruce* (1967) and *The Almost Unpublished Lenny Bruce* (1984). He also released several phonograph records. (See also RED SCARE.)

For additional reading, see Gale's *Encyclopedia of American Humorists*.

Buchwald, Art A JOURNALIST and writer of SATIRE. Born in 1925, Buchwald served in the Marine Corps during World War II. He worked as a Paris correspondent for *Variety* magazine in 1948 and on the editorial staff of the Paris edition of the *New York Herald-Tribune* from 1949 to 1962, when he moved to Washington, D.C. to continue writing his syndicated column, "Art Buchwald," which he had begun in Paris. By the end of the Cold War, the column appeared in some 550 newspapers, and in 1986 the American Academy and Institute of Arts and Letters inducted him as a member. Buchwald's rather mild satire extends to virtually every aspect of American culture and society, including Cold War politics. A 1956 article that was republished in the February 1957 *Reader's Digest* purportedly describes the Hungarian Revolution from the communist point of view. In this account, Soviet tanks stood helplessly by while counter-revolutionaries beat them with their fists, until the tanks were forced to fire "several friendly rounds of ammunition which exploded harmlessly in crowds, kill-

ing no more than 300 or 400 people." Another article spoofs the agonizingly slow pace of disarmament talks. When the American ambassador at the 12,654th plenary session of the Geneva talks sneezes, the Soviets are at a loss as how to respond. One adviser suggests, "We could say 'Gesundheit,' " but his superior counsels, "Yes, but how do we know the sneeze wasn't a trap to make us say 'Gesundheit?' " After weighing the propaganda consequences of refusing to say "Gesundheit" the Soviet ambassador decides to say "Gesundheit" with reservations. "If it's trap, we can always renounce it." In Buchwald's Cold War Washington, "accidental peace" remains a continual threat, and the American Communist Party is on the verge of being taken over by FBI informants. The danger from this development would be that, unlike regular party members, the informants would actually pay their dues and thus might enable the Communist Party to gain political strength. During the Cold War Buchwald published over 30 books of political satire, including *A Gift From the Boys* (1958), *And Then I Told the President* (1965), *Getting High in Government Circles* (1971), *Washington Is Leaking* (1976), *I Am Not a Crook* (1977) and *While Reagan Slept* (1983).

For additional reading, see Gale's *Encyclopedia of American Humorists*.

"Buck Rogers" a TELEVISION SCIENCE FICTION SHOW that ran on ABC in 1950–51, based on a 1928 novelette called *Armageddon—2419*, which had previously been adapted for a comic strip, comic books, radio and the movies. NBC revived it from 1979 to 1981 as "Buck Rogers in the 25th Century." The 1950–51 show starred Kem Dibbs and then Robert Pastene as the title character; the revival featured Gil Gerard in that role. Like THE ADVENTURES OF SUPERMAN (syndicated, 1951–57), "Buck Rogers" brought to television a character who had been popularized in other media in an earlier time. Unlike Superman, however, Rogers relied on scientific gadgetry and cleverness instead of superhuman powers to foil interstellar villains intent on destroying the peaceful inhabitants of the universe. Likewise, the hero of "Buck Rogers in the 25th Century" employed the American virtues of cleverness, wit, intelligence, charm, technological know-how and brute strength to overcome evil and powerful enemies.

Buckley, William F., Jr. A JOURNALIST, NOVELIST, NONFICTION WRITER, founder and editor of the *National Review* MAGAZINE and host of the television talk show FIRING LINE. Buckley was born in New York in 1925 to a devout Catholic family led by William F. Buckley Sr., a Texas lawyer who built the family fortune from his significant holdings in Mexican oil. The elder Buckley actively opposed the Mexican revolution, and after the revolution's success, the new leftist government confiscated all of his holdings in 1922. Though he was able to restore the family's wealth through oil investments in Venezuela, William Sr. instilled in his 10 children a profound hatred of revolution and communism.

William Jr. attended private schools in England and France and joined the family on a 1939 tour of Italy, which was then under the fascist control of Mussolini. Like his isolationist father, the young Buckley originally opposed U.S. intervention in World War II on Britain's behalf. While

William F. Buckley Jr. Courtesy William F. Buckley Jr.

attending Millbrook, a Protestant preparatory school, Buckley befriended and became influenced by Albert Jay Nock, a brilliant essayist who distrusted egalitarian democracy. However, Buckley rejected Nock's anti-Semitism and consistently sought to purge American conservatism of its anti-Semitic tendencies throughout his career. He joined the army in 1944 and reached the rank of second lieutenant.

In 1946 Buckley enrolled at Yale University, where he became editor of the student paper and an outspoken critic of what he saw as the faculty's attraction to left-wing causes and intellectual positions. Though chosen to speak at the 1950 Alumni Day ceremonies, Buckley was removed from the program because the administration objected to the harsh criticisms he planned to issue against the faculty. In response, he decided to write a book exposing what he saw as the faculty's anti-capitalist and anti-religious positions, which Buckley believed were inappropriate for a university that had been founded as a religious institution and had benefited from American capitalism. *God and Man at Yale: The Superstitutions of "Academic Freedom"* appeared in October 1951, on the university's 250th anniversary. Though the book received many negative reviews, including one in the *Atlantic Monthly* by future national security adviser McGeorge Bundy, the surrounding controversy unexpectedly propelled it to the best-seller lists. Richard Condon alludes to it THE MANCHURIAN CANDIDATE (1959) when one of the characters describes right-wingers as renting their opinions from "Mr. Sokolsky, Mr. [David] Lawrence, Mr. [Westbrook] Pegler, and that fascinating younger fellow who had written about men and God at Yale." In 1951

Buckley was accepted into the CIA and after completing his training he was stationed in Mexico City. He coauthored his second book, *McCarthy and His Enemies: The Record and Its Meaning* (1954), with his brother-in-law Brent Bozell. This defense of Senator Joseph McCarthy (R, Wisconsin), issued the same year as the ARMY-MCCARTHY HEARINGS, which led to the right-wing senator's fall from power, received only one review in the mainstream press, a negative one in the *New York Times*. In 1962 Buckley also published a defense of the HOUSE COMMITTEE ON UN-AMERICAN ACTIVITIES entitled *The Committee and Its Critics.* (See also RED SCARE.)

The failure of the McCarthy book to receive attention in the national press convinced Buckley of the need for a magazine that would provide a forum for conservative views and for reviewing politically conservative books that were otherwise being overlooked. With the support of Willi Schlamm, a Jewish Austrian emigre and a former communist who had turned decidedly anti-communist, Buckley raised funds and hired an editorial staff for a new publication, the *National Review.* William Casey, the future director of the CIA, drew up the legal papers. In addition to providing a new forum for conservatives, Buckley and Schlamm hoped to redefine American conservatism to liberate it from the anti-Semitic and isolationist tendencies that were characteristic of the right-wing through the early 1950s. The first issue appeared on November 14, 1955, with Buckley serving as editor-in-chief and publisher. He remained publisher until 1957, when William Rusher took over that position, but stayed as editor-in-chief until 1990, when he stepped down to become editor-at-large. Among the initial senior editors were James Burnham, a former Trotskyite and a CIA consultant who had fallen into disfavor among the liberals because of his refusal to denounce McCarthy without reservation. Buckley offered an editorial position to Whittaker Chambers, who had achieved national fame in 1948 for accusing Alger Hiss of espionage and had published an autobiographical account of his years with the Communist Party in the 1930s, WITNESS (1952). However, Chambers turned down the post due to differences of political opinion. Unlike Buckley, Chambers supported the more moderate positions of President Eisenhower. Chambers did join the editorial staff briefly in the late 1950s, and in 1957 he contributed a review of Ayn RAND's novel *Atlas Shrugged* that attacked her philosophy of "objectivism" because it was not rooted in religious values. According to Chambers, Rand's apparently right-wing materialism differed little from the atheistic materialism of Karl Marx. The review, which outraged Rand's conservative followers, demonstrated the importance of religion to Buckley's vision of American conservatism. In 1987 Buckley commemorated Chambers in *Odyssey of a Friend: Whittaker Chambers' Letters to William F. Buckley, Jr., 1954–1961.*

In the early 1960s Buckley expanded his efforts to promote the conservative cause while remaining active with the *National Review.* In 1962 he began a syndicated newspaper column, "A Conservative Voice." His later column "On the Right" appeared in more than 200 newspapers. Buckley helped found such conservative organizations as Young Americans for Freedom and the Conservative Party of New York. Meanwhile his politics moderated somewhat. Buckley reversed his earlier defense of racial segregation in the

South, though he differed with integrationists over the means for achieving their goals. And he led the efforts to dissociate the ultra-right-wing John Birch Society from mainstream conservatism. Nonetheless, he opposed President Nixon's overtures to China and the U.S.S.R. in the early 1970s. In June 1974 Buckley called for Nixon's resignation over the Watergate scandal despite his fears of the damage this would cause the Republican Party.

In 1965 Buckley ran as the Conservative Party's candidate for mayor of New York City and surprised even himself by gaining 13.4% of the vote. When asked about the first thing he would have done had he been elected, Buckley replied with characteristic wit that he would have demanded a recount. He describes his campaign in *The Unmaking of a Mayor* (1966). Partly as a result of his exposure in the mayoral election, he was given the opportunity to do his own television discussion show, "Firing Line" (syndicated PBS, 1966–continuing). Initially featured on a single New York television station, the program was soon nationally syndicated and ran throughout the Cold War. It featured debates between Buckley and prominent liberals and other political advocates as well as discussions with like-minded conservatives. Among those who appeared on "Firing Line" were Presidents Nixon, Ford and Reagan, British prime minister Harold Macmillan, failed presidential candidates Barry Goldwater and George McGovern, and writers Norman MAILER, Claire Booth Luce and John Kenneth Galbraith. The show won a special Emmy Award in 1969 for Outstanding Program Achievement. In 1989 Buckley published *On the Firing Line*, excerpts from transcripts of his more memorable shows. The program established his reputation for quick wit, expansive vocabulary and erudition.

In addition to his activities as a political activist in the print and broadcast media Buckley also stands out as an author of best-selling SPY NOVELS featuring a JAMES BOND-like superhero, Blackford Oakes. These include *Saving the Queen* (1976), *Stained Glass* (1978), *Who's on First* (1980), *Marco Polo, If You Can* (1982), *The Story of Henri Tod* (1984), *See You Later Alligator* (1985), *High Jinx* (1986), *Mongoose, R.I.P* (1987) and *Tucker's Last Stand* (1990). More than most works of Cold War fiction, these novels deal with actual historical events, such as the power struggle in the Kremlin after Stalin's death (*High Jinx*), the Hungarian Revolution and the beginnings of the space race (*Who's on First*), the second Berlin Crisis (*Henri Tod*) and the 1960 U-2 incident (*Marco Polo*).

For additional reading, see *Dictionary of Literary Biography* (vol. 137, *American Magazine Journalists*).

"Bullwinkle Show, The"   A television cartoon show that ran on NBC from 1961 to 1964 and on ABC from 1964 to 1973. A sequel to "Rocky and His Friends" (1959–1961) "The Bullwinkle Show" featured the exploits of Rocky, a flying squirrel, and his pal Bullwinkle, a moose. They were frequently pursued by Russian agents, Boris Badenov and Natasha Fatale. The cartoon series satirized TELEVISION SPY SHOWS and SPY FILMS as well as government bureaucracy. It was as popular among adults as it was among children. (See also TELEVISION SHOWS FOR CHILDREN.)

Burdick, Eugene   A NOVELIST. Burdick is best known for his best-selling POLITICAL NOVEL, THE UGLY AMERICAN (1958), coauthored with William LEDERER, and FAIL SAFE, a best-selling 1962 MILITARY NOVEL he coauthored with Harvey Wheeler. Director Sidney Lumet adapted *Fail Safe* into a MILITARY FILM in 1964. *The Ugly American* also appeared as a 1961 play and a 1962 POLITICAL FILM starring Marlon Brando. Set in Sarkhan, a fictional Southeast Asian country similar to Vietnam, the story focuses on the American ambassador, whose failure to understand and appreciate local history and customs undermines the well-intentioned American efforts to improve Sarkhan's standard of living with advanced technology and improved agricultural methods. The novel criticizes State Department bureaucrats and political hacks who fail to learn native languages and customs, insult local leaders, inhibit the constructive efforts of private individuals working with the villagers and allow their own egos and career aspirations to dominate their decisions. A sequel, *Sarkhan*, appeared in 1965, the year the United States introduced combat troops into the Vietnam War. It describes the efforts of an American businessman and a professor to prevent a communist takeover. Like *The Ugly American*, it attacks U.S. government bureaucrats for their ignorance and ineptitude and contrasts the tactics used by the communist opposition. For all its explicit and implicit criticism, however, the novel does not question either the basic good intentions of the American involvement or the Cold War assumptions that underlie it.

Fail Safe, originally serialized in the *Saturday Evening Post*, appeared the same month as the Cuban Missile Crisis, October 1962. The subject is the fate of the world after a mechanical malfunction sends a group of nuclear-armed U.S. bombers from their "fail-safe" positions outside of Soviet air space to attack Moscow. When combined U.S. and Soviet efforts fail to stop the warplanes, the U.S. president realizes he can forestall all-out nuclear warfare only by ordering a nuclear attack on New York as compensation for the destruction of the foremost Soviet city. *Fail Safe* dramatizes the then-current debate between some right-wing, militant anti-communists and centrist and liberal pacifists. The hardliners rejected the strategic stalemate concept of Mutually Assured Destruction (MAD) and argued that, since nuclear war with the Soviet Union was inevitable anyway, the United States should launch a preemptive strike. The pacifists, on the other hand, maintained that the United States must never be a nuclear aggressor; they accepted MAD and sought to achieve "peaceful co-existence" with the Soviets. The story also presents the tension between old-school humanists and a class of emerging "pragmatic" technocrats. Ironically, the humanists must perform the nuclear dirty work and make the greatest personal sacrifices.

Other political novels by Burdick include *The 480* (1964) and *Ninth Wave* (1956). *The 480* centers on the 1964 Republican convention and describes a "new underworld" of American politics "made up of innocent and well-intentioned people who work with slide rules and calculating machines" and who employ the science of demographics. *Ninth Wave* is about the rise and fall of a California politician who learns that fear and hatred are sources of power. Though the literary establishment did not regard him as a "serious" writer, Burdick joins such popular writers as Lederer, Fletcher KNEBEL, James MICHENER and Leon URIS who directly address the Cold War in their fiction.

By Dawn's Early Light   A 1990 APOCALYPTIC FILM starring James Earl Jones, Martin Landau, Rip Torn, Peter Mac-Nichol and Rebecca De Mornay, directed by Jack Sholder. The plot follows the course of a disaster that begins when a nuclear missile from an unknown source in the Middle East detonates in the Soviet Union. The ensuing events lead to global destruction. Though compared to DR. STRANGELOVE (1964) and FAIL-SAFE (1964) because of its scenario of nuclear doom, the Bush-era film seems anachronistic because it appeared the year the Cold War ended, when the threat of worldwide annihilation was at its lowest since the 1950s. On the other hand, by placing the source of the disaster in the Middle East the movie reflected the growing perception that that region was the new source of the greatest danger to peace.

Cabrera Infante, Guillermo A Cuban EXILED WRITER (to the United States) now living in London. A graduate of the University of Havana's School of Journalism, Cabrera Infante translated works of Mark Twain, William FAULKNER, Ernest Hemingway, James Joyce and other prominent writers into Spanish during the 1950s. In 1960 he published in Spanish a collection of short stories about life in Cuba under the dictator Fulgencio Batista, and he supported the new revolutionary government of Fidel Castro. Appointed editor of *Lunes,* the literary magazine of the Cuban revolution, Cabrera Infante was fired when he protested the official banning of a documentary film about Havana's nightlife. His 1964 novel, *Tres Tristes Tigres* (published in English in 1971 as *Three Trapped Tigers*), describes the exploits of three young men in Havana in 1959, on the eve of Castro's revolution. The book was banned by the communist government, even though it was not overtly political. However, it celebrates individuality, a message that the collectivist-oriented Cuban government considered destructive to the society it was trying to build. As Cabrera Infante himself put it, "Perhaps that is the reason and unreason of this prohibition: all freedom is subversive. Totalitarian regimes are more afraid of individual liberty than vampires are of crosses." *Infante's Inferno* (1974; published in English, 1978) also describes Havana during the Batista years, portraying it as a violent, decadent world characterized by poverty and eroticism and populated by pimps, prostitutes and pederasts. Like his earlier work, the novel is not explicitly political; however, its playful spirit and indulgence in artistic liberties and formal experimentation implicitly repudiate the restrictions on personal freedoms in Castro's Cuba. In essays and interviews Cabrera Infante has vigorously and explicitly denounced the Castro regime.

For additional reading, see Tucker's *Literary Exile in the Twentieth Century.*

Cafe Flesh A 1960s pornographic film. Set in the postnuclear-war period, the story involves nuclear-fallout-created mutants who can enjoy sex only vicariously because physical touching nauseates them. Consequently they patronize live sex shows featuring people who do not have the affliction. The film's bizarre premise gave it the appeal of a campy FILM COMEDY. (See also APOCALYPTIC FILMS.)

Call for the Dead A 1961 SPY NOVEL by John LE CARRÉ (U.S. edition, 1962). Written while the author was still working for the British intelligence organization MI6, *Call for the Dead* was le Carré's first novel and the basis for the 1967 SPY FILM, DEADLY AFFAIR. The story introduces George Smiley, a spymaster for the intelligence branch called the Circus, who appears prominently in several of le Carré's novels, notably the trilogy THE QUEST FOR KARLA, which includes *Tinker, Tailor, Soldier, Spy; The Honourable Schoolboy;* and *Smiley's People.* Unlike Ian Fleming's virile, dashing and suave hero JAMES BOND, Smiley is, in the words of his ex-wife, "breathtakingly ordinary" yet "enigmatically attractive." Smiley had been a student of literature when his tutor "wisely guided [him] away from the honours that would undoubtedly have been his" and into espionage. His scholastic skills of observation and rigorous analysis are well suited for intelligence work, but the humane values of truth, beauty and goodness expressed in the literature he studies are not, and the contrast between literature and espionage provides the moral tension that animates the Smiley novels.

Smiley's first assignment for the Circus had been to recruit potential agents while teaching in a provincial German university, and in that capacity he induced Dieter Frey, a German student, to become a British agent. The story begins several years later when Frey has abandoned the West for ideological reasons and become an East German spymaster. Acting on orders from Matson, his inept and politically motivated superior, Smiley investigates a young clerk, Fennan, who has been accused of treason. Smiley clears Fennan, but soon the clerk is found dead. Matson induces Smiley to cover up the incident by alleging a suicide and then, fearful that the investigation might reveal security breaches in the Circus, he betrays Smiley's inquest. The outraged Smiley resigns, but his sense of loyalty forbids him from accepting the determination that Fennan had killed himself. His subsequent investigation leads him back to Frey, whom he finally kills at the book's conclusion. However, the Circus's corrupt internal politics contrast with Frey's more idealistic ideological motivations, and the book concludes on a morally ambiguous note. As Lynn Dianne Beene states in *John le Carré*, "The action of *Call for the Dead* emanates from doubling contrasts that induce crisis: past political facts (specifically, the Holocaust and the Nazis' military aggressiveness) compete with present ones (interagency rivalries and . . . the cold war), duty and loyalty ambivalently become crime and perfidy, ultimate betrayal masquerades as unselfish love, and, most of all, grim realities replace imperfect dreams."

For additional reading, see Beene's *John le Carré* and Cawelti and Rosenberg's *The Spy Story*.

"Campaign and the Candidates, The"

An NBC TELEVISION NEWS show that covered the 1960 presidential campaign between John F. Kennedy and Richard M. Nixon. Frank McGee acted as the show's host and coordinator. Cold War issues included Kennedy's charge of a "missile gap" and the candidates' responses to threats by the People's Republic of China against the islands of Quemoy and Matsu.

Canticle for Leibowitz, A

A 1959 APOCALYPTIC NOVEL by Walter M. Miller. *A Canticle for Leibowitz* is frequently cited by critics as one of the first and best examples of the subgenre of apocalyptic novels that imagine humanity returning to an anti-intellectual, religion-dominated Dark Age in the aftermath of a NUCLEAR APOCALYPSE before eventually re-evolving a rational, science-based society. It was published during the second Berlin Crisis, when nuclear war seemed an imminent possibility. This was one of the most intense periods of the Cold War: Two years after launching *Sputnik I* and successfully testing intercontinental missiles, the Soviets were erroneously believed to enjoy missile superiority. The book originally appeared as three stories in *Fantasy and Science Fiction* magazine: "A Canticle for Leibowitz" (1955), "And the Light Is Risen" (1956) and "The Last Canticle" (1957); these

became the three sections of the novel: "Fiat Homo," "Fiat Lux" and "Fiat Voluntas Tua."

Miller sets the story in three postnuclear periods 600 years apart, from about 2600 to 4300 A.D. The tale begins with a nuclear armageddon and concludes with a spaceship leaving for the stars. In the interim, humanity reverts to a new Dark Age in which the landscape is desolate and the few clusters of human society are isolated from each other. Monks live in monasteries and occasional wanderers provide tenuous links among them. The book begins when Brother Francis of Utah discovers an ancient fallout shelter while fasting in the desert for Lent. Though he concludes that a "fallout" was a demonic, salamander-like creature born in the "Flame Deluge," he enters the shelter anyway and discovers the blueprint of an electrical circuit design. Deciding the blueprint is a holy relic, he dedicates several years to reproducing it in his cell, just as medieval monks reproduced religious texts. Unlike his medieval predecessors, however, Brother Francis belongs to an order started by the nuclear physicist Leibowitz following the Flame Deluge, a period when survivors were executing the political leaders and scientists who had brought about the destruction. These survivors also destroyed books and other repositories of human knowledge, as they likewise held these accountable for nuclear war. Leibowitz founded his order to "preserve human history for the great-great-great-grandchildren of the children of the simpletons who wanted to destroy it." But by the time Brother Francis is initiated, the preserved knowledge has become arcane and incomprehensible. As in the first Dark Ages, no central governments exist and travel is extremely dangerous. Thus, after spending 15 years conscientiously copying the circuit diagram, Francis loses it when a band of mutants robs him. The drawing is not destroyed, but because it is not recognized as an electrical design, it is transformed from a text in a technical language into a piece of art. Miller thus underscores the double-sidedness of nature and artifice: The code describing the electrical pathway is both a scientific communication and an aesthetic form with spiritual value.

The novel picks up 600 years later as a new Renaissance is about to begin. This section replicates the emergence of science at the end of the Middle Ages and reconsiders the dilemmas it causes. The discovery of Leibowitz's ancient documents parallels the discovery in the early Renaissance of the lost works of Plato. As neo-Platonism informed and shaped the rise of modern science in the 16th and 17th centuries, Leibowitz's documents promise to spark a new era of scientific and technological advancement.

A great scholar named Thon appears as a second Newton, but his sponsor is a barbarian warlord presumably positioned to employ the fruits of Thon's research. Thus the Cold War debate over scientists' responsibility for their discoveries reemerges in Miller's imagined second Renaissance. An abbot asks, "But you promise to begin restoring Man's control over Nature. But who will govern the use of the power to control natural forces? Who will use it? To what end? How will you hold him in check? Such decisions can still be made. But if you and your group don't make them now, others will soon make them for you. Mankind will profit, you say. By whose sufferance? The sufferance of a prince who signs his letters *X*?"

Thon replies, "What you really suggest . . . is that we wait . . . Keep science cloistered, don't try to apply it, don't try to do anything about it until men are holy. Well, it won't work . . ." Thon goes on to insist that "the freedom to speculate is essential." The abbot counters, "But to abuse the intellect for reasons of pride, vanity, or escape from responsibility, is the fruit of that same tree [the Tree of Knowledge whose fruit was forbidden to Adam and Eve in the Garden of Eden]." The section concludes with the monastery preparing to defend itself from an attack by Thon's sponsor.

In the last section, history again replays itself, as computers, space satellites and nuclear bombs provide the backdrop for human life. Excessive pride remains a fundamental human characteristic even in the distant future, and it continues to condemn the human race to repeating its mistakes. As one of the abbots asks, "Is the species congenitally insane . . . [and subject to] an unending sequence of rise and fall?" Thus Miller proposes a cyclic view of history that replays the historic tension between science and religion and between the forces of progress and restraint. Much of the final section is devoted to an argument between a committed doctor and an equally committed monk over the appropriateness of mercy killings in the aftermath of a nuclear attack. Miller leaves that question open but suggests that religion requires scientific open-mindedness and inquiry while science needs a greater sense of religious humility and responsibility. Finally, the cycle of history is broken, offering hope not for Earth but "for the soul and substance of Man somewhere": Several clerics flee the planet in a reinvented rocketship. Walker Percy sums up *Canticle* thus: "Shiva destroys, but good things come of it." Miller was working on a sequel when he died, *St. Leibowitz and The Wild Horse Woman.* Terry Gibson has completed it, and it is scheduled for publication in 1997. (See also SCIENCE FICTION NOVELS.)

For additional reading, see Dowling's *Fictions of Nuclear Disaster,* Anisfield's *The Nightmare Considered* and Scheick's "Continuative and Ethical Predictions: The Post-Nuclear Holocaust Novel of the 1980s."

Capable of Honor A 1967 POLITICAL NOVEL by Allen DRURY. Part of a series that began in 1959 with ADVISE AND CONSENT, *Capable of Honor* focuses on the decision of President Harley Hudson to stand up to communist aggression in a fictional Third World country, Grotoland, despite attacks from liberals and the liberal news media. Written while the Vietnam War was escalating and protests against it were becoming increasingly strong and occasionally violent, the book affirms the necessity of adhering to the U.S. Cold War containment policy of opposing communist aggression throughout the world. Hudson, who had been vice president in *Advise and Consent,* is loosely based on Lyndon Johnson. One of the novel's less appealing characters is the liberal journalist "Wonderful Walter," who is based on Walter LIPPMANN, one of the earliest critics of the U.S. military involvement in Vietnam. The novel, which spent 41 weeks on the *New York Times* best-seller list, is dedicated to "all the many sincere and objective newspaper men and women . . . who are not part of Walter's World."

For additional reading see Kemme's *Political Fiction, The Spirit of the Age, and Allen Drury.*

"Captain Video and His Video Rangers" A TELEVISION SHOW FOR CHILDREN that ran on the DuMont network from 1949 to 1955 and in syndication in 1956. The very popular show, produced on an extremely low budget, brought to television the genre of the handsome, dedicated protagonist who fights for freedom against an evil genius. Captain Video was originally played by Richard Coogan and later by Al Hodge (who had been the voice of radio's "Green Hornet"). A private citizen and a scientific wizard, he lived in the 21st century and worked atop a mountain, from which he controlled a widespread network of "Video Rangers" who assisted him against such adversaries as Mook the Moon Man, Heng Foo Seeng and Dr. Pauli, who headed the evil Astroidal Society and possessed a scientific aptitude almost equal to Captain Video's. The fact that Captain Video's major adversary shared the last name of the pioneering atomic theorist and Nobel Prize winner Wolfgang Pauli was probably coincidental, but the major role of science on both sides of the Cold War reflected contemporary reality. Produced during the era of the first atomic and hydrogen bombs, the show featured many exotic high-tech devices that actually anticipated later real-life weapons developed during the Cold War. These included an indestructible robot, an "Opticon Scillometer" that enabled its user to see through things, an atomic rifle, and a miniature long-range radio that fit into the palm of the user's hand. The special effects were quite primitive by 1990s standards, or even by the modest standards of STAR TREK (NBC, 1966–69), but they spoke to the evolving Cold War belief that scientific and technological superiority would determine the fate of the world. "Captain Video" demonstrated to its young viewers that science and technology could serve both virtuous and evil masters.

cartoons Both mainstream and "underground" cartoonists addressed the Cold War. Among the mainstream Cold War-related cartoon strips that appeared on the comic pages of newspapers were Walt Kelly's *Pogo* (1949–1975), Al Capp's *Li'l Abner,* Garry Trudeau's *Doonesbury* (1968–present) and Berke Breathed's *Bloom County. Pogo* featured animals living in the Okefenokee Swamp who commented on contemporary domestic and worldwide politics. Its enduring line was "We have met the enemy and they is us." *Li'l Abner,* which first appeared in 1934 and was made into a Broadway play and later a movie, was populated by backwoods hicks from Dogpatch and reflected Capp's conservative politics. It took an especially hard line against the Vietnam War protesters, labeling FOLK SINGER/protester Joan BAEZ "Little Joanie Phonie."

Pogo and *Li'l Abner* were in print in the early stages of the Cold War (*Pogo* took on the RED SCARE) and satirized Joseph McCarthy at the height of his power, but *Doonesbury* debuted in 1968. The cast of characters were students at Walden (Yale) University and lived in an off-campus commune, but when Trudeau graduated and syndicated the column nationally, they also graduated and became more or less integrated into mainstream American life. Among the more notable characters are Mark Slackmeyer, the campus radical who later came out and became a gay activist; B.D., the gung-ho, all-American quarterback who served in Vietnam (based on Yale quarterback Brian Downing, it is

Trojan Horse

Joseph Parrish, Trojan Horse, *1949.* Copyright © Chicago Tribune Company; all rights reserved, used with permission.

said); Calvin, the black activist; Zonker Harris, who smoked marijuana and cultivated his tan; Joanie Caucus, the feminist; Zonker's Uncle Duke, a sleazy, unscrupulous drug abuser who held various important positions including that of ambassador (based loosely on Hunter S. Thompson); Phred, the Viet Cong soldier who befriends B.D. and later appears at the United Nations; and Michael Doonesbury, bemused Ivy League everyman, standing in, more or less, for Trudeau himself. Though Trudeau used and continues to use these characters to satirize the American establishment, he also satirizes the characters themselves. His strongest political barbs were directed against the Vietnam War, the Watergate scandal and the Reagan presidency, though leftists and Democrats were also his targets from time to time. A sample cartoon from 1972 makes fun of U.S. government doublespeak. It shows B.D. and another soldier in a Vietnamese jungle discussing a recent bombing raid. B.D., a war supporter, declares, "That wasn't a bombing raid! It was a protective reaction strike." His companion states, "They drop bombs in both cases. There's no difference." But B.D. insists, "There's a *big* difference, fellah! A protective reaction strike means not having to say you're sorry." In 1975 President Ford declared, "There are only three major vehicles to keep us informed as to what is going on in Washington: the electronic media, the print media, and *Doonesbury* . . . not necessarily in that order." That year *Doonesbury* became the first comic strip ever to receive the Pulitzer Prize.

Bloom County first appeared in the last decade of the Cold War. It too satirized Cold War politics and Presidents Reagan and Bush. Its cast of characters included Opus, the penguin who bemoans his large nose; Bill the Cat, a reprobate alley cat who once dated UN Ambassador Jeane Kirkpatrick; and various humans. One of the *Bloom County* books, *Tales Too Ticklish to Tell* (1987), contains an introduction supposedly by Soviet president Mikhail Gorbachev and features a cover drawing of President Bush holding Opus. The volume contains a satire on former defense secretary Caspar Weinberger who was largely responsible for the arms buildup in the early 1980s. Opus recites a poem in tribute to him: "The wind doth taste so bittersweet. / Like jasper wine and sugar. / I bet it's blown thru others' feet / Like those of Caspar Weinberger."

In addition to cartoon strips, political cartoons also appeared on the editorial pages of newspapers. Syndicated political cartoonists addressed virtually every facet of the Cold War, most notably Jules FEIFFER, Bill Mauldin, Pat Oliphant, Herb Block, Don Wright, Charles G. Werner and Richard Q. Yardley. "Underground" comics also had a strong political, antiestablishment dimension, and they sometimes depicted America as a totalitarian state akin to the communist regimes. Read by members of the COUNTERCULTURE, among others, they brutally satirized the Vietnam War, nuclear weaponry and other aspects of the Cold War. Robert Crumb was one of the leading underground comic artists, and Zap Comix one of the most prominent publishers. Underground comics also presented sexually oriented material and frequently celebrated the drug culture of the 1960s and 1970s. Raymond Briggs' WHEN THE WIND BLOWS 1982 was a British comic book that reflected the common citizen's sense of impotence in his or her inability to affect the course of events and deter an apparently inevitable nuclear war. The cartoon follows James and Hilda, a hard-working English middle-class couple who feel helpless before "the Powers That Be [which] will get us in the end." Briggs represents the nuclear attack by doing violence to the comic strip medium itself, slicing off the strip in mid-drawing and leaving a blank page shaded bright pink and red. (See also SATIRE.)

For additional reading see the Foreign Policy Association's *A Cartoon History of the United States Foreign Policy;* Estren's *A History of Underground Comics;* Inge's *Comics as Culture.*

Castro Convertible   A fold-out sofa bed. The Castro company—no relation to the Cuban leader—invoked the Cold War space race in its promotional jingle, "Who was the first to conquer space? / It's incontrovertible. / The first to conquer living space / Was the Castro Convertible." (See also CONSUMER GOODS.)

"Cat in the Hat for President, The"   A 1968 short story by Robert COOVER published in *The New American Review.* The BLACK HUMOR story appeared during a year of social and political unrest in the United States that culminated in the divisive Democratic convention in Chicago. The convention's infamous "police riot" featured antiwar demonstrators and others being beaten before television cameras both inside and outside the convention hall. The Cat in the Hat, protagonist of popular children's stories by Dr. Seuss, was satirically portrayed by Coover as the ideal presidential candidate because of his easy ability to transform himself continually. The politically astute narrator points out that ambiguity is a politician's greatest asset. The Cat in the Hat is on the verge of winning the election when he is martyred. He then emerges as a Christ-figure who is crucified, roasted and eaten. His sacrifice serves to unite America as those present fall into a great orgy: "While the Cat burned, the throng fucked in a great conglobation of races, sexes, ages and convictions; it was the Great American Dream in oily actuality." They feast on the Cat's carcass and share a psychedelic vision of American history.

> The whole hoopla of American history stormed through our exploded minds, all the massacres, motherings, couplings, and connivings, all the baseball games, PTA meetings, bloodbaths, old movies, and piracies . . . We saw everything, from George Washington reading the graffiti while straining over a constipated shit . . . [to] Johnson and Kennedy shooting it out on a dry dusty street in a deserted cowtown . . . It was all there . . . all the flag-waving, rip-staving, truck-driving, gun-toting, ram-sqauddled, ringtail roaring, ass-licking, bronc-breaking, A-bombing, dragracing Christ-kissing, bootlegging, coffee-drinking, pig-fucking tale of it all.

Coover's language and imagery render America a psychedelic experience reminiscent of an LSD-induced hallucination, characterized by vivid colors, striking figures, distortions of reality and tremendous creative energy. Coover's exaggeration and exuberant technique rejoice in a playful, animated, creative energy, the underlying life force that, like the Hindu god Shiva and American society itself, is simultaneously Creator and Destroyer. Coover later proposed a similar vision of American history in his fictional account of the Rosenberg execution in THE PUBLIC BURNING (1976). (See also SATIRE.)

Catch Me a Spy A 1971 SPY FILM starring Kirk Douglas, Trevor Howard, Tom Courtenay and Marlene Jobert and directed by Dick Clement. It is based on the novel by George Marton. Set in Bucharest and Scotland, the story involves a British agent who smuggles Russian manuscripts into England and falls in love with the wife of a Soviet spy.

Catch-22 A 1961 MILITARY NOVEL by Joseph Heller. In 1970 director Mike Nichols adapted it into a MILITARY FILM starring Alan Arkin, Richard Benjamin, Orson Welles, Anthony Perkins, Paula Prentiss, Martin Balsam and Jon Voight. Though the film version lacks the intricate wordplay that characterizes the novel, it nonetheless communicates something of Heller's powerful, funny absurdist worldview. Made during the Vietnam War, the film was directed against the military mentality per se; in the novel, on the other hand, Heller uses the military as a metaphor for the social and economic structure of postwar America whose bureaucratic institutions were perpetuating the Cold War. Students, antiwar activists and members of the COUNTERCULTURE championed the book for its antimilitary, antiauthoritian positions.

One of the literary masterpieces of 20th-century American literature, *Catch-22* shows institutional bureaucracy to be the ordinary person's most pernicious enemy. Set in Mediterranean Theater during World War II, the largely comic novel centers on Captain Yossarian, a U.S. bombardier who is terrified during every mission, has already flown a large number of missions and wants to go home. But he is thwarted and assaulted at every turn by the army bureaucracy, in which intra-service rivalries and superior officers' unmitigated quest for personal power and wealth are the determining factors behind high-level decisions and policies, not the war effort or the soldiers' well-being.

Heller plays with language, logic and a nonlinear plot to communicate further the disoriented paradoxical sensibility that comes from Yossarian's having to fight two wars simultaneously—one against the Germans and the other against his commanding officer, Colonel Cathcart, and the army bureaucracy. Every time Yossarian approaches the number of missions necessary for rotation home, Cathcart raises the quota, hoping thereby to impress his superiors with how tough he is. Cathcart endangers Yossarian's life even more directly when he orders an air strike against his own squadron's airfield. Cathcart and his supply officer, Lieutenant Milo Minderbinder, had contracted with the Germans to perform this job for them. In return the Germans agreed to save Cathcart and Minderbinder's black-market syndicate by purchasing its shares of devalued Egyptian cotton, which had become a sudden liability on the international commodities market. Cathcart and Milo defend their action by pointing out that preserving the integrity of business contracts is, after all, why the United States is fighting the war. When their actions become public, they escape punishment because they open their books and show the profit they made, even after reimbursing the government for its losses.

In the film version Cathcart orders the air attack only after Milo first tries to unload the cotton by coating it with chocolate and feeding it to the soldiers. In the novel a chef mashes bars of GI soap into the sweet potatoes to show the men they have the taste of Philistines. Eventually the practice stops, but not for the obvious rational reasons. The men do not reasonably reject the soap as unfit for human consumption. Instead, in their enthusiasm for the delicacy they eat too much and become sick. Here again, human behavior is shown to be fundamentally irrational.

"Catch-22" became a familiar term in the Cold War vocabulary to refer to circular, self-contradictory situations. The army policy stated that if Yossarian was crazy, he did not have to fly any more missions. He merely needed to report himself insane. However, there was a catch, Catch-22: The very act of reporting himself insane demonstrated that Yossarian was sane enough to want to preserve his own life. Therefore, he could not be insane and so he had to fly more missions. Later in the book, Catch-22 becomes the official justification for every capricious and malicious action the ranking officers undertake. Heller also shows the absurdity and irrationality of RED SCARE-inspired loyalty oaths, which were increasingly popular when Heller was working on the book's first draft in the middle 1950s. In the novel, the military comes to a standstill as officers compete to prove their patriotism by demanding a plethora of signed loyalty oaths before their units will perform any work. Consequently, even food service is slowed to a crawl as each soldier must sign a new loyalty oath at every stop of the chow line. Elsewhere, Heller satirizes McCarthy-like inquisitions and heavy-handed FBI investigations.

Repeatedly throughout the novel, Heller shows that human situations are governed by illogical behavior. The disparity between declared motives and actual motives especially contributes to an illogical, contradictory, insane environment in which basic moral values and humane instincts become inverted. Yossarian receives a medal for causing his squadron to drop its bombs in the sea rather than demolish an Italian town with no military significance. But his reward comes not because of his humanitarian common sense but because his superiors thought it would be less embarrassing than court-martialing one of their officers. Like "spin-doctors" in the last stages of the Cold War, Cathcart and his adviser Colonel Korn praise the squadron's "tight bombing pattern" as they decorate Yossarian. In this respect, *Catch-22* may have anticipated the 1983 U.S. invasion of Grenada, in which an unprecedented number of medals (more medals than there were troops) was awarded for a bloody attack against a small force of lightly armed soldiers and construction workers.

Toward the book's conclusion, Heller changes his tone from playful to shocking, as the military's inverted logic and perverted values lead to calamity instead of mere confusion. In one powerful scene, Yossarian tries to cope with the fact that his friend Aarfy has raped and killed an Italian girl while on leave in Rome. He tries to make Aarfy recognize the horror of what he has committed, but Aarfy fails to acknowledge any wrongdoing: "I only raped her once." Then he condescendingly points out that he had to kill her, because "I couldn't very well let her go around saying bad things about us, could I?" To Yossarian's frantic protestations that he will be sent to prison, Aarfy calmly maintains that "They aren't going to put good old Aarfy in jail. Not for killing *her*." And when Yossarian points out that her body is lying in the street, Aarfy sanctimoniously replies, "She has no right to be there . . . It's after curfew." To Yossarian and to readers, Aarfy seems to be in a state of total denial—completely disconnected from reality. But in the world of *Catch-22*, the world of bureaucratic logic, Aarfy proves correct and Yossarian is the one who is out of touch. When the MPs arrive, they ignore the girl's body in the street, apologize to Aarfy for the intrusion, and arrest Yossarian for being in Rome without a pass.

While on a bombing mission in an earlier part of the story, Yossarian panics when he reaches for his parachute and finds instead a stock certificate; Milo's syndicate had traded the silk parachutes for other commodities. Because Yossarian is in no real danger, his horror appears comic. However, the situation replays later as tragedy when Yossarian reaches for morphine to comfort a dying comrade and instead finds another stock certificate. This leads to the culminating moment when Yossarian looks down at Snowden, who has literally spilled his guts over the airplane floor. "It was easy to read the message in his entrails. Man was matter, that was Snowden's secret . . . The spirit gone, man is garbage. That was Snowden's secret. Ripeness was all." By alluding in the final sentence to *King Lear*, Heller invokes the questions about mortality that Shakespeare's most existential play explores. At the same time, the pun on *ripeness* diminishes Shakespeare's more uplifting suggestions of maturity, self-acceptance and endurance, replacing them with spiritually empty, viscerally offensive associa-

tions of rotten garbage and the fermenting stewed tomatoes that lie undigested in Snowden's stomach. Yet, because the very act of describing Yossarian's deepest despair occurs in a pun, the book simultaneously affirms creativity and play. In this respect, Heller shares with such other experimental NOVELISTS as John BARTH, Thomas PYNCHON, Robert COOVER and Kurt VONNEGUT Jr. the practice of generating life-affirming vitality and creativity from the same process by which he logically demonstrates the meaninglessness and horror of existence. In a logical, rational world, Yossarian's conclusion that humans are merely garbage would seem irrefutable. But the very irrationality of Yossarian's experiences permits hope that once again logic will be turned on its head. If logic cannot provide meaning, perhaps meaning exists experientially in the book's humor and creative spirit. Thus the BLACK HUMOR in *Catch-22* itself produces the spirituality without which "man is garbage," suggesting that "man" can be more than the world of *Catch-22* allows him to be.

Cat's Cradle A 1963 APOCALYPTIC NOVEL by Kurt VONNEGUT Jr. Published a year after the Cuban Missile Crisis—the point when the Cold War seemed most likely to lead to outright war between the United States and the Soviet Union—*Cat's Cradle* presents a vision of worldwide apocalypse resulting from the achievements of science. It imagines a unique isotope, *ice-nine*, which reconfigures water molecules so that water freezes at 114 degrees Fahrenheit, instead of 32 degrees. Dropped into the ocean, a single crystal of ice-nine can solidify the entire sea, and touched to someone's lips, it freezes the blood and kills the individual. Felix Hoenikker, the inventor of the atomic bomb, has developed the isotope. When he dies, Hoenikker leaves a piece to his three maladjusted children, who divide it among themselves. They never speak of its moral implications or even of the propriety of treating it as personal property. Eventually they give away their chips for personal gain and pay little attention to the potential consequences. When Frank, the mechanical genius who is wanted by the police, gives his piece to "Papa" Monzano, the dictator of the Caribbean island of San Lorenzo, he replies to his horrified siblings, "I bought myself a job, just like you [the daughter] bought yourself a tomcat husband, just the way Newt [a midget] bought himself a week on Cape Cod with a Russian midget." From this statement, the reader can infer that both the United States and U.S.S.R. have also acquired ice-nine, a fact that the narrator bemoans: "What hope can there be for mankind . . . when there are such men as Felix Hoenikker to give such playthings as *ice-nine* to such short-sighted children as almost all men and women are." "Papa" Monzano is at odds with Bokonon, a black leader on the island who, having failed to combat poverty and disease through social reform, has invented a religion of reduced aspirations. Bokonon's playful, cynical pronouncements, such as "History . . . read it and weep!" contribute to the novel's tone of BLACK HUMOR. "Papa" Monzano commits suicide by touching ice-nine to his lips, and during his burial ceremony, a series of unplanned events causes his body to fall into the sea before he can be cremated. Immediately, the ocean turns to ice and apocalypse follows. Thus Vonnegut warns that science will inevitably be abused because human nature will drive people to treat it carelessly and apply it to selfish ends. Moreover, the unpredictability of nature ensures that the best efforts to control the dangerous products of science will inevitably fail. Nonetheless, the novel's playfulness and its pleasure in creative imagination render this bleak theme palatable, even fun.

Cat's Cradle served in lieu of a master's thesis in anthropology for Vonnegut in 1971, an effort to replace the 1947 thesis, "Fluctuations Between Good and Evil in Simple Tales," that had been unanimously rejected by the anthropology department at the University of Chicago. Hoenikker was patterned after Dr. Irving Langmuir whom Vonnegut knew when he worked at General Electric. The first scientist from private industry to win a Nobel Prize, Langmuir had imagined something like ice-nine and suggested it H. G. Wells. According to Vonnegut, "Wells was uninterested, or at least never used the idea. And then Wells died, and then, finally, Langmuir died. I thought to myself: 'Finders, keepers—the idea is mine.'" (See also SCIENCE FICTION NOVELS.)

For additional reading, see *Dictionary of Literary Biography* (vol. 2, *American Novelists Since World War II*).

Ceremony A 1977 APOCALYPTIC NOVEL by Leslie Marmon Silko. Released during a period of U.S.-Soviet détente, *Ceremony* was one of the few novels about the nuclear threat published in the mainstream press by a Native American. (Other Native American authors who addressed nuclear themes include Wendy Rose, Linda Hogan, Paula Gunn Allen, Stephen Popkes and Martin Cruz Smith, who wrote STALLION GATE.) Like *Stallion Gate*, *Ceremony* views nuclear weaponry as the logical culmination of the European-American Empirical, scientific world view that values technology above all else. Both novels likewise address the impact of the development of the atomic bomb in New Mexico on the Native Americans who populate the region. *Ceremony* centers on Tayo, a World War II veteran who is returning to his tribe after being released from a Japanese prison camp. According to Helen Jaskoski in *The Nightmare Considered*, "The novel follows his healing journey, centering on traditional Pueblo and Navajo beliefs and ceremonial practices through which he becomes cured of the maladies of psychological disintegration, guilt and despair contracted during the war." The conflict between the tribe's world view and that of the atomic scientists plays a central role in the novel. Tayo's native rituals express reverence for the Earth, and their rich language is pitted against the stark, data-filled language of the atomic scientists who want to desecrate the Earth with their nuclear experiments. Silko reconciles the two opposite orientations somewhat by introducing Pueblo myths that seemingly predict the coming of the bomb.

For additional reading, see Anisfield's *The Nightmare Considered*.

Chaplin, Charles A British-born FILM ACTOR and FILM DIRECTOR who flourished in Hollywood before being driven into exile to Switzerland during the 1950s RED SCARE. One of the world's most popular and well-known performers during the first half of the century, Chaplin was born in

Charles Chaplin as Monsieur Verdoux, 1947. Courtesy AP/ Wide World.

London in 1889. He grew up in poverty, laboring in a workhouse when his father refused to support him. In 1913 he joined the Keystone Film Company in Hollywood and made his debut in *Making a Living* (1914). Soon after he developed his enduring "Little Tramp" character, whose good heart, sad eyes, graceful movements, self-respect and indomitable spirit in the face of adversity was soon beloved by silent picture viewers throughout the world.

Most of Chaplin's films center around down-and-out characters, and several have implicit or explicit political content. One of his funniest movies, *Modern Times* (1936), centers on an unemployed factory worker during the Depression. In that film, a heartless industrialist treats his employees as machines, even monitoring their bathroom breaks through closed-circuit television. (Chaplin was accused of plagiarizing Fritz Lang's *Metropolis* [1926] because of such scenes.) The police serve the capitalists' interests, and the well-off middle class seems insensitive to the plight of the poor. In *The Great Dictator* (1940), Chaplin ridicules Adolf Hitler and Benito Mussolini and concludes with an impassioned plea for peace and human cooperation. MONSIEUR VERDOUX (1947) also concludes with a moralizing speech, an anti-capitalist commentary that accuses society of adopting brutal means to achieve its ends.

In the late 1940s, Chaplin criticized American foreign policy, defended the civil liberties of American communists and supported the 1948 presidential aspirations of populist candidate Henry Wallace, whom the American Communist Party also endorsed. At the same time, Chaplin always denied that he was a communist, and no evidence has surfaced to prove that he ever actually belonged to any Communist Party, despite an FBI file almost 2,000 pages long. Nonetheless, accusations about Chaplin's alleged communist affiliations abounded in the columns of such influential gossip columnists as Hedda Hopper and Louella Parsons. Accusations about Chaplin even appear in the FBI file on Albert Einstein, whom an unnamed informant accused of collaborating with Chaplin to take over Hollywood. Though the FBI spent many hours investigating these and other charges against Chaplin, all of the accusations remained unsubstantiated. Despite the failure of the FBI to demonstrate either communist affiliation or illegal activity, Chaplin's socialist inclinations and his sexual involvements with underaged women led to his investigation by Senator Joseph McCarthy (R. Wisconsin) and the HOUSE COMMITTEE ON UN-AMERICAN ACTIVITIES (HUAC). Though HUAC announced its plans to have Chaplin testify, it repeatedly postponed calling him as a witness and finally declined to do so at all.

In 1947 Chaplin telegrammed HUAC to claim that he had never "joined any political organization in my life." Nevertheless, while the actor was aboard the luxury liner *Queen Elizabeth* en route to England for the 1952 premiere of his film *Limelight,* Attorney General James McGranery revoked his entry permit, citing the U.S. code that allowed for the exclusion of aliens based on "morals, health, or insanity, or for advocating Communism or associating with Communist or pro-Communist organizations." (Chaplin had remained a British citizen and was therefore subject to deportation or exclusion.) Responding to accusations from such right-wing figures as Senator Richard Nixon (R. California) that he had mismanaged the Chaplin case, the Democratic attorney general ordered Chaplin to appear before hearings of the Immigration and Naturalization Service to ascertain whether he was eligible for readmission to the United States. In response, Chaplin refused to return to the United States until 1972, when he received a special Oscar award and was honored at the Lincoln Center Film Society in New York. Instead, he lived briefly in London before immigrating to Switzerland. In 1954 he lunched with China's foreign minister Chou En-lai during the Geneva peace conference that arranged the French exit from Vietnam, and in 1956 he met with Soviet leaders Khrushchev and Bulganin in London. In 1962 Oxford University awarded him an honorary degree, and Queen Elizabeth II knighted him in 1975.

Throughout the late 1940s and early 1950s, Chaplin's films came under attack because of the actor's political beliefs and sexual affairs. Attempts to ban *Monsieur Verdoux* failed, but picketing by the American Legion outside of the theaters where it was screened caused the film to be removed prematurely from circulation. In 1952 the legion also picketed *Limelight,* even though that film contained no political or "unwholesome" themes. The legion and the Catholic War Veterans also persuaded theater owners and some television stations not to screen Chaplin's earlier silent films from the teens, twenties and thirties. In 1957 Chaplin

responded to his treatment during the Red Scare with his British-made film A KING IN NEW YORK, about a deposed European monarch who immigrates to America. The movie satirizes American culture when the destitute king is reduced to earning a living by making television commercials. However, the king falls afoul of HUAC when he befriends a runaway boy whose parents are suspected of communism. Tarnished by guilt-by-association, the king must appear before the committee, but he makes literal the metaphorical farce of the hearings when he accidentally turns a fire hose on his interrogators. The film was not shown in the United States until 1976. Chaplin died in Switzerland in 1977. (See also EXILED WRITERS [from the United States].)

For additional reading, see Tucker's *Literary Exile in the Twentieth Century,* Whitfield's *The Culture of the Cold War.*

Chase, Richard A NONFICTION WRITER and proponent of the NEW LIBERALISM. In his 1949 study of Herman Melville, Chase sought to contribute to

> a movement which may be described . . . as the new liberalism—that newly invigorated secular thought at the dark center of the twentieth century which, whatever our cultural wreckage and disappointment, now begins to ransom liberalism from the ruinous sellouts, failures, and defeats of the thirties. The new liberalism must . . . present a vision of life capable, by a continuous act of imaginative criticism, of avoiding old mistakes: the facile ideas of progress and "social realism," the disinclination to examine human motives, the indulgence of wish-fulfilling rhetoric, the belief that historical reality is merely a question of economic or ethical values, the idea that literature should participate directly in the economic liberation of the masses, the equivocal relationship to communist totalitarianism and power politics.

In a 1952 essay in *The Kenyon Review,* Chase put forward the New Liberal position that political ideas can benefit from literature:

> I once advanced the opinion that if one had read and understood Melville one would not vote for [Progressive Party nominee] Henry Wallace . . . because Melville presents his reader with a vision of life so complexly true that it exposes the ideas of Henry Wallace as hopelessly childish and superficial. Literature tells us that life is diverse, paradoxical, and complicated, a fateful medley of lights and darks . . . It warns us that the tendency of modern liberal politics has been to bleed political ideas white, to deny them their roots in natural reality, to deny them their extension over the possible range of human experience.

For further reading, see Schaub's *American Fiction in the Cold War.*

chess Because the Cold War relied so much on political strategies and diplomatic maneuvering, it was often cast in terms of a chess match between the superpowers. The chess metaphor suggested that success in the Cold War depended upon the strategic abilities and the intelligence of each side's

World chess championship match, 1970; Boris Spassky (l.) and Bobby Fischer. Courtesy AP/Wide World.

political leaders. In the United States, the Soviets were often depicted as exploiting every slight advantage in the arena of treaties and international diplomacy and were thus likened to highly skilled chessmasters, many of whom did, indeed, come from Russia. The blunt heavy-handedness of the nuclear threat lurking behind the refined diplomatic strategies may actually have rendered the chess metaphor inappropriate; nonetheless it persisted throughout the Cold War, especially during its earlier stages, when direct Soviet involvement in or influence over the international communist movement was more common. Thus, the argument that the Soviets were coordinating a chess-like global political/military assault against the West was easier to make. As divisions among the communist nations surfaced, first in Yugoslavia in 1948 and then in China in the late 1950s, the metaphor lost some of its vitality. Similar cracks in the West's unified front, such as the U.S. opposition to the joint French-British action in the Suez in 1956 or France's withdrawal from the integrated NATO military command in 1966, further weakened the notion of a carefully coordinated Western strategy. Nonetheless, the tendency persisted to

conceive of the Cold War as a highly cerebral chess match filled with clever traps, misdirections and moves signaling ambiguous intentions and possibilities. This metaphor gave special significance to the two great U.S.-Soviet chess rivalries of the Cold War era: the 1972 meeting between American Bobby Fischer and Russian Boris Spassky and the 1978 and 1981 matches between Soviet defector Viktor Korchnoi and Soviet citizen Anatoly Karpov.

The Fischer-Spassky matched was played in Reykjavik, Iceland, between July 11 and September 1, 1972. It was accompanied by considerable media hype for several reasons. Fischer was known to be a moody, idiosyncratic and demanding loner. During the 1968 Chess Olympiad in Lugano, for instance, he demanded special lighting and a private playing room apart from spectators. When officials refused, he quit the American team and went into isolation "to plot my revenge if I ever come back." He remained out of active competition for 18 months before agreeing in 1970 to play in a new chess event: the Soviet Union versus the World, in which 10 players from throughout the world challenged the best 10 Soviet players. Fischer nearly led the world players to victory, although the Soviet team finally won, as chess experts had predicted.

After arrangements had been finalized for the 1972 championship match with Spassky, Fischer added new demands. He insisted that he receive half the profits from the event and complained in *Life* magazine that "Iceland, with all due respect, is just too small and primitive a country to handle an event of this size. Their hall is inadequate and so is their lighting . . . But the worst thing of all is that there is no way to telecast the match from Iceland to the United States or even to Europe. That's why the Russians picked Iceland. They know they're going to lose the match, so they figure they might as well bury it." After being given 72 hours to accept the Iceland match with Spassky, the reigning world champion, or to be replaced by another challenger, Fischer agreed to play but then backed out again at the last minute because the prize money was too small. He relented two days after the first match had been scheduled to be played when an English donor doubled the purse to $250,000. The match did not begin for another week, until Fischer formally apologized to Spassky.

Fischer lost the first game despite having the advantage of the white pieces (which enable a player to move first), and he forfeited the second game when he refused to show up due to a dispute over the television cameras. He arrived at the last moment before the third game, which he demanded be played in a small back room normally reserved for Ping-Pong. Spassky, who quite probably could have provoked Fischer to forfeit the entire tournament by declining the unusual request, magnanimously agreed to play there just once, and Fischer went on to win his first game. Fischer then proceeded to dominate the next several games until Spassky began to play him nearly even at the end. Fischer eventually won $12\frac{1}{2}$ points to $8\frac{1}{2}$. Spassky gained respect for his gentlemanly behavior, which contrasted with Fischer's arrogance. Many observers believed that Fischer's demands were a psychological ploy designed to throw Spassky off his game. Yet despite the personal differences that made Spassky appear a more attractive individual, the first-time American defeat of a Soviet for the world championship stirred patriotic sentiments in the United States and caused concern for the Soviet ideologues who had long maintained that their chess dominance reflected the superiority of their social system. After his defeat Spassky was permitted to live abroad without losing his citizenship.

Fischer forfeited his title in 1975 when he refused to play Soviet challenger Anatoly Karpov, who then became the reigning world champion. In 1974 Viktor Korchnoi, still a Soviet citizen, had lost to Karpov in his bid for the right to play against Fischer, but he believed that the Soviet chess authorities had decided Karpov should prevail and had therefore exerted formal and informal pressure against him. Korchnoi's discontent eventually became public and his permission to travel internationally was temporarily suspended. However, in 1975 he was again allowed to travel abroad, and in July 1976 he defected after winning a tournament in Holland. Afterward he continued to win chess matches and to demand that his wife and son be allowed to emigrate from the Soviet Union. As a defector, he faced Karpov for the championship in 1978 but lost in an extremely close match that, like the 1972 Fischer–Spassky tournament, was enmeshed in rumor, propaganda and intrigue. Korchnoi lost again in 1981. Then in 1985 Karpov lost the title to his younger countryman Gary Kasparov, who remained the chess champion of the world through the end of the Cold War.

Other major chess players who defected from communist countries include Pal Benko, who left Hungary after the 1956 Hungarian Revolution; Soviets Anatoly Lein, Vladimir Liberzon, Gennadi Sosonko and Leonid Shamkovich; and Czechs Lubomir Kavalek and Ludek Pachman.

Children's Television Programming See TELEVISION SHOWS FOR CHILDREN.

Chill of Dust A 1964 APOCALYPTIC NOVEL by Stephen Minot. Published two years after the Cuban Missile Crisis, *Chill of Dust* follows the evolution of a postapocalyptic society through humanist, religious and pagan phases. The novel finally concludes that a successful society requires elements from each world view. The first leader portrayed by the book is a teacher who hopes to prevent a cultural regression to barbarism. He insists that the children of the planet's 21 surviving families keep alive as much of Western humanist culture as possible, even making them memorize a surviving fragment from *Paradise Lost*. However, the teacher's instruction proves inadequate for dealing with the lawless outside world. A band of criminals kills and rapes some of the children, who never learned how to protect themselves, and in despair, the teacher ignites his remaining books and tries to immolate himself. The social authority then passes to a priest, and finally to a hobo, who represents a pagan love of nature and a down-to-earth, practical ability. Minot suggests that each leader contributed some of the elements needed for long-term survival and meaningful life: the teacher's humanistic learning, the priest's religious faith and humility, and the hobo-pagan's practical know-how.

For additional reading, see Dowling's *Fictions of Nuclear Disaster*.

"China Beach" A TELEVISION MILITARY DRAMA that ran on ABC from 1988 to 1991. "China Beach" and "TOUR OF DUTY" (CBS, 1987–90) were the only two television series set in the Vietnam War. Unlike other shows about warfare, however, "China Beach" centered on women: nurses, USO entertainers and prostitutes near the U.S. military base at Da Nang. Though many of the plotlines featured the romantic relationships of Nurse Colleen McMurphy (Dana Delany), the show was pervaded with a sense of the harsh reality of warfare. It included elements of BLACK HUMOR, especially through the comments of Private Sam Beckett (Michael Boatman) who ran the morgue and Red Cross worker Holly the Donut Dolly (Ricki Lake). The series combined graphic portrayals of the war with harsh, Vietnam-era ROCK AND ROLL and allusions to the U.S. civil unrest that the Vietnam War spawned. One of the regular characters, Cherry White (Nan Woods), was killed during the 1968 Tet Offensive. Another character, K. C. Koloski (Marg Helgenberger), was a prostitute and heroin addict, and one of the men fathered an

Amerasian child. Like M*A*S*H (CBS, 1972–83), "China Beach" presented a strong antiwar viewpoint. Unlike "M*A*S*H," which was produced during the Vietnam War, "China Beach" aired during the waning days of the Cold War, when the communist regimes in Eastern Europe and the Soviet Union were crumbling.

China in Revolution: 1911–1949 A 1988 FILM DOCUMENTARY directed by Susan Williams. Partially funded by the National Endowment for the Humanities, the film traces the establishment of the Chinese communist state from the fall of the boy emperor Pu Yi to the birth of the communist People's Republic of China under Mao Zedong.

Chinese Boxes A 1984 British and West German-made SPY FILM starring Will Patton, Gottfried John, Adelheid Arndt and Robbie Coltrane and directed by Christopher Petit. The story centers on an American (Patton) in West Berlin who becomes enmeshed in a complex situation involving drugs and international politics. The film uses the bewildering, ambiguous Cold War context to explore a theme of alienation.

"Chronoscope" A TELEVISION TALK OR DEBATE SHOW that ran on CBS from 1951 to 1955. Moderated initially by Frank Knight and then in turn by William Bradford Huie, Edward P. Morgan and Larry Le Sueur, "Chronoscope" covered current events by featuring an expert on some issue of immediate interest, including such Cold War topics as the Korean War and domestic politics. Two journalists would then discuss the topic and its implications for America.

Clancy, Tom A NOVELIST. The author of MILITARY NOVELS, Clancy wrote during the later phases of the Cold War, and his books are known for their precise details about military hardware and advanced technology. His first novel, HUNT FOR RED OCTOBER (1984), appeared during the most intense period of U.S.-Soviet confrontation since the 1962 Cuban Missile Crisis. The MILITARY FILM adaptation appeared in 1990, just as the Soviet Union was collapsing and the Cold War was coming to an end. The story centers on U.S. efforts to deal with a renegade, top-secret Soviet submarine that is heading toward the United States—possibly to defect, but possibly for other, more hostile purposes. The U.S. military leaders must facilitate the defection without unduly risking U.S. security. *Red Storm Rising* (1986) addresses the problem of Islamic fundamentalism, which added a new twist to the Cold War in the 1980s. Written while the Soviet Union was fighting a war in Afghanistan, the novel begins with Muslim terrorists destroying a major Soviet oil refinery. Faced with a serious oil shortage, the Soviets initiate a ground war in the Persian Gulf to seize the region's oil deposits. NATO and the United States fight back, and the book's action chronicles the war. The story is based on Convoy '84, an actual military war game predicated on fighting a war with conventional weapons. Clancy received praise for the depth of his research and his knowledge of military procedure and technology. The reviewer for *Time* noted:

> For too much of *Red Storm Rising*, the humans are obscured by the afterburn of the weapons systems.

Oddly enough, it is this very flaw that enhances the [novel's] credibility . . . World War III . . . is not likely to involve a grand Tolstoyan sweep of personal valor. Arsenals and tactics might indeed be set in motion by the frailties of flesh-and-blood players, but once launched the lethal machines would take on a life of their own—almost like characters in a novel. That possibility, vividly rendered, is what gives Clancy's book such a chilling ring of truth.

Cardinal of the Kremlin (1988) also features warfare between the superpowers. Published toward the end of the Cold War, when Gorbachev had been in power for three years, the book again centers on high technology as a Soviet laser on the Afghanistan border attacks a U.S. space satellite. The use of the laser as a space weapon points to President Reagan's proposed Strategic Defense Initiative (SDI—popularly known as STAR WARS). Other contemporary features include sensory-deprivation tanks in a KGB prison, Afghani guerrillas armed with U.S.-supplied Stinger anti-aircraft missiles, and U.S.-Soviet disarmament talks. *Patriot Games* (1987) deals with the aftermath of an attack by the Irish Republican Army on the British royal family. Clancy's last novel from the Cold War era, *Clear and Present Danger* (1989), likewise turns away from the Cold War, focusing instead on the danger to U.S. security posed by the drug barons of South America.

Cleaver, Eldridge An exiled American political activist and NONFICTION WRITER. Born in Arkansas in 1935, Cleaver became attracted to the Black Power movement while he was imprisoned in California during the 1960s. His essays from this period, *Soul on Ice* (1968), call for liberating black Americans by overthrowing the social, military and economic institutions of the government. He also proposed rape as a strategy of racial liberation, as black men could attack white men through "their" women. In response to the persecution of the militant Black Panther Party and to divisions among the Black Muslims, he adopted a Marxist position, which appears in *Post Prison Writings and Speeches* (1969). Under the threat of arrest and reincarceration for parole violations, Cleaver fled first to Cuba and then to Algeria. While exiled in Algeria he wrote an introduction to *Do It!* (1970) by the Yippie antiwar activist, Jerry Rubin. In that introduction, Cleaver sees American history as encapsulated in a single word, *blood,* and calls on American youth to smoke marijuana, listen to good music and reject authority as a means of undermining what he and Rubin both saw as a racist, capitalist system: "I can unite with Jerry around hatred of pig judges, around hatred of capitalism, around the total desire to smash what is now the social order in the United States of Amerika." (The use of *K* to spell America was a reference to the German spelling, linking the United States with Nazi Germany.)

At their invitation, Cleaver visited North Vietnam, North Korea and the People's Republic of China. There, he concluded that Marxist ideals had been betrayed by what he saw as tyrannical governments, and he became disillusioned with communism. Subsequently, he and his wife, Kathleen Neal, settled in France, where he began to reconsider his political stance. His Christian-oriented account of the events

Eldridge Cleaver, 1968. Courtesy AP/Wide World.

that led to his voluntary return to the United States appears in *Soul on Fire* (1978). Upon his return, he stood trial and was sentenced to more than 2,000 hours of community service in California, where he now resides. (See also EXILED WRITERS [from the United States].)

For additional reading, see Tucker's *Literary Exile in the Twentieth Century.*

Cliburn, Van American classical pianist who, at age 23, was awarded first prize in the 1958 Tchaikovsky competition in Moscow. The competition took place at the beginning of the three-year second Berlin Crisis, one of the most intense periods of the Cold War. The *New York Times* ran a hopeful front-page headline proclaiming that Cliburn's victory had created "an artistic bridge between the U.S. and Russia." Cliburn later became a personal friend of President Johnson and performed at the president's Texas ranch for visiting West German chancellor Ludwig Erhard, as well as at the White House for other visiting heads of state.

Closely Watched Trains A 1966 Czechoslovakian FOR-EIGN FILM starring Vaclav Neckar, Jitka Bendova and Josef Somr and directed by Jiri Menzel. The film was distributed internationally during the 1968 Prague Spring—a brief period of liberalization in Czechoslovakia under the short-lived administration of Alexander Dubcek. The story centers on the several initiations of a young man stationed at a remote train depot during World War II, while the Germans were occupying Czechoslovakia. *Closely Watched Trains* thus contained a subtext about the de facto Soviet occupation during the Cold War. Of the films shown in America during the Prague Spring, *Closely Watched Trains* was probably the most widely seen and most profitable, and it won an Academy Award for the best foreign film. Along with the Academy Award–winning *The Shop on Main Street*, directed in 1965 by Czechs Jan Kadar and Elmar Klos, *Closely Watched Trains* represented one of the few instances during the early Cold War when a film made "behind the Iron Curtain" gained relatively wide circulation and popular and critical acclaim within the United States.

Van Cliburn meets Nikita Khrushchev, Tchaikovsky Competition, 1958. Courtesy *Soviet Life.*

"Close-Up!"   See BELL & HOWELL CLOSE-UP!

Cobb, Lee J.   A FILM ACTOR. After a promising musical career as a violinist and virtuoso harmonica player was destroyed by a broken wrist, Cobb began his acting career in California and New York during the 1930s. In the Group Theater he befriended Alvah BESSIE and other members of the Communist Party, though he never joined or contributed to the party himself. In 1947 he achieved considerable prominence for his performance as Willy Loman in Arthur MILLER's *Death of a Salesman*, which Elia KAZAN directed, and for which Cobb was acclaimed as one of the major talents of American theater, "the next Barrymore." However, he was blacklisted in 1951 (see BLACKLISTING) after Larry PARKS named him as a communist before the HOUSE COMMITTEE ON UN-AMERICAN ACTIVITIES (HUAC). On principle, Cobb resisted testifying before HUAC for two years, during which time he ran out of work and money and his wife was institutionalized for alcoholism. Finally, in 1953 he appeared before the committee, naming 20 people as communists and accusing Philip LOEB and Sam Jaffe of controlling the Forum, a left-wing caucus within Actors Equity, though he emphasized that "I never knew them to be Communists." Cobb also described how party theorist John Howard LAWSON wanted to "rewrite the precepts of Stanislavski's method on acting, to try as far as possible to color it by the prevailing Communist ideologies." Shortly after testifying, Cobb suffered a massive heart attack for which Frank Sinatra paid the hospital bills and "saved my life." After his testimony, Hollywood considered Cobb to be politically rehabilitated, and he renewed his acting career. In 1954 he starred with Marlon Brando in ON THE WATERFRONT. The film celebrates the courage of a longshoreman who testifies against corrupt former friends, and it was also written (Budd SCHULBERG) and directed (Elia Kazan) by men who had named names before HUAC.

Cobb has said that if he had not been reduced to dire circumstances and abandoned by the friends he was being asked to protect, he would not have cooperated with HUAC:

> When the facilities of the government of the U.S. are drawn on an individual it can be terrifying. The blacklist is just the opening gambit—being deprived of work. Your passport is confiscated. That's minor. But not being able to move without being tailed is something else. Phone taps are expected, but the interception of the grocery bill? After a certain point it grows to implied as well as articulated threats, and people succumb. My wife did, and she was institutionalized. I had two babies then . . . No one has held out, that's my profound discovery. I discovered that what I thought was thoroughly principled resistance really wasn't that at all . . . I still have contempt for my former cronies . . . I didn't act out of principle. I wallowed in unprincipledness. One of my closest friends pleaded with me not to do a thing like this, as he ran to catch the boat for England. He was fleeing the country, but I was the coward. We haven't spoken since . . . My friends had the attitude I would rather eulogize you dead than have you as an imperfect contemporary alive.

Cobb has also commented on the breach among himself, Kazan and Miller caused by the politically motivated HUAC hearings:

> In the theater the odds are so remote, but then comes the miraculous coincidence of a Kazan, Miller, and Cobb being contemporaries. If you spit in the face of that kind of good fortune it is unforgivable. If for so-called political reasons the breach is widened, that it is deserving of criminal prosecution.

For additional reading, see Navasky's *Naming Names.*

"Code Name: Foxfire"   A TELEVISION SPY SHOW that ran on NBC during the winter of 1985. This short-lived, Reagan-era show reflected the penchant for covert operations that the Reagan administration later became known for. A cross between a James Bond movie and "Charlie's Angels" (ABC, 1976–81), "Code Name: Foxfire" described the exploits of a covert-operations team headed by former CIA agent Liz "Foxfire" Towne (Joanna Cassidy). The team answered directly to the president's brother, Larry Hutchins (John McCook), who employed it to carry out especially sensitive counterespionage work. The series began when Hutchins secured Foxfire's release from prison, where she had already served four years for a crime she did not commit. Her partners were Maggie "The Cat" Bryan, a reformed thief from the streets of Detroit, and Danny "The Driver," a clever ex-cabbie from York. Street-wise and tough, the group could also be suave and elegant when those qualities were called for. The show seemed to suggest that both polish and toughness were needed to fight the Cold War and that circumventing the law to achieve a patriotic goal was both acceptable and necessary.

Codrescu, Andrei A Romanian EXILED WRITER (to the United States) and radio commentator. Born in Transylvania on the Hungarian-Romanian border, Codrescu claims he "could see the barbed wire all through my infancy." He left Romania for Hungary in 1965 during a brief period of liberalization in Eastern Europe that concluded with the Soviet repression of Czechoslovakian reforms in 1968. He studied briefly at the University of Bucharest but was expelled because he was considered a Jew. After living in Italy and France for a year, Codrescu moved to the United States in 1966. He has published 16 books of poetry, three works of fiction and two autobiographical books, including *Comrade Past and Mister Present: New Poems and a Journal* (1986), *Monsieur Teste in America and Other Instances of Realism* (1987) and *Raised by Puppets: Only to Be Killed by Research* (1989). He is also commentator for National Public Radio's "All Things Considered," and he edited the now-defunct literary journal *Exquisite Corpse*. A professor at Louisiana State University, Codrescu visited Romania in 1990 as a correspondent for National Public Radio to report on the fall of the communist regime of Nicolae Ceausescu.

For additional reading, see Tucker's *Literary Exile in the Twentieth Century*.

Cold War Killers A 1986 British-made SPY FILM starring Terence Stamp and Michael Culver and directed by William Braine. The plot centers on the discovery of an airplane that had disappeared 30 years earlier. A British agent (Stamp) must work to keep its secret cargo from the Soviets.

Cole, Lester A SCREENWRITER and member of the HOLLYWOOD TEN. An outspoken hard-line communist, Cole had written 36 films and was running for reelection to the Screen Writers Guild executive board when he was subpoenaed to testify at the 1947 HOUSE COMMITTEE ON UN-AMERICAN ACTIVITIES (HUAC) hearings on communist influence in Hollywood films. Prior to his appearance Ayn RAND, a "friendly" witness and self-proclaimed expert on identifying communist messages in the movies, accused Cole of planting a subversive sentiment in a movie in which a football coach tells his players, "It is better to die on your feet than live on your knees." She believed the sentence alluded to a statement made by the Spanish communist La Pasionaria during the Spanish Civil War. After citing his First Amendment rights and refusing to testify, Cole was cited for contempt of Congress and eventually sentenced to prison. He was also blacklisted and never wrote another screenplay, except for HOLLYWOOD ON TRIAL, a 1976 FILM DOCUMENTARY about the RED SCARE in the film industry. In 1948 Cole filed a lawsuit against MGM's parent company, Loew's, charging breach of contract and conspiracy to blacklist. His intent was to break the blacklist, but his initial victory was reversed on appeal and he dropped the case in 1952. His autobiography was entitled *Hollywood Red* (1981). Cole died in 1985. (See also BLACKLISTING.)

For additional reading see Navasky's *Naming Names*.

Collins, Richard A SCREENWRITER. Collins cowrote *The Song of Russia* (1944), a World War II-era film that its star, Robert Taylor, and a self-proclaimed expert, Ayn RAND, criticized as pro-communist propaganda in their 1947 testimony before the HOUSE COMMITTEE ON UN-AMERICAN ACTIVITIES (HUAC). Collins, a ranking member of the Communist Party at the time, had been subpoenaed to testify as one of 19 "unfriendly" witnesses, but unlike the HOLLYWOOD TEN who preceded him, Collins was never called before the 1947 committee. He was thus spared the prison sentences incurred by the Ten, but like them, he was blacklisted by the film studios. About a year prior to his HUAC subpoena, Collins became disenchanted with the party, especially with its dogmatic policies on artistic expression and its intolerance for independent thought. He claimed that when the party forced Albert MALTZ to recant a controversial article attacking socialist realism, he became further disillusioned, and that he disagreed with the party's refusal to unequivocally support the United States in the event of a war with the Soviet Union. Nonetheless, he would have suffered the fate of the Ten had he been called to testify because, "At that time it seemed to me that purely on American democratic constitutional grounds there was a question of the propriety of asking a man his political beliefs."

Eventually his disaffection for the party led him to become an FBI informant, an act supported by former communist Edward DMYTRYK, one of the Ten. Collins was summoned before HUAC in 1951 when the committee opened its second round of Hollywood hearings. The Supreme Court had by then upheld the contempt of Congress convictions of the Ten, who had unsuccessfully invoked their First Amendment constitutional protection. Collins's choices were thus to go to prison for contempt of Congress, invoke the Fifth Amendment protection against self-incrimination or cooperate with the committee. Collins, whose position within the party enabled him to know the names of virtually all of its Hollywood members, chose to cooperate because "There had been a marked change in the world situation since 1947, and there had been as great a change in me. It is hard to tell where one thing begins and the other ends." Moreover, he said:

> The Party is really a religious operation, and if you have religion it's fine to suffer for it, and if you don't, well maybe you don't want to. But I'm not taking any moral positions on that, because I never felt that it was a marvelous thing to do. I think it took a certain amount of guts. In a sense it was harder to be cooperative than not.

Collins claimed that in order to avoid harming anyone's career, his strategy was to name only party members who had died, those who had already testified "because we figured that they were stuck already," and those who had long before left the party. Naming the third group was "my mistake . . . I had no idea that they would be bounced as hard as they were. I figured that having been out for ten years . . . [Budd] SCHULBERG for instance, that everybody would see that they *had* left. It was a tremendous mistake . . . " Schulberg, a prominent novelist, appeared on the front-page headline of the *New York Times* after Collins named him. In turn, Schulberg named additional names.

Though his career was rehabilitated in 1953 because of his testimony, Collins maintained that getting off the blacklist was not his primary motivation and that he had no reason to expect that cooperating with the committee would affect his employment status. Prior to Collins's appearance, Larry PARKS had been the only Hollywood communist to identify party members. Parks was subsequently pilloried in the press, and his career was ultimately ruined. According to Collins, "The primary consideration was that I just thought it was ridiculous to go through life as a member of the Party—which taking the Fifth in effect said publicly you were doing—when I wasn't." Collins's first post-blacklist work was *Riot in Cell Block 11* (1954). He also wrote for television, including Ronald REAGAN'S GENERAL ELECTRIC THEATER (CBS, 1953–62). He and Reagan had at least one dispute over the representation of communism when "Reagan had a scene he wanted to put in, some idiot thing where the Communist mother slaps her child because she finds him praying or something like that." (See also BLACKLISTING; RED SCARE.)

For additional reading, see Navasky's *Naming Names*.

Comaneci, Nadia   A Rumanian gymnast who defected to the United States in 1989. When she was 14, Comaneci participated in the 1976 OLYMPIC GAMES. She won three gold, two silver and one bronze medal and achieved a perfect score in two events, something no one had ever accomplished before. As a result, and because she was young and charming, she became a much-loved worldwide celebrity. Comaneci also won two gold medals in the 1980 Olympics. Her technical execution and the difficulty of her routines raised the level of performance in women's gymnastics. Comaneci defected in 1989, claiming she had been abused and essentially imprisoned by Rumania's communist president Nicolae Ceausescu. (Ceausescu was overthrown by the army and executed on Christmas Day, 1989 after being hastily convicted of genocide and gross misuse of power.) The post-Cold War Rumania named an athletic arena for Comaneci on the fifth anniversary of her defection. (See also SPORTS.)

"Combat"   A TELEVISION MILITARY DRAMA that ran on ABC from 1962 to 1967. Starring Vic Morrow as Sergeant Saunders and Rick Jason as Lieutenant Hanley, "Combat" was one of the more successful World War II television dramas. The show featured the exploits of a U.S. Army platoon during the last year of the war as the soldiers fought across France. More realistic than sensational, "Combat" celebrated the accomplishments and sacrifices of American infantrymen without unduly glamorizing them or turning them into superheroes. It often called on the soldiers to exercise proper judgment and to live by their true values. The show premiered a week before the Cuban Missile Crisis and continued through the buildup of American troops in Vietnam. Significantly, it went off the air in August 1967, at a time when the U.S. antiwar movement was becoming large and increasingly vocal. Soviet soldiers—America's allies in WWII—were rarely, if ever, depicted on the show. On the other hand, the German enemies were not shown to have identifiably "communist" traits and behaviors, as sometimes happened in propagandistic shows that tried to make the

audience transfer their feelings about a past enemy onto the current one. Therefore, contribution of "Combat" to the Cold War was largely to reaffirm such American values as courage, loyalty, sacrifice, toughness, honesty, prudence and respect for authority. The challenge to these values by the COUNTERCULTURE and the antiwar movement during the middle and late 1960s may also account for the show's demise in 1967.

Come Nineveh, Come Tyre   A 1973 POLITICAL NOVEL by Allen DRURY. Written as the United States was preparing to extricate itself from the unsuccessful Vietnam War and as President Nixon was undergoing the Watergate Crisis, the book appeared on the *New York Times* best-seller list for 26 weeks between 1973 and 1974. The story, which plays out a conservative's worst fears, explores what would happen if a liberal who was "soft" on communism were elected president. Ted Jason is the novel's well-intentioned U.S. leader who comes to power after his running mate, the conservative presidential candidate Orrin Knox, is assassinated. Jason genuinely hopes to do good for the nation and the world, reducing military spending in order to finance social programs at home. However, when he refuses to vigorously oppose Soviet action in Grotoland (Vietnam) and Panama, Jason compromises the U.S. political position throughout the world and his weakness inadvertently brings the planet to the brink of nuclear war. Ironically, Robert Leffingwell, the rejected liberal candidate for secretary of state in Drury's earlier novel, ADVISE AND CONSENT (1959), reappears here in the same position but with a more conservative political outlook. However, the liberal president refuses to accept Leffingwell's advice. Eventually both President Jason and his vice president choose to commit suicide rather than live with the consequences of their actions. In addition to holding liberal politicians responsible for the decline and possible demise of the country, Drury also faults an irresponsible liberal press. The book's title comes from Rudyard Kipling's "Recessional," which laments the downfall of the British Empire: "Lo, all our pomp of yesterday / Is one with Nineveh and Tyre."

In THE PROMISE OF JOY (1975) Drury provides an alternative ending to the six-part political series that began in 1959 with *Advise and Consent*. In that story Jason, not Knox, is assassinated, and Knox survives to lead the country through a time of crisis, despite opposition from liberal politicians, antiwar activists and the liberal press.

For additional reading, see Kemme's *Political Fiction, The Spirit of the Age, and Allen Drury*.

Coming Home   A 1978 VIETNAM WAR FILM starring Jane FONDA, Jon Voight and Bruce Dern and directed by Hal ASHBY. The film centers on Sally Hyde (Fonda), the wife of a Marine captain (Dern) who leaves to fight in Vietnam in 1968. She does her bit by volunteering at the veteran's hospital, where she meets Luke Martin (Voight), a bitter paraplegic who had been wounded in combat. Eventually, Martin opens to Sally's warmth and optimism; in return she becomes receptive to his liberal, antiwar, feminist political perspective. Their friendship and mutual compassion grow until, despite his handicaps, they become passionate lovers. However, soon they must deal with Captain Hyde, who returns from the war wounded silent, angry and potentially violent. Nominated for eight Oscars, including best picture and best director, *Coming Home* won three: best actor, best actress and best original screenplay.

Made five years after the U.S. exit from Vietnam, *Coming Home* is an extension and perhaps a justification of Fonda's earlier antiwar activities. These culminated in a much-vilified trip to North Vietnam during which she labelled U.S. soldiers as killers and war criminals and pleaded with them to disobey their orders to fight. *Coming Home,* by contrast, sympathizes with individual soldiers, even with Captain Hyde, who has been wounded emotionally and spiritually, as well as physically. But the film steadfastly indicts the war that created both his wounds and Martin's, attributing it to the insane drive for power of cynical and venal men. Sally's personal evolution comes as Martin expands the boundaries both of her sexuality (with him, she achieves her first orgasm) and her political vision.

"Command Post"   An instructional television show that ran on CBS during the winter and spring of 1950. The U.S. Army produced it and CBS broadcast it as an eight-week course for training reservists. Subjects included combat theory and technique, self-defense and plans of attack. The show ran opposite NBC's extremely popular "Milton Berle Show" (1948–53).

communications satellites (COMSAT)   Spacecraft launched to relay radio, television and telephone signals from points of origin on Earth back to points of reception on other parts of Earth. Launched in August 1960, the first communications satellite, Echo, could only passively reflect sounds and pictures. In 1962, the United States launched Telstar, the first satellite to relay television signals. INTEL-SAT, the International Telecommunications Satellite Consortium, was founded in 1964 as an 18-nation joint venture. In 1965, INTELSAT launched its first satellite, Early Bird, which actively received, amplified and transmitted signals. Communications satellites, which evolved from the Cold War Space Race, facilitated the spread of American music, television programming and other aspects of U.S. culture throughout the world during the Cold War.

Confession, The   A 1970 French and Italian-made POLITICAL FILM starring Yves Montand, Simone Signoret, Gabriele Ferzetti and Michel Vitold, directed by Constantin COSTA-GAVRAS. Based on a true incident in Czechoslovakia, the film centers on Gerard (Montand), a communist official in an unidentified Eastern European country in 1951. A confirmed communist, Gerard had fought for the Loyalist side during the Spanish Civil War. When he observes that he is being followed, he mentions his fears to friends who had also supported the anti-fascist cause and who likewise suspect they are being watched. Soon he is arrested. Kafka-like, he is held without being told of the charges against him, while his captors psychologically torture him and try to extract a confession for crimes they will not identify. Throughout the ordeal Gerard tries to take comfort in the fact that his tormentors are also dedicated communists who are doing what they believe is best for their mutual cause. Eventually

he appears in a highly publicized war trial. The film was significant for the participation of Costa-Gavras, Montand and Signoret, all of whom were well-known leftists who had never before publicly criticized the communist cause.

consumer goods   Many consumer products and technologies were developed in conjunction with the space and arms races that characterized the Cold War. The Cold War was also characterized by claims that the much greater variety and superior quality of consumer goods in the West was proof of the superiority of capitalism over communism. The 1959 Kitchen Debate between Vice President Richard M. Nixon and Premier Nikita Khrushchev at the American National Exhibition in Moscow foregrounded this argument. In that encounter, Khrushchev repeatedly predicted that the Soviets would supersede the United States in world influence, while Nixon pointed out the superiority in quality and variety of American commodities like color televisions and washing machines. During the 1970s such American goods as blue jeans became highly popular behind the IRON CURTAIN and commanded considerable sums on the black market.

Computers were perhaps the most important technological development related to the Cold War. Improvements in the computer were essential for the development of the hydrogen bomb in 1952, and the invention first of the transistor (which replaced the hot and energy-intensive vacuum tube) and then of the microchip made possible the development of the computer and an entire industry surrounding it. Although the Soviet Union pioneered computer technology in the 1950s, the United States soon took the lead, in part because of Soviet anxieties about control over information. Computer technology not only revolutionized military communications and weapons systems, it also changed the way American companies conducted business and made possible a vast array of new services and products, from credit cards and travel services to word processing and electronic mail, from information processing and billing procedures to specially targeted mailing lists to digital recordings, video games and children's toys—to name just a few.

Among the other technologies developed directly or indirectly in conjunction with the Cold War were lasers, which not only guided missiles but also made possible compact disc players, scanning devices for cash registers, new surgical procedures and precision industrial manufacturing, and which first appeared before the American public in the James Bond SPY FILM, GOLDFINGER. Other Cold War–related technologies included digital displays; such appliances as microwave ovens; new plastics, ceramics and adhesives with special properties of hardness, strength, flexibility and endurance; weather satellites; robotics; and fiber optics, among many others. COMMUNICATIONS SATELLITES, which were first developed for their military applications, eventually led to improved and expanded cable television and long-distance telephone service. Even the threat of NUCLEAR APOCALYPSE was translated into a consumer product, a cinnamon-based candy called ATOMIC BOMBS because it burned the mouth. Arguably, consumer demand and the working of the free market would have led to the development of many of these new technologies, but the extensive funding in research and development that came directly from the Defense Department, NASA and other Cold War–related government agencies played an important and often central role.

Coover, Robert A NOVELIST. Born in 1932, Coover was an adolescent when the Cold War began, and his writing reflects his concern with NUCLEAR APOCALYPSE and other manifestations of human insanity. Like John BARTH, Thomas PYNCHON, Kurt VONNEGUT Jr. and other BLACK HUMOR writers, Coover writes with spirit and imagination about horrific themes and events. In this way he both acknowledges the desperate nature of the Cold War era and offers energy, vitality, and creativity as means of coping with it, if not overcoming it. Coover's interest in apocalyptic themes appears in his first novel, *The Origin of the Brunists* (1966), in which a religious cult springs up around the survivor of a mining accident. The book climaxes when the members of the cult await the end of the world. However, just before the anticipated Second Coming, as members wait at the top of a hill, their children rush home so they can watch the event on television, where it will be more real to them. In *The Universal Baseball Association* (1968), Coover plays out the evolution of human society through baseball. A remarkable tour de force, the book seems to have been inspired by

Robert Coover. Courtesy Stathis Orphanos.

Einstein's declaration that he refused to believe God plays dice with the universe. In response, Coover created J. Henry Waugh, an accountant who invents a baseball game that he plays with dice. As Waugh names his imaginary ballplayers, he endows them with personalities and social concerns. Thus Waugh becomes a godlike figure who keeps track of the league's history, retires and kills off the ballplayers as they age, and oversees their off-field efforts at creating society. At the end of the book, Waugh apparently goes crazy and disappears from the scene. Only the ballplayers remain, and they, like their counterparts in the real world, ask the big existential questions common to the Cold War era: Is there a God? If so, does he care about the efforts of humanity? Is he sane? Coover concludes by acknowledging that these questions can never be adequately answered, but he suggests that the game itself (i.e., life) has intrinsic joy and value.

Coover's short story THE CAT IN THE HAT FOR PRESIDENT (1968) likewise celebrates the life force. Written while the country was in the midst of race riots and anti-Vietnam War protests, the story presents the Dr. Seuss character, the Cat in the Hat, as a viable contender for the U.S. presidency. The Cat's ability to ridicule his opponents and change his appearance at will makes him an especially effective candidate. In THE PUBLIC BURNING (1977), Coover presents a surrealistic account of the 1953 execution of Julius and Ethel Rosenberg, the "atomic spies" who were convicted amid worldwide controversy in 1951, at the height of the Korean War, of having passed the "secret" of the atomic bomb to the Soviet Union. The novel is narrated by Richard Nixon and Uncle Sam, and the execution takes place not at Sing Sing Prison but in Times Square. The story concludes with a remarkable explosion suggestive of a nuclear bomb. Throughout his work and especially in "The Cat in the Hat for President" and *The Public Burning,* Coover questions the nature of history and humans' need for myth-making.

For additional reading, see *Dictionary of Literary Biography* (vol. 2, *American Novelists Since World War II*).

Corso, Gregory A POET. Corso viewed poetry as a means of changing society by energizing the individual will. Born in 1930, he joined with Allen GINSBERG and Jack Kerouac in 1951 to become an early member of the BEAT MOVEMENT. His poetry from the 1950s and early 1960s reveals a concern for death and destruction, which, if not always directly pointing to the Cold War, reflects the underlying apocalyptic sensibility spawned by it. For instance, "Don't Shoot the Warthog" from his collection *Gasoline* (1958) represents society eating its young as cannibals do—an image that mirrors Ginsberg's representation of Moloch in his 1956 masterpiece, "Howl."

> The child trembled, fell,
> and staggered up again,
> *I screamed his name!*
> And a fury of mothers and fathers
> sank their teeth into his brain.
> I called to the angels of my generation
> on the rooftops, in the alleyways,
> beneath the garbage and stones,
> *I screamed the name!* and they came
> and gnawed the child's bones.

"Bomb," which appears in Corso's later volume *The Happy Birthday of Death* (1960), takes up the Cold War more directly. The title refers to nuclear warfare, and parts of the poem depict the immense violence implicit in a nuclear war: "Turtles exploding over Istanbul/ The jaguar's flying foot/ soon to sink in arctic snow/ Penguins plunged against the sphinx/ The top of the Empire State/ arrowed in a broccoli field in Sicily." In addition to denouncing the hydrogen bomb, Corso attacks the emotionally detached, scientific thinking that allows people even to contemplate using such weapons of mass destruction. He advocates replacing what he calls "calculative thinking" with a more subjective, emotional and humanistic attitude, which would produce the "restructuring of the world."

Other poems in *The Happy Birthday of Death,* such as "Police" and "1953," criticize militarism, oppression and authoritarianism in the West. Corso elaborates on this theme in *Elegiac Feelings American* (1970), in which he celebrates the radical American revolutionaries Thomas Paine and Samuel Adams over their more bourgeois colleagues Thomas Jefferson, Benjamin Franklin and George Washington. He attacks Jefferson for owning slaves, the "black losers of liberty," and Franklin for offering bounties on the scalps of American Indians. And he claims that Cold War America has become even worse: "The state of Americans today compared to the/ Americans/ of the 18th century proves the nightmare—/Not Franklin not Jefferson who speaks for America/ today/ but strange red-necked men of industry/ and the goofs of show business." The last reference ostensibly alludes to Ronald REAGAN, who was then governor of California. Thomas McClanahan argues in the *Dictionary of Literary Biography* that "For Corso, America's promise, its hope for authentic freedom, is soured by hypocrisy." But McClanahan adds that in overlooking Jefferson's attempts to liberate his slaves and Samuel Adams's raids against Indian villages, Corso presents a simplistic view of history. And he claims that, "As in the case with most occasional verse, Corso's social protestations are no longer stylish or even interesting to most readers. But . . . [in] his attempts to 'kick against the pricks' there is a power of honest sentiment that withstands cultural considerations."

For additional reading, see *Dictionary of Literary Biography* (vol. 5, *American Poets Since World War II*).

Costa-Gavras, Constantin   A Greek-born FILM DIRECTOR. Costa-Gavras is best known for his POLITICAL FILMS, which constitute the majority of his works. Due to his father's activities in the Greek underground during World War II, Costa-Gavras was unable to pursue his education in Greece when the right-wing government came to power there. His personal and family experiences no doubt informed the anti-rightist, anti-totalitarian sentiment that predominates in his films. Unable for political reasons to obtain a visa to study in the United States, Costa-Gavras attended the Sorbonne in Paris. As a directorial trainee in 1958, he studied with René Clair and other important filmmakers. His first film, a detective thriller, was followed by *Shock Troops* (1967), a highly political film about the French Maquis that was shown in the 1967 Moscow Film Festival and was later reedited with a happy ending for release in the United States (1969). Costa-Gavras achieved international promi-

nence in 1969 with *Z*, a political thriller based on the real-life assassination in Greece of a liberal reform politician. The film, which won the jury and best actor prizes at the Cannes Film Festival as well as the Academy Award for best FOREIGN FILM, was banned in Greece. Like many of Costa-Gavras's more famous films, *Z* starred Yves Montand. THE CONFESSION (1970), which alludes to Kafka's *The Trial*, is also based on a true incident. It attacks totalitarian repression and torture in Eastern European communist regimes. Otherwise Costa-Gavras's most common villains are agents of right-wing dictatorships that are aided in their cruelty by U.S. government officials. Such is the case in STATE OF SIEGE (1973), which describes the fate of a U.S. AID agent whom leftist guerrillas believe is actually the person responsible for introducing new, sophisticated means of torture into their country. MISSING (1982) is set in an unnamed Latin American country shortly after a military coup leads to the imprisonment, torture, execution and disappearance of thousands of civilians. The story centers on the search for a leftist expatriate American writer who is among the missing, and it reveals the duplicity of both the dictatorship and the U.S. government officials who support it. Like *State of Siege*, *Missing* is based on a real-life figure; it points to the U.S.-backed military coup that deposed Chile's Marxist president Salvador Allende in 1973. *Missing* has been called the most significant U.S.-made political thriller since THE MANCHURIAN CANDIDATE (1962). Later films include *Betrayed* (1988), which explores the rise of racist, right-wing, survivalist politics in the American West, and *The Music Box* (1989), about an alleged Hungarian war criminal who has been a U.S. citizen for 40 years.

For additional reading, see Monaco's *The Encyclopedia of Film*.

Countdown to Zero   A 1966 TELEVISION DOCUMENTARY produced by Fred FREED. It premiered as an *NBC White Paper*, a sequel to Freed's earlier documentary, *The Decision to Drop the Bomb: A Political History*. Made when nuclear proliferation was a growing concern, the film establishes the point that "the bomb is very easy to make, very inexpensive." Narrator Chet Huntley opens the film by commenting, "In the next hour we are going to talk about what no one wants to talk about; to think about the unthinkable," and the film goes on to imagine what might occur if ten or twenty nations possessed nuclear weapons. However, despite an ample budget and access to such experts in international politics as Ralph Lapp and Herman Kahn, author of ON THERMONUCLEAR WAR, the film was unsuccessful, even according to Freed, who later criticized it for "a failure of reporting. We didn't investigate with any depth. The real feeling of those countries without the bomb wasn't carefully analyzed as to whether they were actually going to build it . . . We simply accepted conventional wisdom." See also APOCALYPTIC FILMS.

For additional reading, see Shaheen's *Nuclear War Films*.

Counterattack: Facts to Combat Communism   An anti-communist MAGAZINE that began publication in 1947 and continued through 1971. *Counterattack* was published by American Business Consultants, a corporation formed by three former FBI agents, Theodore Kirkpatrick, John G.

Keenan and Kenneth M. Bierly, who were frustrated by the FBI's policy of refusing to make public its files on suspected communists and communist sympathizers. They began *Counterattack* as a newsletter and hired free-lance writer Sam Horn (whose pen name was Andrew Avery) to write it while they handled the business end and made policy. In 1952, the magazine's circulation was about 4,000 copies per issue, at a subscription price of $24 a year. The magazine ran articles identifying alleged communists and fellow travelers. Its greatest effect on Cold War culture, however, was its publication of a special report entitled RED CHANNELS, which listed people within the entertainment industry who had been identified in any of a variety of sources as having communist past or present affiliations. *Red Channels* quickly became a major source for BLACKLISTING in the television and radio industries during the RED SCARE.

For additional reading, see Cogley's *Report on Blacklisting.*

counterculture American Cold War ideology championed capitalism as the bulwark against communism, and the free market came to symbolize the other individual freedoms in the West that were curtailed behind the IRON CURTAIN. Thus the emergence of an American anti-capitalist counterculture during the 1960s and 1970s not only highlighted the dissatisfaction of a minority of mostly younger citizens with the culture of consumerism, it also challenged several of the premises behind the Cold War itself. The term *counterculture* alludes to a loosely defined range of largely unaffiliated people who rejected "establishment" values in a variety of ways. In general, their politics were essentially left-of-center, though many were apolitical and repudiated politics altogether as part of society's process of corrupting and co-opting liberated human creativity and joy. Among those included in the counterculture were HIPPIES, some feminists, and individuals who moved to communes to live off the land and "get back to nature." The counterculture emerged in conjunction with opposition to the Vietnam War, and it typically rejected militarism and the politics of political domination, seeing itself as celebrating life within a larger society that glorified death. Many members of the counterculture sympathized with the sentiments expressed by the BEAT MOVEMENT and by such later poets as Robert BLY who sought to revitalize human spirituality within a culture seen as materialistic and militaristic.

The counterculture's disaffection with capitalism stemmed from a belief that the Vietnam War and Cold War politics were largely motivated not by a much-proclaimed defense of freedom but rather by the need for Western corporations to create and control worldwide markets and generate vast profits through military spending. Moreover, the counterculture frequently opposed the waste implicit in consumer capitalism, which encouraged material rather than spiritual values, produced pollution and otherwise despoiled the environment. Many members of the counterculture thus became involved in the nascent environmentalist movement of the 1970s. Others attributed capitalistic domination of nature and society to the nation's patriarchal social structure and supported the second-wave feminist movement of the 1970s.

Members of the counterculture often adopted so-called "alternative life-styles," rejecting corporate and industrial life in favor of communes on small farms or livelihoods based on art and craft. These life-styles reflected a predilection for creativity, imagination and the unconventional and sought to avoid the demands for conformity imposed by corporate and middle-class America. Attire was often unconventional—blue jeans and T-shirts frequently replaced the corporate suit and tie, and men and women often dressed similarly. On the other hand, some of the fashions harkened back to pre-industrial cultures in which women wore long skirts and favored hand-made clothing made from natural fibers. Many men grew their hair and beards long. Elements of the counterculture also explored their creativity through such "mind-expanding" drugs as marijuana, peyote and LSD, though certainly not all drug users from the period were members of the counterculture and not all members of the counterculture used drugs. Indeed, many rejected the ingestion of any chemicals and eschewed not only narcotics but also prescription drugs, diet drinks containing additives, processed foods and virtually anything else that was not considered organic. Some illegal drug users did consider marijuana and peyote natural while rejecting additives and other artificial products.

The quest for purity of mind and body led some to reject television and what they believed to be other violent and debased forms of American popular culture, and to practice yoga, meditation and other disciplines associated with Eastern religion. Alternately, some members of the counterculture embraced ROCK AND ROLL, electronic music and other aspects of high technology. Again, some in the counterculture reconciled both. Thus a considerable range of attitudes and practices existed in what we call the counterculture, which absorbed many contradictory elements. What these elements had in common, however, was a belief that mainstream American culture was misguided and life-denying in its Cold War politics and consumer capitalism. In response, the counterculture sought, with varying degrees of success, to affirm life through nurturing, noncompetitive life-styles and economies. The conclusion of the Vietnam War in 1973 eliminated the common rallying point of the counterculture, elements of which either petered out, became an exercise in nostalgia or went on to acquire new focus and shape.

Cousins, Norman A JOURNALIST. Born in New Jersey in 1915, Cousins graduated from Columbia University Teacher's College in 1933. In 1934 he served as education editor for the *New York Evening Post* and then as book critic, literary editor and managing editor of *Current History* from 1935 to 1940, when he became executive editor of *The Saturday Review of Literature*. In 1942 he became editor and renamed the MAGAZINE *The Saturday Review*. He effectively held the post until 1977. As editor, Cousins expanded the publication's scope to include current events, science, the arts, education, travel and other matters of general interest. He contributed articles as well as editorials and took an active role in engaging the *Saturday Review* in the politics of the day. Soon after the conclusion of World War II, he called for readers to support a "moral adoption" program to aid children orphaned by the atom bomb. The fund-raising efforts he sponsored cared for and educated 440 Japanese children. Cousins also led efforts to bring to the United

States for medical treatment 24 "Hiroshima maidens" who had been deformed by the atom bomb, as well as 35 Polish women known as the "Ravensbruck Lapins," who had been brutalized by Nazi medical "experiments." (John Hersey's HIROSHIMA [1946] describes the experiences of the Hiroshima women.)

In the late 1940s and early 1950s, Cousins used the magazine to advocate nuclear nonproliferation and international efforts to promote peaceful uses of atomic energy, and he was a founder of the Committee for a Sane Nuclear Policy in 1957. He addresses nuclear energy and the need for disarmament in his NONFICTION books *Who Speaks for Man?* (1953) and *In Place of Folly* (1961). A member of the United World Federalists, Cousins in 1961 proposed empowering the United Nations so it could "define and carry out a program of orderly and enforceable disarmament under proper safeguards," and in a July 1962 editorial he argued that "the human imagination has not yet expanded to the point where it comprehends its own essential unity. People are not yet aware of themselves as a single interdependent entity." He further argued that national interest had to yield to a "world consciousness" predicated upon a "collective identity."

In 1960 Cousins helped begin a series of dialogues between U.S. and Soviet scientists called the Dartmouth Conferences. These took place in the United States and the Soviet Union between 1960 and 1964, one of the most intense periods of the Cold War, spanning the second Berlin Crisis and the Cuban Missile Crisis. Cousins criticized the Soviets' resumption of aboveground nuclear testing at the height of the Berlin Crisis in late August 1961, declaring in a September editorial, "Any nation that engages in atmospheric testing has in effect declared war on the human race." He likewise criticized the United States when it resumed atmospheric testing a few months later. In 1962 Cousins employed shuttle diplomacy among Kennedy, Khrushchev and Pope John XXIII to secure the release of Ukrainian Archbishop Josef Slipyi, whom the communists had imprisoned for 18 years. The line of communication Cousins established between the White House and the Kremlin helped make possible the 1963 Nuclear Test Ban Treaty. At Kennedy's request, Cousins helped establish the Citizens Committee for a Nuclear Test Ban, which lobbied for Senate confirmation of the treaty. Cousins traveled throughout the globe to meet with world leaders, among them President Kennedy, Soviet premier Nikita Khrushchev, Indian prime minister Nehru, and head of the Palestine Liberation Organization (PLO), Yasir Arafat. He discusses his observations from these and other meetings in *Human Options* (1981). Cousins also took editorial positions against the Vietnam War and in favor of space exploration, as well as stands on such non-Cold War topics as racial discrimination, pollution, television violence and cigarette advertising.

He left the magazine in 1971 when new owners planned to divide it into four separate monthlies, but after that plan failed and the new ownership filed for bankruptcy, Cousins returned as editor and chairman of the board of the company that took over the publication under the new title, *Saturday Review/World*. Within a year, the magazine resumed the title *Saturday Review* and again became profitable, and Cousins won the Magazine Publishers Association's 1973

award for publisher of the year. He sold the magazine in 1977 and became editor emeritus when it was resold in 1980. The *Saturday Review* finally went out of business in 1982. Cousins published some 18 books and edited several others. His articles published in *The Saturday Review* cover developments in Laos (1961), nuclear war (1961), fallout shelters (1961), Cuba (1962), General Douglas MacArthur (1964), his visit with Khrushchev (1964), the Vietnam peace process (1969) and Watergate (1974), among other topics. In addition to addressing social and political issues, he wrote about medicine in *The Healing Heart: Antidotes to Panic and Helplessness* (1983), a book that was occasioned by his own near-fatal heart attack and his belief in the power of vitamin C and "large doses of love, hope, faith, laughter, confidence and the will to live." He died in 1990.

For additional reading, see *Dictionary of Literary Biography* (vol. 137, *American Magazine Journalists 1900–1960, Second Series*).

"Cover Up" A TELEVISION SPY SHOW that ran on CBS in 1984–85. This Reagan-era show tried to combine espionage and sex appeal. Mac Harper (Jon-Erik Hexum) was a handsome male model, and Danielle Reynolds (Jennifer O'Neill) was a beautiful fashion photographer. Together, they traveled the world on assignment, going from photo shoots to fashion shows with scantily clad models. Under their professional cover, however, they served as secret agents working for a mysterious U.S. government agency. A former Green Beret, Mac was a master of karate, chemical interrogation and foreign languages. Danielle, the widow of a secret agent, also had special skills and knowledge. The title, "Cover Up," punned by merging the "plausible deniability" surrounding the secret assignments with the show's numerous, scantily clad models who needed to "cover up." The short-lived show combined the glamour and glitz of the Reagan years with the Cold War concerns that underlay the era.

Crack in the World A 1965 SCIENCE FICTION FILM starring Dana Andrews, Janette Scott and Kieron Moore and directed by Andrew Marton. This film presents the possibility of nuclear apocalypse when a dying scientist fires a missile into the Earth's core and nearly destroys the planet. (See also APOCALYPTIC FILMS.)

Crazy Iris and Other Stories of the Atomic Bomb, The A 1984 collection of eight Japanese short stories edited by Kenzaburo Oe. These stories chronicle the impact of the atomic bombings of Hiroshima and Nagasaki on the lives of a spectrum Japanese citizens, including peasants, professionals, artists, children and others. (See also APOCALYPTIC NOVELS.)

Cronkite, Walter A television correspondent and anchor of "The CBS Evening News." He joined CBS in 1950 and in 1952 covered the first televised presidential nominating conventions. He anchored the CBS weekend show "The Week in Review" from 1951 to 1962, when he replaced Douglas Edwards as the managing editor and anchorman of the "CBS Evening News." Cronkite held that post until his retirement in 1981. In addition to his work as a news anchor, he covered political conventions and narrated several documentary and informational shows for CBS, including AIR POWER (1956–57), "*Eyewitness to History*" (1960–63), THE FACTS WE FACE (1950–51), *The 20th Century* (1957–67), "*The 21st Century*" (1967–69), "*Universe*" (1980–82) and YOU ARE THERE (1953–57, 1971–72). Appearing on CBS television continuously for over 30 years, Cronkite became one of the most trusted figures in America. Through his reporting and in his role as anchorman and managing editor, he played a significant role in determining how the Cold War was presented to America. In February 1968, after returning from Vietnam during the Tet Offensive, he rejected the official U.S. government forecasts of eventual victory, declaring in his February 27 broadcast that it seemed "more certain than ever that the bloody experience of Vietnam is to end in a stalemate." Cronkite's change in attitude about the war has been credited with significantly helping to reshape the American consensus about fighting the war; it certainly helped fuel the arguments of the antiwar movements, as well as creating a category of liberal thought that saw the war as unwinnable whether or nor it was considered well-intentioned. Cronkite concluded each of his broadcasts with his signature, "That's the way it is," though in his final broadcast in 1981 he undermined that statement by describing the inevitable manipulation that accompanies the presentation of the news. (See also TELEVISION NEWS SHOWS and TELEVISION DOCUMENTARIES.)

Crossing in Berlin A 1981 POLITICAL NOVEL by Fletcher KNEBEL. Published a year after the disintegration of the 1970s U.S.–Soviet détente and during a resurgence of the environmental movement, the novel centers on Mike Simmons, a middle-aged American businessman who comes to East Germany as a subcontractor for a Swedish company contracted to build a hotel in Leipzig. His son is a military helicopter pilot stationed in West Germany. The book opens with a bleak picture of Leipzig, where newspaper headlines give a distorted anti-capitalist spin to the news and the number-one pastime is to search for the few consumer goods that occasionally appear on the store shelves. Stern government bureaucrats supervise individual activities, and a visiting Soviet official observes that "capitalist women had a sexual sheen that he had failed to spot among females of the Socialist Bloc." East Germany's opera, on the other hand, can compete with the best in the United States. The book's anti-communist orientation becomes further evident in the tension between East Berliners and the Soviets because, "ever since the Polish labor confrontation [with the Solidarity trade union] startled the world the previous year, new anxieties complicated the usual tension between the Soviet Union and the small countries it had corralled for Communism at the close of World War II." Now East Germans feared that their "benefactor's tanks might come calling in their neighborhoods." The book's expository section also reminds readers of the Berlin Wall, the U.S.-Soviet confrontation at the Brandenburg Gate in 1961 and the "forty miles of the armed, mined, raked, fenced, electrified, gunned, trapped, patrolled, and dog-guarded" East German frontier.

Early in the novel, Simmons takes an East German lover, a chemist named Gisela, who seeks his assistance in arranging her defection. She desires to leave because "I have

learned something that leaders of the West must be told." After telling Simmons that he is "an American, naive about world politics and about what it means to be a prisoner in one's own country . . . [and] without appreciation for the ambivalent feelings of a woman," Gisela reveals that her secret involves a colleague's research on the greenhouse effect. His findings show that the dangers from air pollution by burning oil, coal and other fossil fuels are far more imminent than currently believed in the West. But East German officials have suppressed the information and imprisoned her colleague, as the data threaten to undermine their efforts to increase industrial production and export coal. Eventually, the officials detain Gisela as well, and the plot then centers on Simmon's efforts to gain Gisela's freedom and her entry into the West. Although Knebel had written earlier political best-sellers, including SEVEN DAYS IN MAY (1962) and NIGHT OF CAMP DAVID (1965), *Crossing in Berlin* received scant critical attention and was not widely reviewed.

Crucible, The A 1953 play by Arthur MILLER. Though Miller has consistently resisted attempts to read *The Crucible* as an allegory of the HOUSE COMMITTEE ON UN-AMERICAN ACTIVITIES (HUAC), the RED SCARE and BLACKLISTING, most commentators continue to perceive it as such. Presumably Miller's concern is that this interpretation limits the scope of the play to a single historical moment, depriving it of applications that extend beyond the 1950s congressional inquests into the political activities of the entertainment industry. As he said in 1965, "McCarthyism may have been the historical occasion of the play, not its theme." He amplifies in the introduction to his *Collected Plays*: "It was not only the rise of McCarthyism that moved me, but something which seemed more weird and mysterious. It was the fact that a political, objective, knowledgeable campaign from the far Right was capable of creating not only a terror, but a new subjective reality, a veritable mystique which was gradually assuming even a holy resonance." Miller began writing the play shortly after his former collaborator, film director Elia KAZAN testified before HUAC and, despite Miller's efforts to dissuade him, named past and current members of the Communist Party. Miller, who had not been a communist, was subpoenaed to testify before HUAC in 1956. By that time he had already been blacklisted in Hollywood. He stated his willingness to tell the committee about his own activities and beliefs, but he refused to discuss anyone else or identify anyone he believed to be a communist, citing his First Amendment protection. Since the Supreme Court had already upheld the contempt of Congress citations issued against the HOLLYWOOD TEN, who likewise had invoked the First Amendment, Miller risked a one-year prison sentence by taking this stand. However, he was fined only $500 and given a 30-day suspended sentence.

The play dramatizes the 17th-century Salem witch hunts and centers around John Proctor, a good but flawed man who goes to his death rather than indict innocent people before a tribunal. Like the hearings conducted by HUAC and Senator Joseph McCarthy (R, Wisconsin), which were motivated by political agendas that extended beyond their ostensible fact-finding missions, the witch hunts in *The Crucible* also have ulterior motives. They allow wealthy citizens to obtain the land of the tribunal's victims, while other citizens pursue vendettas against personal enemies. Thus one of the heroes in the play is Giles Corey, who elects to be crushed to death rather than enter a plea of either innocent or guilty, thereby circumventing the legal machinations by which his property would have become forfeit and his family left destitute. Proctor's wife, Elizabeth, is also implicated by someone with personal motives. She realizes that her former servant, Abigail, whom she cast out of the house after Proctor had an affair with her seven months earlier, "thinks to kill me, then to take my place." Witnesses called to testify before HUAC could clear themselves by admitting to past communist affiliations and naming others who had been party members, thereby clearing themselves while subjecting others to blacklisting and other forms of persecution. Likewise, after one of Abigail's cohorts accuses Proctor of being "the Devil's man," in order to cover up her own earlier mendacity, Proctor can escape harm only by confessing his guilt and then implicating others as witches. Proctor tries to save himself by making a false spoken confession, but he refuses to name others: "I speak for my own sins; I cannot judge another. I have no tongue for it." He asks how he can teach his children to "walk like men in the world, and I sold my friends?" He finally refuses to sign his confession in order to preserve his good name, going to his death rather than betraying his values and his soul. "I do think I see some shred of goodness in John Proctor," he says finally. (See also THEATER.)

For additional reading, see Hughes' *Plays, Politics and Polemics*.

"Crusader, The" A TELEVISION SPY SHOW that ran in syndication from 1955 to 1956. One of the most direct expressions of the Cold War in television drama, "Crusader" depicted the dedication of free-lance writer Matt Anders (Brian Keith) to the cause of helping people oppressed by communism. Holding the communists responsible for the death of his mother, whom Polish officials had incarcerated in a labor camp, Matt employed every means possible to free others from communist tyranny. Aired at the end of the first Eisenhower administration, "Crusader" reflected the popular American concern with Eastern Europe. The show coincided with Secretary of State John Foster Dulles's advocacy of a never-enacted "liberation policy" whose ultimate goal was the liberation of Eastern European countries from communist control.

Cuba A 1979 FILM COMEDY starring Sean Connery, Brooke Adams and Jack Weston and directed by Richard Lester. Made during the Carter presidency, when rapprochement with Cuba was considered possible and a slightly more sympathetic view of Castro was beginning to emerge in the United States, *Cuba* satirizes the island's pre-Castro military dictatorships and its revolutions. Connery stars as a British mercenary who has been recruited to help crush Castro's revolution. The satire emphasizes how the selfishness and corruption of dictator Fulgencio Batista, his cohorts and American businessmen contributed to Castro's success.

Cuba, Si! A 1968 play by Terrence McNally. The story centers on a female supporter of Fidel Castro named Cuba who has established a "beachhead" for the revolution in Central Park, where she delivers pro-Castro diatribes to anyone who will listen. She captures the attention of a newspaper reporter and they discuss politics. The lively girl is engaging and fun-loving, so when she "dispatches" (kills) a would-be infiltrator of her camp she shocks both the audience and the reporter, to whom she declares, "That's revolutionary politics, sweetheart. You think because I laugh I play games?" To some extent she may also be speaking for McNally, whose playful writing style masks a serious political purpose. (See also THEATER.)

For additional reading, see *Dictionary of Literary Biography* (vol. 7, *Twentieth-Century American Dramatists*).

Cuban Thing, The A 1968 play by Jack Gelber. Gelber is best known for his experimental play *The Connection*, produced by the LIVING THEATER in 1959, which introduced jazz-inspired improvisation to theater and collapsed the distance between the audience and the actors. Gelber had visited Cuba in 1963 and 1967 and conceived *The Cuban Thing* as a part of a HAPPENING, a Cuban Action Night that would also include Cuban music, food and other cultural and political events centering on Cuba. However, he was unable to raise the financial support for the project, so he opened the play by itself at Henry Miller's Theater in New York in 1968. *The Cuban Thing* presents the accomplishments of the revolution as viewed by a middle-class Cuban family. Considered pro-Castro, it was violently attacked in the Cuban-American press (dominated by anti-Castro exiles) and on Spanish-speaking television and radio even before it opened. Gelber and some of the actors received threats, and on the preview before opening night the theater was bombed. Five men were later convicted for the attack, which used sophisticated powder bombs. The play ran for only one evening, as audiences were afraid to attend it. Moreover, reviewers criticized the play as poorly researched, though supporters of the play believed those criticisms were actually excuses for a political rejection of the play. (See also THEATER.)

For additional reading, see *Dictionary of Literary Biography* (vol. seven, *Twentieth-Century American Dramatists*).

Cultural and Scientific Conference for World Peace
A 1949 international peace conference held in New York and sponsored by the National Council of Arts, Sciences and Professions. Among those participating were Arthur MILLER, Norman MAILER, Charles CHAPLIN, Thomas MANN, Leonard Bernstein, Dorothy Parker, Lillian Hellman, Langston Hughes, Mark van Doren, F. O. Matthiessen, Adam Clayton Powell, Susan B. Anthony II and sculptor Jo Davidson. Held in the early days of the RED SCARE, the peace conference, which advocated disarmament and reconciliation among the superpowers, was attacked by right-wing anti-communists for serving a communist agenda. For instance, on April 4, 1949, Henry LUCE's *Life* magazine ran a highly critical article claiming that the conference was "dominated by intellectuals who fellow-travel the Communist line." The article featured pictures of 50 personalities who attended, describing them as "Dupes and Fellow Travelers" and stating that they ranged from "hard working fellow travelers to soft-headed do-gooders."

Damnation Alley A 1977 FILM DRAMA starring Jan-Michael Vincent, George Peppard and Dominique Sanda and directed by Jack Smight. It was based on the 1969 novel by Roger Zelazny. The story centers on four survivors of World War III who attempt to reach a colony of other survivors. (See also APOCALYPTIC FILMS.)

dance As in other forms of modern artistic expression such as ART and MUSIC, the Eastern and Western societies differed on the role of dance within their societies and on the degree to which individual expression should be encouraged or tolerated. Because communism was predicated on the belief that the individual found his or her fullest expression through the collective, the communist regimes often discouraged or even forbade styles of art that were primarily expressionist, that is, whose main goal was to express an individual's emotions or idiosyncratic vision. In these societies, individual's emotions were considered to be of secondary importance, and the expression of personal passions might divert attention or commitment from the needs of the entire society. George ORWELL had an additional theory: As he suggested NINETEEN EIGHTY-FOUR, (1949) controlling personal expression was a means of maintaining power. Finally, Russian art had always focused more on social or religious themes, and even before the Revolution, abstract and expressionistic work had been considered "European" and foreign. For a variety of reasons, then, in the visual arts the Soviet Union and its allies behind the IRON CURTAIN discouraged abstract expressionism and instead promoted socialist realism, whose purpose was to celebrate and promote the Soviet people as a whole—the collective—shifting emphasis from the identity and individuality of the artist.

Similarly, the communist countries rarely encouraged experimentation in dance, preferring either traditional folk dances, which emphasized group performance and national tradition over individual virtuosos and personality, or traditional ballet in which the Bolshoi and Kirov Ballets had gained international renown. The free-spirited, loosely styled and sexually suggestive Western dances associated with ROCK AND ROLL and Western discotheques were denounced as decadent and/or obscene.

Many American religious figures and conservatives also condemned rock music and the dancing it engendered on similar grounds. However, the U.S. Constitution severely limited any attempts to censor music and dance, since both art forms were held to be forms of personal expression protected under the First Amendment. In general, the Western democracies protected artistic expression to a much greater extent than did the communist states. Moreover, free-market capitalism gained vitality by permitting, if not always encouraging, a wide range of personal expression. Thus abstract art and new musical forms such as JAZZ and rock and roll thrived in the West—and created new, lucrative markets for investors and entrepreneurs—while they were suppressed behind the Iron Curtain. Similarly, Western forms of expressionist modern dance blossomed during the Cold War, in contrast to the more conservative and traditionalist approach to dance taken in the communist countries. Prevalent in the West were the sexually suggestive dances that accompanied rock music and that were often favored by teenagers, such as the Twist, the Hully Gully and many variations in which dancers move sensuously or provocatively to sometimes pulsating music. Popular audiences also watched and danced to such free-style exuberant steps as the Freddy, a dance more joyous, humorous and absurd than sexual. Another Western dance innovation was break-dancing, a 1980s form of street dance that imitated machinery in precise, jerky movements.

Professional dance companies also experimented with expressionism as they developed new strains of modern dance. Among the more well-known modern dance choreographers in the Cold War era were Martha Graham, Merce Cunningham, Alvin Ailey, Twyla Tharp, Antony Tudor, Jerome Robbins and Kenneth MacMillan. Soviet emigré George Balanchine, the artistic director of the New York City Ballet, abandoned many of the restraints imposed by the traditional bodily symmetry of 19th-century ballet and pioneered new, expressionistic movements and choreography that Soviet dance companies were not allowed to develop. Balanchine's work was also featured by the Robert Joffrey Ballet (later briefly called the City Center Joffrey Ballet), which additionally performed pieces choreographed by Ailey and Tudor on their tours of Europe, Asia and the Soviet Union. The American Ballet Theater (ABT) encouraged experimentation and featured works by these choreographers as well.

The opportunities for a greater range of artistic expression appealed to several of the leading Soviet dancers who, though they received special, luxurious treatment from their government, felt frustrated by the limited range of what they were allowed to perform. Thus during the Cold War, several important Soviet dancers defected to the West in search of artistic freedom rather than to escape political persecution. (However, some critics claimed that many of these dancers were actually in pursuit of the greater economic opportunities in the West, where some continued to dance the same classical repertoire that they had in the Soviet Union.) Most notable of the Soviet emigré dancers were Rudolf NUREYEV (1961), Natalia MAKAROVA (1970), Mikhail BARYSHNIKOV (1974) and Alexander GODUNOV (1979). They all went on to receive acclaim in the West for both classical and modern dance. Nureyev danced with England's Royal Ballet from 1962 to 1979 and was frequently paired with Margot Fonteyn. He directed the Paris Opera Ballet from 1983 to 1989 and died in Paris in 1993. Makarova danced with the ABT before moving to London to perform with Nureyev in Europe. She also encouraged Baryshnikov to dance with the ABT shortly after his defection. He did so and went on to become the company's artistic director from 1980 to 1990. Godunov also danced with the ABT for three years before leaving due to artistic differences with Baryshnikov. He then performed on television and film before dying in 1995. Dance critic Nancy Goldner's review of Makarova's performance in Alvin Ailey's jazz-like dance *The River* describes the passion behind these artists' need to gain their artistic freedom: "As I was watching Makarova cavort, swing her hips, smile brazenly at the audience, and pout à la Bardot at Bruhn [her partner], I thought, so

this is what this lady came to America for . . . She won her point."

"Danger Man"   A TELEVISION SPY SHOW that ran on CBS in 1961. Starring Patrick McGoohan, who later starred in SECRET AGENT, this British-made show featured the exploits of internationally famous security investigator John Drake, who worked only for democratic governments or highly placed government officials. Affiliated with NATO, Drake was as comfortable with native tribes in the African jungles as he was with posh European high society. Produced at the beginning of the Kennedy administration, just as the United States and the United Nations were expanding their involvement in such countries as Vietnam, Laos and the nations of central Africa, the show's broad international setting suggested that the threats to national security were worldwide.

"Dangerous Assignment"   A TELEVISION SPY SHOW that ran in syndication in 1952. Starring Brian Donlevy as undercover agent Steve Mitchell, this was among the first "secret agent" television shows to feature intense violence in an international setting. "Dangerous Assignment" began as a radio show in 1940, prior to the U.S. entry into World War II.

Dark December   A 1958 APOCALYPTIC NOVEL by Alfred Coppel. Published at the outset of the most threatening period of the Cold War, 1958–62, *Dark December* considers who should lead a postapocalyptic society and what that society's values and aspirations should be. Specifically, the novel celebrates Major Gavin, an officer who launched missiles from an underground silo in the nuclear war and, having survived the retaliation, vows never to kill again. But Gavin must reconcile his new humanist attitude with a lawless society predicated on rule by the strongest. His antagonist is Captain Collingwood, a brutal and bloodthirsty madman who nonetheless accurately points out that he has killed far fewer people than Gavin has. In the postnuclear world, competing social orders, values and figures of authority vie for power. Reflecting contemporary blue-collar resentment of the emerging class of technocrats that was assuming power in Cold War America, Collingwood accuses, "You button pushers. For a while you had it all your own way. You could hide in your holes and let the computer and the rockets do your fighting for you. But not any more . . . You've made us important again. A man with a bayonet and a gun fighting for a piece of ground." In response Gavin thinks, "My God . . . The world smashed and burned and bleeding and here it was ready to start all over again. Here was the face of the real enemy. The man with a bayonet eager to kill." In a triumph for enlightened liberalism, Gavin ultimately prevails and expresses his hope that humanity will be able to recommence its progression up the evolutionary ladder. With his new lover and adopted son he hopes to begin a new race of humans that will elevate the species "as Cro-Magnon did over Neanderthal."

For additional reading, see Dowling's *Fictions of Nuclear Disaster*.

"David Susskind Show, The"   A TELEVISION TALK OR DEBATE SHOW that ran in syndication from 1961 to 1987. It was originally titled "Open End" because the show had no set time limit, although eventually time limits were imposed. The liberal and erudite Susskind spoke with articulate and controversial guests. He interviewed Nikita Khrushchev in 1960, when the Soviet premier visited the United States. The show was aired on educational and public broadcast stations in many areas.

Davy A 1964 APOCALYPTIC NOVEL by Edgar Pangborn. Published two years after the Cuban Missile Crisis, the novel is set in the fourth century after the Age of Confusion ("Old Time" abruptly ended in 1993 following a brief but devastating nuclear war). A new medieval society has evolved in which a repressive church denies access to books and outlaws the manufacture of gunpowder "or any other substance that may . . . be reasonably suspected of containing atoms." But the protagonist, Davy, rebels: "I say to hell with the laws that forbid most Old-Time books or reserve them to the priests." He vows to find and publish the forbidden *Book of John Barth,* a reference to the writer JOHN BARTH, a contemporary of Pangborn's known for his BLACK HUMOR, exuberant writing style, ornate narrative structure and self-conscious narrators. Like Barth's hero Todd Andrews in *The Floating Opera* (1956) Davy is also a self-conscious storyteller who worries about the inherent contradictions in narration. Though others have speculated about the effect of a NUCLEAR APOCALYPSE on language, Pangborn's interest in the shape of postnuclear literature and the artistic challenges that would befall a postnuclear storyteller appears to be unique. Like other apocalyptic novels, *Davy* reaffirms the importance of retaining the best of the Western humanistic tradition, including its arts and letters. But where other authors are intent on preserving such past masterpieces as *Paradise Lost* and Plato's *Dialogues,* Pangborn reminds us that many contemporary authors also deserve to be preserved. Other related novels by Pangborn include *The Judgment of Eve* (1966), *The Company of Glory* (1975), and *Still I Persist in Wondering* (1978).

For additional reading, see Dowling's *Fictions of Nuclear Disaster.*

Davy Crockett, King of the Wild Frontier A 1955 MILITARY FILM starring Fess Parker, Buddy Ebsen and Basil Ruysdael and directed by Norman Foster. Spliced together from episodes of the Walt DISNEY television show, the story celebrates the heroics, wisdom, determination and good values of the American frontiersman who died fighting at the Alamo in 1836. As in other Cold War–era Disney enterprises, like Disneyland and Disney World, *Davy Crockett* reinforced an American mythology about its frontier past (and ignored unpleasant facts such as his support for slave-owning interests that wanted to annex Texas). In that mythology, heroic figures like Congressman Crockett embodied Disney's version of the American ideal: big and strong, respectful, clear about right and wrong, certain of men's and women's roles, and totally committed to doing the right thing. Though not brilliant, he has common sense in abundance and can be shrewd when necessary. According to this mythology, these qualities are responsible for America's success, and they form the basis of its security during the Cold War. Crockett was an especially inviting choice for mythologizing since he already existed in American popular culture as the larger-than-life legendary figure who could thaw out the sun and get it moving on a freezing cold day. Spin-offs from the film included the popular "Ballad of Davy Crockett" and a short-lived fashion fad featuring Crockett-style coonskin caps. Parker and Ebsen made a sequel in 1956, *Davy Crockett and the River Pirates.*

Day After, The A special TELEVISION DOCU-DRAMA AND MINI-SERIES that aired on ABC in 1983. Coinciding with the nuclear buildup of the first Reagan administration, *The Day After* graphically enacted the devastation that a nuclear attack might wreak upon a "typical" midwestern city, in this case, Lawrence, Kansas. Accused by conservatives of presenting a liberal, pacifist message, *The Day After* seemed to respond to statements by high-ranking Reagan administration officials suggesting that a nuclear war was winnable and that WITH ENOUGH SHOVELS Americans could adequately protect themselves in the event of a nuclear attack. Reagan administration statements represented a dramatic change in attitudes about nuclear warfare, which during the preceding era of détente had been represented as MAD—Mutually Assured Destruction. Broadcast over two consecutive nights, the controversial, widely viewed film not only depicted the physical devastation that the attack itself might cause, it also portrayed the difficulties of surviving after the war was over and the city had been destroyed. The program graphically portrayed the breakdown in law enforcement, medical support, communication technology and social services, as well as people's inability to procure food, clean water, medical supplies and other essential resources. Moreover, the film showed the outbreak of disease and radiation poisoning that would presumably characterize the aftermath of a nuclear attack. *The Day After* has been compared to the British-made pseudo-documentary THE WAR GAME (1966), another bleak depiction of a hypothetical attack on a population center. Some commentators felt that ABC's airing of the mini-series AMERIKA in 1987 represented an effort by the network to appease conservative critics who had objected to *The Day After*. *Amerika* enacts the fate of a United States that had become unwilling to fight against Soviet expansionism and that consequently fell under Soviet rule. (See also APOCALYPTIC FILMS.)

Day The Earth Caught Fire, The A British-made 1961 SCIENCE FICTION FILM starring Edward Judd, Janet Munro and Leo McKern and directed by Val Guest. This film was shot during the height of the second Berlin Crisis, as the Soviets were ending their three-year moratorium on nuclear testing by exploding a bomb 300 times more powerful than the one that leveled Hiroshima, and not accidentally, the film deals with the real and imagined dangers of nuclear testing. In a plea for international cooperation, the movie shows scientists from East and West working together to avert the imminent destruction of the planet after simultaneous U.S. and Soviet nuclear tests knock the Earth from its axis and send it out of its orbit toward the sun's gravitational field. The scientists attempt to restore the Earth to its proper orbit by simultaneously exploding four nuclear bombs near the equator. The film maintains an ambiguous ending, with the audience remaining unsure about whether the protagonists succeed. (See also APOCALYPTIC FILMS.)

For additional reading, see Shaheen's *Nuclear War Films.*

Day the Earth Stood Still, The   A 1951 SCIENCE FICTION FILM starring Patricia Neal, Michael Rennie and Hugh Marlowe and directed by Robert Wise. The film, which appeared during the Korean War, is set in a Washington, D.C., whose residents are gripped by fear of imminent atomic war. When a spaceship lands on the Washington Mall, the U.S. Army surrounds it and greets it with suspicion, despite the proclamation by spaceman Klaatu that "We have come to visit you in peace." When a soldier shoots Klaatu, Gort, an indestructible machine with a death ray, threatens to annihilate the entire city, but Klaatu calls off Gort just in time. Klaatu recovers from his wound and tries to call a summit meeting of the heads of state, but though all are in principle willing to meet, they cannot agree on an acceptable site. U.S. president Truman offers to speak with the spaceman alone but Klaatu declines, not wanting to drawn into the bickering. Finally, the spaceman gains access to an international community by befriending Professor Barnhardt, a scientist who resembles Albert Einstein. Klaatu tells him, "Soon one of your nations will apply atomic energy to spaceships—that will threaten the peace and security of other planets." So Klaatu shuts down energy sources throughout the world to demonstrate his own capacity to destroy the planet and arranges to speak before an international body of scientists. Afterward, he is once again shot by the authorities. But Gort revives the body, and Klaatu gives his farewell speech, "At the first sign of violence, your earth will be reduced to a burned-out cinder. Your choice— join us and live in peace, or face obliteration."

The film provided a kind of wish fulfillment for anxious audiences who felt that only well-intended, extraterrestrial intervention could solve the Cold War stalemate and end the world's seemingly inexorable progress toward nuclear war. The unwillingness of world leaders to compromise even over such insignificant issues as the meeting site with a space alien conveyed the great powers' intransigence and the consequent deadlock that seemed to characterize the Cold War. *The Day the Earth Stood Still* provided a rare liberal point of view of the RED SCARE: Since the audience sees from the start that Klaatu is well-meaning, the hysteria against him, like the Red Scare it suggests, is shown to be both dangerous and absurd. Pacifist intellectuals, who were in many cases victims of the Red Scare, are depicted sympathetically as the world's best hope for survival. For instance, the conference of scientists that Klaatu summons evokes the international 1949 CULTURAL AND SCIENTIFIC CONFERENCE FOR WORLD PEACE, which was attacked viciously in *Life* magazine and elsewhere as a subversive act of cooperation with the communists. In this film, however, the international dialogue appears as an intelligent attempt to end an absurd and dangerous course of human self-destruction. And the film depicts pacifism as the only sane solution to the Cold War, rather than as the subversive communist plot or dangerous weakness that more right-wing critics considered it. The association of Barnhardt with Einstein, an outspoken

pacifist, also creates somewhat left-wing sympathies, as does the film's central theme—that the world's countries must either seek peace or be destroyed. Moreover, like other contemporary science fiction films, *The Day the Earth Stood Still* represents scientists as the best hope for the human race, not only because of their knowledge but also because their intellect transcends their fears. Moreover, scientists already function as an international community and so represent a successful model for other cooperative human societies.

For additional reading, see Biskind's *Seeing Is Believing.*

Day the Fish Came Out, The   A 1967 Greek and British-made FILM SATIRE starring Tom Courtenay, Candice Bergen and Sam Wanamaker and written, produced and directed by Michael Cacoyannis. The story satirizes the military's attempts to retrieve nuclear material dropped near a Greek island. Cacoyannis is better known for directing *Electra* (1961), *Zorba the Greek* (1964) and *Iphigenia,* (1977), a powerful film about the beginning of the Trojan War that points to contemporary Greek politics. (See also APOCALYPTIC FILMS.)

Day the Hot Line Got Hot, The   A 1968 FILM COMEDY starring Charles Boyer, Robert Taylor and Marie Dubois and directed by Etienne Périer. This SPY FILM SPOOF shows a Soviet and an American spy being duped by their go-between.

Day Miami Died, The   A 1950s pseudo-TELEVISION DOCUMENTARY produced by the CBS affiliate in Miami and narrated by news commentator Ralph Renick. Part of a "For Your Information" (FYI) series produced by Miami's WTVJ, *The Day Miami Died* depicts what Miami would be like under communist control. Reported in documentary style, it shows police and government officials being taken before a firing squad for resisting the communist "take over." Renick points out that while these events did not actually happen in Miami, they did occur in Eastern Europe and, he says, they *could* happen here. In the program, Florida senator George Smathers speaks about the importance of preserving democracy, which he says requires remaining committed to truth, participating in civic matters, supporting schools, maintaining a belief in God and respecting everyone's right to worship God in whatever way they see fit. Other cities ran similar programs during the 1950s.

Day the Sun Blowed Up, The   A 1976 British-made FILM DOCUMENTARY directed by Stephen Peet and produced for the BBC. The film examines the Manhattan Project, which developed the atomic bomb during World War II, and it features recollections by and about many of the project's principal figures, including J. Robert Oppenheimer, Enrico Fermi and project director General Leslie Groves. Among the more interesting anecdotes is the claim that Oppenheimer had wagered a $10 bet that the bomb would fail its first test at Los Alamos. (See also APOCALYPTIC FILMS.)

Day the World Ended, The   A 1955 SCIENCE FICTION FILM starring Richard Denning, Lori Nelson and Adele Jergens and directed by Roger Corman. The story centers on survivors of a nuclear war who take refuge in the mountains but must fight off mutant three-eyed cannibals. (See also APOCALYPTIC FILMS.)

Deadly Affair A 1967 British-made SPY FILM starring James Mason, Simone Signoret, Lynn Redgrave and Maximilian Schell and directed by Sidney Lumet. Based on John LE CARRÉ's 1961 SPY NOVEL, CALL FOR THE DEAD, the story centers on the investigation of an apparent suicide by a British government employee and features international Cold War intrigue.

Deal of the Century A 1983 FILM COMEDY starring Chevy Chase, Sigourney Weaver and Gregory Hines and directed by William Friedkin. The film satirizes the international arms market of the early 1980s, when President Reagan initiated a dramatic U.S. arms build-up and a corresponding international weapons race. (See also FILM SATIRE.)

Dean's December, The A 1982 POLITICAL NOVEL by Saul Bellow. The story follows the experiences of Albert Corde, a former newspaperman, now an academic, who has traveled to Hungary to be with his wife who is caring for her dying mother. In Budapest he becomes entangled in the communist bureaucracy. At the same time, back home in Chicago, his involvement in a student murder scandal entangles him in controversy. The story thus contrasts two major cities on opposite sides of the Cold War. Chicago is characterized by anarchy, violence, racial discord, a rampant drug culture and poverty, whereas totalitarian Budapest imposes a repressive and stultifying order. Bellow, a Nobel Prize winner, thus mourns the shortcomings of both societies, one an example of individual liberties run wild, the other, a demonstration of individuals subordinated to the state. The reviewer for *Newsweek* called the book "Bellow's dourest, most dispirited book after *Mr. Sammler's Planet* (1970)," which had presented Bellow's despairing response to America's social and political anarchy of the late 1960s.

Death in Life: Survivors of Hiroshima A 1968 NONFICTION book by Robert Jay Lifton. Published during the early stages of the East-West détente, *Death in Life* studies the long-term psychological consequences of the atomic bombing on the survivors of Hiroshima, concluding that the nuclear event had severe long-term social and psychological consequences. The book thus provided a case study that informed Cold War discussions about the impact of nuclear war. Lifton was a psychologist who worked in Japan for several years before he began this study in 1962. He pointed out that the Japanese themselves had avoided such studies while other researchers who had begun them had become dispirited and abandoned the enterprise. Lifton therefore discusses the profound impact that performing the research had upon him, too.

Lifton interviewed 75 survivors for this landmark book: 33 whom he chose at random and 42 selected because of their prominence in nuclear and atomic politics. Lifton notes that the survivors, known as *hibakusha* ("explosion-affected persons") in Japanese, were treated like lepers in Japan, where they were frequently shunned for fear they might contaminate others. They were often denied employment because they tired easily and lacked motivation. They also held themselves in low self-esteem, suffering from persistent neuroses.

The book was generally praised for its powerful treatment of this frightening topic. *Newsweek* compared it to Bruno Bettelheim's study of World War II concentration camp survivors, *The Informed Heart* (1960). However, the more critical *New York Review of Books* called it a treatise on how to master death and complained that Lifton robbed the *hibakusha* of the unique, spiritual aspects of their experience in order to argue his own interpretation "and incidentally to denigrate any insight and discourage any action they may have initiated from it. Put crudely, not in the always considerate style of the author, they are a bunch of neurotics and therefore cannot get out of their box. Aggressive responses like revenge or political action are put down as mere spite or quite impractical (as well as being Communist-inspired)." *Death in Life* inspired TO DIE, TO LIVE, Robert Vas's 1976 FILM DOCUMENTARY about Hiroshima. Vas, a Hungarian concentration camp survivor, intercuts between black-and-white shots of Hiroshima immediately after the bombing in 1945 and color footage of Hiroshima in 1975 to show how the survivors reacted to their experience and how the experience continues to affect them. In his earlier work, HIROSHIMA (1946), John Hersey also presents the stories of atomic survivors.

"Decision: The Conflicts of Harry Truman" A TELEVISION NEWS show that ran in syndication during 1964. Former president Truman discussed the major events of his administration and gave background information about his most difficult and controversial decisions. Discussed within the 26 episodes were his ascension to the presidency, the Potsdam Conference and the beginning of the Cold War, Truman's decision to use the atomic bomb against Japan, the 1946 Soviet attempt to take over Iran, the Marshall Plan, the Berlin airlift, the recognition of the State of Israel, the RED SCARE and the Korean War, and Truman's firing of General Douglas MacArthur.

Decision to Drop the Bomb, The A 1965 TELEVISION DOCUMENTARY produced by Fred FREED. Narrated by Chet Huntley, it premiered as an "NBC White Paper." The film shows interviews with many of the major figures who helped decide to drop the atomic bomb on Hiroshima and Nagasaki. In addition to documenting the decision-making process, the film includes footage of the devastation at Hiroshima.

For additional reading, see Shaheen's *Nuclear War Films*.

Deer Hunter, The A 1978 VIETNAM WAR FILM starring Robert De Niro, Christopher Walken, John Savage and Meryl Streep and directed by Michael Cimino. The story follows a group of steelworker friends who fight together in Vietnam, where they are captured by the Viet Cong and made to play Russian roulette with a loaded pistol. They manage to break free and escape, but Steven (Savage) is badly wounded and Nick (Walken) is destroyed emotionally. De Niro plays Michael, the powerful, life-affirming friend (the Deer Hunter) who engineers their escape. He later goes back to Saigon just before its fall in 1975 in order to retrieve Nick, who had returned after the U.S. military withdrawal to pursue his new obsession with gambling and Russian roulette. The film thus shows a range of responses to the brutal experience of the war, from Steven's disability and embitterment to Nick's mental derangement to Michael's underlying sanity, which stems from his physical and emotional strength and his commitment to his own personal values. Streep plays Linda, Nick's girlfriend, who remains at home but is also affected by the war.

Critics of the film pointed out that it attributes actual U.S. and South Vietnamese military behavior to the North Vietnamese. The Viet Cong are shown to stage a My Lai-type massacre, to put their prisoners in tiger cages and to force prisoners to play Russian roulette—all actions actually taken by the United States and its allies.

Def-Con 4   A 1985 MILITARY FILM starring Tim Choate, Kate Lynch and Lenore Zann and directed by David L. Rich. This Reagan-era vision of NUCLEAR APOCALYPSE centers on a crew of astronauts who are orbiting the Earth when a major nuclear war breaks out. Eventually they return to a post-apocalyptic nightmare. One of the crew is eaten by cannibalistic teenagers; the survivors must deal with a crazed survivalist and a neofascist sadist. (See also APOCALYPTIC FILMS.)

Defector, The   A 1966 French and West German-made SPY FILM starring Montgomery Clift, Roddy McDowall, Jean-Luc Godard and Hardy Kruger and directed by Raoul Levy. The film is based on Paul Thomas's novel, *The Spy*, the story of an American physicist in East Germany who becomes involved in espionage.

"Defenders, The"   A TELEVISION DRAMA that ran on CBS from 1961 to 1965, during Kennedy's New Frontier and Johnson's Great Society, bringing new attention to social causes and civil rights. Starring E. G. Marshall and Robert Reed as father-and-son partners in the law firm Preston & Preston, "The Defenders" took on a range of social and political issues at a time when most television shows avoided such controversy. In addition to episodes about mercy killing and abortion, the show also touched on Cold War themes. One episode addressed the right of the U.S. government to restrict travel to unfriendly countries. Another, entitled *Blacklist* (January 1964), starred Jack Klugman and addressed the practice of BLACKLISTING in the television industry during the 1950s RED SCARE. Klugman and writer Ernest Kinoy won Emmy awards for the *Blacklist* episode.

Deighton, Len   A British NOVELIST. One of the more popular and critically acclaimed authors of SPY NOVELS, Deighton adapts the anti-hero to spy fiction. In this respect his work is similar to that of John LE CARRÉ, though Deighton's vision is more comic and less bleak. His first novel, THE IPCRESS FILE (1962), appeared in the year of the Cuban Missile Crisis and was made into a popular 1965 SPY FILM. The story centers on an out-of-shape, near-sighted British intelligence agent who traces a missing scientist and discovers that one of his own superiors is a spy. In contrast to the flashy, sexy James BOND—popular hero of novels and films during throughout the Cold War—Deighton's un-

named spy (Harry Palmer in the films) is an anti-hero who entered a career in espionage to avoid imprisonment for black marketeering while he was a sergeant stationed in Berlin. The novel's action, which involves double, triple and quadruple agents with apparently indiscernible loyalties, takes the unassuming hero to the Near East, a nuclear test site in the Pacific, and possibly behind the IRON CURTAIN. One reviewer points out that Deighton "recognizes that the spy—whose survival depends on his guile, cunning, and adaptability—is today's *picaro*," so that the Cold War spy genre becomes an occasion for updating one of the oldest forms of literary narrative.

The Ipcress File had two less successful sequels, *Funeral in Berlin* (book 1965, film 1965) and *Billion Dollar Brain* (book 1966, film 1967). *Funeral in Berlin* centers on efforts to smuggle a Russian scientist out of East Berlin with the aid of a Russian security officer. It too involves a complex plot and features double and triple agents. In *Billion Dollar Brain* Palmer delivers a mysterious canister to Finland and becomes enmeshed in an American megalomaniac's attempt to win control of the world.

Throughout the 1970s, Deighton showed that spying continued among the superpowers even during détente. *Spy Story* (1974) focuses on another reluctant anti-hero in a story centering on nuclear submarines and the possible defection of a Soviet admiral. *Yesterday's Spy* (1975) is the story of a "retired British agent of distinguished achievement" with the French Resistance who may have gone to work for Egypt. *Catch a Falling Spy* (1976; English title, *Twinkle, Twinkle, Little Spy*) recounts efforts by British and American agents to protect an idiosyncratic defecting Soviet scientist. The action characteristically takes the team throughout the world, from the Sahara to New York to France to Miami Beach. In the waning days of the Cold War, Deighton wrote three more spy stories, *Spy Hook* (1988), *Spy Line* (1989) and *Spy Sinker* (1990), all in his characteristic style.

"Delphi Bureau, The"   A TELEVISION SPY SHOW that ran on ABC in 1972–73. Starring Laurence Luckinbill as Glenn Garth Gregory and Anne Jeffreys as Sibyl Van Loween, a high society hostess and Gregory's contact at the super-secret Delphi Bureau, this Nixon-era show offered the standard espionage-story fare: coded messages, hidden islands and free-wheeling agents from countries throughout the world. The Delphi Bureau itself was ostensibly a research agency; in fact, its operations were so secret that the bureau's office was in a moving limousine. The limousine projected qualities of affluence and mobility while suggesting the extremely sensitive and dangerous nature of the bureau's work. In many ways, the qualities associated with the limousine reflected the way Americans often pictured themselves vis-à-vis the Soviets: sleek, affluent, on the move, possessed of the most expensive and up-to-date equipment, and enjoying the good life while playing the tricky and deadly game of the Cold War in order to protect their prized way of life.

DeMille, Cecil B.   A FILM DIRECTOR. One of the pioneers of the film industry, DeMille played an important role in developing the classic Hollywood style of filmmaking and in shaping the structure of the Hollywood studio system.

Cecil B. DeMille. Courtesy Paramount Pictures.

Diplomatic Courier A 1952 SPY FILM starring Tyrone Power, Patricia Neal and Karl Malden and directed by Henry Hathaway. Critically well received, the film features U.S. and Soviet agents trying to outmaneuver each other on a train from Salzburg to Trieste.

Disney, Walt An animator, film studio owner, and television producer. The creator of the highly popular Mickey Mouse, Disney testified as a friendly witness in the 1947 HOUSE COMMITTEE ON UN-AMERICAN ACTIVITIES (HUAC) hearings on communist influence in Hollywood films. His testimony included an accusation that communists were attempting to subvert Mickey by taking over the Cartoonists Guild. He also alleged that the Communist Party had instigated a strike at his studio, and he identified several people he believed to be communists. During the 1950s and early 1960s, Disney films frequently championed patriotic causes. His idealized treatment of American pioneers and historical figures also reinforced the Cold War view of Americans dedicated to freedom and virtue, as in the film DAVY CROCKETT: KING OF THE WILD FRONTIER (1955). Crockett is big and strong, clear about right and wrong, certain of men's and women's roles, and totally committed to doing the right thing. Though not brilliant, he has common sense in abundance and can be shrewd when necessary. In Disney's mythology, these qualities are responsible for the success of the American nation, and they are the basis of America's security during the Cold War. These themes are also found in his entertainment parks Disneyland and Disney World and in Disney's popular television show, "Walt Disney Presents (ABC/NBC/CBS 1954–83, 1986–90)", which ran under

DeMille was strongly anti-union—in 1945 he quit a successful radio show that he had hosted and directed for nine years rather than join a radio union—and during the late 1940s and 1950s, he emerged as a leader among Hollywood's right wing. His Cecil B. DeMille Foundation regularly provided information to the HOUSE COMMITTEE ON UN-AMERICAN ACTIVITIES (HUAC) and other bodies investigating communist influences in Hollywood, and in 1950 he led a key battle within the Screen Directors Guild to require a loyalty oath of all members.

DeMille's EPIC FILMS celebrated Christian and democratic values, which he saw as the first line of defense against communism. His prologue before the 1956 remake of THE TEN COMMANDMENTS made explicit his view of the relationship between his epic films and the Cold War: "The theme . . . is whether men are to be ruled by God's law—or whether they are to be ruled by the whims of a dictator . . . Are men the property of the state? Or are they free souls under God? This same battle continues throughout the world today." The epic's enormous cast, vast sets and expensive props, as well as the huge scope of epic films were also seen as proof of the superiority of capitalism: No films made behind the IRON CURTAIN could even approach the seemingly endless store of resources in America.

Walt Disney, 1955. Courtesy AP/Wide World.

different titles for 29 consecutive seasons—the longest run of any prime-time television series.

Disneyland (opened 1955) and Disney World (opened 1971) both celebrate the American past, especially its frontier and small-town heritage, and their exhibits illustrate how corporate capitalism has aided technological progress, improved the quality of life, and secured a bright future for the United States. James Monaco suggests in *The Encyclopedia of Film* that, along with George Lucas and Jim Henson, Disney did more than anyone "to establish the gallery of characters who now populate contemporary childhood." These characters reflected his Cold War values.

For additional reading see Fjellman's *Vinyl Leaves: Walt Disney and America; The Encyclopedia of Film;* Dorfman and Mattelhart's *How to Read Donald Duck: Imperialist Ideology in the Disney Comics.*

Dmytryk, Edward   A FILM DIRECTOR and member of the HOLLYWOOD TEN. Between 1929 and 1949 Dmytryk directed 24 films including *Crossfire* and *Hitler's Children,* both critiques of anti-Semitism. He had been a member of the Communist Party but left in 1945. In 1947 he was called to testify at the HOUSE COMMITTEE ON UN-AMERICAN ACTIVITIES (HUAC) hearings on alleged communist influences within Hollywood films. Like the other members of the Hollywood Ten, Dmytryk refused to testify, citing his First Amendment right of free speech. As a result, he was fired from RKO and subjected to BLACKLISTING in Hollywood. Subsequently he went to England to make two films but was arrested for contempt of Congress when he returned to the United States to have his passport renewed. He received a six-month prison term, which he served in 1950.

Dmytryk claims that even before his imprisonment he had considered breaking away from the Ten, with whom he had ideological differences, but he decided to wait until after he had served his sentence so people would not think he was simply trying to avoid jail. While in prison, however, he issued a statement saying that although he believed he was correct to refuse to testify before HUAC, he was not then or now a party member and that he recognized the United States as the only country to which he was loyal. This statement enabled his agent to negotiate for new projects with Columbia after Dmytryk completed his jail term. At fellow-Ten member Herbert BIBERMAN's request, Dmytryk agreed to sign a petition supporting the parole applications of the remaining Ten who were still imprisoned, on the condition that he receive no publicity for doing so. However, Dmytryk's cooperation *was* widely publicized and as a result, his contract with Columbia was scuttled. Dmytryk therefore felt betrayed by the rest of the Ten, and shortly thereafter he decided to "rehabilitate" himself by writing an anti-communist article in 1951 for the *Saturday Evening Post* entitled "What Makes a Hollywood Communist." Then he reappeared before HUAC and identified 26 people who had been in the party while he was an active member. All had been previously identified by other witnesses, and all were already blacklisted. Dmytryk told HUAC that he was changing his position because of developments in world events, including the Korean War and the Alger Hiss case and that he would support the United States in a war against the Soviet Union.

Commenting in 1973 on his 1951 testimony he asserted, "With me it was [that] defending the Communist Party was something worse than naming the names. I did not want to remain a martyr to something that I absolutely believed was immoral and wrong. It's as simple as that." After testifying, Dmytryk was removed from the blacklist, and he went on to direct many notable films, including *The Caine Mutiny* (1954), *The Young Lions* (1958), *Walk on the Wild Side* (1962) and THE HUMAN FACTOR (1975). He also appeared in HOLLYWOOD ON TRIAL, a 1976 FILM DOCUMENTARY about the RED SCARE in the film industry, directed by fellow Hollywood Ten member Lester COLE. Dmytryk's autobiography, *It's a Hell of a Life But Not a Bad Living,* appeared in 1979.

For additional reading, see Navasky's *Naming Names.* For a partial transcript of Dmytryk's testimony before HUAC, see Bentley's THIRTY YEARS OF TREASON.

Dr. No   A 1958 SPY NOVEL by Ian Fleming and a 1962 British-made SPY FILM starring Sean Connery, Ursula Andress and Jack Lord and directed by Terence Young. The first of a highly successful series of James BOND films, *Dr. No* introduced the suave, sexy and skillful secret agent who saves the world from nuclear blackmail by the fiendish Dr. No, who plans to blow up a space rocket being launched from Cape Canaveral. In addition to the fancy gadgetry, the story introduces the collaboration between Her Majesty's Secret Service and the CIA. The book appeared the year after the Soviets' Sputnik I became the first human-made satellite to enter outer space, and the film appeared the year after the first human space flights and in the same year that John Glenn became the first American to orbit the Earth. Both book and film thereby tapped into the excitement surrounding the superpowers' fledgling space programs.

Dr. Strangelove: Or How I Learned to Stop Worrying and Love the Bomb   A British-made 1964 FILM SATIRE starring Peter SELLERS, George C. Scott, Slim Pickens and Sterling Hayden and directed by Stanley KUBRICK. It is based on a 1958 MILITARY NOVEL, RED ALERT, by Peter George, a retired Royal Air Force pilot. The book portrays a psychotic general who sends a squadron of American planes to attack Russia. Kubrick, George and Terry SOUTHERN wrote the screenplay. Before beginning to make the film, Kubrick had spoken with nuclear strategists and read some 70 books about the bomb, including *Red Alert.* Kubrick decided to make the film "because it's the only social problem where there's absolutely no chance for people to learn anything from experience." However, he said, "As I kept trying to imagine the way in which things would really happen, ideas kept coming to me which I would discard because they were so ludicrous. I kept saying to myself: 'I can't do this. People will laugh.' But . . . I began to realize that all the things I was throwing out were the things which were most truthful." Finally he concluded "the only way to tell the story was as a black comedy, or better, a nightmare comedy, where the things you laugh at most are really the heart of the paradoxical postures that make a nuclear war possible."

The epitome of Cold War BLACK HUMOR, *Dr. Strangelove* depicts the crisis that ensues when insane U.S. Air Force general Jack D. Ripper orders a nuclear strike against the

Peter Sellers as Dr. Strangelove, 1963. Courtesy AP/Wide World.

Soviet Union, and bumbling, sex-crazed American and Soviet leaders are unable to prevent a Soviet Doomsday machine from going off in retaliation. Sellers plays three roles: U.S. president Merkin Muffley; British group commander Lionel Mandrake, assigned to Ripper's command; and top ex-Nazi scientist and current U.S. presidential adviser, Dr. Strangelove. Pickens plays a resourceful, highly professional and competent "redneck" Air Force pilot, Major T. J. "King" Kong, whose multiethnic, multiracial crew valiantly flies its nuclear-armed B-52 to its target inside the Soviet Union. Scott plays the sexually obsessed chief of the U.S. Air Force, General "Buck" Turgidson, who must unwillingly help the Soviets try to shoot down Kong in order to prevent the automatic detonation of the Doomsday device.

Dr. Strangelove's comic incongruity derives from the contrast between its black-and-white documentary style and its absurd dialogue ("No fighting in the War Room"; "You'll have to answer to the Coca-Cola Company"), its visual jokes (iubiquitous signs on the air force base saying "Peace Is Our Profession") and occasional slapstick on the part of the generals, advisers and diplomats. The film suggests that, despite their public images as serious and responsible men, the leaders on both sides who control the destiny of the world are at best ineffectual and at worst criminally insane; virtually all are dominated by their sex drives, which are ultimately more responsible for political policy than either logic or the national interest.

In *Dr. Strangelove*, sex lies at the core of the Cold War, not ideology, economic philosophy or national security. The opening shots introduce this theme by showing a bomber's midair refueling as though the two planes are mating. The film concludes with men in the War Room planning a post-nuclear civilization to be populated by survivors who will take shelter in mine shafts. The strategists conclude that for the species to have its best chance of survival, the ratio of women to men must be extremely high; women must be chosen for their sex appeal, and men for their intelligence, while male monogamy must be eliminated in light of the pressing need for repopulation. In other words, the countries' leaders have subconsciously created a nuclear scenario that fulfills their greatest sexual fantasies. Throughout the film, the hovering threat of nuclear armageddon acts like an aphrodisiac upon these powerful men whose sexual appetites become deformed by their strange love for the enormous power and destructive capability of the hydrogen bomb. The title character, Dr. Strangelove, is a cripple who cites studies from the "Bland Corporation" (a reference to the Rand Corporation, a Cold War think-tank) and dispassionately calculates the millions of deaths that will ensue from the nuclear encounter. He may have been based loosely on Herman Kahn, a military planner for the Rand Corporation whose ON THERMONUCLEAR WAR (1960) was the first widely read popular book to employ statistics and other scientific methodologies to calculate the precise consequences of a major nuclear war. He also seems to refer to Werner von Braun, a German rocket scientist formerly employed by the Nazis and then brought to the United States to work on the space program. (See also APOCALYPTIC FILMS; FILM COMEDIES.)

For additional reading, see Whitfield's *The Culture of the Cold War.*

Dr. Zhivago A 1957 novel by Boris PASTERNAK and a 1965 FILM DRAMA starring Omar Sharif, Geraldine Chaplin, Julie Christie and Tom Courtenay and directed by David Lean. Pasternak began the novel about the impact of the Russian Revolution on a middle-class doctor shortly after Stalin died in 1953. Since the Soviet Union banned its publication, the novel first appeared in Italy. It was published in English in 1958. The story centers on Dr. Yuri Zhivago (Sharif), a married man who falls in love with Lara (Christie), another man's mistress, during World War I. The story becomes a tale of frustrated love as the hardships they endure because of the 1917 Russian Revolution keep Yuri and Lara apart. Because of its unflattering portrayal of communism, the book was outlawed in the Soviet Union and highly praised in the United States. It received international acclaim and helped Pasternak win the 1958 Nobel Prize in literature. Though he initially accepted the prize, the Soviet authorities later pressured him into renouncing it before consigning him to internal exile in an artist community near Moscow. The film's musical theme, "Lara's Theme," became a popular song in the United States.

Don't Drink the Water A 1966 play by Woody Allen and a 1969 FILM COMEDY starring Jackie Gleason, Estelle Parsons, Ted Bessell and Joan Delaney and directed by Howard Morris. Allen directed a 1994 television remake starring himself, Julie Kavner, Michael J. Fox and Dom De Luise. The Cold War creates the circumstances and lingers on the fringers of this story about a Jewish caterer from New Jersey and his family. They take refuge in the American Embassy in an unidentified IRON CURTAIN country after the vacationing caterer is mistaken for a spy because his tourist photos inadvertently include military installations in the background. Allen derives humor by juxtaposing the concerns of the Cold War with those of a Jewish family whose daughter is supposed to marry in two weeks. Instead of subordinating family issues to the urgent international crisis they have created, the caterer and his wife carry on about the wedding and dismiss the urgent pleas of the embassy staff. A crazy Orthodox priest who has taken refuge in the embassy for several years and mastered magic tricks during his stay contributes to the absurd mixture of characters, as does the developing romance between the engaged daughter and the ambassador's inept son, who has been left in charge during his dad's absence. Though most of the action occurs within the embassy, the communist officials who have accused the caterer also become targets of Allen's barbs. They appear humorless and their ruthlessness is acknowledged but never shown. They therefore become suitable comic villains and are ultimately the biggest losers in the story. (See also THEATER.)

Doomsday Warrior A 1984 APOCALYPTIC NOVEL by Ryder Stacy. Along with its 1984 sequel, *Doomsday Warrior No. 2: Red America*, the novel presents the vision of right-wing survivalists of the 1980s. The books appeared during the most intense period of the Cold War since the Cuban Missile Crisis, when the Reagan administration was accusing the Soviet Union of preparing to prevail in a nuclear war and was therefore advocating a policy of winnable nuclear war for the United States. In this story, the Soviets launch an unprovoked first strike against the United States. Their "killer" satellites—a reference to Reagan's controversial Strategic Defense Initiative—enable them to conquer America and enslave most of the survivors. However a group of Freefighters led by "Ultimate American" Ted Rockson, a survivalist, fights to "restore the dream the way the people back there failed to do. The original dream." Like Reagan, who wanted to revitalize Secretary of State John Foster Dulles's 1950s liberation policy, Rockson ultimately wants to "spread freedom" to the Soviets too. In their quest, the Freefighters come across various other surviving communities, including the "Macy's folk," who inhabit a large shopping mall, and the Technicians, who develop sophisticated weaponry. In return for learning practical survival skills, the Technicians give the Freefighters a secret weapon "as powerful and awesome as the atomic bomb itself, the twentieth century's gift of extinction. But now the twenty-first century as well had its weapon of superdeath." Thus, rather than underscore the folly of the nuclear arms race, as many postnuclear works do, these survivalist novels retain their faith in weaponry and advanced technology even as they insist on the importance of mastering practical survival skills.

For additional reading, see Dowling's *Fictions of Nuclear Disaster.*

Dovlatov, Sergei A Soviet EXILED WRITER (to the United States). Born in 1941 in Bashkiria, U.S.S.R., Dovlatov worked as a newspaper journalist and satirist during the Brezhnev years and as a guard in a labor camp. In 1978 his satiric jabs at Soviet policy provoked government officials to make him choose between prison or exile; he chose the latter and came to the United States. His first work of fiction published in America was translated by a student, Ann Frydman, and appeared in *The New Yorker.* His memoir, *Ours: A Russian Family Album* (1989), describes his family life in the Soviet Union: His mother had been a powerful editor at a literary house; his grandfather was shot as a spy because he had hosted one of Dovlatov's friends from Belgium, ironically, a supporter of Stalin who had come to the U.S.S.R. to celebrate communism; his cousin chose a life of crime to escape the confining Soviet way of life. While in the United States, Dovlatov worked as an announcer in New York for Radio Free Europe in addition to writing fiction. He died in 1990.

For additional reading, see Tucker's *Literary Exile in the Twentieth Century.*

Down to a Sunless Sea A 1979 APOCALYPTIC NOVEL by David Graham (aka Wilbur Wright). Published in London during the waning days of détente, the novel was first published in the United States in 1981, when U.S.-Soviet relations were deteriorating. *Down to a Sunless Sea* revives the postapocalyptic subgenre that had been largely dormant since the mid-1960s. The story follows the fates of the passengers and crew of a jumbo jet who survive because they are airborne when nuclear war breaks out. The plane lands at a NATO base in the Azores where a "clean" neutron bomb has killed all the people but left the facilities intact. (President Carter had canceled development of the neutron bomb during the 1970s.) The pilot, Captain Scott, learns from radio broadcasts that a base in Antarctica is receiving refugees from the radiation. Like an Old Testament patriarch, Scott leads his passengers to the new world, where they are joined by a plane full of Russian women. Like many of the postapocalyptic novels from the 1950s in which the nuclear bomb is transformed from an instrument of destruction into a purifying agent, *Down to a Sunless Sea* appears to suggest that a new and better world will emerge from the ruins of the old one, especially since the nuclear explosions have reconfigured the Earth's axis, so that Antarctica now promises to become a fertile region.

However, the author appends a final statement that undercuts the promise of regeneration. The "epilogue/prologue" reveals a radioactive cloud moving toward Antarctica: Unbeknounst to themselves, the survivors are doomed. Thus in this post-Vietnam novel, the many religious references and suggestions of possible salvation prove empty. Critic William Scheick points out that in Graham's view, "all ideologies, not just authoritative ones, are pernicious to human survival and engender a hell on earth, a hell most manifest . . . [in] the nuclear war resulting from the clash of American and Russian ideologies." In his 1983 novel, *Carter's Castle,* the author rejects even the United Nations because it is controlled by U.S. and Soviet ideologies.

For additional reading, see Dowling's *Fictions of Nuclear Disaster* and Scheick's "Continuative and Ethical Predictions: The Post-Nuclear Holocaust Novel of the 1980s."

Drury, Allen A NOVELIST. Drury wrote several popular political novels between 1959 and 1990, most notably ADVISE AND CONSENT (1959), which won the 1959 Pulitzer Prize. *Advise and Consent* inaugurated a six-part series of novels about the struggle between liberals and conservatives over whose ideology should guide the nation through the Cold War. Each book in the series appeared on the *New York Times* best-seller list for at least 19 weeks; *Advise and Consent* was on it for 102 weeks, from August 1959 to July 1961. That book centers on the political battle surrounding the confirmation of Robert Leffingwell, a liberal nominee for secretary of state loosely based on Alger Hiss. Leffingwell and several other characters go on to play major roles throughout the series, which includes A SHADE OF DIFFERENCE (1962), CAPABLE OF HONOR (1967), PRESERVE AND PROTECT (1968), COME NINEVEH, COME TYRE (1973) and THE PROMISE OF JOY (1975).

A politically conservative writer, Drury explained that one of his central themes was "the continuing argument between those who use responsible firmness to maintain orderly social progress and oppose Communist imperialism in its drive for world domination; and those who believe [that] in a reluctance to be firm, in permissiveness and in the erosion of the law lie the surest path to world peace and a stable society." In *Political Fiction, The Spirit of the Age, and Allen Drury*, Tom Kemme identifies several other fundamental beliefs that characterize Drury's political fiction: There are only two major American ideologies—liberal and conservative. Liberals control the media and thereby influence the public to support their causes and reject conservativism; views opposed by the liberal media will inevitably be distorted; liberals are intellectually shallow and fail to truly grasp the insidious nature of communist methods; liberals undermine patriotism by attacking American ideals, goals, and accomplishments; U.S. power is decreasing and the U.S. commitment to protect its foreign interests is waning; communist power and commitment to its objectives is increasing; liberals believe in accommodating communism; the growing fear of nuclear war is leading many Americans to prefer a communist America to the destruction of the United States and the world; and African and Asian countries, which require the good will of the United States and United Nations to flourish, nonetheless adopt policies that alienate the United States and threaten to destroy the United Nations.

Drury's other political novels include *That Summer* (1966), *Throne of Saturn: A Novel of Space and Politics* (1971), *Anna Hastings, The Story of a Washington Newsperson!* (1977), *Mark Coffin, U.S.S: A Novel of Capitol Hill* (1979), *The Hill of Summer* (1981), *Decision* (1983), *Pentagon* (1986) and *Toward What Bright Glory* (1990). His NONFICTION includes his private diary, *A Senate Journal: 1943–1945* (1963), and *Courage and Hesitation: Notes and Photographs of the Nixon Administration* (1971). In addition, Drury wrote *A Very Strange Society: A Journey to the Heart of South Africa* (1967) and two novels about the Egyptian pharaoh Akhenaton, *God Against the Gods* (1976) and *Return to Thebes* (1977).

For additional reading, see Kemme's *Political Fiction, The Spirit of the Age, and Allen Drury*.

Druzhnikov, Juri A Soviet EXILED WRITER (to the United States). Born in Moscow in 1933, Druzhnikov immigrated to the United States in 1987, after waiting 10 years to secure a permit to leave the Soviet Union. While in the Soviet Union he published eight books and had two plays produced. However, Soviet authorities altered each of his works. His novel *Wait till Sweet Sixteen* (1976) was cut in half and the ending was changed, and officials banned one of his plays during its premiere run. A 1974 article in *Izvestia* accused Druzhnikov of possessing a "harmful philosophy" and distorting the character of the Soviet people. While in the United States he published *The Myth of Pavlik Morozov* (1988), his account of the murder of a boy who had become a hero in the Soviet Union by reporting his father to the police. Druzhnikov's literature in exile includes a collection of short stories, *A Crack in the Pink Lampshade* (1989), and a novel, *Angels on the Head of a Pin* (1989), which describes the Soviet repression of independent thinkers before and just after the Soviet intervention in Czechoslovakia in 1968.

For additional reading, see Tucker's *Literary Exile in the Twentieth Century.*

Dylan, Bob A FOLK SINGER and a singer of ROCK AND ROLL. Dylan was born in 1941 as Robert Allen Zimmerman to Jewish parents in Hibbing, Minnesota, where he experienced anti-Semitism growing up. This background made him feel alienated as an adolescent, and his songs of personal alienation came to reflect the sentiments of many young people who also felt out of step with mainstream America. Dylan's early musical influences came from such singers of country music and rhythm and blues as Hank Williams, Muddy Waters, B.B. King and Jimmy Reed. But after reading Woody Guthrie's autobiography, *Bound for Glory*, he became particularly enamored of the folk singer— the champion of the people who, in Guthrie's words, "do all of the little jobs and the mean and dirty hard work in the world." Dylan eventually traveled to New York, where he visited Guthrie during his dying days. Dylan began performing in coffeehouses and at hootenannies where he sang his own songs of social protest. His girlfriend at the time, Suze Rotolo, was a secretary for the civil rights group CORE. She encouraged him to write about social issues and probably influenced him to compose "The Ballad of Emmet Till," about the lynching of an African-American teenager.

Dylan's first album, *Bob Dylan*, appeared in late 1961; his second album, *Freewheeling* (1963), includes "Blowin' in the Wind" which became a theme song for the civil rights movement, and "Oxford Town," a song about James Meredith, the black student who integrated the University of Mississippi. During this period Dylan also wrote about the Cold War. "A Hard Rain's A-Gonna Fall" is about the Cuban Missile Crisis and the prospect of NUCLEAR APOCALYPSE, though it was also seen as a prediction of social upheaval. "Talking World War Three Blues" provides a BLACK HUMOR view of life after a nuclear war, and "Masters of War" attacks complacent, middle-class citizens for permitting American militarism: "You fasten the triggers for others to fire/ Then you sit back and watch when the death count gets higher." On May 12, 1963, Dylan canceled a performance on the Ed SULLIVAN television show when he was forbidden to perform "Talking John Birch Society Blues," a humorous song that makes fun of the ultra-right-wing political organization and the RED SCARE.

Dylan was an early critic of the Vietnam War, and he used his music to voice his opposition. In 1964 he performed with his girlfriend Joan BAEZ at peace concerts, and together they were known as the King and Queen of Folk Rock. However, in 1965 Dylan began to withdraw from politics, claiming in a *Newsweek* interview, "I've never written a political song. Songs can't save the world. I've gone through all that. When you don't like something, you gotta learn to just not need that something." He subsequently turned to music that was more personal and less political in nature, though in early 1974 he participated in a concert organized by Phil OCHS in tribute to Salvador Allende, the president of Chile who was assassinated in a U.S.-assisted coup. And in 1982 he performed with Baez, Tom Petty, Stevie Wonder, Linda Ronstadt, Bonnie Raitt, Bette Midler, David Crosby, Stephen Stills, Graham Nash and others in a concert that raised over $250,000 for the anti-nuclear-weapons movement.

For additional reading, see Orman's *The Politics of Rock Music;* Szatmary's *Rockin' in Time;* Ward et al.'s *Rock of Ages: The Rolling Stone History of Rock & Roll.*

Eastern Europe A Cold War term used to identify the central European nations within the Soviet sphere of influence, including Poland, Hungary, Czechoslovakia, East Germany (the German Democratic Republic), Yugoslavia, Romania, Bulgaria and Albania. The term *Eastern Europe* came into use after World War II to emphasize the demarcation between the Western allied nations and the Soviet Union, a part of which occupied the eastern-most portion of the European continent. Prior to the Cold War those countries were known as *Central Europe,* a designation to which the State Department officially returned in 1994. In 1946, Winston Churchill warned of an IRON CURTAIN descending on Europe to separate the Soviet-dominated countries from the rest of the continent. Subsequently the Eastern European nations also became known as the "Iron Curtain countries." (See also LANGUAGE.)

"Emerald Point N.A.S." A TELEVISION DRAMA that ran on CBS in 1983–84. Combining elements of the military film STRATEGIC AIR COMMAND (1955) and the television soap opera "Dallas" (CBS, 1978–91), "Emerald Point" presented the sordid interplay between the military and big business at a U.S. naval air station. Dennis Weaver starred as the widowed commanding officer, Rear Admiral Thomas Mallory. He was joined on the base by his three daughters: one married to a brilliant military lawyer, one to a former navy pilot who was discharged after being charged with manslaughter, and one a recent Annapolis graduate. Harlan

Adams (first Patrick O'Neal and then Robert VAUGHN) was the unscrupulous businessman whose honorable son was a navy pilot. The admiral's beautiful sister-in-law craved power and wealth and sought to marry him but became involved with a KGB agent instead. In short, "Emerald Point N.A.S." brought the sleaziness and greed of "Dallas" and "Dynasty" (ABC, 1981–89) to a domestic, Cold War military base.

End of the World A 1984 play by Arthur Kopit. The Broadway cast starred John Shea, Barnard Hughes, Linda Hunt, and David O'Brien. *End of the World* appeared during the most intense period of the Cold War since the 1962 Cuban Missile Crisis, when all-out nuclear-war once again seemed possible, even likely. A BLACK HUMOR comedy, the play centers on Michael Trent, a playwright who has accepted the seemingly impossible task of treating the concept of Mutually Assured Destruction (MAD) and the bleak realities behind nuclear deterrence as subjects for THEATER. The story begins as a *film noir* parody in which the trench coat–wearing Trent imitates the style of the hard-boiled detective. As in *The Maltese Falcon,* the protagonist must ascertain the exact nature of a deeply disturbing truth, which his secretive sponsor, tycoon Philip Stone, reluctantly reveals only in disjointed fragments.

However, after interviewing top-level nuclear policy planners Trent comes to a profound recognition—Within the framework of MAD, the very existence of nuclear weapons implies their eventual use in a nuclear war, since MAD relies on fear as its primary deterrent: "Deterrence is dependent upon strength—well, that's obvious; the stronger your nuclear arsenal, the more the other side's deterred. *However*, should deterrence *fail* for any reason, your strength *instantly* becomes your greatest liability, *inviting* attack *instead* of preventing it." Thus MAD requires that the balance of fear be maintained. "By the way, that's the problem with a nuclear freeze: to the extent that it makes people feel safer it raises the chances of war." However, "discontinuities"—unexpected, fluke occurrences—ensure that eventually the nuclear balance will be thrown off, forcing the stronger nation to launch a defensive first strike. Consequently, every long-term projection from the MAD scenario points to inevitable nuclear war. Moreover, any attempt to break out of MAD will also result in nuclear war.

As though these dismal projections for MAD were not bad enough, Trent discovers something even more disheartening: the seductive nature of doom. Humans are drawn to the awesome power of the bomb and are thrilled as well as horrified by the prospect of their own destruction. (In this respect Kopit elaborates on a theme Bernard Wolfe and William Golding introduced in their 1950s APOCALYPTIC NOVELS, LIMBO '90 (1953) and LORD OF THE FLIES (1954), and which Stanley KUBRICK addresses in his FILM SATIRE, DR . STRANGELOVE (1964).) As Trent's sponsor declares, "There's a glitter to nuclear weapons. I had sensed it in others and [while observing a nuclear test] *felt it in myself*." This psychological attraction to the bomb and its destructive power also fuels MAD, and it gives nuclear planning an emotional component that drives everyone involved. Indeed, this emotional aspect of the issue, which rarely figures in policy analyses or public debate, has occasioned the sponsor to commission Trent's play in the first place: "Because the theater, sir, alone among the arts, engages, in equal measure, the emotion and the intellect. And both must be touched here if we are to survive."

As a playwright, Trent's task is to communicate both intellectually and emotionally the reality of the nuclear situation while leaving the audience with something more uplifting than the despair that comes from knowing they are doomed by MAD, doomed by human nature itself. Trent feels hopeless before this task, just as the policy planners feel hopeless about ultimately preventing nuclear war. Kopit, however, manages to succeed where Trent fails. Kopit communicates the dismal facts about nuclear war while using black humor, irony and paradox to generate a humor that transcends despair. The laughter, in effect, becomes the palliative, if not the antidote, for the doom that Kopit identifies but cannot alter. Moreover, Kopit's success in his seemingly impossible task provides a modicum of hope for success in the other seemingly impossible task of avoiding nuclear war. In a play that highlights the breakdown of logic and reason, hope comes from the wild-card possibilities of unpredictable and irrational discontinuities (as indeed the sudden and unexpected collapse of the Soviet Union proved to be).

Among the works Kopit consulted in his research were Herman Kahn's ON THERMONUCLEAR WAR (1960) Jonathan Schell's THE FATE OF THE EARTH (1982), the writings of George Kennan and Robert Scheer's WITH ENOUGH SHOVELS (1982), which provided the basis for one of the major speeches in

the play. (See also NUCLEAR APOCALYPSE and APOCALYPTIC FILMS.)

For additional reading, see Anisfield's *The Nightmare Considered.*

End of the World, The A 1962 APOCALYPTIC NOVEL by Dan Owen. It became the basis for the 1962 FILM DRAMA, PANIC IN YEAR ZERO. Published immediately after the resolution of the second Berlin Crisis and the same year as the Cuban Missile Crisis, *The End of the World* presented scenarios that its readers could recognize as real possibilities for their own lives. The story centers on the Baldwin family, which is leaving Los Angeles for a fishing trip when a nuclear attack begins. The father, Harry, decides to continue into the wilderness and quickly casts off the shackles of civilized behavior in his effort to ensure that his family survives. His wife criticizes him for "robbing and mauling people, like some kind of cheap hoodlum," as he holds up stores to gain provisions, but his every-man-for-himself sensibility seems justified by the circumstances. However, when the family finally establishes itself within a cave in the woods, Harry orders them to return to traditional "civilized" routines and values: The men must shave, the women must attend to their appearance and the son must not rob people. Harry even frees a trio of men who try to run him over. Ironically, in this survivalist novel, Harry's act of compassion proves to be a weakness for which the family is severely punished. The roving trio returns to kill some neighbors and abduct and rape Baldwin's daughter. Harry and his son finally rescue her and mete justice to the rapists, and soon after the son and another rape victim initiate a romance. But Harry blames himself for the violence done to his daughter and neighbors: "Oh, if he only had it to do over again. To have stood, shotgun in hand, as they climbed out of the rusted Chevy after trying to run him down. To have cut loose with the shotgun and ended it right there, before it had ever started." Though the book concludes with the family's rescue by the army and their eventual return to the remnants of civilization, the focus is primarily on the breakdown of civilized behavior in the aftermath of a nuclear war, with its replacement by a sort of Hobbesian law of the jungle in which life is "nasty, brutish and short." In *Nuclear War Films* Jack Shaheen criticizes this premise, which both the book and movie share: "The easy philosophy of becoming barbaric to survive . . . [fails to acknowledge that] the new beginning is the old belief in technology and the ethos of the gun." (See also NUCLEAR APOCALYPSE.)

For additional reading, see Dowling's *Fictions of Nuclear Disaster.*

End of the World News, The A 1982 APOCALYPTIC NOVEL by Anthony Burgess. Inspired by a photograph of President Carter watching three television sets simultaneously, Burgess presents in "visual counterpoint" three 20th-century visions of apocalypse. In the first, set in Nazi Germany, Freud expresses his belief that when the mind liberates itself from subconscious neuroses, "the world will come to an end and then start all over again—a new world. Men and women will know themselves for what they are, for the first time. It will be a terrible shock for the world." In the second, Trotsky imagines the final synthesis of Marx's dialectic when the classless society is achieved and history ends. The third apocalyptic vision begins with natural disasters and concludes when a devastating comet strikes the Earth. This last scenario presents an ironic and playful takeoff on earlier SCIENCE FICTION NOVELS AND STORIES, with a science fiction writer organizing the construction of a space ship and the departure of a group of settlers to begin a new world elsewhere in the universe.

The first two apocalyptic visions are affirmative and evolutionary, and even the third is somewhat hopeful, although the settlers' children quickly forget the myths they were supposed to remember and pass along to future generations. But, as David Dowling points out in *Fictions of Nuclear Disaster*, "Just as Freud's new world was mocked by the Jewish Holocaust, and Trotsky's by his assassination, so the apocalypse of any fiction will be mocked by the final, real end, whatever it may be. Readers are desperate for myths, and Burgess fabricates one as suavely as any other science fiction writer, but it has nothing to do with 'reality' . . . Fiction, like the ideas of Freud and Trotsky, can appeal to the imagination, but history takes care of itself."

For additional reading, see Dowling's *Fictions of Nuclear Disaster*.

"Enterprise"   A TELEVISION DOCUMENTARY series that ran on ABC from 1952 to 1958. Sponsored by various major U.S. corporations, the shows celebrated American industry. They were introduced with an unabashed Cold War message: "These films, presented in cooperation with such industries as Bethlehem Steel and General Electric, will point out that America is out to prove democracy in industry and to fight Communism in industry."

epic films   A category of FILM that treats stories from antiquity and employs vast sets, spectacular scenes and "casts of thousands." During the Cold War, epics frequently established parallels between ancient despotism and contemporary communist tyranny. In both eras, the epics suggested, protagonists had to assert their Judeo-Christian religious values in a struggle against oppression. In fact, epic films frequently presented Judeo-Christian values as the principle weapon against tyranny, while the suppression of those values was what defined tyranny. Cecil B. DEMILLE, a strong anti-communist, was one of the most prominent producers of epic films. His prologue before the remake of THE TEN COMMANDMENTS (1956) made explicit the general relationship between most epic films and the Cold War: "The theme . . . is whether men are to be ruled by God's law—or whether they are to be ruled by the whims of a dictator . . . Are men the property of the state? Or are they free souls under God? This same battle continues throughout the world today." Enormous casts, vast sets, expensive props and the huge scope of epic films demonstrated America's seemingly endless store of resources. No films being made behind the Iron Curtain could rival the excesses of Hollywood epics. Thus the ability of the capitalist-based Hollywood film industry to produce such spectacular movies also presented the audience with the apparent superiority of the American way. Among the more prominent Cold War epics were BEN-HUR (1959), QUO VADIS (1951),

SPARTACUS (1960), *The Ten Commandments* and *Samson and Delilah* (1949).

"Espionage"   A TELEVISION SPY SHOW that ran on NBC in 1963–64. Produced in England and filmed on location in Europe, "Espionage" presented an anthology of spy stories from World War I through the Cold War, all based on actual case histories.

Everything We Had   A 1981 NONFICTION book edited by Al Santoli. A collection of 33 oral histories by U.S. men and women who served in the Vietnam War, *Everything We Had* was well received by critics and the public and even appeared briefly on the *New York Times* best-seller list. The book came out at a time when Vietnam War veterans were receiving more attention than they had during the 1970s. The oral histories cover events from 1962, when President Kennedy dramatically increased the number of U.S. military advisers to Vietnam, to the fall of Saigon in 1975. Among the subjects that the veterans discuss are jungle warfare, firefights, major battles, naval patrols, the air war, the 1972 Christmas bombing of North Vietnam, life as a prisoner of war, experiences of minority soldiers, drug use within the military, "pacification" programs and the Phoenix program, whose mission was to assassinate leaders of the Viet Cong within South Vietnamese villages. Also included are accounts by American women nurses, a group whose participation in the war had been largely overlooked. The Vietnam War Memorial opened a year after the book's publication, another indication of the country's growing awareness of Vietnam veterans. (See also VIETNAM WAR LITERATURE.)

exiled writers (from the United States)   Though the vast majority of Cold War literary figures who emigrated for political reasons fled from communist countries to the West, movement did take place in the opposite direction. In the United States, most of the literary exile resulted from the RED SCARE, usually as a result of intimidation by the HOUSE COMMITTEE ON UN-AMERICAN ACTIVITIES (HUAC) and/or Senator Joseph McCarthy (R. Wisconsin). In addition, some African-American writers left the United States partly for political reasons associated with the Cold War and partly to escape the racism they experienced in American society. Notable among these were Richard WRIGHT and Eldridge CLEAVER. James BALDWIN, another prominent African-American literary emigré, left the country both to escape racism and to feel freer to live as a homosexual, and though his writings made significant contributions to American Cold War culture, he is not usually considered a political exile in the traditional sense.

Writers who fled the United States because of the Red Scare include both native and foreign-born authors. In the former category are John Howard LAWSON, Albert MALTZ, Dalton TRUMBO, Carl FOREMAN and Margaret SCHLAUCH. Margaret RANDALL, another native-born writer, was also a political exile, though her emigration was not dirtly related to Red Scare persecution. Foreign-born writers who exiled from the United States because of the Red Scare include Bertolt BRECHT, Stefan HEYM and Thomas MANN. The film artist Charles CHAPLIN was another notable exiled artist from the United States.

From the late 1940s through the mid-1950s, HUAC and other Congressional bodies conducted highly publicized investigations into alleged communist efforts to control the Hollywood motion picture industry. In 1947, with J. Parnell Thomas as its chair, HUAC cited the "unfriendly" witnesses known as the HOLLYWOOD TEN for their refusal to answer the committee's questions about their past involvement with the Communist Party or to name others who had been party members. The Ten refused to answer both because they objected to the political interrogation of U.S. citizens, and because they did not want to betray others who shared their views. Among the Ten were three writers who were to become exiles: Trumbo, Hollywood's highest paid SCREEN-WRITER at the time, Lawson and Maltz.

Trumbo was eventually convicted of contempt of Congress for refusing to answer HUAC's questions. He served 10 months in federal prison, and after his release, he went into exile to Mexico in 1951, where he pseudonymously wrote film scripts that continued to be produced by Hollywood studios. Still subject to BLACKLISTING after his return to the United States in 1953, he continued to write under aliases for a fraction of his earlier salary. Finally, director Otto Preminger announced in 1960 that Trumbo had written the script for his film, EXODUS. Not only was the writer rehabilitated, but also the film blacklist itself was ended. The same year Trumbo received credit for his work on another major film, Stanley KUBRICK's SPARTACUS, which president-elect John F. Kennedy crossed American Legion picket lines to view. In 1970 Trumbo received the Screen Writers Guild's highest honor, the Laurel Award. In his acceptance speech he addressed those who were too young to remember the Red Scare:

> To them I would say only this: that the blacklist was a time of evil, and that no one on either side who survived it came through untouched by evil . . . There was bad faith and good, honesty and dishonesty, courage and cowardice, selflessness and opportunism, wisdom and stupidity, good and bad on both sides; and almost every individual involved . . . combined some or all of these antithetical qualities in his own person, in his own acts . . . In the final tally we were *all* victims because . . . each of us felt compelled to say things he did not want to say . . . none of us— right, left, or center—emerged from that long nightmare without sin.

Lawson, an open Communist Party member, was tried for violation of the 1940 Smith Act, which made it illegal for people to belong to organizations that advocated the overthrow of the U.S. government by force or violence, even though the Communist Party did not officially hold that position and was in fact a legal organization at that time. Lawson was found guilty of contempt of court and served a year in federal prison between 1947 and 1948. Blacklisted and unable to work in Hollywood after his release from jail, Lawson also moved to Mexico and wrote screenplays there under assumed names, also for far less money than he had earlier commanded. His most significant work from that period was the screenplay for the British-made *Cry, the Beloved Country* (1952), which was based on Alan Paton's 1948 novel about South African apartheid. Between 1961

and 1963, Lawson spent time in the Soviet Union and East Germany, where a revision of his play *Parlor Magic* (1939) was produced. Though he was an open communist, Lawson denied interjecting pro-communist lines into his film scripts. He did not believe such simplistic attempts at propaganda were either politically effective or aesthetically defensible.

Maltz, too, was an active member of the Communist Party. He frequently contributed to Marxist periodicals; in fact, one of his articles about socialist realism provoked a major party controversy in 1946. The article criticized the restrictions on freedom of thought within the party, and Maltz, attacked by Lawson, Howard FAST, Alvah BESSIE and others, had to repudiate it in order to remain in the party. After serving a prison sentence in 1950 for contempt of Congress, he went into exile in Mexico from 1952 to 1962, where he pseudonymously wrote several Hollywood films, most notably *The Robe*. Even though the blacklist was broken in 1960, Maltz received no screen credit for any work before 1970, when he wrote *Two Mules for Sister Sara*. Maltz later challenged Trumbo's claim that everyone but the members of HUAC had been equally a victim of the Red Scare; by contrast Maltz, maintained that the Ten's refusal to name names was a morally superior position, as opposed to what he considered to be the generally immoral act of betraying others and giving in to HUAC.

Besides the Hollywood Ten, Brecht was also called to testify before the 1947 HUAC hearings. A Marxist playwright who began writing in Berlin, Brecht is best known to U.S. audiences for *The Threepenny Opera*, on which he collaborated with composer Kurt Weill in 1928. This German writer who had often been linked to Communist Party causes though never known to be a member, came to the United States in 1941 to avoid Nazi persecution and took employment as a Hollywood screenwriter. In his appearance before HUAC, Brecht denied ever having been a member of the Communist Party, either in Germany or in the United States. Although HUAC cleared him of any criminal charges, the former exile from Nazism fled the country immediately after testifying and settled in East Germany, whose government provided him with his own theater and a generous subsidy to continue his work. Ironically, the Marxist playwright was responsible for the longest-running musical up to that time in American history, a revival of *The Threepenny Opera* that enjoyed over 2,000 performances in Greenwich Village from 1954 to 1961.

Carl Foreman is best known for writing the Academy Award–winning films HIGH NOON (1952) and THE BRIDGE ON THE RIVER KWAI (1957). Foreman had been a member of the Communist Party but resigned in 1942. He claimed to have written *High Noon* to express his sense of abandonment by the film community when he was subpoenaed to testify before the HUAC in 1952. Foreman refused to inform on people he had met during his years as a communist and was subsequently blacklisted.

Foreman went into exile in England in 1952 and had his passport revoked by the State Department. While living in exile, he earned his living by writing "black-market screenplays," that is, screenplays that could not appear under his own name. Most notably he wrote but did not receive screen credit for *The Bridge on the River Kwai*. In 1956 Foreman's attorney, Sidney Cohn, arranged for him to testify in private session before a HUAC subcommittee of one person, Congressman Francis Walter. Walter had agreed that Foreman could testify only about himself; he would not be asked to report on others. Cohn wanted to try a strategy that might allow other blacklistees also to testify about themselves without informing on others. In this way, he hoped to break the blacklist—at least for those who were no longer communists. The strategy did succeed for Foreman, but because of political repercussions for Walter it did not extend to anyone else. After his testimony, Foreman returned to work in Hollywood. John WAYNE, president of the strongly anti-communist MOTION PICTURE ALLIANCE FOR THE PRESERVATION OF AMERICAN IDEALS, asserted in 1977 that, "I'll never regret having helped run Foreman out of this country."

Charlie Chaplin was perhaps the most beloved and most famous performer in the world between the world wars. His Little Tramp character, who always retained his bravado and dignity however far his fortunes had fallen, had endeared him to audiences everywhere. Born in England, Chaplin remained a British citizen despite living and working in Hollywood from 1913 to 1952. His films typically championed the "little man," and several criticized capitalists and the dehumanizing aspects of industrialism. Chaplin supported such left-wing causes as former vice president Henry Wallace's third-party presidential campaign for the Progressive Party. In the late 1940s, Chaplin criticized American foreign policy and openly defended the civil liberties of American communists. Though HUAC announced its plans to have Chaplin testify, it repeatedly postponed calling him as a witness before finally declining to do so at all. In 1947, Chaplin sent a telegram to HUAC, claiming that he had never "joined any political organization in my life," and no evidence has ever surfaced to prove that he was a member of any communist party, despite extensive investigations by the FBI.

Nevertheless, while the actor was en route to England for the 1952 premiere of his film *Limelight,* the Democratic U.S. attorney general, acting in response to criticism from such Republicans as Senator Richard Nixon, revoked Chaplin's permit to reenter the country, citing the U.S. code that allowed for the exclusion of aliens based on "morals, health, or insanity, or for advocating Communism or associating with Communist or pro-Communist organizations." In response, Chaplin refused to return to the United States until a visit in 1972, when he received a special Oscar award and was honored at the Lincoln Center Film Society in New York. In 1957, he retaliated against HUAC in his British-made film A KING IN NEW YORK, which depicts a deposed European monarch who immigrates to America. The movie satirizes American culture as the destitute king is reduced to earning a living by making crass television commercials. The king falls afoul of HUAC when he befriends a runaway boy whose parents are suspected communists. Tarnished by guilt-by-association, the king must appear before the committee, but he reveals the farcical nature of the hearings when he accidentally turns a fire hose on his interrogators. The film did not premiere in the United States until 1976.

Margaret Schlauch was a distinguished American-born linguist and literary scholar. She disappeared from her office at New York University after receiving a subpoena from HUAC, which she believed would lead to persecution for her communist beliefs. She later reappeared in Warsaw, where she received political asylum.

Like Brecht, Thomas Mann was a German who came to the United States to avoid Nazi persecution. In 1930 in Germany, he supported the Social Democratic Party in opposition to Hitler, though he did not join it. After Hitler's parliamentary victory in 1933 and the subsequent Nazi book burnings of the same year, Mann immigrated to Czechoslovakia. He happened to be in the United States in 1938, when Germany annexed Austria, and he elected to remain in North America rather than return to Europe. He supported the U.S. war effort and became a U.S. citizen in 1944. He was very popular during the war, but afterward he received criticism for his socialist leanings. Concerned over the Red Scare, he went into exile in Switzerland in 1952. His disenchantment with America during this period appears in *The Black Swan* (1953; in English, 1954) in which America is portrayed as an appealing source of rejuvenation that ultimately proves to be both corrupted and corrupting.

Stefan Heym was yet another German-born refugee from the Nazis. He also fled to Czechoslovakia in 1933 and came to the United States a few years later on a special scholarship from the University of Chicago for "brilliant students whose education had been interrupted by the coming of National Socialism to Germany." After receiving his master's degree in 1936, he edited an anti-fascist weekly newspaper and wrote *Nazis in the U.S.A.: An Exposé of Hitler's Aims and Agents in the U.S.A.* (1938). During World War II, Heym served in the psychological warfare division of the U.S. Army while he continued writing. Afterward he participated in the reeducation program in the U.S. Occupied Zone in Germany and later served as chief of the American delegation at the 1950 World Peace Conference in Warsaw.

Heym's popular novels from the immediate postwar period had a wide readership. They include *The Crusaders* (1948) and *The Eyes of Reason* (1951), both of which reflect his socialism. In 1952 he was transferred back to the United States to face an investigation into his alleged communism. In response to further accusations by Senator McCarthy, Heym renounced his U.S. citizenship and moved to East Germany (the German Democratic Republic, or GDR) where his "socialist literature" was warmly received. There he wrote editorials, reports and articles praising East Germany and its relationship to the Soviet Union, as well as children's stories. However, in 1965 Heym fell into disfavor with the East German government after publishing an article describing the decline of Stalin's importance and its impact on communism. Subsequently, most of his writing became illegal in East Germany until 1989, though he was published in West Germany, England and the United States. His English-language best-selling novels include *Uncertain Friend* (1969), *The King David Report* (1972) and *Five Days in June* (1977). *Uncertain Friend* deals with the conflict between intellectual integrity and the power of a personality cult; *Five Days in June* describes the 1953 popular uprising against the East German regime. Heym was expelled from the German Democratic Republic Writers Guild in 1979, as were those writers who rose to his defense. However, he continued to live in and to defend the GDR.

Richard Wright, the son of a Mississippi sharecropper and a schoolteacher, dropped out of high school and ran away, first to Memphis and then to Chicago. There Wright became attracted to Marxism. He joined the Communist Party in 1932. During this period, he began to publish free-verse poems about racism, poverty and socialism in such radical magazines as *The New Masses*. Also during the 1930s, Wright worked in two New Deal programs to help writers, the Federal Experimental Theater and the Federal Writers' Project. In 1937 he went to New York to work on *The Daily Worker*, the Communist Party newspaper. He published his first book in 1938, a collection of stories entitled *Uncle Tom's Children*. In 1940 he won a Guggenheim fellowship to write *Native Son*, the best-selling story of the capture, trial and execution of a black man who accidentally kills his employer's daughter. *Native Son* established Wright's reputation as a leading American writer. Though Wright quickly became disenchanted with the party's tactics and discipline, he remained a Marxist until 1944 when *The Atlantic Monthly* published his recantation of his Communist Party affiliation, "I Tried to Be a Communist." (It was later republished in a collection of essays by former communists, THE GOD THAT FAILED (1949).) The essay criticizes the Communist Party for exploiting black Americans for its own purposes and subordinating to the party's strategic interests such black issues as the segregation of the Armed Forces and of Red Cross blood banks. In 1945 Wright published his autobiography *Black Boy*.

Even after he left the party, Wright faced harassment because of his outspoken political and social beliefs. Angered by the way government and establishment figures shunned him, Wright and his family moved to Paris shortly after World War II. He lived there until his death in 1960, mingling with such figures as philosopher Jean Paul Sartre and other members of the French intelligentsia, who received him far more warmly than had American intellectuals. In 1953, Wright wrote *Black Power*, a call for African unity in which he dedicated himself to the cause of Pan-Africanism. However, his efforts were not well received either by whites or by Africans. Other works from his later years include an existential novel, *The Outsider* (1953), and an unpublished novel, *Island of Hallucination*, about an expatriate writer who is kept under CIA surveillance because of his Marxist writings. This novel expressed Wright's own sense of persecution by the CIA during the Cold War.

Eldridge Cleaver was born in Arkansas in 1935. He became attracted to the Black Power movement while he was imprisoned in California during the 1960s. His essays from this period, *Soul on Ice* (1968), call for liberating black Americans by overthrowing the social, military and economic institutions of the government. He also proposed rape as a strategy for attacking white men through "their" women. In response to the persecution of the militant Black Panther Party and to divisions among Black Muslims, the two major political groups that were specifically African-American, Cleaver adopted a more international Marxist position, which he elaborates in *Post Prison Writings and Speeches* (1969). Under the threat of arrest and re-incarceration for parole violations, Cleaver fled first to Cuba and then to Algeria. While exiled in Algeria he wrote an introduction to *Do It!* (1970) by more internationalist Yippie antiwar activist Jerry Rubin. In that introduction he encapsulates American history into a single word, *blood,* and calls on American youth to rebel against a racist capitalist system by smoking marijuana, listening to good music and rejecting authority. At their invitation, Cleaver visited North Vietnam, North Korea and the People's Republic of China, but his observations of the betrayal of Marxist ideals by those tyrannical governments disillusioned him about communism. Subsequently, he and his wife, Kathleen Neal, settled in France, which he found more congenial. While in France, Cleaver began to reconsider his political stance. His Christian-oriented account of the events that led to his voluntary return to the United States appears in *Soul on Fire* (1978). Upon his return, he stood trial for the old parole violations and was sentenced to some 2,000 hours of community service in California.

Margaret Randall lived in New York from 1958 to 1961, holding a variety of jobs and writing articles supporting Castro and the Cuban revolution. In 1961 she moved to Mexico with her 10-month-old son. There she married Sergio Mondragon, a Mexican poet, and gave up her American citizenship in order to gain the right to work in Mexico. From 1962 to 1968, she and Mondragon coedited *El Corno Emplumado* (The Plumed Horn), a bilingual literary journal that was influential in both Latin America and the United States. In 1967 and 1968 Randall traveled to Cuba to attend cultural congresses there, which inspired a still-greater devotion to the Cuban revolution and other social causes. When she returned to Mexico in 1968, she and poet Robert Cohn became lovers as well as coeditors of *El Corno Emplumado*. Fearing political assassination by the Mexican police or by right-wing terrorists because of their open support of the Mexican student uprisings of 1968, Randall and Cohn went into hiding. In 1969, they settled in Cuba, where Randall became deeply involved in building that nation, in women's issues and in the politics of other Latin American countries. In 1979 she moved to Nicaragua to write about women who had taken part in the Sandinista overthrow of the Somoza dictatorship. In 1981 she published *Sandino's Daughters: Testimonies of Nicaraguan Women in Struggle*.

In 1984 Randall returned to Albuquerque, New Mexico, on a visitor's visa, married writer Floyce Alexander and began teaching at the University of New Mexico. However, when Randall applied for permanent residency later that year, the U.S. Immigration and Naturalization Service (INS) denied her request, and she was asked to leave the country in 1985. She appealed the decision, and her cause was supported by a range of human rights activists, civic groups and literary associations. Nonetheless, in 1986 the INS ordered her deportation because, "her writings advocate the economic, international, and governmental doctrines of world Communism." Her appeal was supported by a letter to Attorney General Edwin Meese sent by the PEN American Center and signed by Norman MAILER, Susan Sontag, William Styron, Kurt VONNEGUT and John Irving, among others. The letter argued that Randall's ideas were being punished and that the decision to deport her abridged the American right to free expression. Randall won the first round of appeals and was allowed to remain in the United States while the case continued. In 1989 an INS review board voted that she had always remained an

American citizen, which freed her to remain in her native country.

For additional reading, see Navasky's *Naming Names*; Tucker's *Literary Exile in the Twentieth Century*.

exiled writers (to the United States) Writers who, for political reasons, left communist countries to immigrate to the United States. (Or, in the case of South Korea, writers who fled to the United States from an oppressive government aligned with the United States during the Cold War.) The literary emigrés who had the greatest impact on American Cold War culture came from the Soviet Union and Eastern Europe, though writers from China, Vietnam, South Korea and Cuba also contributed significantly to the American experience of the Cold War. In addition, a relatively small number of writers left the United States for political reasons, and their writings also helped shape Cold War culture. (See EXILED WRITERS [exiled from the United States].) Only works that were either written in or translated into English during the Cold War were accessible to the mainstream of American readers. Therefore, writers whose work did not appear in English at that time are omitted from this discussion.

The primary impact of exile literature was to reinforce the American impression of ongoing tyranny under the various communist regimes. Since most of the exiled writers were victims of political oppression, they were able to communicate their firsthand experiences in detailed and moving ways. For instance, Arthur KOESTLER's fictional account of Stalinist show trials in *Darkness at Noon* (1941) was read widely throughout the Cold War. The book recounts Koestler's involvement in and subsequent denunciation of communism, also the subject of his essay in Richard Crossman's 1950 anthology of essays by former communists, THE GOD THAT FAILED (1949). Other works by exiles include realistic accounts, such as Nobel Prize winner Aleksandr SOLZHENIT-SYN's well-documented *Gulag Archipelago* (1974), which contains the testimony of 227 witnesses of torture and abuse in the Soviet camps for political prisoners. Other works were highly expressionist or surreal depictions of life under highly bureaucratized socialist regimes, such as Tamas AC-ZEL's novel *Illuminations* (1981), which comically depicts life in Hungary, or Andrei AMALRIK's collection of absurdist plays, *Nose! Nose? No-se! and Other Plays* (1973). Indeed, for many emigré Eastern European writers, the ability to leave behind the restrictions of communist-sanctioned "social realism" and to engage in formal experimentation and expressionist wordplay represented the kind of freedom that had been denied them in the East. By giving free play to their imaginative and comic spirits, they demonstrated what was missing in the homelands they saw as repressive. Other writers, such as the Cuban Poet Armando VALLADARES and the Vietnamese exile TRAN THI NGA used the medium of poetry to express both political and personal sentiments.

Though many exiled writers reveled in their newly acquired freedom, some, such as Yuz ALESHKOVSKY and Dorin TUDORI, also expressed disappointment in what they believed to be the superficial nature of the highly materialistic American society or the unjust policies of the U.S. government.

Some of the most compelling accounts of life under communist regimes are autobiographies. Soviet authors whose autobiographies were published in English include Vassily Pavlovich AKSYONOV, Amalrik, Sergei DOVLATOV and the poet Irina RATUSHINSKAYA. Some describe brutal treatment while in prison; others recount their early attraction to and then disaffection from communist ideology. Accounts of prison life include Ratushinskaya's *Grey Is the Color of Hope* (1988) and Amalrik's *Involuntary Journey to Siberia* (1970). Amalrik also wrote *Notes of a Revolutionary* (1982), an account of his last 10 years in the U.S.S.R. Dovlatov's *Ours: A Russian Family Album* (1989) describes his family life in the Soviet Union. His mother had been a powerful editor at a literary house; his grandfather was shot as a spy because he hosted one of Dovlatov's friends from Belgium, a supporter of Stalin who had come to the U.S.S.R. to celebrate communism; his cousin chose a life of crime to escape the confining Soviet way of life. Aksyonov's *In Search of Melancholy* (1987) presents the "story of my emigration, alienation, and acceptance of a new home." The Polish writer Aleksandr WAT describes his intellectual journey to and from communism in his memoir *My Century: The Odyssey of a Polish Intellectual* (1977; in English, 1988) which is based on a series of interviews Wat gave his fellow emigré Czeslaw MILOSZ. Milosz, winner of the 1980 Nobel Prize, received international acclaim for *The Captive Mind* (1953), which he described as "an analysis of the mental acrobatics Eastern European intellectuals had to perform in order to give assent to Stalinist dogmas."

Other NONFICTION accounts by emigré writers include Solzhenitsyn's *Gulag Archipelago*, Amalrik's historical essay *Will the Soviet Union Survive Until 1984* (1970); Joseph BRODSKY's collection of autobiographical and literary essays *Less Than One* (1976) and Igor YEFIMOV's KENNEDY, OSWALD, CASTRO, KHRUSHCHEV (1987). Based on four years of research, Yefimov's book concludes that the Cuban leader hired the Mafia to kill Kennedy in response to efforts by Kennedy to have the CIA assassinate Castro. Mark POPOVSKY's *Manipulated Science* (1979) describes how the Soviet Communist Party tried to subjugate science to political ends, distorting experimental results and conclusions; he warns of the possible destruction of Soviet science. Juri DRUZHNIKOV published *The Myth of Pavlik Morozov* (1988), an account of the murder of a boy who had become a hero in the Soviet Union by reporting his father to the police. From an alternate political perspective, South Korean emigré Kyung Jae KIM wrote a three-volume exposé of the activities of the Korean CIA within the United States entitled *Revolution and Idol* (1979).

Emigré fiction writers have also represented life under communism. Solzhenitsyn's early novel, *One Day in the Life of Ivan Denisovich* (1962), is a fictional account of the daily routine in a Soviet prison camp. Written in the third person, it is a composite of Solzhenitsyn's own experiences and those he observed while incarcerated. *Cancer Ward* (1968) depicts a conflict in values between two hospitalized patients, a former political prisoner who, like Solzhenitsyn, suffers from abdominal cancer, and a high party official with neck cancer. The doctors and hospital staff represent a cross-section of Soviet society. *First Circle* (1968) is the story of scientists forced to work in a Stalinist research center. Solzhenitsyn's other fiction includes a series of novels, still in progress, based on events that led to the Russian Revolution. He calls the projected tetralogy *The Red Wheel*. So far, the series includes his earlier, historical novel *August 1914* (1972) and the more recent sequels, *October 1916* (1984; in English, 1991) and *March 1917* (unpublished).

Other prominent emigré NOVELISTS include the Russian Vladimir NABOKOV and the Pole Jerzy KOSINSKI. Nabokov immigrated to the United States in 1940. Though his work rarely addresses the Cold War directly, it often includes Cold War references and themes, featuring, say, a Slavic country or a totalitarian regime. Moreover, Nabokov questions how we can ascertain truth with any meaningful degree of certainty, given the basic unreliability of all sources of fact. In a Cold War environment in which both sides have produced revisionist histories and rewritten textbooks, Nabokov's concern with the difficulty of distinguishing fact from fiction resonates significantly.

Jerzy Kosinski's novels contrast sharply to Nabokov's playful and apparently apolitical work. Based closely on his own life experiences in Poland and the United States, Kosinski's fiction depicts life as a struggle. *The Painted Bird* (1965) describes the harrowing experiences of a young boy, a Jew or Gypsy, whose urban parents leave him with ignorant peasants in order to protect him from the concentration camp that they imagine is their fate after the Nazi occupation begins. The boy progresses through a series of abusive situations in the Polish countryside and, like Kosinski, becomes mute after a particularly traumatic experience, though he finally reacquires his power of speech. Ironically, German soldiers and those in the liberating Red Army are the only ones to treat the boy compassionately. *Cockpit* (1975) continues Kosinski's fictionalized autobiographical account, describing how the protagonist, an accomplished photographer like Kosinski himself, secures permission to leave communist Poland by forging documents and a dossier of official correspondence pertaining to his request for an exit visa. Kosinski claimed that this is how he himself managed to emigrate in 1957.

Episodes from other novels describe a Kosinski-like man's experience as a new immigrant living in a tough New York neighborhood, as well as his rise to international acclaim as a writer and his membership in the fashionable "jet set" of worldwide travelers. Kosinski also satirized American politics in BEING THERE (1970), a novel about a mentally deficient man named Chance who knows about the world only from television and his work as a gardener. Through a chain of accidents and misunderstandings, Chance becomes attached to a wealthy and politically powerful family and gains influence. The media and members of the political inner circle come to regard him as a man of great wisdom, able to communicate effectively to the nation through what they believe to be parables based on gardening. Kosinski won an Academy Award for writing the screenplay for the film version of *Being There* (1979). He has also published two books pseudonymously under the pen name Joseph Novack. *The Future Is Ours, Comrade* (1960) is a socio-psychological analysis of a totalitarian state. *No Third Path* (1962) also addresses totalitarianism.

Other emigré fiction writers include Aleshkovsky (U.S.S.R.), Druzhnikov, Arkady LVOV (U.S.S.R.), Sacha SOKOLOV (U.S.S.R.), Milosz (Poland), Janusz GLOWACKI (Poland), Guillermo CABRERA INFANTE (Cuba), Roberto FERNANDEZ

(Cuba) and Hsin-yung PAI (China). Aleshkovsky's *The Hand, or the Confession of an Executioner* (1980; in English, 1990) describes the brutality of the Stalinist regime and the efforts of a victim to achieve revenge against his tormentors by becoming a KGB agent himself. Druzhnikov's *Angels on the Head of a Pin* (1989) describes how Soviet officials repress independent thinkers before and just after the Soviet intervention in Czechoslovakia in 1968. When he emigrated, Lvov smuggled out the manuscript of *The Courtyard* (1989) by hiding it in a shoeshine kit. Set during the Stalinist era, 1936–1953, the novel presents several families in a tenement building that serves as a microcosm of Soviet society. The book criticizes Stalin's rule as well as government-sanctioned anti-Semitism. Sokolov wrote *School for Fools* (1976) while still in the Soviet Union. The détente-era novel was well received in the West, where critics welcomed its innovative style and humorous treatment of the Soviet bureaucracy. However, the reception was not so warm in the Soviet Union, and after much harassment, Sokolov immigrated to America in 1978. He has since published *Between the Dog and the Wolf* (1980) and *Astrolabia* (1989), the fictional memoirs of a hermaphroditic Soviet bureaucrat.

Milosz's prize-winning novel, *The Seizure of Power* (1953; in English, 1955) describes the communist takeover of Poland. Much of Milosz's work concerns his feelings for Poland and his native Lithuania—for example, *The Issa Valley* (1955; in English, 1981) and *Native Realm: A Search for Self-Definition* (1968). Glowacki's novel *Give Us This Day* (1981; in English, 1983) portrays members of the Solidarity movement and the hostility they endure from Polish military and government officials. Although the novel was officially banned in Poland, it was first published there as an underground book and then smuggled abroad, where it was translated into several languages.

Cabrera Infante writes primarily of Havana before Castro's takeover in 1959. *Three Trapped Tigers* (1964; in English, 1971), written while he was still in Cuba, was banned by the communist government even though it was apparently apolitical. However, the novel does celebrate individuality, and according to Cabrera Infante, "Perhaps that is the reason and unreason of this prohibition: all freedom is subversive. Totalitarian regimes are more afraid of individual liberty than vampires are of crosses." *Infante's Inferno* (1974; in English, 1978), written in exile, also describes Havana during the pre-Castro years. Fernandez provides a wild, comic and surreal account of Miami's Cuban enclave in *Raining Backwards* (1988). Pai's story collection, *Wandering in the Garden, Waking from a Dream: Tales of Taipei Characters* (1971; in English, 1982) describes the plight of Chinese exiles who fled to Taiwan from the communist regime on the mainland.

Emigré poets who have drawn upon their Cold War experiences include the 1987 Nobel Prize winner Joseph Brodsky, Ratushinskaya, Milosz, Andrei CODRESCU (Romania), Pablo MEDINA (Cuba) and Tran Thi Nga. Brodsky wrote poetry in the Soviet Union before coming to the United States. Though he had difficulty publishing in the U.S.S.R., his poetry was well received in America, where it first appeared in the 1968 anthology *Poets on Street Corners*. After Brodsky was anthologized in *The Living Mirror: Five Young Poets from Leningrad* (1972), Soviet officials exiled him abroad. His *Selected Poems* (1973) earned the praise of W. H. Auden, among other prominent literary figures: His *A Part of Speech* (1980) was translated into English by such leading poets as Derek Walcott and Richard Wilbur. Brodsky's themes range from the metaphysical to the political, including a 1980 poem expressing his reaction to the Soviet invasion of Afghanistan, as well as others dealing with individual human suffering.

A writer of short stories, Ratushinskaya also excelled as a poet. Poems written while she was imprisoned in the Soviet Union won the highest honors in the 1986 Poetry International Festival in Holland. After she emigrated, a volume of her prison poems was translated and published under the title *Beyond the Limit* (1987). According to one of the translators, Frances Brent, the poems were "written with a sharpened matchstick on a bar of soap. When they were memorized, the poet washed her hands and the palimpsest was erased. The poems were composed sporadically over a period of 14 months."

Milosz's volume *Daylight* (1953) consists of poems collected and published in exile, including the poem, "You Who Have Wronged a Simple Man." That poem was chosen to be inscribed on a monument in Gdansk celebrating the Solidarity movement before the labor union was outlawed and martial law imposed.

During the Cold War, Codrescu published 16 books of poetry, three works of fiction and two autobiographical books. His titles include *Comrade Past and Mister Present: New Poems and a Journal* (1986), *Monsieur Teste in America and Other Instances of Realism* (1987) and *Raised by Puppets: Only to Be Killed by Research* (1989). He also hosted a program of commentary for National Public Radio's "All Things Considered" and edited the now-defunct literary journal, *Exquisite Corpse.*

Medina's *Pork Rind and Cuban Songs* (1975) was the first English-language collection of poems published by an exiled Cuban writer. The collection, which explores the family and the self, also criticizes the oppressive regimentation of Castro's government. With Wendy Wilder Larsen, Tran Thi Nga coauthored the best-selling SHALLOW GRAVES (1986), a collection of poems modeled on the Vietnamese *truyen,* a novel in verse. Written between 1980 and 1985, *Shallow Graves* addresses the lives of women and non-combat personnel during the Vietnam War. (See also VIETNAM WAR LITERATURE.)

Notable emigré playwrights include Brodsky, Amalrik and Glowacki. Brodsky's play *Democracy* was performed in London in 1990. Amalrik's absurdist, experimental plays led to his surveillance by the KGB and his eventual arrest in the mid-1960s. The plays were published in the West in 1973. Glowacki's most powerful play, *Cinders* (1981), was written in Poland but later published in the United States. It portrays a Polish filmmaker trying to document a production of *Cinderella* in a girls' reform school. As part of the documentary, the director compels the girls to describe their own tales of woe. The more extreme and sensational their stories are, the better they are for his cinematic purposes. All the girls but one comply, embellishing their stories for greater effect. Cinders, the girl who refuses to lie for the camera, becomes the protagonist of the play, which pits the desire to preserve truth against those who would manipu-

late it for their own purposes. Glowacki has written two full-length plays since coming to the United States, *Fortinbras Gets Drunk* (1985) and *Hunting Cockroaches* (1986), as well as two shorter plays: "Journey to Gdansk" and "Flashback" both, of which deal with the dilemmas of exiled writers who must decide whether to return to Poland to report on the strike of shipyard workers in Gdansk. If they go, they risk imprisonment or other personal losses; if they stay, they must live with what they see as their own cowardice.

Though most literature by exiles from communist countries condemns the oppressive regimes of their homelands, the West also receives criticism. In particular, Aleshkovsky and Tudoran (Romania) have eloquently expressed dissatisfaction with aspects of Western politics and/or culture. An extremely harsh critic of the Soviet system, Aleshkovsky has declared his dissatisfaction with the West as well—for allegedly "surrendering . . . to world totalitarianism."

Tudoran observed during the Cold War that Western governments and media used exiled Eastern European writers for political exploitation; thus the quality of their literature mattered less in the West than the current political attitude toward the particular country whence the writer was exiled. Moreover, when writers did not come from currently "fashionable" oppressed countries, their work was likely to be ignored, regardless of its merit. Ironically, Tudoran argued, art for art's sake could exist in socialist states because of bureaucratic toleration, condescension and ignorance on the part of government officials. Poets enjoyed wide readership in Romania because the audience understood and responded to sentiments implied; however, the audiences were not free to act upon the writer's message. By contrast, in the West audiences were free to act, but few people read poetry, which had no viable economic base. Thus, for poets in the West freedom of expression mattered little because there was no audience to hear their words and no economic support to enable them to write.

For additional reading, see Tucker's *Literary Exile in the Twentieth Century.*

Exodus A 1958 novel by Leon URIS and a 1960 FILM ABOUT COLD WAR EVENTS starring Paul Newman, Eva Marie Saint, Peter Lawford and Lee J. COBB, and directed by Otto PREMINGER. *Exodus* presents the developments leading up to the formation of the state of Israel in 1948 and the war with its Arab neighbors that immediately followed. The action centers on the leader of the Israeli independence movement and his love affair with a Christian woman. Pat Boone wrote the theme song, which became a popular hit. Though more a consequence of the dissolution of the British Empire than of the Cold War, the emergence of the Jewish state went on to become an important feature in Cold War Middle Eastern politics.

The film's major contribution to Cold War American culture, however, was that it was the film that broke the RED SCARE practice of BLACKLISTING FILM ACTORS, SCREENWRITERS and FILM DIRECTORS who had allegedly had ties to the Communist Party or who had otherwise expressed communist sympathies. The screenplay was written by Dalton TRUMBO, one of the HOLLYWOOD TEN, "unfriendly" witnesses who had gone to prison for refusing to testify before the HOUSE COMMITTEE ON UN-AMERICAN ACTIVITIES (HUAC) in 1947. Trumbo had been compelled to write under aliases throughout the 1950s, but Preminger publicly credited him for the script of *Exodus,* an act that drew front-page coverage from the *New York Times.* After this announcement, Trumbo was also credited with writing the script of Stanley KUBRICK'S SPARTACUS (1960). The public acknowledgment of Trumbo's role in these films signaled the end of the blacklist and made it possible for other blacklisted writers and performers to work again in the Hollywood film industry. (See also LITERATURE ABOUT COLD WAR EVENTS.)

"Face the Nation" A TELEVISION NEWS show that ran on CBS from 1954 throughout the Cold War. The show featured interviews with well-known politicians, foreign dignitaries and other public figures. Its most famous moment during the Cold War was in 1957, when a panel of three reporters conducted an hour-long interview of Soviet premier Nikita Khrushchev. The network was heavily criticized for failing to conform to the established practice of following a communist spokesperson with anti-communist commentators. The decision by an American television network to give unanswered air time to a communist leader provoked considerable controversy, including a demand by the commander of the Catholic War Veterans that CBS cancel the show. President Eisenhower also objected, calling the interview a stunt and stating that "a commercial firm in this country [is] trying to improve its commercial standing." CBS president Frank Stanton defended the interview, claiming that "Khrushchev and his views are of great importance to our world and the world of our children. The less this man . . . remains a myth or a dark legend or a mystery to the American people, the more certain they are to size him up correctly." Rival networks NBC and ABC declined to defend CBS's right to broadcast the show.

For additional reading, see Whitfield's *The Culture of the Cold War.*

Facial Justice A 1960 APOCALYPTIC NOVEL by L. P. Hartley. Published in England and written during the most threatening period of the Cold War, 1958–62, the novel is set in "the not very distant future, after the Third World War." From the ashes of the nuclear war emerges a new society that embraces a totalitarian dictatorship. The survivors welcome the Dictator, who implements the caste system of "Facial Rearmament," permanently assigning people to a social class on the basis of their faces. For instance, those with *alpha* and *beta* faces are at the bottom of society and are given the names of famous murderers. The virtue of the seemingly capricious system is that it provides a social stability that had been absent in the prewar democracies. As in George Orwell's NINETEEN EIGHTY-FOUR (1949), the Dictator reconstructs and simplifies language to lessen the possibility of political resistance. The story centers on a woman who tries to challenge the Dictator and his repressive language, which she regards as "a storehouse of dead metaphors." But ultimately, the system proves too strong.

For additional reading, see Dowling's *Fictions of Nuclear Disaster.*

"Facts We Face, The" A TELEVISION NEWS show that ran on CBS in the summers of 1950 and 1951. It was moderated in 1950 by Bill Shadel and in 1951 by Walter Cronkite under a new title, "Open Hearing." "The Facts We Face" was intended to inform the public about how the mobilization for the Korean War would affect their lives. The show covered such topics as the draft, resource allocations and production goals, manpower and civil defense.

Fail-Safe A 1962 MILITARY NOVEL by Eugene Burdick and Harvey Wheeler and a 1964 MILITARY FILM starring Dan O'Herlihy, Henry Fonda, Edward Binns, Larry Hagman and Walter Matthau and directed by Sidney Lumet. The novel, which became a best-seller, was originally serialized in the *Saturday Evening Post;* it appeared the same month as the Cuban Missile Crisis (October 1962). Produced by Max Youngstein, a member of the anti-nuclear organization SANE, and written by the formerly blacklisted writer Walter Bernstein, the film version closely follows the novel. Often paired with DR. STRANGELOVE (1964), which treats a similar story line with BLACK HUMOR, *Fail-Safe* is a tense, serious drama that centers on the fate of the world after a mechanical malfunction sends a group of nuclear-armed U.S. bombers from their "fail-safe" positions outside of Soviet air space to attack Moscow. When combined U.S. and Soviet efforts fail to stop one of the warplanes, the U.S. President (Fonda) realizes he can forestall all-out nuclear warfare only by ordering a nuclear attack on New York as compensation for the destruction of the foremost Soviet city. His anguish becomes even more personal because his beloved wife is visiting New York, and he does not have time to warn her.

Stanley KUBRICK, who directed DR. STRANGELOVE, threatened the producers with a plagiarism lawsuit but was appeased when Columbia agreed to release his film first. *Fail-Safe* begins with a disclaimer that ". . . it is the stated position of the Department of Defense and the United States Air Force that a rigidly enforced system of safeguards and controls insure[s] that occurrences such as those depicted in this story cannot happen." In fact, the Positive Control System in Omaha, which oversaw the airborne bombers from the Strategic Air Command (SAC), was set so that a computer failure would abort an air strike, not initiate one. Despite the disclaimer, the Air Force refused to cooperate with the making of the movie.

Fail-Safe presents the then-current debate between rightwing "hawks" and centrist and liberal "doves." The hawks rejected the stalemate of Mutually Assured Destruction (MAD) and argued that, since a nuclear war with the Soviet Union was inevitable anyway, the United States should launch a preemptive strike. The doves, on the other hand, maintained that the United States must never be a nuclear aggressor; they accepted MAD and sought to achieve "peaceful co-existence" with the Soviets. The story also presents the tension between old-school humanists and a class of emerging technocrats who value pragmatism above all else. The humanists, like General Black (O'Herlihy), who appears early on as a tender and devoted husband, insist upon retaining ultimate human control over military systems. They also see personal interaction as the ultimate basis for professional conduct. Thus Colonel Grady (Binns), who flies the bomber that destroys Moscow, values the personal bonds that fliers formed in the old days and objects to the new generation of fliers who show no emotion, form no attachments, and follow orders mechanically. Likewise, the president tries to establish a personal bond of mutual trust with the Soviet premier as they work together to avert the full-scale nuclear war that would create NUCLEAR APOCALYPSE.

By contrast, Professor Groeteschele (Matthau), a political scientist, views the Cold War purely in statistical terms and coldly advocates strategies predicated entirely upon their efficiency and utilitarian value. When the president announces his decision to bomb New York, Groeteschele dispassionately calculates that millions of people will die immediately and millions more deaths will follow in the coming weeks, but that rescue efforts must concentrate on retrieving important documents from the international corporate headquarters in New York, since the national economy depends upon them. Groeteschele also favors making military systems entirely dependent on machines and computers since these are less prone to error than humans. Furthermore, he argues that since the bombers cannot be recalled, the president should authorize a full-scale attack against the Soviet Union; otherwise the United States will be annihilated. Groeteschele appears to have been at least partly based on Herman Kahn, the author of ON THERMONUCLEAR WAR (1960).

However, mechanical, not human, error creates the disaster: "a tiny knob of burnt carbon on top of the disabled condenser." And New York's last chance for salvation vanishes when Grady subordinates his human instincts and obeys a standing order to disregard commands given vocally after he has left his fail-safe point. Grady thus denies his strong, human impulse to believe the voices of the president and of his own wife, who explain about the mechanical error and plead with him to abort the mission. Ironically, the humanists perform the nuclear dirty work and make the greatest personal sacrifices: Grady drops the bombs on Moscow and dies soon after off-camera; Black drops the bombs on New York and immediately kills himself with a lethal injection, knowing he has killed his wife in New York, and the president must accept responsibility for destroying his nation's most important city and for killing his own wife as well. The film thus highlights the new type of moral dilemmas introduced by the Cold War and underscores the feeling in the early 1960s that the world was on a nuclear hair-trigger that comparatively innocent events could set off. (See also APOCALYPTIC FILMS; APOCALYPTIC NOVELS.)

Falwell, Jerry A television evangelist and founder of the politically conservative Moral Majority. Falwell began hosting a religious show in 1971; he remained on the air throughout the Cold War. Originally his show was entitled "The Old-Time Gospel Hour"; it was later listed simply as "Jerry Falwell" (syndicated, 1971–present). In the 1980s, he headed the politically influential Moral Majority, an organization somewhat to the right of Ronald REAGAN. Abolishing legal abortions and reinstituting prayer in the public schools were its main issues, but the organization was also associated with other right-wing, Cold War positions, notably opposition to communism, (See also RELIGIOUS TELEVISION PROGRAMMING.)

Far From Vietnam A 1967 French-made FILM DOCUMENTARY about the Vietnam War. Eleven internationally acclaimed directors contributed to this documentary view of the war, which by then was extremely unpopular in France.

Among the participating directors were Jean-Luc Godard, Claude Lelouch, Alain Resnais, Joris Ivens and Agnes Varda. (See also VIETNAM WAR FILMS.)

Farnham's Freehold A 1965 SCIENCE FICTION NOVEL by Robert Heinlein. Published just as the Vietnam War was escalating, the novel imagines alternative apocalyptic endings to NUCLEAR APOCALYPSE. The protagonist is a survivalist who believes that the next war will probably be an "ABC war—atomic, biological, and chemical . . . That's why I stocked that bottled breathing. Aerosols. Viruses. God know what. The communists won't smash this country if they can kill us without destroying our wealth." But a nuclear war does take place, and a nuclear explosion propels the protagonist into a distant future. When he emerges from his bomb shelter, he enters an idyllic parallel universe where the last war occurred long ago. But he learns that this new paradise is also subject to new nuclear war, and he must take shelter in a mine shaft while the apocalypse repeats itself. Heinlein characterizes the relationship between scientists and the ruling military and government leaders in terms of bright boys who are subservient to dull boys. "The bright boys made it possible, and the dull boys they worked for had not only never managed to make the possibility unlikely but had never really believed it when the bright boys delivered what the dull boys ordered." (See also APOCALYPTIC NOVELS.)

For additional reading, see Dowling's *Fictions of Nuclear Disaster*.

Fast, Howard A NOVELIST and NONFICTION WRITER. Born in New York in 1914, Fast served with the Office of War Information during World War II before becoming a war correspondent in the China-Burma-India Theater in 1944–45. He wrote his first novel when he was 18, the first of several books set in the American Revolution. Fast joined the American Communist Party in 1943 and remained a member until 1956. Thus he was a communist during the most intense period of the RED SCARE and one of the most intense parts of the Cold War. Though at the time he maintained that he resisted party demands to eliminate "politically incorrect" and "bourgeois" passages from his writing, his work from this period reflects his Marxist values, and he later claimed that he "sold his soul" to the communists and submitted to their demands for changes in his play *Thirty Pieces of Silver* (1954). In 1946 Fast was among those who stridently attacked Albert MALTZ for publishing an article in *New Masses* advocating greater artistic latitude for communist writers. Though Maltz capitulated and renounced the article, the savagery of the attacks against him provoked several others to leave the party. Fast's writing from his communist period includes *Freedom Road* (1944), about whites and blacks during Reconstruction; *The American* (1946), about John P. Altgeld, the governor of Illinois who pardoned three of the anarchists convicted in the 1886 Haymarket bombing (John F. Kennedy treats the same subject in *Profiles in Courage*, 1956); *Clarkton* (1947), about a Massachusetts mill town; and SPARTACUS (1951), about the slave revolt against the Romans in 71 B.C.

The communists had adopted Spartacus as one of their historical heroes whose efforts symbolized the universal fight against oppression, and Fast's fictional account was probably the basis for his receiving the Stalin Peace Prize in 1954. He wrote the book in federal prison while serving a sentence for contempt of Congress as a result of his refusal in 1950 to give the HOUSE COMMITTEE ON UN-AMERICAN ACTIVITIES (HUAC) the names of anti-fascists who had contributed to a Spanish hospital in which Fast had worked during the Spanish Civil War. Fast founded the Blue Heron Press to publish *Spartacus* himself after the originally contracted publisher and six others turned it down. *Spartacus* became a best-seller, and it was the basis for the 1960 EPIC FILM directed by Stanley KUBRICK. Screenwriter Dalton TRUMBO, one of the original HOLLYWOOD TEN who also served a prison term for refusing to comply with HUAC, adapted the novel for the film. Kirk Douglas, who produced as well as starred in the movie, thus deliberately challenged the practice of BLACKLISTING by presenting a film written by one of the Hollywood Ten and based on a novel by a prominent communist, though Fast had disavowed his communism by the time the film was made. Douglas' announcement that Trumbo wrote the screenplay, along with Otto Preminger's crediting Trumbo for writing EXODUS, set the precedent that destroyed the practice of blacklisting former communists and communist sympathizers. President-elect John Kennedy and his brother Robert crossed American Legion picket lines to see the movie.

Fast also wrote NONFICTION during his party days, including *Tito and His People* (1948), about the communist leader of Yugoslavia; *Peekskill, USA* (1951), about his own role in resisting anti-communist rioters and police during Paul ROBESON's 1949 concert in Peekskill, New York; and *The Passion of Sacco and Vanzetti* (1953), about the anarchist rebels. *The Naked God* (1957) describes his decision to leave the party in 1956. Fast continued to write fiction after renouncing communism, especially historical fiction, but he never regained the reputation he had earned in the 1930s and 1940s. In 1990 he published his autobiography, *Being Red*.

For additional reading, see *Dictionary of Literary Biography* (vol. 9, *American Novelists 1910–1945*).

Fat Man and Little Boy A 1989 FILM DRAMA starring Paul Newman, Dwight Schultz, John Cusack and Laura Dern and directed by Roland Joffe. It also appeared under the tile *Shadow Makers*. The story centers on the Manhattan Project and the creation of the first two atomic bombs, which scientists called Fat Man and Little Boy. (See also APOCALYPTIC FILMS.)

Fate of the Earth, The A 1982 NONFICTION book by Jonathan Schell. It was published in three installments in *The New Yorker* magazine shortly before its publication in book form. The widely read analysis of possible outcomes of a nuclear war appeared during the first Reagan administration, when Cold War tensions were rising to their highest levels since the 1962 Cuban Missile Crisis and government officials were attempting to reverse the assumptions of Mutually Assured Destruction (MAD) in favor of winnable, limited nuclear war. Schell analyzes the technical and strategic properties of nuclear weapons and speculates on several possible scenarios for nuclear war. He then describes the consequences of a massive nuclear exchange, which, he maintains, would reduce the Earth to a wasteland and introduce a nuclear winter by creating massive clouds that would block out the sun. He also considers the philosophical consequences of a broad nuclear war and the fallacies of the notion of a limited nuclear war. Schell discusses the strategies of deterrence and retaliation and concludes with a call for sharp reduction in strategic arms and a freeze on building new nuclear weapons. The *New York Times Book Review* praised *The Fate of the Earth* for accomplishing "what no other work has managed to do in the 37 years of the nuclear age. It compels us—and compel *is* the right word—to confront head-on the nuclear peril in which we all find ourselves." The reviewer for the *New Republic* said, "My guess is that Jonathan Schell's book . . . will become the classic statement of the emerging consciousness [about the nuclear peril]," and *Saturday Review* called it the most important general work on nuclear war since Linus Pauling's 1958 volume, NO MORE WAR!

"Father Knows Best" A TELEVISION SITUATION COMEDY that ran on CBS in 1954–55, NBC in 1955–58, CBS in 1958–62 and ABC in 1962–63. The last original episodes appeared in the 1959–60 season; thereafter the networks ran reruns. Along with LEAVE IT TO BEAVER (CBS/ABC, 1957–63), "The Donna Reed Show" (ABC, 1958–66) and other situation comedies of the mid-1950s to the mid-1960s, "Father Knows Best" presented television's view of the ideal American family during the first half of the Cold War. The nuclear family was headed by a competent, level-headed, compassionate, but authoritative father, Jim Anderson (Robert Young), who provided adequately, but not extravagantly, for his family on his single income as an insurance agent. Though their passion was certainly restrained, Jim clearly cared for and respected his wife, Margaret (Jane Wyatt), who spent her days caring for their three children and dealing with domestic concerns. Margaret was intelligent and generally competent within her domestic domain, and she held authority over her children. But Jim was clearly the family's head and final decision-maker; he also possessed considerable wisdom, presumably gained from his experience in the corporate world, which he judiciously applied to the problems at home. As the ideal husband and father, he was both thoughtful and decisive. He genuinely loved his family and exercised his authority to do what was best for them, individually and collectively. Jim seemed to have few passions, needs or intense desires of his own. By contrast, most of the problems at home arose when other family members strongly desired something and either employed inappropriate methods to achieve it or were frustrated in their legitimate efforts. Jim projected the professional's belief that a calm, rational approach could resolve most problems in ways that were fair to all concerned. It is significant that this idealized parent works as a professional for a large corporation, where he seems to prosper and enjoy job security. Thus he is accustomed both to working within a framework of authority, which he respects, and to acting independently on his own judgment. The show's run coincided with the postwar rise of professional workers who employed scientific and rational methods on their jobs and acquired new levels of influence during the 1950s and 1960s.

Though the show rarely dealt directly with Cold War issues, it helped shape the view of the American way of life, which the Cold War was ostensibly being fought to preserve. This picture of the American way centered around the nuclear family who lived in a small, non-ethnic city in a house that they owned. Their major daily concerns were not about survival or anything that had life-threatening consequences; instead they addressed problems of child-rearing and relationships with friends and neighbors.

"Father Knows Best" did play a more active role in the Cold War in 1959, when the U.S. Treasury Department commissioned a special episode to promote the sale of savings bonds. The episode, "24 Hours in Tyrant Land," showed the children attempting to live for a day under the rule of a make-believe dictator. Though never broadcast, the episode was distributed to churches, schools and civic organizations to demonstrate the need for maintaining a strong American democracy.

Faulkner, William A NOVELIST. Faulkner wrote his masterpieces *Absalom, Absalom!* (1936), *As I Lay Dying* (1930), *Light in August* (1932) and *The Sound and the Fury* (1929) before World War II, and his Cold War-era fiction was generally apolitical. However, in his 1950 Nobel Prize acceptance speech, Faulkner described his view of the impact of impending NUCLEAR APOCALYPSE on literature:

> Our tragedy today is a general and universal fear so long sustained by now that we can even bear it. There are no longer problems of the spirit. There is only the question: When will I be blown up? Because of this, the young man or woman writing today has forgotten the problems of the human heart in conflict with itself which alone can make good writing because only that is worth writing about, worth the agony and the sweat.

"F.B.I., The" A TELEVISION DRAMA that ran on ABC from 1965 to 1974. It overlapped the Vietnam War and its accompanying protest, the civil rights and Black Power movements, and Richard Nixon's law-and-order presidential campaigns, and it left the air a month after Nixon resigned from the presidency. Starring Efrem Zimbalist Jr. as FBI inspector Lewis Erskine, a man whom *Total Television* describes as "of impeccable integrity and little humor," the show claimed to be based on actual FBI cases. Some plots involved such Cold War threats to U.S. security as spying by communists and bombings by radicals opposed to the Vietnam War. In other episodes, the FBI investigated illegal but nonpolitical acts, such as counterfeiting, extortion and the deeds of organized crime. Real-life FBI director J. Edgar Hoover endorsed the show, which depicted the bureau in a very positive light. Hoover not only permitted the producers to film some background scenes at the FBI headquarters in Washington, D.C., and to open and close each episode with a shot of the FBI seal, but he also inaugurated each new season with a personal appearance. In return for the FBI's active cooperation, ABC producer Quinn Martin gave the bureau complete power to approve scripts, sponsorship and all personnel who worked on the show. Each episode concluded with an expression of gratitude to "J. Edgar

Hoover and his associates for their cooperation in the production of this series."

The show was neither violent nor risqué. As Hoover commented in a 1972 *TV Guide* interview, "Perhaps we are inclined toward Puritanism in an increasingly permissive world, but foremost in our minds from the beginning episode has been the fact that *The F.B.I.* is telecast into American homes at a 'family hour' on a 'family evening.'" The show thus endorsed law and order and traditional American values by showing the calm, highly professional law enforcement agents defeat those who would undermine the America way of life, whether through crime, communism or permissiveness. Moreover, it suggested that America's best protection came not from violent, glamorous and individualistic secret agents like James BOND, but from rational, dispassionate, "corporate" professionals. Likewise, citizens who did not share corporate values were suspected of being anti-American, or at least unduly permissive. (See also TELEVISION SPY SHOWS.)

Feiffer, Jules A playwright and political cartoonist. Born in 1929, Feiffer served from 1951 to 1953 in the army, which he detested. In 1956 he began drawing political CARTOONS for the avant-garde newspaper, *Village Voice*. As the paper became more widely circulated, Feiffer's national recognition rose with it, and by 1959 he was publishing in PLAYBOY magazine, being syndicated nationally and gaining a following for his witty SATIRE of American politics and society. In 1961 he won an Academy Award for *Munro*, an animated film based on a character he had created while in the army. His first theatrical production, a musical revue called *The Explainers*, was also performed that year by the Second City in Chicago. *Crawling Arnold* is a 1961 one-act comedy that appeared amidst the tension of the second Berlin Crisis. It premiered at the prestigious Festival of Two Worlds in Spoleto, Italy. *Crawling Arnold* is the story of a 35-year-old businessman who begins behaving like an infant. His parents, caricatures of conservative, middle-class Americans, arrange for him to be visited by attractive social workers. Unlike Arnold, the parents are vigorous and athletic despite being in their seventies. Their bomb shelter appears in *Good Housekeeping* magazine, and they occupy themselves with civil defense drills and talking about the communist menace. Their maid is a black activist who wants her own bomb shelter.

Feiffer published two short plays in popular MAGAZINES that satirize the Kennedy administration: *Interview* (in *Harpers*, June 1962) and *You Should Have Caught Me At the White House* (in *Holiday*, June 1963). However, these lost their appeal after Kennedy was assassinated in November 1963. In 1967 Feiffer produced his first full-length original play, *Little Murders*, about an all-American family victimized by random violence. Though most of the play is comic, its violent ending shocked American audiences, and it closed after seven Broadway performances. However, when the Royal Shakespeare Company produced it later that year in England, it won the London Theatre Critics Award. In 1969 Alan Arkin directed an Off-Broadway production that ran for 400 performances and won two major awards. Feiffer suggests that the assassinations of Robert Kennedy and Martin Luther King that intervened between the first Ameri-

can performance and the play's 1969 revival may have made it appear more appropriate and powerful.

Feiffer's play *God Bless* (1968) takes place amidst revolutionary activity in Washington, D.C., and expresses cynicism about those who exercise power. The play was never produced in New York and did not do well in England when the Royal Shakespeare Company staged it, perhaps because the references to American politics were too oblique for British audiences. *The White House Murder Case* (1970) imagines a Vietnam-like war with Brazil and presents the secret machinations of the president and his administration. Like *Little Murders,* it combines humor with gruesome horror to create BLACK HUMOR effects. The play won the 1970 Outer Circle Critics Award. In 1973 Feiffer and eight other playwrights satirized President Nixon in *Watergate Classics*. Feiffer's other major plays include *Carnal Knowledge* (1971), which Mike Nichols directed as a controversial film (1971), and *Knock Knock* (1976) about two contemporary hermits who have given up on the outside world until they are visited by Joan of Arc. *Hold Me!* (1977) is composed of Feiffer's cartoons remade into theatrical sketches.

While writing for the stage Feiffer continued to draw his political cartoons, which were syndicated in newspapers throughout the country. He also published several books of his cartoons, including *Pictures at a Prosecution: Drawings and Text from the Chicago Conspiracy Trial* (1971) about the trial of antiwar protestors who were arrested for disrupting the 1968 Democratic Convention, and *Feiffer on Nixon: The Cartoon Presidency* (1974). His cartoons are known for their ironic perspective that revealed underlying ambiguities and contradictions in the positions and attitudes of his subjects, who ranged from political figures from the East and West to 1950s beatniks and corporate men to 1960s radicals and professors to common citizens grappling with the complexities of their times and with the angst spawned by them. (See also THEATER.)

For additional reading, see *Dictionary of Literary Biography* (vol. 7, *Twentieth-Century American Dramatists*).

Ferlinghetti, Lawrence A POET and publisher. Born in 1920, Ferlinghetti emerged as one of the leaders of the BEAT MOVEMENT when he opened the City Lights Bookstore in San Francisco in June 1953.

Ferlinghetti received a bachelor's degree from the University of North Carolina and a master's degree from Columbia University in 1948. He was in the naval reserve from 1941 to 1945 and served as a command officer during the Normandy invasion in World War II. After the war, he worked for *Time* magazine and received a Doctorat de l'Université in 1951 from the Sorbonne in Paris.

In addition to featuring the works of the Beat poets, City Lights became the first major bookstore in the country to specialize in paperback books; it also sold radical magazines that were unavailable in more traditional outlets. It soon became a center for leftist intellectuals and university students and offered jazz performances and poetry readings. It thus served as an unofficial headquarters for many experimental poets and political radicals.

In 1955, Ferlinghetti turned to publishing, and in addition to issuing his own work, City Lights Books featured volumes by such major poets and novelists as Allen GINSBERG,

Gregory CORSO, Denise LEVERTOV, Jack Kerouac, Frank O'Hara and Robert Duncan. Ferlinghetti was arrested in 1957 on obscenity charges for publishing Ginsberg's *Howl and Other Poems* (1956), but the court ruled the work was not obscene. The ruling established a precedent that enabled other writers to employ images and language hitherto absent from American literature. In recognition of Ferlinghetti's sponsorship of radical literature, Ginsberg later asserted that Ferlinghetti "ought to receive some sort of Pulitzer Prize for publishing." Ferlinghetti's publishing efforts were a deliberate attempt to provide an alternative to government-sponsored funding of poetry, which he condemned in a footnote in *Tyrannus Nix* (1969), a work attacking President Richard Nixon. "Many American poets do in fact help the government in sanctioning a *status quo* which is supported by and supports WAR as a legal form of murder . . ."

Like the works of other Beat poets, Ferlinghetti's own poetry is intended to alter society. In 1958 he declared that poetry should move "back into the street where it once was, out of the classroom, out of the speech department, and—in fact—off the printed page." However, while promoting poetry performances and criticizing the academic nature of poetry in the Cold War era, Ferlinghetti did not repudiate the written word. In fact, he criticized the radicals of the 1960s for eschewing literature in favor of the "psychedelic and visual and oral": "I hope the next time the young go out for an intellectual rebellion, they will think to try the library. It's still the most subversive building in town, and it's still human headquarters. And even rebels can find it useful to know something, if only to learn to sit still with a book in hand."

Ferlinghetti's first book of poems, *Pictures of the Gone World* (1955), was the first publication of City Lights Books. It criticizes unimaginative and emotionally disconnected leaders as "a few dead minds/ in higher places" capable of delivering "a bomb or two/ now and then/ in your up-turned faces." The general aim of that volume is to subvert the capitalistic system, which Ferlinghetti believes is dehumanizing. His second and third volumes, *Tentative Description of a Dinner Given to Promote the Impeachment of President Eisenhower* (1958) and *A Coney Island of the Mind* (1958), also have strong political agendas. *A Coney Island of the Mind* attacks the religious hypocrisy in America that permits the rampant commercial exploitation of Christ while remaining unmoved by the human suffering caused by U.S. political policies. In that book, Ferlinghetti also attacks nationalism and the nation-state itself, since warfare and the nuclear bomb are their logical/ outgrowths. Published at the outset of the second Berlin Crisis, when nuclear war among the superpowers seemed almost inevitable, *A Coney Island of the Mind* depicts nuclear destruction: "Oh it was a spring/ of fur leaves and cobalt flowers/ when cadillacs fell through the trees like rain/ drowning the meadows with madness/ while out of every imitation cloud/ dropped myriad wingless crowds/ of nutless nagasaki survivors."

An early and outspoken critic of the Vietnam War, Ferlinghetti attacked the American leaders at public rallies and in his poetry. *Where Is Vietnam* (1965) lambastes President Johnson as "Colonel Cornpone" who callously orders the suffering and death of people on the other side of the earth.

Tyrannus Nix (1969) accuses President Nixon of promoting the "nazification" of America and points to Nixon's role in the 1950s RED SCARE. Ferlinghetti claims, "I am thinking Old Sick Dick in you we finally see no face at all behind the great seal of the United States." *The Secret Meaning of Things* (1969) expresses Ferlinghetti's pain at the assassinations of John and Robert Kennedy, which he believes were also products of the violence that arises from nationalism, and "A World Awash with Fascism and Fear" (1971) attacks all aspects of American society, "the left and the Right/ not to mention the unsilent center." In *The Mexican Night: Travel Journal* (1970) and *Who Are We Now?* (1976) Ferlinghetti further rejects nationalism in favor of universal brotherhood. Like his literary predecessor Walt Whitman, to whom he sometimes alludes, Ferlinghetti concludes "I AM YOU."

In 1984, while President Reagan was sponsoring the revolution by contras against the leftist Sandinista government in Nicaragua, Ferlinghetti traveled to that country at the invitation of the Nicaraguan government. Subsequently, he published SEVEN DAYS IN NICARAGUA LIBRE (1984), an account of his journey with photographs by Chris Felver. In contrast to the picture of oppression painted by the Reagan administration, Ferlinghetti represents Nicaragua under the Sandinistas as a country dedicated to sincerely motivated social reform and equal rights for women, a country that values poetry and elevates poets to high positions within the government. (See also VIETNAM WAR LITERATURE.)

For additional reading, see *Dictionary of Literary Biography* (vol. 5, *American Poets Since World War II*).

Fernandez, Roberto G. A Cuban EXILED WRITER (to the United States). As a child, Fernandez fled from Cuba with his family in 1961. A professor of Hispanic literature at Florida State University, he published three books of fiction in Spanish between 1975 and 1985. In 1988 he released the English-language novel *Raining Backwards,* which describes Miami's Cuban exile community in a frenetic, absurdist style.

Fields of Fire A 1978 novel by James Webb, a highly decorated Vietnam War veteran who won the Navy Cross, the Silver Star and two Bronze Stars; was wounded in the fighting; and later became secretary of the navy. This work of VIETNAM WAR LITERATURE is set during the height of the war and follows a platoon of Marines through months of jungle warfare. In this respect, it applies a standard formula for World War II fiction to the Vietnam conflict as it depicts the private struggles and motivations of each member of a diverse combat unit. The central character is Will Goodrich, a Harvard student mistakenly assigned to combat after enlisting in the Marine Band. Other characters include Lt. Hodges, who is maintaining his family tradition of fighting for America; Snake, who uses combat to express his basic aggression; Phony, who resents traditional Marine discipline; and Senator, who tries to serve as the platoon's conscience. The book was generally well received. The reviewer for *Time* states that

> Webb is a shrewd storyteller who seems to have gone through Viet Nam with a cassette recorder in his inner ear . . . [The] book has the unmistakable sound of

truth acquired the hard way. His men hate the war; it is lethal fact cut adrift from personal sense. Yet they understand that its profound insanity, its blood and oblivion, have in some way made them fall in love with battle and with one another. Back in 'the World' they would never again be so incandescently alive. The point is as old as Homer, of course, but Webb restates it with merciless precision.

Webb also wrote a later Vietnam War novel, *A Sense of Honor* (1981).

film Along with other forms of storytelling, such as TELEVISION, THEATER and LITERATURE, films communicated attitudes, values, world views and ideologies to Cold War viewers. As the Cold War progressed, the world view it embodied also altered and so did its influence on film. For instance, such early films as I WAS A COMMUNIST FOR THE F.B.I. (1951), THE RED DANUBE (1950), THE IRON CURTAIN (1948), BIG JIM MCCLAIN (1952), JET PILOT (1957), WALK EAST ON BEACON (1952), MY SON JOHN (1952), THE RED MENACE (1949), Samuel FULLER'S PICKUP ON SOUTH STREET (1953) and Alfred HITCHCOCK'S NORTH BY NORTHWEST (1959) portray a world in which devious, emotionally detached communists engage in illegal activities in order to weaken the United States and advance their own cause of world domination. Cumulatively, these films reinforced the American Cold War world view that depicted the superpower confrontation in terms of good and evil, represented Americans as law-abiding and Soviets as lawless, and portrayed the U.S. military, its intelligence agencies and, for the most part, its government as capable organizations headed by responsible men of European descent (never women or ethnic minorities) who were sincere, incorruptible, fully committed, rational, professional and self-sacrificing.

In the 1960s and early 1970s, however, this cinematic portrait of the Cold War began to change in the wake of such events as the Cuban Missile Crisis, the assassinations of John and Robert Kennedy and civil rights leader Martin Luther King, the Vietnam War and Nixon's resignation after the Watergate scandal. The Cuban Missile Crisis made the threat of worldwide nuclear war seem imminent and raised the possibility that defeating the communists "at all costs" might not be worth the price. The assassinations, the war and the Watergate scandal undermined public confidence in the government's competence, honesty and commitment to democracy. Though communism never achieved mainstream approval, for many it faded into the background as confidence in the U.S. government waned and the country became increasingly divided over the war, civil rights, race riots, Watergate and the burgeoning feminist movement, which also pointed to the absence of women in the offices where Cold War policy originated. Consequently, though some 1960s and 1970s films retain the 1950s Cold War world view, others depict a more cynical vision of world politics in which the U.S. government and the Western Allies are as likely to be a source of danger as the communists, and in which both sides are motivated primarily by power, greed and self-interest rather than by truth, justice or ideology. Among the films from the 1960s and 1970s that provide this more cynical view are SEVEN DAYS IN MAY (1964), DR.

STRANGELOVE (1964), THE BEDFORD INCIDENT (1965), THE SPY WHO CAME IN FROM THE COLD (1965), THE KREMLIN LETTER (1970), THE HUMAN FACTOR (1979), THREE DAYS OF THE CONDOR (1975), THE IPCRESS FILE (1965), *Marathon Man* (1976) and the Vietnam War films COMING HOME (1978) and APOCALYPSE NOW (1979).

This shift in attitudes appears in sub-genres such as westerns, science fiction and epics, none of which directly depicts Cold War issues but many of which play out Cold War themes. For instance, such earlier Westerns as HIGH NOON (1952), *Gunfight at the O.K. Corral* (1957) and *My Darling Clementine* (1946) typically celebrate lawmen who enforce the law against violent criminals and thereby civilize the frontier. In this respect, the protagonists mirror the popular image of the United States protecting Western civilization by standing tall against communist grabs for land and power. In the 1960s and 1970s, however, the U.S. role as the world's policeman became more complicated, costly and morally ambiguous, while modern technology seemed to relegate the American frontier to the distant past; consequently, Westerns lost much of their appeal. Though John WAYNE could still make a traditional film like *True Grit* in 1969, a bleaker view of frontier society emerged in Robert Altman's *McCabe and Mrs. Miller* (1971) two years later. Moreover, while Westerns from the 1950s and early 1960s consistently glamorized lawmen and showed that crime does not pay, later films often portrayed outlaws such as Billy the Kid, Butch Cassidy and the Sundance Kid, Cat Ballou and the more recent criminals Bonnie and Clyde as sympathetic protagonists.

In the 1950s, SCIENCE FICTION FILMS typically associated invaders from outer space and monsters who had mutated from nuclear testing with communists. In INVASION OF THE BODY SNATCHERS (1956), for instance, the aliens behave like Senator Joseph McCarthy's representation of communist subversives during the RED SCARE. They look just like everyone else, display no emotions, attempt to take control of the government and military from within, and try to convince the world that their accusers are crazy. In that film, which takes a particularly right-wing perspective, the FBI saves the country from the aliens. In more centrist films, dedicated, competent, highly rational male military officers and/or scientists protect the world from the aliens/communists, though these films often take sides over who is best qualified to fight the menace: soldiers or scientists. In such film epics from the early Cold War as BEN-HUR (1959), QUO VADIS (1951), SPARTACUS (1960), THE TEN COMMANDMENTS (1956) and *Samson and Delilah,* (1949) protagonists asserted their Judeo-Christian religious values in their struggle against oppression. Cecil B. DEMILLE made explicit the general relationship between most epic films and the Cold War in his prologue to *The Ten Commandments:* "The theme . . . is whether men are to be ruled by God's law—or whether they are to be ruled by the whims of a dictator . . . Are men the property of the state? Or are they free souls under God? This same battle continues throughout the world today." The ability of the capitalist-based Hollywood film industry to produce spectacular epics with casts of thousands, opulent sets and exotic costumes also demonstrated the apparent superiority of the American way. FOREIGN FILMS always seemed stark and impoverished by contrast. As the Red Scare abated around 1960 and the terms of the Cold War began to change shortly afterward, these sub-genres also lost popularity and largely disappeared.

In many respects, the 1980s re-instituted the 1950s view of the Cold War as President Ronald REAGAN decried the Soviet Union's "evil empire." But the cynicism of the previous decade did not entirely vanish, and movies from the Reagan and Bush eras reflect both sets of values. Chuck NORRIS and Sylvester STALLONE star in several films that depict the United States to be unequivocally on the side of justice and freedom, while cruel and duplicitous communists serve nefarious causes. SAKHAROV (1984), WHITE NIGHTS (1985) and GORKY PARK (1983) also depict the U.S.S.R. negatively. On the other hand, during the détente of the 1970s and in the early years of the Reagan presidency, Constantin COSTA-GAVRAS was able to portray U.S. duplicity in his political films STATE OF SIEGE (1973) and MISSING (1982), as well as showing the dangers of right-wing America and the duplicity of the FBI in his later film *Betrayed* (1988).

Films addressed the Cold War, in a variety of ways: by portraying important historical moments, acting out political situations based on actual events, satirizing politicians and events, creating imaginary military and/or espionage engagements among Cold War enemies, depicting postnuclear war scenarios and embedding Cold War subtexts within seemingly unrelated genres. Among the prominent Cold War events featured in films were the Cuban Missile Crisis, the Korean and Vietnamese wars, coups and attempted coups in South America and Southeast Asia, the development of the atom bomb and the Kennedy assassination. Nonetheless, such dramatic historical moments as the Berlin Airlift; the anti-communist uprisings in East Germany, Hungary and Czechoslovakia; the second Berlin Crisis; President Nixon's trips to China and the Soviet Union; the Soviet invasion of Afghanistan; and U.S. invasion of Grenada were rarely treated in mainstream films, though they received somewhat more substantial treatment in FILM DOCUMENTARIES, especially in made-for-television documentaries by such directors as Fred FREED and David WOLPER. Though diplomacy and political intrigue were rarely the subjects of smash hits at the box office, after the Red Scare abated, several notable POLITICAL FILMS appeared. In the early and middle 1960s, political orientations at the movies ranged from such conservative works as ADVISE AND CONSENT (1962), in which the Senate refuses to confirm a liberal nominee for secretary of state; to the centrist THE UGLY AMERICAN (1962), which endorses U.S. involvement in Southeast Asia but criticizes the State Department's handling of the job; to *Seven Days in May* and THE MANCHURIAN CANDIDATE (1962), both of which show the greatest threat to American democracy as coming from the political right wing, rather than from communism. Later political films include *The Kremlin Letter,* in which the United States and the Soviet Union conspire to destroy China; ALL THE PRESIDENT'S MEN (1976), about the Watergate scandal; and *JFK* (1991), Oliver STONE's controversial film about the Kennedy assassination, and his *Nixon* (1995). Both of those films appeared shortly after the Cold War concluded.

During the Red Scare, making fun of the government or of American institutions could result in charges of being "un-American" or pro-communist, as playwright George S.

Kaufman discovered to his chagrin in the only movie he directed, the 1947 film comedy THE SENATOR WAS INDISCREET. Consequently, apart from such British-made films as THE MOUSE THAT ROARED (1959), and MODESTY BLAISE (1956), few FILM SATIRES appeared in America before the 1960s. Charles CHAPLIN's 1957 British-made A KING IN NEW YORK fiercely satirizes the HOUSE COMMITTEE ON UN-AMERICAN ACTIVITIES (HUAC) which had helped drive the actor/director from the country. However, the film was not released in the United States until 1976, 19 years after it was debuted. Thus, perhaps the first major political film satire was *Dr. Strangelove,* which appeared in 1964, only two years after the Cuban Missile Crisis. Combining realistic photography with comically exaggerated acting and incongruous dialogue, the film undermines the public perception of the world's leaders as sober, responsible citizens and depicts them instead as insane, sex-crazed maniacs for whom the nuclear bomb is a kind of aphrodisiac. During the Vietnam War, several antiwar films satirized both politics and warfare, notably M*A*S*H (1970), CATCH-22 (1970), HAROLD AND MAUDE (1971) and the French/Italian-made KING OF HEARTS (1967).

In addition to Korean and Vietnam War films (see separate entries), MILITARY FILMS depicted other aspects of the Cold War military confrontation. During the 1950s those military films not related to the Korean War often dealt with the preparations for nuclear warfare. STRATEGIC AIR COMMAND (1955) depicts an air force unit whose nuclear-armed bombers hover in "fail safe" positions close to their Soviet targets; INVASION U.S.A. (1952) imagines what New York City would be like during an atomic attack; and ON THE BEACH (1959) depicts members of a U.S. submarine crew in Australia after a nuclear war has destroyed the entire Northern Hemisphere and created a lethal nuclear cloud that is drifting toward them. Several military films from the middle 1960s depict failures in command that lead to inadvertent nuclear strikes against the U.S.S.R., notably FAIL-SAFE (1964), *The Bedford Incident* and *Dr. Strangelove.* A GATHERING OF EAGLES (1963), also focuses on the nuclear deterrent in its depiction of the Strategic Air Command. From the later 1960s, ICE STATION ZEBRA (1968) centers on a U.S. submarine sent to the North Pole.

During the détente of the 1970s, fewer military films were made, apart from VIETNAM WAR FILMS. However, THE MISSILES OF OCTOBER (1974) reenacted the Cuban Missile Crisis, and PATTON (1970) celebrated the American World War II hero who had advocated an immediate attack against the Soviet Union after Germany was defeated. When the Cold War reintensified during the Reagan era, on the other hand, the number of Cold War-related military films increased. RED DAWN (1984) portrays an underground of teenagers who fight against the communist occupying force after a limited nuclear war. THE BEAST (1988) vilifies the Soviet war in Afghanistan, while TOP GUN (1986) glamorizes the lives of navy fighter pilots. The Bush-era HUNT FOR RED OCTOBER (1990) describes how the U.S. Navy arranges the defection of a state-of-the-art Soviet submarine.

Apart from the Korean War, when U.S. soldiers fought Chinese communists, the armies of the superpowers did not fight against one another. Consequently, the Cold War was played out mostly through proxy wars, diplomacy and spying. Not surprisingly, the spy genre flourished during this period. In some SPY FILMS, especially those adapted from SPY NOVELS by Mickey SPILLANE and Ian Fleming's James BOND stories, the lines between good and evil are clearly drawn. Western spies are fundamentally moral, while communist spies are cold, cynical, merciless agents working for an evil empire. James Bond became the prototypical secret agent for the Cold War era, and he appeared in over 15 films as well as inspiring characters in other films. As a superior man armed with state-of-the-art technology, Bond showcases the virtues of consumer capitalism over communism. While Bond never loses touch with his animal nature, which makes him strong and virile, he balances it with the refinement and high fashion that are the pride of Western achievement, along with its superior technology. In this regard, the Bond stories create images of success and masculine desirability similar to those cultivated by PLAYBOY magazine, which, like the Bond novels, first appeared during the early 1950s. By contrast, in the film adaptations of John LE CARRÉ's *The Spy Who Came in from the Cold* and DEADLY AFFAIR (1967) and Graham GREENE's *The Human Factor* antiheroic spies become victims of their own governments' duplicities and self-serving strategies.

Later films present an even more cynical view of Western intelligence agencies. *Three Days of the Condor* shows the CIA turning against its own agents, as do HOPSCOTCH (1980) and *The Ipcress File*. Because of their heroics and spectacle, spy films became the subject of several British SPY FILM SPOOFS, including *Modesty Blaise* and THE SECOND BEST SECRET AGENT IN THE WHOLE WIDE WORLD (1965), which make fun of the suave, sophisticated superspy, and *Casino Royale* (1967), which parodies the Bond character directly. OUR MAN IN HAVANA (1960) ridicules the British Secret Service when a would-be Cuban spy with no military information sends back technical diagrams of vacuum cleaner parts. James Coburn starred in several American-made spoofs: OUR MAN FLINT (1966) and its sequel and THE PRESIDENT'S ANALYST (1967), in which a psychologist who treats the president becomes the object of kidnapping and assassination attempts. THE IN-LAWS (1979) centers around a fast-talking CIA agent who manages to drag his unwilling brother-in-law, a successful but highly nervous dentist, into a scheme to overthrow a Latin American dictatorship.

In addition to incorporating Cold War views of the communist threat into their story lines, FILM DRAMAS also addressed the threat of NUCLEAR APOCALYPSE, which hovered over the world throughout most of the Cold War. Notable apocalyptic dramas from the 1950s include *On the Beach* and THE WORLD, THE FLESH AND THE DEVIL (1959), which envisions a postnuclear repopulation of the Earth via interracial and non-monogamous sexual coupling. The French- and Japanese-made HIROSHIMA, MON AMOUR (1959) deals with the effects of an actual nuclear bombing as it portrays a Japanese architect and a French actress who have a brief love affair in Hiroshima after the war. Notable 1950s foreign films that allude indirectly to the nuclear threat include Akira Kurosawa's THE SEVEN SAMURAI (1954) and Ingmar Bergman's THE SEVENTH SEAL (1956) and *Shame* (1968). More direct portrayals of nuclear politics were produced in the 1960s. *Fail Safe* dramatizes the agony of a president who must respond to an unauthorized U.S. attack against the

Soviet Union, while the British-made LADYBUG, LADYBUG (1963) and LORD OF THE FLIES (1963) portray children during the threat of an imminent nuclear war. The 1970s and 1980s saw the reemergence of APOCALYPTIC FILMS as the nuclear arms buildup continued and the Cold War reintensified during the Reagan era. Among these were the cult films MAD MAX (1979), *The Road Warrior* (1982), A BOY AND HIS DOG (1975), and AMAZING GRACE AND CHUCK (1987), in which a boy leads a protest against nuclear weapons.

The Red Scare deeply affected the film industry, partly because the American Communist Party had been active in Hollywood, especially among SCREENWRITERS and FILM DIRECTORS and in some of the unions, and partly because of the sensational headlines created by investigations into the political lives of FILM ACTORS AND ACTRESSES. HUAC conducted hearings into alleged communist influence in the film industry in 1947, when the HOLLYWOOD TEN refused on constitutional grounds to answer questions about their political activities. After the Supreme Court denied the Ten's claim to protection under the First Amendment, HUAC resumed its hearings in 1951 and continued periodically throughout the decade to question hundreds of workers in the film industry. Friendly witnesses cooperated fully with the committee and named names of individuals they knew or believed to be communists. Witnesses who refused to name names either invoked their Fifth Amendment protection against self-incrimination or risked prison sentences for contempt of Congress, such as those that had been served by the Hollywood Ten. Individuals identified as communists in these hearings, as well as those who pled the Fifth Amendment, were immediately subject to BLACKLISTING in film and television. Though the Hollywood studio owners claimed they did not maintain a specific list of individuals to be denied employment, RED CHANNELS and other publications by virulently anti-communist organizations such as the American Legion served as de facto blacklists.

The blacklists were effective partly because of the militant anti-communism of several studio owners, union leaders, including Ronald Reagan and Roy BREWER, and film stars, such as John Wayne and Robert Taylor, all of whom supported the principle of keeping communists and communist sympathizers out of American films. Even those less predisposed to political blacklists were subject to political and economic pressures. Boycotts and picketing by the American Legion, the Catholic War Veterans, the American Jewish League Against Communism and other anti-communist groups could potentially destroy a film's ability to make a profit; even threats of a boycott could dissuade banks from lending the funds necessary to make a movie with a blacklisted star or a suspect theme. Consequently, it was safer and probably more profitable to accept the blacklist and to work around other Red Scare-induced constraints. The Red Scare thus denied the film industry the services of many of its most gifted creative talents and created a "chilling effect" that kept filmmakers from taking on social and political issues of any kind.

For all of Hollywood's unwillingness to deal with the issue, the Red Scare inspired some fascinating films. STORM CENTER (1956), about a librarian who is harassed and fired because she refuses to remove a copy of *The Communist Dream* from the shelves of her small-town library, stands out as the only major film of the time that actually attacked the Red Scare. Elia KAZAN's ON THE WATERFRONT (1954) celebrates an act of informing and is often read as the director's defense of his cooperation with HUAC. In the early 1950s, Hollywood Ten member Herbert BIBERMAN and producer Paul Jarrico formed an independent production company whose goal was to hire blacklisted talent and draw "from the living experiences of people long ignored in Hollywood—the working men and women of America." Their efforts to make SALT OF THE EARTH (1954) on location in rural California were impeded by the unions under control of AFL leader Roy Brewer; by local residents who fired on the crew while they were filming; by the Immigration and Naturalization Service, which deported the Mexican lead actress before the filming was completed; and by U.S. congressmen who denounced the film-in-progress and charged that it was "a new weapon for Russia" that might somehow instigate copper miners to strike and thereby block the production of weapons for the then-current Korean War. (The film celebrated a strike by New Mexican copper miners.) Though critically acclaimed abroad, *Salt of the Earth* appeared briefly in only 10 U.S. cities when it was made, though it had renewed life in political and feminist circles in the 1970s. Made in the 1970s, THE WAY WE WERE (1973) vilifies the Red Scare, as does the 1970s enactment of Senator Joseph McCarthy's life in TAIL GUNNER JOE (1977). (See also FILMS ABOUT COLD WAR EVENTS; FILMS ASSOCIATED WITH THE RED SCARE; FILM WESTERNS; EPIC FILMS; FILM COMEDY; KOREAN WAR FILMS.)

film actors and actresses   Film performers contributed to Cold War culture by appearing in stories dealing with Cold War issues and by taking public political stands. Notable in the first category are Charles CHAPLIN, Chuck NORRIS, Peter SELLERS, Sylvester STALLONE and John WAYNE. Wayne, Norris and Stallone starred in highly popular films that glorified the United States and showed valiant Americans fighting for the cause of good against evil communist villains. Wayne was a major Hollywood figure during the 1950s and 1960s, and his films dealing directly with the Cold War include JET PILOT (1957), about a pilot who resists the seduction of a female Soviet spy, and BIG JIM MCLAIN (1952), about an investigator for the HOUSE COMMITTEE ON UN-AMERICAN ACTIVITIES (HUAC). Wayne also produced, directed and starred in THE ALAMO, which celebrates American history and the willingness of brave Americans to resist a tyrant even in the face of overwhelming odds. The film was released during the second Berlin Crisis, when American troops in Berlin were surrounded by hostile Warsaw Pact forces. Wayne also directed and starred in a VIETNAM WAR FILM, THE GREEN BERETS, a pro-war movie that appeared shortly after the pivotal 1968 Tet Offensive. In addition to his film efforts, Wayne contributed to Cold War politics by actively supporting right-wing positions. He was president of the politically conservative MOTION PICTURE ALLIANCE FOR THE PRESERVATION OF AMERICAN IDEALS, and he supported the BLACKLISTING that kept communists, suspected communists and "Communists sympathizers" from working in Hollywood.

Though they did not achieve Wayne's dominant stature, Norris and Stallone in the late '70s and '80s made the kind of super-patriotic action films that Wayne had made earlier in the Cold War. Both Norris and Stallone starred in several films that celebrated Vietnam War veterans who returned to Vietnam to defeat elements of the North Vietnamese Army. In this respect, the films provided a form of revisionist history that made the American failure in Vietnam more palatable after the fact, suggesting that American might, unhampered by liberals' constraints, *could* have won the war in Vietnam. Norris's Vietnam War films include *Missing in Action* (Parts 1–3, 1984, 1985, 1988) and *Good Guys Wear Black.* (1979). In another Cold War film, INVASION U.S.A. (1985), Norris saves the United States from an invasion of Soviet-backed terrorists. Stallone's highly successful RAMBO series (1982, 1985, 1988) also features a war veteran who returns to fight his former enemies. The hero's willingness to go in and do what was necessary, to act outside the law no matter how much violence was required, was intended to appeal to the right-wing image of a U.S. military hamstrung during the war by international law and political constraints. President Reagan, who saw the first Rambo film shortly after 39 Western hostages were released in Lebanon, drew on Rambo's appeal in a public statement "Boy, I saw *Rambo* last night. Now I know what to do the next time this happens." In the ROCKY series, Stallone portrays a boxer who succeeds through hard work, dedication and the love of a good woman. In *Rocky IV* (1990) he defeats a larger Russian fighter in a title bout between representatives of the superpowers.

On the other side of the political spectrum, the British-born actors Chaplin and Sellers made FILM COMEDIES and FILM SATIRES that ridiculed U.S. and Soviet behavior during the Cold War. An extremely popular star from the days of silent pictures, Chaplin made several films with socialist sentiments. Because of his attacks on capitalism and his sexual affairs with underaged women, the American Legion picketed MONSIEUR VERDOUX (1947), which Chaplin claimed was his response to the atom bomb, as well as *Limelight* (1952), even though that film contained no political or "unwholesome" themes. In the late 1940s, Chaplin criticized American foreign policy, defended the civil liberties of American communists and supported the 1948 presidential aspirations of Progressive candidate Henry Wallace. At the same time, Chaplin always denied that he was a communist, and no evidence has surfaced to prove that he ever was one, despite an FBI file almost 2,000 pages long. Nonetheless, accusations about Chaplin's alleged communist affiliations abounded in columns by such influential gossip writers as Hedda Hopper and Louella Parsons. While the actor was aboard the luxury liner *Queen Elizabeth* en route to England for the 1952 premiere of *Limelight,* U.S. attorney general James McGranery revoked his entry permit. Chaplin then went into exiled in England and Europe and refused to reenter the United States until 1972, when he was given a special Oscar award and was honored at the Lincoln Center Film Society in New York. In 1957 Chaplin made the biting satire A KING IN NEW YORK, his response to HUAC and the RED SCARE that drove him from the United States.

Sellers did not suffer political persecution, and his satires are directed more at specific policies and at general human shortcomings, rather than presenting a political critique of capitalist ideology. Notable among his Cold War–related films are THE MOUSE THAT ROARED (1959), about a small country that declares war on the United States in hopes of losing quickly so it can enjoy the fruits of foreign aid; DR. STRANGELOVE (1964), about a nuclear attack against the Soviet Union launched by an insane U.S. Air Force general; *Casino Royale* (1967), a James BOND spoof; and BEING THERE (1979), about a mentally retarded man obsessed with gardening and television who becomes an influential political adviser to the president. Sellers also starred with Ringo Starr, the drummer from the ROCK AND ROLL band the Beatles, in the film version of Terry SOUTHERN's *The Magic Christian* (1969), which spoofs greed and the lust for money.

Among the film performers whose contribution to Cold War culture appeared more in their personal political activities than on screen were Ward Bond, Charlton HESTON, Lee J. COBB, Jane FONDA, John GARFIELD, Zero MOSTEL, Larry PARKS and Ronald REAGAN. All but Fonda were involved in the Red Scare. Bond, Heston and Reagan were among the more vocal anti-communist activists who supported the blacklist. Like Wayne, Bond was a prominent member of the Motion Picture Alliance, and he was influential in helping to "clear" individuals who had been blacklisted but who were willing to demonstrate their anti-communist sympathies through various public acts of contrition—usually by identifying any members of the Communist Party known to them. In 1951 Parks became the first person to "name names" of communists before HUAC, though his reluctance to do so made him suspect to the political right, and his career was ruined by his appearance before the committee. After being blacklisted and living in poverty for two years, Cobb named names in 1953, and his career was rehabilitated shortly afterward. He appeared in Elia KAZAN's ON THE WATERFRONT (1954), a film that celebrates an act of informing. Because he had not been a communist, Garfield had no names to name; consequently, clearing himself of accusations that he was a communist sympathizer was more problematic. He died of a heart attack while still trying to get off the blacklist. Mostel refused to name names and remained on the blacklist until the 1960s. In 1976 he appeared in the tribute to the victims of the blacklist, THE FRONT (1976), written and directed by former blacklistees Martin Ritt and Walter Bernstein, and costarring Woody Allen.

In addition to appearing in COMING HOME (1978), an antiwar film, Fonda was an outspoken public critic of the Vietnam War. When Fonda traveled to North Vietnam in 1972, she gave radio broadcasts encouraging American soldiers to disobey orders to fight, so many Americans considered her traitor who had aided the enemy. She thus acquired the popular nickname "Hanoi Jane", an allusion to the World War II radio broadcasts by Tokyo Rose, who likewise urged Allied soldiers to quit fighting. Reagan, of course, became the most political of all Hollywood performers. As a spokesman for General Electric, a defense contractor, he publicly espoused a strong anti-communist position that later helped him to win two terms as governor of California and two terms as U.S. president.

Bob HOPE's contribution to the Cold War came primarily from his patriotic USO shows for U.S. troops overseas; Marilyn MONROE's came from her alleged sexual alliances with President Kennedy and other powerful men and from her marriage to Playwright Arthur MILLER, whose autobio-graphical *After the Fall* (1963) includes a character based on Monroe. Moreover, as a Hollywood sex icon she became an international symbol of what many Americans embraced as the pursuit of happiness and communists rejected as decadent. She was featured as a character in Nicholas Roeg's *Insignificance* (1985), a British-made film that imagines her, her husband Joe Dimaggio, the baseball star, and Albert Einstein exploring the nuclear threat.

Robert VAUGHN appeared in political film and television thrillers, most notably "THE MAN FROM U.N.C.L.E." (NBC, 1964–68). He was also one of the most significant observers of the HUAC hearings. His book *Only Victims*, based on his 1972 Ph.D. dissertation, studied the hearings' effects on THEATER and film during the Cold War.

film comedy The ability to spin comedy from superpower confrontation and the prospect of imminent NUCLEAR APOCALYPSE was one of the more life-affirming aspects of the Cold War experience. Frequently such comedies invoked BLACK HUMOR to enable audiences to laugh, albeit sometimes uncomfortably, at the realization of their own worst fears. Foremost of the black humor films was Stanley KUBRICK's DR. STRANGELOVE (1964), starring Peter SELLERS. Filmed in a highly realistic fashion, the 1964 film depicts an insane air force general who orders a surprise attack on the Soviets, leaving sex-crazed generals, diplomats and politicians to deal with the crisis, which threatens to set off a Soviet Doomsday device. Darker and more gruesome than *Dr. Strangelove*, Robert Altman's M*A*S*H (1970) generates humor even as the camera shows spurting blood and vivid images of carnage. Like *Dr. Strangelove*, *M*A*S*H* depicts a world run by insane, sexually crazed, sexually frustrated and/or perverted men (and to a lesser extent, women), but the horror behind its humor is more immediate and more frightening. *Dr. Strangelove* appeared in 1964, a relatively benign period in the Cold War after U.S.-Soviet tensions had subsided from the Cuban Missile Crisis and before the major U.S. escalation in Vietnam. On the other hand, *M*A*S*H*, though set during the Korean War, was made in 1970 at the height of the Vietnam War, when TELEVISION NEWS shows were regularly sending home pictures of dead and wounded Americans. Its antiwar message thus had a more direct target. Another powerful black humor film from 1970 was CATCH-22, starring Alan Arkin. Like *M*A*S*H* and an earlier FOREIGN FILM, KING OF HEARTS (1967), *Catch-22* uses a setting from an earlier conflict (World War II) to depict warfare as an insane enterprise run by power-hungry men with twisted values. Hal Ashby's HAROLD AND MAUDE (1971) is another black humor film of the era that celebrates COUNTERCULTURE values and implicitly attacks the war.

Post-apocalyptic film and LITERATURE flourished during the 1980s, when the Reagan administration reinvigorated the arms buildup, proposed the Strategic Defense Initiative (SDI—popularly known as STAR WARS, after another film) and replaced the premise of Mutually Assured Destruction (MAD), with the possibility of winnable, survivable nuclear war. Though most film and literary treatments of possible nuclear holocaust were serious during this period of renewed superpower tensions, some movies were funny. Earlier apocalyptic comedies included A BOY AND HIS DOG (1975) and CAFE FLESH (1960s). RADIOACTIVE DREAMS (1986) was a

Reagan-era black-humor comedy about life after a nuclear holocaust. All of those films echo THE ATOMIC KID, a 1954 comedy starring Mickey Rooney, about a man who survives a nuclear war but becomes radioactive. The Reagan-era film documentary THE ATOMIC CAFE (1982) pairs scenes from 1950s Civil Defense films with actual footage from nuclear tests to create black humor. The editing underscores the preposterous nature of 1950s government assurances about nuclear war. Moreover, it implicitly suggests that 1980s claims of survivable nuclear war are equally absurd. Set during the Cuban Missile Crisis, the Bush-era WAITING FOR THE LIGHT (1990) also spawns black humor, though the historical setting reassures audiences that the apocalypse will be averted. Released during the collapse of communism, in the final stage of the Cold War, *Waiting for the Light* appeared when the nuclear threat seemed more distant than it had since 1945. In DEAL OF THE CENTURY (1983), Chevy Chase spoofs the international arms trade that fueled the proliferation of sophisticated weaponry during the early and mid-1980s, and in SPIES LIKE US (1985) he poked fun at the efforts of U.S. intelligence agencies in Afghanistan and other parts of Asia. Other Cold War film comedies that spoofed or referred to SPY FILMS included MODESTY BLAISE (1956), THE IN-LAWS (1979), HOPSCOTCH (1980), THE PRESIDENT'S ANALYST (1967), OUR MAN FLINT (1966), OUR MAN IN HAVANA (1960), THE TROUBLE WITH SPIES (1987) and *The Fiendish Plot of Dr. Fu Manchu* (1980).

A few films spoofed politics itself, though in the late 1940s this was a surprisingly dangerous thing to do. THE SENATOR WAS INDISCREET (1947), the only movie directed by writer George S. Kaufman, was criticized for lampooning a corrupt and inept politician on the grounds that such criticism undermined public confidence in the government. U.S. representative Clare Boothe Luce demanded to know, "Was this picture made by an American?" The American Legion attacked the film as un-American propaganda, and the Motion Picture Association of America prohibited the film from being shown overseas. Ironically, Kaufman went on to write the 1955 Broadway musical play SILK STOCKINGS, which became the basis for the 1957 film musical by the same title. A remake of the 1939 Greta Garbo movie *Ninotchka*, *Silk Stockings* celebrates the virtues of capitalism over communism.

Charles CHAPLIN was also the target of boycotts in the late 1940s and early 1950s because of the anti-capitalist themes in his films and because of his affairs with under-aged women. His MONSIEUR VERDOUX (1947) was boycotted and quickly withdrawn, and his 1957 comic attack on the HOUSE COMMITTEE ON UN-AMERICAN ACTIVITIES (HUAC), A KING IN NEW YORK (1957), was not released in the United States until 1976.

Though not overtly political, BABY DOLL (1956) was also the target of boycotts because of its then-racy sexual content, which some believed undermined the American character and American values. THE FRONT (1976), directed and written by blacklisteds Martin Ritt and Walter Bernstein and starring Woody Allen and former blacklistee Zero MOSTEL, later chronicled the RED SCARE practice of BLACKLISTING. The film included other actors who had also been blacklisted in the 1950s.

Not until after the Red Scare subsided with the 1960 election of John Kennedy did political satires and critiques begin to appear in U.S. films, though the British-made satire THE MOUSE THAT ROARED was widely viewed in the United States in 1959. Starring Peter Sellers, *The Mouse that Roared* tells the story of a small country that wages war on the United States with the intention of losing immediately, so it can quickly begin receiving foreign aid—much as Germany and Japan were funded after World War II. Sellers plays three roles, as he did in *Dr. Strangelove*. The British-born actor also starred in *The Fiendish Plot of Dr. Fu Manchu* and BEING THERE, (1979). Based on the novel by Jerzy KOSINSKI, *Being There* centers on a mentally deficient man who knows the world only through his gardening and from watching television. By accident he is befriended by a powerful family and quickly becomes a leading political figure. Some viewers believed the Sellers character was loosely based on Ronald REAGAN, who was campaigning for president when the movie was released.

CUBA (1979), MOON OVER PARADOR (1988), *Our Man in Havana* and Woody Allen's BANANAS (1971) all spoofed Western involvement in Latin American dictatorships. *Bananas* satirizes Fidel Castro's 1959 Cuban revolution as well as the U.S. efforts to undermine it. Greek director Michael Cacoyannis satirizes the military in THE DAY THE FISH CAME OUT (1967). In THE RUSSIANS ARE COMING! THE RUSSIANS ARE COMING! (1966) a Soviet submarine accidentally runs aground off Nantucket Island, convincing some of the local reactionaries that the Soviet invasion has finally begun. The film satirizes the American Legion in ways that probably would not have been possible during the Red Scare seven or eight years earlier. The sentiment of the film anticipates Nixon-era détente by advocating peace and good will between U.S. and Soviet citizens. Made during the second Berlin Crisis, ONE, TWO, THREE (1961) portrays the meeting of East and West as a Coca-Cola executive assigned to West Berlin must deal with an East German communist beatnik whom his boss's daughter has rashly married. BASIC TRAINING (1986) adds a 1980s feminist dimension to the Cold War, as a clever secretary of defense appoints to the Pentagon a woman who outsmarts both the top Soviet and U.S. brass. (See also FILM SATIRES and SPY FILM SPOOFS.)

film directors Film directors contributed to Cold War culture either by making films about Cold War issues or by taking political stands. Among the former were Samuel FULLER, Hal ASHBY, Constantin COSTA-GAVRAS, Cecil B. DE-MILLE, Alfred HITCHCOCK, Stanley KUBRICK, Otto PREMINGER, Oliver STONE and such directors of FILM DOCUMENTARIES as Fred FREED, David WOLPER and Frederick Wiseman. A fervent anti-communist who also condemned American chauvinism and racism, Fuller wrote and directed two KOREAN WAR FILMS, THE STEEL HELMET (1951) and *Fixed Bayonets* (1951) and an early VIETNAM WAR FILM, *China Gate* (1957). He also wrote and directed PICKUP ON SOUTH STREET (1953), a FILM DRAMA about a small-time criminal who inadvertently steals atomic secrets intended for communist spies, and he collaborated on the screenplay for its 1967 remake set in South Africa, *The Capetown Affair*. He also wrote and directed *Hell and High Water* (1954), about a privately owned, scientifically equipped submarine that sails to Alaska to thwart a plot by the Chinese communists. Ashby directed several FILM

COMEDIES, including THE RUSSIANS ARE COMING! THE RUSSIANS ARE COMING! (1966), about the reception given the crew of a Soviet submarine that runs aground off Nantucket Island; HAROLD AND MAUDE (1971), an antiwar BLACK HUMOR comedy about the 1960s COUNTERCULTURE; and BEING THERE, a 1979 FILM SATIRE about a mentally retarded man with a short attention span who is obsessed by gardening and television and who becomes an influential political adviser to the president. Ashby also directed *Bound for Glory*, the 1976 biography of left-wing FOLK SINGER Woody Guthrie, and COMING HOME (1978), a powerful anti–Vietnam War film.

Costa-Gavras achieved international prominence with *Z*, a political thriller based on the real-life assassination in Greece of a liberal reform politician. His THE CONFESSION (1970), also based on a true incident, attacks totalitarian repression and torture in Eastern European communist regimes. Otherwise Costa-Gavras's most common villains are agents of right-wing dictatorships that are aided in their cruelty by U.S. government officials, such as in STATE OF SIEGE (1973) and MISSING (1982). *Missing* has been called the most significant U.S.-made political thriller since THE MANCHURIAN CANDIDATE (1962).

A staunch anti-communist, DeMille produced several EPIC FILMS whose lush sets and "casts of thousands" showcased the vast resources and capabilities of American capitalism. These films typically promoted Judeo-Christian values, which DeMille believed to be the strongest defense against communism. He made this clear in his introduction to THE TEN COMMANDMENTS (1956) "The theme . . . is whether men are to be ruled by God's law—or whether they are to be ruled by the whims of a dictator . . . Are men the property of the state? Or are they free souls under God? This same battle continues throughout the world today." Hitchcock's NORTH BY NORTHWEST (1959) and TORN CURTAIN (1966) center on Cold War spying (see SPY FILMS), and TOPAZ (1969), which is based on the novel by Leon URIS, provides one of the surprisingly few cinematic treatments of the 1962 Cuban Missile Crisis.

Kubrick's black humor satire DR. STRANGELOVE (1964) is one of the funniest yet most insightful treatments of nuclear brinkmanship and the men who practiced it. Kubrick also directed *2001: A Space Odyssey* (1968), which grew out of the Cold War-inspired space race, and FULL METAL JACKET (1987), a bleak Vietnam war film. His *A Clockwork Orange* (1971), though not directly about the Cold War, portrays the violence in Cold War–era Western society. Kubrick's SPARTACUS (1960), written by HOLLYWOOD TEN member Dalton TRUMBO, helped end the blacklist; president-elect Kennedy crossed American Legion picket lines to see it in 1960. Preminger also helped break the blacklist at about the same time when he announced—reported by the *New York Times* on its front page—that Trumbo had written his upcoming film EXODUS (1960). Preminger also directed several POLITICAL FILMS, including ADVISE AND CONSENT (1962), *The Court-Martial of Billy Mitchell* (1955) and THE HUMAN FACTOR, (1979) based on the novel by Graham GREENE. Stone, a Vietnam War veteran who came to prominence as a director during the Reagan era, was perhaps the most consistently political Hollywood director during the Cold War. His films include the realistic Vietnam War film, PLATOON (1986), which was informed by his own war experiences. He later wrote, directed, produced and acted in BORN ON THE FOURTH OF JULY (1989), a more overtly antiwar piece about the fate of a gung-ho, all-American athlete who serves in Vietnam. The film criticizes both American politics and the machismo that fuels it. Other Cold War–related films by Stone include *Salvador* (1986), about an American photo-journalist in Central America, and *JFK* (1991), a revisionist account of the Kennedy assassination centering on the investigations of New Orleans district attorney Jim Garrison. Stone's *The Doors* (1991) documents Jim Morrison and his rock band from the 1960s, and *Nixon* (1995) depicts the former president.

Notable for their personal politics were Herbert BIBERMAN, Walt DISNEY, Edward DMYTRYK, Elia KAZAN, Leo McCarey and Robert ROSSEN. Disney and McCarey were strong anti-communists who testified as friendly witnesses in the 1947 hearings of the HOUSE COMMITTEE ON UN-AMERICAN ACTIVITIES (HUAC). In 1952 Kazan, a former Communist Party member, also cooperated with the committee and named names. Considered one of the major directors of the 1940s and 1950s, Kazan directed numerous films and plays known for their social content and liberal orientation. Before his testimony, he had directed *Gentleman's Agreement* (1947), a film about anti-Semitism; *Pinky* (1949), concerning racial discrimination; and VIVA ZAPATA (1952), about revolution and land reform in Mexico. Kazan also directed Arthur MILLER's play *Death of a Salesman* (1949), which starred Lee J. COBB. Miller and Cobb were both later called before HUAC. Of his experience with the Communist Party, Kazan told HUAC, "I had enough regimentation, enough of being told what to think and say and do . . . I had a taste of police-state living and I did not like it." Kazan's informing and his widely publicized defense of it in a *New York Times* advertisement provoked a rift with Miller, who shortly afterward wrote THE CRUCIBLE (1953), an allegorical treatment of HUAC and the RED SCARE based on the Salem witch trials. In 1954, Kazan directed and Cobb starred with Marlon Brando in ON THE WATERFRONT, which celebrates an act of informing. Cobb and Budd SCHULBERG, the movie's SCREENWRITER, had also named names by then. Kazan was among the more harshly criticized informers because his stature and his presumed ability to work in live theater even if he were banned from Hollywood made him less vulnerable to the blacklist. Critics felt that Kazan should have refused to testify and thereby attempted to break the blacklist by forcing the studio owners to forgo one of their brightest and most profitable talents. Nonetheless, Kazan steadfastly defended his testimony throughout the years.

Many critics feel that Miller's 1955 Broadway play *A View from the Bridge*, depicting a man whose life was ruined by a single act of informing, was the playwright's response to his colleagues' defection. In 1963 Kazan and Miller were reconciled when they were named resident director and playwright for the premiere season of New York's Lincoln Center. For that season, Kazan directed Miller's autobiographical *After The Fall*, (1963) the story of a former communist who breaks with a friend about to inform before a congressional committee.

Biberman and Dmytryk were among the Hollywood Ten who appeared in the 1947 HUAC hearings but refused to testify, citing their First Amendment protection. Like the other members of the Ten, they were cited for contempt of Congress and forced to serve a prison sentence when the Supreme Court denied their First Amendment claim and upheld the citation. They were also blacklisted. Biberman never again directed in Hollywood, although he did make SALT OF THE EARTH (1954), an independently produced docudrama about a strike by Mexican-American zinc workers. The internationally acclaimed film was the first and only attempt by Biberman and blacklisted producer Paul Jarrico to create an independent film company to employ blacklisted artists and to draw "from the living experiences of people long ignored in Hollywood—the working men and women of America." On the other hand Dmytryk, who had left the Communist Party prior to his appearance and had strong ideological differences with the other members of the Ten, later rehabilitated himself by writing an anti-communist article in 1951 for the *Saturday Evening Post* and by reappearing before HUAC and identifying 26 people who had been party members while he was an active member. All had been previously identified by other informers. After testifying, Dmytryk was removed from the blacklist, and he went on to direct many notable films, including *The Caine Mutiny* (1954), *The Young Lions* (1958), *Walk on the Wild Side* (1962) and THE HUMAN FACTOR (1975), about a NATO planner's run-in with terrorists (not to be confused with the 1979 film of the same title directed by Preminger).

Rossen had been scheduled to testify in HUAC's 1947 hearings along with the Ten, but he was not called then. However, he was called in 1951, when he tacitly admitted that he was a member of the Communist Party but refused to name others who had also belonged. He was subsequently blacklisted. After suffering unemployment and social ostracism, Rossen left the party and testified again before HUAC in 1953. He told the committee, "I don't think, after two years of thinking, that any one individual can even indulge himself in the luxury of individual morality or pit it against what I feel today very strongly is the security and safety of this nation." He then identified some 50 communists and provided a detailed account of Communist Party practices. Afterwards Rossen was able to resume his career in Hollywood.

Roman POLANSKI was a Polish director who moved to the West after his first feature-length film, *Knife in the Water* (1962), was poorly received by the Polish government but was greeted enthusiastically in Western Europe and the United States, receiving an Academy Award nomination in 1962. In 1979, Polanski was arrested for having sexual relations with a 13-year-old girl. After spending 42 days in prison under observation, he was released. Shortly afterward he fled the country and continued working in Europe, including Poland. The husband of actress Sharon Tate, whom Charles Manson's cult murdered in 1969, Polanski was also a childhood friend of Jerzy KOSINSKI.

Among the better known directors of FILM DOCUMENTARIES were Frederick Wiseman, Fred FREED and David WOLPER. Freed and Wolper specialized in made-for-television documentaries, and many of Wiseman's films were also aired on television. Wiseman's Cold War films are MISSILE (1988), about a training program for air force officers in charge of the nuclear-armed Minuteman missile silos, and BASIC TRAINING (1970), a Vietnam War–era film that focuses on the U.S. Army Training Center at Fort Knox, Kentucky. Freed made several "NBC White Papers" and special programs for "NBC Reports." Wolper worked as an independent producer and director. He produced the syndicated television series BIOGRAPHY (1962–64) and "Men in Crisis" (1965), as well as TELEVISION DOCUMENTARIES on the space race, the atom bomb, the American Communist Party, Berlin, the Korean War, China and refugees who fled from communist countries.

film documentaries   Nonfiction FILMS that attempt to provide accurate renderings of the situations or events they present. Some documentaries may have a social or political agenda with the FILM DIRECTOR setting out to make a particular point—say, that communism is bad, or that poverty is a serious problem, as evidenced by the incidents portrayed in the film. Other directors see themselves more as observers, believing that they simply allow the underlying dynamics of the situation to reveal themselves. Nonetheless, no matter how objective and detached documentary makers wish to be, what they look for, what they see, and how they interpret events is inevitably influenced by their own beliefs and backgrounds.

During the Cold War, documentaries rarely appeared in first-run commercial theaters because they lacked the audience appeal of Hollywood films. Some, such as those by Fred FREED, David WOLPER and Frederick Wiseman, were first shown on television. Others were made by organizations for educational viewings or to raise money for political causes. Civic and religious groups often rented 16mm copies of films made by the U.S. government and private companies for educational purposes. Universities also screened documentaries in the classrooms and in public showings. Film festivals and movie houses specializing in foreign and "art films" also showed documentaries. A notable exception was THE ATOMIC CAFE (1982), which had a fairly wide commercial distribution. Made when the Reagan administration was promoting the idea of survivable nuclear war, *The Atomic Cafe* presents archival footage from 1950s U.S. civil defense and military documentaries to expose the government's ludicrous claims that greatly minimized the dangers of nuclear testing and likewise maximized the prospects for surviving a nuclear attack.

Most Cold War–related documentaries address nuclear weaponry and military defense, particularly the development and use of the atom bomb. ATOMIC POWER (1946) and THE DAY THE SUN BLOWED UP (1976) document the Manhattan Project, the team of U.S. scientists who constructed the atom bomb at the end of World War II. *The Atomic Café* also contains some documentary footage on that subject. Made for television 20 years after the Hiroshima bombing, THE DECISION TO DROP THE BOMB (1965) presents the political and military concerns that led to that controversial action. HIROSHIMA: A DOCUMENT OF THE ATOMIC BOMBING (1970), HIROSHIMA–NAGASAKI (1970) and HIROSHIMA–NAGASAKI—AUGUST, 1945 (1968) all provide views of the bomb's destruction, and each contains archival footage taken by a Japanese camera crew only hours after the explosion. That footage had been confiscated by the U.S. occupying army, which classified it as secret for some 23 years before releasing it in 1968. A THOUSAND CRANES: CHILDREN OF HIROSHIMA (1962) was made in the same year as the Cuban Missile Crisis. Its stated purpose was "To inform American children what it is like to be a child in Hiroshima . . . to make a plea for peace." TO DIE, TO LIVE (1976), a British and Canadian-made film written and directed by Robert Vas, a Hungarian concentration-camp survivor, is based on the nonfiction book DEATH IN LIFE, Dr. Robert Jay Lifton's 1962 study of survivors' psychological responses to the Hiroshima bombing.

Other films dealing with the nuclear threat include Wiseman's MISSILE (1988), about a training program for air force officers in charge of the nuclear-armed Minuteman missiles silos; the BBC-produced RUMOURS OF WAR (1972), also about Minutemen missiles; and FOOTNOTES ON THE ATOMIC AGE (1969), a made-for-television film critical of U.S. nuclear testing practices. Documentaries addressing the aftermath of a nuclear attack include PATTERN FOR SURVIVAL, a 1950 film intended to prepare the United States for a possible atomic attack by "an aggressor nation," and THE WAR GAME, (1966) a BBC-produced simulation of a nuclear attack in England. Like the Reagan-era television docu-drama THE DAY AFTER, *The War Game* is not truly a documentary as it dramatizes events rather than records them. Nevertheless, it received the 1967 Academy Award for best feature documentary. Its accolades notwithstanding, the BBC refused to air the film, which was considered "too horrifying" and unsuitable for family viewing. Other documentaries related to nuclear war include the U.S. Army films *The Atom Strikes* and *A Tale of Two Cities,* and the short films *H-Bomb Over U.S., A Short Vision, The Hole* and *23 Skidoo.*

A number of Cold War documentaries had explicit political agendas. THE BELL was made in 1950 to encourage movie-goers to purchase savings bonds. Produced by the Crusade for Freedom, which was chaired by General Lucius Clay, USA (retired), the former high commissioner for Germany, and made in cooperation with the Defense Department, it includes footage from the Berlin Airlift and depicts the evils of communism and the dangers of Soviet aggression. The film was released in coordination with a nationwide radio address by then-General Eisenhower in support of the Crusade for Freedom. ONLY THE STRONG (1972) was produced by the politically conservative Institute for American Strategy, an arms lobby directed by former high-ranking military officers and representatives of defense contractors. Made during the détente negotiated by President Richard M. Nixon and his adviser Henry Kissinger and aired shortly after the signing of the antiballistic missile treaty in 1972, the film represents Soviet military strength as superior to U.S. strength and claims that peace can be ensured only by a strong, well-armed U.S. military. None of the major television networks would air the film, which rival organizations and newspaper editorials attacked as self-serving propaganda rather than the public service program it purported to be. Nonetheless, church groups, veterans organizations, service clubs and schools extensively screened the 16 mm prints made available for a nominal fee. The film was also aired on over 400 local and independent stations as a public service show.

Vietnam was also the topic of many Cold War documentaries. Wiseman's BASIC TRAINING (1970) provides a view of the U.S. Army Training Center at Fort Knox, Kentucky, during the Vietnam War. FAR FROM VIETNAM (1967) is a French-made documentary about that war. Eleven internationally acclaimed directors contributed, including Jean-Luc Godard, Claude Lelouch, Alain Resnais, Joris Ivens and Agnes Varda.

Communist China fascinated many documentary filmmakers. RETURN FROM SILENCE: CHINA'S REVOLUTIONARY WRITERS (1982) concerns five politically active Chinese writers. CHINA IN REVOLUTION: 1911–1949 (1988) traces the establishment of the Chinese communist state from the fall of the boy emperor Pu Yi to the birth of the communist People's Republic of China under Mao Zedong. Both films were partially funded by the National Endowment for the Humanities in the 1980s.

The RED SCARE figures prominently in SEEING RED, (1983) a partial oral history of the American Communist Party, and in HOLLYWOOD ON TRIAL (1976), about the film industry's response to the hearings conducted by the HOUSE COMMITTEE ON UN-AMERICAN ACTIVITIES (HUAC). These 1970s films criticize HUAC, which in 1960 had commissioned OPERATION ABOLITION, an attempt to prove that anti-HUAC demonstrators at a San Francisco hearing were sponsored by communists and traitors. Also in response to the Red Scare and the ensuing blacklisting, Herbert BIBERMAN, one of the black-listed HOLLYWOOD TEN, made the independently produced SALT OF THE EARTH, (1954) a docu-drama about a strike by Mexican-American zinc workers. Although the entire film is fictionalized and scripted, it uses actual strikers as actors. *Salt of the Earth* was attacked as the work of communists even before it was completed. The female lead, Rosaura Revueltas, was deported by the Immigration and Naturalization Service for a minor passport violation before the shooting was finished. She was subsequently blacklisted in both the United States and Mexico and never made another film. Though it was acclaimed internationally, *Salt of the Earth* appeared only briefly in 10 U.S. cities when it was released in 1954. However, it was re-released and more widely distributed in 1965, when it became a rallying point for COUNTERCULTURE activism and later for feminism.

The Academy Award–winning WOODSTOCK (1970) documented the ROCK AND ROLL music festival that took place in upstate New York in 1969. The rock festival, which was billed as a celebration of peace, occurred while the U.S. involvement in Vietnam was still considerable; the film came to symbolize the links between the peace movement and counterculture. Notable performers were Joan BAEZ; Jimi Hendrix, Arlo Guthrie; Richie Havens; Joe Cocker; Melanie; Blood, Sweat and Tears; the Jefferson Airplane; Ravi Shankar; The Who; Crosby, Stills, and Nash; and Country Joe McDonald and the Fish. FROM MAO TO MOZART: ISAAC STERN IN CHINA (1980) is a far different sort of musical documentary; it covers the classical violinist's 1980 trip to China. (See also VIETNAM WAR FILMS; TELEVISION DOCUMENTARIES AND SPECIAL REPORTS.)

For additional reading, see Einstein's *Special Edition: A Guide to Network Television Documentary Series and Special News Reports, 1955–1979;* Suid's *Film and Propaganda in America: A Documentary History,*

film drama Film dramas typically addressed Cold War issues by incorporating them into their storylines. Several films from the early days of the Cold War deal with the threat from domestic communism, notably BIG JIM MCCLAIN (1952),which features John WAYNE as an investigator for the HOUSE COMMITTEE ON UN-AMERICAN ACTIVITIES (HUAC), I MARRIED A COMMUNIST (1949), I WAS A COMMUNIST FOR THE F.B.I., (1951) THE IRON CURTAIN, (1948) WALK EAST ON BEACON (1952) MY SON JOHN (1952), THE RED MENACE (1949), PICKUP ON SOUTH STREET (1953), *Conspirator* (1949), *The Whip Hand* (1951) and THE FOUNTAINHEAD, (1949) based on Ayn RAND's novel. These films typically reinforce the right-wing viewpoints current during the RED SCARE. Also from that era, THE ATOMIC CITY (1952) and THE ATOMIC MAN (1956) deal with possible threats to and from atomic scientists. In 1951, Ronald REAGAN starred in STORM WARNING, playing a district attorney who encourages townspeople to testify against a Ku Klux Klan murderer. *Storm Warning* alludes directly to the HUAC hearings, which Reagan supported as president of the Screen Actors Guild. In the movie the hero, like HUAC, insists that the guilty parties must be revealed. On the other hand, the villainous townspeople protect the Klan by invoking verbatim the arguments used by the Committee for the First Amendment in support of the HOLLYWOOD TEN. Thus the film implicitly endorses HUAC and vilifies the unfriendly witnesses who would not cooperate with its quest to identify members and sympathizers of the Communist Party working in Hollywood.

Likewise, ON THE WATERFRONT, a 1954 film about union corruption, celebrates an act of informing. Elia KAZAN directed it and Budd SCHULBERG wrote the screenplay; both men as well as costar Lee J. COBB named communists in their testimony before HUAC, and the film is often seen as their statement of vindication. Prior to *Waterfront*, Kazan had directed VIVA ZAPATA! (1951), about the Mexican revolutionary war hero—the only major Hollywood film made during the Red Scare that sympathetically treats such issues as land reform and peasants' rights. STORM CENTER (1956) stands out as the only major film of the time that actually attacked the Red Scare. The 1956 movie stars Bette Davis as a librarian who is harassed and fired because she refuses to remove a copy of *The Communist Dream* from the shelves of her small-town library. Made in 1973, THE WAY WE WERE also vilifies the Red Scare, as does the 1977 enactment of Senator Joseph McCarthy's life in TAIL GUNNER JOE.

Other early Cold War dramas deal with the prospects for nuclear war and survival afterward. (See APOCALYPTIC FILMS.) Made two years after the bombing of Hiroshima, THE BEGINNING OR THE END (1947) dramatizes the building of the first atomic bomb in 1945. (The Bush-era FAT MAN AND LITTLE BOY (1989) also tells that story.) Made seven years after the development of the hydrogen bomb, ON THE BEACH (1959) follows the lives of people in Australia awaiting the arrival of a lethal nuclear cloud that has already destroyed the Northern Hemisphere. The French- and Japanese-made HIROSHIMA, MON AMOUR (1959) is the story of a Japanese architect and a French actress who have a short love affair in Hiroshima after the war. The film intercuts documentary footage of the destruction caused by the atomic bomb with tender shots of the protagonists' love-making, both with each other and with lost lovers from the war. Other notable 1950s FOREIGN FILMS that indirectly allude to the nuclear threat include Akira Kurosawa's THE SEVEN SAMURAI (1954)

and Ingmar Bergman's THE SEVENTH SEAL (1956) and *Shame* (1968).

The Red Scare created a "chilling effect" on Hollywood's willingness to make POLITICAL FILMS. But with the election of John Kennedy in 1960 the Red Scare abated, and in the early and mid-1960s several film dramas depicted Cold War issues. FAIL SAFE (1964), a MILITARY FILM, tells of an accidental U.S. nuclear strike against the U.S.S.R. The movie is often paired with DR. STRANGELOVE, (1964), a FILM SATIRE that treats the same subject through BLACK HUMOR. THE BEDFORD INCIDENT (1965) likewise depicts an accidental U.S. attack that presumably triggers a nuclear war. The character responsible is partly based on the 1964 Republican nominee Barry Goldwater, whose bellicose campaign rhetoric advocated "extremism in defense of liberty." Inspired by the 1962 Cuban Missile Crisis, LADYBUG, LADYBUG (1963) explores the emotional turmoil suffered by a group of schoolchildren who are sent home from school in anticipation of a nuclear attack that ultimately does not come. The British-made LORD OF THE FLIES (1963) also focuses on children. Based on the novel by Nobel Prize–winning author William Golding, the film shows upper-class British school boys degenerating into barbarism when they are marooned on an island after being evacuated in expectation of a nuclear war. The story suggests that all of human society would similarly degenerate in a postapocalyptic world without law and other civilizing social constraints.

Like *Fail-Safe*, SEVEN DAYS IN MAY (1964), ADVISE AND CONSENT (1962), THE MANCHURIAN CANDIDATE (1962) and THE UGLY AMERICAN (1962) are all based on best-selling POLITICAL NOVELS. *Seven Days in May* features a narrowly averted coup by right-wing officers in the U.S. military. *Advise and Consent* centers on Senate confirmation hearings for a liberal nominee for secretary of state. *The Manchurian Candidate* tells about the stepson of a right-wing senator whom the communists capture during the Korean War, brainwash and turn into a mind-controlled assassin. The figure of the senator clearly alludes to Joseph McCarthy, and the film suggests that McCarthyites and others behind the Red Scare pose a stronger danger to U.S. democracy than do the communists. The film also seems to anticipate the Kennedy assassination, which occurred a year after *The Manchurian Candidate* appeared. Frank Sinatra, who starred in the movie and owned part of the rights to it, was so disturbed by the parallels that he blocked the film's re-release for some 25 years. Like THE QUIET AMERICAN (1958) that preceded it in the 1950s, *The Ugly American* anticipates the debacle in Vietnam. It depicts a well-meaning but arrogant U.S. ambassador in a fictitious Southeast Asian country that communist insurgents are winning over through dedication, hard work, self-sacrifice and ideological commitment. The book appeared in 1958 and the film debuted in 1962, when communist insurgency in Laos was a current concern and the U.S. military involvement in Vietnam was just beginning to intensify.

Made in 1969, Alfred HITCHCOCK'S TOPAZ centers on U.S.-French relations and the 1962 Cuban Missile Crisis, which THE MISSILES OF OCTOBER reenacted on television (ABC) in 1974. The Reagan-era WARGAMES tells of a nuclear war almost instigated by youthful computer hackers who tap into a defense computer network, which they mistake for a challenging computer game. Like *Fail-Safe*, if warns of the danger of nuclear war triggered by a technological accident; like *Dr. Strangelove,* it features a crazed right-wing military figure.

Several other dramas enact life after a major nuclear confrontation. These include FIVE (1951), DAMNATION ALLEY (1957), THE WORLD, THE FLESH AND THE DEVIL (1959), THE LAST WOMAN ON EARTH (1960), PANIC IN YEAR ZERO (1962), PLANET OF THE APES (1968) and its sequels, GLEN AND RANDA (1971), and MAD MAX (1979) and its sequels, *Road Warrior* (1982) and *Mad Max Beyond Thunderdome* (1985). The controversial made-for-television movie THE DAY AFTER (1982) is also a key apocalyptic film drama. Conservatives answered the liberal *Day After* with another made-for-television movie, AMERIKA (1987), about life in a Soviet-occupied United States. *The World, the Flesh and the Devil* was particularly notable in this genre, because it pointed out the likelihood of interracial mixing among the survivors of a nuclear holocaust.

Early anti-Soviet film dramas include THE RED DANUBE (1950), about a romance between a British military officer and a Russian ballerina in occupied Vienna, where the communists compel citizens to return to the U.S.S.R. against their will. THE THIRD MAN (1950) is also set in occupied Vienna. Based on the novel by Graham GREENE, who also wrote the screenplay, the 1950 film deals with black-marketing and the uneasy collaboration among the superpowers' police forces in the divided city. Other early anti-Soviet films include NEVER LET ME GO (1953), a story about a newspaper correspondent trying to smuggle his wife out of the U.S.S.R.; JET PILOT (1957), in which a female Soviet spy tries to lure John Wayne to into defecting but is herself converted to the American cause by her love for him; *The Red Nightmare;* and *Red Snow.* Soviet-related dramas from the 1960s include THE KREMLIN LETTER, (1970) about a diplomatic proposal for the United States and the U.S.S.R. to cooperate in the annihilation of China, and DR. ZHIVAGO (1965), about a Russian doctor at the time of the 1917 Russian Revolution. *Dr. Zhivago* is based on the 1957 novel by Nobel Prize winner Boris PASTERNAK, who was sentenced to internal exile for writing it.

The 1970s détente inspired few dramas dealing with the Soviet Union, but the renewed intensification of the Cold War in the early and mid-1980s brought the U.S.S.R. back to Hollywood films. Dramas from the Reagan era include SAKHAROV (1984), about the Soviet atomic scientist who became a human rights advocate; NINETEEN EIGHTY-FOUR (1984), presenting George ORWELL's vision of a totalitarian future; MOSCOW ON THE HUDSON (1984), a comic drama about a Soviet circus artist who defects to the United States; WHITE NIGHTS (1985), which stars Mikhail BARYSHNIKOV and Gregory Hines as dancers trapped in the U.S.S.R.; *Rocky IV,* which plays out the U.S.–Soviet competition via a boxing match between Sylvester STALLONE and a Russian fighter; and GORKY PARK, a 1983 anti-Soviet spy story that the Soviets refused to allow to be filmed on location. By contrast THE RUSSIA HOUSE, made as communism was collapsing in 1990, was shot on location in Moscow and St. Petersburg. Like its 1950s predecessor *Anastasia* (1956), the 1986 drama ANASTASIA: THE MYSTERY OF ANNA is an anti-Soviet drama about the missing daughter of the deposed Russian czar.

Prominent dramas depicting Cold War events in Asia, apart from the Korean and Vietnam wars, include THE YEAR OF LIVING DANGEROUSLY (1982, Indonesia), THE KILLING FIELDS (1984, Cambodia) and LOVE IS A MANY-SPLENDORED THING (1955, Korea and Hong Kong). Particularly powerful dramatic treatments of Vietnam War veterans include COMING HOME (1978), THE DEER HUNTER (1978) and BORN ON THE FOURTH OF JULY (1989). (See also KOREAN WAR FILMS and VIETNAM WAR FILMS.)

The Eisenhower-era THE MAN IN THE GRAY FLANNEL SUIT (1956) addresses the situation of veterans returning from World War II and entering Cold War America. ZABRISKIE POINT (1970) presents the antiwar counterculture during the Vietnam War. THE PRESIDENT'S PLANE IS MISSING (1967) centers on the disappearance of the presidential plane, Air Force One, at a time when Chinese communists are threatening nuclear war. ALL THE PRESIDENT'S MEN (1976) dramatizes the discovery of the Watergate cover-up. Constantin COSTA-GAVRAS directed several political dramas in the 1970s and 1980s, including THE CONFESSION (1970), STATE OF SIEGE (1973), and MISSING (1982). (See also FILM COMEDY; FILMS ABOUT COLD WAR EVENTS; NUCLEAR APOCALYPSE; SCIENCE FICTION FILMS; SPY FILMS.)

film satires Film satires parodied various aspects of the Cold War. During the RED SCARE of the late 1940s and 1950s, making fun of the government or of anti-communist activities was often attacked on the grounds that such satire assisted the communist cause, so few satirical films appeared during that time. THE SENATOR WAS INDISCREET (1947) illustrated the kind of response that even an innocuous political spoof could generate. Made in 1947, the same year that the HOUSE COMMITTEE ON UN-AMERICAN ACTIVITIES (HUAC) opened its first hearings into communist influences in the film industry, *The Senator Was Indiscreet* was essentially a screwball comedy. The only film ever directed by George Kaufman, a comic writer whose screen credits include Marx Brothers movies, *Senator* spoofs a bumbling and unabashedly corrupt U.S. senator. However, the parody outraged some members of Congress when it premiered. Critics claimed that the unflattering depiction of a U.S. senator would undermine the public's confidence in their country's government. They argued that since the Congress was leading the fight against communism, any attempt to ridicule members of congress was in effect striking a blow for communism. Senator Joseph McCarthy called the film "traitorous," and Representative Clare Boothe Luce demanded to know, "Was this picture made by an American?" An editorial warned, "The picture will be recommended highly by [the official Soviet newspaper] *Pravda* and the party line," and the Motion Picture Association of America banned the film from being shown overseas.

Charles CHAPLIN's A KING IN NEW YORK (1957) was his personal response to the Red Scare in general and to HUAC in particular. Chaplin wrote, directed and starred in the film, which he made in England five years after Attorney General James McGranery had revoked his re-entry permit to the United States in 1952. *A King in New York* depicts a deposed European monarch who immigrates to America. The movie satirizes American culture as the destitute king is reduced to making television commercials. However, the king falls afoul of HUAC when he befriends a runaway boy whose parents are suspected communists. Tarnished through guilt by association, the king must appear before the committee, but he makes literal the metaphorical farce of the hearings when he accidentally turns a fire hose on his interrogators. Subsequently, however, the committee intimidates the boy into becoming an informer who identifies several of his parents' political colleagues.

Peter SELLERS appeared in three roles in THE MOUSE THAT ROARED, a 1959 British-made satire about a small country that invades the United States in hopes of losing quickly and subsequently receiving foreign aid. Unfortunately, its invasion force accidentally captures a new secret weapon and it is the United States that surrenders.

Sellers also played three roles in DR. STRANGELOVE (1964), which spoofs both the U.S. and the Soviet leadership who were conducting the Cold War. Made two years after the Cuban Missile Crisis of 1962, the BLACK HUMOR film depicts the crisis that ensues when an insane U.S. Air Force general orders a nuclear strike against the Soviet Union, and bumbling, sex-crazed officials are unable to prevent a Soviet Doomsday machine from going off in retaliation. The film suggests that, despite their public images as serious, rational and responsible men, the leaders on both sides who control the destiny of the world are at best mentally unbalanced and at worst criminally insane; virtually all are dominated by their sex drives, which are ultimately more responsible for their decisions than are logic, reason and national interest. Throughout the film, the hovering threat of nuclear armageddon acts like an aphrodisiac upon these powerful men, whose sexual appetites become accentuated and deformed because of their strange love for the hydrogen bomb and the enormous power and destructive capability it represents. Ultimately, the world's leaders subconsciously create a nuclear scenario that fulfills their greatest sexual fantasies.

Sellers also starred in BEING THERE, a 1979 film about a mentally retarded man with a short attention span who is obsessed by gardening and television and who becomes an influential political adviser to the president. Less overtly political satires in which Sellers appeared include *I Love You, Alice B. Toklas,* (1968), about a middle-class man who becomes caught up in the 1960s marijuana-smoking, hippie COUNTERCULTURE; *Casino Royale* (1967), a James Bond SPY FILM SPOOF; and *The Magic Christian* (1970), based on a novel by Terry SOUTHERN, which lampoons human greed and the perverse amusements of the very wealthy.

THE DAY THE FISH CAME OUT (1967) spoofs attempts by the military to retrieve nuclear material dropped near a Greek island. The French- and Italian-made KING OF HEARTS (1967) appeared at the height of the Vietnam war. It highlights the inherent insanity of warfare in a story set during World War I. Robert Altman's M*A*S*H (1970) was another Vietnam-era, antiwar satire; the black humor film, which inspired the immensely popular TELEVISION SITUATION COMEDY, is set in an army hospital during the Korean War. Another black humor, antiwar film from the Vietnam War era was CATCH-22 (1970), based on Joseph Heller's MILITARY NOVEL. A BOY AND HIS DOG (1975) became an underground cult film. Based on a science fiction story by Harlan Ellison, it is set in a postnuclear-war wasteland, and it centers around a survivor and his dog. The film manages to walk a thin line between serious drama and self-parody until the end, when it gives in completely to black humor. Made when the Reagan

administration was promoting the idea of survivable nuclear war, THE ATOMIC CAFE (1982) uses archival footage from 1950s U.S. civil defense and military documentaries to highlight the ludicrous government claims of the time: Like those of the Reagan administration, they greatly minimized the dangers of nuclear testing and vastly maximized the prospects for surviving a nuclear attack. Though primarily a FILM DOCUMENTARY, *The Atomic Cafe* is also a type of satirical black humor. DEAL OF THE CENTURY (1983) satirizes the international arms market during the early 1980s, at a time when Reagan had initiated a dramatic U.S. arms buildup and a corresponding international weapons race.

OUR MAN IN HAVANA (1960), which was based on the novel by Graham GREENE and filmed in Havana a year after Castro's 1959 revolution, satirizes Cold War intelligence operations and the popular literary genres that describe them. The story centers on a vacuum cleaner salesman who agrees to spy for the British in order to finance his daughter's private schooling. Since he has no real information to pass along, he submits enlarged schematics of vacuum cleaner technology, claiming they describe enemy installations. The Johnson-era THE PRESIDENT'S ANALYST (1967) satirizes mindless bureaucracy, psychoanalysis, liberalism and the Cold War itself as it features attempts by various organizations to kidnap the man privy to the president's deepest secrets, his psychiatrist. Woody Allen's BANANAS (1971), a Nixon-era film, satirizes Castro as well as U.S. intelligence agencies, the U.S. justice system and American popular culture. Made during the Carter presidency, when rapprochement with Cuba was considered possible and a slightly more sympathetic view of Castro was beginning to emerge in the United States, CUBA (1979) satirizes the island's pre-Castro military dictatorships as well as its revolutions. Sean Connery stars as a British mercenary who has been recruited to help crush Castro's revolution. The satire emphasizes how the selfishness and corruption of dictator Fulgencio Batista and his cohorts contributed to Castro's success.

From the same era, THE IN-LAWS (1979) spoofs the CIA as rogue agent Peter Falk manages to drag his unwilling brother-in-law, a successful but highly nervous dentist (Alan Arkin), into a scheme to overthrow a Latin American dictatorship. (Arkin also starred in *Catch-22.*) Alex's Cox's 1987 surreal political film WALKER presents William Walker, the 19th-century American adventurer who invaded Nicaragua with 58 men and became that country's ruler from 1856 to 1857. Made with the complete cooperation of Nicaragua's Sandinistas, who were then resisting efforts by the CIA and U.S.-backed contras to overthrow them and who had feared a seemingly imminent U.S. invasion only a few years earlier, the film focuses on the outlandish bravado of a power-crazed American who once took over the country. Made just before the congressional hearings into the Iran-contra affair, the film benefited from the timeliness of those hearings and from unanticipated comparisons between William Walker and Colonel Oliver North. The Bush-era MOON OVER PARADOR (1988) also spoofs Latin American dictators. (See also SATIRE; TELEVISION SATIRE; FILM COMEDY.)

film Westerns Western heros typically stood tall against those who would break the law, greedily grab power and wealth for themselves, and violate the established social order, just as the United States was perceived to be standing tall against the expansion of a communist empire that used its Red Army to seize power for itself and support its advocacy of worldwide revolution. In this respect, Westerns reaffirmed U.S. commitment to fighting for its values and for freedom. John WAYNE starred in several such Westerns, notably *Fort Apache* (1948) and *True Grit* (1969). *Gunfight at the O.K. Corral* (1957) and *My Darling Clementine* (1946) both championed family values while celebrating the legendary lawman Wyatt Earp. HIGH NOON (1952) also shared traditional American values, though it was more controversial. The plot centers around Will Kane, a lawman who must stand alone against a trio of killers seeking revenge against him. Initially, he assumes he can count on the help of the townspeople, but they all desert him, including his pacifist bride. Screenwriter Carl FOREMAN claimed to have written *High Noon* to express his sense of abandonment by the film community when he was subpoenaed to testify before the HOUSE COMMITTEE ON UN-AMERICAN ACTIVITIES (HUAC) in 1952. The film was attacked by both the left and the right. The official Soviet newspaper *Pravda* dismissed *High Noon* as "a glorification of the individual," while Wayne, the president of the MOTION PICTURE ALLIANCE FOR THE PRESERVATION OF AMERICAN IDEALS, condemned the depiction of the cowardly middle-class townspeople as "the most un-American thing I've ever seen in my whole life."

A very popular genre during the 1940s, 1950s and early 1960s, the appeal of Westerns diminished when the U.S. role as "policeman of the world" began to become more complicated, costly, and morally ambiguous, and as Cold War technology increasingly relegated the American frontier to the distant past. Likewise, whereas Westerns from the 1950s and early 1960s glamorize lawmen and show that crime does not pay, later films favorably portray outlaws, such as Billy the Kid, Butch Cassidy and the Sundance Kid and the more recent criminals Bonnie and Clyde. At the same time, the COUNTERCULTURE that rose from the antiwar movement spawned new attitudes denouncing violence as an unacceptable means even for a desirable end and criticizing policies that sent the U.S. Army to fight against indigenous peoples on their own territory. Thus films from the late 1960s and 1970s such as Robert Altman's *McCabe and Mrs. Miller* (1971) sought to deglamorize the frontier West and the violence associated with it. In the same vein, this era's new critique of racism inspired more sensitive and sympathetic treatments of North American Indians in such films as *Little Big Man* (1970). Finally, the morally ambiguous Vietnam War inspired critical views of the U.S. Army that fought the 19th-century Indian Wars, and of the civil authorities and corporate interests that ran the frontier settlements. The comedy *Cat Ballou* (1965) was one such critical look, as was Kevin Costner's 1990 *Dances with Wolves*, the last great film Western of the Cold War era.

films about Cold War events The pivotal events of the Cold War attracted surprisingly little interest from the film industry. This may have been because, as a "cold war," so much of the superpower confrontation took the form of diplomatic maneuvers, proxy wars and attempts to influence the political situations in far-off parts of the world.

Though not untreatable subjects, these do not have the immediate market appeal of heavy action, "hot war" films that feature American protagonists fighting for an easily identifiable and universally acceptable cause. Even when the cause is not so identifiable or acceptable, war films contain violence and destruction and fit readily into an established genre that already has a large following. On the other hand, conflicts that center on diplomatic resolutions of political situations share neither of those qualities; thus they are less attractive investments for filmmakers and financiers. Therefore, such dramatic historical moments as the Berlin Airlift; the anti-communist uprisings in East Germany, Hungary and Czechoslovakia; the second Berlin Crisis; the Cuban Missile Crisis; Nixon's trips to China and the Soviet Union; the Soviet invasion of Afghanistan; and the Grenada invasion were rarely treated in mainstream films. Indeed, the two full-scale wars the United States fought during the Cold War account for far more films than all of the other Cold War events combined. (See KOREAN WAR FILMS and VIETNAM WAR FILMS.)

Two films dramatized the development of the atomic bomb, THE BEGINNING OR THE END (1947) and FAT MAN AND LITTLE BOY (1989). *Daniel* (1983), Sidney Lumet's adaptation of E.L. Doctorow's THE BOOK OF DANIEL, presents the arrest, trial, and execution of convicted atomic bomb spies Julius and Ethel Rosenberg. EXODUS (1960) centers on the formation of the state of Israel in 1949, an event influenced by Cold War politics though these are not treated directly in the film. Based on popular POLITICAL NOVELS, THE QUIET AMERICAN (1958) and THE UGLY AMERICAN (1962) depict the political situation in Southeast Asia. *The Quiet American*, which appeared in 1957, reverses the anti-Americanism of Graham GREENE's original book and supports the U.S. efforts there. *The Ugly American* criticizes State Department bureaucrats and political hacks who fail to learn the native languages and customs, insult local leaders, inhibit the constructive efforts of private individuals working the villages, and allow their own egos, self-interest and career aspirations to dominate their decisions. The film appeared in 1962, when the number of American advisers in Vietnam increased from 700 to 12,000. FRANCIS GARY POWERS (1975) presents the biography of the pilot of the U.S. U-2 spy plane that was shot down on a reconnaissance mission over the Soviet Union in May, 1960. The incident scuttled a Paris summit conference that had been convened to resolve the on-going Berlin crisis. The situation in Berlin then rapidly deteriorated over the following year and a half, until it climaxed in October 1961 in one of the most dangerous U.S.-Soviet showdowns of the Cold War. TOPAZ (1969) is a SPY FILM that culminates with the Cuban Missile Crisis, which THE MISSILES OF OCTOBER reenacted in 1974. THE YEAR OF LIVING DANGEROUSLY (1982) centers on an imminent communist coup in Indonesia in 1965, and it highlights the repressive response taken by President Sukarno. Anthony Page's PUEBLO stars Hal Holbrook as the captain of the U.S. spy ship captured by North Korea in January 1968.

Constantin COSTA-GAVRAS directed several POLITICAL FILMS based on actual Cold War events. His Kafkaesque THE CONFESSION (1970) portrays a political show trial behind the "Iron Curtain," while STATE OF SIEGE (1973) and MISSING (1982) depict the right-wing repression of U.S.-backed Latin

American dictatorships. *Missing* alludes to the 1973 military coup that, with covert aid from the United States, overthrew the freely elected government of Marxist president Salvador Allende. Made during the eighth year of the Soviet occupation of Afghanistan, THE LIVING DAYLIGHTS (1987) features Afghani rebels who help James BOND fight against a rogue Soviet general. An earlier Bond film, *Octopussy,* (1983) centered on an evil Afghani prince attempting to plunder treasures that once belonged to the czar. THE BEAST (1988) focuses on a Soviet tank crew in Afghanistan that becomes increasingly confused about its mission and the purpose of the war. One crew member becomes sympathetic to the rebel cause and eventually fights against his own tank. *Rambo III* (1988) also highlights the war in Afghanistan as Sylvester STALLONE saves a friend who is captured by communists while fighting for the U.S.-backed Afghani rebels. A year after the Cold War ended, Oliver STONE made *JFK* (1991), a revisionist history of the Kennedy assassination. In its portrayal of NASA's Mercury program, *The Right Stuff* (1983) shows how the United States's first manned flights into outer space were motivated by competition with the Soviet space program. Based on the book by Tom Wolfe and filmed in 1983, the movie appeared while renewed Cold War tensions were at their highest since the Cuban Missile Crisis. It appealed to patriotic sentiments by celebrating the courage and physical endurance of the early astronaut corps and the military test pilots who were the first Americans to leave the earth's atmosphere. At the same time *The Right Stuff* also shows how personal and political opportunism played a role in the space program. (See also FILMS ASSOCIATED WITH THE RED SCARE.)

films associated with the Red Scare   The RED SCARE, which lasted from the late 1940s and finally abated with the election of John Kennedy in 1960, influenced American filmmaking in a number of ways. The Red Scare practice of BLACKLISTING banned from the movie industry all current and all unrepentant former communists. It drove from Hollywood many SCREENWRITERS, FILM DIRECTORS, and FILM ACTORS AND ACTRESSES who had knowingly participated in communist-backed causes during the 1930s and 1940s, as well as several individuals who had unknowingly been involved with suspected communist front organizations or who simply had made public their objections to the hearings conducted by the HOUSE COMMITTEE ON UN-AMERICAN ACTIVITIES (HUAC). Consequently, one influence of the Red Scare was to reduce the pool of talent and thereby limit the range of cinematic possibilities in 1950s Hollywood. Many of the blacklisted people whose talents Hollywood lost during the Red Scare were among the most gifted in the film community. These included directors Herbert BIBERMAN and Joseph Losey; writers Dalton TRUMBO, John LAWSON, Arthur MILLER, Ring LARDNER Jr., Carl FOREMAN and Lillian Hellman; actors Charles CHAPLIN, Zero MOSTEL, Larry PARKS, Will Geer and Academy Award winners Anne Revere and Gale Sondergaard; and musicians Leonard Bernstein and Aaron Copland. Others who had to "clear" themselves before becoming eligible again for work included performers Lee J. COBB, John GARFIELD, Jose Ferrer and Judy Holliday and directors Edward DMYTRYK, Elia KAZAN, Robert ROSSEN and John Huston.

In addition to diminishing the talent pool, blacklisting very actively discouraged writers and directors from making films about subjects with serious social content, especially if the topic could be construed as criticizing American government, military, business or other institutions. In 1948 the MOTION PICTURE ALLIANCE FOR THE PRESERVATION OF AMERICAN IDEALS published Ayn RAND's A SCREEN GUIDE FOR AMERICANS, which became the basis for the film industry's movie code. Warning that the communists were trying to "*corrupt our moral premises by corrupting non-political movies . . .* making people absorb the basic principles of Collectivism *by indirection and implication,*" the *Screen Guide* insisted that American films not "smear" industrialists, success or the free enterprise system, "deify the common man," "show that poverty is a virtue" or suggest that "failure is noble." (The emphasis is Rand's.)

In an environment so hostile to criticism of the status quo, comparatively few films attempted to probe social inequities or even to acknowledge the Red Scare itself. Even such an innocuous FILM COMEDY as George S. Kaufman's 1947 THE SENATOR WAS INDISCREET, which lampooned a bumbling and corrupt U.S. senator, was attacked for undermining public confidence in the integrity of the U.S. Congress. U.S. representative Clare Boothe Luce demanded to know, "Was this picture made by an American?" The American Legion attacked the film as un-American propaganda, and the Motion Picture Association of America prohibited the film from being shown overseas. The American Legion and Catholic War Veterans demonstrated outside of movie theaters showing Chaplin's MONSIEUR VERDOUX (1947), which criticized both capitalism and war. The picket lines succeeded in forcing the film to be withdrawn from circulation. This kind of intense attack on the few films that took on social issues may also account for the paucity of Red Scare–era movies dealing with racial inequities in the United States, especially since many powerful people on the right, including FBI director J. Edgar Hoover, maintained that the civil rights movement was communist-controlled.

The American Legion and other fervently anti-communist groups boycotted films not just for political content but also because of who made or appeared in them. For instance, the legion demonstrated against Chaplin's *Limelight* (1952) even though that film had no objectionable political content. By then Chaplin had been smeared, inaccurately, as a communist, and his sexual alliances with underaged girls had also become public. The legion also picketed John Huston's *Moulin Rouge* (1952) until Huston and star José Ferrer met with a Legion officer and "indicated that they will go all the way with us in fighting Communism." The Catholic War Veterans picketed *Born Yesterday* (1950) and *The Marrying King* (1952), which starred Judy Holliday, whom the group called "the darling of [the Communist Party publication] *The Daily Worker,*" until she cleared herself before the Senate Internal Security Subcommittee. Francis Cardinal Spellman ordered a Catholic boycott of BABY DOLL (1956), whose then-daring sexuality he believed would undermine the moral values that supported America's fight against communism.

SALT OF THE EARTH (1954) encountered both union censorship and union sponsorship. The independently made film sympathetically portrayed a 1951–52 strike by Mexican-

American zinc workers. It was directed by a blacklisted member of the HOLLYWOOD TEN (Biberman) and employed other blacklisted individuals. The film's sponsor, the International Union of Mine, Mill and Smelter Workers, which conducted the strike, had been expelled from the CIO in 1950 on charges that it was controlled by communists. Consequently, technicians in other unions refused to perform post-production work as did laboratories, and members of Roy BREWER's International Alliance of Theatrical Stage Employees (IATSE) were also prohibited from participating in the film. The Immigration and Naturalization Services even deported the female lead for a minor passport violation before the shooting was finished. *Salt of the Earth* was eventually completed—but even then, the American Legion threatened to picket theaters showing the film and IATSE projectionists refused to screen it. *Salt of the Earth* appeared only briefly in 10 U.S. cities after it was made, although it was later revived in political and feminist circles in the mid-1960s and 1970s.

When Dalton Trumbo openly received credit for writing EXODUS (1960) and SPARTACUS (1960), he broke the blacklist and signaled the decline of the influence of the Red Scare on American film. Trumbo had been a member of the Hollywood Ten, had gone to prison for refusing to comply with HUAC, and had been banned from writing for Hollywood studios (at least under his own name—he wrote many scripts anonymously). His official acceptance back into Hollywood introduced a new era of greater social and political expression that would soon make possible such political films of the early 1960s as THE MANCHURIAN CANDIDATE (1962), ADVISE AND CONSENT (1962), *To Kill a Mockingbird* (1962), SEVEN DAYS IN MAY (1964), FAIL SAFE (1964) and DR. STRANGELOVE (1964). When president-elect Kennedy and his brother Robert crossed the picket line to see *Spartacus,* they signaled the end of the American Legion's power to dictate to the film industry. This was too late for Chaplin's 1957 British-made attack on HUAC, A KING IN NEW YORK, which did not premiere in the United States until 1976.

Very few films treated the Red Scare directly while it was going on. Those that did, endorsed the Red Scare by depicting the dangers posed by American communists and the valiant efforts to combat them undertaken by private citizens and the FBI. Prominent among those films were BIG JIM MCCLAIN (1952), featuring John WAYNE as a HUAC investigator; I WAS A COMMUNIST FOR THE FBI (1951); THE IRON CURTAIN (1948); WALK EAST ON BEACON (1952); MY SON JOHN (1952); RED MENACE (1949); PICKUP ON SOUTH STREET (1953); *Conspirator* (1949); and *The Whip Hand* (1951). In 1951 Ronald REAGAN starred in STORM WARNING (1951) as a district attorney who encourages townspeople to testify against a Ku Klux Klan murderer. *Storm Warning* alludes directly to the HUAC hearings, which Reagan supported as president of the Screen Actors Guild. In the movie the hero, like HUAC, insists that the guilty parties must be revealed. On the other hand, the villainous townspeople protect the Klan by invoking verbatim arguments used by the Committee for the First Amendment in support of the Hollywood Ten. Thus the film implicitly endorses HUAC and vilifies the unfriendly witnesses who would not cooperate in indentifying Hollywood communists.

STORM CENTER (1956) stands out as the only major film of the time that actually attacked the Red Scare while the Red Scare was going on. The 1956 movie stars Bette Davis as a librarian who is harassed and fired because she refuses to remove a copy of *The Communist Dream* from the shelves of her small-town library. A communist plot to use a right-wing politician patterned after Senator Joseph McCarthy (R. Wisconsin) as its dupe is the focus of *The Manchurian Candidate* (1962). Several films from the 1970s condemned the Red Scare. THE WAY WE WERE (1973) uses it as an important plot element; THE FRONT (1976), made by blacklisted actors, writers and directors, criticizes the blacklist; TAIL GUNNER JOE (1977) exposes McCarthy as a demagogue; and *Marathon Man* (1976) uses a past injustice from the Red Scare first to inhibit and then to motivate the protagonist. FILM DOCUMENTARIES that address the Red Scare include OPERATION ABOLITION, which HUAC commissioned in 1960; HOLLYWOOD ON TRIAL (1976); THE TRIALS OF ALGER HISS (1980); and SEEING RED (1983), a partial oral history of the American Communist Party.

The Red Scare also appears metaphorically in such 1950s SCIENCE FICTION FILMS as INVASION OF THE BODY SNATCHERS (1956), THE THING (1951), THEM! (1954), INVADERS FROM MARS (1953), THE BLOB (1958) and THE DAY THE EARTH STOOD STILL (1951). Peter Biskind points out in *Seeing Is Believing* that there were Cold War subtexts in many 1950s films that featured creatures from outer space or mutations caused by atomic testing. The subtexts, which associated communism with the alien life forms, extend across the political spectrum. *It Came from Outer Space* (1953) and *The Day the Earth Stood Still* feature pacifist sentiments, value independent thought and intellectual achievement, and maintain that the aliens/communists should be listened to and not feared. The right-wing *Invasion of the Body Snatchers,* on the other hand, echoes McCarthy's charges that aliens/communists have already taken control of the government and military. More centrist films, such as *The Thing, Them!, Invaders from Mars* and *Forbidden Planet* (1956), accept the premise that the alien creatures pose a genuine threat, but they also reject McCarthy's claim that the government is already co-opted. Instead, these films depict the civil authorities working actively and successfully to combat the menace. Within the centrist films, a competition for authority sometimes emerges between the scientists and the military. In such films as *Them!,* for instance, the military is unable to defeat giant mutant ants without the assistance of a brilliant but socially inept scientist. On the other hand, in *The Thing,* the scientist's intellectual curiosity induces him to act "soft" toward the carnivorous vegetable, and the world is spared only because an air force officer overrules him. The tough military man fortunately destroys the Thing, from which the "duped" scientist had hope to learn "secrets hidden from mankind."

These conflicts between scientists and the military play out the nation's differing attitudes about the roles of intellect and military force in the national defense against communism. Given that Adlai Stevenson, the 1952 and 1956 Democratic presidential candidate, was branded an "egghead" intellectual and that his successful opponent, Dwight Eisenhower, had been a war hero, these films also seem to reflect presidential politics. Moreover, the 1950s saw the rise of a technocracy within the United States, a cadre of well-educated experts who were trained in science and assumed positions of authority in government and business. The tension in science fiction films between traditional, "straight-thinking," task-oriented military personnel and more innovative and imaginative scientists thus reflects the larger tension within the society between those who welcomed new scientific approaches as the universal key to success and those who resisted change, distrusted the claims made on behalf of experts, and regarded the insurgent technocracy as a threat to their own authority. Indeed, much of the anti-intellectualism that characterized the Red Scare can be viewed as a conservative attempt to retain or reclaim power within the culture by attacking members of the well-educated, generally liberal technocracy.

Two films from the early 1950s, HIGH NOON (1952) and ON THE WATERFRONT (1954) can be read as the statements about the filmmakers' own roles in the HUAC investigations of Hollywood. *High Noon,* which stars Gary Cooper as a Western sheriff who must face a vengeful gang alone, reflected screenwriter Carl Foreman's sense of abandonment by the film community when he was summoned to testify before HUAC in 1952. The film was in production while Foreman was preparing for his committee appearance, and he found a tremendous lack of support from friends and associates within the film community, including Stanley Kramer, his business partner and the film's producer. In his committee testimony, Foreman refused to name names of people he had met during his years as a communist, before 1942. He was subsequently blacklisted and he went into exile in England until 1956.

On the Waterfront, on the other hand, was an attempt at vindicating the testimonies of director Elia Kazan, a former communist who named 16 names before HUAC in 1952; writer Budd SCHULBERG, also a former communist, who had named 15 names in 1951; and actor Lee J. Cobb. Cobb, who had been close to the Communist Party but not a member, refused to testify in 1951 but, after suffering in poverty from being blacklisted, he reappeared before HUAC in 1953 and named names. The film glorifies an ex-boxer who heroically alienates his friends and community and risks his life by testifying against the vicious and corrupt union boss who runs the harbor. Arthur Miller, an unfriendly HUAC witness who was fined and received a suspended sentence for refusing to cooperate with the committee, had earlier collaborated with Kazan on *The Hook,* a screenplay about union corruption in the longshoreman's union. However, Miller withdrew from the project after Columbia Pictures' president Harry Cohn, at the suggestion of union leader Roy Brewer, insisted on changing the villains from union figures to communists. There were no direct references to communism in *On the Waterfront,* however. Miller went on to write THE CRUCIBLE (1953) at least partly in response to Kazan's testimony; and Miller's play *A View from the Bridge,* which also centers on an act of informing, is often considered to be his response to *On the Waterfront. After the Fall* (1964) the autobiographical play that Miller wrote and a newly reconciled Kazan directed, tells of a broken friendship between the play's protagonist and an ex-communist colleague who is about to name names.

For additional reading, see Sayre's *Running Time;* Na-vasky's *Naming Names;* Whitfield's *The Culture of the Cold War;* Biskwind's *Seeing Is Believing.*

"Firing Line" A syndicated TELEVISION TALK OR DEBATE SHOW hosted by conservative commentator William F. BUCKLEY Jr. from 1966 throughout the Cold War. Buckley started the show after attracting a following from his 1964 campaign as the Conservative Party's nominee for mayor of New York City. The first show aired on April 30, 1966. Initially featured on a single New York television station, WOR, the program was soon nationally syndicated. It featured debates between Buckley and prominent liberals and other political advocates as well as discussions with like-minded conservatives. PBS produced the show between 1971 and 1976, after which it went back into syndication. Buckley, editor of the conservative MAGAZINE *National Review,* would engage guests of various political persuasions in discussion of current political issues, including many pertinent to the Cold War, such as foreign policy and domestic antiwar protest. Buckley, whom Stephen Whitfield has described in *The Culture of the Cold War* as [Senator Joseph] "McCarthy's classiest defender," was known for his wit, detached demeanor and extensive vocabulary. The show won a special Emmy Award in 1969 for outstanding program achievement. In 1989, Buckley published *On the Firing Line,* excerpts from transcripts of his more memorable shows. Included are interviews with presidents Nixon, Ford and Reagan, British prime minister Harold Macmillan, failed presidential candidates Barry Goldwater and George McGovern, Norman MAILER, Clare Booth Luce and John Kenneth Galbraith.

First Blood See RAMBO.

Fiskadoro A 1985 APOCALYPTIC NOVEL by Denis Johnson. Published toward the end of the most intense period in the Cold War since the 1962 Cuban Missile Crisis, *Fiskadoro* suggests that the state of the world results from collective human consciousness and that storytelling and myth-making can constructively reshape human perceptions of reality. Fiskadoro, a bright 13-year-old African-American boy, lives in the Florida Keys with a postapocalyptic fishing tribe. They dwell in shanties, listen to garbled news reports and old ROCK AND ROLL on Cuban radio, and practice voodoo. MUSIC plays an important role in their lives, and Fiskadoro, a Pan-like, Christ-like figure, is a devotee of the clarinet. After Fiskadoro's father drowns and his mother contracts "killme," a cancer caused by radioactive fallout, the Quraysh tribe of quasi-Islamic swamp-dwellers, kidnaps him in order to replace one of their own boys who drowned during a wild orgiastic ceremony. They initiate Fiskadoro into the tribe in a drug-induced shamanic ritual that leaves him without his long-term memory, rendering him similar to the other men in the tribe. The mystical experience gives him shamanic powers and inner vision and allows for the full integration of his psyche. As he discovers the intuitive, feminine side of his soul, his anima and animus harmonize, and Fiskadoro completes his integration into the collective unconscious of the human race. In *The Nightmare Considered,* Millicent Lenz likens Fiskadoro's transformation to the developing of human consciousness represented in mythology by stories of the questing mythic hero: "He passes through the three stages of [Joseph] Campbell's monomyth of heroic adventure: separation, initiation, and return." But, "Fiskadoro's transformation of consciousness and myth-making powers are bought at the price of his individual identity."

If Fiskadoro embodies the developing human consciousness, his tutor A. T. Cheung exhibits "an historical/mystical consciousness," according to Lenz. "He seeks meaning and coherence in the attempt to recover historical knowledge." The book's third major character, Grandmother Wright, represents the intuitive, dream-filled unconscious. Her life has encompassed the Vietnam War, the nuclear holocaust known as "The End of the World," and postnuclear society. She sees "the filament of time . . . never tangled . . . a deep red event" when she stares at the flame in the kitchen stove: Through these three major characters, Johnson explores the different states of psychic evolution in a postapocalyptic environment. Moreover, as William Scheick suggests, nuclear destruction "becomes an opportunity for mankind to begin again. Just as a person tends to forget his dreams upon awakening, so too can the race forget its past as humanity evolves out of the holocaust. This is the meaning of Fiskadoro's severe memory loss, from which he never recovers."

For additional reading, see Anisfield's *The Nightmare Considered* and Scheick's "Continuative and Ethical Predictions: The Post-Nuclear Holocaust Novel of the 1980s."

Five A 1951 FILM DRAMA starring William Phipps, Susan Douglas and James Anderson and written and directed by Arch Oboler. Based on Oboler's radio drama THE WORD, *Five* was Hollywood's first postapocalyptic film. The story centers on the sole survivors of an atomic war, a culturally diverse group comprised of an idealistic college graduate; an hysterical, pregnant young woman; an African-American bank worker; an elderly cashier; and a fascist sportsman-explorer. The cashier dies quickly from his injuries, and the black man is murdered by the sportsman, who soon after succumbs from radiation poisoning. The college student and young woman remain to repopulate the Earth. Unusual for a Hollywood film during the RED SCARE, *Five* portrays the black man sympathetically and the neo-fascist negatively. By pointing out the possibility that the few survivors of a nuclear war might come from different racial backgrounds, the film anticipated the more popular and more respected 1959 film, THE WORLD, THE FLESH, AND THE DEVIL. But by killing off the black man, *Five* evades the question of interracial relations raised by the later film. (See also APOCALYPTIC FILMS).

For additional reading, see Shaheen's *Nuclear War Films.*

"Five Fingers" A TELEVISION SPY SHOW that ran on NBC in 1959–60. Based very loosely on the 1952 Joseph Mankiewicz film of the same name, "Five Fingers" features the exploits of Victor Sebastian (David Hedison), an American counterspy posing as a communist agent. The movie starred James Mason as a well-placed Albanian valet who sold secret World War II military plans to the Nazis. But the television show updated the setting to the Cold War and reversed the spy's role from an antagonist to protagonist,

as Sebastian feeds information on communist activities in Europe back to his American contact.

Fleming, Ian See BOND, JAMES.

Flight from Vienna A 1956 SPY FILM starring Theodore Bikel, John Bentley and Adrienne Scott and directed by Denis Kavanagh. Made during the same year as the Hungarian Uprising, this film centers on a Hungarian official who wishes to defect. However, to demonstrate the sincerity of his intentions, he must first assist in the defection of a Hungarian scientist.

folk singers especially during the early 1960s, folk songs were a popular form of social protest in the Cold War. Initially, many of the most popular songs centered on the civil rights movement; however, they also included anti-nuclear sentiments, representing the growing peace movement that accompanied the escalation of the Vietnam War. Woody Guthrie, a folksinger who flourished during the Depression and expressed left-wing, pro-union sentiments, inspired many of the early Cold War–era folk singers, notably Pete SEEGER, Bob DYLAN and Guthrie's own son, Arlo. During the 1950s, Guthrie's ballad about America, "This Land Is Your Land," was popular nationwide, but the stanzas critical of private property were commonly excluded.

In 1948, Seeger founded the folk group the Weavers. They reached number one in the charts for their rendition of "Good Night Irene" but soon became victims of BLACKLISTING after being listed in RED CHANNELS and attacked by nationally syndicated JOURNALIST Walter WINCHELL. The group subsequently broke up. (Tom Glazer was another blacklisted folk singer listed in *Red Channels.*) In 1955, Seeger was convicted on 10 counts of contempt of Congress for his refusal to cooperate with the HOUSE COMMITTEE ON UN-AMERICAN ACTIVITIES (HUAC); however, the convictions were overturned in 1962. In the interim, Seeger remained the most visible singer of pro-union and anti-racist folk songs during the 1950s.

In 1961, Seeger helped found and fund Sis Cunningham's *Broadside,* a biweekly magazine of songs about contemporary social issues. *Broadside* furnished a previously missing forum for left-wing, socially conscious music, publishing songs by Dylan, Phil OCHS, Tom Paxton, Less Chandler and Peter La Farge. Seeger was thus a vital force in the rising interest in folk music during the early 1960s.

Most notable among the younger generation of folk singers who came into prominence in the early 1960s were Dylan, Joan BAEZ, Phil Ochs, Tom Paxton, the Kingston Trio, the Chad Mitchell Trio, and Peter , Paul and Mary (Peter Yarrow, Noel Paul Stookey and Mary Travers). Dylan and Baez, who were romantically involved at the time, became known as the King and Queen of Folk Rock, and they had enormous influence. Both focused on the civil rights movement and pacifism in their songs. Dylan's Cold War music includes "Hard Rain's A-Gonna Fall," about the Cuban Missile Crisis, and the prospect of NUCLEAR APOCALYPSE; "Talking World War Three Blues," which provides a BLACK HUMOR view of life after a nuclear war; and "Masters of War," which attacks complacent, middle-class citizens for permitting American militarism. However, by 1965, Dylan withdrew from political music, and he and Baez broke up. Baez continued to be active in the peace movement and became a vocal critic of the Vietnam War.

Ochs, too, was an early critic of the war. Among his antiwar songs are "Talking Vietnam," "Is There Anybody Here?" "White Boots Marchin' in a Yellow Land" and "The War Is Over." His other Cold War music includes his first song, "The Ballad of the Cuban Invasion," about the failed Bay of Pigs invasion; "Talking Cuban Crisis"; "The Ballad of William Worthy," about a black journalist who ran afoul of the State Department when he traveled to Cuba without a passport; "Thresher," about the nuclear submarine that was lost at sea; "Love Me, I'm a Liberal," which attacks the hypocrisy of liberals; and "Cops of the World," which attacks U.S. imperialism. Tom Paxton's 1965 album *Ain't That News* features such protest songs as "Lyndon Johnson Told the Nation," "Buy a Gun for Your Son," "We Didn't Know" and "Ain't that News." According to Paxton, ". . . when after the long sleep of the Eisenhower years you find heated dialogues and demonstrations throughout the country—that's news."

Peter, Paul and Mary's contribution to the folk music movement includes popular recordings of peace songs "Where Have All the Flowers Gone," which Seeger translated, and "If I Had a Hammer," which Seeger wrote with Lee Hays. They also popularized Dylan's "Blowin' in the Wind," which became an anthem for the civil rights movement. Arlo Guthrie was less popular, but his long, comic ballad about the draft, "Alice's Restaurant," attracted a wide audience in the late 1960s and became the basis of the 1969 film by the same name. Guthrie stopped performing the song after the war concluded and the draft was ended; however, he began singing it at concerts in the 1980s after draft registration was reinstituted. During that time, he and Seeger toured together.

The protest aspect of folk singing spread to ROCK AND ROLL and helped create a mixed genre, folk rock. Among the popular practitioners of this new form were Judy Collins, Joni Mitchell, Melanie (Melanie Safka), Don McLean, Laura Nyro, James Taylor and Leonard Cohen. Many folk and folk-rock singers became active in the 1980s nuclear freeze movement, and performed in the series of well-attended concerts in June 1982 that were timed to coincide with the opening of the United Nations conference on nuclear disarmament. Among those who performed were Baez, Dylan, Taylor, Collins, Tom Petty, Linda Ronstadt, Bonnie Raitt, David Crosby, Stephen Stills, Graham Nash, Jackson Browne and John Denver.

For additional reading, see Orman's *The Politics of Rock Music;* Ward et al.'s *Rock of Ages: The Rolling Stone History of Rock & Roll.*

Fonda, Jane A film actress and political activist. The daughter of Henry Fonda, an actor associated with liberal causes, Fonda starred in several political and socially oriented films. An outspoken activist against the Vietnam War, her second marriage was to another prominent war protestor, Tom Hayden. Along with others from the film industry, Fonda participated in the organization called Entertainment Industry for Peace and Justice. Civilian and military audiences at home and abroad warmly received

this group's production, *Free the Army* (1970), which received an Obie award after its New York performance. However, when Fonda traveled to North Vietnam for two weeks in 1972, many Americans felt she was a traitor who was aiding the enemy, especially because she allowed herself to be filmed wearing a military helmet while sitting on an anti-aircraft gun aimed toward American planes, and because in her broadcast on Hanoi radio she labeled U.S. soldiers killers and war criminals and pleaded with them to disobey their orders to fight. She thus acquired the popular nickname "Hanoi Jane," an allusion to the World War II radio broadcasts by Tokyo Rose, who had likewise urged Allied soldiers to quit fighting. Years later Fonda apologized for her "thoughtless and careless" behavior, but the antagonism she generated persisted into the 1990s, especially among POWs who claimed they were tortured for refusing to participate in photo sessions with her. During that trip, Fonda also directed a film account of her experience of the war, *Viet Nam Journey.*

The 1978 film COMING HOME was her strongest film statement against the war, and she won a best actress Academy Award for her performance in it. The film features an affair between a bitter, paralyzed war veteran who has turned against the war and a middle-class housewife (Fonda) married to gung-ho officer still fighting in Vietnam who helps out in the V.A. hospital. During the 1970s, Fonda protested nuclear power. The 1979 release of *The China Syndrome* (1979), centering on a possible meltdown in a nuclear power plant, coincided with the Three Mile Island accident, which consequently attracted considerable attention to the film. Fonda's other socially aware films include *Klute* (1971); *Julia* (1977), which is based on a story by Lillian Hellman; *No Nukes* (1980), a filmed rock concert protesting nuclear power; and *The Old Gringo* (1989), about writer Ambrose Bierce's experiences during the Mexican revolution. During the 1980s, Fonda became a prominent promoter of physical fitness and exercise routines. She divorced Hayden and subsequently married the cable television innovator Ted Turner. Fonda was the subject of a BBC biography filmed in 1977, and aired in the United States in 1979.

For additional reading, see the Sterns' *Encyclopedia of Pop Culture.*

Footnotes on the Atomic Age A 1969 FILM DOCUMENTARY narrated by Tom Pettit and produced for television by NBC. *Footnotes* takes a critical look at the nuclear arms industry, pointing out some of the less well-known dangers of nuclear testing and nuclear policy. It presents the case history of Patrick Stout, an army veteran who was ordered to stand for 12 minutes on an atomic testing site in 1945, two months after a bomb had been detonated there. He eventually contracted leukemia and, after several appeals, was finally granted disability pay in 1969, less than three months before his death. The film goes on to point out that some 5,000 military personnel participated in "close-in operations" following atomic tests in 1951 and 1952 and leaves open the question of whether these men risked Stout's fate. It also notes that no follow-up study was ever conducted.

Footnotes also addresses some of the projected peaceful uses of atomic energy. It shows a segment from *Project*

Plowshare, a film by the Atomic Energy Commission (AEC) that advocates using nuclear devices to widen the Panama Canal. A critic of the plan points out that tens of thousands of Panamanian Indians would be endangered or displaced by it. Moreover, *Footnotes* describes the inherent dangers involved in making nuclear weapons. It documents the fire that contaminated a plutonium plant in Rocky Flats, Colorado, one of the most serious accidents in the nuclear weapons program during the Cold War. And the film addresses the financial interests at stake within the nuclear armaments industry. Finally, it intercuts scenes from the 1964 film satire DR. STRANGELOVE against interviews with former defense secretary Robert McNamara and the "father" of the hydrogen bomb, Edward Teller. (See also APOCALYPTIC FILMS.)

For additional reading, see Shaheen's *Nuclear War Films.*

foreign films Most of the foreign films viewed by U.S. audiences during the Cold War came from Great Britain. For instance, all of the highly popular James BOND films were British-made, as were such other SPY FILMS as COLD WAR KILLERS (1986), DEADLY AFFAIR (1967), THE IPCRESS FILE (1965), THE SELLOUT (1975), THE SPY WHO CAME IN FROM THE COLD (1965), STATE SECRET (1950) and THE THIRD MAN (1950), and such SPY FILM SPOOFS as OUR MAN IN HAVANA (1960), MODESTY BLAISE (1965) and THE SECOND BEST SECRET AGENT IN THE WHOLE WIDE WORLD (1965). Charles CHAPLIN's anti-capitalist MONSIEUR VERDOUX (1947), as well as A KING IN NEW YORK (1957), his attack on the RED SCARE and the HOUSE COMMITTEE ON UN-AMERICAN ACTIVITIES (HUAC), were also British-made, as were the film satire THE MOUSE THAT ROARED (1959) and DR. STRANGELOVE (1964), starring British actor Peter SELLERS, and the antiwar military and Vietnam War films KING OF HEARTS (1967), FULL METAL JACKET (1987), TELL ME LIES (1968) and THE KILLING FIELDS (1984). NINETEEN EIGHTY-FOUR (1984) was the British film adaptation of George Orwell's POLITICAL NOVEL. RUMOURS OF WAR (1972), TO DIE, TO LIVE (1976), THE WAR GAME (1966) and THE DAY THE SUN BLOWED UP (1976) were British FILM DOCUMENTARIES dealing with nuclear weapons and NUCLEAR APOCALYPSE. THE DAY THE EARTH CAUGHT FIRE (1961), which was made during the tense second Berlin Crisis, was a British SCIENCE FICTION FILM that also deals with the consequences of nuclear bombs. (See also APOCALYPTIC FILMS.)

Notable foreign films about the Cold War from Western Europe include THE DEFECTOR (1966, French and West German) about an American physicist in East Germany; Ingmar Bergman's THE SEVENTH SEAL (1956, Sweden), in which the bubonic plague of the Middle Ages serves as a metaphor for nuclear destruction; Bergman's *Shame* (1968, Sweden), about the deterioration of the marriage and individual personalities of a couple caught up in a brutal war; Constantin COSTA-GAVRAS' THE CONFESSION (1970), about a show trial behind the "Iron Curtain"; Costa-Gavras' STATE OF SIEGE (1973), about U.S. support for a Latin American dictatorship; the French-made antiwar documentary FAR FROM VIETNAM (1967), which features contributions from 11 internationally known directors; and the French-Japanese-made HIROSHIMA, MON AMOUR (1959). The Japanese films GODZILLA (1954) and RODAN (1957) are science fiction films featuring monsters that metaphorically equate powerful and destructive mon-

sters with the atom bombs dropped on Japan. In later sequels, however, these monsters change from Japan's nemesis to its protector, much as the U.S. nuclear force that destroyed Hiroshima and Nagasaki went on to protect Japan from possible threats from North Korea and the U.S.S.R. Set in an earlier time, when rifles were beginning to challenge the superiority of the samurai's sword, Akira Kurosawa's THE SEVEN SAMURAI (1954) likewise contains a nuclear-based subtext, in which rifles symbolize nuclear weapons. HIROSHIMA: A DOCUMENT OF THE ATOMIC BOMBING is a 1970 Japanese film documentary that intercuts contemporary scenes of Hiroshima with then-recently discovered film footage shot by Akira Iwasaki soon after the atomic bombing of that city. The footage, which the U.S. Department of Defense suppressed in 1945, first appeared in 1968.

American audiences rarely saw films made behind the IRON CURTAIN, though there were some exceptions. Made in 1958 in Poland, when that nation was permitting new freedoms and greater individuality to its film directors, Andrzej Wajda's ASHES AND DIAMONDS studied the conflicts among Poland's political factions just after World War II. The film appeared in the United States during the second Berlin Crisis. The Czech film CLOSELY WATCHED TRAINS (1966) was distributed internationally during the 1968 Prague Spring—a brief period of liberalization in Czechoslovakia under the short-lived administration of Alexander Dubcek; the film contains a subtext about the de facto Soviet occupation during the Cold War. Based on the SCIENCE FICTION NOVEL by Polish writer Stanislaw Lem, the Soviet film SOLARIS (1972) appeared in the United States in 1972, the same year that Nixon went to China and the U.S.S.R. and established détente among the superpowers. *Solaris* tells the story of cosmonauts exploring a planet that is, in fact, alive. Another Soviet-made film, MOSCOW DOES NOT BELIEVE IN TEARS (1979), was made at the end of détente and released in the United States in the early 1980s. The film depicts three working women in Moscow who remember romances from 1958.

"Foreign Intrigue" A TELEVISION SPY SHOW that ran in syndication from 1951 to 1955. Filmed on location, "Foreign Intrigue" featured the exploits of Robert Cannon (Jerome Thor), an American wire service correspondent whose foreign assignments took him across Europe and pitted him against political provocateurs, neo-Nazis and other threats to the new postwar order. After the first two seasons, the protagonist changed twice, first to Michael Powers (James Daly), another correspondent, and then to Christopher Storm (Gerald Mohr), a hotel owner in Vienna.

Foreman, Carl A blacklisted Hollywood SCREENWRITER. He is best known for writing the Academy Award-winning films, HIGH NOON (1952) and THE BRIDGE ON THE RIVER KWAI (1957). Foreman had been a member of the Communist Party but resigned in 1942. He claimed to have written *High Noon* to express his sense of abandonment by the film community when he was subpoenaed to testify before the HOUSE COMMITTEE ON UN-AMERICAN ACTIVITIES (HUAC) in 1952. The film was in production while Foreman was planning strategy for his testimony; *High Noon* reflects his discovery that no one would stand up with him against HUAC.

According to Foreman, even Stanley Kramer, his business partner and the film's producer, turned on him: "I got kicked out of my own company by Kramer . . . If Stanley had had the guts to ride it out we might have won . . . But Stanley was scared. In the crunch he was not prepared to have his career destroyed by my misguided liberalism." Kramer recounted the episode differently and maintained that Foreman had never told him all the facts of his involvement.

Eventually Foreman refused to inform on people he had met during his years as a communist and so he was subsequently blacklisted. John WAYNE, president of the MOTION PICTURE ALLIANCE, found the film "un-American" because it portrayed middle-class townspeople as cowards, desecrating the badge of a U.S. law enforcement officer. Wayne asserted as late as 1977 that, "I'll never regret having helped run Foreman out of this country." Foreman went into exile in England in 1952 and had his passport revoked by the State Department. While living in exile, he remarried and earned his living by writing black-market screenplays. Most notably, he wrote but did not receive credit for the Academy Award-winning script of *The Bridge on the River Kwai.* Pierre Boulle, author of the original novel, received the screen credit, even though he could not write in English. Of Boulle, Foreman said, "He had the good taste not to return in person to accept the Academy Award."

In 1956 Foreman's attorney, Sidney Cohn, arranged for him to testify in private session before a HUAC subcommittee of one person, Congressman Francis Walter. Cohn wanted to try a strategy that would allow Foreman and then others to testify about themselves without informing on others. In this way, they might break the blacklist. The strategy succeed for Foreman, but because of political repercussions for Walter, no one else was able to use it. There were rumors of a $25,000 bribe to the congressman that Foreman denied. In 1973, he added, "But don't get me wrong—I would have been happy to pay $25,000 to go back to work. I would have paid fifty thousand without batting an eyelash." Subsequently, the blacklist against Foreman was lifted. He returned to work in Hollywood, and his passport was reinstated. (See also EXILED WRITERS [from the United States].)

For additional reading, see Navasky's *Naming Names;* Whitfield's *The Culture of the Cold War.*

Fountainhead, The A 1943 novel by Ayn RAND and a 1949 FILM DRAMA starring Gary Cooper, Patricia Neal, and Raymond Massey and directed by King Vidor. The story celebrates Howard Roark, an individualist architect modeled after Frank Lloyd Wright. The film so strongly reflects Rand's fiercely pro-capitalist, anti-communist sentiments that in *Seeing Is Believing,* film critic Peter Biskind calls it "a Wagnerian soap opera for the radical right . . . Hollywood's *Triumph of the Will."* The film defines heroism as the individual resisting the collective will. Roark, who was expelled from architecture school because his ideas were "too original," cannot find work because he refuses to comply with the generally accepted notion that "artistic value is achieved collectively, by each man subordinating himself to the majority," an aesthetic philosophy that Rand portrays as dangerously close to communism. Fiercely self-reliant, Roark

reflects right-wing isolationism, insisting that "I don't give or ask for help." Like the radical right, Roark is also unyielding in his principles; for him, compromise is synonymous with selling out. The film depicts an inherent communist threat in the ever-present financial and social pressures for conformity that Rand believed threatened American society. The book, which sold two million copies by 1952, was frequently required or recommended for public school students during the 1950s and 1960s and was held up as a paean to the virtues of capitalism.

For additional reading, see Biskind's *Seeing Is Believing.*

Fourth Protocol, The A 1984 SPY NOVEL by Frederick Forsyth and a 1987 British-made SPY FILM starring Michael Caine, Pierce Brosnan and Joanna Cassidy and directed by John Mackenzie. Forsyth also wrote the screenplay. The story centers on a competition between British and Soviet master spies who narrowly forestall a nuclear disaster.

Francis Gary Powers: The True Story of the U-2 Spy Incident A 1976 made-for-television MILITARY FILM starring Lee Majors, Nehemiah Persoff, and Noah Beery, directed by Delbert Mann. The film presents the biography of the pilot of the U.S. U-2 spy plane that was shot down on a reconnaissance mission over the Soviet Union in May 1960. The incident scuttled a Paris summit conference that had been convened to resolve the on-going Berlin crisis. The situation in Berlin then rapidly deteriorated over the following year and a half, until it climaxed in October 1961 in one of the most dangerous U.S.-Soviet showdowns of the Cold War.

Powers, a Lockheed employee working for the CIA, survived the downing and was subsequently tried for espionage and sentenced to prison by the Soviets. He was criticized in the United States for allowing himself to be captured alive. In 1962 Powers returned to the United States in exchange for Soviet spy Rudolf Abel. (See also FILMS ABOUT COLD WAR EVENTS.)

Free World A Cold War term referring to the portions of the world not under communist domination, especially the democracies in the United States, Canada, Great Britain and Western Europe. (See also LANGUAGE.)

Freed, Fred An award-winning writer and producer of FILM DOCUMENTARIES for television. Freed made several "NBC White Papers" and special reports for "NBC Reports" addressing Cold War subjects. Prominent among these are KHRUSHCHEV AND BERLIN (1961); *Red China* (1962); *The Death of Stalin* (1963); *The Rise of Khrushchev* (1963); *Cuba: Bay of Pigs* (1964); THE MISSILE CRISIS (1964); THE DECISION TO DROP THE BOMB (1965); *United States Foreign Policy* (1965); COUNTDOWN TO ZERO (1966); *Pueblo: A Question of Intelligence* (1969), about the North Korean capture of the U.S. intelligence ship *Pueblo; Vietnam Hindsight* (1971); *The Energy Crisis* (1973); and a show about the nuclear arms race entitled AND NOW THE WAR IS OVER . . . THE AMERICAN MILITARY IN THE 1970s (1973).

For additional reading, see Einstein's *Special Edition: A Guide to Network Television Documentary Series and Special News Reports, 1955–1979.*

From Mao to Mozart: Isaac Stern in China A 1980 FILM DOCUMENTARY directed by Murray Lerner. Made eight years after President Nixon established cultural ties with China, the film documents violinist Isaac Stern's visit during which he gave master classes to promising young Chinese performers. It also provides impressive visual sequences of China and its citizens.

From Russia, With Love A 1957 James Bond SPY NOVEL by Ian Fleming and a 1963 SPY FILM starring Sean Connery and Daniela Bianchi, directed by Terence Young. The plot centers around a plan by S. P. E. C. T. R. E., an international organized crime syndicate, to play off the British Secret Service against S. M. E. R. S. H., the Soviet Secret Service. In so doing S. P. E. C. T. R. E., intends to acquire a sophisticated Soviet deciphering machine while simultaneously eliminating Bond, who had earlier caused them grief. A high-ranking S. M. E. R. S. H. official, whose defection to S. P. E. C. T. R. E. was not advertised to the rank and file, arranges for an attractive female clerk in the Soviet Embassy in Istanbul to offer the deciphering machine to the British. The clerk, assuming she is acting on behalf of the U. S. S. R., demands an amorous tryst with Bond in return. With the help of pro-Western Turkish agents, Bond and the clerk steal the machine, though several Soviet and Turkish agents kill each other in the interim. As Bond and the female agent make their way by train from Turkey through Yugoslavia, a S. P. E. C. T. R. E. agent waylays them to steal the deciphering device and kill Bond. However, Bond frustrates him and succeeds in delivering the machine to the British Home Office. As is typical in the discrepancy between Bond novels and films, the Bond character in the novel is less at peace with himself and more affected by the unsavory actions he must commit. For example, as he begins the assignment, The literary Bond regards himself as a "pimp for England" and wonders how his 17-year-old self would have viewed the person he has become. The film character has no such scruples. Made only a year after the Cuban Missile Crisis, the film's Turkish setting brings to mind the fact that Kennedy had agreed to remove U.S. medium-range Jupiter missiles from Turkey as part of the crisis resolution.

Front, The A 1976 FILM COMEDY starring Zero MOSTEL, Woody Allen, Andrea Marcovicci and Joshua Shelley, directed and produced by Martin Ritt. A tribute to the writers, directors and performers who faced BLACKLISTING during the 1950s RED SCARE (among them Mostel, Ritt and Walter Bernstein, who received an Academy Award nomination for writing the screenplay), *The Front* centers on the complicated situations that arise when a man (Allen) with little writing talent agrees to "front" for a blacklisted television writer by submitting the writer's work under his own name. Mostel plays a formerly active "communist sympathizer" who wants desperately to continue with his acting career, but who is told by a man from a RED CHANNELS-type organization that he must spy on Allen to clear himself. Loosely based on Philip LOEB, the Mostel character commits suicide.

Fu Manchu The subject of SPY FILMS and a TELEVISION SPY SHOW that lasted for 39 episodes in 1955 and 1956. Based on the character from Sax Rohmer's stories written in the early part of the 20th century, Fu Manchu was a brilliant Chinese scientist committed to the destruction of Western democracies. Often aligned with criminals, Fu Manchu employed his virtually unlimited resources and his scientific genius in diabolical plots for waging germ warfare, subverting peace conferences, undermining U.S. currency, extorting state secrets from U.S. diplomats and performing other acts detrimental to the West. Scotland Yard's Sir Denis Nayland-Smith succeeded in each episode in foiling the evil scientist's schemes but could never apprehend him.

One of the few villains ever to be the main character in an American television show, Fu Manchu also appeared throughout the century in numerous silent and sound films and on radio. In the 1960s Christopher Lee starred in five spy films based on the character: *The Face of Fu Manchu* (1965), *The Brides of Fu Manchu* (1966), *The Vengeance of Fu Manchu* (1967), *The Blood of Fu Manchu* (1968) and *The Castle of Fu Manchu* (1968). The 1980 FILM COMEDY, *The Fiendish Plot of Dr. Fu Manchu*, featured Peter SELLERS in the title role.

Though the television series played down the racist "Yellow Peril" aspect of the novels, which Rohmer wrote during the anti-immigration agitation prior to World War I, in the Cold War context the image of a powerful Chinese villain bent on undermining Western democracies inevitably resonated with Mao Zedong's bellicose anti-Western rhetoric. Thus the show both exploited and reinforced current, widespread political fear. The Korean War, in which the Chinese Army had effectively battled American troops, had ended in an inconclusive truce only two years before the show's premiere, and fighting constantly threatened to resume. In the show, Scotland Yard's continued success in thwarting Fu Manchu's schemes conveyed a message that democracy would win out in the end. On the other hand, Nayland-Smith's failure to capture Fu Manchu and eliminate his evil designs reflected the public's frustration with the sense that this was a seemingly interminable Cold War—with enemies who could never be decisively defeated.

Fuentes, Carlos A Mexican NOVELIST who lived in the United States, France and Mexico during the Cold War. Fuentes was born in 1928 in Mexico City, the son of a career diplomat. A prolific writer, he is frequently mentioned as a candidate for the Nobel Prize in literature. Given to wordplay and formal experimentation, Fuentes's work rarely addresses the Cold War directly. However, he has been an outspoken critic of U.S. foreign policy toward Mexico and Central America, dating back to when, as an 11-year-old child, he shouted at a movie about Sam Houston and the Alamo, "Death to the gringos! Viva Mexico!" More recently, his Third World spy thriller about international oil transactions, *The Hydra Head* (1978), criticizes both superpowers. Fuentes has also expressed support for the Castro regime in Cuba. *The Old Gringo* (1985), about the American writer/JOURNALIST Ambrose Bierce, addresses the U.S. role in suppressing the populist rebellion of Pancho Villa. Its subtext suggests that the Reagan administration's policies toward Mexico play a similar repressive role. Among other publications, Fuentes' Cold War work appeared in GROVE PRESS's *Evergreen* magazine.

For additional reading, see Tucker's *Literary Exile in the Twentieth Century*.

Full Metal Jacket A British-made 1987 VIETNAM WAR FILM starring Matthew Modine, Adam Baldwin and Vincent D'Onofrio and produced, written and directed by Stanley KUBRICK. Made during the Iran-contra scandal some 14 years after the Vietnam War had concluded, *Full Metal Jacket* appeared the year Ronald REAGAN and Mikhail Gorbachev signed the INF treaty, as U.S.-Soviet tensions began to ease considerably. The film depicts the deliberate dehumanizing process that American soldiers in Vietnam underwent before and during combat. The first section of the film follows a group of Marine recruits as they progressively lose their personal identity under the supervision of a sadistic, foul-mouthed drill sergeant. The second part follows one of them, Joker (Modine), a *Stars and Stripes* reporter who becomes caught in the 1968 Tet Offensive. The film's tone is dark and unrelenting; it undermines any notion of military glory or commitment to a worthwhile cause.

Fuller, Samuel a FILM DIRECTOR and SCREENWRITER. Though a fervent anti-communist, Fuller also took strong stands against racism and American chauvinism, an unusual combination of values in American movies. Fuller worked as a newspaper journalist in the 1930s and then as a screenwriter, before enlisting in the infantry during World War II. He fought in the European theater and earned several decorations. The first two films he directed were Westerns, *I Shot Jesse James (1949)* and *The Baron of Arizona* (1950). His next film, THE STEEL HELMET (1951), was the first KOREAN WAR FILM to be made in Hollywood. Fuller wrote the screenplay in a week and filmed the movie in 10 days; it was released just six months after the beginning of the Korean War. Considered one of the better war films from the 1950s, it presents the Korean War as a grim, confusing and dehumanizing experience in which becoming desensitized becomes necessary for survival, and being caring and compassionate can lead to death. The soldiers' and audience's inability to distinguish friendly Koreans from hostile ones reflects the confusion over the purpose of the war, which was somewhat unpopular at home. Overall, the film renders the war as an exercise in ongoing madness. The final credit reads, "There is no end to this story." Fuller wrote and directed a second Korean War film, *Fixed Bayonets* (1951), about a corporal who must assume command in a rear-guard action as his superiors are killed.

Fuller also wrote and directed PICKUP ON SOUTH STREET (1953), a *film noir* FILM DRAMA starring Richard Widmark as a small-time criminal who accidentally steals a roll of microfilm with atomic secrets intended for communist agents. The crook finally puts aside his cynicism and works with the FBI to thwart the enemy spies. Fuller helped write the screenplay for *The Capetown Affair* (1967), a remake of *Pickup* set in South Africa. He wrote and directed *Hell and High Water* (1954), about a privately owned, scientifically equipped submarine that sails to Alaska to thwart a plot by the Chinese communists. *The China Gate* (1957), which Fuller produced as well as wrote and directed, was an early VIETNAM WAR FILM in which a female Eurasian saloon keeper helps a squad of soldiers from the French Foreign Legion destroy a communist supply depot. It was the first film to show American soldiers fighting in Vietnam, though they do so under the auspices of the French. The movie, which stars Angie Dickinson and features Nat King Cole, attacks both the Vietnam communists and American racism.

For additional reading, see Server's *Sam Fuller: Film is a Battleground*.

games and toys The Cold War was reflected in the games and toys that were popular among children and sometimes among adults. G.I. JOE was probably the most popular Cold War toy. It began in 1964 as a foot-tall toy soldier marketed along the lines of the popular Barbie Doll, who required a seemingly endless supply of accessories. Joe was compiled from a composite of 20 Medal of Honor winners and was fully jointed, with 21 moving parts that enabled him to crouch, salute, and assume protective postures. He appealed to both boys and girls. The many changes he underwent throughout the Cold War mirrored domestic politics. During the 1980s Joe was also featured in television cartoon shows, comics, videotapes and games, in all of which he was marketed as "a Real American Hero."

More traditional board games such as Risk had centered on world conquest for decades, and the ever-popular Monopoly, whose capitalist orientation dates back to the 1930s, continued to flourish during the Cold War. Computer video games first appeared in the late 1970s and were sometimes criticized as a waste of time for young people, though on one occasion President Reagan praised them for developing the reflexes of future fighter pilots. Pinball games, video games and other arcade games also featured topical Cold War enemies. For instance, during the early 1980s, when the United States was supporting the anti-communist government in El Salvador and anti-Sandinista contras in Nicaragua, game soldiers frequently had a Central American look and wore jungle uniforms.

CHESS also played a role in the Cold War. Indeed, the Cold War itself was often represented as a chess match between the superpowers in which each side employed subtle gambits in their quest to gain advantage in a global competition. The metaphor is of dubious accuracy, but its prevalence in the United States suggested a clever and relentless enemy ready to pounce on any American error in diplomacy or international politics. The Soviets dominated international chess competitions throughout the Cold War, and Soviet propagandists used this fact to demonstrate their claim of the superiority of their social system. That claim was undermined in 1972, when the American chess genius Bobby Fischer defeated reigning Soviet world champion Boris Spassky in a highly publicized tournament. When Fischer refused to agree to the terms for a match with Soviet challenger Anatoly Karpov in 1975, he forfeited his title and Karpov reigned until his Soviet countryman Gary Kasparov defeated him in 1985. In the interim, Karpov twice defeated highly publicized challenges in 1978 and 1981 by Viktor Korchnoi, a Soviet chessmaster who in 1976 had defected from the U.S.S.R. to live in the West. Several other chessmasters defected from behind the IRON CURTAIN during the Cold War, including Pal Benko, who left Hungary after the 1956 Hungarian Revolution; Soviets Anatoly Lein, Vladimir Liberzon, Gennadi Sosonko and Leonid Shamkovich; and Czechs Lubomir Kavalek and Ludek Pachman.

Garcia Marquez, Gabriel A Colombian NOVELIST and winner of the 1982 Novel Prize for literature. Born in Colombia in 1928, Garcia Marquez fled to Paris in 1955 in fear of reprisal for a series of articles embarrassing to Colombian dictator Gustavo Rojas Pinilla. In 1957 he moved to Venezuela before returning to Colombia in 1959. He affiliated with Prensa Latina, the official press agency of Castro's Cuba, for which he worked first in Bogota, then in Havana, then in New York. In 1961, he moved to Mexico City, where he currently resides. His fiction, characterized by magical realism, ranges from overtly political to political in very subtle ways, and he has remained an outspoken supporter of Castro and other socialist causes. As a result, the United States has refused him unrestricted entry. Garcia Marquez is best known for his monumental novel, *One Hundred Years of Solitude* (1970). Other important works include *No One Writes to the Colonel and Other Stories* (1958; in English, 1968), *The Autumn of the Patriarch* (1975), *Chronicle of a Death Foretold* (1981; in English, 1982) and *Love in the Time of Cholera* (1985; in English, 1988).

Garfield, John A FILM ACTOR. The son of immigrants who raised him in slums, Garfield began his acting career in the left-wing Group Theater in New York and then moved to Hollywood. Between 1938 and 1951 he frequently played tough anti-heroes in films that often showed sympathy for working-class protagonists. In 1946 he cofounded Enterprise Productions to support artists with liberal and left-wing viewpoints, though he himself was not a member of the Communist Party. He then starred in Robert ROSSEN's *Body and Soul* (1947), Elia KAZAN's *Gentleman's Agreement* (1947) and Abraham POLONSKY's *Force of Evil* (1948). Garfield's career was curtailed in 1951 when he was blacklisted for his political activities. In an effort to get off the blacklist, he tried to avail himself of a limited offer by the HOUSE COMMITTEE ON UN-AMERICAN ACTIVITIES (HUAC) to allow people who were incorrectly identified as communists to clear themselves. Naming members of the Communist Party was the accepted method for achieving clearance, and Garfield, not having been a communist, declared himself unable to identify party members. Another requirement for gaining clearance was an act of public contrition. Since Garfield sometimes played boxers, his apology, which appeared as an article in *Look* magazine, was entitled "I Was a Sucker for a Left Hook." He was still in the process of gaining clearance when he suffered a heart attack and died. Most of those around him believed that the problems surrounding his BLACKLISTING triggered his heart attack. Garfield was one of the figures on which the protagonist of Conrad Bromberg's *The Dream of a Blacklisted Actor* (1969) was based.

Gathering of Eagles, A A 1963 MILITARY FILM; the story of a young air force colonel who whips a sub-par wing of the Strategic Air Command (SAC) into shape. Starring Rock Hudson, Mary Peach and Rod Taylor and directed by Delbert Mann, this film was a favorite of Curtis LeMay, the air force chief of staff and former chief of SAC, who believed that it was the most realistic film depiction of the service. In many ways the film vindicates SAC and LeMay from the criticisms that had been leveled in 1957 by a presidential commission investigating military preparedness. The film does expose problems with morale, family life and alcoholism on the military base, and the dedicated commander must make tough, unpleasant decisions in order to ensure

the wing's combat readiness and high-quality performance. Ultimately the film shows that the nation's defense must outweigh all other considerations, including family and friendship.

"General Electric Theater" An anthology of TELEVISION DRAMAS that ran on CBS from 1953 to 1962. Though the dramas had little political content, ranging from adventure stories and light comedies to Westerns and melodramas, the show was a notable contribution to Cold War culture in that from 1954 to 1962 it provided national exposure to its host and sometime star, Ronald REAGAN.

"Get Smart" A TELEVISION SITUATION COMEDY that ran on NBC from 1965 to 1969 and on CBS in 1969–70. Developed and written by Mel Brooks and Buck Henry and starring Don Adams as CONTROL agent Maxwell Smart, Barbara Feldon as agent 99, and Edward Platt as the chief of CONTROL, "Get Smart" parodied the SPY FILMS and TELEVISION SPY SHOWS popular during the 1960s. CONTROL, a U.S. government agency patterned after the CIA, was involved in counter-espionage, especially against its opposite organization, KAOS. Like the James BOND films, "Get Smart" featured high-tech gadgets, but on this show the gadgets were unlikely, absurd or completely dysfunctional; e.g., the Cone of Silence was intended to keep high-level CONTROL conversations confidential but in fact rendered all attempts at communication impossible. Smart, who fancied himself a suave, debonair agent à la Bond, was in fact a bumbler who nonetheless always managed to stumble upon success. In this respect he was similar to Inspector Clouseau, Peter SELLERS's character in the *Pink Panther* movies from about the same time. In 1969 "Get Smart" received the Emmy award for outstanding comedy series.

G.I. Joe A toy soldier conceived in 1964. Joe was inspired by the success of Mattel's Barbie Doll, which had appeared in 1959 and created a market not only for the basic doll but also for a seemingly endless number of accessories. Hassenfeld Bros. Inc., a Rhode Island toy company that later changed its name to Hasbro, developed a toy soldier that it could sell to both boys and girls, along with accompanying uniforms, weapons, medical supplies, vehicles and companion dolls to serve as enemies and allies. The list of Joe's accessories eventually grew to include a bazooka that shot plastic shells, a flamethrower that spouted water, karate uniforms and accompanying break-apart bricks, and an astronaut suit and space capsule. Before G.I. Joe, no dolls were produced in America specifically for boys, and Joe's manufacturers were careful to market him not as a doll but as a foot-tall "action soldier" and "America's Movable Fighting Man." His rugged face, which bore a scar on the right cheek, was based on a composite of 20 Medal of Honor winners, and he was fully jointed with 21 moving parts that enabled him to crouch, salute and assume protective postures. Joe came wearing army, navy, Marine, air force and Green Beret (in 1965) uniforms. In 1965, manufacturers also added a black G.I. Joe, which they marketed only in the North. A talking G.I. Joe appeared in 1967 and issued such battlefield commands as "Medic, get that stretcher."

G.I. Joe, 1964. Courtesy Hasbro Toy Group.

Joe's companions were slightly smaller and less rugged. They wore the uniforms of Germany, Japan, England, France, Australia and the U.S.S.R. For a short time in 1967 a G.I. Joe Nurse was marketed to tend to Joe's wounds. By 1967 Joe led sales among toys for five-to-twelve-year-olds, since he appealed to girls as well as boys. According to a *New York Times* article at the time, the girls were "smitten with the snappy Annapolis and West Point models." Michigan psychiatrist Norman Westland attempted to reassure parents who were concerned that their sons were playing with dolls, explaining that Joe was "a virile, masculine figure" and that "Boys never dwell on the word 'doll.' "

As opposition to the Vietnam War increased during the late 1960s, G.I. Joe became a target for antiwar organizations and others who believed that the toy soldier was teaching children that violence could be fun. For instance, one antiwar mother demanded, "If we're going to have toys that teach our children about war, why not have them *really* true to life? Why not have a G.I. Joe who bleeds when his body is punctured by shrapnel, or screams when any of his twenty-one movable parts are blown off, or vomits at the smell of burning flesh after a napalm attack?" Though it did not go to such extremes, the manufacturer did reduce the doll's military orientation, replacing the label "America's Movable Fighting Man" with "America's Movable Adventure Man." Accessories for this new approach included underwater equipment for hunting treasure, safari outfits, mountain climbing gear, bomb-disposal tools for combating terrorists, and a trench coat and attaché case for espionage.

In Joe's fan club bulletin, the *Command Post News,* the term *action adventure* replaced *war.* However, during the early 1980s, as the Cold War reintensified and the United States dramatically increased its military budget and worldwide military presence under the leadership of President Reagan, Joe once again became a soldier. After being reduced to eight inches in 1976, he was shrunk down to three inches in 1982 and sold as part of a Mobile Strike Force that emphasized teamwork over individual heroism; he was now marketed as "a Real American Hero." During the 1980s he was also featured in television cartoon shows, comics, videotapes and games. For additional reading, see the Sterns' *Encyclopedia of Pop Culture.*

Giles Goat-Boy A 1966 POLITICAL NOVEL by John BARTH. The story presents an elaborate Cold War allegory focusing on the metaphor of the universe as university. Thus, the United States is the West Campus; the U.S.S.R. is the East Campus; the new West Campus chancellor alludes to John Kennedy, his predecessor represents Eisenhower, and so on. Within this framework is another allegory depicting the journey of the mythic hero as described by Carl Jung and Joseph Campbell. The novel tells the story of a modern hero, a Grand Tutor (New Messiah) who appears at the height of Cold War tensions to save the Campus from the threat of imminent annihilation by the great computer that controls the entire university. Mixing BLACK HUMOR, Jungian archetypes, existentialism and an Eastern philosophy that sees the world in terms of paradox, Barth depicts the primary Cold War anxieties of the middle 1960s: a world on the brink of self-destruction, technology gone dangerously out of control, flawed leaders motivated by a variety of personal and political interests, and a population desperately seeking salvation or simply escape. The novel concludes that the answers for living meaningfully in such a volatile world must come bottom-up from each individual, and not top-down from governments and leaders. Each person must find his or her own answers through an ongoing process of self-scrutiny and growth. Moreover, the novel suggests that we must come to accept the chaos and competition of power politics as part of the energy of life, and so find ways to live harmoniously with power politics instead of rejecting or fearing it. Barth consequently finds some virtue in the balance of power between superpowers. In this respect, the novel anticipated Nixon and Kissinger's policy of détente by some six years. (See also LITERATURE ABOUT COLD WAR EVENTS; SCIENCE FICTION NOVELS AND STORIES; SATIRE.)

Gilligan's Island A TELEVISION SITUATION COMEDY that ran on CBS from 1964 to 1967. The show featured the misadventures of a cross-section of American society that had been stranded on an ocean island. Mr. and Mrs. Howell (Jim Backus and Natalie Schafer) were millionaires who insisted upon being treated as aristocracy, and the others largely complied. The Professor (Russell Johnson) provided the technical know-how to build various labor-saving devices as well as machines that were supposed to help the group get off the island. Ginger (Tina Louise) was the glamorous, sexy movie star, and Mary Ann (Dawn Wells) was the sweet, naive country girl. Alan Hale Jr. played the

Skipper, the boat's captain, and Bob Denver starred as the well-intentioned but inept crewman, Gilligan. An extremely successful show, "Gilligan's Island" showed the various members of Cold War American society working together and resolving conflicts in order to survive. Social peace was shown among the upper caste (the millionaire Howells), the working class bumbling (Gilligan), a manager (the Skipper) a scientist from the professional class, a movie starlet and a "farm girl." Interestingly, the upper-class couple, though retaining considerable authority on the island, was portrayed as naive and almost helpless, while the "egghead" professor was often impractical. Finally, the island castaways relied on Gilligan and the Skipper, who, though clumsy and sometimes ignorant, did the necessary work to maintain the island society.

Ginsberg, Allen

Ginsberg, Allen A POET and founder of the BEAT MOVEMENT. Ginsberg was born in Newark, New Jersey, to a Jewish family in 1926 and died April 5, 1997. Among his formative childhood experiences was his mother's paranoid fear of political persecution for her leftist beliefs. Naomi Ginsberg was institutionalized for three years during Allen's adolescence and then permanently later in life; his poem "Kaddish" describes the effect of her mental illness upon him. Ginsberg's father was an English teacher and poet, though unlike Allen, his personality as well as his poetry celebrated order and personal restraint. Thus Allen appears to have rebelled against his father's conservatism and embraced his mother's radical sympathies while simultaneously deriving from her his appreciation for the outcast and insane. Ginsberg attributed his homosexuality to the "usual oedipal entanglement."

Ginsberg received a bachelor's degree from Columbia University in 1948. He had befriended William Burroughs and Jack Kerouac in 1944 and with them became a major figure in the literary and social movement known as Beat. Finding conventional middle-class American society unimaginative, unduly repressive and spiritually confining, they pictured themselves as social outcasts and advocated the spontaneous and free expression of libidinal impulses. The Beat movement reflected despair over a world gone mad with nuclear weapons and other forms of mass destruction and with an apparently insatiable need to impose conformity and deny creativity. Ginsberg's most powerful expression of these sentiments appears in his famous poem "Howl" (1956), which was inspired by his incarceration in the Columbia Psychiatric Institute in 1949 and dedicated to Carl Solomon, a fellow inmate whom Ginsberg called a "lunatic saint." Beginning "I saw the best minds of my generation destroyed by madness, starving hysterical, naked,/ dragging themselves through the negro streets at dawn looking for an angry fix," "Howl" depicts corporate, industrial American society as the ancient god Moloch "within whose brazen image living children were . . . burned as sacrifices." Ginsberg's poem was reportedly inspired by a peyote-induced vision of San Francisco's Sir Francis Drake Hotel as the pagan Canaanite god. In 1957 Lawrence FERLINGHETTI was arrested on obscenity charges for publishing the poem, but the court finally ruled that the work was not obscene. The ruling helped establish a precedent that enabled other writers to employ images

and language hitherto absent from American literature. In recognition of Ferlinghetti's sponsorship of radical and non-traditional literature, Ginsberg later asserted that Ferlinghetti "ought to receive some sort of Pulitzer Prize for publishing." The GROVE PRESS's *Evergreen Review* reprinted "Howl" in 1957.

During the 1960s, Ginsberg experimented with LSD and other drugs to heighten his consciousness and to draw upon unexplored aspects of his subconscious. He also traveled widely. Between 1961 and 1963 he visited France, Morocco, Greece, Israel, India, Vietnam and Japan. He met philosopher Martin Buber in Israel and Hindu holy men in India, achieving a spiritual transformation that he felt allowed him to become more accepting of the universe with all its horror, change and irrationality—i.e., to accept the effects of the Cold War. Buber counseled Ginsberg to concentrate on personal relationships, while the holy men advised him to focus on matters of the heart rather than the mind and to seek contentment within his own body. While traveling in Japan in 1963, the meaning of their advice became suddenly clear to him. Ginsberg describes his spiritual transformation in his poem "The Change."

In 1965 Ginsberg visited several communist countries including Cuba, Poland, Czechoslovakia and the Soviet Union. The Czechs initially greeted him warmly, but after he advocated artistic spontaneity and freedom of expression, the Czechoslovakian government expelled him. That experience caused him to reject Marxist-Leninism. On his return to the United States, Ginsberg became involved with the nascent Vietnam War protest movement and helped originate the concept of "flower power" as a means of achieving peace. He participated in a 1967 "life festival" that offered chanting, ROCK AND ROLL, and poetry readings as alternatives to war and was arrested with Dr. Benjamin Spock for blocking access to a military induction center. He continued his social criticism in *Planet News* (1968), a collection of poetry written from 1961 to 1967, and in *The Fall of America* (1972), which won the National Book Award.

In 1971 Ginsberg met CIA director Richard Helms at a reception before a poetry reading. Ginsberg claimed that

Allen Ginsberg, 1966. Courtesy AP/Wide World.

the CIA was involved in opium trading in Southeast Asia but Helms denied the charge. Ginsberg then proposed a wager: He would give Helms his *vajra*, a Buddhist-Hindu ritual instrument, if he was wrong, but Helms would agree to meditate an hour every day for the rest of his life if Ginsberg proved to be right. Ginsberg appears to have been correct, but Helms apparently declined the bet. A year later Ginsberg wrote Helms before attending the Democratic national convention in Miami. He advised the director to meditate daily or, "If this is too much, try sitting cross-legged, back straight, on soft rug . . . use no mantra eyes open Zen style . . ."

Until recently the CIA file on Ginsberg was unavailable. (Normally the Freedom of Information Act does not release information on living subjects except to themselves.) But part of Ginsberg's FBI file has become public; it shows that in 1965, FBI director J. Edgar Hoover sent the Secret Service information on Ginsberg because the bureau regarded him as a potential threat to President Johnson. Hoover noted that Ginsberg was a subversive who met all three of the following criteria: "(a) Evidence of emotional instability . . . or irrational or suicidal behavior; (b) Expressions of strong or violent anti-U.S. sentiment; (c) Prior acts . . . of conduct or statements indicating a propensity for violence and antipathy toward good order and government." Following the 1968 Democratic convention the FBI office in Chicago reported that Ginsberg had "chanted unintelligible poems" in Grant Park on 8/28/68; however, officials declined prosecution of Ginsberg. The chanted poem was William Blake's "The Grey Monk."

Ginsberg takes up the Cold War directly in his 1956 poem "America," which links mass-market consumerism and middle-class attitudes with the RED SCARE and threat of nuclear war, so that his personal insanity is the result of a nation gone mad in the name of reason. The poem begins, "America I've given you all and now I'm nothing./ America two dollars and twentyseven cents January 17, 1956./ I can't stand my own mind./ America when will we end the human war?/ Go fuck yourself with your atom bomb." Later he states, "I'm obsessed by Time Magazine. . . . It's always telling me about responsibility. Businessmen are serious. Movie producers are serious. Everybody's serious but me." Ginsberg describes how his mother took him to communist cell meetings as a child, how he ate garbanzos and "everybody was angelic." He then comments ironically on the Red Scare, "Everybody must have been a spy." Finally, echoing James Joyce's *Finnegans Wake* in his play with sound, meaning and syntax, Ginsberg adopts the voice of Middle America, which he perceives as chauvinistic, paranoid and, like him, crazy.

America you don't really want to go to war.
America it's them bad Russians.
Them Russians them Russians and them Chinamen.
  And them Russians.
The Russia wants to eat us alive. The Russia's
  power mad. She wants to take our cars from
  out our garages.
Her wants to grab Chicago. Her needs a Red
  Readers' Digest. Her wants our auto plants

in Siberia. Him big bureaucracy running our
  fillingstations.
That no good. Ugh. Him make Indians learn read.
  Him need big black niggers. Hah. Her make us
  all work sixteen hours a day. Help.
America this is quite serious.
America this is the impression I get from
  looking in the television set.
America is this correct?
I'd better get right down to the job.
It's true I don't want to join the Army
  or turn lathes in precision parts factories,
  I'm nearsighted and psychopathic anyway.
America I'm putting my queer shoulder to the
  wheel.

Ginsberg again took up the Cold War in his 1982 collection, *Plutonium Ode*, in which he declares a pox on both Cold War houses. In "Capitol Air" he declares:

No hope Communism no hope Capitalism Yeah
Everybody's lying on both sides Nyeah nyeah nyeah
The bloody iron curtain of American Military Power
Is a mirror image of Russia's red Babel-Tower.

Paul Berman, the critic for the *Village Voice*, observed in a review of *Plutonium Ode*, "The words to discuss this [nuclear] calamity seem not to exist. Language fails us . . ." Berman also points to a greater level of despair in *Plutonium Ode* than in Ginsberg's earlier work. In "America" Ginsberg still offered hope for the future: "America when will you be angelic?" But in *Plutonium Ode* such hope no longer exists.

For additional reading, see Hyde's *On the Poetry of Allen Ginsberg*.

"Girl from U.N.C.L.E., The" A TELEVISION SPY SHOW that ran on NBC from 1966 to 1967. A spin-off of the more successful MAN FROM U.N.C.L.E., this series also parodied James BOND-type spy stories. April Dancer (Stefanie Powers) and Mark Slate (Noel Harrison) teamed to combat the efforts of U.N.C.L.E.'s rival organization, T.H.R.U.S.H. As in the original series, the plots were playfully outlandish and farfetched.

Glen and Randa A 1971 FILM DRAMA starring Steven Curry and Shelley Plimpton and written and directed by Jim McBride. Set 50 years after an atomic war, the story centers around a young couple as they wander throughout the country seeking remnants of civilization but finding only its ruins. (See also APOCALYPTIC FILMS.)

Glowacki, Janusz A Polish EXILED WRITER (to the United States). Born in 1938, Glowacki was active in the Polish Union of Writers and a strong supporter of Lech Walesa's Solidarity movement. His novel *Give Us This Day* (1981; in English, 1983) describes the lives of members of the Solidarity movement and the hostility toward them exhibited by the Polish military and government officials. Banned in Poland, it was first published there as an underground book and then smuggled abroad where it was translated into several languages. In 1985 it was published in the United

States, where it found critical success. His most powerful play, *Cinders* (1981), was also published in the United States in 1985. It describes efforts by a Polish film maker to document a production of *Cinderella* in a girls' reformatory school. As part of the documentary, the director compels the girls to describe their own tales of woe. The more extreme and sensational their stories, the better suited they are for his cinematic purposes. All the girls but one comply, embellishing on their stories for greater effect. Cinders, the girl who refuses to lie for the camera, becomes the protagonist of the play, which pits the desire to preserve truth against those who would manipulate events for their own purposes. Martial law was declared in Poland while Glowacki was in London attending the play's 1981 premiere there. Rather than return, Glowacki remained in England and then came to the United States in 1982, where he taught at Bennington College and the University of Iowa before moving to New York's Lower East Side. In addition to two full-length plays, *Fortinbras Gets Drunk* (1985) and *Hunting Cockroaches* (1986), Glowacki has also written two shorter plays while in America. "Journey to Gdansk" and "Flashback" both deal with the dilemmas of exiled writers who must decide whether to return to Poland to report on the strike of shipyard workers in Gdansk. If they go, they risk imprisonment or other personal loss; if they stay, they must live with what they believe to be their own cowardice. Glowacki has also written over 10 books, 20 radio plays and four produced screenplays, as well as journalistic articles and essays. See also THEATER.

For additional reading, see Tucker's *Literary Exile in the Twentieth Century*.

Go Tell the Spartans

A 1978 VIETNAM WAR FILM starring Burt Lancaster, Craig Wasson and Marc Singer and directed by Ted Post. The film is based on Daniel Ford's novel *Incident at Muc Wa* (1967). Made five years after the U.S. military withdrawal from Vietnam, the film centers on American military advisers during the initial period of the Vietnam War and depicts the basic problems inherent in the U.S. attempt to conduct the war. As in David HALBERSTAM's 1967 Vietnam War novel ONE VERY HOT DAY, *Go Tell the Spartans* represents the futility of the war effort with images of endless circularity. As Lancaster tells a young draftee who wants to see what war is actually like, "Shame we couldn't have shown you a better war, like Anzio, or Bataan; this one's a sucker's tour, going round and round in circles."

For additional reading, see Lanning's *Vietnam at the Movies*.

God That Failed, The

A 1949 NONFICTION collection of essays by former communists and communist sympathizers edited by Richard Crossman. The book contains personal accounts by three prominent ex-communist intellectuals, Arthur KOESTLER, Richard WRIGHT and Louis Fischer, and three "fellow travelers," Ignazio Silone, Andre Gide and Stephen Spender. It was commonly cited by anti-communists as firsthand evidence of communism's failings and hypocrisies. The volume was inspired by Koestler's comment to Crossman: "It's the same with all you comfortable, insular, Anglo-Saxon anti-Communists. You hate our Cas-

sandra cries and resent us as allies—but when all is said, we ex-Communists are the only people on your side who know what it's all about." Crossman then challenged Koestler to write his own account of why he turned to and departed from communism.

Anti-communists often cited *The God that Failed* as evidence of how the Communist Party demanded intellectual conformity that ultimately proved empty and even dangerous. Crossman also urges readers to understand why communism attracted these exceptional thinkers and to consider what that attraction suggests about the shortcomings of Western democracy: "The only link . . . between these six very different personalities is that all of them—after tortured struggles of conscience—chose Communism because they had lost faith in democracy and were willing to sacrifice 'bourgeois liberties' in order to defeat Fascism. Their conversion, in fact, was rooted in despair—a despair of Western values." He adds, "These six pieces of autobiography should at least reveal the dangers of . . . this facile anti-Communism of expediency. That Communism, as a way of life, should . . . have captured the profoundly Christian personality of Silone and attracted individualists such as Gide and Koestler, reveals a dreadful deficiency in European democracy. That Richard Wright, as a struggling Negro writer in Chicago, moved almost as a matter of course into the Communist Party, is in itself an indictment of the American way of life." Crossman adds that Fischer and Spender turned to communism because Western democracy had disillusioned them and its appeasement of Hitler nauseated them. Because all six "had a premonition of catastrophe [ie.: the failure of liberal faith in progress], they looked for a philosophy with which they could analyze it and overcome it—and many of them found what they needed in Marxism."

Crossman continues, "The intellectual attraction of Marxism was that it exploded liberal fallacies—which really were fallacies. It taught the bitter truth that progress is not automatic, that boom and slump are inherent in capitalism, that social injustice and racial discrimination are not cured merely by the passage of time, and that power politics cannot be 'abolished,' but only used for good or bad ends . . . The choice seemed to lie between an extreme Right, determined to use power in order to crush human freedom, and a Left which seemed eager to use it in order to free humanity." Crossman also suggests that communism enjoyed greater success in Catholic countries because "The strength of the Catholic Church has always been that it demands the sacrifice of [spiritual] freedom uncompromisingly, and condemns spiritual pride as a deadly sin. The Communist novice . . . felt something of the release which Catholicism also brings to the intellectual, wearied and worried by the privilege of freedom. Once the renunciation has been made, the mind, instead of operating freely, becomes the servant of a higher and unquestioned purpose. To deny the truth is an act of service . . . Any genuine intellectual contact which you have with [a Communist] involves a challenge to his fundamental faith, a struggle for his soul."

Koestler amplifies Crossman's analogy of communism to religion: "A faith is not acquired by reasoning. One does not fall in love with a woman, or enter the womb of a church, as a result of logical persuasion . . . All true faith involves a revolt against the believer's social environment, and the projection into the future of an ideal derived from the remote past." Koestler describes how a childhood guilt complex about enjoying good fortune prepared him intellectually and emotionally for communism. As a middle-class child in Budapest, his family fell into dire economic straits, and he thereafter felt guilty whenever his parents gave him gifts or later, when he was supporting them, whenever he bought something for himself. "I developed a strong dislike of the obviously rich; not because they could afford to buy things (envy plays a much smaller part in social conflict than is generally assumed) but because they were able to do so without a guilty conscience. Thus I projected a personal predicament onto the structure of society at large." He adds that during the Depression his situation was common throughout Europe: "It was the beginning of Europe's decline . . . The pauperized bourgeois became rebels of the Right or Left . . . Those who refused to admit that they had become déclassé, who clung to the empty shell of gentility, joined the Nazis and found comfort in blaming their fate on Versailles and the Jews. Many did not even have that consolation; they lived on pointlessly . . . members of a class displaced by history. The other half turned Left . . ."

Koestler left the French party's central committee after refusing to let party officials dictate the content of a speech about Spain he gave to the German Emigré Writers' Association in Paris. He fully disassociated himself from communism "the day when the swastika was hoisted on Moscow Airport in honor of Ribbentrop's arrival." He concludes, "I served the Communist Party for seven years—the same length of time as Jacob tended Laban's sheep to win Rachel his daughter. When the time was up, the bride was led into his dark tent; only the next morning did he discover that his ardors had been spent not on the lovely Rachel but on the ugly Leah."

Each of the other two former party members describes his experiences with the party. Their departures also stem from an unwillingness to subordinate personal beliefs to the party line. Moreover, Wright tells how white communists physically evicted him when he tried to march in a May Day parade after leaving the party, and the formerly sympathetic non-member Silone describes how he became disillusioned after being ordered to condemn a statement by Trotsky that he was not permitted to read beforehand.

The other fellow travelers also condemn communism for its self-serving perversion of truth. Gide, who had once praised the communist experience in the Soviet Union, now concludes: "The Soviet Union has deceived our fondest hopes and shown us tragically in what treacherous quicksand an honest revolution can founder. The same old capitalist society has been re-established, a new and terrible despotism crushing and exploiting man, with all the abject and servile mentality of serfdom."

Fischer was first drawn to communism when, after serving in World War I, he began studying that war's causes. He became attracted to arguments that the expansionist intentions of czarist Russia, Austria-Hungary, Germany, France and England had been the primary reasons for the worldwide conflict: "All these great powers had, by secret treaties, agreed to carve up and share small, helpless nations. This expansionist urge of one set of countries ultimately brought them into conflict with another set of expanding countries, and then came war. Liberal New York weekly magazines now charged that the Versailles Peace Conference had worked on the same, evil imperialistic principle . . . My attitude toward the War and the peace made me receptive to Bolshevik criticism of the West."

Like Koestler, Fischer's final falling out with the party came when Stalin signed the 1939 nonaggression pact with Hitler, though evidence that the Soviets were purging communists who had served the Loyalist cause in the Spanish Civil War precipitated his disillusionment. He states, "I have not changed my attitude to the dangers of excessive [capitalist] power. But I now realize that Bolshevism is not the way out because it is itself the world's biggest agglomeration of power over man . . . Stalin's Russia is condemned as a 'police state.' That is a fraction of the evil. The Kremlin holds its citizens in subjugation not only by police-and-prison power but also by the greater power inherent in the ownership and operation of every economic enterprise in the nation. Capitalism's trusts and cartels and monopolies are pygmies compared to the one mammoth, political-economic monopoly which is the Soviet State." Fischer concludes that "All goals . . . are nothing in the abstract. They only have meaning in relation to the interests of living men, women, and children who are the means through which everything on earth is achieved . . . I thought, in my Soviet phase, that I was serving humanity. But it is only since then that I have really discovered the human being."

Spender, an Englishman, had written *Forward from Liberalism* in 1936, arguing that liberals "must put the cause of freedom on the side of social justice. They must transplant individual freedom from the capitalist to the workers' interest." Afterward, he was invited to join the British Communist Party to show his support for the anti-fascist Loyalists in Spain, and he agreed on the condition that he could also publish in *The Daily Worker* an article criticizing Stalin's show trials and purges. However, after a few weeks he allowed his membership to lapse and never paid any dues. He points out that "For the intellectual of good will, Communism is a struggle of conscience. To understand this, explains many things. Amongst others, that Communists, who act in ways which may seem to the non-Communist unscrupulous, may nevertheless be perfectly sincere." Before joining the party, Spender had traveled to Gibraltar, Oran and Tangier as the Spanish Civil War was beginning. "Everywhere . . . where I came in touch with Communist groups, I was impressed by their confidence and their decency." By contrast he formed bad impressions of the officials and businessmen who represented the interests of the Western countries and generally supported Franco. However, later communist treachery in Spain and subsequent denial of it disillusioned Spender. He came to believe that communist support for Spain was not given in good faith but only to form "united fronts in order then to seize control of them from within." He concludes: "Thus when Communists talk of unity they mean unifying various deviating groups and showing them the correct line of historic development. In order to achieve this, they emphasize that they are the party of democracy which wants all the forces of progress to unite." Spender's post-communist position is that "my duty is to state what I support without taking sides. Neither side, in the present alignment of the world, represents what I believe to be the only solution to the world's problems. This is: for the peoples and nations who love liberty to lead a movement throughout the world to improve the conditions of the millions of people who care more for bread than for freedom, thus raising them to a level of existence where they can care for freedom. The interests of the very few people in the world who care for the values of freedom must be identified with those of the many who need bread, or freedom will be lost."

God's Grace A 1982 APOCALYPTIC NOVEL by Bernard Malamud. The book was published during the most intense period of the Cold War since the 1962 Cuban Missile Crisis, when the Reagan administration was speaking of winnable nuclear war and implementing a massive military buildup. The novel imagines the aftermath of a NUCLEAR APOCALYPSE in which Calvin Cohn, a paleologist and the son of a rabbi, functions as a modern Noah, despite the fact that "God has allowed violent, insufficient humankind to incinerate itself at last" and will permit "No Noah this time, no exceptions, righteous or otherwise." Shipwrecked on an ocean island with Buz, an experimental chimpanzee who speaks, Cohn tries to create an improved race of human-chimps that will regain God's love. Initially he meets success but then his efforts go awry, suggesting that humans are finally incapable of creating peaceful, successful societies.

Godunov, Alexander A DANCE performer and Soviet defector. Born in the Soviet Union, Godunov danced for 13 years with the prestigious Bolshoi Ballet before defecting to the United States in August 1979. He was touring the United States with the Bolshoi when he attracted worldwide news coverage by requesting political asylum, claiming he was artistically restrained in the Soviet Union. His wife Lyudmilla Vlasova, a soloist with the Bolshoi, elected to return to the U.S.S.R., and they divorced in 1982. After his defection, Godunov danced with the American Ballet Theater for three years before leaving due to disagreements with artistic director Mikhail BARYSHNIKOV, an earlier Soviet defector with whom Godunov had been a fellow dance student in the Soviet Union. Subsequently, Godunov starred in his own television show, "Godunov: The World to Dance In," which ran in 1983–84. He then turned to film, debuting as an Amish farmer in *Witness* (1985) and later performing in *The Money Pit* (1986) and *Die Hard* (1988). Godunov became a U.S. citizen in 1987 and died of natural causes at age 45 in 1995.

Godzilla, King of the Monsters A 1954 Japanese-made SCIENCE FICTION FILM starring Raymond Burr, Takashi Shimura and Momoko Kochi and directed by Inoshiro Honda. Originally released in Japan as *Gojira*, the American version cut 20 minutes and added footage of Burr as a reporter and commentator who witnesses the rampage of an ancient sea monster that rises from the sea and destroys everything in its path. *Gojira* was among the biggest popular and critical hits in Cold War Japan. Like Akira Kurosawa's

THE SEVEN SAMURAI (1954), which also treats the atomic bomb through allegory, *Godzilla* metaphorically equates the powerful, destructive monster with the atom bombs dropped on Japan. *Godzilla* appeared during the same year that fallout from a massive U.S. nuclear test on the BIKINI atoll fell on a Japanese fishing boat, giving the crew radiation sickness, contaminating their catch, and causing widespread panic in Japan.

In the 1959 sequel to the film, *Godzilla Raids Again*, atomic testing reawakens the monster, who goes on to devastate the city of Osaka. However, in later sequels, Godzilla changes from Japan's nemesis to its protector, much as the U.S. nuclear force that destroyed Hiroshima and Nagasaki was later seen as protecting Japan from possible threats from North Korea and the U.S.S.R. By showing the wholesale destruction of major cities, the *Godzilla* films mimicked the potential consequences of a nuclear war, which remained an active possibility throughout the Cold War but was most strongly felt in the 1950s. The attraction held by scenes of massive carnage and destruction may thus have responded to audiences' alternating fascination with and repulsion by images of their own doom. (See also APOCALYPTIC FILMS.)

"Goldbergs, The" A TELEVISION SITUATION COMEDY that ran on CBS from 1949 to 1951 on NBC from 1952 to 1953, on the DuMont network in 1954, and in syndication in 1955–56. Based on a popular radio show for which Abraham POLONSKY wrote in the late 1930s, "The Goldbergs" featured the adventures of a middle-class Jewish family from the Bronx. The show starred Gertrude Berg as housewife Molly Goldberg. Though the program had no political content, it is relevant to the Cold War because of the BLACKLISTING of Philip LOEB, who played Molly's husband from 1949 to 1951. Loeb had been named as a communist symphatizer in RED CHANNELS, a publication that listed alleged communists and fellow travelers in the radio and television industry. Loeb denied any communist affiliations, but despite Berg's declaration that it was "un-American" to fire anyone on the basis of unproven charges, General Foods threatened to withdraw its sponsorship of the show if Loeb remained. CBS official Frank Stanton tried to work out a mutually acceptable solution, and meetings were held every 13th week to review the situation. But after the 1951 season, General Foods dropped its sponsorship. The show moved to NBC, but without Loeb, who was replaced first by Harold J. Stone and then by Robert H. Harris. The radio-television reporter for the New York *Journal-American* revealed in his August 25, 1951, column that "The Goldbergs" had lost its sponsor because of Loeb. He further declared that Loeb left the show "after a long and luxurious hiatus in [CBS's] pink-tinged boudoir." Four years later Loeb committed suicide. He was the basis for Zero MOSTEL's character in the THE FRONT.

Golden Days A 1987 APOCALYPTIC NOVEL by Carolyn See. The book was published during the second Reagan administration, when the threat of nuclear war had diminished somewhat from his first administration but was still very much present and when the country was embracing both a materialistic life-style and a New Age belief in unlimited personal power. The novel centers on Edith Langley, a 38-year-old woman who accepts the notion that money is power and participates in the "golden days" of Reaganomics until the nuclear war brings that time to an apparently disastrous end. However, Edith survives the disaster in sunny Southern California along with a cast of bizarre characters who continue to apply pop psychology and Eastern mysticism to cope with their new situation. The reviewer for the *New York Times Book Review* states, "In its weird way, this may be the most life-affirming novel I've ever read." The title comes from book three of Milton's *Paradise Lost,* in which God refrains from destroying humanity after Jesus offers himself as sacrifice: "The world shall burn, and from her ashes spring/ New heaven and earth, wherein the just shall dwell,/ And after all their tribulations long/ See golden days . . ."

Goldfinger A 1960 SPY NOVEL by Ian Fleming and a British-made 1964 SPY FILM starring Sean Connery, Gert Frobe, Honor Blackman and Shirley Eaton and directed by Guy Hamilton. One of the best James BOND films, *Goldfinger* also provides one of the most interesting treatments of the Cold War. The story centers on a plot by Goldfinger, a rich and powerful man obsessed with gold, to detonate an atomic bomb inside the U.S. gold depository at Ft. Knox, Kentucky. By rendering the entire U.S. gold supply radioactive, Goldfinger plans to increase the value of his own private hoard of gold. Communist China has supplied Goldfinger with the bomb because his action will destabilize its most powerful enemy, and leaders of organized crime have facilitated the bomb's transportation to Tennessee. A muscular North Korean, Oddjob, is Goldfinger's personal bodyguard. After discovering Goldfinger's plan, Bond successfully thwarts it—just seconds before the bomb's scheduled detonation. Along the way, the secret agent has several harrowing experiences, which he survives with the aid of the clever high-tech gadgetry that characterizes all the James Bond stories. Likewise, he seduces various beautiful women, including Pussy Galore, the leader of a corps of tough-but-sexy women pilots in Goldfinger's employ. Thus, *Goldfinger* shows some women to be highly competent, disciplined and accomplished, though others are completely passive or incompetent when attempting traditionally male tasks. On the other hand, even tough-minded women are shown to be ruled by their libidos, as Pussy switches sides after making love to Bond. The film concludes that virility—which assures the cooperation and ultimate domination of women—is an important weapon in the Cold War.

Made in 1964, *Goldfinger* reflects the new shape of the Cold War after the 1962 Cuban Missile Crisis. In the aftermath of that nuclear showdown, tensions lessened between the United States and the U.S.S.R., as both sides fought the Cold War more through proxy states than in direct confrontation. On the other hand, in 1964, China exploded its first nuclear device. Its leader, Mao Zedong, who was preparing for his Cultural Revolution, threatened war, criticizing Soviet premier Khrushchev for his reforms and attempts to reconcile with the West. Consequently, *Goldfinger* replaces the Soviets, who had been the enemy in such earlier works as FROM RUSSIA WITH LOVE (book 1957, film 1963), with Chinese and North Koreans. It also reinforces the alleged collusion between communism and organized crime that often appeared in 1950s films. Moreover, the film added a scene, absent in the novel, which memorably introduced millions of Americans to the then-new laser technology that 20 years later would become the basis of President Reagan's Strategic Defense Initiative (SDI—more popularly known as STAR WARS). The film first shows Goldfinger impressively using the laser to slice bars of gold. But the new technology made a more lasting impact when Goldfinger turned the laser on Bond, who was tied down, spread-eagled, watching helplessly as the powerful beam inched up between his legs. Whether viewed as attempted castration or, as John Cawelti and Bruce Rosenberg suggest in *The Spy Story,* Goldfinger's symbolic effort to rape Bond, the scene reinforced the notion that the Cold War was finally a struggle for male dominance. (See also APOCALYPTIC FILMS.)

For additional reading, see Cawelti and Rosenberg's *The Spy Story.*

Good Morning Vietnam A 1987 FILM COMEDY starring Robin Williams, Forest Whitaker and Tung Than Tran and directed by Barry Levinson. The story centers on frenetic radio disk jockey Adrian Cronauer who hosts a morning show in 1965 for the American military forces in Saigon. He befriends some South Vietnamese civilians, encountering some conflicts of interest as a result. The protagonist is based on an actual disk jockey named Adrian Cronauer who began his show by shouting, "Good morning, Vietnam," though the real Cronauer stated in an interview that he would not have been allowed to undertake the antics Williams performs in the film. (See also VIETNAM WAR FILMS.)

For additional reading, see Lanning's *Vietnam at the Movies.*

Gorky Park A best-selling 1981 SPY NOVEL by Martin Cruz Smith and a 1983 SPY FILM starring William Hurt, Lee Marvin, Brian Dennehy and Joanna Pacula and directed by Michael Apted. The novel was written and the film was produced during the first Reagan administration, when Cold War tensions had reintensified after the 1970s détente. The story centers on a police investigation of the deaths of three people discovered in Moscow's Gorky Park. The trail leads to an American fur trader (Marvin) and a young Soviet dissident (Pacula). The movie, which presents a stark view of life behind the IRON CURTAIN, was filmed in Helsinki after the Soviet government refused to allow it to be shot in the U.S.S.R.

Graham, Billy A television evangelist who flourished throughout the Cold War. Graham's rise to national prominence occurred during a Protestant revival he was holding in Los Angeles in the fall of 1949. The revival coincided with President Truman's announcement that the Soviets had exploded their first atomic bomb, and Graham played upon Americans' resulting anxieties by merging old-fashioned fire and brimstone with Cold War anti-communism: "God is giving us a desperate choice, a choice of either revival or judgment. There is no alternative! . . . The world is divided into two camps! On the one side we see Communism . . . [which] has declared war against God, against Christ, against the Bible, and against all religion! . . . Unless the Western world has an old-fashioned revival, we cannot last." Later he declared, "My own theory about Communism is that it is master-minded by Satan . . . I think there is no other explanation for the tremendous gains of Communism in which they seem to outwit us at every turn, unless they have supernatural power and wisdom and intelligence given to them." This formula of combining fundamentalist Christianity with anti-communism became the cornerstone of Graham's appeal throughout the Cold War.

In the fourth week of Graham's 1949 revival, the vehemently anti-communist publisher William Randolph Hearst sent his editors a succinct memo, "Puff [promote] Graham." With the support of Hearst publicity, Graham emerged as a major figure in Cold War American culture. The Los Angeles revival attracted some 350,000 patrons by the year's end, and even Hollywood became interested in him. Director Cecil B. DEMILLE, also known for his intense hatred of communism, offered Graham a screen test. Graham's next revival was held in Columbia, South Carolina. The right-wing governor Strom Thurmond and former secretary of state James Byrnes attended and endorsed Graham, and MAGAZINE publisher Henry LUCE flew down to meet him. Over the next five years, Graham's picture adorned the cover of Luce's *Life* magazine four times. He was also featured on the cover of *Newsweek* six times. By 1958, the Billy Graham Evangelistic Association was receiving over 10,000 letters a week and collecting over $2 million a year. Throughout the 1950s, Graham repeatedly appeared in magazine lists of the 10 most admired men in America.

In addition to writing a nationally syndicated newspaper column, Graham was among the first ministers to employ the new medium of the postwar era, TELEVISION. Between 1951 and 1954, his Billy Graham Evangelical Association sponsored "Hour of Decision," a series of regular Sunday night talks on ABC. Between 1957 and 1959 Graham held four widely viewed television "crusades," during which he held services every Saturday night for two to three months.

Though he was originally a registered Democrat, Graham became a religious "adviser" to two Republican presidents, Eisenhower and Nixon. His publicly stated views on foreign policy reflected those of the political right wing. In a sermon on "The Sin of Tolerance," which he twice delivered on the air and published as a pamphlet, Graham equated the term "tolerance" with "liberal" and criticized what he labeled American appeasement of the Soviet Union. He accused Presidents Roosevelt and Truman of selling out in the Teheran, Yalta and Potsdam conferences and, echoing Secretary of State Dulles' Liberation Policy, he called for the Eisenhower administration to promote armed rebellion against communist regimes in EASTERN EUROPE and to unleash Chiang Kai-shek and his "crack troops" against Mao Zedong's government on the Chinese mainland. Graham's domestic politics were also right-wing. During the winter of 1950–51 he warned that "over 1100 social sounding organizations . . . are communist or communist operated in this country" and that "the infiltration of the left wing" had damaged American religious and educational culture "almost beyond repair." Graham supported Senator Joseph McCarthy's demand that witnesses testifying before his committee not be allowed to invoke their Fifth Amendment rights against self-incrimination. He also endorsed the implied link between communism and homosexuality that often appeared in right-wing rhetoric, as he praised the

congressional investigators "who, in the face of public denouncement and ridicule, go loyally on in their work of exposing the pinks, the lavenders, and the reds who have sought refuge beneath the wings of the American eagle." Taking an anti-union stand, Graham declared that Adam and Eve in Eden had "no union dues, no labor leaders, no snakes, no disease."

Though he condemned America's growing materialism, he favored a strong economy and spoke as though capitalism and Christianity were inextricably fused. In sum, he anticipated the Religious Right of the Reagan and Bush eras by representing right-wing political views as the true Christian position and by projecting fundamental Christianity as the essence of American patriotism: "Only as millions of Americans turn to Jesus Christ at this hour and accept him as Savior, can this nation possibly be spared the onslaught of a demon-possessed communism . . . If you would be a true patriot, then become a Christian. If you would be a loyal American, then become a loyal Christian."

Toward the end of the Cold War Graham's positions modified. After Mikhail Gorbachev introduced reforms in the Soviet Union that eventually dismantled the Communist Party and the U.S.S.R., Graham voiced opposition to nuclear warfare and advocated policies predicated on peace. He was the first outside religious figure to legally preach in the officially atheistic Soviet Union. He visited five times between 1982 and 1991. (See also RELIGIOUS TELEVISION PROGRAMMING.)

For additional reading, see Whitfield's *The Culture of the Cold War.*

"Grandpa Goes to Washington" A TELEVISION SITUATION COMEDY that ran on NBC from 1978 to 1979. A Carter-era show that poked fun at Washington insiders and special-interest politics, "Grandpa Goes to Washington" evoked recollections of the popular, folksy 1939 Jimmy Stewart movie, *Mr. Smith Goes to Washington.* The show centered on the exploits of Senator Joe Kelley (Jack Albertson), a former political science professor who ran independently for the Senate after being forced to retire from the university at age 66. Elected when the nominees from both parties were both exposed as crooks, Senator Kelley represented the common people and fought for honesty in government. Like President Carter, Kelley made a point of publicly eschewing the trappings of power. He drove a Volkswagen, played drums for relaxation and relied on a network of "friends in low places" to feed him important political information. He referred to his son, an empty-headed air force general, as "my son, the fathead." The show reflected the post-Watergate, anti-establishment values that contributed to Carter's election. Made during the period between the Vietnam War and the Reagan presidency, it depicted the U.S. military as bureaucratic and unenlightened—a view that was relatively rare in American television during the Cold War.

Great American Novel, The A 1973 novel by Philip Roth. An absurdist critique of revisionist history, *The Great American Novel* purports to describe the Patriot League, a third major league that, according to the narrator, has been excised from all accounts of professional baseball. The story centers on the fate of the hapless Rupert Mundys, whose owners sold the stadium to the army during World War II, thereby reducing the team to the status of permanent visitors in other clubs' ballparks. They are thus likened to the Jews wandering in the desert after the exodus from Egypt. The plot meanders in many directions, but by intermingling improbable truths (such as the appearance in professional baseball of a midget and a one-armed player) with probable fiction (such as Aunt Jemima's attendance at a game in a Negro league) Roth uses the baseball context to question how we record history and to convey the uncertainty implicit in our daily assumptions about the nature of truth. At the same time, Roth insists on the importance of remembering history. Writing at a time when the HOUSE COMMITTEE ON UN-AMERICAN ACTIVITIES (HUAC) was interrogating Vietnam War protestors, Roth reminds us of HUAC's outrages of 20 years earlier.

The book culminates with a series of HUAC investigations reminiscent of those during the RED SCARE. Several Mundy players, "the Mundy 13," are implicated in an alleged communist conspiracy. Some confess and name the names of other conspirators rather than face BLACKLISTING; others go to jail, like the HOLLYWOOD TEN. Like other blacklistees, one commits suicide; another appears as a single, double or possibly triple agent. The narrator himself is sentenced to jail for refusing "to participate in this lunatic comedy in which American baseball players who could not locate Russia on a map of the world—who could not locate *the world* on a map of the world—denounce themselves and their teammates as Communist spies out of fear and intimidation and howling ignorance, or . . . out of incorrigible human perversity and curdled genes." Thus, despite our inevitable uncertainty over basic historical facts, Roth still makes us feel moral outrage over the abuses from the Red Scare. *The Great American Novel* admonishes us to learn from history, as well as to notice who is included or excluded from historical accounts. Nevertheless, the book's satirical nature allows us to enjoy political corruption even while asking us to despise it. (See also SATIRE.)

For additional reading, see Schwartz's, "Postmodernist Baseball."

Green Berets, The

A 1965 best-selling novel by Robin Moore and a 1968 VIETNAM WAR FILM starring and directed by John WAYNE, with David Janssen, Richard Pryor and Jim Hutton. The title song, "The Ballad of the Green Berets" by Sergeant Barry Sadler, became a popular hit in 1966. Sadler, who was wounded in Vietnam while serving as a medic with the Special Forces, appeared on the ED SULLIVAN television show and was featured in *Life* magazine after his song displaced the current ROCK AND ROLL hits and topped the pop chart for five consecutive weeks. His picture appeared on the cover of the paperback edition of Moore's novel, which sold one and a half million copies and inspired a 200,000-member fan club. A patriotic film that endorsed the U.S. military effort in Vietnam, *The Green Berets* attempts to update Wayne's World War II film heroics to the Vietnam War. The book was published the same year as the first U.S. combat troops were introduced into the war. Its action centers on American military advisers to the South Vietnamese Army. The movie appeared shortly after the pivotal Tet Offensive, during the height of the U.S. involvement in Vietnam. It was the first film to try to depict accurately the combat between the South Vietnamese Army and the Viet Cong, and its portrayal of an attack against a U.S. Special Services (Green Beret) outpost is essentially realistic. *The Green Berets* includes a rare depiction in American films of a brave and loyal South Vietnamese officer. (See also VIETNAM WAR LITERATURE.)

For additional reading, see Lanning's *Vietnam at the Movies.*

Greene, Graham

A British NOVELIST. Born in 1904 and educated at Oxford University, Greene's greatest contribution to Cold War LITERATURE was as a writer of SPY NOVELS. His earliest treatment of the Cold War appears in THE THIRD MAN (1949), which is set in occupied Vienna after World War II. The plot, which centers on efforts by British military police to catch a black marketeer, depicts the lack of cooperation between the Soviets and the Western allies, suggesting that American naiveté is out of place in postwar Europe. Greene also wrote the screenplay for the critically acclaimed 1950 film adaptation.

In 1952 Greene was a victim of the RED SCARE when he was denied a visa to the United States because he had joined the Communist Party for a month in 1923. Greene blamed the action on President Truman's attorney general, James McGarnery. *Commonweal* editorialized, "That it could be seriously thought that Graham Greene would carry the contagion and infect us is a fair measure of the intelligence and the precision of the authors of the McCarran Act. McCarran and McCarthy might sacrilegiously have met Mr. Greene on his arrival, with bell and book and candle to drive from his spirit the last few traces of germs." In response to similar problems experienced by Charles CHAPLIN in the same year, Greene published "The Return of Charlie Chaplin: An Open Letter," attacking McCarthy and the HOUSE COMMITTEE ON UN-AMERICAN ACTIVITIES (HUAC) and urging British writers and actors to refuse to participate in films sponsored by organizations that included "these friends of the witch-hunter." Greene eventually received a visa, but some reviewers have suggested that the anti-American position in THE QUIET AMERICAN (1955), Greene's novel implicitly condemning the early U.S. involvement in Vietnam, stemmed from these Red Scare experiences. Greene also wrote a NONFICTION piece on Vietnam for the *New Republic* entitled "Indo-China" (1954).

In *The Spy Story*, John Cawelti and Bruce Rosenberg call Greene's SATIRE, OUR MAN IN HAVANA (1958), "the greatest burlesque of the spy story ever penned." The story centers on a Cuban vacuum cleaner salesman who agrees to spy for the British in order to finance his daughter's private education. Since he has no real information to pass along, he submits enlarged schematics of vacuum cleaner technology, claiming they describe military installations. Greene also wrote the screenplay for the film. The novel appeared before Castro's communist revolution, spoofing the regime of Castro's predecessor, Fulgencio Batista. The film, on the other hand, appeared after Castro came to power and thus acquired a new slant.

THE HUMAN FACTOR (1978) presents a more serious spy story that may have been based on Greene's friend Kim

Philby, a British intelligence officer who defected to the U.S.S.R. in 1963, though Greene denied the connection. (Greene served with Philby in British intelligence during World War II and wrote "Reflections on the Character of Kim Philby" for *Esquire* in 1968, as well as the introduction to Philby's memoirs.) Cawelti and Rosenberg consider *The Human Factor* one of the finest spy novels ever written. The story centers on Maurice Castle, a British intelligence agent who specializes in African affairs and has married a black South African woman he once used as an agent. His loyalty to her and to Africa leads him to pass information to the Soviets. Greene depicts a morally ambiguous world in which almost no one has a full picture of the machinations of any side and in which everyone is manipulated for someone else's purposes. Finally, no one can be trusted. Castle's fundamental uncertainty about the overall picture renders problematic his ability to make moral decisions or take responsible action. The communists do not represent an attractive alternative, but neither does the West, which supports the racist South African regime in order to retain access to that country's gold, diamonds and uranium.

For additional reading, see Cawelti and Rosenberg's *The Spy Story; The Dictionary of Literary Biography* (vol. 15, *British Novelists, 1930–1959*).

Grove Press A publishing house established in New York in 1949 by John Balcomb and Robert Phelps. Barnet Lee Rosset Jr. acquired it for $3,000 in 1952 and decided to concentrate on publishing European literature. In the early 1950s, he introduced American readers to works by Samuel BECKETT, Bertolt BRECHT, Jean Genet and Simone de Beauvoir. In 1959 the press published D. H. Lawrence's *Lady Chatterley's Lover,* which postal inspectors soon impounded on the grounds of obscenity. A U.S. district court ruled the work was not obscene, however, and the decision helped open the American market to a wider range of sexual expression. The novel was also the press's first major financial success. Grove further expanded the boundaries of legally acceptable literature when it successfully defended its publication of Henry Miller's *Tropic of Cancer* in 1964 against obscenity charges. Rosset later published such authors as Eugene Ionesco, Alain Robbe-Grillet, Jorge Luis Borges, Octavio Paz, Jean Cocteau, Harold Pinter, Tom Stoppard, William Burroughs and Jack Kerouac, as well as the poets Charles Olson, Robert Duncan, Imamu A. Baraka (LeRoi Jones) and Allen GINSBERG. He also revived such works of 19th-century erotica as *My Secret Life* and *A Man with a Maid.*

The overall thrust of Grove's booklist was to provide an outlet in America for avant-garde writers, many of whom held socialist or other anti-capitalist, anti-bourgeois views that were considered suspect during the RED SCARE. The press also provided a forum for advocates of Castro's regime in Cuba by publishing *Che Guevara Speaks* (1967) and Regis Debray's *Revolution in the Revolution?* (1967). Grove angered the CIA by publishing *My Silent War* (1968), the memoirs of Kim Philby, the British spy who defected to the U.S.S.R. In July 1968, anti-Castro Cubans bombed the offices of the publishing house, apparently in response to its publication of the pro-Castro books. Grove alleged that the CIA had tapped its phones, infiltrated its offices and been a party to

the bombings, and in 1975 it unsuccessfully sued the agency for damages and access to the CIA's files.

In 1957 the press introduced *The Evergreen Review,* which became a leading voice of radical and avant-garde writing in America. (See also MAGAZINES.) *Evergreen* reprinted Ginsberg's poem "Howl," which Lawrence FERLINGHETTI had first published a few months earlier in his City Lights press. Among those also published in *Evergreen* were Beckett, Jean-Paul Sartre, Ferlinghetti, Carlos FUENTES, Denise LEVERTOV, Terry SOUTHERN and Baraka, who reported on a 1960 trip to Castro's Cuba he had made with several other African Americans. The magazine also published portions of Che Guevara's journals. Financial difficulties forced Grove to discontinue *Evergreen* in 1973 and to dramatically scale back the number of new publications it offered. In 1968 it had been able to issue 136 titles, but in 1979 it offered only 45. In 1985, the Wheatland Corporation acquired the Grove Press for $2 million. Subsequently, Grove Press became an independent publishing house again but more mainstream and less political.

For additional reading, see *Dictionary of Literary Biography* (vol. 46, *American Literary Publishing Houses 1900–1980*).

"Guide Right" A television variety show that ran on the DuMont network in 1952–53. This Korean War-era show was designed to help the U.S. military recruit volunteers. Employing both military and civilian performers, the show sometimes originated directly from military bases. In addition to featuring the Airmen of Note and the Singing Sergeants, "Guide Right" included an October 1952 performance by PFC Eddie Fisher, the nation's most popular singer at the time.

"Gunsmoke" A TELEVISION WESTERN that ran from 1955 to 1975. American television's longest-running series with a continuing cast of characters, "Gunsmoke" was the first adult Western to appear on American television and the last Western to remain on the air. Set in Dodge City, Kansas, in 1873, "Gunsmoke" featured the adventures of U.S. Marshal Matt Dillon (James Arness), his first deputy, Chester (Dennis Weaver, who left the show in 1964), his second deputy, Festus (Ken Curtis), and his friends, Doc Adams (Milburn Stone), Quint Asper the blacksmith (Burt Reynolds) and Miss Kitty the saloon proprietor (Amanda Blake). The show began as a radio program in 1952 starring William Conrad. John WAYNE was the first choice for the starring role on television. He declined but recommended Arness for the part. However, Wayne did introduce the first episode.

Though the show did not directly address the Cold War, it reflected the American view of itself in the postwar era, as Marshal Dillon strived to impose order and justice in the unruly frontier town. Dedicated to law and order, Dillon also tried to be fair-minded and compassionate. But he was always ready to stand up to anyone who might violate the rights of law-abiding citizens or otherwise endanger the security of Dodge City. Some of the shows from the 1960s addressed such current social issues as minority rights and social protest.

Gyorgyey, Clara A Hungarian EXILED WRITER (to the United States). Born in Budapest in 1938, Gyorgyey has been the president of the Writers in Exile chapter in America of PEN International, a writer's organization. Her own plays have been performed off-Broadway, as has her translation of Istvan Orkeny's *Cats Play*. In 1987 she published a collection of criticism, *With Arrogant Humility,* and she has written a definitive study of the works of her fellow exiled (from the Nazis) Hungarian writer, Ferenc Molnar. (See also THEATER.)

For additional reading, see Tucker's *Literary Exile in the Twentieth Century.*

"Hail to the Chief"   A TELEVISION SITUATION COMEDY that ran on ABC for only seven episodes in 1985. Starring Patty Duke as Julia Mansfield, the president of the United States, "Hail to the Chief" was created by Susan Harris who also created the soap opera spoof, "Soap." Like "Soap," "Hail to the Chief" featured wild, improbable plot complications in which the president confronted an ongoing string of crises ranging from a lunatic major's threatening to start World War III to equally insane hot-line threats from the Russian premier to blackmail the president's husband, whom the KGB had caught in a compromising position with a female spy. However, the Reagan-era show was unable to garner sufficient ratings to sustain itself.

Hair   A 1968 musical play written by Galt MacDermot and conceived by Gerome Ragni and James Rado and a 1979 VIETNAM WAR FILM starring John Savage, Treat Williams and Beverly D'Angelo and directed by Milos Forman. The antiwar musical appeared at the height of the Vietnam War, originally opening in New York's Cheetah discotheque before producer Michael Butler brought it to Broadway four months before the riotous 1968 Democratic Convention in Chicago. Possessing a distinct psychedelic flavor, the play celebrates the culture of life as represented by HIPPIES and members of the COUNTERCULTURE. The thin plot line centers around a student who joins a hippie commune to avoid the military draft, which represents the culture of death. The story also addresses the generation gap in which children and parents are divided over their feelings about the war,

portraying the difficulties each generation had in understanding the other. The title song, "Hair," praises the practice by many men in the counterculture of growing their hair long as a way to celebrate individuality and oppose the "establishment." "Aquarius," another popular number from the musical, expresses hope for a new era of peace. The play ran on Broadway through the end of the war. Director Tom O'Horgan borrowed a shock technique from Off-Off-Broadway by having the cast stand nude at the end of act one as the lights dimmed, the first use of nudity on the Broadway stage. The ostensible reason for the nudity was to induce middle-class viewers to question their system of values in which nudity was disturbing but napalm was acceptable. Furthermore, the nudity contributes to the self-acceptance and celebration of sex, life and love that the play advocates. (See also THEATER.)

Halberstam, David   A JOURNALIST, NOVELIST and NONFIC-TION WRITER. As a reporter for the *New York Times*, Halberstam reported from Washington and the Congo before going to Vietnam in 1962. At that point, the war was not going well for South Vietnam's president, Ngo Dinh Diem, despite a substantial increase in U.S. military advisers and economic aid, and he was cracking down on journalists who painted a negative picture of the situation. Just before Halberstam's arrival Diem had expelled *Newsweek*'s François Sully for writing an article critical of his powerful sister-in-law, Madame Ngo Dinh Nhu. Nonetheless, Halberstam, Malcolm Browne of the Associated Press and Neil Sheehan of the

Hair. Courtesy AP/Wide World.

sordid activities concealed by official [rhetoric]." At the same time, Halberstam acknowledged Vietnam's strategic value to the United States, declaring ". . . it is perhaps one of only five or six nations in the world that is truly vital to U.S. interests."

In 1965 the *Times* assigned Halberstam to its Warsaw bureau, but he was expelled less than one year later after his reporting upset Polish authorities. Shortly afterward he left the *Times* to become a contributing editor to *Harper's* magazine. After writing political profiles on national security adviser McGeorge Bundy and Secretary of Defense Robert McNamara, Halberstam decided to write a more comprehensive study on the staff of presidential advisers who had promoted and escalated the Vietnam War. In THE BEST AND THE BRIGHTEST, the 1972 best-seller that resulted from that study, Halberstam points out how Kennedy chose for his advisers the most brilliant and intellectually accomplished men in their areas. Halberstam explores how such intelligent men ultimately produced what he believed was an inept and inhumane war policy. (Mary MCCARTHY reviewed it in her 1974 book, *Seventeenth Degree*.)

In 1967 Halberstam published a novel, ONE VERY HOT DAY. It describes the despair of a middle-aged U.S. military adviser who is frustrated by the bureaucracy and illogic of the war. In the afterword Halberstam explain, "I wanted to portray the frustrations, and the emptiness of this war. It was after all a smaller and, I think, less tidy war than Americans were accustomed to, and almost nothing that happened in it fit the preconceptions of Westerners." Halberstam also wrote *Ho* (1971), about North Vietnam's popular leader, Ho Chi Minh; *The Powers that Be* (1979), which chronicles the news media in the postwar era; *Amateurs* (1985); and a post–Cold War study of the 1950s entitled *The Fifties* (1993). (See also VIETNAM WAR LITERATURE.)

United Press International began reporting on the deteriorating situation in the critical Mekong Delta and on Diem's insensitivity to the needs of the South Vietnamese people. They also reported sympathetically on Buddhist dissident groups that opposed Diem. Government officials and such pro-war journalists as Joseph ALSOP tried to discredit or dismiss their reporting. However, Halberstam gained considerable recognition for his account of the battle of Ap Bac in January 1963. In this first major battle of the war's American era, the South Vietnamese Army performed poorly, and Halberstam described how three U.S. advisers died while trying to get reluctant Vietnamese soldiers to fight.

As a result of his account of Ap Bac, the Pentagon began monitoring Halberstam's sources and keeping track of his whereabouts and telephone conversations. President Kennedy's White House press secretary, Pierre Salinger, labeled Halberstam's articles "emotional and inaccurate," and Kennedy personally but unsuccessfully intervened to have Halberstam transferred out of Vietnam. In 1964, Halberstam and Browne shared the Pulitzer Prize for their Vietnam reporting, and in 1965 Halberstam published *The Making of a Quagmire*, a widely read personal account of his 15 months in Southeast Asia. According to a commentator in *The Nation*, ". . . it had an electrifying effect on a new generation of dissenters. It opened the eyes of a wider public to the

Hamburger Hill   A 1987 VIETNAM WAR FILM starring Anthony Barrile, Michael Boatman and Don Cheadle and directed by John Irvin. Filmed in a highly realistic style, *Hamburger Hill* avoids making judgments about the politics behind the war and concentrates instead on the dirty business of combat. The story centers on a squad from the 101st Airborne Division, which is trying to capture Hill 937 in the Ashau Valley. The film depicts the ferocity of the struggle, as well as providing intense private moments as soldiers receive letters from home, argue with each other and seek out prostitutes. *Hamburger Hill* strikes a middle ground between Stanley KUBRICK's cynical and nihilistic FULL METAL JACKET (1987), made the same year, and John WAYNE's 1968 THE GREEN BERETS, which glorified valor and self-sacrifice in combat. *Hamburger Hill* also avoids the more expressionistic effects found in such other Vietnam War films as APOCALYPSE NOW (1979).

For additional reading, see Lanning's *Vietnam at the Movies*.

happenings   A form of THEATER that developed between 1959 and 1963, primarily among artists and sculptors associated with the Reubens Gallery in New York. A spontaneous form of art that was influenced by the BEAT MOVEMENT and political activism in Europe, happenings called upon performers to appear as themselves at the particular moment of their performance. Sometimes used as a form of political protest, particularly against nuclear weapons, happenings included MUSIC, FILM, poetry and action recordings. Prominent Americans who participated in happenings included musician John Cage, dancer Merce Cunningham, artist Robert Rauschenberg and pianist David Tudor. The best-known happening took place in Paris in the early 1960s when Jean-Jacques Lebel performed and filmed two nearly nude women wearing masks of President Kennedy and Soviet premier Khrushchev who entered "an international bloodbath"—a tub filled with chicken blood and water. That happening also featured huge papier-mâché phalluses and a political collage. Like the 1964 film satire DR. STRANGELOVE, it suggested that sexual dynamics underlay the international power struggle. American derivatives of happenings, sometimes called Theater of the Apocalypse, were produced periodically during the later 1960s as protests of the Vietnam War and the capitalist society that waged it. For instance, in 1967 Yippie activist Jerry Rubin led a political happening in which protestors entered the balcony of the New York Stock Exchange and threw money onto the floor. In his book *Do It* (1970), Rubin describes the brokers climbing all over each other for the money "like wild animals." (Terry SOUTHERN's novel *The Magic Christian* [1960] and the 1969 film based upon it include a similar scene in which people wade into a pool of excrement to collect money.) The massive antiwar protests in Washington in 1967 and in Chicago in 1968 before the Democratic national convention featured street theater that derived from happenings. Also linked to happenings was guerrilla theater, in which antiwar protestors would enter shopping malls and other public places and enact scenes of soldiers killing civilians or other scenes that would require citizens to respond.

"Happy Days" A TELEVISION SITUATION COMEDY that ran on CBS from 1974 to 1984. Providing a retrospective look at the 1950s, "Happy Days" originally focused on the exploits of two high-school boys in Milwaukee, Richie Cunningham (Ron Howard) and Potsie Weber (Anson Williams). However, a third teenager, drop-out motorcyclist Fonzie Fonzarelli (Henry Winkler) soon came to dominate the show. Centering on the relationship between middle-class Richie and working-class Fonzie, "Happy Days" looked back nostalgically on life in America during the 1950s, as the boys learned about tolerance, love, respect and other qualities that would eventually lead to their maturation. The Cold War is notable for its complete absence from this highly popular reminiscence about the "happy days" that in fact coincided with the height of Cold War tensions. The public's fears of nuclear war, creeping communism and internal subversion do not appear in this representation of the good old days gone by.

Harold and Maude A 1971 FILM COMEDY starring Ruth Gordon, Bud Cort and Vivian Pickles and directed by Hal ASHBY. Cat Stevens sang the background music. The story centers on the romance between Harold, a wealthy young man in his early twenties who is fascinated by death, and Maude, an 80-year-old flower child and concentration camp survivor who is equally powerful in her joyous celebration

of life. They meet while sitting in on a stranger's funeral, and Maude eventually opens Harold to celebrating his inner spirit. In addition to expressing many of the COUNTERCULTURE's life-affirming sentiments, the film also satirizes the army and implicitly attacks the Vietnam War, which was still raging at the time. (See also FILM SATIRE.)

Havana A 1990 FILM DRAMA starring Robert Redford, Raul Julia, Lena Olin and Alan Arkin and directed by Sydney Pollack. The story is centered on the final days of Fidel Castro's successful Cuban revolution, which culminated in his assumption of power on New Year's Day, 1959. Set in Havana and rural Cuba, and made during the final days of the Cold War as communism was collapsing everywhere but in Cuba, China and North Korea, the film tries to walk a fine line between depicting the atrocities of the Batista dictatorship and avoiding sympathy for Castro.

Heston, Charlton A FILM ACTOR and FILM DIRECTOR. Heston was active in anti-communist activities in Hollywood during the 1950s. As a six-term president of the Screen Actors Guild, he earned a reputation as a staunch Republican. He later served as co-chair of Ronald REAGAN's Task Force on the Arts and Humanities. Heston's characters typically exhibited physical prowess, strength of character, virtue, and righteousness, and he projected these qualities onto the right-wing cause when he lent his presence to politics. His 1950s EPIC FILMS, such as THE TEN COMMANDMENTS (1956) and BEN-HUR (1959), contain strong implicit and explicit messages about the moral superiority of democratic societies, establishing parallels between ancient despots and contemporary communist tyranny. They also portray the victory of Judeo-Christian religious values in the struggle against oppression. Moreover, the epic-sized cast, vast sets, expensive props and enormous scope of the epics demonstrate the seemingly endless store of resources in capitalist America. Heston also starred in THE OMEGA MAN (1971), about a survivor of germ warfare, and narrated *Vietnam! Vietnam!* a 1966 documentary produced by John Ford for the United States Information Agency (USIA) to help convince foreign audiences that the U.S. participation in the Vietnam War was moral and necessary. *Vietnam! Vietnam!* was not released until 1971, however, and it failed to have the impact its sponsors desired. (See also VIETNAM WAR FILMS.)

Heym, Stefan A German NOVELIST and EXILED WRITER (from the United States). Born in 1913 in Germany to Jewish parents, Heym was an early opponent of Hitler and Nazism, from which he fled to Czechoslovakia in 1933. He came to the United States a few years later when the University of Chicago offered him a scholarship intended for "brilliant students whose education had been interrupted by the coming of National Socialism to Germany." After receiving his master's degree from the University of Chicago in 1936, Heym edited an antifascist weekly newspaper and wrote *Nazis in the U.S.A.: An Expose of Hitler's Aims and Agents in the U.S.A.* (1938). His first English-language novel, *Hostages* (1942), addressed the Nazi occupation of Prague. During World War II he served in the psychological warfare division of the U.S. Army while he continued his writing. His novel *Of Smiling Peace* (1944) contributed to his reputation as a popular writer in English. At the end of the war, Heym participated in the reeducation program in the U.S. Occupied Zone and later served as chief of the American delegation at the 1950 World Peace Conference in Warsaw. Heym's popular novels from the immediate postwar period, including *The Crusaders* (1948) and *The Eyes of Reason* (1951), expressed his belief in socialism.

In 1952 Heym was transferred back to the United States to face an investigation into his alleged communist inclinations. In response to further accusations by Senator Joseph McCarthy, Heym renounced his U.S. citizenship and moved to East Germany, where his socialist-oriented literature was warmly received. There, he wrote editorials, reports and articles praising East Germany and its relationship to the U.S.S.R., as well as children's stories, including the English-language collections *The Cannibals and Other Stories* (1953) and *Shadows and Lights* (1960). However, in 1965 Heym fell into disfavor with the East German government after publishing an article describing the decline of Stalin's importance and its impact on communism. Subsequently, most of his writing became illegal in East Germany until 1989, though he was published in West Germany, England and the United States. His English-language best-selling novels include *Uncertain Friend* (1969), *The King David Report* (1972) and *Five Days in June* (1977). *Uncertain Friend* deals with the conflict between intellectual integrity and the power of a personality cult; *Five Days in June* describes the 1953 popular uprising against the East German regime. Heym was expelled from the German Democratic Republic Writers Guild in 1979, as were those writers who rose to his defense. In 1994, at the age of 81, he was elected to the parliament of the reunited Germany, as a candidate of the reform Communist Party of Democratic Socialism.

For additional reading, see Tucker's *Literary Exile in the Twentieth Century.*

High Noon A 1952 FILM WESTERN starring Gary Cooper and Grace Kelly, directed by Fred Zinnemann and written by Carl FOREMAN. Cooper won an Academy Award for his portrayal of Will Kane, a lawman who must stand alone against a trio of killers who are arriving on the noon train to seek vengeance against him. Initially, he assumes he can count on the assistance of the townspeople, but they all desert him. SCREENWRITER Carl Foreman, who had quit the Communist Party in 1942, claimed to have written *High Noon* to express his sense of abandonment by the film community after he was subpoenaed to testify before the HOUSE COMMITTEE ON UN-AMERICAN ACTIVITIES (HUAC) in 1952. The film was in production while Foreman was planning strategy for his testimony, and *High Noon* reflects his feeling that no one would stand up with him against HUAC. According to Foreman, even Stanley Kramer, his business partner and the film's producer, turned on him by forcing him from his own company. (Kramer recounted the episode differently.) Foreman refused to inform on people he had met during his years as a communist and was subsequently subjected to BLACKLISTING.

The film, which symbolically attacks HUAC, celebrates such traditional American values as courage, integrity and standing up for what is right. Perhaps for that reason, the official Soviet newspaper *Pravda* attacked *High Noon* as "a glorification of the individual." Ironically, John WAYNE, the president of the MOTION PICTURE ALLIANCE, also vilified the film, condemning its depiction of the cowardly townspeople as "the most un-American thing I've ever seen in my whole life." Wayne also objected strongly to the final scene, in which Will Kane throws down his badge and squashes it with his foot: "That was like belittling a Medal of Honor."

For additional reading, see Biskind's *Seeing Is Believing;* Navasky's *Naming Names;* Whitfield's *The Culture of the Cold War;* Sayre's *Running Time.*

hippies A bohemian segment of the COUNTERCULTURE that emerged in San Francisco in the mid-1960s. They first made national news in a series of articles Michael Fallon wrote for the *San Francisco Examiner* in 1965. That was the year the United States first sent combat troops to Vietnam, and the hippie movement, which espoused peace and love, opposed the war. Most hippies were less than 30 years old, so hippie men were subject to the military draft. They typically dressed in blue jeans, T-shirts and old clothes; smoked marijuana or took other "mind-expanding" drugs such as peyote and LSD, which was still legal in the mid-1960s; and rejected conformist, middle-class life-styles in favor of individual expression. As part of their celebration of life and rejection of a culture of death, many hippies advocated sexual promiscuity, which they labeled "free love." The hippie movement, which was originally centered in San Francisco's Haight-Ashbury neighborhood, spread rapidly throughout the country, attracting a small but visible minority—and an enormous number of imitators.

The hippie movement was a powerful though ultimately unrealistic and unsuccessful attempt to create a culture of innocence in the face of the Cold War, the Vietnam War and other manifestations of militarism and imposed conformity. The hippie movement culminated in the 1967 "Summer of Love," based in San Francisco. After that summer, the culture of peace and love began to give way to the "Days of Rage," as opponents of the war and social oppression within the United States vented anger at an allegedly repressive government. Nonetheless, hippies were still able to turn out in force at the WOODSTOCK rock festival in 1969, where a number of antiwar musicians sang songs advocating peace and love, while thousands of audience members camped out in the adjoining field, made love, shared food, took drugs and enjoyed the music despite the rain and mud. Associated with hippies were the peace sign, two fingers held up in the shape of a V (the same sign Winston Churchill used to signal victory during World War II) and the peace emblem, a circle divided into thirds. The peace emblem was often worn on clothes, drawn on walls and classroom chalkboards, pictured on record covers and otherwise used in public ways.

For additional reading, see the Sterns' *Encyclopedia of Pop Culture.*

Hiroshima A 1946 NONFICTION book by John Hersey. *Hiroshima* originally appeared as articles in the *New Yorker* MAGAZINE, and then as a book published within a year after the atomic bombing of Hiroshima. (Hersey updated the book in 1985.) The book presents the experiences of six survivors and gives a firsthand account of nuclear devastation. Though highly descriptive, Hersey's narration is neither emotional nor judgmental, e.g.: "In a city of two hundred fifty thousand, nearly a hundred thousand people had been killed or doomed at one blow, a hundred thousand more were hurt. At least ten thousand more made their way to the best hospital in town," which Hersey explains, had only 600 beds and one physician. We learn the physician's story as well as those of a priest, a Protestant minister, a seamstress, an office worker and another doctor. They describe the practical difficulties of surviving a nuclear attack: finding safe haven from the firestorms that engulf the city following the blast; treating the wounded when hospitals have been destroyed, supplies are scarce and most doctors and nurses are dead or wounded; being rescued when pinned beneath fallen furniture and collapsed buildings; obtaining accurate information and helpful guidance; and communicating with family and friends within the city and beyond. Hersey's 1985 update for the 40th anniversary of the Hiroshima bombing coincided with a period of renewed Cold War hostilities and concerns about U.S.-Soviet nuclear war. By drawing renewed attention to the actual experience of a nuclear attack, the revised edition cautioned against nuclear warfare.

Hiroshima: A Document of the Atomic Bombing

A 1970 Japanese-made FILM DOCUMENTARY written and directed by M. Ogasawa. The film intercuts contemporary scenes of Hiroshima with then-recently discovered film footage shot by Akira Iwasaki soon after the bombing of Hiroshima. That footage, which the U.S. Department of Defense had suppressed, first appeared in 1968 as HIROSHIMA–NAGASAKI—AUGUST, 1945. The intercutting shows how the effects of the bombing continued 25 years later, partly by following some of the survivors, notably a woman who was three years old at the time of the attack and who died 32 years later from stomach cancer. Iwasaki's footage includes melted teacups and watches, a railway schedule burned into a surface by the atomic blast, and wounded and disfigured survivors. *Hiroshima* concludes by reminding viewers that the hydrogen bombs of 1970 are 2,500 times more powerful than the one that destroyed the Japanese city. (See also APOCALYPTIC FILMS.)

For additional reading, see Shaheen's *Nuclear War Films.*

Hiroshima, Mon Amour

A 1959 French- and Japanese-made FILM DRAMA starring Emmanuelle Riva and Eiji Okada, directed by Alain Resnais and written by Marguerite Duras. The story centers on a Japanese architect and a French actress who have a short love affair in Hiroshima after the war. The film intercuts documentary footage of the destruction caused by the atomic bomb with tender shots of the protagonists' love-making, both with each other and with lost lovers from the war. As the film recalls the pain of World War II, it also makes both characters and audience aware of the physical and emotional devastation another nuclear war would cause. The film appeared during the three-year span from 1958 to 1961 that included the second Berlin Crisis, a period that saw both overtures to peace—such as Khrushchev's 1959 visit to the United States—and renewed military escalation. *Hiroshima, Mon Amour* thus tapped into both the desires and fears occasioned by the Cold War during the late 1950s. (See also APOCALYPTIC FILMS.)

Hiroshima-Nagasaki

A 1970 FILM DOCUMENTARY produced for television by National Educational Television (NET). The film appears in three segments. The first shows public reaction to a 1970 New York photographic exhibit commemorating the 25th anniversary of the atomic bombings. The horror and fear on the viewers' faces establish the mood for the rest of the film. The second segment was a film originally produced by Dr. Erik Barnouw, who discovered film footage shot by Akira Iwasaki soon after the bombing of Hiroshima, footage that had been confiscated by the occupying U.S. Army and classified as secret for 23 years before being released from the National Archives in 1968. Barnouw had edited the remnants of the original 150 minutes of footage as the 16-minute film HIROSHIMA–NAGASAKI—AUGUST, 1945; the remaining footage had "probably been destroyed during the conversion from acetate to safety film," according to the Defense Department. The final segment is an edited version of a 1967 BBC documentary, *The Building of the Bomb,* which chronicles the development of the atomic bomb that destroyed the two cities. *Hiroshima-Nagasaki* was shown only once. Additional screenings, including closed-circuit viewings in college classrooms, have not been allowed, and as of 1978, only the master copy remained extant. (See also APOCALYPTIC FILMS.)

For additional reading, see Shaheen's *Nuclear War Films.*

Hiroshima-Nagasaki—August, 1945

a 1968 FILM DOCUMENTARY edited by Dr. Erik Barnouw and directed by Akira Iwasaki. Paul Ronder wrote the script and narrated it along with Kazuko Oshima. The 16-minute film is all that remains of Iwasaki's original documentation of the destruction at Hiroshima. Although Iwasaki's film crew had shot several hours of film footage soon after the atomic attack, it was all confiscated by the U.S. occupying army and kept for 23 years at the National Archives in Washington, D.C., labeled "Secret" and "Not to be released without approval of the Defense Department." By 1968, only 16 minutes of film remained; the rest of it had "probably been destroyed during the conversion from acetate to safety film," according to the Defense Department. Barnouw, a professor at Columbia University, discovered and obtained the surviving footage. Ronder added a sound track that includes Robert Oppenheimer repeating the words he quoted from the *Bhagavad-Gita* upon seeing the first atomic test, "Now I am become death, the destroyer of worlds." The soundtrack also has background music that suggests wailing air-raid sirens. According to Iwasaki, the documentary, "is an appeal or warning from man to man for peaceful reflection—to prevent the use of the bomb ever again . . . It was not the kind of film the Japanese thought the Americans would produce." Released in 1970, 25 years after the atomic bombings, *Hiroshima-Nagasaki—August, 1945* was screened most widely at universities, and it was integrated into the National Educational Television documentary, HIROSHIMA-NAGASAKI. Iwasaki's suppressed footage led Barnouw to question U.S. censorship: "What else lies silent and sealed in the vaults of the Defense Department?" he asked. (See also APOCALYPTIC FILMS.)

For additional reading, see Shaheen's *Nuclear War Films.*

Hitchcock, Alfred   A British-born FILM DIRECTOR. Known for his psychological thrillers, Hitchcock directed several SPY FILMS with a Cold War backdrop, just as he had frequently employed anti-Nazi sentiment in his World War II–era films. One of Hitchcock's finest movies, NORTH BY NORTHWEST, (1959) stars Cary Grant as a businessman whom Soviet spies mistake for a U.S. government agent. The culminating scene atop Mt. Rushmore shows Grant and the communists fighting upon the carved faces of America's most revered presidents. The film reveals the Soviets to be sophisticated but ruthless, and only Grant's determination and resourcefulness enable him to succeed. TORN CURTAIN (1966) centers on an American scientist (Paul Newman) who pretends to defect while at an international conference. And TOPAZ (1969), which is based on the 1967 SPY NOVEL by Leon URIS, provides one of the surprisingly few cinematic treatments of the 1962 Cuban Missile Crisis. Hitchcock's recurring situation—ordinary people removed from the safety of their middle-class lives and compelled to rely on their own resources to extricate themselves from potentially disastrous situations—also reinforces the traditional notion of American self-reliance.

Hollywood on Trial   A 1976 FILM DOCUMENTARY directed by David Helpern Jr. and written by Lester COLE, a blacklisted writer who had been one of the HOLLYWOOD TEN. Using such archival material as print and radio interviews, film footage and other original documents from the RED SCARE, the film centers on the hearings about the Hollywood film industry conducted by the HOUSE COMMITTEE ON UN-AMERICAN ACTIVITIES (HUAC). Included in the film are such figures as Walt DISNEY, Dalton TRUMBO, Gary Cooper, Jack

Warner, Adolphe Menjou, Robert Taylor and Louis B. Mayer. (See also BLACKLISTING.)

Hollywood Ten, The   A group of 10 "unfriendly" witnesses who in 1947 refused to answer questions by the HOUSE COMMITTEE ON UN-AMERICAN ACTIVITIES (HUAC) about their alleged communist affiliations. Most—perhaps all—of the Ten were or had been members of the Communist Party. The Ten consisted of SCREENWRITERS Alvah BESSIE, Lester COLE, Ring LARDNER Jr., John Howard LAWSON, Albert MALTZ, Sam ORNITZ and Dalton TRUMBO; FILM DIRECTORS Herbert BIBERMAN and Edward DMYTRYK; and writer-producer Adrian SCOTT. Screenwriter and Playwright Bertolt BRECHT was the 11th unfriendly witness who appeared before HUAC in 1947, but unlike the others, he testified.

The 1947 HUAC hearings were ostensibly held to investigate the alleged communist influence on the content of Hollywood films, though credible evidence exists that HUAC's deeper purpose was to break the left in general and the Communist Party in particular, as well as to establish parameters for acceptable film content in terms of political values, attitudes toward capital and labor, and other sentiments that could potentially render a film "un-American." In her analysis of film content, "Communism and the Movies: A Study of Film Content," Dorothy Jones found little evidence of communist propaganda in the films written by Communist Party members and others under suspicion. Among the committee members were chairman J. Parnell Thomas and Congressman Richard M. Nixon.

The committee called 25 friendly and 11 unfriendly witnesses. Eight other unfriendly witnesses were scheduled but were never actually called to testify in the 1947 hearings. Attending the hearings to lend moral support to the Ten were members of Hollywood's Committee for the First Amendment, including Humphrey Bogart, Lauren Bacall,

The Hollywood Ten (and two attorneys). First row, left to right: Herbert Biberman, Martin Popper (attorney), Robert W. Kenny (attorney), Albert Maltz, Lester Cole. Second row: Dalton Trumbo, John Howard Lawson, Alvah Bessie, Samuel Ornitz. Third row: Ring Lardner Jr., Edward Dmytryk, Adrian Scott. **Courtesy AP/Wide World.**

Groucho Marx and Frank Sinatra (although Sinatra later became very conservative, he was then on the left). On the other side were prominent friendly witnesses, including Jack Warner of the Warner Brothers film company; Louis B. Mayer of MGM; FILM ACTORS Ronald REAGAN, Gary Cooper, George Murphy, Adolphe Menjou, Robert Taylor and Robert Montgomery; writer Ayn RAND; animator and studio-owner Walt DISNEY; director Leo McCarey; and union leader Roy BREWER.

In addition to identifying individuals they believed to be communists, friendly witnesses were commonly asked if they believed Hollywood should make anti-communist films to reveal "the dangers and intrigue of the Communist Party here in the United States" and if they believed that the United States should outlaw the Communist Party. Thomas permitted the friendly witnesses to read introductory statements prior to their testimony because he deemed them pertinent to the inquiry.

On the other hand, Thomas ruled that introductory statements from most of the unfriendly witnesses were inadmissible because they were "not pertinent." These unfriendly statements attacked the committee and its right to conduct hearings into the political beliefs of individual citizens. The unfriendly witnesses refused to answer committee questions about their alleged membership in the Communist Party, citing protection under the guarantees of the First Amendment. They were then removed from the witness stand (in Lawson's case, forcibly) and consequently were unable to refute or comment upon the subsequent allegations of their communist affiliations, which the committee read into the *Congressional Record.* HUAC later cited all 10 for contempt of Congress.

Some historians believe that by calling the unfriendly witnesses, refusing to admit their introductory statements and reading the allegations against them into the record, HUAC was deliberately attempting to create an official list of names that could become the basis for BLACKLISTING. Whether or not this was the case, the HUAC listings did function like a blacklist. After the Supreme Court upheld the contempt citations, the Ten were convicted and imprisoned for periods ranging from six months to a year. All were blacklisted, though after his release from prison Dmytryk reversed his position, named names of former communist associates, and was enabled to resume his career almost immediately. Likewise, director Robert ROSSEN, one of the eight scheduled unfriendly witnesses who had not been called, was blacklisted after refusing to testify in later hearings in 1951, but was cleared when he finally named some 50 names in 1953. The 208 signers of a Committee for the First Amendment petition on behalf of the Hollywood Ten, as well as other supporters who contributed their names to an *amicus curiae* brief asking the Supreme Court to review the contempt citation, were also blacklisted. Some of the Ten's original supporters later renounced their position, either to clear themselves from possible blacklisting, because they were put off by the Ten's aggressive and confrontational performance before the committee, because they had changed their minds about communism and the left, or for all three reasons. The revelation that many of the Ten were, indeed, communists may also have influenced their decision. Bogart, for instance, cleared himself by writing to

influential right-wing columnist George SOKOLSKY, "I went to Washington because I thought fellow Americans were being deprived of their constitutional rights, and for that reason alone. That trip was ill-advised, even foolish . . . At the time it seemed like the right thing to do. I have absolutely no use for Communism nor for anyone who serves that philosophy."

Some of the Ten, like Trumbo, Lawson and Maltz, went into exile and continued to write films under assumed names, at much reduced salaries. (See also EXILED WRITERS [from the United States.]) Writers who submitted scripts under assumed names were later portrayed in the 1976 FILM COMEDY, THE FRONT.) Cole, Lardner, Maltz and Trumbo wrote some plays for live THEATER, though Lawson's play about life in the black ghetto, *Thunder Morning,* was never produced. In 1954, Biberman and blacklisted producer Paul Jarrico made SALT OF THE EARTH, a pro-union docu-drama about a strike by Mexican-Americans. They employed several other blacklisted individuals in their first effort to create an independent production company that would hire blacklistees. However, *Salt of the Earth* was the only film they made.

In 1948 Cole filed a lawsuit against MGM's parent company, Loew's Inc., charging breach of contract and conspiracy to blacklist. His intent was to break the blacklist, but his initial victory was reversed on appeal and he dropped the case in 1952. Eventually Trumbo broke the industry blacklist in 1960 when he was publicly credited for writing the screenplays for *EXODUS* (1960) and *SPARTACUS* (1960). Personal accounts of their experiences with HUAC include Bessie's *Inquisition in Eden* (1965) and his autobiographical novel *The Un-Americans* (1957); Cole's autobiography *Hollywood Red* (1981); and some sections of Edward Dmytryk's *It's a Hell of a Life But Not a Bad Living* (1979). Trumbo's pamphlet "Time of the Toad" (1949) lashes out against what he believed were the underlying motives behind the blacklist. In 1976, Cole wrote the film documentary HOLLYWOOD ON TRIAL, which portrayed Hollywood's responses to the HUAC hearings. Eric Bentley and Robert VAUGHN provide commentary and portions of the Ten's testimony before HUAC in THIRTY YEARS OF TREASON (1971) and *Only Victims* (1972), respectively. Testimony of the Ten also comprises part of the dialogue in Bentley's 1972 play about the HUAC hearings, ARE YOU NOW OR HAVE YOU EVER BEEN?.

Bertolt Brecht was the 11th of the unfriendly witnesses called to testify during the 1947 HUAC hearings. However, unlike the Ten, Brecht agreed to answer the committee's query because, "I am a guest in this country and do not want to enter into any legal arguments." He then went on to assert that he had never been a member of any Communist Party. Brecht, whose lifelong commitment to communism was apparent throughout his literary career (though there is no evidence that he was actually a member), fled the country immediately after testifying and ultimately settled in East Germany, where he was given his own theater and a generous subsidy to create new work. At the time of his testimony, he had been preparing a revised production of *Galileo* (1938–39), which addresses the failure of individuals to confront an unjust, repressive and unimaginative authority. "Pity the land that has no heroes," says one of the characters after the astronomer's capitulation. "Pity the land that *needs* a hero," answers the astronomer. (See also RED SCARE.)

For additional reading, see Whitfield's *Culture of the Cold War;* Navasky's *Naming Names;* Vaughn's *Only Victims;* Goodman's *The Committee: The Extraordinary Career of the House Committee on Un-American Activities;* and Jones's "Communism and the Movies: A Study of Film Content." For partial transcripts of testimonies before HUAC, see Bentley's THIRTY YEARS OF TREASON.

Honorable Rocky Slade, The A 1957 POLITICAL NOVEL by William Wister Gaines. Published the year of Senator Joseph McCarthy's death, the novel presents an unflattering account of the early career of a politician intended to parallel McCarthy, the man most closely associated with the RED SCARE. The novel is set in 1947 in a small Midwestern town, three years before McCarthy inaugurated his anti-communist crusade and rose to national prominence. Thus Rocky Slade creates his demagoguery around highway construction, not communism, but he shares with McCarthy a history of family poverty, an exaggerated and inauthentic war record, dubious financial dealings, womanizing and the nickname of "Joe." The plot concerns a contest for the same woman's affection between Slade and the narrator, and the book concludes with the narrator winning the woman as Slade goes off to represent his constituency in Washington, where he presumably will elevate his bombastic style to new levels. (See also SATIRE.)

Hook, The A 1963 KOREAN WAR FILM starring Kirk Douglas, Robert Walker and Nick Adams and directed by George Seaton. The story centers on the ethical dilemma faced by a sergeant and private who are ordered to execute a North Korean prisoner of war. Such executions, though prohibited by the Geneva Convention, apparently took place on both sides during the Korean conflict. In the film, the POW threatens the safety of a UN ship. Like such other Korean War films as Samuel Fuller's STEEL HELMET (1951), WAR HUNT (1962) and WAR IS HELL (1964), *The Hook* depicts the moral quagmires that engulfed U.S. Cold War military actions in such Third World countries as Korea and Vietnam. *The Hook* appeared about a year after President Kennedy increased the number of U.S. advisers in Vietnam from 700 to 12,000 and at a time when Laos and other countries in Southeast Asia were also becoming focal points in U.S. foreign policy.

Hope, Bob A FILM ACTOR and comedian. Though his films were apolitical comedies, Hope was known for his patriotism. During World War II and the Korean and Vietnam wars, he brought USO shows to soldiers overseas. In World War II and Korea he was widely lauded for this; in the Vietnam War the reception was more ambiguous. He was also well known for his support of President Nixon and his virulent opposition to the antiwar movement.

Hopscotch A 1980 FILM COMEDY starring Walter Matthau, Glenda Jackson and Sam Waterston and directed by Ronald Neame. Brian Garfield wrote both the screenplay and the novel upon which the film was based. Though the novel was a serious spy thriller, Matthau transformed the film into a comedy through his blustery portrayal of an ex-CIA agent who decides to write his memoirs, which threaten to expose the entire intelligence world. Aided by the very considerable wit of his mistress (Jackson), he enters into a game of wits with a young agent (Waterston) who was once his protégée. The film appealed to post-Watergate cynicism about government intelligence agencies by depicting the CIA as driven by petty internal politics and power struggles, not by dedication to the cause of freedom. (See also SPY FILMS.)

Horne, Lena A black singer who was listed 11 times in RED CHANNELS, a publication issued by the anti-communist magazine COUNTERATTACK, which listed people who had been identified as having communist affiliations. Horne's scheduled 1950 appearance on Ed SULLIVAN's "Toast of the Town" television show led to an attack on CBS by Jack O'Brian, the radio columnist for the New York *Journal-American,* the week before the show. O'Brian wrote, "It was no secret . . . that the sponsor and advertising agency were considerably perturbed about what was believed would be certain public resentment [over Horne's appearance] . . . Amazing, isn't it, that so many of these pink teas seem to 'just happen' to the Columbia Broadcasting System?" CBS responded by pointing out that Horne had also appeared prominently on NBC and that Sullivan's anti-communist credentials were well known. Horne threatened to sue if she was removed from the show, and her union, the American Guild of Variety Artists, threatened to remove other performers if she was replaced. She appeared on the Sullivan show as scheduled, and CBS received few or no complaints. A few weeks later, Horne met with *Counterattack's* Theodore Kirkpatrick and received "a clean bill of health." According to her agent, she had not promised to change "her opposition to Jim Crow and oppression" and made no other commitments, "despite the fact that the ex-FBI man usually requires a signed statement, recanting past associations and promising to espouse only anti-Communist statements." (See also BLACKLISTING; RED SCARE; MUSIC)

For additional reading, see Miller's *The Judges and the Judged.*

House Committee on Un-American Activities (HUAC) A congressional committee that held hearings on the film and entertainment industries in 1938, 1947, 1951–52, 1953–55 and 1957–58. The committee also looked into alleged pro-communist activities of teachers, professors and other individuals and organizations. Congress has two recognized constitutional reasons for holding hearings and subpoenaing witnesses: to obtain information useful for crafting legislation and to oversee the executive branch of government. Since no significant legislation grew out of these hearings and no executive oversight was involved, widespread claims that these investigations were politically motivated and self-serving possess considerable credence. In particular, critics of HUAC have charged that its actual objective was to destroy the Communist Party and the left while enabling committee members to benefit from the national publicity that accompanied the testimony of celebrities. Furthermore, the hearings routinely punished liberals and leftists who refused to inform on former associates who had been accused of no illegal activity (even membership in the Communist Party was, in fact, legal), but whose careers would be ruined if they were identified as present or former members of the Communist Party. Liberals who cooperated with the committee were often forced to apologize publicly for their political past and to participate in a distasteful process of informing on others in order to preserve their own livelihoods. Thus another effect of the HUAC hearings was the public humiliation of prominent liberals before a committee comprised largely of right-wing conservatives.

In 1938, under the chairmanship of Martin Dies, HUAC investigated the New Deal Works Progress Administration's Federal Theater Project, which it found to be dominated by communists. The 1947 HUAC hearings were ostensibly held to investigate alleged communist influences on the content of Hollywood films, though credible evidence exists to substantiate claims that HUAC's deeper purpose was to break the left, as well as to establish parameters for acceptable film content in terms of political values, attitudes toward capital and labor, and other sentiments that could potentially render a film "Un-American." In her analysis of film content, "Communism and the Movies: A Study of Film Content," Dorothy Jones found little evidence of communist propaganda in the films written by Communist Party members and others under suspicion. Among the committee members were chairman J. Parnell Thomas and Congressman Richard M. Nixon.

The 1947 committee called 24 "friendly" and 11 "unfriendly" witnesses. Eight other scheduled unfriendly witnesses were never called to testify. The MOTION PICTURE ALLIANCE FOR THE PRESERVATION OF AMERICAN IDEALS, an anti-communist, pro-free enterprise political group, furnished most of the friendly witnesses who identified instances of alleged communist activity in Hollywood. In addition to commenting on perceived communist influences in the film content, they also identified alleged communists and communist sympathizers. The friendly witnesses included Jack Warner of the Warner Brothers film company and Louis B. Mayer of MGM; FILM ACTORS Gary Cooper, George Murphy, Adolphe Menjou, Robert Taylor and Robert Montgomery; SCREENWRITER and NOVELIST Ayn RAND and screenwriter Robert Hughes; animator and studio-owner Walt DISNEY; FILM DIRECTOR Leo McCarey; and union leader Roy BREWER. Lela Rogers, the mother of actress Ginger Rogers and a supposed expert on detecting communist themes latent within films, also testified.

Chairman Thomas permitted the friendly witnesses to read introductory statements before their testimony because he deemed them pertinent to the inquiry. In addition to identifying individuals they believed to be communists, friendly witnesses were commonly asked if they believed Hollywood should make anti-communist films to reveal "the dangers and intrigue of the Communist Party here in the United States," and if they believed that the United States should outlaw the Communist Party. The friendly testimony included such problematic assertions as Lela Rogers' claim that Trumbo's World War II–era *Tender Comrade* (1943) included such "Communist sentiments" as "Share and share alike, that's democracy." Jack Warner identified as communist several non-communists, including Howard Koch (Screenwriter of *Casablanca*), who had provoked War-

ner's ire by participating in a 1945 strike at Warner Brothers. Robert Taylor identified Howard Da Silva as a possible communist on the grounds that "He always seems to have something to say at the wrong time."

Thomas also ruled that introductory statements from most of the unfriendly witnesses were inadmissible because they were "not pertinent" to the inquiry. These statements attacked the committee and its right to conduct hearings into the political beliefs of individual citizens. The unfriendly witnesses, who came to be known as the HOLLYWOOD TEN, refused to answer committee questions about their alleged membership in the Communist Party, citing protection under the First Amendment. Eventually, they were convicted of contempt of Congress and imprisoned for periods ranging from six months to a year. Upon their release from prison all were blacklisted. Bertolt BRECHT, the 11th unfriendly witness, did testify before the committee. He denied that he had ever been a communist and fled the country immediately after his appearance.

The 1947 HUAC hearings established a blacklist, promoted the production of anti-communist films (which were typically unprofitable), and created a climate of political fear in Hollywood. However, they revealed very little communist influence in the content of Hollywood movies—the announced purpose of the investigation. Thus the 1951–52 HUAC hearings, under the chairmanship of John Wood, changed their focus to the prestige, power and money that the Communist Party acquired in Hollywood. In these mass hearings—HUAC called 90 witnesses in 1951, almost all of them well-known figures—people who had past communist affiliations were compelled not only to testify about their own activities but also to "name names" of others who had participated. For example, screenwriter Martin Berkeley identified 162 people as past members of the Communist Party. Many witnesses were willing to discuss their own activities but refused to name the names of others. However, after the Supreme Court ruled that individuals could not invoke the Fifth Amendment if they had already testified about themselves, witnesses had to choose between explaining their own past actions and being compelled to implicate other people. Thus a witness's price for using a committee hearing as a forum for defending his or her views was either to inform on friends and colleagues or to face a jail sentence for contempt of Congress. Otherwise, witnesses had to invoke the Fifth Amendment from the outset and thereby lose the opportunity to make a case for themselves. "Fifth Amendment Communists," as Senator Joseph McCarthy labeled them, were routinely denied employment within the entertainment industry.

Among those who refused to name names were playwright and screenwriter Lillian Hellman, writer-producer Carl FOREMAN, director Robert ROSSEN, actors Lee J. COBB and José Ferrer, and playwright Arthur MILLER who, because he did not invoke a constitutional right, was cited for contempt of Congress, fined $500 and given a 30-day suspended jail sentence. Like Hollywood Ten member Edward DMYTRYK, Rossen and Cobb later reversed their positions and named names before the committee. Among those cooperating with the committee were actor Larry PARKS, director Elia KAZAN and screenwriters Richard COLLINS and Budd SCHULBERG. Blacklisted actor John GARFIELD also attempted to cooperate with the committee, but, not having been a member of the party, he claimed to have no names to name, and was therefore unable to clear himself through a ritual act of contrition. He died from a heart attack believed to have been brought on from the experience.

HUAC's 1952 and 1953 annual reports released 212 names of individuals in the movie industry named by cooperative "friendly" witnesses as having been communists. Evidence suggests that in having witnesses name their associates, HUAC was trying to create a blacklist—the list of names in the public record. (See *Report on Blacklisting*, vol. 1, re: testimony of Larry Parks.) Whether or not this was the case, the HUAC listings did function like a blacklist, as all 212 people listed lost their livelihoods in Hollywood by having their contracts either canceled, bought up or not renewed. Once without a contract, they were unable to get new work in the Hollywood studios under their own names for several years unless they publicly repented and gained "clearance."

HUAC's suppressed Appendix Nine was also employed in the creation of blacklists. In 1944 J. B. Matthews and Benjamin Mandel prepared Appendix Nine for a subcommittee of HUAC. This appendix was a seven-volume compilation of some 2,000 pages listing thousands of people who participated in alleged communist-front organizations between 1930 and 1944. The first six volumes identify and document some 245 organizations; the last volume contains 22,000 names of individuals. According to Mandel, the inclusion of a name in Appendix Nine did not necessarily indicate the person was subversive; however, the document itself contains no disclaimer to that effect, or any other explanation of its purpose or proper use. When the full committee learned of the report, it ordered that Appendix Nine be restricted and that all existing copies be destroyed. Consequently, during the RED SCARE, there were no copies in the Library of Congress or in any public library. However, before the committee's order, several of the 7,000 printed copies had been distributed to private individuals or organizations, including the editors of RED CHANNELS, as well as to such government agencies as the FBI, the State Department and army and navy intelligence. Thus people cited for inclusion in Appendix Nine usually had no access to it, even to verify that they were actually listed in the document or to review the source behind the accusation.

Between 1953 and 1955, under the chairmanship first of Harold H. Velde and then of Francis Walter, HUAC conducted hearings into other aspects of the entertainment industry, and it investigated the *Report on Blacklisting* made by John Cogley for the Fund for the Republic. Chairman Walter attacked Cogley's well-documented and generally evenhanded report as a "partisan, biased attack on all persons and organizations who are sincerely and patriotically concerned in ridding the movie industry and radio and television of Communists and Communist sympathizers." Rossen, Cobb, bandleader Artie Shaw and choreographer Jerome Robbins appeared at these hearings as friendly witnesses. Unfriendly witnesses included actor Lionel Stander, television and theater director Mortimer Offner and songwriter Jay Gorney. Lucille BALL testified that she had signed an electoral petition for a Communist Party candidate in 1936 to please her grandfather, but that she now fully repudiated communism, as she had always been apolitical anyway. Jean MUIR testified that she had been blacklisted from television.

In 1958, still under the chairmanship of Francis Walter, HUAC held its last hearings on the entertainment industry. Prominent witnesses included Arthur Miller and Paul ROBESON, whose passports had been denied. Robeson was belligerent and took the Fifth Amendment. Miller testified, answering questions about THE CRUCIBLE, *A View from the Bridge* and *You're Next*, a play attacking HUAC. He did not inform on anyone else, however.

Notable among personal accounts of experiences with HUAC are Hellman's SCOUNDREL TIME (1976); Kazan's *Elia Kazan, A Life* (1988) and several works by members of the Hollywood Ten. These include Alvah Bessie's *Inquisition in Eden* (1965) and his autobiographical novel, *The Un-Americans* (1957), Lester Cole's *Hollywood Red* (1981) and sections of Dmytryk's *It's a Hell of a Life But Not a Bad Living* (1979). Cole also wrote HOLLYWOOD ON TRIAL, a 1976 FILM DOCUMENTARY about Hollywood's response to the HUAC hearings. Eric Bentley's 1972 play ARE YOU NOW OR HAVE YOU EVER BEEN? dramatizes the HUAC hearings using portions of the committee transcripts for the dialogue. In 1960 HUAC produced its own documentary film, OPERATION ABOLITION, which attempts to prove that anti-HUAC demonstrators at a San Francisco hearing were sponsored by communists and traitors. HUAC answered criticism of the film in an article entitled "The Truth about *Operation Abolition*," which appears in *Film and Propaganda in America* (vol. 5). In addition to defending the film, the article identifies other contemporary works of anti-communist propaganda.

A few studies of the HUAC investigations of the entertainment industry appeared during the Cold War. John Cogley's 1956 *Report on Blacklisting* extensively documents the nature and practice of BLACKLISTING in the television and film industries. HUAC subsequently interrogated Cogley and condemned the report. Eric Bentley presents edited and annotated transcripts from HUAC hearings dating from 1938 to 1968 in THIRTY YEARS OF TREASON (1971): Actor Robert VAUGHN published his doctoral study of the HUAC investigations of the entertainment industry, *Only Victims* (1972). In 1980 Victor Navasky, editor of the left-liberal magazine *The Nation*, published *Naming Names*, a study of the whole process of informing or refusing to inform before HUAC.

For additional reading, see Goodman's *The Committee: The Extraordinary Career of the House Committee on Un-American Activities;* Jones's "Communism and the Movies: A Study of Film Content"; Vaugn's *Only Victims;* Navasky's *Naming Names;* Suid's *Film and Propaganda in America;* and William F. BUCKLEY Jr.'s *The Committee and Its Critics.* For partial transcripts of testimony by major figures, see Bentley's THIRTY YEARS OF TREASON.

Howe, Irving A NONFICTION WRITER and literary critic. Born in 1920 to Jewish immigrants, Howe became a socialist at age fourteen. He received his bachelor's degree from the City College of New York in 1940 and joined the faculty at Brandeis University in 1953. He left Brandeis in 1961 and taught for two years at Stanford before accepting a position as Distinguished Professor of English at City University of New York. In 1954 he founded the literary journal *Dissent,* a publication dedicated to democratic socialism. Howe rejected the politically neutral tenets of the New Criticism, the dominant school of literary criticism in the 1950s and early 1960s, maintaining that those whose interests are purely literary cannot write good criticism. His early work addressed such figures as Sherwood Anderson, William FAULKNER, Arthur KOESTLER and George ORWELL. In *A World More Attractive* (1963), which contains essays on Richard WRIGHT and Norman MAILER among others, Howe criticizes the tendency of postwar American authors to turn from social issues to what he calls personal "troubles." His conception of democratic socialism departed significantly from the ideas propounded by the New Left during the late 1960s, and in *Decline of the New* (1970) he articulates those differences. The most influential essay in that volume is "The New York Intellectuals," which first appeared in the conservative journal *Commentary* in 1968. The essay addresses the work of such critics as Lionel TRILLING, Philip Rahv and Alfred Kazin, and attacks the new "adversary culture" championed by Susan Sontag that was bringing about "modernism in the streets." Howe also attacks the emerging art of the time that, he charged, sought pure sensory experience "as unarguable as orgasm."

Howe founded *Dissent* to keep socialist thought alive during the RED SCARE, and throughout the Cold War he published several works intended to keep socialism intellectually viable. Among his books dealing with socialist and communist issues and personalities are *The American Communist Party: A Critical History, 1919–1957* (1957; coauthored with Lewis Coser), *Leon Trotsky* (1978), *Celebrations and Attacks: Thirty Years of Literary and Cultural Commentary* (1979) and *Socialism and America* (1985). Howe also edited *Basic Writings of Trotsky* (1963), *The Radical Papers* (1966), *Student Activism* (1967), *The Radical Imagination: An Anthology from Dissent Magazine* (1967), *Poverty: Views from the Left* (1968; coedited by Jeremy Larner), *A Dissenter's Guide to Foreign Policy* (1968), *Beyond the New Left* (1970) and *Essential Works of Socialism* (1970). (See also MAGAZINES.)

For additional reading, see *The Dictionary of Literary Biography* (vol. 63, *American Literary Critics and Scholars*).

Human Factor, The (1)   A 1975 British-made SPY FILM staring George Kennedy, John Mills and Rita Tushingham and directed by former HOLLYWOOD TEN member Edward DMYTRYK. The story centers on the aftermath of a terrorist killing in Italy of the family of a NATO war planner.

Human Factor, The (2)   A 1978 SPY NOVEL by Graham GREENE and a 1979 British-made SPY FILM starring Nicol Williamson, Richard Attenborough, Derek Jacobi, Robert Morley and John Gielgud, written by Tom Stoppard and directed by Otto Preminger. Considered one of the finest spy novels ever written, the story centers on Maurice Castle, a British intelligence agent who specializes in African affairs. While stationed in South Africa, ostensibly as a junior diplomat, he falls in love with Sarah, a black woman whom he had used as an agent there. After the South African police agency BOSS discovers their affair, which is illegal under apartheid, Castle is transferred. Sarah narrowly escapes death in a South African prison when a friendly communist agent smuggles her out of the country through Marxist Mozambique. In gratitude, Castle agrees to supply the Soviets secret information about Africa, but not about Europe. When the British discover the leak in his section, they suspect Castle's partner and poison him. Castle decides to stop leaking information, but when he learns of a South African-British-U.S.-West German plan to use tactical nuclear weapons against South African revolutionaries, he feels morally compelled to pass on that information as well.

Greene depicts a morally ambiguous world in which almost no one has a full picture of the machinations of any political entity and in which everyone is manipulated for various purposes. Finally, no one can be trusted. Castle's fundamental uncertainty about the overall picture renders problematic his ability to make moral decisions or take responsible action. The communists do not represent an attractive alternative, but neither does the West, which supports the racist South African regime in order to retain access to that country's gold, diamonds and uranium. Some critics argue that the story is based on Greene's friend Kim Philby, a British intelligence officer who defected to the U.S.S.R. in 1963, though Greene denied any connection between Philby and Castle, pointing out that he had begun the book prior to Philby's defection and suspended work on it specifically to avoid the comparison.

For additional reading, see Cawelti and Rosenberg's *The Spy Story.*

Hunt for Red October, The   A 1984 MILITARY NOVEL by Tom CLANCY and a 1990 MILITARY FILM starring Sean Connery, Alec Baldwin and James Earl Jones and directed by John McTiernan. The story centers on U.S. efforts to deal with a renegade top-secret Soviet submarine that is heading toward the United States possibly to defect—but possibly for other, more hostile purposes. Though the film appeared during the worldwide collapse of communism, *The Hunt for Red October* is set half a decade earlier, "shortly before Gorbachev came to power," when tensions between the superpowers were especially high and President Reagan was accelerating the U.S. buildup, endorsing the Strategic Defense Initiative (SDI—popularly known as "Star Wars") and changing the official nuclear strategy from Mutually Assured Destruction (MAD) to "winnable nuclear war." Within this context, the U.S. military leaders must ascertain the submarine's real intentions and, when satisfied that the Soviet captain wants to defect, they must facilitate the defection without unduly risking U.S. security. Appearing just before the collapse of the Soviet Union, the film reflected the challenge of encouraging the new ostensibly peaceful intentions of the Soviet Union without jeopardizing national security.

"Hunter"   A TELEVISION SPY SHOW that ran on CBS for four months in 1977. Like other more successful spy shows, this one featured a male–female team that traveled throughout the world, fighting communists and underworld crime syndicates. Occasionally they even confronted other U.S. intelligence agencies. "Hunter" starred James Franciscus as James Hunter and Linda Evans as his partner, Marty Shaw. They reported to the head of federal intelligence, General Baker (Ralph Bellamy).

"Hunter, The"   A TELEVISION SPY SHOW that on CBS in 1952 and on NBC in 1954. "The Hunter" featured the adventures of Bart Adams (Barry Nelson), a wealthy, handsome American businessman who traveled throughout the world. A master of disguises, Bart spent most episodes rescuing people from communist agents or thwarting communist plans to undermine the Free World.

"Huntley-Brinkley Report, The"   A TELEVISION NEWS show that ran on NBC from 1956 to 1970. Like their competitor Walter CRONKITE, NBC's Chet Huntley and David Brinkley were among the first superstars in television news. Reporting from New York, the somber Huntley provided a counterpoint for the wry, bemused Brinkley, who broadcast from Washington, D.C. Together they reported on many of the defining moments of the Cold War, as well as on other items of national and international interest. They also covered national political conventions. Their show opened with the dramatic beginning of the second movement of Beethoven's Ninth Symphony, and it ended with their famous signature, "Good night, Chet . . . Good night, David." A poll in 1965 showed that more adults recognized the names of Huntley and Brinkley than those of Cary Grant, James Stewart or the ROCK AND ROLL group the Beatles.

I Led Three Lives   A best-selling 1952 NONFICTION book by Herbert A. PHILBRICK and a TELEVISION SPY SHOW that ran in syndication from 1953 to 1956. Philbrick's book described his experiences as a U.S. government infiltrator into the American Communist Party. An undercover agent since 1940, Philbrick had risen to the party's middle ranks, eventually becoming a member of a secret cell and one of the education directors for the New England region. At the same time, he retained his profession as a Boston advertising executive. Thus he led three lives: a businessman and ordinary citizen, a Communist Party member and an FBI counterspy. Philbrick's affiliation with the Communist Party abruptly concluded in 1949, when he testified at the trials that convicted eleven top communist leaders of violating the 1940 Smith Act, which outlaws advocating the violent overthrow of the U.S. government.

The book's prose is not polemical, and Philbrick comes across as a thoughtful and competent person. He explains the methods by which the Communist Party would sometimes infiltrate other causes and the way it would create so-called "front" organizations, often without the knowledge of those organizations' members. However, although Philbrick portrays the Communist Party as cynical, hypocritical, rigid, rigorous in its exercise of discipline, devoid of warmth and good cheer, and willing to commit dirty tricks, he does not reveal any instances of actual plotting by the Communist Party to commit or incite specific acts of violence as part of an attempt to overthrow the U.S. government. (He does point out that after Earl Browder was ejected from the

American Communist Party leadership in 1945, the organization took a more hard-line stance against cooperating with capitalist governments and that party-sponsored classes in communist theory then began to stress the inevitable necessity of violent revolution by the working class.) Much of Philbrick's testimony against the Communists convicted in the Smith Act trials centered on the educational material covered in Communist Party study groups, rather than on actual statements or actions of the accused leaders. Apart from two instances of hearsay, *I Led Three Lives* does not document any instances of the Communist Party harming informers or individuals who have renounced the party. Neither Philbrick nor his family were threatened or harmed after he testified.

I Led Three Lives provides other details of the Communist Party's day-to-day operations. Philbrick expresses shock and distress at how people he least suspected of communist membership belonged to the party, and how, therefore, no one can ever be sure whether a friend, relative or acquaintance is a communist. This widely shared uncertainty fueled the RED SCARE, which Philbrick deplores but which his book nonetheless contributed to. He does insist that not all communist front organizations were the same (he describes four distinct kinds) and that "Blanket condemnations [such as those of the HOUSE COMMITTEE ON UN-AMERICAN ACTIVITIES], which black-list entire organizations because of the presence of a few Communists, frequently harm innocent persons. Guilt by association merely strengthens the hand of agitators in their attacks upon the infringements of civil liberties."

Philbrick opposes the proposed Mundt-Nixon bill to outlaw the Communist Party because he fears that driving the party underground will make it more difficult to infiltrate and monitor. He concludes, "The most important single thing is to avoid behaving the way a Communist says the individual must behave in a capitalist society. If the Communist had his way, he would force all non-Communists to the extreme right, toward fascism and state control . . . thus creating the demand for a violent revolution as the only possible cure . . . If we adhere to our traditional American dream of a society of freedom, of personal rather than state responsibility . . . of civil rights rather than rigid civil controls, then we will have disproved the Communist theory of the inevitability of capitalist deterioration."

The television show based on Philbrick's book claimed that each episode was based on fact, though the names, dates and places had been changed "for obvious reasons." However, the television plots were far more sensational than Philbrick's field reports to the FBI had been. Television's Philbrick (played by Richard Carlson) was constantly being called on to participate in communist schemes to undermine the United States, ranging from acts of sabotage, espionage and dope-smuggling to infiltrating labor unions, university faculties and even churches in order to spread the party line. In one episode, "Philbrick" tracked down a communist art dealer who had been polluting a teenaged couple with pacifist thoughts. When the girl began stating her hatred of bombing and warfare, her mother asked, "Where did my daughter get the outrageous ideas she's been expressing?" Moreover, the Philbrick character was in constant danger. On the one hand he risked death if his Communist Party colleagues discovered him; on the other hand, friends and neighbors were always wondering if "Maybe he is . . . a Communist." Nonetheless, his work paid off in regular FBI arrests of communist agents.

The show had the support of FBI director J. Edgar Hoover. Moreover, Philbrick himself, an ex-FBI agent, reviewed all of the scripts, acted as a consultant and was otherwise closely involved in the show's production. Nonetheless, in the later episodes, as the writers began to run out of material, the plots became increasingly farfetched. In one episode, for instance, communist agents plotted to sabotage the U.S. guided-missile program by converting vacuum cleaners into bomb launchers. Despite the improbability of some of the scripts, the show was taken seriously as a patriotic effort. In fact, people would write in and ask the show to investigate communists in their own neighborhoods. The producers passed those letters on to the FBI. Local sponsors of the series received promotional information stating that they were members of "the businessman's crusade" against international communism. Breweries were the show's primary sponsors, but banks, utilities and oil and steel companies sponsored reruns into the 1960s in order to enhance their patriotic image.

I Married a Communist   A 1949 FILM DRAMA starring Laraine Day, Robert Ryan and Janis Carter, directed by Robert Stevenson. It is also known by the title *The Woman on Pier 13*. The story of communist longshoreman who tries to leave the party, *I Married a Communist* attacks reform union leader Harry Bridges and depicts the West Coast

Longshoremen's and Warehousemen's Union as under communist control. As in other anti-communist films of the era, communists are portrayed in terms that audiences associated with organized crime: corrupt, cold-blooded murderers capable of drowning an informer without a trace of compassion. Their ideological goals prove to be mere cover for their ruthless pursuit of power and wealth.

Time magazine declared *I Married a Communist* "a celluloid bullet aimed at the U.S.S.R." Because of the film's strong anti-communist message, those who participated in its production were able to clear themselves from possible blacklisting. On the other hand, Joseph Losey was blacklisted apparently because he declined to direct the movie when RKO offered him the opportunity.

For additional reading, see Sayre's *Running Time*.

"I Spy"   A TELEVISION SPY SHOW that ran on NBC from 1965 to 1968. "I Spy" stands out from other spy/adventure shows in that it paired a white man and a black man as U.S. government agents. In fact, in his role as Alexander Scott, Bill Cosby became the first African-American performer on American television to have a starring role in a regular dramatic series. Scott's partner in espionage was Kelly Robinson (Robert Culp), a top-seeded tennis player and former Princeton law student who traveled around the world participating in tournaments. Scott was his trainer and traveling companion, a graduate of Temple University and a Rhodes scholar with a handy knowledge of many languages. The characters were more fully and more realistically developed than on most spy shows. They combined a serious dedication to their work with an ironic detachment that interjected an element of humor into each episode. Produced during the Johnson administration, "I Spy" reflected many topical issues and attitudes. Johnson's Great Society was heavily committed to advancing civil rights for racial minorities; Cosby's prominent role seemed consistent with that agenda. Also coincidental with the show's run were the violent race riots of the middle 1960s, and it is likely that in featuring Cosby as a loyal, successful, resourceful, well-educated black man, the producers were hoping to present a more positive image of black Americans and to provide a role model for them. The outstanding academic credentials that both protagonists possessed reflected the exceptional respect for intellectuals that characterized both the Kennedy and Johnson administrations. (David HALBERSTAM discusses the attraction to intellectuals in THE BEST AND THE BRIGHTEST.) Finally, the show also coincided with the major escalation of the Vietnam War and the corresponding increase in antiwar protest. "I Spy" reflected the problematic nature of the American involvement in Vietnam by having its protagonists question the motives behind some of their assignments. Whereas in most other spy shows before 1970 the U.S. government is always properly motivated and morally correct, "I Spy" presented a somewhat morally ambiguous arena within which its heros had to operate.

I Was a Communist for the F.B.I.   A 1951 SPY FILM starring Frank Lovejoy and Dorothy Hart, directed by Gordon Douglas and based on a 1950 *Saturday Evening Post* article ghost-written for Matt Cvetic, who had been an FBI operative for seven years. In 1952 *I Was a Communist for the*

F.B.I. became a radio spy show starring Dana Andrews. All three versions purport to portray Cvetic's experiences as an FBI informer who had infiltrated the Communist Party at the behest of FBI director J. Edgar Hoover. In general, all three painted the standard right-wing portrait of the Communist Party: Communists are shown to be cynical, self-serving and power-hungry, with no genuine feeling for the plight of the worker. They fear the HOUSE COMMITTEE ON UN-AMERICAN ACTIVITIES (HUAC) and cynically support liberals and others who use the Bill of Rights to thwart the committee's mission. To them, the Bill of Rights is valuable not because it guards individual liberties but because it can protect communist agents who are trying "to deliver America to Russia as a slave." Liberals, intellectuals, African Americans and other ethnic minorities who are attracted to the party appear as misguided dupes. Soft-hearted liberals receive little sympathy either from the communists, who treat them as chumps to be used and discarded, or from plain-spoken, working-class Americans like Cvetic himself, who can recognize the communist danger when it stands clearly before them. As Ralph Ellison does in his powerful 1952 novel, *Invisible Man,* the movie suggests that the communists cynically manipulate race riots on orders from the Soviet Union: "When blacks died they never knew that their death warrants were signed in Moscow." Likewise, the communists manipulate Jews for their own ends, even though Jews are among their supporters. For instance, they beat non-striking workers with steel bars wrapped in a Jewish newspaper, so Jews will be blamed for the violence. Though the *New York Times* critic Bosley Crowther found the film "horrendous" because of its "reckless 'red' smears," *I Was a Communist for the F.B.I.* seemed so authentic that it received an Academy Award nomination for best feature-length documentary in 1951.

As a weekly series, the radio show had to continually invent new story lines to sustain dramatic interest. Consequently, each week Cvetic had to neutralize a new danger to national security without revealing his true identity. To help radio audiences distinguish between Cvetic's FBI and Communist Party personas, Andrews spoke in different tones; his FBI voice sounded proud, powerful and confident, while his communist voice seemed slower and more clumsy.

In *I Was a Communist for the F.B.I.,* Cvetic anticipated Herbert PHILBRICK, whose 1952 I LED THREE LIVES was a bestselling NONFICTION book and a popular TELEVISION SPY SHOW (syndicated, 1953–56). Philbrick, also an FBI infiltrator, testified at the 1949 Smith Act trials of Communist Party leaders. Cvetic, on the other hand, proved to be a less enduring spokesperson for the anti-communist cause. Though he joined the national lecture circuit, made 63 appearances before different official committees and named some 300 individuals as communists, his record of alcoholism and mental illness soon discredited him. Among those he identified were several U.S. congressmen from both parties, and among his accusations was that "the Communist is not only plotting murder, he's plotting mass murder. Communists plan to liquidate one-third of the American population, mostly the oldsters." He also charged that the U.S.S.R. planned to invade the United States via Alaska and that all UN representatives from Soviet-bloc governments were spies. Cvetic, who eventually joined the ultra-right-wing

John Birch Society, even blamed his own alcoholism on "constant harassments and smears by Communists." (See also RED SCARE; FILMS ASSOCIATED WITH THE RED SCARE.)

For additional reading, see Whitfield's *The Culture of the Cold War* and Sayre's *Running Time.*

Ice Station Zebra A 1968 MILITARY FILM starring Ernest Borgnine, Rock Hudson and Patrick McGoohan and directed by John Sturges. The story centers on a secret mission in which a U.S. submarine goes to the North Pole to gather missile data being beamed down by a Soviet space satellite.

In Country A 1985 novel by Bobbie Ann Mason and a 1989 VIETNAM WAR FILM starring Emily Lloyd, Bruce Willis and Joan Allen and directed by Norman Jewison. The story centers on Samantha, a graduating high school senior in small-town Kentucky whose father died in Vietnam shortly after she was conceived in 1965, soon after U.S. combat troops were first introduced into the war. "Sam's" transition into adulthood and her ability to assume her own identity become enmeshed in her need to learn more about her father and the war; however, her friends, family and the veterans she knows cannot or do not want to talk about those issues. Only through examining her father's actions and her nation's past and by coming to terms with the war are she and her uncle, a Vietnam vet, able to move forward in life. Published 12 years after U.S. troops evacuated from South Vietnam, the story attempts to effect both personal and national reconciliation over the highly divisive war.

The novel reveals popular culture to be the medium of this teenager's consciousness. Sam dates events according to which rock concerts were playing at the time; she interprets her life through television shows and commercials, and her only frame of reference for comprehending the Vietnam War is the television situation comedy M*A*S*H (CBS, 1972–83). Pointedly, she begins to find her identity and expand her frame of reference at the end of the story after she touches the hard granite of the Vietnam War Memorial. (See also VIETNAM WAR LITERATURE.)

In the Court of Public Opinion A 1957 NONFICTION book by Alger Hiss. The book provides Hiss's account of the 1949 trial in which he was convicted of perjury after Whittaker Chambers accused him of having spied for the Soviet Union in the 1930s. (The statute of limitations for espionage had expired, so the government prosecuted Hiss for lying before a grand jury about his past communist affiliations.) Hiss had been a ranking member of the Roosevelt administration, advised the president during the Yalta Conference and was instrumental in the founding of the United Nations. In this book, he reviews the evidence from the trial and makes the case for his innocence in a dispassionate and legalistic manner. However, except for some new evidence about his typewriter, which had allegedly been used to type stolen information that was then passed on to the Soviets, Hiss adds little new information beyond that presented at the trial. Most contemporary reviewers found his account interesting but not compelling. Moreover, some criticized Hiss for omitting facts detrimental to his defense. Chambers, a repentant ex-communist, testified before the HOUSE COMMITTEE ON UN-AMERICAN ACTIVITIES

(HUAC) in 1948 and at Hiss's trial; he also presents his version of the Hiss affair in his 1952 autobiography, WITNESS.

The Hiss conviction played a major role in the RED SCARE since it appeared to confirm charges by Senator Joseph McCarthy and others that communists had infiltrated the government, especially the State Department, and were working to undermine the United States. However, documents from the Soviet Union released after the Cold War have thus far failed to support Chambers' charge that Hiss had ever been either a communist or a Soviet agent.

In Like Flint   See OUR MAN FLINT.

In the Matter of J. Robert Oppenheimer   A 1968 play by East German playwright Heimar Kipphardt. Based on the transcripts of the 1954 Atomic Energy Commission (AEC) hearing that led to the denial of Oppenheimer's security clearance, the play attacks the prejudice and viciousness behind the RED SCARE. Oppenheimer had led the successful World War II effort to create the atomic bomb and headed the AEC from 1946 to 1952. He angered right-wing conservatives by advocating international control of atomic energy and by opposing the development of hydrogen bombs. Thinly supported right-wing accusations that Oppenheimer had had communist associations during the 1940s led to his dismissal from the AEC, an act that created public controversy.

Kipphardt depicts Oppenheimer as a martyr to an unjust witch hunt, and from a historical perspective the charges against him do appear to have been fabricated and/or exaggerated. However, Kipphardt misleadingly suggests that the AEC inquisition left the gifted Oppenheimer a broken man. The physicist went on to head the Institute for Advanced Study at Princeton University, where he remained active in the field of nuclear physics. He also served on many government committees and met with influential lawmakers, generals and even presidents. In 1963, four years before his death, Oppenheimer received the Fermi Award from President Johnson. His own response to Kipphardt's play was that the playwright had "tried to convert a farce into a tragedy." (See also THEATER.)

Inchon   A 1982 KOREAN WAR FILM starring Sir Laurence Olivier, Jacqueline Bisset and Ben Gazzara and directed by Terence Young. The film showcases the U.S.-led surprise landing at Inchon. Devised by General Douglas MacArthur, the attack is considered one of the finest examples of strategy in military history. *Inchon* depicts the landing as the turning point of the war. The film was financed by The Reverend Sun Myung Moon's Unification Church.

Incredible Shrinking Man, The   A 1957 SCIENCE FICTION FILM starring Grant Williams, Randy Stuart and April Kent and directed by Jack Arnold. The film draws on 1950s Cold War fears of nuclear fallout as it describes the fate of a man who begins to shrink after an atomic cloud contaminates him while he is on vacation. Apart from the literal effects of the radiation, his shrinking suggests the increasing impotence of the average citizen in the face of the nuclear threat.

"Industries for America"   A TELEVISION DOCUMENTARY that ran on ABC intermittently from 1951 to 1952 and then during the summer of 1957. The show's central theme was "American Industry on Parade," and it featured documentary films about such major industries as lumber, steel and cement. Though the episodes did not directly address the Cold War, the superiority of American industry to its Soviet counterpart and the role of American industry in the defense of the United States gave the program Cold War relevance.

In-Laws, The   A 1979 FILM COMEDY starring Alan Arkin and Peter Falk and directed by Arthur Hiller. Falk plays a fast-talking CIA agent who may or may not have been removed from the agency. His son is marrying Arkin's daughter. Falk manages to drag the unwilling Arkin, a successful but highly nervous dentist, into a scheme to overthrow a Latin American dictatorship. The show spoofs Cold War spy agencies and covert actions, especially as neither the audience nor Arkin is ever completely certain whether Falk is sane or is actually backed by the CIA.

Inquest: A Tale of Political Terror   A 1970 play by Donald Freed. Based on the 1965 study *Invitation to an Inquest* by Walter and Miriam Schneir, the Vietnam War–era play dramatizes the arrest and conviction of atomic bomb spies Julius and Ethel Rosenberg and argues for their innocence. The prologue recreates the social and political atmosphere of the early 1950s, culminating with the voice of FBI director J. Edgar Hoover commanding his agents, "The secret of the atomic bomb has been stolen. *Find the thieves!*" A film then shows the arrest of David Greenglass, Ethel's brother, after which Julius and Ethel are taken into custody. The main part of the play takes place in the courtroom where the Rosenbergs are on trial, and the dialogue is taken from the trial transcripts and original documents, though the play also features "reconstruction(s) from actual events." Interspersed among the trial scenes are flashbacks that purport to reenact the Rosenbergs' loving and joyous relationship. Other elements of the dramatic treatment underscore the Rosenbergs' innocence and the sense of an anti-Semitic government witch hunt directed against them.

The play has been criticized for being heavy-handed and one-sided. Julius and Ethel appear as a typical fun-loving couple, and their radical past and real-life communist membership are omitted. *Inquest* also overlooks the fact that the judge and members of the prosecution were, like the victims, Jewish, and the play omits the sense of public uncertainty that then clouded the case and presents the trial as an unequivocal miscarriage of justice. (After reviewing documents from the former Soviet Union released in the 1990s the Schneirs have concluded that Julius, at least, engaged in espionage. In 1997, Alexander Fekislov, a former KGB official, maintained that Julius spied for the Soviets but was not directly involved in stealing secrets about the atomic bomb. He also claimed that Ethel was entirely innocent.) (See also THEATER.) For additional reading, see Hughes' *Plays, Politics and Polemics.*

Intensive Care A 1970 APOCALYPTIC NOVEL by Janet Frame. Published during the Vietnam War, before the beginning of the U.S.-Soviet détente, the novel imagines a post-nuclear scenario set in New Zealand. Frame, a New Zealand author, rejects the assumption shared by Aldous Huxley and others that New Zealand would escape nuclear destruction because of its remote location in the Southern Hemisphere. As one reviewer describes it, "The novel presents a number of fleeting episodes, moving back and forth in time and interlarded with epigraphs of free-verse poetry, snatches of songs, flashes of dreams, glimpses of letters and diaries, and intonations of refrains." The reviewer for *Time* magazine adds, "Characters compulsively chase their dreams back to the nightmare garden where Miss Frame magically transforms personal obsessions into her climactic vision of general apocalypse."

The initial part of the book centers on survivors from World War II, reminding readers that New Zealand was involved in earlier world conflicts and will likely be affected by any new one. The story then shifts to the future, in which a nuclear war has destroyed the rest of the world and damaged New Zealand. In the aftermath of the disaster, a dehumanized totalitarian government emerges. Many survivors are deformed by the radiation, and the government passes a "Human Delineation Act" to separate functioning humans from the mutilated and wounded. On "Classification Day," computers designate everyone as either human or animal. Those classified as animals are consigned to be recycled as useful products. In this respect Frame evokes actual practices during World War II, when Nazis extracted gold from the teeth of concentration camp prisoners and made lampshades and soap from their bodies. The novel contains vivid descriptions of the postapocalyptic experience, much of which appears in the journal of an autistic woman who is later exterminated. The entire story is meant as a cautionary tale to the world. As Milly, the autistic narrator, writes, "If you think I paint a grim picture of what will happen, then I can only say that you who are reading this are lucky not to be living in the time I write of. Do not be deceived—you may be living in it and not know, because two times can live together and one doesn't know that the other time is living because if you're in one time whatever would make you want to think another is there."

For additional reading, see Dowling's *Fictions of Nuclear Disaster*.

Intrigue A 1988 SPY FILM starring Scott Glenn, Robert Loggia, William Atherton and Eleanor Bron and directed by David Drury. Made during the waning days of the Cold War, the story centers on an attempt by an American undercover agent to smuggle a defector out from behind the Iron Curtain.

Invaders from Mars A 1953 SCIENCE FICTION FILM starring Arthur Franz, Helena Carter and Jimmy Hunt and directed by William Cameron Menzies. Tobe Hooper directed a 1986 remake starring Karen Black, Laraine Newman and Bud Cort. The story centers on a boy who realizes that his father has been possessed by space aliens. The original version anticipated INVASION OF THE BODY SNATCHERS (1956), which also depicts creatures who possess humans and turn them into emotionless automatons dedicated to serving the alien cause. Both films focus on the frustration of protagonists who cannot get their fellow citizens to recognize the danger that is right before them. But *Invaders from Mars* ultimately shows the government and the military defeating the space invaders, while *Invasion of the Body Snatchers* reveals those authorities to be already controlled by aliens; only J. Edgar Hoover's FBI can save the country. (See also FILMS ASSOCIATED WITH THE RED SCARE.)

For additional reading, see Biskind's *Seeing Is Believing*.

Invasion of the Body Snatchers A 1956 SCIENCE FICTION FILM directed by Don Siegel and starring Kevin McCarthy and Dana Wynter; remade in 1978, directed by Philip Kaufman and starring Donald Sutherland and Brooke Adams; remade again in 1993 under the title *Body Snatchers*, directed by Phil Neilson and starring Terry Kinney and Meg Tilly. The story is based on Jack Finney's 1955 SCIENCE FICTION NOVEL, *The Body Snatchers*. The original film is about a small California town whose inhabitants are taken over by seed pods from outer space and transformed into unfeeling automatons. It contains a subtext that plays out Senator Joseph McCarthy's right-wing claims about communists taking over American institutions. Like the extreme political right wing, which believed that it saw events accurately and was unfairly being branded insane and paranoid for shouting the truth, film protagonist Miles Bennel, M.D., opens the movie arguing before a disbelieving audience of doctors and psychiatrists that he is fleeing from treacherous "pod people." Moreover, the pod people possess characteristics that the right associated with communists: They are emotionless, motivated entirely by their cause, and immune to the attachments of family or love; they come from large pods, which are seed cells, just as fifth-column communists were known to work in revolutionary cells for security reasons. More important, the pod people work at the local level in ways that the right wing believed communists worked at the national level. Like the communists, who, according to McCarthy and his supporters, were trying to dominate the world by first infiltrating the top levels of the U.S. military and government, the pods seize control of the local community by transforming the mayor and police force into unfeeling pod people dedicated to pod domination. Right-wing distrust of psychiatry also plays a role in the film. In the end, the right-wing fantasy is justified: Dr. Bennel is proven correct, and J. Edgar Hoover's FBI has been called in to save the day.

Whereas the original appeared during a relatively bellicose stage of the Cold War (the Hungarian Revolution had occurred in October 1956) and during the later stages of the RED SCARE, the 1978 remake appeared during the later stages of détente and in the post-Watergate era, when abuses by federal agencies such as the FBI were still in the public mind. Consequently, the right-wing subtext, while still present in the remake, does not appear as well suited to the times as in the original. (See also FILMS ASSOCIATED WITH THE RED SCARE.)

For further reading, see Biskind's *Seeing Is Believing*.

Invasion U.S.A. (1) A 1952 FILM DRAMA starring Dan O'Herlihy, Gerald Mohr and Peggie Castle and directed by Alfred E. Green. The story centers around a hypnotist in a New York bar who helps patrons imagine what might happen to them in an atomic war. As they feel the stress of the imagined combat, the patrons become militaristic; in the final moments, the protagonists rush to convert tractor plants into tank factories. The film relies heavily on stock film footage from World War II to suggest the damage that an atomic attack might cause. (See also APOCALYPTIC FILMS.)

For additional reading, see Shaheen's *Nuclear War Films.*

Invasion U.S.A. (2) A 1985 MILITARY FILM starring Chuck NORRIS, Richard Lynch and Melissa Prophet and directed by Joseph Zito. The action centers on Norris, whose heroics save the United States from an invasion of Soviet-backed terrorists. The highly patriotic anti-Soviet film appeared during one of the most intense and bellicose moments in U.S.-Soviet relations since the early 1960s.

Investigator, The A phonograph record that satirized Senator Joseph McCarthy and the RED SCARE. It appeared during the height of McCarthy's power, and Reuben Ship, the Canadian who made the SATIRE, faced deportation hearings in 1953 because of it. (See also MUSIC.)

"Invisible Man, The" (1) A TELEVISION SPY SHOW that ran on CBS from 1958 to 1960. The British-produced show featured the exploits of Dr. Peter Brady (Jim Turner), an English scientist who had discovered how to make himself invisible but then couldn't regain his visibility. Making the best of a bad situation, he offered his services to British intelligence, which used him as a secret agent to thwart enemies in Europe. The Invisible Man was never seen on screen; he was either covered in bandages or heard off-screen.

"Invisible Man, The" (2) A TELEVISION SPY SHOW that ran on NBC from 1975 to 1976. This update of the H. G Wells story featured the exploits of Dr. Daniel Westin (David McCallum) who had discovered how to make objects, including people, invisible. However, when he learned that the government planned to use his discovery for military purposes, he memorized his formula, destroyed his equipment and turned himself invisible to escape. Unable to make himself visible again, he had a friend make him a wig, a face mask and plastic hands so he could interact in human situations. He then took a job with the KLAE Corporation, for whom he participated in dangerous security missions while trying to develop a formula for restoring his visibility. Westin's fear that the military would expropriate and misuse his scientific discovery reflects a change in American Cold War attitudes. Made in the aftermath of the U.S. withdrawal from Vietnam, President Nixon's resignation due to the Watergate scandal, and the Church Committee's revelations before the Senate of abuses by U.S. intelligence agencies, the show's premise reflects the growing popular distrust of the government and the military during the mid-1970s. Whereas most shows from the 1950s and 1960s depicted the U.S. government as well-intentioned and committed to using its military power only for just

causes, shows from the mid-1970s sometimes presented a more cynical view of the government and its covert operations.

Ipcress File, The A 1962 SPY NOVEL by Len DEIGHTON and a 1965 British-made SPY FILM starring Michael Caine, Nigel Green and Sue Lloyd and directed by Sidney J. Furie. The story centers on an out-of-shape, nearsighted British intelligence agent who is unnamed in the novel but called Harry Palmer in the film. Palmer traces a missing scientist and discovers that one of his own superiors is a spy. In contrast to the flashy and sexy James BOND, the hero of popular novels and films throughout the Cold War, Palmer is an anti-hero who enters a career in espionage to avoid imprisonment for black marketeering he undertook when he was a sergeant stationed in Berlin. *The Ipcress File* had two less successful sequels, *Funeral in Berlin* (book and film 1965), based on Deighton's *The Berlin Memorandum,* and *Billion Dollar Brain* (book and film 1967), based on the novel of that name by Deighton.

Iron Curtain A term used to describe the communist countries in EASTERN EUROPE. In a speech in Fulton, Missouri, on March 5, 1946, Winston Churchill warned, "From Stettin in the Baltic to Trieste in the Adriatic an iron curtain has descended across the continent of Europe. The Communist parties . . . have been raised to preeminence and power far beyond their numbers and are seeking everywhere to obtain totalitarian control . . . Whatever conclusions may be drawn from these facts—and facts they are—this is certainly not the liberated Europe we fought to build up. Nor is it one that contains the essentials of permanent peace." The Iron Curtain offered a powerful image of communist oppression that dominated the Cold War. Its concrete manifestation came 15 years later in the cement and barbed wire of the Berlin Wall. Some critics objected to the term, however, as presenting too uniform and monolithic a view of what were in fact diverse societies. (See also LANGUAGE.)

Iron Curtain, The A 1948 FILM DRAMA starring Dana Andrews and Gene Tierney and directed by William Wellman. The first major anti-communist Cold War movie, *The Iron Curtain* was based on the story of Igor Gouzenko, a Russian who helped the Royal Canadian Mounted Police break a communist spy ring. The film was made under tight security: Visitors were barred from the set and those working on the movie were essentially quarantined. Bosley Crowther of the *New York Times* called the film "highly inflammatory" and "dangerous" and likened it to a "mild spy melodrama." (See also FILMS ASSOCIATED WITH THE RED SCARE.)

For additional reading, see Sayre's *Running Time.*

Iron Dream, The A 1972 SCIENCE FICTION NOVEL by Norman Spinrad. The novel imagines a parallel universe in which Adolf Hitler is a fascist science fiction writer instead of dictator. He writes a 1950s science fiction novel entitled *Lord of the Swastika* in which a motorbike gang from Heldon escapes the effects of a nuclear war they have waged by cloning themselves and colonizing space. Hitler, the writer, describes the settlers leaving the Earth aboard a spaceship:

"The seed of the Swastika rose on a pillar of fire to fecundate the stars." In the postnuclear world imagined by Hitler, there are neither women nor natural landscapes. Acquiring and exercising power is the chief concern of the new race, which is drawn to technology instead of nature. Hitler's text is followed by a debate in which fictional critics interpret the story. One describes it as an allegory of Germany and the Soviet Union, another claims it is the product of a neurotic mind. In its literary form, *The Iron Dream* adapts the ironic literary framing devices pioneered in the 18th century by Jonathan Swift and employed by such contemporary writers as John BARTH and Vladimir NABOKOV.

Spinrad gave similarly free rein to his imagination in his short story "The Big Flash," which appeared in the collection *No Direction Home* (1969). In that story, a rock band named the Four Horsemen acts like the Sirens of myth on the missile control crew of a Polaris submarine, bewitching and intoxicating the sailors with their video countdown to orgasm. (See also APOCALYPTIC NOVELS; NUCLEAR APOCALYPSE.)

For additional reading, see Dowling's *Fictions of Nuclear Disaster.*

Iron Triangle, The   A 1989 VIETNAM WAR FILM starring Beau Bridges, Haing S. Ngor and Liem Whatley and directed by Eric Weston. The film is based on the diary of an unknown Viet Cong soldier. Appearing over 15 years after the American withdrawal from Vietnam, *The Iron Triangle* presents the war from the perspective of the Viet Cong. The story centers on an American company commander (Bridges) who is captured by two Viet Cong soldiers, one of whom is cruel and the other sympathetic. The film depicts the Viet Cong's organization and motivation and represents life as the Viet Cong experienced it in the jungle and underground. The captured soldier learns to "understand that on the other side of the gun was a man like me."

For additional reading, see Lanning's *Vietnam at the Movies.*

"It Takes a Thief"   A TELEVISION SPY SHOW that ran on ABC from 1968 to 1970. Alexander Mundy (Robert Wagner) had been a stylish and adept professional thief before he was finally caught. While in prison he agreed to work for the U.S. spy agency, SIA, in return for his freedom. In his new capacity as a government thief, he travels throughout Europe romancing beautiful women, enjoying the good life, and stealing secrets for the United States. The Mundy character was based on the protagonist in the Alfred HITCHCOCK film, *To Catch a Thief,* which starred Cary Grant.

jazz A popular form of MUSIC that first appeared in the late 19th century as an outgrowth of African-American spirituals combining African rhythms and European-style melodies. It evolved throughout the 20th century and experienced significant growth and transformation throughout the Cold War. One of the few musical forms indigenous to the United States, Cold War–era jazz was pioneered by Charlie Parker, John Coltrane, Dizzy Gillespie, Thelonius Monk and Miles Davis. Though not necessarily political per se, jazz embodies the personal expression and experimentation that were often not permissible behind the IRON CURTAIN. Thus, like ROCK AND ROLL, abstract art and other artistic forms of expressionism, jazz was often banned in the Soviet Union, where it was denounced as decadent. The freedom of musicians to play jazz in the West thus became one of the important cultural differences between the Western democracies and communist-dominated Eastern Europe. However, partly because of its close connection to the culture of black Americans and partly because of its bold experiments in instrumentation, harmony, melody and rhythm, some conservatives during the RED SCARE labeled jazz subversive. Jazz was not performed at the White House until November, 19, 1962, when the PAUL WINTER JAZZ SEXTET performed for President Kennedy—as it happened, some three weeks after the conclusion of the Cuban Missile Crisis.

Jenny: My Diary A 1981 APOCALYPTIC NOVEL by Yorick Blumenfeld. Published shortly after the demise of détente, when the U.S.-Soviet rivalry was re-intensifying and the Reagan administration was beginning to speak of winnable nuclear war, *Jenny: My Diary* revived the postnuclear subgenre that had been largely dormant since the mid-1960s. Presented as a diary whose text is handwritten for verisimilitude, the book chronicles the experiences of a mother who takes refuge in a communal shelter with her two children just before a nuclear attack. The sexually promiscuous postnuclear society that develops underground initially repels her, "as if this shelter were some kind of suburban swapclub." Eventually she becomes more tolerant, and her antipathy for "life forces" disintegrates when she finds a Jewish lover with whom she can discuss the Holocaust. The ending suggests that a successful, new society can be rebuilt from the ashes.

For additional reading, see Dowling's *Fictions of Nuclear Disaster*.

Jet Pilot A 1957 SPY FILM starring John WAYNE and Janet Leigh and directed by Josef von Sternberg under the auspices of Howard Hughes. Leigh plays a Soviet pilot and spy who tries to lure Wayne into defecting, but she is herself converted to the American cause by her love for him. Then they arrange her defection.

For additional reading, see Rogin's *Ronald Reagan the Movie*.

journalists Along with TELEVISION NEWS reporters, newspaper and MAGAZINE journalists presented the Cold War to the American citizenry and thus helped shape public perceptions of this historical period. In the early years of the Cold War, most journalists supported the emerging view that the Soviet Union was a growing threat to U.S. and Western world interests and that the United States should take steps to oppose it. Although by 1949 this was a widely held view, before the late 1940s it had been subject to debate, and even the 1948 candidacy of Progressive Party presidential nominee Henry Wallace, a former vice president, cast doubt on the assumption that the U.S.S.R. was a de facto enemy. Thus the press, acting in concert with the Truman administration and members of Congress, was instrumental in helping to convince the public that the United States was, in fact, engaged in a Cold War. Among the journalists who took a strong, anti-communist stand from the beginning were Joseph and Stewart ALSOP, Walter LIPPMANN and Henry LUCE, the owner of *Time* and *Life* magazines, who used his considerable prestige to support the sagging fortunes of the Nationalist government in China under Chiang Kai-shek.

The Luce journals and the so-called China Lobby exerted pressure to maintain U.S. aid to Chiang, even when Secretary of State George Marshall and other members of the State Department concluded that Chiang would be unable ever to prevail against the communists. Prior to assuming office, Marshall, a World War II hero, had gone to China as a special envoy of President Truman and concluded that the United States would "virtually [have] to take over the Chinese government" in order to preserve Chiang's rule. "It would involve a continuing [U.S.] commitment from which it would practically be impossible to withdraw." *Time*'s China correspondent T. H. White gradually came to similar conclusions, and he was frustrated by the attempts of the editorial staff, including Alger Hiss' later accuser, Whittaker Chambers, to revise his dispatches to provide a pro-Chiang slant. Though White and Luce had enjoyed a special relationship based on their mutual passion for China, they parted ways in 1945. In 1946 White published THUNDER OUT OF CHINA, a best-seller that attacked Chiang as venal and corrupt. (White went on to serve as a senior editor of *The New Republic* and then political correspondent for *Collier's* magazine, and he wrote the best-selling *Making of the President* books after the 1960, 1964, 1968 and 1972 elections.)

When the communist revolution finally succeeded in 1949, Luce was in the forefront of those who attacked the State Department for "losing China." He later exerted pressure that helped preclude President Kennedy from agreeing to communist China's admission to the United Nations, which therefore did not occur for another decade. Like Luce, the Alsop brothers detested the Chinese communists. In 1962 Joseph Alsop attacked a suggestion by Supreme Court Justice William O. Douglas to send aid to China in order to avert a widespread famine: "Sentimentalists are beginning to talk of feeding starving China, which would simply mean getting Mao Tse-tung off his self-created hook."

By contrast, I. F. STONE was one of the few journalists to question the fundamental assumptions behind the Cold War, and he attacked the Truman administration and subsequent administrations from a left-wing point of view that was rare in American journalism, especially during the late 1940s and 1950s. Stone's ability to reach an audience was considerably more limited than that of the more conserva-

"Dr. Lippmann wants to amputate, but Dr. Alsop says to take more shots."

Bill Mauldin, "Dr. Lippmann wants to amputate." Reprinted with permission, Chicago Sun-Times; copyright © 1995.

tive mainstream press. While Luce's magazines were read by literally millions of Americans and the Alsops were nationally syndicated, Stone's weekly newsletter had an initial subscription of only 5,000. It grew to some 70,000 by 1971, when Stone ceased publication, but its influence was minuscule compared to that of *Time* or *Life.*

Norman COUSINS, who promoted a liberal point of view in his *Saturday Review,* which he edited and later owned, was considerably closer to the political center than Stone. He pressed for nuclear disarmament in the late 1950s and early 1960s and helped establish lines of communication with the Kremlin that made possible the 1963 Nuclear Test Ban Treaty, which he actively supported. Walter Lippmann also established ties with Moscow, and won two Pulitzer Prizes for his interviews with Soviet premier Khrushchev.

Allen DRURY patterned the unsympathetic antiwar journalist "Wonderful Walter" after Lippmann in his political novel CAPABLE OF HONOR (1967). Drew PEARSON likewise interviewed Khrushchev during the Kennedy years, and he too attempted to convince the president to modify his harsh stand against the Soviets. Pearson, who pioneered the field of investigative journalism, also advised President Johnson. In the final 10 years of his life, Pearson was joined by a new partner, Jack Anderson, who took over his syndicated column when Pearson died.

Both Lippmann and Cousins, though supporters of Kennedy, were early opponents of the Vietnam War. David HALBERSTAM was another early and forceful critic of the war. A Saigon correspondent for the *New York Times,* he gained considerable recognition for his account of the battle of Ap Bac in January 1963. In this first major battle of the war's American era, the South Vietnamese Army performed poorly, and Halberstam described how three U.S. advisers died while trying to get reluctant Vietnamese soldiers to fight. As a result of this account, the Pentagon began monitoring Halberstam's sources, keeping track of his whereabouts and telephone conversations. Kennedy's White House press secretary Pierre Salinger labeled Halberstam's articles "emotional and inaccurate," and Kennedy personally but unsuccessfully intervened to have Halberstam transferred from Vietnam. In 1964, Halberstam and Malcolm Browne shared the Pulitzer Prize for their Vietnam reporting, and in 1965 Halberstam published *The Making of a Quagmire,* a widely read personal account of his 15 months in Southeast Asia. He is best known for his 1972 bestselling NONFICTION book THE BEST AND THE BRIGHTEST, which describes the process by which the United States became involved in the war as well as the personalities responsible for that process. He also wrote *The Powers That Be* (1975), about the American news media in the postwar era and a 1967 novel, ONE VERY HOT DAY, which expresses the futility of the Vietnam situation.

By contrast, the Alsop brothers supported the war and Joseph accused Halberstam, Browne, and Neil Sheehan of painting a "dark, indignant picture" of the situation in Southeast Asia. Alsop compared the three to the journalists in the 1940s who had called Mao an "agrarian reformer." Sheehan later wrote A BRIGHT SHINING LIE (1988) about Colonel John Paul Vann's experiences in Vietnam.

TRAN THI NGA was the only woman working for *Time* magazine's Vietnam bureau between 1968 and 1975. With Wendy Wilder Larsen she coauthored the best-selling SHALLOW GRAVES (1986), a collection of poems modeled on the Vietnamese *truyen,* a novel in verse.

William F. BUCKLEY was a prominent, conservative, anticommunist journalist. He founded and edited the *National Review* in 1955 to provide a forum for his right-wing views, and he emerged as an important voice for conservative politics during the later stages of the Cold War. In 1962 Buckley began a syndicated newspaper column, "A Conservative Voice." His later column, "On the Right," appeared in more than 200 newspapers, and in 1966 he began to host the syndicated television talk show FIRING LINE, in which he debated liberal-minded guests and conversed with conservative ones. ("Firing Line" remained on the air into the 1990s.) Buckley objected to détente and criticized President Nixon's overtures to China and the U.S.S.R. in the early 1970s. In June 1974, Buckley called for Nixon's resignation over the Watergate scandal despite his fears of the damage this would cause the Republican Party. Buckley was also an early defender of Senator Joseph McCarthy and of the HOUSE COMMITTEE ON UN-AMERICAN ACTIVITIES (HUAC) during the RED SCARE, and he wrote books supporting each. Walter WINCHELL, an influential gossip columnist and radio news

broadcaster, was another defender of McCarthy, as was Hedda Hopper, a California-based gossip columnist who reported on the political affiliations of Hollywood personalities. When Larry PARKS reluctantly became the first man in Hollywood to "name names" before HUAC, accurately noting that he was probably destroying his career in the process, Hopper wrote, "The life of one American soldier is worth all the careers in Hollywood. We must be careful lest we give sympathy to those who do not deserve it—and Parks certainly does not."

Winchell, Hopper, Victor Riesel, Jack O'Brian and Hearst newspaper columnist George SOKOLSKY all used their columns as forums for ex-communists or fellow travelers willing to admit the error of their former ways, thereby removing themselves from the blacklists that kept them from working. In addition to renouncing their past beliefs, the blacklisted individuals routinely had to demonstrate their good faith by identifying other people who had communist affiliations. Sokolsky, in particular, played a major role in helping penitent television and film personalities clear themselves.

Ed SULLIVAN was another anti-communist columnist. He wrote a nationally syndicated newspaper column entitled "Little Old New York," as well as serving as master of ceremonies in 1948 for the early television show *"The Toast of the Town,"* which later achieved prominence as "The Ed Sullivan Show" (CBS, 1948–71). In 1950, Sullivan publicly cheered the publication of RED CHANNELS, the document that became the unofficial basis for BLACKLISTING in the entertainment industry. He wrote in his syndicated column:

> With television going into its third big year . . . the entire industry is becoming increasingly aware of the necessity to plug all Commie propaganda loopholes. Networks and station heads, with a tremendous financial stake, want no part of Commies or pinkos. Sponsors, sensitive in the extreme to blacklisting, want no part of Commies or their sympathizers. Advertising agencies held responsible by sponsors for correct exercise of discretion in programming, want no controversy of any kind. For that reason, [the] *Red Channels* listing of performers who, innocently or maliciously, are affiliated with Commie-front organizations will be a reference book in preparing any program.

By contrast, Pearson and the Alsop brothers actively opposed the Red Scare in their columns. In response to a verbal attack by Pearson, McCarthy once kicked the reporter in the groin and later boasted about it. In 1953 the Alsops coauthored *We Accuse!* a denunciation of the Atomic Energy Commission's refusal to reinstate the security clearance of J. Robert Oppenheimer, who had headed the commission from 1946 to 1952 and had previously directed the wartime Manhattan Project, which developed the atomic bomb. (See also IN THE MATTER OF J. ROBERT OPPENHEIMER, 1968.) However, by the 1960s, Joseph Alsop had come to believe that domestic communists had infiltrated the civil rights movement and were fomenting the racial strife that was erupting throughout the nation.

New Hampshire newspaper publisher William LOEB, an arch-conservative known for his vicious attacks on his political enemies, was another McCarthy supporter. He endorsed the unsuccessful Republican candidates Thomas Dewey and Barry Goldwater in 1948 and 1964, respectively, and actively opposed Presidents Kennedy and Johnson. He reluctantly supported President Nixon but rejected Nixon and Henry Kissinger's policies of détente in the early 1970s. Loeb is best known for his role in subverting the presidential candidacy of Maine's Democratic senator, Edmund Muskie, in 1972, when Loeb's newspaper *The Manchester Union Leader* participated in a Watergate-related "dirty trick" by publishing a letter allegedly by a Florida youth that accused Muskie of making ethnic slurs against New Hampshire's French-speaking population. The youth was never found and the letter later proved to originate in the Nixon White House. The day after publishing the letter, Loeb attacked Muskie's wife, and the senator cried before television cameras while defending her. His public display of tears is generally credited with derailing his bid for the Democratic nomination.

William LAURENCE was the only journalist permitted to cover the Manhattan Project. The science editor of the *New York Times* and winner of two Pulitzer Prizes, he wrote *Dawn Over Zero* (1946) and *Hell Bomb* (1951), about the atomic and hydrogen bombs. He also wrote *Men and Atoms* (1959) and appeared in PATTERN FOR SURVIVAL, a 1950 instruction film designed to ease fears about atomic warfare and advise viewers about how to prepare for an atomic attack.

William Worthy Jr. was an African-American journalist who fell into trouble with U.S. officials for traveling to Cuba and China without a passport in the early 1960s. The FBI file on James BALDWIN records that the prominent NOVELIST was among those who signed a petition calling for the Kennedy administration to stop harassing Worthy. Worthy was also the subject of "The Ballad of William Worthy," a protest song by FOLK SINGER Phil OCHS. Other Key Cold War journalists include *Washington Post* reporters Carl Bernstein and Robert Woodward, who broke the Watergate story through their investigative reporting. The story of their effort appears in their book ALL THE PRESIDENT'S MEN (1974) and in Alan Pakula's 1976 POLITICAL FILM of the same title.

From 1962 through the end of the Cold War Art BUCHWALD wrote a syndicated humor column that satirized American politics, including Cold War politics. (See also SATIRE.) His column appeared in some 550 newspapers, and in 1986 the American Academy and Institute of Arts and Letters inducted him as a member. Liberal columnists during the Cold War include James Reston, Tom Wicker, Joseph Kraft, Marquis Childs and Nicholas Von Hoffman; among the conservative columnists were James Kilpatrick, Gary Will, Robert Novak and Cal Thomas. In addition, journalists representing extreme positions on the left and right appeared in less widely read, alternative publications. *The*

Daily Worker was the official newspaper of the American Communist Party.

For additional reading, see Halberstam's *The Powers That Be* and Aronson's *The Press and the Cold War.*

Journey Beyond Tomorrow

Journey Beyond Tomorrow A 1962 APOCALYPTIC NOVEL by Robert Sheckley. Published the same year as the Cuban Missile Crisis, this absurdist story centers on Joenes, a young man raised on a low-tech Pacific island who inadvertently initiates a nuclear war when he visits North America. Due to a labyrinthine bureaucracy that only one character, Theseus, can successfully navigate, the U.S. military performance is woefully inept, and half the American missiles fall on U.S. soil. Accompanied by a beatnik named Lum, Joenes returns to his Pacific island, where he disappears into the mountains with maps of the prewar world. Stories of an old man studying papers in a remote cave give rise to a new religion, and eventually Joenes is deified, a development that critic David Dowling claims "is just one more satirical example of man's desperate quest for signposts in a bewildering world."

For additional reading, see Dowling's *Fictions of Nuclear Disaster.*

Judas Time, The

Judas Time, The A 1946 POLITICAL NOVEL by Isidor Schneider. A rare American pro-communist book, *The Judas Time* centers on Calvin Cain, a college instructor and party member who betrays the communist cell at his university in return for promotion to assistant professor. As evidence of his moral deterioration, Cain sinks to consorting with fascists and Trotskyites. The book, which attacks intellectuals who have turned against the party, was criticized in the mainstream press for its heavyhanded treatment of the characters. Yet one reviewer noted, "Although *The Judas Time* is so oversimplified that it loses much of its potential effectiveness, it has considerable interest, not as a novel but as a document of our time . . . With such a steady and violent stream of books written by the men whom Mr. Schneider looks on as traitors, it is valuable to hear the other side for a change."

Judgment Day

Judgment Day A 1955 SCIENCE FICTION STORY by L. Sprague de Camp. Published in the August issue of *Astounding Science Fiction*, the story centers on a nuclear scientist who feels persecuted by humanity. Consequently, when he discovers the secret to nuclear fission and foresees that humans will inevitably employ it to build highly destructive nuclear weapons, he decides to reveal the formula as a way of gaining revenge against the species. (See also APOCALYPTIC NOVELS and NUCLEAR APOCALYPSE.)

For additional reading, see Dowling's *Fiction of Nuclear Disaster.*

Kazan, Elia A Turkish-born FILM DIRECTOR and THEATER director. The son of Anatolian Greeks, Kazan immigrated to the United States when he was four years old. He worked his way through Williams College and Yale Drama School as a waiter, an experience that provoked an "antagonism to privilege, to good looks, to Americans, to Wasps" that ultimately led him to join the Communist Party in 1934. Kazan left the party in 1936, when it wanted him to take over the Group Theater. Of this experience Kazan told the HOUSE COMMITTEE ON UN-AMERICAN ACTIVITIES (HUAC), "I had enough regimentation, enough of being told what to think and say and do . . . I had had a taste of police-state living and I did not like it." Along with Lee Strasberg, in 1947 Kazan founded the famed Actors Studio, which introduced Stanislavski-based "method" acting. The Actors Studio featured such performers as Lee J. COBB, Marlon Brando, Julie Harris and James Dean. Considered one of the premier directors of the 1940s and 1950s, Kazan directed numerous films and plays known for their social content and liberal orientation. In 1947 he directed Brando in *A Streetcar Named Desire,* and in 1949 he directed the highly successful Broadway debut of Arthur MILLER's *The Death of a Salesman* in which Cobb received rave reviews. During that period, Kazan also directed the films *Gentleman's Agreement* (1947), about anti-Semitism, *Pinky* (1949), about racial discrimination, and VIVA ZAPATA (1952), about revolution and land reform in Mexico.

In 1952 Kazan was subpoenaed to testify before HUAC. Because of his stature and his presumed ability to work in live theater even if he were banned from directing films, many felt that Kazan should have refused to testify and tried to break the blacklist by forcing the studio owners to forgo one of their brightest and most financially remunerative talents. (See also BLACKLISTING.) Miller personally tried to dissuade Kazan from cooperating with the committee and broke with him for several years after Kazan testified anyway. In his testimony, Kazan identified several communists. He also included a list of the 25 productions he had directed, followed by discussions defending the political content of each. The day after his testimony was released, he took out a large ad in the *New York Times,* explaining that he had informed because communism represented a grave danger to democracy. Moreover, he urged others also to recognize their patriotic duty to cooperate with HUAC. Both Kazan's testimony and his ad moved many on the left to condemn Kazan. Some saw Kazan's move as self-serving, motivated by a desire to work and to become politically acceptable. Others felt he had betrayed his ideals by joining with the right to condemn communism in such terms.

In 1954 Kazan directed ON THE WATERFRONT. SCREENWRITER Budd SCHULBERG, who had also named names before HUAC, wrote the screenplay. The film's sympathetic treatment of an informer has led many critics to interpret the story as an allegory justifying those who cooperated with the committee. In *On the Waterfront,* the cause of justice and integrity is served by informing, not by standing silent and permitting dangerous crimes to go unpunished. Ironically, the original idea for *On the Waterfront* had come from *The Hook,* Miller's

1951 screenplay. However, when Miller and Kazan tried to interest Columbia Pictures, *The Hook* was turned down because Miller would not change the corrupt union officials to communists. Many critics feel that Miller's 1955 Broadway play *A View from the Bridge,* which depicts a man whose life was ruined by a single act of informing, was the playwright's response to *On the Waterfront.* One story maintains that when Miller finished the play, he sent a copy to Kazan. Kazan responded that he would be honored to direct it, and Miller supposedly replied, "I didn't send it to you because I wanted you to direct it. I sent it to you because I wanted you to know what I think of stool pigeons."

In 1963 Kazan and Miller reconciled when they were named resident director and resident playwright for the premiere season of New York's Lincoln Center. Kazan directed Miller's autobiographical *After the Fall,* whose protagonist is a former communist who breaks with a friend about to inform before a congressional committee. The female lead was a beautiful, vulnerable blond character modeled after Miller's former wife, MARILYN MONROE. According to one reviewer, "*After the Fall* seeks to understand, not to judge." On the other hand, many other prominent figures who had stood up to HUAC never forgave Kazan. Zero MOSTEL never ceased to refer to him as "Looselips," and Dalton TRUMBO derided him because he "carried down men much less capable of defending themselves than he . . . who had much more to lose than he and much less ability to function than he." In 1988 Kazan published his autobiography, *Elia Kazan, A Life.*

For additional reading, see Navasky's *Naming Names.* For a partial transcript of Kazan's testimony before HUAC, see Bentley's THIRTY YEARS OF TREASON.

"Keep Posted" A TELEVISION NEWS show that ran on the DuMont network from 1951 to 1953. Moderated by Martha Rountree and including Lawrence Spivak as a regular panelist, this Washington-based show featured a panel of citizens questioning leading public figures. A notable episode included an appearance by Senator Richard Nixon, whose topic was "Fighting Communism."

Kennedy, Oswald, Castro, Khrushchev Igor YEFIMOV's 1987 NONFICTION documentary study of the Kennedy assassination. After four years of research, Yefimov, a Soviet emigré, concluded that the Cuban leader hired the Mafia to kill Kennedy in response to Kennedy's efforts to have the CIA assassinate Castro.

Kennedy–Nixon Debates See NIXON–KENNEDY DEBATES.

K.G.B.: The Secret War A 1986 SPY FILM starring Sally Kellerman, Michael Billington and Denise DuBarry. The plot centers on a female U.S. agent (Kellerman) attempting to thwart a KGB spy who steals computer secrets in order to make a deal with the CIA.

Khrushchev and Berlin A 1961 TELEVISION DOCUMENTARY produced by Fred FREED. It premiered as an "NBC White Paper" on December 26, 1961, about two months after the peak of the second Berlin Crisis, when U.S. and Soviet tanks faced each other across Checkpoint Charlie.

Kill Castro A 1980 SPY FILM starring Robert VAUGHN, Stuart Whitman and Caren Kaye and directed by Chuck Workman. Made as the U.S.-Soviet détente of the 1970s was ending, the film centers on a Key West boat captain (Whitman) who is hired by a renegade CIA agent (Vaughn) to assassinate the Cuban leader. The plot also involves drugs and the Mafia. The linking of the drug trade and organized crime reflected contemporary charges that Cuba was involved in drug trafficking and that the CIA had recruited the Mafia to assassinate Castro during the early 1960s. The film also appeared under the titles *Assignment Kill Castro, Cuba Crossing, Key West Crossing, The Mercenaries* and *Sweet Dirty Tony.*

Killing Fields, The A 1984 British-made FILM DRAMA starring Sam Waterston, Haing S. Ngor and John Malkovich and directed by Roland Joffe. The film is based on the experiences of *New York Times* reporter Sydney Schanberg (Waterston) who was in Phnom Penh in 1975 when Cambodia fell to the communist Khmer Rouge led by Pol Pot. Early in the film Schanberg and his photographer (Malkovich) are saved by their interpreter, Dith Pran (Ngor), who is subsequently sent to a "reeducation camp," which he barely survives. In the process of escaping to freedom, Dith discovers the "killing fields," which contain the remains of some three million Cambodians whom the Khmer Rouge had murdered. Schanberg reveals the story to the world after he reunites with Dith. Prior to his acting career, Ngor had been a Cambodian physician whose real-life experiences were similar to those described in the movie. Malkovich made his film debut in *The Killing Fields.* (See also VIETNAM WAR FILMS.)

Kim, Kyung Jae A South Korean EXILED WRITER (to the United States). Born in 1942 in Soonchun, South Korea, Kim studied political science at the National University of Seoul. In 1960, while still a student, he participated in the April Revolution that deposed the government of President Syngman Rhee. In 1971 he became the press secretary for opposition leader Kim Dae Jung's unsuccessful presidential campaign against the leader of the military government, Park Chung Hee. Shortly thereafter, military police arrested Kim and tortured him while he was in detention. When the Park government reversed its policy of detaining dissidents, Kim was freed and ordered into immediate exile. He arrived in the United States in 1972. In 1974 he collaborated with Kim Hyung Wook on an exposé of the clandestine operations of the Korean CIA within the United States. *Revolution and Idol,* a three-volume study, was based on numerous secret documents and taped interviews. Though completed in 1976, its publication depended upon the approval of Kim Hyung Wook, former chief of the Korean CIA. Therefore, Kim released the book in 1979, only after Kim Hyung Wook disappeared in Paris. The South Korean government banned *Revolution and Idol,* but Kim persuaded a publisher there to issue 150,000 copies. Subsequently, the government suspended the publishing house's license, and the publisher fled into hiding. In addition to short stories and essays written while he lived in South Korea, Kim published *The Midnighters* (1977), a realistic novel describing the treatment of farmers, laborers and intellectuals living in a right-wing dictatorship. He also edited and published the *Korean Independent Monitor,* a New York-based weekly newspaper.

For additional reading, see Tucker's *Literary Exile in the Twentieth Century.*

Kim, Richard A South Korean EXILED WRITER (to the United States). Born in 1932 in Hamhung City, Korea, Kim served as an officer in the South Korean Army during the Korean War. He immigrated to the United States in 1954 and became a U.S. citizen in 1964. His best-selling military novel, THE MARTYRED (1964), tells the story of a South Korean Army captain who investigates the fates of 14 Christian ministers whom the North Koreans had captured. In the process of the investigation, the captain confronts evidence that compels him to rethink his own notions of right and wrong, belief and hypocrisy, and patriotism and treason. Kim, a professor at the University of Massachusetts at Amherst, has also published *The Innocent* (1968) and a collection of stories, *Lost Names: Scenes from a Boyhood in Japanese-Occupied Korea* (1988). (See also NOVELISTS)

For additional reading, see Tucker's *Literary Exile in the Twentieth Century.*

King in New York, A A 1957 British-made FILM COMEDY starring Charles CHAPLIN, his son Michael Chaplin, and Dawn Addams. Chaplin also wrote and directed the film, which he made in England five years after Attorney General James McGranery revoked his reentry permit to the United States. (Chaplin was a British citizen, even though he had lived in the United States since 1913.) In *A King in New York,* Chaplin clearly responds to the right-wing factions that smeared him and drove him from the United States in 1952. These included the HOUSE COMMITTEE ON UN-AMERICAN ACTIVITIES (HUAC), Senator Richard Nixon and JOURNALIST Hedda Hopper.

A King in New York depicts a deposed European monarch who immigrates to America. The movie satirizes American culture, as the destitute king is reduced to earning a living by making television commercials. However, the king falls afoul of HUAC when he befriends a spirited runaway boy whose parents are suspected communists. Tarnished through guilt by association, the king must appear before the committee, but he makes literal the metaphorical farce of the hearings when he accidentally turns a fire hose on his interrogators. Subsequently, however, the committee intimidates the boy into becoming an informer who identifies several of his parents' political colleagues. By the end of the film, the once-spirited boy has been clearly traumatized and has become withdrawn.

The reviewer for the *London Evening Standard* described *A King in New York* as Chaplin's most bitter film, "a calculated, passionate rage." It was not shown in the United States until 1976, and Chaplin banned all American members of the news media from its Paris premiere.

For additional reading, see Whitfield's *The Culture of the Cold War.*

King of Hearts A 1967 French- and Italian-made MILITARY FILM starring Alan Bates, Pierre Brasseur and Genevieve Bujold and directed by Philippe de Broca. Set during World War I, *King of Hearts* was released during the height of the Vietnam War, and for many it served as an antiwar parable that underscored the innate insanity of warfare. Bates stars as Private Charles Plumpick, a specialist in homing pigeons who is mistakenly sent to locate and defuse a powerful bomb that the retreating Germans had planted in a clock tower of a small French town. Because of the bomb, the townspeople have fled, leaving behind only the inmates of a mental institution. The inmates escape, assume the roles of the townspeople and welcome Plumpick as their returning ruler, the King of Hearts, while he desperately searches for the explosives. A very warm and often funny film, *King of Hearts* eventually concludes that the inhabitants of the mental institution are more sane than the warriors from the outside world, who pointlessly kill each other. The film was popular during the war and enjoyed a consistent cult following for many years thereafter. (See also FILM SATIRE.)

Kiss Me Deadly A 1952 bestselling detective novel by Mickey SPILLANE and a 1955 SPY FILM starring Ralph Meeker, Albert Dekker and Cloris Leachman and directed by Robert Aldrich. The film version introduced an element of atomic radiation not found in the novel. The plot centers on detective Mike Hammer's failed attempt to save a helpless woman fleeing from killers and his subsequent revenge. Hammer must track down a stolen box containing radioactive material that burns and disfigures people even slightly exposed to it. One of the most brutal spy films of its era, in which the protagonist viciously kills the Communist spies, *Kiss Me Deadly* became a cult film.

For additional reading, see Rogin's *Ronald Reagan, The Movie* and Darby's *Necessary American Fictions.*

Knebel, Fletcher A NOVELIST and JOURNALIST. An author of POLITICAL NOVELS, Knebel is best known for SEVEN DAYS IN MAY (1962), which he coauthored with Charles W. Bailey II. NIGHT OF CAMP DAVID (1965) also attracted a great deal of critical attention, as opposed to CROSSING IN BERLIN (1981), a later Cold War novel, which was relatively ignored. The best-selling *Seven Days in May,* which was made into a 1964 POLITICAL FILM directed by John Frankenheimer, describes an attempted military coup by outraged right-wing U.S. generals after the signing of a nuclear disarmament treaty with the Soviets. It was one of the earliest Cold War stories to suggest that powerful officers in the U.S. military might be irresponsible, pernicious and/or insane and out of control, and it suggests that the greater danger to U.S. democracy comes not from communist subversion but from the super-patriotic, self-righteous political right wing that regards the Constitution as a hindrance to protecting national security. The story also singles out the nuclear bomb as the underlying cause of the nation's hysteria and even of the coup itself. Thus, like the 1959 film ON THE BEACH, *Seven Days in May* takes an antinuclear position without arguing for unilateral disarmament.

Night of Camp David centers on Jim MacVeagh, a senator who learns in a mysterious meeting with the president that he is under consideration as a vice presidential candidate in the forthcoming election. Over time, however, MacVeagh realizes that the president is extremely paranoid with delusions of persecution and grandeur. The president's crucial upcoming meeting with Soviet leaders leaves MacVeagh wondering if the U.S. head of state can be deposed before he invokes nuclear war. *Crossing in Berlin* focuses on efforts by an American businessman to effect the defection of an East German chemist who has discovered that her government has suppressed important but politically unpleasant research on the greenhouse effect. Published a year after the collapse of the U.S.-Soviet détente, the novel blames communism for the economic deprivation and the political and personal restrictions of East Germany.

Knebel's other political novels include *No High Ground* (1960), about the development of the atomic bomb; *Convention* (1964), which was also coauthored with Bailey and is about the 1964 Republican convention; *Vanished* (1965), about a friend of the president who suddenly disappears; *Zinzin Road* (1966), about a Peace Corps volunteer who becomes involved in the internal politics of the host country; and *Dark Horse* (1972), about a populist commissioner of the New Jersey Turnpike Authority who is selected as the presidential candidate when the elected candidate dies three weeks before the election. The book is a kind of portrait of the radicalism and political chaos of the early 1970s. The candidate's top advisers are his uncle from a small town in Arkansas, a former college roommate who works for the Rand Corporation, an African-American woman activist and a college radical. Though the literary establishment did not regard him as a serious writer, Knebel joins such other popular writers as William LEDERER, Eugene BURDICK, James MICHENER and Leon URIS who directly address the Cold War in their fiction and had an enormous influence on popular perceptions.

Koestler, Arthur A Hungarian-born NOVELIST and JOURNALIST. Born in Budapest in 1905, the descendant of a chief rabbi in Prague, Koestler grew up in Vienna, where his family moved when he was nine years old. He studied science and linguistics, but after he became attached to the cause of militant Zionism, he dropped out of the university and moved to Palestine, where he performed menial labor. In 1927, Koestler began a career as a journalist serving as a science editor and correspondent for papers in Paris and Berlin. At the end of 1931 he joined the German Communist Party. Shortly thereafter, he was fired from his job because of that affiliation. He moved briefly to the Soviet Union and then to Paris, where he worked for international communism from 1933 to 1935. He reported on the Spanish Civil War during 1936 and 1937, providing a left-wing point of view on that conflict. Franco's army captured him in Malaga and sentenced him to death. However, British protest on his behalf saved his life.

Disillusioned by the failure of the communists to strongly protest his death sentence, Koestler resigned from the Communist Party in 1938. In 1940, while he was working on *Darkness at Noon* in Paris, French police arrested him and consigned him to a camp for aliens. Once again, British objections secured his release. Before the German occupation of Paris, Koestler fled to England, where the English transla-

tion of *Darkness at Noon* (1941) was a critical success. Widely read in the West throughout the Cold War, the novel recounts Koestler's attraction to, his involvement with, and his denunciation of communism. Set in 1937, the story centers on a former Soviet revolutionary who is asked to confess to crimes he did not commit. It condemns the Stalinist purges and portrays the Soviet regime as brutal and unreasonable. In 1951, Sidney Kingsley adapted the novel for live THEATER, and the play ran for 186 performances on Broadway. Immediately after World War II, Koestler's passion for Zionism rekindled. He served as a correspondent for the *London Times* in order to witness the situation in Palestine. *Thieves in the Night* (1946) is a pro-Zionist novel, and *Promise and Fulfillment: Palestine 1917–1949* describes the history of the formation of the state of Israel.

During the Cold War, Koestler maintained his strong anti-communist stand, appearing on panels and seminars with other intellectuals to discuss Cold War issues. Koestler participated in a famous debate with existentialist philosophers Jean Paul Sartre and Simone de Beauvoir, who were sympathetic to communism. With ORWELL and others, Koestler attempted to form a League for the Rights of Man to further promote the anti-communist cause. His contribution to Richard Crossman's anthology of essays by former communists, THE GOD THAT FAILED (1950), further elaborates on his disaffection for Marxism. His essay provoked a wide range of intense responses. Koestler also wrote a SCIENCE FICTION NOVEL *The Age of Longing* (1951).

Koestler's later work remained political but also moved on to issues beyond communism in his nonfiction. *Reflections on Hanging* (1956), for instance, objects to capital punishment. In *The Lotus and the Robot* (1961), he expands his concerns to include parapsychology, psychology and the creative process. Later in life, Koestler contracted leukemia and Parkinson's disease. He did not want to suffer from the terminal illness, and he and his wife, Cynthia Jefferies, committed a double suicide in their London apartment in 1983. (See also EXILED WRITERS [to the United States].)

For additional reading, see Tucker's *Literary Exile in the Twentieth Century*.

Korean War See KOREAN WAR FILMS; MILITARY NOVELS; TELEVISION DOCUMENTARIES; TELEVISION MILITARY DRAMAS.

Korean War films The Korean War (1950–53) was fought to enforce President Truman's Cold War containment policy, and it provided an early test of the U.S. resolve to stop the spread of communism everywhere in the world. The Korean War was the only instance during the Cold War when armies of two major powers (China and the United States) actually fought directly against each other. Though it never generated the public dissent provoked by the Vietnam War, the Korean War was not nearly as enthusiastically supported as World War II had been. To most Americans, Korea was a remote and unfamiliar country with mysterious customs and political history. And the war's purpose—to contain an ideology—was far more abstract than the threat from Germany and Japan had been. Moreover, it was difficult for the public to imagine the "bad" North Koreans overrunning the "good" South Koreans when, in the words of a character from THE STEEL HELMET (1951), the only way to tell them apart was, "If he's running with you, he's a South Korean. If he's running after you, he's a North Korean."

Many Korean War films reflect the underlying ambivalence and confusion surrounding that "police action." Though typically respectful of the ground soldiers who actually fought the war, these movies often cast doubt about how and why the war was waged. For instance, in *The Steel Helmet,* which appeared six months after the war began, writer/director Samuel FULLER employs a set and special effects calculated to create a claustrophobic atmosphere in which everything seems vague, hazy and ambiguous. The effect is to render the war as an exercise in ongoing madness; its final credit reads, "There is no end to this story." Fuller's *Fixed Bayonets* (1951) follows a corporal who must assume command of a rear-guard action when his superiors are killed. PORK CHOP HILL, (1959) another grimly realistic film, portrays a valiant but absurd struggle over a meaningless hill hours before the armistice is signed. The soldiers perceive only the futility of dying to gain control of an apparently worthless mound. However, the film ultimately vindicates the soldiers' sacrifice: U.S. negotiators are shown to need the hard-won victory to convince the communists of the West's unyielding resolve to stand up to aggression at every turn. Likewise, Brubaker, the protagonist in THE BRIDGES AT TOKO-RI (1954), has initial misgivings about the war. Like the hero in *I Want You* (1951), he is a World War II veteran who resents this second interruption of his life to serve his country, especially since he is now starting a family. However, by the film's conclusion, he has become reconciled to the war and the sacrifices he must make.

During the Vietnam War, many films were set in the Korean War, criticizing the later war via a portrayal of the earlier one as cruel and/or absurd. The films WAR HUNT (1962) and WAR IS HELL (1964) depict the capacity of war to cause soldiers to lose their perspective as well as their fundamental humanity. *War Hunt* is based on an actual Marine who would go off for days by himself to kill the enemy. Robert Altman employs BLACK HUMOR in M*A*S*H* (1970), his Vietnam War-era FILM SATIRE that highlights the insanity that he saw as permeating virtually every aspect of the Korean War.

On the other hand, several films made during and shortly after the Korean War take a strong and uncritical patriotic stand, including *I Want You* (1951), *Mission Over Korea* (1953), *Sabre Jet* (1953), *Men in War* (1957), *Marines, Let's Go!* (1961), *Hold Back the Night* (1956), *The Hunters* (1958), *Take the High Ground* (1953) and *Submarine Command* (1951). Made during the war, *Bright Victory* (1951) focuses on a blinded soldier who tries to adjust to civilian life. The Reagan-era documentary-like INCHON (1981) also celebrates the Korean War, occasion for one of the most brilliant military maneuvers in the history of warfare. *Cease Fire* is another Korean War documentary.

Several postwar films from the middle and late 1950s center on patriotic biographies of Korean War heroes. These include Sterling Hayden's portrayal of a one-legged admiral in *The Eternal Sea* (1955), Alan Ladd's depiction of a jet fighter pilot in *The McConnell Story* (1955) and Rock Hud-

son's enactment in *Battle Hymn* (1957) of a preacher who is also an air force pilot.

A number of Korean War films bring romance to the combat zone. Sometimes the women are damsels in distress, caught in the wrong place at the wrong time (*Operation Dames* [1959] and *The Nun and the Sergeant* [1962]). In other films, they have chosen or been assigned to dangerous situations (*Tank Battalion* [1958], *Target Zero* [1955] and *Jet Attack* [1958]). By contrast, part of the drama in ONE MINUTE TO ZERO (1952) centers on a U.S. colonel forcing his romantic interest, a UN official, to evacuate. The same colonel is ultimately forced to bomb fleeing refugees. SAYONARA (1954) and *Japanese War Bride* (1952) both address the Korean War-related phenomenon of romances and marriages between Japanese women and the U.S. servicemen assigned to Japan because of the war. Official U.S. military policy forbade such marriages. LOVE IS A MANY-SPLENDORED THING (1955) centers on a mixed-race romance between a male U.S. war correspondent and a female Eurasian doctor. The conflicts between the communist and Nationalist Chinese forms part of the background, in addition to the war in Korea.

Several Korean War films center on prisoners of war (POWs). Although prohibited by the Geneva Convention, executions of POWs apparently took place on both sides during the Korean conflict. Moreover, for the first time in history, U.S. POWs were accused of widespread collaboration with their captors, and no U.S. POW ever escaped from a permanent internment camp in North Korea. THE HOOK (1963) revolves around the ethical dilemma faced by a sergeant and private who are ordered to execute a North Korean prisoner of war. THE MANCHURIAN CANDIDATE (1962) uses the Korean War as a powerful backdrop to a compelling anti-McCarthy drama in which communists brainwash a captured U.S. soldier so they can recall him as an assassin at a future date.

Made the year following the cease-fire, Ronald REAGAN's PRISONER OF WAR (1954) paints a rosier picture of U.S. soldiers in captivity. Most of them sarcastically defy their captors, and the only soldier who cooperates proves to be planting misinformation to fool the enemy. *The Bamboo Prison* (1955), whose script the Defense Department found unacceptable and which was turned down by the Memphis, Tennessee, Board of Censors, employs a similar theme. Likewise, in *Time Limit* (1957) Richard Basehart's apparent collaboration with the enemy is ultimately vindicated, as is Lee Marvin's in *Sergeant Ryker* (1968). Only in *The Rack* (1956) is Paul Newman, a career officer, found guilty. The penitent Newman tells the camera, "Every man has a moment in his life when he has to choose. If he chooses right, then it's a moment of magnificence. If he chooses wrong, then it's a moment of regret that will stay with him for the rest of his life. I wish that every soldier . . . could feel the way I feel now . . . they'd know what it's like to be a man who sold himself short, and who lost his moment of magnificence."

Other Korean War films include *Battle Circus* (1952), *Battle Zone* (1952), *Flight Nurse* (1953), *Hell's Horizons* (1955), *The Glory Brigade* (1953), *Retreat, Hell!* (1952), *Sniper's Ridge* (1961), *Tokyo File 212* (1951, about combating Japanese communist subversives during the war), *A Yank in Korea* (1951) and *The Young and the Brave* (1963). (See also MILITARY NOVELS; TELEVISION MILITARY DRAMAS.)

For additional reading, see Smith's *Looking Away*.

Kosinski, Jerzy A Polish emigré. NOVELIST and EXILED WRITER (to the United States). Born in Lodz, Poland, in 1933, Kosinski led an extraordinary life before his suicide in 1991. He drew heavily on his personal experiences in his novels. *The Painted Bird* (1965), for example, describes the harrowing experiences of a young boy, a Jew or gypsy, whose urban parents leave him in the custody of ignorant peasants in order to protect him from incarceration in a concentration camp. The boy progresses through a series of abusive situations in the Polish countryside, where the superstitious peasants fear his darker complexion. Like Kosinski, the boy becomes mute after a particularly traumatic experience, though he reacquires his power of speech at the book's end after a skiing accident, when he regains the will to communicate. Ironically, German soldiers and those in the liberating Red Army are the only ones to treat him compassionately. In this and subsequent novels, the protagonists must learn to survive in a hostile, amoral world, often through guile and cunning and by adopting violent behavior of their own. *Cockpit* (1975) continues the autobiographical account, describing how the protagonist, an accomplished photographer like Kosinski himself (he exhibited throughout Poland), secures permission to leave communist Poland by forging documents and a dossier of official correspondence pertaining to his request for an exit visa. Kosinski claimed that this was how he himself managed to leave Poland in 1957, though some people doubt the authenticity of his account.

Episodes from other novels describe the autobiographical protagonist's survival as a new immigrant living in a tough New York neighborhood (*Steps*, 1968, a National Book Award winner) and his rise to international acclaim as a writer and member of a fashionable "jet set" of worldwide travelers. A childhood friend of FILM DIRECTOR Roman PO-LANSKI, Kosinski was scheduled to be a guest in the house of Polanski's actress wife, Sharon Tate, on the night Charles Manson and his followers murdered her and her companions. Kosinski was spared because he had to remain in New York to wait for luggage lost on the first leg of his flight from Paris to California. This episode is also recounted in his fiction, as is his marriage to Mary Hayward Weir, the widow of the founder of one of the nation's largest steel companies. A prominent literary figure, Kosinski served as president of the PEN American Center, a writers' organization.

In addition to describing life in communist Poland, Kosinski also satirized American politics. The novel BEING THERE (1970), for example, concerns a mentally deficient man named Chance who knows about the world only from television and from his work as a gardener. Through a chain of accidents and misunderstandings, Chance becomes attached to a wealthy and politically powerful family and gains enormous political influence. The media and members of the political inner circle come to regard him as a man of great wisdom, able to communicate effectively to the nation through what they believe to be parables, but which are in fact Chance's literal descriptions of gardening. Kosinski won an Academy Award for the 1979 screenplay of *Being There*, which starred Peter SELLERS. The release of the movie coincided with the presidential campaign of Ronald REAGAN, to whom many viewers found parallels with Chance, whether or not these comparisons were intended. Kosinski published two books pseudonymously under the pen name Joseph Novack. *The Future Is Ours, Comrade* (1960) is a socio-psychological analysis of a totalitarian state. *No Third Path* (1962) also addresses totalitarianism. Kosinski also acted, appearing as Soviet Communist Party chief Grigory Zinoviev in Warren Beatty's highly praised film REDS (1981), which told the story of the radical American journalist John Reed, feminist Louise Bryant and their involvement in the early days of the Russian Revolution.

For additional reading, see Tucker's *Literary Exile in the Twentieth Century*.

Kremlin Letter, The A 1966 POLITICAL NOVEL by Noel Behn and a 1970 POLITICAL FILM starring George Sanders, Max von Sydow, Bibi Andersson and Orson Welles and directed by John Huston. The novel appeared two years after China exploded its first atomic bomb, at the beginning of Mao Zedong's Cultural Revolution, when both the United States and the Soviet Union had increasingly strained relations with the Asian nation. The movie was filmed at the beginning of the U.S.–Soviet détente, during the final stages of the Cultural Revolution but before the thawing in the Sino-U.S. relationship. The action centers on a diplomatic proposal from the United States to the U.S.S.R. that the two "superpowers" cooperate in the annihilation of China.

Kubrick, Stanley A FILM DIRECTOR. Born in the Bronx, New York, in 1928, Kubrick entered adulthood just as the Cold War was beginning. Throughout the Cold War, he explored a range of military and political issues in powerful and imaginative ways. After graduating from high school, Kubrick worked for four years as a photographer for *Look* magazine; his first film was a short based on a photostudy about a boxer he had made for *Look*. RKO Radio Pictures released the film in 1952 in its This is America series. His first feature film was *Fear and Desire* (1953), an independently produced story about a group of soldiers on patrol. *Paths of Glory* (1957) depicts the execution of three sympathetic French privates during World War I. The film's representation of the abuses of power by high-ranking Allied officials was one of the few highly critical film treatments during the Eisenhower years of the military institution of a friendly country.

As director of Kirk Douglas's production of SPARTACUS (1960), Kubrick helped to end the film industry's practice of BLACKLISTING directors, producers, SCREENWRITERS and FILM ACTORS AND ACTRESSES accused of having pro-communist sentiments. Douglas based the film on a book by former communist Howard FAST, who had written it while in jail for refusing to cooperate with the HOUSE COMMITTEE ON UN-AMERICAN ACTIVITIES (HUAC). Moreover, Douglas publicly credited the screenplay to blacklisted writer Dalton TRUMBO, a member of the HOLLYWOOD TEN who had also served a prison sentence for refusing to testify before HUAC.

Trumbo's credits for *Spartacus* and EXODUS (1960) were the first instances since the late 1940s when the Hollywood blacklist was blatantly, even defiantly ignored by a film production. When president-elect John Kennedy and his brother Robert crossed American Legion picket lines to see *Spartacus,* they further signaled that right-wing censoring groups could no longer impose their will on Hollywood. In 1962, Kubrick again became involved in controversy when he directed the film adaptation of Vladimir NABOKOV's *Lolita* (1958), about a middle-aged man who falls in love with a teenaged girl (preteen in the book), a "nymphet." That film stars Peter SELLERS, James Mason, Sue Lyon and Shelley Winters.

In the early 1960s, Kubrick conducted extensive research into the nuclear arms race, a political development that troubled him deeply. His studies led him to RED ALERT (1958), a novel about nuclear confrontation that became the inspiration for the film satire DR. STRANGELOVE (1964), one of the funniest yet most insightful and thought-provoking treatments of nuclear brinkmanship and the men who practice it. The story centers on the decision of an insane U.S. Air Force general to launch a surprise nuclear attack against the Soviet Union. The officer believes that once he has initiated the attack, the United States will have no option but to continue into full-scale war, since to do nothing would invite disaster. What he doesn't know is that the Soviets have a "Doomsday Machine" that will destroy the entire world in the event of an attack. Kubrick decided to make the film "because it's the only social problem where there's absolutely no chance for people to learn anything from experience." In *Dr. Strangelove,* sex lies at the core of the Cold War—not ideology, economic philosophy or national security—as the world's leaders subconsciously create a postnuclear scenario that fulfills their greatest sexual fantasies—underground bomb shelters populated with far more women than men. Throughout the film, the hovering threat of nuclear armageddon acts like an aphrodisiac upon these powerful men, whose sexual appetites become accentuated and deformed because of their strange love for the hydrogen bomb and the enormous power and destructive capability it represents. Kubrick's comic treatment of such men dealing with a nuclear crisis represents one of the best examples of BLACK HUMOR to emerge from the Cold War. In *Dr. Strangelove,* Kubrick again worked with Sellers, who starred in three roles.

2001: A Space Odyssey (1968), made while the United States was approaching its goal of putting a person on the moon, celebrates Cold War–driven space-age technology. It suggests that the human race might be on the verge of a gigantic leap in consciousness akin to that it experienced when a *homo sapiens* first employed technology by using an animal bone as a weapon. Kubrick captures thousands of years of evolution, from prehistoric days to the near future, with a single match cut in which the primitive club, spinning

through the air, suddenly becomes a space station twirling through space. The film shows the influence of psychedelic drugs popular during the late 1960s, as well as the emerging interest in metaphysical solutions to human problems. By contrast, Kubrick's much darker *A Clockwork Orange* (1971), based on the novel by Anthony Burgess, presents a surreal, brutal depiction of urban violence and the politicians and behavioral scientists who try to control it. Though the film does not directly deal with the Cold War, it reflects contemporary distrust of the government and expresses the common Cold War sentiment that civilization was falling apart. In 1987 Kubrick directed FULL METAL JACKET, a VIETNAM WAR FILM that depicts the deliberate dehumanizing process that soldiers underwent before and during combat. Its vision, too, is extremely bleak.

For additional reading, see *Dictionary of Literary Biography* (vol. 26, *Screenwriters*); Kagan's *Cinema of Stanley Kubrick.*

Kundera, Milan A Czech NOVELIST. Born in 1929 in Czechoslovakia, Kundera joined the Czech Communist Party after World War II but was expelled from it in 1948 when the U.S.S.R. incorporated that country into its sphere of influence. He taught at the Prague Institute of Advanced Cinematographic Studies from 1958 to 1968 but was fired after the Soviet invasion in 1968 because of his activities during the preceding period of liberalization under Alexander Dubcek, whom the Soviets deposed. The new regime banned Kundera's work in 1971, and copies of his first novel, *The Joke* (1968), and story collection, *Laughable Loves* (1968; in English, 1978), were removed from Czech libraries. In 1975 Kundera accepted an offer to teach in France, where he remained throughout the Cold War. The Czech government stripped him of citizenship in 1979.

Kundera became best known in the United States for *The Joke* and *The Unbearable Lightness of Being* (1982). Set in his homeland, these books depict the many levels of absurdity that emanate from living in a restrictive, highly bureaucratic society. *The Joke* describes the tragic fate of a man whose playful comment on a postcard leads to his undoing at the hands of literal-minded bureaucrats. In *The Unbearable Lightness of Being,* the Soviet invasion of Czechoslovakia functions as a background that permeates all aspects of personal life. Other novels relevant to the Cold War include *The Book of Laughter and Forgetting* (1978), which depicts the power of the bureaucracy to erase all sense of history and cultural identity, and *The Farewell Party* (1976), a SATIRE in which Kundera contrasts elegant prose with the ponderous and oppressive language of government. Throughout his career, Kundera has employed a graceful, free-flowing literary style to protest the linguistic and political restrictions of a repressive government and the conformity of politically prescribed social realism.

For additional reading, see Tucker's *Literary Exile in the Twentieth Century.*

Ladybug, Ladybug A 1963 British-made FILM DRAMA directed by Frank and Eleanor Perry. Inspired by the 1962 Cuban Missile Crisis, the story explores the emotional turmoil suffered by a group of schoolchildren who are sent home from school in anticipation of a nuclear attack that ultimately does not come. One boy must deal with his senile grandmother as he tries to prepare for the attack. A brother and sister are taken downstairs by their mother, who leads them in prayer. The little boy then asks if God made the bomb. Another girl dies after taking refuge in an abandoned refrigerator because her friends will not admit her into their fallout shelter, for fear that an extra person will mean insufficient food, air and water for everyone. The children thus exhibit a range of responses, from apathy and disbelief, to greed and jealousy, to religious fervor, to heroism. (See also APOCALYPTIC FILMS.)

For additional reading, see Shaheen's *Nuclear War Films*.

language The Cold War influenced the language by introducing many new terms into it. The term *Cold War*, itself, emerged to describe the hostile relationship between the United States and the U.S.S.R., who largely avoided direct military confrontation. Bernard Baruch introduced the term in 1947, when he stated, "Let us not be deceived. We are today in the midst of a cold war. Our enemies are to be found abroad and at home." Former (and future) British prime minister Winston Churchill introduced the earliest, most powerful and most enduring Cold War image in 1946, when he warned of an IRON CURTAIN descending on Europe

to separate the Soviet-dominated countries from the rest of the continent. The region "behind the Iron Curtain" had been known as *Central Europe* prior to World War II, but during the Cold War, the State Department began calling it EASTERN EUROPE to emphasize the demarcation between the Western allies and the Soviet Union, part of which occupied the easternmost portion of the European continent. In 1994, the State Department officially readopted the designation Central Europe.

In contrast to the "Iron Curtain" countries of "Eastern Europe" was the FREE WORLD, which consisted of the United States and its allies, notably the democracies in Canada, Australia, Great Britain and "Western Europe." Thus, the United States considered itself the leader of the *free world*—any countries that did not have communist or socialist governments. The combined impact of this terminology was to sustain an impression that people living under *communist domination* were essentially imprisoned in their own homelands, while those in the Western democracies were free. The Berlin Wall, erected by the Soviets and East Germans (German Democratic Republic) in 1961, literally became a concrete manifestation of these metaphors.

The development of nuclear weaponry and the threat of nuclear war gave rise to new industries. At the end of his presidency, Dwight Eisenhower warned of the power of the emerging *military-industrial complex* to exert an undue force on American politics. The presence of nuclear weapons also spawned new terminology, especially slang. Thus to deploy a nuclear strike became the verb *to nuke*, as in "Nuke them back to the Stone Age," a suggestion made by General Curtis LeMay during the Vietnam War. The general was sometimes known among his more irreverent critics as "Nuke" LeMay. When microwave ovens allowed consumers to heat food through a form of radiation, the process also employed the verb *to nuke:* "Let's nuke a frozen dinner." Among drug users, the term ATOM BOMB was slang for a potent mixture of heroin and marijuana, and ATOMIC BOMB was the name of a cinnamon-based candy that burned the mouth. Somebody who lost emotional control and became enraged might be said to have *gone ballistic,* a reference to the ballistic missiles deployed by the superpowers in the Cold War.

As Carol Cohn points out in *"Slick 'Ems, Glick 'Ems, Christmas Trees, and Cookie Cutters: Nuclear Language and How We Learned to Pat the Bomb,"* the specialized language employed by nuclear planners did not contain a word for peace. The closest approximation was "a state of *permanent pre-hostility.*" Civilian casualties were referred to as *collateral damage,* since planning strategies centered on the protection of missiles and other weapons systems, not people. This focus was intended to ensure that the United States would retain the capacity to retaliate against a *first strike,* (the first use of a nuclear weapon) and thus maintain a *credible deterrent* (a believable reason *not* to attack). The term collateral damage was actually used in the reporting of the 1991 Gulf War and thus entered the mainstream discourse.

The *nuclear stalemate* that persisted through much of the Cold War created a *balance of power* that afforded some degree of stability and arguably deterred a major war among the superpowers. The stalemate was predicated on a policy of Mutually Assured Destruction, more commonly known by its acronym *MAD,* which inadvertently alluded to the underlying insanity of a policy based on mutual annihilation. (Similarly, *CREEP,* the acronym for the 1972 Committee to Re-Elect the President, seemed to allude inadvertently to President Nixon, whose reelection campaign was punctuated by White House–orchestrated "dirty tricks" and the Watergate scandal.)

The RED SCARE also gave rise to new terminology. Those who sympathized with *commies* or *reds* but were not party members might be called *pinkos* or *fellow travelers.* Liberal intellectuals who entertained left-wing ideas from the comfort of their middle-class homes were *parlor pinks* in the 1940s and 1950s. In the more explosive late 1960s and early 1970s, they were considered to partake of *radical chic,* a term Tom Wolfe coined for Leonard and Felicia Bernstein and their guests at a party they gave for the Black Panthers.

Hard-liners warned of *creeping communism,* an image treated metaphorically in the science fiction film THE BLOB (1950). They often accused *liberal dupes* of being *soft* on communism. Such language implied that those who remained *firm* in their *hard* opposition to communism possessed a sexual potency that was not shared by cerebral *eggheads* and feminine pinkos and *do-gooders,* some of whom may have been the victims of MOMISM—overly nurturing mothers who raised weak and sometimes homosexual sons.

The Red Score produced other linguistic innovations. President Truman used the term RED HERRING to denounce Whittaker Chambers's accusations before the HOUSE COMMITTEE ON UN-AMERICAN ACTIVITIES (HUAC) that State Depart-

ment employee Alger Hiss had been a communist. Truman used the term to mean that the charges were a deliberately conceived distraction and sleight-of-hand intended to produce an erroneous impression. During the HUAC investigations into domestic communist activity, people who had opposed Hitler and Franco in the 1930s Spanish Civil War, and had supported the legally elected communist-backed government instead, were sometimes called *prematurely antifascist.*

Because Congress never officially issued declarations of war, the Korean War was known as a *police action* and the Vietnam War was an *intervention,* while the invasion of Cambodia was an *incursion.* When the Johnson administration was caught lying about the progress of the war, it began to suffer from a *credibility gap* that widened along the lines of the *generation gap,* since young people were more likely to question authority and to oppose the war than were their elders (with significant exceptions). Both terms point back to the *missile gap* of the late 1950s, when some politicians, including then-Senator John Kennedy, maintained that the Soviets possessed missile superiority over the United States. Shortly after Kennedy was elected president, the CIA deployed satellites that were better able to assess Soviet missile capacity, and the missile gap proved not to exist. In fact, the satellites demonstrated that the United States had significant missile superiority. Illegal U.S.-sponsored *covert actions* throughout the Cold War also created credibility gaps, though these became somewhat institutionalized during the 1980s Iran-contra affair, when Colonel Oliver North spoke openly of the policy of *plausible deniability* that accompanied illegal government activities. North described the standard operating procedure of creating a plausible cover story so the government could deny wrongdoing. In fact, as far back as 1948 the National Security Council had authorized the CIA to conduct covert operations with the proviso that the operations remain secret and that the government be able to plausibly deny their existence. Members of the Reagan administration also spoke of using lies—*misinformation* and *disinformation*—to confuse domestic and foreign enemies. All administrations worked to create a positive *spin* on any political development, though Michael Deaver and other members of the Reagan White House elevated the practice to an art and became known as *spin doctors.*

Attempts by both the United States and Soviet Union to revise versions of historical events in order to support current policies were known as *revisionist history.* George ORWELL's influential novel NINETEEN EIGHTY-FOUR (1949) describes how those in authority manipulate both history and language as a means of maintaining political power. Though written as an attack on Stalinism, the book later also became identified with abuses by the U.S. government. Thus *Big Brother* became a synonym for big, intrusive government, and *doublespeak* became a synonym for lies.

For additional reading, see Hilgartner et al.'s *Nukespeak;* Lutz's *Doublespeak;* Cohn's *"Slick 'Ems, Glick 'Ems, Christmas Trees and Cookie Cutters: Nuclear Language and How We Learned to Pat the Bomb."*

Lardner, Ring, Jr. A SCREENWRITER and NOVELIST and a member of the HOLLYWOOD TEN. Born in 1915, the son of humorist and journalist Ring Lardner, Ring Lardner Jr. attended Princeton University and worked briefly for the *New York Daily Mirror* before going to Hollywood and signing a contract with David O. Selznick. There he met Budd SCHULBERG with whom he worked on some minor projects and collaborated on two unfilmed screenplays. They also made a small contribution to *A Star Is Born* in 1937. That year Lardner married Silvia Schulman, with whom he had two children. He also began attending Marxist study groups with Schulberg and his wife, Virginia. In 1938 Lardner joined the Warner Brothers studio, where he worked on an adaptation of a story by Dalton TRUMBO for *The Kid from Kokomo* (1939). Lardner left Warner Brothers shortly afterward. His first major screen contribution came in 1942 when, with Michael Kanin, he wrote *Woman of the Year,* which starred Spencer Tracy and Katharine Hepburn and earned an Academy Award for the two writers, as well as a major salary increase. In 1944 they wrote *The Cross of Lorraine,* about the defeat of the French Army and the commitment of some captured French soldiers to continue the fight against fascism. *Tomorrow the World* (1944), which Lardner wrote with Leopold Atlas, also dealt with defeating Nazism, this time in the form of a German teenager indoctrinated with Nazi beliefs who comes to the United States after his parents have been killed in a concentration camp. That year Lardner also worked on the scripts for *Laura* (1944) and Fritz Lang's *Cloak and Dagger* (1946). In 1945 Lardner divorced; in 1946 he married film actress Frances Chaney, with whom he had a son.

In 1947 Lardner was among those summoned to testify before the HOUSE COMMITTEE ON UN-AMERICAN ACTIVITIES (HUAC), which was conducting politically charged hearings about alleged communist influences upon Hollywood films. When committee chairman J. Parnell Thomas asked him to testify about his political activities, Lardner refused. Like the other members of the Hollywood Ten, he cited his First Amendment constitutional protection of freedom of speech. He added famously, "I could answer the way you want, Mr. Chairman, but I'd hate myself in the morning." Subsequently, Lardner served nine months of a one-year sentence for contempt of Congress in 1950–51.

After his release from federal prison in Danbury, Connecticut, Lardner became a subject of BLACKLISTING and was unable to write screenplays under his own name. While imprisoned he began a novel, *The Ecstacy of Owen Muir* (1954), which he had to publish abroad. The book concerns the pressures to conform in American culture and touches on the blacklist. Afterward Lardner wrote or contributed pseudonymously to several films and television scripts. In 1965 he received screen credit, along with Terry Southern, for the script of *The Cincinnati Kid,* his first credit under his own name since Trumbo broke the blacklist in 1960. In 1970 Lardner won an Academy Award and the Writers Guild Award for his screenplay of the Korean War Film M*A*S*H. In 1988 he appeared in *My Name Is Bertolt Brecht–Exile in U.S.A.* (Brecht had been the eleventh of the unfriendly witnesses called before HUAC in 1947.)

For additional reading, see *Dictionary of Literary Biography* (vol. 26, *Screenwriters*). For a partial transcript of his testimony before HUAC, see Bentley's THIRTY YEARS OF TREASON.

Last Day, The A 1959 APOCALYPTIC NOVEL by Helen Clarkson. According to Paul Brians in *The Nightmare Considered, The Last Day* is the best-researched postapocalyptic novel prior to Whitley Strieber and James Kunetka's best-selling *Warday* in 1984. Clarkson wrote the novel in reaction to Nevil Shute's best-selling ON THE BEACH (1957). It appeared during one of the most bellicose moments in the Cold War, when a global nuclear exchange seemed not only possible but also imminent. Like Judith Merril's SHADOW ON THE HEARTH (1950) and Philip Wylie's TOMORROW! (1954), *The Last Day* presents a before-and-after view of a community struck by a nuclear attack. However, unlike Wylie, Clarkson presents a feminine, if not feminist, perspective on events. Clarkson makes the well-being of children her foremost concern and rejects MOMISM, Wylie's belief that over-nurturing mothers were responsible for the country's problems. Clarkson claims that Americans require more nurturing love, not less. The protagonist takes exception to a *Life* Magazine editorial that declares that "the only people who wanted to end nuclear testing were 'scared mothers, fuzzy liberals and weary taxpayers.' In other words: mothers are a lunatic fringe, a minority group." Clarkson also points out that women were the most vocal protestors of the nuclear accident in which radioactive fallout from a Pacific test contaminated a Japanese fishing boat in 1954.

Unlike most apocalyptic novels, *The Last Day* provides a detailed political analysis of the events leading up to the war. The secretary of state is based on John Foster Dulles, Eisenhower's secretary of state who advocated a "liberation policy" to "free" EASTERN EUROPE and who died the year of the book's release. Another character is a scientist who, like J. Robert Oppenheimer, loses his security clearance. He lives next door to the protagonist and is the target of a security investigation because he has quit his job rather than develop nuclear weapons.

For additional reading, see Ansfield's *The Nightmare Considered.*

Last Plane Out, The A SPY FILM starring Jan-Michael Vincent, Lloyd Batista and Julie Carmen and directed by David Nelson. The story is set in the final days of the Somoza government in Nicaragua. It involves intrigue between the supporters of Nicaraguan dictator Anastasio Somoza and the revolutionaries who went on to overthrow the dictator and establish a socialist government.

Last Woman on Earth, The A 1960 FILM DRAMA starring Antony Carbone and Betsy Jones-Moreland and directed by Roger Corman. The story centers on a love triangle in which two men compete for the only woman to survive a nuclear war. The trio has survived because they had been deep-sea diving with special aqualungs. (See also APOCALYPTIC FILMS.)

"Laugh-In" A TELEVISION comedy variety show that ran on NBC from 1968 to 1973. Hosted by Dan Rowan and Dick Martin, the show featured a montage of skits, one-liners, comic poems, monologues, SATIRE, DANCE, body painting, blackouts and a "joke wall" that closed the show. Regular performers included Ruth Buzzi, Judy Carne, Goldie Hawn, Arte Johnson, Henry Gibson, Jo Anne Worley, Lily Tomlin and Richard Dawson. Guest stars included Tiny Tim, a long-haired man who sang "Tiptoe through the Tulips" in a falsetto voice and President Nixon, who mispronounced the stock "Laugh-In" phrase, "Sock it to me." Despite its obvious vaudeville roots, the show's fast pace, lack of traditional structure and topical references reflected the quick tempo and iconoclastic developments of U.S. political and social culture of the Vietnam War era. (See also TELEVISION SATIRE.)

Laurence, William L. A JOURNALIST and NONFICTION WRITER. Laurence, winner of two Pulitzer Prizes, was the science editor for the *New York Times*. The only journalist permitted to cover the entire atomic bomb project, he wrote *Dawn over Zero* (1946) about the atomic bomb, *Hell Bomb* (1951) about the hydrogen bomb, and *Men and Atoms: The Discovery; The Uses, and The Future of Atomic Energy* (1959). He also published *Suicide or Survival: a Summons to Old and Young to Build a United, Peaceful World* (1948) and *Reminiscences of William L. Laurence* (1972). Laurence appeared in PATTERN FOR SURVIVAL, a 1950 instruction film designed to ease fears about atomic warfare and advise viewers about how to prepare for an atomic attack.

Lawson, John Howard An American SCREENWRITER, playwright, literary theorist and communist social critic who is best known as a member of the HOLLYWOOD TEN. Born in New York in 1894, Lawson served in the American armed services during World War I. Afterward he wrote several experimental plays that drew heavily upon German expressionism before he began his career as a Hollywood screenwriter. Lawson worked on over 20 film scripts and wrote the screenplay for Cecil B. DEMILLE's first sound film, *Dynamite* (1929). Lawson also wrote for the THEATER and had four plays successfully produced. These include *Roger Bloomer* (1923), the first American-written expressionist play. Lawson was the founding president of the Screenwriters Guild.

From the late 1920s onward, Lawson's left-wing political orientation became increasingly prominent in his plays. *Gentlewoman* (1934) attacks the decadent excesses in America, and *Marching Song* (1937) casts the capitalist owners in a company town as unequivocal villains while the proletariat workers are equally unequivocal heroes. On the other hand, his film scripts from the same period were far less ideologically driven, as fuller character development replaced easy political stereotypes. Films from this period include *Babes in Arms* (1939), *Action in the North Atlantic* (1943), *The Jolson Story* (uncredited, 1946) and *Smash-Up: The Story of a Woman* (1947).

In 1946 Lawson was among those who viciously attacked future Hollywood Ten member Albert MALTZ for publishing an article in *New Masses* calling for greater artistic freedom for communist writers. Though Maltz capitulated and renounced the article, the savagery of the attack, and the rejection of artistic freedom drove others from the party and in some cases, served as justification for their informing on party members before the HOUSE COMMITTEE ON UNAMERICAN ACTIVITIES (HUAC). In 1947 Lawson appeared before HUAC as one of 10 so-called unfriendly witnesses in its investigation of communist influences within the motion picture

industry. Lawson refused to comply with the committee's interrogation, insisting instead on his constitutional right to freedom of expression. Immediately after his appearance before HUAC, Lawson was tried for violation of the 1940 Smith Act, which made it illegal for members of organizations to advocate the overthrow of the U.S. government by force or violence. He was found guilty of contempt of court and served a year in federal prison between 1947 and 1948. While in prison he wrote a historical study, *The Hidden Heritage: A Rediscovery of the Idea and Forces that Link the Thought of our Time with the Culture of the Past* (1950). Lawson suffered from BLACKLISTING and was unable to work in Hollywood after his release from jail. Therefore, like Dalton TRUMBO, another member of the Ten, he moved to Mexico and wrote screenplays there under assumed names for a fraction of his earlier salary. His most significant work from that period was the screenplay for the British-made *Cry, the Beloved Country* (1952), which was based on Alan Paton's 1948 novel about apartheid in South Africa. Between 1961 and 1963 Lawson spent time in the U.S.S.R. and East Germany, where a revision of his play *Parlor Magic* (1939) was produced. His play about life in the black ghetto, *Thunder Morning,* was never produced.

Lawson had been a member of and theorist for the Communist Party, and anti-capitalist sentiments did figure strongly in his plays. But the charge that he sought to promote the Soviet Communist Party line through his film scripts does not hold up well. The only "overt act" mentioned in his trial was a pamphlet he had written, *Grasp the Weapon of Culture,* which asserts that cultural activity is an important aspect of the Communist Party's work. An analysis of his screenplays by Dorothy Jones revealed considerable independence from the party line dating from the 1939 nonaggression pact between Hitler and Stalin. Moreover, Lawson did not believe that movie dialogue was a suitable medium for achieving political goals. Responding to a *New York Times* article claiming that Lawson "used to give his colleagues tips on how to get the Party viewpoint across in his dialogue," Ring LARDNER Jr., another of the Hollywood Ten, replied in a letter to the editor, "Actually he regarded anything of that sort as a puerile approach to the politicization of screenwriting." Lardner, writing after Lawson's death, added that Lawson believed that effective, meaningful revolutionary films required both the interdependence of form and content and the profound exploration of human character, especially within groups of people whose characters were typically not well developed in the movies e.g., workers and minorities.

Lawson, who had been attracted to expressionism since the beginning of his career, also rejected the Soviet insistence on socialist realism. In an interview with Victor Navasky, he stated, "I thought it was idiotic to talk about realism, for instance in the Soviet Union, where they make a whole issue of socialist realism yet the art they admire is the Russian ballet, which is not realistic at all and which is of an aristocratic origin, obviously." Lawson died in 1977. (See also EXILED WRITERS [from the United States].)

For additional reading, see Tucker's *Literary Exile in the Twentieth Century;* Navasky's *Naming Names;* Jones's "Communism and the Movies: A Study of Film Content"; *Diction-*

ary of Literary Biography (vol. 26, *Screenwriters*). For a partial transcript of Lawson's testimony before HUAC, see Bentley's THIRTY YEARS OF TREASON.

Lear, Norman A television producer who introduced socially relevant and controversial TELEVISION SITUATION COMEDIES to American television. His first big hit was the long-running ALL IN THE FAMILY (CBS, 1971–91), which starred Carroll O'Connor as Archie Bunker, a working-class New Yorker with a range of ethnic and racial prejudices and a conservative political viewpoint. He was surrounded at home, however, by his liberal daughter and son-in-law and by neighbors of different ethnicities. (In 1979 the show changed its title to "Archie Bunker's Place" and its setting to a bar.) Lear-produced spin-offs from "All in the Family" included "Maude" (CBS, 1972–78), which starred Bea Arthur as Archie's liberal and liberated female in-law, and "The Jeffersons" (CBS, 1975–85), which portrayed Archie's black neighbors after they had become rich and moved to the Upper East Side. Lear followed "All in the Family" with another hit, "Sanford and Son" (NBC, 1972–77), about an elderly, black junk dealer (Redd Foxx) and his son (Demond Wilson) living in the deteriorated Watts section of Los Angeles. Lear also produced the short-lived "A.K.A. Pablo" (ABC, 1984), about a struggling Mexican-American comedian; "The Baxters" (Syndicated, 1979–80), in which the studio audience determined how the middle-class characters would handle such situations as whether to commit a parent to a nursing home or how to react to the revelation that their son's teacher is homosexual; a satirical soap opera, "Mary Hartman, Mary Hartman" (Syndicated 1976–78). "Fernwood 2-Night" (Syndicated, 1977–78), a spin-off of "Mary Hartman, Mary Hartman" that spoofed late-night talk shows; "Good Times" (CBS, 1974–79), a spin-off from "Maude" centering on Maude's black maid, Florida Evans (Esther Rolle), and her family; "Hanging In" (CBS, 1979), a short-lived spin-off from "Maude" centering on university politics; "Hot L Baltimore" (ABC, 1975), a controversial comedy that employed racy dialogue and considerable sexual innuendo, featuring characters living in a run-down Baltimore hotel, among them a prostitute and a homosexual couple; "The Nancy Walker Show" (ABC, 1976), about the wife of a navy officer who must suddenly deal with her husband's retirement; "Palmerstown, U.S.A." (CBS, 1980–81), a drama coproduced with Alex Haley about a black and white pair of nine-year-old friends growing up in a small Southern town during the Depression; "A Year at the Top" (CBS, 1977), a short-lived comedy about two would-be rock stars who entertain an offer from the Devil; and "Sunday Dinner" (CBS, 1991), a semi-autobiographical show about a man in his mid-fifties who marries a 30-year-old environmental activist attorney.

Lear won Emmy awards for "All in the Family" for three consecutive years, 1971 to 1973. A major force in Cold War–era network television, Lear brought to the medium a willingness to experiment in both form and content, as well as a proclivity for addressing social concerns, race, feminism, homosexuality, politics and other controversial subjects from which American television notoriously shied away. "Maude" and "All in the Family," in particular, presented the responses of working and professional-class men and women to both domestic politics and foreign policy.

"Leave It to Beaver" A TELEVISION SITUATION COMEDY that ran on CBS from 1957 to 1958 and on ABC from 1959 to 1963. Like FATHER KNOWS BEST (CBS/NBC/ABC, 1957–63), "Leave It to Beaver" was one of several situation comedies from the late 1950s and early 1960s that presented an idealized view of the American family. Shown mostly from the point of view of the Beaver (Larry Mathers), a seven-year-old, it presented American life as a series of minor trials and challenges, all of which were learning experiences. Beaver's parents, Ward and June Cleaver (Hugh Beaumont and Barbara Billingsley), provided guidance and insisted that their children always strive to do the right thing. As with "Father Knows Best," the father was a caring, if somewhat distant authoritarian figure, but the mother was also intelligent, competent and loving. Made during the height of Cold War tensions (the show's run coincided with the Berlin and Cuban Missile crises), "Leave It to Beaver" ignored the existence of Cold War threats or any childhood anxieties that might have emanated from them.

le Carré, John (pseudonym for David Cornwall) A British NOVELIST. One of the foremost authors of Cold War SPY NOVELS, le Carré was born in 1931 in Somerset, England. He served in the Army Intelligence Corps from 1949 to 1950 and graduated from Oxford University in 1956, earning first honors in modern languages with a specialty in German. Afterward he tutored at prestigious Eton College from 1956 to 1958. Le Carré served in Britain's Foreign Office from 1959 to 1964, and from 1964 to 1966 he was its consul in Hamburg, Germany. During this time he was also a member of MI6, Britain's military intelligence agency. His experiences thus provided the necessary background for his fiction, which is highly detailed and realistic. In fact, le Carré wrote his first novels while still working for MI6. Le Carré maintains that the requirements of bureaucratic writing did much to create the sparse, direct literary style characteristic of his earlier novels. A Foreign Office prohibition against publishing under his real name led Cornwall to adopt his pseudonym.

As LynnDianne Beene points out in *John le Carré*, the novelist's fiction centers on acts of betrayal: "Betrayal of and by security institutions, bureaucracies, ideologies, or country is expected but seldom excusable; betrayal of individuals or self is unforgivable. Yet both are understandable and predictable, and both guarantee wrenching loneliness." She adds, "In each of his novels, le Carré warns that, as countries and their agents cautiously gauge their alliances, people must warily confront relationships. Like spies, all people fear insincerity, conspiracy, and betrayal yet must embrace love if they are to survive. Individuals may espouse moral attitudes to which they 'subscribe perhaps intellectually, but not emotionally.' These attitudes, however, concurrently alienate by minimizing the chance of emotional commitments and, ironically, protect by suggesting rationales for inexplicable betrayals." Thus much of le Carré's fiction concerns the moral dilemmas and human needs experienced by agents of unfeeling bureaucracies and government institutions.

Le Carré's first novel, *Call for the Dead* (1961; U.S. edition, 1962), introduces George Smiley, a spymaster who appears prominently within several of his books. Unlike the virile, dashing and suave James BOND, hero of Ian Fleming's spy novels, Smiley is, in the words of his ex-wife, "breathtakingly ordinary." Smiley had been a student of literature before becoming a spy. His scholastic skills of observation and rigorous analysis are well-suited for intelligence work, but the humanistic commitment to truth, beauty and goodness expressed in the literature he studies are a positive hindrance. The contrast in values between the world of literature and that of espionage provides a moral tension that animates the Smiley novels. *Call for the Dead* requires Smiley to investigate charges of treason against a clerk in his agency, the Circus. After Smiley clears him of wrongdoing, the clerk is found dead, and Smiley is ordered to cover up the death by alleging suicide. Smiley's superior then betrays Smiley in order to forestall revelations of incompetence within the Circus. Eventually, Smiley tracks down the man responsible for the murder, an agent named Frey whom Smiley had once recruited but who has since gone over to the East Germans for ideological reasons. Though Smiley ultimately "eliminates" Frey, the Circus's corrupt internal politics contrast with Frey's less selfish motivations, and the book concludes on a morally ambiguous note. In *A Murder of Quality* (1962; U.S. edition, 1963), le Carré's second novel, Smiley solves a murder, but this book does not have Cold War significance.

THE SPY WHO CAME IN FROM THE COLD (1963; U.S. edition, 1964), le Carré's first major success, tells the story of Alec Lemas, a British agent who poses as a defector in order to entrap Mundt, a former Nazi and the current head of East German intelligence. Unknown to Lemas, however, Mundt is actually a British double agent. The Circus uses Lemas's East German girlfriend to discredit Lemas; it thereby foils the efforts of Mundt's second-in-command, a Jew, who had been trying to prove Mundt's treasonous alliance with the British. The story underscores the cynicism of the Cold War intelligence agencies for whom the ends justify any means, and Lemas finally chooses death with the woman he loves over life without her in such a cruel world. Shortly before their deaths, he likens the superpowers to two large trucks speeding along a highway and converging indifferently to crush a car filled with innocents trapped between them. This image serves as metaphor for the entire story. THE LOOKING GLASS WAR (1965) further depicts the cynical and self-serving nature of the intelligence community as interoffice politics prompts a British spymaster to send ill-prepared, under-equipped agents to their deaths in his effort to show up a rival agency. A SMALL TOWN IN GERMANY (1968), le Carré's bleakest Cold War novel, shows British officials working in cooperation with a powerful former Nazi who has become the chancellor of West Germany. The British diplomats willingly sacrifice any moral qualms in order to secure Britain's entry into the Common Market.

Collected as a trilogy in 1982, THE QUEST FOR KARLA consists of *Tinker, Tailor, Soldier, Spy* (1974), *The Honourable Schoolboy* (1977) and *Smiley's People* (1980). In the trilogy Smiley, now an old man, eliminates double agents who

have infiltrated the Circus and finally forces the Soviet spymaster Karla, Smiley's opposite, to defect to the West. His success, however, comes at a high moral cost, and the trilogy reiterates le Carré's dark view of the espionage profession. THE RUSSIA HOUSE (1989) is set during the waning days of the Soviet Union and centers on efforts by Western agents to ascertain the authenticity of claims by a Soviet scientist that the Soviet military-industrial complex is hopelessly corrupt, inept and grossly mismanaged. The claim threatens the Western agents because it suggests that the entire Cold War has been a farce, a possibility that undermines the necessity for their work.

Several of le Carré's novels have been made into SPY FILMS, including *The Spy Who Came in From the Cold* (1965), *Call for the Dead* (1967, under the title DEADLY AFFAIR), *The Looking Glass War* (1969), and *The Russia House* (1990). The BBC produced *Tinker, Tailor* (1979, shown in United States on PBS in 1980), *Smiley's People* (1982) and *A Perfect Spy* (1986–87). These were broadcast on public television in the United States.

For additional reading, see Beene's *John le Carré* and Cawelti and Rosenberg's *The Spy Story.*

Le Guin, Ursula A NOVELIST. Because of their futuristic settings in other galaxies, Le Guin's books are typically classified as SCIENCE FICTION NOVELS, though her influences come more from such literary figures as Tolstoy, Chekhov and Virginia Woolf. Born in 1929, Le Guin graduated from Radcliffe College in 1951 and received a master's degree from Columbia University in 1952. Her field of concentration was medieval Romance literature. Of her many novels *The Left Hand of Darkness* (1969), *The Dispossessed* (1974) and ALWAYS COMING HOME (1985) deal most directly with the Cold War. Told in the first person by the protagonist, *The Left Hand of Darkness* centers on Genly Ai, an Earthling who comes as an envoy to inform the inhabitants of the planet Gethen that they are not alone in the universe. Also known as Winter because of its extremely cold climate, Gethen has produced a civilization that has evolved to approximately the level of Earth's, with merchants, entertainers and electric cars. Most strikingly, its inhabitants are androgynous. They do not know until the act of mating whether they will assume male or female roles, and all are capable of bearing children. Anticipating the women's movement of the 1970s, the book presents a society in which all citizens are capable of child-bearing, and in which attitudes, values and social policies are deeply affected by this sexual equality. The planet has two cultures, Karhide, whose inhabitants live in harmony with nature, and Orgoreyn, which is modeled on Le Guin's view of Stalinist Russia and which features secret police, an oppressive bureaucracy and remote prison camps in the frozen wilderness. The story thus pits the feminine values of harmony and cooperation against the masculine values of dominance that are reflected both by the Stalinist police state and by the Earthly visitor to the planet, who represents American materialism and machismo as well as American innocence and optimism.

The Dispossessed presents three civilizations. Two correspond to Cold War–era capitalism and communism. The third represents an anarchist utopia. The relatively open capitalist society offers much that is elegant and beautiful but suffers from social and sexual hierarchies and from the fact that everything is owned. The anarchist society, on the other hand, has closed itself off from the wealthy capitalist world for fear of contamination and restricts individual thought. The plot centers on Shevek, a mathematician from the anarchist society who has discovered the work of a scientist who corresponds to Einstein. This work allows Shevek to complete his theory of simultaneity, which permits the construction of a device that allows instantaneous communication among all the societies. In so doing he becomes a political outcast, but the enhanced communication opens his society and brings about the possibility of cooperation among the different cultures.

In her 1972 short story, "The Word for World Is Forest" (collected in a volume by that title in 1976), Le Guin also takes up such Cold War issues as the Vietnam War, exploitation of planetary resources, and cultural domination of one group by another. "The New Atlantis" (1975) presents a grim view of the United States in the near future. In that story, American society has devolved into something akin to a Stalinist state in which intellectuals, radicals and other suspect groups are imprisoned in Rehabilitation Camps, and the FBI maintains widespread surveillance. *Always Coming Home* presents the conflict between two postnuclear societies: one matriarchal and one patriarchal.

For additional reading, see *The Dictionary of Literary Biography* (vol. 8, *Science Fiction Writers*).

Lederer, William a NOVELIST and NONFICTION WRITER. Lederer's biggest contribution to Cold War literature is the best-selling political novel THE UGLY AMERICAN (1958), which he coauthored with Eugene BURDICK. In 1965 they published a sequel, *Sarkhan*. *The Ugly American* also appeared as a 1961 play and a 1962 POLITICAL FILM starring Marlon Brando. Set in Sarkhan, a mythical Southeast Asian country similar to Vietnam, the story centers around on American ambassador whose failure to understand local history and customs undermines well-intentioned U.S. efforts to improve the local standard of living with advanced technology and improved agricultural methods. The novel criticizes the State Department bureaucrats and political hacks who fail to learn the native languages and customs, insult local leaders, inhibit the constructive work of private individuals working the villages, and allow their own egos, self-interest and career aspirations to dominate their decisions. The sequel appeared the year the United States introduced combat troops into the Vietnam War. It describes the efforts of an American businessman and a professor to prevent a communist takeover. Like *The Ugly American*, it attacks U.S. government bureaucrats for their ignorance and ineptitude and presents the more effective tactics used by the communist opposition.

Lederer also criticizes U.S. government behavior—in Vietnam more for being ineffective than for being wrong—in his NONFICTION books A NATION OF SHEEP (1961) and its sequel *Our Own Worst Enemy* (1968). Lederer attacks the U.S. government and press for misinforming the American public and concludes by offering suggestions on how to remedy U.S. foreign policy. One reviewer criticized *A Nation of Sheep* for its "faith in an exploded dogma, the assumption of the Enlightenment and of nineteenth-century liberalism that man is a perfectly rational being whose errors are

due solely to ignorance." *Our Own Worst Enemy*, published during the height of the Vietnam War, reiterates and expands upon the theses in *A Nation of Sheep*. Lederer argues that the United States is simultaneously fighting—and losing—several wars in Vietnam: a large-scale bombing war, a guerrilla war, a political war aimed at winning the loyalty of the Vietnamese people, and a moral war. This book was not as well received as the original. Like Burdick, Fletcher KNEBEL, Leon URIS and James MICHENER, Lederer was not regarded as a serious writer by the literary establishment, but he was one of relatively few authors to address the Cold War directly.

Lehrer, Tom A performer of satirical MUSIC. Born in 1928, Lehrer was a child prodigy at the piano and in mathematics. He received his bachelor's degree in mathematics from Harvard at age 18 and his master's degree the following year. He continued his graduate work at Harvard and Columbia and taught statistics and mathematics at several other universities, including the Massachusetts Institute of Technology and the University of California at Santa Cruz, where he also taught courses in musical theater. Despite his success as a performer and satirist, he considers himself foremost a teacher. During the Korean War, Lehrer spent time at the atomic test site in Los Alamos, New Mexico, while employed for the Baird-Atomic company. He was drafted into the army in 1955 and served with the National Security Agency until 1957.

Lehrer's musical career began when the Harvard Law School sponsored a quartet contest. After his group won,

Tom Lehrer, 1959. Courtesy AP/Wide World.

Lehrer began singing his own offbeat songs at smokers and dance intermissions. He first appeared before the general public in 1951 on a weekly television satire program that cartoonist Al Capp hosted in Boston. During the 1950s and early 1960s, Lehrer performed at coffeehouses and on college campuses. His first record album, which appeared in 1953, includes references to nuclear testing in "The Wild West Is Where I Want to Be": Western "scenery's attractive," but "the air is radioactive." His second album appeared in 1959 and includes "It Makes a Fellow Proud To Be a Soldier," a spoof on the U.S. Army that Lehrer introduces by remarking that he has been mustered out and is now a member of the Radioactive Reserves. Lehrer performed on national television in 1964 on the television satire THAT WAS THE WEEK THAT WAS where he sang his BLACK HUMOR songs, including a 1959 song about nuclear apocalypse, WE WILL ALL GO TOGETHER WHEN WE GO. ("When the air becomes uranious, we will all go simultaneous. We will all go together when we go.") The show aired some two years after the Cuban Missile Crisis when humanity had indeed come dangerously close to nuclear extinction. Following President Johnson's decision to send troops to the Dominican Republic in 1965 to quell a pro-communist insurrection, Lehrer performed a song parodying U.S. gunboat diplomacy, "Send the Marines." A famous anti–Cold War song on his last album, "Who's Next?" (1965), describes nuclear proliferation: "First we got the bomb, but that was good, 'cause we love peace and motherhood; Then Russia got the bomb, but that's okay, 'cause the balance of power's maintained that way . . ." Other Tom Lehrer songs are less political but equally macabre, such as "Poisoning Pigeons in the Park." Lehrer has published an illustrated collection of his songs, *Too Many Songs by Tom Lehrer with Not Enough Drawings by Ronald Searle* (1981) and issued three record albums, *Songs by Tom Lehrer* (1953), *An Evening With Tom Lehrer* (1959) and *That Was the Year that Was* (1965). Jeremy Bernstein's interview with Lehrer, "Tom Lehrer: Having Fun," appears in *The American Scholar* (Summer 1984).

For additional reading, see Gale's *Encyclopedia of American Humorists*.

Level 7 A 1959 APOCALYPTIC NOVEL by Mordecai Roshwald. Written during one of the tensest moments of the Cold War, during the second Berlin Crisis, with the United States and Soviet Union threatening nuclear war, and with fallout shelters in fashion, *Level 7* presents the diary of a man 4,400 feet below the surface of the Earth in the deepest section of an underground command post. The entries range over a five-month period in the future, presenting the events leading up to the nuclear war, the war itself and the nature of survival underground. By the time the novel begins, Mutually Assured Destruction (MAD) has enabled the Cold War to continue for so long that its causes are no longer remembered or deemed important. The warring countries are never identified because their identities are irrelevant: "Each of us wanted to rule the world, or save it (both formulas amount to the same thing now)." To make the nuclear deterrent more reliable, the technocratic society has placed nuclear policy entirely in the hands of computers, and sociopaths are deliberately placed in charge of launching an attack because only people who are detached from

their feelings and emotionally disconnected from their fellow humans could obey the command to blow up the world. These are the people who inhabit Level 7. By accident one person, X-117, has retained some degree of compassion; when the order to launch comes, he declares, "I can't kill my mother!" and refuses to initiate the strike. He is soon removed, and a nuclear war immediately breaks out. Within days, the world's population drops to 2,500 and those are all doomed, even the ones on Level 7, since the radiation has penetrated the underground shelter and is seeping down, level by level.

The final entries chronicle the slow and tortuous deaths that come, ironically, not from the bomb but from a leak in the shelter's nuclear reactor. The diarist writes, "It is strangely ironical that we, PBX Command, should be killed by a gadget making a peaceful use of atomic energy. It does not seem fair. Divine justice, I always thought, was eye for eye, tooth for tooth. It should be bomb for bomb. Instead we are being killed by a piece of faulty machinery. Not really a warrior's death." He goes on to speculate on the religious implications of this irony. "Perhaps God intended it as a sort of joke. 'You killed with bombs . . . You will be killed by peaceful radiation.' Or maybe he is a Christian God, and Christian charity inspires his acts: 'You killed with atomic missiles . . . but I shall help you over to the other side with a reactor.'" But he rejects these religious musings as self-delusion and stoically embraces the spiritually denuded scientific world view that has guided his entire life: "What am I talking about? God? Reactor?" Like Nevil Shute's ON THE BEACH (1957), *Level 7* shows that full-scale nuclear war will extinguish the human race. It further maintains that in the long run, MAD is doomed to fail, and war will inevitably ensue. Finally, *Level 7* suggests that nuclear war becomes possible when the completely empirical and pragmatic sensibility of a mechanistic, technocratic, scientifically oriented society succeeds in detaching people from their emotions.

For additional reading, see Dowling's *Fictions of Nuclear Disaster* and Anisfield's *The Nightmare Considered*.

Levertov, Denise A POET. Born in England in 1923 to a Welsh mother and Russian-Jewish father who converted to Christianity and became an Anglican minister, Levertov became one of the more prominent poets of the Cold War era. She grew up in England but moved to the United States in 1948 after marrying an American soldier, NOVELIST Mitchell Goodman. Subsequently, Levertov adopted the American idiom and is identified as an American poet. In the early 1950s, she befriended such poets as Robert Creeley and Robert Duncan and published in *Black Mountain Review,* the organ of the so-called Black Mountain School led by Charles Olson. Her poetry later appeared in such MAGAZINES as *Evergreen,* published by GROVE PRESS. Her work addresses a wide range of topics including city life, nature, life in Mexico, marital relationships and other human affairs. Though her political poems are not generally regarded as her best work and are sometimes criticized for their didacticism, Levertov was among a small but significant group of U.S. poets to forcefully protest the Vietnam War in both her poetry and her personal life. She participated in antiwar demonstrations and eventually traveled to Hanoi. Her husband was a codefendant with Dr. Benjamin Spock in a highly publicized trial of draft resisters.

Levertov's first war poetry appeared in the final section of *The Sorrow Dance* (1967), entitled "Life at War." The poems evoke powerful images of the innocent victims of the war and express Levertov's rage at those who perpetrate the horror: "You who go out on schedule/ to kill, do you know/ there are eyes that watch you,/ eyes whose lids you burned off"; "the scheduled breaking open of breasts whose milk/ runs out over the entrails of still-alive babies." That year Levertov also edited *Out of the War Shadow: An Anthology of Current Poetry,* published by the War Resisters League. *Relearning the Alphabet* (1970) addresses such contemporary issues as the Vietnam War and war resisters, starvation in Biafra, and race riots in Detroit. *To Stay Alive* (1971) collects Levertov's antiwar poetry to date within a single volume so those poems might serve "as a document of some historical value, a record of one person's inner/outer experience in America during the '60s and the beginning of the '70s." Most of her subsequent poetry became less overtly political after the war ended, though part of *The Freeing of the Dust* (1975) contains reflections on the trip to Hanoi during the war. In particular, "The Pilots" describes her mixed emotions on meeting with the captured American pilots who dropped bombs on North Vietnamese civilians. (See also VIETNAM WAR LITERATURE.)

For additional reading, see *Dictionary of Literary Biography* (vol 5, *American Poets Since World War II*).

Lewis, R. W. B. A NONFICTION WRITER. As a literary critic, Lewis challenged the pessimism of NEW LIBERALISM in his 1955 collection *American Adam,* calling it "something which began as a valuable corrective to the claims of innocence in America [but] which has declined into a cult of original sin." The epilogue, entitled "Adam as Hero in the Age of Containment," nonetheless recognizes a vital dynamic between innocence and sin.

"Life Is Worth Living" A television religious talk show that ran on the DuMont network from 1952 to 1955, and on ABC from 1955 to 1957. It was also a 1953 best-selling NONFICTION book by the same title. Hosted by a Catholic bishop, Fulton J. SHEEN, "Life Is Worth Living" was probably the most widely viewed religious series during the Cold War. Bishop Sheen, who had long been heard on radio, regularly presented a stridently anti-communist stand. The show was highly rated, beating out even the extremely popular program of Milton Berle in head-to-head competition. By 1954, Sheen was reaching some 25 million Americans each week. In one of his most memorable shows, he gave a dramatic reading of the burial scene from Shakespeare's *Julius Caesar,* replacing the names of Caesar, Cassius, Antony and Brutus with those of Stalin, Beria, Malenkov and Vishinsky. Sheen declared that "Stalin must one day meet his judgment." Three days later the Soviet leader suffered a sudden stroke; he died the following week. Though the press widely reported the coincidental timing, Sheen never commented on it. The show was canceled after Sheen fell out with his superior, Cardinal Francis Spellman. In 1953 Sheen published a best-selling book based on the television show, also entitled *Life Is Worth Living.* This fol-lowed his 1948 publication of *Communism and the Conscience of the West* in which he argued that "modern Christians have truth but no zeal; the Communists have zeal but no truth." Sheen returned to the air from 1961 to 1968 in a new syndicated show, "The Bishop Sheen Program," which was virtually indistinguishable from "Life Is Worth Living," though not nearly as popular. (See also RELIGIOUS TELEVISION PROGRAMMING.)

For additional reading see Whitfield's *The Culture of the Cold War.*

Limbo '90 A 1953 APOCALYPTIC NOVEL by Bernard Wolfe. Published in London the year Stalin died, the Korean War ended and the Soviet Union exploded its first hydrogen bomb, the novel centers on Dr. Martine, a surgeon who is on an island lobotomizing natives when the war breaks out in 1990. He returns home to a land of mutilated people who, in the words of critic Brian Dowling, deify him in "a religion of prostheses." Martine is horrified when the people misinterpret his notebooks and promote the voluntary amputation of their limbs in an attempt to excise the human proclivity for destruction by eliminating body parts:

> I can slice up the worst homicidal maniac's prefrontal lobes and give you a lamb of a pacifist . . . but he's not a human being anymore, just a lump! . . . There's only one thing . . . that has any chance of saving man before he's annihilated through his own masochism, it's to get behind his shows of violence and pound it home to him that 99 per cent of them are phony, masochistic in inception and masochistic in aim, born of death and striving for death. That'll work, and only that, all the rest is suicide disguised as science and humanitarianism.

Wolfe thus suggests that the nuclear threat stems from deep, unconscious forces pulling humanity toward self-destruction. In this respect he anticipates William Golding's LORD OF THE FLIES (1954) and Arthur Kopit's play END OF THE WORLD (1984).

Wolfe is greatly aware of the Western literary tradition and especially shows the influence of James Joyce, to whose *A Portrait of the Artist as a Young Man* he alludes in Joycean word play, "Old myth-mother, old artificialer, stand me now and forever in not too bad stead." Like *Finnegans Wake,* *Limbo '90* treats the power of language to shape reality, and it is deeply concerned with the power of the unconscious mind. Because words can mediate between the conscious and unconscious, language itself emerges as an important element of the book. The wordplay lightens the tone of an otherwise demoralizing subject and thus endows the novel with elements of BLACK HUMOR. The new religion is predicated on puns: "arms means armaments, legs mean marching order," and even the title presents a sick pun on body parts—limb-o. According to Dowling, "Wolfe's message seems to be that we must accept the whole of life, man's stupidity and capacity for self-mutilation and self-destruction as well as his nobility, if we are to avoid the reification of his worst fantasies. The most effective way to open up the imagination and keep it supple and alive is playing with language . . . and *Limbo '90,* for all its bombast, is a brilliant example of the verbal imagination at play."

For additional reading, see Dowling's *Fictions of Nuclear Disaster.*

Lippmann, Walter A JOURNALIST. Born in 1889 to an affluent German-Jewish family, Lippmann studied at Harvard from 1906 to 1910, where he was influenced by the pragmatism of William James and George Santayana's advocacy of an "aesthetic aristocracy." He also joined Harvard's Socialist Club and became active in social reform. In 1914 he joined the staff of the newly founded progressive MAGAZINE, the *New Republic,* which supported the notion of an activist president propounded by Theodore Roosevelt and Woodrow Wilson. During World War I Lippmann served as an assistant to the secretary of war and played a major role in developing Wilson's plan for postwar Europe. His work formed the basis of much of Wilson's Fourteen Points address to Congress outlining the president's vision of a peaceful world in which every nationality would be allowed its own homeland. In the 1920s, Lippmann edited the liberal *New York World* and wrote several books that revealed his growing dissatisfaction with democracy. In 1931 he began his column "Today and Tomorrow" in the Republican *New York Herald-Tribune* and was syndicated nationally until 1971. During the Depression, Lippmann opposed President Franklin Roosevelt's New Deal because he feared underlying totalitarianism.

By 1937 he had become absorbed by foreign affairs and urged the United States to prepare for war. After Hitler invaded Poland in 1939, Lippmann advocated sending U.S. assistance to France and England as the best way to keep the United States out of the European war. After the fall of France, he proposed working out a settlement with Japan so the United States could concentrate its efforts against Germany, if necessary. Following the attack on Pearl Harbor, Lippmann traveled to the West Coast and concluded that it should be considered a combat zone in which civil liberties might be curtailed. According to his biographer, Ronald Steel, "This argument, coming from such a prestigious and normally calm observer, gave powerful impetus to the demand for relocation [of Japanese-American citizens], and may even have intensified the panic." In 1943, Lippmann published the best-selling book *U.S. Foreign Policy,* which advocated the formation of postwar alliances against aggression. According to Steel, "Lippmann's formula of great power cooperation seemed a realistic alternative both to bankrupt isolationism and to wishful universalism." Though initially skeptical about the formation of the United Nations (UN), in 1945 Lippmann persuaded Senator Arthur Vandenberg, the leading voice for postwar isolationism, to endorse the organization. Nonetheless, Lippmann retained his skepticism about the ability of the UN to sustain international peace.

Following the war, Lippmann emerged as the preeminent American journalist and enjoyed close ties to the nation's power brokers. Though he believed that Dwight Eisenhower's vision was simplistic, vague and disjointed, Lippmann nonetheless supported the general's candidacy for president in 1952 because he believed that Eisenhower could end the Korean War, curtail the RED SCARE activities of Senator Joseph McCarthy and unify the nation. According to Steel, throughout the Eisenhower presidency, Lippmann sensed that

"America's cold war policies were essentially defensive, that it had acquired its informal empire by 'accident,' and that the problem was primarily one of execution rather than conception. He criticized the policy makers, but rarely what lay behind their policies." In 1958 Lippmann traveled to the Soviet Union. He received his first Pulitzer Prize for the series of articles he wrote about his experiences and observations on that trip.

Lippmann strongly supported John Kennedy and became an administration insider following Kennedy's 1960 election. In 1961, his close ties to the president garnered Lippmann another invitation to the Soviet Union, where he was warmly welcomed. Lippmann was also granted an interview with Premier Nikita Khrushchev, who spoke about the need for a peace treaty that would recognize the post-World War II boundaries of Eastern Europe—something the United States refused to do until the 1975 Helsinki agreements provided implicit recognition. Lippmann won his second Pulitzer Prize for his three articles based on that trip. Despite his close ties to the Kennedy administration, Lippmann criticized Kennedy's economic policies and the U.S. role in the 1961 Bay of Pigs invasion of Cuba, but he defended Kennedy's handling of the 1962 Cuban Missile Crisis. That year, Lippmann joined the *Washington Post,* which offered him a lucrative contract and reduced workload.

Following Kennedy's assassination, Lippmann supported President Johnson's civil rights legislation and regarded Johnson as an attractive alternative to the hawkish, ultra-conservative Republican candidate Barry Goldwater in the 1964 election. However, Lippmann fell out with Johnson over the president's decision to send troops to Vietnam in 1965; Lippmann believed that it was foolish to fight a land war in Asia. He helped convince the *Post's* publisher Katharine Graham to reverse the paper's prowar position and became increasingly embittered by the Johnson administration, which he felt had used him. Allen DRURY patterned the unsympathetic, antiwar journalist "Wonderful Walter" after Lippmann in his political novel CAPABLE OF HONOR.

In addition to writing newspaper articles, Lippmann wrote several NONFICTION books addressing Cold War issues, including *The Cold War: A Study in U.S. Foreign Policy* (1947), *Commentaries on Far Eastern Policy* (1950), *Essays in the Public Philosophy* (1955), *The Communist World and Ours* (1959), *The Confrontation* (1959), *The Coming Tests with Russia* (1961) and *The Nuclear Era: A Profound Struggle* (1962).

For additional reading, see Ronald Steel, *Walter Lippmann and the American Century* (1960); *Dictionary of Literary Biography* (vol. 29, *American Newspaper Journalists 1926–1950.*)

literature Cold War literature typically deals with the threat of nuclear warfare and/or political repression in the West or "behind the IRON CURTAIN." Consequently, its tone is usually bleak, except when writers turn to SATIRE or BLACK HUMOR to generate an uncomfortable comic sensibility to cope with situations and events that seem out of control. Like much post–World War II literature, Cold War literature frequently contains elements of existentialism and often employs anti-heroes to reflect the authors' sense of impotence about political situations that appear irrational, absurd and out-of-control. Existentialism, which has its roots in the work of 19th-century philosopher Friedrich Nietzsche and which was developed by such postwar French writers as Jean-Paul Sartre and Albert Camus, posits an absurd universe that has no intrinsic meaning. The philosophy therefore calls on each individual to create meaning for his or her own life by adopting a personal set of values and acting upon them. Thus when Sartre declares "Man is condemned to be free," he means that the burden of forging a meaningful, authentic life falls on every person, that the terms of a worthy and fulfilling existence must come from each individual and not from religion, government or other social institutions, all of which appear to the existentialists to have proven inadequate in the face of the massive devastation of World War II and the looming threat of NUCLEAR APOCALYPSE in the Cold War.

At its best, living by an existentialist philosophy can create highly ethical, motivated, spiritually fulfilled and politically active citizens. However, if not tied to a moral system that respects life and other human values, existentialism can lead to self-centeredness and anarchy, on the one hand, or to unrestricted quests for power and domination on the other hand. Thus terrorism and fascism are possible negative outgrowths of unmitigated existentialism. Consequently, the problem of establishing the proper relationship of the individual to society was of great concern to authors during the Cold War. Such concern is particularly evident in such diverse works as George ORWELL's novel, NINETEEN EIGHTY-FOUR (1949); the novels of John BARTH, Thomas PYNCHON, Robert COOVER, Norman MAILER, Mary MCCARTHY, Kurt VONNEGUT Jr., Richard WRIGHT, Ayn RAND, and Joseph Heller; the poetry of Denise LEVERTOV, Daniel BERRIGAN and the POETS of the BEAT MOVEMENT; the literature centering on the Korean and Vietnam wars; the survivalist literature of the 1980s; the plays of Arthur MILLER, Arthur Kopit and Joeph Heller and even the stand-up comedy of Lenny BRUCE and Mort SAHL.

The problem of defining the proper relationship between the individual and society became even more complicated during the later stages of the Cold War, when the Vietnam War and the Watergate scandal undermined public confidence in government and challenged the general consensus over the value of fighting the Cold War. Even before then, such prominent works as Heller's novel CATCH-22 (1961) had underscored the irrational world-view that emanates from a society run by bureaucracies, in which the personal goals of the individual administrators often contrast with the stated goals of the institutions they serve. Moreover, given the large amount of secrecy demanded in the name of Cold War national security, individuals had to choose their loyalties, base their actions and cast their votes, in situations about which they were never fully informed. Modernist thought from earlier in the century had already proposed that no view of any situation was ever complete and that values, assessments and even basic facts would change depending on point of view. For instance, depending on one's perspective, the North Vietnamese communists might be fighting a civil war, a war of national liberation or an aggressive war to conquer a sovereign state, while the United States was either fighting to defend a deserving ally or waging an imperialistic battle to extend its influence. Each one of these interpretations of the war could be supported by credible arguments. Likewise, the nuclear buildup might be viewed either as an insane act that could potentially annihilate humanity or a necessary act that prevented war by forestalling communist invasions of Western Europe and elsewhere.

And the internal danger from domestic communism was either significant or greatly exaggerated to promote a political point of view. Even the determination of which actions or beliefs were "un-American" and which posed significant threats to national security was problematic. Much Cold War literature thus deals with the problem of acting in an irrational universe in which access to all of the necessary facts is incomplete and no consensus exists on the interpretation of political reality. Greene's THE HUMAN FACTOR (1978) and Le Carré's THE SPY WHO CAME IN FROM THE COLD (1963) take up this problem within the spy genre; Arthur Kopit addresses it in his play END OF THE WORLD (1984) and Barth and Pynchon deal with it throughout their fiction. Likewise, though many works continued to portray human behavior as intrinsically rational, or at least saw it as effectively serving self-interest, other works such as End of the World, William Golding's LORD OF THE FLIES (1954) and Bernard Wolfe's LIMBO '90 (1953) see humans as basically irrational, following Freud's belief that the two strongest human impulses are toward sex (procreativity) and death (destruction). They thus consider the subconscious human impulse for our own destruction to be part of the Cold War scenario. Stanley KUBRICK's black humor film satire DR. STRANGELOVE (1964) handles this theme in an especially complex and comprehensive manner.

In the face of such overwhelmingly complex situations, perceptions and motivations and in response to the threat of nuclear annihilation, U.S. society was seized by a widespread desire for some extra-human form of salvation. Not surprisingly, church attendance reached its highest levels of the century at the end of the 1950s, as Cold War tensions peaked. Television evangelists such as Billy GRAHAM thrived during the Cold War, and sales of the Revised Standard Version of the Bible reached over 26 million within a year of its publication in 1952; it remained on the best-seller list for several years following. In the late 1940s and 1950s, Bishop Fulton J. SHEEN also appeared on best-seller lists with his anti-communist, religious books: Peace of the Soul (1947), which argues that communism is the antithesis of Roman Catholicism; Communism and the Conscience of the West (1948), which maintains that communism is a kind of secular religion that evokes great dedication from its adherents; and LIFE IS WORTH LIVING (1953), a spin-off from Sheen's popular television show by the same title (DuMont/ABC, 1952–57). (See also RELIGIOUS TELEVISION PROGRAMMING.) Arthur C. Clarke's science fiction novel Childhood's End (1953) and his later 2001 (1968) express the wish that salvation might come from an alien society from outer space, as do the science fiction films THE DAY THE EARTH STOOD STILL (1951), RED PLANET MARS (1950), and the FILM on which Clarke based his novel, 2001: A Space Odyssey (1968). Barth's novel GILES GOAT-BOY (1966) likewise pictures a society desperately seeking a savior, though the novel ultimately endorses a more existentialist point of view.

A number of literary works dealt with domestic Cold War politics. Typically these were written by such popular writers as Allen DRURY, Eugene BURDICK, William LEDERER, Fletcher KNEBEL, Leon URIS and James MICHENER. Drury took a strong conservative stand that advocated a hard line against communism, while Knebel and Charles W. Bailey II depicted the dangers of right-wing extremists in the military in SEVEN DAYS IN MAY (1962). Richard Condon does likewise in THE MANCHURIAN CANDIDATE (1959). Burdick and Lederer support the United States' basic goals in Southeast Asia in THE UGLY AMERICAN (1958) but criticize how those goals are implemented by arrogant and self-serving State Department bureaucrats. These popular writers were among the relatively few writers to integrate Cold War events into their work, except within the genre of spy fiction. Perhaps more than any other genre, spy fiction addressed actual Cold War situations, especially the novels by William F. BUCKLEY Jr. and Watergate conspirators E. Howard Hunt, G. Gordon Liddy, and John Ehrlichman. The MILITARY NOVELS of Tom CLANCY constitute a related sub-genre.

Literature dealing with the RED SCARE includes firsthand, nonfiction accounts by Alger Hiss (IN THE COURT OF PUBLIC OPINION, 1957); his accuser Whittaker Chambers (WITNESS, 1952); Owen Lattimore, who was a target of Senator Joseph McCarthy (ORDEAL BY SLANDER, 1950); and Lillian Hellman, who confronted HUAC before taking the Fifth Amendment (SCOUNDREL TIME, 1976). On the other hand, William F. Buckley Jr. defends McCarthy (*McCarthy and His Enemies: The Record and Its Meaning*, 1954) and HUAC (*The Committee and Its Critics*, 1962). HOLLYWOOD TEN member Alvah BESSIE describes his experience with HUAC and BLACKLISTING in *Inquisition in Eden* (1965) and his autobiographical novel *The Un-Americans* (1957). Other members of the Ten to write about their experiences and the underlying issues were Dalton TRUMBO ("Time of the Toad," a 1949 pamphlet), Lester COLE (*Hollywood Red*, 1981) and Edward DMYTRYK (*It's a Hell of a Life But Not a Bad Living*, 1979).

Fictional treatments of the Red Scare include William Wister Gaines's THE HONORABLE ROCKY SLADE (1957), which parodies McCarthy's early career, and Earnest Frankel's TONGUE OF FIRE (1960), which likewise denounces McCarthy. Philip Roth's THE GREAT AMERICAN NOVEL (1973) concludes by satirizing HUAC. Roth also satirizes Richard Nixon's participation in the Red Scare as well as his activities as president in OUR GANG (1971). Arthur Miller's play THE CRUCIBLE (1953) is commonly read as an allegory about the Red Scare, while *After the Fall* (1963), portrays Miller's own life during that time. E. L. Doctorow and Robert COOVER treat the execution of the convicted atomic bomb spies Julius and Ethel Rosenberg in their novels THE BOOK OF DANIEL (1971) and THE PUBLIC BURNING (1978), respectively. The Rosenbergs' sons, Robert and Michael Meeropol, provide a NONFICTION account of events in WE ARE YOUR SONS (1975). Donald Freed's 1970 play INQUEST is based on Walter and Miriam Schneir's 1965 review of the case, *Invitation to an Inquest*, while Louis Nizer contradicts the Schneirs' claim for the Rosenbergs' innocence in his 1973 study, *The Implosion Conspiracy*. Other literary and artistic responses to the Rosenberg case appeared in a 1988 exhibition of ART and literature: *Unknown Secrets: Art and the Rosenberg Era*, which was part of the Rosenberg Era Art Project. Project director Rob A.

Okun published the contents of the exhibition in *The Rosenbergs: Collected Visions of Artists and Writers* (1988); Margaret RANDALL wrote the introduction. FBI director J. Edgar Hoover, who led the efforts to break the spy ring the Rosenbergs were accused of leading, describes the dangers of domestic communism and ways to combat them in MASTERS OF DECEIT (1958).

In the late 1950s the GROVE PRESS began publishing anti-establishment and left-wing domestic and foreign literature that had had difficulty finding outlets during the Red Scare. It also provided a forum for pro-Castro writings. On the other hand, a number of writers who were in exile in the United States from communist countries describe political oppression behind the Iron Curtain.

The threat of nuclear war is the other dominant theme in Cold War literature. Relevant nonfiction books include John Hersey's HIROSHIMA (1946); Robert J. Lifton's DEATH IN LIFE: SURVIVORS OF HIROSHIMA (1968); OUR NUCLEAR FUTURE (1958) by the "father of the hydrogen bomb," Edward Teller; NO MORE WAR! (1958) by Nobel Prize–winning scientist Linus Pauling, who opposes Teller's view; Herman Kahn's ON THERMONUCLEAR WAR (1960), which was the first book to employ scientific methods to calculate the actual effects of a large-scale nuclear war and which concludes such a war is survivable; and Jonathan Schell's THE FATE OF THE EARTH (1982), which projects the impact on the planet of a nuclear war some 24 years after Kahn's book and concludes that a massive nuclear exchange would reduce the Earth to a wasteland and introduce a nuclear winter by creating massive clouds that would block out the sun.

Fiction involving nuclear warfare and its aftermath ranges from Nevil Shute's ON THE BEACH (1957), which predicts the end of humanity, to Pat Frank's ALAS, BABYLON (1959) and Philip Wylie's TOMORROW! (1954), which view the bomb as a sort of spiritual cleansing agent that will allow survivors to create a new and better society. Wylie uses his book to promote civil defense and attack MOMISM, which he saw as the weakening of American society by overbearing, over-nurturing, emasculating mothers. On the other hand, Judith Merril's SHADOW ON THE HEARTH (1950), Helen Clarkson's THE LAST DAY (1959) and Yorick Blumenfeld's JENNY: MY DIARY (1981) imagine nuclear war from the viewpoint of housewife-mothers. Many critics view Walter Miller's A CANTICLE FOR LEIBOWITZ (1959) as the prototypical postnuclear story, with human society reverting initially to a new Middle Ages before undergoing a new Enlightenment in which it learns to harness the power of science more responsibly. Typically, in apocalyptic literature, society devolves into lawless anarchy, medieval feudalism or fascistic dictatorships. The strongest poetic statements about the bomb come from Beat poets Allen GINSBERG, Lawrence FERLINGHETTI and Gregory CORSO, though Robert Lowell, Adrienne Rich, Charles Gullans and Mark Strand also address the prospects of nuclear holocaust.

Though the body of Cold War literature is considerable, it remains somewhat surprising that the dominant political circumstance of the postwar era did not attract even more attention, especially from the leading "serious" writers of the time. The number of women and minorities who directly address the Cold War is scant, and few poets or playwrights wrote about it. Such major American NOVELISTS as John

Updike, Saul Bellow, John Cheever, Chaim Potok, Flannery O'Connor, Eudora Welty, Donald Barthelme, Raymond Carver, Ishmael Reed, Joyce Carol Oates, Marge Piercy, Truman Capote, Toni Morrison, Alice Walker, Jack Kerouac, John Steinbeck, James BALDWIN and Vladimir NABOKOV treat it only tangentially or not at all. Their omission of the Cold War does not imply any criticism of their work—they were pursuing other legitimate artistic goals. However, it does illustrate how the dominant literary response to an overwhelming political situation that seemed beyond anyone's control was simply to ignore it. Consequently, the major trend in post–World War II America was to move away from social and political literature in favor of writing that permitted personal introspection and exploration; analyzed relationships among lovers, friends, husbands and wives; and otherwise addressed the more private sphere of activities as the only area in which individuals were able to exert a meaningful influence. (See also APOCALYPTIC NOVELS; LITERATURE ABOUT COLD WAR EVENTS; NEW LIBERALISM; NONFICTION WRITERS; POLITICAL NOVELS AND STORIES; SCIENCE FICTION NOVELS AND STORIES; SPY NOVELS; VIETNAM WAR LITERATURE; EXILED WRITERS [from the United States]; EXILED WRITERS [to the United States]; THEATER.)

literature about Cold War events There are surprisingly few literary treatments of such major Cold War events as the 1949 Berlin Airlift, the Berlin uprising against the communist regime in East Germany (1953), the Hungarian Revolution (1956), the second Berlin Crisis (1958–61), the 1960 U-2 incident, the U.S. commitment of troops to Lebanon in 1958 and 1983, the Cuban Missile Crisis (1962), the overthrow of leftist governments in Guatemala and Chile (1954 and 1973), the Soviet Union and Warsaw Pact nations' crushing of the Prague Spring and Czechoslovakia's short-lived reform government (1968), President Nixon's historic trip to China (1972), the 1970s civil wars in Angola and elsewhere in Africa, the U.S. involvement in the 1980s civil wars in Nicaragua and El Salvador, the Soviet downing of the Korean passenger plane carrying a conservative U.S. congressman (1983), the U.S. invasion of Grenada (1983), the Polish Solidarity Movement of the 1980s, the Soviet war in Afghanistan in the 1980s or the collapse of communism in the late 1980s. The Korean and Vietnam Wars, on the other hand, were the subjects of many books and stories.

The nuclear bombing of Japan received surprisingly little literary attention as well. John Hersey's nonfiction HIROSHIMA (1946) provides firsthand accounts by survivors of the atomic bombing of Hiroshima, the event that concluded World War II and introduced the nuclear age. Almost 20 years later, Robert J. Lifton reported the results of his study of the long-term psychological consequences of that nuclear attack in DEATH IN LIFE: SURVIVORS OF HIROSHIMA (1968).

Reviews of the relatively little prose literature that deals directly with Cold War events follow. Novelist Leon URIS treats the U.S.-Soviet occupation of Germany and the Berlin Airlift in ARMAGEDDON (1964). In TOPAZ (1968), Uris develops a tale of espionage set against the Cuban Missile Crisis and the deteriorating relations between France and the United States. His best-selling novel EXODUS (1958) describes the founding of the state of Israel, an event that had important Cold War consequences. Exiled writer (from the United States) Stefan HEYM wrote *Five Days in June* (1977), a novel about the 1953 Berlin uprising. Irving Wallace's THE PLOT (1967) interweaves the Kennedy assassination, the split between China and the U.S.S.R., and the beginnings of détente, also treating such figures as Dwight Eisenhower, Alger Hiss and Christine Keeler, a central figure in a major British sex scandal. Robert Kennedy's nonfiction THIRTEEN DAYS (1969) provides a firsthand account of the Cuban Missile Crisis from the viewpoint of one of the major players. James MICHENER's THE BRIDGE AT ANDAU (1957) documents the Hungarian Revolution and its immediate aftermath, while Michener's *Kent State: What Happened and Why* (1971) is a highly acclaimed study of the 1970 incident in which the Ohio National Guard killed protesters and bystanders at a demonstration against the Cambodia "incursion" of the Vietnam War. The 1950–51 trial and 1953 execution of Julius and Ethel Rosenberg, who were convicted of passing secrets about the atomic bomb to the Soviets, are treated in the political novels THE BOOK OF DANIEL (1971) by E. L. Doctorow and THE PUBLIC BURNING (1978) by Robert COOVER, and in Donald Freed's 1970 play INQUEST, which is based on Walter and Miriam Schneir's nonfiction *Invitation to an Inquest* (1965), which Louise Nizer countered in *The Implosion Conspiracy* (1973). The Rosenbergs' sons, Robert and Michael Meeropol, provide their account in WE ARE YOUR SONS (1975). *The Rosenbergs: Collected Visions of Artists and Writers* (1988) also treats the subject.

Some poetry was also inspired by specific Cold War events. Lawrence FERLINGHETTI's *A Coney Island of the Mind* (1958) was published at the outset of the second Berlin Crisis, when the prospects for nuclear war among the superpowers seemed not only possible but also almost inevitable. It depicts the probable nuclear destruction of people, nature and machines: "Oh it was a spring/ of fur leaves and cobalt flowers/ when cadillacs fell through the trees like rain/ drowning the meadows with madness/ while out of every imitation cloud/ dropped myriad wingless crowds/ of nutless nagasaki survivors." Gregory CORSO's poem "Bomb" (1960), which also appeared during the Berlin Crisis, likewise describes the immense damage to nature that nuclear war would create: "Turtles exploding over Istanbul/ The jaguar's flying foot/ soon to sink in arctic snow/ Penguins plunged against the sphinx/ The top of the Empire State/ arrowed in a broccoli field in Sicily." In "Fall, 1961" Robert Lowell expresses his sense of frustration and impotence during the Berlin Crisis: "All autumn, the chafe and jar/ of nuclear war;/ we have talked our extinction to death./ I swim like a minnow/ behind my studio window." And in "Gunnery Practice, Seaside, Oregon, August 16, 1961," Charles Gullans, writing about the same crisis, expresses frustration at the inability to stop what appears to be an unfolding disaster: "Nations rearm with steel and with cold nerve./ I sit here doing nothing."

The following year saw the Cuban Missile Crisis, when the two nuclear superpowers confronted each other "eyeball to eyeball." Mark Strand declared in "When the Vacation Is Over for Good,"

It will be strange
Knowing at last it couldn't go on forever,
The certain voice telling us over and over

That nothing would change . . .
. . . unable, to know just what it was
That went so completely wrong, or why it is
We are dying.

The Missile Crisis also inspired Dave Smith's "Cuba Night," which was written after President Kennedy had declared that the United States would risk war to prevent a Soviet Cuba. In the same vein, David Ingatow's 1964 poem "Simultaneously" imagines U.S. and Soviet nuclear missiles passing en route to their respective targets. (See also POETS.)

Cold War events appear most prominently in SPY NOVELS. William F. BUCKLEY Jr., for example, invokes the politics behind such Cold War events such as the power struggle in the Kremlin following Stalin's death (*High Jinx*, 1986), the Hungarian Revolution and the beginnings of the space race (*Who's on First*, 1980), the second Berlin Crisis (*The Story of Henri Tod*, 1983) and the 1960 U-2 incident (*Marco Polo If You Can*, 1982). Watergate conspirator E. Howard Hunt's *The Berlin Ending* (1973) depicts Willy Brandt and other advocates of détente as Soviet agents, while his *The Kremlin Conspiracy* (1985) derides the politics of European "peaceniks" who pressure the Nobel Prize committee to give the Peace Prize to a man who is secretly a Soviet agent. The prizewinner then uses his influence to force NATO to withdraw its missiles from Europe. Another Watergate conspirator and former top White House aide, John Ehrlichman, centers *The Company* (1976) on rivalries among the CIA, FBI and other intelligence agencies. The unflattering portrayal of the president is apparently based on Richard Nixon, whom Ehrlichman served as a top domestic adviser until Nixon fired him during the Watergate scandal. Ehrlichman also wrote *The China Card* (1986), which suggests that Nixon's historic trip to China actually resulted from the activities of a spy working on behalf of Zhou En-lai, the Chinese premier.

More respected authors of spy fiction include Graham GREENE, whose 1978 novel, THE HUMAN FACTOR, deals with superpower rivalries in South Africa, Angola and Mozambique. Tom CLANCY's military novel *Cardinal of the Kremlin* (1988) makes prominent use of the Soviet war in Afghanistan. John LE CARRÉ sets his 1989 spy novel, THE RUSSIA HOUSE, during the waning days of the Soviet Union, when Premier Gorbachev's new economic policies and social reforms were taking effect. The novel centers on efforts by Western agents to find out whether the Soviet military-industrial complex is indeed hopelessly corrupt, inept and grossly mismanaged, as a Soviet agent alleges. The claim threatens the Western agents because it suggests that the entire Cold War has been a farce, a possibility that undermines the necessity for their work.

Exiled writers (to the United States) also wrote about Cold War events. Nobel Prize winner Czeslaw MILOSZ describes the communist seizure of Poland in *The Seizure of Power* (1953; in English, 1955). In *Angels on the Head of a Pin* (1989), Juri DRUZHNIKOV describes the behavior of Soviet government officials in Moscow and their repression of independent thinkers in the Soviet Union before and just after the 1968 Soviet intervention in Czechoslovakia. Janusz GLOWACKI's novel (1981; in English, 1983) *Give Us This Day* describes the lives of members of the Solidarity movement and the hostility exhibited toward them by the Polish military and government officials. Banned in Poland, the novel was first published there as an underground book and then smuggled abroad, where it was translated into several languages. (See also MILITARY NOVELS; POLITICAL NOVELS; VIETNAM WAR LITERATURE; FILMS ABOUT COLD WAR EVENTS; EXILED WRITERS [from the United States]; EXILED WRITERS [to the United States].)

Living Daylights, The   A 1987 SPY FILM starring Timothy Dalton, Maryam d'Abo and Jeroen Krabbe and directed by John Glen. The British-made James BOND film presents an ambivalent attitude toward the U.S.S.R. that reflects the more conciliatory Western feelings about the Soviet Union under Gorbachev, who had been in power for two years when *The Living Daylights* was released. Here the villain is a rogue Soviet general who pretends to defect in order to play the British Secret Service against his superiors in the KGB. His ultimate plan is to make a fortune selling weapons, diamonds and opium. The film features a daring rescue when the defector is placed in a capsule and shot through the then-new gas pipeline between Russia and Western Europe, a product of the 1970s détente. When Bond realizes the defector has been using Her Majesty's Secret Service to assassinate a ranking Soviet officer for whom the British have held a grudging respect, he works in limited cooperation with that KGB officer to foil the defector. The action takes Bond to Afghanistan, where anti-Soviet Afghani rebels assist him. Except for its military involvement in Afghanistan, ongoing when the film appeared, the U.S.S.R. itself is not vilified for its sinister intentions, as it was in earlier Bond films. Instead, the top-level Soviet officials appear responsible and even somewhat compassionate, while the danger comes from their inability to control a wayward subordinate. Along with THE BEAST (1988) and *Rambo III* (1988), *The Living Daylights* is one of the few mainstream films to address the Soviet war in Afghanistan, a pivotal Cold War event that ended the U.S.-Soviet détente in December 1979. (See also FILMS ABOUT COLD WAR EVENTS.)

Living Theater, The   A leftist New York THEATER group founded in 1946 by Julian Beck and Judith Malina. The Living Theater's aim was to encourage political, social and theatrical experimentation with the objective of changing society. In the 1950s it presented works by Bertolt BRECHT, Jean Cocteau, and Luigi Pirandello. It promoted pacifism in such works as its 1963 performance of Kenneth Brown's *The Brig*, which depicted the growing militaristic tendencies of the United States. Because the theater premises had been seized by the Internal Revenue Service for nonpayment of taxes, and doors padlocked, audiences for *The Brig* had to enter through an open window in the building. The group left the United States for Europe shortly after that performance closed.

Loeb, Philip   A TELEVISION PERFORMER who was blacklisted in 1951. Loeb starred as Jake Goldberg from 1949 to 1951 in the popular television situation comedy, THE GOLDBERGS (CBS/NBC/DuMont, 1949–54). In the summer of 1950, RED CHANNELS listed him as a communist sympathizer. After receiving four letters of protest, the show's sponsor,

General Foods, expressed concern. In meetings with CBS and General Foods officials, the show's star, Gertrude Berg, declared that it was "un-American" to demand that Loeb be fired on the basis of unproven charges. Loeb refused to publicly clear his name by refuting the accusations, though he later denied under oath that he was a communist. He argued that any public statement would lend credibility to those who made the undocumented charges in the first place. Loeb remained on the show until the end of the 1951 season, when General Foods threatened to cancel its sponsorship if he continued. In fact, General Foods did withdraw its sponsorship, and the show moved to NBC, but without Loeb. The columnist for the New York *Journal-American* reported that Loeb departed "after a long and luxurious hiatus in [CBS's] pink-tinged boudoir."

In 1952 Loeb reached a contract settlement with Berg, but he felt that the real issue, his BLACKLISTING, remained unresolved. In a memo to the national board of the Television Authority he stated, "I did not come to my union for a financial settlement . . . I came for truth and justice. I am still seeking truth and justice . . . I am deprived of work because of a cowardly, furtive smear campaign . . . I claim that although innocent I have been ousted from my work and hounded from my profession by a dirty, undercover job." After his departure from "The Goldbergs," Loeb worked in the THEATER, appearing in the Broadway production of *Time Out for Ginger*. When he went on tour with the show, Edward Clamage of the American Legion protested Loeb's appearance and tried to organize a boycott of the Chicago production. However, the boycott failed to materialize, and the play ran for 10 months. In subsequent years, Loeb became embittered and depressed, feeling victimized by the self-appointed protectors of the Republic. He also experienced family problems. In September 1955 he committed suicide by taking an overdose of sleeping pills. The character played by Zero MOSTEL in THE FRONT was loosely based on Loeb.

For additional reading, see Cogley's *Report on Blacklisting*, vol. 2.

Loeb, William A JOURNALIST. Born in 1905 to President Theodore Roosevelt's private secretary, Loeb grew up in Oyster Bay, New York, and graduated from Williams College in 1927. He held a variety of newspaper jobs in the 1930s and 1940s before purchasing a string of small New England papers in the 1940s and 1950s. In 1948 he gained full control of the *Manchester Union Leader*, the only New Hampshire newspaper with a statewide circulation. As the *Union Leader*'s publisher, Loeb acquired considerable influence within the state and in the New Hampshire presidential primary. Since that primary is the first national primary, it has assumed importance beyond what the state's relatively small population would otherwise command. Thus Loeb, an arch-conservative, was able to play a significant role in national politics during the Cold War. His front-page editorials supported the presidential bid of conservative Republican Robert Taft in 1948 and endorsed the RED SCARE activities of Senator Joseph McCarthy during the 1950s. He opposed Senator John Kennedy's successful bid for the 1960 Democratic nomination, claiming Kennedy was "soft on Communism"; he supported instead a virtually unknown ball-point

pen manufacturer from Chicago, Paul C. Fisher. Fisher's relatively strong showing in the New Hampshire primary (13% of the Democratic vote) is regarded as a testament to Loeb's influence. Shortly before the general election, Loeb denounced Kennedy in an editorial. Kennedy waited until the day before the election to respond, so Loeb would not have time to reply in turn. Though Kennedy fared better in New Hampshire than any previous Democratic candidate, he nonetheless failed to carry the state, and Loeb later denounced him as "the No. 1 liar in the United States." He remained at odds with Kennedy throughout his presidency.

In 1964 Loeb supported conservative Barry Goldwater, first against his more moderate Republican opponent, Nelson Rockefeller, and then against Democrat Lyndon Johnson. Loeb levied his characteristic personal attacks against both men. For example, he dubbed Rockefeller a "wife swapper" because he had divorced to remarry a younger woman. In 1968 Loeb labeled President Johnson "Snake Oil Lyndon" and called peace candidate Eugene McCarthy "a skunk's skunk" while endorsing Richard Nixon. However, even Nixon's foreign policy proved too liberal for Loeb, who denounced his moves toward normalizing relations with communist China. In the 1972 presidential election, Loeb announced that his paper would endorse only a candidate who would restore national defense and "support a foreign policy designed to preserve the security and honor of the United States"—therefore, he failed to endorse either candidate.

Loeb's greatest impact in the 1972 election came when he published a letter purportedly from a Florida youth who claimed that Edmund Muskie, a formidable Democratic candidate, had made an ethnic slur against French-speaking Canadian Americans. Since this group constitutes a significant political force in New Hampshire, the charge had serious implications. The 1974 Watergate investigations later revealed that the letter had been one of the White House "dirty tricks," written by Nixon aide Ken Clawson. Reportedly, Clawson had been in contact with the *Union Leader*'s editor-in-chief at the time the letter appeared. The day after the letter appeared, Loeb attacked Muskie's wife. On February 26, nine days before the primary, Muskie delivered a speech in front of the newspaper office defending himself against Loeb's charges. However, he broke down in tears when he alluded to the accusations against his wife, and the nationally televised image of him crying destroyed his candidacy. Loeb later viciously attacked the Democratic nominee, Senator George McGovern, a peace candidate who opposed the Vietnam War. In July, he published a series of articles charging McGovern with cowardice while he was a bomber pilot during World War II. The charges proved completely false.

Loeb initially called for Nixon's resignation after the Watergate scandal but then reversed himself on the grounds that the resignation would "take control of the nation away from the voters and give it to a small group of arrogant self-appointed rulers in the form of radio and TV commentators and newspaper publishers." In 1976 he rejected the candidacy of Republican president Gerald Ford, which he characterized as "dead as a dodo," and instead backed independent candidate George Wallace.

Long Tomorrow, The A 1955 APOCALYPTIC NOVEL by Leigh Brackett. Written three years after the development of the hydrogen bomb, *The Long Tomorrow* is initially set in a Mennonite community in the aftermath of a NUCLEAR APOCALYPSE. The novel addresses the proper role of science in a postnuclear society. The story follows Len, a boy whose grandfather has told him about the war. Knowledge about science and the past is considered dangerous, and Len's father beats him for studying physics and American history and exploring technology in the form of a radio. Thereafter Len leaves the insulated Mennonite community and enters the larger, postnuclear world, which is populated by religious fanatics akin to medieval flagellants, self-serving capitalists and a group of scientists working at a secret site called Bartorstown. The scientists are developing a nuclear reactor that will create a force-field capable of nullifying the fission-fusion process necessary for making nuclear bombs. Thus their goal is to employ atomic energy to free humanity from the threat of atomic disaster. Initially Len rejects the reactor as essentially satanic: "Behind it is the reactor. Behind it is evil and night and terror and death." However, he eventually concludes, "I guess it makes better sense to try and chain the devil up than to try keeping the whole land tied down in the hopes he won't notice it again."

Like other postapocalyptic SCIENCE FICTION, such as A CANTICLE FOR LEIBOWITZ (1959), *The Long Tomorrow* pictures human recovery from a nuclear apocalypse as a progression: from a new Dark Ages in which the dominant religious authority is capricious, superstitious and hostile to science, to a new age in which science is finally used responsibly.

For additional reading, see Dowling's *Fictions of Nuclear Disaster.*

Looking Glass War, The A 1965 SPY NOVEL by John LE CARRÉ and a 1969 British-made SPY FILM starring Christopher Jones, Anthony Hopkins, Pia Degermark and Ralph Richardson and directed by Frank R. Pierson. The action centers on attempts by a British intelligence unit to gain information about a communist missile site on the border between East and West Germany. However, the larger conflict is between that agency—a behind-the-times remnant from World War II called the Department—and the more dominant, more professional and better funded Circus, for which George Smiley works. Trying to recapture the Department's glory days from the Second World War, the agency's head, Leclerc, nearly causes a commercial airliner to be shot down when he authorizes it to fly over and photograph the missile site. Inept, inadequately trained and poorly equipped agents make three subsequent efforts to retrieve the film. Leclerc plays upon the agents' human weaknesses to recruit them, and he treats the agents as expendable pawns in his futile effort to show up the Circus. Thus the noble cause for which the agents believe they are making sacrifices becomes subordinated to the political ambitions of bureaucrats engaged in inter-office rivalries. (Joseph Heller addresses the same theme through BLACK HUMOR in his 1961 novel, CATCH-22.)

For additional reading, see Beene's *John le Carré* and Cawelti and Rosenberg's *The Spy Story.*

Lord of the Flies A 1954 APOCALYPTIC NOVEL by William Golding and a 1963 British-made FILM DRAMA starring James Aubrey, Tom Chaplin and Hugh Edwards and written and directed by Peter Brook. Harry Hook remade the film in 1990, starring Balthazar Getty, Chris Furth and Danuel Pipoly. The story is set just before the expected outbreak of an atomic war—a premise that was not far-fetched either in 1954, when the book appeared two years after the development of the hydrogen bomb, or in 1963, when the film was released, the year after the Cuban Missile Crisis (though it was remote when the remake appeared in 1990, when communism was collapsing throughout Eastern Europe). The story focuses on a group of British schoolboys whose plane crashes on an isolated Pacific island while they are flying to a safe haven. No adults survive. Initially the boys behave as their upper-class, British upbringing has trained them to, but soon the thin veneer of civilization wears off, and they degenerate into a primitive society led by the dominant male. Golding, a British Nobel Prize winner, may have had an eye on the U.S. RED SCARE as he depicted the ritual hunting down and killing of Piggy, a social outcast and a physically weak but humane and compassionate intellectual. The story suggests that human civilization is a fragile arrangement, and that the species is quick to revert to its primitive instincts if the basic rules for civilized behavior are not externally enforced. This bleak assessment of the human condition refers both to the inherent barbarism of nuclear blackmail and power politics, and to Golding's vision of a postnuclear society. *Lord of the Flies* suggests that postnuclear humans would probably revert to primitive, brutish behavior and social patterns, with rule by reason giving way to tribal rituals and superstition.

The story also posits the inability of a rational world view to succeed in a barbaric environment and suggests the death of a social ego that mediates between communal desires for order and the human species' basic impulse toward violence and destruction. Before Piggy's death, Ralph, the group's original leader, functions as an ego mediating between the urges of the id, as embodied by the brutal Jack, and the superego, as embodied by the cerebral, future-oriented, rule-oriented Piggy. Once Piggy dies, however, Ralph feels compelled to assume the role of the superego, and no mediating middle ground remains between him and the visceral, primal Jack. Ralph embraces democracy and insists that the boys perform the unappealing chores necessary to provide food, shelter and hope for rescue. He is fundamentally concerned with survival. But the forces of the id soon overwhelm those of the superego as Jack wrests the leadership from Ralph by promising immediate excitement and creating a hierarchical society based on brute force.

The "Lord of the Flies" is actually the severed head of a pig that the boys have ritualistically killed, and it too is associated with the violent, libidinal impulses of the id. One of the boys, Simon, stumbles upon the "obscene thing" on a stick and has a visionary experience that underscores the primacy of the libido: " 'Fancy thinking the Beast was something you could hunt and kill,' said the head. For a moment or two the forest and all the other dimly appreciated places echoed with the parody of laughter. 'You knew, didn't you. I'm part of you. Close, close, close!

I'm the reason why it's no go. Why things are as they are.' "

Finally Ralph, the story's second voice of reason, is also hunted down and nearly murdered by Jack's troop of hunters, who are motivated by bloodlust rather than by a desire to survive and be rescued. According to Freud the two strongest libidinal impulses are toward sex (procreativity) and death (destruction). Since sex does not occur on the all-male island, the boys' subconscious impulses point toward death. Golding thus suggests that the human subconscious drive for destruction is a central aspect of the Cold War scenario. (In this respect, like Bernard Wolfe in LIMBO '90 [1953], he anticipates Arthur Kopit's 1984 play, END OF THE WORLD, which views the subconscious death wish as the final guarantor that Mutually Assured Destruction [MAD] will inevitably devolve into nuclear war. Stanley KUBRICK also addresses the themes of sex and death in his 1964 BLACK HUMOR film satire DR. STRANGELOVE.)

The conclusion of *Lord of the Flies* underscores the central place of irrationality in Golding's world view. No ship ever sees the smoke from the small fire Ralph struggled to maintain as the group's best logical hope to be noticed, but a blaze intended to kill Ralph engulfs most of the island and draws the attention of a passing navy ship. The fire, inspired by Jack's bloodlust, seems to serve the unconscious death wish, since it consumes the community's supply of food and fuel. But it also inadvertently succeeds where all of Ralph's rational planning and responsible behavior have failed—the boys are rescued because of it. In an irrational world, improbable occurrences can lead not only to disaster—as in FAIL-SAFE (book 1962, film 1964), where a poorly timed mechanical failure leads to NUCLEAR APOCALYPSE—they can also bring salvation.

A Jungian reading also suggests Golding's fascination with the subconscious's dual capacity to save and destroy. In such a reading, Jack may subconsciously perceive the presence of the ship. Thus his impulsive decision to set the island aflame would represent a subconscious gesture directed simultaneously toward destruction *and* salvation. In this reading, the figure of the Lord of the Flies represents the full range of subconscious impulses, not simply the destructive ones. The human inability to rid itself of the Lord of the Flies, or the subconscious, thus appears more hopeful than a reading that simply identifies the pig's head with libidinous impulses toward violence and death. (See also APOCALYPTIC FILMS.)

Love Is a Many-Splendored Thing A 1955 FILM DRAMA starring Jennifer Jones and William Holden. The story retells the Madame Butterfly tale in a Korean War setting, portraying the love affair between a male U.S. war correspondent and a beautiful female Eurasian doctor against a background of the struggle between the Chinese communists and Chinese Nationalists. The film's theme song became an enduring popular hit.

Luce, Henry A JOURNALIST. Born in Tengchow, China, in 1898 to Presbyterian missionaries, Luce was raised in China until the age of 15, when he attended the Hotchkiss School in Lakeville, Connecticut. His childhood experiences spawned a lifelong love of China that shaped his politics

during the Cold War. He entered Yale University in 1916 and graduated in 1920. After working briefly for the Chicago *Daily News* and the *Baltimore News,* he and his schoolmate Briton Hadden started *Time* MAGAZINE in 1923. Luce became editor-in-chief of *Time,* which in turn became the prototypical news magazine, then a new type of publication in America. To promote the magazine, Luce and Hadden sponsored "March of Time," a radio show on current events. By 1927 the venture was financially stable, and the founders were millionaires. Hadden died of streptococcus infection in 1929, but in 1930 Luce went on with their plan to publish a high-priced magazine for business, entitled *Fortune.* In 1935, Luce divorced his wife and married Clare Booth Brokaw, an editor at Condé Nast's *Vanity Fair* and *Vogue.* His bride took his name, and Clare Booth Luce became a major force in developing a new picture magazine, *Life,* which debuted in 1936. She was also active in Republican politics and served in the House of Representatives from 1943 to 1947. President Eisenhower named her ambassador to Italy in 1953.

Henry Luce strongly endorsed the U.S. entry into World War II. At the end of the war he established Time-Life International to distribute *Time* and *Life* overseas. In the 1950s he also introduced *Architectural Forum* and *House & Home* to capitalize on the postwar housing boom, but these did not prove profitable, and Luce sold *House & Home* and suspended publication of *Architectural Forum* in 1964. (*Architectural Forum* was taken over by the nonprofit American Planning and Civic Association and resumed publication in 1965.) On the other hand, *Sports Illustrated,* which Luce introduced in 1954, proved a great success.

As a Cold War publisher, Luce was strongly anti-communist, a fervent opponent of Mao Zedong's communist revolution, and an avid supporter of Chiang Kai-shek, the leader of the Chinese Nationalists, with whom Luce had a close personal relationship. Luce used his personal resources and prestige to support the so-called China Lobby that called for continued support to the Nationalist Chinese government in the late 1940s even while many State Department officials, including Secretary of State George Marshall, had concluded that Chiang was corrupt and ineffectual. Luce thus led the voices that condemned the Truman administration for "permitting" the fall of China to the communists in 1949. Four years earlier, Luce had had a falling out with Theodore White, his star foreign correspondent in China whose anti-Chiang reports *Time* editors softened or even revised to support Chiang. White finally resigned in 1945 and published his own view in THUNDER OUT OF CHINA (1946), a bestseller that was later banned in State Department libraries overseas and was actually burned during the RED SCARE by two aides of Senator Joseph McCarthy, Roy Cohn and David Schine.

Life supported Vice President Nixon in the 1960 presidential election, despite Luce's close ties to John Kennedy's family. Throughout the Kennedy administration, his publications were lukewarm on Kennedy's performance, which was too "soft on Communism" for Luce's tastes. Luce did approve of Kennedy's demotion of Undersecretary of State Chester Bowles, whom Luce found too conciliatory toward the communists, and *Time* praised Kennedy's handling of the Cuban Missile Crisis, which, "In sharp contrast to frustration in Vietnam, murkiness in Laos and stalemate in Berlin" represented "action with honor." Luce also helped pressure Kennedy into retaining the U.S. policy of opposing communist China's entry into the United Nations, and Luce publications were early supporters of the Diem government in South Vietnam, which the United States also supported in the early 1960s. According to W. A. Swanberg, editors at *Time* frequently altered reports from their Saigon bureau to remove criticisms of Diem and provide a more positive outlook on the progress of the war.

On the other hand, despite his strong stand against international communism, Luce took a lead in investigating domestic right-wing extremism, and *Time* was the first to expose the right-wing John Birch Society. However, when *Life* was faced with an advertising boycott in 1961 after criticizing Dr. Fred Schwarz's Christian Anti-Communist Crusade, Luce ordered *Life* publisher C. D. Jackson to appear at a rally and apologize for the magazine's "oversimplified misinterpretation" of the organization. Luce stepped down as editor-in-chief of Time, Inc. in 1964, but as editorial chairman he exercised control over editorial policy until his death in 1967.

For additional reading, see *Dictionary of Literary Biography* (vol. 91, *American Magazine Journalists 1900–1960*); Halberstam's *The Powers that Be.*

Lvov, Arkady   A Soviet EXILED WRITER (to the United States). Born in the U.S.S.R. in 1931, Lvov published 16 novels in the Soviet Union before immigrating to the United States in 1976. When he left the U.S.S.R., he smuggled out a microfilm of *The Courtyard* by hiding it in a shoeshine kit. In the 800-page novel set during the Stalinist era, 1936–53, several families in a tenement building serve as a microcosm of Soviet society. The novel criticizes Stalin's rule and what Lvov saw as government-sanctioned anti-Semitism. *The Courtyard* was published in the United States 13 years later, in 1989.

MacBird A 1966 play by Barbara Garson, produced Off-Off-Broadway. The Vietnam War-era work parodies Shakespeare's *Macbeth*, likening the assassinated John F. Kennedy to King Duncan; Lady Bird Johnson to Lady Macbeth; and President Johnson to Macbeth himself. The play, which vilified Johnson, found favor among opponents of the war who had come to detest him. (See also THEATER; SATIRE; VIETNAM WAR LITERATURE.)

Mad Max A 1979 Australian-made SCIENCE FICTION FILM starring Mel Gibson, Joanne Samuel and Hugh Keays-Byrne and directed by George Miller. The film creates a postapocalyptic setting in which society has essentially disintegrated, and chaos and violence are normal characteristics of daily life. The violent story centers on a good policeman who decides to quit his hopeless and dangerous job but resumes his career after his wife and child are kidnapped and murdered. The film's depiction of a civilization falling apart expresses a common Cold War theme. The aridity of the land and the lawlessness of the community also suggest the depths to which civilization might descend after a nuclear war. Two sequels were made, *The Road Warrior* (1982) and *Mad Max Beyond Thunderdome* (1985). (See also APOCALYPTIC FILMS.)

magazines Magazines influenced and were influenced by the Cold War in several ways. Political magazines discussed Cold War policies and current events, often from distinct political perspectives. For instance, I. F. STONE

founded *I. F. Stone's Weekly* in 1953 to provide an otherwise absent forum for his left-wing perspective on the Cold War and other contemporary events. The four-page subscription newsletter ran through December 1971. William F. BUCKLEY Jr., on the other hand, founded the *National Review* in 1955 to create an outlet for the right-wing views he was having difficulty airing in the mainstream press. The *National Review* eventually became an important conservative voice that helped the rise of Ronald REAGAN and the more extreme form of conservatism he and his followers represented. The magazine retained Buckley's belief that religion is a necessary component of American conservatism; it once ran a book review by Whittaker Chambers, Alger Hiss's accuser, criticizing the right-wing Ayn RAND's novel *Atlas Shrugged* (1957) because her philosophy of "objectivism" was essentially atheistic. Buckley also used the *National Review* to disassociate his own variety of right-wing conservatism from the ultra-right-wing John Birch Society, and to criticize the efforts of the more moderate conservatives, President Richard Nixon and Secretary of State Henry Kissinger, to promote détente with the U.S.S.R. in the 1970s.

COUNTERATTACK was an even more extreme right-wing journal that began publication in 1947. It was founded by three former FBI agents who were frustrated by the FBI's policy of refusing to make public its files on suspected communists and communist sympathizers. The magazine ran articles identifying alleged communists and "fellow travelers." Its greatest effect on Cold War culture, however, was the publication of a special report, RED CHANNELS, which listed people in the entertainment industry who had been identified as having communist affiliations in the present or past. *Red Channels* quickly became a major source for BLACKLISTING in the TELEVISION and radio industries. Over the course of the Cold War, *Commentary,* published by the American Jewish Committee, took an increasing right-wing conservative stand, bringing to prominence such Jewish conservatives as Irving Kristol, Norman Podhoretz and Gertrude Himmelfarb. Likewise, *The New Republic,* which had long been a liberal magazine, acquired an ever more conservative orientation under new ownership later in the Cold War.

On the other hand, *The Nation* remained a consistent left-liberal voice. It opposed the RED SCARE and supported Democratic candidates over Republicans, though it often expressed frustration with the Democrats for being too similar to the Republicans. It advocated arms control and reduction, opposed the Vietnam War and government attempts to suppress the antiwar movement, reported on government investigations of such politically active figures as Albert Einstein, and generally sought some degree of reconciliation among the superpowers. Its editor-in-chief after 1978, Victor Navasky, wrote *Naming Names,* a 1980 study of the liberals, leftists and conservatives who informed on former friends and colleagues as part of the investigations of the entertainment industry by the HOUSE COMMITTEE ON UN-AMERICAN ACTIVITIES (HUAC) during the Red Scare.

The Bulletin of the Atomic Scientists focused on the scientific and technological aspects of the Cold War and generally advocated responsible arms reduction and dialogue with the Soviets. It was especially known for the "doomsday clock" on its cover, set to a few minutes before midnight to symbolize that time was running out for humanity as the prospects for nuclear war intensified. Throughout the Cold War, the editors moved the clock closer to 12:00 as the threat of nuclear war increased, setting it farther back when tensions significantly lessened.

Although leftist intellectuals rarely prevailed in American politics, they flourished in several literary journals. *The Partisan Review,* which was taken over by Philip Rahv and William Phillips in 1934, provided a forum for such literary figures as Saul Bellow, Paul Goodman, Bernard Malamud, Norman Podhoretz, and Lionel TRILLING. Other "New York intellectuals" who contributed included Mary MCCARTHY, Edmund WILSON, Irving HOWE, Dwight Macdonald, James Agee, James T. Farrell and Delmore Schwartz. The journal had broken with Stalinism at the time Rahv and Phillips took it over; through the mid-1940s it retained a Trotskyist-Marxist orientation politically, but grew increasingly conservative thereafter. During the 1950s it attacked both New Criticism and the myth criticism of Northrop Frye on the grounds that they removed works of literature from their historical context.

In 1954 Howe, a socialist since the age of 14, founded the political journal *Dissent,* a publication dedicated to democratic socialism. Howe rejected the apolitical tenets of the New Criticism, the dominant school of literary criticism from the 1940s to the early 1960s, maintaining that writers whose interests are purely literary cannot produce good criticism. His conception of democratic socialism varied

significantly from ideas propounded by the New Left during the late 1960s, and in his book *Decline of the New* (1970) he articulates those differences.

Starting in 1957 the GROVE PRESS issued *The Evergreen Review,* which ran pieces by such leftist, anti-establishment and/or avant-garde writers as Samuel BECKETT, Jean-Paul Sartre, Lawrence FERLINGHETTI, Allen GINSBERG, Carlos FUENTES, Denise LEVERTOV, Terry SOUTHERN and Imamu A. Baraka (LeRoi Jones), who reported on a 1960 trip to Castro's Cuba he made with several other black Americans. The magazine also published portions of Che Guevara's journals.

In 1958 Paul Krassner founded *The Realist,* a magazine that emerged as a voice for 1960s antiestablishment radicals, anti-Vietnam War activists and the COUNTERCULTURE. It published pieces by Lenny BRUCE, Jules FEIFFER, Kurt VONNEGUT Jr., Joseph Heller, Terry Southern, Abbie Hoffman and Jerry Rubin, as well as articles with such provocative titles as "Fuck Communism!" "Un-American Activities in My Own Home," "The Sex Life of [FBI Director] J. Edgar Hoover," and "Why Was [wife of U.S. attorney general John Mitchell] Martha Mitchell Kidnapped?"

Margaret RANDALL coedited *El Corno Emplumado* (The Plumed Horn), a leftist, bilingual, Mexican literary journal that was influential in both Latin America and the United States. The journal introduced U.S. readers to the works of prominent Latin American writers, including Ernesto Cardenal, who later became the minister of culture in Nicaragua's Sandinista government, and Octavio Paz, who won the 1990 Nobel Prize for literature. It also brought to the attention of Latin American readers the works of such North American writers as Allen Ginsberg, Denise Levertov and Diane DiPrima, among others.

Norman COUSINS edited the *Saturday Review,* which examined arts and letters and other aspects of American culture from a more mainstream, centrist position. Cousins did use the magazine to pursue a liberal agenda that promoted a responsible program of nuclear disarmament, peace-oriented dialogues among U.S. and Soviet scientists, and a strong United Nations capable of subordinating nationalism. Cousins also took editorial positions against the Vietnam War and in favor of space exploration, as well as stands on such non-Cold War topics as racial discrimination, pollution, television violence and cigarette advertising.

Such large-circulation, mainstream news and general-interest magazines as Henry LUCE's *Time* and *Life; Newsweek; U.S. News and World Report; Harper's; Collier's;* and *Look* were more conservative than the literary journals, though not as far right as the *National Review.* Their reporting was more likely to highlight the abuses of the Soviet Union, China, Cuba and other communist countries and less likely to depict the United States as a nation employing foreign policy in pursuit of its own selfish interests or to analyze the impact of corporations and consumer capitalism on U.S. political behavior and social developments. In short, they more readily accepted the basic premises of the Cold War, which the leftist journals often questioned: the need for nuclear weapons and a large defense budget, a foreign policy predicated on containing worldwide communism, and a distrust of domestic communists and left-wing activists. Especially during the first half of the Cold War, these mainstream journals tended to provide positive representations of the U.S. government and its allies and negative depictions of its enemies. For example, most mainstream magazines supported the Vietnam War at least through the late 1960s.

Luce was fervently anti-communist, and his magazines, *Time* and *Life,* reflected that position. *Life* ran pictures of 50 "Dupes and Fellow Travelers" who had participated in the 1949 Cultural and Scientific Conference for World Peace, an international conference of artists, writers, musicians and others who were ostensibly trying to reduce the growing Cold War tensions and effect world peace. The conference was sponsored by the U.S. National Council of Arts, Sciences and Professions, an organization that *Life* claimed was dominated by "intellectuals who fellow-travel the Communist line." Stating that the American participants ranged from "hard working fellow travelers to soft-headed do gooders," the article criticized such nationally prominent figures as Arthur MILLER, Charles CHAPLIN, Thomas MANN, Leonard Bernstein, Dorothy Parker, Langston Hughes, Lillian Hellman and sculptor Jo Davidson. A *Life* editorial two weeks later praised *God's Underground,* a book about the Christian underground in communist Russia. And a 1952 *Life* article by Chester Wilmot entitled "Allies Handed Stalin His Victory" attacked the 1945 Yalta agreement, a favorite scapegoat of the political right.

Time's editorials and reporting also typically reflected a hard line against the Soviet Union and especially against the People's Republic of China. Luce, who grew up in China (his parents were missionaries), had been an ardent supporter of Chiang Kai-Shek in the 1940s, and he blamed the Truman State Department for the fall of China to the communists, citing its failure to support Chiang fully. The *Time* editorial staff repeatedly revised dispatches critical of Chiang to provide a more sympathetic slant. T. H. White, *Time's* China correspondent, became increasingly disenchanted with Chiang and finally left the magazine in 1945 because it would not publish his view of the situation in China. One of White's editors was Whittaker Chambers, the former communist turned fervent anti-communist whom Luce hired to control the liberalism of his reporters. Chambers became famous in 1948, when he accused Alger Hiss of spying for the Soviets.

The other mainstream magazines also typically endorsed the Cold War as necessary for U.S. national security and for protecting the remaining "free world" that had not yet been "enslaved" by communism. For instance, a 1951 issue of *Collier's* featured a panel of "experts" who contemplated a war with the U.S.S.R. They presented a scenario in which the United States would prevail after sending airborne troops into the Ural mountains to destroy the Soviet arsenal of atomic bombs. As independent leftist JOURNALIST I. F. Stone pointed out in a critique of the article, the article's overall effect is to make atomic war with the Soviets appear to be an acceptable idea, since the United States would surely prevail. The *Collier's* experts also suggested that the Soviet regime was a "rule of terror" that would quickly be rejected by its oppressed citizens once they were given a chance to do so. According to Stone, "The impression *Collier's* creates is that Russia is one vast slave labor camp where we need only shoot the guards and wreck the gates to be hailed as liberators."

Somewhat more liberal than the other mainstream, general-interest magazines, though still in the political center, the *New Yorker* occasionally ran pieces that questioned Cold War assumptions. It published John Hersey's HIROSHIMA (1946) before its publication as a book, thus allowing readers to consider the destructive power of nuclear weaponry from the perspectives of actual survivors. It also ran Jonathan Schell's THE FATE OF THE EARTH in 1982, a series of articles that appeared during the arms buildup of the first Reagan administration warning that a major nuclear war would threaten all life on Earth. The *New Yorker* was also critical of the FBI, thereby provoking its ire. The entry in the FBI file on James BALDWIN from July 30, 1964, reads:

> . . . *The New Yorker* has over the years been irresponsible and unreliable with respect to references concerning the Director and the FBI. New York has previously been instructed to follow the publication of this book [allegedly planned by Baldwin for publication in the *New Yorker*] and to remain alert to any possibility of securing galley proofs for the Bureau.

Men's magazines such as PLAYBOY, *Esquire* and later *Penthouse* had a twofold influence on Cold War culture. First, they embodied fundamental differences between the democratic, capitalistic Western societies that published them and the communist governments that banned them. Not only did the communists object to the publication of nude photos and sexually oriented material, which they regarded as morally degenerate, they also decried the promulgation of a "decadent" consumer culture that promoted luxury items and middle-class attitudes and tastes. By contrast, though many conservatives and religious figures agreed with the communist critique, the very fact that the United States and other democracies permitted the publication of the controversial magazines illustrated the considerably greater freedom the press enjoyed in the West. Moreover, especially during the Kennedy years, many American men and women were attracted to *Esquire* and *Playboy*'s image of the modern, successful man as tasteful, knowledgeable, cultured, urbane, well-accoutered and frankly open about his sexuality. This vision of the ideal man clashed with the proclaimed communist ideal of the upright laborer in work clothes who is dedicated to serving the cause of the people. Likewise, *Playboy*'s ideal woman contrasted with the idealized Soviet woman. Whereas the *Playboy* woman was a sexy toy for men, dressed in expensive lingerie and adorned with cosmetics, the ideal Soviet woman was unconscious of her appearance, hard-working and selflessly devoted to both her family and her society.

In addition to highlighting basic differences between capitalist and communist cultures, *Playboy* also influenced domestic politics by promoting liberal political positions. Early issues of the magazine criticized the House Committee on Un-American Activities (HUAC) and J. Edgar Hoover while defending the America Civil Liberties Union. Later issues criticized the Vietnam War and supported the sexual revolution. *Playboy*'s fiction and essays included pieces by and about respected writers, thinkers and creative artists, among them Vladimir NABOKOV, Norman MAILER, Terry Southern, Jean-Paul Sartre, Federico Fellini, Bertrand Russell and Miles Davis. The magazine also endorsed JAZZ and other artistic forms favored by avant-garde sophisticates that were banned behind the IRON CURTAIN. It provided an outlet to middle America for many figures who otherwise typically reached a narrower, more liberal, and comparatively better-educated audience. Often attacked by conservatives for promoting degenerate sexual values and by feminists for depicting women as mere sexual objects, the men's magazines provided a dramatic contrast between the capitalist and communist cultures.

Comic and satirical magazines also touched upon the Cold War and American Cold War–era politics. Among these *Mad Magazine,* the *National Lampoon* (an offshoot of the *Harvard Lampoon*) and *Spy* stand out. All primarily satirized American culture, but they sometimes satirized politics and Cold War hypocrisy as well. First published in 1952 by William Gaines, *Mad* paved the way for the later satirical magazines and such early *Mad* imitators as *Cracked* and *Sick*. It originally employed a comic-book format, but in 1955 it adopted a magazine format after the 1954 Comics Code effectively censored it as a comic book. In 1955 Al Feldstein replaced founding editor Harvey Kurtzman. Among the first writers for the newly formatted *Mad* were Ernie Kovacs, Carl Reiner, Jean Shepherd and Roger Price, while artist Don Martin joined founding artists Will Elder, Wally Wood and Jack Davis. During the Red Scare, *Mad* was sometimes accused of having communist influences, primarily because of its irreverent attitude toward authority and its cheerful willingness to debunk the pristine image of the American family and American way of life then commonly featured on TELEVISION SITUATION COMEDIES. Its absurdist parodies sometimes featured BLACK HUMOR, and its targets ranged from government, business, the entertainment industry and other establishment institutions to the ultra-right-wing John Birch Society, the Ku Klux Klan, black militants and the New Left. Presidents Kennedy, Johnson, Nixon and Bush were among those satirized, as was Dr. Frederick Wertham, whose book SEDUCTION OF THE INNOCENT (1954) charged that comic books were corrupting American youth.

Jack Davis' "What's My Shine" satirized the ARMY-MCCARTHY HEARINGS when *Mad* was still in its comic book format (issue 17). The episode depicted the hearings as a television panel show based on the then-popular show "What's My Line?" and alluded to Senator Joseph McCarthy's aide, David Schine, who was at the center of the controversy that sparked the hearings. The 1958 anniversary issue featured a spoof magazine, *Caveman's Weekly,* that satirized the arms race in an article entitled, "Is the Stone-Ax the Ultimate Weapon?" Antonio Prohias, one of Cuba's most influential cartoonists, who fled the island in 1960 because of his anti-communist cartoons, contributed *Spy vs. Spy,* a regular feature that debuted in January 1961 and spoofed Cold War–era spying. Though its ridicule was often antiestablishment, *Mad* was eventually taken over by the very establishment Time Warner corporation, and its circulation eventually grew to 800,000. (Maria Reidelbach's *Completely Mad* analyzes the satirical content, reproduces every cover, provides a history of virtually every issue, and profiles every artist and staff writer.) Between 1963 and 1973 the *Satire Newsletter* provided academic and political satire, articles about satire and examples of satire in Eastern Europe, Germany, France and the U.S.S.R. (See also SATIRE.)

For additional reading, see Halberstam's *The Powers that Be;* Sloane's *American Humor Magazines and Comic Periodicals.*

Mailer, Norman   A NOVELIST and NONFICTION WRITER. Born in Long Branch, New Jersey, to a Jewish family, Mailer grew up in New York City and graduated from Harvard in 1943 with a degree in engineering. He served in the army during World War II, and his experiences formed the basis of his first novel, *The Naked and the Dead* (1948). Set in a Pacific campaign, the novel follows the exploits of a reconnaissance platoon comprised of a cross-section of Americans. It also explores the differences in background, personal styles and philosophies of a conservative general and his liberal aide. The ambitious General Cummings believes in efficacy of power and argues that victors acquire the characteristics of the nations they defeat, so the United States will become more fascistic and militaristic after the war. The more idealistic Lt. Hearn disagrees. A highly effective strategist, Cummings is denied credit for the American victory when the Japanese defense crumbles while is he away and his unimaginative second-in-command obtains their surrender. Meanwhile, Hearn is killed when a resentful sergeant sets him up on a patrol. Historical events prove to be less subject to individual control than either man had assumed.

In Mailer's second novel, *The Barbary Shore* (1951), the rational universe breaks down even further. The amnesiac narrator cannot distinguish fact from fiction or memory from imagination. He rents a room in a boardinghouse where the fellow boarders prove to be spies, double agents and former communists. The communist power struggle between Trotsky, a Jew, and Stalin, portrayed as an anti-Semite, provides a backdrop for the political and sexual liaisons that the novel centers on. Communism proves bankrupt in the book, but so does American culture, and the protagonist must find meaning beyond the failed institutions of politics and religion. Mailer claimed to be attempting to bridge Marx and Freud, insisting on the connection between sex and politics, as well as on the importance of representing history in personal terms. He addresses similar themes in his next novel, *The Deer Park* (1955).

Mailer takes up politics more directly in *The Armies of the Night* (1968) and *Miami and the Siege of Chicago* (1968). In the *The Armies of the Night*, he describes his personal experiences at a massive anti-Vietnam War demonstration in Washington, D.C., pairing them with more objective reporting about events he did not personally witness. As one of the protesters, he is arrested and jailed. Even in this account of a public event, Mailer retains his awareness of the sexual energy underlying political protest. He observes that the day spent marching, chanting and being beaten by riot police will unleash libidos, and many of the protesters will yield to a strong desire to have sex in the evening. *Miami and the Siege of Chicago* reports on the 1968 presidential nominating conventions. Together the books introduce Mailer's attempt to write "history as a novel." In *Some Honorable Men: Political Conventions, 1960–1972* (1976), Mailer continues his study of the American political process.

In 1965 Mailer described President Johnson as "alienated from the self by a double sense of identity . . . [Johnson exhibits] the near insanity of most of us, and his need for action is America's need for action; not brave action, but action; any kind of action . . . A future death of spirit lies close and heavy upon American life." For Mailer, the Vietnam War was a manifestation of this need for action and of this spiritual emptiness. *Why Are We in Viet Nam?* (1967) reflects these sentiments in the narration of a Texas teenager who "sees through [the] shit" of adult society while recounting his observations and experiences, including a high-tech hunting trip to Alaska replete with advanced weaponry and helicopters. In *Of a Fire on the Moon* (1970), Mailer regards the need for action in terms of the U.S. space program. Subsequently, his attention turned to responding to feminist attacks on his work, and he became less directly concerned with Cold War–related issues. Nonetheless, his interest in violence and male aggression can be viewed in terms of his quest for meaning and personal validation in a spiritually empty Cold War society.

Makarova, Natalia A DANCE performer and Soviet defector. Born in Leningrad in 1940, she attended the famous Vaganova Ballet, the training school for the Kirov Ballet. She became the favorite pupil of Natalia Dudinskaya, a former prima ballerina and the wife of the Kirov's director. Upon graduating, Makarova entered the Kirov and quickly rose to prominence. To compensate for the 1961 defection of Rudolf NUREYEV, the Kirov allowed her to perform the title role of *Giselle* when the company performed in London soon afterward. She later told a reporter, "They wanted to put on a show which would offset to some extent the effect of his action." Her performance was outstanding. She impressed Western critics and audiences again in the fall of 1961 when the Kirov made its first tour in the United States, and once more in 1964 when she also performed in the United States and again received rave reviews. Makarova defected on September 4, 1970, at the conclusion of a six-week season the Kirov had performed in London. Two weeks later she explained her decision in several articles for the London *Sunday Telegraph*: "I want to be free—free to dance as I please, free to develop my art, free to work with whom I want to work . . . In the Soviet Union there is no experimenting with new styles, new techniques, new choreography, such as there is in the West . . . I would dance the old, classical roles to the end of my dancing years, and that would be that. Some ballerinas are ready to accept that fate. For me, it was artistic death." Makarova exemplified her point by noting how the Kirov had suppressed a new version of *Romeo and Juliet* because the directors deemed it too erotic. She had worked on the ballet for a year before its cancellation.

On October 11, 1970, Makarova signed a contract with the American Ballet Theater (ABT). Prior to her ABT debut she danced with Nureyev in a performance televised by the BBC and then appeared on the Ed SULLIVAN show in November. She premiered with the ABT on December 22, when she performed Giselle. Soon after she appeared in *Coppélia* and *Lilac Garden*, which were choreographed by the contemporary choreographer Antony Tudor. In 1970 she won a Tony award for her performance in the musical comedy *On Your Toes*. In 1971 she further broadened her dance repertoire when she appeared in Alvin Ailey's *The River*, a jazz-influenced duet that she performed with Erik Bruhn. She also performed an expressionist interpretation of Bela Bartok's *The Miraculous Mandarin* and danced Juliet in Tudor's new interpretation of *Romeo and Juliet*. The critics appreciated not only her dancing but also her reasons for defecting. Nancy Goldner wrote in *Dance News*, "As I was watching Makarova cavort, swing her hips, smile brazenly at the audience, and pout a la Bardot at Bruhn, I thought, so this is what this lady came to America for . . . She won her point." When her ABT contract expired in 1972, Makarova moved to London so she could dance throughout Europe with Nureyev, but she continued to make guest appearances with the ABT and helped convince Mikhail BARYSHNIKOV to dance with that company after he defected in 1974. She had earlier danced with Barynshnikov in his New York debut on July 27, 1974, before a sold-out audience at Lincoln Center. The performance was an enormous success. In 1980 Makarova published her autobiography, *Defected from Russia*.

Malevil A 1973 APOCALYPTIC NOVEL by Robert Merle. One of the comparatively few novels to address NUCLEAR APOCALYPSE during the U.S.-Soviet détente of the 1970s, *Malevil* tells the story of old friends who are attending a reunion in the castle inherited by the protagonist, Emmanuel. They are in the wine cellar when the nuclear attack comes, and the friends survive by immersing themselves in the wine vats. The book then describes the postnuclear society they construct. Emmanuel, whose name alludes to Jesus, emerges as the communal leader, retaining his sense of spirituality despite the horror of the apocalypse. Emmanuel establishes a form of agrarian collectivism and establishes policies on the distribution of food, defense, religion and sex (the group contains only one woman). The conclusion suggests that the fledgling society will survive by pursuing enlightened policies that are informed by responsibility.

For additional reading, see Dowling's *Fictions of Nuclear Disaster*.

Maltz, Albert A SCREENWRITER, playwright and short-story writer. Considered one of the most talented of the HOLLYWOOD TEN, Maltz was an active member of the Communist Party. He frequently contributed to Marxist periodicals, and his article in *New Masses* about socialist realism provoked a major party controversy in 1946. That essay criticized the restrictions on freedom of thought within the party, and Maltz was viciously attacked by Alvah BESSIE, John Howard LAWSON, Howard FAST and others. He eventually had to repudiate it in order to remain a communist; however, the savagery of the attack provoked others to leave the party, and several cited it as one of their reasons for informing on communists before the HOUSE COMMITTEE ON UN-AMERICAN ACTIVITIES (HUAC). Before his 1947 testimony before HUAC, Maltz wrote several screenplays, including such patriotic wartime films as *Destination Tokyo* (1943) and *Pride of the Marines* (1945). He worked on but did not receive screen credit for *Casablanca* (1942). Along with the nine other "unfriendly witnesses," Maltz was called to speak about alleged communist influences in Hollywood films. The Ten refused to testify, citing their First Amendment protection under the Constitution. Maltz, like the others, was cited for contempt of Congress. After his appeals were denied, Maltz was sentenced to a prison term, which he served in 1950. He was also blacklisted, though he pseudonymously wrote several Hollywood films, most notably *The Robe* (1953) while living in Mexico from 1952 to 1962 (See also BLACKLISTING and EXILED WRITERS [from the United States].) The blacklist was broken in 1960 when fellow Hollywood Ten member Dalton TRUMBO was credited for SPARTACUS and EXODUS, but Maltz did not receive any screen credits until 1970, when he wrote *Two Mules for Sister Sara*. He also appeared in HOLLYWOOD ON TRIAL, Lester COLE's 1976 FILM DOCUMENTARY about the RED SCARE in Hollywood. During the 1970s, Maltz challenged Trumbo's public assertion that everyone but HUAC was equally a victim of the Red Scare, even those who had informed on others; by contrast, Maltz remained adamant about the moral superiority of the Ten's refusal to name names. He also publicly supported Alexander SOLZHENITSYN, who was then still living in the U.S.S.R. and "suffering blacklist" there.

For additional reading, see Navasky's *Naming Names*.

"Man Called Sloane, A"   A TELEVISION SPY SHOW that ran on NBC in 1979–80. Reminiscent of James BOND, "A Man Called Sloane" presented the adventures of Thomas Remington Sloane (Robert Conrad), who worked for the counterintelligence team UNIT, which was accountable only to the U.S. president. The highly intelligent, urbane and ultra-sophisticated Sloane traveled throughout the world, using his romantic charms as one of his espionage tools. Sloane was accompanied by Torque, a tall agent whose stainless-steel hand could be adapted to various detachable gadgets. As in the Bond movies, the spies were supported by a high-tech lab that provided them with exotic but useful devices. A highly sophisticated computer named "Effie," which spoke in a sexy female voice, also contributed to the effort to preserve national security.

"Man Called X, The"   A TELEVISION SPY SHOW that ran in syndication from 1955 to 1956. Based on real government files and supervised by Ladislas Farago, a former agent of the U.S. Office of Naval Intelligence, the show featured the exploits of American secret agent Ken Thurston (Barry Sullivan), whose code name was "X." Thurston traveled throughout the world to such locations as Prague, Teheran and Nepal in order to rescue brilliant scientists and beautiful women. A radio version of the show ran from 1944 to 1952.

"Man from U.N.C.L.E., The"   A TELEVISION SPY SHOW that ran on NBC from 1964 to 1968. The show featured the exploits of two agents, American Napoleon Solo (Robert VAUGHN) and Russian Illya Kuryakin (David McCallum), who worked for the secret organization U.N.C.L.E. (United Network Command for Law and Enforcement) in its battle against the international crime syndicate T.H.R.U.S.H. The suave, sophisticated Solo played counterpoint to the shy but handsome Kuryakin. Solo was patterned after James BOND; in fact, producer Norman Felton had consulted with Bond's creator, Ian Fleming, and secured permission to use the name of a minor character from GOLDFINGER (1964) as Solo's namesake. As in the Bond movies, the U.N.C.L.E. characters traveled the world and employed high-tech gad-

gets. As the show progressed, the plots became increasingly farfetched until they ultimately parodied the spy genre. The cooperation between an American and a Russian anticipated the U.S.–Soviet détente that began shortly after the show was terminated. The collaboration may have appealed to desires for a reconciliation of the Cold War following the tense moments of the Cuban Missile Crisis in October 1962.) The show generated the spin-off series: THE GIRL FROM U.N.C.L.E. (1966); a made-for-television movie, *The Return of the Man from U.N.C.L.E.* (1983); and several SPY FILM spin-offs that were shown in movie houses. These include *To Trap a Spy* (1966), *The Spy with My Face* (1966) and *One Spy Too Many* (1968).

For additional reading, see McNeil's *Total Television*.

Man in the Gray Flannel Suit, The   A 1955 novel by Sloan Wilson and a 1956 FILM DRAMA starring Gregory Peck, Jennifer Jones, and Fredric March and directed by Nunnally Johnson. This story about a returning World War II veteran explores many of the social changes of the 1950s that occurred during one of the most intense periods of the Cold War. Among the issues covered are the development of the suburbs, the rise of the advertising industry, child support for illegitimate war babies fathered overseas, problems for veterans trying to adapt to postwar America, and the growing phenomenon of divorce.

"Man Who Never Was, The"   A TELEVISION SPY SHOW that ran on ABC from 1966 to 1967. Filmed on location in Berlin, Munich, London, Athens and other European cities, the show featured the exploits of the American spy Peter Murphy (Robert Lansing), who in the first episode narrowly escapes from East Berlin when enemy agents kill his double, millionaire playboy Mark Wainwright. Murphy assumes Wainwright's identity, which he uses as a cover for his espionage activities throughout Europe. He is accompanied by Wainwright's wife, Eva (Dana Wynter), who recognizes Murphy as an impostor but goes along with him in order to retain the family fortune.

Manchurian Candidate, The   A best-selling 1959 POLITICAL NOVEL by Richard Condon and a 1962 POLITICAL FILM starring Frank Sinatra, Laurence Harvey and Angela Lansbury and directed by John Frankenheimer. The story tells how communists brainwash a company of captured American soldiers during the Korean War. One of the soldiers, Sergeant Raymond Shaw (Harvey), is programmed to obey the orders of his controller whenever he sees the queen of diamonds in a deck of playing cards. He and the other captured soldiers are then made to forget their brainwashing and released. They have been programmed to believe that Shaw saved their company through heroic efforts, and based on their reports, he receives the Medal of Honor. Shaw returns to civilian life, where he again encounters his mother (Lansbury) who, unbeknownst to him or anyone else, is a top Soviet spy—the controller who uses him to commit political assassinations. She has remarried and is now the wife of Senator John Iselin, a right-wing demagogue and vice presidential candidate whom the audience identifies with Senator Joseph McCarthy. The communists plan to program Shaw to shoot Iselin's running mate with a high-powered rifle, thereby elevating Iselin to the presidency. The plot takes a new turn, however, when another soldier from the company, Major Marco (Sinatra), recognizes that he has been brainwashed, reprograms himself and, with the assistance of the FBI, CIA and military intelligence officers, works to thwart the assassination.

Both the book and film present an anti-RED SCARE perspective, though the book takes harder shots at the political right wing, which expresses "opinions they rented that week from [right-wing columnists] Mr. SOKOLSKY, Mr. [David] Lawrence, Mr. [Westbrook] Pegler, and that fascinating younger fellow that had written about men and God at Yale [William F. BUCKLEY Jr.]." However, both the film and book make the connection between Iselin and McCarthy evident and satiric. Like McCarthy, Iselin has fabricated his war background, attacked the State Department and arbitrarily invented the specifics behind his accusations. Like McCarthy, he keeps altering the number of communists he alleges to be in the State Department because, as Mrs. Iselin explains, the confusion shifts the focus of attention to the number of communists in government and away from the question of whether any communists are there at all. The story's ultimate irony is that the communists prefer to have men like Iselin in power because they undermine U.S. democracy and thereby advance the communist cause more than anyone else.

The story depicts communists as cynical, insensitive and ideologically driven. It also explores the dangers of a dominating mother whose son is unhealthily—and resentfully—attached to her. In this respect it fits in with other films from the early Cold War, which also point to unhealthy manifestations of motherly love as a Cold War danger. (See MOMISM.) Here the domineering mother is literally a Soviet agent who indirectly causes her son to be brainwashed and turned into an unknowing assassin under her control. In the book she literally rapes him while he is under her hypnotic control just before his final assignment; in the film she merely kisses him suggestively on the lips. However Sergeant Shaw asserts his spiritual freedom, his underlying sense of patriotism, and his male liberation by assassinating her instead of his assigned target, the presidential nominee.

The story also contrasts two forms of mind control and distortion of reality, a recurrent Cold War theme. *The Manchurian Candidate* attacks both the communists' scientifically induced brainwashing and McCarthy's fear-induced hysteria as pernicious national security risks. Cynical, emotionally restrained, highly cerebral, cruel and perverse communist scientists perform the brainwashing by which they hope to seize control of American politics. On the other hand, an easily manipulated, shallow alcoholic and his shrewd, bitter, vindictive wife create the anti-communist hysteria by which they plan to gain personal and political power. Frankenheimer recalled that "at one stage we were going to be picketed by both the American Legion and the Communist Party at the same time, which we tried to encourage of course; after all, the whole point of the film was the absurdity of any type of extremism."

A year after the film's release, an ex-military man who had recently returned from a communist country used a high-powered rifle to assassinate President John Kennedy. The parallels between art and reality so disturbed Sinatra,

a personal friend of Kennedy, that he blocked the re-release of *The Manchurian Candidate* for some 25 years.

For additional reading, see Rogin's *Ronald Reagan: The Movie.*

Maniac's Dream, The   A 1946 SCIENCE FICTION NOVEL by F. H. Rose. Rose claimed it was "the first novel about the atomic bomb," *The Maniac's Dream* appeared the year after the bombing of Hiroshima and Nagasaki. It alludes to Conrad's *Heart of Darkness:* A detached narrator observes Thara, a mad scientist at work deep in a tropical jungle. The Faustian scientist who suffers from hubris heretically likens himself to God: "Mankind harnessing to his own uses the power of Atomic Energy, will prove once and for all, that there is no other God but Man, and that he himself is God." Through a special camera obscura, Thara reveals what appears to be the destruction of the Western world, but this later proves to be literally a projection of his fantasy. Initially, however, neither the narrator nor the reader has reason to doubt the destruction on the screen: "The atomic Bomb fell somewhere between Westminster and St. Paul's . . . surely London could not be wiped out by that one bomb which we saw flash down upon it through the lovely golden hazes of that Autumn day." Eventually the native tribesmen turn against Thara, who brings about a localized NUCLEAR APOCALYPSE when he throws a nuclear bomb down a nearby volcano. In the words of the narrator, "I knew that this was no flame of fire such as ever had belched from the jaws of a volcano. It was the flame of vast, mysterious Atomic radiations which were rushing up from the bowels of the earth and pouring down with terrible and remorseless power upon the world around us." The author's postscript makes explicit his admonition about science gone amok. He condemns "the ruthlessness with which Science goes forward in its search for truth, brushing aside every obstacle, and caring for nothing but to search and find . . . Does not his [Thara's] attitude toward God and Man typify the attitude, and foretell the doom, of all men and nations who exalt Man and despise God?" (See also APOCALYPTIC NOVELS.)

For additional reading, see Dowling's *Fictions of Nuclear Disaster.*

Mann, Thomas   A German NOVELIST and winner of the 1929 Nobel Prize for literature. Born in Germany in 1875, Mann was the son of a sensitive artistic mother from southern Germany and a respectable merchant father from the north. Throughout his literary career, Mann sought to reconcile the creative artist with the social responsibilities of the bourgeoisie. Though he supported German nationalism and the German war effort during World War I, he supported socialism and the Weimar Republic after the war. As early as 1930, he opposed Hitler and the rise of Nazism by publicly supporting the Social Democratic Party, although he did not actually join it. Mann was in Switzerland in 1933 when he learned of the burning of the Reichstag, the Nazi book burnings (in which his books were spared) and Hitler's landslide victory in parliamentary elections on March 5. Consequently, he remained abroad. After a three-year public silence, he openly denounced the Nazi regime in 1936, for which action he and his family were deprived of German citizenship. Mann became a Czech citizen in 1936. He was in the United States when Germany annexed Austria in 1938. Foreseeing subsequent events in Europe, he elected to accept a chair as part-time lecturer at Princeton University and remain in America. Mann assisted other German emigrés and toured the United States to promote America's entry into World War II. Mann became a U.S. citizen in 1944, and throughout the war his work was well received in America. To many he exemplified the best of German humanism.

However, after the war, critics derided his highly autobiographical novel, *Doctor Faustus* (1947; in English, 1948). Because of his disappointment in this reception and his concern over the RED SCARE, which threatened to affect him because of his socialist proclivities (he had never been a communist), Mann went into exile in Switzerland in 1952. His disenchantment with America during this period appears in *The Black Swan* (1953; in English, 1954), in which the United States appears to be a source of rejuvenation but is actually both corrupt and corrupting. In the novella, an older woman comes to believe that her love for a young American man has renewed her menstrual cycle; in fact, she dies from cancer of the womb. Though most of Mann's literary output deals with the soul of Europe and with Nazism, his decision to flee the United States because of the Red Scare makes him a Cold War figure. (See also EXILED WRITERS [from the United States].)

For additional reading, see Tucker's *Literary Exile in the Twentieth Century.*

Marcuse, Herbert A Jewish-German EXILED WRITER (to the United States), Marxist philosopher and NONFICTION WRITER. Born in Berlin in 1889, Marcuse was a student of Edmund Husserl and Martin Heidegger during the 1920s. The left-wing, non-communist intellectual group known as the Frankfurt School, which espoused so-called Critical Theory, became attracted to his writings in 1932, and Marcuse joined their Institute of Social Research in Geneva in 1933. In 1934 he moved to New York, where he helped formulate the "Critical Theory of Society," which revitalized Marxism and social theory within U.S. intellectual circles. In 1964 Marcuse published *One-Dimensional Man*, which describes advanced industrial civilization as inherently unfree and oppressive and which calls upon citizens to make the "Great Refusal" to cooperate with it. A vehement opponent of the Vietnam War, Marcuse found a receptive audience among college-aged men and women who also opposed the war. His works were highly influential in shaping the thought of the New Left, which put itself forward as a non-communist, anti-capitalist movement interested in liberating humanity's sexual and creative energies as well as remaking social and economic institutions.

For additional reading, see Tucker's *Literary Exile in the Twentieth Century.*

"Marshall Plan in Action, The" A TELEVISION NEWS show that ran on ABC from 1950 to 1953. A series of documentary films prepared by the U.S. government and introduced by a statement from federal administrator Paul G. Hoffman, the show presented the results of the Truman administration's Marshall Plan, which helped reconstruct Western Europe after World War II. The show's run coin-

cided with the Korean War. At the end of 1951, its title was changed to "Strength for a Free World."

Martyred, The A 1964 best-selling MILITARY NOVEL by South Korean emigré Richard E. KIM. (See also EXILED WRITERS [to the United States].) *The Martyred* tells the story of a South Korean Army captain who investigates the fates of 14 Christian ministers whom the North Koreans had captured. In the process of the investigation, the captain confronts evidence that compels him to rethink his own notions of right and wrong, belief and hypocrisy, patriotism and treason.

M*A*S*H A 1968 MILITARY NOVEL by Dr. Richard Hooker; a 1970 FILM COMEDY starring Donald Sutherland, Elliott Gould, Sally Kellerman and Robert Duvall and directed by Robert Altman; and a TELEVISION SITUATION COMEDY that ran on CBS from 1972 to 1983, starring Alan Alda, Loretta Swit, Wayne Rogers, Mike Farrell, Larry Linville, David Ogden Stiers, McLean Stevenson and Harry Morgan. SCREENWRITER Ring LARDNER Jr., a previously blacklisted member of the HOLLYWOOD TEN, won an Academy Award for the screenplay for the film, which received four other Academy Award nominations including best film, best director and best editing. The television show became one of the most popular and longest-running sitcoms in the history of the medium; its final episode was a nationally reported event viewed by the largest audience ever to watch a single television program.

The novel provides a series of amusing pranks based on those actually played by surgeons in a Mobile Army Surgical Hospital (MASH) during the Korean War. The author, a doctor who served in that war, employed the pseudonym Hooker in order not to compromise his medical standing. Though it gives a rare, comic view of the war, the novel is not as artfully crafted as either the film or the television episodes; nor does it have the deeper emotional resonances that the other treatments provide.

All three versions depict life in a surgical hospital stationed just behind the front lines in Korea. Working under extremely difficult conditions, the medical staff treats a seemingly endless stream of casualties that constantly arrive fresh from the battlefield. Altman's film, which appeared just as the U.S. buildup in Vietnam had crested, provides a BLACK HUMOR view of warfare and army life in general. Like the film treatment of CATCH-22 (book 1961, film 1970), Altman's *M*A*S*H* reveals the army bureaucracy to be a greater threat than the enemy, as ranking U.S. officers routinely issue orders designed primarily to satisfy their individual cravings for power, wealth and sex, regardless of what is best for their units. To the men in the highest echelons of power, inter-unit football games matter most of all. The film contained much more gore than did the television show; for instance in one scene, Altman's camera focuses on a geyser of blood spurting from a wounded man's artery. The television show often implies that wounds are serious, even grotesque, but it rarely presents detailed shots of the carnage. Within the gruesome wartime setting, the characters in both media manage to generate considerable humor through their wit and their pranks, often played at the expense of the unpleasant and incompetent Major

Frank Burns (Duvall/Linville) and/or his equally sanctimonious paramour, Major "Hot Lips" Houlihan (Kellerman/Swit). However, the effect is different in the film, which steers more toward black humor precisely because it compels the audience never to lose sight of the carnage that forms an ever-present backdrop for the characters' lives and their laughter. The film's dark comedy, ostensibly about the Korean War, actually served as a strong anti–Vietnam War statement.

The television show, which lasted more than three times longer than the Korean War, was less overtly political than the film, and its edge was less sharp. Nonetheless, it also seemed to carry an antiwar message when it debuted in the final years of the Vietnam War. Its protagonists were softer and more compassionate; ultimately they conformed more to such conventional American values as honesty, responsibility and loyalty to the American cause than did their cinematic counterparts.

These values became dominant in 1975, when clean-cut B.J. Hunnicut (Farrell) replaced scruffy Trapper John (Rogers) as sidekick to the scampish but heart-of-gold protagonist, Hawkeye Pierce (Alda). Also in that year, Morgan's wise, authoritative, regular-army Colonel Potter replaced Stevenson's zany, unscrupulous, adulterous and incompetent Colonel Blake, a reservist. The 1975 cast alterations changed the show's earlier fraternity house ambiance to a more mature and adult atmosphere. As America's Baby Boomers grew up in the aftermath of Vietnam, leaving college and assuming the full responsibilities of adult life, the new cast enabled "M*A*S*H" to grow up along with them. In the process, the show's tone became less rebellious and its values more middle-class and accepting of authority.

For instance, whereas the Vietnam-era trio of Hawkeye–Trapper John–Colonel Blake had seen itself as apart from and superior to the military establishment, the post-Vietnam crew of Hawkeye–Hunnicut–Colonel Potter more readily accepted and conformed to conventional authority. And whereas Trapper John had been an irreverent wise guy, an alcoholic and an adulterous womanizer, Hunnicut remained a dedicated family man who rarely lost sight of his values or drank excessively. Potter, also a loyal husband, replaced another officer with loose sexual mores. Even Hawkeye began to clean up his act with alcohol and women, as the show reflected influences of the then-current woman's liberation movement and the 1980s anti-drug backlash to the COUNTERCULTURE of the late 1960s and early 1970s. In many ways Hunnicut and Potter functioned as a stabilizing center of sanity and clear perspective against which Hawkeye's emotional outbursts could be judged. Hunnicut and Potter also respected army discipline and establishment values, albeit reluctantly at times; whereas their predecessors, Trapper John and Colonel Blake, openly ridiculed procedure, rules and regulations. As Hawkeye came to respect Potter and Hunnicut, and to ally with them, the show's perspective shifted from that of the rebellious, youthful outsider to the viewpoint of a mature, if often exasperated, insider. When they acted in unison, the team of Hawkeye–Hunnicut–Potter brought a strong sense of moral authority and righteous indignation to their cause. In this respect, the television show replaced the film's nihilism

with a strong set of traditional values based on right action, discipline, responsibility, compassion, honesty and fair play.

Though stressed out and often discouraged, television's Hawkeye Pierce never becomes as jaded as the corresponding character in the film (Sutherland). Indeed, Sutherland's character had a demonic and perverse side that most of the time was barely under control. That side is absent in Alda's more fundamentally decent character. The show, which also outlasted the U.S.-Soviet détente of the 1970s, generally encouraged audiences to view situations compassionately and remain open to heartfelt communications, even from the communist enemy. Unlike the more cynical film, the television show suggests that individual people could get along compatibly if only their governments would stop acting in ridiculous or self-serving ways and genuinely seek peace.

One specifically Cold War–related episode of the television show featured a HUAC investigator who demanded that Major Houlihan (by then called "Margaret" rather than "Hot Lips," reflecting the show's feminism) name names. It was revealed that Margaret had known some fun-loving boys in college whom the HUAC investigator reveals to have been communist sympathizers, unbeknownst to her. She refuses to inform on her old friends, and her coworkers stand by her, devising a prank to foil the investigator.

Masters of Deceit: The Story of Communism in America and How to Fight It A 1958 best-selling NONFICTION book by FBI director J. Edgar Hoover. Written toward the end of the RED SCARE and at the beginning of the second Berlin Crisis, one of the most intense periods of the Cold War, the book sold some 250,000 copies in hardback and two million copies in paperback. It was ghostwritten by Louis B. Nichols, head of FBI public relations, and went through 29 printings over 12 years. The book was frequently required reading in mandatory high school courses on Americanism versus communism. Hoover's foreword begins, "Every citizen has a duty to learn more about the menace that threatens his future, his home, his children, the peace of the world—and this why I have written this book." He claims to draw on "Party statements, resolutions, platforms, news accounts, manifestoes, the very first documents of American communism. I studied also the writings of Marx, Engels, and Lenin as well as the activities of the Third International." He quotes Soviet premier Khrushchev and William Z. Foster, former national chairman of the American Communist Party, who assert that the grandchildren of contemporary Americans will grow up in a communist United States. Hoover tries to make the case that American communists, aided by the Soviet Union, are actively and illegally acting to impose communism on America. He adds that these statements

> are confirmed, day after day, by documented reports from areas where communists have already taken over: Hungary, East Germany, Bulgaria, Poland, Roumania, Czechoslovakia, Red China, and others. When you read such reports, do not think of them as something happening in a far-off land. Remember, always, that "it could happen here" and that there are thousands of people *in this country* now working in secret

J. Edgar Hoover. Courtesy the Federal Bureau of Investigation.

to make it happen. But also, thank God, there are millions of Americans who oppose them. If we open our eyes, inform ourselves, and work together, we can keep our country free.

The book then goes on to provide a history of communism and to explain the basic precepts of Marxism-Leninism, claiming that Stalin employed mass terror, suspicion, illegal arrests and a cult of personality to consolidate and maintain his power. Hoover then describes the history of communism in the United States, arguing that

Party influence is exerted through the communist device of thought control . . . The Party's objective is to drive a wedge, however slight, into as many minds as possible. That is why, in every conceivable way, communists try to poison our thinking about the issues of the day: social reforms, peace, politics, veterans', women's and youth problems . . . Top Party officials have a definite assignment: to capture positions of power. They are the Party's front-line commanders. Communism is at war with America. The United States is a vast battlefield. A school, a labor union, a civic group, a government official, a private citizen—all are important in the never-ending struggle for power.

Hoover presents five types of people who work on behalf of the communists: acknowledged party members, secret party members, fellow travelers, opportunists and "dupes." He describes how the American Communist Party is organized and how it operates, its strategies and its tactics, which, he claims, include mass agitation, infiltration, front organizations, appeals to minorities and a "malicious" attempt to create a myth that "persons of the Jewish faith and communists have something in common." He then depicts a communist underground that practices espionage and sabotage, citing the activities of Harry Gold and Klaus Fuchs, Julius and Ethel Rosenberg, and Rudolf Abel. He acknowledges that

The Communist Party, USA, has not reached the point where preparations for sabotage are vital to its future plans. Its small numbers, fear of FBI penetration of its inner discussions, and the existence of federal laws against sabotage and insurrection militate against such plans. So far the communists have carefully refrained from any show of terrorism. Any such act, even random sorties, the communists realize, would cause more harm to the Party by counter prosecutive action than any damage achieved by violence.

But, he warns, "Never must we forget . . . that even though acts of sabotage are not now part of the Party's program, they may become so in the future," and he describes the party's practice of "colonization," in which members are concealed in strategic positions in basic industries and defense facilities so they will be poised to strike at the appropriate moment.

Finally, Hoover concludes that individual Americans can fight against communism by becoming aware of and resisting communist attempts to make them innocent dupes; by learning to spot deceptive communist fronts; by exposing and opposing communist efforts to infiltrate trade unions and civic organizations; and by exposing any attempts at espionage and/or sabotage of which they become aware. He encourages citizens to contact the FBI about suspicious activities, citing the example of a man who alerted the bureau to suspicious garbage left by roomers who had recently moved. The garbage enabled the FBI to secure the membership records of a complete section of the party. Hoover cautions citizens to avoid rumors, stick to basic facts, and refrain from performing investigations themselves, but he urges everyone to remain alert and not disregard even small pieces of information that might seem too trivial to bother with. Hoover concludes that religion represents the strongest bulwark against atheistic communism. "All we need is faith, *real faith* . . . The truly revolutionary force of history is not material power but the spirit of religion." Though ABC bought the rights to *Masters of Deceit,* it never produced a television version. However, it later produced the television drama, THE F.B.I. (1965–74), which Hoover introduced each season in a personal appearance.

"Max Headroom" A TELEVISION SCIENCE FICTION SHOW that ran on ABC in 1987. Set "twenty minutes into the future," the show featured the exploits of investigative television reporter Edison Carter (Matt Frewer), who has been digitized by the child computer genius Bryce Lynch (Chris Young) and manifest as video character Max Headroom, who appeared intermittently on a pirate television station. In the world of "Max Headroom," television had essentially replaced government, and ratings, which were all-important, were reported every second. The show provided a cynical view of television and society and may have alluded to President Reagan, whose mastery of the television medium was legendary. Garry Trudeau satirized Reagan in this manner in the comic strip *Doonesbury* through the video character Ron Headrest.

McCarran Internal Security Subcommittee, The A Senate committee that investigated the TELEVISION and radio industries during the 1950s. The committee also originated the 1950 McCarran Internal Security Act, which established concentration camps for communists in Pennsylvania, Florida, Oklahoma, Arizona and California, though these were never used. The legislation also required all communist and communist-dominated organizations to provide the federal government with the names of all of their members and contributors. (See also RED SCARE.)

McCarthy, Mary A NOVELIST and NONFICTION WRITER. Born in 1912, McCarthy graduated from Vassar College in 1933 and soon thereafter began writing for the *Nation* and the *New Republic*. During the Depression she associated with left-wing intellectuals but remained aloof from the Communist Party, which she attacked after World War II,

Mary McCarthy. Photo by Cecil Beaton; courtesy AP/Wide World.

having become closer to Trotskyism. In 1938, McCarthy married Edmund WILSON but divorced him in 1946 and married Bowden Broadwater, who worked for the leftist but anti-communist magazine *Partisan Review*. Her novel *The Oasis* (1949) satirizes a group of liberals who try to create an ideal society atop a mountain. It was republished in England in 1950 under the title *A Source of Embarrassment*. Based on McCarthy's experiences and acquaintances, the award-winning novel presents a debate between two idealistic factions. The group finally recognizes its inability to live up to its own principles after it drives away a group of people who had been innocently picking strawberries from a particularly desirable patch, and the wizened liberals recognize that utopia is impossible. *The Groves of Academe* (1952) was written and set during the RED SCARE, and it too satirizes liberals. Here the targets of McCarthy's satire are members of a college community who oppose the firing of a former communist, Henry Mulchay. Their knee-jerk defense of Mulchay blinds them to his dishonesty and incompetence and leads them to oppose the liberal and honest college president. Thus the very institution that promotes reason and truth becomes corrupted by its passionate politics.

In 1959 the State Department sponsored McCarthy on a tour of Poland, Yugoslavia and Britain for which she developed lectures on "The Fact in Fiction" and "Characters in Fiction," later collected in *On the Contrary* (1961). During this period, her marriage to Broadwater dissolved, and in 1961 she married James West, a State Department officer whom she had met during the tour. He was soon thereafter transferred to Paris, where the couple went to live. McCarthy twice visited Vietnam during the 1960s to gain a firsthand view of the war, which she always actively opposed. The books *Vietnam* (1967), *Hanoi* (1968) and *Medina* (1972) resulted from her experiences. She collected these in *The Seventeenth Degree* in 1974. Her observations on the Watergate scandal first appeared in the *London Observer* and were then collected in *The Mask of State: Watergate Portraits* (1974). In 1979, the year of the Iran hostage crisis, McCarthy treats international terrorism in her novel *Cannibals and Missionaries*, which centers on the hijacking of an airplane carrying a committee flying to Iran to investigate charges of torture and civil rights violations against the shah. In 1985 McCarthy published her memoirs, *How I Grew*. She died in 1989.

McCarthyism The term was first used by *Washington Post* editorial cartoonist Herbert Block in March 1950. In 1954 it was defined for the first time, in the *American College Dictionary*, as "(1) public accusation of disloyalty . . . unsupported by truth, (2) unfairness in investigative technique." See also ARMY-MCCARTHY HEARINGS.

McDonald, Walter A POET. Born in 1934 in Lubbock, Texas, McDonald received his bachelor's degree in 1956 and his master's degree in 1957 from Texas Technological College (now Texas Tech University), where he also served in the Reserve Officers Training Corps (ROTC) and later joined the faculty. From 1969–70 he served as an air force pilot in the Vietnam War, and he is best known for his poetry dealing with the war. One of his earlier war poems is "For Kelly, Missing in Action," an erudite poem in which the protagonist uses James Joyce's *Dubliners* to understand his experience. "When you disappeared/ over the North/ I pulled down Dubliners./ What strange counterparts,/ You and the Cong./ You, who said no one would make/ General/ reading Joyce,/ named your F-4 'The Dead'. . . / I never knew what launched/ the search for Araby in you,/ that wholly secular search/ for thrills." His first collection of war poems appears in *Burning the Fence* (1981), a book that mostly deals with life in west Texas but also collects five pieces about the war. "Al Croom" is about a pilot who was always "daring the Russian/ rockets/ to do him in" but "When they shipped him home/ it took triple straps/ to bind him." And "Veteran" describes an ex-soldier with aluminum legs who imagines that "leaves lie in the park/ like tiny bombs/ ready to explode. Someday/ someone raking/ will strike a fuse. We'll all be killed."

McDonald's next several books deal primarily with Texas, but *After the Noise of Saigon* (1988) again takes up the war. The volume, which won the University of Massachusetts Juniper Prize, includes "The Food Pickers," which describes the Vietnamese civilians who would scavenge for food remains. "War Games" depicts men who played with imaginary dice while "rockets that crashed down/ on the base always killed somebody else." James Hoggard describes the characters in these poems as "never macho or hawkish, [since] the poet is . . . concerned with ordinary men thrust into nightmarish danger." *Night Landings* (1989) also treats the war, though most of the poems return to Texas for their subject matter. (See also VIETNAM WAR LITERATURE.)

For additional reading, see *Dictionary of Literary Biography* (vol. 105, *American Poets Since World War II, Second Series*).

Medina, Pablo A Cuban EXILED WRITER (to the United States). Born in Havana in 1948, Medina went into exile in the United States with his parents in 1961, the year of the failed Bay of Pigs invasion and two years after Fidel Castro assumed power on the island. In 1975 Medina published *Pork Rind and Cuban Songs*, the first English-language collection of poems published by an exiled Cuban writer. The collection, which explores the family and the self, also criticizes the oppressive regimentation of Castro's government. It received a warm critical reception in the United States. In one poem from the collection, "To the Cuban Exiles to Make Much of Time," Medina plays off the 17th-century British seduction poem by Robert Herrick, "To the Virgins to Make Much of Time." Instead of promoting a sexual liaison, however, Medina's poem ironically calls for celebrating the amenities of American middle-class comfort. In 1990 Medina published his second volume of poetry, *Arching into the Afterlife*, a surrealistic study of an America that has failed to achieve its potential, in which "Freedom [is] more alive than you." He also published a novel, *The Marks of Birth*, in 1989. According to Carolina Hospital, editor of *Cuban American Writers* (1989), Medina has served as "a strong role model" for other exiled Cuban writers.

For additional reading, see Tucker's *Literary Exile in the Twentieth Century*.

"Meet the Press" A TELEVISION NEWS show that began in 1947 on NBC and is still running on that network. Featuring moderators Martha Rountree (1947–53) and Ned Brooks (1953–65) and regular panelists Lawrence Spivak

and Bill Monroe, the NBC show presented members of the press interviewing major newsmakers, both American politicians and foreign dignitaries. From 1965 to 1975 Spivak was the moderator. He was replaced by Marvin Kalb (1984–87), Chris Wallace (1987–88) and Garrick Utley (1988–end of the Cold War).

Michener, James A NOVELIST and NONFICTION WRITER. Born in 1907, Michener first achieved popular success for *Tales of the South Pacific* (1947), his account of the Pacific theater in World War II. His Korean War novels, THE BRIDGES AT TOKO-RI (1953) and SAYONARA (1954), were both made into KOREAN WAR FILMS. *The Bridges at Toko-Ri* centers around Lieutenant Harry Brubaker, a World War II veteran and Navy Reserve pilot who is called up to serve in the Korean War. Though he feels he has already done more than his share in the service of his country, and though he deeply resents this second intrusion into his family life, Brubaker nonetheless subordinates himself to military authority and does his share to fight the war. *Sayonara* addresses the American racial prejudice directed at the Japanese, especially the U.S. military policy forbidding marriages between American military personnel and Japanese women. During the war, Japan housed crucial U.S. military bases, and so the frequent pairing of American soldiers and Japanese women was virtually inevitable. *Sayonara* explores the ramifications of the official policy against this form of interracial marriage, which some 10,000 American servicemen knowingly violated. Since Michener, himself, was among those who took a Japanese bride, the story reflects autobiographical concerns.

THE BRIDGE AT ANDAU (1957) is a NONFICTION account of the 1956 Hungarian Revolution and its immediate aftermath. It describes how some 20,000 people fled from Hungary into Austria across a frail wooden bridge in the weeks immediately following the revolt. Michener, who calls the Soviet invasion brutal and barbaric, interviewed many of the refugees, visited the sites and helped some of the refugees escape, even carrying one on his back. SIX DAYS IN HAVANA (1989), also nonfiction, describes a visit that Michener and photographer John Kings made to Cuba in 1988. Though it generally avoids politics, the photographs reveal the deterioration of the island's capital city since Castro's communist revolution, while the text presents a sympathetic account of the Cuban people and points out that the children are well fed and well educated. *Six Days in Havana* stemmed from Michener's work on *Caribbean*, a 1989 novel that traces the Caribbean Sea from the year 1310 to the present and features a fictitious dialogue between Castro and a political refugee in exile in Miami. The communist leader and the exile discuss differences between Cuba and the United States, the different Latino communities within the United States, and the possible consequences of renewed relations between the two countries. In the end, the refugee declares that his allegiance is now with the United States. *Kent State: What Happened and Why* (1971) is a nonfiction account of the Ohio National Guard's killing of students protesting the Vietnam War. Considered one of the most comprehensive studies of the incident, the book includes interviews with eyewitnesses, police, administrators, students, radicals and others. *Space* (1982) offers a fictional presentation of the U.S.

space program. *Poland* (1983) provides a series of vignettes of a Polish village from the 1200s to the 1980s, but does not highlight the Cold War era. In 1992 he published his memoirs, *The World is My Home*.

Though scholars and literary critics rarely regard Michener as a writer of serious fiction, his historical novels are uniformly well researched and the prolific novelist commanded a large popular readership throughout the Cold War. Moreover, along with other popular but not critically acclaimed authors such as Leon URIS, Fletcher KNEBEL, Eugene BURDICK and William LEDERER, Michener addressed the Cold War more directly than most writers held in higher esteem by the literary establishment.

Middle of the Journey, The   A 1947 POLITICAL NOVEL by Lionel TRILLING. Trilling's first novel, it was reissued in 1975 with a new introduction by the author discussing the influence of Whittaker Chambers on the book. *The Middle of the Journey* expresses Trilling's disaffection from communism. It follows John Laskell, a communist intellectual who becomes disillusioned while recovering from an illness at the Connecticut farm of some friends who are also communists. The book was praised for its insight and deep treatment of moral dilemmas, in spite of its limited action. One of the main characters, Gifford Maxim, is based on Whittaker Chambers, whom Trilling knew slightly when both were students at Columbia University in the middle 1920s. The novel appeared a year before Chambers gained international attention by accusing Alger Hiss of working with him in a communist spy ring during the 1930s. Hiss had been a ranking member of the Roosevelt administration who played important roles at the Yalta Conference and in the formation of the United Nations. Chambers had been part of the party's secret governing apparatus in the early 1930s, and he claimed that he had received classified information from Hiss at that time. He left the party in 1936 and, fearing for his life, went underground. (See also his 1952 autobiography WITNESS). Chambers later claimed he kept incriminating documents Hiss furnished as insurance against party attempts to murder him. Eventually Chambers surfaced and in 1939 became an editor for *Time* magazine, but he retained his furtive habits.

Trilling based Maxim on the pre-Hiss-trial Chambers. He behaves in a melodramatic and paranoid fashion, but Trilling portrays the threat to his life as apparently genuine. Like Chambers, Maxim needs to reassert his presence in society, since "A man who does not exist can be got rid of easily." Trilling conceived of the character as a tragic comedian who accurately attests to the empty and pernicious nature of communism but becomes almost buffoonish in his fear of the party. Maxim's defection from the party ultimately awakens Laskell's dormant dissatisfaction with communism. Maxim functions almost as a priest or psychoanalyst who, through skillful use of questioning, helps his patient achieve a heightened sense of awareness and deeper insight and revelation, in this case, helping Laskell recognize unpleasant truths about communism that he has always seen but never acknowledged.

military films   Apart from the Korean and Vietnam wars, U.S. soldiers saw limited combat in the Cold War. Conse-

quently, relatively few military films were made about Cold War–related events except for KOREAN WAR FILMS and VIETNAM WAR FILMS. Those 1950s military films not related to the Korean War often deal with the preparations for and possibilities of nuclear warfare. STRATEGIC AIR COMMAND (SAC), a 1955 film, depicts the air force unit whose nuclear-armed bombers hover in "fail-safe" positions close to their Soviet targets, and it showcases the newest jets in the 1950s fleet. The film also suggests that the U.S. nuclear fleet is in responsible hands and that SAC's capacity for retaliation leaves the nation relatively secure from attack. INVASION U.S.A. (1952) imagines what New York City would be like during an atomic attack. It concludes on a highly militaristic note as the protagonists rush home to convert tractor plants into tank factories. ON THE BEACH (1959) depicts members of a U.S. submarine crew in Australia after a nuclear war has destroyed the entire Northern Hemisphere and created a lethal radioactive cloud that is drifting toward them.

Several military films from the middle 1960s picture failures in command that lead to inadvertent attacks by the United States, notably THE BEDFORD INCIDENT (1965), FAIL-SAFE (1964) and the film satire DR. STRANGELOVE (1964). A GATHERING OF EAGLES (1963) also focuses on nuclear deterrence and human failings in its 1963 depiction of SAC. SEVEN DAYS IN MAY (1964) describes an attempted military coup by outraged right-wing U.S. generals after the signing of a disarmament treaty with the Soviets. ICE STATION ZEBRA (1968) centers on a U.S. submarine sent to the North Pole to gather secret missile data being beamed down by a Soviet space satellite.

During the détente of the 1970s, comparatively few military films were made (apart from Vietnam War films). However, in 1973, the year the Vietnam War ended, Hal Holbrook starred in PUEBLO, a drama about the U.S. spy ship that had been captured in North Korean waters in 1968. Antiwar military films from the Vietnam era include KING OF HEARTS (1967), CATCH-22 (1970), M*A*S*H (1970) and THE DAY THE FISH CAME OUT (1967). FRANCIS GARY POWERS (1975) presents the biography of the pilot of the U.S. U-2 spy plane that was shot down on a reconnaissance mission over the Soviet Union in May, 1960. The incident scuttled a Paris summit conference that had been convened to resolve the on-going Berlin crisis. The situation in Berlin then rapidly deteriorated over the following year and a half, until it climaxed in October, 1961 in one of the most dangerous U.S.-Soviet showdowns of the Cold War. THE MISSILES OF OCTOBER (1974) reenacts the 1962 Cuban Missile Crisis. PATTON (1970) celebrates the American World War II hero who advocated an immediate attack against the Soviet Union after Germany was defeated. George C. Scott won an Academy Award for his portrayal of General George Patton. The film also won the 1970 Academy Awards for best picture, best script (Francis Ford Coppola) and best director (Franklin Schaffner).

The Cold War reintensified during the Reagan era, and the number of Cold War-related military films increased. RED DAWN (1984) imagines a partly successful atomic attack against the United States, portraying an underground army of teenagers who fight against the communist occupying force. Made when the United States was supporting the anti-communist government in El Salvador and the anti-communist contras in Nicaragua, and when President

Reagan was publicly claiming that the communist forces in Latin America were only a day's drive from Texas, the film suggests that the United States is, indeed, vulnerable to an attack from communists in Latin America. THE BEAST (1988) vilifies the Soviet war in Afghanistan. TOP GUN (1986) glamorizes the lives of navy fighter pilots and the military service. DEF-CON 4 (1985) imagines the fates of astronauts who return to Earth after a nuclear war has devastated the planet, while the Bush-era HUNT FOR RED OCTOBER (1990) describes how the U.S. Navy manages the defection of a state-of-the-art Soviet submarine. Made as the Iran-contra scandal was still unfolding, AIR AMERICA (1990) satirically depicts the illegal operations of a CIA front organization in Southeast Asia during the Vietnam War.

Some military films with non–Cold War settings were nonetheless relevant to the Cold War. Elia KAZAN's VIVA ZAPATA! (1951) provides a rare RED SCARE-era liberal viewpoint in its depiction of the Mexican Revolution hero and its championing of land reform. Many films celebrated American valor in earlier wars. World War II films made in the 1950s and 1960s typically pictured an American military capable of doing whatever was necessary to preserve democracy. These reminders of the still-recent victory over fascism thus reassured viewers concerned about the "Communist threat." On the other hand, THE BRIDGE ON THE RIVER KWAI (1957) explores the conflict between an officer's duty to undermine the enemy and his innate need to do a job as well as it can be done. Working well is a military value that Colonel Nicholson, the ranking British officer in a Japanese prisoner-of-war camp, rigidly imposes in order to maintain order and preserve sanity among his troops; ironically, Nicholson's means of building morale also provides military support to the enemy. Through this conflict, the story implicitly questions the ultimate results of military values, showing the contradictions that ensue when they become an end in themselves. Such criticisms were rare in the 1950s, when military values were popularly seen to be a bulwark against communist tyranny. For example, THE ALAMO (1960), starring John WAYNE, celebrated the famous final stand of outnumbered Texans in 1836, just as Warsaw Pact forces were surrounding American troops during the second Berlin Crisis in 1960. DAVY CROCKETT, KING OF THE WILD FRONTIER (1955) had celebrated the Alamo five years earlier in a similar patriotic gesture.

Another Cold War film with a pre–Cold War setting is THE SAND PEBBLES (1966). The story centers on a U.S. Navy gunboat cruising China's Yangtze River during Chiang Kai-shek's 1926 Nationalist rebellion. Starring Steve McQueen and Candice Bergen, the powerful and critically acclaimed film portrays how the U.S. vessel and crew, though trying to maintain neutrality, are manipulated by political forces and drawn into the conflict. (See also FILM DOCUMENTARIES and MILITARY NOVELS.)

military novels Because the Cold War was largely "cold," the superpowers never directly fought one another, except when the troops of the United States and its Western allies faced Chinese armies during the Korean War. Apart from the Korean and Vietnam wars, the U.S. military was not openly engaged during the Cold War, except for more limited expeditions in Lebanon (1958 and 1983), the Domini-

can Republic (1965) and Grenada (1983), and the 1975 rescue of crew members of the cargo ship *Mayaguez*, who were held in Cambodia. Thus, although the U.S. armed forces remained in a high state of preparedness, U.S. political objectives were pursued either through diplomacy; covert military actions overseen by the CIA, the National Security Council and/or other intelligence agencies; or proxy wars in which the United States supplied and advised allies. Consequently, there are few Cold War military novels apart from those dealing with the Korean War and Vietnam War. (See also VIETNAM WAR LITERATURE.)

Notable within Korean War literature are two novels by James MICHENER, THE BRIDGES AT TOKO-RI (1953) and SAYO-NARA (1954), both of which were made into films. *The Bridges at Toko-Ri* appeared the year the armistice ended the fighting. The story centers on Lieutenant Harry Brubaker, a World War II veteran and Navy Reserve pilot who is called up to serve in Korea. Though he feels he has already done more than his share in the service of his country, and though he deeply resents this second intrusion into his family life, Brubaker nonetheless subordinates himself to military authority and does his share to fight the war. The book ultimately affirms the importance of the intervention in Korea and the Cold War itself. *Sayonara*, an updated version of the opera *Madame Butterfly*, deals with the racial prejudice of the U.S. military toward the Japanese, at a time when the United States was occupying Japan and using it as a staging area for the Korean War, and when U.S. soldiers, like Michener himself, were falling in love with but officially forbidden to marry Japanese women.

Also published in the early 1950s, Kurt VONNEGUT Jr.'s ALL THE KING'S HORSES (1953) treats the diplomatic problems of dealing with communist-backed, rogue Asian warlords who operated independently of any nation. Vonnegut later updated the story in a Latin American setting in a post–Cold War television special featuring dramatizations from his 1968 story collection, *Welcome to the Monkey House*. Richard Condon's THE MANCHURIAN CANDIDATE (1959) portrays a communist effort to use sophisticated psychological methods to "brainwash" captured American prisoners-of-war (POWs), with one POW "programmed" to assassinate political enemies on command. Exiled writer Richard E. KIM's best-selling novel, THE MARTYRED (1964), tells the story of a South Korean Army captain who investigates the fates of 14 Christian ministers whom the North Koreans had captured. In the process of the investigation, the captain confronts evidence that compels him to rethink his own notions of right and wrong, belief and hypocrisy, patriotism and treason.

Dr. Richard Hooker's M*A*S*H (1968) details a series of amusing pranks based on those actually played by surgeons in a Mobile Army Surgical Hospital (MASH) during the Korean War. The author, a doctor who served in that war, employed the pseudonym Hooker in order not to compromise his medical standing. Though the book gives a rare, comic view of the war, the novel is not as artfully crafted as the FILM COMEDY and TELEVISION SITUATION COMEDY based upon it; nor does it have the deeper emotional resonances that the other treatments provide. All three versions depict life in a surgical hospital stationed just behind the front lines in Korea. Working under extremely difficult conditions, the medical staff treats a seemingly endless stream of casualties that constantly arrives fresh from the battlefield. The book, film and television show all appeared during the Vietnam War, and their antiwar, anti-military sentiment made them popular among those who opposed that war.

Chaim Potok's THE BOOK OF LIGHTS (1981) is set shortly after the conclusion of the Korean War. The story centers on Gershon Loran, a quiet Jewish seminary student who is drawn to study the mystical writings of the Kabbalah, and his moody roommate Arthur Leiden, the unforgiving son of a brilliant physicist who helped make the atomic bomb. All of the seminarians are coerced into joining the military services as chaplains, and Loran is assigned to a front-line medical unit in South Korea, where Americans still patrol to maintain the armistice. The responsibilities he assumes in this hostile environment mature him, give him new self-confidence, and allow him to integrate his understanding of the Kabbalah more fully into his life.

Norman MAILER's *The Naked and the Dead* (1948) uses World War II to present insights relevant to the Cold War. The novel follows the exploits of a reconnaissance platoon comprised of a cross-section of Americans. It also explores the differences in background, personal styles and philosophies of a conservative general and his liberal aide. The ambitious General Cummings believes in the efficacy of power and argues that victors acquire the characteristics of the nations they defeat, so the United States will become more fascistic and militaristic after the war. The more idealistic Lt. Hearn disagrees. A highly effective strategist, Cummings is denied credit for the American victory when Japanese defenses crumble while he is away and his unimaginative second-in-command obtains their surrender. Meanwhile, Hearn is killed when a resentful sergeant sets him up on a patrol. Both men learn that historical events are less subject to individual control than they had assumed.

One of the masterpieces of 20th-century American literature, Joseph Heller's CATCH-22 (1961) also employs a World War II setting. It shows institutional bureaucracy to be a far more pernicious enemy than any military opponent. Like *M*A*S*H*, the work was championed by the opponents of the Vietnam War, even though it is set in a different conflict and was, in fact, written before extensive U.S. involvement in Vietnam. (Mike Nichols did adapt the novel into a MILITARY FILM in 1970, while the Vietnam War was ongoing.) Set during World War II, the BLACK HUMOR novel centers on Captain Yossarian, a U.S. bombardier who is terrified during every mission, has already flown a large number of missions, and wants to go home. But he is thwarted and assaulted at every turn by the army bureaucracy, in which intra-service rivalries and superior officers' unmitigated quest for personal power and wealth are the determining factors behind all decisions, not the war effort or the soldiers' well-being. Heller plays with language, logic and a nonlinear plot to further communicate the disorienting, paradoxical sensibility that comes from Yossarian's having to fight two wars simultaneously—one against the Germans and the other against his commanding officer and the army bureaucracy. The title, *Catch-22*, became a familiar term in Cold War vocabulary to refer to circular, self-contradictory situations. Army policy stated that if Yossarian was crazy he did not have to fly any more missions. He merely needed to report himself insane. However, there was a catch—Catch-22—which stated that the very act of reporting himself insane demonstrated that Yossarian was sane enough to want to preserve his own life. Consequently, he must not be insane, and so he must fly more missions.

Heller also shows the absurdity and irrationality of RED SCARE–inspired loyalty oaths, which were increasingly popular when he was working on the novel's first draft in the mid-1950s. The military comes to a standstill as officers compete to prove their patriotism by demanding signed loyalty oaths before their units will perform any work. Elsewhere Heller satirizes McCarthy-like inquisitions and heavy-handed FBI investigations. Repeatedly throughout the novel, Heller depicts situations that are the result of illogical behavior by bureaucrats and superior officers. The disparity between declared and actual motives creates an insane environment in which basic values and instincts become inverted. Yossarian receives a medal for causing his squadron to drop its bombs in the sea rather than demolish an Italian town with no military significance. But his reward comes not because of his humanitarian common sense, but because his superiors thought it would be less embarrassing than court-martialing one of their officers. (See also SATIRE.)

The period between 1958 and 1962 was the most intense in the Cold War, when nuclear war seemed not only possible but also at times likely. Consequently, several novels deal with the danger of a single irresponsible officer pushing the world into nuclear war. Peter George's novel RED ALERT (1958), which appeared at the beginning of the second Berlin Crisis, was the basis for Stanley KUBRICK's black humor film, DR. STRANGELOVE (1964), which, like *Catch-22*, provides an absurdist world view. The novel itself presents a more serious and straightforward drama, in which a crazy air force general launches an unauthorized nuclear attack against the Soviet Union. Published the same year as the Cuban Missile Crisis, Mordecai Roshwald's A SMALL ARMAGEDDON (1962) also depicts the possibility of nuclear disaster that could arise from a field commander going out of control. It centers on a submarine captain who holds all humanity hostage by aiming his nuclear missiles at major cities throughout the world. His demands include visits from striptease dancers whose vibrating body parts are compared to nuclear reactors. Mark Rascovich's THE BEDFORD INCIDENT (1963) also deals with the possibilities of a field-level commander becoming mentally unstable and ordering an unauthorized nuclear attack.

On the other hand, Eugene BURDICK and Harvey Wheeler's FAIL-SAFE (1962) considers the possibility of a mechanical failure accidentally leading to a nuclear strike. (*Fail-Safe* and *The Bedford Incident* were released as films in 1964 and 1965, respectively.) An even earlier work that deals with unauthorized use of nuclear weaponry is David Divine's *Atom at Spithead* (1953), in which the enemy uses a military review of the Royal Navy to sneak a nuclear device aboard an impostor ship. Fletcher KNEBEL's best-selling SEVEN DAYS IN MAY (1962), coauthored with Charles W. Bailey II, shows a different kind of danger caused by nuclear weapons. It describes an attempted coup by the U.S. military in response to a president's decision to sign a treaty with the Soviets banning nuclear weapons. It too became a popular film. Nevil Shute's ON THE BEACH (1957) deals with the consequences of nuclear war. It portrays the crew of an American submarine, the sole surviving vessel in the U.S. Navy, which awaits the arrival in Australia of a lethal radioactive cloud that has already killed everyone in the Northern Hemisphere. Stanley Kramer directed the popular film adaptation in 1959.

The détente of the 1970s diminished the interest in military fiction, though THE THIRD WORLD WAR, a 1978 novel by General Sir John Hackett and other top-ranking NATO generals and advisers, projects detailed military and political scenarios based on the state of the Cold War during the Carter administration. Part of their purpose was to alert the public to what they saw as the dangers inherent in allowing U.S. and NATO military forces to fall behind those of the Soviets and Warsaw Pact countries. The authors wrote a 1982 sequel, *The Untold Story*, in which they warn, "If you want nuclear peace prepare for non-nuclear war: but be ready to pay the price." The price, in their view, is vulnerability to a conventional Soviet attack in Europe that can be repelled only by tactical nuclear weapons or extreme good luck.

Détente collapsed at the end of 1979 when the Soviets invaded Afghanistan, and the early 1980s saw renewed tensions among the superpowers. Maintaining that the Soviets were preparing to prevail in a nuclear war, the Reagan administration began to reverse U.S. policies predicated on Mutually Assured Destruction (MAD) in favor of those based on winnable nuclear war. In 1979, under the Carter administration, the United States had placed intermediate-range nuclear missiles in Europe over the strong protests of the antinuclear groups in Britain and Germany, and throughout the early 1980s the United States implemented a massive arms buildup. In 1983 Reagan proposed the Strategic Defense Initiative (SDI—more popularly known as STAR WARS after a popular SCIENCE FICTION FILM of the time). Though Reagan promoted it as a defensive weapon capable of shooting down incoming missiles, SDI had offensive capabilities that deeply worried the Soviets. Some Cold War planners consequently feared that the U.S.S.R. might therefore be driven to launch a preemptive first strike. (See also END OF THE WORLD.) After the Soviets shot down a Korean passenger plane in September 1983, tensions escalated further, and Soviet foreign minister Gromyko cautioned that "The world situation is now slipping toward a very dangerous precipice. Problem number one for the world is to avoid nuclear war."

Within this context, Tom CLANCY emerged as the preeminent military novelist of the 1980s. His first novel, THE HUNT FOR RED OCTOBER (1984, film 1990), describes the political considerations in determining whether an approaching state-of-the-art renegade Soviet submarine intends to defect or to attack. *Red Storm Rising* (1986), written while the Soviet Union was fighting a war in Afghanistan, begins with Muslim terrorists destroying a major Soviet oil refinery. Faced with a serious oil shortage, the Soviets initiate a ground war to seize the oil deposits of the Persian Gulf. NATO and the United States fight back, and the novel chronicles the war, which is fought with high-tech weaponry

that Clancy describes in detail. The story is based on "Convoy '84," a military war game predicated on fighting a war with conventional weapons. *Cardinal of the Kremlin* (1988) also features warfare between the "superpowers." Published toward the end of the Cold War, when Gorbachev had been in power for three years, the book likewise centers on high technology as a Soviet laser on the Afghan border attacks a U.S. space satellite. The use of the laser as a space weapon alludes to SDI. The novel also describes sensory-deprivation tanks in a KGB prison, Afghan guerrillas armed with U.S.-supplied Stinger anti-aircraft missiles, and U.S.–Soviet disarmament talks. Clancy is generally known for his detailed descriptions of weapons systems and of military considerations.

Millennium A 1983 APOCALYPTIC NOVEL by John Varley and a 1989 film starring Kris Kristofferson and Cheryl Ladd, directed by Michael Anderson. Varley wrote the film script, which was based on his 1977 story "Air Raid." The novel appeared during the most intense period of the Cold War since the Cuban Missile Crisis, when the Reagan administration was accusing the Soviet Union of preparing to prevail in a nuclear war and therefore advocated a policy of winnable nuclear war for the United States. A small group of survivors in the "Last Age" tries to save the human race after it has been fatally contaminated by nuclear accidents and 19 limited nuclear wars. Their plan—"a last-ditch, hopeless effort to salvage something from the human race"—is to go back in time to rescue people who had been killed in airplane accidents, since these uncontaminated individuals presumably will not disrupt the unfolding of history. The rescued group will then be sent to the stars to colonize other planets and propagate the species, with the hope that their descendants will eventually be able to return to Earth. Sometimes compared to Walter Miller's classic postnuclear novel, A CANTICLE FOR LEIBOWITZ (1959), this novel questions human free will in the nuclear era, asking whether it is a "salient fact" that "events tend toward their predestined pattern."

For additional reading, see Anisfield's *The Nightmare Considered* and Scheick's "Continuative and Ethical Predictions: The Post-Nuclear Holocaust Novel of the 1980s."

Miller, Arthur A playwright. Miller's first Broadway success was *All My Sons*, a 1947 tragedy about a corrupt wartime defense contractor. In 1949 Elia KAZAN directed and Lee J. COBB starred in the premiere of *Death of a Salesman*, a tremendous success that is considered Miller's finest work. The tragedy centers on a good but flawed, hard-working salesman whose family is destroyed because of his sexual infidelity and misplaced value of popularity and salesmanship over hard work. In 1951, Miller and Kazan tried to interest Columbia Pictures in his screenplay *The Hook*, but the studio turned it down when Miller refused to change the corrupt union officials to communists.

Miller's collaboration with Kazan came to an end in 1952 when Kazan cooperated with the HOUSE COMMITTEE ON UN-AMERICAN ACTIVITIES (HUAC), naming former and current members of the Communist Party. Miller had tried to dissuade Kazan from testifying; shortly thereafter he began writing THE CRUCIBLE (1953), an allegory about HUAC and the RED SCARE that is played out in Salem's 17th-century witch hunts.

Ironically, *The Hook* later inspired Kazan's film ON THE WATERFRONT (1954), which is often taken as Kazan's defense of informing. Miller responded with his next play, *A View From the Bridge* (1955), a tragedy about an immigrant who informs on an illegal alien and dies because of it. Supposedly, when Miller finished the play, he sent a copy to Kazan. Kazan responded that he would be honored to direct it. Miller replied, "I didn't send it to you because I wanted you to direct it. I sent it to you because I wanted you to know what I think of stool pigeons."

Miller, who had not been a communist, was himself subpoenaed to testify before HUAC in 1956. By that time he had already been blacklisted by Hollywood and even by the New York Board of Education, which canceled a contract for him to write a film about street gangs. Miller stated his willingness to tell the committee about his own activities and beliefs but refused to discuss anyone else or identify anyone he believed to be a communist, citing his First Amendment protection. Since the Supreme Court had already upheld the contempt of Congress citations issued against the HOLLYWOOD TEN, who had likewise invoked the First Amendment, Miller risked a one-year prison sentence by taking this stand. However, he was fined only $500 and given a 30-day suspended sentence. When asked why the Communist Party had produced *You're Next*, his satire about HUAC, Miller replied, "I take no more responsibility for who plays my plays than General Motors can take for who rides in their Chevrolets." Of his own brief association with organized communism, Miller stated, "I have had to go to hell to meet the devil." Lillian Hellman, who disagreed with Miller's decision even to talk about himself to the committee, later retorted that he must have gone tourist class. In 1958 Miller reappeared before the committee, along with Paul ROBESON, whose passport had been revoked. Robeson was belligerent and took the Fifth Amendment. Miller testified, answering questions about *The Crucible, A View from the Bridge* and *You're Next* but, again, not about anybody else.

In 1963 Kazan and Miller reconciled when they were named resident director and resident playwright for the premiere season of New York's Lincoln Center. Kazan directed Miller's autobiographical *After the Fall* (1963), the story of a former communist who breaks with a friend about to inform before a congressional committee. The female lead was a beautiful, vulnerable blonde woman modeled after Miller's former wife, Marilyn MONROE. According to one critic at its debut, "*After the Fall* seeks to understand, not to judge." Subsequent plays include *Incident at Vichy* (1964), *The Price* (1968) and *The Creation of the World and Other Business* (1972). In 1969 Miller wrote *In Russia*, a book about the U.S.S.R. in the late 1960s, accompanied by photographs taken by his third wife, Inge Morath. (See also THEATER.)

For additional reading, see Navasky's *Naming Names*, Vaughn's *Only Victims; Dictionary of Literary Biography* (vol. 7, *Twentieth-Century American Dramatists*). For a partial transcript of Miller's testimony before HUAC, see Bentley's THIRTY YEARS OF TREASON.

Milosz, Czeslaw   A Lithuanian/Polish EXILED WRITER (to the United States) and recipient of the 1980 Nobel Prize for literature. Born in 1911 in Seteiniai, Lithuania, then part of the Russian Empire, Milosz grew up in Wilno (Vilna), which was part of the restored Polish state created between the world wars. In 1931 he cofounded the avant-garde literary group, Zagary. He left Wilno in 1940, after the U.S.S.R. incorporated Lithuania, and spent World War II in occupied Warsaw, where he secretly wrote and edited collections of anti-Nazi poems and essays. In 1945, after the war, he published *Rescue*, a volume of poetry that includes a cycle entitled "Voices of Poor People" honoring the victims of oppression. The cycle includes poems on the destruction of Warsaw and the Warsaw Jewish ghetto.

Milosz served in the Polish consular delegation to New York in 1945, as a cultural attaché in Washington in 1947, and as a secretary in the Polish embassy in Paris in 1950. His poems from this era express indignation over the intellectual and political climate in postwar Poland and the world. Collected and published in exile, *Daylight* (1953) includes the poem, "You Who Have Wronged a Simple Man." It was chosen to be inscribed on a monument in Gdansk, celebrating the Solidarity Movement before the labor union was outlawed and martial law imposed.

When socialist realism became Poland's official artistic policy in 1951, Milosz asked for and received political asylum in France, where he lived as a free-lance writer. He received international acclaim for *The Captive Mind* (1953), which he describes as "an analysis of the mental acrobatics Eastern European intellectuals had to perform in order to give assent to Stalinist dogmas." His prize-winning novel from the same time, *The Seizure of Power* (1953; in English, 1955), describes the communist seizure of Poland. Much of Milosz's work attempts to communicate the nature of, and his feelings for, Poland and his native Lithuania. Among the most prominent of these books are *The Issa Valley* (1955; in English, 1981) and *Native Realm: A Search for Self-Definition* (1968). Milosz moved to Berkeley, California, in 1960 and accepted a position at the University of California as professor of Slavic literature. While holding that position he interviewed his fellow Polish exile and faculty member Aleksander WAT about his experiences with communism. These interviews were published 10 years after Wat's death under the title, *My Century: The Odyssey of a Polish Intellectual* (1977; in English, 1988).

For additional reading, see Tucker's *Literary Exile in the Twentieth Century.*

Missile   A 1988 FILM DOCUMENTARY produced, directed and edited by Frederick Wiseman. The film was shot in 1986, when Cold War tensions between the United States and U.S.S.R. were still high and Reagan administration officials were speaking publicly about winnable nuclear war and first-strike capabilities. The film premiered at the U.S. Film Festival in Utah in 1988, when East–West relations were considerably smoother, and was broadcast on public television later that year. *Missile* documents the training program for the air force officers in charge of the nuclear-armed Minuteman missile silos. The film's highlights include a discussion among the officers on the concept of "only following orders." *Missile* was filmed at the Strategic Air Command Center at Vandenberg Air Force Base, California. (See also APOCALYPTIC FILMS.)

Missile Crisis, The   A 1964 TELEVISION DOCUMENTARY produced by Fred FREED. The film, which documents the Cuban Missile Crisis, first appeared as the second installment of a two-part "NBC White Paper" on Cuba; the first installment covered the failed Bay of Pigs invasion of 1961. *The Missile Crisis* was broadcast on February 9, 1964, some 15 months after the resolution of the nuclear showdown that proved to be the most dangerous moment of the Cold War. (See also APOCALYPTIC FILMS.)

For additional reading, see Shaheen's *Nuclear War Films.*

Missiles of October, The   A 1974 made-for-television MILITARY FILM starring William Devane, Martin Sheen and Ralph Bellamy and directed by Anthony Page. Made 12 years after the Cuban Missile Crisis, during the détente of the 1970s, *The Missiles of October* presents President Kennedy in a favorable light as it reenacts the 1962 confrontation between the United States and U.S.S.R., in which the two superpowers stood "eyeball to eyeball" on the verge on nuclear warfare. (See also APOCALYPTIC FILMS.)

Missing   A 1982 POLITICAL FILM starring Jack Lemmon, Sissy Spacek, Melanie Mayron and John Shea and directed by Constantin COSTA-GAVRAS. *Missing* was the first Hollywood-produced film by Costa-Gavras, who had also directed such powerful political films as Z (1969), STATE OF SIEGE (1973) and THE CONFESSION (1970). Closely based on the fate of U.S. expatriate writer Charles Horman (Shea), the film apparently takes place in Santiago, Chile, after the U.S.-backed 1973 military coup. Though the Latin American country is never explicitly identified, Horman is named. Horman disappears shortly after the coup topples the left-leaning government, and the plot centers on the efforts of his leftist wife (Spacek) and conservative father (Lemmon) to ascertain his whereabouts. The wife and father are drawn closer together as they encounter growing evidence of a cover-up by both Chilean and U.S. authorities, who have executed Horman as part of the brutal repression that accompanied the coup. *Missing* provoked a categorical denial of U.S. complicity in the coup from Secretary of State Alexander Haig.

"Mission Impossible"   A TELEVISION SPY SHOW that ran on CBS from 1966 to 1973. It was later revived on ABC between 1988 and 1990. This show featured the adventures of the Impossible Missions Force, a group of highly unique government agents who specialized in covert activities. They were led by Daniel Briggs (Steven Hill) in the first season and then by James Phelps (Peter Graves) for the rest of the show's run. Phelps's assignments were always given to him on a self-destructing tape recording that concluded, "As always, should you or any member of your I.M. Force be caught or killed, the secretary will disavow any knowledge of your actions." Phelps would then look through a portfolio of possible operatives and choose those he deemed most appropriate for the task. In addition to occasional guest stars, the team Phelps assembled always included the

same members: Cinnamon Carter (Barbara Bain), a sophisticated, sexy woman; Rollin Hand (Martin Landau), a master of disguise; Barney Collier (Greg Morris), an African-American electronics wizard; and Willie Armitage (Peter Lupus), the strongman who handled the heavy lifting. At the end of the 1968–69 season Martin Landau and Barbara Bain, who were married to each other in real life, left the show over a contract dispute. Bain was replaced by Lynda Day George and Landau was replaced by Leonard Nimoy, whose STAR TREK show had recently been canceled.

The I.M. Force was chiefly used to disrupt the nefarious activities of small, foreign powers—frequently communist countries—that were intent on undermining the Free World or blackmailing the United States. The team's plans always required split-second timing, sophisticated gadgetry, quick-witted improvisation and the complete array of talents that each member brought to the effort. Better acted and scripted than most spy shows, "Mission Impossible" also stands out because it showed the Cold War to be fought by highly trained professionals who functioned cooperatively as a team. Moreover, the opening caveat that the U.S. government would disavow any knowledge of their actions explicitly acknowledged that the government sometimes publicly lied in order to carry out its policy objectives. During the Iran-contra hearings Colonel Oliver North would later give this practice a name, "plausible deniability," and speak of it as standard operating procedure, but in 1966, most audiences did not expect government dishonesty to be a matter of policy. In fact, it was during this period, as the Vietnam War was beginning to escalate, that President Johnson was first beginning to experience the "credibility gap" that helped undermine his presidency, as U.S. citizens suspected Johnson of not telling the whole truth about the war.

Modesty Blaise   A British-made 1966 FILM COMEDY starring Monica Vitti, Terence Stamp and Dirk Bogarde and directed by Joseph Losey. Losey was blacklisted in 1951 and went into exile in England after being identified as a former communist in hearings conducted by the HOUSE COMMITTEE ON UN-AMERICAN ACTIVITIES (HUAC). The film spoofs the SPY FILM genre through the activities of sexy super-spy, Modesty Blaise. (See also SPY FILM SPOOFS; BLACKLISTING.)

momism   A term popular in the 1940s, 1950s and early 1960s; used to describe overbearing, emasculating mothers. Philip Wylie first popularized the concept in his best-selling book, *Generation of Vipers* (1942), which argues that middle-class industrial-age mothers, freed from their preindustrial chores, had become self-centered manipulators who demanded excessive attention, adulation and material support from men. Selected by the American Library Association in 1950 as one of the most important works of NONFICTION in the first half of the 20th century, *Generation of Vipers* depicted the middle-class American mother as self-righteous, self-absorbed, hypocritical and sexually repressed, a member of "a matriarchy in fact if not in declaration" in which "the women of America raped the men." According to Wylie, American middle-class mothers dominated their sons and husbands. As Michael Rogin observes in *Ronald Reagan, the Movie,* for Wylie, a typical, overbearing mother "elicited [her son's] adulation to repress his sex and transferred the desire that ought to go to another woman into sentimentality for herself." As a result, the sons of these mothers typically grew into weak, often homosexual, men lacking the requisite character, self-knowledge and mental toughness to resolutely confront a dangerous enemy.

Though the notion of momism clashed with the more traditional picture of the American mother as a loving, self-sacrificing, nurturing figure, it had a huge impact in Cold War culture, especially in novels and films from the 1950s and 1960s. In these representations, momism serves communism by creating a generation of men who are "soft," unable to effectively oppose the communist menace. In MY SON JOHN (1952) the bookish, intellectual son whom the mother coddles becomes a communist spy, while his athletic brothers who play football with their dad grow up to serve their country admirably. In THE MANCHURIAN CANDIDATE (book 1959, film 1962), the domineering mother is herself a Soviet agent who causes her son to be brainwashed and turned into an unknowing assassin under her control. In the book, she literally rapes him while he is under her hypnotic control; in the film, she merely kisses him suggestively on the lips. However, he asserts his spiritual freedom, his underlying patriotism and his latent manhood by assassinating her instead of his assigned target. In the 1952 KOREAN WAR FILM *Retreat, Hell!*, made while the fight was ongoing, an overprotective mother attempts to keep her son from combat. James Dean's popular film about misunderstood youth, *Rebel Without a Cause* (1955), holds momism directly responsible for teenagers' alienation and delinquency.

Wylie's own 1954 novel, TOMORROW!, celebrates both nuclear armament and civil defense. Among the antagonists are three domineering mothers who oppose the civil defense program, largely because they resent the disruption of their shopping routines and social engagements. The two who are still married dominate their husbands; the widow controls her son and, through him, the town. When the nuclear attack comes, none takes shelter and each is duly punished and humbled: The face, breast and stomach of one are "sliced to red meat." The second survives but only because the baby she is pressing against her absorbs the blast; the child is "almost torn apart" after receiving a pound of glass in her back. The woman's other children also die horrible deaths. The widow, who coordinated a campaign against the civil defense program, is ignobly rescued and carried through the streets in a wheelbarrow. In Alfred HITCHCOCK's spy film NORTH BY NORTHWEST (1959), the protagonist, played by Cary Grant, is dominated by his mother as the movie opens. Then Soviet agents mistake him for an American spy and frame him for a murder. The act of clearing his name, fighting for his survival and combating the communists produces a change in his character that enables him to assert his independence from his mother and emerge as a worthy mate for the beautiful blonde secret agent whose life he saves.

On the other hand, Helen Clarkson explicitly rejects momism in her 1959 novel, *The Last Day*. Clarkson makes the well-being of children her foremost concern, rejects Wylie's belief that over-nurturing mothers are responsible for the country's problems, and argues that Americans require more nurturing love, not less. The protagonist takes exception to a *Life* magazine editorial that declares that "the only people who wanted to end nuclear testing were 'scared mothers, fuzzy liberals and weary taxpayers.' In other words: mothers are a lunatic fringe, a minority group."

As the feminist movement developed throughout the 1960s and 1970s, the arguments about momism became absorbed into the larger debate over gender roles. Traditionalists like Wylie directly and indirectly associated with communism strong mothers and independent women, especially women who were sexually liberated. They argued that women should not have careers but should rather dedicate themselves to supporting their husbands and nurturing their children. Yet they also believed women should not dominate or overly protect their sons. On the other hand, feminists attacked the charges of momism and its association with communism as a RED HERRING designed to subordinate women to men. They suggested that conservatives' equation of strong mothers and sexually liberated women with communism indicated the extent to which these men felt threatened by strong women. Ironically, feminists sought to free women from the state of idleness that Wylie described, to involve them in interests that might make them less emotionally dependent on their children and less economically dependent on men.

For additional reading, see Rogin's *Ronald Reagan, the Movie*.

Monroe, Marilyn A FILM ACTRESS. Born Norma Jean Mortenson in 1926, Monroe was a leading sex symbol during the 1950s and early 1960s. She appeared as the first nude centerfold in the premiere issue of PLAYBOY magazine in 1953. She was married to baseball player Joe DiMaggio and playwright Arthur MILLER and was posthumously the basis for Maggie in Miller's play, *After the Fall*. She was also the subject of a book by Norman MAILER. Her interest as a Cold War figure derives from her alleged affairs with President Kennedy and other powerful and influential men of the era. Moreover, as a Hollywood sex icon she became an international symbol of what many Americans embraced as glamour and the pursuit of happiness and communists rejected as decadent. The subject of famous pictures by Andy Warhol, Monroe was also featured as a character in Nicholas Roeg's *Insignificance* (1985), a British-made film that imagines her, her baseball-player husband Joe DiMaggio, Albert Einstein and a U.S. senator exploring the nuclear threat.

Monsieur Verdoux A 1947 FILM COMEDY starring Charles CHAPLIN and Martha Raye and directed by Chaplin. The film tells the BLACK HUMOR story of an unemployed bank clerk who marries rich widows and then kills them so he can use their money to support his crippled wife and their child. The film, which Chaplin claimed was his response to the atomic bomb, questions the relationship between virtuous goals and the immoral methods sometimes used to achieve them. It concludes with a moralizing speech, an anti-capitalist commentary accusing society of adopting brutal means to achieve its proclaimed noble objectives. Attempts to ban *Monsieur Verdoux* failed, but picketing by the American Legion outside of the theaters where it was screened caused the film to be removed prematurely from circulation.

Moon Over Parador A 1988 FILM COMEDY starring Richard Dreyfuss, Raul Julia, Sonia Braga, Jonathan Winters and Sammy Davis Jr., and directed by Paul Mazursky. The film spoofs late 1980s Latin American politics as Dreyfuss plays an actor who impersonates a dictator who has died.

Moonraker A 1955 SPY NOVEL by Ian Fleming and a 1979 British-made SPY FILM starring Roger Moore, Lois Chiles, Michel Lonsdale and Richard Kiel and directed by Lewis Gilbert. *Moonraker* brings the space race to the spy story. The book was written before the 1957 Soviet launching of Sputnik I, the first human-made satellite to orbit the Earth, but by the time the film appeared, the United States had sent astronauts to the moon and was talking about space stations and space shuttles. The film literally takes the suave James BOND and his fancy gadgets to outer space, where he thwarts the plans of an evil scientist to replace the Earth's population with a super race he has developed inside a huge space station. The vision of outer space as a possible base for an enemy attack both harkens back to the SCIENCE FICTION FILMS of the 1950s and anticipates by a few years President Reagan's Strategic Defense Initiative (SDI—more popularly known as STAR WARS).

Moscow Does Not Believe in Tears A 1979 Soviet-made FILM DRAMA directed by Vladimir Menshov; it is also known as *Moscow Distrusts Tears*. Made at the end of the 1970s U.S.–Soviet détente and distributed in the United States in the early 1980s, the film features three working girls from Moscow who, 20 years afterward, reminisce about their romances in 1958.

Moscow on the Hudson A 1984 FILM DRAMA starring Robin Williams, Maria Conchita Alonso and Cleavant Derricks and written and directed by Paul Mazursky. The comic drama centers on a Soviet circus artist who defects to the United States after a visit to Bloomingdale's, a trendy department store. His image of the United States becomes tarnished, however, when he experiences the less savory aspects of life in New York City. Finally, the emigré learns to embrace American liberties and material bounty.

Mostel, Zero A FILM ACTOR. Known for his wit, Mostel was blacklisted after he refused to cooperate with the HOUSE COMMITTEE ON UN-AMERICAN ACTIVITIES (HUAC) during his 1951 testimony. To Congressman Donald Jackson's claim that by performing at a benefit for *Mainstream* magazine Mostel had aided the Communist Party, Mostel countered that he had only done "an imitation of a butterfly at rest. There is no crime in making anybody laugh. I don't care if you laugh at me." Jackson did not concur. After his blacklisting Mostel asserted, "I am a man of many faces, all of them blacklisted." However, in the 1960s he exceeded his former popularity in live THEATER, starring in *A Funny Happened on the Way to the Forum* and *Fiddler on the Roof*. In 1976, Mostel starred in a film about the victims of the blacklist, THE FRONT, playing a character loosely based on Philip LOEB. He also appeared that year in HOLLYWOOD ON TRIAL, a documentary about the RED SCARE in Hollywood written by HOLLYWOOD TEN member Lester COLE.

For a partial transcript of Mostel's testimony before HUAC, see Bentley's THIRTY YEARS OF TREASON.

Motion Picture Alliance for the Preservation of American Ideals An anti-communist, pro–free enterprise political group founded by Sam Wood in 1944 to combat "the growing impression that this [movie] industry is made up of, and dominated by Communists, radicals and crackpots." The Motion Picture Alliance (MPA) endorsed the controversial findings of Senator Jack Tenney's California Un-American Activities Committee, and it cooperated fully in the 1947 HOUSE COMMITTEE ON UN-AMERICAN ACTIVITIES (HUAC) hearings investigating communist influence in Hollywood films. The MPA furnished most of the "friendly" witnesses who identified instances of alleged communist activity in Hollywood. In addition to commenting on perceived communist influences in film content, they also publicly identified alleged communists and communist sympathizers. Prominent among the MPA witnesses were SCREENWRITER Robert Hughes, a founder of the alliance; Lela Rogers, mother of Ginger Rogers; actor Robert Taylor; union leader Roy BREWER; and writer Ayn RAND, who had written a "Screen Guide for Americans" that the MPA published and distributed and that the *New York Times* and other publications reprinted. The guide admonished filmmakers not to smear the free enterprise system, glorify failure, deify the common man, glorify the collective or smear success. "It is the *moral* (no, not just political but *moral*) duty of every decent man in the motion picture industry to throw into the ashcan where it belongs, every story that smears industrialists as such."

Brewer, president of the AFL's International Alliance of Theatrical Stage Employees (IATSE), was also president of the MPA during much of the RED SCARE. Ward BOND succeeded him in 1955, after Brewer left the industry. Both Brewer and Bond were influential in helping to "clear" individuals who had been blacklisted but who were willing to demonstrate their anti-communist sympathies through various public acts of contrition. (See also BLACKLISTING.)

For additional reading, see Cogley's *Report on Blacklisting*, vol. 1.

Mouse that Roared, The A British-made 1959 FILM COMEDY starring Peter SELLERS and Jean Seberg and directed by Jack Arnold. As in DR. STRANGELOVE (1964), Sellers plays three roles in this FILM SATIRE, which centers on the efforts of the tiny and financially desperate duchy of Grand Fenwick to unsuccessfully invade the United States. The invasion has been planned by the grand duchess (Sellers) and prime minister (Sellers) with the expectation that Tully Bascombe's (Sellers) expeditionary force will immediately surrender. Afterward, they plan, Grand Fenwick will quickly begin receiving foreign aid, much as vanquished foes Japan and Germany received U.S. aid to rebuild their industrial base and become Cold War bastions against communism. However, by a fluke, Tully's army of 20 men—wearing armor and equipped with bows and arrows—arrives in New York during an air raid drill, and they inadvertently capture the prototype of the mighty Q-Bomb. Suddenly, Grand Fenwick is the most powerful country on Earth. This satire on U.S. foreign policy and nuclear politics was one of the earliest in the Cold War.

Muir, Jean   A TELEVISION PERFORMER who was blacklisted in 1950. Muir had been contracted to join the cast of the situation comedy, "The Aldrich Family" (NBC, 1949–53), which was about to begin its second season. However, after RED CHANNELS listed her as a communist sympathizer, the show's sponsor, General Foods, and its advertising agency, Young & Rubicam, had her dropped from the series. As a result, the first episode of the series was never aired and Muir was fired, despite her protests that she was not a communist and that she had never been given an opportunity to defend herself. Muir was paid the full amount that her contract stipulated and was replaced by Nancy Carroll in the role of Alice Aldrich. Prominent among Muir's accusers were Theodore Kirkpatrick, an editor of the anti-communist publication COUNTERATTACK, and Rabbi Benjamin Schultz of the Joint Committee Against Communism in New York. Schultz claimed to represent two million Americans. However, according to Merle Miller's 1952 report, *The Judges and the Judged*, a General Foods spokesman stated that

> Less than 40% [of the people questioned in a survey the company had commissioned] had ever heard of the Muir affair. And of those that had, less than three percent could relate the name of General Foods or the product involved, Jell-O, with the name of Muir. They tied up the name of Muir hazily with General Mills, even the Bell Telephone Company . . . We telephoned

Jean Muir, 1950. Courtesy AP/Wide World.

several General Foods sales offices in other cities like Chicago. We asked "How has the Muir publicity affected our sales?" The answer invariably was, "Muir? Who's Muir?"

Muir, who was celebrating her 20th year in show business on the day she was fired, did not appear again on television. She later became a social worker. Her firing was the first directly attributable to *Red Channels*. Muir died in 1996. (See also BLACKLISTING.)

For additional reading, see Cogley's *Report on Blacklisting*, vol. 2; Miller's *The Judges and the Judged*.

Mumford, Lewis   A NONFICTION WRITER. One of the most influential social critics during the early Cold War, Mumford criticized the traditional liberal notion of progress both for its inability to oppose fascism before World War II and for its postwar equation of progress with increased wealth and advanced technology. Though not opposed to science and technology per se, Mumford believed that these must be subordinated to human spiritual development. *The Conduct of Life* (1951) and *In the Name of Sanity* (1954) criticize the development of the atomic bomb, arguing that the destruction of Hiroshima and America's Cold War use of methods employed by the Nazis indicate that Hitler had actually "won" World War II. His earlier work, *Values for Survival* (1946), insists on the necessity of accompanying technological development with moral wisdom based on the ethics of the great religions. Mumford criticizes 20th-century writers and artists whose objective is mainly to illustrate the fragmentation and dehumanization of the modern world. Instead, he argues, the purpose of contemporary art should be to provide the wholeness and harmony that industrial society lacks: writers have a "responsibility to be sane," and their literature should provide "healing forces," a "cleansing greatness of spirit" and a "scheme of ideal values" through which the society can lift itself from its spiritual wasteland.

Mumford's numerous writings on architecture likewise propose that city planning and building design transcend the restrictions of mere efficiency and profitability, rather addressing the challenge of creating living spaces to enhance human interaction and spiritual fulfillment. Writing at a time when most of the country regarded capitalism as the only viable alternative to communism, Mumford objected to the pursuit of capitalism without regard to its impact on human needs. In *The Urban Prospect* (1968), he opposes the Cold War–era practice of building large skyscrapers and bringing massive highways into the inner cities, since these pack cities too densely, destroy parks and neighborhoods, and make society too dependent on cars. According to Mumford, the net effect of all these developments is to depersonalize urban life.

Mumford's early opposition to the Vietnam War won the support of antiwar activists who agreed with his charge in *The Myth of the Machine* (1967) that the "military-industrial scientific" complex circumvented democratic control in its prosecution of the war. Moreover, Mumford argued that both the United States and Soviet Union represented totalitarian forces of destruction that employed nuclear weapons, mass culture, propaganda and centralization to extinguish human subjectivity.

For additional reading, see *The Dictionary of Literary Biography* (vol. 63, *American Literary Critics and Scholars*).

Murrow, Edward R. A CBS radio and television journalist. Often regarded as the elder statesman of American television journalism, Murrow first gained national prominence during World War II for his live radio broadcasts during the Nazi bombings of London. In November 1951, along with producer Fred Friendly, he introduced the half-hour TELEVISION NEWS show SEE IT NOW (CBS, 1951–58), proclaiming "For the first time in the history of man we are able to look out at both the Atlantic and Pacific coasts of this great country at the same time . . . no journalistic age was ever given a weapon for truth with quite the scope of this fledgling television." At a time when American television was reluctant to engage in political controversy or to challenge the practices of Senator Joseph McCarthy or other practitioners of the RED SCARE, Murrow frequently did so. In 1953, for example, he presented the case of Lieutenant Radulovich, an officer whose resignation had been requested by the air force because his father and sister were considered security risks for reading communist newspapers and participating in activities the air force deemed questionable. Quoting the Bible, Murrow asserted, "We believe that 'the son shall not bear the iniquity of the father,' even though that iniquity be proved; and in this case, it was not." Five weeks later, "See It Now" showed the secretary of the air force restoring Radulovich to duty. In 1956 Murrow interviewed China's premier, Chou En-Lai, and in 1957 he interviewed Yugoslavia's Marshal Tito. In both instances he deflected possible criticism by following the interviews with

Edward R. Murrow, at the time of his appointment to head the USIA, 1961. With Murrow are Senators George McGovern (l.), Hubert Humphrey (c.). Courtesy Library of Congress.

panel discussions featuring such prominent anti-communists as T. F. Tsiang, the Nationalist Chinese delegate to the United Nations; former congresswoman Clare Booth Luce, then the U.S. ambassador to Italy; and Hamilton Fish, the editor of *Foreign Affairs*.

Murrow's most significant contribution to the Cold War was the March 9, 1954, installment of "See It Now" entitled, *A Report on Senator Joseph R. McCarthy*. Primarily a collection of film clips showing the senator contradicting himself and making inaccurate statements and accusations, the show was the first time that network television directly addressed McCarthy's reckless demagoguery. The following week, the senator received free air time to respond; however, rather than address the contents of Murrow's show, McCarthy attacked the broadcaster personally, calling him a communist and "the leader and the cleverest of the jackal pack which is always at the throat of anyone who dares expose individual Communists or traitors." Murrow's *Report on Senator McCarthy* has since come to be regarded as one of the high points in television journalism. At least one critic calls it "the most important show in the history of television."

Immediately after the McCarthy report aired, however, a CBS poll showed that more Americans found McCarthy more credible than Murrow, and after McCarthy's rebuttal, a third of those polled believed Murrow to be either a communist or a communist sympathizer. CBS broadcast Murrow's *Report on McCarthy* reluctantly, running no advertisements to promote it and refusing to let Murrow and Friendly use the CBS logo in ads that they had paid for personally. The CBS public relations department also gave advance notification of the show to FBI director J. Edgar Hoover. In the aftermath of the broadcast, CBS president Fred Stanton told Fred Friendly of his fears that political pressures could influence the Federal Communications Commission to take action against them: "You may have cost us the network." In fact, such action never materialized. Alcoa, the show's sponsor, received considerable hate mail but continued to sponsor the show for another year, after which it withdrew. Afterward, the show received only partial or occasional sponsorship, had its hours reduced and its time slot changed. CBS separated Friendly and Murrow and then canceled "See It Now" in 1958.

In 1959 Murrow spoke out: "The timidity of television in dealing with this man [McCarthy] when he was spreading fear throughout the land is not something to which this art of communication can point with pride, nor should it be allowed to forget it." Murrow later helped defeat the television and radio blacklist by donating $7,500 to a 1955 libel suit that Texas raconteur John Henry Faulk brought against Vincent Harnett and Laurence Johnson, whose Aware, Inc. had mistakenly identified Faulk as having communist associations, leading to his blacklisting. After seven years, a jury awarded a large sum to Faulk, and put Aware, Inc. out of business, implying new dangers for would-be blacklisters. (See also BLACKLISTING.)

After the demise of "See It Now," Murrow remained for another year, hosting "Person to Person," a show he inaugurated on CBS in 1953. He would interview various celebrities who were sitting in their homes while Murrow was in his studio. Interviewees included Fidel Castro,

Speaker of the House Sam Rayburn, Senator John F. Kennedy, and such movie stars as Marilyn MONROE and Zsa Zsa Gabor. In CBS's "Small World" (1958–60), Murrow held four-way telephone conversations with political and cultural figures throughout the world. In one show about U.S. prestige in Asia, Murrow interviewed U.S. Information Agency director George Allen, Manila's Mayor Arsenio Lacson, and Eugene BURDICK, coauthor of THE UGLY AMERICAN (1958) and FAIL-SAFE (1962). Murrow left CBS in 1961; *Crossroads Africa: Pilot for a Peace Corps* was his final assignment. He then headed the U.S. Information Agency from 1961 to 1964. A chain-smoker, Murrow died of cancer in 1965 at the age of 57. His career was the subject of *Murrow,* a 1986 made-for-television movie starring Daniel J. Travanti, Dabney Coleman and Edward Herrmann, directed by Jack Gold. (See also TELEVISION DOCUMENTARIES.)

For additional reading, see Whitfield's *The Culture of the Cold War*; Einstein's *Special Edition: A Guide to Network Television Documentary Series and Special News Reports, 1955–1979.*

music Overt concern with politics did not play a large role in most mainstream, Cold War–era American music, except in ROCK AND ROLL and folk music, though several performers and conductors of classical music fled communist regimes to the United States. Notable among them was Rafael Kubelik who conducted the Czech Philharmonic from 1941 until the communist takeover in 1948 and then went on to become the principal conductor for several major Western orchestras, including the Chicago Symphony. His successor in Chicago, Sir Georg Solti, fled Hungary during World War II but remained in the West partly to avoid the communist regime in his homeland. The Takacs Quartet, a string quartet comprised entirely of exiles from communism, also performed to acclaim before Western audiences, as did the Tchaikovsky Chamber Orchestra which was founded by Lazar Gosman, the former music director of the Leningrad Chamber Orchestra. In 1958 classical pianist Van CLIBURN won first prize in the 1958 Tchaikovsky competition, which was judged by 16 Moscow jurors. The *New York Times* ran a front-page headline proclaiming that Cliburn's victory had created, "an artistic bridge between the U.S. and Russia." John Adams's 1987 opera NIXON IN CHINA enacts the five days of President Nixon's historic visit to China in February 1972. Adams and librettist Alice Goodman conceived the work as a heroic opera.

The indigenous American musical form of JAZZ continued to evolve during the Cold War. The form was pioneered during the late 1940s, 1950s and 1960s by Charlie Parker, John Coletrane, Dizzy Gillespie, Thelonius Monk and Miles Davis. Though not usually explicitly political, jazz facilitates the personal expression and experimentation that were not permissible "behind the IRON CURTAIN." Thus, like rock and roll, abstract art and other forms of expressionism, jazz was generally banned in the Soviet Union, where it was denounced as decadent. The freedom of musicians to play jazz in the West thus became one of the important cultural differences between the Western democracies and communist-dominated Eastern Europe. The PAUL WINTER JAZZ SEXTET became the first group to perform jazz at the White House when they gave a concert in November 1962, a few weeks

after the Cuban Missile Crisis. Singer Celia Cruz, the "Queen of Salsa," and band leader Tito Puente were notable among early Cuban exiles who performed their lively mixture of Caribbean music and jazz before American audiences. In the 1980s Gloria Estefan, who was exiled from Castro's Cuba as a child, achieved immense popularity by fusing Latin rhythms with rock and roll.

Tom LEHRER and Mark RUSSELL performed songs of political SATIRE during the Cold War. Lehrer's WE WILL ALL GO TOGETHER WHEN WE GO (1959), for instance, is a BLACK HUMOR number about NUCLEAR APOCALYPSE. Following President Johnson's decision to send troops to the Dominican Republic in 1965 to quell civil unrest, Lehrer performed a song parodying U.S. gunboat diplomacy, "Send the Marines." He also wrote "Who's Next?" about nuclear proliferation and a satirical ballad about Werner von Braun, the Nazi rocket scientist who ended up working for the U.S. space program.

Country music often expressed patriotic sentiments. Some 1950s country songs also addressed the nuclear threat directly, such as those featured in the 1982 film documentary THE ATOMIC CAFE, including "The Hydrogen Bomb" (Al Rogers and His Rocky Mountain Boys), "The Cold War With You" (Floyd Tillman), "I'm No Communist" (Carson Robinson), "Jesus Hits Like an Atom Bomb" (Lowell Blanchard with the Valley Trio), "Atom Bomb Baby" (The Five Stars), "When the Atom Bomb Falls" (Karl and Harty) and "When They Drop the Atomic Bomb" (Jackie Doll and the Pickled Peppers).

On the other end of the political spectrum, the song OLD MAN ATOM, a 1950 "talking blues number" by Los Angeles newspaperman Vern Partlow, warned against the possibility of nuclear apocalypse. It acquired a significant degree of popularity before Rabbi Benjamin Schultz and his Joint Committee Against Communism led a successful boycott against it, pressuring radio stations to stop playing it. Among the musicians who fell victim to BLACKLISTING during the RED SCARE were Paul ROBESON, Lena HORNE, Hazel SCOTT, Pete SEEGER, the Weavers, composer Aaron Copland, performer Gypsy Rose Lee, band leader Artie Shaw and harmonica player Larry Adler. ED SULLIVAN publicly apologized for allowing Adler and tap dancer Paul Draper to appear on his television variety show in the early 1950s, and their careers in the United States were effectively ruined.

FOLK SINGERS were among the most politically engaged performers of the Cold War era. Though much of their earlier work centered on the 1950s civil rights movement, in the early 1960s they began addressing the Cold War as well. They almost universally advocated peace and sang out against U.S. militarism, nuclear weapons, government suppression of dissent, and the U.S. military involvement in Vietnam and Southeast Asia. Despite being blacklisted, Pete Seeger continued singing pro-union songs and other leftist numbers throughout the 1950s Red Scare, mostly in concerts performed at college campuses, union halls, churches and libraries. He became known for encouraging audience participation, a practice that became common among American folk singers. In late 1961 Seeger helped found and fund Sis Cunningham's *Broadside*, a biweekly magazine of songs about contemporary social issues. *Broadside* furnished a previously missing forum for this kind of left-wing music, and among those who published in it were

Bob DYLAN, Phil OCHS, Tom Paxton, Les Chandler and Peter La Farge. Seeger's efforts were thus instrumental in creating the rising interest in folk music during the early 1960s.

Ochs had a particularly extensive repertoire of songs about the Cold War, including "The Ballad of the Cuban Invasion" about the failed Bay of Pigs invasion; "Talking Cuban Crisis"; "The Ballad of William Worthy," about a black JOURNALIST who ran afoul of the State Department when he traveled to Cuba without a passport; "Thresher," about a nuclear submarine that was lost at sea; and "Talking Vietnam," an early song of Vietnam War protest. He remained actively opposed to the war and went on to compose such antiwar ballads as "Is There Anybody Here?" "White Boots Marchin' in a Yellow Land," "Draft Dodger Rag" and "The War Is Over." Dylan, too, wrote about the Cuban Missile Crisis in "Hard Rain's A-Gonna Fall." "Talking World War Three Blues" provides a black humor view of life after a nuclear war, and "Masters of War" attacks complacent middle-class citizens for permitting American militarism.

In 1964, Dylan performed with his girlfriend Joan BAEZ at peace concerts, and together they were known as the King and Queen of Folk Rock. However, in 1965 Dylan began to withdraw from politics, claiming in a *Newsweek* interview, "I've never written a political song. Songs can't save the world . . ." He subsequently turned to music that was more personal and less political. Baez, on the other hand, remained political throughout the Cold War. Other prominent folk singers include Tom Paxton, the Kingston Trio, and Peter, Paul and Mary (Peter Yarrow, Noel Paul Stookey and Mary Travers). The protest aspect of folk singing eventually spread to rock and roll and helped create a mixed genre, folk rock. Among the popular practitioners of this new form were Judy Collins, Joni Mitchell, Melanie (Melanie Safka), Don McLean, Laura Nyro, James Taylor and Leonard Cohen. Many folk and folk-rock singers became active in the 1980s nuclear freeze movement.

Rock and roll did not become significantly politicized until 1965, the year when the United States first sent combat troops to Vietnam. That year, Barry McGuire's rendition of "Eve of Destruction" became a number-one hit. (Nineteen-year-old P. F. Sloan wrote the song). As the title suggests, the song laments the current state of worldwide affairs, and the refrain repeatedly asks its audience to deny that "we're on the eve of destruction." Most political rock music attacked the war and the American establishment that prosecuted it. The 1968 rock musical HAIR centers on a young man who joins a COUNTERCULTURE commune in order to avoid the draft. Among the many popular singers and groups to sing out against the war were Donovan, the Beatles, John Lennon, the Rolling Stones, Jim Morrison and the Doors, Eric Burdon, Grace Slick, Creedence Clearwater Revival, Frank Zappa's Mothers of Invention, Blind Faith, the Allman Brothers, and MC5.

The 1969 WOODSTOCK rock festival brought together several of these artists under a kind of tacit antiwar aegis; other rock concerts and "festivals of life" from the period also suggested or stated opposition to the war. One of the best known antiwar songs of the time was Country Joe McDonald's "I-Feel-Like-I'm-Going-To-Die Rag," which incorporates elements of black humor as its chorus asks, "1-2-3,

What're we fightin' for?/ Don't ask me, I don't give a damn/ Next stop is Vietnam./ And it's 5-6-7, open up the pearly gates./ Ain't no time to wonder why/ Whoopee! We're all bound to die." After the war, rock music became less idealistically motivated and generally less overtly political, though during the late 1970s and 1980s some punk rock took on brutal neo-fascist overtones. In 1989 Billy Joel reviewed the entire Cold War in his song/music video "We Didn't Start the Fire," which traces a family from the 1950s through the Vietnam War and beyond.

For additional reading, see Orman's *The Politics of Rock Music*; Denisoff's *Sing a Song of Social Significance*; Szatmary's *Rockin' in Time: A Social History of Rock and Roll*; Nite's *Rock On Almanac*; Ward et al.'s *Rock of Ages: The Rolling Stone History of Rock & Roll*; Ramet's *Rocking the State: Rock Music and Politics in Eastern Europe and Russia*.

My Son John A 1952 FILM DRAMA starring Helen Hayes, Robert Walker and Van Heflin and directed by Leo McCarey. In *Running Time* Nora Sayre calls this "By far the most feverish of the anti-Communist films" made during the RED SCARE. McCarey had directed the Marx Brothers in *Duck Soup* and Bing Crosby in *Going My Way*. A staunch anticommunist, he had been an extremely cooperative witness in the 1947 hearings held by the HOUSE COMMITTEE ON UN-AMERICAN ACTIVITIES (HUAC). In 1950 he supported Cecil B. DEMILLE's demand that all members of the Screen Directors Guild take a loyalty oath. In *My Son John*, he portrayed the anti-intellectualism, fear of homosexuality and fear of women—especially strong mothers—that several scholars have shown to be integral aspects of Red Scare sensibility.

Helen Hayes plays the overly protective mother who clings to her third and youngest son. Consequently, while the older brothers grow up to be "real men" who play football with their American Legionnaire father, fight bravely in Korea and respect their Christian beliefs, John remains inside studying: "He has more degrees than a thermometer." When he goes off to college, he becomes first in his class. But he also returns with homosexual traits, disdain for his father's patriotism, and disregard for religion. Eventually, his mother suspects that her worst fears might be true—her favorite son may be a communist. She travels to Washington, D.C., and discovers that John's "girlfriend" is actually a spy. She returns and interviews John before an FBI agent, hoping he will confess. She tells him to "get in this game and . . . carry the ball yourself."

But Hayes has urged her son to take the ball too late. She should have done so when he was a child. John ignores the football reference and the apparent suggestion that he should become like his patriotic, ball-playing brothers. Seeing that John is hopeless, his mother collapses onto a sofa and tells the FBI agent to "Take him away! He has to be punished."

Eventually John changes his mind and agrees to confess, but communist agents assassinate him on his way to FBI headquarters. John dies at the foot of the Lincoln Memorial, but his rediscovered patriotism lives on after him in a tape recording of his valedictorian speech. A heavenly ray of light shines on the empty podium as the graduating class hears how "I was going to help to make a better world" and how the communists' recognition of his intellectual achievement flattered him and led him to defy the only authorities he had ever known: "my church and my father and mother." He declares that "Even now, the eyes of Soviet agents are on some of you" and concludes by confessing his guilt: "I am a living a lie, I am a traitor . . . Communist. Spy. And may God have mercy on my soul."

My Son John thus presents a Red Scare view of the domestic communist menace in which intellectuals, soft-hearted liberals and homosexuals were liable to become communist dupes—however unwittingly—and thereby to betray the nation. The film's closing speech highlights the ways that excessive intellectual pride can blind a bright young person, rendering him a tool for cynical communists to exploit. On the other hand, super-patriots who are not bright or intellectually inclined but who respect religion, family values, and loyalty to one's country will prove to be America's salvation. As we see in such other 1950s films as *Rebel Without a Cause*, a mother's excessive nurturing causes her son to behave in a deviant fashion—sexually, emotionally, socially, politically or all of the above. The contrast between "manly" sports, which are associated with patriotism and American values, and "feminine" intellectual and aesthetic pursuits, which are associated with communism, illustrates how anti-intellectualism and fear of feminine traits were incorporated into the anti-communist message. (See also MOMISM and FILMS ASSOCIATED WITH THE RED SCARE.)

For additional reading, see Sayre's *Running Time;* Whitfield's *Culture of the Cold War.*

Nabokov, Vladimir A Soviet EXILED WRITER (to the United States). Born in St. Petersburg in 1899, Nabokov was the son of aristocratic gentry in czarist Russia. They reputedly lost their fortune when their estates were confiscated during the 1917 Russian Revolution. Nabokov and his brother immigrated to Germany with their father, an important liberal politician who was assassinated at a political rally in Berlin in 1923, although the bullet was intended for another political leader. After graduating from Cambridge University, Nabokov returned to Berlin in 1923. He worked as a private tutor and published literary works in Russian under the pseudonym he used through 1940, V. Sirin.

In 1940 Nabokov moved to the United States, where he taught college. With his immigration to the United States he began writing in English under his real name. In 1947 he published *Bend Sinister*. Set in a Slavic country, the novel describes how an absolutist, totalitarian environment creates universal mediocrity. Also written during his American period were *Pnin* (1957), a loosely autobiographical novel about a Russian emigré professor in the United States, and *Lolita* (1958), a comic novel describing a middle-aged professor's infatuation with a preadolescent girl, a "nymphet." The book's comic intention was not always appreciated, and it became highly controversial. In 1962, Stanley KUBRICK directed the successful film version, starring Peter SELLERS, James Mason, Sue Lyon and Shelly Winters. *Lolita* won Nabokov considerable recognition and made his fortune, allowing him to retire from teaching and move to a hotel suite in Montreux, Switzerland, in 1961. He remained there until he died in 1977, though he always retained his U.S. citizenship.

Notable from Nabokov's Swiss period are *Pale Fire* (1962) and *Ada* (1969). A wicked satire of academic literary criticism, *Pale Fire* contains a 999-line poem by the character John Shade. Framing the poem is a critical apparatus written by an insane editor who believes he is the exiled king of a mythical Balkan country and who improbably suggests that the poem is actually about his life. An elaborate network of cross-referenced footnotes makes the highly tenuous connections between the poem and the editor's experiences, including a humorous episode set during a communist revolution in which loyal subjects make possible the king's escape by dressing in pajamas to look like him. Living in a world of personal and political ambiguities, Nabokov populates his books with ambiguities of many sorts. As in *Ada* and much of his other work, Nabokov questions how we can ascertain truth with any meaningful degree of certainty, given the basic unreliability of all sources. This concern frequently appears as a dominant issue in both Eastern and Western literature throughout the period. Nabokov rarely addresses the Cold War directly. (See also NOVELISTS.)

For additional reading, see Tucker's *Literary Exile in the Twentieth Century*.

Nation of Sheep, A A 1961 NONFICTION book by William LEDERER. Something of a sequel to THE UGLY AMERICAN (1958), a best-selling POLITICAL NOVEL that Lederer coauthored with Eugene BURDICK, *A Nation of Sheep* criticizes the United States for its support of regimes in Laos, Thailand, Formosa and South Korea. Lederer attacks the U.S. government and press for misinforming the American public and concludes by offering suggestions on how to remedy U.S. foreign policy. Though mixed, the reviews for this work were generally favorable. The book did receive some criticism for overstating its case but was praised for its thesis that the government is often inexcusably ill-informed. The reviewer for the *Atlantic* points out that the book "is weakened throughout by his [Lederer's] faith in an exploded dogma, the assumption of the Enlightenment and of nineteenth-century liberalism that man is a perfectly rational being whose errors are due solely to ignorance."

Lederer's *Our Own Worst Enemy* (1968), published during the height of the Vietnam War, expands upon the theses in *A Nation of Sheep*. He argues that the United States is simultaneously fighting and losing several wars in Vietnam: a large-scale bombing war, a guerrilla war, a political war aimed at winning the loyalty of the Vietnamese people, and a moral war. This book also received mixed reviews. One critic points out that Lederer skirts the most central question of why the United States is in Vietnam at all but that it "escapes the faults of reiteration because we have never listened to what he had to say." Most reviewers fault the book for its overly polemical style.

"Navy Log" An anthology of TELEVISION MILITARY DRAMAS that ran on CBS in 1955–56 and on ABC in 1957–58. Based on official navy files and produced with the cooperation of the Navy Department, "Navy Log" featured reenactments of events that actually took place. The show focused on individual seamen or airmen, usually in a battle setting but sometimes addressing personal issues such as the plight of a mentally disturbed veteran. One episode featured an account of the sinking of John F. Kennedy's *PT-109* in the South Pacific. Kennedy, a senator at the time, appeared as a special guest. The show's celebration of America's navy during one of the more tense periods of the Cold War helped bolster the public's confidence in the U.S. military.

Never Let Me Go A 1953 FILM DRAMA starring Clark Gable and Gene Tierney and directed by Delmer Daves. The story centers on the efforts of a newspaper correspondent to smuggle his wife out of the Soviet Union.

For additional reading, see Rogin's *Ronald Reagan, the Movie*.

new liberalism A Cold War political philosophy that emerged in the late 1940s and early 1950s in opposition to the "old liberalism" of the teens, '20s and '30s, especially as embodied by the Progressive movement and other movements ideologically sympathetic to socialism and communism. Consistent with President Truman's Cold War policies, the new liberalism recognized limitations to America's power to change conditions throughout the world. Thus new liberalism endorsed containment and the implicit acceptance of superpowers' spheres of influence inherent in the Yalta agreements. Sobered by revelations of Stalin's abuses, the new liberalism explicitly disassociated itself from communism and even socialism. The new liberals

accused their predecessors of believing that good intentions alone were sufficient for foreign and domestic policy. They presented themselves as pragmatists who rejected ideology in favor of simply "doing what worked." Their critics claimed that this rejection of ideology was in itself an ideological attack on the left.

The new liberalism was most effectively expressed by such literary critics as Lionel TRILLING and Richard CHASE and such intellectual figures as Reinhold Niebuhr and Arthur Schlesinger Jr. They replaced the inherently optimistic assumptions of Progressivism, which held that enlightened social policies can create a better world, with a more pessimistic outlook that saw the irrational forces of the id as frequently dominating human behavior. In this way they pushed liberalism in a more traditionally conservative direction. Trilling thus wrote in *The Liberal Imagination*, "Some paradox of our natures leads us, when once we have made our fellow men the objects of our enlightened interest, to go on to make them the objects of our pity, then of our wisdom, ultimately of our coercion. It is to prevent this corruption . . . that we stand in need of the moral realism which is the product of the free play of the moral imagination."

R. W. B. LEWIS challenged the pessimism of new liberalism in his 1955 collection, *American Adam*, calling it "something which began as a valuable corrective to the claims of innocence in America [but] which has declined into a cult of original sin."

The propensity of the new liberalism to replace ideology with pragmatism and to view life as morally and socially ambiguous provided a political context for such apparently apolitical intellectual endeavors as New Criticism, which largely separates literature from its historical context and celebrates levels of ambiguity within poetry and fiction.

For further reading, see Schaub's *American Fiction in the Cold War*.

Night of Camp David A 1965 POLITICAL NOVEL by Fletcher KNEBEL. The story centers on Jim MacVeagh, a senator who learns in a mysterious meeting with the president that he is under consideration as a vice presidential candidate in the forthcoming election. Over time, however, MacVeagh realizes that the president is extremely paranoid with delusions of persecution and grandeur. The president's upcoming meeting with Soviet leaders leaves MacVeagh wondering whether the U.S. head of state can be deposed before he invokes nuclear war. One reviewer commented, "I respect Mr. Knebel for refusing to hoke up his material for the sake of effect, for avoiding the apocalyptic ending in favor of one that is quite credible. I am equally certain that although his resolution is entirely within character, it will be a distinct let-down to most readers."

Nineteen Eighty-Four A 1949 POLITICAL NOVEL by George ORWELL and a 1984 British-made POLITICAL FILM starring John Hurt, Richard Burton and Suzanna Hamilton and written and directed by Michael Radford. Thomas Dolby wrote the sound track, which he released as a popular musical recording. One of the most famous and powerful anti-communist works, the book was written at the outset of the Cold War. It projects a time in the near future when, after a series of limited atomic wars, England is ruled by the Communist Party, which maintains absolute control over its citizens. (Orwell chose the futuristic date by reversing the last two digits of the year in which he wrote the novel, 1948.) Not only does the party employ terror and raw power to maintain control, it also uses extensive, highly developed technology to monitor each individual's spoken words and actions. A daily, public, two-minute "hate session" directed against an enemy of the state, public executions and an ongoing state of war among the world's three remaining superpowers create a state of continuous panic that renders citizens more malleable. (Scholars in the 1980s used the term "panic culture" to describe contemporary societies that employ hysteria to manipulate their citizens.)

The party also practices a sophisticated form of thought control by altering language itself in order to limit what people can think. Its bureaucratic "newspeak" radically limits the vocabulary available for forming new thoughts. The party not only controls the present but, through a systematic and ongoing revision of all historical documents, it alters the past as well, in order to make the past always appear consistent with current party actions. The Stalin-like revisions of history are important because the party recognizes that whoever controls the past controls the present, and whoever controls the present controls the future.

The bleak story centers around Winston Smith, a minor party official who seeks to acquire a modicum of individual thought and feeling but who is ultimately completely suppressed. Orwell provides an astute and somewhat prophetic view of the emerging Cold War and the methods that the superpowers would employ to control their domestic populations. The Cold War itself is one of those methods, since it contributes to panic culture. Orwell argues that whereas power was primarily viewed by kings and capitalists as a means to a self-gratifying end, in the advanced communist state run by technocrats, power is an end in itself. Many of the novel's elements refer directly to such actual communist leaders as Joseph Stalin (the party's paternal leader Big Brother) and Leon Trotsky (Goldstein, the enemy of the state) and to actual events, such as Soviet political purges of the 1930s, the operations of the secret police, and Stalinist revisions of history. The book's superpowers roughly correspond to the then-emerging NATO alliance, the Soviet empire in EASTERN EUROPE and a then-emerging Chinese empire in Asia.

Throughout most of the Cold War, *Nineteen Eighty-Four* loomed as a stark prophecy of a future in which huge centralized governments would employ technology and distort language to repress freedom, restrict thought and gain control over their citizens. During the Vietnam War era, the book became popular among antiwar activists, who saw analogies to U.S. government attempts to manipulate the public and exercise thought control. In the year 1984, the book attracted considerable national attention as academic forums, television panels of experts, and other groups widely discussed the accuracy of Orwell's forecast. Since 1984, the novel has ceased to be a prediction of the future and is now set completely in the past. Thus even though the words have remained the same, *Nineteen Eighty-Four* has changed significantly over time. Anthony Burgess also published a sequel, *1985* (1978). The Hungarian Gyorgy

Dalos also imagined a sequel entitled *1985* (1983). His presented a cynical view of the communist-sponsored reforms in Eastern Europe: Members of the Outer Party gain some freedoms, but the hopes of would-be dissidents like Winston Smith are shown to be futile. (See also APOCALYPTIC NOVELS.)

Nixon in China   A 1987 opera by John Adams. Alice Goodman wrote the libretto, and Peter Sellars directed the first production. The lyrics are written in couplets, and the MUSIC is in the minimalist tradition pioneered by Adams, Philip Glass, and Steve Reich. The action celebrates the five days of President Nixon's historic visit to China in February 1972.

Adams and Goodman conceived this work as an heroic opera. The first scene is set at the airfield outside Beijing: A Chinese military chorus sings "The Three Main Rules of Discipline and the Eight Points of Attention" as Nixon's plane taxis from the runway. After greeting Premier Zhou En-lai, Nixon sings of his excitement and fears. In the next scene Nixon meets with Chairman Mao Zedong. According to Goodman's notes, "Mao's conversational armory contains philosophical apothegms, unexpected political observations, and gnomic jokes, and everything he sings is amplified by his secretaries and the Premier. It is not easy for a Westerner to hold his own in such a dialogue." The first act then concludes with a banquet scene in which Nixon, National Security adviser Henry Kissinger and Zhou toast each other.

The second act begins with Mrs. Nixon's tour of Beijing and is followed by a performance of "The Red Detachment of Women," a ballet devised by Mao's wife, Chiang Ch'ing. According to Goodman, "The ballet entwines ideological rectitude with Hollywood-style emotion," and the Nixons are quite moved by the performance. The act concludes with Chiang's aria, "I am the wife of Mao Zedong," which finishes with full choral backing.

The final act takes place in a single scene depicting the Nixons' last night in Beijing. *Nixon in China* is one of the few major artistic works to treat this pivotal moment in the Cold War.

Nixon-Kennedy Debates, The   A series of televised debates between Senator John F. Kennedy and Vice President Richard M. Nixon during the 1960 presidential election. These were the first televised debates between U.S. presidential candidates, and Kennedy's youthful looks and greater ease before the television cameras are often credited with making a significant difference in the close election. Nixon is remembered for his heavy beard, a "five o'clock shadow" that, along with his sweating, made him appear sinister and unattractive under the television lights. One key result of these debates was that future candidates became immensely more conscious of their appearance and their ability to project an image. From then on, television became an increasingly important factor in U.S. electoral politics.

The candidates debated on both foreign and domestic issues. The foreign issues, especially, had Cold War significance as both candidates proposed to take a tough line against communism and as Kennedy accused the Republican Eisenhower administration of allowing a "missile gap" to develop between the U.S.S.R. and the United States.

The Nixon-Kennedy Debates, 1960. Courtesy Library of Congress.

No More War!   A 1958 NONFICTION book by Linus Pauling. Pauling, a Nobel Prize–winning scientist, calls for international agreements to end nuclear bomb testing and reduce the possibilities of nuclear war. He describes the biological effects of radiation and other hazards of radioactive fallout, presenting a scientist's perspective on the Cold War's nuclear threat. Pauling also calls for the establishment of a World Peace Research Organization to discover the "recipe" for peace, just as science found the recipe for penicillin. He further predicts that when communist China joins the United Nations, the UN "will become more powerful and the international law system more effective." The appendix to *No More War!* includes the Mainau Declaration of Nobel Laureates, a list of petitioners to the United Nations seeking peace, and appeals by Albert Einstein and Albert Schweitzer for the public to deal with the nuclear threat.

Pauling's pacifist proposals were not well received. They came during the RED SCARE and at the beginning of the second Berlin Crisis, when the possibilities for a major nuclear war were intensifying. A congressional committee concluded that Pauling was "primarily engrossed in placing his scientific attainment at the service of a host of organizations which have been in complete subservience to the Communist Party," and various reviewers expressed skepticism over Pauling's political suggestions, even while admiring his scientific work. Physicist Edward Teller, who headed the project to develop the hydrogen bomb, presented an opposite perspective the same year in OUR NUCLEAR FUTURE (1958).

nonfiction   An enormous amount of nonfiction dealing with the Cold War appeared between 1945 and 1990, much of it directed to popular audiences. In addition to memoirs by presidents, cabinet officers, generals, ambassadors and other key players in the Cold War, scholars, activists and others interpreted Cold War events and attempted to forecast future developments. Most of these works are beyond the scope of this study, though Robert Kennedy's personal account of the 1962 Cuban Missile Crisis, THIRTEEN DAYS (1969), is included.

The early days of the Cold War were characterized by a growth of interest in organized religion. In the face of the overwhelmingly complex postwar world, and in response to the new threat of nuclear annihilation, widespread desires emerged for some extra-human form of salvation. Not surprisingly, church attendance reached its highest levels of the century at the end of the 1950s as Cold War tensions peaked; television evangelists such as Billy GRAHAM thrived during the Cold War. Sales of the *Revised Standard Version of the Bible* reached over 26 million within a year of its publication in 1952; it remained on the best-seller list for several years following. Nonfiction by such religious leaders as Bishop Fulton J. SHEEN also attracted substantial audiences. In the late 1940s and 1950s, Sheen appeared on best-seller lists for his anti-communist, religious books: *Peace of the Soul* (1947), which argues that communism is the antithesis of Roman Catholicism; *Communism and the Conscience of the West* (1948), which maintains that communism is a kind of secular religion that evokes great dedication from its adherents; and LIFE IS WORTH LIVING (1953), a spin-off, from Sheen's popular television show by the same title (DuMont/ABC, 1952–57). (See also RELIGIOUS TELEVISION PROGRAMMING.)

The fear of domestic communism played a large role in mobilizing the American public to support the Cold War and accept restrictions on personal freedoms and privacy. During the RED SCARE of the late 1940s and 1950s, the dangers of domestic communism appeared in such works as THE GOD THAT FAILED (1949), a collection of personal testimonies by former communists or communist sympathizers who had become disaffected with communism. The collection, edited by Richard Crossman, includes personal accounts by ex-communists Arthur KOESTLER, Richard WRIGHT and Louis Fischer, and "fellow-travelers" Ignazio Silone, Andre Gide and Stephen Spender. It was often cited by anti-communists as firsthand evidence of communism's failings and hypocrisies. (Polish exiled writer Aleksander WAT also describes his initial attraction to and subsequent disaffection from communism in his memoir, *My Century: The Odyssey of a Polish Intellectual* [1977; in English, 1988]. The book is based on a series of interviews Wat gave to his Berkeley colleague Czeslaw MILOSZ.)

Whittaker Chambers's WITNESS (1952) reiterates the author's 1948 charges before the HOUSE COMMITTEE ON UN-AMERICAN ACTIVITIES (HUAC) that Alger Hiss, a ranking member of President Roosevelt's State Department and a founder of the United Nations, had spied for the Soviets in the 1930s. It also detailed the workings of the American Communist Party from the perspective of a formerly highly placed (though now disaffected) member. Though documents released from the Soviet Communist Party archives since the collapse of the Soviet Union corroborate some of Chambers's claims about domestic communism, they do not indicate that Hiss had ever been a Soviet agent. Hiss, who was convicted and imprisoned for perjury on the basis of Chambers's testimony, later presented his defense in IN THE COURT OF PUBLIC OPINION (1957). Owen Lattimore, whom Senator Joseph McCarthy had accused of being the top

Soviet espionage agent in the United States, describes his experiences in ORDEAL BY SLANDER (1950). Although McCarthy introduced unsubstantiated testimony from former ranking members of the U.S. Communist Party, a Senate panel chaired by Millard Tydings cleared Lattimore after finding no evidence that he had ever been a Soviet agent. Later criminal charges against Lattimore were eventually dropped for lack of evidence. Matt Cvetic and Herbert Philbrick describe their experiences as F.B.I. infiltrators in I WAS A COMMUNIST FOR THE F.B.I. (1950) and I LED THREE LIVES (1952), respectively.

BLACKLISTING was a common practice during the Red Scare, especially within the TELEVISION and FILM industries. RED CHANNELS: THE REPORT OF COMMUNIST INFLUENCE IN RADIO AND TELEVISION, a 1950 publication issued by the right-wing magazine COUNTERATTACK, served as the basis for much of the blacklisting. *Red Channels* listed 151 men and women who the editors claimed were linked with a variety of "Communist causes," either formerly or currently. Among the victims of blacklisting to write about their own experiences and the blacklist were Lillian Hellman, who confronted HUAC before taking the Fifth Amendment (SCOUNDREL TIME, 1976), and HOLLYWOOD TEN members Dalton TRUMBO ("Time of the Toad" a 1949 pamphlet), Lester COLE (*Hollywood Red*, 1981), Edward DMYTRYK (*It's a Hell of a Life But Not a Bad Living*, 1979) and Alvah BESSIE (*Inquisition in Eden*, 1965). Bessie also addressed his experiences in his autobiographical novel *The Un-Americans* (1957). HUAC interrogated *Commonweal* editor John Cogley because of his heavily documented and critical 1956 study of blacklisting and HUAC's role within it, *Report on Blacklisting*. Eric Bentley presents transcripts from the HUAC hearings and other related documents in THIRTY YEARS OF TREASON (1971) and includes portions of witnesses' testimony as the dialogue in his play about HUAC, ARE YOU NOW OR HAVE YOU EVER BEEN? (1972). Robert VAUGHN also studies the HUAC investigations in his doctoral study published in 1972 as the book *Only Victims*. In *Naming Names* (1980), Victor Navasky, later editor and now publisher of the *Nation,* studies the motivations of those who informed or refused to inform against their colleagues in the film industry. *Fear on Trial* (1964) describes the ordeal of John Henry Faulk, whose successful lawsuit ended the radio and television blacklists. On the other hand, William F. BUCKLEY Jr. defended both HUAC and Senator McCarthy.

FBI director J. Edgar Hoover outlined the practices and beliefs of domestic communists, as well as describing the threat they posed, in his best-selling book, MASTER OF DECEIT (1958). The work was used in high school courses on Americanism versus communism and was otherwise widely circulated. In 1950, the same year Hiss was convicted, the FBI cracked a spy ring that had passed secrets about the development of the atom bomb to the Soviet Union during World War II. The alleged ringleaders were Ethel and Julius Rosenberg, who denied their guilt and whose convictions remained controversial throughout the Cold War and beyond. Louis Nizer reviewed the evidence and concluded in *The Implosion Conspiracy* (1973) that the Rosenbergs were, indeed, guilty, despite claims to the contrary in Walter and Miriam Schneir's *Invitation to an Inquest* (1965). (Documents released in the 1990s from the former Soviet Union have

since led the Schneirs to conclude that Julius passed along some relatively unimportant information to the Soviets. In 1997 Alexander Feklisov, a former KGB official, claimed that Julius had passed on information, but nothing concerning the atomic bomb. He also maintained that Ethel had nothing to do with spying.) In WE ARE YOUR SONS (1975), Robert and Michael Meeropol, the Rosenbergs' sons, argue for their parents' innocence and describe their own personal ordeals growing up as children of convicted atomic spies. Their book received considerable criticism and was generally viewed as unconvincing.

The CIA is the U.S. agency responsible for international intelligence gathering and covert operations. Allen Dulles, who helped create the CIA and directed it under President Eisenhower, wrote *The Craft of Intelligence* (1963) and *Great True Spy Stories* (1968) to explain and justify his creation. Former CIA agent Philip Agee later wrote *Inside the Company: CIA Diary* (1975), a critical post-Watergate exposé of the agency's illegal activities that the government tried unsuccessfully to suppress.

The threat of nuclear war was a dominant fear throughout the Cold War. The only instances when nuclear weapons were actually deployed against human beings were the U.S. bombings of Hiroshima and Nagasaki at the end of World War II. Reports of those attacks and their consequences thus helped people imagine the effects of nuclear war. John Hersey's HIROSHIMA (1946) appeared about a year after the attack and included personal accounts by several survivors. Over 20 years later, Robert Jay Lifton presented the first study of the long-term psychological effects of the Hiroshima bombing in DEATH IN LIFE: SURVIVORS OF HIROSHIMA (1968). Lifton notes that the survivors, known as *hibakusha* (explosion-affected persons) among the Japanese, were treated as zombies or lepers in Japan, where they were frequently shunned for fear they might contaminate others. He found they were often denied employment because they tired easily and lacked motivation, and that they held themselves in low esteem and suffered from neuroses from which they had difficulty recovering.

The year 1958 saw the beginning of the second Berlin Crisis, which inaugurated an intense three-year period of the Cold War. Nuclear war among the superpowers suddenly appeared almost inevitable. That year, two leading scientists published popular books presenting opposite assessments of nuclear weaponry. Edward Teller's OUR NUCLEAR FUTURE (1958) described how atomic energy works, assessed the radioactive fallout from previous nuclear tests and insisted on the necessity of continued testing if the United States was to prevail in the Cold War. Teller was known as the "father of the hydrogen bomb," which seemed to give his opinions additional weight. He and his coauthor Albert Latter argued that the fallout from nuclear testing did not pose a serious threat to human life and favorably compared the risks to ordinary dangers in everyday life, such as the possibility of developing lung cancer from smoking. The book was widely praised for its clear description of how atomic energy works, but received mixed reviews for its political assessments. By contrast, in NO MORE WAR! (1958), Nobel Prize winner Linus Pauling called for international agreements to end nuclear testing and to reduce the possibilities of nuclear war. Pauling described the biological effects of radiation and other hazards of radioactive fallout, presenting another scientific perspective on the Cold War nuclear threat. Pauling also called for the establishment of a World Peace Research Organization to discover the recipe for peace, just as scientists found the recipe for penicillin. He too received mixed reviews.

Herman Kahn's ON THERMONUCLEAR WAR (1960) was the first academically informed book published for popular audiences that attempted to calculate the actual effects a nuclear war might create. Based on three lectures Kahn gave at Princeton University's Center for International Studies in March 1959, *On Thermonuclear War* employs statistics, mathematics and other scientific tools to conclude that with proper air and civil defense, the United States could survive nuclear war, even if 20 to 40 million Americans were to die and all major U.S. cities were destroyed. In this regard, Kahn repudiated the conventional wisdom that an all-out nuclear war would destroy not only the nation-state but also human civilization. He thus set the stage for later Cold War planners in the 1970s and 1980s, who rejected the strategy of Mutually Assured Destruction (MAD) in favor of attempting to win a nuclear war. In his day, Kahn was both praised and vilified for "thinking the unthinkable" in this book.

Jonathan Schell's THE FATE OF THE EARTH (1982) projected the impact on the environment of a nuclear war some 24 years later, when Cold War tensions were at their highest since the 1962 Cuban Missile Crisis. Schell analyzes the technical and strategic properties of nuclear weapons and speculates on several possible nuclear war scenarios. He then describes the consequences of a massive nuclear exchange, which, he maintains, would reduce the Earth to a wasteland and introduce a nuclear winter by creating massive clouds that would block out the sun. Schell also considers the philosophical consequences of a broad nuclear war and the fallacies inherent in the notion of a limited nuclear war. Schell concludes with a discussion of the strategies of deterrence and retaliation and a call for sharp reductions in strategic arms and a freeze on building new nuclear weapons. Also published in 1982, Robert Scheer's WITH ENOUGH SHOVELS documents how the Reagan administration was abandoning MAD in favor of preparing for winnable nuclear war, a policy that the administration claimed the Soviets had already adopted.

The Vietnam War attracted considerable commentary both during the fighting and after its conclusion. Even before the major U.S. military commitment in Southeast Asia, William LEDERER, who had earlier coauthored the novel THE UGLY AMERICAN (1958) with Eugene BURDICK, attacked U.S. policy, the State Department and the media in A NATION OF SHEEP (1961). Lederer concludes by offering suggestions on how to remedy U.S. foreign policy. In 1968, the year U.S. forces reached their highest level at some 540,000 troops, Lederer published a sequel entitled *Our Own Worst Enemy*. In 1971 Daniel Ellsberg published *The Pentagon Papers*, a collection of secret government papers from the Johnson administration documenting the decision-making process by which the war was escalated and revealing instances in which the government had lied to the public about its plans and actions in Vietnam. The Nixon administration, then in power, fought the publication of this work, but a Supreme Court decision permitted it. Subsequently, Ellsberg was placed on Nixon's "enemies list," and the burglary of his psychiatrist's office by White House "plumbers" trying to obtain information to discredit him became part of the Watergate scandal. (Carl Bernstein and Robert Woodward describe how they investigated the Watergate crimes in ALL THE PRESIDENT'S MEN [1974].)

David HALBERSTAM's THE BEST AND THE BRIGHTEST (1972) also appeared while the war was going on. It documents the history of the U.S. involvement in Vietnam and describes the people in the Kennedy and Johnson administrations responsible for formulating and implementing policy. The title is an indictment of the liberal tradition dating back to the 18th-century Enlightenment, which maintained that virtually any problem could be resolved by the appropriate application of knowledge, reason and scientific methodology. Halberstam goes to great lengths to show how Kennedy and Johnson indeed employed "the best and the brightest" men in America to formulate policy in Vietnam, men who came from the faculties of Harvard and other leading universities. However, these brilliant men's work was confused, misguided and ineffective. Moreover, Halberstam suggests, hubris and self-deception contributed to the failure of the Americans' efforts. Former defense secretary Robert McNamara, who figures prominently in the book, concurred with many of Halberstam's judgments in his 1995 assessment of the war, *In Retrospect: The Tragedy and Lessons of Vietnam*, in which he admits that the war was a mistake and that U.S. policies had been confused and improvised almost from the beginning.

During the war, NOVELIST James Jones visited Vietnam, meeting with soldiers and the U.S. military command. He published his impressions a year after the U.S. withdrawal in VIET JOURNAL (1974). Philip Caputo's *A Rumor of War* (1977) was one of the first autobiographical accounts by a war veteran. EVERYTHING WE HAD (1981) presents 33 oral histories by U.S. soldiers who fought in the war. Among those included are American women nurses, a group whose participation in the war had been largely overlooked until the 1980s. These women's experiences also appear in Lynda Van Devanter's *Home Before Morning* (1983), Myra MacPherson's *Long Time Passing: Vietnam and the Haunted Generation* (1984) and D'Ann Campbell's *Women at War with America: Private Lives in a Patriotic Era* (1984). Stanley Karnow's best-selling *Vietnam: A History* (1983) claims to be the first complete account of the war and was the basis of Richard Ellison's widely viewed Vietnam War television documentary VIETNAM: A TELEVISION HISTORY (1983). Neil Sheehan's A BRIGHT SHINING LIE (1988) presents the biography of Lt. Colonel John Paul Vann, an American officer who first went to Vietnam in 1962 as a military adviser to the South Vietnamese Army. Originally convinced of the appropriateness of the U.S. mission, Vann became increasingly disillusioned and began to speak out against the ineffective U.S. strategy and the brutality it entailed. Even though Vann resigned from the military in 1963 so he could speak out publicly against the way the war was fought, by 1971 he was, according to Sheehan, the most important American in South Vietnam after the ambassador and commanding general in Saigon, and his control as a civilian over U.S. military troops was unprecedented. Vann was killed in a helicopter crash shortly after turning back a major North Vietnamese offensive in 1972.

Other key Cold War nonfiction includes T. H. White's THUNDER OUT OF CHINA (1946), which criticizes U.S. support for the Chinese Nationalist leader Chiang Kai-Shek, whom White characterizes as corrupt, incompetent and venal. The best-selling book came under strong attack from the right-wing, pro-Chiang "China Lobby," and in 1953 McCarthy aides Roy Cohn and David Schine actually burned copies of this and other objectionable books they found in the Berlin office of the International Information Agency, prompting a denunciation of book burning from President Eisenhower. Frederick Wertham's SEDUCTION OF THE INNOCENT (1954) charged that comic books were corrupting American youth and undermining their values. Congressional hearings followed its publication, and ultimately a Comics Code certified the magazines' adherence to a standard of morality and decency. James MICHENER's BRIDGE AT ANDAU (1957) describes the failed 1956 Hungarian Revolution and its immediate aftermath, and his SIX DAYS IN HAVANA (1989) chronicles his visit to communist Cuba. Michener also wrote *Kent State: What Happened and Why* (1971), a highly acclaimed study of the 1970 incident in which the Ohio National Guard killed protesters and by-standers at a demonstration against the Vietnam War.

During the détente of the 1970s, when rumors suggested the United States and Cuba might reestablish relations, Howard Senzel published BASEBALL AND THE COLD WAR (1977), which chronicles the role baseball played in his life as he grew up in the 1950s and suggests that the resumption of diplomatic relations be initiated with the completion of the last baseball game between the Havana Sugar Kings and the minor-league Rochester Red Wings. The game had been suspended when a Red Wings player was shot in the head shortly after Castro came to power. Lawrence FERLINGHETTI's SEVEN DAYS IN NICARAGUA LIBRE (1984) describes the POET's week-long visit to Nicaragua in January 1984 at the invitation of the socialist Sandinista government. Ferlinghetti's apparent purpose in publishing his travelogue was to give Americans a view of the Sandinistas' alternative to the Reagan administration's depiction of them as oppressive and brutal. (See also NONFICTION WRITERS.)

nonfiction writers Though writers of NONFICTION abounded throughout the Cold War, those who made the greatest impact on the arts, letters and popular culture were primarily literary critics, philosophers and other literary writers. The Cold War had a strong impact on the U.S. left-wing intelligentsia. Though some, like Irving HOWE, remained committed to the basic tenets of socialism, World War II had disillusioned many others about the promise of enlightened progress. Lewis MUMFORD criticized the traditional liberal notion of progress both for its inability to effectively oppose fascism before World War II and for its postwar equation of progress with increased wealth and advanced technology. Though not opposed to science and technology per se, Mumford believed that these must be subordinated to human spiritual development. In *The Conduct of Life* (1951) and *In the Name of Sanity* (1954) Mumford criticized the development of the atomic bomb and argued

that the destruction of Hiroshima and America's Cold War use of methods employed by the Nazis meant that Hitler had actually "won" World War II. Mumford's earlier work, *Values for Survival* (1946), had insisted on the necessity of shaping technological development with moral wisdom based on the ethics of the great religions.

The disillusionment created by World War II led other liberals to create a NEW LIBERALISM that saw itself as pragmatically serving U.S. interests in the world as it was, rather than ideologically creating policies to improve the world. Among the founders of the new liberalism were Richard CHASE, Lionel TRILLING, Reinhold Niebuhr and Arthur Schlesinger Jr. They replaced the inherently optimistic assumptions of Progressivism, which held that enlightened social policies can create a better world, with a more pessimistic outlook that saw the id as dominating human behavior. Trilling thus wrote in *The Liberal Imagination*, "Some paradox of our natures leads us, when once we have made our fellow men the objects of our enlightened interest, to go on to make them the objects of our pity, then of our wisdom, ultimately of our coercion. It is to prevent this corruption . . . that we stand in need of the moral realism which is the product of the free play of the moral imagination." R. W. B. LEWIS challenged the pessimism of new liberalism in his 1955 collection *American Adam*, calling it "something which began as a valuable corrective to the claims of innocence in America [but] which has declined into a cult of original sin."

A more conservative critic, Edmund WILSON had become disenchanted with Marxism well before World War II though he had some use for Marxist-oriented literary criticism. Wilson's major work during the postwar era, *Patriotic Gore* (1962), is a study of the Civil War that attacks the American drive for power, centralized government and nationalistic aggression. Its view of human nature is extremely bleak, and it concludes that the American notions of order, national unity and justice are based on an underlying desire for power. Wilson's former wife, Mary MCCARTHY, was both a NOVELIST and writer of nonfiction. She too used fiction, literary criticism and philosophical essays to criticize the Soviet Union and the left. In 1959, the State Department sponsored her tour of Poland, Yugoslavia and Britain, in which she developed lectures on "The Fact in Fiction" and "Characters in Fiction." She later collected these essays in *On the Contrary* (1961). McCarthy twice visited Vietnam during the 1960s to gain a firsthand view of the war, which she actively opposed. The nonfiction works *Vietnam* (1967), *Hanoi* (1968), and *Medina* (1972) resulted from her experiences. She collected these in the single volume *The Seventeenth Degree* in 1974. McCarthy's observations on the Watergate scandal first appeared in the *London Observer* and were later collected in *The Mask of State: Watergate Portraits* (1974).

William LEDERER, David HALBERSTAM and Norman MAILER are other author/JOURNALISTS who opposed the war. Lederer, who coauthored the political novel THE UGLY AMERICAN in 1958, published A NATION OF SHEEP in 1961. That nonfiction book and its 1968 sequel, *Our Own Worst Enemy*, criticize U.S. policy in Southeast Asia. Halberstam's THE BEST AND THE BRIGHTEST (1972) traces the process by which the United

States became involved in Vietnam and provides biographical sketches of the men responsible for formulating policy. Mailer covered antiwar protest in *Armies of the Night* (1968) and *Miami and the Siege of Chicago* (1968).

Best-selling novelist James MICHENER also wrote several important pieces of nonfiction about the Cold War, including THE BRIDGE AT ANDAU (1957), about the 1956 Hungarian Revolution and its aftermath; *Kent State: What Happened and Why* (1971), a highly acclaimed study of the 1970 incident in which the National Guard killed protesters and bystanders at a demonstration against the Vietnam War; and SIX DAYS IN HAVANA (1989), about his visit to communist Cuba.

A member of the Communist Party until 1956, best-selling novelist Howard FAST wrote several nonfiction works that reflected his changing political beliefs, notably *Tito and His People* (1948), about the communist leader of Yugoslavia; *Peekskill, USA* (1951), about his role in resisting anti-communist rioters and police during Paul ROBESON's 1949 concert in Peekskill, New York; and *The Passion of Sacco and Vanzetti* (1953) about the falsely accused anarchist leaders. *The Naked God* (1957) describes his decision to leave the party. Fast also published his autobiography in 1990, *Being Red*. Nonfiction about the Communist Party was also produced by Herbert PHILBRICK, an FBI informer and infiltrator of the American Communist Party. Philbrick wrote of his experiences in I LED THREE LIVES (1952), which later became a popular TELEVISION SPY SHOW.

William LAURENCE was the only journalist permitted to cover the entire atomic bomb project. Among his books are *Dawn Over Zero* (1946) and *Hell Bomb* (1951), about the atomic and hydrogen bombs, respectively.

A number of EXILED WRITERS (from the United States) also wrote nonfiction related to the Cold War. Margaret RANDALL went into exile from the United States to Mexico, where she coedited *El Corno Emplumado* (The Plumed Horn), a bilingual literary journal that was influential both in Latin America and the United States. In 1967 and 1968 Randall traveled to Cuba to attend cultural congresses there; subsequently, her devotion to social causes intensified. In 1979, she moved to Nicaragua to write about women who helped the Sandinistas overthrow the Somoza dictatorship. Her volume, *Sandino's Daughters: Testimonies of Nicaraguan Women in Struggle* (1981), documents the role of women in the Nicaraguan revolution. She also published several other books of writings by and about Cuban and Latin American women. Black power leader Eldridge CLEAVER wrote *Soul on Ice* in 1968, a call for liberating black Americans by overthrowing the social, military and economic institutions of the government. In response to the persecution of his Black Panther Party and to divisions among the Black Muslims, he adopted a Marxist position, which appears in his *Post Prison Writings and Speeches* (1969). To escape arrest for parole violations, he went into exile first in Cuba and then in Algeria. However, after visiting North Vietnam, North Korea and the People's Republic of China, he became disillusioned by communism and settled in France before returning to the United States, where he published an account of his conversion to a more Christian perspective, *Soul on Fire* (1978).

Nonfiction writers who went into exile in the United States to escape either communism or fascism and subsequently published in America include Tamas ACZEL, Sergei DOVLATOV, Kyung Jae KIM, Herbert MARCUSE, Mark POPOVSKY, Armando VALLADARES, Aleksandr WAT and Igor YEFIMOV. (See also EXILED WRITERS [to the United States].)

Norris, Chuck   A FILM ACTOR. In addition to starring in a number of karate and martial arts films, Norris appeared in several patriotic, anti-communist films during the Carter and Reagan years. *Missing in Action* (Parts 1–3, 1984, 1985, 1988; Part III is also entitled *Braddock*) and *Good Guys Wear Black* (1979) deal with U.S. prisoners-of-war (POWs) in postwar Vietnam. In INVASION U.S.A. (1985), Norris saves the United States from an invasion of Soviet-backed terrorists. In *The Delta Force* (Parts 1 and 2, 1986, 1990), he fights more contemporary foes of Western civilization—international terrorists and drug barons. (See also VIETNAM WAR FILMS.)

North by Northwest   A 1959 SPY FILM starring Cary Grant, Eva Marie Saint, James Mason, Martin Landau and Leo G. Carroll and directed by Alfred HITCHCOCK. The story centers on George Kaplan (Grant), an American advertising executive whom Soviet spies (Mason and Landau) mistake for a nonexistent espionage agent invented by members of a secret U.S. government agency. Framed for an assassination he did not commit, Kaplan flees and is assisted by Eve Kendall (Saint), a beautiful double agent who pretends to be in the service of the communists but who actually works for the United States. The professor (Carroll) who heads the U.S. agency takes advantage of the communists' confusion and is coldly willing to sacrifice Kaplan's life to foil their assault on national security. Left to his own devices, Kaplan eventually outwits his pursuers, helps break up the communist spy ring, and wins the love of the worldly and seductive Eve. The film contains several memorable scenes, including one of a crop-dusting airplane trying to kill Kaplan in the cornfields outside Chicago and another of enemy agents chasing Kaplan and Eve across the faces of the U.S. presidents on Mt. Rushmore. The title comes from *Hamlet,* whose protagonist cautions that he is "but mad north-northwest; when the wind is southerly I know a hawk from a handsaw."

North by Northwest also embodies MOMISM, a belief popularized by Philip Wylie in his 1942 best-seller, *A Generation of Vipers*. Momism depicted the middle-class American mother as self-righteous, self-absorbed, hypocritical and sexually repressed, a member of "a matriarchy in fact if not in declaration" in which "the women of America raped the men." According to Wylie, American middle-class mothers dominated their sons and husbands. As Michael Rogin observes in *Ronald Reagan, the Movie,* for Wylie a typical, overbearing mother "elicited [her son's] adulation to repress his sex and transferred the desire that ought to go to another woman into sentimentality for herself." As a result, the sons of these mothers typically grew into weak men lacking the requisite character, self-knowledge and mental toughness to resolutely confront a dangerous enemy. At the outset of *North by Northwest*, George Kaplan is such a son. However, the need to clear his name, fight for his survival and combat the communists produces a change in his character that enables him to assert his independence from his mother and emerge as a worthy mate for the beautiful woman whose life he saves. Thus Kaplan's accidental and unwilling immersion into the seamy underside of Cold War politics actually builds character while bolstering national security.

novelists Among the major "serious" writers who address the Cold War in their fiction, John BARTH is the only one to take up the Cold War itself as the only subject of a novel. His 1966 allegorical comedy, GILES GOAT-BOY, tells the story of a modern mythic hero, a new messiah in a universe represented by a university. The new messiah, a Grand Tutor, appears at the height of Cold War tensions to save the Campus, which is under the threat of imminent annihilation from the great computer that controls the entire University. Drawing on Jungian archetypes, existentialism, BLACK HUMOR and an Eastern world-view that sees life in terms of paradox, Barth depicts the key Cold War anxieties of the early 1960s: a world on the brink of self-destruction, technology gone dangerously out of control, flawed leaders motivated by a variety of personal and political interests, and a citizenry desperately seeking salvation or simply escape.

Kurt VONNEGUT Jr. is another author who addresses Cold War fears of apocalypse in comic, exuberant fiction. Vonnegut has written several APOCALYPTIC NOVELS about technology gone amok including CAT'S CRADLE (1963), *Player Piano* (1953), *Dead-eye Dick* (1982) and *Galapagos* (1986). He collected several of his early short stories from the 1950s and early 1960s in *Welcome to the Monkey House* (1968), which includes ALL THE KING'S HORSES, a 1953 story dealing with a renegade communist warlord in Asia; "Manned Missiles," which features the correspondence between the fathers of a U.S. astronaut and a Soviet cosmonaut who were killed in an accident in outer space; and "Harrison Bergeron," which attacks government attempts to create literal equality by handicapping anyone with exceptional talent. *Slaughterhouse Five* (1969) is an antiwar book that was extremely popular during the Vietnam War. It moves back and forth between an alien society in another galaxy and the firebombing of Dresden during World War II, an event at which Vonnegut himself was present as a prisoner of war. Though Joseph Heller published CATCH-22 in 1961, four years before the United States sent combat troops into Vietnam, he too later gained considerable popularity among the antiwar movement for his criticisms of the military and bureaucracy in that novel.

Like Vonnegut, Ursula LE GUIN uses science fiction to explore Cold War themes and other contemporary social and political issues. (See also SCIENCE FICTION NOVELS AND STORIES.) *The Dispossessed* (1974), for instance, presents two civilizations that correspond to Cold War–era capitalist and communist societies, as well as an anarchist utopia. The book considers the virtues and limitations of each. Robert COOVER, another exuberant writer of nonrealistic fiction, presents a surreal account of the execution of Julius and Ethel Rosenberg in THE PUBLIC BURNING (1976) and satirizes American politics in THE CAT IN THE HAT FOR PRESIDENT (1968).

Though Thomas PYNCHON rarely addresses the Cold War directly, his fiction treats the social, emotional and psychological climate spawned by Cold War technology and politics. His most important work, *Gravity's Rainbow* (1973), suggests that the Cold War human condition celebrates death. Part of the plot centers on efforts to track the relationship between WWII's German V-2 rocket and the sexual exploits of a main character, Tyron Slothrop. Toward the end of the book someone charges that Slothrop "might be in love, in sexual love, with his, and the race's death." In this respect *Gravity's Rainbow* shares the basic premise of Stanley KUBRICK's film satire, DR. STRANGELOVE: OR HOW I LEARNED TO STOP WORRYING AND LOVE THE BOMB (1964). Pynchon's frenetic and somewhat surreal story reveals the growing divisions between the Soviets and Western democracies that eventually became the Cold War. Its thematic concerns address such Cold War issues as the role of multinational corporations, the constant possibility of a sudden apocalypse against which no defense exists ("the rocket can penetrate, from the sky, at any given point"), and the untrustworthiness of governments that are obsessed by technology, secrecy and death.

William FAULKNER, a Nobel Prize winner, was also concerned with the danger to the human spirit posed by nuclear weapons, of which he warned in his 1950 Nobel acceptance speech:

> Our tragedy today is a general and universal fear so long sustained by now that we can even bear it. There are no longer problems of the spirit. There is only the question: When will I be blown up? Because of this, the young man or woman writing today has forgotten the problems of the human heart in conflict with itself which alone can make good writing because only that is worth writing about, worth the agony and the sweat.

The atomic bomb also plays a significant role in Chaim Potok's THE BOOK OF LIGHTS (1981), partly set in Korea shortly after the Korean War. Potok's *My Name Is Asher Lev* (1972) deals indirectly with another Cold War issue: the problems of reestablishing Jewish communities in communist Eastern Europe after World War II.

Nobel Prize winner Saul Bellow writes of Cold War–related social and political anarchy in the United States during the 1960s in *Mr. Sammler's Planet* (1970) and again in THE DEAN'S DECEMBER (1982), where he contrasts American "disorganization" to the political repression "behind the Iron Curtain." Another realist, Norman MAILER, likewise deals with the failure of both communist and capitalist ideologies in his early fiction. Later, Mailer describes in almost journalistic fashion the U.S. space program and protests of the Vietnam War.

Eugene BURDICK and William LEDERER were early critics of U.S. diplomatic behavior in Southeast Asia in their bestselling novel THE UGLY AMERICAN (1958). Burdick also coauthored FAIL-SAFE (1962), about an accidental U.S. nuclear attack against the Soviet Union that results from a failure in technology. Novelist Mary MCCARTHY also writes about the Vietnam War, which she actively opposed, in her nonfiction trilogy *The Seventeenth Degree* (1974), based on her travels to North and South Vietnam. Her novels from the late 1940s and early 1950s deal with the Cold War by satirizing liberal intellectuals and leftist academics. (See also SATIRE.)

Lionel TRILLING, though best known as a NONFICTION WRITER, also authored THE MIDDLE OF THE JOURNEY (1947), an early Cold War novel about an intellectual's disaffection with communism. One of the central characters is based on Whittaker Chambers, the accuser of Alger Hiss. On the other hand, the 1949 NONFICTION book, THE GOD THAT FAILED, contains personal accounts by three prominent ex-communist novelists (Arthur KOESTLER, Richard WRIGHT and Louis Fischer) and three "fellow-traveling" novelists (Ignazio Silone, Andre Gide and Stephen Spender).

Ayn RAND, author of the best-selling novels THE FOUNTAINHEAD (1943) and *Atlas Shrugged* (1957), was an ardent supporter of capitalism who glorified individual initiative and enlightened self-interest and denounced anything hinting of socialism. Howard FAST, on the other hand, was a member of the Communist Party until 1956, and his fiction from the early Cold War reflects those values. He wrote the best-selling SPARTACUS (1951)—about a slave revolt against the Roman Empire—while in jail for refusing to testify before the HOUSE COMMITTEE ON UN-AMERICAN ACTIVITIES (HUAC) during the RED SCARE.

Other best-selling novelists who wrote about Cold War events and issues include Leon URIS, James MICHENER, Fletcher KNEBEL and Allen DRURY. Uris's ARMAGEDDON (1964) takes place during the Berlin Airlift of the late 1940s and deals with U.S. and Soviet relations with German citizens in Occupied Germany as the Cold War was just beginning. His TOPAZ (1967) merges a fictional account of the real-life Soviet infiltration of the French intelligence agency with the unfolding of the 1962 Cuban Missile Crisis, highlighting the problems of U.S.–French relations during the early 1960s.

Michener's Korean War novels, THE BRIDGES AT TOKO-RI (1953) and SAYONARA (1954), were both made into KOREAN WAR FILMS. His THE BRIDGE AT ANDAU (1957) is a nonfiction account of the 1956 Hungarian Revolution and its immediate aftermath. His *Kent State: What Happened and Why* (1971) presents a nonfiction account of the National Guard's killing of Ohio students protesting the Vietnam War. His SIX DAYS IN HAVANA (1989) describes a visit he and photographer John Kings made to Cuba in 1988. *Space* (1982) offers a fictional account of the U.S. space program.

Knebel is best known for SEVEN DAYS IN MAY, a 1962 novel coauthored with Charles W. Bailey II. It portrays an attempted coup by the U.S. military in response to a president's decision to sign a treaty with the Soviets banning nuclear weapons. Knebel also wrote NIGHT OF CAMP DAVID (1965), about a power-crazed, deranged U.S. president, and CROSSING IN BERLIN (1981), about East German attempts to suppress crucial research on global warming.

Drury's 1959 ADVISE AND CONSENT inaugurated a six-part series of novels dealing with the struggle between liberals and conservatives over whose ideology should guide the nation through the Cold War. Every book in the series appeared on the *New York Times* best-seller list for at least 19 weeks. Drury's fiction promotes conservative political values and attacks the liberal press. He maintains that one of his enduring themes was "the continuing argument between those who use responsible firmness to maintain orderly social progress and oppose Communist imperialism in its drive for world domination; and those who believe [that] in a reluctance to be firm, in permissiveness and in the erosion of the law lie the surest path to world peace and a stable society." The other five books in the series, following American politics through the mid-1970s, are A SHADE OF A DIFFERENCE (1962), CAPABLE OF HONOR (1967), PRESERVE AND PROTECT (1968), COME NINEVEH, COME TYRE (1973) and THE PROMISE OF JOY (1975). Drury also wrote *That Summer* (1966), *Throne of Saturn: A Novel of Space and Politics* (1971), *Anna Hastings, The Story of a Washington Newsperson!* (1977), *Mark Coffin, U.S.S: A Novel of Capitol Hill* (1979), *The Hill of Summer* (1981), *Decision* (1983), *Pentagon* (1986) and *Toward What Bright Glory* (1990).

American authors of SPY NOVELS include Mickey SPILLANE, William F. BUCKLEY Jr., Robert Ludlam and Watergate conspirators E. Howard Hunt, G. Gordon Liddy and John Ehrlichman. Spillane's protagonist, private detective Mike Hammer, fights domestic communists in *One Lonely Night* (1951). The novels of the others deal with international spying. Buckley's spy fiction, centering on his superhero Blackford Oakes, invokes the politics behind such Cold War events as the post-Stalin power struggle in the Kremlin (*High Jinx*, 1986); the Hungarian Revolution and the beginnings of the space race (*Who's on First*, 1980); the second Berlin Crisis (*The Story of Henri Tod*, 1984); and the 1960 U-2 incident (*Marco Polo If You Can*, 1982). Hunt's 1973 *The Berlin Ending* depicts Willy Brandt and other advocates of détente as Soviet agents. His 1985 novel, *The Kremlin Conspiracy,* derides the politics of European "peaceniks," who pressure the Nobel Prize committee to give the peace prize to a man who is secretly a Soviet agent. The prizewinner then uses his influence to force NATO to withdraw its missiles from Europe. Ehrlichman's *The Company* (1976) centers on rivalries among the CIA, FBI and other intelligence agencies. The unflattering portrayal of the president is apparently based on Richard Nixon, whom Ehrlichman served as a top domestic adviser until Nixon fired him during the Watergate scandal. Ehrlichman also wrote *The China Card* (1986), which suggests that Nixon's historic trip to China actually resulted from the activities of a spy working on behalf of Zhou Enlai, the Chinese premier.

Much of the best and most popular Cold War spy fiction came from Great Britain. Ian Fleming's James BOND novels were extremely popular in their own right as well as inspiring at least 15 SPY FILMS. Bond became the prototype for the Cold War superspy—smart, strong, virile, technologically adept and extremely sexy. By contrast, John LE CARRÉ, Graham GREENE and Len DEIGHTON wrote of spies who were anti-heroes, ordinary people in unusual circumstances. Le Carré and Greene depict spying and the Cold War itself as morally ambiguous, and their characters are often challenged to determine the proper action in situations where they have either limited or distorted knowledge.

South Korean emigré writer Richard KIM wrote about the Korean War in THE MARTYRED (1964). Among the many novelists who wrote VIETNAM WAR LITERATURE from the soldiers' perspective are David HALBERSTAM, Irwin BLACKER, Robert Stone, Bruce McAllister, Tim O'Brien, Robin Moore (author of THE GREEN BERETS, 1965) and James Webb (author of the 1978 FIELDS OF FIRE), a highly decorated officer who later became secretary of the navy. Bobbie Ann Mason deals with veterans' and civilians' difficulties after Vietnam in her

1985 novel, IN COUNTRY, and in her short stories, notably the Big Bertha stories. Tom CLANCY became a best-selling writer of MILITARY NOVELS in the 1980s. His fiction centers on the renewed possibilities of U.S.-Soviet warfare that became a genuine fear after the collapse of détente in the 1970s.

Novelists who were investigated and/or prosecuted for their political beliefs during the Cold War include Richard Wright and James BALDWIN, black Americans who went into exile from the United States, and Stefan HEYM, a German who came to the United States during World War II and served with the U.S. military in that war. In response to accusations by Senator Joseph McCarthy, Heym renounced his U.S. citizenship and moved to East Germany, where his socialist literature was warmly received. There, he wrote editorials, reports and articles praising East Germany and its relationship to the U.S.S.R. However, in 1965 Heym fell into disfavor with the East German government after publishing an article describing the decline of Stalin's importance and its impact on communism. Subsequently, most of his writing became illegal in East Germany until 1989, though he was published in West Germany, England and the United States. His English-language best-selling novels include *The King David Report* (1972); *Uncertain Friend* (1969), which addresses the conflict between intellectual integrity and the power of a personality cult; and *Five Days in June* (1977), which describes the 1953 popular uprising against the East German regime. Like Heym, Thomas MANN came to the United States to escape the Nazis but left in response to the Red Scare. After the poor U.S. reception of his novel *Dr. Faustus* (1947), he went into exile in Switzerland, where he expressed his disenchantment with America by writing *The Black Swan* (1953). In that novel, the United States appears as an outwardly appealing source of rejuvenation but actually proves to be corrupt and corrupting. Dalton TRUMBO and Alvah BESSIE were novelist/SCREENWRITERS who, as members of the HOLLYWOOD TEN, were blacklisted from the Hollywood film industry and served prison terms for refusing to testify before HUAC in 1947. Bessie wrote about his experiences in his semi-autobiographical novel *The Un-Americans* (1957). Other novelist/screenwriters who dealt with aspects of the Cold War include Budd SCHULBERG and Terry SOUTHERN.

EXILED WRITERS who came to the United States as a result of communist persecution during the Cold War include novelists Jerzy KOSINSKI and Czeslaw MILOSZ. Vladimir NABOKOV and Isaac Bashevis SINGER had gone into exile to the United States before the Cold War, but deal slightly with Cold War issues in their work. Nobel Prize winners Aleksandr SOLZHENITSYN and Boris PASTERNAK suffered internal exile in the Soviet Union, though their work was widely read in the United States. Solzhenitsyn eventually immigrated to the United States, though he returned to Russia after the disintegration of the Soviet Union. Other novelists who went into exile in the United States from communist countries include Tamas ACZEL, Vassily AKSYONOV, Yuz ALESHKOVSKY, Guillermo CABRERA INFANTE, Andrei CODRESCU, Juri DRUZHNIKOV, Janusz GLOWACKI, Kyung Jae KIM, Arkady LVOV, Hsin-yung PAI and Sacha SOKOLOV.

Prominent foreign writers who addressed Cold War issues and were widely read in the United States include British writer George ORWELL, whose NINETEEN EIGHTY-FOUR (1949) indicts what he saw as Stalinist-communist mind control. Other foreign writers about the Cold War include the Mexican Carlos FUENTES, Columbian Nobel Prize winner Gabriel GARCIA MARQUEZ, the Czech Milan KUNDERA, the Peruvian Mario VARGAS LLOSA—a prominent critic of the Castro regime—and Isabel ALLENDE, the niece of the Marxist Chilean president whom the Nixon administration helped depose. (See also POETS; LITERATURE; LITERATURE ABOUT COLD WAR EVENTS; BLACKLISTING.)

Nuclear Age, The A 1985 APOCALYPTIC NOVEL by Tim O'Brien. Published just after the most intense period of the final part of the Cold War, the novel centers on William, who grew up in the 1950s, opposed the Vietnam War and joined the COUNTERCULTURE in the 1960s, and now in the 1980s cannot shake his awareness that "THE BOMBS ARE REAL," that they are more than the evocative words used to describe the nuclear process: "uranium is not a figure of speech." ("Fission," "Fusion" and "Critical Mass" are the titles of the book's sections, and the chapters have such titles as "Quantum Jumps.") Continually aware of the ever-present nuclear threat, William is unable to commit to a creative, life-affirming existence. Instead he retrenches by giving up political activism, breaking off with his enthusiastic, activist girlfriend, becoming more introverted, and eventually marrying a flight attendant named Bobbi. One of the book's main concerns is the psychological impact of living in the nuclear age. The fear induced by the nuclear threat, even if not consciously acknowledged, causes people to direct their energies inwardly toward survival instead of outwardly toward improving the world. William applies his energy to digging a fallout shelter, which, as Lee Schweninger points out in *The Nightmare Considered*, becomes associated with his subconscious and gradually assumes control over him. The hole declares, "I am all there is . . . I am what happened to the dinosaurs. I am the ovens at Auschwitz, the Bermuda Triangle, the Lost Tribes . . . I am the uncaused cause, the unnamed source . . . I am you, of course. I am your inside-out."

Eventually William's obsession with survival alienates and nearly destroys the wife and child he is intent on protecting. And as he digs, he begins to question his own sanity, which he is indeed losing. But he maintains that his behavior is not crazy: "If you're sane, you're scared; if you're scared, you dig; if you dig, you deviate." To ensure his wife and daughter's safety, he drugs them and places them sleeping inside the hole that he has wired with dynamite. He then sits up all night with his hand on the plunger as apocalyptic visions from the *Book of Revelations* go through his head. Finally, however, his daughter awakens and convinces him of the importance of finding another way to deal with the nuclear threat. David Dowling concludes in *Fictions of Nuclear Disaster*:

William's extreme experiment, like our experience of reading the book, is cathartic. Having visited the nuclear age in word and deed, we must knowingly retreat to the fiction of a happy ending. Imagined disasters keep us sane, and there is a sense of communal confession and affirmation as we join with William in acknowledging that even when it happens we "will hold to a steady orthodoxy, confident to the end that E will somehow not quite equal $mc,^2$ that it's a cunning metaphor, that the terminal equation will somehow not quite balance."

For additional reading, see Dowling's *Fictions of Nuclear Disaster;* Anisfield's *The Nightmare Considered.*

nuclear apocalypse the threat of a nuclear war that would kill all or most of human and animal life on Earth was a dominant and unique aspect of the Cold War. The cultural responses to this threat appear in several mass-market media, notably APOCALYPTIC NOVELS and APOCALYPTIC FILMS. A sampling of apocalyptic novels includes ALAS, BABYLON (1959), TOMORROW! (1954), SHADOW ON THE HEARTH (1959) LEVEL 7 (1959) and THE THIRD WORLD WAR (1978), in addition to a vast number of novels about survival in a postnuclear world. Written during the second Berlin Crisis, German author Hans Hellmut Kirst's SCIENCE FICTION NOVEL *The Seventh Day* (1959) castigates both the United States and the U.S.S.R. as it chronicles six days of failed diplomatic negotiations that culminate in a massive nuclear war. Tim O'Brien's novel THE NUCLEAR AGE (1985) explores the impact on the Baby Boom generation of living continuously under the threat of nuclear annihilation: "If you're sane, you're scared; if you're scared, you dig [a bomb shelter]; if you dig, you deviate." Among the most notable apocalyptic films are ON THE BEACH (1959) and FAIL-SAFE (1964) (which were originally best-selling novels in 1957 and 1962 respectively), and the made-for-television movie THE DAY AFTER (1983). Several FILM DOCUMENTARIES also deal with nuclear apocalypse, notably THE ATOMIC CAFE (1982) and made-for television documentaries dealing with the Hiroshima bomb and the nuclear arms race.

Science fiction literature and SCIENCE FICTION FILMS also imagine nuclear apocalypse, as do such works of literary NONFICTION as John Hersey's HIROSHIMA (1946) Edward Teller's OUR NUCLEAR FUTURE (1958) Linus Pauling's NO MORE WAR! (1958), Herman Kahn's ON THERMONUCLEAR WAR (1960), Nigel Calder's *Nuclear Nightmares* (1979), Robert Scheer's WITH ENOUGH SHOVELS (1982) and Jonathan Schell's THE FATE OF THE EARTH (1982). POETS Robert Lowell, Adrienne Rich and Charles Gullans wrote about the 1962 Cuban Missile Crisis, when the United States and U.S.S.R. came closest to waging nuclear war. Others, such as Beat poets Allen GINSBERG, Lawrence FERLINGHETTI and Gregory CORSO, wrote more generally about the nuclear threat. (See the BEAT MOVEMENT.) Other poetry about nuclear war (discussed in Anisfield's *The Nightmare Considered,* 1991) includes the anthologies *Meltdown: Poems From the Core* (1980), *Peace Is Our Profession: Poems and Passages of War Protest* (1981) and *Nuke-Rebuke* (1983). Merritt Clifton's prose journal *Samisdat* (1973–89) also deals with war and peace.

Plays such as Arthur Kopit's END OF THE WORLD (1984); MUSIC, especially ROCK AND ROLL; CARTOONS, including WHEN THE WIND BLOWS (1982); and ART also took up the problem of nuclear war. For instance, in the late 1950s and 1960s, the March Gallery Group, also known as the Doom artists, presented exhibits in New York on the theme of nuclear destruction. Henry Moore's bronze sculpture *Nuclear Energy* (1965) commemorates the first sustained atomic chain reaction at the University of Chicago's Stagg Field, now the site of the Regenstein Library. The piece evokes the characteristic image of the atomic bomb's mushroom cloud while also referring to a human skull.

Songs about nuclear war include OLD MAN ATOM, "Eve of Destruction," WE WILL ALL GO TOGETHER WHEN WE GO, "Atom Bomb Baby," "The Hydrogen Bomb," Bill Haley's "Thirteen Women" and "99 Red Balloons" by Nena, a West German singer. "Old Man Atom," a 1950 "talking blues number" by Los Angeles journalist Vern Partlow, warns: "Here's my thesis; Peace in the world, or the world in pieces." Though the song was initially popular, it was driven from radio by Rabbi Benjamin Schultz and his Joint Committee Against Communism. They maintained that the message was subversive and echoed the sentiments expressed in the Stockholm peace petition, which the communists were then circulating. Partlow stated, "I thought that [the song's message was] the policy of the United Nations and of our government." Such FOLK SINGERS as Phil OCHS, Bob DYLAN and Tom Paxton also wrote about the Cuban Missile Crisis and the threat of nuclear destruction.

In addition to works that address the nuclear threat directly or contemplate life in a postapocalyptic society, practitioners of BLACK HUMOR in a variety of media found ways to laugh at the nuclear threat while simultaneously pointing out its horror. The 1964 film satire DR. STRANGELOVE represents the epitome of Cold War black humor: An insane U.S. Air Force general orders a nuclear strike against the Soviet Union, while bumbling, sex-crazed, high-ranking officials are unable to prevent a Soviet Doomsday machine from going off in retaliation and destroying the entire world. The treatment of nuclear war as a bad LSD trip in Brian Aldiss's novel, BAREFOOT IN THE HEAD (1969), also provides elements of black humor, as do Kopit's play *End of the World* and Tom LEHRER's 1959 song, "We Will All Go Together When We Go." Black humor also appeared in Cold War fashions during the 1970s and 1980s in the form of T-shirts with Pop art drawings. One shows a woman sobbing, saying, "Nuclear War?! There Goes My Career!" Other black-humor T-shirts displayed such slogans as "One Nuclear Bomb Ruins Your Whole Day," "Cobaltone . . . For the Tan of Your Life," and the exit line from the Looney Tunes cartoons, "That's All, Folks!"

For additional reading, see Anisfield's *The Nightmare Considered.*

Nureyev, Rudolf A DANCE performer and Soviet defector. Born in 1938 on a train en route to Vladivostok, where his soldier father was stationed, Nureyev was descended from Tatars, an ethnic group he characterized as volatile, passionate and sensuous with "a curious mixture of tenderness and brutality." He began studying ballet at age 11 and in 1955 was accepted into the Leningrad Ballet School, which trained dancers for the Kirov Ballet. At the end of his third year, he won a national contest in classical ballet, and upon his graduation he was offered the rank of soloist in both the Kirov and Bolshoi ballets. He chose the Kirov because he believed the Bolshoi lacked passion and because its policies were too conservative. In June 1960 he performed before Soviet premier Nikita Khrushchev. In 1961, he toured England, where he was a great success. However, he fell into trouble with the authorities at the Kirov because he was an apolitical loner. He refused to join the Communist Youth League, associated with visiting foreign artists, and criticized the company's artistic choices as too old-fashioned.

While preparing to return home after performing in Paris in June 1961, Nureyev learned that he was to be sent to Moscow to be disciplined for insubordination, "non-assimilation" and dangerous individualism. On the spur of the moment he decided to defect and jumped over an airport railing to escape the Soviet security agents. The French police then protected him. Subsequently, Nureyev joined the International Ballet of the Marquis de Cuevas and gave his first post-defection performance in Paris on June 23, when he danced Florimund in *The Sleeping Beauty*. He toured Israel and Italy with the company but did not renew his contract because of artistic differences. On November 2, 1961, Nureyev made his London debut at a gala benefit for the Royal Academy of Dancing. He came at the invitation of Margot Fonteyn, who became his dancing partner at the Royal Ballet from 1962 to 1979. He made his North American debut in the spring of 1963 and received an enthusiastic welcome for both his immense talent and his politically popular defection from the Soviet Union. Nureyev directed the Paris Opera Ballet from 1983 to 1989. He died in Paris in 1993.

For additional reading, see his autobiography, *Nureyev* (1963); Watson's *Nureyev: A Biography.*

Ochs, Phil A FOLK SINGER. Ochs became nationally known in the 1960s for his songs that supported such COUNTERCULTURE issues as ending government censorship, legalizing marijuana, curbing U.S. imperialism and protesting the Vietnam War. The son of a Jewish army physician, Ochs won his first guitar while a student at Ohio State University when he bet on John Kennedy to win the 1960 presidential election. His first song was "The Ballad of the Cuban Invasion" about Kennedy's failed Bay of Pigs invasion. Ochs subsequently joined a radical singing group known sometimes as the Sundowners and sometimes as the Singing Socialists. He dropped out of Ohio State in 1962 over a dispute about freedom of the press for the school paper and moved to New York to begin his career as a folk singer. Ochs's first breakthrough came at the Newport Folk Festival in 1963, when he performed with Bob DYLAN, Joan BAEZ and the Freedom Singers. In 1964 he released his first album, *All the News That's Fit to Sing*—a reference to the motto of the *New York Times*, "All the news that's fit to print." The album contains such Cold War-related pieces as "Talking Cuban Crisis"; "The Ballad of William Worthy," about a black JOURNALIST who ran afoul of the State Department when he traveled to Cuba without a passport; "Thresher," about a nuclear submarine that was lost at sea; and "Talking Vietnam."

Later songs include "Love Me, I'm a Liberal," which attacks the hypocrisy of liberals who champion the Bill of Rights but cheer when "the Commies were thrown out from the AFL-CIO"; who send money but will not participate in the great causes of their time; and who lose their concern for human rights and civil liberties "when it comes to Asian guerrillas." "Cops of the World" attacks U.S. imperialism:

> We've got to protect all our citizens fair/ So we'll send a battalion for everyone there/ . . . And dump the Reds in a pile, boys, dump the Reds in a pile./ . . . We'll smash down your doors; we don't bother to knock./ We've done it before so why all the shock,/ . . . We own half the world, oh say can you see. And the name for our profits is democracy. So like it or not you will have to be free/ 'Cause we're the cops of the world, boys, we're the cops of the world.

"Santo Domingo" protests the 1965 invasion of the Dominican Republic by U.S. Marines.

However, Ochs is best known for his Vietnam War protest songs that ridiculed the American war effort. Ochs pointed out, "I was writing about Vietnam in 1962, way before the first antiwar marches. I was writing about it at a point where the media were really full of shit, where they were just turning the other way as Vietnam was being built." Among his antiwar songs are "Is There Anybody Here?" "White Boots Marchin' in a Yellow Land," "Draft Dodger Rag" and "The War Is Over."

After the U.S. withdrawal from Vietnam in 1973, Ochs remained politically active. In 1974 he helped organize a concert in tribute to Salvador Allende, the president of Chile who was toppled in a U.S.-assisted coup. In 1975 he performed at a rally in Central Park to celebrate the final

Phil Ochs. Courtesy AP/Wide World.

conclusion of the Vietnam War on May 11. According to Ochs, "It's a paradox inside my head to laugh at something and at the same time take it seriously and deal with it . . . it's not enough to know the world is absurd and restrict yourself merely to pointing out that fact. To me this was the essential flaw of the fifties, great perception leading to inaction. If there is to be any hope for the world this perception must lead to action." Apparently Ochs eventually lost all hope, because he hanged himself in April 1976.

A month after his death, the FBI, which had been monitoring him since 1963, still considered Ochs potentially dangerous. In May 1976, FBI director Clarence Kelley forwarded Ochs's name to the Secret Service as a potential threat to the president's safety. The FBI's treatment of Ochs as a presidential security risk dated back to a 1969 complaint by a woman in Little Rock, Arkansas, who maintained the song "Pretty Smart on My Part" included lyrics threatening the president's life. As early as 1968, the FBI had erroneously begun to describe Ochs as a communist on the basis of testimony from a single informer; however, in 1971 FBI director J. Edgar Hoover corrected the mistake in Ochs's file.

For additional reading, see Ochs's book, *The War Is Over*; as well as Orman's *The Politics of Rock Music* and Szatmary's *Rockin' in Time: A Social History of Rock and Roll.*

"Old Man Atom"   A topical song about the atomic bomb. Written as a "talking blues number" by Los Angeles journalist Vern Partlow, the song resulted from Partlow's interviews with scientists and government officials shortly after the Hiroshima and Nagasaki bombings. The song includes the following lyrics,

. . . If you're scared of an A Bomb
Here's what you gotta do:

You gotta gather all the people in the world with you
Because if you don't get together and do it, well-uh
The first thing you know we're gonna blow the world
   plumb to-uh- . . .

The song concludes by saying "Here's my thesis; Peace in the world or the world in pieces."

"Old Man Atom" was originally recorded by a small record company on the West Coast and its initial impact was minimal. However, in 1950 Martin Block played it on his "Make-Believe Ballroom" radio show in New York and it became an overnight hit. Columbia Records bought the rights to the original recording and rereleased under its own label, and RCA-Victor issued a new recording of the song. Both were successful, and "Old Man Atom" was frequently played by radio stations. However, both record companies withdrew the song from circulation and radio stations stopped playing it on the air after receiving complaints from members of the Joint Committee Against Communism, headed by Rabbi Benjamin Schultz. According to Rabbi Schultz, several members agreed that the song should be banned because its message was subversive, for it echoed the sentiments expressed in the Stockholm peace petition, which communists were then circulating. Officials of the record companies declined comment. However, Partlow stated, "I thought that [the song's message was] the policy of the United Nations and of our government." (See also MUSIC; NUCLEAR APOCALYPSE; RED SCARE.)

For additional reading, see Miller's *The Judges and the Judged.*

Olympic Games   The SPORTS rivalry in the Olympic Games has carried over into politics ever since the games began in ancient Greece. In the modern era, national rivalries have played a role in the Olympic Games both as part of the sports competitions and vis-à-vis power politics. For instance, Hitler used the 1936 Berlin Olympics to showcase the Third Reich, though his attempt to demonstrate Aryan supremacy was undermined by the brilliant performance of the African-American runners Jesse Owens and Ralph Metcalf. Because of World War II, the 1940 and 1944 games were canceled. The first Cold War-era Olympics was held in London in 1948, though the 1952 Summer Olympics held in Helsinki, Finland, was the first postwar games in which the Soviet Union participated.

Politics intruded noticeably into the Olympics during the Cold War era. In 1952 a single team consisting of athletes from West Germany represented Germany, but from 1956 to 1964, athletes entered from both East and West Germany. Even though they participated on the same team, these athletes are identified in the record books as being East or West German. In 1968, East and West Germany began entering separate teams, a practice that continued throughout the Cold War. China also competed in 1952, but the communist People's Republic of China (PRC) left when the International Committee subsequently recognized Taiwan. The PRC did not return to Olympic competition until the 1980 Winter Games at Lake Placid, New York. They also competed in the 1984 Summer Games at Los Angeles, which the Soviets and Warsaw Pact countries boycotted. For its part, Taiwan has competed under the name of China (1956), Taiwan

(1960–72) and Chinese Taipei (1984). It did not participate in the 1976 Games or the 1980 Summer Games in Moscow.

In the 1968 Summer Olympics in Mexico City, Tommie Smith and John Carlos, America's gold and bronze medal winners of the 200-meter track race, created controversy when they raised their hands in a black power salute during the U.S. national anthem. In 1972, pressure from predominately black countries led to the exclusion of Rhodesia (now Zimbabwe), which had recently broken from the British Commonwealth to form a white supremacist government. The same year, Palestinian terrorists entered the Olympic Village and fired on the dormitory in which the Israeli team resided. They killed two Israeli athletes and took nine more as hostages. In the showdown with police that followed, five of the terrorists and all of the hostages were killed.

In response to the Soviet Union's 1979 invasion of Afghanistan, President Carter ordered a U.S. boycott of the 1980 Summer Games that were held in Moscow. The Soviets and their Warsaw Pact allies participated in the Winter Olympics in Lake Placid later that year but boycotted the 1984 Summer Olympics in Los Angeles. However, both superpowers participated in the 1988 Summer Olympics in Seoul, South Korea. The 1988 Winter Games in Calgary, Canada, were the last ones held before the dissolution of the Soviet Union and the conclusion of the Cold War, and both the United States and the Soviet Union participated.

In the games themselves, a fierce rivalry grew between the United States and the U.S.S.R., especially in basketball—in which the United States won the gold medal every year but two while the Soviets frequently placed second—and in hockey, a sport that the Soviets came to dominate but did lose to the United States in 1960 and 1980. The U.S. upset victory in 1980 had special significance because it followed the U.S. boycott of the Moscow Olympics and came as the Cold War was beginning to reintensify following the dissolution of the 1970s détente.

Following is a review of every significant Cold War Olympics: In the 1952 Summer Olympics, the United States defeated the Soviet team in the basketball finals, and middleweight U.S. boxer Floyd Patterson, a future world champion, defeated Rumanian and Bulgarian challengers to win the gold medal. The Soviets dominated the men's and women's gymnastic events, rowing, wrestling and the women's discus throw. The United States dominated men's track and field, including the 3,000-meter steeplechase, in which Horace Ashenfelter defeated Soviet Vladimir Kazantsev and broke Kazantsev's world record in the process. Neither country dominated in the 1952 Winter Olympics in Oslo.

The American hockey team beat the U.S.S.R. team for the gold medal at the 1980 Winter Olympics in Lake Placid, New York.
Courtesy AP/Wide World.

In the 1956 Summer Olympics at Melbourne, the United States, led by future Boston Celtic stars Bill Russell and K. C. Jones, again defeated the U.S.S.R. for the gold medal in basketball, and American Pete Rademacher knocked down Soviet Lev Moukhin three times in the first round to win the gold medal for heavyweight boxing. The Soviets again dominated the men's and women's gymnastics. Both countries won gold medals in track and field and came in first and second in several of the weightlifting divisions. American Harold Connolly defeated Soviet Anatoly Krisvonosov for the gold medal in the hammer throw and then went on to marry Olga Fikotova, the Soviet women's discus champion, whom he courted during a much publicized romance in the Olympic Village. However, they divorced after nine years. In the Winter Olympics in Cortina, Italy, the Soviets won most of the speed-skating competitions and began their dominance of hockey by defeating the second-place U.S. team.

In 1960 at Rome, the United States once again won the gold medal in basketball, while the U.S.S.R. won the silver. U.S. players included future NBA stars Oscar Robertson, Jerry Lucas, John Havlicek and Jerry West, and the group is considered by some to be the greatest Olympic basketball team ever to compete. Future world champion Cassius Clay (who later changed his name to Muhammad Ali) won the light-heavyweight boxing division, though boxers from the IRON CURTAIN countries fared well in the other divisions. The United States won several events in women's and men's swimming and track and field, while the Soviets prevailed in gymnastics, rowing, shooting, fencing, wrestling and women's track and field. They also won the men's speed skating in the Winter Olympics at Squaw Valley in the United States. However, the United States won gold medals in hockey and figure skating.

In 1964, the Summer Olympics were played in Tokyo, and the United States and U.S.S.R. again placed first and second in basketball, respectively. Future NBA stars Bill Bradley, Walt Hazzard and Joe Caldwell led the U.S. team to its sixth consecutive undefeated tournament. Future world champion, the American Joe Frazier, won the heavyweight boxing division despite fighting with a broken hand; Soviets Stanislav Stepashkin and Boris Lagutin won the featherweight and light-middleweight divisions. The Soviet women again dominated gymnastics, but the men fell second to the Japanese, who also prevailed in judo. American Lones Wigger defeated Soviet Velichko Valichkov and set world records in the small-bore rifle competition despite never having performed before an audience before. The United States dominated in men's and women's swimming and in men's track and field. In the Winter Olympics in Innsbruck, Austria, the Soviets resumed their dominance of hockey, but American Terry McDermott won the 500-meter speed-skating competition.

In the 1968 Summer Olympics held in Mexico City, the U.S. basketball team won again, led by Jo-Jo White and Spencer Haywood, while the Soviets fell to third place behind Yugoslavia. The Soviet men also fell second to the Japanese in gymnastics, but the Soviet women defeated Czechoslovakia for the gold. The U.S. men and women dominated the swimming and track and field events, while the Soviets prevailed in volleyball and weightlifting and

made a strong showing in wrestling. In the Winter Olympics in Grenoble, France, the Soviets won their third gold medal in hockey by defeating Canada.

The 1972 Summer Games in Munich were delayed for 34 hours to pay tribute to the murdered Israeli athletes. The Soviets handed the U.S. basketball team its first Cold War–era defeat after an official's controversial ruling pushed the clock back three seconds instead of one, thereby allowing the Soviets time to in-bound the ball and shoot the winning basket. The final score was 51-50, giving the Soviets the gold medal, the United States the silver and Cuba the bronze. American Ray Seales won the light-welterweight boxing medal, and a Soviet boxer won the middleweight division; otherwise, Cuba prevailed in boxing as Teofilo Stevenson won the gold medal in the heavyweight class. East and West Germany faced each other for the gold medal in the 4,000-meter team pursuit cycling competition; West Germany won by three seconds. The Soviets won the cycling team time trial and also fared well in fencing and gymnastics. The Soviet women won the gold medal for team combined gymnastic exercises, but the men finished second once again to Japan. Soviet teams won gold medals for the modern pentathlon and single-scull rowing, though West Germany upset East Germany in the four-oared shell competition. The United States dominated the men's swimming events as Mark Spitz won seven gold medals and broke several world records. U.S. women also dominated their competition. Athletes from both superpowers fared well in the men's track and field events, with Soviet women winning several gold medals. The Soviets also prevailed in weightlifting, though the United States won two of the three wrestling categories, with the third going to the Soviets. The Soviets won their third consecutive medal in ice hockey in the Winter Olympics in Sapporo, Japan.

In Montreal's 1976 Summer Olympics, the U.S. men's basketball team regained the gold medal and the Soviets placed third, but the Soviets won the first gold medal in the newly created women's basketball competition, while the Americans captured the silver. In boxing, future champions Sugar Ray Leonard, Michael Spinks and Leon Spinks won their respective divisions while representing the United States as light welterweight, middleweight and light heavyweight, respectively, but the Cuban Teofilo Stevenson won the gold medal for heavyweight boxing, becoming the first heavyweight fighter to win back-to-back Olympic championships. The Soviets and Japanese dominated the men's gymnastics, with the Japanese winning the team combined exercises. Despite an outstanding personal performance by Rumanian Nadia COMANECI, a future defector, the Soviets won the women's team combined exercises and excelled in several individual categories. Nevertheless, the 14-year-old Comaneci became a media darling who won instant fame, recognition and affection throughout the world, though the U.S.S.R.'s Lyudmila Tourischeva won four gold medals and five additional medals. The Soviet men and women dominated the team handball competition, and Soviet competitor Sergei Novikov won the heavyweight judo title. The Soviets also prevailed in weightlifting and heavyweight wrestling, though John Peterson became only the second American to win the middleweight freestyle wrestling division. Americans Lanny Bassham and Margaret Murdock won the gold and silver medals for small-bore rifle shooting as Murdock became the first woman ever to win an Olympic shooting metal. Americans also dominated the men's swimming competition, though the East Germans and Soviets prevailed in the women's categories. Neither superpower dominated the track and field events, though Americans won the men's 400-meter hurdles, the relay races, the long jump and the discus throw, and the Soviets won the triple jump and hammer throw. The East Germans prevailed in the women's track and field events. American Bruce Jenner gained fame when he set a new world record while winning the gold medal for the decathlon. In the Winter Olympics at Innsbruck, Austria, American Dorothy Hamill won the women's figure-skating competition, but Soviets Irina Rodnina and Aleksandr Zaitsev won the figure-skating pairs division. The Soviet men and women prevailed in cross-country skiing, and the Soviet men dominated the 500-meter speed-skating event. They also won their fourth consecutive gold medal in ice hockey.

The 1980 and 1984 competitions were marred by boycotts in response to the Soviet invasion of Afghanistan in 1979. No Americans and only a limited number of other Westerners participated in the 1980 Summer Olympics held in Moscow, and no Soviet or Eastern Europeans competed in the 1984 Summer Olympics in Los Angeles. Both superpowers did compete in the 1980 Winter Olympics at Lake Placid, New York, where the Soviets again won the pairs competition for figure-skating and the 30-kilometer cross-country skill event. But American Eric Heiden won all five speed-skating events, an unprecedented achievement, and the United States hockey team upset the greatly favored Soviet team to win the gold medal in that event. The hockey victory was widely celebrated in the United States.

The 1984 Winter Olympics was held in Sarajevo, Yugoslavia, where Bill Johnson became the first American man ever to win the gold medal for alpine skiing. Debbie Armstrong became the first American to win the women's alpine competition since 1952; another American, Christin Cooper, placed second. Twin brothers Phillip and Steven Mahre captured the gold and silver medals in the men's slalom competition for the United States. The American Scott Hamilton won the men's figure-skating event, though the Soviets again prevailed in the pairs competition. They also won the 10,000-meter speed-skating event and the 30-kilometer cross-country skiing competition and regained the gold medal in ice hockey.

In the 1988 Summer Olympics in Seoul, the U.S. women's basketball team again prevailed, but the men's team placed third behind the U.S.S.R. and Yugoslavia in its worst Olympic performance ever. Otherwise, the American men prevailed in boxing and performed well in the swimming events as Greg Louganis won his fourth gold medal in diving. Janet Evans won three gold medals for the United States in the women's swimming competition. Led by runner Carl Lewis, the American men won several of the track and field events, though the Soviets garnered gold medals in the high jump, pole vault and hammer throw. Lewis won the 100-meter track race when Canadian Ben Johnson, the apparent winner, was disqualified after testing positive for drugs. Americans won six events and Soviet women won five as the superpowers dominated the women's track and

field events. The American men and Soviet women prevailed in volleyball, while Soviet men dominated weightlifting and wrestling. In the Winter Olympics at Calgary, Brian Boitano became the only American man to win a gold medal when he won the men's figure-skating competition. American Bonnie Blair won the gold medal in the 500-meter women's speed-skating race. The Soviets won the two-person bobsled competition, the figure-skating pairs event, the 30-kilometer men's and 20-kilometer women's cross-country skiing events, and the ice hockey competition.

For additional reading, see Jarrett's *Timetables of Sports History: The Olympic Games.*

Omega Man A 1971 FILM DRAMA starring Charlton HES-TON, Rosalind Cash and Anthony Zerbe and directed by Boris Sagal; it is based on Richard Matheson's novel, *I Am Legend.* Whereas the novel and its earlier film treatment, *The Last Man on Earth* (1964), describe the plight of a survivor of a vampire plague, *Omega Man* concerns a survivor (Heston) of a plague caused by germ warfare. Set only six years into the future, the film relies on images of a deserted Los Angeles in which the Omega Man fights against the hateful carriers of the disease. The film appeared at a time when germ warfare was a topical subject, as both the United States and U.S.S.R. were increasing their arsenals. (See also APOCALYPTIC FILMS.)

On the Beach A 1957 MILITARY NOVEL by Nevil Shute and a 1959 MILITARY FILM starring Gregory Peck, Ava Gardner, Fred Astaire and Anthony Perkins and directed and produced by Stanley Kramer. *On the Beach* was written and filmed during an intense period of the Cold War, when both sides had nuclear warheads and intercontinental ballistic missile systems (ICBMs), and the Eisenhower administration's declared policy was to threaten "massive retaliation" against the U.S.S.R. in response to communist aggression anywhere in the world. The Soviet Union had launched Sputnik I, the first human-made satellite, and had tested its first ICBM the year the book appeared. Moreover the still-unresolved Berlin Crisis, which lasted from 1958 to 1961, made nuclear war at times seem imminent as both superpowers threatened to use their nuclear weapons.

Set in 1964, the story depicts the aftermath of an all-out nuclear confrontation—not an improbable scenario in the late 1950s. *On the Beach* follows the fates of people in Australia who helplessly await the cloud of radioactive fallout that has already killed everyone in the Northern Hemisphere and is drifting south. Dwight Towers (Peck) commands a U.S. nuclear submarine that was submerged when the bombing took place and found safe haven in Melbourne. He meets Peter Holmes (Perkins), an officer in the Australian Navy with a wife, Mary, and infant girl. Holmes, in turn, introduces Towers to Moira Davidson (Gardner), with whom he begins an unconsummated romantic relationship. Towers and Holmes sail to California to investigate a radio transmission, hopeful that someone has survived the NUCLEAR APOCALYPSE. But the signal proves to be merely an empty Coke bottle banging against a telegraph transmitter, and San Francisco and San Diego are ghost towns. The submarine then returns to Australia, where the romantic subplots end with death or the promise of impending death. In the book, Holmes injects his infant with a lethal serum and then administers suicide pills to Mary and himself. In the film, he only remarks on the uniquely cruel nature of his situation: "How do you tell a woman you love that she has to kill herself and her baby?" Towers, on the other hand, leaves Moira behind as his final moments are spent in the service of the navy of his now-defunct nation.

The story highlights the different kinds of denial that each victim practices. Mary refuses to think of or tolerate talk about the impending disaster; Towers limits his relationship with Moira because he cannot acknowledge his wife's death; Moira and others drink excessively. Even the business-as-usual behavior of the Royal Navy and the Australian townspeople is shown as a form of denial. The story also raises questions about whether impending doom should alter traditional loyalties, values and ethics. Tower's middle-class American virtues—his patriotism and family loyalty—become problematic qualities after his country and his wife have been wiped out. His decision to leave Moira for his submarine at the end of their lives seemingly affirms his values; but under the circumstances, the decision appears both absurd and sado-masochistic, an empty gesture to a no-longer existent country that denies both him and Moira the final comfort their love might have offered. Though neither Shute nor Kramer seem to have intended this, the story questions whether cultural priorities that value men's love of country over their love of women might in fact be responsible for the armageddon.

More explicitly, the nuclear bomb itself appears as a culprit. Various characters blame the scientists who built the bomb, and even Julian Osborn (Astaire), the resident scientist, accepts part of the responsibility. When explicitly asked who is responsible he first replies, "Albert Einstein," but then goes on to maintain that there are no simple explanations. He concludes that their present situation stems from Cold War policies making national security dependent on weapons that must never be used. The book informs us that the war started with fighting between the U.S.S.R. and China, but as Holmes explains to Mary, "Some kinds of silliness you just can't stop . . . if a couple of hundred million people all decide that their national honour requires them to drop cobalt bombs upon their neighbour, well, there's not much that you or I can do about it. The only possible hope would have been to educate them out of their silliness." Holmes suggests that newspapers could have provided that education, but "We all liked our newspapers with pictures of beach girls and headlines about cases of indecent assault, and no government was wise enough to stop us having them that way."

The film ends slightly more optimistically as the final shot of Melbourne, now a ghost town, focuses on a religious banner stating, "There's still time." That message is just wishful thinking for the characters in the story, and it provides a deeply ironic, even sarcastic conclusion to their story. But the banner also admonished the 1959 viewing audience. Though *On the Beach* never explicitly advocates unilateral nuclear disarmament, it does imply that the hope for salvation from the bomb lies in creating a national defense that does not require nuclear weapons. The film premiered in 18 cities located in all seven continents. The

Australian folk song "Waltzing Matilda" became popular in the United States after being featured in the film. (See also APOCALYPTIC FILMS.)

On Thermonuclear War A 1960 NONFICTION book by Herman Kahn. A staff member of the Rand Corporation, Kahn here presents three lectures he gave at Princeton University's Center for International Studies in March 1959: "The Nature and Feasibility of Thermonuclear War," "The Formulation and Testing of Objectives and Plans" and "World War I through World War III." His appendices also include plans for a civil defense program. Kahn gave his lectures and published the book during the second Berlin Crisis (1958–61), one of the most volatile periods of the Cold War in which a major nuclear war between the United States and U.S.S.R. appeared likely. The book became quite controversial because Kahn ventures to "think the unthinkable," imagining the pursuit of nuclear war as a viable option, and because he dispassionately contemplates the details of massive human annihilation, attempting to calculate with scientific precision the approximate nature of the destruction that would ensue from a major nuclear war. Kahn concludes that with proper air and civil defense, the United States could survive such a war, even if it were to kill 20 to 40 million Americans and destroy all major U.S. cities. In this regard, Kahn repudiates the conventional wisdom that an all-out nuclear war would destroy not only the nation but also human civilization itself, and he thus sets the stage for later Cold War planners in the 1970s and 1980s who argued in favor of rejecting scenarios of Mutually Assured Destruction (MAD) in favor of policies predicated on winning a nuclear war.

Kahn's closely argued, highly rational methodology received both praise and criticism. His supporters, such as the reviewer for *Foreign Affairs*, praised him for "thinking concretely and imaginatively about a range of questions too frequently avoided in much discussion of the prospects for war and peace." Likewise, *Library Journal* maintains that "His theses are closely argued and sometimes involved, but they are so lucidly presented that his meaning is always clear," and the *New York Times* lauds Kahn for using data on genetics, economics, sociology and political science to draw his conclusions: "Above all, the work is valuable because the author has taken off the blinders of self-deception and has faced up to the stark realities of thermonuclear war."

On the other hand, the reviewer for the *Nation* complains, "If *On Thermonuclear War* were concerned with the destruction of 100 million or more dogs, anti-vivisection societies, sportsmen and dog lovers generally would raise a howl of protest . . . But because the subject matter is the incineration, poisoning and starving of women, children, and perhaps a few combatants, this book has been hailed as the important work of a thoughtful and dedicated man." *New Statesman* attacks the scientific premises of Kahn's presentation: "In the United States . . . a new science, or rather pseudo-science, has been developed by the Rand Corporation . . . I call the work of the Corporation a pseudo-science for the simple reason that its exponents have no means of verifying their conclusions by experiment. Apart from the two bombs dropped on Japan, they do not know what really happens when nuclear weapons are used." And *The Saturday Review* concludes, "Mr. Kahn and his fellow theorists have done something to convince me that a substantial part of the human race may survive World War III; they have not convinced me that mankind deserves to survive if it is capable of the horrors of destruction for which we prepare ourselves."

By contrast, the generally positive discussion in the *Yale Review* praises Kahn for "demolishing the nihilism of the security policy the United States has pursued during the past few years," but points out that he neglects to take into account the Soviets' belief that the battle for Europe could decide the outcome of a protracted nuclear war with the United States. And the *Times* of London complains,

> It is sensational because it is the first published study to examine seriously the question of how a nuclear war would be conducted; provocative, because Mr. Kahn employs techniques of mathematical analysis which, the farther he takes them, the farther they take him from the real world . . . The result is a major, if baroque, work of military thought . . . Russia never figures in his book as anything but a simple, monolithic military power deterred from using armed force to conquer the world only by the maintenance of American military strength . . . What is absent from the thinking of most American military intellectuals— and it is their lack which spoils much even of their purely strategic thinking—is the slightest consideration of the possibility that Russian policy consists of a great deal more than Marxist doctrine plus Soviet economic potential . . . or that Russia has at least as good historic grounds for fearing attack by the West as the West has for fearing attack by her.

This range of response to *On Thermonuclear War* reflects the growing split in Western Cold War culture between traditional humanists—who took into account such subjective, nonquantifiable human experiences as pain, suffering, grief and a sense of loss—and a growing class of technocrats and social scientists who viewed world events more or less dispassionately and assessed situations primarily in quantifiable terms.

Kahn appears to have served as a model for Professor Groeteschele, a political scientist in the MILITARY NOVEL and military film FAIL-SAFE (1964) who views the Cold War purely in statistical terms and coldly advocates strategies predicated entirely upon their efficiency and utilitarian value. He may also have been a partial model for the title character in Stanley Kubrick's DR. STRANGELOVE (1964), who likewise dispassionately calculates the likely deaths of millions of Americans and refers to recent studies conducted by the "Bland Corporation." (The former Nazi scientist then working in the U.S. space program, Werner von Braun, was another source for Strangelove.)

On the Waterfront A 1954 FILM DRAMA starring Marlon Brando, Lee J. COBB, Karl Malden, Rod Steiger and Eva Marie Saint, directed by Elia KAZAN and written by Budd SCHULBERG, who subsequently wrote the novel *Waterfront,* based on his own screenplay. Leonard Bernstein wrote the musical score. The story centers on Terry Malloy (Brando),

an ex-boxer who works at the loading docks and belongs to a union run by the corrupt boss Johnny Friendly (Cobb). Friendly has always treated him well, but Malloy falls in love with the sister of a man Friendly had murdered to keep him from testifying in a criminal investigation. Despite a virtually inviolable code against informing on others, Terry eventually concludes that, in this case, informing is the proper thing to do. He testifies, breaking Friendly's grip on the union by asserting his right to work.

The depiction of union ties to organized crime alluded to the closely followed 1950–51 Kefauver Senate investigations, the first congressional hearings to be widely televised. The story can be taken solely at face value as a drama about fighting corruption. In fact, the screenplay was based on Malcolm Johnson's series of Pulitzer Prize–winning articles in the *New York Sun* about corruption on the docks of New York harbor.

However, the film's sympathetic treatment of an informer has led several critics to interpret the story as an allegory justifying those "friendly witnesses" who cooperated with the HOUSE COMMITTEE ON UN-AMERICAN ACTIVITIES (HUAC) and named the names of colleagues with past or current communist associations. Among those friendly witnesses were former Communist Party members Schulberg and Kazan, who in 1951 and 1952 collectively named 31 names. Thus, in *On the Waterfront* they portray the cause of justice as served by informing, not by standing silent and permitting violent crimes to go unpunished. Malloy's informing on Friendly is shown to be a heroic deed that threatens to cost Malloy his friends and possibly his life. (In Schulberg's novel, he loses both.) Cobb, too, eventually named names.

Though both Kazan and Schulberg continued to consider themselves progressive members of the anti-Stalinist Left, they felt comfortable about equating the political "crimes" of the Communist Party of America with the murders, extortion, theft and other violent practices of organized crime. In an interview with Nora Sayre, Schulberg stated, "I thought they [American Communists] were accessories to murder," referring to the Stalinist purges of the 1930s and 1940s. He also believed that American communists were capable of similar purges if they ever came to power. After his testimony before HUAC, Kazan took out a full-page ad in the *New York Times* stating that, "Firsthand experience of dictatorship and thought control left me with an abiding hatred of these," and that citizens who knew the actual facts about communism "had an obligation to make them known, either to the public or to the appropriate Government agency."

Ironically, the original idea for *On the Waterfront* came from Kazan's one-time collaborator, playwright Arthur MILLER—an unfriendly witness who had defied HUAC and refused to name names, thereby risking imprisonment. (He actually received only a fine and suspended 30-day sentence.) Miller severed his relationship with Kazan after the director testified in 1952. But in 1951, Miller had written *The Hook,* based on the life and death of Peter Panto, a dock worker who had tried to organize a rank-and-file protest in his local branch of the International Longshoremen's Association. Miller and Kazan had presented the script to Harry Cohn, the president of Columbia Pictures, who showed it Roy BREWER, the president of the AFL-affiliated

International Alliance of Theatrical Stage Employees. Brewer, whose union of projectionists had the power to keep a movie from being screened, objected to the presentation of union corruption, which he maintained did not exist to the extent Miller had portrayed it. Brewer asserted that no loyal American could have written the script, which he feared could cause "turmoil" in New York harbor from which supplies were being shipped to fight the Korean War. Brewer suggested that Miller rewrite the story "so that instead of racketeers terrorizing the dockworkers, it would be the Communists." However, Miller refused, arguing that the communist presence on the docks was very slight and that to exaggerate the communist influence would make the racketeers appear as patriots. He then withdrew from the project, which was shelved until Kazan invited Schulberg to work with him on it. (Harry Cohn's response to Miller was to send a telegram: "Strange how the minute we want to make the script pro-American you pull out.") Many critics feel that Miller's 1955 Broadway play *A View from the Bridge,* which depicts a man whose life was ruined by a single act of informing, was the playwright's response to *On the Waterfront.*

For additional reading, see Sayre's *Running Time;* Navasky's *Naming Names;* Whitfield's *The Culture of the Cold War.*

One Minute to Zero   A 1952 KOREAN WAR FILM starring Robert Mitchum and Ann Blyth and directed by Tay Garnett. The story centers on a romance between a U.S. colonel and a female UN official whom he must evacuate against her will. Eventually, the colonel is forced to bomb refugees.

One, Two, Three   A 1961 FILM COMEDY starring James Cagney, Horst Buchholz and Pamela Tiffin and directed by Billy Wilder. Cagney stars as a Coca-Cola executive who brings his family to Berlin. Much to his embarrassment—and to the possible detriment of his career—his boss's daughter falls in love with a scruffy anti-capitalist from East Berlin. The plot provided a comic view of the Cold War, East German beatniks, Coca-Cola's transnationalism and other subjects during one of the most critical moments of the Cold War, the second Berlin Crisis. The ongoing Berlin Crisis had begun in 1958, when Khrushchev demanded that the United States, France and Great Britain leave Berlin. The crisis peaked in 1961 when Khrushchev ended a three-year voluntary moratorium on nuclear testing and ordered the erection of the Berlin Wall that summer, so that U.S. and Soviet tanks faced off at Checkpoint Charlie, dividing East and West Berlin, in October.

One Very Hot Day   A 1967 novel by David HALBERSTAM. Published during the height of U.S. involvement in Vietnam, the novel takes a cynical view of the war as it traces a day in the life of an American military adviser on patrol in 1963. The protagonist, Sergeant Beaupre, is a veteran of World War II and the Korean War who is frustrated by his limited role:

> He wished the troops would go faster . . . and he wished he were a real officer, someone who could give commands and then see them obeyed, who could send a patrol here and another there, could make the troops go fast, go slow, be brave, be strong; wished to be hated, to be feared, even to be loved, but to be an officer and in charge.

Instead, he must restrict himself to instructing his young South Vietnamese lieutenant and accommodate himself to the lack of straightforward progress in this different sort of warfare. The circularity of his patrols emerges as a metaphor for the war itself, which seems to defy resolution and which refuses to provide any sense of accomplishment:

> We didn't know how simple it was, and how good we had it [during World War II]. Sure we walked, but in a straight line. Boom, Normandy beaches, and then you set off for Paris and Berlin . . . No retracing; no goddam circles, just straight ahead. But here you walk in a goddam circle, and then you go home, and then you go out the next day and wade through a circle, and then you go home and the next day you go out and reverse the circle you did the day before.

In the novel's afterword Halberstam claims, "I wanted to portray the frustrations, and the emptiness of this war. It was after all a smaller and, I think, less tidy war than Americans were accustomed to, and almost nothing that happened in it fit the preconceptions of Westerners." Halberstam, who also wrote the Vietnam NONFICTION books THE BEST AND THE BRIGHTEST (1972), *The Making of a Quagmire* (1965) and *Ho* (1971), had reported on the war in the early 1960s for the *New York Times* and won a Pulitzer Prize for his coverage, despite efforts by the Kennedy administration to have him transferred out of Southeast Asia. (See also VIETNAM WAR LITERATURE.)

Only the Strong   A 1972 FILM DOCUMENTARY produced by the politically conservative Institute for American Strategy (IAS) and sponsored by the American Security Council of Culpepper, Virginia, an organization that had campaigned since the early 1960s to prevent arms limitation agreements with the Soviet Union. The IAS was an arms lobby directed by former high-ranking military officers and representatives of defense contractors. Made during the Nixon-Kissinger détente of the 1970s and aired shortly after the completion of the antiballistic missile treaty that limited U.S. and Soviet defensive capabilities, the film represents Soviet military strength as superior to U.S. strength and claims that peace can be ensured only by a strong, well-armed U.S. military. None of the major television networks would air the film, which newspaper editorials and other organizations had attacked as self-serving propaganda instead of the public service program it purported to be. Nonetheless, church groups, veterans organizations, service clubs and schools screened it extensively, using 16mm prints that were available for a nominal fee. In addition, over 400 local and independent television stations broadcast it as a public service show. It was aired over 800 times, mostly during prime time. Liberal organizations responded by demanding time to reply under the provisions of the Federal Communications Commission's Fairness Doctrine.

The film was strongly attacked for overstating Soviet strength and American military weakness. For instance, it points out that "the Russians have about five times as much missile megatonnage as we have, and thus could divide theirs into five times as many warheads as we have." But the film failed to indicate that the United States had twice as many warheads and was projected to have a 4:1 advantage by 1977, or that U.S. warheads were considered far more accurate. The film was also criticized for omitting the arsenals of the other NATO countries from its calculations of nuclear strength and for treating the U.S.S.R. and China as a single communist monolith, instead of the adversaries they had already become by 1972. (In fact, Nixon's historic trip to China that year was designed to take advantage of the schism between the communist "superpowers.") The film concludes with a "Peace Poll": Responses in sympathy with the opinions of the film's producers were sent to Congress and the president; less sympathetic respondents received literature intended to change their views. (See also APOCALYPTIC FILMS.)

For additional reading, see Shaheen's *Nuclear War Films.*

Open Theater, The An experimental THEATER group in New York founded by Joseph Chaikin to succeed the LIVING THEATER. Chaikin had been a member of the Living Theater but remained behind when it left the country after performing Kenneth Brown's *The Brig* in 1963. More professional in its approach to drama, the Open Theater produced experimental and politically provocative plays including Megan Terry's VIET ROCK (1966) and Jean-Claude van Itallie's *American Hurrah* (1966), which includes an attack on the Vietnam War as part of a larger critique of American culture. Its comic, somewhat absurdist style is influenced by pop art, and both plays turn to elements of American popular culture and news and entertainment media to make their critiques of the war. The Open Theater became part of the populist Off-Off-Broadway, a form of low-budget, alternative theater that originated in California and was directed primarily against racism and the Vietnam War. (See also ART.)

Operation Abolition A 1960 FILM DOCUMENTARY produced by the HOUSE COMMITTEE ON UN-AMERICAN ACTIVITIES (HUAC). *Operation Abolition* attempts to prove that anti-HUAC demonstrators at a San Francisco hearing were sponsored by communists and traitors. Included within *Operation Abolition* is footage unrelated to that demonstration. HUAC answered criticism of the film in an article entitled "The Truth about *Operation Abolition,*" which appears as Document M-561 in the microfiche supplement to *Film and Propaganda in America.* In addition to defending the film, the article also identifies other works of anti-communist propaganda which were distributed throughout the United States.

For additional reading, see Suid's *Film and Propaganda in America.*

"Operation Information" A TELEVISION NEWS show that ran on the DuMont network during the summer of 1952. The Korean War–era show was designed to inform war veterans of their benefit rights.

Ordeal by Slander A 1950 NONFICTION book by Owen Lattimore. A China scholar who had supported agrarian reform and attacked Chiang Kai-shek for being corrupt and insufficiently democratic, Professor Lattimore was the target of accusations by Chiang supporter Senator Joseph McCarthy during the RED SCARE. In 1950, McCarthy accused Lattimore of being pro-communist and of sabotaging U.S. aid to Chiang's Nationalist government. He labeled Lattimore the top Soviet espionage agent in the United States and introduced unsubstantiated testimony from former ranking members of the U.S. Communist Party. However, a Senate panel chaired by Millard Tydings cleared the professor after finding no evidence that Lattimore had ever been a Soviet agent. This book provides Lattimore's defense of himself and describes the ordeal he went through. He relates how he was working in Afghanistan with the United Nations Technical Aid Mission when McCarthy first accused him of being a communist; presents his wife's account of what happened in the United States until he arrived back home; describes his testimony before the congressional subcommittee; and tells what happened to the friends who came forward to defend him.

The book was well received. The reviewer for *American Political Science* described it as "a masterpiece of factual exposition, a social document of first-rate importance. Over and above that, it is a tremendously stirring human drama." And *The New Yorker*'s reviewer stated, "Anyone who really wants to know the facts of the entire case can and should read *Ordeal by Slander.* Indeed, Americans owe it to Lattimore—and even more to themselves—to get the story here in one connected narrative, with the falsities exposed and the methods laid bare." That year Lattimore also published *Pivot of Asia: Sinkiang and the Inner Asian Frontiers of China and Russia,* a scholarly work that analyzes the political dynamics of that region of Asia.

Orion Shall Rise A 1983 APOCALYPTIC NOVEL by Poul Anderson. The novel appeared during the most intense period of the Cold War since the 1962 Cuban Missile Crisis, when the Reagan administration was accusing the Soviet Union of preparing to prevail in a nuclear war and was therefore advocating a policy of winnable nuclear war for the United States. Anderson envisions the world a century after the "War of Judgment." By that time, distinct societies have emerged on the different continents, and they are again competing for global domination. Eventually a new world war breaks out involving left-over nuclear and chemical weapons. Ironically, peace is finally achieved when a nuclear-powered spaceship carrying a deadly solar weapon imposes a new order. Unlike many earlier apocalyptic novels that hold science responsible for the disaster and reject it in the future, this vision of postapocalyptic society gives science and technology an important if problematic role in the salvation of the race. Anderson also wrote earlier stories dealing with technology and chemical and nuclear energy in postnuclear society. These include "Vault of the Ages" (1952), "Progress" (1962) and "Tomorrow's Children" (1947), a story written two years after Hiroshima about the effects of a worldwide atomic war. (See also SCIENCE FICTION NOVELS.)

For additional reading, see Dowling's *Fictions of Nuclear Disaster.*

Ornitz, Sam A SCREENWRITER and NOVELIST and member of the HOLLYWOOD TEN. Best known for his novel *Haunch,*

Paunch and Jowel (1923), Ornitz had written the screenplays for over 20 films before he was called to testify at the 1947 HOUSE COMMITTEE ON UN-AMERICAN ACTIVITIES (HUAC) hearings on communist influences in Hollywood films. After citing their First Amendment rights and refusing to testify, Ornitz and the nine other "unfriendly" witnesses were cited for contempt of Congress and eventually sentenced to prison. They were also blacklisted in Hollywood. In preparing to take their stand before the committee, Ornitz advised the other members of the Ten, "Let us at least be as brave as the people we write about." (See also BLACKLISTING.)

Orwell, George a British NOVELIST. Best known for his two anti-communist books, *Animal Farm* (1945) and NINE-TEEN EIGHTY-FOUR (1949), Orwell was born in 1903 in Burma as Eric Blair, the son of a British civil servant. He attended Eton, and his painful awareness of the class differences between himself and the upper-class boys at the school, as well as his feelings of guilt over British colonialism in Burma, led him to adopt a socialist point of view, though he never joined a political party. He went to Spain in 1936 to support the Loyalists against Nazi-backed Franco during the Spanish Civil War and afterward returned to England, where he wrote *Homage to Catalonia* (1938). That book criticized the communists, who had also opposed Franco, for what Orwell saw as their attempt to destroy any allies who did not adhere to a strict Stalinist position. *Animal Farm* takes his attack on Stalin even further by presenting the Russian Revolution and its aftermath as an allegory about farm animals who overthrow the farmer but replace him with power-hungry pigs who eventually sell out the promise of freedom and equality that had inspired their revolt. The two leading pigs stand for Stalin and Trotsky.

In 1946 Orwell wrote the influential essay, "Politics and the English Language," which analyzes modern political uses of language. After pointing out how modern writing often obfuscates instead of clarifies by using "dying metaphors," "operators or verbal false limbs," "pretentious diction" and "meaningless words," Orwell notes that "Orthodoxy, of whatever colour, seems to demand a lifeless, imitative style" and that "if thought corrupts language, language can also corrupt thought." These premises play a prominent role in Orwell's masterpiece, *Nineteen Eighty-Four*, in which a totalitarian one-party government uses "newspeak" to control its citizens by limiting their vocabulary for thinking original thoughts or other ideas that might challenge the party. Published a year before Orwell's death from tuberculosis, *Nineteen Eighty-Four* imagines a futuristic society in which communists have gained total control. They employ terror, technology, mob psychology and strict control of language in order to sustain power, which is their sole goal. And because whoever controls the past controls the present, and whoever controls the present controls the future, they also practice ongoing revisionist history, in which books, newspapers and other documents from the past are continuously updated to support current party positions. The book also features a power struggle among superpowers that anticipates the Cold War stalemate and shows how the party uses the existence of an external enemy to keep its citizens in line. Orwell directed the book against Stalin, who practiced virtually all of these techniques for maintaining power. In the earlier days of the Cold War, *Animal Farm* and *Nineteen Eighty-Four* were used in the West to illustrate the dangers of communism. However, during the later stages of the Cold War, domestic critics of the U.S. government also saw *Nineteen Eighty-Four* as an analysis of "Orwellian" aspects of U.S. social and political institutions, including the FBI, the CIA and advertising agencies, whose uses of language were often compared to newspeak.

"O.S.S." A TELEVISION MILITARY DRAMA that ran on ABC in 1957–58. Based on the public files describing the CIA's predecessor agency, the Office of Strategic Services (O.S.S.), this show presented accounts of the activities of U.S. intelligence teams during World War II. Though the show dealt exclusively with events from the Second World War, it appealed to a Cold War interest in covert intelligence operations.

Osterman Weekend, The A 1972 SPY NOVEL by Robert Ludlum and a 1983 SPY FILM starring John Hurt, Burt Lancaster, Dennis Hopper and Rutger Hauer and directed by Sam Peckinpah. The story centers on a powerful television journalist whose trusted friends are Soviet agents.

Our Gang A 1971 SATIRE by Philip Roth. *Our Gang* satirizes President Richard Nixon in general and his stand on the Vietnam War in particular. It begins by quoting Nixon's opposition to abortion on the grounds of the sanctity of human life. When an interviewer congratulates the president on his position, Nixon states, as he had actually said to contemporary war protesters, that he could have "done the popular thing" and opposed the sanctity of life, but he would rather stand up for his beliefs and be a one-term president than violate them and win a second term. The interviewer then asks him about the conviction of Lieutenant William Calley, who was responsible for American soldiers murdering 22 Vietnamese civilians at My Lai. Nixon replies that he could have done the popular thing by seeking the conviction of the dead civilians, but he would rather be a one-term president than review the question of their guilt. He continues to support Calley, whom he actually called a hero, even though Calley's troops may have unwittingly performed abortions by killing pregnant women. The exchange continues to highlight the incongruity between Nixon's declaration in his belief in the sanctity of life and his prosecution of the war: Nixon explains that any My Lai abortions would have been inadvertent, since Vietnamese women wore "pyjamas" that would have hidden pregnancy. Nixon later defends Vice President Agnew and Secretary of Defense Laird against criticism on the grounds that, as former unborn Americans, they deserved the protection accorded to fetuses. He dismisses the wounded Vietnam veterans who had turned in their medals in protest to the war as "a bunch of malcontents who had lost arms and legs and so on, and so had nothing better to do with their time than hobble around feeling sorry for themselves." He later adds, "Gentlemen, you can go to war without Congressional consent, you can ruin the economy and trample on the Bill of Rights, but you just do not violate the moral code of the Boy Scouts of America and expect to be reelected to the highest office in the land!" Elsewhere Nixon explains his failure to produce the secret peace plan he had campaigned on by stating that he left it in the pocket of his other suit.

Roth also satirizes Nixon's earlier political opportunism by having the president thank Alger Hiss for all he had done to promote Nixon's career. Moreover, Nixon says, in a reference to the "kitchen debates" he had had with Soviet premier Nikita Khrushchev as Eisenhower's vice president, "I would actually have forgiven Khrushchev himself, yes, right there in that kitchen, if it had been politically expedient to do so." The book continues in this vein throughout, including a section where the president blames baseball player Curt Flood for the nation's woes because Flood had challenged the legality of the "reserve clause" in the standard major league contract, which prevented players from selling their services to the teams of their choice. Anthony Burgess called *Our Gang* "Brilliant satire in the real Swift tradition," and the reviewer for *Newsweek* described it as "the funniest and most complex exercise in sustained political satire since *Animal Farm.*"

Our Man Flint   A 1966 FILM COMEDY starring James Coburn, Lee J. COBB and Gila Golan and directed by Daniel Mann. The film spoofs the suave, technologically proficient James BOND spy films popular at the time, as Flint (Coburn) foils the plans of an evil organization intent on seizing control of the world by manipulating the weather. Sequels included *In Like Flint* (1967) about a diabolical plan by a group of women to sieze control of the world, and *Our Man Flint: Dead on Target*, a 1976 made-for-television production. Coburn also starred in the 1967 spy film spoof, THE PRESIDENT'S ANALYST. (See also SPY FILM SPOOFS.)

Our Man in Havana   A 1958 SPY NOVEL by Graham GREENE and a 1960 British-made FILM COMEDY and FILM SATIRE starring Burl Ives, Alec Guinness, Ernie Kovacs, Noël Coward and Maureen O'Hara and directed by Carol Reed. Greene wrote the screenplay. The novel, a SATIRE that John Cawelti and Bruce Rosenberg call "the greatest burlesque of the spy story ever penned," centers on Jim Wormold (Guinness), a vacuum-cleaner salesman who agrees to spy for the British in order to finance his daughter's private schooling. Since he has no real information to pass along, he submits enlarged schematics of vacuum cleaner technology, claiming they describe enemy installations. The plot continues onto a complicated series of twists, based on espionage organizations' willingness to believe even absurd claims if those claims fit their paranoid world-views. The film was made in Havana shortly after Castro's Revolution. Both it and the novel satirize Cold War intelligence operations as well as the popular genres that reverently portray them. (See also SPY FILM SPOOFS.)

For additional reading, see Cawelti and Rosenberg's *The Spy Story.*

Our Nuclear Future: Facts, Dangers and Opportunities   A 1958 NONFICTION book by Edward Teller and Albert Latter. Writing at the beginning of the second Berlin Crisis, one of the most intense periods of the Cold War, Teller, the "father of the hydrogen bomb,"and Latter, also a nuclear physicist, explain to lay audiences what they see as the potential dangers and opportunities of nuclear physics. They describe how atomic energy works, assess the radioactive fallout from previous nuclear tests, and insist on the necessity of continued testing if the United States is to prevail in the Cold War. They argue that the fallout from nuclear testing does not pose a serious threat to human life and favorably compare its risks to ordinary dangers in everyday life, such as the possibility of developing lung cancer from smoking. The book was widely praised for its clear description of how atomic energy works, but it received mixed reviews for its political assessments.

The Chicago Sunday Tribune, which criticized Linus Pauling's pacifist arguments in NO MORE WAR from the same year, applauds Teller and Latter. However, the reviewer for the *New York Times* points out that the analogy to cigarette smoking is faulty, since individuals can choose whether to accept that risk, whereas they have no control over the risks from nuclear fallout. Moreover, the reviewer adds, "The fact is that bomb tests are not the issue . . . The real worry . . . is the danger of nuclear bombs being used in earnest." And the reviewer for the *San Francisco Chronicle* questions the authors' rosy assessment of the limited dangers from the fallout, pointing to the fate of the Japanese fishermen who contracted radiation poisoning after a nuclear test, and raising questions about the bomb's effect on weather. *Our Nuclear Future* thus joined the scientific debate over the safety and desirability of further developing nuclear weapons.

"Our Secret Weapon—The Truth"   A TELEVISION TALK OR DEBATE SHOW that ran on the DuMont network during the 1950–51 season. Originally a radio propaganda program during World War II, the show was revived for television during the Korean War. Panelists Leo Cherne and Ralph de Toledano appeared each week to rebut "Communist lies about us" with facts and testimony from special guests.

Paar, Jack A TELEVISION TALK show host. Paar took over NBC's TONIGHT SHOW after the departure of its originator, Steve Allen. Known for his displays of emotion, Paar involved the show in Cold War issues more than any of its other hosts. Paar interviewed presidential candidates John Kennedy and Richard Nixon during the 1960 campaign. Before Fidel Castro's assumption of power in Cuba in 1959, Paar attacked the Cuban dictator Batista on the air and praised Castro's revolutionary efforts. In 1961, after the CIA-sponsored Bay of Pigs invasion by Cuban exiles failed to overthrow the Castro regime, Paar tried to arrange a trade of tractors for prisoners. With the actress Peggy Cass, he originated several broadcasts from the Berlin Wall. One broadcast prompted an inquiry by the Defense Department when a detachment of U.S. soldiers was positioned in the background as Paar was filmed at the Brandenburg Gate. Paar was accused in the press of inflaming the situation, though he maintained that his efforts relieved tensions.

Pai, Hsin-yung An EXILED WRITER (to the United States). Born in China in 1937, Pai fled to Taiwan in 1949 with his politically prominent family after the communist takeover of mainland China. In the early 1960s he cofounded and became a major contributor to *Modern Literature,* a principal organ of exiled Chinese writers in Taiwan. Pai moved to Santa Barbara, California, in 1963. His story collection, *Wandering in the Garden, Waking from a Dream: Tales of Taipei Characters* (1971; in English, 1982), describes the plight of Chinese exiles who fled to Taiwan from the communist regime on the mainland.

For additional reading, see Tucker's *Literary Exile in the Twentieth Century.*

Panic in Year Zero A 1962 FILM DRAMA starring Ray Milland, Jean Hagen, Mary Mitchell and Frankie Avalon, directed by Milland and based on Dean Owen's 1962 apocalyptic novel THE END OF THE WORLD. Made during the same year as the Cuban Missile Crisis, *Panic in Year Zero* follows a middle-class American family through the aftermath of a nuclear attack. Harry (Milland), the dominating father in this nuclear family, quickly decides that their greatest peril comes from looters, not from fallout. He quickly and easily slips into a mode that emphasizes survival of the fittest and every man for himself. "We can start with one basic fact—us," he declares. His son, Rick (Avalon), echoes his sentiments: "We are on our own, Ma. No rules, regulation or laws." Though the mother, Ann (Hagen), prefers a more humane and moral approach to their situation, she dutifully complies with her husband's decisions. When her daughter is raped, Ann becomes a more forceful advocate of violence and revenge; then, toward the film's end, the males regain some of their compassion. Ultimately, Rick falls in love with a kidnapped girl he and his father rescue, and the family returns home to Los Angeles where the U.S. Army is imposing order. The film thus ends on an upbeat note, suggesting that a healthy new society can emerge from the ashes of the

Jack Paar. Courtesy AP/Wide World.

nuclear holocaust. (See also APOCALYPTIC FILMS; APOCALYPTIC NOVELS.)

For additional reading, see Shaheen's *Nuclear War Films*.

Parallax View, The   A 1974 SPY FILM starring Warren Beatty, Hume Cronyn, William Daniels and Paula Prentiss and produced and directed by Alan J. Pakula. It is based on the 1970 novel by Loren Singer. The story centers on the mysterious Parallax Corporation, which recruits disaffected, violent and alienated individuals and trains them to become professional assassins. Though not explicitly about the Cold War, the film alludes to the Kennedy assassination and to the factual ambiguities that surround it. The film also reflects the political cynicism of the mid-1970s and the conspiracy theories popular at the time.

Parks, Larry   A FILM ACTOR. Parks was among the original 19 so-called "unfriendly" witnesses who had indicated their intention to refuse to testify at the 1947 HOUSE COMMITTEE ON UN-AMERICAN ACTIVITIES (HUAC) hearings on communist influences in the film industry. But unlike the HOLLYWOOD TEN, Parks was never actually called before the 1947 committee. He was thus spared the prison sentences incurred by the Ten, but like them, he was blacklisted by the film studios and his career was destroyed. When the hearings reopened in 1951, Parks was the first person summoned. The Supreme Court had by then upheld the contempt-of-Congress convictions of the Ten, who had unsuccessfully invoked their First Amendment constitutional protection. Parks' choices were thus to go to prison for contempt of Congress, invoke the Fifth Amendment protection against self-incrimination, or cooperate with the committee. He reluctantly chose to coop-erate atter begging the committee, "Do not make me crawl through the mud like an informer." Parks concluded his testimony with a prophetic observation: "It is doubtful whether, after appearing before this Committee, my career will continue." Despite his public contrition, Parks remained on the blacklist, partly because he had testified so reluctantly. Newspaper columnist Hedda Hopper wrote, "The life of one American soldier [in the Korean War] is worth all the careers in Hollywood. We must be careful lest we give sympathy to those who do not deserve it—and Parks certainly does not." The *Los Angeles Times* also criticized him, comparing him unfavorably to Whittaker Chambers, who had testified against Alger Hiss. In 1953 Parks again tried to rehabilitate himself by writing to HUAC and expressing not only his anti-communist sentiments but also his approval of the committee's work and his willingness to assist it. Between that time and his death in 1976, Parks appeared in only three more movies, all in supporting roles.

For additional reading, see Navasky's *Naming Names*. For a partial transcript of Parks' testimony before HUAC, see Bentley's THIRTY YEARS OF TREASON.

Passion of Josef D., The   A 1964 play by Paddy Chayefsky. The play was inspired in part by a visit Chayefsky made to the Soviet Union in 1959 under the auspices of the State Department and Union of Soviet Writers, during a thaw in the tensions occasioned by the ongoing second Berlin Crisis. Chayefsky was reported to be "almost uncontrollably angry in the discussion of writing and censorship," and *The Passion of Josef D.* presents a harsh view of Stalin and Soviet communism. The story centers on the 1917 Russian Revolution and its aftermath. It depicts the communist state substituting a new form of oppression and brutality for that of the czar whom it replaced. The central characters are Josef Stalin and his wife Nadya, and the action reveals Stalin's growing and increasingly violent desire for power. Even Nadya, who helped lead the Revolution, becomes victimized by the Soviet leader's brutality, but her love for him precludes her from retaliating. In the beginning of the play, Stalin is cynical and nihilistic, but he admits "I cannot endure to live without god." Lenin thus emerges as a god figure for him, because Lenin can "make one feel significant. That's all any man needs a god for." Ironically, Lenin dies believing that the Revolution has failed to change the basic beliefs of the people, concluding that it has been a meaningless illusion, a futile attempt to impose some sense of significance on life. The play concludes with Stalin coming to power and offering a prayer to Lenin. Thus the earlier worship of the czar has been replaced by worship of a new god figure. The play enjoyed only 15 performances on Broadway before closing. Chayefsky stated in a 1964 letter to Harold Taubman, "It is entirely possible that man will destroy himself in order to preserve his own identity. That was just what my play was about." (See also THEATER.)

For additional reading, see *Dictionary of Literary Biography* (vol. 7, *Twentieth-Century American Dramatists*).

Pasternak, Boris Leonidovich   A Soviet NOVELIST and POET. Born in 1890, Pasternak worked in the library of the Soviet Commissariat of Education after the 1917 Russian

Revolution. During that time he also wrote poetry, including his most important volume *My Sister, Life* (1922). His refusal to support the execution of Soviet generals in the early 1930s during one of the Stalinist purges led him to fear for his life, though in fact he suffered no repercussions. Nonetheless, he stopped writing poetry and turned instead to translation. In addition to translating into Russian works by writers from other nationalities in the U.S.S.R., Pasternak also translated literature by Goethe, Paul Verlaine, Ben Jonson, Shelley and Shakespeare. He returned to poetry in the 1940s when he wrote verse celebrating the Soviet successes against the Nazis. His novel DR. ZHIVAGO was originally accepted and then rejected by the official State Publishing House. The story centers on Dr. Yuri Zhivago, a married man who falls in love with Lara, another man's mistress, during World War I. The story becomes a tale of frustrated love as the hardships they endure because of the Russian Revolution keep Yuri and Lara apart. Before the Soviet rejection of *Zhivago*, its foreign rights had been sold to a publisher in Milan, who issued an Italian translation in 1957. Because of its unflattering portrayal of communism, the book was outlawed in the U.S.S.R. and highly praised in the United States, where it was published in English in 1958. In 1965 David Lean directed its adaptation into a FILM DRAMA starring Omar Sharif, Geraldine Chaplin, Julie Christie and Tom Courtenay.

Pasternak was awarded the 1958 Nobel Prize for literature but was not allowed to travel to Sweden to accept it. Instead, he was expelled from the Soviet Writers Union and denounced as a traitor in official publications. To avoid being exiled from the U.S.S.R., he refused to accept the Nobel Prize and wrote to Soviet Premier Nikita Khrushchev acknowledging his political weakness. He thus endured internal exile at the writers' colony in Peredelkino, near Moscow, until his death in 1960. He was later officially rehabilitated under Gorbachev.

Pattern for Survival A 1950 FILM DOCUMENTARY intended to prepare the United States for a possible atomic attack by an aggressor nation. Produced by the Cornell Film Company, the film is narrated in part by William L. LAURENCE, a Pulitzer Prize–winning science writer for the *New York Times*, the only newspaper JOURNALIST officially assigned to cover the development of the atomic bomb. The film describes how the bomb works and demonstrates its three forms of destruction: the shock wave, the heat wave and radioactive fallout. It then gives instructions for surviving an atomic attack and preparing a fallout shelter. The two-reel film was distributed in 16mm format for use by community, church and educational organizations.

Patton A 1970 MILITARY FILM starring George C. Scott, Karl Malden and Michael Bates and directed by Franklin J. Schaffner. Francis Ford Coppola wrote the screenplay, which was based on Ladislas Farago's biography, *Patton: Ordeal and Triumph* (1963), and General Omar Bradley's 1951 autobiography, *A Soldier's Story*. The Vietnam War–era film presents a complex biographical study of one of World War II's most successful, most feared and most controversial generals, George S. Patton Jr. (Scott). *Patton* depicts the general's career throughout the war: his victory over Germa-

ny's Field Marshal Erwin Rommel in North Africa; his invasion of Sicily, when he disobeyed orders to reach Messina before the British; his public humiliation for slapping a soldier suffering from battle fatigue; and his great successes in Europe after the 1944 D-Day invasion of Normandy—especially his rescue of the surrounded 101st Airborne Division during the Battle of the Bulge. The film concludes with Patton advocating that the United States should next invade the Soviet Union, whom he sees as our major postwar enemy. Shortly after the war's victorious conclusion, Patton dies in a car accident surrounded by suspicious circumstances.

Apart from the questions it raises about the soundness of Patton's proposals for the postwar era, *Patton* must also be considered in terms of its Vietnam War context. Made while President Nixon was reducing U.S. troop strength from its Johnson-era peak, but while the war was still being earnestly waged, the film takes a complex look at war, politics and leaders. It lets the audience weigh Patton's virtues against his shortcomings, depicting "Old Blood and Guts" to be a man of tremendous inner strength, determination and loyalty who could also be arrogant, cruel, impulsive and narrow of vision. In this respect, Scott's Patton approaches tragic dimensions; he is a great but flawed man capable of incredible achievements but also capable of destroying an entire civilization. Both prowar and antiwar critics found commendable sentiments in *Patton*. For instance, even though Scott considered it an antiwar film, President Nixon reportedly admired it greatly and saw it twice before ordering the 1970 U.S. invasion of Cambodia. *Patton* won six Academy Awards, including best director, best screenplay, best art, and best sound and film editing. Although Scott was chosen best actor, he declined to accept the award, having previously announced his opposition to such competitions. In 1986 Scott starred in a television sequel, *The Last Days of Patton*.

Paul Winter Jazz Sextet The group that gave the first White House JAZZ performance, on November 19, 1962. President Kennedy attended. Shortly before, the group had toured Central and South America under the State Department's Cultural Exchange Program, and their White House program included several pieces that incorporated Latin American influences, including the Brazilian bossa nova and a "Toccata" that Argentinean pianist Lalo Schiffrin had written for Dizzy Gillespie. Though the program had been planned before the nuclear showdown, it happened that the debut of jazz at the White House came only three weeks after the October Cuban Missile Crisis. The joyous Latin flavor of the MUSIC must have acquired special significance for Kennedy and other Missile Crisis veterans in the audience.

Pau-Llosa, Ricardo An EXILED WRITER (to the United States). Born in Havana in 1954, Pau-Llosa left Cuba as a child when his family immigrated to the United States to escape the Castro regime. A POET, literary critic and art historian, he taught at Florida International University in Miami and became senior editor of *Art International*. In 1973, he published a bilingual volume of poetry, *Twenty-Five Poems*. In 1983, he published in English another volume, *Sorting Metaphors*.

For additional reading, see Tucker's *Literary Exile in the Twentieth Century.*

Peacemakers, The   A 1960 APOCALYPTIC NOVEL by C. S. Casewit. Written during the middle of the second Berlin Crisis, one of the most threatening moments of the Cold War, the story centers on Rick Ames, a nuclear physicist who joins a group of scientists taking refuge on a secluded island from a global nuclear war. The fascist General Puckett rules the island, but Ames employs his scientific talents to overthrow him. However, unlike the hydrogen bomb that Ames helped develop, Ames's new weapon is not lethal. Thus the scientist has learned from the NUCLEAR APOCALYPSE to be more responsible for what he develops. (See also SCIENCE FICTION NOVELS AND STORIES.)

For additional reading, see Dowling's *Fictions of Nuclear Disaster.*

Pearson, Drew   A JOURNALIST. Pearson was a pioneer of investigative journalism. Born in 1897, he attended the Phillips Exeter Academy and graduated from Swarthmore College in 1918. He then served for two years in Siberia with the American Friends Service Committee. In 1925 Pearson became foreign editor of the *United States Daily,* which eventually became *U.S. News and World Report.* He later joined the Washington bureau of the *Baltimore Sun,* where he met Robert S. Allen of the *Christian Science Monitor.* In 1931 the two men anonymously published *Washington Merry Go-Round,* a book containing gossip about Washington figures. They published a sequel in 1932. These became the basis of the syndicated newspaper column they began that year after losing their jobs when their authorship of the popular books finally became known. Originally distributed to only 12 papers, by 1942, the year Allen left to join the army, *Washington Merry Go-Round* appeared in over 350 newspapers, and the columnists were featured on radio. Some 600 papers ran the column by the time of Pearson's death in 1969.

Pearson drew the ire of politicians across the political spectrum. President Roosevelt called him a "chronic liar" and President Truman labeled him an "S.O.B." On the other hand, Pearson was among the first journalists to openly attack Senator Joseph McCarthy and his RED SCARE tactics. McCarthy literally attacked him back, once kicking him in the groin and then later boasting about it. Pearson reported that Attorney General Robert F. Kennedy had authorized electronic surveillance of civil rights leader Martin Luther King Jr., and his investigative reporting revealed information that led to the censure of Senator Thomas Dodd and the removal of Congressman Adam Clayton Powell for their improper financial dealings. During the Kennedy administration, Pearson interviewed Soviet premier Nikita Khrushchev and attempted to convince the president to modify his harsh stand against the Soviets. Pearson also advised President Johnson. In the final 10 years of his life, Pearson was joined by Jack Anderson, who took over the column when Pearson died.

"Pentagon"   A TELEVISION NEWS SHOW that ran on the DuMont network from 1951 to 1952. This show featured interviews with high-ranking Pentagon officials, who discussed the progress of the Korean War with reporters. "Battle Report," which ran from 1950 to 1952, provided similar war coverage for NBC.

"Pentagon U.S.A."   A TELEVISION MILITARY DRAMA anthology that ran on CBS during the summer of 1953. Appearing just a few months after the conclusion of the Korean War, the dramas presented cases adapted from the files of the U.S. Army's Criminal Investigation Division. Robert Pastene starred as the Colonel.

People to People Program   A program established by the Eisenhower administration to promote cultural exchange. In addition to bringing foreign artists to the United States, the program encouraged American performers to enter foreign competitions. That policy's notable success occurred in 1958, when Van CLIBURN entered and won the Tchaikovsky competition in Moscow.

"Phil Silvers Show, The"   A TELEVISION SITUATION COMEDY that ran on CBS from 1955 to 1959. This comedic representation of the American peacetime army featured the exploits of conniving Sergeant Ernie Bilko (Phil Silvers), who ran the motor pool at Fort Baxter, Kansas. A con man who could talk his way out of almost anything, Bilko bullied his subordinates into participating in his various, wild money-making schemes. He was a constant irritant to the fort's strait-laced commander, Colonel John Hall (Paul Ford). The show's original title, "You'll Never Get Rich," became the subtitle after the first two months. The name Bilko was reputed to have been taken from the Chicago Cubs baseball player, Steve Bilko, a favorite of the show's creator, Nat Hiken. It also, of course, evoked the word *bilk.* In 1996, the show became the basis of a movie, *Sergeant Bilko,* starring Steve Martin.

Philbrick, Herbert   A NONFICTION WRITER of the best-selling book, I LED THREE LIVES (1952), and the star character in the syndicated TELEVISION SPY SHOW by the same name, which ran from 1953 to 1956. Philbrick's book describes his experiences as a U.S. government infiltrator into the American Communist Party. An undercover agent since 1940, Philbrick had risen to the party's middle ranks, eventually becoming a member of a secret communist cell and one of the education directors for the New England region. At the same time, he retained his profession as a Boston advertising executive. Thus his three lives were as a businessman and ordinary citizen, a Communist Party member and an FBI spy.

I Led Three Lives provides a detailed firsthand account of how the Communist Party manipulated and took over front organizations, as well as other details of the party's day-to-day operations. Philbrick expressed shock and distress at how people he least expected to be communists belonged to the party. Therefore, he concluded, no one could ever be sure whether a friend, relative or acquaintance was a communist. This widely shared uncertainty fueled the RED SCARE, which Philbrick deplored but to which his story nonetheless contributed. Philbrick cautions anti-communists that not all communist front organizations are the same (he describes four distinct kinds) and that "Blanket condemnations such as those of the [HOUSE COMMITTEE ON UN-AMERI-CAN ACTIVITIES], which black-list entire organizations because of the presence of a few Communists, frequently harms innocent persons. Guilt by association merely strengthens the hand of agitators in their attacks upon the infringements of civil liberties." Philbrick opposed the Mundt-Nixon bill to outlaw the Communist Party because he feared that driving the party underground would make it even more difficult to infiltrate and monitor. He concludes the book by asserting,

> The most important single thing is to avoid behaving the way a Communist says the individual must behave in a capitalist society. If the Communist had his way, he would force all non-Communists to the extreme right, toward fascism and state control . . . thus creating the demand for a violent revolution as the only possible cure . . . If we adhere to our traditional American dream of a society of freedom, of personal rather than state responsibility . . . of civil rights rather than rigid civil controls, then we will have disproved the Communist theory of the inevitability of capitalist deterioration.

Philbrick's courtroom testimony and the highly popular book and television show contributed significantly to the popular perception that a large body of communist subversives were actively seeking to undermine the U.S. government and American institutions, even though party membership had dropped from 80,000 immediately after World War II to about 5,000—and so many of those were FBI agents that in 1957 FBI director J. Edgar Hoover considered taking control of the party by having all of his informants support one faction at the Communist Party national convention.

Philbrick gave up his cover in 1949 when he testified against 11 Communist Party leaders who were being tried under the Smith Act for conspiring to advocate violent revolution. In all his years as an FBI informer, Philbrick had never discovered any violent or criminal acts; nor had he met any of the 11 defendants at the Foley Square trial in New York. However, like other prosecution witnesses, he read passages from Lenin to support the claim that the defendants advocated violence against America. Stating that Lenin's *State and Revolution* had been used in classes he had attended, Philbrick excerpted a passage for testimony: "The replacement of the bourgeois by the proletarian state is impossible without violent revolution." Despite the prosecution's failure to demonstrate the "clear and present danger" that was the established standard, the defendants were found guilty, and the Supreme Court upheld their convictions despite dissenting opinions by Associate Justices William O. Douglas and Hugo Black. Subsequently Philbrick wrote *I Led Three Lives* and lectured throughout the country on such topics as "The Red Underground Today," "Christianity versus Communism" and "Communism and Youth." He also wrote a regular column for the *New York Herald-Tribune,* published a monthly newsletter and became an American hero. Boston even held a parade to honor him. Philbrick died in 1996.

The television show claimed that each episode was based on fact, though the names, dates and places had been changed "for obvious reasons." However, the plots were far more sensational than warranted by Philbrick's actual field reports to the FBI. As a party member, Philbrick (played by Richard Carlson) was constantly being called on to participate in schemes to undermine the United States, ranging from acts of sabotage, espionage and dope-smuggling to infiltrating labor unions, university faculties and churches to spread the party line. The Philbrick character was in constant danger. On the one hand he risked death if his Communist Party colleagues discovered him; on the other hand, friends and neighbors were always wondering if he might be a communist. Philbrick himself reviewed all of the scripts, acted as a consultant and was otherwise closely involved in the show's production.

For additional reading, see Whitfield's *The Culture of the Cold War* and Navasky's *Naming Names.*

Pickup on South Street A 1953 FILM DRAMA starring Richard Widmark, Jean Peters, Richard Kiley and Thelma Ritter, written and directed by Samuel FULLER. Filmed in *film noir* style, the plot centers on a pickpocket who unintentionally steals a microfilm intended to provide atomic secrets to the Soviets. The pickpocket then becomes the target of communist agents so brutal that ordinary criminals look honorable by comparison. Eventually the cynical criminal sides with the FBI to thwart the enemy spies. Fuller collaborated on the screenplay of *The Capetown Affair,* a 1967 remake of *Pickup.* (See also FILMS ASSOCIATED WITH THE RED SCARE.)

For additional reading, see Server's *Sam Fuller: Film is a Battleground.*

Pink Floyd The Wall A 1982 British-made film musical starring Bob Geldof, Christine Hargreaves, James Laurenson and Bob Hoskins and directed by Alan Parker. Roger Waters wrote the screenplay and the MUSIC; Gerald Scarfe was the animation designer; the ROCK AND ROLL band Pink Floyd performed the music. A kind of rock opera, *The Wall* tells the story of Pink, a burnt-out rock star who grew up alienated, neglected and unloved during World War II. (His only friend is a pet rat, who dies.) By the time Pink becomes a young adult and a rock star, he has encased himself within an emotional wall—one of the many uses of the wall metaphor throughout the film. After a nearly lethal drug overdose, he pulls himself together to go on stage and lead a neofascist hate rally. The film mixes live action with animation to criticize middle-class institutions, especially public schools, whose severe and hypocritical teachers attempt to mass-produce conformist, dispirited citizens. The schools themselves are described as "just another brick in the wall" in the hit song "We Don't Need No Education." The animation also effectively portrays the chain of human violence going from World War II, when Pink's father was killed, to neo-fascist behavior by contemporary working-class and unemployed citizens. The sound track became a best-selling album that remained popular throughout the Cold War. Though the film does not directly address Cold War conflicts, it powerfully projects the emotional carnage wrought by war-oriented, violence-prone, industrialized postwar society. Pink Floyd performed *The Wall* live at the Berlin Wall after East Germany deposed its communist government in 1989.

Planet of the Apes, The A 1968 SCIENCE FICTION FILM starring Charlton Heston, Roddy McDowall and Kim Hunter, directed by Franklin J. Schaffner and written by Michael Wilson and Rod Serling. Based on the 1963 novel by Pierre Boulle, the author of THE BRIDGE OVER THE RIVER KWAI (1952), the film portrays the human crew of a spaceship that has been gone for many years on an extended voyage. But before they can complete their mission, they crash onto an unidentified planet. The survivors discover what appears to be a tribe of Stone Age humans foraging for food. To the astronauts' surprise, however, the dominant species is a militarized, fascistic society of intelligent apes who have subjugated the planet's human inhabitants. The ensuing plot requires the astronauts to try to escape. But as Heston rides away, he sees the remnants of the Statue of Liberty sinking into the sand; he and the audience realize that the planet of the apes is the long-term result of a nuclear war. Therefore, no ultimate escape is possible.

The film appeared at a time when fears of nuclear warfare had subsided considerably from earlier in the decade. However, the Vietnam War was still escalating when the film was released, and its pacifist message gave the film some antiwar appeal. *The Planet of the Apes* also drew on the growing interest in the space race, since by 1968 the Apollo missions were on the verge of placing a person on the moon. (See also APOCALYPTIC FILMS.)

Platoon A 1986 VIETNAM WAR FILM starring Tom Berenger, Willem Dafoe and Charlie Sheen and written and directed by Oliver STONE, a Vietnam veteran. The film centers on Chris (Sheen), a recruit who arrives in Vietnam and quickly finds his new platoon divided by deep personal differences. One group is led by Sergeant Barnes (Berenger), who is immoral, cynical and corrupt but a very skilled fighter. The other group coalesces behind Sergeant Elias, an equally effective soldier who has retained a considerably greater degree of compassion and humanity. For the members of Chris's platoon, the enemy thus becomes not only the Viet Cong but also their comrades-in-arms. Chris feels caught in a "battle for possession of my soul."

The first of the third wave of Vietnam War films, *Platoon* does not take a strong ideological position on the war itself. However, it depicts the combat and jungle experience in exquisite detail and reveals heroism to be motivated more by terror and desperation than by dedication to a noble cause. In casting Sheen as a central character, Stone invited comparison to APOCALYPSE NOW, which starred Charlie's father, Martin.

For additional reading, see Kagan's *The Cinema of Oliver Stone.*

Playboy A men's MAGAZINE founded by Hugh Hefner in 1953. In the 1970s, *Playboy* had over six million subscribers, and in 1990, at the end of the Cold War, management estimated that one in nine American men read it. The magazine features photos, including a centerfold pinup poster of nude women ("Playmates") as well as humor, sex-oriented cartoons, fiction, feature articles and interviews on a range of social, political and cultural issues. The magazine contains upscale advertising and appeals to affluent, cosmo-

Playboy, *March 1964.* Reproduced by special permission of *Playboy* magazine; copyright © 1964 by *Playboy.*

politan tastes. Marilyn MONROE was the Sweetheart of the Month in the premiere issue.

Playboy's influence on Cold War culture was twofold. First, it represented fundamental differences between the open capitalistic Western societies where it was published (there are a number of foreign editions) and the authoritarian communist governments that banned it. Not only did the communists object to the publication of nude photos and sexually oriented material, which they regarded as morally degenerate, they also decried the magazine's promulgation of a "decadent" consumer culture that promoted luxury items and bourgeois attitudes. By contrast, though many conservatives and religious figures agreed with the communist critique, the very fact that the United States and other democracies permitted the publication of the controversial magazine illustrated the considerably greater freedom of the press enjoyed in the West.

Moreover, especially during the Kennedy years, many American men and women were attracted to *Playboy*'s image of the modern man as tasteful, knowledgeable, cultured, urbane, well dressed and coiffed, open about his sexuality. Hefner cultivated that image for himself, as did the men depicted in advertisements and featured in the articles. This vision of the ideal man clashed with the proclaimed communist ideal of the devoted laborer in work clothes who is dedicated to serving the cause of the people. Likewise, *Playboy*'s ideal woman is sexually active and also active during sex, which she unabashedly enjoys. She feels confident about herself sexually and has her own interests, goals and aspirations. Although she subordinates herself to men, she is neither passive nor dull. During the Cold War, she was seen to contrast with the idealized Soviet woman, who was revered for her ability to work hard, nurture her children, and partner her mate as both strove to build a better society. These idealized *Playboy* men and women found counterparts in the James Bond SPY NOVELS first published by Ian Fleming in 1953, the year of *Playboy*'s first issue. Fleming later published original Bond stories in the magazine. (James Bond SPY FILMS likewise fit this image.)

In addition to highlighting basic differences between capitalist and communist cultures, *Playboy* also influenced domestic politics by promoting liberal values and positions. Early issues criticized the HOUSE COMMITTEE ON UN-AMERICAN ACTIVITIES (HUAC) and J. Edgar Hoover and defended the American Civil Liberties Union. Later issues criticized the Vietnam War and supported the sexual revolution. In a 1970s issue, Jimmy Carter, a born-again Christian, acknowledged that he had lusted after women "in his heart," a controversial pronouncement that drew criticism from the right and mockery from the left. The magazine has been criticized on both the left and right for its nude photos and sexual orientation. The right denounced it on moral grounds and accused it of undermining wholesome American values. But leftists and progressives saw it as dangerous consumerist, individualist and shallow. In 1962 a Unitarian minister complained:

> *Playboy* comes close now to qualifying as a movement, as well as a magazine. It strikes me that *Playboy* is a religious magazine. It tells its readers how to get into heaven. It tells them what is important in life, delineates ethics for them, tells them how to relate to others, tells them what to lavish their attention and energy upon, gives them a model of the kind of person to be. It expresses a consistent world view, a system of values, a philosophical outlook.

Hefner endorsed what the minister intended as criticism and later that year began his own column to spell out "The Playboy Philosophy."

Feminists also attacked the magazine during the 1960s and 1970s for exploiting women's bodies and reducing women to sexual objects. Defenders of *Playboy* countered that the magazine celebrated the sexuality and sexual freedom of both women and men. Because the Playmates have identities, describe their intellectual interests, appear happy and enthusiastic, and look confidently at the camera, the defenders claimed that the photos were not degrading. Hefner pointed out in 1967, "We are not interested in the mysterious, difficult woman, the *femme fatale*, who wears elegant underwear with lace. She is sad, and somehow mentally filthy."

Playboy's fiction and essays included pieces by and about the world's most respected writers, thinkers and artists, among them Vladimir Nabokov, Norman MAILER, Jean-Paul Sartre, Terry SOUTHERN, Federico Fellini, Bertrand Russell and Miles Davis. The magazine also endorsed JAZZ and other artistic forms favored by the avant-garde. It thus provided a middle-American audience for many figures who otherwise typically reached a narrower, more liberal, and better-educated audience.

For additional reading, see the Sterns' *Encyclopedia of Pop Culture*.

Plot, The A 1967 POLITICAL NOVEL by Irving Wallace. A best-selling writer known for his steamy romances, Wallace received guarantees for a $60,000 publicity budget for this novel, a Book of the Month Club alternative. The book provides a lurid "behind-the-scenes" view of Cold War politics that depicts the top figures of world power as sensual and self-indulgent and explores the relationships between sexual and international relations. The novel takes place against the background of such events as the Kennedy assassination, the split between China and the U.S.S.R., and the beginnings of détente, and it treats such figures as Dwight Eisenhower, Alger Hiss and Christine Keeler, a central figure in a major British sex scandal of the 1960s. (See also LITERATURE ABOUT COLD WAR EVENTS.)

Poets Though the poetry of other eras routinely regarded politics, warfare and national concerns as appropriate subject matter, the tendency in late 20th-century poetry has been to move away from social and political issues toward personal expression. Ironically, this trend came at a time when the restrictions on poetic diction and subject matter had been almost entirely removed. When a federal court ruled in 1957 that Allen GINSBERG's "Howl" was not obscene, it finally eliminated legal prohibitions against foul language and subject matter. The GROVE PRESS, which reprinted "Howl," further extended the limits of acceptable language when it successfully defended its publication of D. H. Lawrence's *Lady Chatterley's Lover* in 1959 and Henry Miller's *Tropic of Cancer* in 1964.

Yet a common response of postwar writers to the horrors of the age was to turn away from the depressing and overwhelming social and political matters over which they held no control and to turn instead to personal expression and self-exploration, areas where they could imagine making a difference. Poets were especially likely to focus on the personal; hence, there is relatively little Cold War–related poetry, except for work from the BEAT MOVEMENT. Throughout the 1950s and early 1960s, Beat poets rejected what they saw as growing U.S. militarism, bureaucracy, social conformity and government intrusion. They also objected to the way corporations and the emerging class of technocrats were eroding traditional humanistic and moral values in favor of what Gregory CORSO called "calculative thinking"—the attempt to quantify experience and to value only what stands up to statistical analysis and cost-benefit ratios. According to the Beats, such calculative thinking permitted atrocities and gave rise to such military adventures as the Vietnam War, as well as stifling sexuality and dulling the creative powers of the unconscious, which are the ultimate source of each individual's greatest spiritual fulfillment and are thus the best hope for a dynamic, invigorated and invigorating society.

The Beat poets rebelled against the constraints of formal poetry and fiction as a means of overcoming the social and political restrictions of middle-class American society. Whereas modernist literature from the earlier part of the century was highly cerebral and often celebrated social order and political conservatism (Ezra POUND's sestinas and his support of fascism represent the extreme of the modernist call for order), the Beats celebrated a liberal outpouring of emotion unfettered by structure or analysis, and they generally endorsed leftist political positions. In many ways, Beat literature harkens back to the Dadaism of the early 20th century, though it is more concerned with attacking the culture of calculative thinking than with assaulting meaning per se. Like the Dadaists, the Beats favored poetry readings in addition to publishing their work in written form, and they sought to bring poetry to ordinary citizens. Their "performance poetry" led to the HAPPENINGS of the later 1960s in which poets and artists made political statements through theatrical gestures. Ginsberg and NOVELIST Jack Kerouac were among the Beat movement's earliest founders. Other prominent Beat poets included Corso, who joined the Beats in 1951, Lawrence FERLINGHETTI and Kenneth Rexroth.

The United States tested its first hydrogen bomb in 1952, and nuclear weapons became a frequent target of the Beat poets. Ginsberg employed the coarse language of obscenity to express his feelings about the bomb, which he saw as far more obscene than any word or image in existence. Refined or rational language is simply inadequate for conveying what he wants to communicate. Thus in "America" (1956) he declares, "Go fuck yourself with your atom bomb." Ferlinghetti's *A Coney Island of the Mind* (1958), published at the outset of the second Berlin Crisis when the prospects for nuclear war among the superpowers seemed virtually inevitable, depicts the probable nuclear destruction of people, nature and machines: "Oh it was a spring/ of fur leaves and cobalt flowers/ when cadillacs fell through the trees like rain/ drowning the meadows with madness/ while out of every imitation cloud/ dropped myriad wingless crowds/ of nutless nagasaki survivors." Corso's poem "Bomb" (1960), which also appeared during the Berlin crisis, likewise describes the immense damage to nature that nuclear war would create: "Turtles exploding over Istanbul/ The jaguar's flying foot/ soon to sink in arctic snow/ Penguins plunged against the sphinx/ The top of the Empire State/ arrowed in a broccoli field in Sicily."

Though the Beats were more political than any other group of early Cold War American poets, they were not the only ones to consider nuclear issues and the prospects for war. As early as 1947, Richard Wilbur wrote about the way war creates a disastrous momentum of its own in "Grace": "Even fraction-of-a second action is not wrecked/ By a graceful still reserve. To be unchecked/ Is needful then: choose, challenge, jump, poise, run . . ./ Nevertheless, the praiseful graceful soldier/ Shouldn't be fired by his gun." And in 1951, Adrienne Rich admonished in "The Uncle Speaks in the Drawing Room": ". . . Let us only bear in mind/ How these treasures handed down/ From a calmer age passed on/ Are in the keeping of our kind./ We stand between the dead glass-blowers/ And murmurings of missile-throwers." In "Fall, 1961," Robert Lowell expressed his sense of impotence during the second Berlin Crisis, when U.S. and Soviet tanks faced each other, the Soviets ended

their voluntary moratorium on nuclear testing, and East Germany and erected the Berlin Wall: "All autumn, the chafe and jar/ of nuclear war;/ we have talked our extinction to death./ I swim like a minnow/ behind my studio window." And in "Gunnery Practice, Seaside, Oregon, August 16, 1961," Charles Gullans, writing about the same crisis, expressed frustration at the inability to stop what appears to be an unfolding disaster:

> The heavy guns that shudder through the day,
> Miles up the coast, are not so far away.
> Nations rearm with steel and with cold nerve.
> I sit here doing nothing. I observe:
> The beach, fine rubble, detritus of war
> Between the assaulting water and the shore;
> Guns that as pointlessly assault the air,
> Precisely mimicking what they prepare,
> Terror of battles that erode mankind.

The following year saw the Cuban Missile Crisis, when the two nuclear superpowers confronted each other "eye to eye." Mark Strand considered the situation in "When the Vacation Is Over for Good":

> It will be strange
> Knowing at last it couldn't go on forever,
> The certain voice telling us over and over
> That nothing would change . . .
>
> When, in a flash
> The weather turned, and the lofty air became
> Unbearably heavy, the wind strikingly dumb
> And our cities like ash . . .
>
> And even then,
> Because we will not have changed much, wondering what
> Will become of things, and who will be left to do it
> All over again,
> And somehow trying,
> But still unable, to know just what it was
> That went so completely wrong, or why it is
> We are drying.

The Missile Crisis also inspired Dave Smith's "Cuba Night," which was written after Kennedy declared the United States would risk war to prevent a Soviet Cuba. In the same vein, David Ingatow's 1964 poem "Simultaneously" imagines U.S. and Soviet nuclear missiles passing en route to their respective targets. (See also LITERATURE ABOUT COLD WAR EVENTS.)

A slightly earlier poem that deals with nuclear weaponry is William Stafford's AT THE BOMB TESTING SITE (1960), which describes an atomic test from the viewpoint of a lizard. *The Nightmare Considered,* a 1991 anthology of nuclear-related literary criticism edited by Nancy Anisfield, includes excerpts from and discussions of poems published in the alternative literary journal *Samisdat,* which Merritt Clifton edited from 1973 to 1989. Among the poets featured in *Samisdat* are Margaret Key Biggs and W. D. Erhardt. Nina Langley and Betsy Shipley edited the antinuclear anthology *Meltdown: Poems From the Core* (1980), and Morty Sklar edited *Nuke-Rebuke* (1983), an anthology that includes work by 65 writers, poets, artists and photographers and features a poem by Hayashi Kyoko, a Hiroshima woman who prayed for deliverance from an impending rape and received it when the atomic bomb exploded immediately afterward. *Peace Is Our Profession: Poems and Passages of War Protest,* a 1981 anthology edited by Jan Barry, also contains poetry dealing with the nuclear threat. Barry discusses the collection in *The Nightmare Considered.* Other nuclear-related poetry includes Howard Nemerov's "Boom," Maya Angelou's "On a Bright Day, Next Week," Nicholas P. Smith's "The Great Nuclear War of 1994" and Peter Porter's "Your Attention Please." John Updike criticizes the U.S. military buildup in his poem "Air Show."

During the 1960s, the Beat movement evolved into or was absorbed by the COUNTERCULTURE, which grew up around the protest to the Vietnam War. Ginsberg, Ferlinghetti and other Beat writers were early, vocal critics of the war. Other antiwar poets include Denise LEVERTOV, Robert BLY and Daniel BERRIGAN. Levertov participated in antiwar demonstrations and eventually traveled to Hanoi. Her husband, Mitchell Goodman, was a codefendant with Dr. Benjamin Spock in a highly publicized trial of draft resisters. Levertov's first antiwar poetry appeared in the final section of *The Sorrow Dance* (1967), entitled "Life at War." The poems evoke powerful images of the innocent victims of the war and express her rage at the perpetrators of the horror: "You who go out on schedule/ to kill, do you know/ there are eyes that watch you,/ eyes whose lids you burned off," and "the scheduled breaking open of breasts whose milk/ runs out over the entrails of still-alive babies." That year Levertov also edited *Out of the War Shadow: An Anthology of Current Poetry* published by the War Resisters League. *Relearning the Alphabet* (1970) addresses such contemporary issues as the war and war resisters, starvation in Biafra and race riots in Detroit. *To Stay Alive* (1971) collected Levertov's war poetry to date within a single volume so those poems might serve "as a document of some historical value, a record of one person's inner/outer experience in America during the '60s and the beginning of the '70s."

Bly, who believes that the warlike expressions of violence stem from spiritual disharmony within the unconscious, also wrote forcefully about the Vietnam War. In 1966 he coedited with David Ray a volume entitled, *A Poetry Reading Against the Vietnam War.* His second book of poetry, *The Light Around the Body* (1967), includes introspective poems that celebrate the unconscious and more explicit attacks on the war and other aspects of American Cold War politics. These latter include "Johnson's Cabinet Watched by Ants," "Those Being Eaten by America," "Listening to President Kennedy Lie about the Cuban Invasion," "The Great Society," "Asian Peace Offers Rejected without Publication," "Hatred of Men with Black Hair" and "Driving through Minnesota during the Hanoi Bombings."

Berrigan, a priest and political activist as well as a poet, served a prison sentence for his role in destroying draft records in Catonsville, Maryland, in 1968. His experiences became the basis for his play, *The Trial of the Catonsville Nine* (1970). After the war he worked with Thich Nhat Hahn, a Buddhist monk, to facilitate a reconciliation between the people of the United States and Vietnam. Throughout the rest of the Cold War he continued to protest nuclear warfare and participate in several demonstrations. His first book to address political issues was *No One Walks Waters* (1966), which includes such poems as "Holy Week, 1965 (The Vietnam Raids Go On)" and "A Pittsburgh Beggar Reminds Me of the Dead of Hiroshima." In 1968, Berrigan published *Night Flight To Hanoi,* which includes "Children in the Shelter," a description of his experience with three children in a Hanoi bomb shelter.

TRAN THI NGA and Wendy Wilder Larsen coauthored the best-selling SHALLOW GRAVES (1986), a collection of poems modeled on the Vietnamese *truyen,* a novel in verse. Written between 1980 and 1985, *Shallow Graves* addresses the lives of women and noncombat personnel during the Vietnam War.

On the other hand, Walter MCDONALD served in the war as an air force pilot, the perspective from which he describes the war. "Al Croom" is about a pilot who was always "daring the Russian/ rockets/ to do him in" but "When they shipped him home/ it took triple straps/ to bind him." And "Veteran" describes an ex-soldier with aluminum legs who imagines that "leaves lie in the park/ like tiny bombs/ ready to explode. Someday/ someone raking/ will strike a fuse. We'll all be killed." McDonald's *After the Noise of Saigon* (1988) includes "The Food Pickers," which describes the Vietnamese civilians who scraped for food remains, and "War Games," which depicts men who played with imaginary dice while "rockets that crashed down/ on the base always killed somebody else."

Other American poets to write against the war include Robert Duncan and James Wright. And other Vietnam War poems are collected in *Vietnam Anthology* (1987) edited by Nancy Anisfield. (See also VIETNAM WAR LITERATURE.)

Among the exiled poets who came to the United States, several wrote movingly about persecution "behind the Iron Curtain." The Soviet poet Irina RATUSHINSKAYA describes her experiences in a labor camp for political prisoners in *Beyond the Limit* (1987). According to one of her translators, the poems were "written with a sharpened matchstick on a bar of soap. When they were memorized, the poet washed her hands and the palimpsest was erased. The poems were composed sporadically over a period of 14 months." Other emigré poets from communist countries who published in English include Nobel Prize winners Joseph BRODSKY (U.S.S.R.) and Czeslaw MILOSZ (Poland), Andrei CODRESCU (Romania) and Dorin TUDORAN (Romania), and the Cubans Pablo MEDINA and Armando VALLADARES. (See also EXILED WRITERS.)

For additional reading, see von Hallberg's *American Poetry and Culture, 1945–1980* and Anisfield's *The Nightmare Considered.*

Polanski, Roman A French-born FILM DIRECTOR. Polanski's family were Polish Jews, and when he was a child they returned to Poland. During World War II, his parents were incarcerated in concentration camps, where his mother died. In 1954 Polanski was accepted into the Lodz Film School, and one of his student films, *Two Men and a Wardrobe* (1958), received international prizes. His first feature-length film, *Knife in the Water* (1962), was poorly received by the Polish government but was greeted enthusiastically in Western Europe and the United States, where it received an Academy Award nomination in 1962. Polanski subsequently moved to England where he made such dark comedies as *Cul-de-Sac* (1966) and *The Fearless Vampire Killers* (1967) whose costar, Sharon Tate, he married in 1968. That year he also made his first American film, *Rosemary's Baby*. The following year, Tate and three of her friends were murdered by members of the Charles Manson cult. Subsequent Polanski films include *Macbeth* (1971), *Chinatown* (1974) and *Tess* (1979). He also acted in *The Magic Christian*, a 1970 FILM SATIRE written by Terry SOUTHERN that stars Peter SELLERS and Ringo Starr and spoofs greed and wealth. In 1979, Polanski was arrested in the United States for an unlawful sexual affair with a 13-year-old girl. After spending 42 days in prison under observation, he was released. Shortly afterward he fled the country. He continued working in Europe, including Poland. Polanski was a lifelong friend of NOVELIST Jerzy KOSINSKI.

political films   Films that explicitly dealt with Cold War ideology and political issues were rarely big successes at the box office; consequently, relatively few appeared before the American public during the Cold War. In this respect, American movies differed considerably from Soviet cinema, which frequently dealt with social issues, rejecting the capitalist notion of film as primarily a vehicle for entertainment via escapist fantasy. Avoiding politics was an especially prudent option during the RED SCARE of the late 1940s and 1950s, when "Share and share alike—isn't that right?" could be credibly cited by an "expert" before the HOUSE COMMITTEE ON UN-AMERICAN ACTIVITIES (HUAC) as evidence of communist values in an American movie (Lela Rogers' testimony in 1947), and when Ayn RAND's widely circulated SCREEN GUIDE FOR AMERICANS cautioned directors not to "smear" industrialists, success or the free enterprise system, "deify the common man," "show that poverty is a virtue" or suggest that "failure is noble." (The *Screen Guide* was originally published by the right-wing MOTION PICTURE ALLIANCE FOR THE PRESERVATION OF AMERICAN IDEALS and then reprinted in the *New York Times* and other leading newspapers.)

Thus during the 1950s, the only political films of note were Elia Kazan's VIVA ZAPATA! (1951), which celebrates the Mexican revolutionary war hero and treats such potentially controversial issues as land reform; THE QUIET AMERICAN (1958), which reverses the criticism of U.S. activities in Southeast Asia found in the original 1955 POLITICAL NOVEL by Graham GREENE; and SALT OF THE EARTH (1954), an independently made docu-drama about a strike by Mexican-American zinc workers. Financed by the striking union itself, *Salt of the Earth* was directed by HOLLYWOOD TEN member Herbert BIBERMAN and employed several black-listed actors. In 1960 HUAC defended itself in OPERATION ABOLITION, a film documentary that attempts to prove that anti-HUAC demonstrators at a San Francisco hearing were sponsored by communists and traitors. Included within *Operation Abolition* is footage unrelated to that demonstration.

As the Red Scare abated with the election of Kennedy in 1960, more films about Cold War political issues appeared. ADVISE AND CONSENT (1962), THE MANCHURIAN CANDIDATE (1962) and THE UGLY AMERICAN (1962) are Kennedy-era films based on best-selling novels. Based on the novel by conservative NOVELIST Allen DRURY, *Advise and Consent* centers on the Senate confirmation hearings on a liberal nominee for secretary of state. *The Manchurian Candidate* tells about the stepson of a right-wing senator whom the communists capture during the Korean War, brainwash and turn into a mind-controlled assassin. The senator clearly alludes to Joseph McCarthy, and the film suggests that McCarthyites and others behind the Red Scare pose a stronger danger to U.S. democracy than do the communists. The film also seems to anticipate the Kennedy assassination, which occurred a year after *The Manchurian Candidate* was released. Like *The Quiet American, The Ugly American* centers on U.S. diplomacy in Southeast Asia. It depicts an arrogant U.S. ambassador in a fictitious Southeast Asian country that communist insurgents are winning over through dedication, hard work, self-sacrifice and ideological commitment. The book appeared in 1958, and the film opened in 1962, when communist insurgency in Laos was a current concern and the U.S. military involvement in Vietnam was beginning to escalate.

The nuclear threat was a frequent topic of Cold War political films. Released the year after Kennedy's death, SEVEN DAYS IN MAY (1964) features a narrowly averted coup by U.S. right-wing military officers. FAIL-SAFE (1964) imagines the diplomacy required after the United States launches an accidental nuclear strike against the U.S.S.R. The FILM SATIRE, DR. STRANGELOVE (1964), also presents an unauthorized U.S. first strike.

Following is a review of other key U.S. films about Cold War politics: THE KREMLIN LETTER was made in 1970, at the beginning of the U.S.-Soviet détente and during the final stages of China's Cultural Revolution but before the thawing in the U.S.-Sino relationship. The film centers on a diplomatic proposal from the United States to the U.S.S.R. that the two superpowers cooperate in annihilating China. THE PRESIDENT'S PLANE IS MISSING (1971), based on the 1967 best-selling novel by Robert Serling, centers on the disappearance of the presidential plane at a time when Chinese communists are threatening nuclear war. Appearing shortly after Nixon's resignation from the presidency, ALL THE PRESIDENT'S MEN (1976) tells the story of how two newspaper JOURNALISTS uncovered the Watergate cover-up. Constantin COSTA-GAVRAS made several Cold War political films during the 1970s and 1980s, notably THE CONFESSION (1970), about a show trial behind the Iron Curtain; STATE OF SIEGE (1973), about U.S. support for a Latin American dictatorship; and MISSING (1982), which alludes to the 1973 military coup that, with covert aid from the United States, overthrew the freely elected government of Marxist president Salvador Allende. NINETEEN EIGHTY-FOUR (1984) depicts George ORWELL's totalitarian nightmare.

Alex's Cox's 1987 surreal film satire WALKER (1987) is the story of William Walker, the 19th-century American adventurer who invaded Nicaragua with 58 men and became that country's ruler between 1856 and 1857. Made with the cooperation of Nicaragua's Sandinistas, who were then resisting efforts by the CIA and U.S.-backed contras to overthrow them and who had feared a U.S. invasion only a few years earlier, the film focuses on the outlandish bravado of a power-crazed American who once took over the country. Made just before the congressional hearings into the Iran-contra affair, the film benefited from the timeliness of those hearings and unanticipated comparisons between William Walker and Colonel Oliver North. During the Bush era, Oliver STONE made *JFK* (1991), a revisionist history of the Kennedy assassination filmed shortly after the Cold War ended, and in 1995 he directed *Nixon,* which also covered Cold War events.

political novels and stories   In many respects, American fiction is more remarkable for its sparing treatment of Cold War politics than for its direct handling of them. With the exception of John BARTH, no major "serious" NOVELIST has taken on the Cold War as the full subject for a novel. Barth's 1966 GILES GOAT-BOY is what Robert Scholes calls a "fabulation," a decidedly fantastic allegory that revels in the pure pleasure of its own storytelling. Barth's novel uses the university as metaphor for the universe with Eastern and Western powers allegorized as the East and West campuses, and the second coming of the Messiah represented by the arrival of a Grand Tutor. The novel features analogues to Presidents Eisenhower and Kennedy and to Albert Einstein and J. Robert Oppenheimer. Embedded within this allegory is another allegory depicting the journey of the mythic hero as described by Carl Jung and Joseph Campbell. In this story of a modern mythic hero, a Grand Tutor appears at the height of Cold War tensions to save the Campus, which is under the threat of imminent annihilation from the great computer that controls the entire University. Mixing Jungian archetypes, existentialism, BLACK HUMOR and an Asian-style philosophy that sees the world in terms of paradox, Barth depicts the primary Cold War anxieties of the early 1960s: a world on the brink of self-destruction, technology gone dangerously out of control, flawed leaders motivated by a variety of personal and political interests, and a citizenry desperately seeking salvation, or simply escape. The novel concludes that the answers for living meaningfully in such a volatile world must come from each individual, not from governments and leaders.

Barth's first novel, *The Floating Opera* (1956), treats the Cold War indirectly by portraying the dangers of emotionally detached reason. The narrator/protagonist is a seemingly likable manic-depressive who decides to blow up most of his community in an act of despair that he masks, even to himself, as a product of pure logic. Thus Barth alludes to the Cold War military and political leaders who predicate their decisions solely on "logical" planning as they dispassionately consider worldwide destruction. The novel also attacks the process of guilt by association used by Senator Joseph McCarthy and the HOUSE COMMITTEE ON UN-AMERICAN ACTIVITIES (HUAC) during the RED SCARE.

Several novels from the late 1940s deal with the dangers and/or failures of American communism. Lionel Trilling's THE MIDDLE OF THE JOURNEY (1947) describes the protagonist's growing disaffection with the Communist Party. One of the book's main characters is based on Whittaker Chambers, whom Trilling knew slightly when both were students at Columbia University in the mid-1920s. The novel appeared a year before Chambers gained international attention by accusing Alger Hiss of working with him in a communist spy ring during the 1930s. (See also Chambers' 1952 autobiography, WITNESS, and Hiss' 1957 self-defense, IN THE COURT OF PUBLIC OPINION.) Lesser known anti-communist novels

from the period include David Dortort's 1949 POST OF HONOR, which presents the disillusionment of a member of the Young Communist League during the seven years before the U.S. entry into World War II. Likewise, Willa Gibb's THE TENDER MEN (1948) criticizes communist methods, portraying an organization in which individuals are expected to subjugate all their rights and beliefs to the party. The 1948 story depicts a Midwestern farm boy who is recruited by the Communist Party but is later sentenced to death by it for failing to follow orders. (More complex and sophisticated accounts of the initial attraction of communism for intellectuals and its subsequent betrayal of them appear in THE GOD THAT FAILED, a 1949 NONFICTION collection of personal accounts by three prominent ex-communist author/intellectuals [Arthur KOESTLER, Richard WRIGHT and Louis Fischer] and three "fellow-travelers" [Ignazio Silone, Andre Gide and Stephen Spender].)

On the other hand, THE JUDAS TIME is a rare pro-communist novel from the period, written in 1946 by Isidor Schneider. It centers on a college instructor and party member who betrays the communist cell at his university in return for promotion to assistant professor. And Merle Miller criticizes the right-wing pressures on the Truman administration to eliminate suspected communists and other leftists from government in his 1949 novel THE SURE THING, which depicts 36 hours in the life of a liberal State Department official who loses his job after an unjust investigation. Miller later wrote *The Judges and the Judged,* a 1952 nonfiction account of BLACKLISTING during the Red Scare.

Some major novelists have addressed other Cold War events. Robert COOVER, who like Barth is an exuberant fantasist, provides surreal accounts of the Rosenberg trial and the politics behind it in THE PUBLIC BURNING (1976). Coover treats American politics more broadly but equally perceptively in his 1968 story, THE CAT IN THE HAT FOR PRESIDENT. E. L. Doctorow provides a more realistic treatment of the politics behind the Rosenberg case in THE BOOK OF DANIEL, which is narrated by the son of a fictional couple based on the famous pair. (The real-life Rosenberg sons, Robert and Michael Meeropol, treated a similar subject four years later in their 1975 nonfiction book, WE ARE YOUR SONS.) Other less well-known books treating aspects of the Red Scare include THE HONORABLE ROCKY SLADE, William Winster Gaines' 1957 SATIRE ridiculing Senator McCarthy's early career, and Earnest Frankel's TONGUE OF FIRE (1960), which also denounces McCarthy. Written in 1955, at the height of the Red Scare, *Tongue of Fire* was suppressed by publishers until 1960. *The Un-Americans,* a 1957 semi-autobiographical novel by Alvah BESSIE, one of the HOLLYWOOD TEN, also describes the Red Scare.

Howard FAST was a member of the Communist Party until 1956. His books did not deal directly with Cold War events but were clearly shaped by the politics and concerns of the times. He wrote SPARTACUS (1951) while in jail for refusing to testify before HUAC. *Spartacus* is the story of a slave revolt against the Romans in 71 B.C. The communists had adopted Spartacus as one of their historical heroes whose efforts symbolized the universal fight against oppression, and Fast's best-selling fictional account was probably the basis for his receiving the Stalin Peace Prize in 1954. Fast's writing from his communist period also includes *The*

American (1946), about the politician who pardoned three of the anarchists convicted in the 1886 Haymarket bombings (John F. Kennedy treated the same subject in *Profiles in Courage*), and *Clarkton* (1947), about a Massachusetts mill town.

Ayn RAND, on the other hand, rejected communism when she left the Soviet Union in 1926 and remained emphatically pro-capitalist ever after. She is best known for her pre–Cold War novel, THE FOUNTAINHEAD (1943), which celebrates individuality and appeared as a film in 1949. Her Cold War–era fiction includes *Anthem* (1946) and the best-selling *Atlas Shrugged* (1957), which presents a futuristic society based on the oath, "I will never live for the sake of another man, nor ask another man to live for mine."

Other major U.S. writers touched only occasionally on Cold War issues. Mary MCCARTHY satirizes American liberals in the fiction she wrote during the Red Scare, *The Oasis* (1949) and *In the Groves of Academe* (1952). Norman MAILER's first novel, *The Naked and the Dead* (1948), suggests that after World War II the United States will become more fascistic. His second novel, *The Barbary Shore* (1951), concludes that both communism and American culture are bankrupt, thus undermining the belief in a rational universe. The power struggle between Trotsky, a Jew, and Stalin, an anti-Semite, provides a backdrop for the political and sexual liaisons of the novel. *Why Are We in Viet Nam?* (1967) features a Texas teenager who "sees through [the] shit" of adult society while recounting his experiences, including a high-tech hunting trip to Alaska replete with advanced weaponry and helicopters. John Updike's ongoing series follows his character Rabbit Angstrom—and through him, American society—throughout the Cold War, dealing in passing with the Vietnam War and antiwar protest. However, the series focuses primarily on the social rather than political developments in American middle-class society. On the other hand, Updike's 1978 semi-comic novel *The Coup* concerns a Western-educated African man who takes over the government of his country and tries unsuccessfully to introduce a form of revolutionary socialism. And in 1992, Updike published *Memories of the Ford Administration,* which pairs the presidencies of Gerald Ford and James Buchanan. THE DEAN'S DECEMBER (1982), Saul Bellow's first novel after winning the 1976 Nobel Prize for literature, contrasts the social anarchy in the West to the social repression of the East by pairing life in Chicago and Budapest. His earlier book, *Mr. Sammler's Planet* (1970), presented Bellow's despairing response to the social and political anarchy in America during the late 1960s.

Less "serious," best-selling writers more frequently took on Cold War political issues directly. Allen DRURY, Fletcher KNEBEL, Eugene BURDICK and William LEDERER stand out among these. Drury's 1959 ADVISE AND CONSENT inaugurated a six-part series dealing with the struggle between liberals and conservatives over whose ideology should guide the nation through the Cold War. Every book in the series appeared on the *New York Times* best-seller list for at least 19 weeks. Drury promotes conservative political values and attacks the liberal press. He later explained that one of his enduring themes was "the continuing argument between those who use responsible firmness to maintain orderly social progress and oppose Communist imperialism in its

drive for world domination; and those who believe [that] in a reluctance to be firm, in permissiveness and in the erosion of the law lie the surest path to world peace and a stable society." The other books in the series, following American politics through the mid-1970s, were A SHADE OF A DIFFERENCE (1962), CAPABLE OF HONOR (1967), PRESERVE AND PROTECT (1968), COME NINEVEH, COME TYRE (1973) and THE PROMISE OF JOY (1975). Drury's other political novels include *That Summer* (1966), *Throne of Saturn: A Novel of Space and Politics* (1971), *Anna Hastings, The Story of a Washington Newsperson!* (1977), *Mark Coffin, U.S.S: A Novel of Capitol Hill* (1979), *The Hill of Summer* (1981), *Decision* (1983), *Pentagon* (1986) and *Toward What Bright Glory* (1990).

Burdick and Lederer are best known for their 1958 novel THE UGLY AMERICAN, which attacks the arrogant and uninformed behavior of the State Department in Southeast Asia. The authors favored U.S. involvement in the region but insisted on the need for U.S. officials to become more directly involved with the local people, live among them, learn their language and support grassroots projects. In this way, they believed, the United States could best use the fruits of Western science to improve the lives of ordinary Asians—and combat communism most effectively. The sequel, *Sarkhan*, appeared in 1965, the year the United States introduced combat troops into the Vietnam War. It describes the efforts of an American businessman and a professor to prevent a communist takeover. Burdick also coauthored with Harvey Wheeler the 1962 military novel, FAIL-SAFE, about an accidental nuclear attack against the Soviet Union.

Knebel coauthored SEVEN DAYS IN MAY with Charles W. Bailey II. The 1962 novel, which John Frankenheimer made into a 1964 POLITICAL FILM, features an attempted military coup by members of the Joint Chiefs of Staff who fear that the president's decision to sign a treaty banning nuclear weapons will gravely endanger U.S. security. It was one of the earliest Cold War stories to suggest that powerful officers in the U.S. military might be irresponsible, insane and out of control, and it suggests that the greater danger to the U.S. democracy comes not from internal communist subversion but from the super-patriotic, self-righteous political right wing that regards the Constitution as a hindrance to protecting national security. The story also singles out the nuclear bomb as the underlying cause of the nation's hysteria and even of the coup itself. Knebel's NIGHT OF CAMP DAVID (1965) centers on a senator who learns in a mysterious meeting with the president that he is under consideration as a vice presidential candidate in the forthcoming election. Over time, however, he discerns that the president is extremely paranoid with delusions of persecution and grandeur. CROSSING IN BERLIN (1981) deals with the efforts of an American businessman to obtain the release from East Germany of an environmental scientist whose crucial research on global warming has been repressed for political reasons.

Other best-selling, popular fiction also addresses Cold War political issues. Philip Wylie's 1954 apocalyptic novel, TOMORROW!, argues for a comprehensive civil defense program. Richard Condon's 1959 THE MANCHURIAN CANDIDATE deals with communist brainwashing and domestic political intrigue as the wife of a dim-witted, alcoholic, McCarthy-like senator proves to be a communist agent who tries to arrange a political assassination in order to secure the presidency for her right-wing husband—ironically, the type of leader who will best serve the communist agenda. Leon URIS's 1964 ARMAGEDDON: A NOVEL OF BERLIN depicts the political and social developments in Berlin from the end of World War II to the end of the Berlin Airlift in 1949. The novel received praise for its journalistic detail but was criticized for its flat characters and other literary failings. Irving Wallace, another best-selling novelist, provides a salacious treatment of Cold War politics in his 1967 novel THE PLOT, which depicts the top figures of world power as sensual and self-indulgent and explores the relationships between sexual and international relations. In 1966, Noel Behn published THE KREMLIN LETTER, which imagines a somewhat plausible collaboration between the United States and U.S.S.R. against China. In Robert Serling's best-selling THE PRESIDENT'S PLANE IS MISSING (1967) Air Force One disappears at a time of particularly hostile anti-American rhetoric by the Chinese communists. Philip Roth satirizes Richard Nixon in OUR GANG (1971) and attacks HUAC in THE GREAT AMERICAN NOVEL (1973).

Surprisingly, the post-Watergate years did not spawn many purely political novels that took up Cold War issues. The U.S.-Soviet détente may account for some of the lack of literary interest in the Cold War during the 1970s, but the renewed tensions in the early 1980s and such events as the Iran-contra scandal would seem to offer rich possibilities for literature. Popular SPY NOVELS and military novels did incorporate such political concerns, however. For instance, William F. BUCKLEY Jr. and convicted Watergate felons E. Howard Hunt, G. Gordon Liddy and John Ehrlichman each gave a prominent role to politics in their spy fiction. Buckley's spy fiction, centering on his superhero Blackford Oakes, invokes the politics behind such Cold War events as the power struggle in the Kremlin following Stalin's death (*High Jinx*, 1986); the Hungarian Revolution and the beginnings of the space race (*Who's on First*, 1980); the second Berlin crisis (*Henri Tod*, 1983); and the 1960 U-2 incident (*Marco Polo*, 1982). Hunt's *The Berlin Ending* (1973) depicts Willy Brandt and other advocates of détente as Soviet agents, and *The Kremlin Conspiracy* (1985) derides the politics of European "peacenicks" who pressure the Nobel Prize committee to give the peace prize to a man who is secretly a Soviet agent. The prizewinner then uses his influence to force NATO to withdraw its missiles from Europe. Ehrlichman's *The Company* (1976) centers on rivalries among the CIA, FBI and other intelligence agencies. The unflaterring portrayal of the president is apparently based on Nixon. Ehrlichman also wrote *The China Card* (1986), which suggests that Nixon's historic trip to China actually resulted from the activities of a spy working on behalf of Zhou En-lai, the Chinese premier.

Military novels also became a popular way of presenting Cold War politics during the 1970s and 1980s. THE THIRD WORLD WAR, a 1978 novel by General Sir John Hackett and other top-ranking NATO generals and advisers, projects detailed and sophisticated military and political scenarios based on the state of the Cold War during the Carter administration. The authors wrote a 1982 sequel, *The Untold Story*, in which they warn, "If you want nuclear peace prepare for non-nuclear war: but be ready to pay the price." The price,

they believe, is vulnerability to a conventional Soviet attack in Europe that can be repelled only by tactical nuclear weapons or extreme good luck. Tom Clancy's THE HUNT FOR RED OCTOBER (1984) describes the political considerations in determining whether an approaching renegade Soviet submarine is intending to defect or attack. His *Red Storm Rising* (1986) treats Middle Eastern politics, and *Cardinal of the Kremlin* (1988) deals with the Afghanistan situation.

Several foreign fiction writers who dealt with Cold War politics also had sizable U.S. audiences. Many of them, such as Samuel BECKETT, Jean Genet and Simone de Beauvoir were first published by the GROVE PRESS. The British writer George ORWELL imagines a bleak world run by futuristic communists in his 1949 masterpiece NINETEEN EIGHTY-FOUR, and he satirizes the Russian Revolution in *Animal Farm* (1945). Graham GREENE's *The Quiet American* (1955) was one of the earliest novels to criticize U.S. policy in Southeast Asia. It appeared a year after the evacuation of the French from Southeast Asia, following their military defeat by the communist-led Viet Minh at Dienbienphu. Greene, who was temporarily denied a U.S. entry visa in 1952 because he had joined the Communist Party for one month in 1923, was accused of writing the book in retaliation. Mexican writer Carlos FUENTES was outspoken in his criticism of U.S. Cold War politics toward Mexico and Central America. His sentiments appear most clearly in his 1978 spy thriller about international oil transactions, *The Hydra Head*, which attacks both superpowers.

The Czech writer Milan KUNDERA's political novels *The Joke* (1968) and *The Unbearable Lightness of Being* (1982) received considerable attention in the United States. Set in his homeland, these books depict the several levels of absurdity that emanate from living in a restrictive, highly bureaucratic society. *The Joke* describes the tragic fate of a man whose playful comment on a postcard leads to his undoing at the hands of literal-minded bureaucrats. In *The Unbearable Lightness of Being*, the Soviet invasion of Czechoslovakia is shown to permeate all aspects of personal life. The Peruvian Mario VARGAS LLOSA, an early supporter of Fidel Castro, retracted his endorsement of the communist Cuban regime after the poet Herberto Padilla was arrested there in 1971. His disaffection with Castro appears in *The War of the End of the World* (1981; in English, 1983). Set in 19th-century Peru, the novel describes a rebellion that began with a utopian vision but turned into a system of demagoguery and repression; it is widely read as being directed against the abuses of Castro's revolutionary government. (See also EXILED WRITERS; MILITARY NOVELS; APOCALYPTIC NOVELS; LITERATURE ABOUT COLD WAR EVENTS.)

For additional reading, see Schaub's *American Fiction in the Cold War*.

"Politics on Trial" A public-affairs TELEVISION TALK OR DEBATE SHOW that ran on ABC during the fall of 1952. The show was presented in a courtroom format and presided over by a real-life judge. Shown during the weeks leading up to the presidential election, it featured a prominent Democrat or Republican presenting his or her party's position on a major issue. The "opposing counsel" would then attack the position, after which the presenter's counsel would defend it.

Polonsky, Abraham   A SCREENWRITER and author. Born in 1910 in New York, the son of Russian immigrants, Polonsky grew up in a Jewish socialist environment, which influenced his creative work throughout his life. He received his B.A. degree from the City College of New York in 1932 and his law degree from Columbia Law School in 1935. During this period, he joined the American Communist Party. In 1937, Polonsky married Sylvia Marrow, with whom he had three children. That year he also went to Hollywood in his capacity as a lawyer to work with the production staff of the radio show, THE GOLDBERGS. He eventually wrote some scripts for that series and as a result dedicated himself to a literary career upon his return to New York. After he published his first novel, *The Enemy Sea* (1943), Paramount Pictures hired Polonsky as a screenwriter. However, shortly thereafter he left for Europe to serve as a civilian volunteer with the Office of Strategic Services during World War II; consequently, his first screenplay was not filmed until 1947. When he returned to the United States in 1945, he worked with the Hollywood Writer's Mobilization, and in 1946 he helped edit the *Hollywood Quarterly*. In 1947, Polonsky earned an Academy Award nomination for his script for *Body and Soul,* a film about a fighter trying to free himself from working-class poverty. Robert ROSSEN directed the film, which starred John GARFIELD. In 1949, Polonsky wrote another screenplay centering on greed and gangsters, *Force of Evil.* Like *Body and Soul, Force of Evil* reveals the untempered profit motive to be the force of evil in American society, as the criminal underworld pointedly reflects corporate capitalism. Polonsky followed with yet another film centering on greed, *I Can Get It for You Wholesale* (1951). After traveling in Europe and obtaining the film rights to Thomas MANN's anti-fascist novella *Mario and the Magician,* he returned to the United States, where he contracted to write and direct for 20th Century-Fox. However, he was blacklisted before beginning work.

In their 1950 testimony before the HOUSE COMMITTEE ON UN-AMERICAN ACTIVITIES (HUAC), screenwriter Richard COLLINS, television producer Meta Rosenberg and film actor Sterling Hayden all named Polonsky as a member of the Communist Party. Called before the committee in April 1951, Polonsky invoked the Fifth Amendment so that he could avoid identifying colleagues and also avoid a contempt-of-Congress jail sentence, such as had been received by the HOLLYWOOD TEN. (The Ten had unsuccessfully taken the First Amendment.) In response, Congressman Harold H. Velde called Polonsky "the most dangerous man in America."

Polonsky was blacklisted as a result of his appearance and did not resume commercial filmmaking under his own name until 1968. In the interim, he wrote fiction, including the novels *The World Above* (1951) and *A Season of Fear* (1956). He also wrote pseudonymously for such television shows as YOU ARE THERE (CBS, 1953–57) and "Danger" (CBS, 1954). He wrote, but did not receive credit for, Robert Wise's film *Odds Against Tomorrow* (1959). He also worked on his pet project, *The Sweet Land,* a never-produced screenplay about black migration from the South after the Civil War. Unlike most blacklisted writers, Polonsky thrived financially during this period in his life, which he described thus: "The guerilla life I pretended to practice in the war I played with

some amusement and frequent disgust in the jungle of TV as a blacklisted writer. Likewise in films." In 1965 Polonsky wrote and received credit for *The Last Clear Chance,* a drama that aired on NBC's "Kraft Suspense Theatre." In 1968 his film blacklisting finally ended when he received credit for *Madigan.* He subsequently wrote and directed *Tell Them Willie Boy Is Here* (1969), a film about a fugitive Indian boy, of which he said, "What particularly interested me is the fact that the Indian is a kind of exile in his own country, and so am I—or was—for a brief period: twenty years." In 1971 he directed but did not write *Romance of a Horse Thief,* the story of Polish Jews plotting against the Cossacks at the turn of the century. For this film Polonsky drew upon tales his grandmother had told him as a child: "It is her voice I hear all through the movie, and it was her voice and her face which toured the locations." (See also BLACKLISTING.)

For additional reading, see *Dictionary of Literary Biography* (vol. 26, *Screenwriters*).

Popovsky, Mark   A Soviet-born EXILED WRITER (to the United States). Born in 1922 in Odessa, Ukraine, Popovsky served as an army medical officer during World War II. He received a degree in philology from Moscow University in 1952, became a member of the Union of Soviet Writers in 1957, and wrote free-lance articles for *Pravda, Izvestia* and other Soviet publications, mostly dealing with Russian scientists, doctors, agronomists and pharmacologists. He also published in the Soviet Union an account of bacteriologist Vladimir Harkin, the man who developed the first vaccines against cholera and the bubonic plague. In 1964, Popovsky began writing for publications outside the U.S.S.R. In 1966, he published in *Space* magazine a portion of his research on the biologist Nicholas Vavilov, who had died of hunger in a Soviet prison. Based on information in secret KGB files, the article earned Popovsky official state censure, and he was unable to publish in the Soviet Union for the next two years. His full account appeared in English as *The Vasilov Affair* (1984), with a foreword by Andrei Sakharov, the "father" of the Soviet atomic bomb who later became a political dissident and exile.

When Popovsky defected from the Soviet Union to the United States in 1977, he smuggled out some 3,000 pages of material describing the peasant followers of Leo Tolstoy, which he published in Russian in 1984. In 1979 he published *Manipulated Science* in English. It describes how the Communist Party distorted supposedly "objective" science within the U.S.S.R. and warns of the possible destruction of Soviet science as a result. He also wrote scripts for Radio Liberty. Popovsky's Russian-language interviews with 250 recent emigrants from the Soviet Union appeared in 1985. (See also NONFICTION WRITERS.)

For additional reading, see Tucker's *Literary Exile in the Twentieth Century.*

Porgy and Bess   George Gershwin's 1935 folk opera about African Americans in New Orleans. The work was revived for a national tour in 1952. According to the *New York Times,* "The purpose of the tour is to show central Europeans that . . . Negro players are not debased or oppressed as the Communist line says." President Truman attended a performance of this production at the National

Theater in Washington that August. The show later toured Europe and the Soviet Union with the primary mission of easing Cold War tensions. It was part of a program of cultural exchange inaugurated in 1954 by President Eisenhower, who had stated, "The exchange of artists is one of the most effective methods of strengthening world friendship." (See also THEATER.)

Pork Chop Hill A 1959 KOREAN WAR FILM starring Gregory Peck, Rip Torn and George Peppard and directed by Lewis Milestone. The action centers on the final days of fighting before the armistice that concluded the Korean War. For Milestone, the film completed a trilogy of films about 20th-century warfare, along with *All Quiet on the Western Front* (1930) and *A Walk in the Sun* (1945). Gregory Peck commands a company that has been ordered to capture an inconsequential but heavily defended hill shortly before the armistice is expected to conclude the fighting. The film depicts the soldiers' honor and dignity as they respond to the pointless but deadly command. Like THE STEEL HELMET (1951), *Pork Chop Hill* initially portrays the Korean War as marked by chaos, confusion, depravity and even insanity. The soldiers perceive only the futility of dying to gain control of an apparently worthless mound. However, the film ultimately vindicates their sacrifice, for the audience sees how U.S. negotiators need the hard-fought victory to convince the communists of the West's unyielding resolve to stand up to aggression at every turn.

Post of Honor A 1949 POLITICAL NOVEL by David Dortort. The story follows Max Gerard, a member of the Young Communist League in 1934 who becomes disillusioned by the Communist Party during the seven years leading up to the U.S. entry into World War II. Gerard believes in the proclaimed communist ideals but begins to change his view when a communist leader deliberately provokes a police attack against a peaceful picket line. He becomes increasingly disaffected as he witnesses communist activity in Harlem and the Spanish Civil War. Though Dortort's sincerity was appreciated by contemporary reviewers, his work was criticized for being "muddled" and overwritten. In the words of one reviewer, "While the author is indisputably on the side of the angels, he cannot be said to have told his story with any special skill or art."

Postman, The A 1985 APOCALYPTIC NOVEL by David Brin. Published toward the end of the most intense period in the Cold War since the 1962 Cuban Missile Crisis, *The Postman* suggests that postapocalyptic society will literally be postman; it will be run by women. The protagonist, Gordon Krantz, wears a mailman's uniform and moves among isolated postapocalyptic communities like a medieval minstrel, exchanging his songs and stories for food. Krantz's stories retain a connection to the preapocalyptic past for people who "long forlornly for a lost shiny age—an era of cleanliness and order and a great nation now lost." Eventually, however, Krantz's accounts of bygone times become distorted. He becomes a kind of con artist telling a hopeful audience only what it wants to hear. Then he has a dream that commands him to substitute the "right myths" for the fabulations he has been foisting upon his listeners. Afterward he joins with a group of women who oppose the return to a male-dominated medieval feudalism and vow "to do anything to end a terrible war." Their efforts fail tragically, but they become martyrs whose sacrifice eventually transforms society and leads to a new, women-led world order that repudiates aggression. The postman wonders whether women will begin killing their sons if they act aggressively, but he concludes that the women themselves would find such behavior too extreme: "That, perhaps, is in the end where our hope lies." Like FISKADORO (1985), RIDDLEY WALKER (1980) and THE WILD SHORE (1984), *The Postman* addresses the role of narrative in the postnuclear world, suggesting the need for creating new myths that will redirect human consciousness.

For additional reading, see Scheick's "Continuative and Ethical Predictions: The Post-Nuclear Holocaust Novel of the 1980s."

Pound, Ezra An American POET. A dominant figure in the modernist literature of the first half of the 20th century, Pound was born in 1885 in Idaho. He worked with such writers as Robert Frost, James Joyce, Ford Madox Ford and Wyndham Lewis. He also made major contributions to T. S. Eliot's seminal modernist poem, "The Waste Land" (1922), which he helped edit and shape. His belief in the necessity of a strong, controlling artist to impose order on chaos found a political correlative in his attraction to fascism. His rabid anti-Semitism also found an appreciative audience among the fascists. Pound lived in Italy from 1925 to 1945 and supported Mussolini during the Second World War. He was brought to the United States after the war to stand trial for treason for his pro-fascist, anti-Semitic wartime radio broadcasts over Rome Radio. His supporters arranged for him to be declared insane so he could escape a jail sentence, and he was consigned to St. Elizabeth's Hospital for the Criminally Insane in Washington, D.C. Largely through the efforts of T. S. Eliot, he received the 1948 Bollingen Prize for his brilliant poetry. However, the fact that the U.S. Library of Congress would award this honor to a legally insane supporter of the fascist war effort who had been indicted for treason created considerable controversy, especially among left-wing writers of a younger generation. Pound's technical virtuosity and his authoritarian politics influenced Cold War–era poets, who either continued his literary program or rebelled against its highly controlled and elitist nature. Released from the hospital in 1958, after 13 years of incarceration, Pound returned to Italy, where he died in 1972.

For additional reading, see *Literary Exile in the Twentieth Century.*

"Powers of Matthew Star, The" A TELEVISION SCIENCE FICTION SHOW that ran on NBC from 1982 to 1983. Matthew Star (Peter Barton) was a high school student who was actually the crown prince from the planet Quadris. After his father was overthrown, Matthew was sent to Earth so he could develop his powers of telepathy and telekinesis, which he was then supposed to use to regain his throne. As these powers developed and new ones accrued, including astral projection and transmutation, Star took time from his normal high school activities to help the U.S. government fight espionage and other crimes. Apart from the espionage theme, this Reagan-era show depicted other-worldly revolutionaries as villains while sympathetically portraying a monarchy. In this respect, it reflected U.S. foreign policy, which typically supported conservative monarchies against communist-sponsored populist revolutions.

Preminger, Otto An Austrian-born FILM DIRECTOR. In addition to directing several films with political content, including ADVISE AND CONSENT (1962), THE HUMAN FACTOR (1979) and *The Court-Martial of Billy Mitchell* (1955), Preminger broke the Hollywood practice of BLACKLISTING in 1960 when he announced—and the *New York Times* reported on its front page—that Dalton TRUMBO had written his upcoming film EXODUS. Trumbo, a member of the HOLLYWOOD TEN, had been among the first members of the film industry to be blacklisted when he refused to testify at hearings conducted by the HOUSE COMMITTEE ON UN-AMERICAN ACTIVITIES (HUAC) in 1947. Preminger also appeared in HOLLYWOOD ON TRIAL, a 1976 FILM DOCUMENTARY about the blacklist written by another member of the Hollywood Ten, LESTER COLE.

Preserve and Protect A 1968 POLITICAL NOVEL by Allen DRURY. A transitional book in the series that begins with ADVISE AND CONSENT (1959) and concludes with THE PROMISE OF JOY (1975), *Preserve and Protect* deals with the caretaker government of Bill Abbott, the speaker of the House who becomes president after the death of Harley Hudson, who had assumed the post at the end of *Advise and Consent* when his predecessor died of a heart attack. Despite violent domestic opposition and criticism from the liberal press, Abbott continues the U.S. policy of opposing communist aggression in Third World countries, much as Lyndon Johnson continued and escalated John Kennedy's Vietnam policy after he assumed the presidency. Written at the height of the Vietnam War, Drury's novel deals with communist activity in Panama and Grotoland, a fictitious version of Vietnam. Of particular interest is the ongoing transformation of Robert Leffingwell, the defeated candidate for secretary of state in *Advise and Consent,* from liberal to conservative. Also significant is the political accommodation between conservative Orrin Knox and liberal Ted Jason. The novel spent 28 weeks on the *New York Times* best-seller list.

For additional reading, see Kemme's *Political Fiction, The Spirit of the Age,* and *Allen Drury.*

President's Analyst, The A 1967 FILM COMEDY starring James Coburn, Godfrey Cambridge and Severn Darden and written and directed by Theodore J. Flicker. A FILM SATIRE of 1960s American culture and international politics, the film centers on Dr. Sidney Schaefer (Coburn), a psychiatrist for the president of the United States. Because he is privy to crucial secret information, Schaefer is targeted for assassination by U.S. agents and for kidnapping by the Soviets. Among the targets of this SPY FILM SPOOF are mindless bureaucracy, psychoanalysis, liberalism and the Cold War itself. In this satire, the telephone company proves to be the ultimate "power behind the power."

President's Plane Is Missing, The A 1967 POLITICAL NOVEL by Robert Serling and a 1971 POLITICAL FILM starring Buddy Ebsen, Peter Graves, Rip Torn and Raymond Massey and directed by Daryl Duke. The story centers on the disappearance of the presidential plane, Air Force One, at a time when Chinese communists are threatening nuclear war. The novel appeared on the *New York Times* best-seller list for 22 weeks.

Prisoner of War A 1954 KOREAN WAR FILM starring Ronald REAGAN and Steve Forrest and directed by Andrew Marton. In order to investigate conditions in a North Korean prisoner-of-war camp and ascertain the veracity of reports the U.S. POWs are collaborating with the enemy, the Reagan character volunteers to infiltrate the prison. He ultimately discovers that the rumors of cooperation are untrue, that most of the soldiers sarcastically defy their captors, and that the only man who cooperates proves to be planting misinformation to fool the enemy. Made a year after the war concluded, *Prisoner of War* attempts to vindicate U.S. POWs who were facing real-life charges of collaboration. Other Korean War films that dealt with the POW issue include *Time Limit* (1957), *Sergeant Ryker,* (1968), *The Rack* (1956) and THE MANCHURIAN CANDIDATE (1962).

Promise of Joy, The A 1975 POLITICAL NOVEL by Allen DRURY. The culminating work in a six-part series that began in 1959 with ADVISE AND CONSENT, *The Promise of Joy* appeared at a bleak moment in U.S. history, a year after President Nixon resigned due to the Watergate scandal, two years after the U.S. military evacuation from Vietnam and the same year that Vietnam and Cambodia fell to communist armies. The book spent 19 weeks on the *New York Times* best-seller list. In the previous novel in the series, COME NINEVEH, COME TYRE (1973), Orrin Knox, the conservative presidential nominee, and Ceil Jason, the wife of his liberal running mate, were assassinated, and Ted Jason became president and presided over the decline of the country. *The Promise of Joy* provides an alternate ending to the series. In this version, Ted Jason and Knox's wife Beth die in the assassination attempt, and Knox goes on to be elected president. In a show of party unity, he offers the vice presidency first to Jason's widow, who declines, and then to Cullee Hamilton, an African-American pro-war congressman from California. In this way, Drury demonstrates his belief that true conservatives are neither inherently anti-female nor anti-black.

Like the conservative president Ronald Reagan, who was elected five years after the book's publication, Knox makes his first order of business the buildup of U.S. military strength, which had been the target of congressional budget cuts. He further orders counterattacks to combat communist offensives in the fictitious Grotoland (Vietnam) and in Panama, where he also blockades the Panama Canal in order to stem the flow of weapons to the communist insurgents. Despite fierce congressional opposition, Knox remains firm in his policies. To circumvent inevitable distortions by the liberal press, he makes a public appearance on television to inform the country that despite the seriousness of these situations and the possibility of nuclear war, U.S. forces must remain in Grotoland and Panama because "counter pressure must be maintained if meaningful negotiations are to come about. Past history, in Vietnam and elsewhere, shows that such negotiations only happen when the Communists face matching strength. They never happen when the Communists face weakness—the negotiations mean nothing but camouflaged surrender to the Communist position." Even after antiwar activists kidnap his son and new wife in order to coerce him to remove the troops, Knox remains adamant and orders an all-out U.S. offensive that leaves the country vulnerable to a Soviet attack. America is spared that fate, however, when nuclear warfare breaks out between China and the Soviet Union. Knox negotiates a temporary truce, but neither country will accede to his demands that they permit an international peacekeeping force on their border, reduce their military strength and renounce their expansionist policies.

After the United Nations (UN) refuses to send troops to the border to impose a peace on the warring communist countries, the liberal press assails Knox once again. Knox vetoes congressional legislation mandating U.S. intervention to aid the U.S.S.R. despite liberal rhetoric insisting that "America must save the civilization of the West from the Godless yellow hordes of Asia." Instead, Knox intends the United States to remain above the fray and restore order later, after the enemies have exhausted their strength. Ultimately, Knox does agree to intercede on the Soviets' behalf in order to maintain the crucial international balance of power. But as he does so, he reminds the country that too many Americans have lost touch with the conservative ideals that made the country great and have been misled by a liberal media that "has consistently denigrated, downgraded, vilified and sabotaged every worthwhile impulse and effort of its country." He also attacks the steady campaign by some churches, schools and the courts "to weaken, destroy, and subvert the laws necessary to maintain [law and order] in our society."

For additional reading, see Kemme's *Political Fiction, The Spirit of the Age, and Allen Drury.*

Public Burning, The   A 1976 POLITICAL NOVEL by Robert COOVER. A surrealist, BLACK HUMOR account of the execution of atomic bomb spies Julius and Ethel Rosenberg, *The Public Burning* satirizes American Cold War politics of the 1950s. Coover's energetic prose; his use of the tall-tale boast and challenge and other frontier humor techniques; his treatment of Uncle Sam as a character who makes a pact with Richard Nixon; and similar elements of fantasy and exaggeration give the book a surreal quality that nonetheless celebrates American vitality, know-how and enthusiasm, even when these are horribly misapplied. Through his very use of these narrative techniques, Coover suggests that libidinal energy underlies Cold War politics, the RED SCARE, racial differences and all human endeavors.

The book culminates when the Rosenbergs, the ultimate un-Americans, are executed in Times Square. Uncle Sam oversees the proceedings, carrying a blinding fireball, which, according to David Dowling in *Fictions of Nuclear Disaster*, "is at once the flame of the Statue of Liberty, the blinding light of racial and religious prejudice, and the atomic bomb itself." Uncle Sam declares:

Philosophers have changed the world . . . it is necessary to CHANGE the world! So hang on to your hats,

folks, cause . . . the Coelestial Light directed here by the Finger of God is gonna drive out the long! long! Night of Heathenish Darkness! I shit you not! Stand back! it's the NEW New Enlightenment.

Uncle Sam's orb then cuts through Time Square

like a sheet of sun, inundating the streets and all the city and nation and oceans beyond with glaring light . . . dragging people to their heads, knees, and elbows, and whipping them as in an orange whirlwind toward the stage, and then—WHOOSH!—the darkness lifts up off the Square like a great mushroom cloud, rising high into the lightening sky and sucking all the fears and phantasms of the people's nighttime up with it—and a lot of the people as well . . . before dropping them back on the sweaty pavements in an exhausted bare-bottomed heap.

Coover's imagery renders Cold War politics and NUCLEAR APOCALYPSE a psychedelic experience, reminiscent of a 1960s LSD-induced hallucination characterized by vivid colors, striking figures, distortions of reality, and tremendous creative energy. As in his 1968 story THE CAT IN THE HAT FOR PRESIDENT Coover's exaggeration and exuberant technique rejoice in a playful, animated, creative energy, the underlying life force, which—like the Hindu god Shiva, Uncle's Sam orb, the hydrogen bomb and American society itself—is simultaneously Creator and Destroyer. (See also SATIRE.)

For additional reading, see Dowling's *Fictions of Nuclear Disaster.*

Pueblo   A 1973 MILITARY FILM starring Hal Holbrook and directed by Anthony Page. The film dramatizes the North Korean seizure of the surveillance ship USS *Pueblo* in January 1968. One U.S. crewman was killed and three were injured when the ship was seized, and its captain and crew of 81 men were captured. The ship was never returned, and the crew was released in December 1968 after the United States simultaneously admitted and denied responsibility for the incident. Commander Lloyd Bucher, whom Holbrook portrays, was subjected to criticism for his handling of the incident. Stanley Greenberg's 1971 play, *Pueblo,* also dramatizes the capture and subsequent court-martial of Commander Bucher.

Pulling Through   A 1983 APOCALYPTIC NOVEL by Dean Ing. The year of the novel's publication was part of the most intense period of the Cold War since the 1962 Cuban Missile Crisis. Détente had disintegrated in December 1979 when the Soviets invaded Afghanistan. When President Reagan came to office in 1981, he branded the Soviet Union an "Evil Empire" and introduced a massive weapons buildup. In March 1983 he proposed the Strategic Defense Initiative (SDI—more popularly known as STAR WARS), which intimidated the Soviets. In September the Soviets shot down a civilian Korean airliner that had strayed over the U.S.S.R., and Reagan and other Western leaders denounced them for their barbarism. On September 8, Soviet foreign minister Gromyko declared, "The world situation is now slipping toward a very dangerous precipice. Problem number one for the world is to avoid nuclear war."

Not surprisingly, *Pulling Through* revives the postnuclear subgenre that had been largely dormant since the mid-1960s. At the same time, it reflects the attitudes of contemporary "survivalists" who were then arming and training themselves to survive in what they envisioned as the lawless and hostile environment that would follow the nuclear war or environmental disaster they saw as inevitable. Its hero, an unsentimental, pragmatic, cheetah-owning bounty hunter named Harve Rackham, relies on his resourcefulness, intelligence and ability to discard liberal nonsense so as to assess situations clearly and astutely. Reflecting the U.S.–Arab antagonisms of the 1980s, the nuclear war that obliterates Harve's town begins when a nuclear-armed Syrian cruise missile capsizes a U.S. supercarrier in the Mediterranean. Ironically, the political reactionary survives in the postnuclear aftermath in part by employing skills he learned from his wife, who herself had learned them during her earlier involvement with the COUNTERCULTURE and its back-to-the-earth efforts during the 1970s. Rackham also makes use of his own no-nonsense attitude and of the technological know-how he gains from the survivalist handbooks he has preserved. One teaches him innovative uses for a bicycle; another urges him to arm himself for personal defense with "a military assault rifle, a reliable combat pistol and a 12-gauge riotgun. You are shooting to *live.*" Most of the book's second half is dedicated to the immediate postapocalyptic situation, where survival of the fittest prevails. However, the final four pages do acknowledge the desirability of renewing civilized society.

For additional reading, see Dowling's *Fictions of Nuclear Disaster.*

Pynchon, Thomas A NOVELIST. Along with fellow BLACK HUMOR writer John BARTH, Pynchon was one of the most celebrated experimental novelists of the Cold War era. *Gravity's Rainbow* (1973) has been called one of the most important novels of the century and compared to James Joyce's *Ulysses* in terms of its contribution to the advancement of the literary form.

Born in 1937, Pynchon majored in engineering at Cornell University, where he graduated in 1958. His knowledge of quantum physics and thermodynamics plays a significant role in his writing, where they are often used as metaphors for the human condition. His short story "Entropy" and his second novel, *The Crying of Lot 49* (1966), allude directly to the second law of thermodynamics, which states that closed systems inevitably lose energy and fall into states of disorder. For Pynchon, individuals and societies who close themselves off from infusions of new energy by limiting their exposure to new ideas become entropic and experience a sort of heat death. *The Crying of Lot 49* suggests that middle America risks this fate in its efforts to isolate itself from the "underclass." Communication is the antidote to entropy, in Pynchon's view. Thus the novel centers on the possibility of a centuries-old alternative postal system used by the dispossessed. Among the bizarre characters who populate this book are members of a secret society that is so right-wing, their values become almost left-wing. In this respect, they mirror the John Birch Society, which, among other positions, opposed the Vietnam War because it believed it was a communist conspiracy to drain U.S. resources and kill American boys. Pynchon's secret society celebrates the first military encounter between U.S. and Russian forces, a Civil War naval exchange between a Confederate and Russian ship in which both sides appeared to retreat and therefore, because of relativity theory, both sides could claim victory.

While at Cornell, Pynchon studied modern literature with Vladimir NABOKOV and met Richard Farina, the promising novelist who died shortly after the publication of his first novel and to whose memory Pynchon dedicated *Gravity's Rainbow.* A literary tour de force, *Gravity's Rainbow* suggests that the Cold War human condition celebrates death. Part of the plot centers on efforts to track the relationship between a German V-2 rocket and the sexual exploits of one of the book's main characters, Tyron Slothrop. Toward the end of the book, someone charges that Slothrop "might be in love, in sexual love, with his, and the race's death." In this respect, *Gravity's Rainbow* shares the basic premise of Stanley KUBRICK's 1964 film satire, DR. STRANGELOVE: OR HOW I LEARNED TO STOP WORRYING AND LOVE THE BOMB. The frenetic and somewhat surreal story features a scene in which Slothrop, searching for a stash of illegal drugs and dressed as Rocket Man, appears at the Potsdam Conference, in which the victorious Allied powers are planning how they will divide and administer Europe. Though mostly set during the Second World War, *Gravity's Rainbow* reveals the growing divisions between the East and West that were eventually manifested as the Cold War. Moreover, its thematic concerns address such Cold War issues as the role of multinational corporations; the constant possibility of a sudden NUCLEAR APOCALYPSE against which no defense exists ("the rocket can penetrate, from the sky, at any given point"); and the untrustworthiness of governments that are obsessed by technology, secrecy (a condition that breeds entropy by restricting communication) and death.

For additional reading, see *Dictionary of Literary Biography* (vol. 2, *American Novelists Since World War II*).

Quest for Karla. The A trilogy of SPY NOVELS by John LE CARRÉ. The 1982 collection consists of three of le Carré's earlier works: *Tinker, Tailor, Soldier, Spy* (1974), *The Honourable Schoolboy* (1977) and *Smiley's People* (1980). In 1980, the BBC produced *Tinker, Tailor* and *Smiley's People* as TELEVISION SPY SHOWS. The highly successful series also appeared in the United States on public television. Collectively, the trilogy presents the efforts by le Carré's long-standing protagonist George Smiley, now in his seventies, to neutralize his counterpart, the Soviet spymaster Karla. LynnDianne Beene points out in *John le Carré* that the trilogy invokes the structure of the medieval romance, in which the questing knight reluctantly journeys into an evil realm to defeat a seemingly invincible enemy in order to revitalize his own community.

Partly inspired by the real-life defection of Kim Philby, a top British intelligence agent who was exposed in 1963, the action centers on Smiley's attempt to find and eliminate a mole—a double agent—in his own intelligence organization, known as Circus. As he becomes absorbed by his quest, Smiley, a former literary scholar, increasingly sacrifices his humanistic values and becomes more and more like his arch-enemy. *Tinker, Tailor, Soldier, Spy* introduces the problem of rooting out the highly placed Soviet mole from the Circus. The book concludes as Smiley uncovers the mole and tolerates his murder by Jim Prideaux, the Circus's premier assassin. In *The Honourable Schoolboy*, Smiley assumes the directorship of the Circus and seeks to identify and eliminate Karla's Chinese mole, so as to finally restore

order to his intelligence operation. Though finally successful in identifying the double agent, Smiley is denied the ultimate victory when agents from the CIA and Drug Enforcement Agency (DEA) capture the man. According to Beene, "Smiley's quest overtakes his sensibilities and compromises his humanity. Against . . . the pressing contemporary political backdrop of the Sino-Soviet split, the American defeat in Vietnam, and the question of Chinese control of Hong Kong, Smiley's covert attempts to rebuild his Round Table complement rather than reform unsavory political realities."

The final novel in the trilogy, *Smiley's People,* is set during the superpower détente of the 1970s. While investigating the murder of an exiled Estonian rebel who had been trying to contact him, Smiley discovers that Karla has been embezzling funds to maintain his unacknowledged illegitimate daughter in a private Swiss psychiatric hospital. Smiley uses this knowledge to force Karla's defection. According to Beene, "Through eight novels Smiley professes an undying belief in the power of Western democracy, in the superiority of moral means over questionable ends, in the permanency of intellectual ideals, and in the salvation possible through love. Yet at every step he fears these decencies are illusions." Thus even Smiley's ultimate victory is a kind of defeat for his high moral ideals.

For additional reading, see Beene's *John le Carré* and Cawelti and Rosenberg's *The Spy Story.*

Quiet American, The A 1955 POLITICAL NOVEL by Graham GREENE and a 1958 POLITICAL FILM starring Michael

Redgrave, Audie Murphy and Claude Dauphin and directed by Joseph L. Mankiewicz. The book was published the year after the French evacuation from Southeast Asia following their defeat at the battle of Dienbienphu. This was two years after Secretary of State John Foster Dulles had warned of a "domino effect" in which, if Vietnam were to fall to the communists, the rest of Southeast Asia would follow. Also at the time the novel was published, the United States was just beginning to take over the French role in Vietnam. The story of *The Quiet American* actually anticipates the U.S. experience in Vietnam. It centers on Alden Pyle, a CIA agent in Southeast Asia whose anti-communist counter-terrorism kills and maims innocent civilians. The narrator describes Pyle as "impregnably armoured by his good intentions and his ignorance." Ultimately Pyle becomes deceived by his own deceptions. Greene based the character partly on a CIA agent, Colonel Edward Lansdale, who also inspired the character of Colonel Edwin Hillandale in Eugene BURDICK and William LEDERER's novel THE UGLY AMERICAN (1958).

The film presents a more sympathetic treatment of American efforts. In that version, Pyle works for a private U.S. aid mission instead of for the CIA, and the ending reverses Greene's critique of Americans into an anti-communist statement. Several reviewers speculated that Greene's attack on U.S. policy was partly motivated by the attorney general's decision to ban him from the United States in 1952 on the grounds that he had briefly joined the Communist Party in 1923. The reviewers may have been unfair in their search for a personal motive for Greene, however, since the novel is certainly consistent with his other political views. Greene also wrote an earlier NONFICTION piece on Vietnam for the *New Republic* entitled "Indo-China" (1954).

For additional reading, see Whitfield's *The Culture of the Cold War.*

Quo Vadis A 1951 EPIC FILM about early Christianity during the reign of Emperor Nero. Filmed in Italy, directed by Mervyn LeRoy and starring Robert Taylor, Deborah Kerr and Peter Ustinov as a convincingly demented Nero, *Quo Vadis* became MGM's second-biggest moneymaker after *Gone With the Wind* (1939). Like such other film epics as BEN-HUR (1959), THE TEN COMMANDMENTS (1956), SPARTACUS (1960) and *Samson and Delilah* (1949), *Quo Vadis* established parallels between ancient despotism and contemporary communist tyranny. And like those epics, the protagonists in *Quo Vadis* asserted their Judeo-Christian religious values in their struggle against oppression. For instance, the opening narration renders Nero's Rome in language often used to describe life behind the IRON CURTAIN: "The individual is at the mercy of the state." As in the Soviet Union, where religion was banned, in *Quo Vadis* Christ was a "rebel against the state." The story revolves around a handsome army commander (Taylor) who falls in love with a Christian woman his forces have captured. Ultimately, she converts him to Christianity, and they both nobly face death in defense of their beliefs at the hands of the cruel and pagan Nero. Audiences could readily infer the Cold War message that Christian values were the strongest weapon against tyrannical communism

and that the fight against communism was being waged to defend those values.

Quotations from Chairman Mao Tse-Tung A 1969 play by Edward Albee. Albee published it in conjunction with another play, *Box*, which he felt was closely related to it. Death is the general subject of these two plays, which are intended to be performed together. In his introduction to the published texts, Albee declares that although these are separate works that were conceived separately and can stand alone, "I feel they are more effective performed enmeshed . . . I have attempted . . . several experiments having to do . . . with the application of musical form to dramatic structure, and the use of *Box* as a parenthesis around *Mao* is part of that experiment." According to Albee, "Whatever symbolic content there may be in *Box* and *Quotations from Chairman Mao Tse-Tung* both plays deal with the unconscious, primarily."

Box consists solely of a large box sitting on stage illuminated by a bright light. A woman's voice speaks from the back of the THEATER describing a variety of subjects in a lyrical tone: the beauty of the box, the deaths of millions of babies, nature, the sea, artistic achievement and loss.

Quotations pairs historical speeches from the Chinese ruler with lines spoken by a long-winded woman, an old lady and a minister. The play appeared toward the end of the Cultural Revolution, in which Chairman Mao consolidated his power in the People's Republic of China. As quoted in the play, Mao's speeches attack capitalism and praise communism, describing the 600 million Chinese as "poor and blank," saying that on "a blank sheet of paper free from any mark, the freshest and most beautiful characters can be written." In the play, Mao always speaks in a reasonable tone to criticize individuality and insist on the necessity of war to cleanse the world. By contrast, the long-winded lady speaks of her husband's demise and her own need to endure both his dying and his death. And the old woman recites a doggerel poem, "Over the Hill to the Poor House," telling of a dedicated woman who raised six children and was a devoted wife but who was placed in the poorhouse after her husband died and was then rejected by her children. The women's speeches thus present concretely the individual suffering that Mao treats abstractly.

According to John MacNicholas in *The Dictionary of Literary Biography*, "Together the two plays present death, revolution, war, societal decline and its corollary of artistic falsification (the mendacity of mere craft) as consequences of self-destroying apathy. Dying (as opposed to death) is not a matter of chronology; rather, it is the immediate result of becoming careless, indifferent, content with blandishments. Both works insist that the opposite of dying is not to be functional but to be vigilant. Each play is designed to appeal to the intuitive rather than to the rational mind, to that sector of the imagination which draws directly on the unconscious." The plays did not attract wide audiences and are not considered to be among Albee's masterpieces, but according to MacNicholas "their originality and lyrical beauty . . . are exceptional."

For additional reading, see *Dictionary of Literary Biography* (vol. 7, *Twentieth-Century American Dramatists*).

Rabe, David   A playwright. Born in 1940, Rabe received a bachelor's degree in 1962 from Loras College, a Catholic college in Iowa, and was working on his master's degree in THEATER at Villanova University in Pennsylvania when he was drafted into the army in 1965. He served for two years in the military, including an 11-month stint in Vietnam. Though he never engaged in combat, he did witness fighting when he served with a hospital support group. He was particularly struck by how young the American soldiers were: "You don't realize how young most of our army is over there until you see them, troops fresh off the line, standing around some bar like teenagers at a soda fountain, talking coolly about how many of their guys got killed in the last battle." Upon returning home, Rabe felt alienated and disoriented because no one seemed to want to talk about the actual war, only about the politics surrounding it and the sensational news of massacres and corruption. He has described the war as being "a carnival—exciting, vulgar and obscene." He completed his master's degree in 1968, married in 1969 and, after a divorce, was remarried to actress Jill Clayburgh in 1979.

Rabe is best known for his three plays dealing with Vietnam: *Sticks and Bones* (1969), *The Basic Training of Pavlo Hummel* (1971) and *Streamers* (1976). As Nancy Anisfield points out in *Vietnam Anthology*, "Each play presents a vision of an America that is permanently poisoned by the war . . . the physically or psychologically wounded veteran is shown ironically as a painful, horrible embarrassment because he represents the ruin of America's myth of heroism and good-

ness. Furthermore, these plays offer an image of the American spirit as a thin veneer of euphemisms and patriotic rhetoric." *Sticks and Bones* centers on David, a blinded veteran who returns to his stereotypical middle-class American home. The family members are named and modeled after the characters from the 1950s TELEVISION SITUATION COMEDY, "Ozzie and Harriet." The play exposes the family's shallow values and their racism as they become scandalized by David's admission that he had had a deeply felt love affair with a Vietnamese girl. Ultimately, when it becomes clear that David and his family can neither understand each other nor accept each others' values Ozzie, Harriet and Ricky convince David to kill himself. The play concludes as he bleeds to death on stage.

Pavlo Hummel centers on a social misfit who begins to come into his own once he passes through basic training and is sent to Vietnam. As a medic, his job is to retrieve the corpses of dead soldiers who have been left to rot in the fields, but he takes to the assignment with enthusiasm and remains in Vietnam even after being wounded three times. Ironically, he dies at the hands of another GI with whom he gets into a fight at a brothel.

Streamers, Rabe's most acclaimed play, is less directly related to the war. It deals with racial and sexual relations among a group of soldiers who are completing their basic training and awaiting assignment to Vietnam. Another Rabe play, *The Orphan* (1973), alludes to the Vietnam War in its representation of the Trojan War. *In the Boom Boom Room*, a study of a young go-go dancer, won a Tony award nomination for best play of the 1973 season. *Hulry Burly* (1984) is about a group of disaffected single men. (See also VIETNAM WAR LITERATURE.)

For additional reading, see *Dictionary of Literary Biography* (vol. 7, *Twentieth-Century American Dramatists*) and Anisfield's *Vietnam Anthology*.

Radioactive Dreams

A 1986 FILM COMEDY starring John Stockwell, Michael Dudikoff and Lisa Blount and directed by Albert F. Pyun. A postapocalypse teen comedy, *Radioactive Dreams* describes the efforts of two boys raised on detective fiction to survive in a postnuclear war environment. The film was made toward the end of Ronald Reagan's first presidential term, when the possibilities of winnable nuclear war were still being publicly discussed.

Rambo

The title character in a series of VIETNAM WAR FILMS starring Sylvester Stallone and Richard Crenna and based on David Morrell's 1972 novel, *First Blood. First Blood* (1982) was also the title of the initial film in the Rambo movie trilogy, which includes *Rambo: First Blood Part II* (1985) and *Rambo III* (1988). All three movies star Stallone as Rambo, a gutsy, straightforward Vietnam veteran who, in *First Blood*, stands up to the sheriff of a small town in which he had been mistreated. In *Rambo II* he returns to Vietnam to save soldiers listed as Missing in Action (MIA), and in *Rambo III* he saves a friend who was captured by the communists while fighting on behalf of Afghani rebels.

The trilogy appeared during Reagan's two terms as president, and Reagan himself invoked it approvingly to applaud the values of loyalty, honesty, commitment and determined action. *Rambo: First Blood Part II* most caught the public imagination as it provided the country with its first unambiguous, larger-than-life cinematic Vietnam War hero since John WAYNE in THE GREEN BERETS (1968). At a time when the Reagan administration was actively trying to reverse the national sense of defeat that follow Vietnam, Watergate and the prolonged Iranian hostage situation (1979–80), *Rambo: First Blood Part II* permitted Americans to indulge in a sort of historical revisionism in which the United States actually defeats the North Vietnamese. The right wing had frequently charged during the Vietnam War and in later hostage situations that bureaucratic, diplomatic and political constraints had handicapped the U.S. military, preventing it from simply going in and "taking out" the enemy. (Other commentators claimed this was a myth, particularly as it applied to Vietnam, pointing out that the U.S. military had indeed made a wholehearted effort to win that war.) Because he acts outside of the government, Rambo is free from those supposed constraints. Thus the character is a vehicle of wish fulfillment for those who wanted to believe in Americans' unlimited military ability. Reagan, who first saw Rambo shortly after 39 Western hostages were released in Lebanon, commented "Boy, I saw *Rambo* last night. Now I know what to do the next time this happens."

Along with THE BEAST (1988) and the James BOND film THE LIVING DAYLIGHTS (1987), *Rambo III* is one of the few films to address the Soviet war in Afghanistan, a pivotal Cold War event that ended U.S.-Soviet détente. Like *Rambo II*, *Rambo III* suggests that the struggle against communism requires direct, forceful and violent action, a popular theme reinforced by Reagan's rhetoric if not always by his deeds. (See also VIETNAM WAR LITERATURE.)

Rand, Ayn

A NOVELIST and SCREENWRITER. Born in St. Petersburg, Russia, in 1905 as Alissa Rosenbaum, Rand came to the United States in 1926, shortly after Stalin had consolidated his power in the fledgling Soviet Union. She found work in Hollywood as a screenwriter in the 1930s before achieving fame for her fiction, which takes a strong pro-capitalist position. Her most famous work is THE FOUNTAINHEAD (1943), which was made into a film of the same name in 1949. The story celebrates Howard Roark, an individualist architect modeled after Frank Lloyd Wright. It attacks conformity and celebrates self-reliance and individualism. The film so strongly reflects Rand's fiercely pro-capitalist, anti-communist sentiments that in *Seeing Is Believing*, Peter Biskind calls it "a Wagnerian soap opera for the radical right . . . Hollywood's *Triumph of the Will*." Though written before the Cold War, *The Fountainhead* was often assigned in the public schools, where it was used to exemplify the virtues of capitalism and the dangers of collectivist thought.

Most of Rand's other literature similarly embodies her rejection of the collective in favor of radical individualism. For example, *Atlas Shrugged* (1957) presents a futuristic society that is based on the oath, "I will never live for the sake of another man, nor ask another man to live for mine." The book sold some 125,000 copies when it first appeared and eventually over two million copies were purchased. Her first novel, *We the Living* (1936), was "as near an autobiography as I will ever write." It is about the impact of the Stalinist Soviet Union on the lives of three individuals. The work remained in print throughout the Cold War. Rand's other works include *Anthem* (1946); *The Virtue of Selfishness* (1964); *Capitalism: The Unknown Ideal* (1966); *The New Left: the Anti-Industrial Revolution* (1971), a critique of the radical politics of the Vietnam War era; and *Night of January 16th*, a play (1933; revised, definitive version, 1968). Rand also helped edit the *Objectivist*, a monthly journal that promoted

Ayn Rand, 1962. Courtesy AP/Wide World.

her theories of objectivism, a policy of rational self-interest (as opposed to self-indulgent hedonism).

Rand also played a significant role during the RED SCARE. In 1947 she testified before the HOUSE COMMITTEE ON UN-AMERICAN ACTIVITIES (HUAC), which was then investigating the alleged presence of pro-communist messages and sentiments in Hollywood films. Unlike the HOLLYWOOD TEN, who refused to cooperate with the committee during those hearings, Rand appeared as a so-called "friendly" witness. She criticized the World War II–era film, *Song of Russia*, for presenting too positive a picture of life in the Soviet Union. When Congressman John McDowell observed, "You paint a very dismal picture of Russia . . . Doesn't anybody smile in Russia any more?" she replied, "Well, if you ask me literally, pretty much no . . . If they do, it is privately and accidentally. Certainly, it is not social. They don't smile in approval of their system." Rand also criticized *The Best Years of Our Lives* (1946) because she believed that by showing a banker refusing a loan to a returning soldier, the movie advanced "the party line of making the returned soldier fear that the world is against him" and "that business is against him."

In 1948 the MOTION PICTURE ALLIANCE FOR THE PRESERVATION OF AMERICAN IDEALS published Rand's A SCREEN GUIDE FOR AMERICANS, which became the basis for the film industry's movie code. Warning that the communists were trying to "*corrupt our moral premises by corrupting non-political movies . . . making people absorb the basic principles of Collectivism by indirection and implication,*" the *Screen Guide* insisted that American films not "smear" industrialists, success or the free enterprise system [Rand's emphasis]. Nor should films "deify the common man," "show that poverty is a virtue" or suggest that "failure is noble." The *New York Times* reprinted the *Screen Guide* on the front page of its entertainment section, and several other newspapers published it as well. Rand credited herself for the virtual elimination of depictions of unscrupulous businessmen in movies from the late 1940s and 1950s.

For additional reading, see Whitfield's *The Culture of the Cold War*. For a partial transcript of Rand's testimony before HUAC, see Bently's THIRTY YEARS OF TREASON.

Randall, Margaret A NONFICTION WRITER and MAGAZINE editor. Born in New York in 1936, Randall grew up in New Mexico. She attended the University of New Mexico, married a wealthy hockey player and lived with him for a year in Spain before the marriage dissolved. She lived in New York from 1958 to 1961, holding a variety of jobs while writing articles supporting Fidel Castro and the Cuban revolution. During this period, she befriended some of the abstract artists and POETS from the BEAT MOVEMENT. In 1961 she and her 10-month-old son moved to Mexico. There she married Sergio Mondragon, a Mexican poet, and gave up her American citizenship in order to gain employment. From 1962 to 1968, Randall and Mondragon coedited *El Corno Emplumado* (The Plumed Horn), a bilingual literary journal that was influential both in Latin America and the United States. The journal introduced American readers to the works of prominent Latin American writers, including Ernesto Cardenal, who later became the minister of culture in Nicaragua's Sandinista government, and Octavio Paz,

who won the 1990 Nobel Prize for literature. It also brought to the attention of Latin American readers the works of such North American writers as Allen GINSBERG, Denise LEVERTOV and Diane DiPrima, among others.

In 1967 and 1968, Randall traveled to Cuba to attend cultural congresses there. As a result, she became increasingly devoted to the Cuban revolution and other social causes. Her marriage to Mondragon ended in 1968, largely because Mondragon's apolitical views were incompatible with Randall's growing social activism. Upon returning to Mexico from Cuba in 1968, she and poet Robert Cohn became lovers as well as coeditors of *El Corno Emplumado*. Fearing political assassination by the Mexican police and/or by right-wing terrorists because of their open support of the 1968 student uprisings, Randall and Cohn went into hiding. They returned to Cuba in 1969, where Randall became deeply involved in building a socialist society, women's issues and Third World politics. In 1979 she moved to Nicaragua to write about the women who had helped the Sandinistas overthrow the Somoza dictatorship. *Sandino's Daughters: Testimonies of Nicaraguan Women in Struggle* (1981) was the result. She also wanted to be with her 11-year-old daughter from her marriage to Mondragon.

In 1984, Randall returned to Albuquerque on a visitor's visa, married writer Floyce Alexander and began teaching at the University of New Mexico. She recorded the impressions of her return to the United States in *Albuquerque: Coming Home to the U.S.A.* (1986). However, when Randall applied for permanent residency in 1984, the U.S. Immigration and Naturalization Service (INS) denied her request, and she was asked to leave the country in 1985. She appealed the decision, and her cause was supported by a range of human rights activists, civic groups and literary associations, including the PEN American Center. Twenty-nine American writers, including Donald Barthelme, E. L. Doctorow and Denise Levertov, cabled the INS on her behalf, objecting to "American officials still impugning writers and intellectuals under the ideological exclusion provisions of the McCarran-Walter Act." Nonetheless, in 1986 the INS ordered her deportation on the grounds that "her writings advocate the economic, international, and governmental doctrines of world communism." Her appeal was supported by a letter to Attorney General Edwin Meese sent by the PEN American Center and signed by Norman MAILER, Kurt VONNEGUT Jr., Susan Sontag, William Styron and John Irving, among others. The letter argued that Randall's ideas were being punished and that the decision to deport her abridged the American right to free expression. Randall won the first round of appeals and was allowed to remain in the United States while the case continued. In 1989 an INS review board voted 3-2 that Randall had always remained an American citizen, and that she was thus free to remain and travel within the United States.

Randall has authored over 40 books, in addition to her work as editor, critic, essayist, poet, translator and photographer. Her publications include *Breaking the Silences: An Anthology of 20th Century Poetry by Cuban Women* (1980), *Women in Cuba, Twenty Years Later* (1981), *Risking a Somersault in the Air: Conversations with Nicaraguan Writers* (1984) and *Women Brave in the Face of Danger: Photographs and Writings by Latin and North American Women* (1985). She also wrote the introduction to *The Rosenbergs: Collected Visions of Artists and Writers* (1988), a collection of literary and artistic responses to the trial and execution of atomic bomb spies Julius and Ethel Rosenberg and to other aspects of the 1950s RED SCARE. (See also EXILED WRITERS [from the United States].)

For additional reading, see Tucker's *Literary Exile in the Twentieth Century.*

Rather, Dan   A TELEVISION NEWS journalist. Rather first came to national attention during the Kennedy assassination, when he coordinated CBS's four-day continuous coverage of the events surrounding the president's murder. After reporting for 10 months in 1964 as White House correspondent, he served for a year in London. Then CBS assigned him to cover the Vietnam War, which he called "the most important story of this generation." He interviewed soldiers in the field, accompanied medical evacuation helicopters and questioned Vietnamese civilians and government officials in an effort to present the war to the American public and to understand the politics that fueled it. Upon returning to Washington in 1966 as White House correspondent, Rather became suspicious of the Johnson administration's attempts to orchestrate the news and misrepresent the progress of the war. Despite CBS's policy of changing White House correspondents when presidential administrations changed, Rather requested to stay on after Richard Nixon came to power in 1969, hoping the new administration would develop a more cordial relationship with the press. Instead, the Nixon White House became increasingly hostile. Nonetheless, Rather accompanied Nixon on his travels to the Mideast, the People's Republic of China and the Soviet Union, and he conducted a rare individual interview with the president which CBS broadcast live from the Oval Office. In 1971, presidential aide John Ehrlichman and H. R. Haldeman accused Rather of being biased and inaccurate. They suggested to CBS that Rather be reassigned, but CBS declined. Many observers believed that the administration had made Rather its media scapegoat.

Rather's tone of reporting subsequently became more adversarial. He established a reputation for his tough and unrelenting questioning of President Nixon during the Watergate scandal. A disrespectful remark to the president in March 1974 generated protests from CBS affiliates demanding his resignation. But as Nixon's guilt became more evident during the summer, Rather's credibility and his following increased. In 1981 he replaced Walter CRONKITE as the anchor for the "CBS Evening News." He remained in that position through the end of the Cold War and beyond.

Rather has published *The Palace Guard* (1974), an account of the events in the Nixon White House that had brought about the Watergate scandal, and his autobiography, *The Camera Never Blinks* (1977). Both were best-sellers. (See also TELEVISION DOCUMENTARIES AND SPECIAL REPORTS.)

For additional reading, see McNeil's *Total Television.*

Ratushinskaya, Irina   A Ukrainian EXILED WRITER (to the United States). Ratushinskaya was born in Odessa, Ukraine, in 1954 into a family that descended from Polish aristocracy. However, her parents, who grew up under communist rule,

discouraged her from identifying with her Polish or Catholic background and forbade her grandparents to speak to her in Polish. Ratushinskaya graduated with honors from Odessa University, where she studied mathematics and physics. In 1977 she received a prestigious appointment to the faculty of the Odessa Pedagogical Institute, but was demoted to a laboratory assistant when she objected to the school's anti-Semitic admissions policies. She was also accused of anti-Soviet tendencies because of a play she had cowritten. The play was banned after its premiere.

Ratushinskaya married Igor Gerashchenko in 1979 and moved to Kiev, where they fell afoul of the authorities by protesting the internal exile of Andrei Sakharov, the eminent physicist and human rights activist who had been the "father " of the Soviet atomic bomb. After Gerashchenko was fired from his position, the couple survived by doing freelance tutoring and menial labor. Ratushinskaya's recollections of this period appear in her story, "Senia the Dream Maker." She was first arrested in 1981 and spent 10 days in a Moscow jail for protesting human rights on Soviet Constitution Day. In 1982 Ratushinskaya and Gerashchenko were arrested for "preparing and distributing anti-Soviet materials," a charge stemming from Ratushinskaya's poetry and articles about the Polish labor movement, as well as her "oral agitation and propaganda" and her possession of "anti-Soviet literature." She was sentenced to seven years in prison and five years of internal exile, during which she was assigned to a special labor colony for political prisoners in Moravia, where guards treated her brutally. During a hunger strike she was force-fed and beaten. One of her beatings caused a concussion, and guards forced liquid down her throat while she lay unconscious, as a consequence of which Ratushinskaya developed kidney disease, dropsy, an inflamed ovary and periodic loss of consciousness. Worldwide protests came from Amnesty International, other human rights groups and such writers' groups as PEN International and the Pen American Center. Though Ratushinskaya was awarded the highest honor of the 1986 Poetry International Festival in Holland, Soviet authorities rejected appeals from PEN on the grounds that she was not a writer. Ratushinskaya continued to write in prison, smuggling her work out for publication abroad.

In 1986 Ratushinskaya was released from prison and allowed to emigrate. She went first to England and then to the United States, where she accepted a post at Northwestern University as poet-in-residence. In that year, a bilingual collection of her short stories appeared, entitled *A Tale of Three Heads,* including a short biography and a description of Ratushinskaya's work. In 1987, a volume of Ratushinskaya's prison poems was translated and published under the title *Beyond the Limit.* According to one of the translators, Frances Brent, the poems were "written with a sharpened matchstick on a bar of soap. When they were memorized, the poet washed her hands and the palimpsest was erased. The poems were composed sporadically over a period of 14 months." Ratushinskaya's autobiographical account of the treatment she and other female prisoners experienced in the prison camps appears in *Grey Is the Color of Hope* (1988). (See also POETS.)

For additional reading, see Tucker's *Literary Exile in the Twentieth Century.*

Reagan, Ronald A FILM ACTOR, TELEVISION PERFORMER, governor of California and president of the United States, from January 1981 to January 1989. Reagan's contributions to Cold War American culture began with his patriotic wartime movies, which extolled the virtues of honesty, strength, loyalty and righteousness and associated them with American causes. He served as president of the Screen Actors Guild from 1947 to 1951 and again in 1959. A liberal Democrat in the 1930s and 1940s, Reagan supported President Franklin Roosevelt, but by the 1950s his political orientation had turned to the right, and he endorsed the Eisenhower–Nixon ticket in 1952. Reagan became a Republican in 1962. As a spokesman for General Electric, he took a strong anti-communist stand. His public exposure from that position, as well as from his films and his television shows— GENERAL ELECTRIC THEATER (CBS, 1953–62; Reagan hosted it from 1954 to 1962) and "Death Valley Days" (syndicated, 1952–75; Reagan hosted it as the Old Ranger in 1965–66)— helped him become governor of California from 1967 to 1975. His 1965 autobiography, *Where's the Rest of Me?* also kept him before the public eye when his acting career was in decline.

A popular second lead in FILM DRAMAS, Reagan also starred in two 1950s MILITARY FILMS. Made the year after the Korean War ended, PRISONER OF WAR (1954) is a propagandistic and stereotyped film about an American officer who volunteers to be captured so he can investigate charges that U.S. POWs are cooperating with the communists. The charges prove erroneous, and the valiant GIs are vindicated. In *Hellcats of the Navy* (1957), Reagan plays a World War II submarine commander fighting against the Japanese. During the early 1950s, Reagan also appeared in *Law and Order*, a 1953 FILM WESTERN about a cowboy who cleans up a corrupt town, and STORM WARNING (1950), about a district attorney who indicts members of the Ku Klux Klan despite the impassioned objections of his community. *Storm Warning* alludes directly to the controversial hearings into the film industry then being conducted by the HOUSE COMMITTEE ON UN-AMERICAN ACTIVITIES (HUAC). As president of the Screen Actors Guild, Reagan supported these hearings. In the movie the hero, like HUAC, insists that the guilty parties must be revealed. On the other hand, the villainous towns-

Ronald Reagan. Courtesy Historical Association of South Florida.

people protect the Klan by invoking verbatim arguments used by the Committee for the First Amendment in support of the HOLLYWOOD TEN's refusal to testify before HUAC. Thus the film implicitly endorses HUAC and vilifies the unfriendly witnesses who would not cooperate with its quest to identify members of the Communist Party working in Hollywood.

As U.S. president, Reagan appointed Charlton HESTON cochair of the Task Force on the Arts and Humanities, and he brought worldwide attention to RAMBO (1985) when he applauded Sylvester STALLONE's forceful methods for freeing captives. Reagan's Strategic Defense Initiative, a proposed orbiting network of antiballistic lasers, became popularly known as STAR WARS, after a Cold War film from 1977.

For a discussion of the influence of Reagan's film career on his performance as a Cold War president, see Rogin's *Ronald Reagan, The Movie.* For a partial transcript of Reagan's testimony before HUAC, see Bentley's THIRTY YEARS OF TREASON.

Red Alert A 1958 MILITARY NOVEL by Peter George, a retired pilot in the Royal Air Force (also known as Peter George Bryant and Bryan Peters). The novel, which appeared just as the Cold War was entering its most dangerous and intense period, 1958–62, is best known for inspiring Stanley KUBRICK's film comedy, DR. STRANGELOVE (1964). (George also worked on the screenplay). However, unlike Kubrick's BLACK HUMOR movie, *Red Alert* presents a serious drama, though both works feature a crazy air force general who launches an unauthorized nuclear attack against the Soviet Union. (See also APOCALYPTIC NOVELS.)

For additional reading, see Dowling's *Fictions of Nuclear Disaster.*

Red Channels: The Report of Communist Influence in Radio and Television A 1950 publication that was widely used as the basis for unofficial BLACKLISTING within the TELEVISION and radio industries. *Red Channels* first appeared as a special report by the right-wing magazine COUNTERATTACK, which was published by American Business Consultants in New York, a corporation formed by three former FBI agents. Vincent Hartnett, who went on to found the anti-communist organization Aware, Inc. and to publish a *Red Channels* sequel, *File 13*, wrote the introduction and claimed responsibility for the publication. Hartnett later became a "talent consultant," running checks on the political backgrounds of people being considered for jobs within the entertainment industry.

Red Channels lists 151 men and women who the editors claim are linked with a variety of "Communist causes," in either the past or present. Those listed include 68 actors, 44 writers, 28 musicians, 18 directors, 11 commentators, three announcers, a music critic, a lawyer and an accountant. (See also TELEVISION PERFORMERS, FILM ACTORS AND ACTRESSES, FILM DIRECTORS, SCREENWRITERS, FOLK SINGERS and MUSIC.) In each instance, the editors cite the alleged communist connection. These include membership in organizations listed as subversive by the attorney general, the House Committee on Un-American Activities (HUAC), the California Un-American Activities Committee and other official and private sources, including various anti-communist groups of the time. For example, *Red Channels* lists performers who belonged to the Stop Censorship Committee, which it cites as a communist front organization formed in 1948. However, the *Counterattack* issue of July 1, 1949, is its only source. It uses similar documentation to identify as "Communist" the CULTURAL AND SCIENTIFIC CONFERENCE FOR WORLD PEACE; its sponsor, the National Council of Arts, Sciences and Professions; the World Peace Congress; the Voice of Freedom; the Committee for Free Political Advocacy; the American Continental Congress for Intellectuals; and the *Book Union Bulletin*. Moreover, *Red Channels* sometimes cites *Counterattack* to document an individual's affiliation with a suspect organization. For instance, *Counterattack* is the sole source for the entry citing radio commentator J. Raymond Walsh's role as chair of the Committee of One Thousand and his appearance as a speaker before the Committee for a Democratic Far Eastern Policy.

Red Channels also listed those cited in HUAC's unreliable Appendix IX, a document that the committee later withdrew and ordered destroyed and that was therefore unavailable to the general public, so that neither the New York Public Library nor the Library of Congress had copies. But since several copies had already been distributed, the editors of *Counterattack* had received some of them.

Red Channels began with a disclaimer stating that those listed may have been free of subversive intentions, and it purported only to report factual information from other sources. Consequently, the publication avoided legal liability for any damage suffered by the people it listed. For example, when Ireene WICKER was able to demonstrate that her *Red Channels* listing had inaccurately shown her to have signed a petition on behalf of a Communist Party candidate, *Counterattack* published her disclaimer of communist affiliation but blamed the inaccurate listing solely on its source, the Communist Party newspaper, *The Daily Worker*. *Counterattack* then reiterated its own position that "*Red Channels* did not call Miss Wicker, or any other person mentioned in the report, a Communist or Communist sympathizer." Nonetheless, Wicker remained banned from the television industry for three years. According to her agent, industry officials would respond to his queries on her behalf, "What about *Red Channels?* We wouldn't touch her with a ten-foot pole."

In practice, most individuals listed in *Red Channels* had to clear their name by demonstrating that they had *not* been affiliated with the named organizations, or they had to demonstrate that those organizations had been free of communist influences. If they could do neither, they faced the cancellation of their contracts and a blacklist on being hired in the broadcast industry for most of the 1950s.

Among those who lost work because of being listed in *Red Channels* were Philip LOEB, Jean MUIR, Hazel SCOTT, Mady Christians, Gypsy Rose Lee, Marsha Hunt and folk singers Pete SEEGER, the Weavers and Tom Glazer, another folk singer. Among the news commentators listed in *Red Channels* were Howard K. Smith and William Shirer. Though Smith has stated that the listing had no impact on his career, Shirer has said that he was the victim of blacklisting. He has also claimed that his three listings in *Red Channels*—which did not accuse him of being a communist or a fellow traveler—were arbitrary and misleading. On the other hand,

Ed SULLIVAN, an early champion of *Red Channels* and industry blacklisting, greeted the publication enthusiastically in his syndicated newspaper column:

> With television going into its third big year . . . the entire industry is becoming increasingly aware of the necessity to plug all Commie propaganda loopholes. Networks and station heads, with a tremendous financial stake, want no part of Commies or pinkos. Sponsors, sensitive in the extreme to blacklisting, want no part of Commies or their sympathizers. Advertising agencies held responsible by sponsors for correct exercise of discretion in programming, want no controversy of any kind. For that reason, [the] *Red Channels* listing of performers who, innocently or maliciously, are affiliated with Commie-front organizations will be a reference book in preparing any program.

For additional reading, see Cogley's *Report on Blacklisting,* vol. 2; Miller's *The Judges and the Judged;* and Whitfield's *The Culture of the Cold War.*

Red Danube, The   A 1950 FILM DRAMA starring Walter Pidgeon, Janet Leigh, Peter Lawford, Ethel Barrymore and Angela Lansbury and directed by George Sidney. Made during the early days of the Cold War, while the communists were consolidating their gains behind the IRON CURTAIN, the story centers on a romance between a British military officer and a ballerina in occupied Vienna, where the communists compel citizens to return to the U.S.S.R. against their will. (THE THIRD MAN [1950] also treats this situation.)

Red Dawn   A 1984 MILITARY FILM starring Patrick Swayze, Thomas Howell and Ron O'Neal and directed by John Milius. *Red Dawn* was made during President Reagan's first administration, when Cold War tensions were at their highest levels since the 1962 Cuban Missile Crisis. At that time the United States was supporting the anti-communist government in El Salvador and the anti-communist contras in Nicaragua; the Soviet Union was fighting an aggressive war in Afghanistan; and Reagan was publicly pointing out that the communist forces in Latin America were only a day's drive from Texas. The film begins shortly after a Soviet–Cuban–Nicaraguan alliance successfully invades the United States from the south and uses limited nuclear strikes to capture a portion of the country. The plot centers on a group of teenagers, led by Swayze, who form a resistance movement and fight back against the communist occupiers. In the process, *Red Dawn* uses many clichés from World War II resistance films. It also presents a right-wing view of the threat to U.S. security posed by communists in Latin America. In this respect, the film reflects what the president was telling the country at the same time.

Red Dawn also embodies the values expressed by many survivalists of the 1980s who opposed gun control and insisted on the importance of wilderness survival training. The first thing the conquering communists do when they seize a town is search the government records for gun registration forms so they can identify the owners and confiscate all weapons. The boys are required to hunt for food and endure winter conditions in the mountains in order to survive and to fight back. The film rejects maternal nurturing in favor of more macho values. The boys rarely mention their mothers but reveal a close bond with their fathers, and they now understand why their fathers had to be tough on them when they were growing up. Elements of class consciousness in the movie celebrate no-nonsense working-class citizens and denigrate wealthy families that are intellectual and "soft." Moreover, the survivalist conditions call for a strong, authoritarian leader who asserts power rather than a democratically chosen official. For instance, the mayor's son, who is also the student government president, initially proposes that the boys surrender. He offers this suggestion as a motion to be voted upon, but he is unable to match the authoritarian leadership of Swayze, a football star who challenges him to a fight. Later the academically inclined student president, who may also exhibit some latent homosexual tendencies, betrays the rebels after he is caught by the communists while violating Swayze's orders.

Thus in this movie, weak-willed, liberal, homosexual intellectuals undermine the cause of freedom, while no-nonsense, authoritarian athletes defend it. The film also likens the American resistance fighters to the Afghani rebels who fought Soviet troops throughout the 1980s. Swayze adopts a winter wardrobe similar to that worn in Afghanistan, and like the Afghani rebels, the boys ride horses across barren country and shoot at Soviet helicopters with hand-held anti-aircraft missiles. The final lines of the super-patriotic movie evoke the Gettysburg Address.

Red Dragon   A 1945 SPY FILM starring Sidney Toler, Fortunio Bonanova and Benson Fong and directed by Phil Rosen. This Charlie Chan story about an attempt to steal a scientist's plans for an atomic bomb was among the first to treat that theme, as it appeared during the same year that the bomb was first tested and used.

Red Heat   A 1985 FILM DRAMA starring Arnold Schwarzenegger, James Belushi and Peter Boyle and directed by Walter Hill. In this violent, Reagan-era film, a Soviet police officer (Schwarzenegger) joins forces with his Chicago counterpart (Belushi) against a Soviet criminal who has fled to the United States. This cinematic example of U.S.-Soviet cooperation coincided with Mikhail Gorbachev's rise to power in the U.S.S.R.

Red Herring   A Cold War term used by President Truman in 1948 to refer to Whittaker Chambers's allegations that Alger Hiss had spied for the Soviets. President Truman denounced the investigation by the HOUSE COMMITTEE ON UN-AMERICAN ACTIVITIES (HUAC) as a deliberate, political distortion and a Republican *red herring*. He used the term to mean that the charges were a deliberately conceived distraction and a sleight-of-hand intended to produce an erroneous impression. In return, Congressman Richard Nixon criticized Truman for his flagrant "flouting of the national interests of the people." (See also LANGUAGE; RED SCARE.)

Red King, White Knight   A 1989 SPY FILM starring Max von Sydow, Tom Skerritt and Helen Mirren and directed by Geoff Murphy. Made while Mikhail Gorbachev was implementing new policies of personal freedom and economic reform in the Soviet Union, this film centers on the efforts of an ex-CIA agent (Skerritt) who returns to duty to prevent Gorbachev's assassination by his internal political enemies.

Red Menace, The   A 1949 FILM DRAMA directed by R. G. Springsteen and narrated by Lloyd G. Davies, an actual member of the Los Angeles City Council. Filmed in quasi-documentary fashion, *The Red Menace* depicts communists as willing to do anything, even use sex, to win converts and get their way. When a potential dupe says to a communist blonde, "I always thought the Commies peddled bunk. I didn't know they came as cute as you," she permits him to kiss her, but only long enough for her to stick a copy of *Das Kapital* into his hand. Elsewhere, communists appear as cynical hypocrites who mock their own rhetoric by deriding blacks and other ethnic minorities. (See also FILMS ASSOCIATED WITH THE RED SCARE.)

For additional reading, see Sayre's *Running Time*.

Red Planet Mars   A 1952 SCIENCE FICTION FILM starring Peter Graves, Andrea King and Marvin Miller and directed by Harry Horner. Set in the near future, the film shows the world to be heading toward nuclear annihilation until religious radio broadcasts from a highly advanced Martian civilization incite a revolution in the Soviet Union. Ultimately, a Voice of America broadcast of the Sermon on the Mount incites the peasants to rip down their posters of Stalin and join with the Orthodox patriarch to drive out the communists, reopen the churches and help their country find its soul. The film provided some wish fulfillment for American audiences hoping to see the oppressed people behind the IRON CURTAIN throw off their chains and overthrow the Communist tyrants. Moreover, like many other Cold War–era films, *Red Planet Mars* shows that the free practice of religion is the best means for opposing atheistic communism. Like science fiction films and EPIC FILMS, *Red Planet Mars* endorses Christianity as both the embodiment of American values and the set of beliefs best suited for defeating communism.

Red Scare, The   Anti-communist fanaticism that flourished in the United States roughly between 1947 and 1960, representing the notion that "Reds"—communists—were an overwhelming present danger to the United States and its citizens. Ironically, the Cold War, waged ostensibly to oppose communist suppression of civil liberties, brought about one of the most politically repressive periods in the history of the U.S. democracy, in which American freedoms of expression, political activism and press were more restricted than at any other time of peace in American history, allegedly in order to combat the "Communist threat." Nonetheless, though deplorable abuses occurred, American society did ultimately reject the worst aspects of the Red Scare, and the courts protected personal, political and press freedoms to a remarkable extent during the rest of the Cold War.

The Red Scare was fueled by right-wing charges concerning American communists, communist sympathizers (called "fellow travelers") and citizens (called "Communist dupes") who were thought to be unwittingly assisting the communist cause in their naive attempts to achieve social justice. According to many on the right, these three groups were subverting the country. The individuals specifically included government officials, political figures, teachers, college professors, members of the entertainment industry and "ordinary" citizens. Many of the accused were intellectuals—writers, academics and the like—who had expressed their desire to enhance opportunities for freedom, justice and dignified work during the Depression and World War II and had become active in liberal or left-wing causes in the 1930s. Thus a resurgent strain of anti-intellectualism—never long absent in American culture—played a significant role in the Red Scare, along with a homophobic association of intellectuals and homosexuals. The Red Scare also had elements of anti-Semitism and racism. Ostensibly a major part of the Red Scare's agenda was to undermine President Roosevelt's New Deal and the philosophy of an activist government that underlay it.

The basic premise of the Red Scare was that Communist agents were infiltrating the US and local governments, the educational system, the entertainment industry and other important social institutions that set policy and shaped public attitudes and beliefs. These charges began in 1947, when the HOUSE COMMITTEE ON UN-AMERICAN ACTIVITIES (HUAC) first began its investigation of SCREENWRITERS and FILM DIRECTORS, who were allegedly introducing pro-communist sentiments into nationally distributed films. Then, in 1948, former Communist Party member Whittaker Chambers accused Alger Hiss, a prominent member of the Roosevelt administration and one of the founders of the United Nations (UN), of having spied for the Soviets in the 1930s. In 1949 Hiss was convicted of lying about his alleged communist affiliations and activities. Though the charges against him remain disputed, his perjury conviction linked New Deal/Fair Deal liberalism with communism in the popular mind. (Chambers later amplified on his charges in WITNESS, his 1952 autobiography about his experiences with the Communist Party in the 1930s. Hiss presented his defense in IN THE COURT OF PUBLIC OPINION (1957).) In 1951, following a highly controversial trial, the government convicted Julius and Ethel Rosenberg for espionage, claiming the couple had delivered atomic bomb secrets to the U.S.S.R. The Rosenbergs were executed in 1953 despite significant national and international protest. The Hiss and Rosenberg convictions seemed to support the right-wing claim that American communists were successfully pursuing a program of infiltration, espionage and subversion. (See also WE ARE YOUR SONS (1975), a defense of the Rosenbergs written by their sons; the political novels THE BOOK OF DANIEL (1971) and THE PUBLIC BURNING (1976); and Donald Freed's 1970 play, IN-QUEST, which is based on Walter and Miriam Schneir's 1965 review of the case, *Invitation to an Inquest*. Louis Nizer contradicts the Schneirs' claim for the Rosenbergs' innocence in his 1973 study *The Implosion Conspiracy*. Since the Schneirs were able to review newly released Soviet documents in 1996, they have contradicted both their critics and their own earlier findings. They now conclude that Julius was a spy though Ethel was not, and that Julius stole no secret of any value. In 1997 Alexander Feklisov, a former KGB official, claimed that Ethel was entirely innocent and that Julius had helped organize a 1940s spy ring and had stolen some military information but did not steal secrets about the atomic bomb.)

The Red Scare occasioned legislative and executive branch action that increasingly restricted the rights of American communists. In 1949 Communist Party leaders were convicted and jailed under the Smith Act. Party members were barred from employment in the U.S. government and forbidden to serve as union leaders. The 1950 McCarran Internal Security Act established concentration camps for communists, though these were never used. It also required all communist and "Communist-dominated" organizations to provide the federal government with the names of all of their members and contributors. Other federal, state and local legislation denied additional rights to communists and required citizens to sign loyalty oaths in order to work for government agencies. In 1952 the State Department, a frequent target of right-wing attacks, imposed travel restrictions to the U.S.S.R. and other IRON CURTAIN countries.

Congress also conducted highly publicized hearings into alleged communist activities. Witnesses who recanted their past activities and identified other communist suspects were labeled "friendly" and were usually exculpated. In fact, several repenting ex-communists became national celebrities and "media experts" on the communist threat, though a relatively small number of "informers" faced discrimination and possible BLACKLISTING once their past left-wing activities became known. On the other hand, witnesses who refused to cooperate with the congressional committees were labelled "unfriendly" and faced imprisonment for contempt of Congress. Notable among these were the screenwriters and directors known as the HOLLYWOOD TEN, who unsuccessfully attempted to invoke their First Amendment protections of free speech in the 1947 HUAC hearings. These ten men were imprisoned for terms ranging from six months to a year. As a result of the HUAC hearings in 1947, 1951–52, 1953–55 and 1957–58, hundreds of FILM ACTORS AND ACTRESSES, writers and directors were blacklisted, unable to work in the film or television industries.

Other witnesses before HUAC and Senator Joseph McCarthy's (R. Wisconsin) Permanent Investigations Subcommittee of the Government Operations Committee who were unable or unwilling to clear themselves of accusations of communist sympathies also suffered from the Red Scare. In addition to losing their standing in their communities and the respect of friends and family, many lost their jobs and were unable to obtain work within their professions for considerable periods, especially workers in the film industry and educators. Some went into temporary or permanent exile in order to practice their professions, including screenwriters Dalton TRUMBO, John Howard LAWSON and Carl FOREMAN, novelist Richard WRIGHT and performers Paul Draper and Larry Adler. German-born playwright Bertolt BRECHT fled to East Germany almost immediately after testifying before HUAC. The German-novelists Thomas MANN and Stefan HEYM also left the United States for fear of Cold War persecution. (See EXILED WRITERS [from the United States].) Historian M. I. Finley, who lost his job at Rutgers University because he had pled the Fifth Amendment before a government committee, moved to England, where he eventually was knighted for his work at Cambridge University. Margaret SCHLAUCH, a distinguished linguist and literary scholar, was another prominent academic who went into exile from the United States after receiving a subpoena from HUAC.

Even those who did not leave the United States suffered from the Red Scare. Professor Owen Lattimore, a China scholar who opposed Chiang Kai-shek and whom McCarthy accused of espionage, describes how he and his supporters were persecuted in ORDEAL BY SLANDER (1950). J. Robert Oppenheimer had been the head of the Atomic Energy Commission. He had directed the Manhattan Project, which developed the atomic bomb during World War II. He lost his security clearance in 1953 as a result of charges that he had had communist affiliations in the 1930s, making him a current security risk. That year, JOURNALISTS Joseph and Stewart ALSOP defended Oppenheimer in their book *We Accuse!* (1953), whose title alludes to Emile Zola's response to the French government's unfair treason conviction of Jewish captain Alfred Dreyfus in 1894. Oppenheimer's ordeal also became the subject of Heimar Kipphardt's 1968 play, IN THE MATTER OF J. ROBERT OPPENHEIMER.

The Red Scare reached its zenith in 1954, when McCarthy accused the secretary of the army of concealing communist espionage. The U.S. military served as the most direct and powerful defense against Soviet aggression. Consequently, McCarthy's accusation represented a declaration by the political right wing that the national leadership was untrustworthy. The nationally televised ARMY–MCCARTHY HEARINGS thus represented a contest for power, authority and public credibility between McCarthy's extreme right wing and President Eisenhower's conservative but more centrist position. The showdown between the army and McCarthy ultimately discredited McCarthy, and the Senate voted to censure him shortly thereafter for his behavior during those hearings and his mismanagement of campaign funds. McCarthy never again commanded the same power to dominate and intimidate.

After McCarthy's fall from power, the Red Scare diminished, though it remained a significant force in American political and professional life at least through 1960, when Democrat John Kennedy was elected president. Kennedy's so-called "Camelot" reversed the Red Scare's anti-intellectualism by placing highly educated intellectuals and scientifically oriented "experts" in positions of new authority. (See David Halberstam's THE BEST AND THE BRIGHTEST, 1972). First Lady Jacqueline Kennedy promoted the high culture of fine arts, classical music and "serious" literature by inviting world-class musicians, artists and writers to the White House. Nonetheless, even in the comparatively liberal 1960s and 1970s, charges of communist sympathy were used to discredit liberals, intellectuals, antiwar advocates, feminists, civil rights advocates and other citizens who were anywhere left of center on the political spectrum or who simply took pacifist positions.

The Red Scare charges of widespread communist subversion have not held up well. Soviet Communist Party files that have become available since the disintegration of the U.S.S.R. have revealed no evidence that Alger Hiss was a Soviet agent. Throughout the Cold War, no American Communist Party members were ever caught engaging in espionage or sabotage, despite their frequent depiction in films, television and radio shows as enemy agents. And despite his accusations of widespread infiltration, McCarthy himself never produced a single bona fide communist employed by the government. While Red Scare rhetoric warned of domestic communist activity, in fact membership in the Communist Party dramatically decreased in the 1950s. Indeed, party membership dropped from 80,000 immediately after World War II to about 5,000 in 1956—and so many of those were FBI agents that Hoover considered taking control of the party in 1957. (Art BUCHWALD facetiously suggests this possibility in one of his SATIRES.)

The image of an active and pervasive threat of communist subversion did not come from politicians and government agencies alone. It was also portrayed by many elements of mainstream popular culture: in MAGAZINES, newspapers and publications of such special-interest groups as the American Legion, the Catholic War Veterans, the Joint Committee Against Communism; in the right-wing journals COUNTERATTACK and RED CHANNELS; in fiction and NONFICTION; and in TELEVISION, THEATER, MUSIC, ART, and FILM.

Moreover, censorship reinforced a very limited picture of the Red Scare and the Cold War. Not only were allegedly pro-communist books banned from local libraries, but also the State Department banned all materials by "any controversial persons, Communists, fellow-travelers, et cetera" from its overseas libraries. In 1953, McCarthy aides Roy Cohn and David Schine toured the libraries of the State Department's International Information Agency and declared that out of the two million books on the shelves, some 30,000 were by "pro-Communist writers." The works of some 40 authors, including Theodore H. White and Dashiell Hammett, were removed from the shelves; some, including White's best-selling THUNDER OUT OF CHINA (1946), were actually burned.

Movies were subject to self-censorship in part to preclude any government move toward official censorship. In 1948, Ayn RAND'S A SCREEN GUIDE FOR AMERICANS became the basis for a movie-industry film code. Published by the anti-communist MOTION PICTURE ALLIANCE FOR THE PRESERVATION OF AMERICAN IDEALS and then republished in the *New York Times* and other major newspapers, Rand's *Guide* admonishes filmmakers not to smear industrialists, success or the free enterprise system, and not to glorify "the common man" or " 'the little people' . . . since it is not the American idea to be either 'common' or 'little.' " Rand also wrote several fiction and nonfiction works extolling the virtues of capitalism and vilifying communism.

Censorship also took the form of prohibiting prominent left-wing performers from reaching a wide public, which undoubtedly had a "chilling effect" on other leftists and even liberals. For example, HUAC frequently referred to Paul ROBESON as a communist or communist sympathizer, despite his public denial of party membership before the California State Legislature. Consequently, Robeson was blacklisted, his records were removed from stores, and newspaper editorials frequently denounced him. In response, Robeson, an African American, reaffirmed his support for the Soviet Union, declaring at the 1949 World Peace Congress in Paris, "It is unthinkable that American Negroes could go to war on behalf of those who have oppressed us for generations against a country [the U.S.S.R.] which in one generation has raised our people to the full dignity of mankind." In 1950, the State Department ordered Robeson—an international concert artist—to surrender his passport. The department refused to issue Robeson a new passport unless he signed an oath declaring that he was not a communist and promised not to give political speeches abroad. Robeson refused and challenged the State Department's action in court. He eventually won in 1958, when the Supreme Court ruled in a similar case that the government's actions were unconstitutional. During the eight-year period of his appeal, Robeson was unable to work abroad, where he could still attract enthusiastic audiences, and was blacklisted at home. Hence he was essentially deprived of opportunities to earn a living, except for poorly paying performances before radical audiences.

Sometimes Red Scare censorship was exercised against particular songs. In 1950, anti-communists successfully drove Vern Partlow's song OLD MAN ATOM from the air by pressuring radio stations not to play it. The "talking blues" number warns of the danger posed by atomic weaponry: "Here's my thesis; Peace in the world, or the world in pieces." According to Rabbi Benjamin Schultz, head of the Joint Committee Against Communism, the song had to be banned because its message was subversive: It echoed the sentiments expressed in the Stockholm peace petition, which communists were then circulating. Likewise, in 1953, at the height of McCarthy's power, Canadian Ruben Ship faced deportation hearings for his phonograph record, THE INVESTIGATOR, a comedy album that satirizes the senator and his hearings.

Earnest Frankel's TONGUE OF FIRE also denounces McCarthy. Its publisher, Putnam's, dropped it three weeks before its scheduled publication in 1955, in what seems to have been the publisher's response to an effort at suppression by McCarthy or his supporters. The book was not released until 1960.

Censorship also extended to certain types of performance that were not explicitly political. During the late 1950s and early 1960s, Lenny BRUCE was arrested several times for his stand-up comedy. The charges generally revolved around accusations of obscenity, although Bruce's irreverent, anti-patriotic and "un-American" satire also provoked arrests, in addition to his frank talk about sex. The fact that Bruce also satirized communism did not defer those who saw him as un-American.

Overall, the Red Scare belief in an active, present danger from domestic communists was given its fullest expression in the print media: magazines, newspapers and nonfiction books. News and general-interest magazines often reflected Red Scare perspectives in their reporting and editorials. For instance, *Life* magazine's article on the 1949 CULTURAL AND SCIENTIFIC CONFERENCE FOR WORLD PEACE declared that the conference was "dominated by intellectuals who fellow-travel the Communist line," and it featured pictures of fifty "Dupes and Fellow Travelers" who ranged from "hard working fellow travelers to soft-hearted do-gooders." Among those shown were Charles CHAPLIN, Arthur MILLER, Leonard Bernstein and Langston Hughes. Such influential journalists as Henry LUCE, who published *Life* and *Time*, George SOKOLSKY, Ed SULLIVAN, Walter WINCHELL, William LOEB, William F. BUCKLEY Jr. and Hedda Hopper articulated a right-wing anti-communist view of the domestic scene.

For example, Buckley defended McCarthy in his 1954 book, *McCarthy and His Enemies,* and attacked critics of HUAC in *The Committee and its Critics* (1962). Sullivan, a nationally syndicated columnist who also hosted a popular television variety show, enthusiastically endorsed the appearance in 1950 of *Red Channels,* which quickly became the basis for the television blacklist. On the other hand, Drew PEARSON and Joseph and Stewart Alsop defended victims of the Red Scare and attacked McCarthy, though they themselves were staunchly anti-communist.

In 1949 Richard Crossman published THE GOD THAT FAILED, an anthology of nonfiction essays by prominent ex-"fellow travelers" and ex-communists including Arthur KOESTLER and Richard WRIGHT. The six authors chart their initial attraction to and their ultimate dissatisfaction with communism. In 1954, Frederic Wertham's THE SEDUCTION OF THE INNOCENT charged that comic books were corrupting American youth and undermining their values. The book provoked congressional hearings and ultimately led to an industry-enforced comics code of morality and decency. Books and articles by J. Edgar Hoover and his former FBI agents, such as Matt Cvetic's I WAS A COMMUNIST FOR THE FBI (1950), Herbert Philbrick's I LED THREE LIVES (1952) and Hoover's own 1958 MASTERS OF DECEIT, were best-sellers. Many were assigned in public schools for such courses as "Americanism versus Communism."

With some exceptions, the Red Scare did not generally capture the imagination of POETS or novelists, though several writers in the BEAT MOVEMENT wrote against it. However, Merle Miller's 1949 novel, THE SURE THING, opposed the Red Scare by criticizing the right-wing pressures on the Truman administration to eliminate suspected communists and other leftists from government. The novel depicts a liberal State Department official who loses his job after an unjust investigation. Miller later wrote *The Judges and the Judged,* a nonfiction account of blacklisting during the Red Scare. Isidor Schneider's 1946 THE JUDAS TIME is a rare pro-communist novel from the period. It centers on a college instructor and party member who betrays the communist cell at his university in return for promotion to assistant professor. One of the sympathetic characters in Judith Merril's 1950 apocalyptic novel SHADOW ON THE HEARTH is a former nuclear physicist who has resigned out of conscience and become a teacher instead. After New York suffers an atomic attack, he is hunted by the police as part of a post-attack Red Scare. Since he not only proves loyal but also saves the protagonists at some risk to himself, the man's role in the book cautions against the abusive extremes of the contemporary Red Scare that was still in its early stages in 1950. On the other hand, we also learn that the threat from internal subversion is genuine, since "fifth-column" collaborators helped guide the Soviet attack.

Howard FAST wrote SPARTACUS (1951) while serving a prison sentence for refusing to testify before HUAC. A communist at the time of his imprisonment, Fast told the story of the legendary Roman slave whom the Communist Party had long used as a symbol for the fight against imperialist oppression. On the other hand, *Spartacus* puts forward an international, multiracial movement as the opposition to Roman imperialism. Philip Wylie's novel TOMORROW! (1954) warns of the international communist threat and promotes civil defense, though it also attacks the right-wing proponents of the Red Scare for exaggerating the danger of domestic communists and underestimating the danger of international communism. As one character puts it, Americans "have refused for more than a decade to face our real fear. We know our world could end . . . The medieval lust of men cowering before the holocaust has been exploited by McCarthy . . ."

At the end of the Red Scare, Senator McCarthy became the basis for a powerful right-wing politician who proves to be a communist dupe in Richard Condon's 1959 novel THE MANCHURIAN CANDIDATE (later a 1962 film). William Wister Gaines's 1957 novel THE HONORABLE ROCKY SLADE parodies McCarthy's early career. John BARTH's novel *The Floating Opera* (1956) refers to the Red Scare when one of the characters temporarily loses his inheritance for contributing to an agency that supported the anti-fascist Loyalists during the Spanish Civil War. A lawyer successfully argues that since the communists also supported that agency and the anti-fascist cause, the contributions demonstrate the character's underlying communist sympathies. Joseph Heller's 1961 military novel CATCH-22 lampoons the practice of demanding loyalty oaths and ridicules investigative committees and other features of the Red Scare. Frederick Pohl's SCIENCE FICTION NOVELS also have anti–Red Scare undertones.

Anti-communist novels from the Red Scare–era include Lionel TRILLING's 1947 political novel THE MIDDLE OF THE JOURNEY, which focuses on the protagonists' disillusionment with the Communist Party. One of the main characters is based on Whittaker Chambers, who became famous for accusing Alger Hiss a year after the book's publication. David Dortort's 1949 POST OF HONOR likewise presents the disillusionment of a member of the Young Communist League during the seven years before the U.S. entry into World War II. Willa Gibb's THE TENDER MEN (1948) criticizes communist methods, portraying a party that expects the individual to subjugate all of his or her rights and beliefs to the party. The novel depicts a midwestern farm boy who is recruited by the Communist Party but is later assassinated for failing to follow orders. *Invisible Man,* Ralph Ellison's critically acclaimed 1952 novel about a black man's struggle for identity in white America, shows communists to be responsible for cynically inciting race riots in Harlem (a theme also presented in *I Was a Communist for the F.B.I.*).

The right-wing themes of the Red Scare found their way into popular fiction of the early Cold War. Allen Drury's ADVISE AND CONSENT (1959) centers on the Senate confirmation hearings of a liberal nominee for secretary of state who is clearly based on Alger Hiss. Detective writer Mickey SPILLANE also depicted the American communist menace. Spillane's protagonist, Mike Hammer, shows that eliminating communists is commendable, indeed, patriotic. In *One Lonely Night* (1951) the private detective boasts, "I shot them in cold blood and enjoyed every minute of it . . . They were Commies . . . They were red sons-of-bitches who should have died long ago . . . They never thought there were people like us in this country. They figured us all to be soft as horse manure."

Although dramatists wrote few plays referring to the Red Scare, there were some exceptions. Most notable are such works by Arthur Miller as THE CRUCIBLE (1953), *A View*

from the Bridge (1955) and *You're Next,* a 1950s satire attacking HUAC. Overall, theater had stronger ties with the left than most other artistic media of the era. Plays relied on individual ticket sales instead of corporate sponsorship. And unlike film producers, theater producers were able to secure bank loans in spite of threatened boycotts by the American Legion and other groups. As a result, theater was generally free from the economic threat of boycotts and pickets, and such blacklisted film actors as Zero MOSTEL and Ruby Dee were able to pursue acting careers on stage. Yet the overall climate of fear created by the Red Scare kept most theaters free of political material.

On the other hand, the television and film industries were highly vulnerable to boycotts and other forms of public protest, and right-wing anti-communists wielded those weapons very effectively. Thus television's response to the Red Scare was to avoid all mention of it whenever possible, since producers did not want to alienate any of their viewers, left or right, because all were potential customers for the sponsors' products. Certainly no regularly scheduled network television show expressed any sentiments objectionable to the political right—or at least, not very often. However, not many shows extolled the Red Scare either. It was simply wiser to remain apolitical.

Some television shows were more concerned with politics, but they generally supported the views of the right and never defended the position of the left. Some TELEVISION NEWS shows, for example, were informed by a right-wing picture of American politics. And some TELEVISION TALK SHOWS allowed guests and hosts to express a (somewhat limited) range of opinion. While right-wing views frequently surfaced on these shows, genuine left-wing positions were rarely if ever voiced. If the Red Scare was mentioned at all, it was usually taken for granted that domestic communism was a serious threat. Viewers frequently saw politicians and public figures calling for the detention of all communists, but never heard serious discussions of a socialist agenda, demands for land reform, advocacy of redistribution of wealth, or even a call for national health insurance.

During the early 1950s Senator McCarthy was considered virtually beyond criticism on television. Edward R. MURROW's television news show SEE IT NOW was the only television show to expose McCarthy when he was at the height of his power. When McCarthy was granted equal time to respond to an episode of Murrow's 1954 show—which mostly consisted of film clips of McCarthy contradicting himself and smearing his enemies—McCarthy levied a vicious personal attack on Murrow, accusing him of being a communist sympathizer.

Eric SEVAREID was also attacked during the Red Scare, by both the left and the right. At the beginning of the Korean War, Sevareid, along with many other liberal and conservative commentators, was criticized by the left-wing Voice of Freedom Committee, which maintained that North Korea had been attacked by South Korea, and that U.S. journalists were distorting the truth. Shortly thereafter, the Voice of Freedom Committee dissolved. Then, as chief of the CBS Washington news staff in 1950, Sevareid made a few paid broadcasts for the government-run Voice of America. As a result, several right-wing "fact sheets" attacked him as a "paid propagandist" for the "pro-Communist" Acheson State Department.

Most other attacks on television journalists came from the right. In 1956 CBS silenced William Worthy's broadcasts from communist China upon the request of the State Department and canceled Sevareid's subsequent commentary, which would have criticized what Sevareid believed to be the Eisenhower administration's effort to preserve American ignorance about the real nature of world events. Among the news commentators listed in *Red Channels* were Howard K. Smith and William Shirer. Though Smith has stated that the listing had no impact on his career, Shirer has said that he was the victim of blacklisting as a result of it. He also claims that his three listings in *Red Channels,* which did not accuse him of being a communist or a fellow traveler, were arbitrary and misleading.

The popular TELEVISION SPY SHOW "I Led Three Lives" (1953–56) also depicted the threat of internal subversion. Based on Herbert PHILBRICK's best-selling book about his years as an FBI informant, it showed communists engaged in various acts of sabotage, which the FBI always managed to thwart at the last minute. SHADOW OF THE CLOAK (1951–52) was another Red Scare–era spy show that dealt with communist efforts at sabotage. Bishop Fulton SHEEN preached strongly against the evils of communism in his long-running, regularly scheduled show LIFE IS WORTH LIVING (1952–57, also the title of his 1953 nonfiction best-seller). Likewise, other RELIGIOUS TELEVISION PROGRAMMING, such as the periodic crusades by the Reverend Billy GRAHAM, made the domestic threat from communism seem imminent and potent. Graham vigorously attacked communism, describing it as Satanic, and both he and Sheen called it the antithesis of Christianity. (Perhaps ironically, during the 1980s Graham called for peace with the Soviet Union and an end to the threat of nuclear war.)

Like television, the film industry generally avoided treatments of social and political issues during the Red Scare, though it did produce several anti-communist films, sometimes at the behest of powerful politicians and interest groups. As a group, these films were not popular, nor were they very profitable. Yet they served to reassure the right of Hollywood's good intentions. Pervasive domestic communist subversion appeared directly in such early FILMS ASSOCIATED WITH THE RED SCARE as BIG JIM MCCLAIN, (1952), I MARRIED A COMMUNIST (1949), *I Was a Communist for the F.B.I.* (1951), PICKUP ON SOUTH STREET (1953), WALK EAST ON BEACON (1952) and THE RED MENACE (1949). IN 1951 Ronald REAGAN starred in STORM WARNING as a district attorney who encourages townspeople to testify against a Ku Klux Klan murderer. *Storm Warning* alludes directly to the HUAC hearings, which Reagan supported as president of the Screen Actors Guild. In the movie, the hero, like HUAC, insists that the guilty parties must be revealed, while the villainous townspeople protect the Klan by invoking verbatim arguments used by the Committee for the First Amendment in support of the Hollywood Ten. Thus the film implicitly endorses HUAC and vilifies the unfriendly witnesses who would not cooperate with its quest to identify members of the Communist Party working in Hollywood.

George S. Kaufman's 1947 film comedy THE SENATOR WAS INDISCREET drew the ire of right-wing politicians who equated its irreverence with un-Americanism. Though the movie is still well regarded, Kaufman never directed another film. *The Senator Was Indiscreet* spoofs a bumbling and unabashedly corrupt U.S. senator. Senator Joseph McCarthy called it "traitorous," and Representative Clare Boothe Luce demanded to know, "Was this picture made by an American?" *Life* magazine, published by Luce's husband, retracted an initial favorable review in a column entitled, "On Second Thought." Editorials in other publications, as well as statements by the American Legion, branded the movie un-American. Units of the Allied Theater Owners asserted that, "The picture will be recommended highly by [the official Soviet newspaper] *Pravda* and the party line . . . We should remember the adverse propaganda of the prewar and early war period that Germany and Italy used against us by presenting *Mr. Smith Goes to Washington, The Grapes of Wrath, Tobacco Road,* and gangster and crime films as true portrayals of American life." The Motion Picture Association of America banned the film from being shown overseas.

Only one 1950's American-made film, STORM CENTER (1956), directly attacked the Red Scare. Bette Davis stars as a librarian who is smeared as a communist because she will not remove an objectionable book from the stacks. Charles Chaplin's A KING IN NEW YORK ridicules HUAC, but the British-made film was not shown in the United States until 19 years after its 1957 release. More indirectly, Carl Foreman's screenplay for HIGH NOON implicitly equates HUAC with a gang of killers, and it implicitly criticizes the Hollywood film community for not supporting those who, like Foreman, stood up to the committee and were blacklisted for it.

Red Scare fears also appear as subtexts in many SCIENCE FICTION FILMS, notably INVASION OF THE BODY SNATCHERS, (1956) THE THING (1951), INVADERS FROM MARS (1953) and the THE BLOB (1958). In many 1950s alien-creature films, the dangerous creatures have traits popularly associated with communism. Like Soviet missiles, they come through the air from outer space. Or they result from mutations caused by Cold War atomic testing. Like stereotypical communist cadres, the aliens are dispassionate; they have no respect for the individual, and they are single-mindedly dedicated to their mission. *The Blob* presents an amorphous, creeping menace that absorbs everything in its path, making literal the Red Scare metaphor of "creeping Communism." In *Body Snatchers*, the aliens work from pod-like "cells," just like communist cadres, and their first achievement is to take over the town's military (police force), government and other institutions of authority, even as communists, were allegedly taking over the U.S. government and military. As in the right-wing view of the Cold War, a hero tries to warn his fellow citizens of the immense danger that is already destroying their community, but no one heeds him, and psychologists (i.e., scientifically trained " experts") hospitalize him for being crazy. However, the FBI—the government institution most trusted by the right—promises to save the day at the end.

On the other hand, a few science fiction films present stories that, although not attacking the Red Scare, celebrate the qualities that the right wing attacked: scientific know-how, liberal tolerance, intellectualism and a willingness to make peace with the aliens (i.e., the communists). Notable among these are THE DAY THE EARTH STOOD STILL (1951), and *It Came from Outer Space* (1953).

The film industry used the film code for self-censorship. Boycotts and picket lines by the American Legion and other organizations also persuaded theater owners not to screen films that the right deemed unpatriotic or un-American. Moreover, due to the mere possibility of such boycotts, banks often declined to finance films that might be controversial. Sometimes film unions refused to participate in movies their leadership found objectionable. For instance, since Roy BREWER's International Alliance of Theatrical Stage Employees (IATSE) included movie theater projectionists and staffers, Brewer could threaten to keep a film from being screened unless he approved content. The right-wing Brewer exercised this censorship when Columbia Pictures' president Harry Cohn, at Brewer's insistence, demanded that Arthur Miller and Elia KAZAN change their villains from union figures to communists in *The Hook*, a 1951 screenplay Miller had written about union corruption on the docks. Miller refused to make the changes, and the film was never produced. However, in 1953 Kazan teamed with fellow friendly witnesses Budd SCHULBERG and Lee J. COBB to produce ON THE WATERFRONT, a movie about union corruption on the docks that vindicates the act of informing.

Herbert Biberman's 1954 film documentary SALT OF THE EARTH also encountered union censorship. The independently made film sympathetically portrays a 1951–52 strike by Mexican-American zinc workers. It was directed by a blacklisted member of the Hollywood Ten and employed other blacklisted workers. The International Union of Mine, Mill and Smelter Workers, which conducted the strike, had been expelled from the CIO in 1950 because of charges that it was controlled by communists. Technicians and laboratories refused to perform post-production work; members of IATSE were prohibited from participating in the film; and the Immigration and Naturalization Services deported the female lead for a minor passport violation before the shooting was finished. *Salt of the Earth* was eventually completed, but then the American Legion threatened to picket theaters showing the film and IATSE projectionists refused to screen it. *Salt of the Earth* appeared only briefly in 10 U.S. cities in the 1950s, though it did enjoy a revival in left and feminist circles in the 1970s.

Much more than TELEVISION PERFORMERS, who generally submerged their political identities, members of the film industry took active stands on both sides of the Red Scare. Among those who endorsed the view that a domestic communist threat was real and dangerous were actors Ronald Reagan, John WAYNE, Charlton HESTON, Ward BOND and Robert Taylor and directors Cecil B. DEMILLE and Leo McCarey. Among those most vocal in opposing the Red Scare were members of the Hollywood Ten and Lillian Hellman, Dashiell Hammett and Arthur Miller. Hellman's SCOUNDREL TIME (1976), provides a firsthand account of her experience with HUAC. Hollywood Ten member Alvah BESSIE describes his experience before the committee and his subsequent blacklisting in his nonfiction account, *Inquisition in Eden* (1965), and in his autobiographical novel, *The Un-Americans* (1957). Other members of the Ten to write about their experiences and their thoughts about blacklisting were

Trumbo ("Time of the Toad," a 1949 pamphlet), Lester COLE (*Hollywood Red*, 1981) and Edward DMYTRYK (*It's a Hell of a Life But Not a Bad Living, 1979*).

In addition to those critics of the Red Scare, other prominent figures from the entertainment industry who were blacklisted include Leonard Bernstein, Aaron Copland, Howard Duff, Will Geer, Tom Glazer, Morton Gould, Lena HORNE, Langston Hughes, Burl Ives, Gypsy Rose Lee, Philip LOEB, Joseph Losey, Burgess Meredith, Arthur Miller, Henry Morgan, Zero Mostel, Jean MUIR, Dorothy Parker, Edward G. Robinson, Hazel SCOTT, Pete SEEGER, Artie Shaw, William SWEETS, Orson Welles, Ireene WICKER and Academy Award winners Anne Revere and Gale Sondergaard. Loeb, Muir and Wicker were driven from television and Sweets from radio.

Sometimes blacklisted or targeted individuals could clear themselves if they vigorously proclaimed their anti-communist credentials. In 1952 Lucille BALL, whose "I Love Lucy" was one of the most popular television shows in America, had to explain to HUAC why she had signed a petition for a Communist Party candidate in 1936. HUAC and the rest of the country accepted her claim to have signed only to "please my grandfather." Her husband, Desi Arnaz, proclaimed to a studio audience shortly after her testimony that Ball's red hair was the "only thing red about her, and even *that's* not legitimate." Other film industry individuals who had to clear themselves in order to continue working included directors John Huston, Robert ROSSEN and Carl Foreman, Hollywood Ten member Edward Dmytryk and performers Judy Holliday, John GARFIELD and José Ferrer.

The most frequent artistic response to the Red Scare was silence. Even as television and film steered clear of controversial political and social issues, literature, art, literary criticism and, to a lesser extent, theater turned to explorations of the individual psyche and away from the social and political themes that had dominated much of the literature of the 1930s and 1940s. Writers like John Cheever and John Updike wrote of personal crises among middle-class suburbanites; Isaac SINGER, Walker Percy and Flannery O'Connor wrote about retaining religious faith in a world gone out of control; Vladimir NABOKOV resurrected the art for art's sake sensibility of the 1920s, reveling in the craft of fine and intricate storytelling and influencing such fabulists as John Barth and Thomas PYNCHON. More social concerns can be found in genre fiction, where science fiction writers like Ray Bradbury and Isaac Asimov took on issues of war, peace, censorship and racism. Likewise, spy fiction treated the international Cold War scene. However, in literary criticism, apolitical approaches were elevated by the New Criticism, which focused exclusively on form, excluding discussion of social or political content as irrelevant or diversionary. The visual arts too eschewed any overtly political content. The major art movement of the time was abstract expressionism, which avoided engaging directly in politics by focusing on abstract form and on the inner emotional life of the artist.

As the Red Scare abated, a limited number of treatments of it appeared in the various media. Such political novels and films from the late 1950s and early 1960s as *The Manchurian Candidate* and SEVEN DAYS IN MAY (book 1962, film 1964)

began treating domestic politics and right-wing agitation in new, more critical ways. Blacklisting is addressed in THE FRONT (1976), directed, written by and starring former blacklistees and featuring a character based on the black-listed actor Philip Loeb. In 1976, former Hollywood Ten member Lester Cole wrote the screenplay for HOLLYWOOD ON TRIAL, a documentary about the HUAC hearings. In 1972, Eric Bentley's play ARE YOU NOW OR HAVE YOU EVER BEEN dramatized the HUAC hearings, using only portions of the actual committee transcripts for the dialogue. In 1980 John Lowenthal directed a FILM DOCUMENTARY on THE TRIALS OF ALGER HISS. Philip Roth's THE GREAT AMERICAN NOVEL (1973) concluded by satirizing HUAC. Roth also satirized Richard Nixon's participation in the Red Scare as well as his activities as president in OUR GANG (1971). The Red Scare also figures prominently in the background story of *Marathon Man* (1974).

A few studies of the Red Scare attacks on the entertainment industry appeared during the Cold War. John Cogley's 1956 *Report on Blacklisting* extensively documents the nature of blacklisting in the television and film industries. HUAC subsequently interrogated Cogley and condemned the report. Eric Bentley presents edited and annotated transcripts from HUAC hearings of 1938–68 in THIRTY YEARS OF TREASON (1971). Actor Robert VAUGHN published his doctoral study of the HUAC investigations of the entertainment industry, *Only Victims* (1972). In 1980, Victor Navasky, soon to be editor of the left-liberal magazine *The Nation*, published *Naming Names*, a study of how various members of the film industry reacted to the HUAC hearings.

It is difficult to assess the extent to which the Red Scare produced a "chilling effect" that discouraged writers and artists from even trying to produce anti–Red Scare works. On the one hand, some works undoubtedly were never produced, published or displayed because of their political content, and other potential political projects were certainly aborted because of Red Scare intimidation. On the other hand, the 1950s brought widespread social and political changes worthy of competing with the Red Scare for a creative person's attention: space exploration, hydrogen bombs, and intercontinental ballistic missiles; international Cold War rivalries; suburban living, middle-class affluence, corporate working environments; the civil rights movement; greater mobility for individuals due to the expansion of the highway network, the greater availability of automobiles and the growth of the airline industry; expanded opportunities for communication; increasing divorce rates; and the introduction of television. So the widespread absence of the Red Scare in literary and artistic media may be attributable to an attraction to other new topics as well as to the reluctance to take on politically sensitive issues.

For additional reading, see Miller's *The Judges and the Judged*; Goodman's *The Committee: The Extraordinary Career of the House Committee on Un-American Activities*; Cogley's *Report on Blacklisting*; Vaughn's *Only Victims*; Navasky's *Naming Names*; Suid's *Film and Propaganda in America*; Whitfield's *The Culture of the Cold War*; May's *Recasting America*; "Kiss Me Deadly: Communism, Motherhood, and Cold War Movies" in Rogin's *Ronald Reagan: The Movie*; and William F. Buckley Jr.'s *The Committee and Its Critics* and *McCarthy*

and His Enemies: The Record and Its Meaning. For partial transcripts of testimonies before HUAC by major figures, see Bentley's THIRTY YEARS OF TREASON.

Red Scorpion A 1989 FILM DRAMA starring Dolph Lundgren, M. Emmet Walsh and Al White and directed by Joseph Zito. This late Cold War film tells the story of a Soviet agent who is sent to assassinate an African leader but instead joins with local residents to drive out the communists.

Reds A 1981 FILM DRAMA starring Warren Beatty, Diane Keaton, Jack Nicholson, Maureen Stapleton, Jerzy KOSINSKI and Edward Herrmann. Beatty also directed, and Kosinski won an Academy Award for the script. Stapleton also won an Academy Award for best supporting actress in her role as Emma Goldman. The story follows real-life newspaper reporter and communist activist John Reed (Beatty) and his wife Louise Bryant (Keaton) before, during and just after the Russian Revolution, which Reed covered in his famous book, *Ten Days that Shook the World* (1919). The movie also portrays Reed and Bryant's activism in the United States and portrays the internal divisions within the American left during the second decade of the century. Rebecca West, Henry Miller and Hamilton Fish are among Reed's real-life contemporaries who provided their reminiscences in cameo appearances intercut with the fictional action. Other real-life personalities represented in the film include Emma Goldman, Eugene O'Neill (Nicholson), Max Eastman (Herrmann) and Communist Party chief Grigory Zinoviev (Kosinski). Made during the early days of the first Reagan administration, when Cold War tensions were quickly heating up again after the 1970s détente, the film provides a complex but generally sympathetic view of the main characters, but ultimately not of their cause. Reed's pathetic death in a communal hospital in Moscow underscores the communist betrayal of his dreams.

religious television programming Because Marxist theory is explicitly atheistic—Marx regarded religion as the "opiate of the people"—religious groups of all denominations strongly opposed communism. Moreover, the persecution of Jews in the Soviet Union, the persecution of Catholics in Eastern Europe and the anti-Christian attitude of China turned ideological differences into more overt confrontations. Consequently, much of the religious programming during the Cold War, especially during the late 1940s and the 1950s, carried a strong anti-communist message. In addition to many local television and radio religious shows, Bishop Fulton Sheen's LIFE IS WORTH LIVING (DuMont/ABC, 1952–57) and the Reverend Billy GRAHAM's television crusades stand out as widely viewed, nationally broadcast shows that carried strong anti-communist messages.

Graham aired four crusades between 1957 and 1959. Each broadcast a religious revival every Saturday night over a two- to three-month period. Between 1951 and 1954, Graham also had a regularly broadcast talk show on ABC "Hour of Decision." He declared communism to be inspired by Satan, and he equated anti-communist patriotism with Christianity. "The world is divided into two camps! On the one side we see Communism . . . [which] has declared war against God, against Christ, against the Bible, and against all religion! . . . Unless the Western world has an old-fashioned revival, we cannot last."

Bishop Sheen likewise bemoaned the West's lack of dedication to its beliefs, as compared to the misguided enthusiasm of the communists. He argued that "modern Christians have truth but no zeal; the Communists have zeal but no truth." Sheen's "Life Is Worth Living" became one of the most highly rated shows of its time, eventually beating out even the highly popular Milton Berle show. Despite his high ratings, Sheen stepped down after a being ordered to do so by his superior within the church, Cardinal Spellman. Sheen did return to the air from 1961 to 1968 in "The Bishop Sheen Program," which was identical to "Life Is Worth Living."

Other notable Christian television evangelists include Jerry FALWELL, who broadcast from 1971 throughout the Cold War, and Pat ROBERTSON, who headed the Christian Broadcasting Network and was on the air from 1976 through the end of the Cold War and beyond. Falwell headed the politically influential Moral Majority during the 1980s. Somewhat to the right of President Reagan, the Moral Majority focused on abolishing legal abortions and reinstating prayer in the public schools. It also was associated with right-wing Cold War positions. Robertson tried unsuccessfully in 1988 to win the Republican Party presidential nomination, but continued to play a powerful role in Republican Party politics.

"Rendezvous" A TELEVISION SPY SHOW that ran on ABC during the winter of 1952. The show centered on the activities of Nikki Angell (Ilona Massey), the beautiful owner of a Parisian nightclub. A member of the French Underground during World War II, Nikki was now engaged in international espionage in Europe and dedicated to thwarting the efforts of communist agents. Massey, a Hungarian-born film star, would sing one or two sultry songs during each episode.

Return from Silence: China's Revolutionary Writers A 1982 FILM DOCUMENTARY directed, produced and written by Joan Chung-wen Shih and sponsored in part by the National Endowment for the Humanities. The film covers five politically active Chinese writers: poet Ai Qing, dramatist Cao Yu, and writers Mao Dun, Ba Jin and Ding Ling.

Riddley Walker A 1980 APOCALYPTIC NOVEL by Russell Hoban. Set over 2,000 years into the future, the novel presents the human society that has evolved following the "Bad Time," the nuclear disaster of 1997. Protagonist Riddley Walker is a master of wordplay in his rudimentary Cockney-like language that grew out of his pretechnological society but retains distorted or absurd references to the long-past industrial world of the Cold War. In its treatment of the nature of postnuclear language, *Riddley Walker* joins such other postapocalyptic novels as Bernard Wolfe's LIMBO '90 (1953). Both Wolfe and Hoban appear indebted to James Joyce's *Finnegans Wake* (1939) and perhaps also to *A Clockwork Orange* (1963), in which Anthony Burgess develops a lower-class slang spoken by urban juvenile delinquents of the future. As in David Brin's THE POSTMAN (1985), the role of storytelling and the nature of language in a nonliterate postnuclear society are major issues. And like THE LONG

TOMORROW (1955) and A CANTICLE FOR LEIBOWITZ (1959), *Riddley Walker* presents a postapocalyptic scenario in which human society eventually evolves from its initial "medieval" opposition to science and technology to an embrace of technology and rational thought. Riddley Walker himself participates in this transformation, which includes the development of gunpowder and presumably, the eventual redevelopment of nuclear technology—though Walker hopes to introduce a spiritual element to the new nuclear world. As Jack Branscomb states in *The Nightmare Considered*, "*Riddley Walker* presents Hoban's vision of a world radically flawed by the human desire for knowledge and power. His solution to its problems lies not in technological knowledge but in Riddley's continual exploration of the meaning of fundamental patterns of human life. It is a hard path, but Riddley says, 'Still I wunt have no other track.' "

For additional reading, see Dowling's *Fictions of Nuclear Disaster* and Anisfield's *The Nightmare Considered*.

Road Warrior, The See MAD MAX.

Robertson, Pat A television evangelist who ran unsuccessfully for the 1988 Republican presidential nomination. In 1972 Robertson took over the daily syndicated religious talk show, "The 700 Club," from Jim and Tammy Faye Bakker, who had inaugurated it in 1966 on Robertson's Christian Broadcasting Network, which was later known as The Family Channel. The show remained on the air throughout the Cold War. Like fellow evangelists Jerry FALWELL and Billy GRAHAM, Robertson attacked what he saw as the moral breakdown of Cold War–era America, and like them, he affiliated with the conservative and right-wing components of the Republican Party. (See also RELIGIOUS TELEVISION PROGRAMMING.)

Robeson, Paul A singer and FILM ACTOR. Born in 1898 in Princeton, New Jersey, Robeson was the son of a former slave who had escaped his master and later joined the Union Army to fight in the Civil War before becoming a Protestant minister. Robeson's mother was a teacher of African, Indian and English heritage. Robeson won a competitive scholarship to Rutgers College (later Rutgers University) in 1915 and became only the third black student in that institution's history. Robeson enjoyed popularity at the school, where he won prizes for his oratory and earned 12 varsity letters in four sports: football, baseball, basketball and track. He was named an All-American end in 1917 and 1918 and gave the commencement address at his graduation. Robeson entered Columbia University Law School in 1920, paying his way by playing professional football. He also began his acting career while in law school, first appearing in amateur college performances and then on the professional stage. He graduated in 1923 and was admitted to the New York bar, but after working for a while at a law firm headed by a prominent Rutgers graduate, Robeson turned instead to theater.

He also developed his singing skills and in 1925–26 toured the United States, England and Europe singing Negro spirituals and international folk songs. He studied the languages of other nations so he could sing their folk songs in the original tongue and eventually mastered more than

Paul Robeson. Courtesy Library of Congress.

20 languages. Robeson released over 300 recordings and toured the world extensively between the world wars. In 1934 he visited the U.S.S.R. for the first time and was impressed by the social experimentation he witnessed there, particularly by what he saw as the opposition to racism and "national chauvinism." He also continued his acting career, winning acclaim for his role as Joe in Jerome Kern's *Showboat*, in which he sang "Ol' Man River." He was also lauded for his performance as Othello, when he first played in 1930. Robeson had major roles in 11 films, but he eventually abandoned the medium because, as he said, "The industry is not prepared to permit me to portray the life or express the living interests, hopes, and aspirations of the struggling people from whom I come."

Robeson was active in left-wing causes. During the 1930s he performed in benefits for Jews and other refugees from fascism. He traveled to Spain during the Spanish Civil War to entertain the Republican troops who were fighting against Franco's fascists. Robeson spent much of this period in England and visited the U.S.S.R. several times, claiming that he loved the Soviet Union more than any other country. He sent his son to school there in order to enable him to grow up in an environment free from racial discrimination. Robeson and his family returned to the United States in 1939 and found that the racial climate had greatly improved. His recording of the patriotic "Ballad for Americans" became an instant hit.

Following World War II, however, Robeson fell victim to the RED SCARE as a result of his left-wing activities and affiliations, which included membership in organizations that later appeared on the attorney general's list of "Communist fronts." He testified to the California State Legislature that he had never been a member of the Communist Party but then refused to answer further questions as a matter of principle. The HOUSE COMMITTEE ON UN-AMERICAN ACTIVITIES (HUAC) frequently referred to Robeson as a communist or communist sympathizer, and consequently he suffered from BLACKLISTING, his records were removed from stores and newspaper editorials frequently denounced him. In response, Robeson courageously reaffirmed his support for the Soviet Union, declaring in the 1949 World Peace Congress in Paris, "It is unthinkable that American Negroes could go to war on behalf of those who have oppressed us for generations against a country [the USSR] which is one generation has raised our people to the full dignity of mankind." He sustained these views throughout the Red Scare, declaring in his autobiography *Here I Stand* (1958), "On many occasions I have expressed my belief in the principles of scientific socialism, my deep conviction that for all mankind a socialist society represents an advance to a higher stage of life."

In August 1949 Robeson sang at a leftist festival in Peekskill, New York, where anti-communist demonstrators began to riot (Howard FAST describes the event in his 1951 NONFICTION book *Peekskill, USA*). Over 100 people were injured, and Robeson became convinced that the United States had become a reactionary country. His feelings were reaffirmed in 1950 when the State Department ordered him to surrender his passport. It refused to issue him a new one unless he signed an oath declaring that he was not a communist and promised not to give political speeches abroad. Robeson refused and challenged the State Department's action in court. He eventually won in 1958, when the Supreme Court ruled in a similar case that the government's actions were unconstitutional. During the eight-year period of his appeal, however, Robeson was unable to work abroad, where he could still attract enthusiastic audiences, and he was blacklisted at home. Hence he was largely deprived of opportunities to earn a living, except for poorly paying performances before radical audiences. Like Arthur MILLER, who was also denied a passport, Robeson appeared before HUAC in conjunction with his efforts to retain his travel privileges. Though Miller testified about himself and his plays, Robeson took the Fifth Amendment. In 1952, the Soviet Union awarded him the Stalin Peace Prize, an honor that made him further suspect in America. Robeson eventually defeated efforts by the Internal Revenue Service to collect taxes on the award when a federal court ruled that it was entitled to the same tax-free status as the Nobel Prize.

Robeson was an outspoken opponent of anti-Semitism in the Soviet Union, and he shocked a Moscow audience in 1949 when he ended a concert with a song celebrating the Jewish Warsaw rebellion against the Nazis in World War II. The audience in Tchaikovsky Hall remained silent when Robeson introduced the song, which he sang in Yiddish, but he received considerable applause when he completed it.

When Robeson regained his passport in 1958, the Red Scare had somewhat subsided, and he was able to give a farewell performance at New York's Carnegie Hall and to make a short tour of the West Coast before leaving the United States. While visiting the Soviet Union in 1959, he fell ill from exhaustion and a circulatory ailment and was hospitalized in Moscow, Eastern Europe and London until his return to the United States in 1963. Robeson refused to speak with the press other than to announce his retirement from public performances, but his wife, Eslanda, denied rumors that he had returned to his native country because he had become disenchanted with communism. In 1975, leaders from the entertainment world and the civil rights movement organized a 75th birthday salute to Paul Robeson at Carnegie Hall. Among those attending were Zero MOSTEL, Harry Belafonte, Sidney Poitier, Coretta Scott King and Angela Davis. Robeson was too ill to attend, but he sent a tape-recorded message stating, "I want you to know that I am still the same Paul, dedicated as ever to the worldwide cause of humanity for freedom, peace and brotherhood." He died on January 23, 1976. (See also MUSIC.)

For a partial transcript of Robeson's testimony before HUAC, see Eric Bentley's THIRTY YEARS OF TREASON and VAUGHN's *Only Victims*.

rock and roll Like TELEVISION, rock and roll developed concurrently with the Cold War, and more than most other forms of MUSIC, it expressed political sentiments related to the Cold War. Though it later came to be appreciated by adults, during the first half of the Cold War, rock was primarily written and performed by and directed to teenagers and young adults.

In its early years, rock and roll was apparently apolitical. Cleveland disc jockey Alan Freed coined the term "rock and roll" in 1951 when he played the music of black rhythm and blues (R&B) performers on an experimental late-night radio show targeted to white teenagers. The show was an instant hit, and Freed went on to promote the music at concerts and dances in New York and elsewhere. The rock phenomenon soon spread throughout the country. It was initially performed by black musicians and then picked up and adapted by white singers. In 1952, Pennsylvania disc jockey Bill Haley became the first white performer to release a major rock hit when his energetic song "Rock the Joint" sold 75,000 records. In 1956, Elvis Presley emerged as the first white artist to successfully combine white and black sounds. Known for the sensual gyrations of his hips when he performed, Presley emerged as the King of Rock and Roll, and even after his death in 1977 he remained a dominant figure in American popular culture. Though condemned by many adults for undermining the moral values of American youth with his overt sexuality, Presley considered himself a patriotic citizen. He served in the army in the late 1950s and regarded FBI director J. Edgar Hoover as one of the country's greatest living men. According to his FBI file, while touring FBI headquarters in 1971 Presley offered his services to the bureau as an undercover informant against the radicals he saw as undermining the nation. In particular, Presley (a heavy user of illegal drugs) blamed the Vietnam War–era civil unrest on illegal drugs and on his rock-and-roll rivals, the Beatles.

Rock was made possible by the development of the electric guitar and other forms of electrically amplified music. Because its loud, driving rhythms often exuded sexuality, communist regimes condemned it as morally degenerate and prohibited it until the late 1970s. Some right-wing American adults agreed with that assessment of the music— but they maintained that rock was part of a *communist* conspiracy to undermine American society by destroying its moral fabric. In fact, most early rock and roll was not overtly political or directly concerned with the Cold War, though in the 1950s Haley performed the humorous "Thirteen Women" about the sole survivors of an atomic attack: one man and 13 women.

In the early 1960s, however, FOLK SINGERS like Phil OCHS, Pete SEEGER, Bob DYLAN, Joan BAEZ, Tom Paxton, and Peter, Paul and Mary performed political songs frequently addressed to college audiences. Much of their music centered on the civil rights movement, the nuclear threat and the Cold War. For instance, in 1961 Ochs wrote "The Ballad of the Cuban Invasion" about the failed Bay of Pigs invasion. His first album in 1964 included "Talking Cuban Crisis" and "Talking Vietnam." Dylan's "Hard Rain's A-Gonna Fall" also referred to the Cuban Missile Crisis.

After the introduction of U.S. combat troops into the Vietnam War in 1965, the folk tradition of political music spread to rock and roll, as many individual performers and groups explicitly sang out against the war and on other Cold War–related issues. Dylan and Baez emerged as the King and Queen of Folk Rock, a hybrid that synthesized folk music and rock and roll. In 1965 Barry McGuire's "Eve of Destruction" became a number-one hit. (Nineteen-year-old P. F. Sloan wrote the song.) As the title suggests, the song laments the current state of worldwide affairs and repeatedly challenges its audience, "Tell me . . . that you don't believe we're on the eve of destruction." Among other early antiwar songs were Donovan's rendition of Buffy Sainte Marie's "Universal Soldier" and Mick Softly's "The War Drags On." Jim Morrison, the lead singer of the Doors, performed the powerful "Unknown Soldier," and Eric Burdon sang "Sky Pilot," which asks how the airmen who bombed civilian targets in Southeast Asia can remain insensitive to the horror of their actions. The group Steppenwolf issued an entire album critical of U.S. politics, while Creedence Clearwater Revival's "Fortunate Son" pointed out how sons of wealthy and influential families remained at home while working-class boys went to war. The group Chicago wrote antiwar music during the late 1960s and early 1970s but became discouraged after President Nixon's landslide reelection in 1972, when lead singer Robert Lamm concluded, "If McGovern could lose by that margin, then I and everybody I know must be nothing." However, Chicago's first album commemorated the peace demonstrations that took place outside the 1968 Democratic Convention in which, according to a grand jury, the police rioted when they assaulted protesters within and outside the convention hall.

Other antiwar, antiestablishment groups from the late 1960s include the Beatles, the Rolling Stones, Frank Zappa's Mothers of Invention, Blind Faith, the Allman Brothers and MC5. The 1968 rock musical HAIR centers on a young man who joins a COUNTERCULTURE commune in order to avoid the draft. The story and music juxtapose the culture of life, represented by the counterculture, against the military's culture of death. The 1969 rock festival at WOODSTOCK brought together several counterculture artists and had a distinct antiwar aspect to it, as did other rock concerts and "festivals of life" from the period. One of the period's best known antiwar songs, sung at Woodstock, was Country Joe McDonald's "I-Feel-Like-I'm-Going-To-Die Rag," which incorporates elements of BLACK HUMOR as its chorus asks, "1-2-3, What're we fightin' for?/ Don't ask me, I don't give a damn/ Next stop is Vietnam./ And it's 5-6-7, open up the pearly gates./ Ain't no time to wonder why/ Whoopee! We're all bound to die." Another verse grimly plays off of 1950s television commercials as it urges parents to "be the first one on your block to have your boy come home in a box."

John Lennon's "Ballad of John and Yoko" describes how he and his wife, Yoko Ono, spent a week in bed to draw attention to their "make love not war" sentiments. Both were active in the antiwar effort, musically as well as politically. Indeed, according to Lennon's FBI file, the Nixon administration tried to have him deported before the 1972 Republican Convention, which they feared he would disrupt. Lennon and Ono's chant-like song, "Give Peace a Chance," became an anthem of the peace movement. Lennon's later song "Imagine" encourages listeners to imagine the possibility of a peaceful world, one not divided by religion or nationalism. The thought was not easy to conjure during the Cold War, but Lennon believed that before the reality of a peaceful world could be manifested, it needed first to exist in people's imagination.

Taking a different approach, virtuoso electric guitarist Jimi Hendrix underscored American militarism by performing a version of the "Star-Spangled Banner" that incorporates the sounds of rockets falling and bombs bursting in air. Other African-American antiwar musicians included Edwin Starr, who sang "War" ("What is it good for? Absolutely nothing!"), which was later sung by Bruce Springsteen, and Freda Payne, who performed "Bring the Boys Home."

Many rock groups of the late 1960s and early 1970s attacked American society and capitalistic values in general. For instance, one Led Zeppelin hit describes a woman who is so wealthy that she purchases the "Stairway to Heaven." The Jefferson Airplane's 1969 Volunteers album contained expressions of antiwar sentiments and radical politics. (The group later became known as the "Jefferson Starship," but by then it was virtually apolitical.) Crosby, Stills and Nash's "Wooden Ships" encourages the younger generation to opt out of the world of conflict. The singer implies the irrelevance of victory in a major nuclear war when he asks, "Who won?" The group, with the addition of Neil Young, also sang about the Kent State massacre in which the Ohio

National Guard killed four students during a 1970 antiwar protest rally. Pink Floyd's song "Us and Them," from its best-selling Dark Side of the Moon album, also addresses the prospect of a major nuclear war in which the question of winning or losing becomes irrelevant. The song attributes the cause of the conflict to economics. Pink Floyd's later album, The Wall, deals with the stifling nature of social institutions. The group performed the album at the fallen Berlin Wall at the end of the Cold War. They also made the album into a 1982 film, PINK FLOYD THE WALL.

In general, the rock of the Vietnam War era (no longer called rock and roll) implicitly or explicitly expressed opposition not only to the war but also to the constraints and the lack of passion in middle-class American society. The era's rock music frequently stated a desire for peace and social justice and opposed both militarism in general and the U.S. military-industrial complex in particular. Moreover, "acid rock"—a type of rock that flourished in the early 1970s—also celebrated the culture of illegal drugs, underscoring an antiestablishment sensibility that extended to Cold War politics.

Post–Vietnam War rock music was often less political, though during the late 1970s and 1980s, some punk rock took on brutal, neo-fascist overtones. In the early 1980s, the British group the Clash promoted a kind of left-wing nihilism that attacked U.S. imperialism. Its 1981 album Sandinista, which attracted many listeners in the United States, supports revolutionary movements in Latin America, notably the Nicaraguan Marxists who had deposed the ruling dictator Anastasio Somoza in 1979 and whose overthrow the CIA was then trying to engineer. The Clash's song "Ivan Meets GI JOE" reflects the renewed U.S.-Soviet tensions of the early 1980s. In 1982 the group issued another album that expressed Cold War tensions, Combat Rock.

Meanwhile rock music responded to the Cold War tensions during the first Reagan administration, reflecting concern over the renewed prospects for nuclear war. Donald Fagen, formerly of Steely Dan, recalls preparations for bomb shelters and nuclear war in "New Frontier," from his 1982 album Nightly. The song's title alludes to the Kennedy administration's name for its overall policy. The West German singer Nena expresses her fear of nuclear destruction in her 1980s hit 99 Red Balloons, in which military leaders are likened to Captain Kirk from STAR TREK as they proceed to destroy a city. Since Germany was considered a likely battle site for a U.S.-Soviet confrontation, the peace movement was particularly strong there, and antinuclear protest music was more common there than in the United States. However, on June 12, 1982, several rock concerts were put on throughout the United States in support of the nuclear freeze movement. These were timed to coincide with the opening of the United Nations disarmament conference, and they attracted hundreds of thousands of concertgoers. Among those who performed were Joan Baez, Bob Dylan, Tom Petty, Stevie Wonder, Linda Ronstadt, Bonnie Raitt, Bette Midler, David Crosby, Stephen Stills, Graham Nash, Bruce Springsteen, Jackson Browne, James Taylor, Judy Collins, Jimmy Buffett, John Denver, Stevie Nicks and Dan Fogelberg.

In 1989, Billy Joel reviewed the entire Cold War in his song/music video "We Didn't Start the Fire," whose lyrics trace the Cold War from the 1950s through the 1980s. Bruce Springsteen's "Born in the U.S.A." (1984) criticizes the U.S. involvement in Vietnam (though many, including Reagan, misunderstood the song as simplistic patriotism.) Springsteen's album of the same name also laments unemployment and factory closings.

For additional reading, see Orman's *The Politics of Rock Music*; Denisoff's *Sing a Song of Social Significance*, Szatmary's *Rockin' in Time: A Social History of Rock and Roll*; Nite's *Rock on Almanac*; Ward et al.'s *Rock of Ages: The Rolling Stone History of Rock & Roll*; and Ramet's *Rocking the State: Rock Music and Politics in Eastern Europe and Russia.*

Rocky A 1976 FILM DRAMA starring Sylvester STALLONE, Burgess Meredith and Talia Shire and directed by John G. Avildsen. Stallone also wrote the script, for which he received an Academy Award nomination while *Rocky* received an Academy Award for best film. Sequels appeared in 1979, 1982, 1985 and 1990. Though not originally related to the Cold War, the first *Rocky* reiterated the traditional American values that frequently characterized film and television during the 1950s and early 1960s but were challenged in the later 1960s and early 1970s. Rocky was made during the Ford administration, when the defeat in Vietnam, President Nixon's resignation over the Watergate scandal, and the Arab oil embargo were still vivid memories. *Rocky* thus appealed to U.S. audiences with its upbeat tale of an underdog boxer (Stallone) who succeeds through hard work, unflagging determination, belief in himself and his dream, and the love of good woman.

Rocky IV (1985) made a much more immediate appeal to Cold War sentiments. Whereas the original appeared during the détente of the 1970s, this sequel was released during one of the more intense periods of the conflict, when both the United States and the Soviet Union were increasing their nuclear arsenals and adopting more bellicose positions. In this film, Rocky takes on an oversized Russian boxer in a match that highlights the nationalistic aspect of their personal grudge match. Though the Soviet fighter is bigger and enjoys other advantages unavailable to Rocky, the American's intractable will and total devotion to his cause enable him to win.

The representation of the Soviet as bigger and stronger than the American reflected a common Cold War stereotype about Soviet might, based partly on the facts that the U.S.S.R. had larger—but less precise—nuclear warheads and that the Warsaw Pact countries enjoyed numerical superiority in conventional troop strength, especially in tank divisions. (In *Alexander Nevsky*, made in 1938, prior to World War II, Soviet filmmaker Sergei Eisenstein similarly showed lightly armed Russians defeating heavily armored Teutonic knights in the 13th century, suggesting that modern-day Soviets would prevail over the Nazi armored panzer divisions.) But the projection of a bigger, stronger enemy also manifested an apparent desire for Americans to perceive themselves as underdogs and victims in the confrontation against the Soviet Union, even while simultaneously proclaiming "We're Number One!" This paradoxical picture of the United States as both stronger and weaker than the U.S.S.R. appeared throughout the Cold War and played a significant role in the politics of appropriations for weap-

onry; for instance, in the nonexant bomber and missile "gaps" of the 1950s and in some of the claims for the Reagan administration's military buildup in the early 1980s.

Rodan A 1957 Japanese-made SCIENCE FICTION FILM starring Kenji Sawara and directed by Inoshiro Honda. Like Honda's earlier film GODZILLA, KING OF THE MONSTERS (1954), *Rodan* metaphorically equates the flying monster with the airborne nuclear threat in the late 1950s. (See also APOCALYPTIC FILMS.)

Rossen, Robert A FILM DIRECTOR who was blacklisted for refusing to cooperate with the HOUSE COMMITTEE ON UN-AMERICAN ACTIVITIES (HUAC) in 1951. Rossen had been scheduled to testify in HUAC's 1947 hearings, along with the HOLLYWOOD TEN; however, he was never called. In his 1951 testimony, he tacitly admitted that he was a member of the Communist Party but refused to name others who also belonged. Prior to his HUAC appearance, Rossen had directed such noteworthy films as *Body and Soul* (1947) and *All the King's Men* (1949). Nonetheless, afterward he was unable to find work either in Hollywood or writing for THEATER in New York. After suffering unemployment and social ostracism, Rossen left the party and testified again before HUAC in 1953. He told the committee, "I don't think, after two years of thinking, that any one individual can even indulge himself in the luxury of individual morality or pit it against what I feel today very strongly is the security and safety of this nation." He then identified some 50 alleged communists and provided a detailed account of communist Party practices, including how it assessed dues from its affluent Hollywood members. (The role of the Hollywood film industry in financing the activities of the Communist Party had been the ostensible focus of the 1951–52 HUAC hearings and some of those that followed.) Afterwards, Rossen was able to resume his career in Hollywood. His most notable post-HUAC film was *The Hustler* (1961). (See also BLACKLISTING.)

For additional reading, see Navasky's *Naming Names.*

Rumours of War A 1972 British-made FILM DOCUMENTARY written and produced by Peter Jones for the BBC. The film explores various aspects of 1970s nuclear culture. Filmed in a low-key manner and narrated by Paul Vaughan, *Rumours* offers a cynical and bleak assessment of the superpowers' nuclear buildup. It opens with a look at one of the officers assigned to a Minuteman missile silo in Albuquerque and documents the procedures that are supposed to ensure that no missile will be launched by mistake or without proper authorization. Two separate control centers house two men apiece. All four must act in harmony in order to launch a nuclear-armed missile. Each carries a gun to shoot his teammate if he tries to take over the control center. And all of the men receive regular psychiatric tests. These safeguards notwithstanding, the narrator asserts that six missiles have failed to perform to standard in selective tests and that, once launched, a Minuteman cannot be recalled. He later adds that one accident occurs every 10 years, thereby creating the possibility that an entire U.S. city might be destroyed by "friendly fire."

An animated cartoon section suggests that arms reduction negotiations are cynically conducted: A Soviet call to halt plutonium production is motivated not by a genuine desire for peace but to nullify the U.S. advantage in plutonium. Likewise, a U.S. plan to eliminate all medium-range bombers would eliminate some 80% of the Soviet fleet while leaving the U.S. fleet largely intact.

The film's title comes from a segment showing a curator at the Sandia Atomic Museum proudly explaining the exhibits to a group of Boy Scouts. After he boasts that "Things are moving so fast . . . they [atomic bombs and hydrogen bombs] will soon be like bows and arrows," one boy declares, "There's meant to be wars. It's unpleasant, but there's meant to be wars." The Scout leader then explains, "That's the boy's religious training coming out . . . In the Bible, it says that there will be wars and rumours of wars." *Rumours* concludes by asserting that, more than the bomb itself, the unrelenting anxiety it fosters is the greatest horror behind the nuclear arms buildup. (See also APOCALYPTIC FILMS.)

For additional reading, see Shaheen's *Nuclear War Films.*

Russell, Mark A political satirist. A would-be successor to Tom LEHRER, Russell wrote satiric songs about contemporary domestic and international politics that he performed on television specials during the 1980s and 1990s to his own accompaniment on the piano. He also appeared in the short-lived "Starland Vocal Band Show" in the summer of 1977 and on "Real People," a comedic, human interest, audience participation show that ran from 1979 to 1984. Unlike Lehrer's biting political satire, Russell's songs seemed calculated not to offend anyone. (See also SATIRE; MUSIC.)

Russia House, The A best-selling 1989 SPY NOVEL by John LE CARRÉ and a 1990 SPY FILM starring Sean Connery, Michelle Pfeiffer and Roy Scheider, written by Tom Stoppard and directed by Fred Schepisi. The complex plot, which contains many unexpected twists and turns, centers on

efforts by U.S. and British agents to establish the credibility of a manuscript detailing Soviet defense systems. The manuscript, which claims that the entire Soviet military-industrial complex is corrupt, grossly mismanaged and inept, threatens the Western spies because, if true, it suggests that the Cold War has been a farce and that their own jobs are unnecessary. Consequently, veteran U.S. and British agents seek to discredit the report. By contrast, the Soviet KGB appears more attractive to the main character because, unlike its Western counterparts, it is able to adjust to radical political change within its bureaucracy and "they don't break their promises." However, the story's end casts doubt on their veracity. Written during the final years of the Cold War, when Premier Mikhail Gorbachev was promoting closer Soviet relations with the West, the book seems to anticipate the collapse of the Soviet Union by emphasizing its inept institutions. The film was shot on location in Moscow and Leningrad.

For additional reading, see Beene's *John le Carré* and Cawelti and Rosenberg's *The Spy Story.*

Russians Are Coming! The Russians Are Coming!, The A 1966 FILM COMEDY starring Alan Arkin, Paul Ford, Carl Reiner, Theodore Bikel, Brian Keith, Jonathan Winters and Eva Marie Saint and directed by Norman Jewison. Arkin stars as the captain of a Soviet submarine that accidentally runs aground in U.S. waters off the coast of Nantucket Island. When he and some of his men go ashore for help, the reactionary islanders, led by American Legionnaire Paul Ford, gather to challenge this "Communist invasion." Made during the lull in U.S.–Soviet tensions that followed the 1962 Cuban Missile Crisis, the film expresses the desire for peaceful coexistence between the citizens of the two "superpowers." In this respect the film anticipates the détente that Nixon, Kissinger and Soviet foreign minister Andrei Gromyko implemented in 1969.

Sahl, Mort A stand-up comedian from the 1950s and early 1960s. Sahl performed at leading nightclubs and posh entertainment spots such as Miami's Fontainebleau and Americana hotels. He poked fun at Democrats and Republicans alike, including President Eisenhower, his Democratic opponent Adlai Stevenson, Vice President Richard Nixon, President John F. Kennedy and others. Sahl spoke about current events as they unfolded, such as the 1961 Bay of Pigs invasion and the ongoing second Berlin Crisis. He also made jokes about the space program and the American Legion's boycott of the films EXODUS (1960) and SPARTACUS (1960), which were written by blacklisted SCREENWRITER Dalton TRUMBO. Commenting on the HOUSE COMMITTEE ON UN-AMERICAN ACTIVITIES (HUAC) Sahl declared, "Every time the Russians throw an American in jail, the committee throws an American in jail to get even." He also stated, "Maybe the Russians will steal all our secrets. Then they'll be two years behind." In the later stages of the Cold War Sahl became known for his preoccupation with the Kennedy assassination and for his apparently incongruous support for Ronald Reagan. His record albums include *A Way of Life* (1960), *Mort Sahl 1960, or Look Forward in Anger* (1960), *The Next President* (1960) and *The New Frontier* (1961). (See also SATIRE.)

Saigon: Year of the Cat A 1983 VIETNAM WAR FILM starring Judi Dench and Frederic Forrest and directed by Stephen Frears. Set during the fall of Saigon in 1975, the film centers on a British bank employee who joins the European community in Saigon and falls in love with a U.S. CIA agent.

Sakharov A 1984 FILM DRAMA starring Jason Robards, Nicol Williamson and Glenda Jackson and directed by Jack Gold. The story centers on Andrei Sakharov, the "father" of the U.S.S.R.'s hydrogen bomb who later fell from favor with the Soviet government because of his international protests against the arms buildup and human rights abuses within the Soviet Union. The film centers on Sakharov's (Robards) internal exile in Gorky and his dedication to his dissident cause, as well as the commitment of his wife, Elena Bonner (Jackson). (Sakharov won the Nobel Peace Prize in 1975 and was exiled to Gorky in 1980.) Ironically, both Sakharov and J. Robert Oppenheimer, the man who headed the U.S. effort to build an atom bomb, were dismissed from positions of power for political reasons after they had made their contributions to nuclear warfare. By focusing on a hero who stands firm against various objectionable Soviet actions, *Sakharov* appealed to the anti-Soviet sentiments promoted by the Reagan administration in the early 1980s.

Salt of the Earth A 1954 independently made POLITICAL FILM starring Rosaura Revueltas, Will Geer and David Wolfe, directed by Herbert BIBERMAN, a member of the HOLLYWOOD TEN, and produced by Paul Jarrico. Made in association with the International Union of Mine, Mill and Smelter Workers (IU), the docu-drama sympathetically portrayed a 1951–52 IU strike by Mexican-American zinc workers. Biberman,

Jarrico, Geer and scriptwriter Michael Wilson had all been blacklisted. Revueltas, the female lead, was deported by the Immigration and Naturalization Services (INS) for a minor passport violation before shooting was completed. She was subsequently blacklisted in both the United States and Mexico and never made another film. Jarrico and Biberman had wanted to create an independent film company to employ blacklisted artists and draw "from the living experiences of people long ignored in Hollywood—the working men and women of America." However, *Salt of the Earth* was their only production.

Filmed in Silver City, New Mexico, *Salt of the Earth* used actual participants from the strike on which it was based. It centers on the workers' struggles and is notable for its inclusion of Chicanos and its depiction of the central role women played in the labor movement. Indeed, in *Running Time*, Nora Sayres claims that the film concentrates more on sexual oppression than class oppression. Both themes were rare in RED SCARE–era American movies.

The film favorably depicts the IU, which had been expelled from the CIO in 1950 on charges that it was controlled by communists. That and the fact that it was made by blacklisted artists prompted widespread charges that *Salt of the Earth* was the work of communists. Even before it was completed, Congressman Donald Jackson, a member of the HOUSE COMMITTEE ON UN-AMERICAN ACTIVITIES (HUAC), argued that the film was "a new weapon for Russia" that might somehow instigate copper miners to strike and thereby block the production of weapons for the then-current Korean War. And Hearst columnist Victor Riesel warned of the dangers of having communists make a film so close to the nuclear research center at Los Alamos.

During the filming, vigilante groups picked fights with crew members and shot at their cars, and many local merchants refused to conduct business with anyone involved with the film. Ultimately, the New Mexico State Police had to protect the crew. After the INS deported Revueltas, a double completed the film. (Some scenes with Revueltas were also filmed in Mexico on the pretext of being test shots for a subsequent movie.) Technicians and laboratories refused to perform post-production work, and members of Roy BREWER's International Alliance of Theatrical Stage Employees (IATSE) were also prohibited from working on the film. Brewer had promised Jackson that he would do everything possible to keep *Salt of the Earth* from being shown. Nonetheless, *Salt of the Earth* was eventually completed. Even then, the American Legion threatened to picket theaters showing the film, and Brewer's IATSE projectionists refused to screen it.

Although it was well received in Europe, *Salt of the Earth* appeared only briefly in 10 U.S. cities. However, it was re-released and more widely distributed in 1965 when it became a rallying point for COUNTERCULTURE activism. In the 1970s it was popular in left and feminist circles. (See also FILMS ASSOCIATED WITH THE RED SCARE; BLACKLISTING.)

For additional reading, see Whitfield's *The Culture of the Cold War*; Sayre's *Running Time*; Monaco's *The Movie Guide*.

Sand Pebbles, The A 1966 MILITARY FILM based on the novel by Richard McKenna. Starring Steve McQueen, Richard Attenborough, Richard Crenna and Candice Bergen and

directed by Robert Wise, the story centers on a U.S. Navy gunboat cruising China's Yangtze River during Chiang Kai-shek's 1926 Nationalist rebellion. The powerful and critically acclaimed film portrays how the U.S. crew, though trying to maintain neutrality, are manipulated by political forces and drawn into the conflict. Though set 40 years in the past, the film echoed the then-current U.S. escalation of the Vietnam War. One critic claimed that Crenna, the ship's captain, "gives a reasonable approximation of what [the U.S. military commander in Vietnam] General Westmoreland might have been like in the '20s." Another called the movie "metaphorically aligned with our current dilemma in the Far East." The film also invited comparison to Mao Zedong's then-current Cultural Revolution. During that period, anti-capitalist sentiment was at its highest, Chinese rhetoric was especially bellicose, China had recently exploded its first nuclear bomb and sympathies for Chiang Kai-shek were high.

satire Somewhat surprisingly, few satires address the Cold War. Indeed, little satire of any kind appeared during the period despite such open invitations to farce as the bumbling in the Watergate and Iran-contra scandals. (White House operatives possessed comically false disguises during Watergate and hid a Bible inside a cake baked for Iranian officials during the Iran-contra Affair.) Some early Cold War satire concentrated on Senator Joseph McCarthy and the HOUSE COMMITTEE ON UN-AMERICAN ACTIVITIES (HUAC), but satirists experienced repercussions for their humor. Reuben Ship, a Canadian, faced deportation hearings in 1953 for making THE INVESTIGATOR, a phonograph record mocking McCarthy and the RED SCARE. Likewise, HUAC interrogated Arthur MILLER for his satirical treatment of the committee in *You're Next*. When asked why the Communist Party had produced the play, Miller replied, "I take no more responsibility for who plays my plays than General Motors can take for who rides in their Chevrolets." THE HONORABLE ROCKY SLADE, a 1957 novel by William Wister Gaines, satirizes McCarthy's early career.

Philip Roth's THE GREAT AMERICAN NOVEL (1973) parodies history itself in its account of a third baseball league that has been written out of the record books. Writing at a time when HUAC was interrogating Vietnam war protesters, Roth reminds readers of the outrages the committee committed 20 years earlier. The book culminates with a series of HUAC investigations reminiscent of those during the Red Scare. Several ballplayers are implicated in an alleged communist conspiracy. Some confess and name names of other conspirators rather than face BLACKLISTING; others go to jail, like the HOLLYWOOD TEN. One commits suicide recalling blacklisted actor Philip LOEB; another appears as a single, double or possibly triple agent. The narrator himself is sentenced to jail for refusing "to participate in this lunatic comedy in which American baseball players who could not locate Russia on a map of the world—who could not locate *the world* on a map of the world—denounce themselves and their teammates as Communist spies out of fear and intimidation and howling ignorance, or . . . out of incorrigible human perversity and curdled genes." Roth's earlier novel, OUR GANG (1971), satirizes Richard Nixon's performance during the Red Scare and while he is president. It especially ridicules the Nixon administration's continued prosecution of the Vietnam War despite the fact that the president campaigned in 1968 on a promise to end the war. In Roth's book, Nixon explains that he left the secret peace plan he had mentioned during the campaign in the pocket of his other suit.

An earlier antiwar satire, Barbara Garson's 1966 play MACBIRD, parodies the Johnson administration by likening it to the cast of characters in *Macbeth*. Several of Jules FEIFFER's plays also satirize Cold War attitudes and events, especially *Crawling Arnold* (1961), *The White House Murder Case* (1970) and *Watergate Classics,* which Feiffer coauthored with eight other writers. Feiffer also drew political cartoons that were nationally syndicated throughout the Cold War.

A number of novelists wrote at least one satirical work during the Cold War. Most of Kurt VONNEGUT's novels have satirical elements. Joseph Heller's BLACK HUMOR novel, CATCH-22 (1961), satirizes government and military bureaucracy as well as loyalty oaths and other elements of the Red Scare. John BARTH satirizes the Cold War in his allegory, GILES GOAT-BOY (1966). Robert COOVER wrote two Cold War Satires, THE CAT IN THE HAT FOR PRESIDENT (1968) and THE PUBLIC BURNING (1976), a surreal treatment of the Rosenberg executions. Mary MCCARTHY's novels *The Oasis* (1949) and *The Groves of Academe* (1952) satirize liberal intellectuals and leftist academics. *The Oasis* presents a group of liberals who try to create an ideal society atop a mountain. Based on the author's personal acquaintances, the award-winning novel presents a debate between two factions. One, led by a character based on Dwight MacDonald, argues that humans can create a utopian society. The leader of the second faction is based on Philip Rahv, one of the founders of the leftist MAGAZINE, the *Partisan Review*. He rejects the possibility of an ideal society. *The Groves of Academe* was written and set during the Red Scare. Its satirical targets are members of a college community who oppose the firing of a former communist, Henry Mulchay. Their knee-jerk defense of Mulchay blinds them to his dishonesty and incompetence and leads them to oppose the liberal and honest college president. Thus the very institution that promotes reason and truth becomes corrupted by its emotional politics. Also from the 1950s, Arthur Hadley's novel *The Joy Wagon* (1958) features a computer that runs for president and outshines its opponents.

Jerzy Kosinski satirizes the relationship between American politics and television culture in BEING THERE (1970), a novel about a mentally deficient man named Chance, who knows about the world only from television and from his work as a gardener. Through a chain of accidents and misunderstandings, Chance becomes attached to a wealthy and politically powerful family and gains enormous political influence. The media and members of the political inner circle come to regard him as a man of great wisdom, able to communicate effectively to the nation through what they believe to be parables based on gardening. Kosinski won an Academy Award for the 1979 screenplay adaptation, which starred Peter SELLERS.

Another EXILED WRITER (to the United States), Sacha Sokolov, published the satiric *School for Fools* in the Soviet Union in 1976. The détente-era novel was well received in the West, where its innovative, imagistic style and humorous treatments of Soviet bureaucracy were appreciated. However, the reception was not so warm in the Soviet Union, and Sokolov immigrated to America in 1978 after much harassment. Sokolov also published the satiric novels *Between the Dog and the Wolf* (1980) and *Astrolabia* (1989), the fictional memoirs of a hermaphrodite Soviet bureaucrat. Soviet writer Vassily AKSYONOV also fell out of favor when he turned his barbs to the U.S.S.R. He went into exiled in the United States after publishing *The Burn* (1980), a mocking portrait of contemporary life in the Soviet Union. Aksyonov had earlier won approval from the Soviet government for his satires of American culture in *Non-Stop Round the Clock* (1976) and *Crimea Island* (1980). His U.S. writings continued to satirize the Soviet Union in such works as *Say Cheese!* (1989) and *In Search of Melancholy* (1987).

Prominent FILM SATIRES include Charles Chaplin's A KING IN NEW YORK (1957), which attacks HUAC and the Red Scare; THE MOUSE THAT ROARED (1959) and DR. STRANGELOVE (1964), which both star Peter Sellers and address the nuclear bomb; DEAL OF THE CENTURY (1983), about international weapons dealers; and the 1982 Film Documentary ATOMIC CAFÉ, which uses actual government films to ridicule claims about survivable nuclear war.

TELEVISION SATIRE was even more rare. Such shows as THAT WAS THE WEEK THAT WAS (NBC, 1964–65), LAUGH-IN (NBC, 1968–73), THE SMOTHERS BROTHERS COMEDY HOUR (CBS, 1967–69), SATURDAY NIGHT LIVE (NBC, 1973–present), SECOND CITY TV (syndicated, 1977–81) and occasional musical specials by Mark RUSSELL did sometimes satirize aspects of the Cold War.

Stand-up comedians from the late 1950s and early 1960s Lenny BRUCE and Mort SAHL both frequently engaged in political satire, though much of their material dealt with domestic matters rather than Cold War issues. Commenting on HUAC, Sahl declared, "Every time the Russians throw an American in jail, the committee throws an American in jail to get even." He also quipped, "Maybe the Russians will steal all our secrets. Then they'll be two years behind." For his part, Bruce suggested that no one had the right to criticize another's loyalty unless the accuser could himself keep secrets while undergoing a hot-lead enema. Bruce also pointed to the link between power, sexuality and the nuclear threat as he has President Johnson declare that the fly on his pants is actually the "button" one pushes for the bomb.

Though better known for his less political work, in 1986 Robin Williams gave a stand-up performance in New York that included some sharp satire directed at President Ronald REAGAN and his Cold War policies. He then released the performance as a nationally distributed record album entitled "Robin Williams, A Night at the Met." Williams claimed Reagan was unable to distinguish between reality and the movies (a point treated in a more scholarly fashion by Michael Rogin in *Ronald Reagan, The Movie*). Williams noted that in a presidential debate, Reagan referred to uniforms as costumes; so, Williams claims, "a war to him is the big film." Williams portrays a discussion of Central America that dissolves into a FILM WESTERN in which the speaker of the House suddenly becomes John WAYNE, declaring in a manly way, "Let's get down to Nicaragua. Kick some ass." Reagan replies in a sidekick's voice, "Well, I'll get the ponies. We'll saddle them up. Come on, we've got them ready right now." The scene then evolves through several other classic films (in one, Defense Secretary Caspar Weinberger becomes Dracula) until Reagan reemerges as the star of STAR WARS (1977, "Star Wars" was also the popular name for Reagan's space-based Strategic Defense Initiative). Williams calls Reagan "Disney's last wish" and portrays Reagan as a creation from Disneyland. Elsewhere in the routine Williams discusses an international summit meeting. "They're talking about partial nuclear disarmament. This is like talking about a partial circumcision."

Such Magazines as *MAD, The National Lampoon, The Realist* and *Spy* also featured satire. So did such men's magazines as PLAYBOY, *Penthouse, Hustler* and Screw. Between 1963 and 1973, the *Satire Newsletter* provided academic and political satire, articles about satire, and examples of satire in Eastern Europe, Germany, France and the U.S.S.R.

Art BUCHWALD, a syndicated JOURNALIST, frequently satirized Cold War developments in his syndicated newspaper column. Garry Trudeau's nationally syndicated CARTOON *Doonesbury* satirized Cold War American politics, as did *Pogo, Li'l Abner* and *Bloom County.* Among the most notable syndicated political cartoonists to address virtually every facet of the Cold War were Jules Feiffer, Bill Mauldin, Pat Oliphant, Herb Block, Don Wright, Charles G. Werner and Richard Q. Yardley. Popular among members of the COUNTERCULTURE, underground comics also had a strong political, antiestablishment dimension, and they brutally satirized the Vietnam War, nuclear weaponry and other aspects of the Cold War. Robert Crumb was one of the leading underground comic artists, and Zap Comix one of the most prominent publishers.

Tom LEHRER's musical performances, especially his songs WE WILL ALL GO TOGETHER WHEN WE GO and "Who's Next," frequently satirized the Cold War, as did the more mild performances by Mark Russell.

During the 1970s and 1980s, T-shirts appeared with Pop art drawings satirizing the possibilities for NUCLEAR APOCALYPSE. One shows a woman sobbing saying, "Nuclear War?! There Goes My Career!" Other black humor T-shirts proclaimed "One Nuclear Bomb Ruins Your Whole Day," "Cobaltone . . . For the Tan of Your Life," and the exit line from the Looney Tunes cartoons, "That's All Folks!"

"Saturday Night Live" A television comedy show that ran on NBC from 1975 through the end of the Cold War and beyond. The show featured the Not Ready For Prime Time Players, who included over the years Chevy Chase, John Belushi, Dan Aykroyd, Gilda Radner, Garrett Morris, Jane Curtin, Laraine Newman, Bill Murray, Al Franken, Tom Davis, Joe Piscopo, Eddie Murphy, Jim Belushi, Billy Crystal, Randy Quaid, Dennis Miller, Dana Carvey, Victoria Jackson and Martin Short, among many others. Each episode would feature a guest host, among whom were Buck Henry, George Carlin, Steve Martin, Elliott Gould, Lily Tomlin, Paul Simon, Ralph Nader, New York's Mayor Ed Koch, and President Ford's press secretary, Ron Nessen. Chevy Chase became known for his imitation of President Ford. Dan Aykroyd imitated Presidents Carter and Nixon, and Dana Carvey imitated President Bush. In addition to specific skits that satirized current events, the show featured Weekend Up-

date, a satirical news broadcast. The humor ranged from straight comedy to political SATIRE to BLACK HUMOR, and its targets included leaders from communist countries as well as from the West. Its politics were more or less liberal in the earlier years but moved more toward the political center and even the right during the 1980s.

Sayonara A 1954 MILITARY NOVEL by James MICHENER and a 1957 KOREAN WAR FILM starring Marlon Brando, Ricardo Montalban, Red Buttons, James Garner, Patricia Owens, Miiko Taka and Martha Scott and directed by Joshua Logan. This updated version of *Madame Butterfly* centers on Lloyd Gruver (Brando), an army major reassigned to Japan during the Korean War. When he supports his friend Joe Kelly (Buttons), who has insisted upon marrying a local woman, Gruver takes an unpopular stand against racial prejudice, since U.S. military policy forbids marriages between American military personnel and Japanese women. Shortly thereafter Gruver himself falls in love with a Japanese dancer and faces the same predicament as Kelly. The U.S. occupation of Japan from 1945 to 1952 and the 1951 U.S.–Japanese security treaty assuring the U.S. defense of Japan in case of external attack permitted the United States to station soldiers in Japan and led to a sizable U.S. military presence in that country. During the Korean War, Japan hosted crucial U.S. military bases. Thus the pairing of American soldiers and Japanese women was a frequent and virtually inevitable occurrence. Within that context, *Sayonara* explores the ramifications of the official policy against this form of interracial marriage, which some 10,000 American servicemen knowingly violated in order to marry according to their own wishes during the U.S. occupation and Korean War.

"Scarecrow and Mrs. King" A TELEVISION SPY SHOW that ran on CBS from 1983 to 1987. Amanda King (Kate Jackson) was a typical suburban divorcee and mother until a mysterious, handsome man pushed a package into her hands at a train station and disappeared. He turned out to be Scarecrow (Bruce Boxleitner), an American agent escaping from Soviet spies. This initial event leads to Amanda's assumption of a double life as housewife and espionage agent when Amanda and Scarecrow become a team.

Schlauch, Margaret An American EXILED WRITER (from the United States). A distinguished linguist and literary scholar, Schlauch was born in Philadelphia in 1898. She went into exile from the United States after receiving a subpoena from the HOUSE COMMITTEE ON UN-AMERICAN ACTIVITIES (HUAC), which she feared would persecute her for her communist beliefs. She disappeared from her office at New York University, where she had taught for decades, then reappeared in Warsaw, where she received political asylum. The Polish government subsequently granted Schlauch several awards for her scholarship. Her works include *English World Literature and Its Social Foundations* (1956) and *Modern English and American Poetry: Techniques and Ideologies* (1956). (See also NONFICTION WRITERS.)

For additional reading, see Tucker's *Literary Exile in the Twentieth Century.*

Schulberg, Budd A NOVELIST and SCREENWRITER. The son of a Hollywood mogul, Schulberg had been a member of the Communist Party during the 1930s but quit in 1940 after being criticized for celebrating individuality in *What Makes Sammy Run?* The reviewer for the communist newspaper *The Daily Worker* initially praised the best-selling novel but then, under pressure from the party, recanted and wrote a highly critical review. In 1950, Schulberg wrote another best-seller, *The Disenchanted*, based on his 1939 screenwriting collaboration with F. Scott Fitzgerald. In his 1951 testimony before the HOUSE COMMITTEE ON UN-AMERICAN ACTIVITIES (HUAC), screenwriter Richard COLLINS identified Schulberg as a former communist who had left the party. Subsequently Schulberg was named in a front-page headline of the *New York Times*. Two days later he telegrammed HUAC confirming his communist membership between 1937 and 1940 and indicating his current opposition to communism and the U.S.S.R. He also offered to cooperate with the committee "in any way I can." Shortly afterward he testified before HUAC, describing the party's attempts to censor his writing and make him submit to party discipline. He explained that the party viewed writers as soldiers who received certain "social commands." Soldiers who failed to follow orders were expelled. Schulberg also identified 15 communist members, all of whom had already been named before the committee.

Schulberg steadfastly defended his testimony. "My guilt is what we did to the Czechs, not to Ring LARDNER. I testified because I felt guilty for having contributed unwittingly to intellectual and artistic as well as racial oppression. In a small way I helped to bring down McCarthy and I can show it." About the literary achievements of the HOLLYWOOD TEN and other blacklisted party members, Schulberg said,

> Get off the idea that these are civil libertarians . . . And don't talk to me about socialist realism. Dalton [TRUMBO] wrote one good novel and that's it. Most of these people never tried to write any social realism . . . There was not a blacklist in publishing . . . [or] theater. They could have written about the forces that drove them into the Communist Party. There was practically nothing written. Nor have I seen these people interested in social problems in the decades since. They're interested in their own problems and in the protection of the Party . . . They question our talking. I question their silence. There were premature anti-fascists but there were also premature anti-Stalinists.

Prior to his HUAC appearance, Schulberg and Arthur KOESTLER cofounded Funds for Intellectual Freedom [FIF], an authors' organization intended to assist writers in totalitarian countries who were being ordered to concentration camps, whether fascist or communist, because their writing was politically unacceptable. Following the 1964 race riots in Los Angeles, Schulberg founded the Watts Writers Workshop to develop the writing talents of young black ghetto writers. He also cofounded the Frederick Douglass Community Arts Center in New York to support African-American artists.

In 1954 Schulberg wrote the screenplay for ON THE WATERFRONT, which was directed by Elia KAZAN, who had also named names before HUAC. Schulberg later wrote the accompanying novel, *The Waterfront.* In *On the Waterfront,* the cause of justice and integrity is served by informing, not by standing silent and permitting violent crimes to go unpunished. The novel celebrates the same ideals but its ending is significantly bleaker.

For additional reading, see Navasky's *Naming Names.* For a partial transcript of Schulberg's testimony before HUAC, see Bentley's THIRTY YEARS OF TREASON.

science fiction films Though the genre extends back to the earliest days of cinema in such works as Meliès' *A Trip to the Moon* (1902), science fiction films flourished during the Cold War when the advancement of science and technology played a central role in world politics. Many SPY FILMS, notably the James BOND series, also featured realistic and fantastic uses of technology. For instance, GOLDFINGER (1964) dramatically introduced the movie public to laser technology. But in those spy films the science, though necessary, was not central to the plot. In science fiction films, science is used to imagine the world differently, usually to illuminate some aspect of the real world. Science fiction films are often set in the future, to more easily justify a plot that revolves around the existence of some technology or some capability that does not currently exist.

Many U.S. Cold War science fiction films show the potential dangers that science—especially nuclear technology—might bring. THE DAY THE EARTH CAUGHT FIRE was made in 1961, during the second Berlin Crisis, when the Soviets ended their three-year moratorium on nuclear testing by exploding a bomb 300 times more powerful than the one that leveled Hiroshima. The film treats the actual and potential dangers of nuclear testing. It shows scientists working cooperatively to avert the imminent destruction of the planet after simultaneous U.S. and Soviet test bombs knock the Earth from its axis and send it off its orbit and toward the sun's gravitational field. CRACK IN THE WORLD (1965) presents the possibility of NUCLEAR APOCALYPSE when a dying scientist fires a missile into the Earth's core and nearly destroys the planet. Set six years into the future, OMEGA MAN (1971) stars Charlton HESTON as a survivor of a plague caused by germ warfare. The postapocalyptic film appeared in the early 1970s when germ warfare was a topical subject and both superpowers were increasing their arsenals. A BOY AND HIS DOG (1975) is a BLACK HUMOR postapocalyptic film based on a story by Harlan Ellison. Other postapocalyptic science fiction films include MAD MAX (1979) and PLANET OF THE APES (1968) and their respective sequels.

The STAR WARS (1977) series dramatically plays out the battle between the forces of good and evil in a high-tech portion of the universe "a long time ago, in a galaxy far, far away." Like its sequels, *The Empire Strikes Back* (1980) and *Return of the Jedi* (1983), *Star Wars* (1977) depicts a hero fighting for freedom and justice against a better-armed evil empire bent on galactic domination. The films appeared during the Carter and Reagan administrations, when conservatives were charging that the Soviet military power had surpassed that of the United States. Reagan invoked the image of the evil empire to label the U.S.S.R. His Strategic Defense Initiative (SDI), which proposed to use laser-armed space satellites to knock out enemy missiles in flight, was popularly labeled Star Wars.

Six STAR TREK movies appeared between 1979 and 1991, starring the major actors from the 1960s TELEVISION SCIENCE FICTION show on which they were based. In this futuristic world, galaxies form military/political alliances similar to NATO and the Warsaw Pact, and Captain Kirk is often hampered by treaty restrictions that his enemies either unfairly exploit or violate—a common public complaint about the United States's situation throughout the Cold War, especially during the Vietnam War. And just as the American public generally viewed their country as working for the cause of peace, justice and international security, the mission of the starship *Enterprise* was an enlightened attempt "to boldly go where no one has gone before" in order to acquire knowledge, protect the frontiers and aid colonies in distress. Of particular interest is the film *Star Trek VI: The Undiscovered Country* (1991), which mirrors the then-current conclusion of the Cold War. In that film, the characters learn to accept the possibility of peaceful coexistence between former enemies and not to be afraid of the future. (The television show usually portrayed the *Enterprise* crew as committed to peaceful coexistence, depicting war as a kind of madness or misunderstanding).

Outer-space invasion films of the 1950s frequently played out Cold War anxieties. The alien creature is typically linked to communism, so that the films become metaphors, if not allegories, for the threat feared from the Red menace. Different films took different positions within the RED SCARE terms of debate. THE DAY THE EARTH STOOD STILL (1951), for example, presents the left-wing argument that the greatest threat to planetary survival comes from those who want to kill the alien/communist without first talking with it and seeking peace, while the right-wing INVASION OF THE BODY SNATCHERS (1956) enacts Senator McCarthy's right-wing vision of America in which the pod-people/communist cadres have already infiltrated and taken over. Like communists, these aliens work in cells (pods); they have no emotions; they are single-minded in their devotion to their cause; and they control police/army and government institutions through internal subversion. Likewise the slimy, slug-like movements of THE BLOB (1958) provide an objective correlative for the right-wing fear of "creeping Communism." In centrist films like THE THING (1951) and INVADERS FROM MARS (1953), the alien/communist indeed poses a genuine threat, but the trustworthy forces of government are actively and competently working to defeat it. Alternately, in RED PLANET MARS (1952), highly advanced Martians inspire the overthrow of the Soviet government via religious radio broadcasts, fulfilling the call of such right-wing religious figures as Bishop SHEEN and Billy GRAHAM, who claimed that religion was the best means by which to defeat communism.

Atomic mutant films comprise another 1950s subgenre. In these films, planetary survival is threatened by monsters, genetic mutations formed by nuclear bomb tests or other sources of radiation. Mutant creatures appear in THEM! (1954, giant ants), ATTACK OF THE CRAB MONSTERS (1956), THE DAY THE WORLD ENDED (1955, three-eyed cannibals), *The Attack of the 50-Foot Woman* (1958), *Attack of the Giant Leeches* (1959) and *The Beginning of the End* (1957, grasshoppers). The

Japanese series GODZILLA (1954) and RODAN (1957) also feature radiation-spawned monsters. As these series progress, the monsters go from destroying the nation to protecting it, just as American nuclear weapons destroyed Hiroshima but were seen as protecting Japan during the Korean War and throughout the Cold War.

Sometimes the radiation produced not dangerous monsters but deformed humans, whose lives were forever ruined by the effects of the radiation. THE INCREDIBLE SHRINKING MAN (1957), and *The Fly* (1958) were films of this type.

Embedded within outer-space invasion and atomic mutant films lies a question of authority: Who is the best equipped to deal with the alien threat: scientists and intellectuals or the government and the military? In many respects, this conflict mirrored an internal power struggle within postwar America over who could best guide the United States through the Cold War. An emerging liberal technocracy that valued science and theoretical approaches to problem-solving was challenging an entrenched conservative establishment of men who saw themselves as practical and straightforward, rather than theoretical, innovative or intellectually curious.

Soviet science fiction films were rarely seen in the United States, but they too engaged in contemporary social issues. Directed by Andrei Tarkovsky, who later came to the West in search of artistic freedom, the 1972 Soviet-made film SOLARIS appeared during the U.S.-Soviet détente and provided American audiences with a rare look at Soviet cinema. Based on the novel by Polish writer Stanislaw Lem, the film portrays cosmonauts who investigate a planet that proves to be sentient and capable of affecting the dreams of humans who visit it. The story reflects experiments with parapsychology that took place within the Soviet Union during the Cold War. Perhaps more profoundly, it reflects concerns with the increasingly mechanized modern world and with humans' loss of connection to the natural world. (See also FILMS ASSOCIATED WITH THE RED SCARE.)

For additional reading, see Sayre's *Running Time* Biskind's *Seeing Is Believing*; Broderick's *Nuclear Movies*.

science fiction novels and stories Most Cold War science fiction imagines the consequences of nuclear war or some other form of mass destruction and is thus treated more fully in the entry on APOCALYPTIC NOVELS. However, the genre is so broadly defined that it can be said to include such mainstream works as the following: George ORWELL's political novel NINETEEN EIGHTY-FOUR (1949), in which science and technology serve as tools of oppression and repression and help those in power construct an easily manipulated citizenry; Richard Condon's THE MANCHURIAN CANDIDATE (1959), which portrays "brainwashing" achieved by advanced forms of hypnosis and other psychological techniques; John Barth's GILES GOAT-BOY (1966), in which a supercomputer controls most aspects of society; Thomas Pynchon's GRAVITY'S RAINBOW (1973); most of the fiction of Kurt VONNEGUT Jr.; Ayn RAND's *Atlas Shrugged* (1957); and virtually any other work with a futuristic setting. On the other hand, most major Cold War science fiction writers—Isaac Asimov, Robert Heinlein, Ray Bradbury, Philip Dick, Frederik Pohl and Arthur C. Clarke—treat the Cold War only tangentially.

One exception is Clarke's *2001: A Space Odyssey,* which was based on the 1968 film by Stanley KUBRICK. The novel has some Cold War implications in its treatment of the link between human violence and technology and of the apparent desire for a new state of human consciousness that might elevate humanity from its Cold War mentality. Clarke wrote a sequel in 1982, *2010: Odyssey Two,* which features a joint U.S.-Soviet expedition to Jupiter. *Childhood's End* (1953) also expresses the desire of Earthlings to find some extraterrestrial source of salvation from their self-destructive tendencies.

Among the more traditional works of science fiction was THE MANIAC'S DREAM (1946). Its author, F. H. Rose, claimed it was the first novel about the atomic bomb. It alludes to Conrad's *The Heart of Darkness* as a detached narrator observes Thara, a mad scientist at work deep in a tropical jungle. The Faustian scientist suffers from hubris and heretically likens himself to God: "Mankind harnessing to his own uses the power of Atomic Energy, will prove once and for all, that there is no other God but Man, and that he himself is God." In 1947 Leonard Engel and Emanuel S. Piller published *The World Aflame: The Russian–American War of 1950.* Narrated by historians in 1955, the futuristic novel provides a right-wing point of view that vindicates Senator Joseph McCarthy's fear of a communist menace and demonstrates that the U.S. monopoly of the atomic bomb is insufficient for a quick, decisive victory over the Soviet Union. Sir General John Hackett and other top-ranking NATO generals and advisers later used a similar narrative framework in their highly detailed 1978 account of THE THIRD WORLD WAR and its 1982 sequel, *The Untold Story.* Both books describe a hypothetical war between NATO and the Warsaw Pact, and both call for the West to upgrade its military arsenal and state of preparedness.

Poul Anderson's 1947 story "Tomorrow's Children," published two years after the Hiroshima attack, also describes the effects of a worldwide atomic war. His 1952 novel *Vault of the Ages* likewise deals with nuclear issues. Bradbury's frequently anthologized story of 1950, "There Will Come Soft Rains," imagines a highly automated house in which only the machines have survived an atomic attack. These eerily seem to take on the functions of living in the absence of their human owners. Bradbury's 1950 *Martian Chronicles* is a collection of stories describing the human colonization of Mars. Though it does not address the Cold War directly, its representation of the human exploitation of its colony parallels the history of Western colonization and raises social issues that played a significant role within the Cold War. Bradbury's *Fahrenheit 451* deals with the rise of a totalitarian society that controls thought by burning books, which ignite at 451 degrees Fahrenheit. Published in 1955, C. M. Kornbluth's *Not This August* imagines a defeated United States occupied by the Soviet Union and communist China until members of an American underground discover a vast cavern containing a nearly completed space vehicle armed with hydrogen and cobalt bombs, which they use to conquer the enemy.

Kornbluth and Pohl write of the dangers of excessive capitalism in *The Space Merchants* (1952), in which the United States is dominated by advertising agencies and a small-business class; everyone else has been reduced to industrial serfdom and become captive consumers. Pohl's *Slave Ship*

(1957), published three years after the French defeat at Dienbienphu in 1954, in some ways anticipates the Vietnam War. It invokes the Domino Theory articulated in 1953 by Secretary of State John Foster Dulles as it imagines the victorious Vietnamese going on to conquer the entire Eastern Hemisphere and forcing a confrontation with the United States and United Nations. A nuclear war is averted by a U.S. mission that relies on telepathic communication with animals—but it then attracts an alien life form that is drawn to telepathy. Asimov's 1956 story "Hell Fire" treats the nuclear theme in a more metaphysical fashion as the careful examination of a film of a nuclear explosion reveals the devil lurking within. There are "dark spots for eyes, with dark lines above them for thin, flaring eyebrows. And where a hairline came down V-shaped a mouth, twisted upward, laughing wildly in the hell-fire. And there were horns."

Other Cold War science fiction from the 1950s includes Arthur KOESTLER's *The Age of Longing* (1951), which depicts totalitarian efforts to enslave Western society; philosopher Bertrand Russell's "Eisenhower's Nightmare: The McCarthy-Malenkov Pact," which appears in his story collection, *Nightmares of Eminent Personalities and Other Stories* (1954); Wilson Tucker's *The Long Loud Silence* (1952), in which the aftermath of a nuclear-biological war that devastates the United States east of the Mississippi involves cannibalism and other primitive means of survival; Tucker's *Wild Talent* (1954), in which government agents try to use and then kill a man who has developed telepathic abilities; Margot Bennett's *The Long Way Back* (1954), about a futuristic expedition of Africans who come to Britain to explore the now-savage country, which they discover was destroyed by nuclear weapons; and Arthur Hadley's satirical *The Joy Wagon* (1958), in which a computer runs for president and outshines its opponents.

The period between 1958 and 1962 encompassed the second Berlin Crisis and the Cuban Missile Crisis and was one of the most intense times of the Cold War, when nuclear war seemed almost imminent. Science fiction from that time includes German author Hans Hellmut Kirst's *The Seventh Day* (1959), which castigates both the United States and U.S.S.R. as it chronicles six days of failed diplomatic negotiations that culminate in a massive nuclear war. In *When the Kissing Had to Stop* (1960), Irish author Constantine Fitz Gibbon imagines the conquest of Great Britain by the Sino-Soviet alliance after extreme left-wing elements gain power in the British Isles. C. S. Casewit's THE PEACEMAKERS (1960) portrays the conflict between a scientist and a fascistic general who have both taken refuge on a Pacific island from a global nuclear war. Eventually, the scientist learns to assume responsibility for his inventions. Daniel F. Galouye's 1961 *Dark Universe* imagines a light-deprived civilization that grows up underground following a nuclear war.

Cold War science fiction from the mid-1960s reflects both concerns over nuclear war and the Vietnam War. British writer Brian Aldiss' *Greybeard* (1964) presents a scenario in which nuclear testing leads to the sterilization of the human race and thus threatens its extinction. The book appeared along with the emergence of the Campaign for Nuclear Disarmament, which advocated Britain's unilateral nuclear disarmament. Aldiss's BAREFOOT IN THE HEAD, a 1969 BLACK HUMOR account of superpower warfare fought with psychedelic drugs instead of nuclear weapons, reflects the interest in "mind-expanding" chemicals that became popular during the Vietnam War era, as well as contemporary reports of CIA tests of LSD on unsuspecting human subjects. Thomas M. Disch's *Camp Concentration* (1968) centers on a political prisoner who is used to test a bacteria, related to syphilis, that is intended to enormously increase IQ levels. Disch also treats Cold War–related topics in his 1982 story collection, *The Man Who Had No Idea.* Kit Reed's *Armed Campus* (1969) presents warfare as an institutionalized method of social control, the inevitable consequence of technological imperatives.

The 1970s brought a temporary détente between the Eastern and Western powers. To some extent, this shaped the type of science fiction that was published at the time, including the new availability of some Soviet and Eastern European science fiction. Published in the United States in 1970, SOLARIS was written in 1961 by the Polish author Stanislaw Lem and made into a 1972 SCIENCE FICTION FILM by the Soviet director Andrei Tarkovsky. The story portrays a planet that is actually a conscious entity that communicates to cosmonauts who land there through the dreams it induces. The story's subject matter thus alludes to the exploration of parapsychology that took place in the U.S.S.R. during the Cold War, as well as to the suggestion that planets are "biospheres," integrated living entities. British author D. G. Compton's *The Steel Crocodile* (1970) shows how two workers at a secret research institute are stymied by a conservatism that impedes both scientific and moral progress. Robert Asprin's *The Cold Cash War* (1977) shows the increasing political importance of multinational corporations, which in his novel form private armies to implement their own foreign policies.

The Cold War reintensified after the Soviet invasion of Afghanistan at the end of 1979, and renewed fears of nuclear war remained strong until Mikhail Gorbachev became the Soviet premier in early 1985. Cold War science fiction from the early 1980s includes British author Kingsley Amis's *Russian Hide and Seek* (1980), in which England has become a Soviet satellite, losing its traditional culture and political freedoms; and Syd Logsdon's *A Sad Farewell to Dying* (1981), in which India emerges as the world's next superpower following a nuclear war. *A Rose for Armageddon* (1982) by Hilbert Schenck centers on a group of aging social scientists whose computer study of the social relationships on a small island offers some hope for the larger world. Hungarian Gyorgy Dalos's *1985* (1983) presents a cynical view of the reforms in Eastern Europe. In this imagined sequel to Orwell's *Nineteen Eighty-Four,* members of the Outer Party gain some freedoms but the hopes of would-be dissidents like Winston Smith are shown to be futile. (Anthony Burgess wrote an earlier sequel in 1978, also entitled *1985.*) British author Bob Shaw's *The Peace Machine* (1985) is an updated version of his 1971 *Ground Zero Man,* portraying a man who must flee for his life after inventing a machine that can destroy stockpiles of nuclear weapons.

Most Cold War-oriented science fiction imagines a postnuclear society. In 1955, three years after the United States developed the hydrogen bomb, Walter Miller published "A Canticle For Leibowitz" in *Fantasy and Science Fiction* magazine. The short story, the first part of his three-part

1959 novel of the same title, became a prototype of postapocalyptic fiction. In such literature, society typically devolves into either lawless anarchy, medieval feudalism or fascistic dictatorship. Whereas many of these stories leave the protagonists stuck in a brutal, capricious, superstitious, male-dominated world, *A Canticle for Leibowitz* suggests that over time, human society will resume its evolution by undergoing a new Enlightenment in which it again embraces science but learns to subordinate it to spiritual values. *Canticle* thus concludes with a futuristic colony of priests taking off for the stars in a spaceship.

John Varley's MILLENNIUM (1983) is often paired with *Canticle.* It features a small group of survivors of a nuclear war who try to save the human race by going back in time to rescue people who had been killed in airplane accidents. Heinlein's FARNHAM'S FREEHOLD (1965) presents a survivalist scenario from the mid-1960s. Published just as the Vietnam War was escalating, the novel imagines alternative apocalyptic endings other than nuclear war. The protagonist is a survivalist who believes that the next war will probably be an "ABC war—atomic, biological, and chemical." When he emerges from his bomb shelter, he discovers he has been blasted into the future when the last war occurred long ago. But he learns that this new paradise is also subject to nuclear war, and he must take shelter in a mine shaft while the apocalypse repeats itself.

Dean Ing's science fiction from the 1980s also reflects the point of view of survivalists who distrusted government and were intent on preparing themselves for the anarchy that they were sure would follow a nuclear war. His books include *Systemic Shock* (1981), in which the United States is ruled by violence and held together by religious cults; *Single Combat* (1983); *Wild Country* (1985); and PULLING THROUGH (1983). Ing's novels recall Dean Owen's earlier survivalist work, THE END OF THE WORLD (1962), which was the basis for the 1962 film drama PANIC IN YEAR ZERO. Ryder Stacy's DOOMSDAY WARRIOR (1984) and its 1984 sequel *Doomsday Warrior No. 2: Red America* also present survivalist scenarios.

Some postapocalyptic science fiction novels project an eventual role for science in postnuclear society, despite its prominent role in creating the nuclear holocaust. These include Stephen Minot's CHILL OF DUST (1964), Leigh Brackett's THE LONG TOMORROW (1955), Poul Anderson's ORION SHALL RISE (1983) and Russell Hoban's RIDDLEY WALKER (1981). Robert Sheckley treats technology in an absurdist manner in JOURNEY BEYOND TOMORROW (1964), and David Skal's *When We Were Good* (1981) shows genetic engineers producing a race of "perfect" hermaphrodites after radiation has sterilized humanity. The protagonist in Sterling E. Lanier's *Hiero's Journey* (1973) travels through a postnuclear world populated by deformed mutants in search of legendary computers that might save the species. Norman Spinrad's 1972 THE IRON DREAM (1972) posits a parallel universe in which Adolf Hitler is a science fiction writer who imagines a Nazi, male-dominated, postapocalyptic motorbike gang that celebrates science and power. The gang escapes the effects of the nuclear war they have waged by cloning themselves and colonizing space. Hitler, the writer, describes the settlers who, like the priests in *Canticle* are leaving the Earth aboard a space ship: "The seed of the Swastika rose on a pillar of fire to fecundate the stars."

By contrast, many books with feminist sympathies depict the dangers of technological violence and sexual inequality and promote a society predicated on female principles of kinship, nurturing behavior and respect for nature. Ursula LE GUIN, a highly respected science fiction writer, published at least two such novels that bear on the Cold War. *The Left Hand of Darkness* (1969) presents a planet where both men and women are capable of child-bearing. The planet has two cultures, Karhide, whose inhabitants live in harmony with nature, and Orgoreyn, which suggests Stalinist Russia, featuring secret police, an oppressive bureaucracy and remote prison camps in the frozen wilderness. An American visitor must learn to deal both with the "Third World" of Karhide and the oppressive Orgoreyn. The story thus pits the feminine values of harmony and cooperation against the masculine values of dominance that are most fully reflected by the Stalinist police state. Le Guin's *The Dispossessed* (1974) presents three civilizations. Two correspond to Cold War–era capitalistic and communist societies. The third is an anarchist utopia. *The Long Tomorrow* and Suzy McKee Charnas's WALK TO THE END OF THE WORLD (1979) also present feminist perspectives. *Walk to the End of the World* appears to have been inspired by the specter of Nazi concentration camps. Women in the postnuclear society become slaves who work underground and are turned into food when they die. "Some man must have designed the process; it was too beautiful, too efficient to be a product of the fems' [women's] own thinking." Charnas wrote a 1981 sequel, *Motherlines*. (See also TELEVISION SCIENCE FICTION SHOWS.)

For additional reading, see Barron's *Anatomy of Wonder: A Critical Guide to Science Fiction*.

Scott, Hazel An African-American pianist and singer whose performances and television appearances were curtailed because of her listing in RED CHANNELS. The publication purported to identify people with communist affiliations. Soon after Scott's name appeared there, the DuMont network dropped Scott's 1950 television program of café favorites and show tunes, though network officials denied that the listing was the reason for canceling her show. The wife of Congressman Adam Clayton Powell, Scott appeared before the HOUSE COMMITTEE ON UN-AMERICAN ACTIVITIES (HUAC) to testify about her listing in *Red Channels*. In her testimony she pointed out that each of the nine mentions of her name was either erroneous or misleading:

> One of these listings is for an appearance—by direction of my employer—an appearance of which I am not ashamed—another was ostensibly a series of benefits for orphaned children. When I found out otherwise, I discontinued such activity. Still another involved the use of my name three years after I had played a benefit. The group later merged with one that developed a bad name . . . A fourth advertised that I was a guest of honor at a dinner I never went to or even heard of. Three others I refused to join. The remaining two I never heard of . . . I did not support [Progressive Party presidential candidate] Henry Wallace, and I voted for Harry Truman. Again this well-known position seems not to have interested the publishers of *Red Channels* . . .

Despite her disclaimers before HUAC, Scott was later dropped from a guest appearance on a network television program, allegedly at the sponsor's insistence. According to the sponsor, her testimony was irrelevant; "She's still listed in that book [*Red Channels*], and we don't want to get involved in any controversy." (See also BLACKLISTING; RED SCARE.)

For additional reading, see Miller's *The Judges and the Judged*.

Scott, Robert Adrian A SCREENWRITER, film producer and member of the HOLLYWOOD TEN. Scott's career was just beginning to blossom when he was called to testify at the 1947 HOUSE COMMITTEE ON UN-AMERICAN ACTIVITIES (HUAC) hearings on communist influences in Hollywood films. After citing their First Amendment rights and refusing to testify, Scott and the other nine "unfriendly" witnesses were cited for contempt of Congress and eventually sentenced to prison. Scott was also blacklisted. He never wrote or produced another Hollywood film after his appearance before the committee. Moreover, his actress wife, who had urged him to cooperate with HUAC, left him after he refused. Scott was among those identified as a communist by director Edward DMYTRYK when Dmytryk, also a member of the Ten, changed his position and testified before HUAC in 1951. Scott had produced two films directed by Dmytryk: *Cornered* (1945), an anti-Nazi movie, and *Crossfire* (1947), a film that attacked anti-Semitism. In 1955, Scott wrote an article for *Hollywood Review* that analyzed the impact of the blacklist on the quality of films made in Hollywood. Comparing the pre–1947 and post–1947 films of such leading non-blacklisted FILM DIRECTORS and screenwriters as Elia KAZAN, John Ford, William Dieterle, Nunnally Johnson and others, Scott concluded that few, if any "have dramatized the humanist, democratic, and antifascist values that illuminated their work in the Roosevelt era. Their talents remain, but the ideas to which they applied their talents have been eroded and forbidden." He died in 1973. (See also BLACKLISTING.)

For additional reading, see Navasky's *Naming Names*.

Scoundrel Time a 1976 NONFICTION book by Lillian Hellman, a playwright and blacklisted SCREENWRITER. The book describes the author's 1952 appearance before the HOUSE COMMITTEE ON UN-AMERICAN ACTIVITIES (HUAC). Her lover, novelist Dashiell Hammett, had joined the Communist Party in the late 1930s, but though Hellman had attended three or four meetings she never became a party member. She claims she found the people at the meetings "unaesthetic," and she complained at a meeting in 1937 that the Soviets had not adequately supported the anti-fascists during the Spanish Civil War, "only enough to keep the Spanish fighting and dying for a cause that was going to be lost." She maintains that "whether I signed a Party card or didn't was of little importance to me. I couldn't have known then what importance would be attached to it a few years later . . . Whatever is wrong with Southerners—redneck or better—we were all brought up to believe we had a right to think as we pleased." Hellman goes on to describe how Hammett was jailed in 1951 for refusing to name the contributors to the bail bond fund of the Civil Rights Congress and how he was financially ruined as a result of living according to his convictions.

Hellman then describes receiving her own subpoena to appear before HUAC in 1952. Much of her prior political work had been directed toward civil rights, and she notes that HUAC chose a black man to deliver the subpoena. " 'Smart to choose a black man for this job. You like it?' " she asked him before slamming the door. She then describes meeting with her lawyers to adopt a strategy for her testimony. The Supreme Court had already upheld the contempt of Congress citations against the HOLLYWOOD TEN, who had unsuccessfully invoked their First Amendment constitutional protections to avoid naming names of alleged communists or communist sympathizers. So to avoid naming names while also avoiding going to jail for contempt of Congress, the only recourse was to invoke the Fifth Amendment protections against self-incrimination. This Hellman was loath to do, since she did not consider herself guilty of anything. She therefore wrote the committee offering to waive her Fifth Amendment protections if the committee, in turn, agreed to question her only about her own political activities and not to ask about other people. In that letter she stated she was "not willing, now or in the future, to bring bad trouble to people who, in my past association with them, were completely innocent of any talk or any action that was disloyal or subversive . . . I cannot and will not cut my conscience to fit this year's fashions." However, HUAC declined her offer and Hellman did ultimately invoke the Fifth Amendment. She thus managed to escape prosecution but was unable to present her own case before the committee. A footnote in her book relates an observation by her lawyer:

> There were three things they [the Committee] wanted. One, names which you wouldn't give. Two, a smear by accusing you of being a "Fifth Amendment Communist." They couldn't do that because in your letter you offered to testify about yourself. [One of the committee members committed the strategic error of introducing her letter into the record.] And three, a prosecution which they couldn't do because they forced us into taking the Fifth Amendment. They had sense enough to see that they were in a bad spot. We beat them, that's all.

However, Hellman points out, the cost for her success was considerable. She had to sell a beloved farm to cover legal expenses, and she was thereafter blacklisted from writing Hollywood screenplays. (See also BLACKLISTING; RED SCARE.)

Screen Guide for Americans, A

A 1948 NONFICTION pamphlet written by Ayn RAND, distributed by the MOTION PICTURE ALLIANCE FOR THE PRESERVATION OF AMERICAN IDEALS and reprinted on the front page of the entertainment section of the *New York Times*. Rand's pamphlet became the basis for a film code promulgated by Roy BREWER, Ronald REAGAN and Eric Johnston, head of the Motion Picture Producers' Association. Rand asserted in her introduction that the communists' objective in Hollywood was "*not* the production of political movies openly advocating Communism," but to "*corrupt our moral premises by corrupting non-political movies . . .* making people absorb the basic principles of Collectiv-

ism *by indirection and implication.*" [The emphasis is Rand's.] Consequently, the *Screen Guide* called on American films not to "smear" industrialists, success or the free enterprise system, and not to "deify the common man," "show that poverty is a virtue" or suggest that "failure is noble." Likewise, the guide instructs filmmakers never to "use lines about 'the common man' or 'the little people.' It is not the American idea to be either 'common' or little." The *Screen Guide* therefore urges that the image of the noble struggles of the downtrodden be seen rather as the "drooling of weaklings."

For additional reading, see Whitfield's *Culture of the Cold War;* May's *Recasting America.*

screenwriters

Film screenwriters contributed to Cold War culture by writing scripts dealing with Cold War issues and events and by taking public political stands. Notable in the first category are Jerzy KOSINSKI, Terry SOUTHERN Samuel FULLER and Oliver STONE. Though best known as a NOVELIST, Kosinski won an Academy Award for his 1979 adaptation of his 1970 novel BEING THERE, a FILM SATIRE about a mentally retarded man who is obsessed by gardening and television and who becomes an influential political adviser to the president.

A major creator of American BLACK HUMOR, Southern provided one of the best treatments of the Cold War nuclear threat in his screenplay for the 1964 film satire DR. STRANGELOVE, about a nuclear attack against the Soviet Union launched by an insane U.S. Air Force general. (The film's director, Stanley KUBRICK, and Peter George, the author of the book on which it is based, also contributed to the screenplay.) Southern also wrote the screenplay *The End of the Road* (1970), adapted from the novel by John BARTH. Other significant film credits include *Easy Rider* (1969); *The Cincinnati Kid* (1965, cowritten with Ring LARDNER Jr.); *Barbarella* (1968), a pacifist SCIENCE FICTION FILM starring Jane FONDA; and *Burroughs* (1983), about writer William Burroughs. He also wrote the screenplays for his novels *Candy* (book 1964, film 1968 and *The Magic Christian* (book 1960, film 1969). Though not exactly an anti-capitalist statement, *The Magic Christian* mocks human greed and portrays the perverse imagination of a very wealthy man.

Better known as a FILM DIRECTOR, Fuller also wrote the screenplays for most of his movies, including his two KOREAN WAR FILMS, THE STEEL HELMET (1951) and *Fixed Bayonets* (1951), his early VIETNAM WAR FILM, *China Gate* (1957); his FILM DRAMA PICKUP ON SOUTH STREET (1953), about a pickpocket who inadvertently steals atomic secrets from Soviet spies; and *Hell and High Water* (1954), about a submarine that thwarts Chinese communists off Alaska. A highly political film director, Stone wrote the screenplays for all of his Cold War films. His two Vietnam War films are the hyperrealistic, Academy Award–winning PLATOON (1986), which was informed by his own participation in the war, and BORN ON THE FOURTH OF JULY (1989) about a Vietnam veteran who comes to oppose the war. Stone's other Cold War–related films include *Salvador* (1986), about an American photojournalist in Central America, and *JFK* (1991), a post–Cold War revisionist account of the Kennedy assassination. *Nixon* (1995) covers several Cold War topics in its portrayal of the former president. *Wall Street* (1987) attacks the greed in the stock market during the Reagan era, and *The Doors* (1991) documents Jim Morrison and his rock band of the 1960s.

Screenwriters known for their own political activity include Ayn RAND, a vehement anti-communist; Lillian Hellman, who wrote SCOUNDREL TIME (1976) about her RED SCARE experiences and the effects of BLACKLISTING and HOLLYWOOD TEN members Alvah BESSIE, Lester COLE, Lardner, John LAWSON, Albert MALTZ, Sam ORNITZ, Robert Adrian SCOTT and Dalton TRUMBO. Most of the Ten were present or past communists who invoked their First Amendment protection of free speech when they refused to testify at the 1947 hearings conducted by the HOUSE COMMITTEE ON UN-AMERICAN ACTIVITIES (HUAC). Those hearings were ostensibly held to investigate alleged communist influences on the content of Hollywood films. However, credible evidence exists to suggest that HUAC's deeper purpose was to break the left in general and the Communist Party in particular, as well as to establish parameters for acceptable film content in terms of political values, attitudes toward capital and labor, and other sentiments that could potentially render a film "Un-American." As film content was the subject of the 1947 hearings, most of those under investigation were screenwriters.

Rand testified as a "friendly" witness at the 1947 hearings. She criticized the World War II–era film *Song of Russia* (1943) for presenting too positive a picture of life in the Soviet Union. She also attacked *The Best Years of Our Lives* (1946) because she believed that by showing a banker refuse a loan to a returning soldier, the movie advanced "the party line of making the returned soldier fear that the world is against him" and "that business is against him." In 1948 the MOTION PICTURE ALLIANCE FOR THE PRESERVATION OF AMERICAN IDEALS, an anti-communist organization that furnished most of the friendly witnesses for the 1947 hearings, published Rand's A SCREEN GUIDE FOR AMERICANS, which became the basis for the film industry's movie code. Warning that the communists were trying to *"corrupt our moral premises by corrupting non-political movies . . . making people absorb the basic principles of Collectivism by indirection and implication,"* the *Screen Guide* insisted that American films not "smear" industrialists, success or the free enterprise system (Rand's emphasis). Nor should films "deify the common man," "show that poverty is a virtue" or suggest that "failure is noble."

The Ten were all cited for contempt of Congress for their refusal to testify and were sentenced to prison terms of six months to a year after the Supreme Court denied their First Amendment claim and upheld the contempt citations. Subsequently, all were subjected to blacklisting. Trumbo, Lawson and Maltz went into exile and continued to write films under assumed names, at much reduced salaries. (Such writers were later portrayed in the 1976 film tribute by and about blacklisted writers, THE FRONT.) Cole, Lardner, Maltz and Trumbo also wrote some plays for live THEATER. Between 1961 and 1963, Lawson spent time in the U.S.S.R. and East Germany, where a revision of his early play *Parlor Magic* was performed.

Trumbo finally broke the blacklist in 1960 when Otto Preminger publicly credited him for writing EXODUS, and when president-elect Kennedy crossed American Legion picket lines to see SPARTACUS (1960), for which Trumbo was also credited. Lardner went on to write M*A*S*H (1970). In 1976 Cole wrote HOLLYWOOD ON TRIAL, a FILM DOCUMENTARY about the Red Scare in the film industry.

Better known as a playwright, Bertolt BRECHT also appeared before HUAC in 1947. He denied being a member of the Communist Party, despite a life-long attachment to communist causes. He fled the country immediately after testifying and ultimately settled in East Germany where he received a subsidy and a theater of his own. Richard COLLINS was scheduled to testify in 1947 too, but he was not called at that time. However, he had allied with the Ten and was prepared not to cooperate with the committee. Consequently, he was also blacklisted. However, when he was summoned before HUAC in 1951, his position changed and he named names of other communists. Subsequently, he was removed from the blacklist, though he credibly maintained that this was not his motivation for informing, since he was the first witness to name names and no precedent existed for how such penitent witnesses would be treated.

Novelist/screenwriter Budd SCHULBERG was another former communist whose politics changed during the early years of the Cold War and who named names before HUAC. In 1954 he collaborated with Elia KAZAN on ON THE WATERFRONT, a film that celebrates an act of informing. On the other hand, Abraham POLONSKY invoked the Fifth Amendment when he was summoned in 1951, an act that enabled him to avoid informing but that also resulted in his being blacklisted. After the blacklist ended, he wrote and directed *Tell Them Willie Boy Is Here*, a 1969 film about a fugitive Indian boy. "What particularly interested me is the fact that the Indian is a kind of exile in his own country, and so am I—or was—for a brief period: twenty years." Carl FOREMAN wrote HIGH NOON (1952) just prior to his HUAC testimony. The FILM WESTERN, about a sheriff who must face a trio of killers alone when the townspeople refuse to help him, expresses Foreman's sense of abandonment by the film community when he was subpoenaed to testify before HUAC in 1952. After he refused to cooperate with the committee, Foreman was blacklisted. He then went into exile in England, during which time his passport was revoked by the State Department. In 1956 Foreman's attorney, Sidney Cohn, arranged for him to testify in private session before a HUAC subcommittee of one person, Congressman Francis Walter. Cohn wanted to try a strategy that would allow Foreman and perhaps others to testify about themselves without informing on others. In this way, they might break the blacklist. The strategy succeeded for Foreman, and after his testimony the blacklist against him was lifted. But because of political repercussions for Walter, the strategy did not extend to anyone else. There were rumors of a $25,000 bribe, which Foreman denied. In 1973 he declared, "But don't get me wrong—I would have been happy to pay twenty-five thousand dollars to go back to work."

For additional reading, see Navasky's *Naming Names.*

Second Best Secret Agent in the Whole Wide World, The

A 1965 British-made SPY FILM SPOOF starring Tom Adams and Karel Stepanek and directed by Lindsay Shonteff. A parody of the popular James BOND movies, this film centers on a secret agent assigned to protect two Swedish physicists who have developed a formula for reversing the effects of gravity. The British spy must defeat Soviet agents who want both the scientists and the formula. The film also appeared under the title *Licensed to Kill*.

"Second City TV" A TELEVISION SATIRE that ran in syndication between 1977 and 1981. The show featured a range of comedy sketches set at the fictional SCTV television studios. Many of the sketches were political or satirical. The actors were from the Toronto-based Second City comedy group, a spin-off of the original Second City improvisational theater group that had formed in Chicago in 1959. The show appeared on network television between 1981 and 1983 under the title "SCTV Network." That version starred John Candy, Rick Moranis and Martin Short, among others.

"Secret Agent" A British-made TELEVISION SPY SHOW that ran on CBS from 1965 to 1966. An expanded version of DANGER MAN, the show featured the exploits of John Drake (Patrick McGoohan), who traveled throughout Europe as a spy working for the British government. His mission was to "preserve world peace and promote brotherhood and better understanding between peoples and nations," but in practice he also had to fight off enemy agents and woo beautiful women. Johnny Rivers sang Phil Sloan and Steve Barri's title song, "Secret Agent Man," which became a popular hit.

Secret Ways, The A 1961 SPY FILM starring Richard Widmark and Sonja Ziemann and directed by Phil Karlson. The story centers on the attempt of a U.S. agent to smuggle an anti-communist leader out of Hungary.

Seduction of the Innocent A 1954 NONFICTION book by Frederic Wertham that charged that comic books were corrupting American youth and undermining their values. The public response to *Seduction of the Innocent* led to congressional hearings and ultimately to a Comics Code defining a standard of morality and decency. Consequently, comic books were largely noncontroversial until the late 1960s, when underground comics disregarded the code. (See also CARTOONS.)

"See It Now" A TELEVISION NEWS show that ran on CBS from 1951 to 1958. Hosted by Edward R. MURROW and produced by Fred Friendly, "See It Now" evolved from that team's radio news program, "Hear It Now," and from their record albums, *I Can Hear It Now*. The show broadcast some of the most controversial and politically daring documentaries of the Cold War. The first broadcast began with Murrow's observation, "We are impressed by a medium through which a man sitting in his living room has been able for the first time to look at two oceans at once . . . no journalistic age was ever given a weapon for truth with quite the scope of this fledgling television." Among the Cold War–related topics and personalities Murrow covered were Presidents Truman and Eisenhower; J. Robert Oppenheimer, the "father of the atomic bomb," who lost his security clearance because of alleged communist affiliations in the 1930s; Secretary of State Dean Acheson, who implemented the containment policy that defined U.S. foreign policy for the first two decades of the Cold War; NATO's supreme commander, General Alfred M. Gruenther; China's Premier Chou En-Lai; and Yugoslavia's Marshal Tito. Murrow also provided shows on nuclear testing, nuclear weapons and radiation; relations among the Western powers; Berlin; the IRON CURTAIN countries; and the 1956 Suez Crisis. During the Korean War, he aired a famous in-person Christmas visit to GIs on the front lines in Korea. *The Case of Lt. Milo Radulovich* (1953) presented the story of an Air Force Reserve officer who was classified a security risk solely because his father and sister read newspapers and engaged in activities that the air force considered subversive or questionable. When CBS refused the publicize the controversial show, Murrow and Friendly paid $1500 of their own money to purchase an advertisement in the *New York Times*. As a result of the show, the air force reversed itself and reinstated Lt. Radulovich.

However, the most famous broadcast of "See It Now" was a 1954 exposé on the practices of Senator Joseph McCarthy. An edited collection of film clips showing the senator contradicting himself and making inaccurate statements, the show was the first time that network television directly addressed McCarthy's reckless demagoguery. The following week, the senator received free air time to respond; however, rather than address the contents of Murrow's show, McCarthy attacked the broadcaster personally, calling him a communist and "the leader and the cleverest of the jackal pack which is always at the throat of anyone who dares expose individual Communists or traitors." That year, "See It Now" contributor Don Hollenbeck committed suicide after being incessantly attacked by pro-McCarthy columnists for his alleged leftist orientation. Murrow's *Report on Senator McCarthy* has since come to be regarded as one of the high points in television journalism. At least one critic calls it "the most important show in the history of television." In 1955, however, "See It Now" lost its sponsor, Alcoa Aluminum, as well as its regular Tuesday night time slot. Between October 1955 and July 1958, it appeared sporadically as a series of 90-minute special reports. (See also TELEVISION DOCUMENTARIES)

For additional reading, see Whitfield's *The Culture of the Cold War*; Rosteck's *See It Now Confronts McCarthyism*; Einstein's *Special Edition: A Guide to Network Television Documentary Series and Special News Reports, 1955–1979*; McNeil's *Total Television*.

Seeger, Pete A FOLK SINGER. Seeger was born in New York City in 1919, the son of a violinist mother and musicologist father. He left Harvard University in 1938 to travel throughout the United States collecting folk songs. On that tour he met Huddie (Leadbelly) Ledbetter and Woody Guthrie, the renowned singer of union and left-wing ballads that celebrate, in Guthrie's words, "the people who do all of the little jobs and the mean and dirty hard work in the world." Seeger entered the military service during World War II and entertained the troops by singing folk songs. In 1948 he organized the folk group the Weavers, which included Ronnie Gilbert, Lee Hays and Fred Hellerman. Their version of "Goodnight Irene" was a number-one hit for 13 weeks in 1950. Seeger and the group were listed in RED CHANNELS, the 1950 publication that was widely used as the basis for unofficial BLACKLISTING within the television and

Pete Seeger. Courtesy AP/Wide World.

radio industries, and they were blacklisted during the 1950s RED SCARE because of their leftist politics. Journalist Walter WINCHELL also made them a target in his nationally syndicated newspaper column. In 1955 the HOUSE COMMITTEE ON UN-AMERICAN ACTIVITIES (HUAC) investigated Seeger, and he was convicted on 10 counts of contempt of Congress for his refusal to cooperate with the committee. However, the convictions were overturned in 1962. In the interim, Seeger remained the most visible singer of folk songs during the 1950s. He recorded several albums for the independent producer Folkways and toured widely, performing at college campuses, unions halls, churches and libraries. He became known for encouraging audience participation and for expressing his populist and leftist views. Seeger's songs were pro-union, anti-racist and pro-peace. They also promoted internationalism, as many were sung in other languages.

In late 1961 Seeger toured England, where he heard many folk songs about contemporary events. Some of these supported the movement to ban the nuclear bomb and others expressed different aspects of the peace movement. When Seeger returned home, he sought to spark a similar trend for topical songs in the United States. He therefore helped found and fund Sis Cunningham's *Broadside,* a biweekly magazine of songs about contemporary social issues. *Broadside* furnished a previously missing forum for this kind of left-wing music, and among those to publish in it were

Bob DYLAN, Phil OCHS, Tom Paxton, Les Chandler and Peter La Farge. Seeger's efforts were thus instrumental in creating the rising interest in folk music during the early 1960s. One outgrowth of that interest was "Hootenanny," a 1963 television show of folk music that aired from a different college campus each week. However, when Seeger would not sign a loyalty oath, ABC executives refused to permit him to appear on the program. In response, many major singers, including Dylan, Joan BAEZ, the Kingston Trio, and Peter, Paul and Mary refused to participate, and the show soon declined. In 1963, Seeger helped host the Newport Folk Festival, which brought together Dylan, Baez, Peter Paul and Mary, and Theodore Bikel.

Seeger was a strong critic of the Vietnam War. Among his more popular peace songs was "Where Have All the Flowers Gone." That song and Seeger and Hays' "If I Had a Hammer" were both recorded and made popular by Peter, Paul and Mary. In 1967 CBS censored Seeger's plans to perform an anti-Vietnam War song, "Waist Deep in the Big Muddy," when Seeger appeared on the SMOTHERS BROTHERS COMEDY HOUR. The appearance was Seeger's first on network television since his blacklisting in the 1950s. He was later permitted to sing the song on a subsequent show. During the Reagan years, Seeger toured with Arlo Guthrie, Woodie's son, and again sang out for peace in the face of the military buildup and reintensification of the Cold War. In 1982 Seeger reunited with the Weavers in a film commemorating their performances during the early part of the Cold War, THE WEAVERS: WASN'T THAT A TIME! He continued to sing his political and folk music—which now also deals with feminism, gay liberation and the environment—throughout the Cold War.

For additional reading, see Ward et al.'s *Rock of Ages: The Rolling Stone History of Rock & Roll;* King's *How Can I Keep from Singing?,* and Seeger's *Where Have All The Flowers Gone?* For a partial transcript of Seeger's testimony before HUAC, see Bentley's THIRTY YEARS OF TREASON.

Seeing Red A 1983 FILM DOCUMENTARY directed by Julia Reichert and James Klein and partially funded by the National Endowment for the Humanities. Made during the first Reagan administration, when Cold War tensions were at their highest since the Cuban Missile Crisis, the film received an Academy Award nomination for its documentation of the American Communist Party. It relies on over 400 interviews with current and former party members and contains archival footage of speeches by Ronald REAGAN, Richard Nixon, Hubert Humphrey and Joseph McCarthy. Also featured are Pete SEEGER, Dorothy Healey, Stretch Johnson and Bill Bailey.

Sellers, Peter A British FILM ACTOR. A highly gifted comic actor, Sellers appeared in several Cold War–related FILM SATIRES, including THE MOUSE THAT ROARED (1959), about a small country that declares war on the United States in hopes of losing quickly so as to enjoy U.S. foreign aid; DR. STRANGELOVE, (1964) about a nuclear attack against the Soviet Union launched by an insane U.S. Air Force general; *Casino Royale;* (1967) a James BOND spoof; *The Fiendish Plot of Dr. Fu Manchu* (1980); and BEING THERE (1979), about a mentally retarded man obsessed by gardening and television who becomes an influential political adviser to the president. Sellers played multiple roles in both *The Mouse that Roared* and *Dr. Strangelove.* He starred in *I Love You, Alice B. Toklas* (1968) about a middle-class man who gets caught up in the 1960s marijuana-smoking, Hippie COUNTER-CULTURE. He also starred in the film adaptation of Terry SOUTHERN's *The Magic Christian* (1969), which lampoons human greed and the perverse amusements of the very wealthy. Ringo Starr, the drummer for the ROCK AND ROLL group the Beatles, costarred. (See also FILM COMEDY.)

Sellout, The A 1975 British- and Italian-made SPY FILM starring Richard Widmark, Oliver Reed and Gayle Hunnicutt and directed by Peter Collinson. The story centers on an effort by U.S. and Soviet agents to lure a double agent to Jerusalem in order to assassinate him.

Senator Was Indiscreet, The A 1947 FILM COMEDY starring William Powell and Ella Raines and directed by George S. Kaufman. This was the only film directed by Kaufman, a comic playwright whose screen credits include Marx Brothers movies. The film spoofs a bumbling and unabashedly corrupt U.S. senator. Described in a 1993 film reference guide as "side-splitting farce comedy," *The Senator Was Indiscreet* outraged some members of Congress when it premiered. Critics claimed that the unflattering depiction of a U.S. senator would undermine the public's confidence in their country's government. They argued that since the Congress was leading the fight against communism, any attempt to ridicule them might strike a blow for communism. Senator Joseph McCarthy called the film "traitorous," and Representative Clare Boothe Luce demanded to know, "Was this picture made by an American?" *Life* magazine, published by Luce's husband, retracted an initial favorable review in a column entitled, "On Second Thought." Editorials in other publications, as well as statements of the American Legion, branded the movie as un-American. A representative of the Allied Theater Owners asserted that, "The picture will be recommended highly by [the official Soviet newspaper] *Pravda* and the party line . . . We should remember the adverse propaganda of the prewar and early war period that Germany and Italy used against us by presenting *Mr. Smith Goes to Washington, The Grapes of Wrath, Tobacco Road,* and gangster and crime films as true portrayals of American life."

The Motion Picture Association of America banned the film from being shown overseas. The film appeared in the same year as the first investigation of the Hollywood film industry by the HOUSE COMMITTEE ON UN-AMERICAN ACTIVITIES (HUAC), and the unexpected volatility of the film's reception may have stemmed from that coincidence. According to Nora Sayre, who witnessed part of the shooting and later interviewed producer Nunnally Johnson, the filmmakers were solely concerned with making comedy, not political statements. Certainly none of their other work had been overtly political in any way. (See also RED SCARE.)

For additional reading, see Sayre's *Running Time.*

Sevareid, Eric A television news journalist. A veteran newsman who held several positions within the CBS news organization, Sevareid delivered regular editorials on the

"CBS Evening News" during the 1960s and 1970s, when Walter CRONKITE was the anchor. At the beginning of the Korean War, along with a host of other liberal and conservative commentators, Sevareid was criticized by the left-wing Voice of Freedom Committee, which maintained that North Korea had been attacked by South Korea and that U.S. journalists like Sevareid had distorted that fact. Shortly thereafter, the Voice of Freedom Committee dissolved.

As chief of the CBS Washington news staff in 1950, Sevareid made a few paid broadcasts for the government-run Voice of America. As a result, several right-wing "fact sheets" attacked him as a "paid propagandist" for the "pro-Communist" Acheson State Department. Of these attacks Sevareid has said, "This sort of thing, the organized pressure and the vituperative letters and calls one sometimes gets, produce a feeling of depression or distress in a man. Any fairly sensitive person cannot help but react." In 1956, CBS silenced William Worthy's broadcasts from communist China upon the request of the State Department and canceled Sevareid's subsequent commentary, which would have criticized what he believed to be the Eisenhower administration's effort to preserve American ignorance about the realities underpinning world events. "Conversations with Eric Sevareid" (1975–77) included interviews with top political figures about Cold War issues. Notable guests were George F. Kennan, Willy Brandt and presidential adviser John McCloy. (See also TELEVISION NEWS; TELEVISION DOCUMENTARIES; RED SCARE.)

For additional reading, see Cogley's *The Report on Blacklisting,* vol. 2.

Seven Days in May A best-selling 1962 POLITICAL NOVEL by Fletcher KNEBEL and Charles Waldo Bailey II and a 1964 POLITICAL FILM starring Burt Lancaster, Kirk Douglas, Fredric March, and Ava Gardner and directed by John Frankenheimer. The Kennedy-era story describes an attempted military coup by right-wing U.S. generals who are outraged at the signing of a nuclear disarmament treaty with the Soviets. Along with DR. STRANGELOVE (1964) which appeared during the same year as the film version, *Seven Days in May* was one of the earliest Cold War stories to suggest that powerful officers in the U.S. military might be irresponsible, power-hungry or insane. The novel's appearance as a major Hollywood film would have been virtually unthinkable during the RED SCARE, which had abated with the election of John Kennedy in 1960. Like Frankenheimer's previous film, THE MANCHURIAN CANDIDATE (1962), *Seven Days in May* shows that the greatest danger to U.S. democracy comes not from internal communist subversion but from the super-patriotic, self-righteous political right wing that regards the Constitution as a hindrance to protecting national security. The film also singles out the nuclear bomb as the underlying cause of the nation's hysteria and even of the coup itself. Thus, like ON THE BEACH (1959), *Seven Days in May* takes an antinuclear position without arguing for unilateral disarmament.

The protagonists are President Lyman (March) and Marine Colonel Casey (Douglas). They are perfectly clear about their personal and professional priorities: Their duty to the Constitution is their greatest priority. The president has signed an unpopular mutual nuclear disarmament treaty, which the Joint Chiefs of Staff oppose. In their view, the treaty entrusts national security to a piece of paper, rather than to military might. Casey agrees with General Scott (Lancaster), his personal hero and the head of the Joint Chiefs. But as a highly responsible and professional military officer, Casey remains aloof from politics. When he figures out that a coup may be in progress, he is duty-bound to subordinate his personal feelings and report his conclusion to the president. Together, Casey, Lyman and trusted presidential friends and assistants subvert the coup. The drama reaches a high point when Scott confronts Casey shortly after he has been foiled. Scott asks Casey if he knows who Judas was. When Casey ignores the question, Scott orders him to reply. Casey declares, "Yes, I know who Judas was. He's a man I worked for and admired until he disgraced the four stars on his uniform."

Afterward, the president takes the moral high road for the good of the country, allowing Scott and the generals to resign gracefully instead of charging them with treason. Moreover, he declines to make use of Scott's incriminating love letters written to his former mistress, Eleanor (Gardner). (In his most distasteful assignment, Casey had earlier romanced the woman in order to secure the letters that could destroy Scott's career.) While other, more pragmatic aides urge the president to employ the letters against Scott, the president refuses to do so unless the fate of the Constitution depends upon it. Casey shares the president's sense of high morality. He genuinely likes and respects Eleanor, though he admonishes her for the excessive drinking that demeans her. It is clear that he would not have toyed with Eleanor's affections except to foil the coup. By contrast Scott, a married man, has treated her arrogantly, disdainfully and abusively. Thus in this film, men who respect women and act with honor and dignity toward them become identified with honorable politics, while Scott's adultery is linked to his willingness to ally with neo-fascists. Ironically, Lyman's decision to act honorably means that Scott might run against the beleaguered president in the next election and, if elected, reverse Lyman's progress toward nuclear disarmament. This, too, affirms democracy and the Constitution, for Lyman refuses to restrict the citizenry's choice in a fair election, even at the cost of his own political well-being.

Seven Days in May presents a debate over the viability in the nuclear era of a slow-moving constitutional process in which civilian nonexperts hold final authority for setting policy and making decisions. General Scott, for instance, objects that there is not time to wait for new elections and that public opinion polls more accurately reflect the national will. He also sincerely believes that the nation's survival requires that nuclear policy be set by military experts. By contrast, Lyman defends his own constitutional authority to lead the country despite his current lack of public approval.

In August 1963, President Kennedy and Soviet premier Khrushchev signed a controversial nuclear test ban treaty that eliminated aboveground testing, providing a significant backdrop for the story. Kennedy gave his support to the film project, which was completed shortly after his assassination in 1963. He had even indicated his willingness to let Frankenheimer shoot scenes in the White House. On the other hand, the film was made without the cooperation of the Defense Department.

The story's depiction of ranking military officers who were hostile to peace had some credibility. The Cuban Missile Crisis occurred the year of the book's publication. In THIRTEEN DAYS, his 1969 memoir of that crisis, Robert Kennedy describes how one member of the Joint Chiefs of Staff had argued in favor of "a preventive attack against the Soviet Union." And when it became clear that the United States had won the showdown and the Soviets would withdraw their missiles from Cuba, "it was suggested by one high military adviser that we attack [Cuba] in any case."

For additional reading, see Whitfield's *The Culture of the Cold War.*

Seven Days in Nicaragua Libre

Seven Days in Nicaragua Libre A 1984 NONFICTION travelogue by POET Lawrence FERLINGHETTI. The book, which contains photographs by Chris Felver, describes Ferlinghetti's weeklong visit to Nicaragua in January 1984 at the invitation of the socialist Sandinista government. During much of the trip, Minister of Culture Father Ernesto Cardenal, a poet and revolutionary, accompanied Ferlinghetti. However, the author privately visited Pablo Antonio Cuadra, also a poet and editor of the opposition newspaper *La Prensa.* Ferlinghetti's apparent purpose in publishing his travelogue was to give Americans an alternate view of the Sandinistas, at a time when the Reagan administration was depicting them as oppressive and brutal.

The book was written while U.S.-backed "contras" were fighting a civil war to depose the Sandinistas and Nicaraguans were fearing an apparently imminent U.S. invasion. *Seven Days* pictures the Sandinista regime sympathetically, but Ferlinghetti does offer some criticism. He goes out of his way to differentiate the Nicaraguan revolution from the Cuban revolution of 1959 but also reports seeing Sandinista soldiers using Soviet weapons and shows children standing beneath a poster bearing a large picture of Che Guevara and excerpts from his poetry. In the anti-Soviet and anti-Cuban climate of 1984 American, these associations would have seemed damning. Ferlinghetti is obviously impressed by poets' positions of authority and by the respect they command within the government. Yet he acknowledges, "The Revolution wanted to bring poetry to the masses; but the masses did not come to poetry." He includes Cuadra's complaints about press censorship and the government's attempts to politicize the arts: "Why if we are in agreement that creative freedom is a requirement of the revolution, does one wish to put literature at its service or impose the arts as weapons of the revolution? As soon as literature begins to be in the service of something it stops being literature and turns into propaganda." But Ferlinghetti follows Cuadra's complaint with an observation by Cardenal defending the Sandinistas' press censorship: "Try and get an article advocating the overthrow of the United States government into any major newspaper in the U.S.—or even try getting a Marxist article in the *New York Times.*" Ferlinghetti reports how Minister of the Interior Tomas Borge walks among the masses in the marketplace, apparently much beloved, but then includes Borge's own admission that the shop owners "really aren't *with* the Revolution. They're putting themselves first. The Revolution is for the consumer, not the merchant."

Still, Ferlinghetti's overall impression of the revolutionary government is highly favorable. The Sandinistas appear compassionate and committed to bringing a better way of life to Nicaragua. The photos show happy peasants and government officials with shining smiles. Even Somoza's imprisoned chauffeur poses with a grin, arm in arm with Cardenal. Ferlinghetti reports that all of the children of Somoza's minister of health are now Sandinistas and recounts how Borge, who had been imprisoned and tortured under Somoza, confronted one of his torturers after the revolution. Borge reportedly declared, "My revenge is to have you shake my hand." (Joan BAEZ was inspired to write a song about the event.) Ferlinghetti meets the top Sandinista leader, Daniel Ortega, who reveals "nothing dictatorial or militarist about him, despite his immaculate uniform" and has a firmer handshake than Castro did after the Cuban revolution. According to Ortega, "We do not want that democracy where barely 30 percent of the population participates in electing its own president; Here we do not want the democracy of the Ku Klux Klan . . . For us democracy is to truly love one another; which is to say, to bury self-centeredness, greed, and the thirst for gold."

Ferlinghetti also depicts the Sandinista regime as committed to respecting women. He notes that over 30% of the soldiers in the revolution against Somoza were women and that the Sandinistas promoted equality. The assistant minister of culture was a woman, and the government enacted legislation forbidding sexist advertising.

Moreover, the Sandinistas are shown as egalitarian. North American officials wear business suits to distinguish themselves from working-class citizens, but Sandinista ministers wear revolutionary military fatigues or, like Father Cardenal, blue jeans. The minister of agriculture appreciates nature and surrounds himself with plants and artifacts from local Indian cultures. Perhaps even more important to the poet Ferlinghetti, the Sandinistas place the arts at the center of their revolution. Ferlinghetti approvingly quotes an official:

Often it is said that the Nicaraguan Revolution is a revolution of poets, and this can be witnessed in the daily lives of the people. We say this is a country of artists . . . For this reason, the Sandinista government insists on the development of cultural activities as a part of the development of the revolutionary process . . . On the day of the victory, the Ministry of Culture was created; the same day a campaign was created which would become the Literacy Campaign, eradicating 80% of the illiteracy in this country . . . We have poetry workshops in the armed forces, state security police, air force and, of course, factories, barrios, and the countryside.

Though not without its flaws, the Sandinista government Ferlinghetti portrays contrasts sharply with Reagan's scathing representation of a repressive regime. Ferlinghetti concludes sympathetically, "The movement toward liberation by the *companeros* and *companeras* of the world, by the wretched of the earth, has been growing since before the French Revolution; and Nicaragua is a part of it. It is an irreversible revolution. *The past will not return.*" However, in 1989, the Nicaraguan people voted the Sandinistas out of office, to be replaced by a U.S.-approved regime.

Seven Samurai, The A 1954 Japanese-made FILM DRAMA starring Takashi Shimura, Toshiro Mifune, and Yoshio Inaba and directed by Akira Kurosawa. Set in the 1600s, the film centers on a group of samurai who agree to defend an unprotected town from marauding bandits in exchange for food. A powerful tale even when taken at face value, *The Seven Samurai* can also be viewed allegorically: The sword-wielding samurai are vulnerable only to a new, superior weapon, the gun, which, serves as a metaphor for nuclear weaponry. The film also reveals the different motivations of the defenders (the samurai) and the defended (the townspeople). It thus raised questions about the relationship between standing Cold War armies and the citizens they served. *The Seven Samurai* appeared during the same year that fallout from a massive U.S. nuclear test on BIKINI atoll fell on a Japanese fishing boat, giving the crew radiation sickness, contaminating their catch and causing widespread panic in Japan. The destruction brought to the village by its Samurai defenders may have recalled that incident for viewers. (See also APOCALYPTIC FILMS; FOREIGN FILMS.)

1776 A 1969 Broadway musical based on the 1964 novel by Peter Stone and a 1972 film musical starring Ken Howard, William Daniels and Blythe Danner and directed by Peter H. Hunt. Sherman Edwards wrote the music and lyrics. This celebration of American independence appeared during the height of the Vietnam War, when the country was especially divided in its thinking about that war and the Cold War in general. The story shows how the Declaration of Independence was forged despite strong differences among the factions represented at the Continental Congress, and it implicitly suggests that national unity can be reforged despite contemporary differences. (See also THEATER; VIETNAM WAR FILMS.)

Seventh Seal, The A 1956 Swedish-made FILM DRAMA starring Max von Sydow, Gunnar Bjornstrand and Bibi Andersson and directed by Ingmar Bergman. Set during the black plague in the Middle Ages, the story centers on the knight Antonius Block (von Sydow) and his squire Jons (Bjornstrand). They have just returned home from the Crusades, which have left them exhausted, jaded and cynical. Death appears before Block, who forestalls the shrouded reaper by challenging him to a game of chess. So long as Block holds off checkmate, he can remain alive. Death agrees, and in this way Block buys time to try to learn the meaning of life, which has eluded him despite all of the carnage he has witnessed. Block also wants to do one meaningful thing before he dies. In contrast to Block is Jons, who speaks disdainfully of trying to understand life's meaning but insists instead on experiencing it completely. Bergman claimed that he used the plague as a metaphor for the nuclear bomb, since during both points in history, death seemed to hover constantly, capable of wiping out entire communities overnight. In such a situation, the film asks, how can individuals give meaning and value to their lives? *The Seventh Seal* contrasts the men's conflicting approaches to living in an apparently absurd universe. When Block meets a young couple in love, he seems to decide that love must be the meaning of life and commits his final meaningful act through a "knight sacrifice" in which he deliberately loses the chess match—and thus his life—in order to distract Death so the young couple can escape. The film exemplifies the angst that frequently appears in 1950s literature. *The Seventh Seal* is also typical of Cold War culture in its concern with religious crises and its reliance on existentialism. (See also APOCALYPTIC FILMS; FOREIGN FILMS.)

Shade of a Difference, A   A 1962 POLITICAL NOVEL by Allen DRURY. The second in a series of political novels centering on the struggle between U.S. liberals and conservatives, *A Shade of a Difference* appeared during the same year as the Cuban Missile Crisis, one of the most tense periods of the Cold War. The civil rights movement was also in full swing during the early 1960s. The book spent 26 weeks on the best-seller list.

Picking up where ADVISE AND CONSENT (1959) left off, the novel begins with former vice president Harley Hudson as president after his predecessor has died of a heart attack. Conservative senator Orrin Knox, from whose point of view much of the story is told, is now secretary of state. The Soviets have launched a space satellite and demanded a summit meeting where they expect to negotiate from a position of strength. Even after the United States has also succeeded in space by landing a man on the moon, the liberal press—which Drury vilifies throughout the entire series—suggests that the United States capitulate to the Soviets. However, Hudson proves stronger than anticipated and refuses to give in to the Soviets' nuclear blackmail. Written as U.S. intervention in Southeast Asia was just beginning to become significant, *A Shade of Difference* also presents communist insurgency in the fictitious Grotoland, a thinly veiled allusion to Vietnam.

The story also deals with political struggles at the UN and with racial prejudice, addressing communist efforts of the 1950s and 1960s to exploit domestic discrimination against African Americans to win over African and Asian allies. The book features Cullee Hamilton, a black congressman from California who will become vice president in the final novel in the series, THE PROMISE OF JOY (1975). Through Hamilton, Drury suggests that, although discrimination exists, black Americans can still succeed through hard work, ambition and self-respect. He also suggests that many white Americans deplore racism and are committed to opposing it; that despite ongoing prejudice, the fortunes of black Americans are considerably better than ever before; and that more good can be accomplished by working within the system than outside it.

For additional reading, see Kemme's *Political Fiction, The Spirit of the Age, and Allen Drury.*

"Shadow of the Cloak"   A TELEVISION SPY SHOW that ran on the DuMont network from 1951 to 1952. "Shadow of the Cloak" was an early espionage series starring Helmut Dantine as Peter House, the chief agent of International Security Intelligence. House had to deal with a variety of spies, traitors and international villains. The inclusion of spies and traitors among the list of antagonists appealed to RED SCARE anxieties. Julius and Ethel Rosenberg had been convicted of passing on atomic secrets to the Soviets shortly before the show's debut, and Senator Joseph McCarthy and the House Committee on Un-American Activities (HUAC)

were at the height of their power during the show's run. Rod Serling, who went on to write for and host THE TWILIGHT ZONE (CBS, 1959–65), was one of the show's writers.

Shadow on the Hearth   A 1950 APOCALYPTIC NOVEL by Judith Merril. Published the year the Korean War broke out, *Shadow on the Hearth* treats postnuclear survival from a female perspective that is rare in early works about NUCLEAR APOCALYPSE. The protagonist is Gladys, a suburban housewife whose life is entirely absorbed by the day-to-day demands of suburban living. She is woefully uninformed about radiation and survival techniques. Her home is far enough away from ground zero not to be harmed when a nuclear attack destroys New York, and her initial response is largely one of denial. However, her teenaged daughter, Virginia, learns the necessary technical information for survival as she awaits the return of her father who, we learn, is safe in another part of town. In the interim, Virginia and her mother acquire survival skills.

One of the book's themes is that women, too, must become knowledgeable about nuclear war in the Cold War era. The women befriend a handsome teacher, a former nuclear physicist who resigned out of conscience and is now being hunted by the police as part of a post-attack RED SCARE. Since he not only proves loyal but also saves the women at some risk to himself, the teacher's role in the book cautions against the abusive extremes of the contemporary Red Scare that was still in its early stages in 1950. On the other hand, we also learn that the threat of internal subversion is genuine, since fifth-column collaborators helped guide the Soviet attack. The book's picture of America after an atomic war differs greatly from the visions of postnuclear society that appeared after the introduction of the hydrogen bomb in 1952: Society, though shaken, still coheres after the atomic bombing, at least in the suburbs. Looting is a problem, but police and government officials perform their duties; the threat of radiation is limited and not too threatening; and prospects appear good that Gladys will eventually reunite with her husband, who is healthy and intact. After the development of the hydrogen bomb, apocalyptic fiction would portray nuclear war as far more devastating and destructive.

For additional reading, see Dowling's *Fictions of Nuclear Disaster* and Anisfield's *The Nightmare Considered.*

Shadows of the Nuclear Age: American Culture and the Bomb   A 1982 radio documentary produced by Steven Shick, sponsored by the antinuclear organization SANE and funded in part by the National Endowment for the Humanities. Made when the Cold War was intensifying, as ranking members of the first Reagan administration were publicly discussing the possibility of winnable nuclear war, the 13-part documentary discusses various aspects of nuclear weaponry. These include the history of the atomic bomb and the decision to use it against Japan; the Cold War phenomenon of nuclear anxiety; the treatment of nuclear warfare in literature and Hollywood films; the language used to describe nuclear warfare; and the impact of the nuclear arms race on the U.S. economy.

Shallow Graves   A best-selling collection of poetry published by poets TRAN THI NGA and Wendy Wilder Larsen in

1986. The poems were written between 1980 and 1985. They were modeled upon the Vietnamese literary form, *truyen*, a verse novel, to describe the lives of women and non-combat personnel in Vietnam. Many poems are based on Tran's personal experiences, such as when she had to destroy her family photographs before leaving the country. Other verses provided ironic commentary on Vietnam's politics. For instance, "Victory" states "After President Thieu won the election/by 99.4% of the vote/we crowned him "Ivory Snow"/99 ⁴⁴/₁₀₀% pure." "Vietnamization" sums up Nixon's policy of turning the war over to the South Vietnamese: "The name of the operation/was changed/from Dewey Canyon II/to Lam Son 719."

For additional reading, see Uba's "Friend and Foe: De-Collaborating Wendy Wilder Larsen and Tran Thi Nga's *Shallow Graves.*"

Sheen, Fulton J. A religious figure, an author of NONFICTION and a television personality. Bishop Sheen's anti-communist credentials dated back to the 1930s, when he equated communism with Nazism during his appearances on the radio show "The Catholic Hour." He supported Franco against the communist loyalists during the Spanish Civil War, arguing that "we cannot breed rats in abundance without being obliged to use rat poison, and so neither can we breed Communists without being obliged to use the poison of fascism." Sheen wrote a vast number of sermons, articles and speeches, as well as 50 books. His *Peace of Soul* rose to ninth on the best-seller list in 1947. A prominent theme that unified Sheen's work was his argument that communism was the antithesis of Roman Catholicism. His *Communism and the Conscience of the West* (1948) maintains that communism is a kind of secular religion that evokes great dedication from its adherents, making it especially difficult to combat, "They have passion but no ideals; we have ideals but no passion."

After presenting "The Catholic Hour" on NBC radio for 22 years, Sheen moved to television in 1952. His highly rated show LIFE IS WORTH LIVING (1952–57) began on the DuMont Network but moved to ABC in 1956, after DuMont folded. By 1954 he had an audience of some 25 million Americans each week. At the show's peak, 170 American stations and 17 Canadian stations broadcast the program. His spinoff book, *Life Is Worth Living* (1953), attained fifth place on the best-seller list. In one of his more dramatic shows, Sheen declared that "Stalin must one day meet his judgment." Three days later, the Soviet leader suffered a sudden stroke; he died the following week. Sheen declined to comment on the coincidence. After a falling out with his superior, Cardinal Francis Spellman, Sheen left the air in 1957 but returned in 1961 on "The Bishop Sheen Program," which ran through 1968. (See also RELIGIOUS TELEVISION PROGRAMMING.)

For additional reading, see Whitfield's *The Culture of the Cold War.*

"Silent Service, The" A syndicated anthology of TELEVISION MILITARY DRAMAS that ran from 1956 to 1958; it was first released in 1957. Hosted by Rear Admiral Thomas M. Dykers (retired), the series presented documentary-style dramas about the U.S. Navy's submarine fleet. The episodes were based on fact and included actual combat footage from navy files. Though most of the episodes were set during World War II, some featured action from the Korean War and the Cold War. The show was made with the full cooperation of the navy, which loaned Admiral Dykers the U.S.S. *Sawfish* for the filming.

Silk Stockings A 1955 musical play written by George S. Kaufman, Leueen McGrath and Abe Burrows and a 1957 musical FILM COMEDY starring Fred Astaire, Cyd Charisse, Janis Paige and Peter Lorre and directed by Rouben Mamoulian. Cole Porter wrote the music and lyrics. Like *Ninotchka*, the 1939 Greta Garbo film on which it is based, *Silk Stockings* celebrates the virtues of capitalism over the deprivations of life behind the IRON CURTAIN. Charisse stars as Ninotchka, a no-nonsense Soviet official who comes to Paris to facilitate the return to the U.S.S.R. of a prominent Russian composer who has agreed to write for a Hollywood film. However, like the three other officials who preceded her in this task, she becomes enchanted by the glamour and luxury of Paris. Moreover, despite her initial contention in song that love is simply a chemical reaction, she falls in love with the film's producer (Astaire). Porter's witty lyrics further underscore the lack of freedom in the Soviet Union and the good life in the West. And a dance sequence set in Moscow shows the average Russian to be willing and anxious to dance to American ROCK AND ROLL when the local authorities are not watching. (See also THEATHER.)

Singer, Isaac Bashevis A Yiddish NOVELIST, an EXILED WRITER (to the United States) and winner of the 1978 Nobel Prize for literature. Born in Poland in 1904, the son and grandson of rabbis, Singer grew up in the Jewish ghetto in Warsaw. From his early childhood he was exposed to his father's "mystical intensity" and his mother's "rational strain," and much of his literature involves trying to integrate these opposites. Despite their father's efforts to confine their education to the Torah and the Talmud, the Singer children were eventually exposed to the secular world. Singer's older brother, Israel Joshua, left religious Judaism to follow the principles of the Enlightenment and became an ardent socialist. He also introduced Isaac to his first "heretical" literature, Dostoyevsky's *Crime and Punishment.* In 1921 Singer enrolled in a rabbinical seminary, but concluded that he could not comply with the demands of organized religion and left without graduating. Seeking greater artistic freedom as well as escape from the ominous European political situation, Singer immigrated to New York in 1935 at the behest of his brother, who was already a prominent Yiddish writer there. Isaac Singer began his personal exodus from Poland during Passover, at the age of 31, bringing with him only two valises of clothing and manuscripts.

In the United States he began writing for a Yiddish newspaper, and he continued to write in Yiddish throughout his career though virtually all of his work has been translated into English. Singer met with critical and popular success in America during the Cold War, first with *The Family Moskat* (1950), which appeared in both Yiddish and English, and then more spectacularly in 1953 with the publication in *Partisan Review* of the short story, "Gimpel the

Fool," translated by future Nobel Prize–winner Saul Bellow. Singer's fiction is typically set in the Jewish urban ghetto or rural shtetl and deals with matters of Jewish identity. Nonetheless, his worldwide popularity suggests that the moral, ethical and spiritual issues he raises were also relevant to Cold War readers, Jewish and gentile alike; like Singer's characters, they too had to find their way in an uncertain, deceitful and frequently hostile world.

For additional reading, see Tucker's *Literary Exile in the Twentieth Century.*

Six Days in Havana   A 1989 NONFICTION book by James MICHENER. In 1989 Michener also published *Caribbean*, a novel that traces life in the Caribbean Ocean from the year 1310 forward to the present. While researching that book, which includes a brief treatment of Castro's Cuba, Michener was denied entry into Cuba by both the U.S. State Department and the Castro government. Then, in the summer of 1988, both countries permitted him to travel to the island with photographer John Kings. *Six Days in Havana* was the resulting documentary. The photos reveal the state of physical decline that Havana has suffered since the U.S. boycott in the 1960s. The automobiles are mostly rusty old American models from before the revolution, and the buildings have deteriorated. The text generally declines to pass judgment on the revolution, but it does describe well-fed and well-educated children and provides a sympathetic view of the Cuban people. It also points out that some Americans remain heroes in Cuba, notably the writer Ernest Hemingway and the Cuban-born baseball star Jose Canseco, who grew up in Miami's Cuban exile community.

Six Days of the Condor   A 1974 SPY NOVEL by James Grady that was the basis for the film THREE DAYS OF THE CONDOR (1975). Written as the Watergate scandal and other revelations of illegal activities by U.S. intelligence agencies were coming to light, the story was a pioneer in a trend among spy novels in which the enemy proves to be the protagonist's own government. This trend reflected a growing cynicism about the morality of the Cold War and the way it was being conducted.

For additional reading, see Cawelti and Rosenberg's *The Spy Story.*

"Six Million Dollar Man, The"   A TELEVISION SPY SHOW that ran on ABC from 1974 to 1978. The show centered on the adventures of Colonel Steve Austin (Lee Majors), a handsome astronaut who had been critically injured while on a test flight in the desert. To save his life, government doctors employed a new operation developed by Dr. Rudy Wells (first Alan Oppenheimer, then Martin E. Brooks), replacing human parts with atomic-powered devices that were better than the human originals. Thus Colonel Austin became a cyborg, part human and part machine. His mechanical legs and right arm endowed him with extraordinary strength and speed, while his "bionic" left eye gave him penetrating vision. Austin then served as an agent for the Office of Scientific Information, for whom he took on mad scientists and international villains, as well as a seven-million-dollar bionic man who had run amok. In addition to showing a U.S. government agent fighting villains intent on undermining American security, the show's Cold War relevance stems from its treatment of science as a means for combating international evil.

Small Armageddon, A   A 1962 MILITARY NOVEL by Mordecai Roshwald. Published the same year as the Cuban Missile Crisis, the most threatening moment in the Cold War, *A Small Armageddon* centers on a submarine captain who holds all humanity hostage by aiming his nuclear missiles at major cities throughout the world. His demands include visits from striptease dancers whose vibrant body parts are compared to nuclear reactors. Roshwald's inclusion of this bizarre sexual element anticipates Stanley KUBRICK's better-known 1964 film satire, DR. STRANGELOVE. (See also APOCALYPTIC NOVELS.)

For additional reading, see Dowling's *Fictions of Nuclear Disaster.*

Small Town in Germany, A   A 1968 SPY NOVEL by John LE CARRÉ. Considered le Carré's bleakest Cold War novel, *A Small Town in Germany* involves the investigation by agent Alan Turner of the disappearance of Leo Harting, a German national who had worked in Britain's West German embassy. The British are anxious to forestall any security breaches that might undermine their efforts to gain admission into the Common Market. Turner's initial admiration for his country's diplomats turns to cynical opposition as they ally with former Nazis in order to achieve their political objectives. The novel invokes German and European political concerns in the aftermath of the second Berlin Crisis (1958–61), as the fictional German chancellor, Dr. Klaus Karfeld, pursues the unification of East and West Germany while using his power to inhibit Britain's quest for entry into the Common Market, purely as a weapon against the British Foreign Office. Unlike Willy Brandt, the real-life socialist foreign minister and chancellor who similarly advocated German reunification in the mid- and late 1960s, the novel's Karfeld is a former Nazi who wrote his doctoral dissertation on the effects of poisonous gas on the concentration camp inmates whom he himself murdered. Turner discovers that only the German Harting has opposed British cooperation with Karfeld; the British diplomats are more concerned with their immediate goals than with the moral implications of dealing with an unrepentant Nazi who still advocates fascism.

For additional reading, see Beene's *John le Carré* and Cawelti and Rosenberg's *The Spy Story.*

"Smothers Brothers Comedy Hour, The"   A TELEVISION SATIRE and variety show that ran on CBS from 1967 to 1969. The show featured the comedy act of Tom and Dick Smothers. Tom was the "stupid" and emotional one who, like Gracie Allen before him, said illogical things that made sense in their own peculiar way; Dick was the calm, rational straight man. The highly popular show quickly became controversial because of its political content. The Smothers Brothers made fun of America's hallowed institutions: motherhood, church, politics and the government. Moreover, it took an increasingly strong stand against the Vietnam War. Pete SEEGER, a folk singer who had long been blacklisted on television, frequently appeared. In fact, on the fall premiere of 1967, in his first network television performance since his BLACKLISTING in the early 1950s, Seeger was forbidden to sing his anti-Vietnam War song, "Waist Deep in the Big Muddy." However, CBS allowed him to perform it on a subsequent show. Other antiwar guests whom CBS censored included Joan BAEZ, draft resistance leader Dr. Benjamin Spock and singer Harry Belafonte. Pat Paulsen's absurdist presidential campaign also disturbed CBS officials who feared they would have to furnish equal time to other (genuine) candidates. Paulsen's campaign slogan echoed President Johnson's speech announcing he would not seek another term in office. Paulsen's motto was, "If nominated I will not run, and if elected I will not serve."

Despite the show's popularity, CBS canceled it in 1969, largely because of the brothers' preference for outspoken, antiwar guests and because of their penchant for keeping their material away from the censors. The program received considerable amounts of hate mail, which especially attacked the frequent appearance of African-American performers. The show was replaced by "Hee-Haw," a country music variety show with cornball humor. "The Smothers Brothers Summer Show" appeared on ABC a year later but did not survive into the fall. In 1975 NBC aired a new version of the variety series, "The Smothers Brothers Show," but this lacked the satiric punch of the original "Comedy Hour" and failed to garner impressive ratings. In 1988 and 1989, CBS brought back the original "Smothers Brothers Comedy Hour," but it too failed.

For additional reading, see McNeil's *Total Television.*

Sokolov, Sacha   A Soviet EXILED WRITER (to the United States). Born in the U.S.S.R. in 1950, Sokolov published the satiric *School for Fools* in 1976. The détente-era novel was well received in the West, where the innovative, imagistic style and humorous treatments of the Soviet bureaucracy were appreciated. However, the reception was not so warm in the Soviet Union, and Sokolov immigrated to America in 1978 after much harassment. He has also published the satiric *Between the Dog and the Wolf* (1980) and *Astrolabia* (1989), the fictional memoirs of a hermaphrodite Soviet bureaucrat.

For additional reading, see Tucker's *Literary Exile in the Twentieth Century.*

Sokolsky, George   A prominent anti-communist and a nationally syndicated JOURNALIST published in the Hearst newspaper chain. An author, lecturer and industrial consultant, Sokolsky wrote several columns about political activities in Hollywood. He helped arrange the "clearance" procedure for evaluating the 300 people named on the American Legion's 1951 list of suspected communists or communist sympathizers, and he became the chief arbitrator for that list, deciding which individuals were acceptable (i.e., were cleared to work) and which still needed to prove their loyalty or be rehabilitated through acts of public contrition. In addition to those on the American Legion list, Sokolsky helped clear other individuals who had been blacklisted, if he felt that they had sincerely repented of their earlier activities. Sokolsky thoroughly disapproved of the practice of other "clearance men" who accepted money for what he himself considered to be the moral task of

helping people rehabilitate themselves. He pointed out that he himself had never blacklisted anyone, but, by assuming the role of de facto judge and jury in blacklisting cases "in the absence of a national policy," he enabled many to return to work.

However, Sokolsky seems to have been quite willing to use his role to reward those whose politics agreed with his own and to dictate both what was politically acceptable and how to interpret political events. For instance, after Humphrey Bogart publicly confessed that his 1947 trip to Washington in support of the HOLLYWOOD TEN was "ill-advised," Sokolsky responded in an open letter in his column:

> Confession is good for any man's soul. And you display great courage and manhood to confess error. Yes that trip was foolish . . . You people out in Hollywood had an idea . . . that this country had an ally during the war . . . Of course that was never true. Soviet Russia was never an ally. Germany's war on Russia coincided, more or less, with our war on Germany . . . They blackmailed us at Teheran and Yalta . . . Only enemies . . . act that way. If you are genuinely contrite for a very foolish bit of exhibitionism, you ought to go further. You might tell us who suggested that trip to Washington. Whose brainchild was it? Who projected you and your wife [actress Lauren Bacall] to take the lead . . . You show first-rate manhood in taking the people who admire you into your confidence. Now do something for your country that is really constructive. Tell us who suggested and organized that trip.

(See also BLACKLISTING; RED SCARE.)

For additional reading, see Cogley's *Report on Blacklisting* (vol. 1, *Naming Names*).

Solaris   A 1961 SCIENCE FICTION NOVEL by Stanislaw Lem and a 1972 Soviet-made SCIENCE FICTION FILM starring Nathalie Bondarchuk, Yuri Yarvet and Donatas Banionis, and written and directed by Andrei Tarkovsky. The novel was translated into English in 1970. The widespread distribution in the United States of a novel by a Polish writer and of a Soviet-made film were among the rare instances during the Cold War when nondissident literature produced behind the IRON CURTAIN found substantial U.S. audiences. The book's translation into English and the production of the movie took place at the beginning of the East-West détente inaugurated by President Nixon and Secretary of State Henry Kissinger and pursued in Europe by West Germany's Chancellor Willy Brandt, who signed 1970 nonaggression pacts with the Soviet Union and Poland. The short-lived 1968 Prague Spring in Czechoslovakia had provided an earlier opportunity for the West to see artistic achievements from Eastern Europe. (See CLOSELY WATCHED TRAINS.) Tarkovsky, who is considered to be one of the finest directors in Soviet cinematic history, eventually left the U.S.S.R. in order to gain greater artistic freedom.

The story centers on a Soviet cosmonaut who travels to a space station on the distant planet, Solaris. His mission is to investigate the strange dreams experienced by other travelers on the planet. Eventually he discovers that the planet itself is a conscious entity that communicates to cosmonauts through the dreams it induces. The story's subject matter thus alludes to the exploration of parapsychology that took place in the U.S.S.R. during the Cold War, as well as to the suggestion that planets are "biospheres"—integrated living entities. This notion, as applied to the Earth, eventually became integrated into the late Cold War and post–Cold War environmental movement. (See also FOREIGN FILMS.)

Solzhenitsyn, Aleksandr A Soviet novelist, EXILED WRITER (to the United States) and winner of the 1970 Nobel Prize for literature. Born in the Caucasus region of the U.S.S.R. in 1918, Solzhenitsyn was christened during the Civil War that followed the 1917 revolution. His father, the son of a peasant, had attended Moscow University and served as an officer in the czar's army during World War I. He was killed in a hunting accident six months before Solzhenitsyn's birth. *August 1914* (1971; in English, 1972, revised and expanded, 1989) depicts the harsh years of Solzhenitsyn's youth, when he and his mother lived in Rostov in a tiny, rotting shack without plumbing. She belonged to a circle of liberal intellectuals whom Solzhenitsyn characterized as "an engineering milieu . . . [filled with] unrestrained and inoffensive humor, freedom, and breadth of thought." According to Solzhenitsyn, they were well

Aleksandr Solzhenitsyn. Courtesy Library of Congress.

educated, possessed good taste and "had the stamp of spiritual nobility on their faces." Though he longed to study literature in Moscow, Solzhenitsyn elected instead to remain with his consumptive mother in Rostov, where he took up mathematics instead of writing. While at the university, Solzhenitsyn met a chemistry student, Natalia Reshetovskaya, whom he married in 1940. They divorced in 1973, and he remarried that same year. During his student days, Solzhenitsyn also became an enthusiastic Marxist-Leninist, though his support for Stalin was qualified.

Within days of his graduation in 1941, Germany broke its nonaggression pact and invaded the U.S.S.R. Solzhenitsyn was called to service a few months later. He served throughout the war, first as a stable boy in a Cossack battalion and later as an artillery officer. Throughout the war he continued his writing, which he had begun in school. He took notes on his observations and experiences, interviewed soldiers, and recorded his thoughts in poems, stories and letters to friends. Many of his wartime experiences also appeared in his later books, including *August 1914, Gulag Archipelago* (1974) and *The First Circle* (1968).

Solzhenitsyn's service in the Red Army ended on February 9, 1945, when he was arrested for anti-Stalinist remarks he had written to a friend on the Ukrainian Front. He remained in prison and in labor camps until April 1956, after Stalin had died and Nikita Khrushchev extended amnesty to political prisoners. Solzhenitsyn's experiences of solitary confinement, interrogation, torture and hard labor became the basis of much of his literature. While he was interned, Solzhenitsyn developed malignant cancers in his lymph nodes and abdomen. He considered his cure, facilitated by intense radiation treatments and his own determination to survive, to be a divine miracle, and the experience restored his childhood faith in Orthodox Christianity.

The short novel *One Day in the Life of Ivan Denisovich,* Solzhenitsyn's first published work, appeared in the November 1962 issue of Moscow's leading literary journal, *Novy Mir* (New World), during the period of Khrushchev's liberalization; the book was approved by the premier himself as well as by the Central Committee. Written in 1959, the novel describes in detail a single day, from morning to night, in the life of an average prisoner in a Stalinist labor camp, including detailed descriptions of menial tasks, body searches, marches to and from the work site, and bricklaying in freezing temperatures, as well as conversations with fellow inmates, transactions for a tobacco purchase, and other social interactions. The timing of the story's publication coincided with Khrushchev's denunciation of Stalin's "cult of personality." Part of Khrushchev's program called for writers to show "the labors and ordeals of our people in a manner that is totally truthful and faithful to life." The novel was a major success: All copies of the journal sold out overnight, the critics praised it and Solzhenitsyn was declared "an exemplary citizen and true helper of the Party." Caspar Wrede directed a 1971 film adaptation, and in 1974 Richard France produced a stage adaptation that ran in the United States. (See THEATER.)

Solzhenitsyn published two more stories in *Novy Mir* during the following January, and in July he published "For the Good of the Cause," a story describing corruption among local party bosses and a factory director. He was voted into the Writer's Union, an affiliation that allowed him to live on the income from his writing without being labeled a parasite.

However, in the aftermath of the Cuban Missile Crisis, Khrushchev lost face and was compelled to make concessions to his hard-line domestic opponents. Consequently, Solzhenitsyn's stories of official abuse became increasingly less well received. The Sovremennik Theater refused to perform his play *The Love-Girl and the Innocent,* and in 1964 the party interceded to keep Solzhenitsyn from winning the Lenin Prize for *A Day in the Life.* Although Aleksandr Tvardovsky, the editor of *Novy Mir,* offered Solzhenitsyn a contract that year for *The First Circle,* a novel about scientists forced to work in a Stalinist research center, the manuscript copies were sequestered in the magazine's office safe. The book was never published in the Soviet Union during the Cold War. Though Solzhenitsyn had begun the manuscript in prison and completed the first draft in 1957, it did not appear in print until its publication in the United States in 1968, first in Russian and shortly thereafter in translation.

Given his difficulties in being published within the U.S.S.R. especially after Khrushchev's fall from power in the coup of October 1964, Solzhenitsyn began smuggling his work abroad for publication. He began work on *Cancer Ward* (1968) during this period and published part one of the novel in Czechoslovakia. The novel addresses the conflict in values between two hospitalized patients, a high party official with neck cancer and a former political prisoner who, like Solzhenitsyn, suffers from abdominal cancer. The doctors and hospital staff represent a cross-section of Soviet society.

Solzhenitsyn began *The Gulag Archipelago* in the winter of 1965 and continued working on it through the summer. However, in September, KGB agents seized his manuscript, which he had hidden at a friend's apartment. Nonetheless, for several years he continued working on this highly autobiographical, novelistic account of the Soviet labor camp, the notes for which he had begun collecting while he was in prison. He often concealed the material in a bottle in his garden to avoid future KGB interference. The novel's first volume was published in France in 1973. In February 1974, the KGB found a copy of the book at his typist's residence. They subsequently took Solzhenitsyn to prison and then deported him to Germany. He moved briefly to Zurich, where he worked on a historical novel, *Lenin in Zurich* (1976), then traveled to Stockholm to receive the Nobel Prize that he had been awarded four years previously but that the Soviet government had not allowed him to claim. Afterward, he traveled throughout Europe before settling in the United States, where he and his family lived secluded within a chain-link fence on their property in Vermont. While living in exile, he continued to write fiction, including *October 1916* (1984; in English, 1991) and *March 1917* (unpublished to date), sequels to his earlier historical novel, *August 1914* (1972). These comprise three-fourths of *The Red Wheel,* a projected tetralogy about the events leading to the Russian Revolution. The published portions of this tetralogy have generated considerable controversy. Solzhenitsyn has been attacked for anti-Semitism and bias against non-Russians and for displaying a prejudiced view of Soviet history; he has also been defended as a creative artist of monumental

talent who is entitled to shape his characters and their actions as he sees fit.

Mikhail Gorbachev became Soviet premier in 1985 and began implementing his program of social reform shortly thereafter. Eventually, Solzhenitsyn was rehabilitated in the Soviet Union. In 1989, he was readmitted to the Union of Soviet Writers from which he had been expelled in 1969. Parts of his 1970 Nobel Prize acceptance speech appeared in *Novy Mir* that year, as did portions of *Gulag Archipelago.* *The First Circle* and *Cancer Ward* were subsequently published, and in 1990 his full Soviet citizenship was restored by direct order of Gorbachev himself. Solzhenitsyn moved back to Russia in 1994, after the dissolution of the Soviet Union.

Solzhenitsyn stands out as a major literary figure in American Cold War culture since his highly detailed and carefully documented accounts of Soviet oppression of political prisoners corroborated the popular U.S. view of the U.S.S.R. as an "evil empire." Soviet refusal to allow Solzhenitsyn to claim his Nobel Prize further reinforced that country's image as a repressive state. Since immigrating to the United States, Solzhenitsyn's harsh commentary upon Western society and the revelation of his anti-Semitism have diminished his popularity somewhat, but he remains an imposing figure in the cultural history of the Cold War.

For additional reading, see Tucker's *Literary Exile in the Twentieth Century.*

Southern, Terry A SCREENWRITER and NOVELIST. A major contributor to American BLACK HUMOR, Southern provided one of the best treatments of the Cold War nuclear threat in his screenplay for the 1964 film satire DR. STRANGELOVE, about a nuclear attack against the Soviet Union launched by an insane U.S. Air Force general. (The film's director, Stanley KUBRICK, and Peter George, the author of the book on which it is based, also contributed to the screenplay.) Southern also produced and wrote the screenplay for the film adaptation of John BARTH's *The End of the Road* (1970). Other significant film credits include *Easy Rider* (1969); *The Cincinnati Kid* (1965, cowritten with former HOLLYWOOD TEN member Ring LARDNER Jr.); *Barbarella* (1968), a pacifist SCIENCE FICTION FILM starring Jane FONDA; and *Burroughs,* about writer William Burroughs. Southern also wrote the novels and screenplays for *Candy* (book 1964, film 1968) and *The Magic Christian* (book 1960, film 1969). Candy is a soft porn spoof of Voltaire's *Candide.* Though not exactly an anticapitalist statement, *The Magic Christian* derives humor from human greed and mocks the perverse imagination of a very wealthy man. The film stars Peter SELLERS and Ringo Starr, the drummer for the ROCK AND ROLL group the Beatles. Southern also published short fiction in *The Realist* and in GROVE PRESS's *Evergreen* magazine.

Spartacus A 1951 POLITICAL NOVEL by Howard FAST and a 1960 EPIC FILM starring Kirk Douglas, Laurence Olivier, Tony Curtis, Jean Simmons, Charles Laughton and Peter Ustinov and directed by Stanley KUBRICK. Fast wrote the novel in 1950 while serving a prison term for refusing to cooperate with the HOUSE COMMITTEE ON UN-AMERICAN ACTIVITIES (HUAC). He published it himself after Little Brown reversed its decision to issue the book and six other publishing houses likewise turned it down. Fast belonged to the Communist Party until he repudiated it in 1956, and he received the Stalin Peace Prize in 1954, probably for writing *Spartacus*. Dalton TRUMBO, who had also served a prison term for refusing to comply with HUAC, adapted the novel for the film. Kirk Douglas, who produced as well as starred in the movie, thus deliberately challenged the practice of BLACKLISTING by presenting a film written by one of the HOLLYWOOD TEN and based on a novel by a prominent ex-communist. (Fast had disavowed his communism in 1956, before the film was made.) Douglas's announcement that Trumbo wrote the screenplay, along with Otto Preminger's crediting Trumbo for writing EXODUS, destroyed the practice of blacklisting former communists and communist sympathizers. President-elect John Kennedy and his brother Robert crossed American Legion picket lines to see the film.

Spartacus tells the story of a slave rebellion against the Roman republic led by the Thracian slave Spartacus. The relationship between the enslaved laborers and the rich Romans who enjoyed the fruits of their labor carried an implicit political message. In the end, the slaves are crucified for challenging the political power of Rome. This can be read in two ways: as Fast's commentary on HUAC and political repression in the United States, or as an allusion to the fate of Eastern Europeans "enslaved" behind the IRON CURTAIN. The historical Spartacus had long been admired by the communists, but most American viewers of the film were probably not familiar with that fact.

For additional reading, see Whitfield's *The Culture of the Cold War*.

"Spies" A TELEVISION SPY SHOW that ran on CBS for six weeks in 1987. George Hamilton spoofed spy shows in his role as Ian Stone, an over-the-hill, womanizing spy who was the idol of his young partner Ben Smythe (Gary Kroeger). Though Smythe had been paired with Stone to keep the older man in line, Stone took pleasure in corrupting his younger counterpart and in slipping away from him to pursue his romantic dalliances.

Spies Like Us A 1985 FILM COMEDY starring Chevy Chase, Dan Aykroyd and Steve Forrest and directed by John Landis. A SPY FILM SPOOF, *Spies Like Us* centers on two incompetent U.S. foreign service agents who unknowingly serve as decoys on a mission that takes them through Asia. The Asian setting reminded audiences of the Soviet war in Afghanistan, which was then current.

Spillane, Mickey A best-selling NOVELIST. Spillane wrote six of the top ten fictional best-sellers of the 1950s; all were detective novels: *My Gun Is Quick* (1950), *Vengeance Is Mine* (1950), *The Big Kill* (1951), *One Lonely Night* (1951), *The Long Wait* (1951) and KISS ME DEADLY (1952). Moreover, his first novel, *I, the Jury* (1947), was even more popular. By 1953, Spillane had sold over 17 million books. His protagonist Mike Hammer, a tough, virile, individualistic ex-Marine, detests criminals, policemen, bureaucrats, intellectuals, communists and fellow-travelers and savagely metes out justice against malefactors.

One Lonely Night most forcefully illustrates Spillane's anti-communism. In that novel, Hammer poses as a Soviet intelligence agent in order to infiltrate a communist cell after becoming involved with an heiress who has joined the party out of boredom. After he seduces her, he assumes "Now that she had a taste of life maybe she'd go out and seek some different company for a change," but when she continues her communist associations, he strips and whips her. Such violence against women, especially against those who are sexually free, is characteristic of Spillane's fiction. Even though Hammer willingly sleeps with several women, the book implies that sexual purity is linked to American values and that women's sexual emancipation undermines America. The chief villain in *One Lonely Night* is both a communist and a psychopath, and the book suggests that a person must be either insane or morally corrupt, or both, to be a party member. When the communist villains abduct and strip Hammer's fiancée, who has remained celibate in order to remain pure for Hammer, he kills everyone who has viewed her naked body and then burns the corpses in a symbolic act of purification. He then states, "I killed more people tonight than I have fingers on my hands. I shot them in cold blood and enjoyed every minute of it . . . They were Commies . . . They were red sons-of-bitches who should have died long ago. They never thought that there were people like us in this country. They figured us all to be soft as horse manure and just as stupid."

Spillane thus appealed to the virulent anti-communist sentiments that abounded during the RED SCARE, which was approaching its height when *One Lonely Night* was published. Hammer's frustration with the legal institutions that protected the rights of communists, his equation of tolerance with softness, and his willingness to administer his own rough justice mirrored the sentiments of Senator Joseph McCarthy, who had emerged as the nation's premier anti-communist in the early 1950s.

For additional reading see Whitfield's *The Culture of the Cold War*; Darby's *Necessary American Fictions*; and Rogin's *Ronald Reagan: The Movie*.

sports The Cold War influenced and was influenced by competitive sports. The OLYMPIC GAMES provided one nonviolent arena in which Cold War competitions could play themselves out. The games resumed after World War II in 1948, but the Soviets did not compete until 1952. That year, a long-lasting rivalry began in basketball, as the United States won the gold medal and the Soviets took the silver. The United States continued to dominate in this sport throughout the Cold War, except for 1972, when the Soviets won in the last second after a referee's controversial ruling gave them extra time to in-bound the ball, and 1988, when the Soviets won and the U.S. team came in third—its worst Cold War–era performance. By contrast, the Soviets dominated the ice hockey competition throughout the Cold War but lost to the United States in 1960 and 1980. The U.S. upset victory in 1980 received special significance because it followed the U.S. boycott of the Moscow Olympics as the Cold War was beginning to reintensify. President Carter had ordered the 1980 boycott in response to the Soviet invasion of Afghanistan. No U.S. and only a few Western athletes competed. The Soviets and other communist countries retaliated in 1984 by boycotting the Summer Olympics in Los Angeles.

In 1976, 14-year-old Rumanian Nadia COMANECI excelled in several individual categories and became a media darling who won instant fame and affection throughout the world. Comaneci won three gold, two silver and one bronze medal and achieved a perfect score in two events, something no one had ever done before. Comaneci defected to the United States in 1989, claiming she had been abused and essentially imprisoned under the regime of Rumania's communist president Nicolae Ceausescu. Other athletes to defect from communist countries were Soviet hockey player Alexander Mogilny, who defected in 1989 and joined the Buffalo Sabres, and Miroslava Nachodska, a 23-year-old Czech skater who defected in 1955.

Table tennis (Ping-Pong) also played a role in the Cold War. On April 10, 1971, the same year that the United States dropped objections to the People's Republic of China's entry into the United Nations, the U.S. table tennis team entered China for a series of matches. As a result, the U.S. press was allowed into China for the first time since the communist takeover in 1949, and the competition helped prepare for the U.S.–Chinese reconciliation that culminated a year later when President Nixon visited China in February 1972.

The Cold War also influenced American sports, especially baseball, which benefited from the immigration of such Cuban exiles as pitcher Luis Tiant, outfielder Tony Perez and home-run hitter Jose Canseco, among other exiles from the Castro regime. The practice of playing spring training exhibition games in Havana ended in March 1960, when the Baltimore Orioles canceled a game scheduled there with the Cincinnati Reds due to political unrest in Cuba. Although Castro had been a promising pitcher before becoming a revolutionary, the U.S. blockade of Cuba severed ties with U.S. professional baseball. As Howard Senzel describes in his memoir BASEBALL AND THE COLD WAR (1977), the last professional game between U.S. and Cuban minor-league teams ended in a draw shortly after Castro's revolution when Frank Verdi, the Rochester Red Wing's third baseman, was shot in the head by a fan in Havana. Secretary of State Henry Kissinger squelched a popular 1975 proposal to complete the Sugar Kings-Red Wings game as a gesture of reconciliation between the United States and Cuba because President Ford feared losing the Cuban vote in the Florida presidential primaries and because Castro had supported an anti-Zionist UN resolution and advocated Puerto Rican independence. However, throughout the Cold War, Cuban teams competed against amateur American teams in the Pan-American Games.

The Cold War also affected the careers of American athletes. For example, the career of Ted Williams, the Boston Red Sox Hall of Fame outfielder who many consider the finest hitter ever to play the game, was interrupted in 1952 and 1953, when he served as an air force pilot during the Korean War. Williams saw combat and had to crash-land on one mission. He played only 43 games during those two years, which occurred while he was still in his prime, and he batted over .400 in those games. By contrast, world champion heavyweight boxer Muhammad Ali lost his title when he protested the Vietnam War by refusing induction into the army. He was only able to resume boxing in 1971, when the Supreme Court upheld his draft appeal on religious grounds. The RED SCARE also influenced baseball

when, on April 9, 1953, the Cincinnati Reds changed their name to the Redlegs to avoid the possible suggestion that they stood for communism. They changed their name back to the Reds a few years later.

spy film spoofs   The spectacle, heroics and high technology of SPY FILMS made the genre readily susceptible to parody. The Cold War spy spoofs MODESTY BLAISE (1956), OUR MAN FLINT (1966) and THE SECOND BEST SECRET AGENT IN THE WHOLE WIDE WORLD (1965) all make fun of the suave, sophisticated James BOND type of superspy, while *Casino Royale* (1967) parodies the Bond films directly. Based on the Graham GREENE novel, OUR MAN IN HAVANA (1960) ridicules the British Secret Service when a would-be spy in Havana sends back technical diagrams of vacuum cleaner parts, since he has no secret information to impart. In the Johnson-era film THE PRESIDENT'S ANALYST (1967), a psychologist who treats the president becomes the object of kidnapping and assassination attempts. Among the targets of this spoof are mindless bureaucracy, psychoanalysis, liberalism and the Cold War itself. Ultimately the telephone company proves to be the greatest power behind the "Free World." From the same period, THE DAY THE HOT LINE GOT HOT (1968) shows a Soviet and an American spy both being duped by their go-between, and the 1966 comedy *Glass Bottom Boat* stars Doris Day as the daughter of a research scientist who is mistaken for a Russian spy. The Carter-era THE IN-LAWS (1979) centers on a fast-talking CIA agent and his son's new father-in-law, a timid dentist. The spy drags the reluctant dentist into a scheme to overthrow a Latin American dictatorship, but neither the audience nor the dentist is ever sure whether the agent is sane or whether his plan actually has the backing of the CIA. Peter SELLERS revitalized the diabolic Chinese scientist FU MANCHU in *The Fiendish Plot of Dr. Fu Manchu* (1980). From the Reagan era, SPIES LIKE US (1985) centers on two incompetent U.S. foreign service agents who unknowingly serve as decoys on a mission that takes them through Asia. The Asian setting reminded audiences of the Soviet war in Afghanistan, which was then current. (See also FILM COMEDIES; FILM SATIRE.)

spy films   The spy story dates back at least to Homer's *Iliad*, in which Odysseus kills some guards, sneaks into Troy, gains information from Helen and steals Athena's sacred Palladian. This ancient genre flourished as never before during the Cold War, however. The Cold War saw the emergence of the CIA, the National Security Council and other intelligence agencies that spied on communist and allied countries, investigated U.S. citizens and conducted various types of legal and illegal covert operations. The FBI also grew during the Cold War, as director J. Edgar Hoover turned the bureau into an anti-communist organization dedicated to thwarting sabotage by communist agents. As the Cold War progressed, intelligence gathering and covert actions became more widely accepted as necessary for fighting communism, and the spy story gained popularity.

Because of their need to betray confidences, spies have always been viewed as morally problematic. In the early part of the Cold War, many films, SPY NOVELS, and TELEVISION SPY SHOWS depicted evil communist spies hard at work in America, trying to steal military and scientific secrets or sabotaging vital U.S. installations. In fact, throughout the Cold War, the number of Soviet agents caught spying in the United States was quite low, and no acts of sabotage were ever attributed to communist foreign agents or so-called "fifth column" American communists working on behalf of the U.S.S.R. Nonetheless, the widespread depiction of ruthless communist spies plotting against America fed the RED SCARE paranoia that communists were undermining the country from within.

RED DRAGON, a 1945 Charlie Chan movie, was the first film to center on a plot to steal secrets for building an atomic bomb. It appeared the same year that the first atomic bombs were tested and used. The first major anti-communist Cold War movie came in 1948, THE IRON CURTAIN, based on the story of Igor Gouzenko, a Russian who helped the Royal Canadian Mounted Police break a communist spy ring. Other early spy films that portray communist agents at work are BIG JIM MCCLAIN (1952), which features John WAYNE as an investigator for the HOUSE COMMITTEE ON UN-AMERICAN ACTIVITIES (HUAC), I WAS A COMMUNIST FOR THE F.B.I. (1951), KISS ME DEADLY (1955), MY SON JOHN (1952), Samuel FULLER's PICKUP ON SOUTH STREET (1953), THE RED MENACE (1949), WALK EAST ON BEACON (1952), Conspirator (1949), and The Whip Hand (1951).

Sometimes the enemy agents worked abroad. STATE SECRET (1950) tells the story of a famous surgeon who is tricked into assisting the leader of a communist police state and then flees the leader's country with the secret police in hot pursuit. JET PILOT (1957) is about a female Soviet agent who tries to seduce an American pilot (Wayne) into defecting, but she is unsuccessful and ultimately defects to the West instead. DIPLOMATIC COURIER (1952) features U.S. and Soviet agents trying to outmaneuver each other on a train to Trieste. Made during the same year as the Hungarian Uprising, FLIGHT FROM VIENNA (1956) centers on a Hungarian official who wishes to defect. During the 1960s Christopher Lee starred in five FU MANCHU movies that depicted the evil machinations of a brilliant Chinese scientist devoted to destroying America and the West.

Because Americans liked to think of themselves as honest, straightforward and just, the role of the treacherous spy was more commonly assigned to the communists. But in 1960, an American U-2 spy plane was shot down over the Soviet Union just before a summit meeting between Eisenhower and Khrushchev. Many Americans were shocked and dismayed to be confronted with the irrefutable truth that the United States also spied on the U.S.S.R. Afterward, however, the practice of spying became more acceptable, and spies began to appear more frequently as protagonists, often with the less disturbing label "secret agent." Many spy films from the 1960s onward celebrated the heroics of Western spies, who were often portrayed as the foot soldiers of the Cold War. Foremost among the spy superheroes was James BOND, the British secret agent who appeared in over 15 films. As a superior man armed with state-of-the-art technology, Bond showcases the virtues of consumer capitalism over communism. While Bond never loses touch with his animal nature, which makes him strong and virile, he balances that virility with the refinement and high fashion that are the pride of Western achievement, along with its superior technology. In this regard, the Bond

stories create images of success and masculine desirability similar to those cultivated by PLAYBOY magazine, which, like the Bond novels by Ian Fleming, first appeared during the early 1950s. Bond's sexual prowess plays a key role in his success over rival agents, and the plots often turn on his ability to seduce and control women, many of whom come to disastrous ends. Among the Bond films related to the Cold War are DR. NO (1962), FROM RUSSIA, WITH LOVE (1963), GOLDFINGER (1964), THUNDERBALL (1965), THE SPY WHO LOVED ME (1977), MOONRAKER (1979), Octopussy (1983) and THE LIVING DAYLIGHTS (1987). The SPY FILM SPOOF Casino Royale (1967) parodies the Bond character.

Other films that champion Western spies against Cold War enemies include COLD WAR KILLERS (1986), INTRIGUE (1988), TELEFON (1977) and K.G.B.: THE SECRET WAR (1986), which features a female protagonist. THE FOURTH PROTOCOL (1984) centers on a competition between two master spies who narrowly forestall a nuclear disaster. CATCH ME A SPY (1971) features a British agent who smuggles Soviet manuscripts into England and falls in love with the wife of a Soviet spy.

Several films reveal an ambivalent view of spies and the governments they serve. Among these are THE SPY WHO CAME IN FROM THE COLD (1965), DEADLY AFFAIR (1967), THE LOOKING GLASS WAR (1969) and THE RUSSIA HOUSE (1990), all based on novels by John LE CARRÉ, and THE HUMAN FACTOR (1979) based on the novel by Graham GREENE. Greene also authored the novel THE THIRD MAN (1949), as well as the screenplay for the 1950 film by the same title. Both the book and film are set in Vienna shortly after World War II and both portray the international rivalries among the occupying powers' police agencies. Made after Watergate and other revelations of illegal U.S. government spying, THREE DAYS OF THE CONDOR (1975) shows the CIA turning against its own agents, as do HOPSCOTCH (1980), THE IPCRESS FILE (1965) and Mikhail Baryshnikov's post–Cold War Company Business (1991). THE SELLOUT (1975) centers on an effort by U.S. and Soviet agents to lure a double agent to Jerusalem in order to assassinate him.

Alfred HITCHCOCK made several Cold War–era spy films. In TORN CURTAIN (1966), an American scientist pretends to defect while attending an international conference. In TOPAZ (1969), French and American agents work together to identify the Soviet nuclear-armed missiles that precipitate the Cuban Missile Crisis, while they simultaneously ferret out a highly placed Soviet spy within the French government. In his 1956 remake of The Man Who Knew Too Much, Hitchcock employs an earlier formula in which the protagonist is an innocent civilian who becomes inadvertently caught up in the machinations of enemy agents. He repeats that formula in NORTH BY NORTHWEST (1959), in which the protagonist becomes involved in a U.S. agency's attempt to catch a cell of Soviet spies. That film culminates with a dramatic fight atop Mt. Rushmore. North By Northwest also embodies MOM-ISM, a belief popularized by Philip Wylie in his 1942 bestseller, A Generation of Vipers. Momism depicted the middle-class American mother as self-righteous, self-absorbed, hypocritical and sexually repressed. According to Wylie, American middle-class mothers dominate their sons and husbands. When North By Northwest begins protagonist George Kaplan is such a dominated son. However, the act of clearing his name, fighting for his survival and combating the communists produces a change in his character that enables him to assert his independence from his mother and emerge as a worthy mate for the beautiful Eve, whose life he saves. Thus Kaplan's accidental immersion into the seamy underside of Cold War politics builds his character as it bolsters the national security. Cold War films by other filmmakers who used the formula of the innocent civilian include ARABESQUE (1966), CHINESE BOXES (1984), THE DEFECTOR (1966) and GORKY PARK (1983).

Spy films alluded to a number of Cold War political issues. *The Day of the Jackal* (1973) centers on an attempt to assassinate French president Charles de Gaulle. THE PARALLAX VIEW (1974) also centers on professional assassins. KILL CASTRO (1980) is about a Key West boat captain who is hired by a renegade CIA agent to assassinate the Cuban leader. THE LAST PLANE OUT (1983) involves intrigue between Somoza sympathizers and the revolutionaries who went on to overthrow the dictator and establish a socialist government in Nicaragua. Another Reagan-era film, THE OSTERMAN WEEKEND (1972), centers on a powerful television journalist whose trusted sources turn out to be Soviet agents. RED KING, WHITE NIGHT (1989) appeared during the Bush era while Soviet Premier Mikhail Gorbachev was being warmly received in the West due to his social and political reforms and his willingness to work with Western leaders. The film tells the story of an ex-CIA agent who returns to duty to prevent Gorbachev's assassination by his internal political enemies.

For additional reading, see Cawelti and Rosenberg's *The Spy Story.*

spy novels

The Cold War furnished the context in which the spy and secret agent story could flourish, for the Cold War depended primarily on clandestine operations and proxy warfare. Also, scientific knowledge and technology played a very large role in the Cold War, more so than in any other international conflict in history, and these were important instruments in real-life espionage work as well as in spy fiction. The Cold War saw the emergence of the CIA, the National Security Council and other intelligence agencies that spied on communist countries and sometimes on allies and U.S. citizens. These agencies also conducted legal and illegal covert operations.

Spy fiction owed a debt to NONFICTION works on espionage. In 1963, former CIA director Allen Dulles published *The Craft of Intelligence,* a popular book of essays describing espionage techniques. In 1968, he published another nonfiction work, *Great True Spy Stories.* The FBI also grew during the Cold War, as director J. Edgar Hoover turned the bureau into an anti-communist organization dedicated to thwarting domestic sabotage by communist agents. Hoover's own best-selling 1958 nonfiction book, MASTERS OF DECEIT, informed citizens how they could assist the FBI's efforts to combat communist espionage and described how communist spy rings operated. I WAS A COMMUNIST FOR THE F.B.I., which became a 1951 film, first appeared as a *Saturday Evening Post* article ghost-written for Matt Cvetic, who had been an FBI operative for seven years. Herbert Philbrick's I LED THREE LIVES (1952) was another autobiographical account of FBI infiltration into the American Communist Party.

Anti-communist spy fiction began early in the Cold War.

In the late 1940s and 1950s, novelist Mickey SPILLANE depicted evil communist spies hard at work in America, trying to steal military and scientific secrets and sabotaging vital U.S. installations. Spillane's protagonist, Mike Hammer, deals with communists most forcefully in the 1951 detective novel *One Lonely Night.* In fact, however, throughout the Cold War, the number of Soviet agents caught spying in the United States was quite low, and no acts of sabotage were ever attributed to communist foreign agents or to so-called "fifth column" American communists working on behalf of the U.S.S.R. Perhaps for this reason, stories centering primarily on domestic espionage do not comprise a large segment of Cold War spy fiction.

Other stories from the early phase of the Cold War portray Western agents working at home and abroad to protect freedom and democracy against the communists. The most notable of these are the James BOND stories. The Bond stories consistently use the time-honored formula of the spy story: The hero penetrates hostile territory, acquires necessary information—often through the assistance of a beautiful woman within the enemy camp—strikes a damaging blow against the enemy and returns safely to his base. Bond, whose appearance in the 1950s coincided with the rise of PLAYBOY magazine, shares many of the traits of the ideal man presented by that publication. He is handsome, refined, sophisticated, intelligent, witty, sexy, physically adept, and proficient with technology. As a superior man, Bond is clearly someone who rose from the masses, not with them, and his attributes and accoutrements showcase the virtues of consumer capitalism over communism. While Bond never loses touch with his animal nature, which makes him strong and virile, he balances it with the refinement and high fashion that are the pride of Western achievement, along with its superior technology.

A special agent in Her Majesty's Secret Service, with a license to kill, Bond first appeared in British writer Ian Fleming's 1953 novel *Casino Royale;* subsequently the James Bond series became the most successful series of spy stories and films in history. In addition to fighting Soviet agents, as in FROM RUSSIA WITH LOVE (1957), Bond frequently combats an international syndicate of criminals. In GOLDFINGER (1960) Bond opposes two enemies of capitalism as the communist Chinese give a sophisticated criminal an atomic device so he can attack Fort Knox and render the U.S. gold reserve worthless. DR. NO (1958), THUNDERBALL (1961) and THE SPY WHO LOVED ME (1962) all deal with the problems that might arise when nuclear weapons or other advanced military technology fall into the hands of villains who operate as individuals instead of as agents of a nation-state. Bond works in close cooperation with the CIA, and his stories leave no doubt about who represents good and who stands for evil. The novels also suggest that female sexuality is a potent but potentially dangerous force that must be safely harnessed. Thus Bond's virility is one of his chief virtues, and his ability to control women through his sexuality plays a significant role in his success—and in the survival of the Western world.

Writers who invoke similar formulas include Donald Hamilton, whose serialized protagonist Matt Helm is in many ways an Americanized and more brutal version of Bond. Robert Ludlum typically invokes enemies with vast resources who have devised broad-ranging conspiracies; his THE OSTERMAN WEEKEND (1972) features Soviet efforts to infiltrate the U.S. media. Other writers who make clear distinctions between the virtuous West and nefarious communists and feature action-packed stories centered on superheros, sexy women and conspiracies include Alistair Maclean, Philip McCutchan, John Gardner, Gavin Lyall, Noel Hynd and Trevanian.

E. Howard Hunt, the former CIA agent and Watergate conspirator, also employs Bond-like protagonists. His books include *The Berlin Ending,* a 1973 novel that depicts Willy Brandt and other advocates of détente as Soviet agents; *The Hargrave Deception* (1980); *The Gaza Intercept* (1981); and *The Kremlin Conspiracy,* a 1985 story in which European "peaceniks" pressure the Nobel Prize committee to give the Peace Prize to a man who is secretly a Soviet agent. The prizewinner then uses his influence to force NATO to withdraw its missiles from Europe. Hunt's protagonist, Neil Thorpe, goes behind the IRON CURTAIN to expose the Soviet villain. (Hunt also wrote a 1973 nonfiction account of the 1961 failed Bay of Pigs invasion of Cuba, *Give Us This Day.*) Hunt's Watergate coconspirator G. Gordon Liddy also writes spy fiction, notably the best-selling *Monkey Handlers* (1990) and *Out of Control* (1979).

The more law-abiding William F. BUCKLEY Jr. was a JOURNALIST, the editor of the *National Review* MAGAZINE, the host of FIRING LINE and an otherwise prominent spokesman for American conservativism; he was also the author of a series of spy novels featuring a Bond-like superhero, Blackford Oakes. The best-selling Oakes novels include *Saving the Queen* (1976), *Stained Glass* (1978), *Marco Polo, If You Can* (1982), *Who's on First* (1980), *See You Later Alligator* (1985), *High Jinx* (1986), *The Story of Henri Tod* (1983) and *Tucker's Last Stand* (1990). More than most works of Cold War fiction, Buckley's center on specific real-life Cold War events, such as the power struggle in the Kremlin following Stalin's death *(High Jinx);* the Hungarian Revolution and the beginnings of the space race *(Who's on First);* the second Berlin Crisis *(Henri Tod);* and the 1960 U-2 incident *(Marco Polo).* Leon URIS also writes of actual Cold War events. (See LITERATURE ABOUT COLD WAR EVENTS.) His spy novel TOPAZ (1967) centers on the cooperation between U.S. agents and a French operative who together expose the placement of the nuclear-armed Soviet missiles in Cuba that gave rise to the Cuban Missile Crisis. At the same time, they ferret out a highly placed Soviet spy within the French intelligence community.

Other writers invent plausible but still fictional events for their spy novels. For example, Frederick Forsyth's *The Day of the Jackal* (1971) presents a credible story about an intelligence group's successful efforts to thwart a secret French military organization's plot to assassinate President Charles de Gaulle. On the other hand, several writers employed the spy genre to suggest that the espionage agencies of all the superpowers had gotten out of hand and lost sight of the ethical values that their countries purportedly endorsed. John LE CARRÉ is the best known and most respected of this group of writers. The author adopted the pseudonym while working in the British Foreign Office and MI6, the British counterpart of the CIA. A Foreign Office prohibition forbade him from publishing under his real name, David Cornwall. Le Carré's novels center on various kinds of betrayal: by individuals, institutions, ideologies and the self. They eschew the high-pitched action of the Bond novels, focusing instead on deep characterizations, intricately woven plots and a somber sense of realism. Le Carré creates a novelistic version of cinema's *film noir* in that virtually everyone seems either amoral or immoral. Characters are rarely able to hold on to their ethical values and still survive.

Thus in THE SPY WHO CAME IN FROM THE COLD (1963), le Carré's first commercial success, espionage is conducted by "seedy little people" with their own agendas, and the British secret service sells out its agent and his girlfriend in order to protect an ex-Nazi who is a highly placed double agent in the East German intelligence agency. When the protagonist finally chooses love over duplicity, it costs him his life. Le Carré's first novel, *A Call for the Dead,* (1961) introduces his recurring character George Smiley, a spymaster who is "breathtakingly ordinary." Smiley had been a student of literature before becoming a spy. His scholastic skills of observation and rigorous analysis are well suited for intelligence work, but the humanistic values of truth, beauty and goodness expressed in the literature he studies are ill-suited to espionage. The contrast between the worlds of literature and espionage provides a moral tension that animates the Smiley novels. These include *Tinker, Tailor, Soldier, Spy* (1974), *The Honourable Schoolboy (1977)* and *Smiley's People* (1980), which le Carré collected in 1982 as the trilogy THE QUEST FOR KARLA. The BBC produced the trilogy as a highly successful television series that appeared in the United States as well as in Britain.

Another writer to invoke le Carré's cynicism is Graham GREENE. In *The Spy Story,* John Cawelti and Bruce Rosenberg call Greene's THE HUMAN FACTOR (1978), which appeared in the waning years of détente, the finest spy novel ever written. The main character may have been based on Greene's former friend Kim Philby, a top British intelligence officer who defected to the U.S.S.R. in 1963—though Greene has denied the connection. Greene served with Philby in the British intelligence service during World War II. In 1968 he wrote "Reflections on the Character of Kim Philby," for *Esquire,* as well as writing the introduction to Philby's memoirs. (The Philby story also serves as part of the inspiration for le Carré's *The Quest for Karla.*) *The Human Factor* centers on Maurice Castle, a British intelligence agent who specializes in African affairs and is married to a black South African woman he once used as an agent. His loyalty to her and to Africa leads him to pass information to the Soviets, since the West appears to be willing to sell out black Africans in order to serve its Cold War needs and protect its access to the uranium and diamonds of white-ruled South Africa. Greene depicts a morally ambiguous world in which almost no one has a full picture of the machinations of any side and in which everyone is manipulated for hidden purposes. Castle's fundamental uncertainty about the overall picture renders problematic his ability to make moral decisions or take responsible action. Greene also wrote a satirical spy novel, OUR MAN IN HAVANA (1958), in which a Cuban vacuum cleaner salesman in need of money pretends to have access to important, secret information during the waning days of the Batista regime. Having no real information to pass along, he forwards technical drawings of vacuum cleaner schematics, which he claims describe military installations.

Len DEIGHTON, another British writer whose books became popular in the United States, also features antiheroes, though his books are more comic than le Carré's or *The Human Factor*. His first novel, THE IPCRESS FILE (1962), appeared the year of the Cuban Missile Crisis. It centers on an out-of-shape, nearsighted British intelligence agent who traces a missing scientist and in the process discovers that one of his own superiors is a spy. The action, which involves double, triple and quadruple agents whose loyalties seem indiscernible, takes the unassuming hero to the Near East, a nuclear test site in the Pacific and behind the IRON CURTAIN. One reviewer points out that Deighton "recognizes that the spy—whose survival depends on his guile, cunning, and adaptability—is today's picaro" and thus suggests that the Cold War spy genre permits the updating of the ancient picaresque, or journey story. Other works by Deighton include *Funeral in Berlin* (1965), *The Billion Dollar Brain* (1966) *Spy Story* (1974), *Yesterday's Spy* (1975), *Catch a Falling Spy* (1976) and, from the final years of the Cold War, *Spy Hook* (1988), *Spy Line* (1989) and *Spy Sinker* (1990).

The political spying in the Watergate scandal led to President Nixon's resignation in 1974 and to the Church Committee's 1975 revelations of other illegal activities conducted by U.S. espionage agencies against U.S. citizens. Several post-Watergate novels portray the U.S. government and its intelligence agencies as villains. John Ehrlichman, the top domestic adviser in the Nixon White House who was convicted for his activities in the Watergate affair, published *The Company* in 1976, a novel about rivalries among the CIA, FBI and other intelligence agencies. In that book, the CIA possesses information implicating the president in the murder of a prominent revolutionary. The unflattering portrayal of the president is apparently based on Nixon. Ehrlichman also wrote *The China Card*, a 1986 novel that suggests that Nixon's historic trip to China actually resulted from the activities of a spy working on behalf of Zhou En-lai, the Chinese premier. In James Grady's 1974 novel *Six Days of the Condor*—the basis for the 1975 film THREE DAYS OF THE CONDOR—CIA agents kill all but one of the members of a special section of the CIA; the action centers on their efforts to assassinate the lone survivor.

William Goldman's *Marathon Man* (1974) features a collusion between a secret U.S. agency and a Nazi war criminal. The RED SCARE figures prominently in the background. Charlie Heller, the protagonist in Robert Littell's *The Amateur* (1981), must overcome not only the communist spies who have killed his fiancée but also the inept and bureaucratic superiors at the CIA who try to kill him. Likewise, the protagonist in Robert Duncan's *Dragons at the Gate* (1976) is a CIA agent who learns that the agency wants to eliminate him. These works of fiction were accompanied by at least one important nonfiction account of the CIA's role in covert operations, *Inside the Company: CIA Diary* (1975). Its author, former agent Philip Agee, overcame the agency's intense efforts to block publication of the book, which later inspired a six-hour documentary film, *On Company Business*.

As the Cold War heated up again during the 1980s, anti-Soviet sentiment reappeared in such works as Martin Cruz Smith's best-selling novel, GORKY PARK (1981). The story centers on a police investigation of the deaths of three people discovered in Moscow's Gorky Park. The trail leads to an American fur trader and a young Soviet dissident and presents a stark view of life behind the Iron Curtain. Concerns about the possibility of nuclear war also intensified during the first Reagan administration, and these surfaced in Forsyth's 1984 novel THE FOURTH PROTOCOL, which presents a competition between two master spies who narrowly forestall a nuclear disaster. Richard Hoyt's *Trotsky's Run* (1982) imagines the quandaries of the CIA and the KGB when the Democrats nominate for president a man who, according to defector Kim Philby, is actually Leon Trotsky. Like much of the rhetoric from the Reagan era, the suggestion that liberals might be duped into supporting a communist harkens back to attitudes common in the 1950s. Le Carré addresses the end of the Cold War in his 1989 bestseller THE RUSSIA HOUSE, set during the waning days of the Soviet Union. It centers on efforts by Western agents to ascertain the authenticity of claims by a Soviet scientist that the Soviet military-industrial complex is hopelessly corrupt, seriously inept and grossly mismanaged. The claim threatens the Western agents because it suggests that the entire Cold War has been a farce and undermines the necessity of their work. With the end of the Cold War the spy genre has had to adapt to a new set of enemies in "the new world order." These include international and domestic terrorists, drug barons, Islamic fundamentalists, corrupt government officials and corporate spies. (See also SPY FILMS; TELEVISION SPY SHOWS.)

For additional reading, see Cawelti and Rosenberg's *The Spy Story* and Beene's *John le Carré*.

Spy Who Came in from the Cold, The a 1963 SPY NOVEL by John LE CARRÉ and a 1965 British-made SPY FILM starring Richard Burton, Claire Bloom, Oskar Werner and Peter Van Eyck and directed by Martin Ritt. The novel was first published in the United States in 1964. Le Carré's third spy novel and his first great financial success, *The Spy Who Came in From the Cold* centers on Alec Lemas (Burton), a burnt-out British spy who pretends to defect to East Germany in a complex plot designed to protect a highly-placed double agent in the East German spy network (Van Eyck). The cynical story obfuscates all distinctions between good and bad agents and good and bad causes and raises the problem of acting morally in a realm of uncertainty. For instance, the double agent Lamas protects is a cruel ex-Nazi, and the man trying to reveal him is a sympathetic Jew working for the communist government (Werner). Moreover, the black-and-white film presents the East and West as visually the same. London and East Berlin are both cold, gray and inhospitable, and life for working-class Londoners appears as bleak and colorless as the world of East Berliners. In the process of unknowingly performing dirty work for the British spy service, Lemas's girlfriend (Bloom) is sacrificed at the Berlin Wall, and Lemas chooses to join her in death rather than seek safety among the cynical and duplicitous British espionage agents. Thus love emerges as the story's only meaningful value.

Elsewhere, the "superpowers" are likened to large trucks moving at high speeds, which merge to crush a family of innocents traveling along the highway between them. The story further depicts the undeclared war between the Eastern and Western intelligence agencies. But in contrast to the highly popular James BOND books and films, this story depicts spies as unglamorous, seedy people who are motivated not by high-minded causes and principles but by their own personal agendas. The book headed the bestseller lists in London and New York and sold over 250,000 copies. Graham GREENE praised it as "the best spy novel I have ever read," and former CIA director Richard Helms criticized it for "undermining the very bedrock of intelligence." Government authorities refused its publication in Poland, and it was criticized in the Soviet Union.

For additional reading, see Beene's *John le Carré* and Cawelti and Rosenberg's *The Spy Story*.

Spy Who Loved Me, The   A 1962 SPY NOVEL by Ian Fleming and a 1977 British-made SPY FILM starring Roger Moore, Barbara Bach, Curt Jurgens and Richard Kiel and directed by Lewis Gilbert. Part of Fleming's popular James BOND series, the novel appeared at the height of the Cold War, during the same year as the Cuban Missile Crisis. By contrast, the film occurred during the more conciliatory détente of the middle 1970s. The film features a collaboration between Bond (Moore), a British spy, and Major Anya Amasova (Bach), a Soviet agent. Together they work to thwart a nefarious free-agent malefactor who has stolen two nuclear-armed submarines. The book played upon the then-current threat of imminent nuclear holocaust, and both the film and movie address the additional fear that control of nuclear weaponry could slip from the superpowers.

Stallion Gate   A 1986 APOCALYPTIC NOVEL by Martin Cruz Smith. *Stallion Gate* was one of the few novels about the nuclear threat published in the mainstream press by a Native American Indian. (Other Native American authors who addressed nuclear themes include Wendy Rose, Linda Hogan, Paula Gunn Allen, Stephen Popkes and Leslie Marmon Silko, who wrote CEREMONY.) Like *Ceremony*, *Stallion Gate* views nuclear weaponry as the logical culmination of the Western empirical, scientific, technologically-driven world view. Both novels address the impact of the development of the atomic bomb in New Mexico on the Native Americans who populate the region.

Stallion Gate centers on Joe Pena, a sergeant who had escaped from the Philippines after the Japanese invasion and is reassigned to serve as J. Robert Oppenheimer's chauffeur and his liaison with the Indians. Pena is cynical and bored with his tribal town. A jazz pianist and prizefighter, he hopes to raise $50,000 so he can purchase a jazz club in Albuquerque. He therefore steals army supplies and promotes and bets on a prize fight scheduled for the evening before the Trinity test. Helen Jaskoski points out in *The Nightmare Considered* that

> *Stallion Gate* emphasizes on every page invasive, objectifying Western empiricism. The apparatus of empirical science obtrudes everywhere; miles of cables, uncounted geiger counters, sensors . . . The Trinity

explosion is to be a gigantic exercise in testing and measurement, for the purpose of which the desert, the atmosphere, and the earth itself are seen as nothing more than a single giant laboratory. In contrast to all this scientific testing and measuring is the epistemology of the elders and clown priests in the Pueblo village.

The clown priests perform a dance mocking the bomb experiment, Oppenheimer and General Leslie Groves, and Oppenheimer himself participates in a ritual that requires him to explode a firecracker that symbolizes the bomb. Even while Oppenheimer feels he has gained the trust and friendship of the Indians, a security officer remains convinced the Indians are spies; both are wrong. The Indian and scientific cultures contrast elsewhere too. Jaskoski points out that "those who engage in wanton destruction belong to the culture of the bomb, and are set in opposition to the people who belong to the land." A scene featuring panicked Mustangs being strafed by airplanes prefigures the novel's ending, in which Pena also runs madly from a weapon.

For additional reading, see Anisfield's *The Nightmare Considered*.

Stallone, Sylvester   A FILM ACTOR and SCREENWRITER. Stallone is most famous for his ROCKY and RAMBO series, both of which contributed to the conservative political and social climate of the 1980s. In addition to starring in *Rocky* (1976), which won the Academy Award for best film, Stallone wrote the script, for which he received an Academy Award nomination. Sequels appeared in 1979, 1982, 1985 and 1990. Though not directly related to the Cold War, the original *Rocky* reiterated the traditional American values of hard work and perseverance that frequently characterized film and television during the 1950s and early 1960s but that were challenged during the later 1960s and early 1970s.

Rocky IV (1985) made a much more immediate appeal to Cold War sentiments. Whereas the original appeared during the détente of the 1970s, *Rocky IV* was released in one of the most intense periods of the superpower conflict when both sides were increasing their nuclear arsenals and adopting more bellicose positions. In this film, Rocky takes on a huge Soviet boxer in a fight that highlights the nationalistic aspect of their personal grudge match. Though the Soviet fighter is bigger and enjoys other advantages unavailable to Rocky, the American's intractable will and total devotion to his cause enable him to win.

In the *Rambo* films, Stallone plays a Vietnam veteran. In the first film in the series, *First Blood*, (1982) the veteran stands up to the sheriff of a small town in which he had been abused. In the sequel, *Rambo* (1985), he returns to Vietnam to save soldiers listed as missing in action. In *Rambo III* (1988), he saves a friend who had been captured by the communists while fighting for Afghani rebels. The trilogy appeared during Reagan's two terms as president, and Reagan himself invoked it approvingly to applaud the values of loyalty, honesty, commitment and determined action. *Rambo: First Blood Part II* most caught the public imagination as it provided the country with its first cinematic Vietnam War hero since John WAYNE in THE GREEN

BERETS (1968). Reagan, who first saw the film shortly after 39 Western hostages had been released in Lebanon, commented, "Boy, I saw *Rambo* last night. Now I know what to do the next time this happens."

Along with THE BEAST (1988) and the 1987 James BOND film, THE LIVING DAYLIGHTS, *Rambo III* is one of the few films to address the Soviet war in Afghanistan, a pivotal Cold War event that ended U.S.-Soviet détente when the Soviet invasion began in December 1979. Stallone also made *Nighthawks* (1981), in which he takes on international terrorists. Along with Chuck NORRIS, Stallone provided movie audiences of the 1980s with the kind of violent, no-nonsense action hero that had been largely missing from Hollywood films made during the previous decade of détente.

"Star Trek" A TELEVISION SCIENCE FICTION SHOW that ran on NBC from 1966 to 1969 and a SCIENCE FICTION FILM series starring William Shatner, Leonard Nimoy, DeForest Kelley and James Doohan. Nimoy directed two and Shatner directed one of the film sequels. The show featured the adventures of the starship *Enterprise,* commanded by Captain James T. Kirk (Shatner). In this futuristic world, solar systems form military-political alliances similar to NATO and the Warsaw Pact. In the films, Captain Kirk was often restrained by treaty restrictions that his enemies either exploit or violate—a common public complaint about the U.S.'s situation throughout the Cold War, especially during the Vietnam War. In the television shown, however, Kirk usually sought peaceful coexistence. And just as the American public generally viewed its country as working for peace, justice and international security, the *Enterprise's* mis-

"Star Trek." 1966. Left to right: Dr. McCoy, Captain Kirk, Mr. Spock. Courtesy AP/Wide World.

sion in both film and television was an enlightened attempt "To boldly go where no one has gone before" in order to acquire knowledge, protect the Federation's frontiers and aid colonies in distress. Kirk was helped by his first officer, Mr. Spock (Nimoy), a pointy-eared half-human from the planet Vulcan who was extremely intelligent, highly rational, mathematically and scientifically inclined and entirely dispassionate. The ship's doctor, Leonard McCoy, and the engineer, a Scotsman nicknamed Scotty (Doohan), were Kirk's other closest advisers. The emotional Dr. McCoy often clashed with the detached Spock, and Kirk had to mediate between the two of them. Likewise, in his own personality Kirk synthesized Spock's reliance on intellect and reason with McCoy's instinctive, emotional values of loyalty, friendship and compassion. In this way the show addressed the conflict in Cold War America between the growing scientific, emotionally detached technocracy and the humanists who advocated national policy predicated on more emotional grounds.

Produced during the height of the Vietnam War, "Star Trek" presented conflicting philosophies about war, pacifism and how to react to dangerous, military enemies. Depending on who wrote each episode, the show either insisted upon the necessity of taking a firm stand and engaging in combat when called upon to do so, or it suggested that nonviolent options were preferable. Thus the program mirrored the division within the United States over these same issues.

Star Trek became even more popular after its demise as a regularly scheduled television show than it was during its three-year run, as a cult of "Trekkies" sprang up around the world. Consequently, a series of six Star Trek movies was made between 1979 and 1991 starring much of the original television cast, including all of the major actors. Of particular interest is the last in the series, *Star Trek VI: The Undiscovered Country* (1991), which mirrored the then-current conclusion of the Cold War. In that film, the characters learn to accept the possibility of peaceful coexistence between former enemies and not to be afraid of the future.

In 1987, a syndicated television sequel appeared, "Star Trek: The Next Generation," starring Patrick Stewart as Captain Jean-Luc Picard, commander of the new, improved starship *Enterprise.* That show was highly rated from the outset. The 1990s saw additional Star Trek sequels with different casts.

Star Wars A 1977 SCIENCE FICTION FILM starring Harrison Ford, Mark Hamill, Carrie Fisher and Alec Guinness and directed by George Lucas. Its two sequels are *The Empire Strikes Back* (1980) and *Return of the Jedi* (1983). Set "a long time ago, in a galaxy far, far away," *Star Wars* dramatically plays out the battle between the forces of good and evil. The plot centers on the efforts of young Luke Skywalker (Hamill), intergalactic smuggler Han Solo (Ford), sage Obi-Wan Kenobi (Guinness) and their robot companions to rescue the Princess Leia (Fisher) and destroy a gigantic Death Star that the better-armed Evil Empire is using to enslave the galaxy. The films appeared during the Carter and Reagan administrations, when conservatives were charging that the Soviets were better armed than the United States. Joseph Campbell, the scholar of comparative mythology, argued that *Star Wars* updates the journey of the mythic hero. As with other such heroes, Luke's growth in self-knowledge enables him to overcome his obstacles. From a Cold War point of view, the conflict between a good and evil empire mirrored both the 1950s and the 1980s American view of the superpower confrontation. In other ways, too, *Star Wars* anticipates Reagan-era Cold War sentiments, even though it was made during the later stages of détente. Traditional values, American ingenuity, courage, commitment, respect and spiritual purity prove to be the qualities necessary for defeating the Evil Empire. The film's state-of-the-art special effects impressively capture the high-tech nature of post-Vietnam warfare. During his presidency, Ronald Reagan alluded to the film in his description of the Soviet Union as an "evil empire," and his Strategic Defense Initiative (SDI) became popularly known as Star Wars because of its reliance on laser weapons orbiting in space.

In *The Movie Guide,* James Monaco suggested that "George Lucas has done more than anyone except Jim Henson (and perhaps Walt DISNEY) to establish the gallery of characters who now populate contemporary childhood." The spin-offs in toys, clothes and advertising gave *Star Wars* enormous cultural impact during the late 1970s and 1980s. In 1978 Ernie Fosselius directed the short parody, *Hardware Wars*. Although children of the 1990s were no longer playing with Star Wars toys, the movies' conventions and its breakthrough use of special effects continue to influence film and popular culture. The *Star Wars* trilogy was enhanced with new computer technology and re-released in movie theaters in 1997. And *Star War* novels remain a staple of science fiction.

For additional reading, see Monaco's *The Movie Guide.*

State of Siege A 1973 POLITICAL FILM made jointly by French, Italian, West German and U.S. production companies. It starred Yves Montand, Renato Salvatori and O. E. Hasse and was directed by Constantin COSTA-GAVRAS. Set in an anonymous Latin American nation that suggests Uruguay, the film focuses on Philip Santore (Montand), an employee of the U.S. Agency for International Development (AID) whom left-wing guerrillas believe is responsible for introducing sophisticated methods of torture into their country and elsewhere. The guerrillas capture Santore and attempt to extract a confession from him before government troops discover their location. The story is allegedly based on real-life AID officer Daniel Mitrione. Upon its release, *State of Siege* was banned from the American Film Institute after its critics complained that it glorified assassination and was violently anti-American.

State Secret A 1950 British-made SPY FILM starring Douglas Fairbanks Jr., Glynis Johns and Jack Hawkins and directed by Sidney Gilliat. The story centers on a famous surgeon who is tricked into assisting the leader of a communist police state and then flees with the secret police in hot pursuit.

Steel Helmet, The A 1951 KOREAN WAR FILM starring Gene Evans and Robert Hutton and directed by Samuel FULLER. Written in a week and filmed in 10 days, *The Steel Helmet* was released just six months after the beginning of the Korean War. The film is considered to be one of the best war films of the 1950s. Like other Korean War films, it refuses to glamorize warfare. Instead, the Korean War appears as a grim, confusing and dehumanizing experience. The film centers mostly on the soldiers' struggle for survival in a brutal situation. The protagonists are survivors of massacred squads who join together to capture a Buddhist temple occupied by a North Korean major. They are accompanied by a South Korean orphan boy who tags along in search of chocolate. In this film, becoming desensitized becomes a key to survival. Caring and compassion can literally lead to death, as in the case of a GI who is blown up while removing the dog tags from a dead soldier. He had ignored the words of the protagonist sergeant, "A dead man is a dead man and nobody cares." The soldiers' and audience's inability to distinguish friendly Koreans from hostile ones reflects the confusion over the purpose of the war, which was somewhat unpopular at home. When a confused soldier asks how to distinguish among Koreans, the sergeant replies, "If he's running with you, he's a South Korean. If he's running after you, he's a North Korean." The set and special effects create a claustrophobic atmosphere in which everything seems vague, hazy and ambiguous. The effect of the film is to render the war as an ongoing exercise in madness. The final credit reads, "There is no end to this story." Fuller also directed another Korean War film, *Fixed Bayonets* (1951), about a corporal who must assume command when his superiors are killed.

For additional reading, see Monaco's *The Movie Guide;* Server's *Sam Fuller: Film is a Battleground.*

Stone, I. F. A JOURNALIST. Born in 1907, Stone began his own newspaper at age 14. Before World War II, he worked for a succession of liberal or radical papers: the *Camden Post,* the *Philadelphia Record* and the *New York Post,* as well as serving as Washington editor for *The Nation* MAGAZINE from 1940 to 1946. During the Truman administration, Stone worked for three New York daily papers, *PM,* the *Star* and the *Daily Compass.* However, each of those left-wing publications went out of business during the RED SCARE. Consequently, in early 1953, Stone founded *I.F. Stone's Weekly,* a four-page weekly newsletter that provided a forum for his left-wing perspective on the Cold War and other contemporary events. Stone sold the newsletter by subscription, initially charging five dollars a year. He received some 5,000 subscriptions the first year from what Stone called "a scattered tiny minority of liberal radicals unafraid in McCarthy's heyday to support, and go on the mailing list of, a new radical publication from Washington." In 1968 he began issuing the paper every other week. Stone ceased publication in December 1971, when he went on to become a contributing editor to *The New York Review of Books.* At the time of its demise, the *Weekly*'s subscription list had grown to over 70,000.

Stone also published several Cold War–related books, including *The Hidden History of the Korean War* (1952), which uses government documents to question the official version of the events that occasioned the outbreak of the war; *The Truman Era* (1953), which compiles Cold War–related newspaper articles Stone wrote between 1945 and 1952; *The Haunted Fifties* (1963); *In a Time of Torment* (1967); *The Killings at Kent State: How Murder Went Unpunished* (1971); and *Polemics and Prophecies* (1971).

In his early Cold War articles, Stone questions whether the United Nations (UN) is truly an organization meant to keep peace and suggests instead that it was established to restrain the Soviet Union. He also criticizes the U.S. lack of a postwar plan for Japan and comments on the events that led to the Cold War and the Red Scare. In one article he attacks a 1951 issue of *Collier's* magazine in which a panel of "experts" contemplates a war with the U.S.S.R. and presents a scenario in which the United States would prevail after sending airborne troops into the Ural Mountains to destroy the Soviet arsenal of atomic bombs. In addition to pointing out specific fallacies in the scenario, Stone suggests that the overall effect of the article is to make an atomic war with the Soviets appear to be an acceptable idea. Stone also criticizes the suggestion by Arthur KOESTLER and others that the Soviet regime is "rule of terror" that will quickly be rejected by the oppressed citizens once they are given a chance to do so. "The impression *Collier's* creates is that Russia is one vast slave labor camp where we need only shoot the guards and wreck the gates to be hailed as liberators." Stone points out that this did not happen either when international armies intervened after the Russian Revolution or when the Nazis invaded the U.S.S.R. during World War II, even though large portions of the Soviet Union were occupied in each instance. Thus Stone concludes that Washington may be "blinded by *its* own propaganda," just as the American press accuses the Soviets of being misled by theirs.

Later, Stone was among the first to go on record against the U.S. decision to send combat troops to Vietnam in 1965. He routinely sustained his positions with research taken from *The Congressional Record,* public hearings and other official documents, often noting incongruities between the evidence introduced and the conclusions drawn and policies made by government leaders. Toward the end of his life, he wrote *The Trial of Socrates,* which appeared in 1989, the year of his death.

Stone, Oliver   A FILM DIRECTOR and SCREENWRITER. During the 1980s and early 1990s, Stone treated Cold War–related subjects and other social and political topics more consistently than any other Hollywood director. He first came to prominence for his Academy Award–winning screenplay of *Midnight Express* (1978), about a young American sentenced to a Turkish prison for drug possession. He also wrote the screenplays for two other popular films, *Conan the Barbarian* (1982) and *Scarface* (1983). Apart from his directorial debut, *Street Scenes* (1970), Stone wrote all of the films he directed during the Cold War.

A Vietnam War veteran, he achieved acclaim for his first Vietnam War Film, PLATOON (1986). *Platoon* shows a U.S. Army as much at war against itself as against the enemy. The protagonist feels as though the opposing factions within his unit are engaged in a "battle for the possession of my soul." The Academy Award–winning film was highly praised for its realism, which starkly contrasted with the expressionism of Francis Ford Coppola's APOCALYPSE NOW (1979). Three years later, Stone wrote, directed, produced and acted in BORN ON THE FOURTH OF JULY (1989) a more

Oliver Stone, 1990. Courtesy AP/Wide World.

overtly antiwar and anti-macho piece about a gung-ho, All-American athlete who enlists in the Marines so he can serve a noble cause in Vietnam. Once over there, however, his world-view breaks down, and when he is wounded and partially paralyzed, he returns home alienated, alcoholic and embittered. Not until he accepts the shortcomings of his earlier beliefs can he pull himself from his abyss. By becoming an antiwar activist, he re-acquires his redeeming sense of commitment to a noble cause. The film is based on the life of Ron Kovic.

Other Cold War–related films include *Salvador* (1986) about an American photo-journalist in Central America, and *JFK* (1991), a revisionist account of the Kennedy assassination centering on the investigations of New Orleans district attorney Jim Garrison. *Wall Street* (1991) attacks the greed and unscrupulous behavior in the stock market during the Reagan era. *The Doors* (1991) documents singer Jim Morrison and his ROCK AND ROLL band of the 1960s. In 1995 Stone released *Nixon,* his portrait of the disgraced president, starring Anthony Hopkins.

For additional reading, see Kagan's *The Cinema of Oliver Stone*

Storm Center   A 1956 FILM DRAMA starring Bette Davis, Brian Keith and Kim Hunter, written and directed by Daniel Taradash. The film tells the story of a feisty small-town librarian (Davis) who refuses to remove a copy of *The Communist Dream* after the local city council bans it from the shelves. The film makes clear that the librarian is a civil libertarian but is neither a radical nor a communist. She becomes branded "a danger to the community" and is shunned for insisting that, although the book is preposterous, it is nonetheless influential and should, like *Mein Kampf*, be available to readers. Her antagonists tend to be not only anti-communist but also anti-intellectual, associating culture with "pinkos." After her opponents denounce the librarian for her membership in World War II–era communist-front groups, she is fired. Eventually a child burns down the entire library.

Storm Center, along with Charles CHAPLIN's British-made A KING IN NEW YORK (1957), was one of the very few 1950s films to directly criticize the Red Scare and to excoriate the practices of censoring books, smearing intellectuals and persecuting liberals for pre–Cold War political activities. The film was written secretly and was made over five years of interrupted filming. It was not completed until after Senator Joseph McCarthy's fall from power.

For additional reading, see Sayre's *Running Time*.

Storm Warning

A 1951 FILM DRAMA starring Ronald REAGAN, Ginger Rogers, and Doris Day and directed by Daniel Fuchs. The story centers on a New York model (Rogers) who visits her younger sister (Day) in the South and discovers that her brother-in-law is a member of the Ku Klux Klan who has committed a murder. District Attorney Rainer (Reagan) encourages knowledgeable citizens to testify against the murderer, but they refuse to cooperate and discourage Rainer from identifying prominent members of the community who are secretly Klan members. Rainer, however, responds that he stands for "law and order" (the title of an earlier FILM WESTERN in which Reagan had recently starred). Eventually Rogers testifies against her brother-in-law, and the cause of justice is served. However, her delay prevents Rainer from protecting her and enables the Klan to brutalize her and kill her pregnant sister.

Storm Warning alludes directly to the controversial hearings into the film industry then being conducted by the HOUSE COMMITTEE ON UN-AMERICAN ACTIVITIES (HUAC). As president of the Screen Actors Guild, Reagan supported these hearings. In the movie, the hero, like HUAC, insists that the guilty parties must be revealed. On the other hand, the villainous townspeople protect the Klan by invoking verbatim arguments used by the Committee for the First Amendment in support of the HOLLYWOOD TEN, who had refused to testify before HUAC. Thus the film implicitly endorses HUAC and vilifies the unfriendly witnesses who would not cooperate with its quest to identify members of the Communist Party working in Hollywood. It further suggests that loyalty to law and order supersedes family loyalty and that by delaying their testimony, citizens endanger themselves and their families as well as their communities.

For additional reading, see Rogin's *Ronald Reagan, the Movie*.

Strategic Air Command

A 1955 MILITARY FILM starring James Stewart, June Allyson, Frank Lovejoy and Barry Sullivan and directed by Anthony Mann. The plot centers on a baseball player (Stewart) who is recalled to active duty in the Air Force. The film showcases the Strategic Air Command (SAC), which always kept nuclear-armed planes in the air near communist targets, ready to respond in the event of a Soviet attack. Prominently featured are the newest air force jets of the 1950s. The highly patriotic film suggests that the U.S. nuclear fleet is in safe and responsible hands and that SAC's capacity for retaliation leaves the nation relatively secure from a nuclear attack.

Sullivan, Ed

A JOURNALIST and TELEVISION variety show host. Sullivan was writing the nationally syndicated newspaper column, "Little Old New York," when he became master of ceremonies for CBS's "The Toast of the Town" in 1948. One of the pioneering television variety shows, it was renamed "The Ed Sullivan Show" in 1955, aired continuously from 1948 to 1971, and held the Sunday 8:00 to 9:00 P.M. time-slot at CBS for 22 years. A television institution, "The Ed Sullivan Show" grew up with the Cold War. Though its content was largely apolitical, the show came to embody and, to some extent, define the tastes of middle America throughout the early and middle years of the Cold War. The tastes it reflected were remarkably diverse, ranging from such highbrow offerings as concert pianists, opera performers and the Bolshoi Ballet, to Broadway show tunes and Las Vegas entertainers, to the June Taylor Dancers, to ROCK AND ROLL, to lesser-known and sometimes eccentric acts. This range of tastes notwithstanding, Sullivan had his limits. For one thing, sexuality was to be restrained. On the show's most famous episode, in 1956, Sullivan had the camera black out Elvis Presley from the waist down rather than show the singer's gyrating hips. Despite the censorship, Sullivan demonstrated that he respected the tastes of teenagers and young adults simply by having Presley appear. Sullivan appealed again to youth when he presented the Beatles in their American television debut in 1964.

In addition to shunning explicit suggestions of sexuality, Sullivan would not tolerate communism. In 1963 Sullivan booked Bob DYLAN to appear, but when CBS officials forbade Dylan to sing "Talkin' John Birch Society Blues," a humorous song that ridicules the RED SCARE, Dylan refused to perform. Moreover, Sullivan praised RED CHANNELS, a private publication that provided lists used to blacklist television entertainers. Upon the booklet's first publication in 1950, Sullivan wrote in his syndicated column:

> With television going into its third big year . . . the entire industry is becoming increasingly aware of the necessity to plug all Commie propaganda loopholes. Networks and station heads, with a tremendous financial stake, want no part of Commies or pinkos. Sponsors, sensitive in the extreme to BLACKLISTING, want no part of Commies or their sympathizers. Advertising agencies held responsible by sponsors for correct exercise of discretion in programming, want no controversy of any kind. For that reason, [the] *Red Channels* listing of performers who, innocently or maliciously, are affiliated with Commie-front organizations will be a reference book in preparing any program.

Sullivan, himself, practiced a policy of excluding alleged communists and sympathizers from his show. When, after their appearance on his show, he discovered that tap dancer Paul Draper and harmonica player Larry Adler were "pro-Communist in sympathy," he gave a public apology.

For additional reading, see McNeil's *Total Television*.

Superman See ADVENTURES OF SUPERMAN, THE.

Sure Thing, The A 1949 POLITICAL NOVEL by Merle Miller. The story presents 36 hours in the life of a liberal State Department official who loses his job after an unjust investigation. He becomes subject to an FBI interrogation, press exposés, political denunciations and betrayal by his friends. Though criticized for its unconvincing characterization and awkward narrative technique, the Truman-era book won some praise for being "a cautionary tale which scarcely could have been published at a better time . . . it may . . . call attention to the prevalence of witch-hunters." (See also RED SCARE.)

Sweets, William A radio director and former national president of the Radio and Television Directors Guild who lost his job due to the RED SCARE. An employee of the Philip Lord agency, which produced radio dramas, Sweets was considered a top director; he was in charge of such popular radio programs as "Gangbusters" and "Counterspy." How-ever, in 1949 the Lord agency received letters from officials at General Foods and Pepsi Cola, sponsors of his shows, charging that Sweets was a communist who discriminated against anti-communists on the job. The Lord agency negotiated with the sponsors for three weeks before deciding that it had to choose between two of its major clients and Sweets. Sweets was allowed to remain with the shows until the season ended, but his right to name his own casting lists terminated immediately. He resigned from the presidency of the Radio Directors Guild after refusing on principle to sign an affidavit stating that he was not a communist. He later stated, "The only unions whose officers are required to sign the affidavit are those which desire the service of the National Labor Relations Board [the Radio and Television Directors Guild did not] . . . My reason for not signing such an affidavit was and is that once people start asking for affidavits, they sometimes don't know when to stop." (See also BLACKLISTING.)

For additional reading, see Cogley's *Report on Blacklisting* vol. 2.

Tail Gunner Joe   A 1977 made-for-television FILM DRAMA starring Burgess Meredith, John Forsythe, Patricia Neal, Jean Stapleton, and Heather Menzies and directed by Jud Taylor. The story follows the rise and fall of Senator Joseph McCarthy, whose name became synonymous with the 1950s RED SCARE. Meredith won an Emmy for his performance.

Telefon   A 1977 SPY FILM starring Charles Bronson, Lee Remick, Donald Pleasence and Patrick Magee and directed by Don Siegel, based on the novel by Walter Wager. Made during the détente of the 1970s, the story centers on a Soviet agent who is ordered to wipe out a ring of hard-line Soviet officials who oppose reconciliation with the West. As in THE MANCHURIAN CANDIDATE (book 1959, film 1962), the plot features an act of mind control. Siegel also directed the original 1956 version of the science fiction film INVASION OF THE BODY SNATCHERS, which also deals with the capacity of one being to "take over" another.

television   The development of television overlapped with the development of the Cold War, and both influenced each other in important ways. The Cold War provided subject matter for the medium, and television shaped the way Americans perceived and responded to the Cold War. The first television broadcast occurred in 1927. In 1928 and 1931, NBC and CBS, respectively, established local stations in New York. Television technology advanced through the 1930s, most importantly via the development in 1937 of the coaxial cable, which allowed long-distance broadcasts and

networking. However, because the Depression made such a luxury item largely unaffordable during the 1930s, and because World War II diverted electronic supplies and other resources, televisions were not widespread and television broadcasts were sporadic until the war ended in 1945. CBS did resume live studio broadcasts in May 1944, when it presented the "CBS Television News" with Ned Calmer. And in August 1945, NBC broadcast the first network-produced, regularly scheduled show, a 15-minute Saturday night roundup entitled "NBC Television Newsreel." In 1946, NBC introduced "Radio City Matinee," an hour-long variety show that appeared on Monday, Wednesday and Friday afternoons—the first live daytime series since World War II. Also in 1946, CBS and the DuMont network introduced broadcasts of college and professional football. The year 1947 saw the introduction of children's programming as DuMont broadcast "The Small Fry Club" and NBC produced "Puppet Television Theater" starring "Buffalo" Bob Smith and his marionette, Howdy Doody. That year, the three networks pooled their personnel and equipment to televise the World Series between the New York Yankees and the Brooklyn Dodgers.

Postwar television programming shifted into a higher gear in 1948, as CBS and DuMont substantially increased their number of broadcasts and ABC returned to the air after a 15-month hiatus. Introduced in 1948 were such hits as Ted Mack's "Original Amateur Hour" (DuMont), "The Texaco Star Theater" (NBC) starring Milton Berle ("Mr. Television") and Ed SULLIVAN's "Toast of the Town" (CBS).

In 1948, DuMont introduced daytime programming between 10 A.M. and 3:30 P.M. Bud Collyer hosted the first television game show, "Winner Take All" (CBS); CBS also introduced a dramatic anthology, "Studio One," and "Arthur Godfrey's Talent Scouts," a showcase of amateur performances, which became a top-rated program; and the Philadelphia Eagles defeated the Chicago Cardinals on live TV as ABC televised the NFL championship game. Between 1948 and 1952, when the last major American city was connected to a coaxial cable hookup, television ownership and programming mushroomed.

In 1950, there were some 3.1 million television sets in the United States; by 1955, the number of televisions had increased tenfold to 32 million. By 1953, half of all U.S. families owned a television set. In the summer of 1948, networks offered no morning, minimal afternoon, and only one to three hours of evening programming on weekday evenings (less on weekends). By fall 1952, the networks were presenting an average of two hours of morning programming, three hours on weekday afternoons, five hours on weekend afternoons, three hours on weekday evenings and four hours on weekend evenings. By fall 1955, mornings were about half filled with network programming, and afternoons were almost entirely filled from 1 P.M. to 7 P.M., with only about an hour or two reserved for local programming. And except for the fading DuMont network, which left the air in 1956, evenings were essentially filled with network shows from 7:30 to 10:30.

The development of television thus coincided with that of the Cold War. In 1947, President Truman articulated the Truman Doctrine, which was designed to contain communism; Eastern European communists took control in Poland, Rumania and Bulgaria; and the HOUSE COMMITTEE ON UN-AMERICAN ACTIVITIES (HUAC) opened its investigation of communist influences in the entertainment industry and tried to interrogate the "unfriendly witnesses" known as the HOLLYWOOD TEN. Both television and the Cold War blossomed in 1948: Much of Eastern Europe, including Czechoslovakia and Hungary, fell under communist rule that year; Chinese communists under Mao Zedong took complete control of Manchuria; the Berlin Airlift began; Truman upset Dewey in the presidential election; and Whittaker Chambers accused Alger Hiss of spying for the Soviets. By the end of 1952, NATO had been in existence for three years; the domestic RED SCARE was in full swing; the Rosenbergs had been convicted of stealing atomic secrets; the Chinese communists were in full control of the Chinese mainland; the Korean War was already two years old; Eisenhower had been elected president; the Soviet Union had exploded its first atomic device; and the United States had detonated its first hydrogen bomb.

Though the Cold War would have evolved even without television, nonetheless the impact of television on Cold War culture was profound. Certainly, television had an enormous ability to shape the public's picture of political reality. At almost any other time in the country's history, Americans would have learned about the state of their world primarily through words: talk among colleagues and neighbors, speeches from local officials, newspaper articles, magazine stories, books and eventually radio broadcasts. Throughout the Cold War, however, Americans increasingly learned about the international conflict from moving images. As Edward R. MURROW said in the first episode of his landmark television series, SEE IT NOW (CBS, 1951–58), "We are impressed by a medium through which a man sitting in his living room has been able for the first time to look at two oceans at once." By 1959, television had become the most relied-upon source of news in the country. In superseding newspapers, radio and magazines as the public's major source of news, television changed the medium through which Americans constructed their views of reality, including their personal pictures of the Cold War. Through television, Americans experienced the Cold War more visually and less verbally than they would have at any other point in history. They also got a more controlled, less diverse picture of events; after all, there were only three networks.

The significance of the change in the citizenry's preferred medium has not been deeply explored. We might compare it to the differences in the way we would understand the Napoleonic Wars if we first rendered an account of them through written histories, speeches, newspaper descriptions, legal documents and narratives, and then represented them solely through visual media: oil paintings, water colors, engravings, drawings, maps and sketches. Both representations of the reality of the Napoleonic Wars could claim validity, and each would possess its own relative strengths and weaknesses. Images can be more concrete than words. They can render experience more graphically, more immediately and often more viscerally. Television, a primarily visual medium, thus lends itself especially well to evoking emotional responses. However, television does not invite the kind of studied, close scrutiny that the written word permits. For instance, viewers watching Cold War developments on television could not refer back to an earlier point in the report to compare it against information that appeared later, or the day before. (Neither could listeners who received most of their news through spoken words: radio, speeches and word of mouth.) The written word thus offers some advantages over television: It is referable, and it encourages readers and writers to deal with abstract concepts and issues with greater subtlety and in greater depth.

However, we should resist the temptations to over-glamorize writing and demonize television. If the written word can more readily facilitate abstract concepts and in-depth explorations, it can also appeal strongly to superficial emotions. The "yellow journalism" that fueled the Spanish-American War, for example, was as shallow, simplistic and lurid as the worst of Cold War–era television reporting; in fact, much of the jingoist newspaper journalism then *and* during the Cold War was considerably more sensational, less objective and less reliable than most Cold War TV news broadcasts. So without making a claim for the superiority of words over images, or vice versa, we should nonetheless be aware that by the mid-1950s, most American citizens were receiving their information and forming their views of "the struggle against Communism" through video images, a fundamentally different medium than Americans had ever employed before.

If the television medium was less well suited than writing for deep scrutiny of facts and logical analysis of premises, it was better suited for conveying the passion and explosiveness that marked most Cold War events and issues.

For example, printed descriptions of Senator Joseph McCarthy's appearances on the Senate floor and quotations from his speeches generally fail to convey how emotionally out of control he could become. Television, however, directly presented his emotional outbursts, bullying style and snide comments. McCarthy's emotional display during the televised ARMY-MCCARTHY HEARINGS, in particular, contributed significantly to his rapid fall from power.

The television medium also projected visual icons that stood for larger, more abstract Cold War situations. On the one hand, these icons tended to render the Cold War in narrow and limited ways. On the other hand, they showed that political concepts were very real. For instance, the intense Cold War rivalry between the superpowers was caught exquisitely in the televised image of Nikita Khrushchev banging his shoe on a United Nations (UN) conference table proclaiming "We will bury you." The televised images both objectified and seemingly made irrefutable the communists' sinister intention to crush and enslave the American people. (However, the image may also have been misleading. Khrushchev was referring not to a Soviet nuclear victory, as was popularly supposed, but to the historical process that he believed would inevitably prove the superiority of the Soviet system. But the dramatic visual image seemed to say otherwise. Of course Khrushchev may also have intended the ambiguity.)

Likewise, the televised pictures of Adlai Stevenson during the Cuban Missile Crisis, leaning forward to declare to the Soviets that he was prepared to wait for an answer "until Hell freezes over" captured visually the tense resolve that culminated when a U.S. naval ship risked nuclear war by turning back a Soviet vessel carrying offensive missiles. Stevenson's adamant tone of voice communicated more than just his words. The video pictures of that showdown also provided a significant symbol of the state of the Cold War in late October 1962.

Other television images that defined key moments for millions of viewers include the tanks rumbling into Hungary in 1956 to suppress an anti-communist revolution; the erection and later the demolition of the Berlin Wall, perhaps the single most forceful symbol of the Cold War; the assassination of President Kennedy; a police officer in Saigon publicly executing a Viet Cong suspect; the many protest marches on Washington; President Nixon's dinner with Zhou En-lai and Mao Zedong; President Carter signing the Camp David Accords with Anwar Sadat and Menachem Begin; the Solidarity dock workers on strike in Poland; poorly armed Afghani rebels fighting against Soviets armed with high-tech weapons; and a single Chinese man facing down a line of tanks in Tiananmen Square. These and other televised images gave the Cold War a unique sense of immediacy, eloquently depicting particular moments in Cold War struggles.

Of course, such depictions not only described historical moments, they also defined them, by establishing the framework through which Americans viewed events. In this respect, television's relationship with the Cold War was interactive. Television selected, edited and interpreted what it presented, and in so doing it played a strong role in setting the national agenda and shaping the terms of debate about Cold War policies.

Television influenced the Cold War in other ways too. The NIXON–KENNEDY DEBATES helped provide the small margin of victory for the more telegenic Kennedy in the 1960 presidential election. Televised pictures of North Vietnamese soldiers occupying the U.S. embassy in Saigon during the 1968 Tet Offensive led many to doubt government claims that there was "a light at the end of the tunnel" and to question the wisdom of pursuing the Vietnam War. (Aware of how television coverage of the Vietnam War undermined popular support for the war, President Bush severely restricted press coverage of the Panama invasion and the Persian Gulf War.) Moreover, after Tet, such respected news commentators as Walter CRONKITE and Eric SEVAREID changed their coverage and editorial commentary in ways that more aggressively challenged official government accounts. This marked the beginning of a shift in television news from coverage that typically accepted and promoted government foreign policy to more aggressive coverage that confronted government officials over foreign and domestic policies, at least to some extent.

Sometimes televised coverage of events made the press and public more willing to support government policies. Popular enthusiasm for space exploration, and the public's consequent willingness to allocate funds for the military space race, was fueled by televised pictures of spectacular rocket launches and views of Earth from outer space, as well as by the thrill of televised broadcasts from the Mercury missions, in which the first Americans left the earth's atmosphere and entered outer space. (Soviet cosmonaut Yuri Gagarin was actually the first person in outer space, on April 8, 1961, but his flight was not televised.) Later, American television audiences watched closely as the Apollo flights orbited and then landed on the moon and as Neil Armstrong became the first human to set foot on the moon.

Gaining influence over the images broadcast by television networks thus became an important aspect of the Cold War. Communist leaders of other countries rarely received opportunities to address American audiences on U.S. television and to explain their perception of world events. When they did in the 1950s, their statements were typically followed by a panel of JOURNALISTS and/or politicians with strong anti-communist credentials. This occurred, for instance, when Murrow interviewed the communist Chinese foreign minister, Zhou En-lai, and Yugoslavia's Marshal Tito. When CBS's FACE THE NATION interviewed Soviet premier Khrushchev in 1957, in an hour-long show without benefit of such a panel, the network was widely criticized: The commander of the Catholic War Veterans demanded that CBS cancel the program, and even President Eisenhower attacked the show, dismissing it as a stunt to improve the network's financial standing. Unlike Saddam Hussein before the 1991 Persian Gulf War, "enemy" leaders—of North Korea, East Germany, North Vietnam, Cuba and Nicaragua—did not have direct access to the American people. Of course, throughout the entire course of history, foreign leaders have rarely been granted such access, and Western leaders were routinely denied access to the government-sponsored television networks in communist countries. The point is that the American picture of communism was presented exclusively by non-communists and often by anti-communists. Conversely, the Soviet, Chinese and

Eastern European perception of Western capitalism was shaped almost exclusively by anti-capitalist non-Westerners. However, the United States did wage an international battle over video images by broadcasting American programming and propaganda to hostile countries. The Television Marti broadcasts to Cuba was a controversial example. (East Germans also received West German TV broadcasts. And generally, U.S. culture was better able to penetrate the communist countries, especially at the end of the Cold War.)

Domestically, the anti-communists succeeded almost completely in keeping even remotely pro-communist or pro-socialist sentiments off the air. They were able either to use the powerful medium to their advantage or to render it neutral by filling it with programs that had little or no social or political content but that implicitly reaffirmed such traditional pro-capitalist values: hard work, private ownership, free trade, maintaining the status quo, and law and order. No regularly scheduled situation comedy, dramatic series, soap opera, Western, spy story, game show or other television format ever seriously presented positions from a communist or socialist agenda: that everyone is entitled to a job, that the nation's resources should be collectively shared, that industry should be nationalized, that the poor are significantly oppressed by the rich or that universal health care is a human right. Before the 1970s, non-news television programming universally refused to acknowledge racial discrimination in the United States, partly because communists routinely accused the United States of being a racist society. Supposedly, if a show suggested that U.S. racism did in fact exist, then that show was validating the communist charge and thereby strengthening the communist cause. Throughout the 1950s and 1960s, FBI director J. Edgar Hoover treated the civil rights movement largely as communist agitation, and FBI agents maintained extensive files and conducted widespread surveillance on civil rights leaders and activists; so writers' and producers' fears about addressing domestic racism were not far-fetched.

Of course, while suspected "Communist influences" were being excluded from American television, communist television excluded a pro-Western perspective. For example, communist countries did not typically air shows illustrating the benefits of entrepreneurial enterprises, celebrating individuals who work hard for private gain or suggesting the desirability of choosing a private doctor. In both communist and capitalist countries, the prevailing ideologies significantly influenced television programming.

From at least 1950, when RED CHANNELS appeared as an unofficial blacklist, through the end of the Cold War, communists, communist sympathizers and people with strong left-wing points of view were essentially eliminated from local and network television including such respected news programs as MEET THE PRESS (NBC, 1947–present), "Washington Week in Review" (PBS, 1967–present), "The McLaughlin Group" (PBS, 1982–present), "The MacNeil-Lehrer News Hour" (PBS, 1983–present) and "Face the Nation" (CBS, 1954–63). For example, during the escalation of the Vietnam War in the middle 1960s pacifists rarely received forums on network television; nor did those advocating unilateral nuclear disarmament or opposing U.S. involvement in Korea, Laos or the Philippines. During the Red Score, to give air time to opponents of the hard line

against worldwide communism, or even to opponents of the Red Scare, would have been considered unpatriotic at best and perhaps even treasonable.

When network employees did not censor themselves, the government and/or network officials often applied pressure. In 1954 Edward R. Murrow broadcast a critical portrait of McCarthy on his news show, "See It Now." CBS president Frank Stanton told "See It Now's" producer Fred Friendly, "You may have cost us the network" after the exposé generated substantial political pressure in Washington to revoke the network's license. Likewise, according to Stephen J. Whitfield in The Culture of the Cold War, open forum programs such as ABC's AMERICA'S TOWN MEETING (ABC, 1948–49, 1952) and NBC's "American Forum of the Air" (NBC, 1950–57) were taken off the air in order to deny opportunities for left-wing non-communists to appear before the public. Even in the 1970s and 1980s, such an articulate, well-credentialed spokesman for the left as Noam Chomsky rarely received opportunities to provide his point of view on current events programs. By contrast, such right-wing figures as William F. BUCKLEY Jr. and Pat Buchanan, and such fervently anti-communist religious figures as Bishop Fulton SHEEN, Reverend Billy GRAHAM and Jerry FALWELL had easy access to the airwaves throughout the Cold War.

During the late 1960s, antiwar leaders realized the importance of gaining access to television so that their protest message would be heard. Most of these activists were in their twenties or early thirties, had grown up with television and understood the medium more readily than the generation that had grown up before World War II. Some war protesters created "media events"—a protest march or creative demonstration that the news media would be compelled to cover. The protesters realized the importance of visual presentation, so they hit on such strategies as guerrilla theater in which, for example, some participants might cover themselves in make-believe blood and lie down on the floor of a shopping mall, while others dressed in military apparel shot them with toy M-16 rifles. Violent protest also videotaped well. Other protest groups followed suit, such as international terrorists, who would highjack airplanes in order to receive television exposure for their cause. By the end of the Cold War several terrorist groups had become quite sophisticated in their management of the medium.

Political outsiders, of course, were not the only ones who deliberately manipulated television. Presidential candidates had long ago learned to select a theme for their campaign—Kennedy's New Frontier or Johnson's Great Society referred back to Roosevelt's New Deal and Truman's Fair Deal—but now they learned to present that theme through televised images. Nixon's 1968 Law and Order campaign was especially effective for its time, though the Reagan administration was the most adept in history at using the television medium to present its view of events. Reagan's 1984 Morning in America reelection advertising campaign made effective use of positive advertising, such as by showing a healthy young blonde woman bicycling on a sunny day, feeling really good about life in Reagan's America.

Negative campaigning was also a key televisual strategy. This type of approach had its first big moment in 1964 when supporters of President Johnson ran an ad showing a little girl holding a flower in a meadow, as a nuclear bomb exploded in the background, under the warlike words of Johnson's opponent, Barry Goldwater. Another visually effective piece of negative television advertising came in 1988, when supporters of George Bush aired pictures of his opponent, Michael Dukakis, driving a tank in circles and looking idiotic. Bush supporters also ran a negative ad that made Governor Dukakis appear to be personally responsible for paroling Willie Horton, a black convicted rapist who repeated his crime after his release. This ad was accused of inflaming racial divisions within the country by appealing to whites' fears about violent crimes committed by African Americans.

By the 1980s, politicians in both parties paid media consultants to help them put the proper "spin" on stories reported by the media. For instance, Michael Deaver, Reagan's media consultant, quite candidly admitted that he did not care how negative the words in a story were so long as the visual images were positive. So he would provide the press with visually strong images designed to show up well on television and flatter the president. The press, which otherwise might not have access to such telegenic images, would often run Deaver's material with their spoken reports. Deaver believed that viewers responded far more to the images than to the words, so that even if the spoken report was critical, the overall effect remained positive.

Political campaigns in the late 1980s and 1990s were widely criticized for negative campaigning and for being dominated by television "sound-bites," short sequences that evoked emotions but actually contained little or no intellectual content. Media critics lamented the way media consultants had apparently begun to dominate the political process, using techniques acquired from years of television advertising and programming. The epitome of the integration of television culture and political culture came in the 1991 Gulf War, which was presented to the American public almost as though it were a made-for-TV docu-drama.

Until the 1970s, Red Scare-induced fears of being blacklisted discouraged writers and producers from addressing social issues. The most innocent or well-intended lines could be twisted to reveal a secret communist message. For instance, when Ginger Rogers' mother appeared before HUAC in 1947 as a "friendly witness" and self-proclaimed expert in detecting hidden communist messages, she pointed to communist influence in this exchange from the film *Tender Comrade*: "Share and share alike—isn't that right?" Another character nods in agreement and adds, "Democracy." In an environment where sharing was branded in Congress as a communist belief, people in the media found it safer to avoid anything that might even hint at controversy. Thus the fear of BLACKLISTING, as well as sponsors' fear of boycotts, contributed to the predominance of apolitical, noncontroversial programming on pre-1970s, U.S. network television.

Sometimes Cold War influences on entertainment programming were obvious and direct, such as in the episode on FATHER KNOWS BEST (CBS/NBC/ABC, 1954–63) where the children pretended to live under a dictatorship for a day, or in the humorous disparity in beliefs between Archie Bunker and his daughter and son-in-law in ALL IN THE FAMILY (CBS, 1971–83). Likewise, in spy stories and action/adventure shows, the villains were sometimes Soviet or communist

agents, while the hero worked on behalf of U.S. interests, frequently in conjunction with the U.S. government. For instance, the "bionic" SIX MILLION DOLLAR MAN (ABC, 1973–78), a product of government scientists, helped out the government on special missions. The MISSION IMPOSSIBLE (CBS, 1966–73) team worked secretly for a government agency whose secretary would disavow knowledge of the team's existence as it sought to foil the plans of communist dictatorships in Third World countries. Even the hero of THE ADVENTURES OF SUPERMAN (syndicated, 1951–57) committed himself to defending "Truth, Justice, and the American way." With rare exceptions, such as in PBS's productions of John LE CARRÉ's spy novels or some episodes of I SPY (NBC, 1965–68), American television shows did not question the morality of the spies' missions or the appropriateness of performing illegal covert actions on behalf of their well-intended government. Television spy and adventure shows rarely considered the possibility that the agent's assignment might have been issued for corrupt or politically motivated reasons, instead of for the legitimate needs of foreign policy and national security. Such themes and possibilities were explored more fully in FILM and LITERATURE. Indeed, during the height of the Red Scare, films and television shows could fall into trouble for even mild criticism of political leaders, on the grounds that a cynical depiction of elected officials would undermine the public's faith in democracy and thereby assist the communist cause. Such was the argument used in 1947 to prohibit the overseas release of the film comedy THE SENATOR WAS INDISCREET.

Science fiction shows and Westerns sometimes explored Cold War antagonisms in settings from the future or the past. For example, STAR TREK's (NBC, 1966–69) Federation, served by the starship *Enterprise*, was associated with NATO, while the enemy "evil empires" suggested the Warsaw Pact and other communist military forces. As the symbolic representatives of the United States, Captain Kirk and his crew were portrayed as spreading peace, order, reason, fairness and equality to realms oppressed by tyranny. Likewise, Western heroes like GUNSMOKE's Matt Dillon (CBS, 1955–75), Wyatt Earp, Jim Bowie or the Cartwright family on "Bonanza" (NBC, 1959–73) all stood tall against those who would violate the law, grab power and wealth for themselves, and upset the established social order, just as the United States was seen as standing tall against the expansion of a communist empire that advocated worldwide revolution and used its Red Army to seize power and territory for itself.

TV drama protagonists embodied the same "American" traits with which the United States identified itself during the Cold War. First, the heroes were often fully committed to their cause. Even when dragged reluctantly into a fight, they stood on the side of goodness. They were typically honest, compassionate, confident in their prowess and committed to fair play. To defeat their enemies, they relied on a combination of physical strength, sexual attraction, technological innovation and quick-wittedness—and occasionally on their accumulated knowledge and good education. Occasionally, heroines possessed the same array of traits, though they were almost always subordinate to men. By contrast, villains were likely to be devious, deceptive, unreliable, opportunistic, cold-blooded and crude, though they could sometimes be elegant. In the Cold War, the U.S.S.R. relied on bigger warheads, more tanks, and greater raw destructive power, while the United States relied on its weapons' superior accuracy, diversity and mobility. Similarly, television villains were often better endowed with muscles than with brains; they were not as quick, accurate or scrappy as the hero.

Situation comedies, family dramas, day and nightime soap operas, and game shows played a more subtle role in Cold War culture. With the exception of shows like Jackie Gleason's "The Honeymooners" (CBS, 1952–57) and the radio carry-over "Amos 'n' Andy" (CBS, 1951–53), most pre-1972 sitcoms and family dramas took place in relatively affluent middle-class settings. Then Norman LEAR introduced "Sanford and Son" (NBC, 1972–77), which was set in the Los Angeles ghetto. Even after the 1970s, the vast majority of shows took place in American suburbs or affluent city neighborhoods, with the protagonists either owning their own homes or living in upscale apartments. These American families rarely worried about being unemployed, being able to secure daily food and shelter, being able to educate their children well, or having a comfortable standard of living. Thus such popular shows as LEAVE IT TO BEAVER (CBS/ABC, 1957–63), "The Adventures of Ozzie and Harriet" (ABC, 1952–66), "The Dick van Dyke Show" (CBS, 1961–66), "The Mary Tyler Moore Show" (CBS, 1970–77), "The Bob Newhart Show" (CBS, 1972–78), "Maude" (CBS, 1972–78), "Dallas" (CBS, 1978–91), "Dynasty" (ABC, 1981–89) and even "Twin Peaks" (ABC, 1990–91) repeatedly communicated that America was affluent, populated mainly by middle-class or rich men and women.

Of course, most Americans did belong to the middle class during the Cold War, so the representation had legitimacy. But even so, television characters tended to be better dressed, more affluent and more financially secure than actual middle-class Americans, let alone poor or working-class people. Consequently, television's aggregate portrayal of the United States allowed Americans to see themselves as better off than citizens of communist countries who, when depicted at all, were shown to be considerably less affluent and comfortable. (This portrayal powerfully affected residents of Eastern and Western Europe as well.) Likewise, game shows, with their abundant prizes of expensive consumer goods and endless selections from the *Spiegel Catalogue,* projected an image of prosperity that contrasted sharply with the media portrayal of communist countries' impoverishment. The makers of these shows were not consciously producing Cold War propaganda. They simply believed that viewers were more attracted to affluence than to poverty, and that audiences found stories of struggle and suffering less than entertaining. Likewise, the popularity overseas of American film and television may be largely attributable to their unabashed presentation of wealth and material abundance. Perhaps television's most profound effect on Cold War culture, at home and abroad, was the way it reinforced Americans' general belief that American life was much nicer than any other kind of life could possibly be. (See also RELIGIOUS TELEVISION PROGRAMMING; TELEVISION ADVENTURE HEROES; TELEVISION DOCU-DRAMAS OR MINI-SERIES; TELEVISION DOCUMENTARIES; TELEVISION DRAMAS; TELEVISION MILITARY DRAMAS; TELEVISION NEWS; TELEVISION

PERFORMERS; TELEVISION QUIZ SHOWS; TELEVISION SATIRE; TELEVISION SCIENCE FICTION SHOWS; TELEVISION SHOWS FOR CHILDREN; TELEVISION SITUATION COMEDIES; TELEVISION SPY SHOWS; TELEVISION TALK OR DEBATE SHOWS; TELEVISION WESTERNS.)

For additional reading, see Whitfield's *The Culture of the Cold War;* Spigel's *Make Room for TV;* Castleman and Podrazik's *The TV Schedule Book;* McNeil's *Total Television.*

television adventure heroes   Television adventure heroes appear mainly in two types of shows, TELEVISION SPY SHOWS and TELEVISION SCIENCE FICTION. With some exceptions—THE BIONIC WOMAN (ABC/NBC, 1976–78), THE GIRL FROM U.N.C.L.E. (NBC, 1966–67), CODE NAME: FOXFIRE (NBC, 1985), WONDER WOMAN (ABC/CBS, 1976–79), SCARECROW AND MRS. KING (CBS, 1983–87) and THE AVENGERS (ABC, 1966–69)—television adventure heroes were men. Sometimes they were loners unwillingly dragged into patriotic service who performed well once involved (like Rick in the 1942 film *Casablanca*). Alternatively, they were heroes actively committed to the cause of freedom and democracy. Reluctant heroes included the A-Team (NBC, 1983–87); Stringfellow Hawke from AIRWOLF (CBS/cable, 1984–88); Alexander Mundy from IT TAKES A THIEF (ABC, 1968–70); and the heroines in "Code Name: Foxfire." More often, heroes were firmly committed to their causes, so much so that their values were sometimes openly declared. For example, the introduction to each episode of THE ADVENTURES OF SUPERMAN (syndicated, 1951–57) explained that the hero fought for "Truth, Justice, and the American Way." STAR TREK's (NBC, 1966–69) Captain Kirk likewise announced at the outset of each show his humanistic mission, which was based on such traditional American values as exploration, conquest of the unknown and repudiation of tyranny.

The hero's commitment to his cause was also apparent in THE CRUSADER (CBS, 1955–56), whose hero, Matt Anders, dedicated his life to helping people oppressed by communism because his mother had died in a communist-run concentration camp. FBI spy Herbert PHILBRICK was clearly motivated by his beliefs in I LED THREE LIVES (syndicated, 1953–56), as was FBI inspector Lewis Erskine in "The F.B.I." These shows tended to project an explicitly anti-communist message. In other shows, the "rightness" of the cause was simply taken for granted, and the shows focused on the action that grew from dangerous situations, which itself implied some external threat to American interests. Often the importance of the cause justified the hero's use of violence and his circumvention of the law.

Superheroes offered an even greater degree of wish fulfillment than heroes, because they represented invincible protectors. As long as Superman or Wonder Woman were around, evil could not possibly thrive. Heroes were portrayed as unwilling to compromise or accept defeat where national security was concerned.

Different heroes manifested different qualities, for defeating enemy agents required a variety of skills. Brute strength was displayed by such heroes and superheroes as Mr. T from "The A-Team," Superman, Wonder Woman, The Bionic Woman, THE SIX MILLION DOLLAR MAN (ABC, 1973–78) and Willie Armitage from MISSION IMPOSSIBLE (CBS, 1966–73). Guile and cunning were the province of Alexander Mundy, Steed from "The Avengers" and the protagonist of

"The Adventures of Fu Manchu" (syndicated, 1956). James BOND imitations had to be sexy, suave, witty and sophisticated, like James West from "The Wild, Wild West" (CBS, 1965–69), Napoleon Solo and Illya Kuryakin from THE MAN FROM U.N.C.L.E. (NBC, 1964–68) and COVER UP's Mac Harper (CBS, 1984–85). GET SMART (NBC/CBS, 1965–70) spoofed all of these characteristics through its protagonist, the bumbling super-agent Maxwell Smart, who nevertheless attempted a suave and sexy persona.

Generational differences in the 1960s and 1970s led to new social attitudes about authority and personal expression. Consequently, television heroes gradually evolved from the strait-laced, middle-class respectability found in FBI inspector Lewis Erskine, "Mission Impossible" team-leader James Phelps and even Captain Kirk, to more colorful, more rambunctious heroes who, like the protagonists of I SPY (NBC, 1965–68), "It Takes a Thief" and MAX HEADROOM (ABC, 1986–87), questioned or were openly cynical about the agencies they served.

television docu-dramas or mini-series Television shows that re-created moments from the Cold War or presented how things might become. A notable re-creation was ABC's THE MISSILES OF OCTOBER (1974), which reenacted the 1962 Cuban Missile Crisis. Many other docu-dramas reenacted other aspects of President Kennedy's life, including a 1983 mini-series aired by NBC. ABC's THE DAY AFTER (1983) and AMERIKA (1987) presented liberal and conservative worst-case scenarios of how things might become. *The Day After,* which is often compared to the BBC production THE WAR GAME (1966), presented the aftermath of a nuclear exchange that targeted Lawrence, Kansas, while *Amerika* imagined life in an America ruled by communists who were able to take over because pacifists surrendered rather than fight. *Amerika* was one of many anti-communist pseudo-documentaries. THE DAY MIAMI DIED was one of the earliest pseudo-documentaries of the 1950s in which local television stations enacted life in their city under communist rule.

Other famous TV docu-dramas include *When Hell Was in Session* (1979), about Commander Jeremiah Denton, USN, an American POW in Vietnam; *Kent State* (1981), about the killing of student war protesters and bystanders by the Ohio National Guard in 1970; *The Final Days* (1989), about the Watergate scandal and Nixon's resignation from the presidency; *Day One* (1989) about The Manhattan Project, and *Challenger* (1990), about the space shuttle that exploded shortly after take-off.

television documentaries and special reports Throughout the Cold War, the networks aired a number of special news reports on topics of particular interest. During the 1950s, the networks produced virtually all of the documentaries aired on American television. Thus the picture of the Cold War presented to American viewers was shaped by the beliefs and perceptions of television journalists and of the networks' upper management. Network-produced shows accounted for the bulk of television special reports throughout the Cold War. However, after independent producer David WOLPER successfully syndicated *The Race for Space* (1960), opportunities for independently produced documentaries began to appear, bringing with them new view-

points and, to some extent, new visual styles. Frederick Wiseman was another notable independent documentary filmmaker whose televised FILM DOCUMENTARIES sometimes addressed Cold War issues. Public television also offered somewhat more room for alternative views and styles.

Among the Cold War–related topics covered in television documentaries and special reports were nuclear warfare; the arms race and military defense; the atomic bombing of Hiroshima; China; the Soviet Union; Cuba; insurgency in the Third World; the Korean War; the Berlin and Cuban Missile Crises; the space race; covert activities by U.S. and foreign intelligence organizations; communism; and the Vietnam War. (See VIETNAM WAR TELEVISION DOCUMENTARIES.)

Documentaries and special reports dealing with nuclear warfare included AIR POWER (1956–58), which became the first regularly scheduled documentary series to explore the ramifications of nuclear warfare. Earlier shows that had presented individual special features about nuclear warfare included the regularly scheduled VISIT WITH THE ARMED FORCES (DuMont, 1950–51); *Three Two One Zero* (NBC, 1954); *Atomic Bomb Blast* and *Atomic Bomb Results* (CBS, 1955), which featured live coverage and follow-up reporting about a nuclear test in Nevada; and *CONELRAD Test* (CBS, 1956) and *Survival Street* (NBC, 1956), about civil defense tests and simulated nuclear strikes on U.S. cities. Later shows about nuclear issues include *This Is Defense* (CBS, 1957); *A Day Called X* (CBS, 1957), which showed Portland, Oregon, responding to a simulated nuclear attack; *Guided Missile* (CBS, 1957); a special episode of Edward R. MURROW's SEE IT NOW entitled *Radiation and Fallout* (CBS, 1958); *Countdown* (CBS, 1958); *Biography of a Missile* (CBS, 1959); *The Year of the Polaris* (CBS, 1960), about Polaris intermediate ballistic missiles and the submarine fleet that carried them; *The Missile Race* (NBC, 1960); *Inside Argonne* (ABC, 1960), about the Argonne National Laboratory, which conducts nuclear research; *The Balance of Terror* (CBS, 1961), a two-part program about the possible aftermath of a nuclear war, and its sequel, *Can We Disarm: Decision at Geneva.*

Minuteman! (CBS, 1961) described the development of the first U.S. solid-fuel intercontinental ballistic missile (ICBM). *Decision to Test* (NBC, 1962) reported on President Kennedy's resumption of nuclear testing during the Berlin crisis. In 1962, CBS's *The Fighting E* and *The President Looks at Our Nuclear Navy* described the nuclear-powered aircraft carrier *Enterprise* and covered Kennedy's inspection of it during maneuvers. *SAC: Aloft and Below* (CBS, 1963) covered the Strategic Air Command's fail-safe policies and its underground missile arsenal. *The Death of the Thresher* (ABC) and *The Loss of the Thresher* (NBC) reported on the U.S. Polaris nuclear submarine that was lost at sea in 1963; *The Meaning of Moscow* (NBC, 1963) and *The Test Ban Treaty* (CBS, 1963) covered progress on the treaty that Kennedy considered his greatest accomplishment in office. *The Missilemen* (ABC, 1964) showed rare footage of test failures as it surveyed the first 10 years of the missile age and followed a Minuteman missile control officer on his daily tasks. *Lost and Found* (CBS, 1966) documented the rescue of a hydrogen bomb that had been lost when a B-52 crashed in Spain. FOOTNOTES ON THE ATOMIC AGE (NBC, 1969) drew on comparisons to the film satire DR. STRANGELOVE, (1964) pointing out some of the less well-known dangers of nuclear testing and nuclear policy. *SAC Make-Believe Nuclear War: Report on Operation Global Shield* (NBC, 1979) described the biggest simulated war since the 1950s (it was an Armed Forces exercise). *Radioactive Fallout* (NBC, 1979) investigated the fates of people who were exposed to radiation as a result of nuclear testing. In 1985, CNN presented *Avoiding Nuclear War*, a roundtable discussion with former presidents Jimmy Carter and Gerald Ford, national security adviser Robert McFarlane and Soviet ambassador Anatoly Dobrynin.

The BBC produced significant shows on the topic of nuclear war, shown in the United States in art-house theaters or on network or public television. THE WAR GAME (1966) was a docu-drama that depicted the horrible deaths and injuries that would ensue from a nuclear strike against a civilian population. Although the film won an Academy Award for best documentary and was otherwise available for limited screening in England and the United States, the BBC declined to broadcast it because it was "too horrifying" and unsuitable for family viewing. The BBC also produced RUMOURS OF WAR (1972), about the men responsible for firing the Minuteman Missiles and TO DIE, TO LIVE (1976), based on DEATH IN LIFE, Dr. Robert Jay Lifton's 1962 study of the survivors' psychological responses to the atomic bombing of Hiroshima.

One of the earliest documentaries about the first atomic bombing of a civilian population center was *Hiroshima* (CBS, 1958). *Hiroshima—20 Years After* (ABC, 1965) commemorated the anniversary of that event. That year Fred FREED produced one of his many "NBC White Papers," THE DECISION TO DROP THE BOMB, followed by a 1966 sequel, COUNTDOWN TO ZERO. National Educational Television (NET) also produced a documentary about the atomic bombing of Japan, HIROSHIMA–NAGASAKI (1970), which included newly released film footage shot by a Japanese crew that came to Hiroshima hours after the explosion. However, *Hiroshima–Nagasaki* was broadcast only once and was not allowed to be shown again, even in private screenings or closed-circuit presentations to university classrooms.

The broader topics of national defense and the arms race were covered in documentaries as well, including *The American Fighting Man: Korea Plus Ten* (NBC, 1960), about the condition of U.S. armed forces; *Arms and the State* (NBC, 1962); *Norstad of NATO: War or Peace* (CBS, 1962), about NATO's supreme commander, General Lauris Norstad; and *The Big Bomber Battle* (ABC, 1963), about the debate over replacing manned bombers with guided missiles. In 1963 Senators Goldwater, Byrd, Dirksen and Fulbright debated *The Nuclear Test Ban Treaty: Delusion or Promise* (ABC). That treaty was also the subject of many special reports. *NATO in Danger* (CBS, 1964) explained differences between the United States and France over an American proposal for a nuclear fleet, and *NATO: The Cracked Shield* (CBS, 1966) explored France's military disaffiliation from NATO. *Anatomy of Defense* (NBC, 1966) and *The ABM* (CBS, 1969) described Nixon's proposed antiballistic missile system (which was later banned in the 1972 U.S.–Soviet ABM treaty). Eric SEVAREID moderated *The Arms Debate* between Senators Goldwater and Proxmire (CBS, 1970). Other special reports included *The Man Who Changed the Navy* (NBC, 1974) about Vice Admiral Elmo Zumwalt, who helped create the "new

navy"; *Who's Ahead? The Debate Over Defense* (CBS, 1977), a détente-era comparison of U.S. and Soviet military preparedness and capabilities; and *The American Army: A Shocking State of Readiness* (ABC, 1978). The 1979 signing of the SALT II treaty and subsequent ratification debates also received considerable coverage, as did later arms limitations and arms reduction talks and various treaties signed during the Reagan and Bush administrations. *The Defense of the United States* (CBS, 1981) provided an in-depth examination of U.S. defenses early in Reagan's first term. President Reagan's 1983 proposal for the controversial "Star Wars" Strategic Defensive Initiative (SDI) was the subject of several special reports throughout the 1980s, as was the IMF treaty Reagan negotiated with Soviet premier Gorbachev.

The money required for the nation's defense was the subject of *A Trillion for Defense: The Military Under Challenge* (NBC, 1969); *The Selling of the Pentagon* (CBS, 1971); ARMS AND SECURITY: HOW MUCH IS ENOUGH? (ABC, 1972); AND NOW THE WAR IS OVER (NBC, 1973); and *The Selling of the F-14* (CBS, 1976). Special reports on cost overruns and corrupt billing practices by defense contractors appeared throughout the 1980s.

The Korean War was the subject of special coverage, including the regularly scheduled THE FACTS WE FACE (CBS, 1950–51), BATTLE REPORT (NBC, 1950–51) and PENTAGON (DuMont, 1951–52). *Korea: The Line* (CBS, 1965) provided an update on Korea 12 years after the ceasefire. *Pueblo: A Question of Intelligence* (NBC, 1969) investigated the North Korean capture of the U.S. intelligence ship *Pueblo* just before the 1968 Tet Offensive in Vietnam. ABC's special report on *The New York Blackout and Korean Crisis* (1977) was in part about the crisis engendered by North Korea's downing of a U.S. helicopter.

The second Berlin Crisis began in 1958 with Khrushchev's demand that the West leave Berlin and peaked in October 1961 when U.S. and Soviet tanks faced each other at Berlin's Checkpoint Charlie. The Soviets had shortly before resumed nuclear testing by detonating a massive 60-megaton bomb. Though the Berlin Crisis subsided shortly afterward, it was politically linked to the Cuban Missile Crisis of 1962 as times when the United States and U.S.S.R. came closest to direct military confrontation. These crises were the subject of the following documentaries: *Berlin: Beleaguered Island* (CBS, 1958) reported on the situation in Berlin immediately following Khrushchev's first ultimatum; *The U-2 Affair* (NBC, 1960) and *Journey to Understanding: Summit Meeting* (NBC, 1960) reported on the aborted Paris summit conference on Berlin and the downing of a U.S. spy plane over the U.S.S.R, which scuttled the conference before it even began; *Berlin: End of the Line* (CBS, 1960); *The Berliners: Life in a Gilded Cage* (CBS, 1960); KHRUSHCHEV AND BERLIN (NBC, 1961); *Berlin: Act of War* (CBS, 1961); and *Berlin: Where the West Begins* (NBC, 1961). Shortly after the Berlin Crisis concluded, NBC presented *Berlin: Christmas 1961* featuring Kennedy and Berlin's Mayor (and future West German chancellor) Willy Brandt, and CBS broadcast *East Germany: The Land Beyond the Wall* (1962). *The Tunnel* (NBC, 1962) described the construction of a tunnel beneath the Berlin Wall a year after it was erected. *The Road to Berlin* (CBS, 1963) appeared less than two weeks before the Kennedy assassination.

The Cuban Missile Crisis was the subject of three special reports as the crisis unfolded: *Quarantine of Cuba* (CBS); *Anatomy of a Crisis* (CBS) and *Clear and Present Danger* (NBC). Each of the crisis' major anniversaries occasioned retrospectives. The 30-year anniversary, which took place after the dissolution of the Soviet Union, spawned several documentaries and interviews with major players, who revealed hitherto unreleased information about the decision-making processes of the various sides.

Documentaries about the communist People's Republic of China (PRC) included *War in China* (CBS, 1958); *The Face of Red China* (CBS, 1958); *China: War or Peace?* (CBS, 1958); and *The Fall of China* (CBS, 1959). *The Great Leap Forward* (NBC, 1959) was reported by John Strohm, the first U.S. reporter allowed by the State Department to travel to China. It was followed by *Red China . . . Update* (NBC, 1959), which used film smuggled out of China by two Swiss businessmen. Both *Red China* (NBC, 1962) and *Inside Red China* (CBS, 1966) used footage shot by German camera crews, since U.S. camera crews were not permitted into the China before President Nixon's visit in 1972. *To Breathe Free: A Profile of Hong Kong* (NBC, 1962) reported on political refugees from China who had fled to Hong Kong. *Encyclopedia of Communism* (NBC, 1963) focused on the differences between the U.S.S.R. and China while *The United States and the Two Chinas* (CBS, 1964) examined U.S. relations with communist and Nationalist China. *Behind the Great Wall* (NBC, 1964) reported on life throughout China. In 1964, both NBC and CBS offered special reports on China's first test of an atom bomb. (China went on to test a hydrogen bomb in 1967.) *Voice of the Dragon* (NBC, 1966) used film shot by a French crew to document the techniques used by the Chinese to convince 700 million Chinese citizens to accept Marxism during Mao Zedong's Cultural Revolution.

Red China: Year of the Gun (ABC, 1966) and *The U.S. and Red China* (CBS, 1966) focused on U.S.–Chinese relations, especially with regard to Vietnam. Filmed by a British camera operator, *Morley Safer's Red China Diary* (CBS, 1967) reported on the American journalist's visit to China. *Triangle of Conflict: China, Russia and the U.S.* (CBS, 1969) addressed the changing political alliances among the "superpowers" after China's Cultural Revolution and Nixon's election. *China Today and Tomorrow* (1969) presented a panel discussion and showed films intercepted from television broadcasts in China. *Journey for Peace* (CBS, 1971) reported on Nixon's upcoming trip to China, which was also the focus of Sevareid's interview with JOURALIST James Reston (CBS, 1971). *China Lost and Found* (NBC, 1972) reported on the history of China, featuring novelist Pearl S. Buck, an American who had grown up in pre-revolutionary China. The show appeared just prior to Nixon's visit, which received extensive live coverage and was the occasion for several additional special reports on China during the winter and spring of 1972. Dan RATHER (CBS) interviewed the president six weeks before the February trip, and ABC featured an interview with Secretary of State Rogers. At the end of 1973, Ted Koppel and Steve Bell presented *The People of "People's China"* (ABC), which showed how the reality of daily life in China differed from government propaganda. President Ford's 1975 visit to China also received substantial coverage, as did President Carter's decision in late 1978 to normalize

U.S.–China relations and the subsequent visit to the United States by China's Vice Premier Teng Hsiao-Ping. China reemerged as a focus of television interest during the 1989 Tiananmen Square uprising.

Documentaries and special reports on the Soviet Union included *Nightmare in Red* (NBC, 1955), a history of communism in the U.S.S.R.; *Fall of Malenkov* (CBS, 1955); and *Comment on Khrushchev* (CBS, 1957), a special edition of FACE THE NATION featuring the Soviet premier—the first time since World War II that a Soviet leader had been interviewed on U.S. television. The network was heavily criticized for failing to conform to the established practice of following a communist spokesperson with anti-communist commentators. Other Soviet-related documentaries included *A Special Report on Soviet Education* (CBS, 1958); *The Ruble War: The Crisis and Beyond* (CBS, 1958), about Soviet expansion into undeveloped countries and its other political uses of trade; and *The Case of Dr. Zhivago* (CBS, 1958), about Boris PASTERNAK and his award-winning novel that was banned in the U.S.S.R. ABC and CBS covered Nixon and Khrushchev's "kitchen debate" during Nixon's tour of Moscow in 1959, and all three networks provided extensive coverage of Khrushchev's trip to the United States that September. *Report from Moscow* (NBC, 1961) addressed disarmament and world security. *Meet Comrade Student* (ABC, 1962) described the Soviet educational system. *Army of the Damned* (CBS, 1962) presented the story of Red Army general Andrei Vlasov, a war hero who organized an army of Russians from Nazi POW camps in order to fight against Stalin.

Other documentaries included *The Death of Stalin* (NBC, 1963); *The Rise of Khrushchev* (NBC, 1963), which appeared four months after the Cuban Missile Crisis; *The Kremlin* (NBC, 1963); *The Rise of Soviet Power* (NBC, 1963); *Soviet Women* (ABC, 1963); *Where We Stand: Ten Years After Stalin* (CBS, 1963), an assessment of the status of the Cold War; *Reflections of a Soviet Scientist* (CBS, 1963), which featured an interview with physicist Igor Tamm filmed in Moscow; *Lenin and Trotsky* (CBS, 1964); *Khrushchev, End of an Era* (CBS, 1964), about the Soviet leader's years in office and his fall from power; *Russia: The New Leadership* (NBC, 1965), about Khrushchev's successors, Leonid Brezhnev and Alexei Kosygin; *Television, Moscow Style* (ABC, 1965); *Siberia: A Day in Irkutsk* (NBC, 1966); *Moscow U* (CBS, 1966), about Soviet university students; *The Russian Sports Revolution* (NBC, 1966); *Khrushchev in Exile* (NBC, 1967); *Ten Days that Shook the World* (NBC, 1967), an account of the 1917 Russian Revolution narrated by Orson Welles; *Ivan Ivanovich* (ABC, 1967), about a typical Soviet family; *Russia in the Mediterranean* (NBC, 1969); *Comrade Soldier* (ABC, 1969); and *Voices from the Russian Underground* (CBS, 1970). Nixon's visit to Moscow in the spring of 1972 received extensive live coverage and was the subject of many special reports and background documentaries.

Brezhnev's 1973 visit to the United States received similar extensive coverage, as did Reagan and Gorbachev's reciprocal visits in the 1980s. During the height of the Watergate crisis, NBC presented a special on *The Russian Connection: Armand Hammer* (1974), about the U.S. industrialist who helped facilitate the U.S.-Soviet détente. *Solzhenitsyn* (CBS, 1974) featured an interview with EXILED WRITER (to the United States) Aleksandr SOLZHENITSYN. The 1983 downing of a Korean passenger plane that had entered Soviet air space was the subject of many special reports analyzing whether the plane had been lost or was spying, as the Soviets claimed. In *Seven Days in the Soviet Union* (CBS, 1987), Bernard Goldberg examined everyday life in the U.S.S.R. *Sex in the Soviet Union* (ABC, 1991) investigated changing sexual mores. Some of the material taken from Soviet television for that show was edited out for American audiences.

Castro's revolution and the subsequent development of a Communist state 90 miles from Key West spawned a number of special reports. *The Rebels of Sierra Maestra— Cuba's Jungle Fighters* (CBS, 1957) and *Cuba in Arms* (CBS, 1958) documented Castro's ongoing revolution in the mountains of Cuba. *Castro: Year of Power* (NBC, 1960), *What Can We Do About Cuba* (CBS, 1960) and *The Cuban Crisis* (NBC, 1960) discussed the growing signs that Castro's revolutionary government was turning communist. The films *90 Miles to Communism* (ABC, 1961) and *Cuba: An Island in Revolt* (NBC, 1961) also dealt with Cuba's political climate. The 1962 return of prisoners from the failed Bay of Pigs invasion by Miami-based exiles occasioned special reports by ABC and CBS. *Picture of a Cuban Family* (ABC, 1963) portrayed a family of Cuban refugees living in Miami. *Cuba: The Bay of Pigs* (NBC, 1964) was paired with a Freed documentary on THE MISSILE CRISIS in a retrospective look at the two major Cuban actions of the Kennedy administration. *Castro and Cuba Today* (ABC, 1964) featured interviews with Castro and Che Guevara, while *Cuba: Ten Years of Castro* (CBS, 1968) reviewed the first decade after the revolution. *Castro, Cuba and the USA* (CBS, 1974) featured Castro's first interview with U.S. reporters since 1968. *Cuba: The Castro Generation* (ABC, 1977) and *Reflections on Cuba '77* (ABC, 1977) focused on the Cuban people, especially the generation of young adults who had grown up under the communist regime. *Fidel Castro Speaks* (ABC, 1977) featured an interview covering Castro's opinions of Kennedy and Nixon, the Cuban military involvement in Angola, U.S.-Cuban relations, and the CIA plots against his life. The 1980 Mariel boatlift occasioned several special reports, and *A Conversation with Castro* (CNN, 1990) featured Ted Turner's interview with the Cuban leader.

Documentaries and special reports about EASTERN EUROPE included *Riot in East Berlin* (CBS, 1958), which used film smuggled out of East Germany to document the 1953 demonstrations that nearly toppled the communist government there; *Hungarian Relief Christmas Day Show* (1956), in which the networks pooled crews to cover the first Christmas in Hungary after the failed anti-communist uprising that autumn; *Revolt in Hungary* (CBS, 1958), about the Hungarian Revolution; *Hungary: Return of Terror* (CBS, 1958), about the current situation there; *Poland on a Tightrope* (CBS, 1959); *Hungary Today* (CBS, 1961), a look at Hungary five years after the uprising; *Czechoslovakia: From Munich to Moscow* (CBS, 1962); *The Changing Face of Hungary* (ABC, 1964); *Yugoslavia: Bridge or Tightrope?* (CBS, 1964), which examined Tito's exceptional communist state that retained ties to both the United States and the U.S.S.R.; *East Europe: Satellite Out of Orbit* (CBS, 1965), television's first examination of the IRON CURTAIN countries after Khrushchev's fall from power; and *Back to Budapest* (NBC, 1966), a report on Hungary 10

years after the uprising. The Soviet invasion of Czechoslovakia in August 1968 was the subject of special reports by all three networks. CBS featured an interview with Yugoslavia's Marshal Tito in 1971. Special reports on Eastern Europe also covered Carter's 1977 trip to Poland; the rise, outlawing and eventual success of the Polish Solidarity labor union; and the other political developments that led to the collapse of communism throughout Eastern Europe in 1989 and 1990.

Middle East politics were a key aspect of the Cold War, and they were the subject of many documentaries and special reports, including *Jordan: Key to the Middle East* (CBS, 1958); *Iran: Brittle Ally* (CBS, 1959); *Summer Incident* (NBC, 1960), about the 1958 landing of Marines in Lebanon; *At the Source: Gamal Abdel Nasser* (CBS, 1961), an interview with the Egyptian champion of pan-Arabism; and *Crisis at Suez* (CBS, 1962), which reviewed the 1956 Suez crisis. The 1967 Six-Day Arab–Israeli war and its aftermath became the topic of several special reports. *Sword or Plowshare* (CBS, 1969) was a three-part report on the Middle East. *Arab Against Arab* (CBS) and *The War in Jordan* (NBC) covered the 1970 war between Jordan and Syria. *Sadat: Action Biography* (ABC, 1974) reported on the Egyptian president a year after the Yom Kippur war with Israel. *What's the Middle East All About* (CBS, 1975) presented a young person's guide to the region's politics. The 1977 reciprocal visits between the leaders of Israel and Egypt received considerable live coverage and generated several special reports, as did the 1979 Carter-brokered Camp David peace accords. CBS commemorated the death of Golda Meir in 1978. The 1978 border war between Israel and Lebanon was the subject of special coverage by all three networks.

No More Vietnams, But . . . (NBC, 1979) discussed the strategic Middle Eastern oil reserves and their role in U.S. foreign policy. The 1979 Iranian Revolution, the subsequent seizure of hostages from the U.S. Embassy in Teheran, and the failed U.S. attempt to rescue them received extensive coverage throughout the duration of the crisis, which lasted over one year. (The Iran crisis also spawned the ABC news program "Nightline," which was hosted by Ted Koppel and which ran throughout the Cold War.) Reagan-era Middle Eastern events that attracted special coverage included the Iran-Iraq war; the landing of U.S. Marines in Lebanon in 1983 and the terrorist bombing that killed 241 of them; the shelling of terrorist camps near civil Lebanese population centers by the USS *New Jersey*; and the Reagan administration's illegal arms sales to Iran, which became known as the Iran-contra affair. The Iran-contra Affair was repeatedly featured on television throughout the Bush administration, as was the 1989 Gulf War.

Communist insurgency and other problems in the Third World countries in Africa, Asia and Latin America were the subject of the following documentaries: *Guatemala* (NBC, 1954); *The Black Star Rises* (CBS, 1957), which covered Vice President Nixon's trip to Africa; *Algeria Aflame* (CBS, 1957), about the Algerian struggle for independence from France; *Freedom for the Philippines* (CBS, 1959); and *Trujillo: Portrait of a Dictator* (CBS, 1960). Other reports included *Crisis in Laos* and *Laos: Time of Decision* (NBC, 1961); *Lumumba: African Martyr* (NBC, 1961), about the death of the Congolese leader; and *The Red and the Black* (ABC, 1961), which explored Soviet influence in Africa. Murrow's final assignment for

CBS was *Crossroads Africa: Pilot for a Peace Corps* (CBS 1961), about a pilot program for a Peace Corps in Africa. Also about the newly formed Peace Corps was *Now . . . In Our Time: The Peace Corps in Tanganyika* (NBC, 1961).

All three networks offered special reports on Kennedy's 1961 trip to South America. Other special reports about the Third World included *Panama—Danger Zone* (NBC, 1961); *Challenge in Laos* (NBC, 1962); *Algeria: Days of Decision* (NBC, 1962); *Pakistan: A Warning to the West* (ABC, 1963); *Our Man in Washington* (NBC, 1964), about Ethiopia's Emperor Haile Selassie's 1963 visit with Kennedy; *Panama* (ABC, 1964); *Malaysia* (ABC, 1964); *Santo Domingo: War Among Friends* (NBC, 1965); and *Santo Domingo: Why Are We There* (CBS, 1965), about the overthrow of Trujillo in the Dominican Republic and the subsequent arrival of the U.S. Marines. *The UN at 20: What Peace Does It Keep?* (ABC, 1965) focused on crises in Iran, Korea, Suez and the Congo. Several reports covered President Johnson's trip to Australia, Thailand and Vietnam in autumn 1966 as well as his 1967 trip to South America. Other documentaries included *Thailand: The New Front* (NBC, 1966), about U.S. involvement in anti-communist efforts in Thailand; *The Undeclared War* (NBC, 1966), about guerrilla warfare in Guatemala, Peru and Columbia; *How to Fight a Guerrilla War* (CBS, 1966), about guerrilla warfare in Malaysia; *The Congo: Victim of Independence* (CBS, 1966); and *Indonesia: The Troubled Victory* (NBC, 1967), about the aftermath of a failed communist coup in late 1966; *Laos: The Forgotten War* (NBC, 1967); *Africa* (ABC, 1967); and *The President Abroad*, about Nixon's 1969 trip to Southeast Asia.

The new decade brought *Laos: America's Not So-Secret War in Asia* (CBS, 1970); *India and Pakistan at War* (CBS, 1971); *Bangladesh* (1972); and *Chile: Experiment in Red* (ABC, 1972), about Chile under the administration of Salvador Allende, its freely elected Marxist president whom the CIA was to help overthrow in 1973. Ford's 1975 trip to Asia a few months after he assumed the presidency also received widespread coverage. Other 1970s documentaries included *Italy, Lebanon and South Africa* (CBS, 1976), about civil unrest in those countries and the implications for U.S. foreign policy; *Who's Got a Right to Rhodesia?* (CBS, 1977); and *The Great Canal Question* (ABC), which appeared in installments throughout 1977 and 1978 as the debate over the Panama Canal treaty evolved. *Central America in Revolt* (CBS, 1982) was one of several Reagan-era special reports that focused on the civil wars in Nicaragua and El Salvador.

Special reports on the CIA, the FBI and espionage-related activities included *FBI* (CBS, 1957); *Brainwashing* (CBS, 1957); *The Hot and Cold Wars of Allen Dulles* (CBS, 1962); *Germany: Red Spy Target* (CBS, 1962); *Red Ships Off Our Shores* (CBS, 1963); *Big Brother Is Listening* (ABC, 1964); *The Science of Spying* (NBC, 1965), which focused on past CIA operations in Guatemala, Laos and at the Bay of Pigs; *The Big Ear* (NBC, 1965); *In the Pay of the CIA: An American Dilemma* (CBS, 1967), about CIA payments to students, union members and broadcasting organizations; *Under Surveillance* (CBS, 1971); *J. Edgar Hoover: 1895–1972* (CBS, 1972); *The CIA* (ABC, 1975); *What's the CIA All About* (CBS, 1975), a young person's guide to the intelligence agency; *Inside the FBI* (CBS, 1976); *Colby of the CIA* (CBS, 1976), about the CIA director; *The CIA's Secret Army* (CBS, 1977) and *Mission:*

Mind Control (ABC, 1979), which interviewed former CIA officials about U.S. efforts to perfect mind control and develop truth drugs.

Special reports on communism included *The Red Sell* (CBS, 1958), a two-part program on communist propaganda; *Fifteen Months in a Red Prison* (NBC, 1962), about camera operator Grant Wolfkill's experiences in a communist jail; *Communist Party, USA* (NBC, 1973), which described the American Communist Party in the aftermath of the 1950s RED SCARE; *What's Communism All About* (CBS, 1975), a young person's guide; and *Friends, Romans and Communists* (CBS, 1976), about the growing influence of communism in Italy.

The space race was the topic of *The First Step into Space* (NBC, 1955), about U.S. plans to launch an orbiting satellite. All three networks did special reports on the Soviets' 1957 launching of Sputnik I; ABC's *The Red Satellite* was the most ominously titled. ABC also presented a special report on Sputnik II later that year. In 1958, all three networks did special reports on the launching of the Jupiter rocket and the Explorer satellite, and NBC followed with *Satellites, Schools and Survival* (1958), about the importance to the space race of public school science education. Subsequent reports included *Reaching for the Moon* (CBS, 1960); *The Space Lag: Can Democracy Compete?* (CBS, 1960); *Why Man in Space?* (CBS, 1960); and *Report from Outer Space* (NBC, 1960). Wolper's independently produced *The Race for Space* (syndicated, 1960) featured rare film footage from both U.S. and Soviet space archives. All three networks offered special reports on the first Soviet and U.S. manned space shots in 1961 and 1962 and featured interviews with both astronauts and cosmonauts. They also offered special reports on the 1962 launching of the COMMUNICATIONS SATELLITE Telstar. Other space-race documentaries included *Beyond the Threshold* (NBC, 1962); *Sixty Hours to the Moon* (ABC, 1962); *109 Days to Venus* (CBS, 1962); *Ask Cape Canaveral* (NBC, 1962), featuring interviews with top space officials; *Ranger 8: Impact on the Moon* and *Ranger 9: Live Moon Pictures* (CBS, 1965), which featured photos from the unmanned flights to the moon; and *T-Minus 4 Years, 9 Months and 30 Days* (CBS, 1965), which examined the U.S. quest to reach the moon by the end of the decade. In 1965, CBS provided background reports on the upcoming Gemini flights, while *The Man Who Walked in Space* (NBC, 1965) and *Major White's Walk* (CBS, 1965) reported on the first Soviet and U.S. space walks. All three networks also offered special reports on the unmanned 1965 Mariner space probe, which was sent to Mars. The 1967 deaths of astronauts Grissom, White and Chaffee occasioned special coverage.

Other space-race reports included *Crossroads in Space* (NBC, 1967), which documented the development of NASA; *Beyond the Sky* (NBC, 1968); *Soviets in Space* (NBC, 1968); *Space '68* (ABC, 1968); *Man at the Moon* (CBS, 1968) and *Man and his Universe: The View from Space* (ABC, 1969), about the Apollo 8 flight; *Two Views from Space* (CBS, 1969), about the Apollo 11 Lunar Mission and Mariner 6's journey to Mars; and *Footsteps on the Moon: The Flight of Apollo XI* (ABC, 1969). Walter CRONKITE's *Man on the Moon: The Epic Journey of Apollo 11* (CBS, 1970) commemorated the first anniversary of the first human landing on the moon, as did *A Day in the Life of the United States* (CBS, 1970), which showed footage from 33 camera teams that surveyed Americans on the day of the lunar landing. The networks also commemorated the tenth and twentieth anniversaries of the moon landing.

After the lunar landings, coverage of the space race diminished but did not die out. *Countdown to 2001* (ABC, 1972) anticipated Skylab, the Space Shuttle, the Viking probe of Mars and the final Apollo missions. *What's Skylab All About?* (CBS, 1973) provided a young person's guide to America's first space station. *Space: A Report to the Stockholders* (CBS, 1974) discussed the costs and achievements of the space program. The 1975 joint U.S.–Soviet Apollo–Soyuz mission attracted widespread coverage and generated several special reports on the scientific and political aspects of the mission. The first shuttle launchings (1977), Skylab's fall to Earth (1979) and the Challenger explosion (1986) also occasioned special reports.

The regularly scheduled shows YOU ARE THERE (CBS, 1953–57; 1971–72) and BIOGRAPHY (syndicated, 1962) documented historical figures and events, including Cold War figures Dwight Eisenhower, George Marshall, Joseph McCarthy, Douglas MacArthur, Josef Stalin, Mao Zedong, Fidel Castro, Eva Peron, Konrad Adenauer, Madame Chiang Kaishek, Charles de Gaulle and Dag Hammarskjöld. INDUSTRIES FOR AMERICA (ABC, 1951–52; 1957) and ENTERPRISE (ABC, 1952–58) documented Cold War contributions by U.S. industry to the fight against communism. Local stations offered simulated documentaries such as THE DAY MIAMI DIED, portraying what might become of a city if it were taken over by communists.

Other Cold War–related documentaries included *As Others See Us* (NBC, 1957), which explored perceptions of Americans by foreigners; Cronkite's "The Twentieth Century" (CBS, 1957–66), which covered historic events throughout the century, such as guided missiles, brainwashing, the FBI, the atomic age, communist propaganda, domestic unrest in Poland and the communist takeover of China; *Project Hope* (CBS, 1961) and *Now . . . In Our Time: The Good Ship Hope* (NBC, 1961) about a U.S. hospital ship at work in Southeast Asia. In 1961, NBC and CBS both ran special reports about the UN secretary general killed on duty in Africa: *I Remember: Dag Hammarskjold* (CBS), *Death of a Hope: The Tragedy of Dag Hammarskjold* (CBS) and *The Death of a Statesman* (NBC). All three networks offered numerous special reports and retrospective documentaries in the immediate aftermath of the Kennedy assassination in 1963. *United States Foreign Policy* (NBC, 1965) presented a three-and-a-half-hour look at U.S. foreign policy since 1945.

The Dissenter: Norman Thomas (CBS, 1965) profiled the outspoken American socialist. *Thunder on the Right* (CBS, 1962) and *Politics: The Outer Fringe* (NBC, 1966) explored such extreme right-wing groups as the Minute Men, the John Birch Society, the Ku Klux Klan and the American Nazi Party. *The Anti-Americans* (CBS, 1966) addressed anti-U.S. sentiment and actions throughout the world. *The Hippie Temptation* (CBS, 1967) investigated the COUNTERCULTURE in San Francisco's Haight-Ashbury district. In *A Conversation with Dean Acheson* (CBS, 1969), Sevareid interviewed Truman's secretary of state about the Korean and Vietnam wars, NATO and the Berlin blockade. In CBS's *Why I Chose Not To Run* (1969), *The Decision to Halt the Bombing* (1970), *LBJ:*

Tragedy and Transition (1970), *Lyndon Johnson Talks Politics* (1972) and *LBJ: The Last Interview* (1973), Cronkite interviewed Lyndon Johnson about decisions made during about his presidency. *The Pentagon Papers: A Conversation with Daniel Ellsberg* (CBS), *Top Secret: Who Draws the Line?* (ABC), *The Pentagon Papers: What They Mean* (CBS) and *June 30, 1971, a Day for History: The Supreme Court and the Pentagon Papers* (NBC) all addressed the Supreme Court's 1971 decision to permit newspapers to publish secret Johnson-era documents about the Vietnam War. *Friends of Harry S. Truman* (CBS, 1972) commemorated America's first Cold War president upon his death; the show featured Johnson, Dean Acheson, Clark Clifford and Hugo Black. All three networks covered Truman's funeral and offered special tributes to him, as they did for Johnson when he died in 1973, a day before the Vietnam peace treaty was announced.

The Watergate investigation, the Senate hearings and Nixon's resignation received substantial live coverage and spawned numerous special reports throughout 1973 and 1974. Juxtaposed against the flurry of Watergate coverage was a retrospective on Kennedy's foreign policy, *JFK: One Thousand Days—And Ten Years* (CBS, 1973). Presented on the tenth anniversary of Kennedy's assassination, the show reassessed his performance on atomic testing, Vietnam and the Berlin and Cuban Missile crises. As the impeachment proceedings against President Nixon were under way, ABC presented *Kissinger: An Action Biography*. The United States was not the only NATO power to change leaders in 1974; *Europe's New Leaders: Giscard and Schmidt* (CBS) reported on the new heads of state in France and West Germany. *Walter Lippmann Obituary* reminisced about the influential Cold War journalist (CBS, 1974). A month after the fall of South Vietnam, CBS broadcast *The Ups and Downs of Henry Kissinger* (1975). David Frost's interview with Nixon (ABC, 1977) provided the former president's first public statement about Watergate since his resignation. In 1979 Frost interviewed Kissinger. *Summer of Judgment* (PBS, 1983) looked back on the Watergate hearings of 10 years earlier; *45/85* (ABC, 1985) reviewed 40 years of U.S. foreign policy; and *Richard Nixon Reflects* (PBS, 1990) offered the former president's thoughts about many Cold War issues and events. (See also TELEVISION NEWS.)

For additional reading, see Whitfield's *The Culture of the Cold War*; Shaheen's *Nuclear War Films*; Einstein's *Special Edition: A Guide to Network Television Documentary Series and Special News Reports, 1955–1979*; McNeil's *Total Television*; Smith's *U.S. Television Network News: A Guide to Sources in English*.

television dramas Plot-oriented television shows that emphasized characters, motivations and issues more than pure action and adventure. Most television dramas were apolitical and made little contribution to the Cold War except in projecting middle-class American values. Most, especially the earlier ones, took for granted that individuals were responsible for their own success or failure, that ownership of private property and accumulation of wealth were worthy aspirations, and that individuals should enjoy the maximum liberty possible. Thus, television dramas reinforced the beliefs that were supposed to distinguish democratic, capitalistic America from its communist enemies.

Among the television dramas that did directly address Cold War issues were THE DEFENDERS (CBS, 1961–65), THE F.B.I. (ABC, 1965–68, 1974), EMERALD POINT, N.A.S. (CBS, 1983–84) and GENERAL ELECTRIC THEATER (CBS, 1953–62). A courtroom drama, "The Defenders" ran from 1961 to 1965, during John Kennedy's New Frontier and Lyndon Johnson's Great Society. The show reflected these presidents' new focus on civil rights and social issues. One Cold War–influenced episode addressed the right of the U.S. government to restrict travel to unfriendly countries. Another, entitled *Blacklist* (January 1964), addressed the practice of BLACKLISTING in the television industry during the 1950s. Actor Jack Klugman and writer Ernest Kinoy won Emmy awards for that episode.

"The F.B.I." ran from 1965 to 1974, during the time of the Vietnam War and its accompanying protest, the Civil Rights and Black Power movements, and President Nixon's Law and Order presidential campaigns; it left the air a month after Nixon resigned from the presidency. The show claimed to be based on actual FBI cases. Some involved such alleged Cold War threats to U.S. security as spying by communists and bombings by radicals opposed to the Vietnam War. In other episodes, the FBI investigated illegal but nonpolitical acts by counterfeiters, extortionists and members of organized crime. Real-life FBI director J. Edgar Hoover endorsed the show, which depicted the bureau in an extremely positive light. The show was neither violent nor risqué. It endorsed law and order and traditional American values by showing calm, highly professional law enforcement agents defeating those who would undermine the American way of life, either through crime, communism or "permissiveness." Moreover, it suggested that America's best protection came not from violent, glamorous secret agents like James BOND, but from rational, dispassionate professionals with corporate sympathies and sensibilities. Citizens who did not share these values were suspect of being anti-American, or at least of opening the door to corruption of various types.

"Emerald Point, N.A.S." was a much shorter-lived drama that ran from 1983 to 1984, during Reagan's first term. Like such other popular dramas as "Dallas" (CBS, 1978–91) and "Dynasty" (ABC, 1981–89), it focused on power, wealth, sex and the intrigue involved in getting them. The setting here was a U.S. military base, and the subterfuge involved spying and making deals with defense contractors.

The content of "General Electric Theater" was less significant for the Cold War than the national exposure it gave its host and sometime star, Ronald REAGAN. From 1965 to 1966 Reagan also hosted "Death Valley Days," an anthology of TELEVISION WESTERNS set in California mining camps of the 19th century. Reagan stepped down from the show after being elected governor of California.

Single-episode television dramas pertaining to the Cold War included David RABE's *Sticks and Bones* (CBS, 1973), a controversial story of a blinded Vietnam veteran; TAIL GUNNER JOE (NBC, 1977), a dramatic biography of Senator Joseph McCarthy; *Friendly Fire* (ABC, 1979), the story of an Iowa couple who struggles to find the truth about how their son was killed in Vietnam; and *A Rumor of War* (CBS, 1980), a TV movie about the Vietnam War.

television military dramas The primary U.S. military actions during the Cold War were the Korean and Vietnam Wars; the Grenada and Panama invasions; the rescue of the crew from the cargo ship *Mayaguez,* which Cambodian communists had captured in 1975; peace-keeping interventions in Lebanon during the Eisenhower and Reagan administrations and in the Dominican Republic during the Johnson administration; the failed attempt to rescue the Iranian-held hostages from the U.S. Embassy in Tehran in 1980. Since the United States achieved only a stalemate in Korea and failed to achieve any of its basic objectives in Vietnam, these conflicts did not readily lend themselves to television, especially when compared to the more successful and unambiguous "good war," World War II. Since sponsor-driven network television has always sought to present an upbeat view, unsuccessful wars, failed rescue missions and problematic military interventions into Third World countries were rarely chosen as settings for Cold War television war shows. Notable exceptions were M*A*S*H (CBS, 1972–83), CHINA BEACH (ABC, 1988–90) and TOUR OF DUTY (CBS, 1987–90).

Set during the Korean War but with obvious reference to the then-current Vietnam War, "M*A*S*H*" hammered home the point that warfare is about misery, not glory. It was one of the few TELEVISION SITUATION COMEDIES ever to feature BLACK HUMOR. Doctors joked, played gags on each other, and sought to bring as much decency and justice as possible to war situations characterized by carnage, confusion and suffering. However, unlike the Robert Altman black-humor film on which the show was based, the doctors did not joke about their patient's wounds, whose grotesque features were largely kept from the cameras. The antiwar television show ran during the last two years of the Vietnam War and for eight years afterward.

"China Beach" and "Tour of Duty" were set during the Vietnam War, but were not made until more than 10 years after the war had ended. Both shows also projected generalized antiwar sentiments, unlike most other network war shows. "China Beach" centered on women—nurses, prostitutes and USO entertainers near the U.S. military base at Da Nang. Though many of the plot lines focused on romance, the show frequently depicted the harsh realities of warfare. Like "M*A*S*H" "China Beach" included elements of black humor, especially through the comments of Private Sam Beckett, who ran the morgue, and the Red Cross worker Holly the Donut Dolly. The show combined graphic portrayals of the war with Vietnam-era acid rock and allusions to the civil unrest back home. "Tour of Duty" also presented the Vietnam War in a tough, realistic fashion that emphasized the realities of fighting an unpopular war in a hostile alien environment.

COMBAT (ABC, 1962–67), NAVY LOG (CBS/ABC, 1955–58), O.S.S. (ABC, 1957–58) and "The Gallant Men" (ABC, 1962–63) were among the World War II shows that flourished during the first half of the Cold War. In general, as the Vietnam War became less popular, so did shows that glorified warfare. By the late 1970s, antiwar sentiment had subsided and World War II was 35 years past and so was not an obvious setting for a television show. Whereas in the 1950s that war had been a major event in the lives of most audience members, by the Reagan era, for fewer viewers remembered it. Consequently, most World War II shows aired during the 1950s and early or mid-1960s. "Combat," one of the better WWII shows, followed an American squad from Normandy into Germany during the last year of the war. The show reaffirmed such American values as courage, loyalty, sacrifice, toughness in the face of adversity, honesty, respect for authority, and prudence. The challenge to these values during the mid- and late 1960s might have accounted for the show's demise in 1967. "The Gallant Men" (1962–63) followed a formula similar to that of "Combat" but was set in Italy instead of France, and the action was viewed from the perspective of a war correspondent. "O.S.S." was a 1950s show based on public files about the World War II American intelligence organization that preceded the C.I.A. "Navy Log" also reenacted events that had actually occurred. One episode featured an account of the sinking of John F. Kennedy's PT-109 in the South Pacific. Kennedy, a senator at the time, appeared on the show as a special guest. THE SILENT SERVICE (syndicated, 1957) was a 1950s-era show about the U.S. submarine fleet. Hosted by Rear Admiral Thomas M. Dykers USN (retired), it included documentary footage from World War II and Korea. In 1953, PENTAGON, U.S.A. (CBS, 1953) presented dramatic adaptations of cases from the criminal investigation files of the U.S. Army. "The Lieutenant" (NBC, 1963–64) and THE PHIL SILVERS SHOW (CBS, 1955–59) provided dramatic and comic treatments of U.S. peacetime troops, respectively. The short-lived show "The Soldiers" (NBC, 1955) was another 1950s sitcom about the peacetime army.

television news   Television news brought the Cold War directly to television viewers through regularly scheduled daily news shows, live coverage of special events, regularly scheduled news reports, panel discussions, press conferences, interviews with newsmakers, and TELEVISION DOCUMENTARIES AND SPECIAL REPORTS.

Television news shows reported on developments as they occurred during the Cold War. Though sometimes accused of holding a liberal bias in domestic matters, most news broadcasts had a strong anti-communist perspective on the Cold War conflict. These perspectives both reflected and reinforced the beliefs of most Americans at the time, beliefs that may, indeed, have been both accurate and legitimate. It is nevertheless useful to recognize the unspoken basic assumptions underlying the news presentations of the Cold War. First, network news shows uniformly accepted as an unquestioned premise that communism represented a genuine threat to the United States and that communist-led countries should be regarded as enemies. They also accepted the premise that the policy of containment should be the basic U.S. response to communism. Conservative broadcasters favored the "liberation policy" of President Eisenhower's secretary of state, John Foster Dulles, in the early 1950s, calling for the West to take an active role in "freeing" EASTERN EUROPE from communist rule. The more moderate containment policy, which the Truman administration formulated in 1947, accepted the status quo but maintained that future communist advances must be checked wherever they occurred. Leftists and pacifists who did not accept

this liberal consensus were virtually shut out of television coverage, especially during the earliest days of the Cold War.

Because news coverage assumed that communist countries were aggressive enemies, it typically emphasized bellicose communist behavior and greeted conciliatory gestures with cynicism. It also tended to highlight communist responsibility for political and military crises while downplaying U.S. responsibility for international tensions. Moreover, apart from coverage of the ITT scandal during the Nixon administration, network news rarely if ever explored the role of U.S. corporate interests in the formation of foreign policy.

Communist leaders rarely had direct access to U.S. audiences. (Nor did U.S. leaders have easy access to airwaves behind the IRON CURTAIN.) When communist leaders did appear on U.S. television during the 1950s, networks typically followed their appearances with panels of anti-communists who commented on the presentation, as when Edward R. MURROW interviewed Yugoslavia's Marshal Tito and communist China's Foreign Minister Zhou En-lai on CBS's SEE IT NOW (1951–58). When CBS's FACE THE NATION (1954–present) interviewed Soviet premier Khrushchev without the benefit of such a panel in 1957, the network was widely criticized. Even President Eisenhower accused it of merely trying to "improve its commercial standing." The year before, CBS had silenced William Worthy's broadcasts from communist China upon the request of the State Department and had canceled the subsequent commentary of Eric SEVAREID, who had planned to criticize what he believed to be the Eisenhower administration's effort to preserve American ignorance of the actual realities of world events.

Later in the Cold War, access to television was less restricted. For instance, in 1967, press conferences by Soviet premier Kosygin and by Josef Stalin's daughter, Svetlana, received live coverage from the major networks. During the 1991 Gulf War the enemy leader, Saddam Hussein, was able to address the American public directly during wartime on CNN (though technically this was after the Cold War had ended).

Throughout the entire Cold War, commentators with communist, socialist or even moderately left-wing political positions were routinely excluded from news broadcasts and news forums such as MEET THE PRESS (NBC, 1947–present), "Washington Week in Review" (PBS, 1967–present), "The McLaughlin Group" (PBS, 1982–present), "The MacNeil-Lehrer News Hour" (now "The News Hour with Jim Lehrer," PBS, 1976–present), "Face the Nation" and others, even though such shows featured discussions on current affairs, presumably from many viewpoints. (See also CHRONOSCOPE (CBS, 1951–55), OUR SECRET WEAPON—THE TRUTH (DuMont, 1950–51) and ABC's "POLITICS ON TRIAL", 1952.) Before the escalation of the Vietnam War in the mid-1960s, pacifists rarely received forums on network television; nor did people who advocated unilateral nuclear disarmament or opposed U.S. involvement in Korea, Laos or the Philippines. In fact, to give air time to opponents of the hard line against worldwide communism, or even to opponents of the RED SCARE, was often considered unpatriotic and perhaps treasonable. For instance, after Murrow's 1954 exposé on Senator Joseph McCarthy, aired on "See It Now," CBS president Frank Stanton told producer Fred Friendly, "You may have cost us the network," for the program had generated substantial political pressure to revoke the network's license. Moreover, according to Stephen J. Whitfield in *The Culture of the Cold War*, open forum programs such as ABC's AMERICA'S TOWN MEETING (1948–49, 1952) and NBC's "American Forum of the Air" (1950–52) were eventually taken off the air in order to deny opportunities for left-wing non-communists to appear before the public. Even in the 1970s and 1980s, such an articulate, well-credentialed spokesman for the left as Noam Chomsky rarely received opportunities to provide his point of view on current events forums. By contrast, such extreme right-wing figures as William F. BUCKLEY Jr., Pat ROBERTSON, and Pat Buchanan and such anti-communist religious figures as Billy GRAHAM and Jerry FALWELL had regular access to news talk shows.

Before the Vietnam War, news reporting was not generally critical of foreign policy, unless to suggest that it was not sufficiently anti-communist. Network news rarely criticized foreign governments supported by the United States or reported sympathetically on communist-backed indigenous movements to overthrow repressive regimes. However, after Walter CRONKITE took a more critical view of the Vietnam War following the 1968 Tet Offensive, news coverage of the war—and subsequently of U.S. foreign policy and US-supported governments—became somewhat more evenhanded. Nonetheless, especially after the Cold War reintensified upon the breakdown of détente in 1979 and the election of Ronald Reagan in 1980, news reporting always hewed to basic Cold War assumptions: that communists were enemies of the United States, and that U.S. foreign policy was being conducted in the general cause of peace and freedom, as well as to protect U.S. interests and national security. Perhaps ironically, the somewhat critical media coverage toward the end of the Vietnam War has been credited for efforts undertaken by the Reagan administration to restrict reporters' access to combat zones during the U.S. invasion of Grenada and by the Bush administration to do the same during its Panama invasion and the Persian Gulf War. Though the restrictions were officially imposed to protect reporters' safety and to safeguard national security, many news professionals believed they were actually government attempts to control how the combat would be reported.

Television crews began covering the Democratic and Republican presidential conventions in 1952. Important early Cold War events that were covered on television included the signing of the NATO pact (1949); the opening session of the Japanese Peace Treaty Conference in San Francisco (1951); Richard Nixon's "Checkers" speech (1952); the ARMY–MCCARTHY HEARINGS (1954); and Nixon and Khrushchev's "kitchen debate" during the vice president's tour of Moscow (1959). By 1960, live television coverage of important events had become routine. Important moments in the Space Race were also televised live, including the Mercury flights in the early 1960s; the Gemini flights and the first space walks (1965); the landing of Apollo 11 on the moon (1969); the U.S.–Soviet Apollo–Soyuz flights (1975); Skylab (1973); the first space shuttle (1977); and the explosion of the space shuttle *Challenger* (1986).

Among the more prominent television newscasters were CBS's Douglas Edwards who anchored the "CBS Evening News" from 1948 to 1962, followed by Cronkite (1962–81) and Dan RATHER (1981–present). Other prominent CBS reporters were Sevareid, Roger Mudd, Harry Reasoner and Daniel Schorr, who broadcast the first radio interview with Khrushchev in 1957, was later expelled from the U.S.S.R. for "adventurism" and was included on Nixon's "Enemies List" in the 1970s. CBS's Bernard Goldberg was also notable for his 1987 broadcast reports from the U.S.S.R. John Cameron Swayze anchored NBC's nightly news program until 1956, when the popular and critically acclaimed HUNTLEY-BRINKLEY REPORT replaced him. The team of New York-based Chet Huntley and Washington-based David Brinkley ran until 1970, after which John Chancellor became anchor until Tom Brokaw succeeded him in 1982. ABC's staffing of the evening news was considerably less stable. H. R. Baukhage and Jim Gibbons anchored a show from 1948 to 1951, to be replaced by the ambitious but unsuccessful "All Star News" (1951–53). Former CBS correspondent John Daly, who also moderated the quiz show "What's My Line" (CBS, 1950–67), anchored from 1953 until 1960. Subsequent ABC anchors included John Cameron Swayze, Ron Cochran, Frank Reynolds, Howard K. Smith, Harry Reasoner, Barbara Walters and Peter Jennings. Though not a regular on the evening news, Ted Koppel emerged as one of ABC's premier journalists during the 1980s when he began hosting the late-night "ABC News Nightline" in 1980.

Regularly scheduled Cold War–related news shows provided background on current Cold War conflicts and developments. News shows from the early days of the Cold War included THE MARSHALL PLAN IN ACTION (ABC, 1950–51), OPERATION INFORMATION (DuMont, 1952, on veterans' benefits), ASIA PERSPECTIVE (CBS, 1966, about China and Vietnam) and the Korean War–related shows THE FACTS WE FACE (CBS, 1950–51), BATTLE REPORT (NBC, 1950–52), VISIT WITH THE ARMED FORCES (DuMont, 1950–51) and PENTAGON (DuMont, 1950–51). "Background" (NBC, 1954–55) featured reports on the military draft; Asian nationalist movements, including those in Indochina, Korea and the Philippines; the rearmament of Germany; the Suez Canal; communist political gains in Italy; the Formosa crisis; the defense buildup; a Czech defector; and the role of Islam in the modern world. NBC replaced "Background" with "Outlook" (1956–58), Chet Huntley's first national assignment. Charles Van Doren, the popular winner of the game show TWENTY-ONE, (NBC, 1956–58), hosted "Kaleidoscope" on NBC from 1958 to 1959 until it was revealed that "Twenty-one" had been fixed. The short-lived "World Wide '60" featured shows on Castro, the missile race, postwar Germany and the space race. From 1958 to 1963, NBC presented "Chet Huntley Reporting," and in 1959 Howard K. Smith anchored CBS's BEHIND THE NEWS. In 1962 and 1963 Smith also hosted "Howard K. Smith—News and Comment." These shows reported on such topical subjects as the workings of the Supreme Soviet; post-revolutionary Iran; the Atlas missile; the rise of French president Charles de Gaulle; the East German economy; the then-current Berlin Crisis; the Bay of Pigs invasion of Cuba; a Tibetan rebellion against communist China; the U.S. State Department; radioactive fallout; the possibilities of Cuba's "going red"; the forthcoming summit conference over the

Berlin Crisis; Khrushchev; and a profile of daily life in Moscow.

From 1959 to 1963, "Eyewitness to History" (CBS) provided in-depth coverage of Eisenhower's trips to Europe, South America and Asia; Khrushchev's visit to the United States; unrest in Africa; communist power in Cuba and Laos; and the space race. "CBS Reports" also began in 1959 and continued beyond the end of the Cold War. In 1961–62 and 1970–71 it was regularly scheduled; otherwise, it became the formal title of most CBS-produced documentaries. "ABC News Close Up" (begun 1973), "NBC White Paper" (begun 1960) and "NBC Reports" (begun 1972) performed similar functions for the other networks. "NBC White Paper" featured several award-winning Cold War documentaries by Fred FREED. From 1961 to 1963, ABC broadcast ADLAI STEVENSON REPORTS, a bi-weekly series centered on the current activities of the United Nations and featuring interviews with Ambassador Stevenson. During the same time, NBC featured "David Brinkley's Journal," which addressed Soviet espionage; Cuban refugees in Miami; the U.S. naval base at Guantanamo, Cuba; and American attitudes about foreign policy, Hiroshima and pacifism.

From 1960 to 1963 ABC presented BELL AND HOWELL CLOSE-UP, which featured special reports on the struggle between communism and democracy in Haiti; the rising influence of communism in Latin America; the growing communist power in Africa; the conversion of Cuba to communism; the war in Algeria; East and West Berlin; Eastern Europe; Italy; Cambodia; the Middle East; and the personal problems facing U.S. ambassadors overseas. These topics were also covered by ABC's "Editor's Choice" (1961–62) and NBC's "Here and Now" (1961) and "Update" (1961–63), a news magazine that also covered the history of the UN, Kennedy's attempts to achieve nuclear disarmament, and the Berlin Crisis. "Sunday Report" (summer 1963) reported on Kennedy's trip to Germany and on the ratification of the nuclear test-ban treaty. David WOLPER's independently produced "Men in Crisis" (1964–65) focused on major figures from critical moments in history, including recent Cold War crises. DECISION: THE CONFLICTS OF HARRY TRUMAN (Syndicated, 1964) featured the former president discussing many Cold War events from his administration, including the Korean War; the Berlin Airlift; the Red Scare; the recognition of Israel; the atomic bomb; the Marshall Plan; and the 1946 Soviet attempt to win control of Iran.

NBC's "Frank McGee Reports" (1965–70) and "First Tuesday" (1969–73) addressed such Cold War issues as chemical and biological warfare; the nuclear defense industry; the Vietnam War; the secret U.S. war in Cambodia; the Soviet invasion of Czechoslovakia; Guatemala; Indonesia; Haiti; the *Pueblo* incident; Soviet involvement in Egypt; military surveillance of antiwar and civil rights activists; and Watergate. CBS's highly popular "60 Minutes" (1968–present) also provided in-depth and investigative reporting from 1968 through the end of the Cold War. In response to "First Tuesday" and "Sixty Minutes," ABC presented "The Reasoner Report" (1973–75), which examined such Cold War topics as Vietnam, Watergate, the FBI, the Philippines and Nixon's trip to Moscow. Beginning in 1978, ABC introduced "20/20" as another competitor to "60 Minutes." It too offered investigative reports on a variety of issues, often

with more of a "feature" than a news focus. "Conversations with Eric Sevareid" (CBS, 1975–77) included interviews with top political figures about Cold War issues. Notable guests were George F. Kennan, Willy Brandt and presidential adviser John McCloy. Throughout the 1980s, Koppel's "Nightline" featured interviews with Cold War political figures, among others.

Some shows provided forums for journalists to exchange views about Cold War issues or to interview political leaders. Among these were ENTERPRISE (PBS), "Meet The Press" (NBC, 1947–present), KEEP POSTED (DuMont, 1951–54), "Face the Nation" and Murrow's "See It Now," best remembered for Murrow's 1954 exposé on McCarthy but also famous for hosting such Cold War figures as Presidents Truman and Eisenhower; NATO supreme commander, General Alfred M. Gruenther; China's foreign minister, Zhou En-Lai; and Yugoslavia's Marshal Tito. Murrow also hosted shows on nuclear testing; nuclear weapons and radiation; relations among the Western powers; Berlin; the "Iron Curtain" countries; the 1956 Suez Crisis; and an in-person Christmas visit to GIs on the front lines in Korea. *The Case of Lt. Milo Radulovich* focused on an air force lieutenant who lost his security clearance because his father and sister read what the air force considered to be subversive newspapers and took part in questionable activities. Murrow also hosted a more informal show, "Person to Person" (CBS, 1953–61), in which he interviewed celebrities and political figures, including Castro; Israel's Ambassador Abba Eban; Federal Civil Defense administrator Val Peterson; and the chief of the U.S. Army missile program, General John B. Medaris. In "Small World" (CBS, 1958–60), Murrow held four-way telephone conversations with political and cultural figures from throughout the world. For instance, in a show about U.S. prestige in Asia, Murrow interviewed U.S. Information Agency director George Allen, Manila's Mayor Arsenio Lacson and Eugene BURDICK, coauthor of THE UGLY AMERICAN (1958) and FAIL-SAFE (1962).

Special panel discussions and interviews appeared on television throughout the Cold War. Typically the networks provided year-end discussions among their correspondents. Between 1954 and 1958, NBC's "Comment" provided round-table discussions about communist China; the different forms of communism throughout the world; European politics; the Middle East; nuclear testing; and the Geneva conference on Indochina and possible U.S. involvement there. "Hot Seat" (1957–59) presented discussions among NBC foreign correspondents and their colleagues back home. Between 1958 and 1963, CBS's "The Great Challenge" addressed foreign policy, the space race and the problems of sustaining a democracy. A notable 1958 episode entitled *What Beliefs Sustain the Free World?* featured theologian Reinhold Niebuhr, historian Arnold Toynbee and philosopher Charles Frankel.

"The Nation's Future" (NBC, 1960–62) claimed to be "the first attempt by television to provide a national debate and discussion service." The show presented debates between atomic physicists Edward Teller and Leo Szilard on disarmament; General Maxwell Taylor and Thomas Lamphier Jr. on the nuclear arms buildup; Representative James Roosevelt and American Legion chairman Martin McKneally on congressional investigations into the loyalty of U.S. citizens;

and geochemist Harrison S. Brown and Herman Kahn, author of ON THERMONUCLEAR WAR (1960), on the prospects for surviving a nuclear attack. From 1963 to 1967, "CBS Town Meeting of the World" used the newly launched COMMUNICATION SATELLITE Telstar to present discussions among leaders and experts from throughout the world. *Human Rights: A Soviet-American Debate* (NBC, 1977) was the subject of a détente-era broadcast that featured Americans and Soviets debating the issues. As one country after another rejected communism in 1990, Koppel moderated a PBS panel discussion about the emerging post–Cold War world, *"World Without Walls."*

For additional reading, see Whitfield's *The Culture of the Cold War*; Einstein's *Special Edition: A Guide to Network Television Documentary Series and Special News Reports, 1955–1979*; McNeil's *Total Television*; Smith's *U.S. Television Network News: A Guide to Sources in English.*

television performers The Cold War affected TELEVISION performers primarily by placing the threat of BLACKLISTING over their heads. In 1950, the right-wing magazine COUNTERATTACK published a special report entitled RED CHANNELS, which listed 151 performers and other industry personnel who had been cited as belonging to or working with organizations alleged to be communist fronts. *Red Channels* quickly became the unofficial industry blacklist, and it affected the careers of many performers. For example, before its publication Ed SULLIVAN had hosted dancer Paul Draper and harmonica-player Larry Adler. After *Red Channels* listed the two men, Sullivan apologized publicly for booking them. Their television careers were ruined by the listing and Sullivan's announcement about it, and both men eventually left the country. Such other television performers as Philip LOEB, Jean MUIR and Ireene WICKER lost roles in regularly scheduled shows because of blacklisting. (Loeb is the model for the Zero MOSTEL character in THE FRONT.) Others, such as Hazel SCOTT, Pete SEEGER, Lena HORNE and Gypsy Rose Lee lost guest appearances—or faced the threat of losing them—due to allegations about their past political activities.

In many instances, the allegations were factually incorrect, such as the charge that Ireene Wicker, a popular children's show host in the late 1940s, had signed a petition on behalf of a communist candidate. Wicker's career was ruined as a result. In 1953, newspaper JOURNALIST Walter WINCHELL revealed that Lucille BALL, "America's top comedienne, has been confronted with her membership in the Communist Party." In fact, in 1952 Lucille Ball had told the HOUSE COMMITTEE ON UN-AMERICAN ACTIVITIES (HUAC) that she had registered to vote as a communist in 1936 "to please my grandfather." HUAC cleared her of the charges, and her sponsor, Philip Morris, continued to support her top-rated show, "I Love Lucy" (CBS, 1951–57), which had been popular enough even to distract attention from the presidential inauguration of her fan Dwight Eisenhower.

Occasionally television performers became identified with a political cause, such as when Jack PAAR supported Castro's revolution in Cuba. As a general rule, however, television performers were either apathetic or politically circumspect. Unlike such FILM ACTORS AND ACTRESSES as John WAYNE or Jane FONDA, television performers were rarely in

the forefront of either right-wing or left-wing political causes. Nor were there many television actors, like Wayne, who were strongly identified with patriotic roles.

However, some performers did become identified with a character role in ways that had some Cold War significance. Ronald REAGAN's role from 1965 to 1966 as the Old Ranger on "Death Valley Days" (syndicated, 1952–70) before his election as governor of California may have contributed to his image as a man of great folk wisdom and common sense who stood on the side of law and order and was associated with a time of clear distinctions between right and wrong. Similarly, as host from 1954 to 1962 of GENERAL ELECTRIC THEATER (CBS, 1952–62) and a public spokesman for G.E., Reagan associated himself with America's future as embodied by the corporate giants of high technology.

Robert Young from FATHER KNOWS BEST (CBS/NBC, 1954–62) and Hugh Beaumont from LEAVE IT TO BEAVER (CBS, ABC, 1957–63) came to stand as archetypal 1950s fathers, and their respective costars, Jane Wyatt and Barbara Billingsley, became archetypal mother figures. These associations reappeared in commercials and subsequent roles, such as Young's Marcus Welby, a wise authoritarian doctor. Young became so identified with the Welby role that he was asked to speak at medical school graduation exercises. The image of strong mother and father figures was desired by a Cold War society characterized by anxiety and uncertainty.

Robert VAUGHN, who starred in the television spy show THE MAN FROM U.N.C.L.E. (NBC, 1964–68), is notable not only for his acting roles but also because he wrote a Ph.D. thesis analyzing the effect of the House Committee on Un-American Activities (HUAC) on the entertainment industry during the Cold War. He published the thesis in 1972 as the book *Only Victims*.

Other notable Cold War television personalities included the TELEVISION NEWS figures Edward R. MURROW, Walter CRONKITE, Dan RATHER, Chet Huntley and David Brinkley (see THE HUNTLEY–BRINKLEY REPORT) and William F. BUCKLEY Jr. Prominent figures in RELIGIOUS TELEVISION PROGRAMMING included the Reverend Billy GRAHAM, Bishop Fulton SHEEN, Pat ROBERTSON, and Jerry FALWELL.

television quiz shows A kind of television game show popular in the 1950s. According to NOVELIST John Updike, "The appeal of the programs, with the rising challenge of Soviet brain power as a backdrop, was ultimately patriotic. The contestants were selected to be a cross-section of our nation just as deliberately as the G.I.'s in a war movie are." Consequently, when in 1959 several popular shows, such as "Dotto" (CBS/NBC, 1958), "The Big Surprise" (NBC, 1955–57), "The $64,000 Question" (CBS, 1955–58) and TWENTY-ONE (NBC, 1956–58) were revealed to be corrupt, a public furor ensued. Several commentators interpreted the dishonesty in these games as evidence of the moral decay of the entire country. U.S. moral fiber, supposedly the basis for the country's survival and for its superiority to the U.S.S.R., had been found to be tainted. Moreover, the betrayal of the public trust by network television, which represented big business, and by "Twenty-One's" Charles Van Doren, who represented Ivy League intellectuals and the WASP "cultural aristocracy" of the United States, exposed a moral lapse in the people and institutions in charge of managing the Cold War. According to Arkansas's Democratic senator William Fulbright, "It has grave possibilities in our international relations . . . What seems to be new about these scandals is the moral blindness or callowness which allows those in responsible positions to accept the practices which the facts reveal." The quiz show scandals were the topic of a post–Cold War movie, *Quiz Show,* linking the scandals to the anti-intellectualism and anti-Semitism that were part of Cold War culture.

For additional reading, see Whitfield's *The Culture of the Cold War.*

television satire   Political SATIRE has never thrived on American television. First, satire is difficult to do well before a mass audience with disparate backgrounds and views. Striking a balance between laughter and bitterness requires an audience with a common sensibility. Also, many viewers turn to television for escape and so do not choose to watch shows that remind them of seemingly unresolvable political problems. Moreover, because television is funded by sponsors who do not want to alienate potential customers, the medium typically avoids controversial material that might offend viewers.

Satire was virtually unknown on American television before 1963, though THE BULLWINKLE SHOW (NBC/ABC 1961–73), a cartoon show mostly directed to children spoofed spies and bureaucracy. During the 1940s and 1950s, Milton Berle and Sid Caesar had highly popular shows built around comedy sketches, but these rarely had political overtones. The proponents of the 1950s RED SCARE had made it clear that fighting communism was no laughing matter. Attempts in any medium to satirize or criticize anti-communist efforts could draw censure from such powerful entities as the HOUSE COMMITTEE ON UN-AMERICAN ACTIVITIES (HUAC). For instance, when Arthur MILLER testified before the committee in 1956, the chief interrogator intimated a connection between Miller and the communists by pointing out that Miller's play criticizing HUAC, *You're Next,* had been reproduced by the Communist Party. In such an accusatory environment, anyone satirizing American anti-communism risked BLACKLISTING. Thus political satire did not come to American television until the Red Scare had clearly passed and it was once again safe to poke fun at the government. THAT WAS THE WEEK THAT WAS (NBC, 1964–65), LAUGH-IN (NBC, 1968–73); THE SMOTHERS BROTHERS COMEDY HOUR (CBS, 1967–69), SATURDAY NIGHT LIVE (NBC, 1975–present), SECOND CITY TV (syndicated, 1977–81) and occasional musical specials by Mark Russell were the major television satires of the Cold War era.

The first significant television satire debuted as a special in November 1963, the month President Kennedy was assassinated. Despite its initial bad timing, "That Was the Week That Was" (also known as *TW3*) ran from January 1964 to May 1965 as a weekly series. The live show employed comedy sketches, musical production numbers, satirical news reports and satirical songs by such figures as Tom LEHRER. Among the regulars were Nancy Ames, Buck Henry, Phyllis Newman, Alan Alda and David Frost. *TW3* was one of the first American television shows to feature BLACK HUMOR, as in Lehrer's cheerful song about nuclear holo-

caust, WE WILL ALL GO TOGETHER WHEN WE GO. Republican presidential candidate Barry Goldwater was a frequent target of the show's satire, and during the 1964 campaign the popular show was repeatedly preempted by low-rated political speeches and documentaries paid for by Republicans. The show failed to regain its momentum after the election, and it was canceled a few months after Lyndon Johnson's presidential inauguration.

"Laugh-In" was a comedy variety show that sometimes included light satire. The show's fast pace and nontraditional structure reflected the quick tempo and iconoclastic developments of U.S. culture during the Vietnam War era. In one of its more notable moments, President Nixon appeared and repeated the "Laugh-In" motto, "Sock it to me," although he mispronounced it by turning it into a question with the emphasis on the final word.

Also a comedy variety show, "The Smothers Brothers Comedy Hour" was decidedly more satiric. The Smothers Brothers made fun of America's most hallowed institutions: motherhood, church, politics and the government. Moreover, it took an increasingly strong stand against the Vietnam War. The show also occasioned folk singer Pete SEEGER's return to network television after over a decade and a half of blacklisting. His anti–Vietnam War song, "Waist Deep in the Big Muddy," landed the Smothers Brothers in trouble with the CBS management, which forbade Seeger to sing it on his first appearance but did allow him to perform it on a later show. Pat Paulsen's absurdist presidential campaign also disturbed CBS officials, who feared they would have to furnish equal time to other candidates. Paulsen's campaign slogan echoed President Johnson's speech announcing he would not seek another term in office: "If nominated I will not run, and if elected I will not serve." Despite the show's popularity, CBS canceled it in 1969, largely because of the brothers' preference for outspoken, antiwar guests and their penchant for keeping their material away from the censors until the last minute. The show was replaced by "Hee-Haw," a country music variety show with cornball humor.

"Saturday Night Live" was another comedy show that sometimes included political satire. Chevy Chase, who began as a regular and later returned as a guest, became known for his imitations of President Ford and later of President Reagan. Dan Aykroyd imitated Presidents Carter and Nixon, and Dana Carvey imitated President Bush. In addition to specific skits that satirized current events, the show featured a regular Weekend Update, a satirical news broadcast. The humor ranged from straight comedy to political satire to black humor, and its targets included leaders from communist countries as well as from the West.

"Second City TV" (1977–81) was an offshoot from Chicago's improvisational comedy club, the Second City. The show featured some political sketches set at the SCTV television studios. It appeared on network television between 1981 and 1983 under the title "SCTV Network." That version starred John Candy, Rick Moranis and Martin Short, among others. (See also FILM SATIRES.)

television science fiction shows   Science fiction shows and Westerns sometimes portrayed Cold War antagonisms in settings from the future or the past. Protagonists embodied the same "American" traits with which the

United States identified itself during the Cold War. For example, STAR TREK's Federation (NBC, 1966–69), served by the starship *Enterprise,* suggested NATO, while the enemy "evil empires" evoked the Warsaw Pact and other communist military powers. Futuristic science fiction shows based on space exploration included *Star Trek,* BATTLESTAR GALACTICA (ABC, 1978–79), BUCK ROGERS (ABC, 1950–51) and CAPTAIN VIDEO AND HIS VIDEO RANGERS, (DuMont/syndicated, 1949–56), an early children's show. These all featured the struggle between forces of good and evil, in which evil was aggressive and repressive, as the communists were believed to be. For instance, "Star Trek's" Captain Kirk and his crew were portrayed as spreading peace, order, reason, fairness and equality to realms oppressed by tyranny. Their opponents lacked compassion, were intent on expanding their empires and relied on military power and duplicity to get their way—just like the popular view of the communists.

Superheroes on science fiction shows offered some degree of wish fulfillment as invincible protectors who could make the world safe for decent, law-abiding Americans. As long as Superman or WONDER WOMAN (ABC/CBS, 1976–79) was around, evil—even in the form of the communist threat—could not possibly thrive. Science fiction shows centering on superheroes with extraordinary powers included THE ADVENTURES OF SUPERMAN, (syndicated, 1951–57), "Wonder Woman" (ABC/CBS, 1976–79) and THE POWERS OF MATTHEW STAR (NBC, 1982–83).

THE TWILIGHT ZONE (CBS, 1959–64) was one of television's most varied and sophisticated science fiction shows. An anthology of dramas, "The Twilight Zone" was on the air during the U-2 incident, the Berlin Crisis, the Cuban Missile Crisis and the Kennedy assassination. It presented offbeat stories that frequently ended with an ironic twist. The show's pervading ironic undertone sometimes provided poetic justice, and its fantastic quality provoked viewers to wonder about the nature of their world. "The Twilight Zone" offered a form of secular mysticism suggesting that everything occurs as part of an unknown design of unknowable but all-powerful purpose. One popular Cold War–inspired episode, entitled *Time Enough at Last,* expressed then-current fears of a major nuclear war with the Soviets. The story featured a bank teller whose only desire was to be left alone to read, but he was always interrupted. One day, while he was spending his lunch hour reading deep in the bank vault, a nuclear attack killed everyone outside. Happy to be alone at last with his books, the far-sighted teller then accidentally broke his reading glasses, upon which he depended completely. It was unusual for American television to suggest that the purpose of the universe might be hostile to, or amused by, human beings.

The short-lived MAX HEADROOM (ABC, 1986–87) was one of the most innovative, astute and technologically aware programs of the second Reagan administration. Set "twenty minutes into the future," the 1987 show featured the exploits of investigative television reporter Edison Carter who has been digitized by the child computer genius Bryce Lynch and manifested as video character Max Headroom, who appears intermittently on a pirate television station. In the world of "Max Headroom," television essentially replaces government, and ratings, which are all-important, are reported every second. The show provided a cynical view of television and society, perhaps alluding to President Reagan, whose mastery of the television medium was legendary.

television shows for children For the most part, children's television programming addressed the Cold War indirectly, by incorporating Cold War images and themes within stories about the struggle between good and evil. The protagonists were usually either superheroes or very strong, smart men who used their talents to save the world from an evil menace. Superheroes included Superman (see THE ADVENTURES OF SUPERMAN syndicated, 1951–57), the Incredible Hulk (CBS, 1978–82) and the cartoon character Mighty Mouse (CBS, 1955–66), whose cape and outfit evoked the American flag. Examples of shows with strong, smart heroes included BUCK ROGERS (ABC, 1950–51) and CAPTAIN VIDEO (DuMont/syndicated, 1949–56). Programming intended for adults drew on the same formula, though in the 1970s they were more likely to include female superheroes such as THE BIONIC WOMAN (ABC/NBC, 1976–78) and WONDER WOMAN (ABC/CBS, 1976–79). Common to all of these shows was the perception that a powerful and malicious enemy who ignores "the rules" threatens world peace and safety. He could only be defeated by protagonists who respected the law and worked cooperatively with authority. These attributes paralleled the respective popular perceptions of the U.S.S.R. and the United States in the Cold War. The protagonists also possessed other traits with which Americans liked to identify themselves: truthfulness, loyalty, cleverness, strength, bravery, ingenuity and mechanical know-how. The shows seemed to reassure children by asserting that strong, trustworthy leaders were in charge of the world.

One exception to the moralism of most children's television was THE BULLWINKLE SHOW (NBC/ABC, 1961–73), which satirized government and TELEVISION SPY SHOWS. Many critics believe this irreverent satire was actually intended for adults. Russian spies Boris and Natash spoofed Cold War fears of evil communists, while Captain Peachfuzz satirized the U.S. military.

Eleven years after Nixon's visit improved U.S. relations with the People's Republic of China, the television special *Big Bird Goes to China* (1983) featured Jim Henson's muppets in that country.

television situation comedies With a few exceptions like Jackie Gleason's "The Honeymooners" (CBS, 1955–56) and the carry-over from radio, "Amos 'n' Andy" (CBS, 1951–53) most situation comedies (sitcoms) took place in relatively affluent middle-class settings before 1972, when Norman LEAR introduced "Sanford and Son," set in the Los Angeles ghetto. Even after the 1970s, the vast majority of sitcoms took place in American suburbs or affluent city neighborhoods where the protagonists either owned their own homes or lived in upscale apartments. These American families rarely worried about being unemployed, being able to secure daily food and shelter, being able to educate their children well, or having a comfortable standard of living. Such popular shows as LEAVE IT TO BEAVER (CBS/ABC, 1957–63), FATHER KNOWS BEST (CBS/NBC, 1954–62), "The Adventures of Ozzie and Harriet" (ABC, 1952–66), "The Dick van Dyke Show" (CBS, 1961–66), "The Mary Tyler Moore Show"

(CBS, 1970–77), "The Bob Newhart Show" (CBS, 1972–78) and "Maude" (CBS, 1972–78) repeatedly communicated that America was affluent and populated mainly by middle-class men and women. Of course, most Americans did belong to the middle class during the Cold War. Nevertheless, the aggregate image of the sitcom world encouraged even poor and working-class Americans to see themselves as better off than citizens of communist countries who, when depicted at all, were shown to live uncomfortable lives in which acquiring even the most basic necessities was a daily struggle.

The makers of situation comedies were not necessarily attempting to produce Cold War propaganda. They did believe that viewers were more attracted to affluence than to poverty and that sponsors preferred their consumer products to be associated with an upbeat image of affluence that would encourage viewers to buy more goods in order to resemble people on TV. Also, programmers perceived that their viewers found stories of struggle and suffering less than entertaining. In fact, the overseas popularity of American film and television may be attributable to their unabashed presentation of wealth and material abundance. Thus, television sitcoms from the Cold War era reinforced the general belief that life under the American system was much nicer than any other way of life.

Most sitcoms revolved around that bastion of American values, the family. These include ALL IN THE FAMILY (CBS, 1971–91), "Father Knows Best," "Leave It to Beaver," THE WONDER YEARS (ABC, 1988), THE GOLDBERGS (CBS/NBC/DuMont/syndicated, 1949–55), HAPPY DAYS (ABC, 1974 to 84) and "I Love Lucy" (CBS, 1951–57). "All in the Family" was a major innovation because it showed that it was possible for family members to hold different political beliefs. It was a significant departure from such shows as "Father Knows Best" and "Leave It To Beaver," which both ran from the mid-1950s through the early 1960s, presenting an idealized view of the American two-parent nuclear family in which the father works and the mother stays home and in which both parents accept responsibility for rearing their children with solid American values. "Happy Days," which ran from 1974 to 1984, was set during the 1950s and attempted, with nostalgia and many anachronisms, to reconstruct the home life of those earlier shows. "The Wonder Years," which premiered in 1988, was likewise set in the 1950s and dealt with similar family situations, but offered a more realistic, even ironic outlook, incorporating a narrator from the present looking back at his childhood. "The Goldbergs" was a family sitcom from the earliest days of television, notable primarily because one of its stars, Philip LOEB, was fired after being listed in RED CHANNELS, the major source for BLACKLISTING in the television industry. (He was the basis for the Zero MOSTEL character in the film THE FRONT). Lucille BALL, star of the very highly rated "I Love Lucy," avoided blacklisting when she admitted to the HOUSE COMMITTEE ON UN-AMERICAN ACTIVITIES that she had signed a Communist Party electoral petition when she was much younger, but only to please her grandfather. HUAC exonerated her after she repudiated communism, and her sponsor, Philip Morris, stood by her.

Those sitcoms not set in the family were usually set in some version of the workplace: M*A*S*H (CBS, 1972–83),

THE PHIL SILVERS SHOW (CBS, 1955–59), BARNEY MILLER (ABC, 1975–82) and even GILLIGAN'S ISLAND (CBS, 1964–67) generated laughs from showing American men and women working together. "M*A*S*H" was an antiwar comedy that, though set in Korea, aired during the Vietnam War. It went on to become one of the most popular television shows ever. Set in a medical evacuation unit close to the front lines, "M*A*S*H" presented an ongoing parade of wounded and dying soldiers, though the comedy stemmed from the interaction of the medical staff as they dealt with stress, exhaustion and cruel circumstances. Whereas the movie of the same title freely employed BLACK HUMOR, the television show rarely invoked that potentially offensive form of comedy. "The Phil Silvers Show" was also set in the military, but in peacetime. It featured the exploits of the scheming Sergeant Ernie Bilko, who ran the motor pool at a midwestern army base, offering a lighthearted look at the U.S. military in which enlisted men are clever, even ingenious, while superior officers are dupes and fools. "McHale's Navy" (ABC, 1962–66) offered a similar view of wartime life in the navy.

"Barney Miller" whose characters were among the most fully drawn in television history, was set in a New York police precinct office. Occasionally the officers had to deal with unusual Cold War developments, such as a defection, a Soviet spy or a college student who had built a nuclear bomb for his class project. "Gilligan's Island" featured a cross-section of American society cast away together on a tropical island. Their little world included an upper caste (the millionaire Howells), a working class (the captain and his bumbling mate, Gilligan), a scientist from the professional class who was the island society's technical innovator, a movie starlet and a small-town young woman. Though the characterizations were heavily stereotyped, the show nonetheless provided a simplistic overview of American society during the Cold War. The wealthy Howells were shown as foolish and incompetent, though the others readily deferred to their sense of entitlement to luxury. The professor commanded respect as the primary problem-solver, but was shown as naive and somewhat out of touch with reality, as "eggheads" often were supposed to be. The Skipper and Gilligan labored hard to take care of the others, doing all the real work, while Ginger and Mary Ann generally acquiesced to whatever was reasonably asked of them and sometimes served as romantic interests.

Politics was the backdrop for comedy in the short-lived GRANDPA GOES TO WASHINGTON (ABC, 1978) and HAIL TO THE CHIEF (ABC, 1985). The former featured a crusading grandfather who was elected to Congress and battled against special interests for the common good. Among those with whom he contended was his dim-witted son, an army general. "Hail to the Chief" starred Patty Duke as the president of the United States. The show featured wild, improbable plot complications in which the president confronted an ongoing string of crises ranging from a lunatic major's threatening to start World War III to the equally insane Soviet premier's hotline threat to blackmail her husband, whom the KGB had caught in a compromising position with a female spy. However, the Reagan-era show was unable to garner sufficient ratings to sustain itself and lasted for only seven episodes in 1985.

television spy shows The Cold War was the logical context for spy and secret agent stories, since fighting the Cold War relied so much upon clandestine operations and proxy warfare. Also, scientific knowledge and technology—used by spies and secret agents—played a vastly greater role in the Cold War than at any other point in history. Thus, the spy story, which arguably dates back to Homer's *Iliad*, evolved into a separate genre during the Cold War, in the form of SPY NOVELS and SPY FILMS as well as television spy or secret-agent shows.

In the *Iliad*, Odysseus sneaks into the Trojan citadel; gains crucial information from Helen; captures the Palladium, which protects the city from capture; and returns safely to his camp. Most spy stories employ similar formulas: The hero penetrates hostile territory; acquires necessary information, often through the assistance of a beautiful woman within the enemy camp; strikes a damaging blow against the enemy's defenses; and returns safely to his base. Spy stories vary, however, with regard to their protagonists' motivations and allegiances, their special skills, their personalities and the values they believe themselves to be serving through their work.

Television secret agents constituted a significant portion of TELEVISION ADVENTURE HEROES, and they shared many of the same traits as other warriors on the side of goodness and justice. Some secret agents were loners unwillingly dragged into patriotic service (like Rick in the pre–Cold War film *Casablanca*): the A-Team, Stringfellow Hawke from AIRWOLF (CBS/cable, 1984–88). Alexander Mundy from IT TAKES A THIEF (ABC, 1968–70), businessman Biff Baker from BIFF BAKER, U.S.A. (CBS, 1952–53) and the heroines in CODE NAME: FOXFIRE (NBC, 1985).

In most instances, however, secret agent heroes were firmly committed to their causes. For instance, FBI spy Herbert PHILBRICK was clearly committed to his profession in the highly popular I LED THREE LIVES (syndicated, 1953–56), which projected a strong anti-communist message by depicting the FBI thwarting the evil machinations of the Communist Party in America. Likewise, the hero of THE F.B.I. (ABC, 1965–68, 1974), Inspector Lewis Erskine, can be described as "a man of impeccable integrity and little humor" (McNeil *Total Television*).

In most spy shows, the "rightness" of the hero's cause was simply taken for granted, and the plots focused on the action that grew from dangerous situations. Of course, the danger itself implied some external threat to American interests or security. Often the importance of the cause justified the hero's use of violence and/or circumvention of the law.

Like other adventure heroes, spies relied on some combination of physical strength, sexual attraction, technological innovation, cleverness and quick-wittedness—and more rarely, on their accumulated knowledge or liberal arts education. Heroines were less frequently seen, but they possessed the same general array of traits.

Sometimes, defeating enemy agents was shown to require a range of skills and attributes. Mr. T from THE A-TEAM (ABC, 1983–87) and Willie Armitage from MISSION IMPOSSIBLE (CBS, 1966–73) possessed a brute strength on which other members of their team could rely. THE BIONIC WOMAN (ABC/NBC, 1976–78) and THE SIX MILLION DOLLAR MAN (ABC, 1973–78) combined all the attributes of a team with their own technologically advanced bodies. In some shows, guile and cunning were more important, as demonstrated by Alexander Mundy, Steed and Mrs. Peel from THE AVENGERS (ABC, 1966–69), and the protagonist of THE ADVENTURES OF FU MANCHU (syndicated, 1956). Having sufficient sex appeal to win over enemy female agents was essential for all James BOND imitations, who also had to be adroit, suave, sophisticated, witty, and good with state-of-the-art gadgetry: James West from THE WILD, WILD WEST (CBS, 1965–69), Napoleon Solo and Illya Kuryakin from THE MAN FROM U.N.C.L.E. (NBC, 1964–68) and COVER UP's Mac Harper (CBS, 1984–85). GET SMART (NBC/CBS, 1965–70) spoofed all of these characteristics through its protagonist, the bumbling super-agent Maxwell Smart who nevertheless presented himself as suave and sophisticated.

By contrast, the villains were likely to possess traits popularly associated with communists. They were devious, unreliable, opportunistic, cold-blooded and crude, though sometimes they were charming, elegant—and decadent. In the Cold War, the U.S.S.R. relied on bigger warheads, more tanks and greater "raw" destructive power, while the United States relied on the greater accuracy, diversity and mobility of its weapons systems. Similarly, television villains were often better endowed with muscles than with brains; they were not as quick-witted, skilled or scrappy as the hero.

As generational differences in the 1960s and 1970s led to new social attitudes about authority and personal expression, television spies lost much of the strait-laced, middle-class respectability found in FBI inspector Lewis Erskine and "Mission Impossible" team-leader James Phelps. More colorful, rambunctious heroes, like the protagonists of I SPY (NBC, 1965–68), began to question the agencies they served or even were openly cynical about them.

Other television shows featuring spies and secret operatives included ASSIGNMENT VIENNA (ABC, 1972–73), BEHIND CLOSED DOORS (NBC, 1958–59), THE CRUSADER (CBS, 1955–56), DANGER MAN (CBS, 1961), DANGEROUS ASSIGNMENT (syndicated, 1952), THE DELPHI BUREAU (ABC, 1972–73), ESPIONAGE (NBC, 1963–64), FIVE FINGERS (NBC, 1959–60), THE GIRL FROM U.N.C.L.E. (NBC, 1966–77), HUNTER (NBC, 1984), THE HUNTER (CBS/NBC, 1952, 1954), THE INVISIBLE MAN (CBS, 1958–59), A MAN CALLED SLOANE (NBC, 1979), THE MAN CALLED X (syndicated, 1956), THE MAN WHO NEVER WAS (ABC, 1966–67), RENDEZVOUS (ABC, 1952), SCARECROW AND MRS. KING (CBS, 1983–87), SECRET AGENT (CBS, 1961, 1965–66), SHADOW OF THE CLOAK (DuMont, 1951–52) and SPIES (CBS, 1987). BBC produced "Tinker, Tailor, Soldier, Spy" (1979; shown in United States, 1980), "Smiley's People" (1982), and "A Perfect Spy" (1986–87), exceptionally good series based on John LE CARRÉ's spy novels.

television talk or debate shows Television talks shows generally concerned personalities or figures from the entertainment world. However, some also ventured significantly into politics. For example, when Jack PAAR hosted THE TONIGHT SHOW (NBC, 1954–present), he publicly supported Fidel Castro's revolution against the Cuban dictator, Fulgencio Batista. He also originated several broadcasts from the Berlin Wall and interviewed presidential contenders John

Kennedy and Richard Nixon. "The Tonight Show's" opening monologues provided a running comic commentary on various aspects of the Cold War from the mid-1950s through the demise of the Cold War. Another significant moment in Cold War television came in 1960, when talk show host David Susskind interviewed Nikita Khrushchev during the Soviet premier's visit to the US. Other talk show hosts who discussed politics included Larry King, Dick Cavett, Jimmy Breslin and William F. BUCKLEY Jr., whose FIRING LINE (syndicated/PBS, 1966–present) featured interviews with Presidents Nixon, Ford and Reagan; British prime minister Harold Macmillan; failed presidential candidates Barry Goldwater and George McGovern; novelist Norman MAILER, Clare Boothe Luce and John Kenneth Galbraith, among others. (See also TELEVISION NEWS.)

Television Westerns The Western is the most American of genres, and the popularity of the Western during the 1950s and early 1960s coincides with that part of the Cold War in which the lines between the United States and the U.S.S.R. were most clearly and emphatically drawn. Prior to the Vietnam era, the Western themes of good versus evil and civilization versus lawlessness paralleled the reasons why most Americans believed it was imperative that the United States fight the Cold War. During the heyday of television Westerns in the 1950s and 1960s lawmen like GUNSMOKE's Matt Dillon, Wyatt Earp, the Lone Ranger and Texas John Slaughter, solid citizens like Roy Rogers, Dale Evans, the Cartwright family on "Bonanza" and the supporting cast on "Gunsmoke," virtuous cowboys like Gene Autry, Sugarfoot, Bronco and the regulars on "Wagon Train," and even drifters with dubious professions like Maverick and Paladin from "Have Gun Will Travel," and reformed outlaws like Johnny Ringo, all stood tall against those who would violate the law, take advantage of weak and unprotected citizens, greedily grab power and wealth for themselves, and upset all norms of established social order, just as the United States was standing tall against the expansion of a communist empire that used its Red Army to take advantage of weak and unprotected countries, seize power for itself, and foment worldwide revolution. In this way traditional Westerns capitalized on the prevailing sentiment in the 1950s and early-to-middle 1960s that the United States, like the Western hero, was shouldering its innate responsibility to do what had to be done to preserve the basic norms of decency and civilization. A somewhat different kind of Western, THE WILD, WILD WEST was a take-off on the JAMES BOND movies set during the Grant administration in the early 1870s. But even though it featured secret government agents instead of cowboys, it too championed the U.S. government and the forces of law and order.

However, after the 1963 Cuban Missile Crisis, the superpowers avoided direct confrontation and pursued their political agendas primarily through proxy wars and revolutions in Asia and Africa. Thus the Cold War confrontation did not loom as large over the socio-political landscape. Moreover, between 1965 and 1973 the increasingly unpopular Vietnam War overshadowed the larger Cold War confrontation between East and West, and the moral ambiguity of the war caused many people to reexamine the underlying values inherent in most Westerns. In particular

some critics claimed that Westerns encouraged resolving differences through violence and that the depiction of Native Americans was stereotypical, dehumanizing and racist. And they argued that those same themes were at work in Vietnam, where the 1968 My Lai massacre, for example, embodied out-of-control American violence and inherent racism toward Vietnamese nationals. Thus, in part because of Vietnam War, in part because outer space was emerging as the new frontier in the 1960s and such TELEVISION SCIENCE FICTION as STAR TREK (NBC, 1966–69) and BATTLESTAR GALACTICA (ABC, 1978–79) were playing out traditional Western themes, and in part because the days of the old West were quickly fading into the past, television Westerns began to lose audiences in the middle 1960s, and by 1975, when "Gunsmoke" left the air, the genre essentially died out. The few post-Vietnam shows set in the old West, such as "Little House on the Prairie" (NBC, 1974–82), stressed domesticity and downplayed violence.

The major television Westerns from the Cold War era include "Bat Masterson" (NBC, 1958–61), "The Big Valley" (ABC, 1965–69), "Bonanza" (NBC, 1959–73), "Broken Arrow" (ABC, 1956–58), "Bronco" (ABC, 1959–60), "Cheyenne" (ABC, 1955–63), "Colt .45" (ABC, 1957–60), "Daniel Boone" (NBC, 1964–70), "Death Valley Days" (syndicated, 1952–60), "The Deputy" (NBC, 1959–61), "The Gene Autry Show" (CBS, 1950–56), "Gunsmoke" (CBS, 1955–75), "Have Gun Will Travel" (CBS, 1957–63), "The High Chaparral" (NBC, 1967–71), "Jim Bowie" (ABC, 1956–58), "Johnny Ringo" (CBS, 1959–60), "Kung Fu" (ABC, 1972–75), "Laramie" (NBC, 1959–63), "Law of the Plainsman" (NBC, 1959–60), "The Lone Ranger" (ABC, 1949–57; CBS ran a Saturday morning cartoon version 1966–69), "A Man Called Shenandoah" (ABC, 1965–66), "Maverick" (ABC, 1957–62), "Nine Lives of Elfego Baca" (ABC, 1958–59), "Rawhide" (CBS, 1959–66), "The Rebel" (ABC, 1959–61), "The Rifleman" (ABC, 1958–63), "Riverboat" (NBC, 1959–61), "The Roy Rogers Show" (1951–57), "The Roy Rogers and Dale Evans Show" (ABC, 1962–63), "Shane" (ABC, 1966), "Sugarfoot" (ABC, 1957–60), "Tales of Texas John Slaughter" (ABC, 1958–59), "Tales of the Texas Rangers" (CBS, 1955–57), "The Texan" (CBS, 1959–60), "The Virginian" (NBC, 1962–70), "Wagon Train" (NBC, 1957–62, ABC, 1962–65), "The Westerner" (NBC, 1960), "The Wild, Wild West" (CBS, 1965–69), "Wild Bill Hickcock" (syndicated, 1951–58), "Wyatt Earp" (ABC, 1955–61), and "Zane Grey Theater" (CBS, 1956–62).

Television's Vietnam: Impact of the Media/ The Real Story A 1985 TELEVISION DOCUMENTARY written, produced and directed by Peter C. Rollins and sponsored in part by the National Endowment for the Humanities. The show responds to Richard Ellison and Stanley Karnow's 1983 PBS documentary, VIETNAM: A TELEVISION HISTORY, exploring the role of the media in creating the perceptions that influenced the conduct and outcome of the Vietnam war.

Tell Me Lies A British-made 1968 VIETNAM WAR FILM starring Glenda Jackson, Peggy Ashcroft, Mark Jones and members of the Royal Shakespeare Company, and produced, directed and conceived by Peter Brook. Made during the height of the U.S. military involvement in Vietnam, *Tell*

Me Lies integrates documentary footage of the war with performances by the cast to create a bitter, mocking attack on the Vietnam War.

Ten Commandments, The A 1956 EPIC FILM starring Charlton HESTON, Yul Brynner, Anne Baxter and Edward G. Robinson and directed by Cecil B. DEMILLE. The film depicts the biblical story of the exodus of the Hebrews from Egypt, Moses's receipt of the Ten Commandments at Mt. Sinai, the people's worshiping of the Golden Calf, their subsequent wandering through the desert and their final arrival at the Promised Land. The theme of resisting tyranny by accepting Judeo-Christian values had strong Cold War overtones, which DeMille made explicit in his personal prologue. Stepping before a white and gold curtain, DeMille states, "The theme of this picture is whether men are to be ruled by God's law—or whether they are to be ruled by the whims of a dictator . . . Are men the property of the state? Or are they free souls under God? This same battle continues throughout the world today." Later in the film a slave articulates the sentiment behind the slogan, "Better Dead Than Red," which was current during the 1950s. The slave proclaims, "Is life in bondage better than death?" Moreover, like other epic films, *The Ten Commandments* communicates American wealth and abundance through its grand scope, spectacular effects and vast scale.

For additional reading, see Sayre's *Running Time*.

Tender Men, The A 1948 POLITICAL NOVEL by Willa Gibbs. The story centers on a Midwestern farm boy who goes to the big city to become a newspaper writer. He is recruited by the Communist Party and undergoes an intense indoctrination. However, when he fails to follow directions the party sentences him to death. The book presents an exposé of communist methods and strategies and portrays a party that expects the individual to subjugate all of his or her rights and beliefs to those of the party. The book was criticized for its poor characterizations and weak narrative structure.

"That Was the Week That Was" A TELEVISION SATIRE that ran on NBC from 1964 to 1965. Based on a British show of the same name, "That Was the Week That Was" (also known as "TW3") first appeared as a special in November 1963, the month President Kennedy was assassinated. It began as a weekly series the following January. The live show employed comedy sketches, musical production numbers, satirical news reports, and satirical songs by such figures as Tom LEHRER. Among the regulars were Nancy Ames, who sang the opening and closing songs and appeared in sketches; Buck Henry; Phyllis Newman; Alan Alda; and David Frost, who had hosted the British version and the second year of the American production. "TW3" was one of the first American television shows to feature BLACK HUMOR, as in Lehrer's cheerful song about nuclear holocaust, WE WILL ALL GO TOGETHER WHEN WE GO (1959). Other episodes featured the "Dance of the Liberal Republicans" and "Send in the Marines," about the 1965 U.S. intervention in the Dominican Republic. Republican presidential candidate Barry Goldwater was a frequent target of the show's satire, and during the 1964 campaign, the popular program was repeatedly preempted by low-rated political speeches and documentaries paid for by Republicans. The show failed to regain its momentum after the election, and it was canceled a few months after Lyndon Johnson's presidential inauguration.

theater The RED SCARE and the Vietnam War were the Cold War issues that attracted the most attention from American dramatists. U.S. playwrights Arthur MILLER, Donald Freed and Eric Bentley and German playwrights Heimar Kipphardt and Bertolt BRECHT dealt directly or indirectly with aspects of the Red Scare. Miller's THE CRUCIBLE (1955), a play about the 17th-century Salem witch hunts, is commonly read as an allegory about the McCarthyite anti-communist "witch hunts" of the late 1940s and 1950s, in which former communists and communist sympathizers were required both to recant their past beliefs and to identify other people who had been involved in communist causes. Refusal to testify could bring about prison sentences and BLACKLISTING, as well as social ostracism. The play was produced in 1953, a year after Miller's collaborator Elia KAZAN identified former communist associates before the HOUSE COMMITTEE ON UN-AMERICAN ACTIVITIES (HUAC), despite Miller's urgings to the contrary. (Kazan's 1954 film drama ON THE WATERFRONT is often taken as Kazan's defense of informing.) Miller's next play, *A View from the Bridge* (1955), is a tragedy about an immigrant who informs on an illegal alien and consequently dies because of it. In 1963 Kazan and Miller reconciled when they were named resident director and resident playwright for the premiere season of New York's Lincoln Center. Kazan directed Miller's autobiographical *After the Fall* (1963), whose protagonist, a former communist, breaks with a friend about to inform before a congressional committee. Miller also wrote a short play, *You're Next*, satirizing HUAC.

Bentley's ARE YOU NOW OR HAVE YOU EVER BEEN? (1972) addresses the HUAC hearings more directly, using portions of the committee transcripts for the dialogue. The testimonies of 18 witnesses, given between 1947 and 1956, are merged into a single session for purposes of dramatic unity. Bentley also wrote THIRTY YEARS OF TREASON (1971), a NONFICTION book that presents edited transcripts from HUAC hearings between 1938 and 1968.

Freed dramatizes the arrest and conviction of atomic bomb spies Julius and Ethel Rosenberg in INQUEST: A TALE OF POLITICAL TERROR (1970). Based on the 1965 study *Invitation to an Inquest* by Walter and Miriam Schneir, the play argues for the Rosenbergs' innocence and presents them as victims of an anti-Semitic political crusade.

Kipphardt, an East German, also used actual hearing transcripts to dramatize political persecution in IN THE MATTER OF J. ROBERT OPPENHEIMER (1968). Kipphardt based the play on the Atomic Energy Commission (AEC) hearing that deprived Oppenheimer of his security clearance due to his alleged communist affiliations in the 1930s. Oppenheimer, who had led the successful World War II effort to create an atomic bomb and who headed the AEC from 1946 to 1952, had angered right-wing conservatives by promoting international control of atomic energy and by opposing for moral and scientific reasons the development of hydrogen bombs. His own response to Kipphardt's play was that the playwright had "tried to convert a [political] farce into a tragedy."

Brecht, a Marxist playwright and screenwriter, was subpoenaed before HUAC in 1947, just as he was preparing to produce his 1938 play *Galileo*, about the religious/political persecution of the famous 16th-century astronomer. *Galileo* addresses the failure of individuals to confront an unjust, repressive and unimaginative authority. Like his character, Galileo, Brecht failed to take a strong stand against his inquisitors, although he tried but was not permitted to read a statement criticizing the hearings. However, unlike other left-wing witnesses, he answered their query about whether he had ever been a member of the Communist Party: "No, no, no, no, no, never" (no evidence exists to suggest that Brecht joined the German Communist Party and he certainly was not a member of the U.S. party). Although HUAC cleared him of any criminal charges, Brecht left the United States immediately after testifying and soon after settled in East Germany, whose government provided him with his own theater and a generous subsidy to continue his work. Ironically, this Marxist playwright was responsible for the longest-running musical up to that time in American history. *The Threepenny Opera* enjoyed over 2,000 Off-Broadway performances in New York from 1954 to 1961, during the height of the Cold War.

The Vietnam War was the other major subject of Cold War–oriented drama in the United States. Megan Terry's VIET ROCK (1966) was the first dramatic production to deal with the war. An experimental work produced the year after U.S. combat troops were introduced into the war, it was produced by the OPEN THEATER, which also presented Jean-Claude van Itallie's *American Hurrah* (1966), which criticizes both the war and American society. Terence McNally's one-act Vietnam War plays dramatize the absurdity of the war and the schism between those fighting it and those at home. These include *Tour* (1967), *Next* (1968), *Botticelli* (1968) and *Bringing It All Back Home* (1969). Barbara Garson's *Macbird* (1966) likens President Johnson to Macbeth in its biting SATIRE of the war and the Johnson administration. Maria Irene Fornes's *A Vietnamese Wedding* (1967) was performed as part of a week-long protest called Angry Arts Week. In that play, the audience becomes involved in a traditional Vietnamese wedding ceremony. Her other war protest play is *The Red Burning Light* (1968). Also in 1968, the Royal Shakespeare Company premiered Peter Brooks' antiwar play *US*. The play's first half describes the situation in Vietnam, featuring a military combat mission, a bombing raid, a U.S. news conference, and a Buddhist monk setting himself on fire to protest the war. The second half presents a debate about the most effective form of domestic protest within Britain. And 1968 also saw Galt MacDermot's musical HAIR, which celebrated the COUNTERCULTURE and the efforts of young man to avoid the draft by joining a HIPPIE commune.

POET and political activist Father Daniel BERRIGAN depicts the trial that resulted from his burning of draft records in Catonsville, Maryland, in *The Trial of the Catonsville Nine* (1970). He drew on a documentary tradition that would be used by other protest plays.

David RABE wrote the most highly acclaimed Vietnam War plays. *Streamers* (1976) shows the range of attitudes toward the war, the military and each other among a group of soldiers who are completing their basic training and awaiting assignment to Vietnam. The play is part of a trilogy that also includes *Sticks and Bones* (1969) and *The Basic Training of Pavlo Hummel* (1971). As Nancy Anisfield points out in *Vietnam Anthology*, "Each play presents a vision of an America that is permanently poisoned by the war . . . the physically or psychologically wounded veteran is shown ironically as a painful, horrible embarrassment because he represents the ruin of America's myth of heroism and goodness. Furthermore, these plays offer an image of the American spirit as a thin veneer of euphemisms and patriotic rhetoric."

As the war continued, other plays began to deal with Vietnam veterans. Lanford Wilson's *The 5th of July* (1978) centers on a veteran who has lost his legs in the war and receives visits from family members and friends. They reminisce about their carefree prewar days and confront what they have done and become since. Emily Mann's *Still Life* (1979) presents a Vietnam veteran, his wife and his woman friend in their own words, based on interviews conducted by the playwright.

Other days dealt with the Cold War by taking on historical incidents. Stanley Greenberg's *Pueblo* (1971) deals with the capture of the U.S. intelligence ship off the coast of Korea in 1968, the congressional inquiry into the event and the subsequent court-martial of Commander Lloyd Bucher. The incident occurred just prior to the communists' Tet Offensive in Vietnam and is believed to have been coordinated with the North Vietnamese as an effort to have the United States redeploy its troops to Korea before Tet. *1776*, a 1969 Broadway musical and 1972 film musical, shows how the Declaration of Independence was forged despite strong differences among the factions represented at the Continental Congress. It implicitly suggested that national unity can be reforged despite contemporary differences.

Though perhaps better known for his political CARTOONS, Jules FEIFFER wrote several plays satirizing American Cold War politics. His one-act comedy *Crawling Arnold* (1961) appeared amidst the tension of the second Berlin Crisis. It centers on Arnold, a 35-year-old businessman who begins behaving like an infant. His parents, who are caricatures of conservative, middle-class Americans, arrange for him to be visited by attractive social workers. Unlike Arnold, the parents are vigorous and athletic despite being in their seventies. Their bomb shelter appears in *Good Housekeeping* magazine, and they occupy themselves with civil defense drills and talking about the communist menace. Their maid is a black activist who wants her own bomb shelter. Feiffer also published two short plays in popular magazines that satirize the Kennedy administration: *Interview* (in *Harpers*, June 1962) and *You Should Have Caught Me At the White House* (in *Holiday*, June 1963). However, these lost their appeal after Kennedy was assassinated in November 1963. In 1967, Feiffer produced his first full-length original play, *Little Murders*, about an all-American family that is victimized by random violence. *God Bless* (1968) takes place amidst revolutionary activity in Washington, D.C., and expresses cynicism about those who exercise power. *The White House Murder Case* (1970) imagines a Vietnam-like war with Brazil and presents the secret machinations of the president and his administration. In 1973, Feiffer and eight other play-wrights satirized President Nixon in *Watergate Classics*.

Paddy Chayefsky's THE PASSION OF JOSEF D. (1964) drama-tizes the brutality of Stalin and the Soviet regime. Edward Albee's QUOTATIONS FROM CHAIRMAN MAO TSE-TUNG (1969), which was published and produced in conjunction with another play, *Box*, pairs historical speeches from the Chinese ruler with lines spoken by a long-winded woman, an old lady and a minister. The play appeared toward the end of the Cultural Revolution in which Chairman Mao consoli-dated his power in the People's Republic of China. The women's speeches present the individual suffering that Mao treats abstractly in his theoretical discourses on capitalism, communism, the necessity of warfare and the evils of indi-viduality.

Some Cold War plays dealt with communist Cuba. Ter-rence McNally's CUBA, SÍ! (1968) centers on a female sup-porter of Fidel Castro named Cuba, who has established a "beachhead" for the revolution in Central Park, where she delivers pro-Castro diatribes to anyone who will listen. Jack Gelber's THE CUBAN THING (1968), inspired by the play-wright's visits to the island, was originally conceived as a part of a HAPPENING, a Cuban Action Night that would also include Cuban music, food, a play about the communist revolution, and other cultural and political events centering on Cuba. *The Cuban Thing* presents the accomplishments of the revolution as viewed by a middle-class Cuban family. Considered pro-Castro, it was violently attacked in the Cuban press and on Spanish-speaking television and radio even before it opened, and at the preview, the theater was bombed. The play ran for only one evening, as audiences feared to attend. Gelber is best known for his experimental play *The Connection*, which the LIVING THEATER produced in 1959, introducing jazz-inspired improvisation to theater and collapsing the distance between audience and actors.

Arthur Kopit's BLACK HUMOR comedy about nuclear plan-ning and policy, END OF THE WORLD (1984), appeared during the first Reagan administration, when Cold War tensions were at their highest since the 1962 Cuban Missile Crisis and administration officials spoke openly of a winnable nuclear war. The play centers on Michael Trent, a playwright who has accepted the seemingly impossible task of writing a play about the 1970s détente-era policy of Mutually Assured Destruction (MAD) and the bleak realities behind nuclear deterrence. The story begins as a *film noir* parody in which the trench coat–wearing playwright imitates the style of a hard-boiled detective. As in *The Maltese Falcon,* much of this *noir* play requires the protagonist to ascertain the exact nature of a deeply disturbing truth, which his secretive sponsor reluctantly reveals only in disjointed fragments. However, after interviewing top-level nuclear policy plan-ners, Trent comes to a profound recognition: Within the framework of MAD, the very existence of nuclear weapons implies their eventual use in a nuclear war. If this dismal conclusion were not bad enough, Trent discovers something even more disheartening: the seductive nature of doom. Humans are drawn to the awesome power of the bomb and are thrilled, as well as horrified, by the prospect of their own destruction. (In this respect, Kopit elaborates on a theme Bernard Wolfe and William Golding introduced in their 1950s apocalyptic novels, LIMBO '90 (1953) and LORD OF

THE FLIES (1954), and which Stanley KUBRICK addressed in his 1964 film satire DR. STRANGELOVE.)

As a playwright, Trent's task is to communicate both intellectually and emotionally the reality of the nuclear situation, while leaving the audience with something more uplifting than the despair that comes from knowing they are doomed by MAD, doomed if they try to extricate themselves from MAD, and further doomed by human nature itself. Trent feels hopeless before this task, just as policy planners feel hopeless about preventing eventual nuclear war. Kopit, however, manages to succeed where Trent fails. Kopit com-municates the dismal facts about the prospects for nuclear war, but he uses black humor, irony and paradox to generate humor rather than despair. The laughter becomes the pallia-tive, if not the antidote, for the doom that Kopit identifies but cannot alter. Moreover, Kopit's success in his seemingly impossible task provides a modicum of hope for success in the other seemingly impossible task of avoiding nuclear war. In a play that highlights the breakdown of logic and reason, hope comes from the wild-card possibilities of un-predictable and irrational discontinuities. Marc Kaminsky's *In the Traffic of a Targeted City* (1986) also deals with nuclear destruction as it moves between present-day New York and 1945 Hiroshima.

An earlier, gentler Cold War comedy is Woody Allen's DON'T DRINK THE WATER (1966), which centers on a Jewish family vacationing in an "Iron Curtain" country. They are forced to take refuge in the American embassy after the father, a caterer, innocently takes pictures of military installa-tions. Allen creates a farce by juxtaposing the concerns of the Cold War with those of a Jewish family whose daughter is supposed to marry in two weeks. The 1955 musical SILK STOCKINGS updates the 1939 film *Ninotchka*, which celebrates capitalism and spoofs communism and Soviet officials. It was written by George S. Kaufman and Leueen McGrath, with songs by Abe Burrows and Cole Porter.

At least three popular Cold War POLITICAL NOVELS were adapted into theater. In 1951 Sidney Kingsley adapted Ar-thur KOESTLER's *Darkness at Noon*. Set in 1937, the play centers on a former Soviet revolutionary who is asked to confess to crimes he did not commit. The play condemns the Stalinist purges and reveals the brutality of the Soviet regime. It ran for 186 performances on Broadway. THE UGLY AMERICAN, Eugene BURDICK and William LEDERER's best-selling 1958 political novel, was produced as a two-act play in 1961. It criticizes American diplomats in Southeast Asia in the years leading up to the Vietnam War. And in 1974, Richard France produced a stage adaptation of *One Day in the Life of Ivan Denisovich*, the 1962 novel by the Soviet dissident and Nobel Prize winner Aleksandr SOLZHENITSYN. The story depicts life in a forced labor camp for political prisoners in the Soviet Union.

PORGY AND BESS, George Gershwin's 1935 folk opera about black Americans, was revived for a national tour in 1952. According to the *New York Times*, "The purpose of the tour is to show central Europeans that . . . Negro players are not debased or oppressed as the Communist line says." President Truman attended a performance of this production at the National Theater in Washington that August. The show later toured Europe and the Soviet Union with the primary mission of easing Cold War tensions.

Among the EXILED WRITERS (to the United States) were dramatists Andrei AMALRIK, Janusz GLOWACKI and Clara GYORGYEY. Amalrik's absurdist, experimental plays led to his surveillance by the KGB in the Soviet Union and his eventual arrest in the mid-1960s. The plays were collected in *Nose! Nose? No-se! and Other Plays* and published in the West in 1973.

Glowacki's most powerful play, *Cinders*, was written in Poland in 1981 and published in the United States in 1985. It describes efforts by a Polish filmmaker to document a production of *Cinderella* in a girls' reformatory school. As part of the documentary, the director compels the girls to describe their own tales of woe. The more extreme and sensational their stories are, the better they are for his cinematic purposes. All the girls but one comply, embellishing on their stories for greater effect. Cinders, the girl who refuses to lie for the camera, becomes the protagonist of the play, which pits the desire to preserve truth against those who would manipulate it for their own purposes.

In addition to two full-length plays, *Fortinbras Gets Drunk* (1985) and *Hunting Cockroaches* (1987), Glowacki has also written two shorter plays while in America, *Journey to Gdansk* and *Flashback*. Both plays deal with the dilemmas of exiled writers who must decide whether to return to Poland to report on the strike of shipyard workers in Gdansk. If they go, they risk imprisonment or other personal loss; if they stay, they must live with what they see as their own cowardice. Gyorgyey's translation of Istvan Orkeny's *Cats Play* has appeared in a run Off-Broadway. The Hungarian playwright has also had some of her own plays produced in smaller productions.

Though he does not address the Cold War directly, Samuel BECKETT was a major force in Cold War theater. His most famous work, *Waiting for Godot* (1952; presented in English, 1954), portrays the desire for an authoritarian god-like figure who is never forthcoming. A major contribution to the Theater of the Absurd, the darkly humorous play depicts an indifferent universe in which human life lacks intrinsic meaning. The characters' unsettling plight of endless waiting for a resolution to their situation parallels the condition of the world caught in an unresolvable stalemate between nuclear-armed superpowers. Like many other literary works of the Cold War, from George Orwell's NINETEEN EIGHTY-FOUR (1949) to John LE CARRÉ's THE SPY WHO CAME IN FROM THE COLD (book, 1963, film 1965) to Kopit's *End of the World* (1984), Beckett's plays question the very terms of sanity and insanity and ask who is in charge of setting those terms. Throughout his career, Beckett showed that the world of human affairs exists on confusing and uncertain terrain, with death always hovering nearby. The desire for redemption is always strong, but God remains absent or at least silent. In 1984, Beckett dedicated *Catastrophe*, a play about political repression, to the Czech dissident playwright Vaclav Havel.

Havel's own *The Memorandum* won the 1967–68 Obie Award for best foreign play when it was produced in New York. *Largo Desolato* (1985; in English, 1987) deals with the struggles of a professor under pressure to deny his writing or face charges of "disturbing the intellectual peace." Havel also wrote *The Garden Party* (1963; in English, 1969) and *Three Vanek Plays* (1990). His plays were banned in Czecho-slovakia in 1969, and he was jailed several times for human rights activism. However, following the fall of communism in 1990, he was elected president of Czechoslovakia. He resigned in 1992 in response to the break-up of the country into the Czech and Slovak federations.

For additional reading, see *Dictionary of Literary Biography* (vol. 7, *Twentieth-Century American Playwrights*); Tucker's *Literary Exile in the Twentieth Century*; and Hughes' *Plays, Politics and Polemics*.

Them! A 1954 SCIENCE FICTION FILM starring James Whitmore, Edmund Gwenn and James Arness and directed by Gordon Douglas. Set in the Mojave Desert, the film features a rampage of giant ants—mutants caused by nearby atomic testing. Impotent before the sugar-crazed creatures, the military turns to a brilliant but socially inept scientist to find a solution and save humanity. The film presents a centrist point of view in which the killer ants, implicitly associated with communism, represent a real threat to U.S. security, and in which the combined efforts of American soldiers and scientists prevail. In this film, the scientist appears as the highest authority and the most indispensable part of the defense against the invaders. Dr. Medford briefs the president and other top officials, commands the full resources of the country and gives orders freely to military personnel.

Ants sometimes provided an image of communism during the Cold War. In the anthill, all workers labor selflessly for the common good, and the individual is entirely subordinated to the collective society. The ants' capacity to swarm evoked recollections of Chinese soldiers who attacked U.S. positions in "swarms" during the Korean War. (See also FILMS ASSOCIATED WITH THE RED SCARE.)

For additional reading, see Biskind's *Seeing Is Believing*.

Thing, The A 1951 SCIENCE FICTION FILM starring James Arness, Kenneth Tobey and Margaret Sheridan, directed by Christian Nyby and produced by Howard Hawks. The 1983 remake, directed by John Carpenter and starring Kurt Russell, was not generally regarded to be as successful as the Korean War–era original. The story centers on the discovery by an Arctic scientific research station of a huge, carnivorous, vegetable-based creature from another world (Arness). The "thing" lives on blood, can reproduce missing limbs, possesses superior wisdom and, like the stereotypical communist cadre, is not "impeded by emotional or sexual instincts." Much of the drama centers on the conflict between Captain Pat Hendry, USAF, who simply wants to destroy an obvious threat to the safety of the entire planet, and Nobel Prize-winning scientist Dr. Carrington, who sports a sinister-looking goatee, wears a Russian-style fur hat and wants to communicate with the Thing to learn new secrets about the universe. But when Carrington tells the Thing, "Listen, I'm your friend," the monster hurls him to the floor. Like the communists, the Thing will only destroy those who try to befriend it. As in many other science fiction films, *The Thing* warns of the possible return of the monster or his friends, concluding with a plea for vigilance, "Watch the skies—everywhere—watch the skies."

The film's right-wing Cold War subtext shows the inherent danger of intellectuals who want to study and understand communism, to establish a dialogue with and ultimately befriend the potentially lethal enemy. Their efforts at friendship will not only kill them, but may destroy everyone else as well, according to the film. The world survives only because a more hard-line military point of view prevails, a viewpoint in which enemies are recognized for what they are and are not tolerated. In *The Thing*, the Faustian dream of knowledge for its own sake must be subordinated to the realities of survival. (See also FILMS ASSOCIATED WITH THE RED SCARE.)

For additional reading, see Biskind's *Seeing Is Believing*.

Third Man, The A 1949 SPY NOVEL by Graham GREENE and a 1950 British-made SPY FILM starring Orson Welles, Joseph Cotten, Alida Valli and Trevor Howard and directed by Carol Reed. Greene also wrote the screenplay. The story is set in Vienna shortly after World War II, when the city was still divided into separate zones controlled by Soviet and Western armies of occupation. The plot focuses on Holly Martins (Cotten), a naive American writer who has come at the behest of his childhood friend Harry Lime (Welles). When he arrives, Martins learns that Lime has been killed in a hit-and-run car accident, but he later discovers that the accident was an elaborate hoax to enable Lime to continue his black-market enterprise of selling diluted and impure medicine to desperate civilians. In the process of investigating Lime's apparent death, Martins falls in love with Lime's girlfriend, who is to be deported from the British sector to the Soviet sector because she is a Czech national. To prevent this, Martins agrees to assist the British officer (Howard) who is trying to arrest Lime. In addition to portraying the politics of policing the divided city, the story shows that innocent Americans must cast off their naivete and recognize and respond to the dirty realities of the postwar situation.

Third World War, The A 1978 MILITARY NOVEL by General Sir John Hackett and other top-ranking NATO generals and advisers. Written toward the end of the 1970s U.S.-Soviet détente, when military planners were complaining that the U.S. arsenal was becoming outdated and military preparedness was suffering, the book imagines a 1985 Soviet attack in Europe that launches World War III. The authors, former ranking NATO officials, project detailed and sophisticated military and political scenarios based on the state of the Cold War during the Carter administration. They show the roots of World War III to reside in the Middle East and Africa, specifically in South Africa and Ethiopia. Direct European fighting between the NATO and Warsaw Pact armies stems from severe unrest in Poland and a Soviet invasion of Yugoslavia. The first major offensive is a Warsaw Pact attack against West Germany, though the fighting quickly spreads throughout the continent and into the North Atlantic. Soviets destroy the English industrial City of Birmingham in the war's first nuclear attack. In retaliation, Britain and the United States launch a devastating nuclear strike against the Soviet city of Minsk. Likewise, the Soviets are the first to employ chemical weapons, though the NATO forces reciprocate.

Told from a NATO point of view, the book clearly identifies communists as aggressors and strongly advocates upgrading NATO weaponry and military readiness. The Soviets choose to launch a war because

> [their] comparatively cautious policy hitherto pursued, which might be described by the slogan "proxy and periphery," had not yet produced the promised results. The attempt to turn the Eurasian landmass into a base for worldwide naval operations had suffered the inescapable setbacks of geography and temperament. The choice now lay . . . between accepting an unwelcome and even humiliating return to previous spheres of influence, and making violent and rapid use of the remaining real Soviet assets in the shape of its truly formidable conventional attack capability in Europe and its ruthless ability to suppress dissent wherever the Red Army was present.

In the 1982 sequel, *The Untold Story*, the authors assert, "If you want nuclear peace prepare for non-nuclear war: but be ready to pay the price." The price, according to this view, is vulnerability to a conventional Soviet attack in Europe that can be repelled only by tactical nuclear weapons or extreme good luck.

For additional reading, see Dowling's *Fictions of Nuclear Disaster*.

Thirteen Days: A Memoir of the Cuban Missile Crisis A 1969 NONFICTION book by Robert F. Kennedy. Published posthumously, *Thirteen Days* provides an account of the most dangerous incident of the Cold War by one of the major players in the 1962 Cuban Missile Crisis. It features afterwords by Richard E. Neustadt and Graham T. Allison of Harvard University and contains an appendix that includes world leaders' public speeches and private communications relating to the crisis. Kennedy, the U.S. attorney general during the crisis and a major adviser to his brother, the president, wrote the memoir in the summer and fall of 1967 while preparing to challenge incumbent president Lyndon Johnson for the Democratic nomination. The Vietnam War was peaking at the time, and it provides an occasional backdrop and point of comparison for Kennedy's observations.

The narrative provides a chronological description of the events that comprised the crisis, beginning with the CIA's formal presentation on October 16 of evidence that the Soviets were placing missiles in Cuba: "I, for one, had to take their word for it. I examined the pictures carefully, and what I saw appeared to be no more than the clearing of a field for a farm or the basement of a house. I was relieved to hear later that this was the same reaction of virtually everyone at the meeting, including President Kennedy." The author expresses his surprise at the development, especially since he had recently met with Ambassador Anatoly Dobrynin, who had indicated Soviet willingness to sign a nuclear test ban treaty and had assured him that the U.S.S.R. would place no ground-to-ground missiles or offensive weapons in Cuba. "Now, as the representatives of the CIA explained the U-2 photographs that morning . . . we realized that it had all been lies, one gigantic fabric of lies . . . the dominant feeling was one of shocked incredulity. We had been deceived by Khrushchev, but we had also fooled ourselves. No official within the government had ever suggested to President Kennedy that the Russian buildup in Cuba would include missiles." In a meeting on the following day, the president's advisers reviewed their options and introduced the possibility of a blockade, the strategy that President Kennedy eventually employed. The Joint Chiefs of Staff had concluded that a surgical air strike was militarily impractical since it would have to include every military installation in Cuba and eventually require an invasion. But it was feared that a blockade of Cuba would incite the Soviets to do the same in Berlin, and that the price of their lifting the Berlin blockade would be the removal of U.S. missiles surrounding the U.S.S.R.

Kennedy goes on to describe other developments, culminating with the Soviet agreement to remove the missiles from Cuba in return for a U.S. pledge not to invade the island. A final section on "some of the things we learned" includes the importance of giving the president multiple perspectives on a crisis situation, including those from many agencies and from people of varying ranks. Kennedy also expresses concern over the U.S. military's limited vision and its assumption that "a war was in our national interest. One of the Joint Chiefs of Staff once said to me he believed in a preventive attack against the Soviet Union. On that fateful Sunday morning when the Russians answered that they were withdrawing their missiles, it was suggested by one high military adviser that we attack on Monday in any case. Another felt we had in some way been betrayed." Kennedy also describes the importance of securing the support of U.S. allies:

> It was the vote of the Organization of American States that gave a legal basis for the quarantine. Their willingness to follow the leadership of the United States was a heavy and unexpected blow to Khrushchev. It had a major psychological and practical effect on the Russians and changed our position from that of an outlaw acting in violation of international law into a country acting in accordance with twenty allies legally protecting their position . . . Even in Africa, support from a number of countries that had been considered antagonistic toward the United States was of great significance.

The final lesson, Kennedy concludes, is the importance of Americans to view situations from the other country's perspective. He emphasizes how President Kennedy made no attempt to embarrass Khrushchev by declaring any kind of victory: "He respected Khrushchev for properly determining what was in his own country's interest and what was in the interest of mankind. If it was a triumph, it was a triumph for the next generation and not for any particular government or people."

Thirty Years of Treason
A 1971 NONFICTION book by Eric Bentley. The book provides portions of transcripts from hearings into the entertainment industry conducted by the HOUSE COMMITTEE ON UN-AMERICAN ACTIVITIES (HUAC) between 1938 and 1968 as well as relevant statements and excerpts from publications by some of the participants. It also includes prepared statements that the committee refused to permit "unfriendly" witnesses to read or enter into the record, as well as speeches and statements from

"friendly" witnesses that the committee did enter. Covered are the 1938 HUAC hearings into the Federal Theater Project; the 1947 hearings on the activities of composer Hans Eisler and his siblings Gerhart and Ruth Fisher; the 1947 hearings on alleged communist influence on the content of Hollywood films, including testimony by the HOLLYWOOD TEN and their accusers; and the hearings on the entertainment industry conducted throughout the 1950s. Among those whose testimony appears are Ronald REAGAN, Ayn RAND, John LAWSON, Edward DMYTRYK, Ring LARDNER Jr., Bertolt BRECHT, Larry PARKS, Budd SCHULBERG, Elia KAZAN, Pete SEEGER, Zero MOSTEL, Arthur MILLER, Paul ROBESON, Adolphe Menjou, Robert Taylor, Gary Cooper, Sterling Hayden, Jose Ferrer, Clifford Odets, Jerome Robbins, Lee J. COBB, Joseph Papp and Lillian Hellman, who published her account of her run-in with HUAC in SCOUNDREL TIME (1976). *Thirty Years of Treason* features additional statements by Richard Nixon, who had been a member of HUAC and was president when the book was published; Dalton TRUMBO; Brecht; Hans Eisler; and Robeson, as well as an excerpt from Alvah BESSIE's *Inquisition in Eden* (1965). (See also BLACKLISTING and the RED SCARE.)

For related reading, see Vaughn's *Only Victims;* Cogley's *Report on Blacklisting* and Navasky's *Naming Names.*

Thousand Cranes: Children of Hiroshima, A
A 1962 FILM DOCUMENTARY written and directed by Betty Jean Lifton. Made the same year as the Cuban Missile Crisis, the film's stated purpose is "To inform American children what it is like to be a child in Hiroshima . . . to make a plea for peace." The title refers to the Japanese saying, "Fold a thousand cranes and they will protect you from illness." After the bombing, sympathizers throughout Japan sent folded paper cranes to friends, relatives and strangers in the hospitals. The film suggests that the power of a thousand well-intended paper cranes could equal that of the atomic bomb. It documents the ceremony created by the Children of the Cranes for the anniversary of the atomic bombing. (See also APOCALYPTIC FILMS.)

For additional reading, see Shaheen's *Nuclear War Films.*

Three Days of the Condor
A 1975 SPY FILM starring Robert Redford, Faye Dunaway, Max von Sydow and John Houseman and directed by Sydney Pollack, based on James Grady's 1974 novel SIX DAYS OF THE CONDOR. Made in the aftermath of Watergate and other revelations of illegal U.S. government spying, the film centers on Joe Turner (Redford), a CIA employee who has a desk job reading works of fiction in search of plausible espionage plots. His sedate job turns dangerous when his entire section is massacred while he is out to lunch. The assassins prove to be other CIA agents, and Turner goes into hiding after they attempt to kill him too. Along the way, he abducts a woman photographer (Dunaway) for assistance. The popular film picked up on current public disenchantment with U.S.-government covert actions that seemed to be out of control.

Thunder Out of China
A best-selling 1946 NONFICTION book coauthored by Theodore H. White and Annalee Jacoby. The Book-of-the-Month Club selection criticizes the U.S.-backed Nationalist Chinese leader Chiang Kai-shek for his

corruption and incompetence. It appeared during the Chinese civil war that followed World War II and eventually culminated in Chiang's defeat and the 1949 communist takeover of mainland China. White had been *Time*'s China correspondent before writing *Thunder*. *Time* publisher Henry LUCE was a powerful supporter of Chiang and the so-called China Lobby, and White's editor, Whittaker Chambers, was the former communist turned passionate anti-communist who later accused Alger Hiss. White quit the MAGAZINE because they distorted his reporting, especially his criticisms of Chiang. In 1953, Senator Joseph McCarthy's aides Roy Cohn and David Schine had copies of *Thunder* removed from the library of the Berlin office of the International Information Agency and actually burned them along with other books the aides had declared pro-communist. President Eisenhower subsequently denounced "book-burners" but did not identify Cohn and Schine by name. (See also RED SCARE.)

For additional reading, see Whitfield's *The Culture of the Cold War.*

Thunderball   A 1961 SPY NOVEL by Ian Fleming and a 1965 British-made SPY FILM starring Sean Connery, Claudine Auger, Luciana Paluzzi and Adolfo Celi and directed by Terence Young. NUCLEAR APOCALYPSE hovers over Miami in this James BOND story, in which the criminal organization SPECTRE steals a nuclear bomb and threatens to blow up the city if a huge ransom is not paid. Though the film appeared during the second Berlin Crisis, a particularly tense moment in Cold War history, the villains are criminals, not communists. The spread of nuclear weapons from ideologically motivated nations to criminals motivated only by greed became a new Cold War concern as the arms race quickened and nuclear proliferation became more widespread.

To Die, To Live   A British and Canadian-made 1976 FILM DOCUMENTARY written and directed by Robert Vas, a Hungarian concentration camp survivor. Based on DEATH IN LIFE, Dr. Robert Jay Lifton's 1962 study of the survivors' psychological responses to the atomic bombing of Hiroshima, it first aired on the BBC. The film intercuts between black-and-white shots of Hiroshima immediately after the bombing in 1945 and color footage of Hiroshima in 1975. Its purpose is to show how the survivors reacted to their experience and how the experience continues to affect them. Survivors recount their experiences and their continuing fears. One woman states, "There is one thing that still burdens my conscience . . . While escaping, I heard a father's cry . . . help! help! . . . If only I had held out a helping hand." A title then appears, "Death Guilt." By labeling the experience, Vas generalizes it into a commonly shared phenomenon. By presenting the woman's anecdote as both a unique, personal story and a widely shared experience, he intensifies its impact. The film also shows how the survivors dealt with the new "A-bomb disease." A different section documents the social ostracism experienced by victims of radiation sickness. Their fellow citizens treated them as though they were contaminated, and they became pariahs. However, their ostracism was sometimes self-imposed. One woman describes how she broke off her engagement

because she was ashamed to have her fiancé see her radiation burns. The final segment is set at Hiroshima's Peace Park, and it urges the viewers "To remember—To forget—To bear witness." (See also APOCALYPTIC FILMS.)

For additional reading, see Shaheen's *Nuclear War Films.*

Tomorrow!   A 1954 APOCALYPTIC NOVEL by Philip Wylie. Wylie served as a consultant to the Federal Defense Administration from 1949 to 1954 and concluded that American defense planning had failed to consider the panic and other psychological consequences that a nuclear attack might create. On the book's dust jacket he states, "Most of our statesmen, military leaders and scientific experts have not studied the subconscious mind . . . There, I believe, is the Achilles heel of an America facing atomic warfare." Dedicated "to the gallant men and women of the federal Civil Defense Administration," *Tomorrow!* excoriates those who discount the communist threat and forcefully advocates a comprehensive civil defense program, including an adequate system of bomb shelters. Wylie also attacks the right-wing proponents of the RED SCARE for exaggerating the danger of American communists and underestimating the danger to the United States of international communism. As one character, a newspaper editor, puts it, Americans "have refused for more than a decade to face our real fear. We know our world could end . . . The medieval lust of men cowering before the holocaust has been exploited by McCarthy . . ."

Wylie sets the story in a small Midwestern town, Green Prairie, in which most people live orderly, routine lives. He devotes the first two-thirds of the book to depicting their community. Consequently, the utter disruption of the townspeople's peaceful lives is one of the bomb's most striking effects, as citizens are reduced to looting and plundering and quickly fall into a mob psychology:

> Here was all that the experts said could never happen. Here was gigantic panic, uncontrolled and hideous . . . [The attack] broke their link with the rest of the nation, with humanity itself. In reaction, they were turning on humanity, on each other, with a final, mindless venting of their stored-up resentments, their hates, their disappointments.

One character watching the blast from an office building observes that the scene looked like "ants in an anthill calamity." However,

> In a part of a second, he was gas, incandescent, hotter than the interior of any furnace. In the same part of a second the proud skyline of River City and Green Prairie smoked briefly, steamed a little, and no shadows were thrown anywhere in the glare. The facades—stone, concrete, brick-glazed—crinkled, and began to slip as they melted. But the heat penetrated, too. The steel frames commenced to sag and buckle; metal, turned molten, ceased to sustain the floors.

The narrator points out that the buildings would have collapsed but gravity was not quick enough: The buildings vaporized before they could fall. "On the sidewalks, for a part of a second, on sidewalks boiling like forgotten tea, were dark stains that had been people, tens of thousands of people . . . The heart of the cities was gone. A third of their people were dead or dying or grievously hurt."

In his 1942 best-seller, *Generation of Vipers*, Wylie describe a phenomenon he labeled MOMISM, "a matriarchy in fact if not in declaration" wherein "the women of America raped the men," in which the typical middle-class mother is self-righteous, hypocritical, sexually repressed and emasculating. In other works, he holds such mothers accountable for America's lack of resolve to stand up against communism. In *Tomorrow!*, three domineering mothers oppose the civil defense program largely because they resent the inconvenience to their shopping routines and social engagements. The two who are still married dominate their husbands; the widow controls her son and, through him, the town. When the nuclear attack comes, none takes shelter and each is duly punished and humbled. The face, breast and stomach of one are "sliced to red meat." The second survives but only because the baby she is pressing against her absorbs the blast. The child is "almost torn apart" after receiving a point of glass in her back. The woman's other children also die horrible deaths, and she becomes like Niobe, the mythical mother whose pride Apollo and Artemis punish by slaying all of her sons and daughters. Minerva Sloan, the fat, influential widow who coordinated a campaign against the civil defense program, is ignobly rescued and carried through the streets in a wheelbarrow.

The Soviets follow their nuclear attack with germ warfare and appear to be on the verge of winning the war. But the president orders the explosion of a secret cobalt bomb in the Black Sea, despite the fears of some scientists that it might destroy the entire world. Instead it destroys only the Soviet Union, and the United States wins the war. In this way, Wylie vindicates the U.S. decision to arm itself with increasingly powerful nuclear weapons. The novel concludes optimistically as the survivors, free of their domineering wives and mothers, work to build a better world under the supervision of those "able to dream and put the dreams on paper." Thus the bomb becomes "no catastrophe at all, but pure benefit. 'End of an era,' they would say. 'Good thing too,' they'd add. 'Can't imagine how they stood those old cities,' they'd assert. 'Barbaric.' 'Positively medieval.' " Moreover, the attack kills Minerva Sloan's odious son, Kittridge, to whom Lenore Bailey, a desirable all-American girl, had been coerced to become engaged. As Jacqueline Smetak points out in *The Nightmare Considered*, "The bomb transforms itself into a rape prevention device, purifying the world of Soviet Reds, Kittridge Sloan, people with bad taste in home furnishing, and keeping the all-American girl safe from all of them."

For additional reading, see Dowling's *Fictions of Nuclear Disaster*; Rogin's *Ronald Reagan, the Movie*; and Anisfield's *The Nightmare Considered*.

Tongue of Fire A 1960 POLITICAL NOVEL by Ernest Frankel. Written in 1955, this fictional account of Senator Joseph McCarthy was originally scheduled for publication that year but was dropped by the publisher, Putnam's, three weeks before its scheduled publication. This may have been an instance of political censorship in which McCarthy or his supporters put pressure on the press. The central character,

Kane O'Connor, resembles McCarthy; he is an Irish Catholic who distorts the truth, employs innuendo and character assassination, misuses campaign funds, widely attacks people whom he consider alleged security risks, and uses televised committee hearings to engineer his rise to power. Like McCarthy, he falls from power after being attacked by a television show based on Edward R. Murrow's SEE IT NOW (CBS, 1951–58) and becoming the subject of a congressional investigation. (See also RED SCARE.)

"Tonight Show, The" A TELEVISION TALK show that has run on NBC from 1953 to the present. Originated by Steve Allen in 1953, "The Tonight Show" has gone through many incarnations as its hosts have come and gone. It has been the dominant show in the 11:30 P.M. time slot. Allen hosted the show through 1957, when Jack PAAR became host, remaining on the show until March 1962. After a six-month hiatus, Johnny Carson took over until he stepped down in 1992, when Jay Leno assumed the position. The show typically began with the host's monologue, which always drew heavily upon topical news headlines, enabling "The Tonight Show" to provide a comic running commentary on various aspects of the Cold War from the mid-1950s through the end of the Cold War. In addition to the monologue, politics was often a discussion topic in the interview section of the program. Sometimes the guests themselves were political figures; for instance, both 1960 presidential candidates, John Kennedy and Richard Nixon, appeared on the show. Entertainers and other popular figures also often expressed their political sentiments.

An early Cold War–related episode of "The Tonight Show" was produced when host Steve Allen convinced the U.S. Marines to stage a nighttime landing on Miami Beach for the show. Because the public had not been adequately notified in advance, many tourists staying at nearby hotels panicked when they saw what they assumed was a real-life invasion taking place on the beach. Paar was particularly outspoken about his own political beliefs, and he involved the show directly in Cold War issues, originating several broadcasts from the Berlin Wall, denouncing Fidel Castro's predecessor, Cuban dictator Fulgencio Batista, and praising Castro's attempt to depose Batista while the revolution was still going on. In 1961 Paar tried to broker an exchange of tractors for prisoners after the failed Bay of Pigs invasion by Miami-based Cuban exiles. On the other hand, Carson, who dominated the show's run, was particularly adept at not revealing his own political opinions; instead he enjoyed poking mild fun at the foibles and ludicrous actions of politicians in general. Under his aegis, the show took on a kind of centrist ironic detachment toward politics.

Top Gun A 1986 MILITARY FILM starring Tom Cruise, Kelly McGillis and Anthony Edwards and directed by Tony Scott. Made during the military buildup of the Reagan presidency, *Top Gun* glamorized the lives of navy fighter pilots. Most praised for its aerial photography, the film centers on Cruise, a self-absorbed individualist who wants to become the navy's best pilot, its "top gun." Not surprisingly, the phrase can also be interpreted in sexual terms, as Cruise strives to become McGillis's "top gun" as well.

Topaz A 1967 SPY NOVEL by Leon URIS and a 1969 SPY FILM starring John Forsythe, Philippe Noiret and Frederick Stafford and directed by Alfred HITCHCOCK. The novel first appeared in *Look* MAGAZINE. Loosely based on French spy Philippe de Vosjoli and the 1962 "Sapphire" scandals that revealed top French officials to be Soviet agents, *Topaz* centers on the defection of a top Soviet intelligence expert and explores the nature of diplomatic and intelligence cooperation between France and the United States. The story culminates in the Cuban Missile Crisis. In this respect, *Topaz* is one of the surprisingly few stories to use the Missile Crisis as the basis for a story. The best-selling book takes a very strong pro-U.S. position, employing stereotypes that highlight the virtues of American democratic, capitalist society and denigrate what it sees as repressive communist society. The book also criticizes Castro's Cuban revolution, though individual Cubans emerge as heroes.

Written just before the second wave of American feminism began, *Topaz* adopts a conservative position on gender, suggesting that if the West is to win the Cold War, men must subordinate themselves to their countries while women subordinate themselves to their men. Though ultimately most sympathetic to the United States, the book also offers insights into the French Cold War position and the World War II experiences that helped shape it. Published a year after Charles de Gaulle withdrew France from NATO and ordered NATO troops from French soil, *Topaz* tries to place into historical perspective the growing rift between the United States and France. The story addresses some of the conflicts that led to bad feelings between these Western allies, including the U.S. delay in supporting de Gaulle during World War II and its opposition to the joint French, British and Israeli invasion of Egypt in 1956 in response to Nasser's nationalization of the Suez canal. (See also LITERATURE ABOUT COLD WAR EVENTS.)

Torn Curtain A 1966 SPY FILM starring Paul Newman, Julie Andrews and Wolfgang Kieling and directed by Alfred HITCHCOCK. The story centers on an American scientist (Newman) who pretends to defect while at an international conference. He is in fact a double-agent, but his mission becomes complicated when his girlfriend (Andrews) follows him to East Germany.

"Tour of Duty" A TELEVISION MILITARY DRAMA that ran from 1987 to 1990. Made over a decade after the United States withdrew from Vietnam without having achieved its military or political objectives, "Tour of Duty" presented the war in a tough, realistic fashion that emphasized the realities of fighting an unpopular war in a hostile, alien environment. The show starred Terence Knox as Sergeant Zeke Anderson, a compassionate, professional company leader whose concern for the safety of his men made him popular. The company commander, Captain Rusty Wallace (Kevin Conroy), and the medic, "Doc" Matsuda (Steve Akahoshi), died within the first six months in order to give the show greater realism. The cast was interracial, multi-ethnic and included both men and women, though most of the regulars were men. Some were pacifists who had been drafted; one character was a surfer; another had a drug addiction that intensified as the situation in Vietnam deteriorated. Once they returned home, platoon members found that civilians were as confused and angry as the soldiers in Southeast Asia. The show's theme song was "Paint It Black," a Vietnam-era number by the ROCK AND ROLL band the Rolling Stones. The dark depiction, relatively unaided by the BLACK HUMOR that uplifted M*A*S*H (CBS, 1972–83) and sometimes CHINA BEACH (ABC, 1988–90), was unique among the portrayals of wartime experiences of U.S. soldiers on American television. That such a dismal and demoralizing picture of American combat soldiers would survive for three full years during the highly patriotic, pro-military Reagan and Bush administrations seems incongruous, but it does illustrate the diversity of tastes and beliefs within American culture.

Tran Thi Nga A Vietnamese EXILED WRITER (to the United States) and JOURNALIST. Born in Kunming, China, in 1927, Tran received a degree in social work in 1966 over the objections of her traditional family. She was the only woman working for *Time* magazine's Vietnam bureau between 1968 and 1975. With Wendy Wilder Larsen, she coauthored the best-selling SHALLOW GRAVES (1986), a collection of poems modeled on the Vietnamese *truyen*, a novel in verse. Written between 1980 and 1985, *Shallow Graves* addresses the lives of women and noncombat personnel during the Vietnam War. Tran's poem "Photographs" describes how she burnt any document that might cause trouble for others when she was preparing to leave Vietnam:

> They warned us not to take too much.
> "They have things in the States,"
> the Big Boss said.
> For days I burnt documents on my terrace,
> papers from when I worked for my government
> papers from when I worked for the Americans.
> I burnt photographs
> of the whole family at Tet,
> year after year
> all of us together
> my father's nine birds . . .
> As the pile of ashes floated away
> I felt I was burning my life.

For additional reading, see Tucker's *Literary Exile in the Twentieth Century*; Uba's "Friend and Foe: De-Collaborating Wendy Wilder Larsen and Tran Thi Nga's *Shallow Graves*."

Trials of Alger Hiss, The A 1980 FILM DOCUMENTARY directed by John Lowenthal. Made the year that Ronald Reagan won his first presidential election, the film describes the difficulties faced by Alger Hiss, the high-ranking State Department official whom Whittaker Chambers and Richard Nixon accused of being a communist agent. (See also FILMS ASSOCIATED WITH THE RED SCARE.)

Trilling, Lionel A NONFICTION WRITER and NOVELIST. Along with Reinhold Niebuhr and Arthur Schlesinger Jr., Trilling helped define the NEW LIBERALISM that emerged after World War II. Trilling's collection of essays, *The Liberal Imagination* (1950), was highly influential in articulating the assumptions of the new liberalism. One critic has referred to the book as "One of those threshold moments marking the transition from Progressive explanations to counter-Progressive ones"; another claimed that *The Liberal Imagination* became "the dominant interpretation of American culture" of its time, while a third described it as marking "the emergence of the New York Intellectuals" into the postwar period.

As depicted in *The Liberal Imagination*, the world is far more complex and morally ambiguous than pre–World War II liberals and leftists had represented it. Trilling rejects the premise that people are inherently rational and inclined to behave in their own best interests. This assumption of rationality dates back to the Enlightenment and had been a primary assumption behind both liberalism and Marxism for over two centuries. By contrast, Trilling advocates Freud's view of human nature as largely irrational, motivated by what Trilling describes as "a kind of hell within him from which rise everlastingly the impulses which threaten his civilization." The change in view led him to a less progressive political philosophy.

Trilling's novel THE MIDDLE OF THE JOURNEY (1947) treats his disaffection with communism. It follows John Laskell, a communist intellectual who becomes disillusioned while recovering from an illness at the Connecticut farm of some communist friends. The book was praised for its insight and deep treatment of moral dilemmas in spite of its limited action. One of the main characters, Gifford Maxim, is based on Whittaker Chambers, whom Trilling knew slightly when both were students at Columbia University in the mid-1920s. The novel appeared a year before Chambers gained international attention by accusing Alger Hiss of participating with him in a communist spy ring during the 1930s. Trilling based Maxim on the pre-Hiss-trial Chambers, who feared assassination and was perhaps overly histrionic and paranoid. Trilling conceived of the character as a tragic comedian who accurately attests to the guilt of communism while becoming almost buffoonish in his anti-communism. Maxim's defection from the party ultimately awakens Laskell's dormant dissatisfaction with communism as Maxim helps Laskell recognize unpleasant truths he has always seen but not acknowledged about communism.

For further reading, see *American Fiction in the Cold War* and *The Dictionary of Literary Biography* (vol. 63, *American Literary Critics and Scholars*).

Trouble with Spies, The A 1987 FILM COMEDY starring Donald Sutherland, Ned Beatty and Ruth Gordon and directed by Burt Kennedy. Made for HBO in 1984, the movie was released by MTV three years later. A SPY FILM SPOOF, *The Trouble with Spies* centers on the exploits of Sutherland, a bumbling secret agent.

Trumbo, Dalton An American NOVELIST and SCREENWRITER. Born in 1905 in Colorado, Trumbo was among the best known of the HOLLYWOOD TEN, a group of so-called "unfriendly" witnesses who refused to testify in the 1947 hearings held by the HOUSE COMMITTEE ON UN-AMERICAN ACTIVITIES (HUAC) on alleged communist influences in the motion picture industry. In 1935, Trumbo published his first novel, *Eclipse*, a satire about small-town America that the *Times Literary Supplement* compared to the writings of Sinclair Lewis. His second novel, *Washington Jitters* (1936),

continues in the satiric vein but contains a more explicitly socialist orientation. Trumbo's most famous novel, *Johnny Got His Gun* (1939), is a pacifist work about a wounded soldier, a quadruple amputee who is unable to hear, speak or communicate in any recognizable way. Essentially a living torso, he eventually comes to perceive through his sense of touch and establishes sexual contact with a nurse. In 1971, Trumbo directed a film version of the novel starring Timothy Bottoms, Jason Robards Jr., Marsha Hunt and Donald Sutherland.

In 1936, Trumbo began working as a screenwriter for Warner Brothers. He eventually became the best-paid writer in Hollywood, earning up to $75,000 per script. He went to work for RKO in 1938, where he further developed his talent for dramatizing the lives of ordinary people. He received an Academy Award nomination in 1940 for his script for *Kitty Foyle*. During World War II, his films took a deeply anti-fascist stand that celebrated American patriotism and the war effort. These include *A Guy Named Joe* (1943), about a dead pilot who comes back from the grave to inspire the next generation, and *Thirty Seconds Over Tokyo* (1944), about the Doolittle Raid against the Japanese home islands early in the war. Other notable Trumbo films from this period celebrate human community. These include *The Human Comedy* (1943), which was based on William Saroyan's novel; *Our Vines Have Tender Grapes* (1945); and *Tender Comrade* (1943), about wives of American servicemen fighting overseas. The film starred Ginger Rogers, whose mother objected before HUAC that the line, "Share and share alike—isn't that right?" represented communist propaganda that Trumbo had somehow snuck into the film. Despite the presumed allusion to communism, the film's title comes from Robert Louis Stevenson's term for a wife.

Attracted to left-wing causes throughout the Depression, Trumbo joined the American Communist Party in 1943. HUAC subpoenaed him to testify in 1947. Rather than cooperate with an investigation he considered unconstitutional, Trumbo, (along with the rest of the Ten) refused to answer the committee's questions, citing his First Amendment right of free speech. As a result, he was convicted of contempt of Congress, for which he served 10 months in federal prison. Trumbo's appearance before HUAC is documented in HOLLYWOOD ON TRIAL, a 1976 FILM DOCUMENTARY directed by David Helpern Jr. and written by Lester COLE, a blacklisted writer who had also been one of the Hollywood Ten. Trumbo describes what he believed were the issues underlying the blacklist in his pamphlet, "Time of the Toad" (1949) and in his collected letters, *Additional Dialogue* (ed. Helen Manfull, 1970). Between 1951 and 1953, he went into exile in Mexico along with Hollywood Ten members John Howard LAWSON, Albert MALTZ and other blacklisted writers. There he worked for a fraction of his previous salary on movie scripts that he submitted pseudonymously to circumvent the blacklist. The approximately 30 screenplays on which he worked this way include *The Prowler* (1951), *Wild Is the Wind* (1957), *The Young Philadelphians* (1959) and *The Brave One* (1956), for which he actually received an Academy Award under the alias Robert Rich. He also employed an alias to rewrite Howard Fast's script for SPARTACUS (1960), but Otto Preminger publicly credited him for that work when he also announced that Trumbo had written

Preminger's EXODUS (1960). Preminger's announcement was a front-page story in the *New York Times*. President-elect John Kennedy and his brother Robert crossed an American Legion picket line to view *Spartacus* in 1960.

In 1970, Trumbo received the Screen Writers Guild's highest honor, the Laurel Award. In his acceptance speech, he addressed those who were not yet born or who were too young to remember the RED SCARE:

> To them I would say only this: that the blacklist was a time of evil, and that no one on either side who survived it came through untouched by evil . . . There was bad faith and good, honesty and dishonesty, courage and cowardice, selflessness and opportunism, wisdom and stupidity, good and bad on both sides; and almost every individual involved . . . combined some or all of these antithetical qualities in his own person, in his own acts . . . in the final tally we were *all* victims because . . . each of us felt compelled to say things he did not want to say . . . none of us— right, left, or center—emerged from that long nightmare without sin.

Elsewhere he reiterated his willingness to forgive those who had informed to the committee, claiming that "to concentrate on them is to forget the enemy. The enemy was the goddamned Committee." Trumbo died in 1976. (See also BLACKLISTING; EXILED WRITERS [from the United States].)

For additional reading, see Tucker's *Literary Exile in the Twentieth Century*; Navasky's *Naming Names*; Sayre's *Running Time*; Vaughn's *Only Victims*.

Tudoran, Dorin A Romanian EXILED WRITER (to the United States), literary editor and radio broadcaster. Born in 1945 in Romania, Tudoran graduated from the University of Bucharest in 1968. After Romanian journals rejected his articles questioning the legitimacy of the Romanian government and criticizing its structure and policies, Tudoran published in the West, where excerpts of his critical work were broadcast over the Voice of America, Radio Free Europe and the BBC. Subsequently, the widely read POET was placed under house arrest for two years. His arrest ended in 1985 after publicity from a 40-day hunger strike persuaded the government to grant him an exit visa. After immigrating to the United States, he worked for the Voice of America, edited the literary journal *Agora, an Alternate Journal of Culture,* and continued to write in Romanian, claiming that a poet cannot change his language.

Tudoran observed during the Cold War that Western governments and media used exiled Eastern European writers for political exploitation, so that the quality of a writer's work mattered less in the West than the West's attitude toward the particular country whence the writer was exiled. When writers did not come from currently fashionable oppressed countries, Tudoran argued, their work was likely to be ignored, regardless of merit. Ironically, he said, art for art's sake could exist in socialist states because of bureaucratic toleration, condescension and ignorance on the part of government officials. Poets enjoyed wide readership in Romania because the audience responded to the sentiments that poetry implied, although they were not free to act upon

the writer's message. By contrast, Tudoran said, in the West, audiences were free to act, but few people read poetry, and poets could not make a living from their work. Thus, freedom of expression was of small benefit to poets in the West because there was only a small audience to hear their words.

For additional reading, see Tucker's *Literary Exile in the Twentieth Century*.

"Twenty-One" A TELEVISION QUIZ SHOW that ran on NBC from 1956 to 1958. Contestants competed to answer trivia questions in fields ranging from history, poetry and opera to baseball and boxing. In 1957, Charles Van Doren, a good-looking, engaging university instructor at Columbia University, defeated reigning champion Herbert Stempel after a series of tense ties, and the show became very successful. For 14 weeks, the popular Van Doren clung to his title as he answered ever more challenging questions. After his success on the show, Van Doren went on to host NBC's TELEVISION NEWS show "Kaleidoscope." However, in 1959, after denying newspaper stories to the contrary, Van Doren confessed to the U.S. House Subcommittee on Legislative Oversight that the games had been dishonest and that the winners were predetermined. Van Doren, who was then working on his Ph.D., claimed he had entered into this deceit because "it was having such a good effect on the national attitude to teachers, education, and the intellectual life."

The revelations of Van Doren's corruption and other instances of dishonesty on such quiz shows as "The Big Surprise" (NBC, 1955–57), "Dotto" (NBC, 1958) and "The $64,000 Question" (CBS, 1955–58) caused a public furor and occasioned several commentators to lament the breakdown of American morals. The Gallup Poll revealed more widespread awareness of fraud than of any other subject about which Americans had ever been interviewed. According to NOVELIST John Updike, "The appeal of the programs, with the rising challenge of Soviet brain power as a backdrop, was ultimately patriotic. The contestants were selected to be a cross-section of our nation just as deliberately as the G.I.'s in a war movie are." For some, therefore, the corruption of such a popular figure as Charles Van Doren, an Ivy League intellectual and teacher from an illustrious family, represented America's fall from innocence. Van Doren was of the American aristocracy, yet he had failed to live up to the standards that America likes to pride itself upon: honesty, skill, fair play and a good, clean competitive spirit. In these game shows, the people and institutions that America relied upon to win the Cold War were revealed to be tainted. Novelist John STEINBECK, for instance, asserted that America was noteworthy "for our wealth, moral flabbiness, uncertainty, and TV scandals," that "on all levels it is rigged" and that "a creeping, all-pervading, nerve-gas of immorality . . . starts in the nursery and does not stop before it reaches the highest offices, both corporate and government . . . I am troubled by the cynical immorality of my country. I do not think it can survive on this basis."

Senator William Fulbright, a Democrat from Arkansas, stated on the Senate floor that "the question of the moral strength of our people is not just an internal domestic matter. It has grave possibilities in our international relations . . .

What seems to be new about these scandals is the moral blindness or callowness which allows those in responsible positions to accept the practices which the facts reveal." As Stephen Whitfield claims in *The Culture of the Cold War,* during the 1950s, there was "the sense that intellect itself had to be drafted into the Cold War . . . Van Doren had come to symbolize the national hope of permanent superiority over the Soviets, and instead he joined the 'phonies' who so repelled Holden Caulfield in *The Catcher in the Rye.* The integrity of American life that was supposed to sharpen the contrast with the Soviet Union thus looked dubious. Nor could the sincerity of American motives any longer be taken for granted as proof of eventual triumph."

For additional reading, see Whitfield's *The Culture of the Cold War.*

"Twilight Zone, The" A TELEVISION SCIENCE FICTION SHOW anthology that ran on CBS from 1959 to 1965. Rod Serling, who had written the television spy show SHADOW OF THE CLOAK (DuMont, 1951–52), created the show and wrote some of the scripts. CBS revived it between 1985 and 1987 and it went into syndication in 1988. In 1985, *Twilight Zone—The Movie* was released.

"The Twilight Zone" appeared during some of the most tense moments of the Cold War, running at the same time as the U-2 incident, the Berlin Crisis, the Cuban Missile Crisis and the Kennedy assassination. It presented unusual, offbeat stories that frequently ended with an ironic twist. Serling originally introduced each episode by saying somberly:

There is a fifth dimension beyond that which is known to man. It is a dimension as vast as space and as timeless as infinity. It is the middle ground between light and shadow, between science and superstition, and it lies between the pit of man's fears and the summit of his knowledge. This is the dimension of imagination. It is an area we call *The Twilight Zone.*

The show's pervading ironic undertone meant that stories sometimes ended in an eerie kind of poetic justice, giving viewers cause to wonder about the supernatural. "The Twilight Zone" offered a form of secular mysticism suggesting that everything occurs for a purpose or as part of a design. The grand design might be benevolent and moral; however, it might be merely perverse or diabolical. The show was especially popular among people interested in science, perhaps because it speculated about other-worldly occurrences without providing definitive explanations or relying on stock religious interpretations. One popular, Cold War–inspired episode entitled "Time Enough at Last," captured the show's irony in a setting that expressed then-current fears of a major nuclear war with the Soviets. The story featured a bank teller whose only desire was to be left alone to read, but he was always interrupted. One day, while he was spending his lunch hour reading deep in the bank vault, a nuclear attack killed everyone outside. Happy to be alone at last with his books, the far-sighted teller then accidentally broke his reading glasses. This episode represented a rare television treatment of NUCLEAR APOCALYPSE during the early 1960s, an era of heightened fears about possible nuclear war.

"Twilight Zone's" suggestion that perhaps the purpose of the universe might be hostile to, or amused by, human beings, fits into a literary tradition going back to the turn-of-the-century Naturalists, like Stephen Crane and Emile Zola, as well as evoking postwar existentialism and the Theater of the Absurd of the late 1940s and 1950s. It is thus linked to the work of such American writers of the 1950s and early 1960s as Norman MAILER, Kurt VONNEGUT Jr. and John BARTH. Serling, an accomplished playwright, would have been familiar with many of his literary forebears. Nonetheless, it was unusual for American television, which usually expressed traditional tastes and values, to treat such controversial themes so ironically. The high quality of the show's writing may have accounted for its ability to transcend the barriers of tradition.

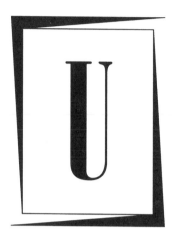

Ugly American, The A best-selling 1958 POLITICAL NOVEL by William LEDERER and Eugene BURDICK; a 1961 play in two acts; and a 1962 POLITICAL FILM starring Marlon Brando, Eiji Okada and Sandra Church and directed by George Englund. Set in Sarkhan, a fictional Southeast Asian country similar to Vietnam, the story centers on an American ambassador whose failure to understand local history and customs undermines well-intentioned U.S. efforts to improve the standard of living with advanced technology and improved agricultural methods. The novel criticizes the State Department bureaucrats and political hacks who fail to learn the native languages and customs, insult local leaders, inhibit the constructive work of individuals working in the villages, and allow their own egos and career aspirations to dominate their decisions. By contrast, the Soviet diplomatic corps is dedicated, modest, self-sacrificing, well informed of local customs, linguistically fluent and focused on its goal. The book extols private Americans working directly with the local people in the villages despite obstacles presented by government officials; these characters anticipate President Kennedy's Peace Corps volunteers. The novel also suggests that supporting small-scale, privately owned businesses within the villages will both improve the quality of life and combat communism in the rural areas. The book was so well known that President Eisenhower read it while on vacation. However, it has been criticized for its shallow understanding of the political situation in Southeast Asia. It largely avoids the moral ambiguities and political pitfalls facing the United States

in the late 1950s, presenting a simplistic world with easy answers. The film appeared in 1962, when the number of American advisers in Vietnam increased from 700 to 12,000.

In 1965, the year the United States introduced combat troops into the Vietnam War, the authors published a sequel, *Sarkhan*. Both a suspense novel and a political tract, *Sarkhan* describes the efforts of an American businessman and a professor to prevent a communist takeover in the mythical Southeast Asian country. Like *The Ugly American*, the sequel attacks U.S. government bureaucrats for their ignorance and ineptitude and presents the tactics used by the communist opposition.

For additional reading, see Whitfield's *The Culture of the Cold War*.

Uris, Leon A NOVELIST. Born in 1924, Uris was one of the few Cold War–era fiction writers to employ significant Cold War events as dramatic settings for his novels. ARMAGEDDON (1964) takes place during the Berlin Airlift of the late 1940s and deals with U.S. and Soviet relations with German citizens in occupied Germany. TOPAZ (1967) draws on fictional account of the real-life communist infiltration of French intelligence as it portrays the events leading up to the 1962 Cuban Missile Crisis. The novel first appeared in *Look* magazine. Loosely based on French spy Philippe de Vosjoli and the 1962 "Sapphire" scandals that revealed top French officials to be Soviet agents, *Topaz* explores the nature of diplomatic and intelligence cooperation between France and the United States. The best-selling book takes a very strong pro-U.S. position, employing stereotypes that emphasize the virtues of American democratic, capitalist society and denigrate what it sees as repressive communist society. Written just before the modern American feminist movement began, *Topaz* adopts a conservative position on gender, suggesting that if the West is to win the Cold War, men must subordinate themselves to their countries while women subordinate themselves to their men. The book also tries to place into historical perspective the growing rift between the United States and France. Published a year after Charles de Gaulle withdrew France from NATO and ordered NATO troops from French soil, the story addresses some of the conflicts that led to this decision, including the allies' disagreement over the joint French, British and Israeli invasion of Egypt in 1956 in response to Nasser's nationalization of the Suez canal. Alfred Hitchcock directed the 1969 film version.

EXODUS (1958), an earlier best-seller, presents the developments leading up to the formation of the state of Israel in 1948 and the war with its Arab neighbors that immediately followed. The action centers on the leader of the Israeli independence movement and his love affair with a Christian woman. Though more a consequence of the dissolution of the British Empire than of the Cold War, the emergence of the Jewish state went on to become an important feature in Cold War Middle Eastern politics. Otto Preminger directed the film version in 1960 and credited Dalton TRUMBO with writing the screenplay. In so doing Preminger effectively ended the RED SCARE practice of BLACKLISTING members of the film industry who had been accused of having communist sympathies.

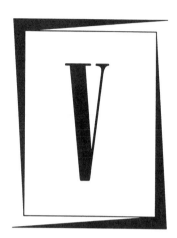

Valladares, Armando   A Cuban EXILED WRITER (to the United States). Born in Pinar del Rio, Cuba, in 1937, Valladares was imprisoned in 1960 for "counterrevolutionary activities" directed against the Castro regime. He denied the charges and refused to submit to "rehabilitation." The brutality and long duration of his 22-year incarceration made him a cause célèbre in the West. In 1982, after Valladares suffered partial paralysis from the rigors of his confinement and inadequate medical treatment while in prison, efforts by the French government succeeded in winning his release. After moving to France for a short time, he came to the United States. He finally moved to Spain after falling out with some of the politically prominent members of Miami's Cuban exile community.

While Valladares was still in prison, his work was smuggled abroad for publication. An account of his prison experience appeared in English translation in a 1983 issue of *Confrontation* magazine. *Against All Hope: The Prison Memoirs of Armando Valladares* appeared in English translation in 1986. Valladares won the 1982 International Prize of the Hispanic-Puerto Rican Pro-Culture Association for artistic achievement in the face of duress.

For additional reading, see Tucker's *Literary Exile in the Twentieth Century*.

Van Doren, Charles   See TWENTY-ONE.

Vargas Llosa, Mario   A Peruvian NOVELIST. Born in 1936, Vargas Llosa joined an underground cell of the banned

Communist Party while he was in college. However, he left the party after about a year because he refused to give up "decadent" literature or to stop reading James Joyce, Andre Gide and William FAULKNER. A strong critic of the Peruvian government, Vargas Llosa voluntarily went into exile in Spain from 1958 to 1975. He became active in international social and human rights issues and served as president of PEN International, a writers organization. He ran for president of Peru in 1989 on the Libertad Party ticket but lost in a run-off election. An early supporter of Fidel Castro, Vargas Llosa retracted his endorsement of the communist Cuban regime after the poet Herberto Padilla was arrested there in 1971. His disaffection with Castro appears in *The War of the End of the World* (1981; in English, 1983). Set in 19th-century Peru, the novel describes a rebellion that began with a utopian vision but turned into a system of demagoguery and repression; it is widely read as being directed against Castro's revolutionary government.

For additional reading, see Tucker's *Literary Exile in the Twentieth Century*.

Vaughn, Robert   A TELEVISION PERFORMER and FILM ACTOR who starred in THE MAN FROM U.N.C.L.E. (NBC, 1964–68) and KILL CASTRO (1980). In addition to appearing in Cold War–related films and television shows, Vaughn published his Ph.D. dissertation as *Only Victims* (1972), a study of the effects that the HOUSE COMMITTEE ON UN-AMERICAN ACTIVITIES (HUAC) had on live theater during the Cold War. Senator George McGovern, the 1972 Democratic presidential nominee, wrote the foreword. The title came from Dalton TRUMBO's 1970 speech of reconciliation before the Screen Writers Guild, when he was presented the Laurel Award, in which Trumbo claimed that there were no heroes or villains among those called before HUAC, only victims. After studying extensive committee testimony, Vaughn concludes:

> We have seen that our culture presented the informer as a moral hero in order to justify the unjustifiable. We have seen how our guilds, trade associations, artists, and lawyers all accepted the illusion of inevitability and in so doing collaborated in the perpetuation of social evil. We have seen how trust, our most cherished of possessions, was dissipated and the possibility of true community polluted by the advent of symbolic betrayal and literal collaboration. Morality, we are told, is a voice of conscience from within in harmony with a voice of authority from without. We have seen what happens when the citizen delegates his conscience to the state.

Viet Journal A 1974 NONFICTION collection of Vietnam War sketches by James Jones. Best known for his novel, *From Here to Eternity* (1951) Jones here describes his one-month tour of Vietnam during the final days of the American involvement in the war. The collection contains 79 short sketches that variously portray the countryside, combat missions and the ranking U.S. military officers whom Jones met. Jones depicts the communists as savage and duplicitous and attacks what he sees as the shallowness of such antiwar activists as Mary MCCARTHY and Frances FitzGerald. He also discusses the costs of the war and U.S. mistakes. Mostly, though, he furnishes accounts of Vietnam steeped with the sights, smells and sounds of the war. One of the most compelling sketches depicts a helicopter mission to resupply a cut-off base. The book concludes with "Hawaiian Recall," an epilogue describing Jones's return to the setting of *From Here to Eternity* for the first time in 31 years.

Viet Rock: A Folk War Movie A 1966 play by Megan Terry. The first play about the Vietnam War ever produced, *Viet Rock* was performed by the OPEN THEATER, the successor group to the LIVING THEATER, a year after the United States introduced combat troops into the war. The antiwar, experimental play contrasts the clichés, media rhetoric and middle-class attitudes that support the war with the harsh realities of the actual fighting. According to Terry, "We used material that bombarded us every day from television and newspapers. We acted out personal stories and tried to get to the roots of our drives toward anger and aggression." The play was praised for its energy and vivid images, though it failed to end the war, as Terry hoped it would. However, it was perceived as so powerful that the CIA and FBI taped the show and interviewed Terry. (See also THEATER; VIETNAM WAR LITERATURE.)

For additional reading, see *Dictionary of Literary Biography* (vol. 7, *Twentieth-Century American Dramatists*).

"Vietnam Report" A TELEVISION DOCUMENTARY series that ran from February 1966 to January 1968 on "ABC Scope," produced by Arthur Holch and anchored by How-ard K. Smith. A total of 97 consecutive weekly features, "Vietnam Report" covered a broad range of aspects about the escalating war, beginning with an outline of the war's progress and its effect on the American public and concluding with "The M-16—What Went Wrong?" about the infantry rifle that was prone to jam. In between, the show ran features on political, personal, logistical and military aspects of the war. Representative features included "Children of War"; "The Champ—Count Me Out," about Muhammad Ali's refusal to be drafted; "Thailand—Counterattack," about the role of Thailand in the anti-communist effort; "Struggle for Power," about internal South Vietnamese politics; "Inside North Vietnam"; and "The Young Veterans," a view of the war from the perspective of four veterans who survived it.

Vietnam: A Television History A 1983 TELEVISION DOCUMENTARY produced by Richard Ellison. Accompanied by a book by Stanley Karnow, the popular 13-part program traces the history of the Vietnam War from World War II to the fall of Saigon in 1975. It was broadcast on PBS and was funded in part by the National Endowment for the Humanities.

Vietnam War See VIETNAM WAR FILMS; VIETNAM WAR LITERATURE; VIETNAM WAR TELEVISION DOCUMENTARIES; TELEVISION MILITARY DRAMAS; TELEVISION SATIRE; SATIRE; THEATER; ART; CARTOONS; FOLK SINGERS; ROCK AND ROLL.

Vietnam War films Over 350 Vietnam War films were made during four periods of the Cold War. The first wave came before 1963, when the number of U.S. military advisers in Vietnam rose from some 700 to 12,000. Several of these early films are set before 1954 when the region was still French Indochina. In 1948, Alan Ladd and Veronica Lake starred in *Saigon,* in which the communist struggle forms part of the background. Also in that year, *Rogue's Regiment* starred Dick Powell as a secret service agent who enlists in the French Foreign Legion and goes to Saigon to track down a Nazi war criminal. In the process of getting his man, Powell finds that the Nazi has now become a Soviet agent who supports the communist guerrillas. Thus this early Cold War film neatly switches national enemies from Nazis to communists by merging them within a single identity. The film also makes clear that the communist rebels have no chance against the French. The Korean War–era *A Yank in Indo China* (1952) features more direct U.S. involvement as it follows two Americans who fly food to French and Vietnamese soldiers combating the communist insurgents. Written by Irving Wallace, *Jump into Hell* appeared in 1955, the year after the decisive French defeat at Dienbienphu. Using newsreel footage and semi-documentary techniques, it follows four French paratroopers assigned to relieve a fort during the battle that led to the French exit from Indochina.

Written and directed by Samuel FULLER, who directed STEEL HELMET (1951), an early KOREAN WAR FILM, *China Gate* appeared in 1957, three years after the French evacuation and the year general elections were to have been held throughout Vietnam. This was the first film to feature Americans in combat, though they officially functioned under the auspices of the French. The film celebrates the heroics of a group of French Legionnaires and foreign mercenaries, all under the expert leadership of a tough U.S. sergeant who never returned from Korea. With the assistance of a Eurasian saloon keeper, Lucky Legs (Angie Dickinson), they demolish a vast communist ammunition depot in 1954. As one of the U.S. soldiers puts it, "What I started out to do in Korea, I didn't finish. There are still a lot of live Commies around." Lucky Legs must choose between her former husband, a U.S. soldier who abandoned her because their child looked too Chinese, and a Eurasian officer serving with the Viet Minh who loves her and promises to take her and her son to Moscow if she will marry him. But her dream is to have her boy grow up in the United States, and, after reconciling with her husband, Lucky Legs dies, making that possible. The film, which shows the Viet Minh leadership answering directly to the U.S.S.R., also criticizes American racism, something rare in 1950s anticommunist movies. Nat King Cole, a popular black singer of the period, sings the title song and stars as one of the commandos.

Joseph L. Mankiewicz's 1958 film version of Graham GREENE's political novel THE QUIET AMERICAN (1958) was filmed in Vietnam. Mankiewicz gives Greene's anti-American story a new and decidedly anti-communist twist that approves the U.S. involvement in Southeast Asia. The film also foresaw the difficulties Americans would face in distinguishing friends from foes in the Vietnamese War. *Five Gates to Hell* (1959) follows the fates of U.S. Red Cross nurses and doctors who are kidnapped by communist guerrillas. Released in 1962 and set in an unnamed Southeast Asian country, *Brushfire* also focuses on the communist kidnappings of an American man and woman. In this film, the communists appear especially brutal, as they ultimately kill the sympathetic husband and rape his wife. THE UGLY AMERICAN (1962) paints a far more confusing and less clear-cut picture, though still generally supportive of U.S. involvement.

The second wave of Vietnam War films appeared while U.S. soldiers were actively involved in the fighting. *A Yank in Viet-Nam,* filmed entirely in Vietnam in 1964, centers on a Marine military adviser whose helicopter is shot down by the Viet Cong. A South Vietnamese patrol rescues him along with a doctor and his daughter, with whom the Marine falls in love. The South Vietnamese are portrayed sympathetically, while the Viet Cong are shown to be hostile and dangerous. Americans are clearly in South Vietnam at that country's behest, and their mission is only to observe and provide advice, fighting only when necessary. Two years after starring in *A Yank in Viet-Nam,* Marshall Thompson appeared again as a U.S. Marine in *To the Shores of Hell* (1966). Here again, the South Vietnamese are sympathetic rescuers while the Viet Cong are brutal rapists who kill children, burn orphanages and torture prisoners. The highly patriotic film concludes when Thompson returns to his faithful girlfriend, whom he marries in a Marine Corps wedding ceremony. *Operation CIA* (1965) stars Burt Reynolds as a CIA operative investigating an assassination plot at the U.S. Embassy in Saigon. The British-made *Some May Live* (1967) stars Joseph Cotten as a U.S. intelligence officer who must discover the communist spy in his unit. *The Lost Command* (1966) stars Anthony Quinn and Alain Delon

as French paratroopers serving in Indochina and Algiers. Charlton HESTON narrated *Vietnam! Vietnam!,* a 1966 documentary produced by John Ford for the United States Information Agency (USIA) to help convince foreign audiences that the U.S. participation in the Vietnam War was moral and necessary. One hundred sixty-one copies were distributed to USIA offices abroad but most were returned without being shown. Divided into two parts, "The Vietnamese People and the War" and "The Debate," *Vietnam! Vietnam!* was not generally released until 1971. However, it failed to have the impact its sponsors desired.

THE GREEN BERETS and TELL ME LIES both appeared in 1968, during the height of U.S. involvement, but they present completely opposite views of the conflict. *The Green Berets* starred and was directed by John WAYNE. It presents the American war as a just and noble cause, and it celebrates the highly skilled and totally committed soldiers who fight it. On the other hand, in the British-made *Tell Me Lies,* director Peter Brook viciously attacks the war by mixing documentary film footage with performances by members of the Royal Shakespeare Company. *The Night Walk* (1972, also known as *Deathdream* and *Dead of Night*) is a Canadian horror movie made during the later stages of the war. The story centers on a soldier who had been killed in action and returns to take revenge on the society that sent him to war.

THE DEER HUNTER (1978), COMING HOME (1978) and APOCALYPSE NOW (1979) spearheaded the third wave of important Vietnam War films. Made half a decade after the last U.S. troops were evacuated from Saigon, these were the first films to deeply explore the war's vast complexities. Though only *Coming Home* takes an overtly antiwar position, all three present the war as a confusing, demoralizing and seemingly pointless experience. *The Deer Hunter,* featuring Robert De Niro in a powerful performance, presents the physical and emotional effects of a horrific war experience on a group of steelworker pals who enlist together, and the war's effects on their families and friends back home. *Coming Home* stars the prominent antiwar activist Jane FONDA as a conventional, prowar military wife who experiences sexual and political awakenings and personal empowerment when she befriends an embittered, partially paralyzed Vietnam veteran who has turned against the war. The most spectacular of all Vietnam War films is Francis Ford Coppola's *Apocalypse Now* starring Martin Sheen and Marlon Brando. The film, which updates Joseph Conrad's *Heart of Darkness* in a Vietnam setting, represents the war as a surreal, almost psychedelic experience completely out of anyone's control. GO TELL THE SPARTANS (1978) centers on the early days of the American involvement and expresses the soldiers' frustration. As an officer tells a young draftee who wants to see what war is actually like, "Shame we couldn't have shown you a better war, like Anzio, or Bataan; this one's a sucker's tour, going round and round in circles."

A decade later, at the end of the Reagan and beginning of the Bush presidencies, came a fourth wave of Vietnam films, including one FILM COMEDY. Directed by Vietnam veteran OLIVER STONE, PLATOON (1986) shows an army as much at war against itself as against the enemy. The protagonist, played by Martin Sheen's son Charlie, feels as though the opposing factions within his unit are engaged in a "battle for the possession of my soul." The Academy Award–

winning film was highly praised for its realism, which starkly contrasts with the expressionism of *Apocalypse Now*. Three years later, Stone directed BORN ON THE FOURTH OF JULY (1989), a more overtly antiwar and anti-macho piece based on the life of antiwar activist Ron Kovic. A gung-ho, all-American athlete, the protagonist, played by Tom Cruise, enlists in the Marines so he can serve a noble cause in Vietnam. Once there, however, his world view breaks down, and when he is wounded in the back and partially paralyzed he returns home an alienated, embittered alcoholic. Not until he recognizes the shortcomings of his earlier attitudes can he pull himself from his abyss. By becoming an antiwar activist, he reacquires his redeeming sense of commitment to a noble cause.

In the year following *Platoon*, Stanley KUBRICK's FULL METAL JACKET (1987) and John Irvin's HAMBURGER HILL (1987) appeared. A dark and cynical film, *Full Metal Jacket* shows that the process of dehumanization is necessary for a soldier's survival, as the soldiers go from boot camp to combat. *Hamburger Hill* largely ignores issues of politics and morality. Instead it renders in detail the experience of the 101st Airborne Division in the A Shau Valley. THE IRON TRIANGLE (1988) centers on an American officer captured by two Viet Cong soldiers, one cruel and the other sympathetic. Based on the actual diary of an unknown Viet Cong soldier, the film presents a perspective of the war from the point of view of the other side. The British-made film THE KILLING FIELDS (1984) depicts the fall of Cambodia in 1975 and the widespread massacres committed by the communist Khmer Rouge regime headed by Pol Pot. SAIGON: YEAR OF THE CAT (1983) is set during the fall of South Vietnam in 1975. The first Vietnam comedy, GOOD MORNING VIETNAM (1987), features Robin Williams as an American disk jockey for Armed Forces Radio in Saigon, where he befriends the South Vietnamese.

War-era FILM DOCUMENTARIES include Frederick Wiseman's BASIC TRAINING (1970) *The Anderson Platoon* (1967) *A Face of War* (1968), *In the Year of the Pig* (1968) and the French-made FAR FROM VIETNAM (1967) which includes antiwar segments by 11 internationally acclaimed directors. *Hearts and Minds* (1974) appeared the year following the U.S. military withdrawal, and the U.S./German-made *Memory of Justice* (1976) appeared the year after the final communist victory. Reagan-era documentaries include *Vietnam: An American Journey* (1981), *Swimming to Cambodia* (1987) and *Dear America: Letters Home from Vietnam* (1987),which premiered on cable television.

Set after the U.S. evacuation from South Vietnam and just before the fall of Saigon, RAMBO revised Vietnam history in 1985 for an America anxious to regain its swagger. In this film, Sylvester STALLONE plays a Vietnam veteran who goes back and almost single-handedly defeats the North Vietnamese who have captured his old buddy. The film showed Reagan-era American audiences what many of them wanted to believe: that if left unencumbered by bureaucrats and politicians, U.S. soldiers could have wiped out the North Vietnamese. Capitalizing on the film's get-tough attitude, Reagan, who first saw the film shortly after 39 Western hostages were released in Lebanon, commented, "Boy, I saw *Rambo* last night. Now I know what to do the next time this happens." An earlier, more cynical story about

a Vietnam vet who returns after the war to rescue POWs was *Good Guys Wear Black* (1979), starring Chuck NORRIS as a vet who is tricked by a high-ranking State Department official into leading a raid on a camp that in fact has no prisoners-of-war (POWs). Made in 1977, when the country was still very conscious of the government betrayals involved in both Vietnam and Watergate, this film shows the U.S. government to be its own worst enemy. Norris's Reagan-era POW films, *Missing in Action* (1984) and *Missing in Action 2—The Beginning* (1985), are less ambiguous in their patriotism. *Braddock: Missing in Action 3* (1988) also follows the aftermath of the war, as Norris returns to Vietnam to rescue his Amerasian child.

In addition to films that treat the war directly, a number of movies address related issues, including returning veterans, the antiwar movement, POWs and MIAs, and the families of men who fought the war. Films dealing with POWs and returning soldiers include *The Born Losers* (1967) and its sequels *Billy Jack* (1971), *The Trial of Billy Jack* (1974) and *Billy Jack Goes to Washington* (1977); *Heroes* (1977); *Rolling Thunder* (1977); *Welcome Home, Soldier Boys* (1972); *The Visitors* (1972); *My Old Man's Place* (1972); *Uncommon Valor* (1983); *Missing in Action* (I and II); *POW—The Escape* (1986); and *First Blood* (1982), the first film in the Rambo series. The Carter-era *Don't Answer the Phone* (1980) features a mentally deranged Vietnam War veteran who rapes and murders his female victims. *Cease Fire* (1985) is a Reagan-era film starring Don Johnson as a veteran suffering from delayed stress syndrome. *Night Wars* (1988) and *Jacobs Ladder* (1990) portray veterans suffering from severe flashbacks about the war.

Though antiwar protest was rarely the primary focus of a major motion picture, it played a significant role in establishing the internal value system of such comedies as *Alice's Restaurant* (1969), HAROLD AND MAUDE (1971), *Getting Straight* (1970) and *I Love You Alice B. Toklas* (1968), starring Peter SELLERS (1970) *Hail, Hero!* (1969), *Homer* (1970), *Getting Straight, Limbo* (1972), *Summertree* (1971), Antonioni's ZABRISKIE POINT (1970) and the film musical HAIR (1979) all treat the impact of the draft on middle-class Americans. *The Strawberry Statement* (1970) focuses on the students takeover of a university administration building in protest to the war. WOODSTOCK (1970), which documents the 1969 rock festival, also contains strong antiwar themes. *The War at Home* documented student protest at the University of Wisconsin at Madison.

The Edge, made during the high point of the war in 1968, depicts a plot to assassinate the president in reparation for the personal loss and suffering caused by the Vietnam War. *Ice* (1970), another war-era film, imagines a similar war in the future—with Mexico—and suggests the role of urban guerrillas who would oppose it. *1776*, a 1969 Broadway musical and a 1972 film musical, shows how the Declaration of Independence was forged despite strong differences among the factions represented at the Continental Congress. It implicitly suggests that national unity can be reforged despite contemporary differences. Adapted from Bobbie Ann Mason's 1985 novel of the same title, the Bush-era IN COUNTRY (1989) also seeks reconciliation as it attempts to resolve past traumas from the war in its celebration of the Vietnam Memorial, which opened in 1982. The film tells the story of Samantha (Sam), a teenaged girl whose father was killed in 1963 before she was born. Her uncle also served and returned emotionally disabled. Through a sometimes painful process of discovering her father's experiences in the war, Sam begins to discover her own identity. Likewise, by confronting and discussing his memories of the war, Sam's uncle begins to get his life in order. (See also VIETNAM WAR TELEVISION DOCUMENTARIES; TELEVISION MILITARY DRAMAS; VIETNAM WAR LITERATURE; THEATER; ART; FOLK SINGERS; ROCK AND ROLL.)

For additional reading, see Smith's *Looking Away*; Searle's *Search and Clear: Literature & Films of the Vietnam War*, Lanning's *Vietnam at the Movies*; Malo and Williams' *Vietnam War Films*; Bates' *The War We Took to Vietnam*.

Vietnam War literature

A large body of Vietnam War literature has developed since the United States first sent a sizable contingent of military advisers to Vietnam during the Kennedy administration. Even before that, Graham GREENE's political novel THE QUIET AMERICAN (1955) criticized U.S. behavior in Vietnam. The book was published the year following the French evacuation from Southeast Asia after their defeat at the battle of Dienbienphu and two years after Secretary of State John Foster Dulles had warned of a domino effect in which, if Vietnam were to fall to the communists, the rest of Southeast Asia would follow. *The Quiet American* centers on Alden Pyle, a CIA agent in Southeast Asia whose anti-communist counterterrorism kills and maims innocent civilians. The narrator describes Pyle as "impregnably armoured by his good intentions and his ignorance." Ultimately, Pyle becomes deceived by his own deceptions.

Greene based the character partly on CIA agent Colonel Edward Lansdale, who also inspired the character of Colonel Edwin Hillandale in Eugene BURDICK and William LEDERER's 1958 novel, THE UGLY AMERICAN. Though more sympathetic than Greene's book to the overall U.S. goal of stopping communism and improving the economic and living conditions of the South Vietnamese, *The Ugly American* also attacks the ignorance and hubris of State Department officials who set and implement U.S. policy in Southeast Asia. The story centers on the American ambassador, whose failure to understand local history and customs undermines well-intentioned U.S. efforts to improve the standard of living with advanced technology and improved agricultural methods. The novel criticizes bureaucrats and political hacks who fail to learn native languages and customs, insult local leaders, inhibit the constructive work of private individuals working in the villages, and allow their own egos and career aspirations to dominate their decisions. By contrast, the Soviet diplomatic corps is portrayed as dedicated, modest, self-sacrificing, well informed of local customs, linguistically fluent and focused on its goals.

Relatively little Vietnam War fiction appeared while the war was going on. In *Vietnam Anthology*, editor Nancy Anisfield suggests that the dearth of wartime fiction stems from three main causes: The war was unpopular, and profit-minded publishers do not seek out unpopular topics; the quality of the earliest writing about the war was uneven because the authors were typically young and had not yet fully developed their craft; and the immediacy of the war had not allowed authors enough time to develop a distance from their topic. By contrast, Anisfield suggests, the renewed patriotism of the 1980s—after the nation had had some time to "put Vietnam behind us"—partly accounts for why so much Vietnam War fiction emerged during the Reagan and Bush administrations. No doubt the unveiling of the Vietnam War Memorial on November 11, 1982, also signaled that the nation was at last willing to reconsider the war. Indeed, the memorial and the need to come to terms with the war play central roles in Bobbie Ann Mason's novel IN COUNTRY (1985), about the search for identity by a girl whose father was killed in Vietnam before she was born.

Of the fiction that did appear during the war, Robin Moore's THE GREEN BERETS (1965) was the first to attract considerable attention, especially after John WAYNE starred in and directed the 1968 film adaptation. The book appeared the same year that U.S. combat troops were first introduced into the war, though the action is set in the war's previous phase, when the United States restricted its role to that of military advisers who helped the South Vietnamese fight against the communist-led Viet Cong. The novel celebrates the efforts of the highly trained U.S. Special Forces, the Green Berets, who served as military advisers and endured combat conditions along with the South Vietnamese. By contrast, David Halberstam's ONE VERY HOT DAY (1967), also set before the introduction of combat troops, centers on a U.S. military adviser and his frustration over his mission's apparent lack of progress and purpose. The protagonist is a veteran of World War II and the Korean War who feels undermined by his limited role. "He wished the troops would go faster . . . and he wished he were a real officer, someone who could give commands and then see them obeyed, who could send a patrol here and another there, could make the troops go fast, go slow, be brave, be strong . . . to be an officer and in charge." The circularity of his patrols emerges as a metaphor for the war itself, which seems to defy resolution and refuses to provide any sense of accomplishment.

In the afterword, Halberstam explains, "I wanted to portray the frustrations, and the emptiness of this war. It was after all a smaller and, I think, less tidy war than Americans were accustomed to, and almost nothing that happened in it fit the preconceptions of Westerners." Halberstam, who also wrote the Vietnam NONFICTION books THE BEST AND THE BRIGHTEST (1972), *The Making of a Quagmire* (1965) and *Ho* (1971), had reported on the war in the early 1960s for the *New York Times* and won a Pulitzer Prize for his coverage of it, despite efforts by the Kennedy administration to have him transferred out of Southeast Asia. David Morrell, a John BARTH scholar, achieved prominence for *First Blood* (1972), which appeared in the final year of U.S. movement in the war. It centers on a gutsy Vietnam veteran who stands up to the sheriff of a small American town in which he has been abused. Morrell's book became the basis for the popular series of RAMBO films starring Silvester STALLONE. Philip Roth's satire OUR GANG (1971) ridicules President Nixon's prosecution of the war and what Roth sees as his hypocritical proclamation of the sanctity of life.

Postwar fiction includes Robert Stone's *Dog Soldiers* (1974), which appeared the year after the U.S. military left

Vietnam. The cynical novel, winner of the 1975 National Book Award, centers on the moral corruption of those who became involved in the Southeast Asian drug trade while they fought the war. In 1978, James Webb published FIELDS OF FIRE. A highly decorated Vietnam War officer who had won the Navy Cross, the Silver Star and two Bronze Stars, Webb was wounded in the fighting and later became secretary of the navy. His novel, follows a platoon of Marines through months of jungle warfare during the height of the war. It applies a standard formula for World War II fiction to the Vietnam conflict by depicting the private struggles and motivations of each member of a diverse combat unit. Webb, who supported the war, also wrote *A Sense of Honor* (1981). Jerome Klinkowitz and John Somer edited *Writing Under Fire* (1978), an early collection of Vietnam War short stories. Other war-related fiction includes Robert Olen Butler's *The Alleys of Eden* (1981), about an American deserter who must decide whether to leave Vietnam when the United States pulls out or remain with the Vietnamese lover who has sheltered him for five years; John Del Vecchio's *The 13th Valley* (1982), about the jungle warfare; Stephen Wright's *Meditations in Green,* about a returned veteran's drug-induced flashbacks of the absurd and violent war; Jeff Danziger's *Lieutenant Kit* (1986), about a well-liked officer who maintains his innocence amidst the corruption surrounding him; and Bruce McAllister's *Dream Baby* (1989), the unusual story of a special team of men and one woman (the narrator) who possess different forms of extrasensory perception and are sent to North Vietnam to secretly blow up the dikes surrounding Hanoi.

Irwin BLACKER also wrote several novels about secret missions behind enemy lines. And female nurses also appear prominently in Patricia Walsh's *Forever Sad the Hearts* (1982), Evelyn Hawkins' *Vietnam Nurse* (1984) and Leonard B. Scott's *Charlie Mike* (1985). Scott's novel also treats Vietnamese women as significant characters, as does *The Alleys of Eden.* Tim O'Brien, a war veteran who also authored THE NUCLEAR AGE (1985), has written four novels about Vietnam soldiers or veterans. His first novel, *If I Die in a Combat Zone* (1973), is a collection of interwoven stories. In 1979 he won the National Book Award for *Going After Cacciato* (1978), a magical-realist work about a group of soldiers who cross Asia, the Middle East and Europe to track down a deserter. O'Brien interweaves a series of short stories about U.S. soldiers in Vietnam in *The Things They Carried* (1990). The title story uses a highly objective, Hemingway-like style to describe the impact of the death of one of their members on a company of soldiers. By focusing on objects and exploring the many uses of the concept of "carrying," O'Brien communicates the shock, horror and alienation experienced by the soldiers. O'Brien's *In the Lake of the Woods* (1994) tells of a Vietnam veteran whose life is still shaped by the horrors of the war.

Most of the poetry responding to the Vietnam War was in protest to the U.S. involvement. POETS from the BEAT MOVEMENT were among the war's earliest and most vocal opponents, notably Allen GINSBERG and Lawrence FERLINGHETTI. In 1965 Ginsberg became involved with the nascent Vietnam War protest movement and helped originate the concept of "flower power" as a means of achieving peace. He participated in a 1967 "life festival" that offered chanting, rock music and poetry readings as alternatives to war and was arrested with Dr. Benjamin Spock for blocking access to a military induction center. Ferlinghetti also attacked American leaders in public rallies and in his poetry. *Where Is Vietnam* (1965) lambastes President Johnson as "Colonel Cornpone," who callously orders the suffering and death of people on the other side of the earth. *Tyrannus Nix* (1969) accuses Nixon of promoting the "nazification" of America and points to Nixon's role in the 1950s RED SCARE. He writes, "I am thinking Old Sick Dick in you we finally see no face at all behind the great seal of the United States."

Other antiwar poets include Denise LEVERTOV, Robert BLY and Father Daniel BERRIGAN. Levertov participated in antiwar demonstrations and eventually traveled to Hanoi. Her husband, Mitchell Goodman, was a codefendant with Dr. Spock in a highly publicized trial of draft resisters. Levertov's first war poetry appeared in the final section of *The Sorrow Dance* (1967), entitled "Life at War." The poems evoke powerful images of the innocent victims of the war and express her rage at the perpetrators of the horror: "You who go out on schedule/ to kill, do you know/ there are eyes that watch you,/ eyes whose lids you burned off," and "the scheduled breaking open of breasts whose milk/ runs out over the entrails of still-alive babies." Also in 1967 Levertov edited *Out of the War Shadow: An Anthology of Current Poetry,* published by the War Resisters League. Her *Relearning the Alphabet* (1970) addresses such contemporary issues as the war and war resisters, starvation in Biafra and race riots in Detroit. *To Stay Alive* (1971) collects her war poetry to date within a single volume so those poems might serve "as a document of some historical value, a record of one person's inner/outer experience in America during the '60s and the beginning of the '70s."

Bly believes that the warlike expressions of violence stem from spiritual disharmony within the individual unconscious. He also wrote forcefully about the Vietnam War and other political issues. In 1966 he coedited with David Ray a volume entitled *A Poetry Reading Against the Vietnam War.* His second book of poetry, *The Light Around the Body* (1967), includes introspective poems that celebrate the unconscious as well as attacks on the war and other aspects of American Cold War politics, including "Johnson's Cabinet Watched by Ants," "Those Being Eaten by America," "Listening to President Kennedy Lie about the Cuban Invasion," "The Great Society," "Asian Peace Offers Rejected without Publication," "Hatred of Men with Black Hair" and "Driving through Minnesota during the Hanoi Bombings."

Berrigan, a priest and political activist as well as a poet, served a prison sentence for his role in destroying draft records in Catonsville, Maryland, in 1968. His experiences became the basis for his play, *The Trial of the Catonsville Nine* (1970). After the war, Berrigan worked with Thich Nhat Hahn, a Buddhist monk, to facilitate a reconciliation between the peoples of the United States and Vietnam. His first book to address political issues was *No One Walks Waters* (1966), which includes such poems as "Holy Week, 1965 (The Vietnam Raids Go On)" and "A Pittsburgh Beggar Reminds Me of the Dead of Hiroshima." In 1968 Berrigan published *Night Flight to Hanoi,* which includes "Children in the Shelter," a description of his experience with three children in a Hanoi bomb shelter.

Many other American poets wrote antiwar poetry. Robert Duncan, James Wright, Tom McGrath and Meridel Lesueur are only some of the poets moved by this aspect of the Cold War.

TRAN THI NGA and Wendy Wilder Larsen coauthored the best-selling SHALLOW GRAVES (1986), a collection of poems modeled on the Vietnamese *truyen,* a novel in verse. Written between 1980 and 1985, *Shallow Graves* addresses the lives of women and noncombat personnel during the Vietnam War. On the other hand, Walter MCDONALD served in the war as an air force pilot, and he describes the war from that perspective. "Al Croom" is about a pilot who was always "daring the Russian/ rockets/ to do him in . . . When they shipped him home/ it took triple straps/ to bind him." And "Veteran" describes an ex-soldier with aluminum legs who imagines that "leaves lie in the park/ like tiny bombs/ ready to explode. Someday/ someone raking/ will strike a fuse. We'll all be killed." *After the Noise of Saigon* (1988) includes "The Food Pickers," which describes the Vietnamese civilians who would scrape for food remains, and "War Games," which depicts men who played with imaginary dice while "rockets that crashed down/ on the base always killed somebody else." Nancy Anisfield collects other Vietnam War poems and stories in *Vietnam Anthology* (1987).

The Vietnam War attracted considerable nonfiction commentary both during and after the fighting. Even before the United States had made a major military commitment in Southeast Asia, William Lederer attacked U.S. policy, the State Department and the media in A NATION OF SHEEP (1961), in which he also offers suggestions of how to remedy U.S. foreign policy. In 1968, the year U.S. forces reached their highest level of some 540,000 troops, he published a sequel entitled *Our Own Worst Enemy.* In 1971 Daniel Ellsberg published *The Pentagon Papers,* a collection of secret government papers from the Johnson administration documenting the decision-making process by which the war was escalated and revealing times when the government had lied to the public about its plans in Vietnam. The Nixon administration, then in power, fought the publication, but a Supreme Court decision upheld it. Subsequently, Ellsberg was placed on Nixon's "enemies list," and the burglary of his psychiatrist's office by White House "plumbers" trying to obtain information to discredit him became part of the Watergate scandal.

Halberstam's *The Best and the Brightest* (1972) is one of the most enduring works of nonfiction published during the war. Written while Richard Nixon was president, it chronicles the history of the U.S. escalation of the war during the Kennedy and Johnson administrations and studies the individuals who were responsible for formulating U.S. policy. The title is an indictment of the liberal tradition, dating back to the 18th-century Enlightenment, which maintained that virtually any problem could be resolved by the appropriate application of knowledge, reason and science. Halberstam goes to great lengths to show that Kennedy and Johnson indeed employed "the best and the brightest" men in America to formulate Vietnam policy. Many of their advisers came from the faculties of Harvard and other leading universities. However, the policy produced by these brilliant men was confused, misguided and ineffective. Moreover, Halberstam suggests, hubris and self-deception contributed to the failure of the American efforts. Former

defense secretary Robert McNamara, who figures prominently in the book, concurred with many of Halberstam's judgments in his own 1995 assessment of the war, *In Retrospect: The Tragedy and Lessons of Vietnam,* in which he admits that the war was a mistake and that U.S. policies had been confused and virtually improvised almost from the beginning.

Many other prominent U.S. authors of nonfiction turned their talent to Vietnam. James MICHENER wrote *Kent State: What Happened and Why* (1971), a highly acclaimed study of the 1970 incident in which the Ohio National Guard killed protesters and bystanders at a demonstration against the Vietnam War. During the war, NOVELIST James Jones visited the soldiers and the U.S. military command stationed in Vietnam and published his impressions a year after the U.S. withdrawal, in VIET JOURNAL (1974). Frances FitzGerald's *Fire in the Lake* (1972) offered a brilliant analysis of how differently the U.S. forces and the Viet Cong operated in Vietnamese villages.

Many veterans wrote or spoke about their own experiences during and after the war. Philip Caputo's *A Rumor of War* (1977) was one of the first important autobiographical accounts by a war veteran. EVERYTHING WE HAD (1981) presents 33 oral histories by U.S. soldiers who fought in the war, including those of female American nurses, a group whose participation in the war had been largely overlooked until the 1980s. Nurses' experiences also appear in Lynda Van Devanter's *Home Before Morning* (1983), Myra MacPherson's *Long Time Passing: Vietnam and the Haunted Generation* (1984) and D'Ann Campbell's *Women at War with America: Private Lives in a Patriotic Era* (1984).

Stanley Karnow's best-selling *Vietnam: A History* (1983) claims to be the first complete account of the war and was the basis of a widely viewed Vietnam War television documentary, VIETNAM: A TELEVISION HISTORY. Neil Sheehan's A BRIGHT SHINING LIE (1988) offers a more specific story, the biography of Lt. Colonel John Paul Vann, an American officer who first went to Vietnam in 1962 as a military adviser to the South Vietnamese Army. Originally convinced of the appropriateness of the U.S. mission, Vann became disillusioned and spoke out against the ineffective U.S. strategy and the brutality it entailed. Even though he resigned from the military in 1963 so that he could speak out publicly against the measures being used to fight the war, by 1971 Vann was the most important American in South Vietnam, after the ambassador and commanding general in Saigon, and his control as a civilian over U.S. military troops was unprecedented. Vann was killed in a helicopter crash shortly after turning back a major North Vietnamese offensive in 1972.

There were relatively few plays about the Vietnam War. The THEATER that did exist generally took an antiwar stand. Two early antiwar plays were Megan Terry's VIET ROCK (1966) and Jean-Claude van Itallie's *America Hurrah* (1966), both of which criticize the Vietnam War as part of a larger critique of American culture. Their comic, somewhat absurdist style was influenced by pop art. Both plays were produced Off-Off-Broadway by the OPEN THEATER, successor to the LIVING THEATER. Maria Irene Fornes's *A Vietnamese Wedding* (1967) was performed as part of a weeklong protest called Angry Arts Week. In that play, the audience becomes involved in a traditional Vietnamese wedding ceremony. Her other war protest play is *The Red Burning Light* (1968). The musical play HAIR (1968) celebrates the COUNTERCULTURE and the efforts of one young man to dodge the draft by joining a HIPPIE commune. Terence McNally's one-act Vietnam War plays dramatize the absurdity of the war and the schism between those fighting it and those at home. These include *Tour* (1967), *Next* (1968), *Botticelli* (1968) and *Bringing It All Back Home* (1969). Barbara Garson's SATIRE *Macbird* (1967) likens President Johnson to Macbeth in its biting satire of the war.

Jules FEIFFER also satirizes the presidential politics behind the war in *The White House Murder Case* (1970), which imagines a Vietnam-like war with Brazil and presents the secret machinations of the president and his administration. In 1968 the Royal Shakespeare Company premiered Peter Brooks's antiwar play *US*. The play's first part describes the situation in Vietnam and features a military combat mission, a bombing raid, a U.S. news conference and a Buddhist monk setting himself on fire in protest to the war. The play's second half presents a debate about what would constitute the most effective form of protest within Britain. Joseph HELLER wrote *We Bombed in New Haven* (1967), which makes use of the BLACK HUMOR he brought to his novel CATCH-22.

David RABE wrote the most highly acclaimed plays about the war. *Streamers* (1976) portrays the range of attitudes toward the war, the military and each other among a group of soldiers who are completing their basic training and awaiting assignment to Vietnam. The play is part of a trilogy that also includes *Sticks and Bones* (1969) and *The Basic Training of Pavlo Hummel* (1971). As Nancy Anisfield points out, "each play presents a vision of an America that is permanently poisoned by the war . . . the physically or psychologically wounded veteran is shown ironically as a painful, horrible embarrassment because he represents the ruin of America's myth of heroism and goodness. Furthermore, these plays offer an image of the American spirit as a thin veneer of euphemisms and patriotic rhetoric."

Other U.S. playwrights took up the Vietnam War after it had ended. Lanford Wilson's *The 5th of July* (1978) centers on a veteran who has lost his legs in the war and receives visits from family members and friends. They reminisce about their carefree prewar days and confront what they have since become. Stanley Greenberg's *Pueblo* (1971) deals with the capture of the U.S. intelligence ship off the coast of Korea in 1968, the congressional inquiry into the event and the resulting court-martial of Commander Lloyd Bucher. The incident occurred just prior to the communists' Tet Offensive in Vietnam and was believed to have been coordinated with the North Vietnamese as an effort to have the U.S. redeploy its troops away from the Vietnam toward Korea. (See also MILITARY NOVELS; POLITICAL NOVELS; VIETNAM WAR FILMS; VIETNAM WAR TELEVISION DOCUMENTARIES; TELEVISION MILITARY DRAMAS; TELEVISION SATIRE; ART; FOLK SINGERS; ROCK AND ROLL.)

For additional reading, see Anisfield's *Vietnam Anthology*; Searle's *Search and Clear*, Bates' *The War We Took to Vietnam*; Searle's *Search and Clear*; Hughes' *Plays, Politics and Polemics*; and Gotera and Brown's special issue of the *Journal of American Culture* on "Poetry and the Vietnam War."

Vietnam War television documentaries   Documentaries about Vietnam did not appear until U.S. involvement there became significant, though *Guerrilla* (CBS, 1961) covered efforts by the army's Special Forces to combat guerrilla warfare in Vietnam and elsewhere, and *The Quiet War* (ABC, 1962) featured life in South Vietnam as well as background on the French–communist war that had concluded with the French defeat in 1954. Former ambassador Henry Cabot Lodge, Dr. Bernard Fall and Colonel John Vann discussed the growing conflict in *South Vietnam* (ABC, 1963; Vann's Vietnam experience was later the subject of a 1988 biography, A BRIGHT SHINING LIE). *Death of a Regime* (CBS, 1963) reported on the military coup that ousted President Diem a few weeks before the Kennedy assassination. Among the early Johnson-era documentaries were *Counterattack in Vietnam* (CBS, 1964); *Vietnam: The Deadly Decision* (CBS, 1964); *Brink in Vietnam* (ABC, 1964); *The Daring American: Letters from Viet Nam* (ABC, 1964), which profiled a U.S. helicopter squadron; and *Vietnam: It's a Mad War* (NBC, 1964).

Direct U.S. military action began in February 1965, when Johnson ordered air raids against the North Vietnam in response to an attack on an American installation. The next month, two Marine battalions sent to defend Danang airfield became the first U.S. combat troops in Vietnam. As the fighting intensified, the number of special reports increased. *Vietnam: Air Strike North* (CBS, 1965) covered the first U.S. bombings of targets inside North Vietnam. The *Battle for the Ia Drang Valley* (CBS, 1965) documented the first major battle fought by U.S. soldiers. In March, CBS featured *Vietnam: The Hawks and the Doves*, a debate between war supporters Sen. Gale McGee and reporter Hanson W. Baldwin and war opponents Sen. George McGovern and diplomat Roger Hilsman. ABC and CBS also reported on the daylong "teach-in" on Vietnam held in May in Washington, D.C. The teach-in included a related debate between Johnson adviser McGeorge Bundy and professor George Kahin. Other special reports from 1965 included *Dilemma in Vietnam* (ABC); *The Berkeley Rebels* (CBS), about the war protest on the University of California campus; *The Agony of Vietnam* (ABC), which looked at the impact of the war on the Vietnamese; *Gas Scare in Vietnam* (ABC), about the use of tear gas by South Vietnamese troops against South Vietnamese war protesters; *Reflections on Vietnam: A Special Report by Frank Reynolds* (ABC); *The Yanks Are Coming* (ABC); *Vietnam: December, 1965* (NBC); *Storm over Vietnam* (ABC), about student protest rallies in the United States; and *Next of Kin* (ABC), about the attitudes of the families of soldiers fighting in Vietnam and their responses to the demonstrations against the war. Several year-end assessments appeared at the conclusion of 1965 and "Vietnam Perspective" (CBS) began a series of 19 episodes about various aspects of the war lasting into 1967.

Vietnam reports from 1966 include *Vietnam: Eric Sevareid's Personal Report* (CBS); *Vietnam Report: A New Phase* (NBC); *Vietnam Crisis* (NBC); *In Search of Peace* (CBS), about the proposed Geneva peace conference; and *Vietnam: The Decision to Bomb* (CBS, 1966). After interviewing citizens throughout the country, a team of ABC news reporters discussed American attitudes in *Vietnam: The Questions America Is Asking*. Other documentaries from that year were *Operation Sea War* (ABC); *Air Rescue: Vietnam* (CBS); *Man of the Month: Ho Chi Minh* (CBS); *Woman Doctor in Vietnam*

(CBS), about physician Pat Smith who treated South Vietnamese tribespeople in the Central Highlands; *To Save a Soldier* (ABC), about battlefield medical treatment; *Man of the Month: The Draftee* (CBS); *The First TV War* (NBC), about the effects of television coverage on the war; *Vietnam: the Senate Hearings* (CBS), which also included an interview with Secretary of State Dean Rusk; and a Morley Safer and Charles Collingwood interview with General William Westmoreland in Saigon at the end of the year. *Vietnam: War of the Ballot* (NBC) analyzed the upcoming South Vietnamese elections to choose a National Assembly that would draft a constitution. Between February 1966 and January 1968, ABC ran 97 consecutive weekly features entitled VIETNAM REPORT, which covered a broad range of aspects about the escalating war. From 1966 through 1967, NBC aired "Vietnam Weekly Review."

In 1967, *The People of Vietnam: How They Feel About the War* (CBS) surveyed South Vietnamese public opinion. *Raymond Burr Visits Vietnam* (NBC) followed the actor who had portrayed TV lawyer Perry Mason as he visited soldiers and gave his impressions of the war. *Where We Stand in Vietnam* (CBS) furnished an updated look at the military and political situation. *Same Mud, Same Blood* (NBC) presented the war from the viewpoint of a black American soldier. *Soldiers' Christmas* (CBS) depicted the Christmas eve celebrations in Vietnam. *The Four Navy Deserters* (CBS) featured four sailors who had deserted from their ships and taken refuge in Sweden.

The 1968 Tet Offensive became a pivotal point in the war, since televised images of enemy soldiers inside the U.S. Embassy in Saigon undermined government assurances that the United States and South Vietnam were on the verge of victory. Broadcast during the offensive, *Viet Cong* (CBS) examined the ideology of the communist guerrilla army as well as focusing on some individuals within it who were fighting to overthrow the U.S.-backed South Vietnamese regime. CBS also aired *Saigon Under Fire,* a special report on the Tet Offensive as it occurred, while NBC pondered *Vietnam and After: What Should We Do?* The most influential Vietnam special report was *Walter Cronkite in Vietnam* (CBS), which did much to change public attitudes about the war. Upon returning from Vietnam at the end of the offensive, CRONKITE concluded that it seemed "more certain than ever that the bloody experience of Vietnam is to end in a stalemate."

The Tet Offensive occasioned offers by the North Vietnamese to conduct peace talks, and these were the subject of several post-Tet special reports in 1968, including *Vietnam Report: Possibilities for Peace* (ABC); *Peace Talks in Paris: The Very First Step* (CBS); and *Peace, Politics and the President* (CBS), which covered President Johnson's decision not to seek reelection and the related prospects for peace in Vietnam. The on-again, off-again talks were the subject of special update reports throughout the duration of the war. That spring, CBS also broadcast *Hanoi: A Report by Charles Collingwood,* and NBC ran *Vietnam This Week.*

The year 1969 was President Nixon's first year in office. Vietnam documentaries and reports from that year included *A Timetable for Vietnam* (CBS), about the "Vietnamization" of the war and the prospects for the success of the South Vietnamese army; *The College Turmoil* (CBS) and *Generations*

Apart: A Profile of Dissent (CBS), about antiwar protests; and *Vietnam Moratorium Day,* in which all three networks covered a nationwide moratorium against the war.

On April 30, 1970, Nixon ordered U.S. troops to attack communist sanctuaries inside Cambodia, an act that provoked student strikes, university closings and massive antiwar protests throughout the United States, including one at the Kent State University, where the Ohio National Guard opened fire and killed four among the protesters and onlookers. These acts prompted several special reports, including *Where We Stand in Cambodia* (CBS), made three days after the Cambodian "incursion"; *Day of Dissent* (ABC); *Campuses in Crisis* (CBS), and *Conversation with the President* (all three networks), in which Howard K. Smith and Eric SEVAREID interviewed Nixon about Cambodia. Between June and early September, some eight additional special war-related reports appeared, most notably John Laurence's Emmy-winning *The World of Charlie Company,* and responses to Nixon from antiwar Senators McGovern, Fulbright and Mathias. Shortly after Christmas, CBS presented *Inside North Vietnam: U.S. Prisoners Speak,* which featured filmed interviews with American prisoners of war (POWs).

The broadening of the war into Cambodia and Laos was also the subject of the first part of CBS's *The Changing War in Indochina* (1971); the second part, *The Waning War in Vietnam,* covered the reduction of U.S. troop strength in Vietnam. *The Court-Martial of William Calley: The Mind of a Juror* (CBS, 1971) and *The Calley Case: A Nation's Agony* (ABC, 1971) reported on the 1968 My Lai massacre and the 1971 conviction of the U.S. lieutenant in charge. *POWs: Pawns of War* (CBS, 1971) addressed the political aspects of the prisoner-of-war question; *Vietnam Hindsight* (NBC, 1971) traced the U.S. involvement in Vietnam and the U.S. role in the assassination of South Vietnam's President Diem. *Escalation in Vietnam* (CBS, 1972) was a series of special reports commenting on recent activities by the president, secretary of state and other ranking government officials. *Can You Go Home Again* (CBS, 1972) reported on draft evaders who fled the country. *American Lives/American Honor* (ABC, 1972) reported on the status of the war just prior to Nixon's trip to Moscow. That autumn, *Hanoi: An Uncensored Report* (CBS) presented a "debriefing" of correspondent John Hart, who had recently returned from North Vietnam. Two weeks before the 1972 presidential election, national security adviser Henry Kissinger announced that a peace treaty was imminent. This occasioned *Kissinger's Vietnam Report* (CBS) and *Peace Is at Hand* (ABC). At the year's end, the still-unresolved peace settlement became the topic of *The Elusive Peace* (CBS). When Nixon announced the final peace settlement on January 23, 1973, all three networks ran special reports on the treaty, the war and the anticipated fates of South Vietnam, draft dodgers, military deserters and POWs.

Between the U.S. military evacuation on March 29, 1973, and the fall of Saigon and the surrender of South Vietnam on April 30, 1975, Vietnam remained a topic of special reports including *POW Interview* (NBC, 1973) and *POWs: The Black Homecoming* (ABC, 1973), which reported on the problems African-American POWs had adjusting to their return home. Perhaps because the country was caught up in the unfolding Watergate drama and was otherwise eager to put Vietnam behind it, 1974 occasioned virtually no documentaries on Vietnam or any related topic. However, as South Vietnam began to fall in 1975, special reports reappeared. *Cambodia: An American Dilemma* (CBS), *Indochina: Savage Springtime* (ABC) and *Indochina 1975: The End of the Road?* (CBS) presented the situations in South Vietnam and Cambodia, which both surrendered to communist forces in April. Broadcast on April 29, when the last Americans evacuated the U.S. Embassy in Saigon, were *7,382 Days in Vietnam* (NBC), *Vietnam: A War that Is Finished* (CBS) and *Vietnam: Lessons Learned, Prices Paid* (ABC).

Though the number of special reports on Vietnam lessened after the war concluded, the networks continued to air them from time to time. *The Class that Went to Vietnam* (ABC, 1977) traced the lives of members of a New Jersey high school graduating class from 1964. *What's Happened in Cambodia?* (CBS, 1978) provided the first television account since the communist revolution had closed the country to Western reporters. *Jane Fonda* (PBS) was a BBC-made biography of the actress/activist filmed in 1977 and aired in the United States in 1979. Made nine years after the United States extricated itself from the war, *The Uncounted Enemy: A Vietnam Deception* (CBS, 1982) alleged that General Westmoreland had overseen a conspiracy to falsify intelligence reports about the events leading to the 1968 Tet Offensive. Westmoreland filed a $120 million libel suit in response. In 1983, PBS broadcast a 13-part documentary tracing the Vietnam War from its earliest days to the fall of Saigon. Entitled VIETNAM: A TELEVISION HISTORY and accompanied by *Vietnam: A History*, a best-selling book by Stanley Karnow, the series provoked a rebuttal documentary by Peter C. Rollins, TELEVISION'S VIETNAM: IMPACT OF THE MEDIA/THE REAL STORY (1985). Other postwar documentaries included *Dear America: Letters Home from Vietnam* (HBO, 1988) and *Two Decades and a Wake-up* (PBS, 1990), which examined the lives of eight veterans with post-traumatic stress disorder. (See also VIETNAM WAR FILMS; FILM DOCUMENTARIES.)

For additional reading, see Einstein's *Special Edition: A Guide to Network Television Documentary Series and Special News Reports, 1955–1979*; McNeil's *Total Television*.

"Visit with the Armed Forces" A TELEVISION NEWS show that ran on the DuMont network in 1950–51. Broadcast during the Korean War, it featured documentary films about the armed forces.

Viva Zapata! A 1951 MILITARY FILM starring Marlon Brando, Jean Peters and Anthony Quinn and directed by Elia KAZAN. John Steinbeck wrote the screenplay, which is based on the 1941 novel *Zapata! the Unconquered* by Edgcumb Pichon. The film tells the story of Emiliano Zapata (Brando), who led a successful peasant rebellion in Mexico between 1911 and 1919. Made during the height of the RED SCARE, *Viva Zapata!* stands out as one of the very few Hollywood films of that era to favorably portray the violent overthrow of landowners and their government by an insurgent movement whose main goal was land reform and redistribution of wealth. Conceivably, the film could have been viewed as giving support to communism although its liberal politics do not in fact go that far. The film appeared the year before Kazan testified before the HOUSE COMMITTEE ON UN-AMERICAN ACTIVITIES (HUAC). By 1951, Kazan considered himself an anti-communist liberal, and he testified before HUAC that *Viva Zapata!* was "an anti-Communist picture. Please see my article on political aspects of this picture in the *Saturday Review* of April 5 [1952], which I forwarded to your investigator . . ."

Vonnegut, Kurt, Jr. A NOVELIST. A writer of science fiction, SATIRE and BLACK HUMOR, Vonnegut was born in 1922 and educated at Cornell and the University of Chicago. There he received a master's degree in anthropology in 1971 after his novel, CAT'S CRADLE (1963), was accepted in lieu of a thesis. Vonnegut began writing in the 1950s. His wry, cynical representation of human society attracted a large following during the Vietnam War era, especially among the COUNTERCULTURE and others who distrusted the U.S. government.

Among Vonnegut's earliest treatments of the Cold War is his 1953 short story, ALL THE KING'S HORSES, which he later collected in *Welcome to the Monkey House* (1968). Published the year the Korean War ended, the story centers on a U.S. military attaché whom a sadistic communist guerrilla shoots down over Asia, along with his wife, two sons and 12 soldiers. Though advised by a Soviet military officer, the guerrilla is autonomous, and because he is not really aligned to any nation, he is essentially immune to outside political pressures. To satisfy his vanity, the guerrilla forces the attaché to participate in a game of chess played on a life-size board, in which the American prisoners are the attaché's chess pieces. Ultimately, the attaché must decide whether to sacrifice one of his sons in order to win the game and gain the release of the rest of the Americans. The story shows the difficulties in conducting foreign policy in a feudalistic Asia, which was how many Westerners then viewed the East. The story also makes use of the stereotypes of Americans and Soviets commonly found in American Cold War culture: The Soviet adviser is a cold, dispassionate professional who cares solely about his mission, while the American is a deeply feeling family man who loves his wife and children but can switch off his emotions and retain his professional cool when crises require it. The American can therefore master his inner anguish and do what he must: Order the sacrifice of his son in order to save everyone else. Ironically, then, the American must become like the Soviet in order for the American community to survive; the difference is that for the American, the suppression of his fatherly love is unnatural and requires a supreme act of will, whereas the Soviet seems to come by it naturally.

Vonnegut's later fiction moves away from the patriotism of "All the King's Horses" and turns against government in general, on the grounds that all governments suppress individuality. "Harrison Bergeron" (1961), also collected in *Welcome to the Monkey House*, expresses this theme most directly by positing a future society in which the government handicaps everyone so that no citizen is in any way superior to anyone else. For instance, the government requires intelligent people to wear in their ears tiny radios that emit loud, irritating sounds every few seconds to distract their concentration; gifted dancers are burdened by sacks of birdshot; and handsome personal features are covered up. Diana Moon Glampers, the Handicapper General, enforces these rules ferociously, and the story climaxes when she suppresses a rebellion of the individual spirit and creative impulse by shooting down in mid-leap a graceful dancer who has thrown off his impediments and begun to perform an exquisite dance. Moreover, in Vonnegut's view, officials often use governmental powers to pursue their own insidious personal agendas. "Manned Missiles" (1961), also in *Monkey House,* features the personal correspondence between the fathers of two astronauts, an American and a Soviet, who were killed when an American rocket accidentally crashed into a manned Soviet satellite. As the politicians in both countries distort the facts and make propaganda of the incident, the fathers write to each other in personal and heartfelt terms. They simply want to communicate their thoughts and feelings and help each other bear the loss of their sons. The story appeared the same year as the first manned space flights.

Vonnegut's novels frequently address the theme of science and technology gone amok. *Player Piano* (1953), for instance, features a super-computer called EPICAC capable of waging totally efficient war. The acronym EPICAC alludes to MANIAC, the computer built to invent the hydrogen bomb, as well as to the vomit-inducing medicine epicac. (The super-computer first appeared in the 1950 short story, "EPICAC," also collected in *Monkey House.*) *Player Piano* climaxes with the destruction of all forms of technology, but even this solution seems inadequate, as humans begin to reconstruct machines out of the wreckage. In *Cat's Cradle* (1963), which appeared a year after the Cuban Missile Crisis, Felix Hoenikker, the father of the atom bomb, has invented *ice-nine.* A unique isotope of ice, ice-nine reconfigures the molecules in water so that they turn solid at temperatures below 114 degrees Fahrenheit, instead of 32 degrees. Dropped into the ocean, a single crystal of ice-nine can solidify the entire sea, and touched to someone's lips it freezes the blood and kills the individual. When he dies, Hoenikker leaves a piece of ice-nine to his three maladjusted children, who divide it among themselves and go out into the world to seek power. Unfortunately their quest leads to the end of the world when ice-nine freezes over the sea and brings about an apocalypse. Thus Vonnegut warns that science will inevitably be abused because it is human nature to treat it carelessly and apply it for selfish reasons. Moreover, the flukes of nature ensure that our best efforts to control the dangerous products of science will inevitably fail. Nonetheless, the novel's playfulness helps to create Vonnegut's characteristic black humor, which renders this bleak theme palatable, even fun.

Billy Pilgrim, the protagonist of *Slaughter-House Five* (1969), moves back and forth among three time periods and locations: 1960s America, Dresden in 1945 and the planet Tralfamadore in the future. The novel describes the Allied fire bombing of Dresden, a city with no military value, an event that Vonnegut witnessed as a prisoner of war and that the Allies kept secret from the American public for years after the war ended. The book's anti-war message and its highlighting of government deception made it popular among Vietnam War protesters.

Deadeye Dick (1982) addresses the question of moral responsibility by contrasting a boy who has accidentally killed a woman with the U.S. government, which may have deliberately destroyed an American city to test the neutron bomb, whose development President Carter had canceled but whose resumed development the Reagan administration was considering. The narrator muses, "My own guess is that the American Government . . . set one off in a small city which nobody cared about, where people weren't doing all that much with their lives anyway, where businesses were going under or moving away. The Government couldn't test a bomb on a foreign city, after all, without running the risk of starting World War Three." In the end, the government suffers no repercussions for its action, while the boy is stigmatized for life and his family is ruined.

Galapagos (1986) also features nuclear destruction. The book begins with an apocalyptic nuclear war and then moves forward a million years to the renewed evolution of the species. However, the laws of natural selection have now reduced human brain size, since excessively large brains were most responsible for the self-destructive nuclear holocaust. The old-time big brains "would tell their owners, in effect, 'Here is a crazy thing we could actually do, probably, but we would never do it, of course. It's just fun to think about.' And then, as though in trances, the people would really do it—have slaves fight each other to the death in the Colosseum . . . or build factories whose only purpose was to kill people in industrial quantities, or to blow up whole cities, and on and on." As Tom Hearron points out in *The Nightmare Considered,* Vonnegut shows that "the essential paradox of our time [is] that people are equipped with such large brains that they have become extremely stupid when it comes to foreseeing the consequences of their action." Elsewhere, Vonnegut might be talking about his own philosophy when he praises the comedy team Bob and Ray: "Man is not evil, they seem to say. He is simply too hilariously stupid to survive." However, in Vonnegut's funny novels, the hilarity has redemptive value in its own right. Like John BARTH, Thomas PYNCHON, Robert COOVER, Terry SOUTHERN and other black humorists, Vonnegut injects a life-affirming spirit of play into the bleak world he perceives. (See also APOCALYPTIC NOVELS.)

For additional reading, see *Dictionary of Literary Biography* (vol. 2, *American Novelists Since World War II;* Anisfield's *The Nightmare Considered;* Dowling's *Fictions of Nuclear Disaster.*

Waiting for the Light A 1990 FILM COMEDY starring Shirley MacLaine and Teri Garr and directed by Christopher Monger. The Cuban Missile Crisis serves as the backdrop to this comedy about an ex-vaudeville magician who is helping her niece put her life back together. In a humorous way, the movie shows the impact of the Cold War on private lives. The title plays the conventional meaning of "waiting for the light" (awaiting illumination) against the expression's Cold War meaning (waiting for the light from a nuclear blast).

Walk East on Beacon A 1952 SPY FILM starring George Murphy and Virginia Gilmore and directed by Alfred L. Werker. The story, told in documentary style, shows the FBI cracking a communist spy ring in Boston. Suggested by FBI director J. Edgar Hoover's *Crime of the Century*, the movie was produced in cooperation with the FBI. It shows FBI agents foiling communist spies trying to steal the results of "an extraordinary experiment" involving a newly developed computer. The communists are both incompetent and cruel. When a member leaves the party because, "I woke up one morning and found I had a Party card . . . [which is like] finding yourself married to a woman you hate," he is soon murdered. As late as 1977, the CIA was leasing 10 copies from Columbia Pictures, apparently for distribution overseas. (See also FILMS ASSOCIATED WITH THE RED SCARE.)

Walk to the End of the World A 1979 APOCALYPTIC NOVEL by Suzy McKee Charnas. Published toward the end of U.S.-Soviet détente, the novel provides a rare feminist treatment of the Cold War that depicts a postnuclear society "in which power is the crucial question, and the struggle of males is the central form that question takes." After the apocalypse, a brutal, fascistic, male-dominated society emerges. Women become slaves who work underground and are turned into food when they die. "Some man must have designed the process; it was too beautiful, too efficient to be a product of the fems' [women's] own thinking." The story centers on Eykar, the ruler's son who falls in love and is inspired to try to reform the racist, misogynistic society. However, his task is complicated by how deeply violence and misogyny are rooted in the culture. For example, the Old Testament is held in high esteem because it celebrates huge battles against unbelievers and authorizes a hierarchical society "with its codes of honour, rigid class divisions, and the subjugation of whole races . . . The problem . . . was that fems had infiltrated and perverted a fine, manly creed." In the sequel, *Motherlines* (1981), a band of roving women who call themselves Mares breed with their stallions, whom they both ride and worship. According to David Dowling, "although Charnas's novels arise from a plausible situation in which men hold women responsible for the nuclear armageddon, the books moved towards an alternative, a vision of the new species of androgynous (wo) mankind."

For additional reading, see Dowling's *Fictions of Nuclear Disaster.*

Walker A 1987 POLITICAL FILM starring Ed Harris, Marlee Matlin, Peter Boyle and Richard Masur and directed by Alex Cox. A surreal satire on U.S.–Nicaraguan relations, *Walker* centers on William Walker, the 19th-century American adventurer who invaded Nicaragua with 58 men and became that country's ruler in 1856 and 1857. The film was made with the complete cooperation of Nicaragua's left-wing Sandinistas, who were then resisting efforts by the CIA and U.S.-backed "contras" to overthrow them and who had feared a seemingly imminent U.S. invasion only a few years earlier.

Filmed just prior to the congressional hearings into the Iran-contra Affair, the movie benefited from the timeliness of those hearings and from unanticipated comparisons between William Walker and Colonel Oliver North. The real-life Walker was a small, egocentric, humorless man who proposed to have the country annexed to the United States as a slave state. He believed in America's "manifest destiny . . . to spread across the continent allotted by Providence for the free development of our yearly multiplying millions," and he worked closely with American business tycoon Cornelius Vanderbilt. The parallels to Cold War American efforts to dictate Nicaraguan politics were readily apparent to film viewers who had been hearing Reagan's anti-Sandinista rhetoric for several years. By introducing such anachronisms as Zippo lighters and helicopters, Cox connects Walker's ambitions to the present and particularly to the Reagan administration. At one point, a modern helicopter rescues Walker's men from near disaster, but the deus ex machina effect further undermines the Americans' credibility. Like Reagan, Walker expresses fine sentiments about freedom, spiritual regeneration and sacred trust, but Walker's actions belie his words. He does nothing to stop his men from pillaging, and he turns to slavery as the answer to the country's economic woes. Moreover, Walker and his men are barely more competent than the inept organizers of the Iran–contra deal. At one point they retreat after they've won a battle.

The overall effect of the film is to expose Walker's grandiose ambitions as the workings of a megalomaniac working in collusion with American robber barons at the expense of the Nicaraguan people. The film's timeliness and anachronisms then silently invite viewers to apply their judgment about Walker and his men to contemporary U.S–Nicaraguan relations. (See also FILM SATIRE.)

Wall, The See PINK FLOYD THE WALL.

War Game, The A 1966 British-made FILM DOCUMENTARY directed by Peter Watkins. It received the 1967 Academy Award for best feature documentary. Using street interviews and simulated newsreels, the film "reports" on the aftermath of a nuclear attack. After the film's first screening, a writer for Britain's *National Observer* declared, "*The War Game* may be the most important film ever made. We are always being told that a work of art cannot change the course of history; I think this one might. It should be screened everywhere." However, after its initial release, the film failed to appear on either British or U.S. television, even though it was produced by the BBC.

The War Game proceeds from a hypothetical political situation in which the United States threatens to use nuclear weapons against Chinese troops that have entered the Vietnam War, much as they actually did during the Korean War. In response, the Soviets threaten to take over West Berlin. A war between NATO and Warsaw Pact troops breaks out in Europe, and Western forces are compelled to employ tactical nuclear weapons against the superior Eastern armored divisions. In response, the U.S.S.R. launches a nuclear attack against military targets in Western Europe. This linkage of targets around the world was an element of Cold War policy on both sides and was the basis of Eisenhower's policy of massive retaliation, which intended a nuclear strike against the Soviet Union in response to communist aggression anywhere on the planet.

The War Game then simulates the aftermath of a Soviet missile strike against England. Supposedly, the strike misses its military target and lands instead in the county of Kent. Panic ensues as the attack is anticipated, but evacuation plans prove inadequate. When the missile finally strikes, the firestorm asphyxiates those who fled to fallout shelters. A windstorm caused by the blast rips a child from its mother's arms and carries it into the flames. In the aftermath, police use their shotguns to put victims out of their misery. Thenceforth, the situation becomes ever more grotesque and horrific. In *Nuclear War Films*, Jack G. Shaheen has noted the similarity to scenes described in John Hersey's account of the atomic attack in HIROSHIMA.

The BBC declined to broadcast *The War Game* because it was fatalistic, bitter, hopeless and cruel—"too horrifying" and unsuitable for family viewing. Watkins quit in protest. Because of its bleak depiction of a hypothetical attack on a population center, ABC's THE DAY AFTER (1983) has been compared to *The War Game*. (See also APOCALYPTIC FILMS.)

For additional reading, see Shaheen's *Nuclear War Films*.

War Hunt A 1962 KOREAN WAR FILM starring John Saxon and Robert Redford and directed by Denis Sanders. *War Hunt* centers on a young soldier (Saxon) in the Korean War who losses his perspective and becomes enamored of killing. Redford, in his film debut, portrays a private who goes through the experience with him. The story is based on an actual Marine who would go off for days by himself to kill the enemy. He was known as "The Candy Bar Kid," because he would take candy as provisions for his killing excursions. Eventually, the Marine Corps removed him from action and sent him to a Veterans Hospital.

For additional reading, see Smith's *Looking Away*.

War Is Hell A 1964 KOREAN WAR FILM starring Tony Russel and Baynes Barron, directed by Burt Topper. The story focuses on a GI who becomes obsessed with gaining "glory" during the Korean War. The obsession causes him to become demented. The film's depiction of grimness and violence emphasized the dehumanizing nature of war.

For additional reading, see Smith's *Looking Away*.

Warday (a.k.a. The Journey Onward) A 1984 APOCALYPTIC NOVEL by Whitley Strieber and James Kunetka. The best-selling book appeared during the most intense period of the Cold War since the 1962 Cuban Missile Crisis, when the Reagan administration was accusing the Soviet Union of preparing to prevail in a nuclear war and was therefore advocating a policy of winnable nuclear war for the United States. Using a pseudo-documentary style, the book presents a first-person account written by an observer who surveys the United States after a small-scale nuclear war. The society has devolved to a pre-industrial level of technology due to the loss of fossil fuel during the war, and a kind of feudalism has emerged as the dominant governing structure within isolated social units, except where anarchy abounds. Nonetheless, the novel concludes optimistically. Like FISKADORO, which appeared the following year, *Warday* suggests that the trauma of NUCLEAR APOCALYPSE might ultimately elevate human consciousness to permit the creation of a new enlightened race: "America is changing, profoundly and probably irrevocably. In a few years there will be . . . few references to us." Later the narrator adds, "Words like *history* have lost their weight. They seem as indefinite as memories and as unimportant." Finally he concludes, "We are not like we were before. Now our habit is more often to accept and heal rather than to reject and punish. Would things have been different if our postwar consciousness had, by some miracle, arisen before the war."

For additional reading, see Anisfield's *The Nightmare Considered* and Scheick's "Continuative and Ethical Predictions: The Post-Nuclear Holocaust Novel of the 1980s."

WarGames   A 1983 MILITARY FILM starring Matthew Broderick, Ally Sheedy and Dabney Coleman and directed by John Badham. Made during the arms buildup in the first Reagan administration, *WarGames* presented a new Cold War threat to world security—the possibility that unauthorized users might gain access to the computer systems controlling the superpowers' arsenals. The plot centers on a teenaged boy who inadvertently gains access to the U.S. nuclear defense system through his computer modem. Believing that he has discovered an exciting new computer game, he begins issuing commands. The resulting crisis gives the film an anti-nuclear theme, as NUCLEAR APOCALYPSE is narrowly averted. In addition to commenting on the intensification of the Cold War in the early 1980s, when Reagan officials were speaking of "winnable nuclear war," *WarGames* also refers to the growing role in American culture of the personal computer. (See also APOCALYPTIC FILMS.)

Wat, Aleksander   A Polish EXILED WRITER (to the United States). Born in Warsaw in 1900, Wat came from a family of Jewish intellectuals. He edited the Polish communist journal *Literary Monthly* from 1929 to 1932, when the right-wing Polish government shut it down. At the beginning of World War II, Wat fled to Lvov, in the Ukraine, to escape the invading German Army, but Soviet authorities arrested him in 1940, and he spent several years in Russian prison camps during the war. In 1946, he returned to Warsaw, where he wrote poetry and prose and mentored other writers. However, Wat became disillusioned by the practices of the communist government and went into exile in Paris in 1959. He came to the United States in 1964 to teach at the University of California at Berkeley but committed suicide in 1967 in despair over his broken health. His memoir, *My Century: The Odyssey of a Polish Intellectual* (1977; in English, 1988), is based on a series of interviews that Wat gave to his Berkeley

colleague Czeslaw MILOSZ. The book describes Wat's initial intellectual attraction to communism and his subsequent beliefs about Soviet corruption and tyranny.

For additional autobiographical accounts of European and American intellectuals who became disaffected with communism after an initial attraction to it, see THE GOD THAT FAILED.

Way We Were, The   A 1973 FILM DRAMA starring Barbra Streisand, Robert Redford and Patrick O'Neal and directed by Sydney Pollack. The story centers on the romance between a communist, working-class, Jewish activist (Streisand) and an apolitical, upper-class writer (Redford) who meet in college during the 1930s and then marry after they meet again during World War II. Their relationship is continuously troubled by the disparity in their politics. Her lack of humor and inability to put politics aside and enjoy life disturbs him; his refusal to stand up for principles upsets her. After the war they move to Hollywood, where he becomes a successful screenwriter. When the HOUSE COMMITTEE ON UN-AMERICAN ACTIVITIES (HUAC) opens its 1947 hearings on communist influences in Hollywood, she helps form the Committee for the First Amendment and travels to Washington in support of the HOLLYWOOD TEN, who refuse to cooperate with HUAC. Though the writer admires his wife's commitment, he feels that it is pointless and self-destructive to fight against the RED SCARE, which he believes will pass in time. These differences finally cause their marriage to dissolve. They meet again in the 1950s, when she is handing out Ban the Bomb leaflets and he is writing for television. Though criticized for its uneven script, the film presents both points of view sympathetically. (See also FILMS ASSOCIATED WITH THE RED SCARE.)

Wayne, John   A Hollywood actor. Born in Winterset, Iowa, in 1907 as Marion Morrison, Wayne was both a major star and a strong spokesman for right-wing anticommunism. As an established star, Wayne typically chose roles that reinforced his view of rugged American individualism. Wayne was a large and physically powerful person, and his characters were strong, emotionally restrained, tough, straightforward, loyal and willing to sacrifice for justice and freedom. They usually possessed a strong, simple sense of morality in which a person was either right or wrong, and they had little patience for those who pondered ethical ambiguities or viewed conflicts in a less clear-cut fashion. In his real-life political dealings, Wayne showed the same attitudes. His films with Cold War significance include BIG JIM MCLAIN (1952), about a communist-fighting investigator for the HOUSE COMMITTEE ON UN-AMERICAN ACTIVITIES (HUAC); JET PILOT (1957), about an American pilot who resists the temptations of a beautiful Soviet spy and wins her to the anti-communist cause instead; THE ALAMO (1960), about the heroic resistance of the vastly outnumbered American fighters at the Alamo; and THE GREEN BERETS (1968), about highly trained U.S. soldiers fighting in Vietnam. Wayne directed *The Alamo* and *The Green Berets*.

As president of the politically conservative MOTION PICTURE ALLIANCE FOR THE PRESERVATION OF AMERICAN IDEALS, Wayne took an active role in trying to ensure that Hollywood films provided a pro-American, anti-communist view.

John Wayne in The Green Berets, *1968.* Courtesy AP/Wide World.

For instance, he supported the alliance's publication of Ayn Rand's A SCREEN GUIDE FOR AMERICANS, which admonished filmmakers not to smear the free enterprise system, glorify failure, deify the common man, glorify the collective, or denigrate success. He objected to the film Western HIGH NOON, (1954) judging it "un-American" because it portrayed middle-class townspeople as cowards. He also thought it desecrated the badge of a U.S. law enforcement officer when, disgusted with the cowardly townspeople, the sheriff hurls the badge to the ground. Carl FOREMAN, who wrote the screenplay, went into exile in England in 1952 after refusing to cooperate with HUAC. In 1977 Wayne asserted that, "I'll never regret having helped run Foreman out of this country." In the 1970s Wayne remained loyal to President Nixon and continued to support the Vietnam War. Though he never served in the armed forces, Wayne's name became synonymous with heroism, bravery and a military ethic.

We Are Your Sons: The Legacy of Julius and Ethel Rosenberg

A 1975 NONFICTION book by Robert and Michael Meeropol. The book argues for the innocence of convicted atomic bomb spies Julius and Ethel Rosenberg, who were also the parents of the authors. (The boys took their stepparents' name after the Rosenbergs were executed in 1953.) *We Are Your Sons* provides many of the Rosenbergs' hitherto unpublished letters from prison and assembles evidence in an effort to prove that they were not guilty of heading a spy ring that passed information about the atomic

bomb to the Soviets during World War II. The Meeropols' conclusions remain controversial and disputed, and the book was criticized for its weak scholarship, unclear references (especially the role of Morton Sobell), simplistic treatment of the Cold War, and attacks on academics who insist on the Rosenbergs' guilt. On the other hand, the book was praised for its description of the impact the case had on the boys' lives after their parents' execution. As of 1995, research into Communist Party archives from the former Soviet Union has revealed no indication of Julius and Ethel Rosenberg's complicity in the theft of the atomic bomb secrets. On the other hand, in July 1995, the CIA released documents from the Venona Project that decoded cables to the Soviet Union from suspected spies in the 1940s. These documents suggest the Rosenbergs' complicity, and Walter and Miriam Schneir, the Rosenbergs' staunchest defenders, have conceded that Julius spied, though the information he passed to the Soviets was far less important than his accusers stated.

"We Will All Go Together When We Go"

A 1959 BLACK HUMOR song by Tom LEHRER. Lehrer wrote the song during the second Berlin Crisis when fears of nuclear war were especially great. He later performed it in 1964, two years after the Cuban Missile Crisis, on the television satire THAT WAS THE WEEK THAT WAS (NBC, 1964–65). Lehrer introduces it on his record album, *An Evening With Tom Lehrer,* as a "survival hymn." The lyrics describe the possibilities of NUCLEAR APOCALYPSE but in a classically black humor mode that generates laughter. The spirited song opens with the observation that death is usually accompanied by grief, but "If the bomb that falls on you/ Gets your friends and neighbors too/ There'll be no one left to grieve when you go." Other lyrics include, "There will be no more misery/ When the world is a rotisserie"; "Just sing out a Te Deum/ When you see that ICBM"; and "When the air becomes uranius/ We will all go simultaneous." The song also comments that, since no one will be able to collect on his or her life insurance, "Lloyds of London will be loaded when we go."

Weavers, The: Wasn't That a Time!

A 1982 film starring Pete SEEGER, Lee Hays, Ronnie Gilbert, and Fred Hellerman and directed by Jim Brown. The Reagan-era film reunites the Weavers, a group of FOLK SINGERS who were blacklisted during the 1950s RED SCARE because of their left-wing sentiments. Seeger organized the group in 1948. Their version of "Goodnight Irene" was a number-one hit for 13 weeks in 1950, but that year they were also listed in RED CHANNELS, the publication that was widely used as the basis for unofficial BLACKLISTING within the television and radio industries. Moreover, JOURNALIST Walter WINCHELL attacked the Weavers in his nationally syndicated newspaper column.

When the Wind Blows

A 1982 CARTOON by Raymond Briggs. An extremely bleak, BLACK HUMOR treatment of a seemingly impending NUCLEAR APOCALYPSE, the book was published in England during the re-intensification of the Cold War which took place during the first Reagan administration. This period involved, among other things, the much-protested placement of U.S. intermediate-range, nuclear-armed cruise and Pershing missiles in bases in England and Western Europe. The cartoon reflects the common citizen's sense of impotence in his or her inability to affect the course of events and deter an apparently inevitable nuclear war. It follows James and Hilda, a hardworking, English middle-class couple who feel helpless before "the Powers That Be [who] will get us in the end." Briggs represents the nuclear attack by doing violence to the comic strip medium itself, slicing off the strip in mid-drawing and leaving a blank page that turns bright pink and red. From that implied carnage, James and Hilda reemerge inside their fallout shelter, where they wait for the Powers That Be to deliver supplies. Later they sun themselves in the contaminated air, and as they begin to decay, James declares with preposterous cheerfulness, "We'll just have to acclimatise ourselves to the Post-Nuclear Area. It could be OK—wiping the slate clean . . . starting afresh—a New Fire of London! The New Elizabethan Age will dawn." The couple dies absurdly, quoting passages from the Bible and "The Charge of the Light Brigade."

For additional reading, see Dowling's *Fictions of Nuclear Disaster*.

White Nights   A 1985 FILM DRAMA starring Mikhail BAR-YSHNIKOV, Gregory Hines, Jerzy Skolimowski and Isabella Rossellini and directed by Taylor Hackford. This Reagan-era film plays on the then-current tension between the superpowers. The story describes what might have been a genuine nightmare for real-life dancer/defector Baryshnikov. Baryshnikov plays a ballet dancer/defector who enjoys stardom as an international performer in the West, where he is free to choose what he will perform and experiment with new dance styles and forms. But when his plane crash-lands in the Soviet Union, he is recognized and taken into custody. In the U.S.S.R. he is regarded not as a naturalized American citizen but as a Soviet criminal. The cosmopolitan Soviet official handling his case appreciates the dancer's talent but cynically wants to use him for propaganda purposes. After serving those purposes, Baryshnikov will become expendable. He is placed with tap dancer Gregory Hines, a disenchanted American exile who came to the U.S.S.R. to escape the Vietnam War, which he believed to be racist and murderous. However, several years after his defection, he is neglected and abused. When the Soviet official, who proves to be as racist as the Americans from whom Hines fled, threatens to separate him from his Russian wife (Rossellini), Hines allies with Baryshnikov. Eventually, after some impressive dancing scenes where the two men match their styles and talents, Baryshnikov and Hines plan their escape. It turns out that Hines has to sacrifice himself so that Baryshnikov and Rossellini can get free. He suffers a cruel imprisonment until Baryshnikov finally arranges his release in exchange for a Soviet spy.

White Nights was unusual for making the open charge that the Vietnam War was racist and for according sympathy to a deserter, especially during the 1980s, when RAMBO and other films were attempting to provide after-the-fact victories over North Vietnam. The charge of racism enables the audience to maintain some sympathy for the black defector until he becomes a co-protagonist. Otherwise, the film reflects Reagan's view of the Soviet Union as an "evil

empire" and depicts Soviet officials as crafty and insidious. The shots of Moscow underscore the inferiority of Soviet consumer goods. For instance, the automobiles are all old models, and Baryshnikov's portable cassette player is a rare and valuable commodity that can command a high price in the Soviet black market. More than anything, however, the film makes the case that artistic freedom is enjoyed in the West but suppressed under communism. Though Baryshnikov came to worldwide prominence as a dancer of classical ballet, in this film he revels in forms of modern dance outlawed by the Soviets. (Twyla Tharp choreographed these scenes.) Hines, too, appears a defeated man until he dances to the forbidden music Baryshnikov has brought with him. Thus, the film argues, by restricting artistic freedom, the cynical communists are attempting to crush the individual spirit, thereby negating the value of individual life and simultaneously maintaining a tighter grip on their power.

Wicker, Ireene   A radio and TELEVISION PERFORMER who was erroneously blacklisted in RED CHANNELS in 1950. After doing children's programming on radio for nearly 20 years, in 1948 Wicker began a popular children's television show, "The Singing Lady." The show featured songs, fairy tales and stories from American history acted out by marionettes. ABC renewed the show in February 1950, but abruptly canceled it that August, after *Red Channels* listed Wicker for allegedly signing a petition on behalf of Benjamin J. Davis, a Communist Party candidate for the New York City Council. Wicker was also listed for having supported a benefit for children who had become refugees during the Spanish Civil War. She met with Theodore Kirkpatrick, an editor of *Red Channels*, and denied signing the Davis petition, which he claimed he learned about from an article in the Communist Party publication, *The Daily Worker*. When asked what she had done to oppose communism, Wicker pointed to several patriotic activities, including sponsoring a children's contest on why "I am glad to be an American," recording a series based on American history entitled "Sing a Song of History" and allowing her son to enlist in the Royal Canadian Air Force in 1940, while the Hitler-Stalin pact was still in effect and American communists opposed U.S. intervention in the European war. However, Kirkpatrick did not find these credentials sufficiently convincing.

Eventually Wicker obtained a court order so that her lawyer could examine all 30,000 names on the Davis petition. When her name was not found among them, COUNTER-ATTACK, the magazine that published *Red Channels*, ran an article that included Wicker's denial of any communist affiliations, shifting the blame for the inaccuracy to *The Daily Worker*, which in turn blamed a news release from the Davis campaign committee. Reiterating its position that *Red Channels* reprinted reports only from other sources, *Counterattack* asserted that it "did not call Miss Wicker, or any other person mentioned in the report, a Communist or a Communist sympathizer." Nonetheless, despite newspaper, radio and television reports of her clearance, Wicker's show was not picked up again. Her agent claimed that the response he repeatedly received was, "What about *Red Channels*? We wouldn't touch her with a ten-foot pole." Wicker's only work during 1951 and 1952 was on a small radio station in Massachusetts. She regained a television show in

1953 and 1954, but by then her popularity had faded, and the show was canceled. She never had a regular show again.

For additional reading, see Cogley's *The Report on Blacklisting,* vol. 2.

Wild Shore, The A 1984 APOCALYPTIC NOVEL by Kim Stanley Robinson. The book appeared during the most belligerent period in the Cold War since the 1962 Cuban Missile Crisis, when officials in the Reagan administration were accusing the Soviets of planning to prevail in a protracted nuclear war and were themselves promoting the notion of winnable nuclear war. The period was also known for its celebration of wealth and materialism. The story centers on the 17-year-old narrator, Henry Aaron Fletcher, who is growing up in an America that has been devastated by a nuclear war and is now quarantined, deprived of technology and overseen by satellites operated by Mexico, Canada and Japan. Robinson explores the generational differences among survivors, as the adults criticize U.S. imperialism and shallow materialism for bringing about the war, while adolescents remember the prewar era as a prelapsarian paradise of high-tech consumer capitalism. Henry joins an underground resistance movement in San Diego but is betrayed by it and everyone else he has come to love and trust. His experiences disillusion him and destroy his belief that the world can be changed for the better. Henry concludes that America has fallen from grace because human nature has been innately corrupted. According to critic William J. Scheick, Robinson's bleak view suggests that "the best one can hope for is not a change in human spirit but a Spenglerian tidal rise and fall, a postlapsarian determined natural rhythm which takes no account of human hope."

For additional reading, see Anisfield's *The Nightmare Considered* and Scheick's "Continuative and Ethical Predictions: The Post-Nuclear Holocaust Novel of the 1980s."

"Wild, Wild West, The" A TELEVISION WESTERN that ran on CBS from 1965 to 1970. James T. West (Robert Conrad) and Artemus Gordon (Ross Martin) were special undercover agents who worked for President Grant. Their assignments typically required them to expose or undermine the nefarious operations of radical, revolutionary or criminal groups. A 19th-century James BOND, West succeeded in his missions through a combination of strength, skill, guts, charm, attractiveness to the opposite sex, good timing and technological gadgetry—the most advanced devices imaginable within the framework of 1860s technology. Essentially, "The Wild, Wild West" applied the formula of the suave, accomplished secret agent to the American frontier. In so doing, it reiterated the definition of the Cold War–era hero as one who can hold his own in high society but can also tough it out with his fists, if necessary. Such a hero is rational and knowledgeable but also very physical. He enjoys romance but subordinates his love interests to his duty. He is dedicated to helping victims and punishing evil, and he serves the interests of law, order and social stability.

Wilson, Edmund A NONFICTION WRITER. Born in 1895, Wilson was educated at Princeton University and was already one of America's best-known literary and social critics by the time the Cold War began. After serving in France at a military hospital during World War I, he decried the failure of Western capitalist institutions and turned toward socialism. He voted for the Communist Party candidate for president in 1932 and traveled to the Soviet Union in 1935 on a Guggenheim Fellowship. He applauded the absence of class distinctions in the U.S.S.R. in his subsequent book, *Travels in Two Democracies* (1936). At the same time, he acquired a distrust of Stalinism and Soviet bureaucracy. In 1938 Wilson married Mary MCCARTHY, but the relationship was tempestuous and they divorced in 1946. McCarthy later accused him of being a drunken wife-beater, while Wilson described her as reckless and unstable. In 1938, Wilson published *The Triple Thinkers: Ten Essays on Literature,* in which he criticizes some aspects of Marxism and the intellectual strategies of left-wing thinkers. The book also suggests how Marxist methodology can be applied to literary and artistic analysis and includes essays on "Marxism and Literature" and "The Historical Interpretation of Literature," criticizing as reductionist the artistic restrictions that Marxist parties imposed on writers. *To the Finland Station* (1940) follows socialist thought and activity through three centuries, culminating with Lenin's arrival at the Finland Station.

Wilson's most direct treatment of the Cold War appears in *The Cold War and the Income Tax* (1963). Inspired by his own difficulties with the Internal Revenue Service (IRS) and written during the early days of U.S. involvement in Vietnam, the book accuses the IRS of employing religious propaganda to justify war and criticizes the use of government funds and power to stifle protest and dissidence. These attitudes also appear in Wilson's major work during the postwar era, *Patriotic Gore* (1962). This study of the literature of the American Civil War attacks the American drive for power, centralized government and nationalistic aggression. Its view of human nature is extremely bleak, and it concludes that the American notions of order, national unity and justice are predicated on the underlying desire for power.

Wilson also published several pieces attacking academic literary criticism and the Modern Language Association, which he believed exercised too much control over literary studies, reducing them to irrelevant "hyphen-hunting." The year before his death, Wilson published *A Window on Russia, for the Use of Foreign Readers* (1971). Though most of his major contributions appeared before World War II, Wilson's writings were widely read throughout the Cold War, and he remained an influence on Cold War–era thought and literature.

For additional reading, see *The Dictionary of Literary Biography* (vol. 63, *American Literary Critics and Scholars*).

Winchell, Walter A JOURNALIST. Born in 1897 in a New York slum, to Russian Jewish immigrants, Winchell pioneered the modern newspaper gossip column. He became a gang leader at an early age and dropped out of school after failing sixth grade three times. At the same time he developed an interest in vaudeville. As an usher and performer, he spent considerable time backstage, where he picked up the racy lingo and acquired a taste for gossip. He served in the navy from 1916 to 1920 but remained in New York throughout World War I. When his career in vaudeville failed, he turned to journalism, writing as a columnist for the *New York Evening Graphic* from 1925 to 1929, the *New York Daily Mirror* from 1929 to 1963 and the *New York Journal-American* from 1963 to 1966. His columns featured insider news about important personalities and contained gossip about romances, divorces and other intimate affairs of the prominent and powerful.

In 1934 Winchell also inaugurated a radio news show for CBS, which he opened each day with the greeting, "Good evening, Mr. and Mrs. America and all the ships at sea, let's go to press!" His staccato delivery and colorful diction made him extremely popular. Winchell's coverage of the Lindbergh kidnapping in 1934 led his reading and listening audiences to believe he had inside knowledge of the FBI investigation, though at FBI director J. Edgar Hoover's request he sacrificed a scoop by withholding an announcement of Bruno Hauptmann's arrest in order to allow agents time to secure important evidence. Winchell cooperated with the FBI on other occasions as well. During the 1930s he avidly supported President Roosevelt and vehemently attacked the rise of Nazism in Germany and was among the first to condemn Hitler. He helped move Americans against isolationism, attacking its proponents as "Assolationists." He served during World War II as a lieutenant commander in the navy.

During the Cold War, Winchell adopted an extreme right-wing position and directed his attacks against communism. He supported the anti-communist crusades of Senator Joseph McCarthy (R. Wisconsin) and the HOUSE COMMITTEE ON UN-AMERICAN ACTIVITIES (HUAC) during the RED SCARE of the late 1940s and 1950s. Among his targets were Folk Singer Pete SEEGER and his group the Weavers. Winchell also joined in the attacks on President Truman, whom Winchell considered a minor figure compared to the much-revered Roosevelt. In 1951, he brought his radio show to ABC, which offered him a lucrative lifetime contract. When the *New York Post* ran a 24–part series attacking Winchell in 1952, the columnist first went into a deep depression and then retaliated by denouncing the *Post* as a communist paper. The *Post* responded with a libel suit against Winchell, ABC, his corporate sponsors and the Hearst Corporation, which ran his syndicated newspaper column. After two years, the *Post* won the suit, and Winchell was forced to retract his statements. When ABC subsequently turned down Winchell's request for increased libel insurance, he resigned, canceling his lifetime contract. To his surprise, the network accepted the resignation. At the same time, McCarthy fell from power following the 1954 ARMY-MCCARTHY HEARINGS and his subsequent censure by the Senate, and Winchell's prestige suffered as a result. His career and influence declined afterward.

By 1960 his column was featured in less than 150 papers, down from a thousand. He continued his public feuds, attacking television talk show host Jack PAAR and party hostess Elsa Maxwell and criticizing the Kennedy administration for attempting to manage the news. He also narrated "The Untouchables," a popular television show that championed the FBI's fight against organized crime in the 1930s. When the *Mirror* stopped publishing in 1963, Winchell joined the *Journal-American*, but his column was shortened and ran less frequently. After the *Journal-American* merged with two other papers in 1966 to form the *World-Journal-Tribune*, his column ran only once a week, and when the *World-Journal-Tribune* folded less than a year later, it ran only in limited syndication. In 1968 King Features, his syndicator, also dropped him. Winchell died in 1972.

For additional reading, see *Dictionary of Literary Biography*, (vol. 29, *American Newspaper Journalists 1926–1950*).

With Enough Shovels A 1982 NONFICTION book by Robert Scheer. The book includes interviews with President Reagan, Vice President (and future president) George Bush and other top administration officials. Scheer's intention was to alert the public to what he believed was a dangerous and misguided approach to Cold War nuclear planning. Written during the arms buildup of the first Reagan administration, the book describes how the administration was shifting policy away from the Mutually Assured Destruction (MAD) of 1970s détente to the notion of winnable nuclear war. Directed to a popular audience, it documents Reagan's long-standing antipathy for MAD, which he believed was a highly dangerous policy, and describes how the conservative Committee on the Present Danger, which reconvened immediately after President Carter's election in 1976, came to dominate nuclear planning during the early 1980s. Scheer claims that when George Bush directed the CIA in 1976, he took the unprecedented step of allowing Team B, a group of conservative outsiders, to review classified agency data on Soviet military activities and to advance the position that the Soviets had abandoned a policy of nuclear parity in favor of attaining nuclear superiority. Many of the members of Team B were prominent opponents of détente, and Bush adopted their conclusions as the official CIA assessment of Soviet policy, over assessments offered by Team A, the regular CIA professionals employed to provide such analysis, who believed the Soviets were pursuing nuclear parity. The idea that the Soviets were attempting to gain a nuclear advantage in order to prevail in a nuclear war thus altered the conventional wisdom that the Soviets had also accepted MAD. It later became a fundamental assumption used by the Reagan administration to justify the arms buildup of the early 1980s, now intended to permit the United States to prevail in a protracted nuclear war.

To promote this new policy, the Reagan administration had to reverse the common perception that nuclear war with the Soviets would be tantamount to suicide. It had to convince the American public that the United States could not only win such a war but also would quickly recover from it. Thus T. K. Jones, deputy undersecretary of defense for strategic and theater nuclear forces, argued that by using primitive fallout shelters, such as those promoted in the Soviet Union, most Americans could survive an attack, and he maintained that the U.S. economy could return to its current levels within six or eight years. The book's title comes from Jones's claim that survival required only digging a hole, "cover it with a couple of doors and then throw three feet of dirt on top . . . It's the dirt that does it . . . If there are enough shovels to go around, everybody's going to make it."

Witness A 1952 NONFICTION book by Whittaker Chambers. *Witness* is the autobiographical account of the former communist who achieved national prominence in 1948 when he accused Alger Hiss of having spied for the Soviet Union during the 1930s. In addition to presenting his version of Hiss' espionage, Chambers describes his activities as a member of the Communist Party, as well as his disaffection and departure from it. He thus provides an insider's view of the workings of the American Communist Party during the Depression. Though praised for the quality of the writing, the book was criticized for not shedding significantly new light on the Hiss case beyond Chambers' testimony at Hiss' trial. Hiss had been a ranking member of the Roosevelt administration who advised the president at Yalta and played a major role in the founding of the United Nations. Thus Chambers' 1948 charges before the HOUSE COMMITTEE ON UN-AMERICAN ACTIVITIES (HUAC) that Hiss had been a member of the Communist Party and had spied for the Soviet Union fueled RED SCARE charges of communist infiltration of the U.S. government, as well as right-wing charges that the UN was a communist plot to disarm the United States. The veracity of Chambers' account has also been attacked. Documents from the Soviet Communist Party released after the Cold War appear to support his contention that the Soviet Union tried to influence U.S. leftwing organizations during the 1930s, but to date they have failed to back up his charge that Hiss was a Soviet agent. IN THE COURT OF PUBLIC OPINION (1957) presents Hiss' own defense.

Wolper, David An award-winning independent producer of TELEVISION NEWS shows and TELEVISION DOCUMENTARIES AND SPECIAL REPORTS. In addition to the syndicated series BIOGRAPHY (1962–64) and "Men in Crisis" (1965), Wolper produced television documentaries on the space race, the atom bomb, the American Communist Party, Berlin, the Korean War, China and refugees who fled from communist countries. His other notable documentaries include *The Making of the President: 1960* and the *Four Days in November,* about the Kennedy assassination. By syndicating *The Race for Space* (1960), Wolper broke the virtual monopoly that the networks had held on producing television documentaries and special reports: When the networks declined to broadcast the documentary, he convinced over a hundred local stations throughout the country to air it and even to cancel network offerings to make room for it in their schedules. The show featured rare film footage from both NASA and Soviet space archives.

For additional reading, see Einstein's *Special Edition: A Guide to Network Television Documentary Series and Special News Reports, 1955–1979.*

"Wonder Woman" A TELEVISION SCIENCE FICTION SHOW that ran on ABC in 1976–77 and on CBS from 1977 to 1979. Based on the comic-book character from the 1940s, Wonder Woman (Lynda Carter) descended from ancient Amazons who had fled to a now-lost island to escape domination by Greek and Roman men. They had discovered a magic substance that, when molded into a golden belt, gave them superhuman strength, and their golden bracelets could deflect bullets. Wonder Woman fell in love with Major Steve Trevor (Lyle Waggoner), an army pilot who crash-landed on the island during World War II. She returned to the United States as Trevor's secretary, but when necessary

would transform herself into Wonder Woman, clad in sexy tights, golden belt and a patriotic-looking cape that suggested the American flag. Initially the show was set during World War II, but in 1977 the producers updated the setting, and the villains changed from Nazis to more contemporary terrorists and subversive elements. A product of the détente period, "Wonder Woman" also emerged during a period of active feminism. And though some considered Lynda Carter's tight-fitting outfit and her submission through love to Major Trevor to be sexist and exploitative, at the same time her Amazon heritage and her amazing strength presented the image of an empowered, assertive woman of the 1970s standing up for her country and helping it defeat its enemies.

"Wonder Years, The" A TELEVISION SITUATION COMEDY that ran on ABC from 1988 through the end of the Cold War. The show provided an adult's reminiscences of growing up in the late 1960s. Set initially in 1968 and narrated by the unseen adult Kevin Arnold (Daniel Stern), the events were presented from the viewpoint of the junior high school-aged Kevin Arnold (Fred Savage). Such Cold War events as the Vietnam War and antiwar protest thus formed a vague background to the young boy's world of school, best friends, girls and adults. The Cold War was largely absent from Kevin's consciousness, but every now and then some aspect intruded upon him: He attended John F. Kennedy Junior High School; he listened to ROCK AND ROLL by the Beatles; his sister wore love beads and engaged in social protest.

Woodstock A ROCK AND ROLL music festival that took place in upstate New York August 15–17, 1969. Michael Wadleigh's Academy Award–winning 1970 film musical *Woodstock* documents the event. The rock festival, which was billed as a celebration of peace, occurred while the U.S. involvement in Vietnam was still considerable; it came to symbolize the beliefs of the peace movement and the COUNTERCULTURE. Some 400,000 people, mostly under the age of 30, camped out for three days in the rain and mud in a pasture in Bethel, New York. Their celebration of life included ample amounts of sex, drugs and rock and roll. Notable performers were Joan BAEZ; Arlo Guthrie; Jimi Hendrix; Richie Havens; Joe Cocker; Melanie; Blood, Sweat and Tears; the Jefferson Airplane; Ravi Shankar; the Who; and Crosby, Stills and Nash. Country Joe McDonald and the Fish sang the antiwar anthem "I-Feel-Like-I'm-Going-To-Die Rag," which incorporates elements of BLACK HUMOR: "1-2-3, what're we fightin' for?/ Don't ask me, I don't give a damn/ Next stop is Vietnam./ And it's 5-6-7, open up the pearly gates./ Ain't no time to wonder why/ Whoopee! We're all goin' to die."

The *New York Times* described Woodstock as "a nightmare of mud and stagnation." Abbie Hoffman was more philosophical in his book *Woodstock Nation,* in which he asks, "God, how can you capture the feeling of being with 400,000 people and everyone being stoned on something. Were we pilgrims or lemmings? Was this really the beginning of a new civilization or the symptom of a dying one? Were we establishing a liberated zone or entering a detention camp?" While on trial with the Chicago 7, Hoffman insisted he was a citizen of the Woodstock nation, "a nation of alienated young people" that existed as a "state of mind, in the mind of myself and my brothers and sisters. It is a conspiracy." Two babies were born during the Woodstock festival, but three people were killed and thousands of others suffered from various injuries stemming from lack of food and water and bad experiences with drugs. Nonetheless, the concert is mostly remembered as a festival of love, which, according to the "CBS Evening News," was characterized by "old-fashioned kindness and caring . . . harmony and good humor." (See also VIETNAM WAR FILMS.)

Word, The A 1940s radio drama by Arch Oboler. An early postapocalyptic story about two survivors from a nuclear war, *The Word* inspired Oboler's 1951 film, FIVE.

World, the Flesh and the Devil, The A 1959 FILM DRAMA starring Harry Belafonte, Inger Stevens and Mel Ferrer and directed by Joseph L. Scanlon. A postapocalyptic film, *The World, The Flesh and the Devil* centers on Belafonte, who appears at first to be the world's sole survivor after poisonous gases have destroyed the rest of humanity. The ensuing plot complications prompted by Stevens' and Ferrer's appearance suggest issues that might confront survivors of a nuclear war, an event that seemed all too possible in 1959. Among the more provocative situations the film envisions is the postnuclear repopulation of the Earth via interracial and non-monogamous sexual coupling. (See also APOCALYPTIC FILMS.)

Wright, Richard An African-American NOVELIST. Born in Mississippi in 1908, Wright was the son of an illiterate sharecropper and a schoolteacher. Raised by his grandmother, a Seventh-Day Adventist, Wright dropped out of high school and ran away, first to Memphis and then to Chicago. The experiences from this portion of his life became the subject of *Black Boy: A Record of Childhood and Youth* (1945). Wright became attracted to Marxism and joined the Communist Party in 1932. During this period he began to publish free-verse propagandistic poems in such radical magazines as *The New Masses.* Also during the 1930s Wright worked in two New Deal programs to help writers, the Federal Experimental Theater and the Federal Writers' Project. In 1937 he went to New York to work on *The Daily Worker,* the Communist Party newspaper. He published his first book in 1938, a collection of stories entitled *Uncle Tom's Children.* He then won a Guggenheim Fellowship to write *Native Son* (1940), the best-selling story of the capture, trial and execution of a black man who accidentally kills his employer's daughter. *Native Son* established Wright's reputation as a leading American writer; it was made into a Broadway play in 1941 and has twice been made into a film, in 1950 and 1986. Wright played the leading role in the low-budget and unsuccessful 1950 adaptation. In 1941 he wrote the text for a cinematic folk history about the black experience in the United States, *Twelve Million Black Voices.*

In 1944, *The Atlantic Monthly* published his recantation of his Communist Party affiliation, "I Tried to Be a Communist." The essay was later republished in a collection of essays by former communists, THE GOD THAT FAILED (1949). Wright criticizes the Communist Party for exploiting black Americans, subordinating such black issues as the segrega-

Richard Wright, 1945. Courtesy AP/Wide World.

tion of the Armed Forces and Red Cross blood banks to the party's own strategic interests. Wright also tells how white communists physically evicted him when he tried to march in a May Day parade after leaving the party. Though Wright had become disenchanted with the party's tactics, he remained a Marxist.

At the invitation of Gertrude Stein, Wright went to Paris in 1946, where he was warmly received by French intellectuals, including Jean-Paul Sartre and Simone de Beauvoir. He was impressed by the greater opportunities black Europeans had for acceptance and recognition. Upset by his harassment in the United States because of his outspoken political and social beliefs and by the way government and establishment figures shunned him as a pariah, Wright and his family moved to Paris, where he lived until his death in 1960. During his years of exile, he wrote *Black Power* (1953), a call for African unity, and dedicated himself to the cause of Pan-Africanism. However, his efforts were not well received either by whites or by Africans. Other works from his later years include an existential novel, *The Outsider* (1953), and an unpublished novel, *Island of Hallucination,* about an expatriate writer who is kept under CIA surveillance because of his Marxist writings.

As an American writer of the Cold War era, Wright had an ambiguous impact on American Cold War culture. On the one hand, his repudiation of the American Communist Party doubtlessly carried some weight, especially among black Americans who may have been attracted to it. On the other hand, his powerful literary descriptions of American racism helped undermine the U.S. claim to moral superiority in the Cold War. Indeed, the Soviets and other communist countries pointed to America's racist practices throughout the Cold War. In calling for Pan-African unity, Wright seemed to be repudiating both superpowers, who in fact went on to use Africa as one of their major battlegrounds shortly after Wright's death. (See also EXILED WRITERS [from the United States].)

For additional reading, see Tucker's *Literary Exile in the Twentieth Century.*

Writing Under Fire: Stories of the Vietnam War A 1978 collection of VIETNAM WAR LITERATURE edited by Jerome Klinkowitz and John Somer. Published five years after the American withdrawal from Vietnam, this collection was one of the earliest publications of Vietnam War literature in book form. It anthologizes 20 stories published during the war that present "the full spectrum of the Vietnam War experience," including stories about combat, the Vietnamese citizens caught up in the war, the peace negotiations, congressional leaders and media coverage. Among the better-known authors represented are J. G. Ballard and Ward Just. The extensive scholarly introduction surveys the existing body of Vietnam fiction and includes discussions of such novels as Robin Moore's THE GREEN BERETS (1965) and David Halberstam's ONE VERY HOT DAY (1967). The editors also include a chronology of the war and a bibliography of Vietnam War literature. The stories deal with the war's ambiguity, questions of political power and morality, the difficulty of coming to terms with death, initiations into manhood and/or humanity, the use of mind-altering drugs during the war and the nature of heroism, among other topics.

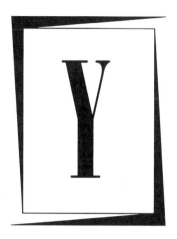

Year of Living Dangerously, The A 1982 FILM DRAMA starring Mel Gibson, Sigourney Weaver and Linda Hunt and directed by Peter Weir. Hunt won the Academy Ward for best supporting actress for her role as a male photographer, Billy Kwan, who works with a newly arrived journalist (Gibson) in Indonesia. Set in 1965, the film depicts the intermingling of politics, private relationships and public affairs. The action centers on a real-life planned communist coup and the actual repressive response of President Sukarno. Billy feels that Sukarno has betrayed Indonesia much as Gibson has betrayed his lover, a woman whom Billy also loves. (See also FILMS ABOUT COLD WAR EVENTS.)

Yefimov, Igor A Soviet EXILED WRITER (to the United States). Born in Moscow in 1937, Yefimov received an engineering degree in 1960 and graduated from the Moscow Literary Institute in 1973. He became a member of the Union of Soviet Writers in the early 1960s and published several novels in the U.S.S.R. Unable to publish other books due to political censorship, Yefimov and his family immigrated to the United States in 1978, the year before détente ended. Yefimov worked for several publishing houses, eventually becoming director of Hermitage Press, which has published over a hundred books by exiled Russian writers. Yefimov published several of his censored works in Russian. One of them, *The Judgment Day Archives* (1982), was translated into English in 1988. Yefimov's greater contribution to American Cold War culture, however, was his 1987 documented study of the Kennedy assassination entitled, KENNEDY, OSWALD, CASTRO, KHRUSHCHEV. Based on four years of research, the book concludes that the Cuban leader hired the Mafia to kill Kennedy in response to efforts by Kennedy to have the CIA assassinate Castro.

For additional reading, see Tucker's *Literary Exile in the Twentieth Century*.

"You Are There" A TELEVISION DOCUMENTARY that ran on CBS from 1953 to 1957 and in 1971–72. Narrated by Walter CRONKITE, "You Are There" presented reenactments of such historical events as the fall of Troy, the Salem witchcraft trials, the Gettysburg Address, the landing of the Hindenburg and the scuttling of the German battleship *Graf Spee* during World War II. Though the emphasis on history precluded direct treatment of the Cold War, nonetheless, part of the show's effect was to strengthen the viewers' identification as Americans by presenting episodes from American history from a largely pro-American point of view. Even accounts from earlier eras or other cultures usually reflected traditional American values in their portrayal of heroes, villains and victims. Abraham POLONSKY, a communist SCREENWRITER who was blacklisted in the Hollywood film industry at the time, wrote some scripts for "You Are There" under an assumed name. (See also BLACKLISTING.)

Zabriskie Point A 1970 FILM DRAMA starring Mark Frechette, Daria Halprin, Rod Taylor and Harrison Ford and directed by Michelangelo Antonioni. The Vietnam-era film centers on a student radical who flees to Death Valley after being identified, accurately or inaccurately, as the killer of a policeman during an antiwar riot. While in the desert he meets a marijuana-smoking secretary with whom he proceeds to share psychedelic and sexual experiences. The film presents the conflict between the COUNTERCULTURE, which uses mind-expanding drugs, advocates free love and opposes U.S. imperialism; and the Establishment, which supports the Vietnam War, drinks alcohol and denounces extramarital sex. (See also VIETNAM WAR FILMS.)

Bibliography

Anisfield, Nancy, ed. *The Nightmare Considered: Critical Essays on Nuclear War Literature.* Bowling Green, Ohio: The Popular Press, 1991.

———, ed. *Vietnam Anthology: American War Literature.* Bowling Green, Ohio: The Popular Press, 1987.

Aronson, James. *The Press and the Cold War.* Indianapolis: Bobbs-Merrill, 1970.

Barron, Neil. *Anatomy of Wonder: A Critical Guide to Science Fiction.* New York: R.R. Bowker, 1987.

Beene, LynnDianne. *John le Carré.* New York: Twayne, 1992.

Benson, Thomas and Carolyn Anderson. *Reality Fictions: The Films of Frederick Wiseman.* Carbondale: Southern Illinois University Press, 1989.

Bentley, Eric, ed. *Thirty Years of Treason: Excerpts from Hearings before the House Committee on Un-American Activities, 1938–1968.* New York: Viking Press, 1971.

Biskind, Peter. *Seeing Is Believing: How Hollywood Taught Us to Stop Worrying and Love the Fifties.* New York: Pantheon Books, 1983.

Blair, Walter and Hamlin Hill. *America's Humor: From Poor Richard To Doonesbury.* New York: Oxford University Press, 1978.

Broderick, Mick. *Nuclear Movies: A Critical Analysis and Filmography of International Feature Length Films Dealing With Experimentation, Aliens, Terrorism, Holocaust and Other Disaster Scenarios, 1914–1990.* Jefferson, N.C.: McFarland & Co., 1991.

Buckley, William F., Jr. *The Committee and Its Critics.* New York: Putnam, 1962.

Buckley, William F., Jr. et al. *McCarthy and His Enemies: The Record and Its Meaning,* Chicago: H. Regnery Co. 1954.

Calder, Nigel. *Nuclear Nightmares.* New York: Viking Press, 1980.

Castleman, Harry and Walter J. Podrazik. *The TV Schedule Book.* New York: McGraw-Hill, 1984.

Cawelti, John G. *Apostles of the Self-Made Man.* Chicago: University of Chicago Press, 1965, rpt. 1988.

———. *The Six Gun Mystique.* Bowling Green, Ohio: Bowling Green University Popular Press, 1971.

——— and Bruce A. Rosenberg. *The Spy Story.* Chicago: University of Chicago Press, 1987.

Cogley, John. *Report on Blacklisting,* 2 vols. New York: Arno Press, 1971 (reprint of 1956 ed.).

Cohn, Carol. "Slick 'Ems, Glick 'Ems, Christmas Trees, and Cookie Cutters: Nuclear Language and How We Learned to Pat the Bomb." *Bulletin of the Atomic Scientists,* 43:5 (June 1987), pp. 17–24.

Cook, Bruce. *Brecht in Exile.* New York: Holt, Rinehart, and Winston, 1983.

Darby, William. *Necessary American Fictions: Popular Literature of the 1950s.* Bowling Green, Ohio: Bowling Green State University Popular Press, 1987.

Denisoff, R. Serge. *Sing a Song of Social Significance.* Bowling Green, Ohio: Bowling Green State University Popular Press, 1972.

Dictionary of Literary Biography. Detroit: Gale Research Co.

Dorfman, Ariel and Armand Mattelart. *How to Read Donald Duck: Imperialist Ideology in the Disney Comics,* tr. David Kunzle. New York: International General, 1975.

Dowling, David. *Fictions of Nuclear Disaster.* Iowa City: University of Iowa Press, 1987.

Einstein, Daniel. *Special Edition: A Guide to Network Television Documentary Series and Special News Reports, 1955–1979.* Metuchen, N.J.: Scarecrow Press, 1987.

Estren, Mark James. *A History of Underground Comics,* 2nd ed. London: Airlift Book Co., 1987.

Fjellman, Stephen M. *Vinyl Leaves: Walt Disney and America.* Boulder, Colo.: Westview Press, 1992.

Foreign Policy Association, Editors of. *Cartoon History of United States Foreign Policy: 1776–1976.* New York: William Morrow, 1975.

Foster, Edward H. *Understanding The Beats.* Columbia: University of S. Carolina Press, 1992.

Gale, Steven H., ed. *Encyclopedia of American Humorists.* New York: Garland Publishing, 1988.

Gallo, Max. *The Poster in History.* New York: NAL, 1975.

Goodman, Walter. *The Committee: The Extraordinary Career of the House Committee on Un-American Activities.* New York: Farrar, Straus & Giroux, 1968.

Gotera, Vince and Theresa Brown, eds. *Journal of American Culture,* 16:3 (Fall, 1993) [special issue on "Poetry and The Vietnam War"]

Halberstam, David. The Best and the Brightest. New York: Random House, 1972.

———. *The Fifties.* New York: Random House, 1993.

———. *The Powers That Be.* New York: Alfred A. Knopf, 1979.

Hellman, Lillian. *Scoundrel Time.* Boston: Little, Brown, 1976.

Hilgartner, Stephen, Richard C. Bell, and Rory O'Connor. *Nukespeak.* New York: Penguin, 1983.

Hoffman, Katherine. *Explorations: The Visual Arts Since 1945.* New York: HarperCollins, 1991.

Hughes, Catherine. *Plays, Politics and Polemics.* New York: Drama Book Specialists/Publishers, 1973.

Hyde, Lewis, ed. *On the Poetry of Allen Ginsberg.* Ann Arbor: University of Michigan Press, 1984.

Inge, Thomas. *Comics as Culture.* Jackson: University Press of Mississippi, 1990.

Jarrett, William. *Timetables of Sports History: The Olympic Games.* New York: Facts On File, 1990.

Jones, Dorothy. "Communism and the Movies: A Study of Film Content," in John Cogley, *Report on Blacklisting (vol. 1, The Movies).* New York: Arno Press, 1971 (reprint of 1956 ed.).

Kagan, Norman. *The Cinema of Oliver Stone.* New York: Continuum, 1995.

———. *The Cinema of Stanley Kubrick.* New York: Holt, Rinehart and Winston, 1972.

Kemme, Tom. *Political Fiction, The Spirit of the Age, and Allen Drury.* Bowling Green, Ohio: The Popular Press, 1987.

King, David. *How Can I Keep From Singing? Pete Seeger.* New York: McGraw Hill, 1981.

Kirk, Elise K. *Music at the White House.* Urbana and Chicago: University of Illinois Press, 1986.

Lanning, Michael Lee. *Vietnam at the Movies.* New York: Fawcett Columbine, 1994.

Lindey, Christine. *Art in the Cold War: From Vladivostok to Kalamazoo, 1945–1962.* London: The Herbert Press, 1990.

Lutz, William. *Doublespeak.* New York: Harper & Row, 1989.

Malo, Jean-Jacques and Tony Williams, ed. *Vietnam War Films: Over 600 Feature, Made-for-TV, Pilot and Short Movies, 1939–1992, from the United States, Vietnam, France, Belgium, Australia, Hong Kong, South Africa, Great Britain and Other Countries.* Jefferson, N.C.: McFarland & Co., 1994.

May, Lary, ed. *Recasting America: Culture and Politics in the Age of Cold War.* Chicago: University of Chicago Press, 1989.

McNeil, Alex. *Total Television.* New York: Penguin, 1991.

Miller, Merle. *The Judges and the Judged.* Garden City, N.Y.: Doubleday, 1952; New York: Arno Press, 1971, (reprint).

Milton, J. Bates. *The War We Took to Vietnam.* Berkeley: University of California Press, 1996.

Monaco, James. *The Encyclopedia of Film.* New York: Perigee, 1991.

———. *The Movie Guide: A Comprehensive, Alphabetical Listing of the Most Important Films Ever Made.* New York: Putnam, 1992.

Navasky, Victor. *Naming Names.* New York: Viking, 1980.

Nite, Norman. *Rock On Almanac.* New York: Harper & Row, 1989.

Nureyev, Rudolf. *Nureyev.* New York: Dutton, 1963.

Ochs, Phil. *The War Is Over.* New York: Collier Books, 1968.

Okun, Rob A. *The Rosenbergs: Collected Visions of Artists and Writers.* New York: Universe Books, 1988.

O'Reilly, Kenneth. *Black Americans: The FBI Files.* New York: Carroll & Graf, 1994.

Orman, John. *The Politics of Rock Music.* Chicago: Nelson-Hall, 1984.

Ramet, Sabrina Petra, ed. *Rocking the State: Rock Music and Politics in Eastern Europe and Russia.* Boulder, Colo.: Westview Press, 1994.

Reidelbach, Maria. *Completely Mad.* Boston: Little, Brown, 1991.

Rogin, Michael. *Ronald Reagan, The Movie.* Berkeley: University of California Press, 1987.

Rosteck, Thomas. *See It Now Confronts McCarthyism: Television Documentary and the Politics of Representation.* Tuscaloosa: University of Alabama Press, 1994.

Salzman, Eric. *Twentieth-Century Music.* Englewood Cliffs, N.J.: Prentice-Hall, 1988.

Sandler, Irving. *American Art of the 1960s.* New York: Harper & Row, 1988.

Sayre, Nora. *Running Time: Films of the Cold War.* New York: Dial Press, 1982.

Schaub, Thomas Hill. *American Fiction in the Cold War.* Madison: University of Wisconsin Press, 1991.

Scheick, William J. "Continuative and Ethical Predictions: The Post-Nuclear Holocaust Novel of the 1980s," *North Dakota Quarterly,* 56 (1988), pp. 61–82.

Schwartz, Richard A. *The Cold War Reference Guide.* Jefferson, N.C. McFarland & Co., 1997.

———. "The F.B.I. and Dr. Einstein." *The Nation,* 237:6 (Sept. 3–10, 1983), 168–173.

———. "Postmodernist Baseball." *Modern Fiction Studies,* 33:1 (Spring, 1987), 135–148.

Searle, William J., ed. *Search and Clear: Literature and Films of the Vietnam War.* Bowling Green, Ohio: The Popular Press, 1988.

Seeger, Pete. *Where Have All The Flowers Gone?* ed. Peter Blood. Bethlehem, Pa.: Sing Out, 1993.

Seitz, William C. *Art in the Age of Aquarius.* Washington, D.C.: Smithsonian Institution Press, 1992.

Server, Lee. *Sam Fuller: Film Is a Battleground—A Critical Study, with Interviews, a Filmography and Bibliography.* Jefferson, N.C.: McFarland & Co., 1994.

Shaheen, Jack G. *Nuclear War Films.* Carbondale: Southern Illinois University Press, 1978.

Sloane, David E. E., ed. *American Humor Magazines and Comic Periodicals.* Westport, Conn.: Greenwood Press, 1987.

Smith, Julian. *Looking Away.* New York: Charles Scribner's Sons, 1975.

Smith, Myron. *U.S. Television Network News: A Guide to Sources in English.* Jefferson, N.C.: McFarland, 1984.

Spigel, Lynn. *Make Room for TV.* Chicago: University of Chicago Press, 1992.

Steel, Ronald. *Walter Lippmann and The American Century.* Boston: Little, Brown, 1980.

Stern, Jane and Michael. *Encyclopedia of Pop Culture.* New York: HarperCollins, 1992.

Suid, Lawrence H., ed. *Film and Propaganda in America: A Documentary History* (vol. IV, *1945 and After*). New York: Greenwood Press, 1991. Volume V is a microfiche supplement that contains additional documents.

Szatmary, David P. *Rockin' in Time: A Social History of Rock and Roll.* Englewood Cliffs, N.J.: Prentice-Hall, 1987.

Thomas, C. David, ed. *As Seen By Both Sides: American and Vietnamese Artists Look at the War.* Boston: University of Massachusetts Press, 1991.

Toropov, Branden. *Cold War Politics.* New York, forthcoming from Facts On File.

Tucker, Martin, ed. *Literary Exile in the Twentieth Century.* New York: Greenwood Press, 1991.

Uba, George. "Friend and Foe: De-Collaborating Wendy Wilder Larsen and Tran Thi Nga's *Shallow Graves*," *Journal of American Culture,* 16:3 (Fall, 1993), 63–70.

Vaughn, Robert. *Only Victims.* New York: G.P. Putnam's Sons, 1972.

von Hallberg, Robert. *American Poetry and Culture, 1945–1980.* Cambridge: Harvard University Press, 1985.

Ward, Ed, Geoffrey Stokes, and Ken Tucker. *Rock of Ages: The Rolling Stone History of Rock & Roll.* New York: Rolling Stone Press 1986.

Watson, Peter. *Nureyev: A Biography.* London: Hodder & Stoughton, 1994.

Whitfield, Stephen. *The Culture of the Cold War,* 2nd edition. Baltimore: Johns Hopkins University Press, 1996.

Index

The entries listed below are additional to those arranged alphabetically in the text. **Boldface** page numbers indicate main entries. The letter *f* indicates illustrations.